Complete baronetage

George E. 1825-1911 Cokayne

Complete Baronetage.

EDITED BY

G. E. C. okayne

EDITOR OF THE

"Complete Peerage."

VOLUME II

1625—1649.

EXETER·
WILLIAM POLLARD & Co Ltd, 39 & 40, NORTH STREET
1902

D.

∠

POLLARD & COMPANY
WILLIAM LIMITED
PRINTERS EXETER
ESTABLISHED. 1781

CONTENTS.

LIST OF SUBSCRIBERS.

Adams, Rev H. W, Normanhurst, Eton Avenue, Hampstead, N W
Aldenham, Lord, St Dunstan's, Regent's Park, N W
Amherst of Hackney, Lord, F S A, per Sotheran & Co, 140, Strand, W C
Anderson, J R, 84, Albert Drive, Crosshill, Glasgow
Annesley, Lieut -Gen A Lyttelton, Templemere, Weybridge, Surrey
Anstruther, Sir R, Bt, Balcaskie, Pillenweena, Scotland
Antrobus, Rev Frederick, The Oratory, South Kensington, S W
Armytage, Sir George, Bt, F S A, Kirklees Park, Brighouse
Arnold, Charles T, Stamford House, West Side, Wimbledon
Assheton, Ralph, Downham Hall, Clitheroe
Astley, John, Moseley Terrace, Coundon Road, Coventry
Athenæum Club, per Jones, Yarrell, & Poulter, Booksellers, 8, Bury Street, S W
Athill, Charles H, F S A, Richmond Herald, College of Arms, E C

Bain, J, Bookseller, 1, Haymarket, S W (4)
Baronetage, The Hon Society of the, per Sotheran & Co, 140, Strand, W C
Batten, H B, Aldon, Yeovil
Beaven, Rev A B, Greyfriars, Leamington
Bedford, Duke of, per Sotheran & Co, 140, Strand, W C
Bell & Sons, York Street, Covent Garden, W C
Boase, F, 28, Buckingham Gate, S W
Bools, W E, Enderby, 13, Vernon Road, Clapham, S W
Boyle, Colonel the Hon R E, 6, Summer Terrace, S W
British Museum, Department of MSS, per Sotheran & Co, 140, Strand, W C
Brooking-Rowe, J, Castle Barbican, Plympton
Bruce Bannerman, W, F S A, The Lindens, Sydenham Road, Croydon, Surrey
Burke, Ashworth P, per Harrison & Sons, 59, Pall Mall, S W
Burke, Henry Farnham, F S A, Somerset Herald, College of Arms, E C
Burnard, Robert, 3, Hillsborough, Plymouth

Carrington, R Smith, F S A , Ashby Folville Manor, Melton Mowbray.
Carlton Club, Pall Mall, per Harrison & Sons, 59, Pall Mall, S W
Carmichael, Sir Thomas D Gibson, Bt , Castlecraig, Dolphinton, N B
Cazenove & Son, C D , Booksellers, 26, Henrietta Street, Covent Garden, W C
Chadwyck-Healey, C E H , F S A , per Sotheran & Co , 140, Strand, W C
Clarke, C L , Homewood, Stevenage, Herts
Clements, H. J B , Killadoon, Cellridge, co Kildare, Ireland
Codrington Library, All Souls College, Oxford
Colyer-Fergusson, T C , Ightham Mote, Ivy Hatch, near Sevenoaks
Conder, Edward, F S A , The Conigree, Newent, Gloucester
Cooper, Samuel J , Mount Vernon, near Barnsley
Craigie, Edmund, The Grange, Lytton Grove, Putney Hill, S W.
Crawford and Balcarres, Earl of per Sotheran & Co , 140, Strand, W C.
Crawley-Boevey, A W , 24, Sloane Court, S W.
Cresswell, L , Wood Hall, Calverley, Leeds
Crisp, F A , F S A , Grove Park, Denmark Hill, S.E.
Crompton, S Douglas, per Sotheran & Co , 140, Strand, W C
Culleton, Leo , 92, Piccadilly, W
Cullum, G M G , 4, Sterling Street, Montpelier Square, S W
Cust, Lady Elizabeth, 13, Eccleston Square, S W

Dalrymple, Hon Hew , Oxenfoord Castle, Dalkeith
Davies, Seymour G P , English, Scottish, and Australian Bank Ltd ,
    Melbourne, Australia
Davison, R M , Grammar School, Ilminster
Douglas, David, 10, Castle Street, Edinburgh
Douglas & Foulis, 9, Castle Street, Edinburgh (6)
Duckett, Sir George, Bt , Oxford and Cambridge Club, Pall Mall, S W
Duleep Singh, His Highness Prince, per Sotheran & Co , 140, Strand, W C
Dunkin, E H W , Rosewyn, 70, Herne Hill, S E

Edwardes, Sir Henry H , Bt , per Harrison & Sons, 59, Pall Mall, S W
Eland, H S , Bookseller, High Street, Exeter
Exeter Royal Albert Memorial Museum, Exeter

Foley, P , F S A , Prestwood, Stourbridge, per A & F Denny, 304, Strand, W C
Foster, Joseph, 21, Boundary Road, N W
Fox, Charles Henry, M D , 35, Heriot Row, Edinburgh
Fox, Francis F , Yate House, Chipping Sodbury, Gloucester, per W
    George's Sons, Top Corner, Park Street, Bristol
Fry, E A , 172, Edmond Street, Birmingham

George, William Edwards, Downside, Stoke Bishop, near Bristol, per
George's Sons, Bristol

George's Sons, William, Top Corner, Park, Street, Bristol

'Gibbs, Antony, Tyntesfield, near Bristol

Gibbs, H Martin, Barrow Court, Flax Bourton, Somerset, per W. George's
Sons, Top Corner, Park Street, Bristol

Gibbs, Rev John Lomax, Speen House, near Newbury, Berks

Gibbs, Hon Vicary, M P, St Dunstan's, Regent's Park, N W

Glencross, R M, The Office of Arms, Dublin Castle, Ireland

Gough, Henry, Sandcroft, Redhill, Surrey

Graves, Robert Edmund, Lyndhurst, Grange Park, Ealing, W. (2)

Green & Sons, W, Law Booksellers, Edinburgh

Guildhall Library (per C Welch), E C.

Hanson, Sir Reginald, Bt, 4, Bryanston Square, W

Hardy & Page, 21, Old Buildings, Lincoln's Inn, W C

Harrison & Sons, 59, Pall Mall, S W (3)

Haslewood, Rev. F G, Chislet Vicarage, Canterbury.

Hatchards, 187, Piccadilly, W (6).

Hawkesbury, Lord, per Sotheran & Co, 140, Strand, W C (2)

Head, Christopher, 6, Clarence Terrace, Regent's Park, N W.

Hesilrige, Arthur G M, 160A, Fleet Street, E C

Hodge, Figgis & Co, Booksellers, 104, Grafton Street, Dublin

Hofman, Charles, 16, Grovenor Street, W

Hovenden, R, F S A, Heathcote, Park Hill Road, Croydon

Hughes of Kimmel, H R, Kimmel Park, Abergele, North Wales, per
Sotheran & Co, 140, Strand, W C

Hull Subscription Library (William Andrews, Librarian), Royal Institution, Hull.

Incorporated Law Society (F. Boase, Librarian), 103, Chancery Lane, W C.

Inner Temple Library, per Sotheran & Co, 140, Strand, W.C.

Iveagh, Lord, F S A, per Sotheran & Co, 140, Strand, W.C

Johnston, G Harvey, 22, Garscube Terrace, Murrayfield, Edinburgh, per
W & A K. Johnston, 5, White Hart Street, Warwick Lane, E C.

Kildare Street, Club, Dublin.

King's Inns Library, Dublin, per Hodges, Figgis & Co., Dublin

Larpent, Frederic de H , 11, Queen Victoria Street, E C

Lawton, William F , Librarian, Public Libraries, Hull

Lea, J Henry, 18, Somerset Street, Boston, Mass , U S A

Lee, W D , Seend, Melksham

Leeds Library (Charles W Thonger, Librarian), Commercial Street, Leeds

Lincoln's Inn Library (A F Etheridge, Librarian), W C

Lindsay, Leonard C C , 87, Cadogan Gardens, S W

Lindsay, W A , K C , F S A , Windsor Herald, College of Arms, E C

Littledale, Willoughby A , F S A , 26, Cranley Gardens, S W

Loraine, Sir Lambton, Bt , 7, Montagu Square, W

Macdonald, W R , Carrick Pursuivant, Midpath, Weston Coates Avenue, Edinburgh

Mackenzie, Sir E M , Bt , Naval & Military Club, Melbourne, Australia

MacLehose & Sons, J , 61, St Vincent Street, Glasgow

Macmillan & Bowes, Cambridge

Maddison, Rev Canon, F S A , Vicars' Court, Lincoln

Magrath, Rev John Richard, D D , Queen's College, Oxford

Malcolm, J W Hoveton Hall, Norwich

Manchester Free Library, per J E Cornish, 16, St Ann's Square, Manchester

Marshall, George W , L L D , F S A , Sarnesheld Court, Weobley, R S O

Marshall, Julian, 13, Belsize Avenue, N W

Marsham-Townshend, Hon Robert, F S A , Frognal, Foots Cray, Kent

Maskelyne, Anthony Story, Public Record Office, Chancery Lane, W C

Mitchell Library (F T Barrett, Librarian), 21, Miller Street, Glasgow.

Montagu, Col H , 123, Pall Mall, S W

Moseley, Sir O , Rolleston Hall, Burton-on-Trent

Murray, Keith W , F S A , 37, Cheniston Gardens, Kensington, W

Myddelton, W M , Spencer House, St Albans

National Library of Ireland, Dublin, per Hodges, Figgis & Co, Dublin

National Portrait Gallery, per Eyre & Spottiswoode, 5, Middle New Street, E C

Newberry Library, Chicago, per H Grevel & Co , 33, King Street, Covent Garden, W C

Nudd, W A., Bookseller, 2, The Haymarket, Norwich.

O'Connell, Sir Ross., Killarney, per Bickers & Son, 1, Leicester Square, W C

Office of Arms, Dublin Castle, Ireland

Oxford & Cambridge Club, Pall Mall, per Harrison & Sons, 59, Pall Mall, S W

Parker & Co , J , Booksellers, 27, Broad Street, Oxford

Paul, Sir James Balfour, Lyon King of Arms, 30, Heriot Row, Edinburgh

Penfold, Hugh, Rustington, Worthing

Phillimore, W P W , 124, Chancery Lane, W C

Pixley, F W , per Sotheran & Co , 140, Strand, W C

Public Record Office, per Eyre and Spottiswoode, 5, Middle New Street, E C

Ramden, J C , Willinghurst, Guildford, Surrey

Ramsay, Sir James H , Bt , Banff, Alyth, N B

Reform Club, Pall Mall, per Jones, Yarrell & Poulter, 8, Bury Street, S W.

Rich, Sir Charles H Stuart, Bt , F S A , Devizes Castle

Richardson, W H , F S A , 2, Lansdown Place, Russell Square, W C

Rimell & Son , J , Booksellers, 91 Oxford Street, W (2)

Royce, Rev David, Nether Swell Vicarage, Stow on Wold, Gloucestershire (2)

Rye, Walter, St Leonard's Priory, Norwich

Rylands, J Paul, F S A , 2, Charlesville, Birkenhead

Rylands Library, The John, Manchester, per Sotheran & Co , 140, Strand, W C

Rylands, W H , F S A , 37, Great Russell Street, Bloomsbury, W C

Schomberg, Arthur, Seend, Melksham

Scott-Gatty, A S , F S A , York Herald and Acting Registrar, College of
    Arms, E C

Seton, Bruce Maxwell, Bt , Durham House, Chelsea, S W

Shadwell, Walter H L , F S A , Trewollack, Bodmin

Shaw, W A , 3, Rusthall Park, Tunbridge Wells

Shelley, Spencer, 37, Bathwick Hill, Bath

Sherborne, Lord, 9, St James's Square, S W

Simpkin Marshall, Hamilton, Kent, & Co , Ltd , 4, Stationers' Hall
    Court, E C

Smith, J Challenor, F S A , Whitchurch, Oxon (2)

Sotheran & Co , 140, Strand, W C (9)

Stevens, Son, & Stiles, Booksellers, 39, Great Russell Street, W C

Stewart, C P , Chesfield Park, Stevenage

Strange, Hamon le, Hunstanton Hall, Norfolk

Stoddart, A R , Fishergate Villa, York

St Leger, James, White's Club, St James's Street, S W

Tempest, Sir Robert T , Bt , Tong Hall, Drighlington, Bradford, Yorks

Tenison, C M , Hobart, Tasmania

Thompson, W N , St Bees, Cumberland.

Tooke Hales J B, Copdock, Ipswich
Toynbee, Paget, Dorney Wood, Burnham, Bucks
Turnbull, Alex H per Sotheran & Co, 140, Strand, W C

United University Club, 1, Suffolk Street, Pall Mall East, London

Wedderburn, Alexander, K C, 47, Cadogan Place, S W
Weldon, William H, F S A, Norroy, College of Arms, London, E C
Were, Francis, Gratwicke Hall, Flax Bourton, Somerset, per George's Sons,
    Bristol
Wilson, Sir S M, Fitzjohn, near Rugby
Wood, F A, Highfields, Chew Magna, Somerset, per George's Sons, Bristol
Wood, H J T, Fingest Cottage, near High Wycombe, Bucks
Woods Sir Albert W, K C B, F S A, Garter, 69, St George's Road, S W

Yarborough, Countess of 17, Arlington Street, Piccadilly, W, per H
    Sotheran & Co, 140, Strand, W C

l

ABBREVIATIONS

USED IN THIS WORK

Besides those in ordinary use the following may require explanation

admon , administration of the goods of an intestate

ap , apparent.

b , born

bap , baptised

bur , buried.

cr , created

d , died

da , daughter

h , heir

m., married

M I , Monumental Inscription

pr , proved.

s , son.

s p , sine prole

s p.m , sine prole masculo

s p m.s , sine prole masculo superstite

s.p.s , sine prole superstite

suc , succeeded.

Baronetcies of England.

1611—1706.

SECOND PART,

VIZ,

CREATIONS BY CHARLES I

27 March 1625 to 30 Jan 1648/9

The number of Baronetcies of England that had been created by James I was 204, not reckoning therein the Baronetcy of Vavasour, which was in fact created by his successor, 22 June 1631, tho' with *the precedency* of 29 June 1611. James had undertaken that the number should not exceed 200, and, allowing for six which had become extinct, they did not exceed 198 at his death "Charles I, however, had not been long on the throne, when, relying on his royal prerogative as the Fountain of Honour, he disregarded the stipulated limitation of the number of Baronets" [*Her and Gen*, vol iii, p 346]

ASHFIELD, or ASHFEILD

cr. 20 June 1626 ;

ex, apparently, March 1713/4.

I   1626   "JOHN ASHFEILD, of Harkestead Netherhall, co Suffolk, Knt., one of the Gentlemen of the Privy Chamber," s of Sir Robert Ashfield, of the same and of Stow Langtoft,(ª) in the said county, by Anne, da of Sir John TASBURGH, of Flixton, Suffolk, was *b.* about 1597, *Knighted*, at Theobalds, 3 June 1615, suc his father, Oct. 1624, entered his pedigree at the Her Visit of London, 1624, was one of the Gentlemen of the Privy Chamber to Charles I, 1637, and was *cr a Bart.* as aforesaid 20 June 1626, being the first person on whom Charles I conferred that dignity. He *m* (Lic Lond 30 April 1627, he 30 and she 27) Elizabeth, widow of Sir James ALTHAM, of Oxey, Herts, da. and h of Sir Richard SUTTON, one of the Auditors of the Imprest. He *d* 1635. Admon. as of St Botolph, Aldersgate, London 30 Nov 1638. His widow *m* 12 Nov. 1655, at St Giles' in the Fields, Sir Richard MINSHALL, widower.

II. 1635   SIR RICHARD ASHFIELD, Bart. [1626], of Harkestead Netherhall aforesaid, s and h , *b* about 1630, *suc to the Baronetcy* in 1635 He was Sheriff of Gloucestershire, 1668 69 He *m.* firstly, in or before 1654, (—), da. and coh of Sir Richard ROGERS, of Eastwood, co. Gloucester He *m* secondly, 20 Feb 1673/4, at St. Mary Mag , Old Fish street, London (Lic Lond 30 Dec 1673, he 44) Dorcas BURCHETT, widow, da of James HORE, of the Mint, in the Tower of London He *d* about 1684 Will pr 1684

(ª) This Sir Robert sold in 1614 the estate of Stow Langtoft (which had belonged to the Ashfield family from the time of Edward III) to Paul D'EWES, ancestor of the D'Ewes, Barts, of that place.

B

III 1684? Sɪʀ John Ashfield, Bart [1626], of Harkestead
to   Netherhall, and of Eastwood, both aforesaid, s and h. by 1st wife ;
1714   *bap* 8 Dec 1654, at Hillesden, Bucks , *suc to the Baronetcy* about
1684 He *m* Anne, da of James Hore abovenamed, being sister
to his stepmother She was *bur.* 13 Dec 1702, at St Giles' in the Fields. He
was living 1692, as was also his son Charles (a minor of the age of 14), but the
estates had been alienated He was *bur.* 9 March 1713/4, at St Giles' aforesaid,
when apparently the *Baronetcy* became extinct,[a] which, it is stated,[b] to have
been before 1727

HARPUR, or HARPER ·

cr 8 Dec 1626 ;

afterwards, since 1808, Harpur-Crewe

I 1626. " Henry Harper, of Calke, co Derby, Esq," 3d s. of
Sɪʀ John Harpur, of Swarkeston, in that co, by Isabel, da of Sɪʀ
George Pierrepont, of Holme, Notts, which John (who *d* 7 Oct 1622), was s and
h of Richard Harpur, one of the Justices of the Court of Common Pleas (*d*
29 Jan 1573), was *b* about 1585, matric at Oxford (Bras Coll) 20 Feb 1595/6, aged
17 , admitted to the Inner Temple, 1598, and was cᵣ a Bart , as above, 8 Dec 1626
He *m* Barbara, widow of Sɪʀ Henry Beaumont, of Grace Dieu, co Leicester, da of
Anthony Faunt, of Foston, by Elizabeth, da of Andrew Noell, of Dalby, both
in co Leicester He *d* 1638 Will pr 1639 His widow *d* 2 July 1649, aged 69,
and was *bur* at All Saints', Derby. M I.

II 1638 Sɪʀ John Harpur, Bart [1626], of Calke Abbey, in
Calke aforesaid, s and h , *b* about 1616 , *suc to the Baronetcy* in
1638 ; Sheriff of Derbyshire, 1641-42 , was sequestrated and fined £110, from May
1646 He *m* , probably about 1640, Susan, da of (—) West, Citizen of London
He *d* 1669, aged 53 Will pr Feb 1670

III 1669 Sɪʀ John Harpur, Bart. [1626], of Calke Abbey aforesaid, s. and h , *b* probably about 1645 ; matric at Oxford (Queen's
Coll), 26 Oct 1660 , *suc. to the Baronetcy* in 1669 and to the estate of Swarkeston,
co Derby, under the will of his cousin, Sɪʀ John Harpur,[c] of Swarkeston, who
d s p. in 1677 He *m.* 17 Sep 1674, at Swarkeston, Anne, 3d da. of William
(Willoughby), 6th Baron Willoughby of Parham, by Anne, da of Sɪʀ Philip
Carey, of Aldenham, Herts She was *b.* at Stansteadbury, Herts, 15 Dec 1652,
her birth being regd at Hunsdon He *d.* 1681. Will pr. 1681

IV. 1681 Sɪʀ John Harpur, Bart. [1626], of Calke Abbey
aforesaid, s. and h , *b.* 23 March 1679 , *suc to the Baronetcy* in
1681 , mat. at Oxford (Mag Coll) 6 July 1697. Sheriff of Derbyshire, 1702
He *m* , in or before 1709, Catherine, yst. da and coheir of Thomas (Crewe), 2nd
Baron Crewe of Stene, by his 2d wife, Anne, da. and coheir of Sɪʀ William Airmyn,

---

[a] " Richard Ashfield, of St Giles' in the Fields, Esq , Bachr, about 22 "
(evidently a yr. s of the 2d Bart), had lic (Vic Gen) 26 Dec. 1677, to marry " Mrs
Mary Gunning, of St Dunstan's in the West, about 22, spinster " This Richard
mat at Oxford (Mag. Coll), 27 Feb 1673/4, aged 17, as " son of Richard, of Eastwood, co. Glouc., Bart ," and became a Barrister of the Middle Temple, 1682
Among the baptisms at St Giles' are some of the children of Sɪʀ Richard Ashfield
and Dame Dorcas, viz., Thomas, 22 Feb 1674/5 ; Charles, 9 Sep 1676 ; and James,
27 Dec. 1677 Among the burials is that of " Charles Ashfield, Esq ," 14 Sep 1694
[b] In Courthope's as well as in Burke's *Extinct Baronetcies.*
[c] This Sɪʀ John had *m* (Lic Fac 3 June 1661) Frances Willoughby, elder sister
to Anne, the wife of his cousin and devisee, the 3d Bart This lady, afterwards
Countess of Bellomont [I], who probably held the principal part of the Swarkeston
estates for life, *d s p.* 25 May 1714, in her 72d year, and was *bur* at Swarkeston.

2nd Bart [1619]   He *d.* suddenly at Calke Abbey, 24 and was *bur* 30 June 1741, at Calke   Will pr 1741   His widow, who was *bap.* 28 Oct 1682 at St Martin's in the Fields, was *bur.* at Calke, 24 Jan. 1744/5   Will pr. 1745

V. 1741   Sir Henry Harpur, Bart [1626], of Calke Abbey, aforesaid, s and h, *b* about 1709 ; matric at Oxford (Bras. Coll), 10 May 1725, aged 16, *suc. to the Baronetcy,* 24 June 1741, M P for Worcester, 1744 47, and for Tamworth, 1747 till his death   He *m* (Spec Lic Fac 2 Oct. 1734) Caroline, da. of John (Manners), 2nd Duke of Rutland, by his 2d wife, Lucy, da. of Bennet, (Sherard), 2nd Baron Sherard of Leitrim [I]   He *d* 7 June 1748   Admon July 1748   His widow *m.,* 18 July 1753, Sir Robert Burdett, 4th Bart [1619], who *d* 13 Feb. 1797   She *d.* 10 Nov 1769, at Foremark, co Derby   Will pr Jan 1770

VI 1748   Sir Henry Harpur, Bart [1626], of Calke Abbey aforesaid, s and h, *suc to the Baronetcy,* 7 June 1748, M P for Derbyshire 1761-68, and Sheriff, 1774-75   He *m* 17 July 1762, Frances Elizabeth, 2nd da of Francis (Greville), 1st Earl Brooke and Earl of Warwick, by Elizabeth, da of Lord Archibald Hamilton   He *d* 10 Feb 1789   Will pr 1789   His widow, who was *b.* 11 May 1744, *d.* 6 April 1825   Will pr May 1825

VII 1789   Sir Henry Harpur, *afterwards,* since 1808, Harpur-Crewe, Bart. [1626], of Calke Abbey aforesaid, s and h, *b* 13 May 1763 ; matric at Oxford (Ch. Ch) 23 June 1781, aged 17, *suc to the Baronetcy,* 10 Feb 1789.   Sheriff of Derbyshire, 1794-95   By royal lic, 11 April 1808, he took the name of Crewe,[a] being that of his great grandmother, the wife of the 4th Bart   He *m*, 4 Feb 1792, at Calke (spec lic), Anne or Nanny Hawkins, of Calke aforesaid, spinster   He *d* 7 Feb 1819, at his residence, Boreham Wood, Elstree, Herts, owing to an accidental fall from his coach box   Admon. April 1819   His widow *d* 20 March 1827, at East Moulsey Park, Surrey, aged 61   Will pr April 1827.

VIII. 1829   Sir George Harpur-Crewe, Bart [1626], of Calke Abbey aforesaid, s and h., *b.* 1 Feb. 1795, entered Rugby School, 30 May 1806, *suc to the Baronetcy,* 7 Feb 1819, Sheriff of Derbyshire, 1820-21 ; M P for South Derbyshire, 1835-43   He *m.,* 9 Sep 1819, Jane, 1st da of Rev Thomas Whitaker, M A, Vicar of Mendham, Norfolk   He *d* at Calke Abbey, 1 and was *bur* 9 Jan 1844, at Calke.   Will pr July 1844   His widow *d* 10 Feb 1880, aged 81, at 13 Queen's Gate Gardens, Kensington, and was *bur* at Calke

IX 1844   Sir John Harpur-Crewe, Bart [1626], of Calke Abbey aforesaid, s and h., *b* there 18 Nov 1824, ed at Rugby and at Ex Coll Oxford ; matric 16 Nov 1843, aged 18 ; *suc to the Baronetcy,* 1 Jan 1844   Sheriff of Derbyshire, 1853   He *m*, 20 Nov 1845, at St. Geo Han sq, his cousin, Georgiana Jane Henrietta Eliza, 2d da of Vice Admiral William Stanhope Lovell, K.H, by Selina, da of Sir Henry Harpur, *afterwards* Harpur-Crewe, 7th Bart. abovenamed   He *d.* 1 March 1886, after a lingering illness, at Calke Abbey, in his 62d year.   His widow living 1900

X 1886   Sir Vauncey Harpur-Crewe, Bart [1626], of Calke Abbey aforesaid, 1st s and h, *b* 14 Oct. 1846, *suc to the Baronetcy,* 1 March 1886   He *m*, 20 April 1876, at Lea Marston, co Warwick, Isabel, 6th and yst da of Charles Bowyer (Adderley), 1st Baron Norton, by Julia Anna Eliza, da of Chandos (Leigh), 1st Baron Leigh of Stoneleigh.   She was *b* 28 Oct. 1852

Family Estates —These, in 1883, consisted of 14,256 acres in Staffordshire, 12,923 in Derbyshire, and 877 in Leicestershire   *Total,* 28,050 acres, worth £36,366 a year   *Principal Residences* —Calke Abbey, Repton Park, and Warslow Hall (near Ashbourne), all in co. Derby.

---

[a] The lic is to take the name of Crewe *only* and to bear the arms of Crewe quarterly with those of Harpur.

SEBRIGHT, or SEABRIGHT

cr 20 Dec. 1626

I   1626   "EDWARD SEABRIGHT, of Besford, co. Worcester, Esq,"
s and h of John SEBRIGHT,(ᵃ) of Blackshall in Wolverley, in that
county, by Anne, da of Richard BULLINGHAM, was b about 1585, matric at Oxford
(Bras Coll), 11 Dec 1601, aged 16, suc his uncle, William SEBRIGHT (Town Clerk
of London, 1573 1612, M P for Droitwich, 1572 83), in the estate of Besford,
27 Oct 1620; was Sheriff of Worcestershire, 1621, and was cr a Bart, as above,
20 Dec 1626, being subsequently,(ᵇ) 10 April 1627, Knighted at Whitehall   He was
a faithful Royalist, and was fined £1,809 by the sequestrators accordingly.   He m
firstly, in or before 1611, Theodocia, da of Gerard WHORWOOD, of Compton, co
Stafford, by Dorothy, da and h of Edward BARBOUR, of Flashbrook   He m
secondly, in or after 1638, Elizabeth, widow of Sir Lewis MANSEL, 2nd Bart [1611],
of Margam, da of Henry (MONTAGU), 1st EARL OF MANCHESTER, by his first wife
Catharine, da of Sir William SPENCER, of Yarnton, Oxon   She d before him   His
admon 11 Feb 1657/8 and 20 Feb 1669

II   1658?   SIR EDWARD SEBRIGHT, Bart [1626], of Besford Court,
in Besford aforesaid, 1st surv s and h (ᶜ) by second wife, b about
1645(ᵈ), suc to the Baronetcy about 1658, matric at Oxford (St John's Coll), 13 Sep
1661, aged 16, cr M A 9 Sep 1661   He m (Lic Lond 15 Feb 1664/5, he 20 and
she 15) Elizabeth, da of Sir Richard KNIGHTLEY, K.B, of Fawsley, co. Northampton,
by 2d wife, Ann, da of Sir William COURTEEN   He d 11 Sep 1679, aged 34, and
was bur. at Besford   His will pr 1679   His widow d. 30 Sep 1685, aged 34   Her
will pr. 1685

III   1679   SIR EDWARD SEBRIGHT, Bart [1626], of Besford Court
aforesaid, s. and h, b 1668, matric at Oxford (Jesus Coll), 7 March
1684/5, aged 17, suc to the Baronetcy, 11 Sep 1679, el Sheriff of Worcestershire,
1685   He m (Lic Lond 24 March 1687/8, he 21 and she 24) Anne, da and h of
Thomas SAUNDERS,(ᵉ) of Beechwood, in Flamsted, Herts, by Ellen, da and h of
Robert SADLEIR, of Sopwell in that county   He d 15 Dec 1702, in his 36th year and
was bur at Besford M I.   Will pr March 1703   His widow, who was b and bap 27
April 1670, at Flamsted, m Charles LYTTELTON (s and h ap of Sir Charles Lyttelton,
3d Bart [1618], of Franckley), who d v p., 16 Aug 1712   She d. 25 Dec. 1718
Will pr. May 1719

IV.   1702.   SIR THOMAS SAUNDERS SEBRIGHT, Bart [1626], of
Beechwood and of Besford Court aforesaid, s and h, b 11 May and
bap 8 June 1692, at Flamsted, matric. at Oxford (Jesus Coll), 3 June 1705, aged 13,
cr M A, 28 April 1708, D C L 19 Aug 1732, having suc to the Baronetcy, 15 Dec.
1702   M P for Herts in four Parls, 1715 till decease   He m. Henrietta, da of Sir
Samuel DASHWOOD, sometime Lord Mayor of London, by Anne, da. of John SMITH, of
Tedworth, Hants   He d 12 and was bur 20 April 1736, at Flamsted   Will pr. 1736.
His widow d 21 and was bur 28 March 1772, at Flamsted.   Will pr March 1772.

V   1736   SIR THOMAS SAUNDERS SEBRIGHT, Bart [1626], of Beechwood and of Besford Court aforesaid, s and h, bap 21 Dec 1723
in London, ed at Westminster School, matric at Oxford (Ch Ch), 10 Feb
1741/2, aged 18, suc to the Baronetcy, 12 April 1736   He d unm 30 Oct, and was
bur. 4 Nov 1761 at Flamsted   Admon 12 Dec 1761

(ᵃ) See Clutterbuck's Herts, vol 1, p. 362
(ᵇ) See vol. 1, p 18, note "c," sub "Tollemache."
(ᶜ) Of his two elder brothers of the half blood (William and John), John was aged
16 in 1627
(ᵈ) He was under age, (his uncle, the Earl of Manchester, being his "curator,")
11 Feb 1657/8, but had attained full age 20 April 1669
(ᵉ) See pedigree in Clutterbuck's Herts, vol 1, p 362, and see also notes in Playfair's Baronetage, under Sebright, as to the families of Saunders and Sadleir

VI. 1761   SIR JOHN SEBRIGHT, Bart [1626], of Beechwood and of
Besford Court aforesaid, br aud h, *bap* 19 Oct 1725 at Flamsted,
ed at Westminster School, *suc to the Baronetcy*, 30 Oct 1761, Colonel of the
18th Regt. of Foot, Lieut Gen in the army, M P for Bath in three Parls 1763 68
He m, 15 May 1766, at St Geo Han sq, Sarah, 3d da of Edward KNIGHT, of
Wolverley, co Worcester, by Elizabeth, da of (—) JAMES of Olton End, co Warwick.
He *d*. 23 Feb, and was *bur* 4 March 1794, at Flamsted Will pr. March 1794 His
widow was *bur*. there 4 Jan 1813 Will pr 1813

VII 1794   SIR JOHN SAUNDERS SEBRIGHT, Bart [1626], of Beechwood and of Besford Court aforesaid, s and h, *b* 23 May 1767 in
Sackville street, St James' Westm, *suc to the Baronetcy*, 23 Feb 1794, M P for
Herts in eight Parls 1807-35; Sheriff of Herts, 1797-98. He *m*, 6 Aug 1793, Harriet,
only da and h of Richard CROFTS, of West Harling, Norfolk, by Harriet, da and
coh of John DARELL, of York street, St James' Westm She *d* Aug 1826
Will pr March 1827 He *d* 15 April 1846 Will pr July 1846

VIII 1846.   SIR THOMAS GAGE SAUNDERS SEBRIGHT, Bart. [1626], of
Beechwood and of Besford Court aforesaid, only s and h *b*. 1802,
suc to the Baronetcy, 15 April 1846 He *m* firstly, 17 Nov 1842, Sarah Anne, 2d
da of (—) HOFFMAN, Capt, R N. She *d*. 14 Feb 1846 He *m*. secondly, in 1850,
Olivia, yst da of John Joseph HENRY, of Straffan, co Kildare, by Emily Elizabeth,
da of William Robert (FITZGERALD), 2d DUKE OF LEINSTER [I] She *d* 27 June
1859, in Wilton crescent, aged 44 He *d* 29 Aug. 1864, at Beechwood, aged 62

IX 1864   SIR JOHN GAGE SAUNDERS SEBRIGHT, Bart [1626], of
Beechwood and of Besford Court aforesaid, s. and h by 1st wife; *b*
20 Aug 1843, in Paris, Ensign 4th Herts Rifle Volunteers, 1860, matric at Oxford
(Ch Ch), 23 May 1861, aged 17, *suc to the Baronetcy*, 29 Aug 1864, Sheriff of
Herts, 1874, Hon Major in the Beds Militia, 1881 He *m*, 27 Aug 1865, Olivia
Amy Douglas, yst da of John Wilson (FITZPATRICK), 1st BARON CASTLETOWN, by
Augusta, only da of Rev Archibald Edward DOUGLAS, Rector of Cootehill, Ireland
He *d* 15 Nov. 1890, at Caddington Hall, Beds, aged 47. His widow *d* 22 May 1895,
at 101 Eaton Place, Midx

X 1890.   SIR EGBERT CECIL SAUNDERS SEBRIGHT, Bart [1626],
of Beechwood aforesaid, only s aud h., *b*. 12 June 1871 in
Chesham place, Midx., *suc to the Baronetcy*, 15 Nov 1890 He *d*, unm, off
Batavia, Java, 1 April and was *bur* 5 June 1897, at Flamsted, aged 25

XI. 1897   SIR EDGAR REGINALD SAUNDERS SEBRIGHT, Bart
[1626], of Beechwood aforesaid, uncle and h, being 2d s (1st s by
the 2d wife) of the 8th Bart, *b*. 27 May 1854; ed at Eton and at Mag Coll,
Oxford, matric 24 Jan 1874, aged 19, sometime Col 4th Batt Beds Militia,
Equerry to H R H the Duchess of Teck, *suc to the Baronetcy*, 1 April 1897

Family Estates.—These, in 1883, consisted of 3,886 acres in Herts; 2,929 in
Worcestershire, 394 in Beds, aud 1 (worth £736 a year) in Surrey *Total*, 7,210
acres, worth £13,567 a year *Residences*—Beechwood, near Dunstable, Herts, and
Besford Court, near Pershore, co Worcester

BEAUMONT.

cr 31 Jan 1626/7,

ex 7 July 1686

I. 1627.   " JOHN BEAUMONT, of Gracedieu [in Belton], co
Leicester, Esq," 2d s, but eventually h male of Francis
BEAUMONT, of Gracedieu Priory, sometime (1592-98) one of the Justices of the
Court of Common Pleas, by Anne, relict of Thomas THOROLD, da of Sir George
PIERREPONT, of Holme Pierrepont, Notts, was *b* about 1582, matric at Oxford
(Broadgates Hall), 4 Feb. 1596/7, aged 14, admitted to Inner Temple, 1598, and suc

to the family estates on the death of his elder br , Sir Henry BEAUMONT, s p m , 13 July 1605, and was *cr. a Bart.*, as above, 31 Jan 1627/8. He was a poet of some merit [a] He *m.* Elizabeth, da of John FORTESCUE He was *bur.* 19 April 1627[b], in Westm Abbey Admon. 3 Jan. 1628/9 His widow was living 16 April 1652

II 1627   SIR JOHN BEAUMONT, Bart. [1627], of Gracedieu Priory aforesaid, s and h , *b.* 21 June 1607 , *suc to the Baronetcy* in April 1627 He, who was a man of extraordinary strength, was a Col in the Army, distinguishing himself in the royal cause He *d.* unm , being slain at the siege of Gloucester, in Sep. 1643 Limited Admon 27 April 1652

III 1643,   SIR THOMAS BEAUMONT, Bart [1627], of Gracedieu
to   Priory aforesaid, br and h , *b.* 29 April 1620 , *suc to the Baronetcy* in
1686   Sep 1643 , was fined £1,190 on 25 Dec 1649 He *m.* Vere, only da of Sir William TUFTON, 1st Bart [I 1622], of Vintners, co Kent, by Anne, da of Cecil CAVE, of Leicestershire He *d* s p m [c], 7 July 1686, aged 66, when the *Baronetcy* became *extinct* His widow *m* George LANE

DERING : [b]

cr 1 Feb. 1626/7

I 1627   " EDWARD DERING, of Surrenden, co Kent, Knt ," s and
h ap of Sir Anthony DERING, of Surrenden Dering, in Pluckley, co. Kent, Deputy Lieut of the Tower of London, by his 2d wife, Frances, da of Sir Robert BELL, Lord Chief Baron of the Exchequer, was *b* 28 Jan 1598, in the Tower of London , ed at Mag Coll, Cambridge ; was *Knighted*, 22 Jan 1618/9, at New market, and was *cr a Bart* , as above, 1 Feb 1626/7 He suc. his father in 1636 , was Lieut of Dover Castle , M P for Hythe, 1629, and for Kent, 1640, till disabled, 2 Feb 1642 He, tho' he had presented a bill for extirpating Bishops, Deans and Chapters, joined the King at Oxford, was sent prisoner to the Tower of London suffered sequestration,[d] and was fined He was well known for antiquarian research and his collection of valuable MS. He *m* firstly, 29 Nov. 1619, at St Dionis Backchurch, London, Elizabeth, da of Sir Nicholas TUFTON, 2d Bart [1611], who, in 1628 (six years after her death) was *cr.* EARL OF THANET, by Frances, da. of Thomas (CECIL), 1st EARL OF EXETER She *d* s p.s , 24 Jan 1622 He *m* secondly, Anne, 3d da of Sir John ASHBURNHAM, of Ashburn-ham, Sussex, by Elizabeth,[e] da. of Sir Thomas BEAUMONT, of Staughton, co Leicester. She *d.* 1628 He *m* thirdly, 16 July 1629, also at St Dionis Backchurch, Unton, da of Sir Ralph GIBBES, of Honington, co Warwick, by Gertrude, da of Sir Thomas WROUGHTON He *d.* 22 June 1644, in his 46th year Inq. p m. at Maidstone 8 Aug 1645 Admon 19 Oct 1648, to his son, Sir Edward Dering, Bart His widow was *bur* 10 Nov 1676

II. 1644   SIR EDWARD DERING, Bart [1627], of Surrenden Dering aforesaid, only s and h , by 2d wife , *b.* 8 Nov 1625, at Pluckley ; *suc to the Baronetcy*, 22 June 1644. M P for Kent, 1660 , for East Retford, Nov. 1670 , for Hythe, 1678 79, 1679 81, and 1681 ; was one of the Lords Commissioners of the Navy He *m*, 5 April 1648, at St Bartholomew's the Less, London,

---

(a) Of his poems " for the first time collected and edited " by the Rev. A. B Grosart, 156 copies were printed for private circulation in 1869 in the " Fuller Worthies Library." His younger brother Francis Beaumont is well known as a dramatist

(b) It has been suggested that this date may be erroneous. Anthony A'Wood and others state his death to have been " in the winter time of 1628."

(c) See as to his five married daughters and coheirs in Nichols' *Leicestershire*, vol iii, p 640, where also is a good account of Gracedieu Priory.

(d) In Wotton's *Baronetage*, vol ii, p 17, etc , is an interesting account of his tergiversations, and a spirited letter in defence of his conduct

(e) This Elizabeth, afterwards wife of L Ch. Justice Sir Thomas Richardson, was (in his lifetime) in 1628 *cr.* Baroness Cramond [S]

Mary, da of Daniel HARVEY,[a] of Coombe in Croydon, Surrey, and of Folkestone, by Elizabeth, da of Henry KYNNERSLEY, of London, merchant He *d* 24 and was *bur.* 28 June 1684 at Pluckley Will dat 24 Feb 1682/3, pr 4 July 1684 His widow, who was *bap* 3 Sep. 1629 at St. Lawrence, Pountney, London, *d* 7 and was *bur* 12 Feb 1703/4 at Pluckley, M I

III   1684.   SIR EDWARD DERING, Bart [1627], of Surrenden Dering aforesaid, s. and h., *b* 1650 , *suc.* to the *Baronetcy*, 24 June 1684 , M P. for Kent, 1678-79, 1679-81, and 1681 He *m* Elizabeth, sister and coh. of Sir Hugh CHOLMELEY, 3d Bart. [1641], 1st da of Sir William CHOLMELEY, 2d Bart , of Whitby, by his 2d wife, Catharine, da of John SAVILE, of Methley, co York He *d* 1689, aged 39, and was *bur* at Pluckley. His widow *d.* 1704, aged 47, and was *bur* there Will pr Dec. 1704

IV   1689   SIR CHOLMELEY DERING, Bart. [1627], of Surrenden Dering aforesaid, s and h , *b.* 23 June, and *bap* 16 July, 1697, at Pluckley , *suc* to the *Baronetcy*, 24 June 1684; matric at Oxford (New Coll), 4 Feb 1696/7, aged 17 , admitted to Middle Temple 1696 M P for Kent, 1705-08 , for Saltash, 1708-10, and for Kent again, 1710-11 He *m.*, 17 July 1704, at St Andrew's, Holborn, Mary, only da and h. of Edward FISHER, of Fulham, co Midx He *d* 9 May 1711, being killed by Richard Thornhill in a duel[b] at Tothill Fields, Westminster Will dat 11 Nov 1707, pr 1 July 1711.

V.   1711   SIR EDWARD DERING, Bart. [1627], of Surrenden Dering aforesaid, s and h , *b* about 1706 , *suc.* to the *Baronetcy*, 9 May 1711 , matric. at Oxford (Oriel Coll), 31 Jan 1721/2, aged 15 , *cr.* M A. 17 Dec 1725 , D C L 3 July 1759 ; M P for Kent in three parls , 1733-54 He *m.* firstly, 24 Feb 1727/8, at St. Geo the Martyr, Queen sq , Midx Mary, da and coh of Edward HENSHAW, of Well Hall in Eltham, Kent, by Elizabeth, da. of Edward ROPER[c], of Well Hall aforesaid and of St. Dunstan's, Canterbury She *d* March 1734/5, and was *bur* at Pluckley He *m.* secondly, 11 Sep 1735, at St Anne's, Soho, Mary (" £30,000 ") widow of Henry MOMPESSON, 1st da and coh of Charles FOTHERBY, Capt R N , of Barham Court, Kent, by Mary, da of George ELCOCKE[d] He *d.* 15 April 1762 Will pr. April 1762, June 1821, May 1835, and Oct. 1843.

VI   1762   SIR EDWARD DERING, Bart [1627], of Surrenden Dering aforesaid, s. and h by 1st wife ; *b.* 28 Sep 1732 , *suc* to the *Baronetcy*, 15 April 1762 ; M P for New Romney (in five parls) He *m* firstly, 8 April 1755, Selina, sister of the half blood and coheir of Sir Henry FURNESE, 3rd Bart [1707], 2d da and coh of Sir Robert FURNESE, 2d Bart , of Waldeshere, Kent, by his 3d wife, Selina, da of Robert (SHIRLEY), 1st EARL FERRERS She *d* 29 March 1757 He *m* secondly, 1 Jan 1765, Deborah, only da. of John WINCHESTER, of Nethersole, Kent, formerly a Surgeon in London He *d* 8 Dec. 1798 Will pr. Dec 1798 His widow *d.* 20 March 1818 Will pr. 1818

VII.   1798.   SIR EDWARD DERING, Bart, [1627], of Surrenden Dering aforesaid, s and h by 1st wife, *b.* 16 Feb 1757 , *suc* to the *Baronetcy* 8 Dec. 1798 He *m.*, 16 April 1782, Anne, da of William HALE, of King's Walden, Herts, by Elizabeth, da. of Sir Charles FARNABY, 1st Bart [1726] He *d* 30 June 1811. Will pr 1811. His widow *d* 17 July 1830. Will pr Aug 1830

(a) See Harvey pedigree in *Mis. Gen. et Her.*, 2d s , vol iii, pp. 329-336, where it is added that this Mary is " said to have clandestinely married (c 1646) her father's apprentice, her second cousin William, son of John Halke, but which marriage was (c. 1647) declared null and void "

(b) This was fought with pistols that were discharged within sword's length. Thornhill was found guilty of manslaughter

(c) He, who was well-known as a sportsman, was the last male of the senior line of the Roper family, of which, on his death (by a fall from his horse when hunting), 24 March 1723/4, aged 84, the Lords Teynham then became the representatives An interesting account, among the Dering MSS. in 1719, of the births, deaths, etc , of the Roper family of Eltham, is printed in Sprots' *Chronica* and reproduced (with notes) in *The Genealogist*, N S , vol. xiii, pp 140-144

(d) See an account of the Fotherby family in Playfair's *Baronetage*, under "Dering."

VIII   1811   SIR EDWARD CHOLMELEY DERING, Bart. [1627], of
Surrenden Dering aforesaid, grandson and h, being s. and h of
Edward Dering, by Henrietta, 1st da and coh of Richard NEVILLE, *formerly*
JONES, of Furnace, co Kildare, which Edward last named was 1st s. and h ap of the
7th Bart, but *d* v p 19 Sep 1808, aged 25. He was *b* 19 Nov 1807 at Barham, co
Kent, *suc to the Baronetcy*, 30 June 1811, matric at Oxford (Ch. Ch), 17 Oct. 1827,
aged 19, was M P. for Wexford, 1829-30 and 1830-31, for Romney, 1831, and for
East Kent, 1852-57 and 1863-68   Lieut Col in the East Kent Yeomanry Cavalry,
1861   He *m*, 10 April 1832, at Haydor, co. Lincoln, Jane, 3d da. of William
(EDWARDES), 2d BARON KENSINGTON [I], by Dorothy, da of Richard THOMAS   He
d 1 April 1896, at Surrenden Dering, aged 89   His widow *d*. 1 Sep 1897, at "The
Ashes," Hothfield, Kent, aged 85

IX   1896   SIR HENRY NEVILL DERING, Bart. [1627], of Surrenden
Dering aforesaid, 4th but 1st surv s and h.[a], *b* 21 Sep. 1839,
ed at Harrow, entered the Diplomatic Service 1859, Chargé d'Affairs, at Coburg,
Sec of Legation at Buenos Ayres, 1882, Sec of Embassy at St Petersburg and at
Rome, Consul Gen in Bulgaria, 1892-94, Minister in Mexico since 1894; **C B**,
1896, *suc to the Baronetcy* 1 April 1896, was sometime Major East Kent Yeomanry
Cavalry   He *m* 20 Oct. 1862, Rosa Anne, da of Joseph UNDERWOOD, of London
and of co Kent

Family Estates   These, in 1883, consisted of 7,280 acres in Kent, worth £12,000 a
year.   *Residence*, Surrenden Dering,[b] in Pluckley, near Ashford, co Kent.

KEMP, *or* KEMPE [c]
cr 5 Feb 1626/7 ;
ex 1667.

I   1627,   "GEORGE KEMPE, of Pentlowe, co Essex, Esq," s and h
to   of John KEMP,[c] of the same, and of Colts Hall, in Cavendish,
1667   Suffolk, by Eleanor, da of John DREWE, of Devon, one of the
Exigenters of the Court of Common Pleas, was *bap*. 12 Nov 1602,
at Finchingfield, Essex, *suc* his father (who *d*, aged 48), 7 Jan 1609, and was *cr a
Bart*, as above, 5 Feb 1626/7   He *m* Thomazine, da of (—) BROOKE   He *d*.
s p m,[d] 1667, when the *Baronetcy* became *extinct*. Will dat 30 March 1663, pr.
22 Jan 1666/7   His wife was living March 1663

BRERETON : [?]
cr. 10 March, 1626/7 ;
ex 7 Jan. 1673/4.

I   1627   "WILLIAM BRERETON, of Hanforde, co Chester, Esq,"
s and h of William BRERETON,[e] of Hanforde, Handforth or Honford
aforesaid, by Margaret, da and coh of Richard HOLLAND, of Denton, co. Lancaster,
was *bap* 1604 at Manchester, *suc* his father 18 Feb. 1610, was adm to Gray's
Inn, 29 Jan 1622/3, and was *cr a Bart*, as above, 10 March 1626/7; M P
for Cheshire, 1628 29, Apr to May 1640, and 1640-53, a zealous Puritan
and an active supporter of the Parl, on whose side he was, in 1642, Com-in-Chief
of the Cheshire Forces against the King, to whose overthrow in those parts he

---

[a] His eldest br, Edward Cholmeley Dering, sometime an officer in the 88th and
44th foot, *m* twice, but *d* s p and v p, 17 Nov 1874, aged 41.

[b] John Dering, of Westbrooke, Kent, who *d* 1425, lineal ancestor of the
1st Baronet, acquired the estate of Surrenden, by his marriage with Christian, da
and coheir of James Hant, of Pluckley, by Joan, da and h of John Surrenden
[Philpot's *Kent*], and this has been inherited by their posterity ever since   The
5th Baronet enclosed the park with a brick wall about 1750

[c] See J J Howard's *Suffolk Visitation*, 156, vol ii, p 1-8

[d] Of his two daughters and coheirs, the younger *m* Sir John WINTER   The estate
of Pentlowe, however, went to his nephew and h. male John KEMPE, who also *d*. s p m

[e] Pedigree in Ormerod's *Cheshire*, vol. iii, p. 644.

greatly contributed. He was appointed one of the King's Judges, but did not act, was on the Council of State, Feb to Dec 1651, and Dec 1652 to April 1653, and was liberally rewarded by various grants, that of Croydon palace (taken from the Archbishopric of Canterbury) being among them (ª) He m firstly, in or before 1627, Susan, da of Sir George BOOTH, 1st Bart [1611] of Dunham, by his 2d wife, Catharine, da. of L Ch Justice Sir Edmund ANDERSON. She d. May 1637, and was bur at Bowdon, Cheshire He m. secondly, Cicely, widow of Edward MYTTON, da of Sir William SKEFFINGTON, 1st Bart [1627], by Elizabeth, da of Richard DERING Her admon, dat 11 Dec 1649 He d. at Croydon palace, 7 and was removed thence 9 April 1661, for burial at Cheadle (ᵇ) Admon 27 July 1661 Will dat 6 April and pr. 27 July 1661, 12 Oct 1677, and 1 May 1678.

II. 1661, SIR THOMAS BRERETON, Bart. [1627], of Honford aforeto said, only s and h, by 1st wife, b. 1632, being aged 32, in the
1674 Her Visit of Cheshire, 1664; suc to the Baronetcy, 7 April 1661
He m. before 1664, Theodosia, 2d da of Humble (WARD), 1st
BARON WARD OF BIRMINGHAM, by Frances, suo jure, BARONESS DUDLEY He
d. s p, 7 Jan 1673/4, and was bur at Cheadle, when the Baronetcy became
extinct Admon 23 March 1677/8 His widow, who was b at the Wren's nest
house, Dudley, and bap 15 May 1642, at St Edmunds, Dudley, m, before Feb 1677,
Charles BRERETON, was living March 1677/8, and d at Brereton after childbirth,
probably not long afterwards, being bur at Cheadle 18 Jan 1678 [1678/9 ?]

RUSSELL :
cr. 12 March 1626/7 ;
ex. 23 Jan. 1705.

I 1627 "WILLIAM RUSSELL, of Wytley, co. Worcester, Esq,"
s. and h. [i e, b ap] of Thomas RUSSELL, Knt," of Strensham in the
same county, by Elizabeth, da of Sir William SPENCER, of Yarnton, Oxon, was b
about 1602; matric at Oxford (Wad Coll) 12 May 1620, aged 18, admitted to
Middle Temple, 1621; to Gray's Inn, 1631, M P for Worcestershire, 1625, and was
cr a Bart, as above, 12 March 1626/7 He was Treasurer of the Navy, 1631, suc
his father, 29 Dec 1632; Sheriff of Worcestershire, 1635-36 and 1642-43, and was a
zealous supporter of the Royal Cause in the Civil Wars, having to compound with
the Sequestrators for £1 800 besides £50 a year At the Restoration, however, his
estate was valued at £3,000 a year, and he was one of the Knights nominated for
the projected order of "the Royal Oak"(ᶜ) He m in or before 1639, Frances,
sister of Sir John READE, 1st Bart, [1642], da of Sir Thomas READE, of Barton,
Berks, by Mary, da. and coh of Sir John BROCKETT, of Brockett Hall, Herts. He
d. 30 Nov. 1669, and was bur at Strensham. M I Admon 28 Dec. 1669.

II. 1669 SIR FRANCIS RUSSELL, Bart. [1627], of Strensham aforeto said, 1st surv. s and h ;(ᵈ) suc to the Baronetcy, 30 Nov 1669; was
1705. M P for Tewkesbury (six Parls), 1673 90 He entered his pedigree
in the Visit. of Worcestershire, 1683, being then 45 He m. (Lic

(ª) The diary of his travels, 1634-35, in England, Ireland, Holland, and the United Provinces, has been published by the Chetham Society.

(ᵇ) There is no entry in the Cheadle registers of such burial, and the tradition is that in crossing a river the coffin was swept away.

(ᶜ) A list of these proposed knights (687 in number) arranged in counties, is given in Dugdale's Ancient usage of Arms [edit 1812, pp 160-172], as also in Burke's Commoners [edit. 1837, vol. i, pp 688-694] The annual value of Russell's estate, £3,000, is much above the average and, though equalled by one person in his own county (Lyttelton, of Franckley, co. Worcester), is exceeded by but eleven out of the 687 persons, viz, Cornwall, of Herefordshire, £6,000, Knightley, of London, and Stawell, of Somerset, each of which three were £5,000; Boscawen, of Cornwall, Legh, of Lyme, co Chester, Freke, of Dorset, Mostyn, of Flintshire; Hall, of Gloucestershire, Carr, of Lincolnshire, Morgan, of Monmouthshire, and Lowther, of Westmoreland, all eight of which were £4,000

(ᵈ) His eldest br, Thomas Russell, d v.p and s p., and was bur. 1 March 1657/8, at St. Peter's, Paul's Wharf, London.

C

Fac 8 July 1662, he 23 and she 20), Anne, da of Sir Rowland LYTTON, of Knebworth, Herts, by his 1st wife, Judith, da of Sir Humphrey EDWARDS, of London   He *d* s p.m , 24 Jan , and was *bur* 2 Feb 1705/6, at Strensham, aged 68, when the *Baronetcy* became *extinct*   Will pr March 1706   The will of his widow pr. June 1710

CURWEN, *or* CURWENN

cr 12 March 1626/7 ,

ex 1664

I.   1627,   "PATRICK CURWENN, of Workington, co Cumberland,
     to   Esq.," s. and h of Sir Henry CURWEN, of the same, sometime
     1664   (1621-22) M P for Cumberland, by his 1st wife, Catherine, da. and
                   coh of Sir John DALSTON , suc his father in 1623 , was M P for
Cumberland, 1625-26, 1628-29, Apr to May 1640 , Nov 1640 till disabled in March 1644 , and 1661 till death, having been *cr* a *Bart* as above, 12 March 1626/7 , Sheriff of Cumberland, 1636 37   He *m.* Isabel, da and coh of George SELBY, of Whitehouse, co Durham   He *d* s p 1664, when the *Baronetcy* became *extinct* (a)

SPENCER ·

cr 14 March 1626/7 ;

ex Sep 1633

I   1627,   "JOHN SPENCER, of Offley, co. Herts, Esq.," s. and h of
    to   Sir Richard SPENCER, of the same, by Helen, 4th da and coh. of Sir
    1633   John BROCKET, of Brocket Hall in that county (which Richard was
                  4th s of Sir John SPENCER, of Althorpe, co Northampton) ; suc his
father in Nov 1624, and was *cr* a *Bart.* as above, 14 March 1626/7   He *m* , in or before 1618, Mary, da of Sir Henry ANDERSON, Alderman, and sometime [1601-02] Sheriff of London, by Elizabeth, sister of Sir William BOWYER, of Denham, Bucks, da of Francis BOWYER, Alderman, and sometime [1577-78] Sheriff of London. She was *bap.* 29 Feb. 1595/6, at St. Olave's, Jewry, London   He *d* s p m. Aug 1633 and was *bur* at Offley, when the *Baronetcy* became *extinct.*(b)   Funeral certificate at Coll. of Arms.

ESTCOURTE :

cr 17 March 1626/7 ;

ex. about 1684.

I   1627.   "GILES ESTCOURTE, of Newton, co. Wilts, Knt ," s. and
                 h of Sir Edward ESTCOURT, of Salisbury, by Mary, da. of John
GLANVILE, of Tavistock, Devon , was *b* about 1601, matric at Oxford (Wad Coll), 8 May 1618, aged 17 ; admitted to Lincoln's Inn, 1618 , *Knighted* 3 Dec 1622, at Newmarket, Sheriff of Wilts, 1626 27, and was *cr* a *Bart.*, as above, 17 March 1626/7.   He was M P for Cirencester, 1628-29.   He *m* Anne, or Amy, da of Sir Robert MORDAUNT, 2d Bart [1611], by Amy, da of Sir Augustine SOUTHERTON

II.   1650?   SIR GILES ESTCOURT, Bart. [1627], of Newton aforesaid,
                 s and h ; *suc to the Baronetcy* on the death of his father   He *d* unm , about 1676, being slain in Italy.   Admon 2 May 1676

(a) The estates passed to his two brothers in succession, and are still (1900) in possession of the heirs male of the body of the younger one
(b) A fresh Baronetcy was, however, granted, 26 Sep 1642, to his only br and h. male, Brocket Spencer, who succeeded to the Offley estate.

III.　1676?　SIR WILLIAM ESTCOURT, Bart [1627], of Newton aforeto　　said, br. and h , *suc to the Baronetcy* about 1676 He *d* unm.,
1684?　being slain in a duel by Henry St John, at the Globe Tavern,
　　　　St Bride's parish, London, about 1684, when the *Baronetcy* became
extinct　Admon. 23 May 1684.([a])

AYLESBURY
cr 19 April 1627 ,
ex. in 1657

I.　1627,　"THOMAS AYLESBURY, Esq., one of the Masters of Re-
to　　quests,"([b]) s of William AYLESBURY, of St. Andrew's, Holborn, London
1657.　(*d* Dec 1620), by his 1st wife, Anne, da of John POOLE, and niece
to Sir Henry POOLE, of Saperton , was *b* in London 1576 , sometime
Master of the Requests and of the Mint ; and was *cr . a Bart* , as above, 19 April 1627.
He fled to Antwerp after the execution of Charles I, and resided there some years
He *m.* (Lic Lond 3 Oct 1611) Anne, widow of William DARELL (*d* 1610), da and
coh of the Rev Francis DENMAN, Rector of West Retford, Notts (1578-95), by Anne,
relict of Nicholas TOWERS and da of Robert BLOUNT, of Eckington, co Derby.
He *d.* at Breda, 1657, aged 81,([c]) in which year the *Baronetcy* become *extinct*
His widow was *bur* 13 Nov 1661 (in the Hyde vault) in Westm. Abbey.

> II.　1657　WILLIAM AYLESBURY, only surv son, *bap.* 13 July
> 1612, at St Margaret's Lothbury, London. He went out to
> Jamaica, as Secretary to the Governor there, in Cromwell's second expedition,
> and *d.* there s p in 1657, but whether shortly before or shortly after his
> father is not certain In the latter case he would, of course, have *suc. to the
> Baronetcy* for a short time In 1657, however, the *Baronetcy* was *extinct*

STYLE:
cr. 21 April 1627.

I　1627　"THOMAS STYLE, of Watringbury [*i.e.*, Wateringbury],
　　　　co Kent, Esq.," s. and h. of Oliver STYLE,([d]) of the same, Alderman
and sometime (July to Nov 1605) Sheriff of London, by Susanna, da. of John BULL,
of London, was *b* 1587 , matric at Oxford (St. Alban Hall), 18 May 1604, aged 17 ;
admitted to Middle Temple, 1606 ; suc his father, 4 March 1621/2, and was *cr a
Bart* , as above, 21 April 1627 Sheriff of Kent, 1632-33 He *m* , in or before 1615,
Elizabeth, da and sole h of Robert FOLKES, of Mountnessing, co Essex He *d.*
18 Oct. 1637, in St John's lane, Smithfield. Will pr. 1637. Funeral certificate
at Coll of Arms His widow *d* 20 May 1660 Both *bur.* at Wateringbury

　　(a) Granted to Sir John Mordaunt, Bart , a creditor , the sisters of the decd
Amy, wife of Alexander Haddon, and Anne Estcourt renouncing
　　(b) Like the previous creation, of Cottington, 16 Feb. 1622/3, no territorial
description is given to the grantee
　　(c) Out of his five children, Frances, *bap* 25 Aug. 1617, at St. Margaret's, Westminster, *m.* Edward (HYDE), 1st EARL OF CLARENDON, by whom she was grandmother of Mary and Anne, Queens of England
　　(d) This Oliver was younger br of Edmund Style, of Langley in Beckenham,
Kent, grandfather of Sir Humphrey STYLE, of Langley, Bart (so *cr* 20 May 1627),
both being sons of Sir Humphrey STYLE, of Langley aforesaid, one of the Esquires
of the body to Henry VIII.

II. 1637   Sir Thomas Style, Bart. [1627], of Wateringbury aforesaid, only s and h , *b.* in St. John's lane, Smithfield, Christmas 1624 , *suc to the Baronetcy,* 18 Oct 1637 , matric at Oxford (Merton Coll), 15 April 1641, aged 15 , M P for Kent, 1656-58 and 1659. He *m* firstly, Elizabeth, da. of Sir William Airmyne 1st Bart [1619], of Osgodby, co. Lincoln, by his 1st wife, Elizabeth, da. of Sir Michael Hicks   She *d* 10 Dec. 1679, and was *bur* at Wateringbury. M I   He *m* secondly, Margaret, da of Sir Thomas Twisden, 1st Bart. [1666], of Bradbourne, by Jane, da. of John Tomlinson   He *d* 19 Nov 1702, in his 78th year   Will pr. 1703   His widow *d.* 5 Dec. 1718 aged 71 Both *bur.* at Wateringbury. M I.

III. 1702   Sir Oliver Style, Bart [1627], of Wateringbury aforesaid, 4th but 1st surv (a) s. and h , by 1st wife , *suc to the Baronetcy,* 19 Nov. 1702   sometime President in Smyrna   He *d* s p , 12 Feb. 1702/3, aged 42, and was *bur.* at Wateringbury   M I   Admon 15 April 1703

IV   1703   Sir Thomas Style, Bart [1627], of Wateringbury aforesaid, br of the half blood, and h., being s of the 2d Bart , by his 2d wife , *suc. to the Baronetcy,* 12 Feb 1702/3, rebuilt the mansion of Wateringbury , was Sheriff of Kent, 1709-10 , M P for Bramber, 1715, till void 1 June   He *m* Elizabeth, 1st da of Sir Charles Hotham, 4th Bart [1622], by his 1st wife, Bridget, da. of William Gee   She *d* , 25 Oct 1737, in Hanover street Midx , aged 43   He *d.* 11 Jan 1769. Will pr 1769.

V. 1769   Sir Charles Style, Bart [1627], of Wateringbury aforesaid, s and h , an officer in the 5th Regt of Dragoons , *suc to the Baronetcy* 11 Jan 1769   He *m.* 7 March 1770, Isabella, da of Richard (Wingfield), 1st Viscount Powerscourt [I], by his 2d wife Dorothy, da of Hercules Rowley   He *d.* 18 April 1774   Will pr April 1774   His widow *d* 24 Sep 1808

VI   1774   Sir Charles Style, Bart. [1627], of Wateringbury aforesaid, s and h , *suc to the Baronetcy,* 18 April, 1774   He *m.,* 29 March, 1794, Camilla, 1st da of James Whatman, of Vintners, in Boxley, Kent, by his 1st wife, Sarah, da of Edward Stanley Sec to H M 's Customs   He *d* 5 Sep 1804   Will pr 1805, in Prerog Court, Dublin   His widow *d* 17 Sep 1829 Admon Oct. 1829

VII   1804.   Sir Thomas Style, Bart [1627], of Wateringbury aforesaid, s. and h, , ed. at the Royal Military College, Marlow , was sometime Ensign in 1st Foot Guards , *suc to the Baronetcy,* 5 Sep 1804   He *d.* unm in Spain, 5 Nov. 1813   Admon. April 1814

VIII   1813.   Sir Thomas Charles Style, Bart [1627], of Wateringbury aforesaid, br and h , *b* 21 Aug. 1797 , *suc to the Baronetcy,* 5 Nov 1813 , Sheriff of co Donegal, 1824 , M P. for Scarborough, 1837-41   He sold the estate of Wateringbury   He *m* , 28 Oct 1822, Isabella, da of Sir George Cayley, 6th Bart. [1661], of Brompton, by Sarah, da of the Rev George Walker, of Nottingham   He *d* s p s 23 July 1879, at 102 Sydney place, Bath, in his 82d year His widow *d.* 27 Dec. 1882, aged 84

IX   1879.   Sir William-Henry-Marsham Style, Bart [1627], of Glenmore, co Donegal, cousin and h. male, being s. and h. of William Style, of Bicester, Oxon, Capt R N , by Charlotte, da. of the Rev the Hon Jacob Marsham, D.D (yr s of Robert, 2d Baron Romney), which William (who *d.* 24 Feb 1868, aged 82) was 2d s. of the Rev Robert Style, Vicar of Wateringbury and Rector of Mereworth, co Kent (*d.* 5 June 1800), who was yr br of the 5th and son of the 4th Bart. He was *b* 3 Sep 1826, at Kirkby Overblow, co York , ed at Eton and Merton Coll , Oxford ; matric 26 June 1844, aged 17 ; B.A , 1848 ; M.A 1852 , Sheriff for co Donegal, 1856 ; *suc. to the Baronetcy,* 23 July 1879   He *m* firstly, 18 Dec 1848, at Bassaly church, Rosamond Marion, da of Charles Morgan Robinson

(a) His elder br., Thomas Style, *m.* (Lic. Vic. Gen 11 Dec. 1671, he 22 and she 16) Mary, da. of Sir Stephen Langham, but *d.* s p s and v p , 30 Aug. 1672

(MORGAN), 1st BARON TREDEGAR, by Rosamond, da of Gen Godfrey Basil MUNDY She *d.* 15 Jan 1883, at the Mansion house, Brecon, aged 53 He *m* 2dly, 2 June 1885, at St Saviour's, Chelsea, Ellen Catherine, widow of Henry Hyde Nugent BANKES and formerly widow of the Rev. Charles Henry BARHAM, da of Edward Taylor MASSY, of Cottesmore, co Pembroke, by Helen, da of Jonathan PEEL, of Cottesmore aforesaid

Family Estates —These, in 1883, consisted of 39,564 acres in co. Donegal, worth £4,000 a year *Residence* —Glenmore, co Donegal

---

CORNWALLIS, *or* CORNEWALLIS
cr. 4 May 1627,
afterwards, 1661—1852, BARONS CORNWALLIS OF EYE,
subsequently, 1753-1852, EARLS CORNWALLIS,
being sometime, 1792—1823, MARQUESSES CORNWALLIS,
ex 21 May 1852

I. 1627. "FREDERICK CORNEWALLIS, of Broomehall, co Suffolk, Esq," 3d s of Sir William CORNWALLIS, of the same, by his 2d wife Jane, da of Hercules MEWTAS, was *b* 14 March 1610, was, when young, in the household of Henry, and afterwards of Charles, Princes of Wales, suc to the family estates on the death of his elder br (or the half blood), Thomas CORNWALLIS, in 1626, and was, in his 17th year, *cr. a Bart* as above, 4 May 1627, being subsequently (a) *knighted* 30 Dec. 1630 ; M P for Eye, April to May 1640, and Nov 1640 till disabled 23 Sep 1642, and subsequently, M.P for Ipswich, Oct to Dec 1660 Opposing the violent measures of the predominant party, he accompanied the King to Oxford and sat among the members assembled there in Jan 1643/4 He distinguished himself in many of the battles against the rebels, particularly in that of Cropredy bridge, Oxon (30 June 1644), where he rescued Lord Wilmot from being made prisoner His estates were consequently sequestrated, he was fined £800 on 21 Feb 1648, and followed Charles II into exile He *m* firstly, about 1630, Elizabeth, da of Sir John ASHBURNHAM, of Ashburnham, Sussex, by Elizabeth, *suo jure* BARONESS CRAMOND [S.], da of Sir Thomas BEAUMONT She *d.* at Oxford and is said to have been *bur* in Christ Church Cathedral there He *m* secondly, before 1641, Elizabeth, sister (of the half blood) to William, BARON CROFTS OF SAXHAM, da of Sir Henry CROFTS, of Saxham, co Suffolk, by his 2d wife, Elizabeth, da of Sir Richard WORTLEY, of Wortley, co York She (who *d* s p m) was living when he, having accompanied the King in his triumphant entry through London 29 May 1660, was *cr* 20 April 1661 (3 days before the coronation) BARON CORNWALLIS OF EYE, co. Suffolk In that peerage this *Baronetcy* then *merged*, the 5th Baron being *cr* 30 June 1753, EARL CORNWALLIS, and the 2d Earl (6th Baron and Baronet) being *cr* 8 Oct 1792 MARQUESS CORNWALLIS This Marquessate became *extinct* 9 Aug 1823, on the death of the 2d Marquess, but the Baronetcy, together with the Earldom and Barony, continued till 21 May 1852, when on the death of the 5th Earl, 9th Baron and Baronet, it, and the other honours became *extinct* See *Peerage*

DRURY, *or* DRURIE
cr 7 May 1627,
ex 27 April 1712

I 1627 "DRUE DRURIE, of Riddlesworth, co Norfolk, Esq," s. and h of Sir Drue DRURY,(b) of Hedgerley, Bucks, and of Linstead, co. Kent, Gentlemen Usher to Queen Elizabeth, by his 2d wife, Catharine, only da and h of William FINCH, of Linstead aforesaid, was *b* 1588 ; suc. his father (who *d*

(a) See vol i, p. 18, note " c," as to these subsequent Knighthoods.
(b) See pedigree of Drury in J J Muskett's *Suffolk Manorial Families.*

aged 99) in 1617 , was M.P for Norfolk, 1621-22, and for Thetford, 1624-25, and was *cr a Bart*, as above, 7 May 1627   He *m.*, 28 June 1608, Anne, 1st da and coh. of Edward WALDEGRAVE, of Lawford, co Essex, by his 1st wife, (—), da. and h. of Bartholomew AVERELL, of Essex   He *d.* 23 April 1632, and was *bur* at Riddlesworth.   M I   Will dat. 23 Jan. 1630, pr 31 Oct 1632   Inq. p m 23 May 1632, at Bury St. Edmunds   His widow *m* (—) GLEANE, of Hardwick, co Norfolk   Her will pr. May 1642.

II.   1632   SIR DRUE DRURY, Bart. [1627], of Riddlesworth aforesaid, 1st s and h , by 1st wife ; *b* 17 Jan 1611 ; *suc. to the Baronetcy*, 23 April 1632   He was fined £957, reduced to £629   He *m* firstly, Susan, da of Isaac JONES, of London, and sister and coh of Sir Samuel JONES, of Courteen Hall, co Northampton   He *m* secondly, 7 Aug 1641, at Maidstone, Mary, widow of John REYNOLDS, da of John BOYS.   He *d* 13 July 1647.   Admon 29 July 1647, and 1 Jan 1650/1.   His widow *d.* 1649   Will dat 10 Nov 1647, pr. 11 Feb 1650/1.

III   1647   SIR ROBERT DRURY, Bart. [1627], of Riddlesworth aforeto   said, s and h , by 1st wife, *suc to the Baronetcy*, 13 July 1647   He
1712   *m* firstly, Elizabeth, da and h of Edward DUNSTON, of Worlingworth and Waldingfield, co Suffolk, by Elizabeth, da. and eventually heir of John MAYHEW   He *m.* secondly, Eleanor, widow of William MARSHAM, of Stratton, co. Norfolk, da. of Samuel HARSNET, of Great Fransham in that county   She was killed in the hurricane of 1703   He *m.* thirdly, Diana, da of George VILET, of Pinkney Hall, Norfolk   He *d.* s p. 27 April 1712, aged 78, when the *Baronetcy* became *extinct* (ᵃ)   M I at Riddlesworth.   His widow living 1736.

SKEFFINGTON

cr 8 May 1627,

afterwards, 1665-1816, VISCOUNTS MASSEREENE [I],

and subsequently, 1756-1816, EARLS OF MASSEREENE [I],

ex. 25 Feb 1816

I   1627   "WILLIAM SKEFFINGTON, of Fisherwicke, co. Stafford, Esq," s and h of John SKEFFINGTON,(ᵇ) of the same, by Alice, da of Sir Thomas CAVE, of Stanford, co Northampton, was *cr a Bart.* as above, 8 May 1627   He *m.*, in or before 1590, Elizabeth, sister of Sir Anthony DERING, of Surrenden Dering, co Kent, by Margaret, da of William TWYSDEN, of East Peckham in that county   He was *bur*. 16 Sep 1635 at St. Michael's, Lichfield.

II   1635.   SIR JOHN SKEFFINGTON, Bart. [1627], of Fisherwick aforesaid, s. and h , *b.* about 1590, being aged 30 in 1619, was M P. for Newcastle under Lyne, 1626 , *suc to the Baronetcy* in Sep 1635   Sheriff of Staffordshire, 1637-38 , was, in Nov. 1650, fined £1,152, reduced to £961   He *m* Cicely, sister and coh of Sir John SKEFFINGTON, of Skeffington, co. Leicester   He *d* 19 and was *bur* 20 Nov 1651, at Skeffington

III   1651.   SIR WILLIAM SKEFFINGTON, Bart. [1627], of Fisherwick and Skeffington aforesaid, only s and h. , *suc to the Baronetcy*, 19 Nov 1651   He *m* Ursula.   He *d.* s p, and was *bur* 7 April 1652, at Skeffington. Admon. 23 June 1652, to Ursula the relict.

IV.   1652   SIR JOHN SKEFFINGTON, Bart. [1627], of Fisherwick aforesaid, cousin and h , being s. and h of Sir Richard SKEFFINGTON, sometime (1646-47) M P for Staffordshire, by Anne, da. of Sir John NEWDIGATE, of

---

(ᵃ) Diana, his only sister and h , *m* Sir William WAKE, 3d Bart [1621], whose descendants inherited, accordingly, Riddlesworth Hall, co. Norfolk, and Courteen Hall, co Northampton

(ᵇ) This John was great grandson of Sir William Skeffington, the well known Lord Deputy of Ireland, *temp* Hen. VIII

Arbury, co. Warwick, which Richard, who had been *Knighted* 24 Aug 1624, and who *d.* 2 June 1647, was yst s of the 1st Bart He *suc to the Baronetcy* in April 1652, was M P [I], for the town of Antrim, 1659, and for co Antrim, 1661-65 He *m*, 20 July 1654, at St. Paul's, Covent Garden, Mary, only child ot John (CLOTWORTHY), VISCOUNT MASSEREENE [I.], by Margaret, da of Roger (JONES), 1st VISCOUNT RANELAGH [I.], which John had been *cr* Viscount Massereene, 21 Nov 1660, with a spec rem (failing heirs male of his body), to his son-in-law, the said Sir John SKEFFINGTON, who, accordingly, on the Viscount's death, s.p.m., 23 Sep 1665, became VISCOUNT MASSEREENE [I] In that peerage, consequently, this *Baronetcy* became *merged*, the 5th Viscount being *cr* EARL OF MASSEREENE [I], which Earldom, together with this *Baronetcy* became *extinct* on the death of the 4th Earl, 8th Viscount and 11th Baronet, 25 Feb. 1816, though the Viscountcy (according to the spec rem in its creation) devolved on his da and heir as heir general

---

CRANE [7]
cr 11 May 1627.
ex. Feb 1642/3

I   1627,   "ROBERT CRANE, of Chilton, co. Suffolk, Knt," s of
to   Robert Crane, of the same (*d* 12 Sep. 1591), by Bridget, da of Sir
1643   Thomas JERMYN, of Rushbrooke in that county, was *Knighted* at
Newmarket, 27 Feb 1604/5, was M P for Sudbury, 1614; for Suffolk, 1621-22, for Sudbury (again) 1624-25 and 1625, for Suffolk (again) 1626 and for Sudbury (again) 1628-29, April to May 1640, and Nov. 1640 till decease, having been *cr. a Bart.*, as above, 11 May 1627, Sheriff of Suffolk, 1631-32 He *m* firstly, 19 Jan. 1606/7, at St. Anne's, Blackfriars, London, Dorothy, 1st da of Sir Henry HOBART, 1st Bart [1611], Lord Chief Justice of the Common Pleas, by Dorothy, da of Sir Robert BELL. She, who was *b.* 14 March 1591/2, *d.* 11 and was *bur.* 13 April 1624, at Chilton He *m* secondly, 21 Sep 1624, at Chilton, Susan da. of Sir Giles ALINGTON, of Horseheath, co Cambridge, by Dorothy, da of Thomas (CECIL), 1st EARL OF EXETER He *d.* s p m,[a] in London, 17 Feb 1642/3, and was *bur.* at Chilton, aged 58, when the *Baronetcy* became *extinct* Will dat 13 and pr 23 Feb 1642/3. His widow *m* Isaac APPLETON, of Waldingfield Parva, co. Suffolk She was *bur.* 14 Sep 1681, at Chilton Her will, dat 18 Aug 1676, pr in Arch Court of Sudbury

---

BRYDGES, *or* BRIDGES : [b]
cr. 17 May 1627,
afterwards, 1676-1789, BARONS CHANDOS OF SUDELEY,
subsequently, 1714-89, EARLS OF CARNARVON,
and finally, 1719-89, DUKES OF CHANDOS ;
ex. 29 Sep. 1789

I.   1627.   "GILES BRIDGES, of Wilton, co Hereford, Esq ," s and h
of the Hon Charles BRYDGES, of Wilton Castle in Bridstow in the said county, by Jane, da. of Sir Edward CARNE, of Ewenny, co Glamorgan, which Charles (who *d* at a great age, 9 April 1619, being 3d but 2d surv s of John, 1st BARON CHANDOS OF SUDELEY) was, presumably, the " Giles Brugges, of co Gloucester, Arm. fil," who matric. at Oxford (St. Alban Hall), 27 Nov 1590, being then aged 17, was M P. for Tewkesbury, 1621 22; for Herefordshire, 1625-29, Sheriff of Herefordshire, 1625-26, and was *cr a Bart.*, as above, 17 May 1627. He *m* Mary, da of Sir James SCUDAMORE, of Holme Lacy, co Hereford, by Anne da of Sir Thomas THROCKMORTON She *d* before Sep. 1634 and was *bur.* at Peterstowe, co Hereford He *d.* 12 Sep 1637 and was *bur.* there Will dat 4 Sep. 1634, pr 22 Nov. 1637. Inq p.m. 31 Oct 1637.

---

[a] Of his four daughters and coheirs (1) Mary *m.* Sir Ralph HARE 1st Bart [1641]; (2) Jane *m.* firstly, 28 Aug. 1649, at Chilton, Sir William AIRMYNE, 2d Bart [1619], and secondly, John (BELASYSE), 1st Baron Belasyse of Worlaby; (3) Susan *m* Sir Edward WALPOLE, K B, and (4) Katherine *m.* Sir Edmund BACON, 4th Bart. [1611].

II. 1637   SIR JOHN BRYDGES, Bart [1627], of Wilton Castle aforesaid s and h , b 1623, matric at Oxford (Bras Coll), 4 May 1638,
aged 14 , suc to the Baronetcy, 12 Sep 1637. His castle at Wilton having been burnt
by the Royalists he took part with their opponents and was instrumental in the
surprise of Hereford by the Parl army He m Mary, only da. and h of James
PEARLE, of Dewsal and Aconbury, co Hereford. He d of the small pox, in Bridges
street, Covent Garden, Midx , 21 Feb 1651/2, and was bur at Peterstowe aforesaid, aged
29 Admon 10 March 1651/2 His widow m , as his 1st wife, Sir William POWELL,
otherwise HINSON, Bart (so cr 23 Jan 1660/61), of Pengethly, co Hereford, who d.
1681 She was bur at Aconbury aforesaid

III 1652   SIR JAMES BRYDGES, Bart [1627], of Aconbury aforesaid,
only s and h , b Sep 1642 , suc to the Baronetcy, 21 Feb 1651/2 ,
matric at Oxford (St. John's Coll), 15 June 1657 , Sheriff of Herefordshire, 1667-68
He m before 1673, Elizabeth, 1st da and coh of Sir Henry BARNARD, of
London, by Emma, da of Robert CHARLTON, of Whitton Court, Salop She was
living, when, on 22 Aug 1676, he suc. on the death of his cousin to the peerage as
8th BARON CHANDOS OF SUDELEY (a Barony cr. 8 April 1554), taking his
seat as such, 15 Feb 1676/7 In that peerage this Baronetcy continued merged ,
the 9th Baron being cr., 19 Oct. 1714, EARL OF CARNARVON, etc , and,
subsequently, 29 April 1719, DUKE OF CHANDOS, etc By the death, 29 Sep
1789, of James, 3d Duke of Chandos, 11th Baron Chandos of Sudeley, and 6th
Baronet, this Baronetcy and all other the said peerage honours became extinct

---

COLEPEPER, or COLEPEPYR
cr 17 May 1627 ,
ex 18 May 1723.

I 1627.   "WILLIAM COLEPEPYR, of Prestonhall [in Aylesford], co
Kent, Esq ," s and h of Sir Thomas COLEPEPER, of the same, by
Mary, da of Thomas PYNNER, of Mitcham, Surrey, Chief Clerk comptroller to Queen
Elizabeth ; was b about 1588 , suc his father, 12 Oct 1604 ; matric at Oxford (St
Alban Hall) 31 Oct. 1606, aged 18 , B A , 11 May 1609 , admitted to Gray's Ion,
1611, and was cr. a Bart, as above, 17 May 1627 ; Sheriff of Kent, 1635 36. He
m Helen, 1st da of Sir Richard SPENCER, of Offley, Herts, by Helen, da of Sir
John BROCKET, of Brocket Hall in that county He d 1651 Will dat 23 Dec.
1648, pr. 5 Nov 1651. The will of his widow, dat 10 Oct 1663, pr. 19 Feb 1678

II 1651.   Sir RICHARD COLEPEPER, Bart [1627], of Prestonhall
aforesaid, s. and h. , suc. to the Baronetcy in 1651 He m , in or
before 1653, Margaret REYNOLDS. He was bur. 10 Jan. 1659/60, at Aylesford Will
pr Sep 1660 His widow was bur. there 26 Sep 1691

III 1660,   SIR THOMAS COLEPEPER, Bart [1627], of Prestonhall
to   aforesaid, only surv s and h , b about 1657 , suc to the Baronetcy,
1723   in Jan 1659/60, matric at Oxford (Mag. Hall), 15 June 1672, aged
15 , Sheriff of Kent, 1703-04 ; M P for Maidstone, in five Parls,
1705-13, and , 1715, till his death He m. Elizabeth (—), of (—). She was bur.
5 Feb 1708, at Aylesford He d. s p (a) at Prestonhall, 18 and was bur. 24 May
1723, at Aylesford, when the Baronetcy became extinct (b) Will dat 16 Feb 1710/1,
pr 27 May 1723

(a) Alice, his sister and sole h , m , for her 4th husband, John MILNER, M D., on
whom she settled Preston Hall She d. s p 1734, and her said husband devised the
estate to the Milner family

(b) The burial, in the Temple church, London, 2 April 1663, of " Sir Cheney Culpeper, Bart. [sic], of the Middle Temple," refers, apparently, to Sir Cheney Colepeper,
of Hollingbourne, co. Kent, Knt , whose admon (to a creditor) is dat 19 Dec. 1666
and 10 March 1690/1.

WINGFIELD, *or* WINGFEILD:
cr. 17 May, 1627;
ex soon after 1727.

I. 1627.   " ANTHONY WINGFEILD, of Godwyns, co. Suffolk, Esq.,"
only s and h of Sir Thomas WINGFIELD, of Letheringham. in that
county, by his 2d wife, Elizabeth, da of Sir Drue DRURY, of Riddlesworth, was *b.*
about 1585 ; suc. his father 22 Jan 1609, and was *cr a Bart*, as above, 17 May 1627.
He was Sheriff of Suffolk, 1637-38   He *m.* Anne, da of Sir John DEANE, of Deane's
Hall, in Great Maplestead, co. Essex, by Anne, da. of Sir Drue DRURY, abovenamed
He *d.* 30 July 1638, aged 53.   Fun certif in Coll of Arms   The will of his widow
pr May 1642.

II. 1638   SIR RICHARD WINGFIELD, Bart [1627], of Letheringham
aforesaid, and of Easton, s and h ; *suc. to the Baronetcy*, 30 July 1638
He *m.* firstly, 11 June 1649, at St Dionis, Backchurch, London, Susanna, da of Sir
John JACOB, 1st Bart [1665], by his 1st wife, Elizabeth, da of John HALLIDAY. He
m secondly, Mary, da of Sir John WINTOUR, of Lidney, co Gloucester, by Mary, da.
of Lord William HOWARD, s. of Thomas, DUKE OF NORFOLK. He *d.* about 1656.
Admon 28 Dec 1656. The will of his widow pr. 1657.

III. 1656?   SIR ROBERT WINGFIELD, Bart. [1627], of Letheringham
aforesaid, 1st s. and h., by 1st wife, *b* about 1652; *suc to the
Baronetcy* about 1656   He *d.* abroad at Strasbourg a minor and unm about 1671
Admon. 17 July 1671, 14 Feb 1671/2, and 18 May 1678

IV. 1671?   SIR HENRY WINGFIELD, Bart [1627], of Easton, co Suffolk
and Letheringham aforesaid, br (of the half blood) and h, being s of
the 2d Bart. by his 2d wife, was *b* about 1655 ; *suc. to the Baronetcy* about 1671. He
m Mary, da of Mervyn (TOUCHET) 4th EARL OF CASTLEHAVEN [I], by Mary, da of
John (TALBOT), EARL OF SHREWSBURY   She *d* 15 Oct 1675, and was *bur* at East
Soham, Suffolk. M I   He *d* abroad in Lorraine, 1677. Admon. 23 June 1677

V 1677.   SIR HENRY WINGFIELD, Bart. [1627], of Letheringham
aforesaid, s. and h ; *b.* about 1673 ; *suc. to the Baronetcy* in 1677.
He sold the estate of Letheringham,(a) and followed James II to France after his
expatriation   He *m.* (—) GUARIGUES, of Toulouse. He *d.* abroad, s p, 1712.

VI. 1712,   SIR MERVYN WINGFIELD, Bart. [1627], br and h. , *b.*
to   about 1675 ; *suc to the Baronetcy* in 1712   He *m* Mary, da. of
1730?   Theobald DALTON, of Greenan, co Westmeath   He *d* s p m (b) after
(probably not long after) 1727, when the *Baronetcy* became *extinct*

KYRLE, *or* KIRLE:
cr. 17 May 1627;
ex. 4 Jan. 1679/80.

I. 1627.   " JOHN KYRLE, of Much Marcle, co Hereford, Esq,"
s and h of Thomas KYRLE, of the same, by Frances, da and h. of
John KNOTSFORD, of Malvern, was *cr a Bart*, as above, 17 May 1627   He was twice
Sheriff of Herefordshire, 1608-09 and 1628-29.   He *m* Sybill, da. and h. of Philip
SCUDAMORE   He *d.* 1650.

(a) The estate of Letheringham had been the chief seat of the head of this most
ancient family for very many centuries.
(b) Mary, his da and h., *m* Francis Dillon, of Proudstown, co. Meath, who was *cr*
a Baron of the Holy Roman Empire in 1767.

D

II. 1670.   SIR SAMUEL HELE, Bart [1627], of Flete aforesaid,
          6th s (by 2d wife) and h ; *suc to the Baronetcy*, 16 Nov. 1670
He *m* 28 April 1668, at St. Martin's in the Fields, Midx , Mary, sister of Sir
Edward HUNGERFORD, K B , da. of Anthony HUNGERFORD, of Farley Castle, Somerset,
by Rachel, da of (—) JONES She *d* in his lifetime He *d* s p m , and was *bur*
18 Jan 1672 at Holberton Will dat 4 March 1671, pr 4 Jan 1675/6, entailing
the Flete estates on the heirs male of his family

III. 1672   SIR HENRY HELE, Bart. [1627], of Flete aforesaid, br and
     to   h. male ; *suc to the Baronetcy* in Jan. 1672. He *m* , 13 July 1676 at
     1677.   St German's, Cornwall, Susan, da of John ELIOT, of Port Eliot, by
             Honora, da of Sir Daniel NORTON, of Southwick, Hants She was
bap 27 April 1648 He *d.* s.p , April 1677, when the *Baronetage* became *extinct.*

On the death of the 3rd Baronet in April 1677 the estate of Fleet passed
under the will of the 2d Baronet to the heir male This was
     RICHARD HELE, only s and h of Richard HELE, by Mary (*m* 16 July 1645
at Holberton) da of Richard HILLERSDON, which Richard Hele last named,
who *d* 1679 was a yr. br of the 1st Bart He *m.* (Lic Exeter 24 May 1678)
Judith, da of George CARY, D D , Dean of Exeter   He is *said to have
assumed the style of Baronet* on succeeding to the estates He *d* 29 July 1682
at Fleet.([a]) His widow *d* May 1784

CARLETON:
cr 28 May 1627 ,
ex 1650

I 1627   "JOHN CARLETON, of Holcum [i e , Holcombe], co Oxford,
           Esq ," s and h ap of George CARLETON, of Holcombe aforesaid, by
Elizabeth, da. and coheir of Sir John BROCKETT, of Brockett Hall, Herts, was B A
Oxford (Ch. Ch), 10 Feb 1609/10, and was *cr a Bart* , as above, 28 May 1627 He
suc his father, 8 March 1627/8, was M P for Cambridgeshire, 1628-29 On the death,
15 Feb 1631/2, of his uncle Dudley (CARLETON), VISCOUNT DORCHESTER, he inherited
the estate of Brightwell, co Oxford , Gent of the Privy Chamber, 1633 ; Sheriff of
Cambridgeshire, 1636 37 He *m* , 1625, Anne, widow of Sir John COTTON, of Lanwade,
co Cambridge, da of Sir Richard HOGHTON, 1st Bart [1611], by Catharine, da of Sir
Gilbert GERARD, Master of the Rolls. He *d* in London, 7 Nov 1637, and was *bur*
at Brightwell Will as of "Cheavley, co Cambridge," dat 21 Sep 1635 to 1 Nov
1637, pr 24 Nov 1637 Inq p m at Oxford, 5 April 1638 His widow *d* 17 May
1671, and was *bur* with her first husband at Lanwade Admon , as "of Cheaveley,
co Cambridge," 5 June 1671, to her son, Sir John Cotton, Bart

II 1637,   SIR GEORGE CARLETON, Bart [1627], of Brightwell and
    to   Holcombe aforesaid, only s. and h , aged 12 on 5 April 1638, having
    1650   *suc to the Baronetcy*, 7 Nov 1637. He *d* unm , 1650, at Cheveley,
             co. Cambridge, and was *bur.* at Brightwell, when *the Baronetcy*
became *extinct.*([b]) Admon 27 Feb. 1650/1, to his sisters Anne, wife of George
Garth, "Esq ," and Catherine Carlton

([a]) He was succeeded in the estates, but not in the assumption of the Baronetcy,
by his only s and h , Richard Hele, sometime M P. for Plympton and for West
Looe, who *d.* Dec 1709 at Fleet, and was suc by his only s. and h , James Modyford
Hele, the last in the male line of the family of Hele of Fleet. He *d.* a minor in
London Aug 1716, when, under the will of his father, the estate passed to James
Bulteel, of Tavistock, an entire stranger in blood to the family

([b]) The estates passed to his two sisters and coheirs, of whom (1) Anne *m.* George
Garth, of Morden, co. Surrey, and *d* 1655, leaving issue ; (2) Catharine, *m* John
Stone, whose son, John Stone, inherited Brightwell, and *d.* 1722 s p , leaving it to his
cousin Francis Lowe, ancestor of the family of Lowndes-Stone, of that place

ISHAM :

cr 30 May 1627.

I 1627   "JOHN ISHAM, of Lamport, co Northampton, Knt," s. and h of Thomas ISHAM, of the same, by Elizabeth, da of Christopher NICHOLSON, of Cambridge, was b. 27 July 1582, suc his father 3 Dec 1605, was *Knighted*, 29 March 1608; was Sheriff of Northamptonshire, 1611-12, and was cr a Bart, as above, 30 May 1627. He m, 19 Oct 1607, Judith, sister to Sir Justinian LEWIN, da of William LEWIN, D C L, Judge of the Prerogative Court of Canterbury, of Ottringden, Kent, by Anne, da of Francis GOULDSMITH, of Crayford, co Kent. She d. 25 June 1625, aged 34. He d 8 July 1651 in his 69th year Both *bur*. at Lamport. M I

II. 1651.   SIR JUSTINIAN ISHAM, Bart, [1627], of Lamport aforesaid, only s and h, b 20 Jan 1610   Fellow Commoner of Christ's College, Cambridge, 18 April 1627   Adm to Middle Temple, 11 Oct 1628   For his zeal in the Royal Cause he suffered imprisonment and had to compound for his estate at Shangton, co Leicester (which he possessed, v p) for £1,106, suc to the *Baronetcy*, 8 July 1651, was M P for Northampton, 1661 till his death. He m firstly, 10 Nov 1634, Jane, da of Sir John GARRARD, 1st Bart [1622], of Lamer, Herts, by his 1st wife, Elizabeth, da. of Sir Edward BARKHAM   She d 8 p m, 3 March 1638, aged 25 years and 10 months, and was *bur* at Lamport   M I. He m secondly, 1653, Vere, da of Thomas (LEIGH), 1st BARON LEIGH OF STONELEIGH, by Mary, da and coheir of Sir Thomas EGERTON, s and h. ap. of Thomas, 1st BARON ELLESMERE and VISCOUNT BRACKLEY   He d at Oxford 2 March 1674/5, in his 65th year, *bur* at Lamport.   M.I. His widow d. 29 Oct 1704.

III 1675.   SIR THOMAS ISHAM, Bart. [1627], of Lamport aforesaid, s. and h, by 2d wife, b. 15 March 1656, matric at Oxford (Ch Ch), 4 June 1675, aged 18, suc. to the *Baronetcy*, 2 March 1674/5   He d. (while on the point of marriage) in London, 26 July 1681, in his 24th year   Admon 31 Oct and 30 Nov 1681.

IV 1681   SIR JUSTINIAN ISHAM, Bart [1627], of Lamport aforesaid, br. and h; b 11 Aug. 1658, matric at Oxford (Ch Ch), 4 Dec 1674, aged 18, adm to Linc Inn, 1677, suc to the *Baronetcy*, 26 July 1681   M P. for Northampton, 1685-87, 1689-90, March to Oct 1695 and 1695-98, for Northants (in eleven Parls), 1698 till his death   He was one of the troop formed at Nottingham as a guard for the Princess Anne of Denmark to enable her to desert her father, James II   He m 16 July 1683, at St. Giles' in the Fields (Lic Fac, he 24 and she 18), Elizabeth, only da of Sir Edmund TURNER, of Stoke Rochfort, co Lincoln, by Margaret, da of Sir John HARRISON, of Balls, Herts   She d 22 Aug 1713, in her 47th year   He d 13 May 1730, aged 72   Both *bur*. at Lamport. M I Will pr 1731

V. 1730.   SIR JUSTINIAN ISHAM, Bart [1627], of Lamport aforesaid, s and h, b 20 July 1687; suc to the *Baronetcy*, 13 May 1730; M P. for Northamptonshire, 1730-37, Commissioner of land and window tax and for the duty on hides.   He was a good antiquary and a great lover of literature   He m Mary, only surv child of Lisle HACKET, of Moxhill, co Warwick, by Dorothy, da. of Sir John BRIDGEMAN, 2d Bart [1660]   He d. s.p suddenly, 5 March 1736/7, in his 50th year, in London.   Will pr 1737   That of his widow pr. 1744

VI 1737.   SIR EDMUND ISHAM, Bart. [1627], of Lamport aforesaid, br and h., b 18 Dec. 1690, ed at Rugby School and at Wadham Coll, Oxford, matric 10 Oct 1707, demy of Magdalen Coll, 1710-20, B A, 1711, M A, 1714, fellow, 1720-36. D C L, 1723, member of the Coll. of Advocates (Doctors Commons), London, 1 Dec. 1724; Judge Advocate for the Court of Admiralty, 1731-41; assessor to the Dep Earl Marshal; suc to the *Baronetcy*, 5 March 1736/7, M P for Northamptonshire (six Parls), 1737 till his death   He m. firstly, in 1734, Elizabeth, 1st da of Edward WOOD, of Littleton, Middlesex, by Elizabeth, da and h of Henry BRIDGER, of Guildford. She, who was *b* 18 Aug 1699, *d* 19 July 1748, aged nearly 49　Admon May 1750　He *m.* secondly, 4 May 1751, at St Geo. the Martyr, Queen's sq , Midx , Philippa, only da of Richard GEE, of Orpington, Kent　He *d.* s p 16 Sep 1772　Will pr. Feb 1773　His widow *d.* 11 Dec 1786　Will pr. Dec 1786.

VII　1772　　　SIR JUSTINIAN ISHAM, Bart. [1627], of Lamport afore-
　　　　　　　said, nephew and h , being s and h of the Rev Euseby ISHAM, D D , Head of Lincoln Coll , Oxford, and Rector of Lamport and Haselbeech, co Northampton, by Elizabeth, da of the Rev Matthew PANTING, D D , Head of Pembroke College, Oxford, which Euseby (who *d* 17 June 1755) was 3d s of the 4th Bart　He was *b* 8 July 1740, and *bap* 1 Aug at All Saints', Oxford , matric at Oxford (Linc Coll), 11 May 1758 , *cr.* M A , 8 July 1763, D C L , 4 July 1793 , *suc to the Baronetcy*, 11 Dec 1772 , was Sheriff of Northants, 1776-77　He *m* 9 Sep 1766, Susanna, da. of Henry BARRET, of London, merchant.　He *d* 1 April 1818　Will pr May 1818 and Feb 1847.　His widow *d.* 31 Jan 1823

VIII　1818　　　SIR JUSTINIAN ISHAM, Bart [1627], of Lamport afore-
　　　　　　　said, and of Elm park, Ireland, s and h , *b* 24 April 1773 , *suc to the Baronetcy*, 1 April 1818　He *m* May 1812, Mary, 1st da of Rev Samuel CLOSE, of Drumbanugher and Elm park, co Armagh by (—), da of Rev Arthur CHAMPAGNÉ, Dean of Clonmacnoise [I.]　He *d* at Lamport Hall, 26 March 1845, in his 72d year　Will pr April 1845 and Jan 1847　His widow *d* 26 Jan 1878, in her 90th year, at Lamport Hall

IX　1845　　　SIR JUSTINIAN VERE ISHAM, Bart [1627], of Lamport
　　　　　　　Hall aforesaid, s and h , *b* 7 Nov 1816 , ed at Eton and at Ch Ch., Oxford , matric 22 Oct 1835 , *suc to the Baronetcy*, 26 March 1845.　He *d* unm., suddenly, 25 Aug 1846, at Cheltenham, in his 30th year.　Will pr Dec. 1846.

X　1846.　　　SIR CHARLES EDMUND ISHAM, Bart [1627], of Lamport
　　　　　　　Hall aforesaid, br and h., *b* 16 Dec 1819, at Lamport , ed at Rugby and at Brasenose Coll , Oxford ; matric 25 Jan 1840 , *suc to the Baronetcy*, 25 Aug 1846　Sheriff of Northamptonshire, 1851　He *m* 26 Oct 1847, at St Geo Han sq , Emily, youngest da of the Right Hon Sir John VAUGHAN, one of the Justices of the Common Pleas, by Louisa, Dowager BARONESS ST JOHN, 1st da of Sir Charles William ROUSE-BOUGHTON, 9th Bart [1641]　She *d* 6 Sep 1898, at Lamport Hall, after a long illness, aged 74

　　Family Estates.—These, in 1883, consisted of 3,112 acres in Northamptonshire and 1,118 in Leicestershire　*Total*—4,230 acres, worth £7,373 a year　*Principal Seat*—Lamport Hall, co Northampton.

- - -

MAPLES,

cr 30 May 1627,

ex 1634/5.

I　1627,　　　"THOMAS MAPLES, of Stowe, co Huntingdon, Esq ," of
to　　　　whom very little seems to be known, was cr a *Bart* as above, 30 May
1635.　　1627.　He *d* s p m s.,(ᵃ) 1634/5, when the *Baronetcy* became *extinct*
　　　　　Will pr 1635

- - -

(ᵃ) His da. and h (or coheir) *m* Edward HINDE, of Madingley, co. Cambridge, and was mother of Jane, who *m* Sir John Cotton, 1st Bart. [1641], of Lanwade

POLLARD, or POLLARDE :
cr. 31 May 1627,
ex June 1701.

I. 1627. "LODOVICK (LEWIS) POLLARDE, of Kings Nimpton, co
Devon, Esq." s and h of Sir Hugh POLLARD,(a) or the same, by his
first wife, Dorothy, da of Sir John CHICHESTER, of Yolston, in that county, was
presumably the "Lewis Pollarde, of Devon, Gent," who matric at Oxford (Broadgates Hall), 12 Dec. 1595, aged 17, and was *cr a Bart*, as above, 31 May 1627 He
m. Margaret, da of Sir Henry BERKELEY, of Bruton co Somerset, by Margaret, da
of William LYGON He *d* after 1641, but before 20 Nov 1657, at which date the
admon. of his widow was granted to her son, George Pollard.

II 1645? SIR HUGH POLLARD, Bart. [1627], of Kings Nympton
aforesaid, s and h, *b* about 1610, *suc to the Baronetcy*, on the death
of his father. He was M P for Berealstone, 19 Nov 1640 till expelled 9 Dec 1641,
as privy to the Army plot, being imprisoned till 1646, M P for Callington, 1660,
and for Devon, 1641, till his death, was a staunch royalist, and held for some time
Dartmouth, of which he was Governor, against the Parliament, and surrendered it
on good terms He was fined £518, by the sequestrators, was P C, 1660, Gov of
Guernsey, Comptroller of the household to Charles II, 1663 till his death, and was
known for his magnificent hospitality, which was the cause of his selling the estate
of Kings Nympton He *m* firstly, Bridget, widow of Francis (NORRIS) EARL OF
BERKSHIRE, da of Edward(DE VERE), EARL OF OXFORD, by his first wife, Anne, da
of William (CECIL), 1st BARON BURGHLEY. He *m* secondly, probably about 1650,
Mary, widow of Henry ROLLE, of Stevenstone, co Devon, da of William STEVENS,
of Great Torrington, by Grace, da and h of John HUDDLE, of the same, Vintner
She, who was *bap* 30 Oct 1619 at Great Torrington, *d* before him Admon. 8 Dec
1657. He *d.* s.p.m, 27 Nov and was *bur.* Dec 1666 in Westm Abbey Admon
18 Dec 1666 to a creditor

III 1666, SIR AMYAS POLLARD, Bart. [1627], br and h male, *b.*
to about 1617, *suc to the Baronetcy* in Dec 1666, but to little, if any,
1701 of the estate He *d.* unm and s p. legit ,(b) in his 85th year, being
bur. 7 June 1701, at Abbots Bickington, when the *Baronetcy* became
extinct M.I

BAGOT.
cr. 31 May 1627 ;
afterwards, since 1780, BARONS BAGOT OF BAGOTS BROMLEY.

I 1627. "HERVEY BAGOTT, of Blithfield, co Stafford, Esq,"
s and h of Walter BAGOT, of the same, by Elizabeth, da of Roger
CAVE, of Stanford, co. Northampton, and Margaret, sister of the well-known
William (CECIL), BARON BURGHLEY, was *b* 8 Feb. 1590/1, matric at Oxford (Trin
Coll), 18 Nov. 1608, suc his father 16 March 1622, was Sheriff of Staffordshire,
1626-27; and was *cr a Bart*, as above, 31 May 1627 He was M P for that county
1628-29 and April 1641, till disabled in Nov. 1642, was a great sufferer in the Royal
cause, being fined £1,340, by the sequestrators reduced to £1,004 He *m* firstly, in or
before 1616, Katharine, da of Humphrey ADDERLEY, of Weddington, co Warwick.
She *d* 16 Feb 1622 and was *bur* at Blithfield. He *m* secondly, Anne, widow of Sir
Thomas DILKE, of Maxtock, co Warwick, da. of Sir Clement FISHER, of Packington,
by Mary, da. of Francis REPINGTON, of Arnington, both in that county He *d*
27 Dec 1660, aged 69, and was *bur* at Blithfield M I.

II 1660 SIR EDWARD BAGOT, Bart. [1627], of Blithfield, aforesaid, s and h by 1st wife, *b.* 23 May 1616 ; matric. at Oxford

---

(a) This Hugh was great grandson to Sir Lewis Pollard, of Kings Nympton, one of
the Judges of the Court of Common Pleas, 1515

(b) Thomas Pollard, his illegit. son, *d* s.p 9 Dec 1710, aged 29, having *m* 25 June
1702, at Encombe, Sarah, da of Jonathan Prideaux

(Trin. Coll.), 20 Feb 1634/5, adm to the Middle Temple, 1635 ; M P. for co Stafford, in the Convention Parl of 1660 , "a true assertor of Episcopacy in the church and hereditary monarchy in the state "(a) , *suc. to the Baronetcy*, 27 Dec 1660 He *m*. 9 May 1641, at Buckingham, Mary, widow of John CRAWLEY, of Someries, Beds , da and h of William LAMBARD, Bailiff of Buckingham He *d* 30 March 1673, in his 57th year His widow (by whom he had 17 children) *d*. 22 Oct 1686, aged 67 Both *bur* at Blithfield M I Her will pr July 1687

III 1673 SIR WALTER BAGOT, Bart [1627], of Blithfield aforesaid, s and h , *b.* 21 March 1644; matric at Oxford (Ch Ch), 26 Nov 1662; adm to the Middle Temple, 1666 : *suc to the Baronetcy*, 30 March 1673 , M P for co. Stafford in six Parls , 1678-81, 1685 90, and 1693-95 ; was a " Noble Promoter " of Plot's *History of Staffordshire* He *m* (Lic Vic Gen , 25 June 1670, he about 22 and she about 20, with the consent of her mother), Jane, da and h of Charles SALUSBURY, of Bachymbydd, co. Denbigh, and Iland Lloyd, co Flint. She *d* 20 July 1695 in her 45th year He *d*. 15 Feb 1704 in his 60th year Both *bur.* at Blithfield M I. His will pr Oct. 1705

IV. 1704. SIR EDWARD BAGOT, Bart [1627], of Blithfield aforesaid, s. and h , *b* 21 Jan 1673/4 , matric at Oxford (Ch. Ch), 15 Dec 1691 , adm to the Middle Temple, 1692 He was M P. for co. Stafford, in five Parls , 1698—1708, having *suc to the Baronetcy*, 15 Feb 1704 He *m* 15 April 1697, Frances, d and h of Sir Thomas WAGSTAFFE, of Tachbrooke, co Warwick He *d* May 1712, and was *bur* at Blithfield Will pr June 1712 His widow *m* her cousin, Adolphus OUGHTON (who, after her death, was, in 1718, *cr a Bart.*), and *d* about 1714. Admon, as of Tachbrooke, 24 July 1714

V 1712. SIR WALTER WAGSTAFFE BAGOT, Bart [1627], of Blithfield aforesaid, only surv s and h , *b.* 23 Aug 1702, *suc to the Baronetcy*, May 1712, matric at Oxford (Mag Coll), 27 April 1720 , D C L. thereof by diploma, 17 May 1737 , M P for Newcastle-under-Lyne, 1724-27 , for co Stafford, in four Parls , 1727-61, and for the Univ. of Oxford, 1762-68 He *m* 27 July 1724, Barbara, 1st da. of William (LEGGE), 1st EARL OF DARTMOUTH, by Anne, da of Heneage (FINCH), EARL OF AYLESFORD She *d* 29 Oct. 1765. He *d* 20 Jan 1768 Both *bur* at Blithfield His will pr 1768.

VI. 1768 SIR WILLIAM BAGOT, Bart. [1627], of Blithfield, aforesaid, s. and h , *b* 28 Feb 1728 ; matric. at Oxford (Mag Coll.), 28 Feb 1746/7, aged 17 ; *cr* M.A , 12 April 1749, and D C L , 2 July 1754 , was M P for Staffordshire, in four Parls , 1754-80, having *suc to the Baronetcy*, 20 Jan. 1768 He *m*. 20 Aug 1760, Elizabeth Louisa, 1st da of John (St John), 2d VISCOUNT ST. JOHN, by his 1st wife, Anne, da and eventually coheir of Sir Robert FURNESE, 2d Bart. [1707] She was living when, on 17 Oct 1780, he was *cr* BARON BAGOT OF BAGOTS BROMLEY, co. Stafford, in which dignity this *Baronetcy* became henceforth *merged*. See *Peerage*.

MANNOCK, *or* MANNOCKE.

cr. 1 June 1627 ;

ex. 3 June 1787.

I 1627 " FRANCIS MANNOCKE, of Gifford Hall, in Stoke juxta Neiland [i e , Neyland], co Suffolk, Esq " s and h of William MANNOCK, of the same, by Etheldred, da of Ferdinando PARYS, of Linton, co Cambridge, *suc* his father, 15 March 1616/7, being then aged above 30, and was *cr a Bart.*, as above, 1 June 1627 He *m* Dorothy, da of William SAUNDERS of Welford, co. Northampton, and of Blofield, Norfolk, by Anne, da. of Rees MORGAN, of Michelchurch. He *d* 20 Nov 1634 and was *bur* in the Mannock Chapel, at Stoke by Neyland Will pr 1634

(a) See his M I at Blithfield

II. 1634.   SIR FRANCIS MANNOCK, Bart. [1627], of Gifford Hall aforesaid, s. and h., *suc to the Baronetcy* in Nov 1634   He *m.* 1636, Mary, 1st da. of Sir George HENEAGE, of Hainton, co. Lincoln, by Elizabeth, da of Francis TRESHAM, of Rushton, co Northampton. By her he had 22 children. He *d.* 26, and was *bur.*, 30 April 1687, in the Mannock Chapel aforesaid   Will dat. 22 April 1687, pr 25 May following, and 24 Jan 1690/1.

III. 1687   SIR WILLIAM MANNOCK, Bart. [1627], of Gifford Hall aforesaid, s and h, *suc to the Baronetcy*, 26 April 1687. He *m* (Lic. Lond., 2 Feb 1672 3, she of Claxby, co. Lincoln, aged 21), Ursula, da. of Henry NEVILL, *otherwise* SMITH, of Holt, co Leicester   He *d* 26 Jan, and was *bur* 1 Feb 1713/4, in the Mannock chapel aforesaid   His widow *bur* there 30 Dec. 1727.

IV 1714   SIR FRANCIS MANNOCK, Bart. [1627], of Gifford Hall aforesaid, s and h., *bap* 20 Jan 1675, at Stoke by Neyland, *suc to the Baronetcy* 26 Jan. 1713/4   He *m* Frances, da and h, of George YEATES, of North Waltham, Hants.   He *d* 27 Aug, and was *bur* 4 Sep 1758 in the Mannock chapel aforesaid   Will pr 1758.   His widow *d* 18 and was *bur.* there 21 May 1761. Her will dat 13 Nov 1758, pr. 30 May 1761.

V 1758.   SIR WILLIAM MANNOCK, Bart. [1627], of Great Bromley Hall, Essex, and of Gifford Hall aforesaid s and h., *suc to the Baronetcy*, 27 Aug. 1758   He *m* firstly, Teresa, da of Anthony WRIGHT, of Wealdside, Essex, and of Covent Garden, Midx, Banker   She *d s p s*, and was *bur.*, 13 July 1750, in the Mannock chapel aforesaid   He *m* secondly, Elizabeth, da and coheir of Robert ALLWYN, of Treford, Sussex.   He *d* 16 March 1764 and was *bur.* in the Mannock chapel aforesaid   Will dat 1 Jan 1762, pr. 18 May 1764.   His widow *d* 1774.   Her will dat 10 Dec 1773, pr 19 Jan 1775

VI 1764   SIR WILLIAM ANTHONY MANNOCK, Bart [1627], of Gifford Hall aforesaid, only surv child and h., by 2d wife, *b.* 28 May 1759 ; *suc. to the Baronetcy*, 16 March 1764, was residing at Liége, in Belgium, in 1775, being then aged 16   He *d.* unm , 24 March 1776.   Will pr March 1776

VII 1776.   SIR FRANCIS MANNOCK, Bart. [1627], of Gifford Hall aforesaid and of Sevington, Hants, uncle and h, *b* 17 Sep., 1710 , *suc to the Baronetcy*, 24 March 1776   He *m.* Elizabeth Mary, 4th da. of Thomas STONOR, of Watlington Park, and of Stonor, Oxon   He *d. s.p*, 17 Sep 1778   Will dat 3 June 1777, and pr 2 Oct 1778   His widow (who was *b* 10 June 1714 at Watlington park aforesaid) *d.* 1789   Her will dat 26 May and 6 Sep. 1789, pr 31 Dec. following.

VIII. 1778.   SIR THOMAS MANNOCK, Bart [1627], of Gifford Hall aforesaid, br and h , *suc. to the Baronetcy*, 12 Sep 1778   He *m* firstly, 1 March 1756, at St Geo , Queen's sq., Midx., Mary, da of George Brownlow DOUGHTY, of Snarford Hall, co Lincoln   She *d s.p*, and was *bur* in the Mannock chapel.   Admon 12 Feb 1781, granted to her husband. He *m.* secondly, 17 April 1780, Anastacia, da. of Mark BROWNE, of Eastbourne, Sussex, by his second wife, Anastacia, da. of Sir Richard MOORE, 3d Bart [1627], of Fawley, Berks   He *d. s p* , 2 Sep 1781.   Will dat. 20 Jan 1781, pr 19 Sep following   His widow, who was *b* 10 May 1749, *d* at Windsor, Berks, 8 April 1814.   Will pr 1814.

IX   1781,   SIR GEORGE MANNOCK, Bart. [1627], of Great Bromley
to   Hall aforesaid, br. and h , *suc to the Baronetcy*, 2 Sep 1781   He *d.*
1787   *s p*, being killed by the overturning of the Dover mail coach, 3 June 1787, when the *Baronetcy* became *extinct* ([a])   Will pr June 1787.

([a]) Of his four sisters, three, *viz.*, Etheldred, Mary, and Anne were unm. in 1761, while the eldest, Ursula, *m* , before 1749, James NIHILL, M.D , of Limerick, to whom she took out admon. in 1753.

E

GRIFFITH :
cr. 7 June 1627 ;
ex. 1656.

I. 1627.   "HENRY GRIFFITH, of Agnes Burton, co York, Esq "
s. and h of Sir Henry GRIFFITH, of the same (admon 2 Oct. 1621),
by Elizabeth, da of Thomas THROCKMORTON, of Coughton, co Warwick, was aged 9
at the Visit. of Yorkshire in 1612, and was cr a Bart, as above, 7 June 1627 ;
Sheriff of Staffordshire, 1633-34. He m Mary, 1st da and coheir of Sir Henry
WILLOUGHBY, Bart [so cr. 1611], of Risley, co Derby, by his 1st wife, Elizabeth,
da and coheir of Sir Henry KNOLLYS. She was b. 24 May 1603 (ª) He d before
Oct 1644

II. 1640 ?   SIR HENRY GRIFFITH, Bart [1627], of Burton Agnes
to   aforesaid s and h , suc. to the Baronetcy,(ª) on the death of his father,
1656.   was fined £7,457, in Oct. 1647. He m. Margaret, da of Sir Francis
WORTLEY, 1st Bart [1611], by his 1st wife, Grace, da of Sir William
BROUNCKER He d. s.p s , 1656, when the Baronetcy became extinct   Admon. 25
June 1656, to " Gustavus Boynton, Esq ," nephew and next of kin.

DYER, or DEYER·
cr. 8 June 1627 ;
ex Nov 1669.

I. 1627,   LODOWICK DEYER [i e., DYER], of Staughton, co
to   Huntingdon, Esq.," s. and h of Sir William Dyer, of the same, by
1669.   Catharine, da and coheir of John DOYLEY, of Merton, Oxon, was
aged 8 at the Visit of co Huntingdon, in 1613 suc his father (who
d. aged 39), 29 April 1621, and was cr. a Bart , as above, 8 June 1627 ; was fined
£1,500 He m., in or before 1637, Elizabeth, da of Sir Henry YELVERTON   He d
s p s (ᵇ) and was bur 15 Nov 1669, at Colmworth, Beds , when the Baronetcy
became extinct.   Nunc will, as " of Colmworth," dat 26 Oct 1669, pr. 4 Feb.
1669/70

STEWKLEY, STEWKELEY, or STUKELEY :
cr. 9 June 1627 ;
ex in 1719.

I. 1627   "HUGH STEWKLEY, of Hinton, co. Southampton, Knt.,"
s and h. of Sir Thomas STEWKLEY, of Marsh, co Somerset, and of
Hinton aforesaid (living 1623), by Elizabeth, da and cob of John GOODWIN, of
Over Wichingdon, Bucks , matric at Oxford (Wadh. Coll), 3 July 1618, aged 14 ;
adm. to Middle Temple, 1621 , was Knighted, at Whitehall 20 June 1626, and was
cr. a Bart., as above, 9 June 1627 ; Sheriff of Hants, 1640-41. He m Sarah, da.
and coheir of Ambrose DAUNTSEY, of Lavington, Wilts. He d 1642   Will pr. Oct
1642.

II. 1642,   SIR HUGH STEWKELEY, Bart. [1627], of Hinton, otherwise
to   Hinton Ampner aforesaid, s and h , suc. to the Baronetcy in 1642;
1719.   Sheriff of Hants, 1661-62 He m firstly, Catherine, da and b of
Sir John TROTT, Bart [so cr 1660] of Leverstoke, Hants, by
Elizabeth, da and coheir of Sir Edmund WRIGHT, sometime (1640) Lord Mayor of
London. Her admon 14 May 1679 to her husband. He m secondly Mary, da of
John YOUNG, of Exton He d s p.m (ᶜ) in 1719, when the Baronetcy became extinct.
Will dat. 17 March 1718/9, pr July 1719 by dame Mary, the relict

(ª) " Henry Griffith, of Agnes Burton, co. York, Bart ," was adm. to Gray's Inn,
16 March 1640/1, being probably, but not certainly, the 2d Bart.
(ᵇ) His only son, Henry, d. an infant, 22 Sep. 1637.
(ᶜ) Charles, s and h ap , living 1686, d. s p and v p Catherine, da by his first
wife, m before 1686, Sir Charles Shuckburgh, 2d Bart [1660]

STANLEY: ⁵⁷

cr 26 June 1627,

afterwards, since 1 Feb. 1735/6, EARLS OF DERBY

I   1627.   "EDWARD STANLEY, of Biggarstaffe, co Lancaster, Esq ,"
s and h of Henry STANLEY, by Margaret (m 26 Sep. 1563), da and
h of Petei STANLEY,(ᵃ) of Bickerstaff, otherwise Biggarstaffe, aforesaid, in the parish
of Ormskirk, suc his father, 23 July 1598, was Sheriff of Lancashire, 1614-15 and
1626-27, of Cheshire, 1627-28, and of Lancashire (again), 1638-39, having been cr a
Bart, as above, 26 June 1627   He m. firstly, Katherine, da of Sir Randal MAN-
WARING, of Over Peovei, co Chester, by his first wife Margaret, da of Sir Edward
FITTON, of Gawsworth   She d. s p m   He m. secondly, in or before 1616, Isabel, da.
and coheir of Peter WARBURTON, of Warburton and Arley, co. Chester, by Mary, da. of
Sir John HOLCROFT, of Holcroft   She was aged 36 at her father's death in 1628.
He d. May 1640.

II   1640.   SIR THOMAS STANLEY, Bart [1627], of Bickerstaffe aforesaid,
s and h, by second wife, bap 22 Oct 1616, at Ormskirk, suc to the
Baronetcy, May 1640   He m, in or before 1643, Mary, da. of Peter EGERTON, of
Shaw, co Lancaster, by Elizabeth, da and coheir of Leonard ASHAWE   He d May
1653   Will pr 1654   His widow m. Capt Henry HOGHTON

III   1653   SIR EDWARD STANLEY, Bart [1627], of Bickerstaffe aforesaid, b. 1643, suc to the Baronetcy in May 1653, matric. at Oxford
(Brasenose Coll , 4 Dec 1661, aged 18 ; M A , 12 Sep 1661.   He m 25 Dec 1663,
Elizabeth, da. and coheir of Thomas BOSVILE, of Warmsworth, co York, by his first
wife, Barbara, da of John BABINGTON   He d 16 Oct. 1671

IV.   1671.   SIR THOMAS STANLEY, Bart. [1627], of Bickerstaffe aforesaid, only s. and h , b 27 Sep 1670, suc to the Baronetcy, in his
infancy, 16 Oct 1671, was M P for Preston 1695   He m firstly, 16 Aug 1688,
Elizabeth da. and h. of Thomas PATTEN, of Preston aforesaid (who d 1697, aged
61), by (—) da. and coheir of (—) DOUGHTY, of Coln Hall, co. Lancaster.   She d
1694   He m. secondly, Margaret, widow of Sir Richard STANDISH, 1st Bart [1677],
da of Thomas HOLCROFT, of Holcroft, co. Lanc.   He d 7 May 1714.   His widow, by
whom he had no issue, d. 14 Oct 1735, at a great age.

V.   1714.   SIR EDWARD STANLEY, Bart [1627], of Bickerstaffe afore-
said, 1st s and h, by 1st wife, b 17 Sep 1689, at Knowsley in
Hayton, co Lancaster, suc to the Baronetcy, on the death of his father, 7 May 1714 ;
Sheriff of Lancashire, 1722-23, M P thereof, 1727-36.   He m. 14 Sep 1714, Elizabeth,
da and h of Robert HESKETH, of Rufford, co Lancaster, by Elizabeth, da of the Hon
William SPENCER, of Ashton Hall, in that county, 3d s. of William, 2d BARON
SPENCER OF WORMLEIGHTON.   She was living when, on the death, 1 Feb 1735/6,
of his 6th cousin, James STANLEY, 10TH EARL OF DERBY, he became EARL OF
DERBY   In that peerage (cr 27 Oct. 1485) this Baronetcy then merged, and
so continues   See Peerage

LITTLETON, or LITLETON:

cr. 28 June 1627,

ex 18 May 1812

I.   1627.   "EDWARD LITLETON, of Pileton [Pillaton] Hall, co
Stafford, Esq.," s. and h ap. of Sir Edward LITTLETON,(ᵇ) of the same,
by Mary da. of Sir Clement FISHER, of Packington, co. Warwick, was b about 1599 ;
mat. at Oxford, 28 March 1617, aged 18, adm. to Inner Temple, 1618, and was cr a
Bart., as above, 28 June 1627.   He suc. his father, 25 Aug 1630; was Sheriff of Stafford-

---

(ᵃ) This Peter was 3d s. of Sir William Stanley, of Hooton, co Chestei, the elder
line of the family of Stanley

(ᵇ) This Sir Edward was fourth in descent from Richard LITTLETON, who m. Alice,
da. and h of William WINESBURY, of Pillaton aforesaid, which Richard, was 2d s
of Sir Thomas Littleton, K.B., of Frankley, co. Worcester, the celebrated Judge

shire, 1636-37 , M P thereof, April to May 1640 and Nov. 1640, till disabled, 4 March 1643/4   He was an ardent Royalist, and had to pay £1,347 6s 8d. to the sequestrators of estates.   He m. Hester, da of Sir William COURTEEN, of London, by his second wife, Hester, sister of Sir Samuel TRYON   He was living 11 June 1649,(a) when he petitions to compound, owning to having "deserted the Parl" and gone to Oxford, which fact precludes the petition from being that of his son   He possibly may be the "Sir Edward Littleton, Knt," who was bur. 3 Aug 1657 at St. Edward's, Romford, and, again, the admon , 5 Feb. 1657/8, of "Sir Edward Littleton, of Ferant, co. Montgomery, Bart," granted, however, to the widow, "Catherine" [sic], may refer to him   His widow is said to have m Thomas THORNE, of Shelrock, Salop, and to have been bur. at Ryton church, Salop, 12 Dec. 1674

II　1657 ?　　SIR EDWARD LITTLETON, Bart. [1627], of Pillaton Hall aforesaid, s and h , suc to the Baronetcy on the death of his father , M P. for Staffordshire, 1663-78   He m. firstly, about 1650, Mary, da of Sir Walter WROTTESLEY, 1st Bart. [1642], by Mary, da. of John GREY of Enville, co Stafford By her he had five children.   He m secondly, before 1674, his cousin, Joyce, da of (—) LITTLETON, of Teddesley Hay   By her he had eight children.   He d in 1709

III　1709　　SIR EDWARD LITTLETON, Bart [1627], of Pillaton Hall aforesaid, grandson and h, being s and h of Edward LITTLETON (Sheriff of Staffordshire, 1680-81, and M P. thereof, 1685-87), by Susannah (m Jan 1670/1), da of Sir Theophilus BIDDULPH, 1st Bart [1664], which Edward last-named was s and h ap of the 2d Bart by his 1st wife, and d. v p. 24 Jan 1704, aged about 55   He suc to the Baronetcy in 1709   He was Sheriff of Stafford-shire, 1712-13   He m Mary, only da of Sir Richard HOARE, Lord Mayor of London (1712-13), by Susanna, da of John AUSTIN, of Brittons, Essex. He d , s p , 2 Jan 1741/2   His widow d 18 April 1761   Will pr 1761

IV　1742,　　SIR EDWARD LITTLETON, Bart. [1627], of Pillaton Hall to　aforesaid, and afterwards of Teddesley Park, near Penkridge, co 1812.　Stafford, nephew and h , being s and h of Fisher LITTLETON, by Frances, 1st da and coheir of James WHITEHALL, of Pipe Ridware, co Stafford, which Fisher was br. of the 3d Bart , and d May 1740   He was b about 1725, and suc. to the Baronetcy 2 Jan 1741/2; was Sheriff of Staffordshire, 1762-63, and M.P. thereof in six Parliaments, 1784-1807   He raised a Company during the rebellion of 1745, being Captain thereof.   He m Frances, 1st da. of Christopher HORTON, of Catton, co. Derby, by Frances, only da and h of Sir Eusebius BUSWELL, Bart., so cr 1718/4.   He d s p 18 May 1812, aged 86, when the Baronetcy became extinct (b)

BROWNE :

cr. 7 July 1627 ;

ex 3 Nov 1690.

I　1697　　"AMBROSE BROWNE, of Bettsworth Castle, co Surrey, Esq ," s and h of Sir Matthew BROWNE, of the same,(c) by Jane, da. of Sir Thomas VINCENT, of Stoke D'Abernon, co Surrey, suc. his father, 4 Aug 1603;

(a) He cannot, therefore, be the Sir Edward Littleton who was slain at Naseby fight (four years before) and bur 19 June 1645, at St Sepulchre's, Northampton.

(b) His estates devolved on his great nephew Edward John WALHOUSE, only s and h of Moreton WALHOUSE, of Hatherton, co Stafford, who was only s. and h of another Moreton WALHOUSE, by Frances, only sister of the said Sir Edward Littleton   He took the name of LITTLETON, and was cr a Peer, 11 May 1835, as BARON HATHERTON

(c) This Matthew was s and h. of Sir Thomas Browne the grandson and h of Sir Matthew Browne, s and h. of Sir George Browne, all of Bettsworth, or Bechworth, Castle aforesaid, the said George being s and h. of Sir Thomas Browne, Treasurer of the Household of Henry VI, by Eleanor, da and h of Sir Thomas Fitzalan, alias Arundel, of Bechworth Castle aforesaid, br of John, Earl of Arundel.   The 4th s. of the said Sir Thomas Browne and Eleanor his wife, was Sir Anthony Browne, Standard Bearer of England, the ancestor of the Viscounts Montagu.

was ed at Jesus College, Cambridge, admitted to Gray's Inn, 12 March 1624/5,
Sheriff of Surrey and Sussex, 1628-29, and was *cr a Baronet*, as above, 7 July 1627.
He was M.P for Surrey, 1628-29, April to May 1640, and Nov 1640, till secluded in
Dec 1648, was one of "the members of the House of Commons that advanced horse,
etc, for defence of the Parl," June 1642 (*N and Q*, 1st S, xii, p. 358), undertaking
to "finde 2 horses well furnisht", was one of the Surrey Sequestrators Committee,
1643 He *m.*, 1 Oct, 1607, at Fulmere, co. Cambridge, Elizabeth, da of William
ADAM, of Saffron Walden, Essex She was *bur* at Dorking, 19 Oct 1657 Admon
19 Dec 1661, to her son, Sir Adam Browne, Bart. He *d* 16 Aug 1661, and was
bur. 23d at Dorking

II   1661,   SIR ADAM BROWNE, Bart [1627], of Bettsworth Castle
     to   aforesaid, s. and h, was fined, 30 June 1648, as a delinquent £60,
     1690.   increased to £240, *suc to the Baronetcy*, 16 Aug 1661 M P for
                Surrey, 1661-79 and 1685-87 He *m*, before 1658, Philippa, da. of
Sir John COOPER, 1st Bart [1622], of Wimborne, by Anne, da of Sir Anthony
ASHLEY, Bart. [1622] He *d s p m s*, and was *bur*, 3 Nov. 1690,(*a*) at Dorking,
when the *Baronetcy* became *extinct* Will pr. Dec 1690. His widow *d* 20 May 1701,
aged 77. Will pr May 1701

CROWE
cr 8 July 1627,
ex 21 June 1706

I.   1627   "SACKVILLE CROWE, of Lanherne [*i e.*, Laugharne], co
                Carmarthen, Esq, Treasurer of the Fleet," s of William Crowe, of
Sacketts, co. Kent, by Anne, da and coh of John SACKVILLE, of Chiddingstone, co
Sussex, was M P for Hastings, 1625, and for Bramber, 1628-29, and *cr a Bart*
as above, 8 July 1627 In April 1648 he was sent as prisoner to the Tower He *m*, in
or before 1674, Mary, sister of John, 8th EARL OF RUTLAND, da of Sir George
MANNERS, of Haddon, co Derby, by Grace, da of Sir Henry PIERREPONT. She was
b 1 Jan 1612 He *d* in the Fleet prison, London, 1683 Admon. 28 May 1683, to
his son John

II   1683,   SIR SACKVILLE CROWE, Bart [1627], of Laugharne afsd.,
     to   s and h, *b* about 1674; *suc to the Baronetcy* in 1683, matric. at
     1706.   Oxford (Jesus Coll), 6 June 1689, aged 15, adm. to Lincoln's Inn,
                1692 He *m* firstly (Lic Worcester, 23 Feb 1670), Ann, da of Sir
[Thomas ?] ROUSE, Bart She *d* 13 Dec 1679, æt 38, and was bur at Langharne (*b*)
He *m* secondly, Elizabeth, widow of Sir Henry Vaughan, of Derwitt, co. Carmarthen,
da. of William HERBERT, of Llangattock, co Monmouth She, by whom he had no
issue, *d*. 6 Aug 1694, æt 56 Admon 13 June 1695, granted to her husband He *d*.
s.p.m.s. 21 June 1706, æt 69, when *the Baronetcy* became *extinct*. Both were *bur* at
Laugharne.

LIVESEY, *or* LYVESEY
cr 11 July 1627,
attainted 1660

I   1627,   "MICHAEL LYVESEY, of Eastchurch, within the Isle of
    to   Sheppy, co Kent, Esq.," only s. and h of Gabriel LIVESEY, of
    1660   Hollingbourne and Minster, in that county, by his second wife Anne,
               da of Sir Michael SONDES, of Throwley, co Kent, was *b* 1611, suc
his father 18 March 1622, and was, when a minor, *cr a Bart*, as above, 11 July

---

(*a*) His son, Ambrose Browne, matric at Oxford (Trin. Coll), 4 Nov. 1673, aged
14, was M P for Bletchingley 1685-87, but *d* unm. and v p, and was *bur*. 24 July
1688, at Dorking. Margaret, the only da and h., *m* in 1691, William Fenwick, but
d s p., and was *bur* 6 May 1726, at Dorking, when the estates of Bechworth passed
by sale, to the families of Tucker, Mildmay, and (in 1798) Peters

(*b*) Sackville Crowe, their only son, *d* unm. and v.p., 15 Feb 1700, aged 28. Their
only da. and h, Jane, *m*. Francis Cornwallis.

1627, was Sheriff of Kent, 1643-44, 1655-56, and 1656-57   At the outbreak of the
Civil War he took an active part against the King, was Col. of Horse in the Parl.
army, and was at the battle of Cheriton Down, 29 March 1644, where, however,
"he deliberately ran away",(ª) was M P for Queenborough in the long Parl. 1645
till its dissolution , was one of the Regicide Judges, attending every day of the
trial and signing the death warrant.   He escaped into the Low Countries at the
Restoration, was one of the thirty living Regicides excluded from the act of oblivion,
was attainted for high treason in 1660, whereby the *Baronetcy* was *forfeited*.   He
m Elizabeth   He was living in Oct. 1663, but *d* probably soon afterwards, presumably s p m (ᵇ)   The admon of his widow as " Dame Elizabeth Livesey, of Maidstone, Kent, widow," was granted 27 Feb 1665/6, to her da , Deborah Livesey.(ᶜ)

BENNETT

cr 17 July 1627,

ex. 21 Aug 1631.

I.   1627,   "SIMON BENNETT, of Benchampton [i e , Beachampton],
      to   co Bucks, Esq.," 2d s and h of Sir Thomas BENNET or BENNETT, of
      1631   the same, sometime (1603-04) Lord Mayor of London, by Mary, da of
                   Robert TAYLOR, of London, mercer, was *b* about 1584 ; matric. at
Oxford (Univ Coll) 15 Oct. 1602, aged 18 , adm. to Inner Temple, 1605, and was
(soon after his father's death, 16 Feb 1626/7), *cr a Bart* , as above, 17 July 1627   He
suc. his elder br , Ambrose Bennett (who apparently was excluded from the family
estates), 22 March 1630/1   He *m* , before Dec. 1624, Elizabeth, da of Sir Arthur
INGRAM, of London, by his 1st wife Susan, da of Richard BROWN, of London   He
d s p 21 and was *bur* 22 Aug. 1631, at Beachampton, when the *Baronetcy* became
extinct. M I (ᵈ)   Funeral certificate at the Coll of Arms   Will dat. 15 Aug , pr.
3 Sep 1631   His widow *d* 13 and was *bur* 30 June 1636, at St. Barth the Great,
London.   Funeral certificate as above

FISHER.

cr. 19 July 1627 ,

ex 7 Oct. 1707.

I   1627   "THOMAS FISHER, of the parish of St Giles, co. Midx ,
                 Knt," only s of Thomas FISHER,(ᵉ) of London, citizen and skinner,
by Susan, da of Sir Thomas TYNDALL, of Hockwold, co Norfolk, suc his father
early in 1613 , was *Knighted* at Whitehall, 12 March 1616/7, and was *cr a Bart*
as above, 19 July 1627.   He *m* , 2 March 1619/20, at Islington, Sarah, 1st da. and
coh of Sir Thomas FOWLER, Bart [1628], of Barnsbury, in Islington, by Elizabeth,
da and h of William PIERSON   He *d* 22, and was *bur* , 25 May 1636, at Islington
Will pr. 1636.   That of his widow, who was living 1649, pr 1666

II.   1636.   SIR THOMAS FISHER, Bart. [1627], of Barnsbury afore-
                 said, s. and h. , *b* about 1623, *suc to the Baronetcy*, 22 May 1636
He *m* , before 1643, Jane, da. of Sir John PRESCOT, of Hoxne, Suffolk.   He was *bur*.
9 Sep 1670, at Islington   Admon 21 Oct 1670   His widow *m*., after Nov. 1671,
(as his 1st wife), the Hon. William MAYNARD, 2d s of William, 2d BARON
MAYNARD, and *d* 1 March 1675.

(ª) *Nat Biogr.*, it being there added that " his cowardice and incapacity made him
generally disliked "
(ᵇ) Said to have been cut to pieces by the Dutch boors on being denounced as one
of the King's murderers [*Hist MSS. Com* , 5th Rep , p. 174]   Gabriel Livesey, M P
for Queenborough, 1657-58, was probably his brother
(ᶜ) Anne, another da , *m* Sir Robert Sprignell, 2d Bart [1641], who *d* s p 1690
(ᵈ) Erected at Beachampton 128 years after his death by Univ. Coll , Oxford, to
which he had been a liberal benefactor.
(ᵉ) See ped. of Fisher in Chester Waters s *Family of Chester of Chicheley*, p 273.

III. 1670.   SIR THOMAS FISHER, Bart. [1627], of Barnsbury afsd., s.
and h , *b.* about 1643 ; *suc to the Baronetcy* in Sep. 1670. He had
lic (Faculty office) dat. 16 Nov. 1666(ª) (he about 23, bachelor, she about 17,
spinster), to marry his cousin Elizabeth, da. of Sir Henry DUCIE, K B., by Sarah, da.
of Sir Thomas FISHER, 1st Bart , but *d.* unm He was *bur* 14 April 1671, at
Islington. Admon. 8 Nov 1671 (as a bachelor) to his uncle Sir Richard Fisher, Bart.

IV. 1671,   SIR RICHARD FISHER, Bart [1627], of Barnsbury afsd ,
to   uncle and h , *bap* 22 Jan. 1629, at Islington, admitted to Middle
1707.   Temple, 1647, *suc to the Baronetcy* in April 1671. He *m.* firstly,
       Anne LEIGH, of St. John's Close, Clerkenwell, spinster   She was *bur*
29 April 1693 at Islington   He *m* secondly (Lic Fac , 31 July 1704), Browne, widow
of Sir George DALSTON, da of Sir William RAMSDEN, of Longley, co. York   He *d*
s.p 7, and was *bur* 14 Oct 1707 at Islington, when the Baronetcy became *extinct* (ᵇ)
Will pr Oct 1707. His widow was *bur.* 24 March 1740 at Islington.   Will pr 1740

BOWYER ·
cr 23 July 1627 ,
ex. Feb. 1679/80

I. 1627   "THOMAS BOWYER,(ᶜ) of Leyghthorne [in North Mund-
ham], co. Sussex, Esq," s. and h. of Thomas BOWYER, of the same,
and of the Middle Temple, London, by his second wife, Jane, da of John BIRCH, one
of the Barons of the Court of Exchequer, was *b.* 28 Nov , and *bap* 4 Dec. 1586, at
Mundham , suc. his father 7 March 1594/5 , was M P. for Midhurst, 1614, and for
Bramber (7 successive Parls), 1621 to 1642, when he was disabled , was Sheriff of
Surrey and Sussex, 1626-27, and was *cr. a Bart*, as above, 23 July 1627 , was fined
£2,033 as a delinquent, 18 May 1650   He *m* firstly, in or before 1610, Anne da and
coheir of Adrian STOUGHTON, of West Stoke, co Surrey, Recorder of Chichester
He *m* secondly, ~~before 1634,~~ Jane widow of Sir George STOUGHTON, and formerly of
Samuel AUSTEN, of Stratford, da and h. of Emery CRANLEY, of co Surrey. She was
bur. 10 April 1640 at North Mundham. He *m.* thirdly, in or before 1642, Anne da and
He was *bur.* 28 Feb ~~1650~~ at Mundham, leaving a widow and thirteen children (ᵈ)
Will dat. 20 Jan. 1648/9, pr 9 April 1652. ✗His widow was *bur* 11 May 1683 at
St Margaret's, Westm.   Will dat 21 March 1682, pr 5 Dec. 1683

II. 1650.   SIR THOMAS BOWYER, Bart [1627], of Leythorne aforesaid, 1st s. and h. by 1st wife ; matric at Oxford (Trin Coll), 9 June
1626, aged 16 , was aged 24 and upwards in 1634 and unm ; *suc to the Baronetcy* in
Feb. 1650. He *m* firstly, Katherine, da and coheir of Richard STANY, of Elston, Sussex,
by Bridget, da. and h of Richard ERNLY, of Rackham. She was living 1648 · He *m*
secondly, Margaret. He *d s p m* ⚓ Will dat 13 June 1659, pr 21 Dec. 1659 by
his widow. Her will as " of Chichester," dat 26 July 1687, pr 22 Nov 1693
she was buried 31 July 1687 at [...] Mundel [...]

III 1659,   SIR JAMES BOWYER, Bart. [1627], of Leythorne aforesaid,
to   brother of the half-blood and h male, being s of the 1st Bart by
1680.   his 3rd wife; *bap.* at North Mundham ; elected a scholar at Win-
       chester in 1656, and then aged 11(ᵉ), *suc to the Baronetcy* in 1659 ;
matric at Oxford (New Coll), 14 Feb. 1661/2, and then aged 17 , Fellow, 1663-65 ;

(ª) In this he is called " Bart.," and " of Islington," yet " Sir Thomas Fisher, the
elder Knt. and Bart of Islington " afsd is therein spoken of as alive   There is,
however, another lic (Vic Gen office), 31 Oct. 1670, of a " Sir Thomas Fisher "
(not however called " Bart "), of St Giles in the Fields, bachelor, about 23 [Qy , if
the same man ?] to marry " Mrs Anne Askew, spinster, about 24."

(ᵇ) Ursula his sister *m* as second wife, Sir William HALTON, 1st Bart [1642], and
her son, the 3d Bart., inherited the manor of Barnsbury, which was devised by his
son, the 4th Bart (*d. s p* , 12 Feb. 1754), to the family of TUFNELL

(ᶜ) *N. and Q.* 7th S., xii, 285 and 422.   See also an article by the Rev. J H.
Cooper, in vol. xlii of the pubs. of the Sussex Arch. Soc.

(ᵈ) Cat. of Compounders, vol. ii, p 833.

(ᵉ) *N. and Q.*, 8th S., i, 137.

adm. to the Middle Temple, London, 1665. Having wasted all his estate, and having no issue, he obtained a new patent of Baronetcy, dated 18 May 1678 (said to have been granted with the precedency of the former creation, on a surrender(a) of the patent of 1627), with rem , failing heirs male of his body, to Henry Goring, of Highden, Sussex (b) He d s p in London, and was *bur.* 28 Feb. 1679/80   Admon. 27 April 1682 to Henry Bellingham, cousin and next of kin   At his death *the Baronetcy,* of 23 July 1627, became *extinct,* but that of the recent creation (18 May 1678) devolved according to the spec rem in the patent thereof   See "Bowyer" Baronetcy, *cr.* 18 May 1678

BACON :
cr. 29 July 1627 ,
merged 30 April 1758
into the Baronetcy of Bacon, *cr* 22 May 1611

I   1627   "Butts Bacon, of Mildenhall, co Suffolk, Esq," yr
           s. of Sir Nicholas Bacon, 1st Bart [1611] of Redgrave, by Anne, da. and h of Edmund Butts, of Thornage, Norfolk, was *cr a Baronet,* 29 July 1627   He *m.* Dorothy, widow of William Jermyn, da of Sir Henry Warner, of Parham and Mildenhall, Suffolk   She *d.* 4 Sep 1655, and was *bur* at Blundeston, Norfolk   He *d* 29 May 1661, and was *bur* there   M I   Will, as of Heringfleet, dat 18 March 1660, pi at Norwich, 30 Jan 1661/2

II   1661   Sir Henry Bacon, Bart [1627], of Heringfleet aforesaid,
           s and h. , *suc* to *the Baronetcy,* 29 May 1661. He *m* Barbara, da. of William Gooch, of Mettringham, Suffolk   He *d.* before 1671.

III.   1670 ?   Sir Henry Bacon, Bart. [1627], of Heringfleet aforesaid
           and of Gillingham, Norfolk, s and h, which last estate he inherited from his sister's husband, Sir Richard Bacon, 3rd Bart [1662] of Gillingham aforesaid , *suc to the Baronetcy* (on the death of his father), about 1670   He *m* , 29 June 1671, at Sturston, Suffolk, Sarah, da of Sir John Castleton, 2d Bart [1641], by Margaret, da and h of Robert Morse, of Sturston aforesaid. He was *bur.,* 13 Jan 1685/6, at Gillingham   His widow *d* 3 and was *bur* 7 Feb 1727, at Gillingham.

IV.   1686   Sir Edmund Bacon, Bart [1627], of Gillingham afore-
           said, s and h   He was *bap* 6 April 1672, at Sturston aforesaid , *suc. to the Baronetcy* in Jan 1685/6 ; M P for Orford (four Parls), 1700-08   He *m* firstly, at Redgrave, about Christmas 1688, Philippa, 4th da and coheir of Sir Edmund Bacon, 4th Bart. [1611] of Redgrave, by Elizabeth, da and coheir of Sir Robert Crane, Bart. [1643]   She, who was *bap* 29 July 1672, was *bur* , 12 July 1710, at Gillingham   He *m* secondly, 16 April 1713, at Raveningham, Norfolk, Mary, da of John Castell, of Raveningham aforesaid   He *d* 10 and was *bur.* 17 July 1721, at Gillingham

---

(a) Such surrender, however would have been invalid, according to the decision, 1678, in the case of the Viscountcy of Purbeck   See note sub "Stonehouse" Baronetcy, *cr* 7 May 1628

(b) This transaction is supposed to have been effected in consequence of a bribe from Goring to the needy baronet, who (save for such bribe), gained nothing whatever by it. There appears to have been no relationship between the parties, and the connection between them is so ludicrously remote as hardly to be worth any consideration. A certain Sir Henry Bowyer married (as her first husband) Dorothy, da of George Goring, of Danny, co Sussex, and died childless in 1606, his widow promptly remarrying   That Henry was great grandson of William Bowyer, from whom, by another of his sons, the grantee of 1678 was a great great great grandson.   The said Dorothy was granddaughter of Sir William Goring, of Burton (*d.* 1553), from whom Henry Goring, the successor to the Baronetcy created in 1678, was (by another son), 4th in descent   Thus James Bowyer, the grantee of 1678 was 2d cousin twice removed to a man who died above seventy years ago, without issue, leaving a *widow,* who was first cousin (also) twice removed to Henry Goring, the remainder man and subsequent inheritor of the Baronetcy thus created.

V. 1721. SIR EDMUND BACON, Bart. [1627], of Gillingham aforesaid, s and h by 1st wife He was b 7 and bap 14 Aug 1693 at Gillingham ; suc to the Baronetcy, 10 July 1721 , M P for Thetford, in 3 parliaments, 1727 to 1738. He m. 7 Nov 1724, at the Chapel Royal, Whitehall, Susan, da of Sir Isaac REBOW, of Colchester He d at Bath 4 and was bur 16 Oct 1738 at Gillingham Will pr 1739 His widow, who was b Sep 1687, was living 1771.

VI 1738 SIR EDMUND BACON, Bart [1627], of Gillingham aforesaid, s and h , b. 7 and bap 17 Aug 1725 at Gillingham , suc to the Baronetcy. 5 Oct 1738 , ed at Westm. School, 1741. He d. unm 6, and was bur 13 April 1750 at Gillingham Admon. 7 June 1750

VII 1750 SIR HENRY BACON, Bart. [1627], of Gillingham aforesaid, uncle and h , being 2d s of the 4th Bart by his 1st wife He was b. 5 and bap 8 Oct 1693 at Gillingham , suc to the Baronetcy, 6 April 1750 He d unm , and was bur 10 April 1753 at Gillingham

VIII. 1753 SIR RICHARD BACON, Bart. [1627], of Colchester, Essex, br and h , being 3d s of the 4th Bart , by his 1st wife. He was b 22 Feb , and bap 5 March 1695, at Gillingham ; suc. to the Baronetcy, 10 April 1753 By the death of his cousin, Sir Edmund BACON, 6th Bart [1611] of Garboldisham, co Norfolk he suc to the Baronetcy, conferred, 22 May 1611, on his ancestor (Sir Nicholas BACON, of Redgrave, co Suffolk), becoming thus the premier Baronet See "BACON," cr 22 May 1611, under the 7th Baronet.

CORBET, or CORBETT

cr 19 Sep. 1627;

ex. 7 May 1750.

43

I 1627. "JOHN CORBETT, of Stoke, co Salop, Esq," s and h. of Richard CORBET,(a) of the same and of Adderley in that county, by Anne, da. of Sir Thomas BROMLEY, Lord Chancellor of England, was bap 20 May 1594, at Ferne, co Salop, and was cr a Bart, as above, 19 Sep 1627 In that same year, however, he was conspicuous in his opposition to the loan required by the King, being, it is said,(b) "one of those five illustrious patriots worthy of the eternal gratitude of their country" who did so. He was Sheriff of Shropshire, 1628 29 ; M.P. for that county 1640 till secluded in 1648, and was one of the Salop Com of Sequestrators, April 1643 He m , in or before 1620, Anne, da of Sir George MAINWARING, of Ightfield, Salop. He d. July 1662, aged 68, having had ten sons and ten daughters, and was bur. at Market Drayton, Salop. M I Admon 1662. His widow, who was known as 'the good Lady Corbet," d. 29 Oct 1682, aged nearly 80, and was bur. with him M.I Her will, dat 28 Oct 1682, proved 31 Jan 1682/3

II. 1662. SIR JOHN CORBET, Bart. [1627], of Stoke and Adderley aforesaid, s and h , b. about 1620 , matric at Oxford (St Alban's Hall), 25 Nov 1636, aged 16 , suc to the Baronetcy in July 1662 (c) He m , in or before 1645, Lætitia, da of Sir Robert KNOLLYS, of Gray's Court, Oxon, by Joanna, da of Sir John WOLSTENHOLME He was bur 24 Feb. 1664/5 at Westminster Abbey. The will of his widow, dat 5 Oct. 1669, was pr 20 July 1670.

III. 1665 SIR JOHN CORBET, Bart. [1627], of Stoke and Adderley aforesaid , s. and h , b. about 1645; suc to the Baronetcy in Feb 1664/5 ; was Sheriff of Shropshire, 1675-76. He m. firstly, 28 Nov. 1658, at Woodford co.

(a) This Richard was s and h of Reynold Corbet, of Stoke, one of the Justices of the Court of Common Pleas, temp Eliz . who was 2d s of Sir Robert Corbet, of Moreton Corbet, Salop, ancestor of the Corbets of that place, cr Barts in 1642 and 1808 respectively

(b) Blakeway. .

(c) He was not the M P. for Bishop's Castle, 1645-53, named as one of the King's Judges. [Ex inform., W D. Pink].

F

1689 till death. He *m*, 3 May 1681, at St. Giles' in the Wood, Florence, da. of Sir John ROLLE, K B, of Marrais, and afterwards of Stevenstone, Devon, by Florence, 1st da of Dennis ROLLE, of Stevenstone aforesaid He was wounded in a duel with James Pound, in May, from the effects of which he *d* 28 July, and was *bur.* 13 Aug 1696, at Tawstock Will, dat. 16 and 18 Aug 1694, pr. 7 June 1697 His wife, living Aug 1694, probably survived him.

V. 1696   SIR BOURCHIER WREY, Bart. [1628], of Tawstock Court aforesaid, s and h ; *b* about 1683, *suc. to the Baronetcy*, 28 July 1696 ; matric at Oxford (Ch Ch), 12 July 1700, aged 17, M.P. for Camelford, 1712-13.   He *m.*, 28 Feb 1707/8, at St Peter's, Cornhill, London (Lic. Fac.), his first cousin, Diana, widow of John SPARKE, of Plymouth, da of John ROLLE, of Stevenstone aforesaid, by Christian, da. of Robert (BRUCE), 1st EARL OF AILESBURY She was *bap.* 12 July 1683 He was *bur* 12 Nov. 1726 at Tawstock

VI. 1726   SIR BOURCHIER WREY, Bart. [1628], of Tawstock Court aforesaid, s and h, *b* about 1715, matric. at Oxford (New Coll), 21 Oct. 1732, aged 17, *suc to the Baronetcy* in Nov 1726, M P. for Barnstaple, 1749-54, Col. of the Devon Militia, 1759 He *m* firstly, 1749, Mary, da. of John EDWARDS, of Highgate, Midx She *d.* s p, and was *bur* 3 Sep. 1751 at Tawstock, aged 27 He *m.* secondly, 1 May 1755, at Chippenham, Ellen, da of John THRESHER, of Bradford, Wilts (who *d* 1741, aged 52), by Ellen, da. of Henry LONG, of Melksham, in that county He *d* 13, and was *bur* 22 April 1784 at Tawstock, aged 69 Will pr May 1784, and in Ireland 1787 His widow *d* Nov. 1813. Will pr. 1814.

VII 1784   SIR BOURCHIER WILLIAM WREY, Bart [1628], of Tawstock Court aforesaid, s and h by 2d wife, *b* 22 and *bap.* 23 Feb 1757 at Tawstock, matric at Oxford (New Coll), 5 Nov. 1774, aged 17 ; Fellow of All Souls' College and, when such, B A., 30 May 1782, M A., 31 Oct 1786; having *suc. to the Baronetcy* 13 April 1784 He *m* firstly, 14 May 1786, at Shottesbrooke, Berks, Ann, da of Sir Robert PALK, 1st Bart [1782], by Anne, da of Arthur VANSITTART She *d* Sep 1791. He *m.* secondly, 1793, Anne, da of John OSBORNE, of Alderley, co Gloucester He *d* 20 Nov 1826 Will pr. March 1827. His widow *d* 26 Jan 1816

VIII 1826   SIR BOURCHIER PALK WREY, Bart [1628], of Tawstock Court aforesaid, s and h. by 1st wife, *b* 10 Dec. 1788, at Haldon House, near Exeter, matric at Oxford (Oriel Coll) 10 June 1807, aged 18 ; Barrister (Linc Inn), 1815, *suc to the Baronetcy*, 20 Nov 1826 He *m* firstly, 14 March 1818, at Christ Church, London, and again 10 July 1832, at St. Geo., Han. sq, Ellen Caroline RIDDLE, widow ([a]) She *d.* s.p m, 23 July 1842, aged 50, and was *bur*, at Tawstock He *m* secondly, 11 Sep. 1843, Eliza COLES, spinster She *d.* s p, 11 May 1875 He *d.* s p m,([b]) 11 Sep. 1879, at Quayfield House, Ilfracombe (of which place he was Lord of the Manor), and was *bur* 18 at Tawstock, in his 91st year

---

([a]) In this last entry she is called "Ellen Caroline Wrey, formerly Riddle," the place and date of the previous marriage being recited, and it being added "doubts having arisen as to the validity of such marriage." In the *North Devon Journal*, 25 Sep. 1879 (quoting the *Western Times* for the 22 and 23 inst), is a long account of the marriages of this Baronet His first wife is stated to have been an Irish woman "of rare beauty, who bore the name of the widow Johnson, *née* Ellen O'Brien," and who was nurse to the eldest child of Mrs. Hartopp, his sister. The marriage of 1818 is said to have been in the belief of the death of the said Ellen's first husband, who had not been heard of for seven years His existence, however, is said to have been afterwards discovered, as also that his name was not Johnson but Riddle : that he had "been a groom to Lord Adare," and that his death took place in 1826 The second wife is said to have been daughter of the lodge keeper at Tawstock and lady's maid to the first There are, apparently, some inaccuracies in this newspaper account, as *e.g*, that the first marriage in 1818 was "at St Anne's, Holborn," the second one "at Brighton," etc

([b]) Ellen Caroline, his 1st daughter, and, eventually, sole heir, *b* 1819, *m* 9 Aug. 1838, Edward Joseph Weld, of Lulworth Castle, co. Dorset, and *d* 13 Oct. 1866, leaving issue, among whom (if the said Ellen can be proved to have been legitimate) the coheirship of the Barony of Fitzwarine is vested.

IX   1879.   Sir Henry Bourchier Wrey, Bart. [1628], of Tawstock Court aforesaid, br of the half blood, and h. male, being s of the 7th Bart. by his 2d wife, b at Tawstock Court, 5 June 1797. Ed. at Eton and at Ball. Coll, Oxford ; matric 11 May 1815, B A , 28 Jan 1819 , M A , 27 June 1821 , in Holy Orders , Vicar of Okehampton, 1822 , Rector of Tawstock, 1840-82 , *suc to the Baronetcy*, 11 Sep 1879   He *m* firstly, 27 Sep 1827, Ellen Maria, only da of Nicholas Roundell Toke, of Godington, Kent   She *d* 1 March 1864   He *m* secondly, 5 Jan 1865, Jane, widow of John Steavenson, of Newcastle-on-Tyne, da. of H Lamb, of Ryton House, co Durham   He *d* 23 Dec 1882, aged 85, at Corffe, near Barnstaple   His widow *d* 26 July, 1889, aged 76.

X   1882   Sir Henry Bourchier Toke Wrey, Bart. [1628], of Tawstock Court aforesaid, 1st s and h , b 27 June 1829, at Sandgate, co Kent, matric at Oxford (Trinity Coll), 3 Nov 1847, aged 18 , B A 1851 , sometime Capt. and Hon Major 4th Batt. of the Devonshire Regiment of Militia , *suc to the Baronetcy*, 23 Dec 1882 , Sheriff of Devon, 1891.   He *m.*, 6 July 1854, Marianna Sarah, da and h of Philip Castell (Sherard), 9th Baron Sherard of Leitrim [I], by Anne, da of Nathaniel Weekes, of Barbadoes.   She *d.*, 16 Feb 1896, at Tawstock Court, aged 68   He *d* 10 March 1900 at Ventnor, Isle of Wight, aged 70.   Will pr at £155,838, the net personalty being £54,253

XI   1900   Sir Robert Bourchier Sherard Wrey, Bart [1628], of Tawstock Court aforesaid, 1st s and h , b 23 May 1855 , served in the Royal Navy ; Lieut , 1879 , Com , 1894 ; served with distinction in the Zulu war, 1879 , in the Egyptian campaign, 1882 , and in Burmah, 1885-86 ; *suc to the Baronetcy*, 10 March 1900.

Family Estates.   These, in 1883, consisted of 7,393 acres in Devon, 373 in Cornwall and 220 in Dorset   *Total*, 7,985 acres, worth £9,269 a year   " By the late Baronet's will the Ilfracombe estate is gone to Mr Weld of Lulworth " [note in Bateman's " Great Landowners," edit. 1883]   *Principal seat* —Tawstock Court, near Barnstaple, North Devon

---

TRELAWNY: 52

cr. 1 July 1628;

afterwards, since 1802, Salusbury-Trelawny.

I   1628   " John Trelawny, of Trelawny, co Cornwall, Esq ," s and h. of Sir Jonathan Trelawny, of the same, sometime Sheriff and M P for that county, by Elizabeth, 2d da of Sir Henry Killigrew, was b at Hall 24 April, and *bap* 7 May 1592, at Fowey, Cornwall , suc his father 21 June 1604 , matric at Oxford (Merton Coll.), 23 Oct. 1607, aged 15 , opposed the validity of the election of Sir John Eliot as M P. for Cornwall, and was accordingly committed to the Tower by the House of Commons, 13 May 1628 , was released by the King, 26 and *Knighted*[a] 29 June 1628, at Whitehall, being, three days afterwards, *cr a Bart* , as above, 1 July 1627, Sheriff of Cornwall, 1630-31 , was (with his son) a Compounder, May 1649   He *m* firstly, in or before 1617, Elizabeth, da of Sir Reginald Mohun, 1st Bart [1611] of Boconnoc, by Philipps, da of Sir John Hele.   She, who was *bap.* 10 Feb 1593 at St. Pinnock, was living Jan 1639   He *m.* secondly, Douglas, widow of Sir William Courtenay, of Saltash, da and coheir of Tristram Gorges, of Budockshead.   She, who was *bap* 13 Sep 1586 at Budeaux, *d.* in or before 1660   Admon 1 Oct 1660   He was *bur* 16 Feb 1664, at Pelynt

II   1664.   Sir Jonathan Trelawny, Bart. 1628, of Trelawny aforesaid, s. and h by 1st wife , b about 1623 , matric at Oxford (Ex Coll), 14 Dec 1640, aged 17 , was fined (with his father) £629, in May 1649 , Gent of the Privy Chamber, 1660 , *suc to the Baronetcy*, 26 Feb. 1664 , M P. for East Looe, 1660 , for Cornwall, 1661-78 , for East Looe, again, 1678-79 and for Liskeard, 1679 81   He is said[b] to have been " sequestered, imprisoned, and ruined for loyalty during the Civil War "   He *m.* Mary, 6th da of Sir Edward Seymour, 2d

---

(a) It will be observed, however, that he was not described as a Knight in the patent of Baronetcy.

(b) *Dict. Nat. Biogr.*

Bart. [1611], by Dorothy, da of Sir Henry KILLIGREW abovenamed   She was *bap.*
19 Dec 1619, at Berry Pomeroy.   He was *bur* 5 March 1680/1, at Pelynt.   Will dat
30 Dec 1680, pr 9 April 1681, in Archd Court of Cornwall

III. 1681.   SIR JONATHAN TRELAWNY, Bart [1628], of Trelawny
aforesaid, 3d but eldest surv s. and h (ª), *b* at Pelynt [*Qy.* if not
at Coldrinick], 24 March 1650 ; ed at Westm School ; matric at Oxford (Ex Coll),
5 Aug. 1668, aged 18 , Student of Ch Ch , 1669 ; B.A. 22 June 1672 , M A , 29 April
1665 ; took Holy Orders, 4 Sep 1673 , Rector of St Ives and Vicar of Southill, co.
Cornwall, 1677 89   He *suc to the Baronetcy* in March 1680/1 , distinguished himself
in his opposition to Monmouth's rebellion in 1685, and was, in that year, made BISHOP
OF BRISTOL, being, as such, one of the seven Bishops committed to the Tower, 8 June
1688, by James II,(ᵇ) and one of the two out of those seven who took the oaths to
William and Mary   He accordingly was made BISHOP OF EXETER in 1689 (the Archdeaconry of Totnes, 1693—1694, and that of Exeter, 1704-1707, being added " *in
commendam* ") and finally, 1707-1721, BISHOP OF WINCHESTER   He *m.* in 1684,
Rebecca, da and coheir of Thomas HELE, of Bascombe, by Elizabeth, da and coheir
of Matthew HALS, of Efford, both in co Devon.   She, by whom he had 12 children,
d. 11 Feb. 1710.   He *d* at Chelsea 19 July and was *bur.* 10 Aug 1721, with his
ancestors, at Pelynt, aged 71   Admon. 6 Dec 1721

IV. 1721   SIR JOHN TRELAWNY, Bart. [1628], of Trelawny aforesaid,
s and h , *b* about 1691, at Trelawny , matric at Oxford (Ch Ch),
26 Jan 1707/8, aged 16 , M P for West Looe, April to Aug 1713 and 1713-15 , for
Liskeard, 1715 22, for West Looe, again, 1722-27, and for East Looe, 1727 34 , *suc
to the Baronetcy*, 19 July, 1721   He *m* Agnes, da of (—) BLACKWOOD, of (—), in
Scotland   He *d.* s p, 1756   Will dat 23 Feb to 26 Nov. 1754, pr. 9 March
1756   His widow *d.* in Edinburgh, 8 April 1777.

V 1756   SIR HARRY TRELAWNY, Bart [1628], of Trelawny aforesaid, cousin and h male, being s and h of Henry TRELAWNY, of
Whitleigh, co Devon, by his 1st wife, Rebecca, da. and coheir of the abovenamed
Matthew HALS, of Efford aforesaid, which Henry, who was Brig General in the Army,
and Governor of Plymouth, and who *d* 1702, was 7th s of the 2d Bart.   He was *bap*
15 Feb 1687, at Egg Buckland , matric. at Oxford 19 Jan 1702/3, aged 15 , was
sometime *Aide-de Camp* to the Duke of Marlborough , M P for East Looe, 1708-10 ,
suc to the Baronetcy, 1756.   He *m* in or before 1720, his cousin(ᶜ) Lætitia, da (whose

(ª) John Trelawny, the eldest son, *d* s p and v p in 1680

(ᵇ) The feeling roused by this arbitrary act is well set forth in a spirited poem by
the Rev Robert Stephen Hawker (41 years Vicar of Morwenstow, Cornwall, *d.* 15 Aug
1875, aged 70), entitled " *The Song of the Western Men*," who (the head of one of
their leading families, being a prisoner) may naturally be supposed to have been
especially affected.   It commences as below—

" A good sword and a trusty hand,
    A merry heart and true,
King James's men shall understand
    What CORNISH LADS can do
And have they fixed the Where and When,
    And shall TRELAWNY die ?
Then twenty thousand Cornish men
    Will know the reason why !
What ! will they scorn TRE, POL and PEN ?
    And shall TRELAWNY die ?
Then twenty thousand underground
    Will know the reason why ! "

The whole of this long passed for an original song dating from 1688, and its author
(when he declared himself) states from local tradition that the *refrain* [" And shall
Trelawny die," etc] was so, but " Hawker's testimony is not quite conclusive   There
is some ground for believing that the cry was first raised in 1628, owing to the fears
of Cornishmen for the life of Sir John Trelawny, 1st Bart., *at the hands of the House
of Commons* " [*Dict. Nat. Biogr*].

(ᶜ) Their ten years' courtship is recounted in the " Love Letters of Myrtilla
and Philander, 1706-36."   The match was opposed by the bride's father.

issue became coheir) of Sir Jonathan TRELAWNY, 3d Bart., by Rebecca, da and coheir of Thomas HELE He d s.p.m.s., 7 April 1762, aged about 75. His widow was *bur.* 6 June 1775, at Egg Buckland Will pr. June 1775.

VI. 1762.   SIR WILLIAM TRELAWNY, Bart. [1628], of Trelawny aforesaid, nephew and h male being s and h of William TRELAWNY, Capt. in the Army (*bap* 13 Nov. 1696, at St Margaret's, Westm), who was br to the last Bart. He, who was sometime of Budshed, in St Budeaux, co. Devon, was a Capt. R N., was M.P. for West Looe, May 1757 61 and 1761-67 , *suc to the Baronetcy*, 7 April 1762, and was appointed Governor of Jamaica, 1767 He *m.*, in or before 1756, his cousin Lætitia, da and sole h of Sir Harry TRELAWNY, 5th Bart , by Lætitia, da. of Sir Jonathan TRELAWNY, 3d Bart , BISHOP OF WINCHESTER She, who was *bap* 16 June 1728, at St Budeaux, *d.* 24 Aug. 1772 He *d.* in Spanish town, Jamaica, 11 and was honoured with a public funeral there (costing 1,000 guineas) 13 Dec. 1772. Will pr May 1773

VII. 1772.   SIR HARRY TRELAWNY, Bart. [1628], of Trelawny aforesaid, only s and heir , *b* at Budshed and *bap* 26 June 1756, at St. Budeaux , ed at Westminster ; *suc to the Baronetcy*, 11 Dec. 1772, matric at Oxford (Ch. Ch), 2 July 1773, aged 17 , B A , 1776 , M A , 1781 , joined the Methodists soon after 1776, and subsequently the Calvinists. He, however, subsequently took Holy Orders in the Church of England , was Preb of Exeter, 1789, Vicar of St Austell, 1791, and of Egloshayle, Cornwall, 1793 He *m* , 28 Feb 1778, Anne, da of Rev James BROWN, Rector of Portishead and Vicar of Kingston, Somerset She *d* 18 Nov 1822 He *d* 24 Feb 1834, at Laveno in Italy (having, apparently, become a Roman Catholic), aged 77 Will pr. June 1834.

VIII. 1834.   SIR WILLIAM LEWIS SALUSBURY-TRELAWNY, Bart. [1628], of Trelawny aforesaid, s and h , *b* at Runcorn, Cheshire, 4 July 1781 ; ed at Westm. ; matric at Oxford (Oriel Coll.) 18 Feb 1799, aged 17. By royal lic , 11 Dec. 1802, he took the name of *Salusbury* before that of *Trelawny*, under the will of his cousin Owen SALUSBURY-BRERETON ; was Sheriff of Cornwall, 1811-12 , M P for East Cornwall, 1832-1837 ; *suc. to the Baronetcy*, 24 Feb 1834 , L Lieut of Cornwall, 1840, and subsequently Custos Rotulorum He *m* , 24 Aug 1807, Patience Christian, da of John Phillips CARPENTER, of Mount Tavy, Devon. He *d.* 15 Nov 1856 at Harewood, near Tavistock, Devon Will pr Jan 1857 His widow *d* 20 June 1857. Will pr. July, 1857.

IX. 1856.   SIR JOHN-SALUSBURY SALUSBURY-TRELAWNY, Bart [1628], of Trelawny aforesaid, s. and h , *b* 2 June 1816, at Harewood aforesaid , ed. at Westm and at Trin. Coll , Cambridge , B A 1839 , Barrister (Mid. Temple), 1841 ; M P. for Tavistock, 1843—1852, and 1857—1865; for East Cornwall, 1868—1874 ; sometime (1840) Capt. Royal Rangers and Dep Warden of the Stannaries He *m.* firstly, 25 Jan. 1842, at St. Ewe, Cornwall, Harriet Jane, 1st da of John Hearle TREMAYNE, of Heligan, in that county She *d.* 5 Nov 1879 He *m* secondly, 19 May 1881, "in London," Harriet Jacqueline, widow of Col E G. W KEPPEL, 5th and yst da of Sir Anthony BULLER, of Pound, co Devon, Judge of the Supreme Court of Bengal, by Isabella Jane, da. of Sir William LEMON, 1st Bart. [1774] He *d.* 4 Aug. 1885, in his 70th year Will pr. 5 Feb 1886, over £7,000. His widow living 1900.

X. 1885.   SIR WILLIAM LEWIS SALUSBURY-TRELAWNY, Bart [1628], of Trelawny aforesaid, only s and h , by 1st wife , *b* 26 Aug 1844, at the Royal Clarence Baths, Devonport , ed at Eton and at Trin. Coll , Cambridge ; sometime Capt Royal Cornwall Rangers Militia ; *suc to the Baronetcy*, 4 Aug 1885 ; Sheriff of Cornwall, 1895. He *m* firstly, 14 July 1868, Jessy Rose Mary, only da. of John MURRAY, of Philiphaugh She *d.* 23 Nov. 1871. He *m* secondly, 17 Dec. 1872, at Morval, co Cornwall, Harriet Buller, 1st da. of the Rev. James Buller KITSON, Vicar of Morval.

Family Estates —These, in 1883, consisted of 8,000 acres in Cornwall, valued at £6,000 a year. *Principal seat.*—Trelawne [or Trelawny], near Liskeard, co. Cornwall.

CONYERS, or CONNIERS

cr. 14 July 1628,

ex 15 April 1810.

I 1628.   " JOHN CONNIERS, of Norden [i e, Horden], in the Bishopric of Durham, gent.," s. and h. of Christopher CONYERS, of the same,
by his 2d wife Anne (m 4 Nov 1586), da of Sir Ralph HEDWORTH, of Harraton, co.
Durham, was cr a Bart., as above, 14 July 1628 In Aug 1648, he was fined £651
He m, about 1606, Frances, da of Thomas GROVES, citizen of York. He was bur
6 Dec 1664, at Easington, co Durham

II 1664.   SIR CHRISTOPHER CONYERS, Bart. [1628], of Horden
aforesaid, 2d but 1st surv. s. and h., bap 28 March 1621, at Easington, admitted to Gray's Inn (with his elder br Richard Conyers), 12 Feb 1637/8,
suc to the Baronetcy, in Dec 1664 He m. firstly, 28 Sep 1648 at Long Ditton,
Surrey, (Lic Fac), Elizabeth (then of Putney, Surrey, aged 19), da of William
LANGHORNE, of London, merchant, and sister (whose issue became heir) of Sir
William LANGHORNE, Bart. [1668] She d in childbed, 27 April, and was bur.
1 May 1654, at St Giles' in the Fields, Midx M I He m secondly (Lic Fac
3 Nov 1666), Julia, widow of Alexander JERMYN, of Lordington, Sussex, da. of
Richard (LUMLEY), 1st VISCOUNT LUMLEY OF WATERFORD [I], by Frances, da. of
Henry SHELLEY. He d Oct 1693. Will pr March 1706.

III 1693.   SIR JOHN CONYERS, Bart. [1628], of Horden aforesaid,
only s and h, by 1st wife, b about 1649, matric at Oxford (New
Inn Hall), 14 Dec 1666, aged 17, suc to the Baronetcy in Oct 1693 He, in Feb
1714, inherited the estate of Charlton, Kent, and other estates from his uncle, the
said Sir William Langhorne, Bart. He m (Lic Vic Gen 9 Nov 1675, he about 26,
she about 22), Mary, 1st da and coheir of Edward NEWMAN, of Folkesworth, Norman
Cross, near Peterborough, by Christian, da of (—) MATTHEWS By her he acquired
the estate of Baldwins in Great Stoughton, co Huntingdon. She was bap. 1 Sep.
1647, at Folkesworth, aud d 24 Oct. 1714, aged 67. He d 14 Sep. 1719, aged 75
Both bur at Great Stoughton. M.I His will pr 1720.

IV. 1719   SIR BALDWIN CONYERS, Bart [1628], of Horden and
Great Stoughton aforesaid, only surv s and h., b. about 1681, suc.
to the Baronetcy, 14 Sep 1719 He m firstly, in or before 1710, Sarah, only da. and
h. of Edward CONYERS, of Blaston, co Leicester, by whom he acquired the manor of
Bradley in that county He m. secondly, Margaret, 1st da. and coh of Henry NEVILL,
otherwise SMITH, of Holt, co Leicester, by Margaret, da of George NAPIER, of Holy-
well, Oxon. He d. s.p.m s,[a] 17 April 1731, in 51st year, and was bur. at Great
Stoughton M I Will pr 1731.[b] His widow living 1741. Her will pr. Jan 1758.

V 1731   SIR RALPH CONYERS, Bart. [1628], of Chester le street,
co Durham, cousin and h male, being s. and h. of John Conyers, of
Chester le street aforesaid, who is stated to have been s of John Conyers [bap. at
Easington 20 Sep. 1622, and d. 1687], who was 2d s of the 1st Bart. He was bap
20 June 1697 at Chester le street, in which town he was afterwards a glazier, and
suc to the Baronetcy, 17 April 1731, but to none of the family estates He m.,
about 1726, Jane, da of Nicholas Blakiston, of Shieldsrow, co Durham, by Jane,
da of (—) PORTER, which Nicholas was br. to Sir Ralph Blakiston, cr. a Bart 1642.
He d 22 Nov. 1767 [c] His widow living 1771.

(a) His only son, John, d 4 Sep 1729 in his 19th year
(b) The estate of Horden was sold by his daughters and coheirs to Rowland BURDON,
while that of Charlton in Kent, went (according to an entail) to the family of GAMES,
and afterwards to that of MARYON, whence it descended to that of Wilson, afterwards
Maryon-Wilson.
(c) In the Chronicon Mirabile there is an entry of the burial of " Sir Ralph Conyers,
Bart," 19 Aug. 1751, at Chester le Street. Query, if this is correct, and if the date
of 22 Nov. 1767 (as given in the text) is an error.

VI. 1767. SIR BLAKISTON CONYERS, Bart. [1628], s. and h., Captain of the Marines, 1757, and Collector of the Customs at Newcastle ; *suc. to the Baronetcy*, 22 Nov. 1767. He *d.* nnm Oct. 1791

VII. 1791. SIR NICHOLAS CONYERS, Bart [1628], br and h , *bap* 27 July 1729, at Chester le Street ; sometime Comptroller of the Customs at Glasgow ; *suc. to the Baronetcy*, in Oct 1791 He *m* (—). He *d.* s.p. 1796. His widow *m* (—) CAMPBELL

VIII. 1796. SIR GEORGE CONYERS, Bart [1628], s and h , *suc. to the Baronetcy* in 1796 He, who is said to have "squandered" his fortune "in scenes of the lowest dissipation,"([a]) *d* s p

IX. 1800? SIR THOMAS CONYERS, Bart. [1628], uncle and h., *bap.* to 12 Sep. 1731, at Chester le Street, *suc. to the Baronetcy* on the death 1810. of his nephew. He *m* Isabel, da. of James LAMBTON, of Whitehall, co. Durham. He *d.* s p m., in great indigence, at Chester le Street, where for many years he had been in the workhouse,([a]) 15 April 1810, aged 79, when the *Baronetcy* became *extinct*.

BOLLES, *or* BOLLE .

cr. 24 July 1628 ,

ex. 23 Dec 1714

I. 1628. "JOHN BOLLES, of Scumpton [*i.e.*, Scampton], co Lincoln, Esq ," s. and h. of Sir George BOLLES, or BOLLE,([b]) sometime [1617-18], L. Mayor of London, by Joan, da and coheir of Sir John HART, of Scampton aforesaid, sometime [1588-89], L. Mayor of London ; was *b* about 1680, and *bap.* at St. Swithin's, London , suc. his father 1 Sep. 1621 , was Sheriff of Lincolnshire, 1626 27, and was *cr. a Bart*, as above, 24 July 1628 He *m* , in or before 1612, Katharine, 1st da and eventually coheir of Thomas CONYERS, of Brodham, co Lincoln, and of East Barnet, Herts. She *d* 20 and was *bur* 21 Sep 1644, at Scampton, aged 55. He *d* 8 and was *bur.* there 9 March 1647/8, aged 67 M I. Will. pr. 1651.

II. 1648. SIR ROBERT BOLLES, Bart [1628], of Scampton aforesaid, 3d but 1st surv s and h , *bap* there 11 April 1619 ; was fined £1,500 in Jan 1646 , *suc. to the Baronetcy*, 9 March 1647/8 , was, in 1661, one of the Grand Jury for trying the Regicides ; M P for Lincoln, 1661 till death , a munificent patron of the fine arts and literature He *m* 14 Oct. 1637, at Honington, co. Lincoln, Mary, da. of Sir Edward HUSSEY, 1st Bart [1611], by Elizabeth, da. of George ANTON He *d* 3 Aug. 1663, aged 44, and was *bur.* (by torch light) at St. Swithin's, London Will dat 8 to 14 July 1663, pr 22 March 1663/4, at Lincoln His widow, who was *bap.* 16 July 1617, at Honington, was *bur* 30 Nov. 1672, at St. Swithin's aforesaid Will pr. 1672.

III 1663. SIR JOHN BOLLES, Bart [1628], of Scampton aforesaid, s. and h , *bap* there 21 June 1641 , *suc to the Baronetcy*, 3 Aug 1663 ([c]) He *m.* firstly, 3 Dec. 1663, at St. Andrew's, Holborn (Lic Vic -Gen , he 23 and she 20), Elizabeth, da. and coheir of John PYNSENT, of that parish, Prothonotary of the Common Pleas She *d* , s p m , and was *bur.* 9 Sep 1664, at St Swithin's He *m* secondly, May 1667, Elizabeth, 1st da of Sir Vincent CORBET, 1st Bart. [1642], by Sarah, *suo jure* VISCOUNTESS CORBET, da of Sir Robert MONSON. She *d*

([a]) See Burke's *Vicissitudes of Families*, 2nd Series, pp. 1-29, for an account of these Baronets. The names of the husbands ("all working men in the little town of Chester le Street ") of the three daughters of the last Bart are there given

([b]) See "anecdotes" of the family of Bolles," in Illingworth's *Scampton, co Lincoln* [4to, 1808], where in some few copies is a folding tabular pedigree

([c]) In Sir Joseph Williamson's account of "*Lincolnshire Families, temp Car II*," his estates there and in Yorkshire are estimated at £3,000 a year. [*Her. and Gen.*, vol ii, p. 120]

at St. Andrew's, Holboro, and was *bur* 8 Aug. 1676, at St. Swithin's aforesaid.
Admon. 18 Aug 1676   He *d* 3 and was *bur* there 8 March 1685/6.   Will dat. 23
Feb 1680, pr March 1687

IV.   1686,   SIR JOHN BOLLES, Bart. [1628], of Scampton aforesaid,
        to   only surv. s and h, by 2d wife, *b.* July 1669, matric at
     1714.   Oxford (Ch Ch), 23 Jan 1682/3, aged 13, admitted to Gray's Inn,
                  1680 ; *suc to the Baronetcy*, 3 March 1685/6 , M P for Lincoln (in
five Parls.) 1690—1702. He is said to have lived in great state. He *d*. unm 23 Dec
1714, aged 44, and was *bur* at St Swithin's aforesaid, when the *Baronetcy* became
extinct   Admon. 29 Jan. 1714/5, to his [only] sister Sarah Bolle.(a)

ASTON ·

cr. 25 July, 1628 ;

ex 22 March 1815.

I.   1628.   "THOMAS ASTON, of Aston [in the parish of Runcorn],
co. Chester, Esq," s and h of John Aston, of the same (Server to
Anne, Queen of James I), by Maud, da. of Robert NEEDHAM, of Shavington,
Salop (which John was s. and h. of Sir Thomas Aston, of Aston aforesaid), was *b.*
29 Sep 1600 in Shropshire ; suc. his father 13 May 1615 ; matric at Oxford (Bras.
Coll.), 28 March 1617, aged 16, B A 8 July 1619, admitted to Lincoln's Inn,
1620, and was *cr* a Bart, as above, 25 July 1628   He was Sheriff of Cheshire,
1635-36 : M P thereof, April to May 1640, Captain of a troop of Horse, which
he raised for the service of Charles I, being a zealous supporter of the
Crown   He was defeated by Sir William Brereton, the Parliamentary General,
near Nantwich, 28 Jan 1642, made a prisoner soon afterwards and brought to
Stafford, where he died, in consequence of a blow received when attempting to escape
from prison   He *m* firstly, in 1627, Magdalen, sister and coheir of John POULTENEY,
of Misterton, co Leicester, da of Sir John POULTENEY, of the same   She *d., s p s ,*
2 June 1635, and was *bur*. at Aston   M I   Admon 30 June 1636, to her husband.
He *m* secondly, in 1639, Anne, widow of the Hon Anchitel GREY, da and coheir of
Sir Henry WILLOUGHBY, Bart [so *cr.* 1611], of Risley, co Derby, being sole heir of his
first wife Elizabeth, da and coheir of Henry KNOLLYS   He *d.* at Stafford (as above-
said), 24 March 1645/6, and was *bur* at Aston. Will pr. 1668   His widow *d.* 2 June
1688, aged 74, and was *bur* (with her father) at Wilne, co. Derby.

II   1646.   SIR WILLOUGHBY ASTON, Bart [1628], of Aston aforesaid,
s. and h, by 2d wife, *b* 5 July 1640, *suc. to the Baronetcy*, 24 March
1645/6 ; aged 22 in 1662, Sheriff of Cheshire, 1680-81 and 1690-91. He built a
magnificent mansion at Aston, a short distance from the old residence. He *m.,* in
or before 1665, Mary, da of John OFFLEY, of Madeley, co Stafford, by Mary, da.
of Thomas BROUGHTON, of Broughton, in that county. He *d.* 14 Dec 1702, and
was *bur* at Aston. M.I   His widow, who was *b* 3 Feb. 1649/50, and by whom he
had eight sons and thirteen daughters, *d.* 22 Jan 1711/2, and was *bur* at Aston. M I.

III.   1702.   SIR THOMAS ASTON, Bart. [1628], of Aston aforesaid,
s and h., *b* 17 Jan 1665/6 ; *suc. to the Baronetcy*, 14 Dec. 1702;
Sheriff of Cheshire, 1723. He *m* (Lic. Lond. 22 Oct 1703, he 30 and she 25),
Catharine, yst da and coheir of William WIDDRINGTON. He *d.* 16 Jan. 1724/5, and
was *bur* at Aston   M.I   Will, dat 6 Feb 1723/4, proved 8 Dec. 1725. His widow,
who was *b* Nov. 1676, *d.* 10 April 1752, and was *bur* at Aston. M I. Will pr
May 1752

IV.   1725   SIR THOMAS ASTON, Bart. [1628], of Aston aforesaid,
only s and h. ; *b*. about 1705 ; matric. at Oxford (Corp. Christi
Coll), 1 March 1721/2, aged 17 ; *suc to the Baronetcy*, 16 Jan. 1724/5, was M.P
for Liverpool, May 1729 to 1734, and for St. Albans, 1734-41   He *m.,* March

---

(a) She *d* unm 7 Nov. 1746, when the Scampton estate devolved on his coheirs
(descendants of the 2d Bart), who in 1749 sold it to William Cayley

1735/6, Rebecca, da of John SHISHE, of Greenwich, Kent. She, who was *b.* 25 Nov. 1717, *d.* 16 May 1737, and was *bur* at Aston M l. He *d.* s p., in France, and was *bur* at Aston, 17 Feb. 1743/4.(ª) Admon. 11 May 1744, to mother, Dame Catharine Aston, widow.

V. 1744.   SIR WILLOUGHBY ASTON, Bart. [1628], of Risley, co. Derby aforesaid, cousin and h , being s and h. of Richard ASTON, of Wadley, Berks, by Elizabeth, da of John WARREN, of Wantage, in that county, and of Priory Court, Oxon, which Richard (who *d* 24 Nov 1741), was 6th s. of the 2d Bart He was *b.* about 1715 ; matric. at Oxford 7 Jan 1729/30 (Oriel Coll), B A. (All Souls' Coll.), 14 Jan 1735 , M A , 20 Oct 1739 , admitted to Linc Inn, 19 Nov. 1731 ; *suc. to the Baronetcy,* 17 Feb 1743/4   He was M P for Nottingham 1754-61 ; Col of the Berkshire Militia 1759   He *m* 14 May 1744, at St Geo the Martyr, Midx., Elizabeth, 4th da of Henry PYE, of Farringdon, Berks, by Anne, sister of Allen, 1st EARL BATHURST, da of Sir Benjamin BATHURST   He *d.* 24 and was *bur.* 27 Aug 1772, at Bath Abbey

VI 1772,   SIR WILLOUGHBY ASTON, Bart. [1628], of Risley aforesaid, to   only s. and h , *b.* about 1748, *suc. to the Baronetcy,* 24 Aug 1772. 1815.   He *m* Jane, 3d da of Robert (HENLEY), 1st EARL OF NORTHINGTON (Lord Chancellor, 1761-66), by Jane, da of Sir John HUBAND. He *d.* s p , 22 March 1815, aged 67, when the *Baronetcy* became *extinct.*   Admon April 1815   The will of his widow pr Feb. 1823.

JENOURE :

cr 30 July 1628 ;

ex 15 Aug. 1755.

I. 1628   " KENELM JENOURE of [Bygotts in] Much Dunmowe, co Essex, Esq," s and h of Andrew JENOURE, of the same, by Crysogona, da and h.of Thomas SMITH, of Campden, co. Gloucester, suc his father in Dec 1622 ; was *cr a Bart,* as above, 30 July 1628   He *m.* Jane, da. of Sir Robert CLARKE, Baron of the Exchequer [1587-1607], by Margaret (relict of Sir Edward OSBORNE), daughter of John MAYNARD. He *d.* in 1629   Will dat. 25 Aug. and pr. 30 Oct. 1629. His widow living 1640.

II 1629   SIR ANDREW JENOURE, Bart, [1628], of Great Dunmow aforesaid, s and h , *suc to the Baronetcy* in 1629. He *m* firstly, in or before 1632, Margaret, da of Richard SMITH, of Strixton, co Northampton, Citizen of London She d s p   He *m.* secondly, 4 March 1678/9, at Roxwell, Essex, Mary, da of Sir John BRAMSTON, K B , of Skreens in that parish, by Alice, da of Anthony ABDY, Alderman of London   His will dat. 26 Feb 1690, pr 9 April 1692 in the Archdeaconry of Middlesex.   His widow, who was *b* 15 Aug 1638, *d* s.p 17 and was *bur* 22 Aug. 1692 at Roxwell   Her will, as of St Ann's, Westm., dat. 12 Aug and pr. 3 Sep. 1692 by her father abovenamed.

III [1692?]   SIR MAYNARD JENOURE, Bart. [1628], of Great Dunmow aforesaid, grandson and h , being s and h. of Andrew JENOURE, by Sarah, da. of Robert MILBORN of Markshall, in Dunmow aforesaid, which Andrew was s and h ap of the 1st Bart by his first wife   He was *b* about 1667, and *suc. to the Baronetcy* about 1692   He *m* (Lic Vic.-Gen , 19 June 1693, he above 21, she about 17) Elizabeth, only da of Sir John MARSHALL, of Sculpons in Finchingfield, Essex, by Dorothy, da and coheir of John MEAD of the same

---

(ª) He devised Aston Hall and other estates to his eldest sister Catherine, wife of Rev. the Hon Henry Hervey, D.D , who took the name of *Aston,* after that of *Hervey,* by Act. of Parl., and in whose descendants they still continue.

H

IV. 1710?   SIR JOHN JENOURE, Bart [1628], s and h, *suc. to the Baronetcy*, on the death of his father. He *m* Joan, da and sole h of Richard DAY, of Northweald, Essex. He *d* 28 April 1739 Will pr 1743. Admon of his widow, as of Great Easton, co Essex, granted 1 Dec 1764 to John Reeve, cousin and next of kin.

V. 1739.   SIR RICHARD DAY JENOURE, Bart [1628], s and h, *b* about 1718 ; *suc. to the Baronetcy*, 17 April 1739 , admitted to Linc. Inn 19 Jan. 1740/1. He *d* s p 23 March 1743/4, aged 26 Will pr 1744

VI 1744,   SIR JOHN JENOURE, Bart, 1628], cousin and h male,(a) being
to   s. and h of Joseph JENOURE, Surveyor Gen. of South Carolina (1731)
1755.   by Anne, da. of John SANDFORD, of Bishops Stortford, which Joseph was 3d s. of the 3d Bart He, who was sometime a Capt. in the Guards, *suc to the Baronetcy* 23 March 1743/4 He *d.* s p (probably unm) 15 Aug. 1755, when the *Baronetcy* became *extinct* Will pr. 1755.

PRYCE, *or* PRICE ·

cr. 15 Aug. 1628 ,

ex. 28 June 1791.

I. 1628.   "JOHN PRYCE of Newtowne, co Montgomery, Esq.," s. and h. of Edward PRYCE, of the same, by Julian, da. of John VAUGHAN, of Llwydyarth in the same county, was cr *a Bart* as above, 15 Aug 1628 He was M P for Montgomeryshire, Nov. 1640, till disabled in Oct 1615 , re-elected 1654-55 , was Gov. of Montgomery Castle, 1643-45 for the Parl , but was accused of intending to betray his trust, his estate being accordingly sequestrated, though freed therefrom 31 March 1652 He *m* Catharine, da of Sir Richard PRYSE, of Gogerddan, co Cardigan, by Gwenllian, da. and h. of Thomas PRYSE, of Aberbychan, co Montgomery. He *d.* in or before 1657 Admon 16 Nov 1657

II. 1657 ?   SIR MATTHEW PRYCE, Bart [1628], of Newtown aforesaid, only surv s and h.(b), *suc. to the Baronetcy*, in or before 1657 He *m.* in or before 1661, Jane, da of Henry Vaughan, of Kilkenain, co Cardigan Will pr. 1674.

III. 1674 ?   SIR JOHN PRYCE, Bart [1628], of Newtown aforesaid, s and h , *b* about 1662, *suc. to the Baronetcy* on his father's death, matric at Oxford (Ch Ch.), 3 May 1679, aged 17 , Sheriff of Montgomeryshire, March to April 1689. He *m* (Lic. Fac 30 June 1680, he about 20), Anna Maria, da. of Sir Edmund Warcup, of Northmore, Oxon. He *d* s p m.s. in 1699 Will dat. 19 June and pr 17 Nov. 1699 That of his widow pr 1732

IV 1699   SIR VAUGHAN PRYCE, Bart. [1628], of Newtown aforesaid, br. and h. male, admitted to Gray's Inn 14 Jan 1680/1 , *suc to the Baronetcy* in 1699 , Sheriff of Montgomeryshire 1708-09 He *m* Ann, sister to Sir Thomas POWELL, Bart. [so cr. 1698] da of Sir John POWELL, of Broadway, near Laugharne, co Carmarthen, one of the Justices of the Court of King's Bench. He *d.* about 1720 Will pr. Nov 1720 That of his widow pr. Oct. 1723

V 1720 ?   SIR JOHN PRYCE, Bart [1628], of Newtown aforesaid, s. and h , *suc to the Baronetcy* about 1720 , Sheriff of Montgomeryshire, 1748-49. He *m.* firstly Elizabeth, da. and eventually sole h of the said Sir Thomas POWELL, Bart. [so cr. 1698], by Judith, da and h of Sir James HERBERT, of Colebrook, co Monmouth She *d.* 22 April 1731 in her 33d year and was *bur* at Newtown. M.I. He *m* secondly, Mary, 1st da. of John MORRIS, of Wern Goch in Beriew, co. Mont

----

(a) See Morant's "*Essex*" vol ii, 426. The late Baronet had a yr. br., John, who, in some accounts, is made to be the "John" who succeeded him in 1744

(b) Edward Pryce, his elder br served with distinction in the Royal army during the Civil War, but *d.* unm and v p being slain in a tumult.

gomery, by Mary, da of Oliver JONES, of Gwern-yr-Ychen, in Llandysail, in that county She *d* s.p.m 3 Aug 1739, aged 24 years, 1 month and 2 days, and was *bur*. at Newtown M.I He *m* thirdly, Eleanor, widow of Roger JONES, of Buckland, Brecon, but by her had no issue He *d* 1761.(a)

VI. 1761. SIR JOHN POWELL PRYCE, Bart [1628], of Newtown aforesaid, only s and h by 1st wife, *suc to the Baronetcy* in 1761. He *m*. Elizabeth, da and h of Richard MANLEY, of Earleigh Court in Sunning, Berks He *d*. 4 July 1776, in the King's Bench prison. Will pr. 1789 The will of "Dame Elizabeth Price" was pr 1805.

VII 1776, SIR EDWARD MAMLEY PRYCE, Bart. [1628], of Newtown
to aforesaid s and h ; *suc*. to the *Baronetcy* 4 July 1776 He *m*. (—),
1791 da of (—) FLINN, of Norfolk street, Strand, Middlesex He *d*. s.p. legit.(b) 28 June 1791, at Pangbourne, Berks, when the *Baronetcy* is presumed to have become *extinct*

BEAUMONT

cr 15 Aug 1628 ;

ex. 28 Oct. 1631.

I. 1628, "RICHARD BEAUMONT, of Whitley, co. York, Knt.," s. and h
to of Edward BEAUMONT, of Whitley Beaumont aforesaid, by Elizabeth,
1631. da of John RAMSDEN, *suc* his father 3 Jan 1574/5, was *Knighted* 23 July 1603, at Whitehall ; was in command of 200 train-band soldiers in 1613 , was M.P for Pontefract 1625 till void 28 May, and was *cr. a Bart.*, as above, 15 Aug 1628 He *d*. unm 28 Oct. 1631, when the *Baronetcy* became *extinct*. By his will, dat 22 Aug. 1631, he devised his estates to his cousin Sir Thomas Beaumont, maternal grandson of his maternal aunt, Rosamond, by (her husband and distant relative) William Beaumont, of Lassells Hall, co York.(c)

WISEMAN :

cr. 29 Aug. 1628

I. 1628 "WILLIAM WISEMAN of Canfeilde Hall, co. Essex, Esq ,"
2d s. of Thomas WISEMAN(d) of the same, by Alice, da. and h of Robert MYLES, of Sutton, Suffolk, *suc* his elder br Robert WISEMAN in the estate of Great Canfield, 1628, and was *cr. a Bart* as above 29 Aug 1628 He was Sheriff of Essex, 1638 39 He *m* 6 Nov. 1628, at Hadham Parva, Herts, Elizabeth, sister of Arthur, 1st BARON CAPELL OF HADHAM, da. of Sir Henry CAPELL, of Hadham, Herts, by his first wife Theodosia, da. of Sir Edward MONTAGU He *d* at Oxford, and was *bur*. 1 July 1643 at St Peter's in the East, in that city Will pr. July 1643 and Nov. 1644 His widow, who was *b* 26 Jan 1612, *d*. 6 April 1660 and was *bur*. at Great Canfield. M.I. Will pr Nov 1660

II 1643. SIR WILLIAM WISEMAN, Bart. [1628(1)],(e) of Canfield Hall aforesaid, s and h , aged 4 years in 1634 (VISIT. of ESSEX) ; *suc to the Baronetcy* in 1643 , Sheriff of Essex, 1659-60. He *m* firstly, 26 Oct. 1659 at St. Mary Magdalen's, Milk street, London, Anne, da and coheir of Sir John PRESCOT, of

---

(a) *Gent Mag* , but Kimber's *Baronetage* says " Oct. 1748."
(b) According to Courthope's "*Extinct Baronetage*" [1835], " Sir Edward left an illegitimate son, who assumed the title "
(c) See Burke's "*Commoners*" (edit 1837), vol. ii, p. 321.
(d) He was grandson of Sir John Wiseman, one of the Auditors of the Exchequer temp. Hen. VIII, who was *Knighted* at the battle of the Spurs.
(e) See vol. i, p. 4, note " a."

Hoxton, and of Bromley, Kent. She *d* s.p , 11 May 1662, aged 24, and was *bur* at Great Canfield. M I. Admon Nov 1662 He *m.* secondly, 18 May 1664, at St. Martin's in the Fields (Lic Fac , he about 33, she about 17), Arabella, sister, of the whole blood, and coheir of George, Viscount Hewett of Gowran [1], 5th da of Sir Thomas Hewett 1st Bart. [1660], by his 2d wife, Margaret, da of Sir William Lytton.   He *d.* 14 and was *bur.* 23 Jan 1684/5, at Great Canfield, aged 55   M I Will pr Feb 1685, That of his widow pr Aug 1705

III   1685   Sir Thomas Wiseman, Bart [1628(¹)], of Canfield Hall aforesaid, s and b by 2d wife ; *suc to the Baronetcy*, 14 Jan 1684/5. He sold the estate of Great Canfield. He *d* unm 1 May 1731   Will pr May 1733.

IV   1731   Sir Charles Wiseman, Bart [1628(¹)], br of the whole blood and h , *bap.* 27 Aug. 1676 at St Andrew's, Holborn, *suc to the Baronetcy*, 1 May 1731. He *d* unm 3 June 1751. Will pr 1751

V. 1751.   Sir William Wiseman, Bart 1628(¹)], nephew and h , being s and h of John Wiseman, of the Temple, London, Barrister, by Penelope, his wife, which John (who was *bap* 14 Dec 1679, at St Andrew's, Holborn), was younger br. of the 3d and 4th Barts.   He *suc to the Baronetcy* 3 June 1751   He was Lieut. Col. of a Company of the Coldstream Guards, 1759   He *d.* s p. 25 May 1774   Will pr June 1774

VI   1774   Sir Thomas Wiseman, Bart [1628(¹)], cousin and h , being only surv. s. and h of Edward Wiseman, of Tewkesbury, by his 1st wife, Mary, da. of (—) Jones, of Worles, which Edward (who was *b* 21 Dec. 1700 and *d* at Jersey about 1767) was s and h. of Edmund W of Tewkesbury (*d.* 1741), the only s of Sir Edmund Wiseman, of London (*d* 8 May 1704, aged 74), who was 2d s of the 1st Bart   He was *b.* 30 Jan 1731 and *suc. to the Baronetcy* 25 May 1774   He *m* firstly, 1 Dec 1757, Mary, da. of Michael Godden, Master Attendant of the Dock Yard at Chatham   She *d* 11 June 1766. He *m.* secondly, 2 Dec 1769, Sarah, da. of Thomas King, of Gravesend, Kent, but by her had no male issue   She *d.* 4 Dec. 1777   He *d* 27 Jan. 1810

VII. 1810.   Sir William Saltonstall Wiseman, Bart [1628(¹)], grandson and h , being s and h of Edmund Wiseman, by Jemima, da of Michael Arne, of London, which Edmund was s and h. ap. of the 6th Bart by his first wife, and *d.* v p. 7 May 1787, aged 28   He was *b* 5 March 1784 and was sometime a Captain R N   He *suc to the Baronetcy* 27 Jan 1810   He *m* firstly, 8 Jan 1812, at Bagdad in Persia, Catharine, 2d da of Right Hon Sir James Mackintosh, Recorder of Bombay. She was divorced by Act of Parl 22 June 1825.   He *m* secondly, 5 April 1827, Eliza, 1st da. of Rev George Davies, B D., Rector of Cranfield, Beds. He *d* 1 July 1845. Will pr July 1845   His widow *d* s p 27 Oct 1862, at Hillingdon End, Uxbridge, aged 74

VIII. 1845.   Sir William Saltonstall Wiseman, Bart. [1628(¹)], s and h. by 1st wife, *b.* 4 Aug 1814 at Bombay ; entered Royal Navy , *suc to the Baronetcy* 1 July 1845 , Capt. R N 1854   Commodore on the Australian station, Vice President Ordnance Select Committee, 1863 ; granted a " good service " pension, 1866, becoming finally (1869) Rear Admiral, and retiring in 1870   C B 1864 , K C B 1867 He *m* 25 Oct 1838, at Widley, Hants, Charlotte Jane, only da of Charles William Paterson, of East Cosham House, Hants , Admiral R.N.   He *d.* suddenly 14 July 1874, in his 60th year, at the Saunders House, St. Joseph Missouri, in the United States of America, and was *bur* in Mount Mora cemetery (ª) His widow *d* 23 May 1891, at 70, Eaton terrace, and was *bur.* in the cemetery at Bedford

IX   1874   Sir William Wiseman, Bart. [1628(¹)], only s and h , *b.* 23 Aug 1845 at Cosham House aforesaid, entered the Royal Navy, 1859, serving in the New Zealand war, 1864-65 , Lieut. 1867 , served in the Niger Expedition, 1869 ; Commander, 1871 , Capt 1882, having *suc. to the Baronetcy*,

----

(ª) See *The Times*, 19 Aug 1874 as to his having registered his name as " William Chambers, Lincoln, Neb "

14 July 1874   He m 20 Sept 1878, at Putney, co Surrey, Sarah Elizabeth, 3d da of Lewis LANGWORTHY, of "Ellesmere," Putney Hill   He d 11 Jan 1893, at 4, Elliot Terrace, Plymouth and was bur in the cemetery at Bedford.   Admon £1,367 gross His widow living 1900

X.   1893   SIR WILLIAM GEORGE EDEN WISEMAN, Bart [1628(¹)], only s and h, b 1 Feb 1885, suc to the Baronetcy 11 Jan 1893

Family Estates —These appear to have been long since alienated, that of Great Canfield was sold about 1710 by the 3d Bart

---

NIGHTINGALE:

cr. 1 Sep. 1628,

dormant (for 70 years), 1722 to 1791

I   1628   "THOMAS NIGHTINGALE, of Newport Pond, co Essex, Esq," as also of Langley in that county, and of Kneesworth in Bassingbourn, co. Cambridge, s and h. of Geoffrey NIGHTINGALE, of Newport Pond aforesaid, Double Reader of Gray's Inn, London, by Katharine, da. and h. of John CLAMPS, of Huntingdon, was admitted to Gray's Inn, 1 March 1591/2, suc his father, 23 Feb. 1619, was Sheriff of Essex, 1627-28, and was cr a Bart, as above, 1 Sept 1628 He m firstly, in or before 1606, Millicent, da of Sir Robert CLERK, of Pleshy and of Newarks in Good Easter, Essex, one of the Barons of the Exchequer, by Dorothy, da. of John MAYNARD   He m secondly, in or before 1617, Catharine, 1st da of Sir Robert CHESTER, of Cockenhatch, Herts, by Anne, da of Sir Henry Capell, of Hadham   She was bur. 3 March 1635/6, at Newport   He m thirdly, Elizabeth, da of (—)   He d Jan. 1644/5.   His will, dat. 4 and proved 24 Jan 1644/5.   His widow d s p m, 23 and was bur 25 Aug 1686, at Newport, Essex, aged 74   M.I

II.   1645   SIR THOMAS NIGHTINGALE, Bart. [1628], of Langley, Essex, and of Stevenage, Herts, grandson and h, being s and h of Robert Nightingale, by Theodosia, 3d da of Sir Robert CHESTER, abovenamed, which Robert Nightingale was s and h ap (by his 1st wife) of the 1st Bart, and d v p 30 April 1636, aged 29   He was b 15 Oct. 1629, and suc to the Baronetcy in Jan 1644/5   He m 30 May 1655, at St Olave's, Southwark, Jane, da of George SHIERS, of London and of Slyfield House in Great Bookham, Surrey, aunt and eventually heir of Sir George SHIERS, Bart so cr 1684   He d s p m s (ᵃ) and was bur. at Newport, Essex, 19 Oct. 1702   Admon 13 Dec 1703, pendente lite between Sir Bridges Nightingale, Bart and others   His widow d 1705   Her will dat. 19 July 1704, proved 22 May 1705

III   1702.   SIR BRIDGES NIGHTINGALE, Bart [1628], of Enfield, Middlesex, nephew and h, being s and h of Geoffrey NIGHTINGALE, of Enfield aforesaid and of Hamburgh, Merchant, by Anne da of John BRIDGES, of St Giles's Cripplegate, London, Citizen, and Pinmaker, which Geoffrey (who was bur at Enfield 23 July 1690), was yr br of the 2d Bart   He suc to the Baronetcy, in Oct. 1702   He d unm and was bur at Enfield.

IV.   1715?   SIR ROBERT NIGHTINGALE, Bart [1628], of Enfield, aforesaid br and h, suc to the Baronetcy on the death of his brother. He was one of the Directors of the East India Company.   He d unm and was bur. 24 July 1722, at Enfield.   Will dat. 23 May, and proved 16 July 1722 (ᵇ)

[After his death the *Baronetcy*, remained *dormant* for about 70 years, the right thereto being as below]

(ᵃ) His only s and h ap Sir Robert Nightingale [often, erroneously said to have suc him in the Baronetcy], was *Knighted* at Whitehall, 12 Dec 1685, Sheriff of Norfolk, 1685-86, d. s p., and v p, 3 and was bur. 11 July 1697, at Newport aforesaid.
(ᵇ) He left his estates to his cousin Robert GASCOYNE, younger s of the Rev. Joseph GASCOYNE, Vicar of Enfield, by Anne, da of Francis THEOBALD, of Barking, Suffolk, and Anne, his wife, sister of Sir Thomas NIGHTINGALE, the 2d Bart.   This Robert GASCOYNE d unm. (of the small pox), 2 Nov 1722 and was bur. at Enfield.

V. 1722.   EDWARD NIGHTINGALE, of Kneesworth aforesaid, cousin and
h male, being s and h of Geoffrey Nightingale, of the same, by his 1st
wife, Elizabeth, da of Sir William LUCKYN, of Essex, which Geoffrey (who *d* 9 May
1681, aged 64), was s of the 1st Bart by his 2nd wife He was *bap.* 27 Aug. 1658
He *suc to the Baronetcy* on the death of his cousin, in July 1722, but *never assumed
the title* He *m.* Anne Charlotte, da. of Sir Arthur SHINGSBY, of Bifrons, 1st Bart
[1657], by his wife, a native of Flanders She was *bap.* 4 Jan 1664, at Patrix-
bourne, in Kent. He *d.* 2 July 1723 Will dat. 20 April 1722, pr 1723.

VI. 1723 ?   GAMALIEL NIGHTINGALE, s. and h , admitted to Gray's Inn,
4 May 1710; mentioned in his father's will April 1722, whom he
probably survived,(a) thereby *succeeding to the Baronetcy*, though *not assuming the
title.* He *d* a lunatic, and unm

VII. 1730 ?   EDWARD NIGHTINGALE, of Kneesworth aforesaid, br and
h ,(a) *b* 1696 , admitted to Gray's Inn, 5 April 1720 His elder br.
having died s p, he *suc. to the Baronetcy* on his (or, possibly, on their father's) death,
but *never assumed the title* He *m* Eleanora, da of Charles ETHELSTON of London.
He *d* at Bath 20 Oct 1750 Will dat. 26 Sep and proved 31 Oct. 1750. His
widow *d.* 14 Sep 1771, aged 71, and was *bur* at Bassingbourne. Her will dat
22 Sep 1765, pr 24 Sep. 1771.

VIII. 1750 ?   EDWARD NIGHTINGALE, of Kneesworth aforesaid, s. and
h , *b* 4 Sept 1726, *suc to the Baronetcy*, presumably on 20 Oct 1750,
but *never assumed the title* He *d.* unm at Town Malling, Kent, July 1782. Admon
1 Aug 1782

IX 1782   GAMALIEL NIGHTINGALE, of Kneesworth aforesaid, br and
h., *b* 15 Feb 1731 Captain R N., was in command of a frigate in
1761, when he captured a French ship of superior force off the Land's End ; *suc to the
Baronetcy* in July 1782, but *never assumed the title* He *m* Maria, da of Peter CLOSSEN,
of Hamburgh, Merchant, a native of Mecklenburg Schwerin. She *d* 20 Feb. 1789,
aged 50, and was *bur.* at Bassingbourne He *d* Jan 1791 Will dat. 20 Aug. 1789,
proved 27 Jan. 1791.

X 1791.   SIR EDWARD NIGHTINGALE, Bart. [1628], of Kneesworth
aforesaid, only s and h, *b* 14 Oct 1760, at Gosport, Hants , *suc to
the Baronetcy* in Jan. 1791, and consequently *assumed the title of Baronet* as heir male
of the body of the 1st Bart , having recorded a pedigree, proving that fact, in the
College of Arms London, which he signed, 12 Aug 1797 He *m* once at Gretna
Green, Scotland, and again at Bassingbourne, Eleanor, da. and sole h of his uncle
Robert NIGHTINGALE, of Kneesworth aforesaid, by (his cousin), Mary, da. of Charles
ETHELSTON, of London He *d* 4 Dec. 1804. Will pr 1805. His widow *d* 20 Jan.
1825 Will pr Feb 1825.

XI 1804.   SIR CHARLES ETHELSTON NIGHTINGALE, Bart [1628], of
Kneesworth aforesaid, 1st surviving s and h , *b* 1 Nov 1784. Lieut.
3d Foot Guards, *suc. to the Baronetcy* 4 Dec 1804 He *m.* Dec 1805, his cousin,
Maria, only da of Thomas Lacy DICKONSON, of West Retford, Notts, by Maria Eleanor,
sister of Sir Edward NIGHTINGALE, 10th Bart. abovenamed He *d.* 5 July 1843, aged
59, at Bath, leaving it was said, all his property to Dr. Greville, his physician.(b) His
widow *d* 8 Dec 1846, at Boulogne sur-mer Admon May 1847.

XII 1843   SIR CHARLES NIGHTINGALE, Bart [1628], s. and h., *b* at West
Retford, 30 April 1809 , sometime a Midshipman in the Royal navy;
served also in Sir de Lacy Evans' brigade in Spain, *suc to the Baronetcy*, 5 July 1843
He *m.* 2 Feb 1829, Harriet Maria, da of Edward Broughton FOSTER, of Ayleston co

---

(a) Whether Gamaliel survived his father, or was himself survived by his brother
Edward, must remain uncertain, till the date of death of Gamaliel is ascertained.
(b) See obituary in *Ann. Reg.* as to the suspicion by his son, of his having been
poisoned The verdict however, after the *post mortem* was "hæmatemis, by the
Visitation of God."

Leicester, and of Kingston-on-Thames, Capt. in the army, niece of Lieut. Gen. TRAPAUD He *d* 17 Sep 1876, aged 67, at Ludham. His widow *d* 22 Dec 1881, aged 81, at Hounslow.

XIII. 1876. SIR HENRY DICKONSON NIGHTINGALE, Bart. [1628], only s and h., *b.* 15 Nov. 1830, at Bruges, in Belgium ; entered the Royal Marines, 1849 , served throughout the Burmese war of 1852 in H M S "Fox" ; First Lieut. 1853 , Captain, 1861 Capt and Paymaster, 45th Foot, 1864 82, retiring as Hon Lieut. Col ; *suc to the Baronetcy,* 17 Sep. 1876 He *m* 14 Aug. 1855, Mary, da of Thomas Spark, Capt R N.

Family Estates.—These appear to have totally alienated, after the death, in July 1843 of the 11th Bart , who for some time resided at Kneesworth Hall He possibly may have disposed of them even in his lifetime

---

JAQUES, *or* JACQUES
cr. 2 Sep. 1628 ,
ex. Jan 1660/1.

I. 1628 "JOHN JAQUES, of (—), co. Middlesex, Esq., one of to H M 's Gentlemen Pensioners," was *b* about 1599, (being, presumably 1661. the "John Jaques, s. and h. of John JAQUES, of Highgate, co. Midx , Esq " who, 20 Oct. 1623, was admitted to Giay's Inn), was *cr a Bart.,* as above, 2 Sep 1628. He was sometime student at Sion College ; was M P for Haslemere, April to May 1640, and Nov. 1640, till void shortly afterwards On 14 Sep 1642 he had lic from the Bishop of London's office (being then of St Helen's, London, about 43, bachelor) to marry Jane DIXON, of Great St. Bartholomew, about 50, widow He apparently *m* (secondly ?) Mary (a) The will of "Dame Mary Jaques " is pr 1657. He *d.* s p and was *bur* 15 Jan. 1660/1, at St Christopher le Stocks, London, when the *Baronetcy* became *extinct.*

VAN LORE, *or* VAULOOR:
cr. 3 Sep. 1628;
ex 1644/5.

I 1628, "PETER VAULOOR [*i e.,* VAN LORE], of Tylehurst,(b) co. to Berks, Esq ," s. of Sir Peter VAN LORE, of Fenchurch Street, 1645 London, Merchant,(c) a Protestant refugee from Utrecht (who with "Jacoba(d) Van Lore, of Ixea [*Qy* Ixem] in Flanders," presumably his wife, had settled in London, being *Knighted,* 5 Nov 1621, at Whitehall, and who *d.* 6 Sep. 1627, aged 80), was probably *b* about 1580, and was *cr a Bart,* as above, 3 Sep. 1628. He *m* firstly, Susan, da. of Laurence BRCKE, of Antwerp He *m.* secondly, Katharine, who survived him He *d.* s p m (e) about 1644/5, when the *Baronetcy* became *extinct* Will dat 18 Aug. 1644, pr 6 March 1644/5, and 1663 His second wife survived him Her will pr 1663

(a) In Courthope's *Extinct Baronetage,* " Mary " is the *only* wife attributed to him

(b) It is stated in Burke's *Extinct Baronetcies* that he " is supposed to have had a temporary interest in the manor of Tylehurst by some alliance with the Kendrick family "

(c) In 1618-19 he was among the wealthy Dutch merchants sued in the Star chamber by James 1 for exporting the large sums made in business from the realm He was fined no less than £7,000. See Moens' introduction to the *Austen Friars Registers.*

(d) She, apparently, is the "Jacomynken" wife of "Pieter Van Loore," living 11 Dec 1608 [Crawley-Boevey's *Boevey Family,* p. 14]

(e) Of his three daughters and coheirs—(1) Jacoba, *m* Henry Alexander, *otherwise* Zinzan, of Tilehurst, and *d* 22 June 1677 ; (2) Susanna, *m* 29 July 1634, at St. Andrew's, Holborn, Sir Robert Crooke , and (3) Mary, *m* Henry (Alexander), Earl of Stirling [S]

DILLINGTON :
cr. 6 Sep. 1628 ;
ex 4 July 1721

I. 1628   " ROBERT DILLINGTON, of [Knighton in the parish
of Newchurch, in] the Isle of Wight, co Southampton, Esq ," only
s. and h of Tristram DILLINGTON, of Newchurch aforesaid, by Jane, da of Nicholas
MARTIN of Achilhampton, co. Dorset, suc his father in Feb. 1593/4, and his uncle,
Sir Robert Dillington, in Dec. 1604, and was cr a Bart, as above, 6 Sep 1628 ; M P
for Isle of Wight, Nov 1654 to 1655   He m. firstly, Mabell, da of Sir Humphrey
FORSTER, of Berks   He m secondly, Catharine [Frances ?] sister of Richard
(GORGES), BARON GORGES OF DUNDALK [I], da. of Sir Thomas GORGES, of Langford,
Wilts, by Helena, Dow Marchioness of Northampton, da of Wolfgang VON SUAVEN-
BURG, of Sweden   He d. 1664.   Admon 31 Oct 1665 to Sir Robert Dillington,
Bart , pendente lite   His relict, " Dame Frances Dillington," was living 7 June, 1688.

II 1664   SIR ROBERT DILLINGTON, Bart. [1628], of Knighton aforesaid, grandson and h , being s and h. of Robert Dillington, of Motti-
stone, in the Isle of Wight (admitted to Gray's Inn, 18 May 1631 , M P. for Newport,
1659 and 1660), who was 2d but 1st surv s and h ap. of 1st Bart by his 1st wife,
and d v.p   He matric at Oxford (Queen's Coll.), 9 Dec 1653 ; was admitted to
Gray's Inn, 1 Nov. 1654, and suc to the Baronetcy in 1664 , was M P for Newport
(Isle of Wight) in four Parls, 1670-81   He m firstly, June, da. of John FREKE,
of Shrowton   She was bur at Newchurch   He m. secondly (Lic. Vic. Gen., 28 May
1678, he about 30, widower, she about 18, spinster), Hunnah, da. of William WEBB,
of Throgmorton street, St Bartholomew, near the Exchange, London, citizen   He
d 25 April 1687, aged 53, and was bur at Newchurch   Will dat 2 Feb 1682/3, pr.
10 June 1687

III 1687 ?   SIR ROBERT DILLINGTON, Bart. [1628], of Knighton aforesaid, s. and h. by 1st wife , was b about 1665 ; matric at Oxford
(Queen's Coll) 1 June 1682, aged 17 ; suc. to the Baronetcy about 1687 , was M P. for
Newport (Isle of Wight) for some months in 1689, till his death   He d. unm
1689, and was bur at Newchurch   Will dat 7 June 1688, pr 17 Dec 1689

IV. 1689   SIR JOHN DILLINGTON, Bart. [1628], of Knighton aforesaid, br. and h ; under 21 in Feb 1682/3, suc to the Baronetcy about
1689.   He d s p 5 March 1705/6, and was bur at Newchurch   Will dat. 9 Nov.
1705, pr 24 July 1712

V. 1706   SIR TRISTRAM DILLINGTON, Bart. [1628], of Knighton
to   aforesaid, half br and h , being s of the 2d Bart. by his 2d wife ; suc
1721   to the Baronetcy about 1706.   He was sometime a Major in the
Guards.   He d s.p., 7 July 1721, aged 43 and was bur at Newchurch, when the Baronetcy became extinct   Will dat. 11 June 1706, pr 5 Sep 1721.

PILE :
cr 12 Sep. 1628 ;
ex. about 1780

I. 1628   " FRANCIS PILE, of Compton [i e., Compton-Beauchamp],
co. Berks, Esq ," s. and h of Sir Gabriel PILE, of Bubton, Wilts,
by Anne, da. of Sir Thomas PORTER, of Newark, co. Gloucester, was b. 15 June 1589 ,
aged 34 in 1623 , suc his father 7 Nov 1626 and, for his service to the Crown, was cr a
Bart as above 12 Sep. 1628   He m , in or before 1617, Elizabeth, 2d da. of Sir
Francis POPHAM, of Littlecott, Wilts, by Amy, da. of John DUDLEY, of Stoke Newington   He d 1 and was bur 8 Dec 1635, at Collingbourne Kingston, Wilts.   Will pr.
1636.   His widow d 7 Oct , and was bur. 5 Nov., 1658, at Collingbourne.   Will pr.
1658

II. 1635.   SIR FRANCIS PILE, Bart. [1628], of Compton Beauchamp aforesaid, s and h, was b about 1617 ; aged 6 in 1623 ; matric. at Oxford (Univ. Coll), 22 Nov 1633, aged 16 ; admitted to Middle Temple, 1637 ; *suc to the Baronetcy*, 1 Dec. 1635. Sheriff of Berks, 1643-45 , M P thereof, July 1646 till death He m firstly, 9 June 1634, Mary, only ds of Samuel DUNCH, of Pusey, Berks, by Dulcibella, his wife She, who was b 25 June 1596, d s p s, Sep 1655, and was bur. at Pusey M I He m. secondly, Jane, said(a) to be da. of John STILL, Bishop of Bath and Wells (1593-1608), by his second wife, Jane, da of Sir John HORNER He d. s p m ,(b) 12 Feb 1648/9. Will pr April 1649 His widow d. 25 July and was bur. 4 Aug 1692, at Collingbourne, aged 80. Will pr 1692.

III. 1649   SIR SEYMOUR PILE, Bart. [1628], of Axford in Ramsbury Wilts, br and h male ; matric (with his brother) at Oxford (Univ Coll), 22 Nov 1633, aged 15 , admitted to Middle Temple, 1635 , *suc. to the Baronetcy*, 12 Feb 1648/9 He m in or before 1661, Elizabeth, 2d da of Sir Henry MOORE, 1st Bart. [1627], of Fawley, by Elizabeth, da of William BEVERLEY, of Kenoe, Beds His widow was living 25 Nov. 1689

IV 1670 ?   SIR FRANCIS PILE, Bart. [1628], of Axford aforesaid, s and h., *suc to the Baronetcy* on the death of his father He m Frances, da of Sir Bulstrode WHITELOCK, of Chilton, Berks, sometime Lord Keeper of the Great Seal, by his 2d wife Frances, da. of William (WILLOUGHBY), 3d BARON WILLOUGHBY OF PARHAM She d before him He d. about 1689 Admon. 25 Nov. 1689

V. 1689 ?   SIR SEYMOUR PILE, Bart [1628], of Axford aforesaid s. and h , *suc to the Baronetcy* about 1689, being then a minor He m Jane, only da of John LAWFORD, of Stapleton, co Gloucester She d. July 1726.

VI. 1730 ?   SIR FRANCIS SEYMOUR PILE, Bart [1628], of North Stone-
to   ham, and of Someley, Hants, s. and h , unm in 1741 ;(c) *suc to the
1761   Baronetcy*, on his father's death He m Anne, widow of Richard FLEMING, da of Sir Ambrose CROWLEY, of GREENWICH, Alderman, and sometime, 1706-07, Sheriff of London, by Mary, da of Charles OWEN The will of "Dame Ann Pill" [sic] is pr. 1761 He d. apparently s p m s , 4 May 1761, when the *Baronetcy*, presumably,(d) became *extinct*

POLE:

cr 12 Sep 1628,

subsequently, 1790-99, *and since* 1874, DE-LA-POLE,

being, *sometime,* 1847-1874, REEVE-DE-LA-POLE

I. 1628.   "JOHN POLE, of Shutt [i.e., Shute], co. Devon, Esq.," s. and h ap of Sir William POLE, of Colcomb in that county, the celebrated Antiquary, by his 1st wife Mary, 1st da and coheir of Sir William PERIAM, Lord Chief Baron of the Exchequer, was M P. for Devon, 1626 ; Sheriff thereof, 1638-39, and was v p cr a Bart , as above, 12 Sep. 1628. He suc. his father (who d. aged 74) 9 Feb. 1635, took arms for the Parl and was one of the sequestrators for

---

(a) In the Bishop's funeral certificate, 4 April 1607, no such da. is mentioned. It is there stated that by Jane his 2d wife he had one son Thomas Still, then 12 years old. The two sons and four daughters (Sarah, Anne, Elizabeth, and Mary) by the 1st wife and their husbands are fully set out. The age of Dame Jane Pile at death is inconsistent with such parentage, as the Bishop died 26 Feb 1607/8 ; possibly it should be 84 or 85, and possibly she was a posthumous child.

(b) Of his three daughters and coheirs by his 2d wife, (1) Ann m Francis (HOLLES), 2d BARON HOLLES OF IFIELD , (2) Elizabeth m. Sir Thomas STRICKLAND, Bart , of Boynton , (3) Jane m , 13 Nov 1672, at Collingbourne, Edward RICHARDS, of Yaverland, Isle of Wight, and their issue inherited Compton Beauchamp

(c) Wotton's *Baronetage*, 1741

(d) According, however, to Kimber's *Baronetage*, 1771, he left a son and successor, Sir Seymour Pile, the present Baronet, who is a minor "

I

Devon, 1643. He *m.* firstly, 5 Jan. 1613/4, at Shute, Elizabeth, da. and h. of Roger How, of London, Merchant, by Jane, da of William SYMES, of Chard, which Jane *m.*, for her 2d husband (as his 2d wife), Sir William POLE abovenamed. He *m.* secondly, Mary, widow of William LOCKLAND, of Bromley St Leonard's, Midx. He *d.* at Bromley aforesaid, 16 April, and was *bur* 13 July 1658, at Colyton. Admon. 24 June 1658, his widow, Mary, being then living.

II 1658   SIR COURTENAY POLE, Bart. [1628], of Shute aforesaid, 2d but 1st surv. s and h male(a); *bap* 17 Feb 1618/9, at Colyton ; adm. to Lincoln's Inn, 16 June 1635 ; took arms for the King, *suc to the Baronetcy* in April 1658 , M P. for Honiton, 1661-79 Sheriff of Devon, 1681-82. He *m.*, in or before 1649, Urith, da. of Thomas SHAPCOTE, of Shapcote He was *bur* 13 April 1695, at Shute

III 1695   SIR JOHN POLE, Bart [1628], of Shute aforesaid, only surviving s. and h. , *b.* and *bap* 17 June 1649, at Allhallows, Goldsmith street, Exeter ; registered at Colyton , M.P for Lyme Regis, 1685-87, and 1689-90 , for Bossiney, 1698-1700 , for Devon, 1701-02 , for East Looe, 1702-05, and for Newport, co Cornwall, 1705-08 , having *suc to the Baronetcy* in April 1695 He *m* Anne, sister of Sir William MORICE, 1st Bart [1661], da. of Sir William MORICE, of Werrington, Devon, Secretary of State to Charles II, by Elizabeth, da. of Humphrey PRIDEAUX, of Soulden in that county He *d* 13 and was *bur.* 20 March 1707/8, at Colyton Will pr. May 1708 His widow was *bur* there 1 March 1713/4 Will pr. March 1714

IV 1708   SIR WILLIAM POLE, Bart. [1628], of Shute aforesaid, s. and h *bap* 17 Aug 1678 ; matric at Oxford (New Coll) 7 July 1696, aged 18 , M.P. for Newport, 1701-02 , for Camelford, 1704-08 , for Newport (again), 1708-10 ; for Devon, 1710-12 , for Bossiney, 1713-15 , for Honiton, 1716-27 and 1731-34 ; having *suc to the Baronetcy*, 13 March 1707/8 Master of the Royal Household, 1713. He is said to have married(b) Elizabeth WARRY or WARREN, of Colyton, spinster, sometimes called da. of Robert WARRY He *d*, of the gout, 31 Dec 1741. Will pr May 1742 His widow was *bur.* 12 April 1758.

V 1741.   SIR JOHN POLE, Bart [1628], of Shute aforesaid, only s and h , *b.* about 1733 , *suc. to the Baronetcy*, 31 Dec. 1741 ; matric. at Oxford (New Coll) 19 April 1750, aged 17 He *m* firstly, Elizabeth, da and coheir of John Mill, of Woodford, Essex She *d.* 10 Aug. 1758, aged 21 He *m.* secondly, Maria, da of Rev. (—) PALMER, of Combe Raleigh, Devon He *d* 19 Feb. 1760, aged 27 Will pr 1760 His widow *m* George CLAVERING (by whom she was mother of Sir Thomas John Clavering, 8th Bart), and *d* in or before 1777 ; admon 2 Aug 1777, as " of St. Marylebone, Midx " granted to her said husband.

VI 1760   SIR JOHN WILLIAM POLE, *afterwards* (1790-99), DE-LA-POLE, Bart. [1628], of Shute aforesaid, only s. and h. by first marriage, *b.* at Salisbury and *bap.* 27 June 1757, at Shute , matric at Oxford (Corpus Christi Coll.), 8 June 1776, aged 18 , *suc to the Baronetcy*, 19 Feb. 1760 Sheriff of Devon, 1782-83 By Royal Lic. 1790, he took the name of DE-LA-POLE in lieu of POLE. M P for West Looe, 1790-96 He *m.*, 9 Jan 1781, Anne, only da of James TEMPLER, of Stover House, Devon. He *d.* 30 Nov. 1799 Will pr. Aug 1800 His widow *d* 12 Feb 1832

VII. 1799   SIR WILLIAM TEMPLER POLE, Bart [1628], of Shute aforesaid, s and h *b* 2 Aug. and *bap.* 20 Sep 1782 at Shute ; ed at Eton , *suc. to the Baronetcy* 30 Nov. 1799 , matric at Oxford (Ch Ch), 24 April 1801, aged 18 , *cr.* M.A., 13 June 1804, and D.C L , 5 July 1810 ; admitted to Lincoln's Inn,

---

(a) Sir William Pole, the eldest s and h ap., was *bap* 6 Dec. 1614, at Colyton , was M P for Honiton, 1640-42 , *Knighted* 19 April 1641 , married two wives and had seven children, of whom the three sons died unm before their grandfather He, himself, *d* v p. and was *bur* 30 Jan 1648/9 at Colyton Admon., as " of Shute, co Devon," 2 Nov 1656, to his principal creditor That of his widow Katherine " as of Burford, Wilts," 18 Feb. 1657/8

(b) The date [presumably in or before 1733] and place of this marriage are unknown, as also are any proofs afforded by settlements or otherwise.

21 Feb 1803 as "POLE," not having availed himself of the licence (to his father) to bear the name of DE-LA-POLE Sheriff of Devon, 1818-19 He *m* firstly, 24 Aug. 1804, Sophia Anne, only da. of his maternal uncle, George TEMPLER, of Shapwick House, Somerset, by Jane, da of Henry PAUL, of West Monckton. She *d* 17 March 1808 He *m* secondly, 31 July 1810, Charlotte Frances, only da. of John FRASER, by (—), sister of John FARQUHAR, of Fonthill Abbey, Wilts. He *d* 1 April 1847, at Shute House, aged 65. Will, as "Pole *alias* De-la-Pole," pr July 1847. His widow *d* 2 Oct. 1877, at Bayford Grange, Herts, in her 91st year

VIII   1847.   SIR JOHN GEORGE REEVE-DE-LA-POLE, Bart. [1628], of Shute aforesaid, s. and h by 1st wife; *b* 21 Jan. 1808 at Shute House, educated at Winchester and at Sandhurst By Royal Lic., 5 Oct. 1838, he took the name of REEVE before that of DE LA POLE in compliance with the will of Anna Maria, widow of Sir George Trenchard, da and coheir of Sir Thomas Reeve He *suc* to the Baronetcy, 1 April 1847 He *m* firstly, 26 March 1829, Margaretta, 2d da of Henry BARTON, of Saucethorpe Hall, co Lincoln She *d* June 1842. He *m* secondly, 2 Feb 1843, Mlle. Josephine Catherine Denise CARRE, of Anse, Rhone, in France He *d*. s.p m., 19 May 1874, in Jermyn street, Midx His widow *m*, 1881, Mons. Antoine Pierre ROUPE and was living at Paris, 1900.

IX.   1874   SIR WILLIAM EDMUND DE-LA-POLE, Bart. [1628], of Shute House aforesaid, br., of the half blood, and h, being s by his 2d wife, of the 7th Bart. He was *b* 3 July 1816 in Weymouth street, Marylebone, ed. at Winchester, matric at Oxford (Ch. Ch), 17 Oct 1833, aged 17, Student, 1834-41, B.A., 1837, M A., 1840, admitted to Lincoln's Inn, 18 Nov 1837; Barrister, 1841; *suc.* to the Baronetcy, 19 May 1874. He *m*, 26 April 1841, Margaret Victoriosa, 2d da. of Admiral the Hon Sir John TALBOT, G C B (son of Margaret, *suo jure* BARONESS TALBOT OF MALAHIDE [I.]), by Juliana, da of James Everard (ARUNDELL), 9th BARON ARUNDELL OF WARDOUR She *d*. 23 Nov 1886, at Colcombe, Mount Ephraim road, Streatham, aged 69 He *d* 21 March 1895, at Shute House, after a long illness. Will pr at £8,604 gross

X.   1895   SIR EDMUND REGINALD TALBOT DE-LA-POLE, *formerly* POLE, Bart [1628], of Shute aforesaid, 1st s and h, *b* 22 Feb 1844, ed at Winchester; *suc* to the Baronetcy, 21 March 1895, on which occasion he assumed the name of *De La Pole* He *m* firstly, 25 Sep. 1877, at South Benfleet, Essex, Mary Ann Margaret, widow of John Ormsby PHIBBS, 3d Hussars, only child of Capt Hastings SANDS, King's Dragoon Guards She *d* 10 May 1878 He *m* secondly, 18 Dec. 1884, Elizabeth Maria. da of Charles RHODES, of "Lyndhurst," in Sidcup, co. Kent

Family Estates—These, in 1883, consisted of 5,846 acres in Devon, valued at £7,416 a year, and of (—) acres in Berks, of the annual value of £370 *Principal Seat*—Shute House, near Axminster, Devon.

66

LEWIS.

cr. 14 Sep. 1628;

ex. 1677.

I   1628,   "WILLIAM LEWIS, of Langors [i e, Llangorse], co Brecon,
    to   Esq," s and h of Lodowick LEWIS, of Trewalter in that county,
    1677   by (—), da. and coheir of William WATKINS, of Llangorse aforesaid,
was Sheriff of Brecon, 1619-20, and again 1636-37, was M P for Petersfield, April to May 1640, and Nov 1640 till (being one of the eleven Presbyterian members impeached in 1647) he was secluded Dec 1648; M.P. for Breconshire, 1606, and for Lymington, 1661 till death, having been *cr a Bart*, as above, 14 Sep 1628. He, who resided principally at Borden, Hants, was Gov of Portsmouth, for the Parl, 1642, served in most of the Parl Committees, and was Commissioner of the

Admiralty in Oct 1645 He *m*, in or after Feb 1621/2, Mary, widow of Sir Thomas NEALE, of Warneford, Hants, da of Robert CALTON, of Goring, Oxon She was *bur* 22 Feb 1635/6, at Warneford aforesaid with her first husband He *d* s p m s,[a] 1677, when the *Baronetcy* became *extinct* Will dat 4 March 1674/5, pr 28 Nov 1677

COLEPEPER, *or* CULPEPER   67

cr 20 Sep 1628,

ex. 28 March 1740

I   1628.   "WILLIAM CULPEPER, of Wakehurst, co. Sussex, Esq," 2d but 1st surv s and h of Sir Edward CULPEPER, *or* COLEPEPER, of the same, by Elizabeth, da of William FERNFOLD, of Nashin, Sussex, was admitted to Lincoln's Inn 1623, and was *cr* a *Bart*, as above, 20 Sep 1628, Sheriff of Surrey and Sussex, 1634-35, M.P. for East Grinstead 1640, till void 24 Dec He *m*., in or before 1629, Jane, da and eventually h of Sir Benjamin PELLETT, of Bolney, Sussex He *d* about 1651 Will pr 1651.

II.   1651?   SIR BENJAMIN COLEPEPER, Bart [1628], of Wakehurst aforesaid, s and h, aged 5 at the visitation of Sussex in 1634; *suc. to the Baronetcy* about 1651 He *m* Catherine, da and coheir of Goldsmith HUDSON. He *d* s p m

III   1670?   SIR EDWARD COLEPEPER, Bart. [1628], of Wakehurst aforesaid, br and h, *b.* about 1632 He *suc to the Baronetcy* on the death of his brother He *m* (—)

IV.   1700?   SIR WILLIAM COLEPEPER, Bart [1628], of Wakehurst
to   aforesaid, grandson and h, being s and h of Benjamin COLEPEPER by
1740   Judith, da of Sir William WILSON, 1st Bart [1660], of Eastbourne, which Benjamin was s and h ap of the late Bart, but *d* v p He was *b.* 23 Nov. 1668, at Wakehurst, *suc. to the Baronetcy* on the death of his grandfather. He *d*, unm 28 March, and was *bur.* 6 April 1740, at St. James', Westm., when the *Baronetcy* became *extinct*.[b]

LAWRENCE, *or* LAURENCE:

cr 9 Oct 1628;

ex. April 1714

I   1628   "JOHN LAURENCE, of [Delaford in] Iver, co Bucks, Knt.," s. and h of Thomas LAWRENCE,[c] of Chelsea, citizen and goldsmith of London (*d* 28 Oct. 1593, aged 54), by Martha, da of Sir Anthony CAGE, of London, was *b* about 1589, matric at Oxford (St John's Coll), 27 May 1603, aged 14, B A. (from Oriel Coll), 29 Oct 1604, M A (from St Edm Hall), 7 July 1615, was *Knighted* at Royston, 26 Jan. 1609/10, and was *cr* a *Bart*, as above, 9 Oct 1628. He *m*, in or before 1610, Grisel, da and coheir of Jarvis GIBBON, of Benenden, co Kent He *d*. 13 and was *bur* 14 Nov 1638, at Chelsea, aged 50 Funeral certificate in Public Record office Will pr 1639 His widow was *bur* 22 March 1675, at Chelsea Will pr. 1679

(a) His only son, Lodowick Lewis, *d* v p, leaving three daughters and coheirs, one of whom was ancestress of the families of Pryse and Loveden, afterwards Pryse, by whom, in 1806, the greater part of the Llangorse estate was sold

(b) In the Temple Church, London, occurs the burial, 2 April 1663, of "Sir Cheney Culpeper, Bart." The word "Bart," however, is clearly a mistake for "Knt" He was of Hollingbourne, co. Kent, matric at Oxford (Hart Hall), 6 Nov. 1618, aged 17, admitted to Middle Temple, 1621 Mar lic (London) 24 Oct 1632, aged 28, and a bachelor. Admon. 19 Dec 1666 and 10 March 1690/1.

(c) See *Coll. Top et Gen.*, vol iii, p. 281.

II. 1638   SIR JOHN LAWRENCE, Bart. [1628], of Chelsea aforesaid,
s and h , b about 1610 , matric at Oxford (St Edm. Hall), aged
17 ; admitted to Inner Temple, 1631, *suc. to the Baronetcy*, 13 Nov 1638 (ª) He *m* ,
in or before 1646, Mary, da of Sir Thomas HAMPSON, 1st Bart. [1642], of Taplow,
Bucks, by Anne, da. and coheir of William DUNCOMBE She was *bur* , 11 Oct. 1664,
at Chelsea He was living 28 Dec 1680, but *d* before 19 Feb 1710/1 (ᵇ)

III. 1690?   SIR THOMAS LAWRENCE, Bart [1628], of Chelsea aforeto   said, s and h, ; b about 1645 , matric. at Oxford (St. John's Coll),
1714.   20 Nov 1661, aged 16 , B A 23 Feb 1664/5 , M A (Univ Coll),
1668 , admitted to Middle Temple, 1664, *suc to the Baronetcy* on his
father's death He, having spent all his estate, emigrated to Maryland, where he was
Secretary to Gov Seymour in 1696 He *m* (Lic Vic Gen 18 May 1674, he about
28 and she about 20) Anne ENGLISH, of St Clement Danes, spinster He *d*
s.p m.s (ᶜ) and was *bur*. at Chelsea, 25 April 1714,(ᵈ) when the *Baronetcy* became
extinct. His widow was *bur*. 2 Nov 1723 at Chelsea

SLINGSBY.

cr 22 Oct. 1628 ,

ex. 1630

I 1628,   ANTHONY SLINGSBY, of Screvin [i e , Scriven], co York,
to   Esq ," s of Peter SLINGSBY,(ᵉ) of the same, being Gov of Zutphen, in
1630   the Low Countries, was cr a *Bart* , as above, 22 Oct. 1628 He *d*
s p. 1630, when the *Baronetcy* became *extinct*

VAVASOUR

cr 24 Oct 1628 ,

ex 27 Jan 1826

I 1628   "THOMAS VAVASOUR, of Hesselwood [i e , Haslewood], co
York, Esq ," s and h of William Vavasour, of the same, by Anne, da
of the Hon Sir Thomas MANNERS, younger s of Thomas, 1st EARL OF RUTLAND, was
cr. a Bart , as above, 24 Oct 1628 He was Knight Marshal of the King's Household
He *m* Ursula, da of Walter GIFFARD, of Chillington, co Stafford, by Philippa da. of
Richard WHITE, of South Warnborough, Hants He *d*. before March 1635,6

II. 1630?   SIR WALTER VAVASOUR, Bart [1628], of Haslewood aforesaid, s and h ; *suc to the Baronetcy* before March 1635/6 He raised
a regiment in the Civil Wars for the service of his King, serving as Colonel under the
Marquess of Newcastle He was, accordingly, nominated in 1660 one of the Knights

---

(ª) In Faulkner's *Chelsea* he is incorrectly identified with Sir John Laurence, of
St Helen's, Bishopsgate, L Mayor of London, 1664-65, who *d.* 26 Jan 1691/2

(ᵇ) His son (in the burial of a child named " Giles ") is spoken of as " Mr Thomas
Laurence, Esq ," 28 Dec 1680, and his son's wife (in the burial of her mother, " Mrs
Elizabeth English "), as " Lady Laurence," 19 Feb 1710/1 See burials of those
dates at Chelsea.

(ᶜ) John Laurence, his s and h ap., was *bap* at Chelsea, 5 Nov 1676 , matric at
Oxford (Univ Coll), 24 May 1694, B A. 26 Feb 1697/8 , *m*. Elizabeth, who was
bur at Chelsea 7 Aug 1701 , sold an estate at Chelsea, 26 March 1706, to William,
Lord Cheyne, and *d* s p m and v.p

(ᵈ) It is, however, stated in *N and Q.* (4th S , xii, 512) that "there is positive
proof that he died in Maryland in 1712," but query if this does not relate to John
Laurence, his son and heir apparent.

(ᵉ) This Peter was s. of Simon Slingsby, a yr. br. of Thomas Slingsby (ancestor of
the family seated at Scriven, who were Baronets [S.] 1635 to 1869), both being sons
of John Slingsby, of Scriven, who *d.* 1513.

of the intended order of the Royal Oak   He m. (Lic Lon , 8 March 1635/6, be 23 and she 18), Ursula, da of Thomas (BELASYSE), 1st VISCOUNT FAUCONBERG OF HENKNOWLE, by Barbara, da of Sir Henry CHOLMLEY, of Whitby   He was living 13 Aug 1666, being then aged 53

III   1670 ?   SIR WALTER VAVASOUR, Bart [1628], of Haslewood afore-
          said, only surv s and h , aged 22 on 13 Aug. 1666, *suc to the Baronetcy* on the death of his father   He m Jane, 2d da of Sir Jordan CROSSLAND, of Newby, co. York, by Bridget, da of John FLEMING   She, who was *bap* at Helmsley, 26 Dec 1649, was living 1696   He *d* s p 16 Feb 1712/3.

IV   1713   SIR WALTER VAVASOUR, Bart [1628], of Haslewood afore-
          said, cousin and h male, being s and h , of Peter VAVASOUR, M D , by Elizabeth, da of Philip LANGDALE, of Lanthorpe, co York, which Peter, who was *bur* at York 26 Nov 1659, was youngest s of the 1st Bart   He was *b* about 1659, and *suc to the Baronetcy*, 16 Feb 1712/3   He *d* unm , May 1740, aged about 80, in Lancashire

V.   1740   SIR WALTER VAVASOUR, Bart. [1628], of Haslewood afore-
          said, nephew and h , being s and h of Peter VAVASOUR, of York, which Peter, who *d* 6 June 1735, aged 68, was next br of the late Bart.   He *suc to the Baronetcy* 10 May 1745   He m. firstly, Elizabeth, da. of Peter VAVASOUR, of Willitoft, in the East Riding, co York   She *d* s.p.s   He m secondly, April 1741, Dorothy, da. of Marmaduke (LANGDALE), 4th BARON LANGDALE OF HOLME, by Elizabeth, da of William (WIDDRINGTON), BARON WIDDRINGTON OF BLANCKNEY   She *d.* 25 April 1751, at Haslewood   He *d* 13 April 1766

VI   1766   SIR WALTER VAVASOUR, Bart. [1628], of Haslewood afore-
          said, s and h by 2d wife , *b* 16 Jan 1744 , *suc to the Baronetcy*, 13 April 1766   He m , Sep. 1797, Jane, only da. and h. of William LANGDALE, of Langthorpe, co York   He *d.* s p 3 Nov 1802, and was *bur* at Haslewood.

VII   1802,   SIR THOMAS VAVASOUR, Bart. [1628], of Haslewood afore-
      to   said, br and h.   He *d* unm , at Haslewood Hall, 20 Jan 1826, aged
      1826   about 80, when the *Baronetcy* became *extinct* (a)

WOLSELEY · ᴵᴵ
cr 24 Nov. 1628.

I   1628   ROBERT WOLSELEY, of Morton, co Stafford, Esq ," Clerk
          of the King's Letters Patent, 2d s (b) of John Wolseley, of Stafford, by Isabella, da of John PORTER, of Chillington in that county, was *b* about 1587, and was *cr a Bart* , as above, 24 Nov. 1628   He was a Col in the King's Army and suffered sequestration accordingly   He m , in or before 1630, Mary, 2d da of Sir George WROUGHTON, of Wilcot, Wilts   He *d* in London, 21 Sep. 1646, aged 59, and was *bur* in Colwich church, co Stafford.   M L

II.   1646   SIR CHARLES WOLSELEY, Bart. [1628], of Wolseley, co.
          Stafford, s and h , *b* about 1630, being aged 33 at the *Visit. of Staffordshire* on 4 April 1663 .   *suc. to the Baronetcy*, 21 Sep. 1646, his (late) father's estate being fined £2,500 in Oct. 1647 , was M P. for Oxon, 1653 ; for Staffordshire, 1654 55 and 1655-58, and for Stafford, 1660   He enjoyed favour with the Commonwealth authorities, and was one of Cromwell's " House of Lords."   He m , in or before 1649, Anne, youngest da. of William (FIENNES), 1st VISCOUNT SAY AND SELE, by Elizabeth, da. of John TEMPLE, of Stow   He *d* 9 Oct. 1714, aged 85, and was *bur.* at Colwich aforesaid.   M I

(a) The Vavasour estates passed, under his will, to his maternal relative, Edward Marmaduke STOURTON, 2d s of Charles-Philip, BARON STOURTON, by Mary, da and coheir of his maternal uncle, Marmaduke (LANGDALE), BARON LANGDALE.   This Edward took the name of Vavasour in 1826, and was *cr a Bart.* 14 Feb. 1828.   He, however, has not any descent from the family of Vavasour.

(b) The elder br , William Wolseley, a Capt. in Ireland, was living 1614 (*Visit. of Stafford*) with a son and h ap named Charles, then five years old.

III. 1714   SIR WILLIAM WOLSELEY, Bart. [1628], of Wolseley aforesaid 4th but 1st surv s and h (ᵃ); b about 1660, *suc to the
Baronetcy*, 9 Oct 1714   He d unm., 8 July 1728, in his 69th year (being drowned
in his chariot, while crossing a brook at Long, near Lichfield), and was *bur.* at Col-
wich aforesaid   M I.

IV 1728.   SIR HENRY WOLSELEY, Bart [1628], of Wolseley aforesaid, br. and h., *suc to the Baronetcy*, 8 July 1728   He d unm
1730   Admon 14 Jan. 1730/1.

V. 1730   SIR WILLIAM WOLSELEY, Bart. [1628], of Wolseley afore-
said, nephew and h, being s. and h (ᵇ) of Capt Richard WOLSELEY,
of Mount Arran, afterwards Mount Wolseley, co. Carlow, by Frances, da and h. of
John BURNESTON of Ireland, which Richard was 6th s. of the 1st Bart   He *suc to the
Baronetcy* in 1730   He *m*, in or before 1740, (—), da of (—).   He d. 12 May 1779.
Will pr. July 1779.

VI. 1779   SIR WILLIAM WOLSELEY, Bart [1628], of Wolseley aforesaid, s and h, b 24 Aug 1740, *suc to the Baronetcy*, 12 May 1779.
He *m.* firstly, 2 July 1765, (—), da. of (—) CHAMBERS of Wimbledon, Surrey.   He
m. secondly, Anna, widow of John WHITLEY, only da of William NORTHEY, of
Compton Bassett, Wilts   He d 5 Aug. 1817   His widow m John ROBINS, and
subsequently (for her 4th husband) (—) HARGRAVE.

VII 1817   SIR CHARLES WOLSELEY, Bart [1628], of Wolseley aforesaid, s and h by first wife, b 20 July 1769, *suc. to the Baronetcy*,
5 Aug 1817   He *m* firstly, 13 Dec 1792, Mary, da of Hon Thomas CLIFFORD, of
Tixall, Salop, by Barbara, da and coheir of James (ASTON), 5th LORD ASTON [S]   She
d. 16 July 1811   He *m* secondly, 2 July 1812, Anne, youngest da. of Anthony WRIGHT,
of Wealdside, Essex, by Anne, da (whose issue become coheir) of John BIDDULPH, of
Biddulph, co Stafford   She d 24 Oct 1838   He d 3 Oct 1846, at Wolseley Hall,
in his 78th year.(ᶜ)   Will pr Oct. 1846.

VIII 1846.   SIR CHARLES WOLSELEY, Bart [1628], of Wolseley aforesaid, s. and h by 2d wife; b 6 May 1813, at Wolseley Hall; *suc to
the Baronetcy*, 3 Oct. 1846   He *m*, 23 Sep 1839, Mary Anne, 1st da. of Nicholas
SELBY, of Acton House, Middlesex   He d 15 May 1854.   Will pr June 1854.   His
widow d. 18 Jan 1873, at the Convent, Kensington square, aged 56

IX. 1854   SIR CHARLES-MICHAEL WOLSELEY, Bart [1628], of Wolseley aforesaid, 2d but 1st surv s and h ; b 4 July 1846 in Paris,
suc. to the Baronetcy, 15 May 1854 ; matric at Oxford (Ch. Ch), 20 Jan 1866, aged
19 ; sometime Lieut in the Staffordshire Yeomanry Cavalry, served with the 9th
Lancers in the Afghan Campaign, 1879   He *m*, 17 July 1883, at the pro cathedral,
Kensington, Anita Theresa, da. of Daniel T. MURPHY, of San Francisco, in California.

Family Estates.—These, in 1883, consisted of 2,111 acres in Staffordshire, worth
£2,789 a year.   *Principal Seat.*—Wolseley Hall, near Rugeley, co Stafford

(ᵃ) His eldest br, Robert Wolseley, aged 14 in 1663; admitted to Lincoln's Inn,
14 May, 1667 ; was by William III sent as envoy at Brussels, and d unm v p 1697
(ᵇ) His yst. br, Richard Wolseley, who inherited the Irish estates of their father,
was *cr. a Bart* [I], 19 Jan 1744, as of Mount Wolseley, co Carlow
(ᶜ) His extraordinary career as a demagogue, his imprisonment for a year, and
subsequently (March 1820) for 18 months, etc, are set forth in the Annual Register
for 1846.

RUDD

cr. 8 Dec. 1628 ,

ex 15 July 1739

I. 1628   "RICHARD RUDD, of Aberglasine [i e, Aberglassney], co
Carmarthen, Esq ," 2d but only son that had issue of Anthony RUDD,
BISHOP OF ST. DAVID'S, 1593 1614 (who purchased a good estate in the parish of
Llangathen, co Carmarthen, erected a mansion thereon called Aberglassney, and d
7 March 1614), by Alice, formerly Alice DALTON his wife, was cr. a Bart, as above,
8 Dec 1628 Sheriff of co Carnarvon, 1636-37 , was a Royalist and was fined £581
in Oct 1648 He m firstly, Jane, da. of Thomas AP RICE, of Richeston, co. Pembroke He m secondly, Elizabeth, sister of Sir John AUBREY, 1st Bart. [1660], da
of Sir Thomas AUBREY, of Llantrithed, co. Glamorgan, by Mary, da and h. of
Anthony MANSELL. She d s p. He d. May 1664.

II 1664.   SIR RICE RUDD, Bart [1628], of Aberglassney aforesaid,
grandson and h , being only s and h of Anthony RUDD, by Judith,
da. and h of Thomas RUDD, of Higham Ferrers, co Northampton, which Anthony
(who matric at Oxford 4 Dec 1635, aged 16) was s and h ap of the 1st Bart , by
his first wife, but d v p He was b about 1643 , suc to the Baronetcy in May 1664 ;
was M P for Higham Ferrers, 1678-79, 1679-81, and 1681 ; and for co Carmarthen
(5 Parls), 1689, till death He m 7 Dec 1661, at St Bartholomew the Less, London
(Lic Fac , each being about 18), Dorothy, da of Charles CORNWALLIS, of High
Holborn He d s p and a widower, July 1701, at St Anne's, Soho Admon
1 Sep. 1701, 9 Feb 1701/2, 26 Feb. 1704/5, and 14 March 1718/9.

III 1701   SIR ANTHONY RUDD, Bart. [1628], of Aberglassney afore-
said, cousin and h male, being s and h of Thomas RUDD, who was
yst. s of the 1st Bart by his first wife He m firstly Magdalen, da of Sir Henry
JONES, Bart. [so cr. 1648], of Abermarles, co. Carmarthen, by Elizabeth, da of Sir
John SALISBURY. She d s p He m secondly, Beatrice, da of Sir John BARLOW,
1st Bart [1677], of Slebech, co Pembroke, sole heir of her mother, his first wife,
Beatrice, da and eventually (1674) heir of Sir John LLOYD, 1st Bart [1662], of
Woking He d 25 Dec. 1725 His widow m Griffith LLOYD, and d. Feb 1735/6
Her will pr 1737.

IV 1725,   SIR JOHN RUDD, Bart. [1628], of Aberglassney aforesaid,
to   s. and h. by 2d wife ; suc to the Baronetcy on the death of his father,
1739   25 Dec 1725 He m Mary, da of (—) He d s p. 15 July 1739,
when the Baronetcy became extinct Admon 9 Aug. 1739 to the
widow. Her will pr 1802.

WISEMAN .

cr. 18 Dec 1628 ,

ex. 1654.

I. 1628,   "RICHARD WISEMAN, of Thundersley, co. Essex, Esq ,'
to   s. and h of Robert Wiseman,(a) of Stondon in that county, by Bar-
1654 ?   bara, da of William BETHELL, was aged 7 in 1608, matric at Oxford
(Wadham Coll), 17 June 1621, aged 20 , admitted to Lincoln's Inn,
1622, and was cr a Bart , as above, 18 Dec. 1628 He was living at Stondon aforesaid, 1634 He d. s p. about 1654, when the Baronetcy became extinct Will pr 1654

(ª) This Robert was 2d s of Sir Ralph Wiseman, of Rivenhall, Essex, and br. of
Sir Thomas Wiseman of the same, whose grandson, William Wiseman, was cr. a Bart
15 June 1660

FERRERS

cr. 19 Dec. 1628 ;

ex 1675.

I. 1628   "HENRY FERRERS, of Skellingthorpe,(ᵃ) co Lincoln,
      Esq.", was *cr. a Bart*, as above, 19 Dec 1628. He resided at
St. Leonard's, Bromley, Midx   He *m* Anne, da. of James SCUDAMORE   He *d.*
1663 (ᵇ)

II. 1663,   SIR HENRY FERRERS, Bart [1628], of Skellingthorpe
   to   aforesaid, s and h , *b.* about 1630, *suc to the Baronetcy*, in 1663
   1675   He *d. s p*, 1675, aged 45, when the *Baronetcy* became *extinct*

ANDERSON.

cr. 3 Jan. 1628/9 ;

ex 1630.

I 1629,   "JOHN ANDERSON, of St. Ives, co. Huntingdon, Esq ,"
   to   yst s. of Sir Francis Anderson,(ᶜ) of Eyworth, Beds (*d* 22 Dec 1615),
   1630.   being only s by his 2d wife, Audrey, 1st da. and coheir of John
(BOTELER), 1st BARON BOTELER OF BRANTFIELD (by Elizabeth, da of
George VILLIERS, and sister to George, the celebrated DUKE OF BUCKINGHAM), was
cr a Bart, as above, 3 Jan. 1628/9   He *d* unm at Apscourt,(ᵈ) in the parish of
Walton upon Thames, Surrey, 1630, when the *Baronetcy* became *extinct*. Admon.
2 Aug 1630 to his mother, Audrey, Lady Baroness Dunsmore.

RUSSELL :

cr 9 or 19 Jan 1628/9(ᵉ) ;

ex, presumably, 25 April 1804

I 1629.   "WILLIAM RUSSELL, of Chippenham, co. Cambridge,
     Knt ," s and h. of William RUSSELL, of Yaverland in the Isle of
Wight, was *Knighted* at Theobalds, 29 April 1618 , M P for Windsor, 1626 , and was
cr a Bart, as above, 9 or 19 Jan. 1628/9 (ᵉ)   He was Treasurer of the Royal Navy,
1618-27 and 1630 39 ; was (as such) admitted to Gray's Inn, 1 March 1630/1, and was
a great benefactor to the church of Deptford, Kent   He *m* firstly, Elizabeth, da. of
Sir Francis CHERRY, of Camberwell, Surrey, by his 1st wife, Margaret, da. of Harry
HAYWARD   She was *bap* 28 July 1588, and *d. s p*   He *m* secondly, in or before 1616,
Elizabeth, da. of Thomas GERARD, of Burwell, co. Cambridge   She was *bur* 14 Oct. 1626
at Chippenham   He *m* thirdly, 12 April 1628, Elizabeth, widow of John WHEATLEY,
of Catsfield, Sussex, Barrister, da and coheir of Michael SMALLPAGE, of Chichester,
by Catharine, da and coheir of William DEVENISH, of Hellingleigh, Sussex. She
probably *d* before him   He was *bur*. 3 Feb 1653/4 at Chippenham. Admon. (to
his son) 16 Feb. 1654/5, and, again, 5 May 1663.

  (ᵃ) "Mrs. Ellinor Ferrers" was buried at Skellingthorpe, 25 Feb 1640/1, and
"William Ferrers, Esq.," 4 Oct. 1646

  (ᵇ) Under the name of "Sir Henry Ferrers, *Knt*," he (or possibly his son) was
indicted for abetting in the murder of "one Stone" by one "Nightingale"   He
pleaded that he was never *Knighted*, and the indictment was made out *de novo* to
"Sir Henry Ferrers, *Baronet*"

  (ᶜ) This Francis was s. and h of Sir Edmund Anderson, Lord Chief Justice of the
Common Pleas, 1582 to 1605, ancestor of the Andersons, of Broughton *cr*. Barts.
1660, and of the Andersons, of Eyworth *cr*. Barts. 1664

  (ᵈ) This was the seat of his mother's 2d husband, Sir Francis LEIGH, Bart.
(*cr* 1618), who was *cr* BARON DUNSMORE, 1628, and EARL OF CHICHESTER, 1644

  (ᵉ) The usual date is "19 Jan.," but "9 Jan." is that given in the "*Creations,
1483-1646*" in ap. 47th Report, D K. Pub Records.

K

II   1654   SIR FRANCIS RUSSELL, Bart [1629], of Chippenham aforesaid, s. and h by 2d wife, *b.* about 1616 ; matric at Oxford (Wadham Coll.), 28 Jan. 1630/1, aged 14, admitted to Gray's Inn, 15 Aug. 1633, and to
the Inner Temple, 1635, was M P for Cambridgeshire, 1645-53, 1654-55, and
1656-58, was a Col in the Parl army, Gov of Ely, 1645, and of Lichfield, and
afterwards, 1648, of the Channel Islands. *suc to the Baronetcy* in Feb 1653/4,
was one of Cromwell's "Upper House" He *m* 19 Sep or Dec. 1631, at Chippenham, Catharine, da and h of John WHEATLEY, by Elizabeth, da and coheir of
Michael SMALLPACE, all abovenamed, the said Elizabeth being the 3d wife of the
1st Bart abovenamed He was *bur* 30 April 1664 at Chippenham (a)

III.   1664   SIR JOHN RUSSELL, Bart [1629], of Chippenham aforesaid, s and h ; *bap* there 6 Oct. 1640, *suc. to the Baronetcy* in April
1664 He *m* (Lic Fac, 22 April 1663, he about 21, bachelor, she of Holy Trinity
London, about 22, widow) Frances, widow of the Hon Robert RICH (who *d s p*,
16 Feb 1657/8, aged 23), yst da. of OLIVER CROMWELL, the "LORD PROTECTOR,"
by Elizabeth, da of Sir James BOURCHIER, of Felstead, co Essex He was *bur*
24 March 1669, at Chippenham Will pr June 1670 His widow, who was *bap*
6 Dec. 1638 at St. Mary's, Ely, *d* 27 Jan. 1720, aged above 80 Will pr 1720.

IV.   1669.   SIR WILLIAM RUSSELL, Bart [1629], of Chippenham
aforesaid, s. and h ; *suc to the Baronetage* in March 1669 He spent
the remainder of what once was a considerable fortune in raising troops at the time
of the Revolution, and sold the estate of Chippenham He *m* Catharine, da of
(—) GORE, of Ireland He, who was latterly of Hampton, co Midx was *bur.*
16 Sep 1707 at Kingston-on-Thames, Surrey. Admon 12 Nov 1707 The admon
of his widow, as of St Anne's, Westm, 18 July 1713, was granted to Dame Frances
Russell, grandmother of her children, then minors.

V   1707   SIR WILLIAM RUSSELL, Bart [1629], s and h ; *suc to
the Baronetcy* in Sep. 1707, was a minor in July 1713 He *d* unm
May 1738, at Passage, near Waterford, Ireland

VI   1738   SIR FRANCIS RUSSELL, Bart. [1629], br. and h ; *suc to
the Baronetcy* in May 1738 ; was one of the Council at Fort William,
in Bengal He *m* in 1725 Anne, da of (—) GEE, merchant

VII   1750?   SIR WILLIAM RUSSELL, Bart [1629], only s. and h ;
suc to the Baronetcy on his father's death ; Lieut. in the 1st Regt of
Foot Guards He *d.* unm 1757. Admon, as of "St Geo Han. sq," 16 Jan 1758.

VIII.   1757   SIR JOHN RUSSELL, Bart. [1629], of Checquers Court, in
Ellesborough, Bucks, cousin and h male, being s. and h of Col
Charles RUSSELL, 34th Foot, by Mary Johanna Cutts,(b) da. of Col. RIVETT,
which Charles (who *d.* 20 Nov 1754, aged 53) was s and h of John RUSSELL,
Governor of Fort Wilham, Bengal (*b*, posthumously, 14 Oct 1670, and *d* 5 Dec
1735), who was 3d s of the 3d Bart He was *b* 31 Oct 1741, *suc to the Baronetcy*
in 1757, matric at Oxford (Ch Ch) 24 May 1758, aged 17 ; B.A. 1762 ; M A 1765,
Barrister (Lincoln's Inn), 1766 He *m* 25 Oct. 1775 Catharine, da, of Gen the
Hon George CARY, of Skutterskelfe, co York (2d s of Lucius Henry, 6th VISCOUNT
FALKLAND [S]), by Isabella, da. and h of Arthur INGRAM She *d* 26 Dec. 1782,
in her 34th year, and was *bur* at Ellesborough M I He *d* 7 Aug 1783 at Sir
Henry Oxenden's house, in Kent, and was *bur* at Ellesborough in his 42d year
M I. Will pr. Aug. 1783.

(a) Elizabeth, their 1st da, *m* Henry CROMWELL, Lord Deputy of Ireland, yst. s. of
the "LORD PROTECTOR."
(b) By her the estate of Checquers came to the Russell family ; her mother,
Johanna, being da. and h of John Thurbane, Serjeant at Law (1689), who had
acquired it by marriage.

IX 1783.   SIR JOHN RUSSELL, Bart [1629], of Checquers Court aforesaid, s. and h , b 6 May 1777 at Knightsbridge, Midx. , *suc to the Baronetcy,* 7 Aug 1738 , matric at Oxford (Ch Ch), 29 Oct 1795, aged 18   He d unm 11 June 1802, and was *bur* at Ellesborough   M I   Will pr 1802

X   1802,   SIR GEORGE RUSSELL, Bart. [1629], of Checquers Court
to   aforesaid, br and h , b 15 April 1780 at Knightsbridge, Midx. ;
1804   matric. at Oxford (Ch Ch), 24 Oct 1798, aged 17 , admitted to Lincoln's Inn, 5 May 1802 ; *suc to the Baronetcy,* 11 June 1802 He d s p 25 April 1804, in London, and was *bur* at Ellesborough   M I   At his death the *Baronetcy* is presumed to have become *extinct* (a)   Will pr. 1804.

POWELL : ⁓7

cr 21 Jan. 1629/30 ;

ex , presumably, about 1700

I.   1630   "THOMAS POWELL, of Berkenhead, co Chester, Esq ," s. and h of Thomas POWELL, of Horsley, co Denbigh, and of the Priory of Birkenhead, co Chester, by Dorothy, da. of Morris WYNNE, of Gwydir, was, presumably, as "Thomas Powell, of co Denbigh, gent," admitted to Lincoln's Inn 23 Oct 1602, was Sheriff of Denbighshire, 1615-16 and 1638-39 ; of Cheshire, 1639-40, having been cr a Bart , as above, 21 Jan 1629/30   He m Margaret (b 2 and bap 6 Sep 1584), da of Sir John EGERTON, of Egerton and Oulton, by Margaret, da of Sir Rowland STANLEY, of Hooton   His burial as " Sir Thomas Powell, Knt ," is registered 25 Sep 1647, both at Long Ditton and at Barnes, co Surrey.

II.   1647 ?   SIR THOMAS POWELL, Bart [1630], of Horsley and Birken-
to   head aforesaid, grandson and h being s. and h. of John POWELL, by
1700 ?   Margaret, da of Edward PULESTON, of Allington, which John was s and h ap of the 1st Bart , but d , v p, Dec 1642   He was b 1631, being aged 18 in 1649 ; he *suc. to the Baronetcy* on the death of his father.   He was Sheriff of Denbighshire, 1656 57   He m firstly, in or before 1650,(b) Mary, da of William CONWAY, of Bodryddan, co Carnarvon   He m secondly, Jane, da of Robert RAVENSCROFT, of Bretton, co. Flint   He was living 1694, aged 63, but d s p.m.s.(c) it is presumed shortly afterwards (1700 ?) certainly before 1710,(d) when the *Baronetcy* appears to have become *extinct*

EVERARD 78

cr. 29 Jan. 1628/9 ,

ex 1745

I   1629   " RICHARD EVERARD, of [Langleys in] Much Waltham, co. Essex, Esq ," s and h ap of Hugh EVERARD, of the same, by Mary, da of Thomas BRAND, *otherwise* BOND, of Great Hormead, Herts (which Hugh

---

(a) In the event of William Russell (who d s p abroad about the same date) having survived him, he would have been entitled to the dignity, as being s of Thomas Russell (b 27 Feb 1724, sometime an officer in the army), s of Francis Russell (bap 19 Jan 1691 at Fordham, co Suffolk), s of William Russell, of Fordham (bur. 26 June 1701), s of Gerald Russell of the same (d. 7 Dec 1682, aged 63), who was a yr. s. of the 1st Bart, by his 2d wife

(b) The date of " 28 May 1629 " [*Qy.* 1649], is given for this marriage in the ped in Ormerod's *Cheshire,* but it is manifestly erroneous   See note " b " below

(c) His only son, Thomas Powell, of Horsley aforesaid, who matric at Oxford (Jesus Coll), 5 July 1667, aged 17 , was Sheriff of Denbighshire, 1683-84, and of Cheshire, April 1689 , m. twice, but d v p before 1694, having had by his 2d wife three daughters, but by his 1st wife ' male issue " [see ped in Ormerod's *Cheshire,* taken from Le Neve's MS. peds. of Baronets], which, presumably, was extinct before the death of his father, the 2d Bart.

(d) In 1710 the estate of Birkenhead Priory was sold to John Cleiveland, presumably after the extinction in the male line of the Powell family.

was next br. and h male (1614) to Sir Anthony Everard, of Langleys aforesaid), was,
v p, cr a Bart, as above, 29 Jan 1628/9 He suc his father, 24 Aug 1637; was
a committee man on the side of the Parl, 1643-45, and for raising and maintaining
the new model, Feb 1645, was Sheriff of Essex, 1644-45 He m firstly, 1 Nov
1621, at St. Barth the Less, London, Joan, da of Sir Francis BARRINGTON, 1st
Bart [1611], by Joan, da of Sir Henry CROMWELL He m secondly, 11 Sep 1653,
at St Anne's, Blackfriars, London, Fiances, widow of Sir Gervas ELWES, of Woodford, Essex, da. of Sir Robert LEE, of Billesley, co Warwick, by Anne, da of Sir
Thomas LOWE, sometime (1604 05), Lord Mayor of London By her, who d in
St Martin's in the Fields and was bur 2 Dec 1676 at St Andrew's, Undershaft,
he had no issue He d. about 1680 His will pr 1680 at the Archdeaconry Court
of Essex.

II 1680 ?   SIR RICHARD EVERARD, Bart [1629], of Langleys aforesaid, s and h by 1st wife, b about 1625; was possibly the
"Sir Richard Everard, Knt." (who, apparently, was of Boreham, Essex), who was
M P for Westm, 1661-78, suc. to the Baronetcy about 1680 He m firstly, in or
before 1654, Elizabeth, 1st da. and coheir of Sir Henry GIBB, Bart. [S 1634], by
Anne, da of Sir Ralph GIBBS, of Honiton, co Warwick He m secondly, Jane,
da of Sir John FINET, Master of the Ceremonies By her he had no issue He
d 29 Aug 1694, aged 69, and was bur at Waltham

III. 1694   SIR HUGH EVERARD, Bart. [1629], of Langleys aforesaid,
only surv s and h by 1st wife, b about 1654 In early life he
distinguished himself in the army in Flanders, was Receiver General of the Land
tax for Essex, suc to the Baronetcy in Aug 1694, but much encumbered his estate
He m in or before 1683, Mary, da of John BROWNE, M D, of Salisbury. He d.
2 Jan 1705/6, aged 51, and was bur. at Waltham Will pr May 1707 His widow
was living 1707.

IV 1706   SIR RICHARD EVERARD, Bart [1629], of Bromfield Green,
co Essex, s. and h, b about 1683, suc to the Baronetcy 10 Jan
1705/6, and sold the estate of Langleys, was Governor of North Carolina, 1724,
under the Lords Proprietor He m (Lic Lond 21 Dec 1705, he aged 22) Susanna,
only child that had issue of Richard KIDDER D D, Bishop of Bath and Wells
[1691-1703] He d 17 Feb 1732/3, in Red Lion street, Holborn Will pr 1733
His widow d 12 Sep 1739 Will pr 1739

V. 1733   SIR RICHARD EVERARD, Bart [1629], of Bromfield Green
aforesaid s and h, admitted to Gray's Inn 14 Aug 1731 suc to
the Baronetcy, 17 Feb 1732/3 He d a widower and s p 7 March 1741/2 Admon,
as of St. Martin's in the Fields, Midx, 11 May 1743, to his br and next of kin as
below

VI. 1742,   SIR HUGH EVERARD, Bart. [1629], only br and h;
to   suc. to the Baronetcy, 7 March 1741/2 He emigrated to Georgia,
1745   where he m Mary, da of (—) He d. s p 1745,[a] when the
Baronetcy became extinct Will dat 2 March 1744/5, and pr 31 Aug.
1745, by his relict and universal legatee

LUCKYN : 14

cr. 2 March 1628/9 ;

afterwards, since 1737, VISCOUNTS GRIMSTON [I];

and subsequently, since 1815, EARLS OF VERULAM [U.K]

I. 1629.   "WILLIAM LUCKYN, of Little Waltham, co Essex, Esq,"
s. and h of William LUCKYN, of Shinges, otherwise Mascalls, in Great
Baddow in that county, by Margaret, da of Thomas JENNY, of Bury St Edmunds,
was b. 1594, suc his father, 13 Dec 1610, was admitted to Lincoln's Inn, 6 Feb.

(a) His sister, Susanna, had m. in Virginia before 1741, (—) WHITE, a considerable
merchant and planter there.

1613/4, and was cr a Bait, as above, 2 March 1628/9, was Sheriff for Essex, 1637-38. He m firstly, in or before 1620, Mildred, 3d da of Sir Gamaliel CAPELL, of Raynes, co Essex, by Jane, da and coheir of Weston BROWNE, of Rookwoods in that county He m secondly, 1 Dec. 1634, at St Bride's, London (Lic Lond, he 30 and she 20), Elizabeth, da of Sir Edward PYNCHON, of Writtle, by Dorothy, da of Sir Jerome WESTON, of Roxwell, both in co Essex His will, dat 2 July 1658, pr 28 Feb 1660/1 His widow d 7 July 1667

II　1660?　　SIR CAPELL LUCKYN, Bart. [1629], of Messing Hall, Essex, s and h. by 1st wife aged 13 in 1634, admitted to Lincoln's Inn, 17 June 1640; Knighted, 2 June 1660, suc to the Baronetcy about 1660, M P for Harwich, April 1648 till secluded in Dec, re-elected 1680 and April 1664-79 He m 20 Jan 1647/8, at Hackney, Midx, Mary, 1st da. of Sir Harbottle GRIMSTON, 2d Bart [1611], of Bradfield Hall, Essex, and afterwards of Gorhambury, Herts, by Mary, da of Sir George CROKE, Justice of the Common Pleas He d about 1680. Will pr 1680 His widow d 18 and was bur. 24 March 1719, at Messing, aged 86

III.　1680?　　SIR WILLIAM LUCKYN, Bart [1629], of Messing Hall aforesaid, surv s and h., suc to the Baronetcy about 1680 He m. 1 Dec 1681, at St Peter's, Cornhill, Mary, da of William SHERRINGTON, Fishmonger and Alderman of London (bur 15 Nov. 1706, at St Peter's aforesaid), by Elizabeth his wife He d about 1708 Admon 11 Feb 1708/9 and 11 Feb 1735/6 His widow, who was bap 4 June 1663, at St. Peter's aforesaid, was bur 24 Nov 1749, at Messing Will pr 1750.

IV　1708?　　SIR HARBOTTLE LUCKYN, Bart [1629], of Messing Hall aforesaid, s and h, bap 16 Jan 1683/4 at St Peter's, Cornhill, London, suc. to the Baronetcy about 1708; was Cupbearer to Queen Anne and to George I and II He d, unm., s p and was bur 15 Feb. 1736/7, at Messing. M I Will pr 1737.

V　1737.　　WILLIAM (GRIMSTON), VISCOUNT GRIMSTON [I] and Bart [1629] br. and h, b. about 1664, suc, in Oct 1700, on the death of his great uncle, Sir Samuel Grimston, 3d Bart [1611], to the estate of Gorhambury, Herts, when he took the name of Grimston in lieu of that of his patronymic of Luckyn; was M P for St Albans, 1710-22 and 1729-34, and was cr, 29 Nov 1719, BARON DUNBOYNE, of co Meath, and VISCOUNT GRIMSTON [I] By the death of his elder br, 4 Feb 1736/7, he suc to the Baronetcy, which has since continued to be united with the Viscountcy of Grimston [I], as also, since 1815, with the Earldom of Verulam, the 4th Viscount having been cr, 24 Nov 1815, EARL OF VERULAM [U K.] See Peerage under "GRIMSTON" and 'VERULAM."

GRAHAM, or GRAHME(a) of Eske, co Cumberland [E.],　8?

cr 29 March 1629,

sometime, 1681-90 and 1690-1739, VISCOUNTS PRESTON [S];

forfeited 1690;

but, possibly, restored in 1691.

I.　1629.　　"RICHARD GRAHAM, of Eske, co Cumberland, Esq," and also of Netherby in that county, 2d s and h male of Fergus GRAHAM, or GRAHME, of Plomp, in that county, by Sibill, da. of William BELL, of Godsbrigg, in Scotland, was Gentleman of the Horse to James I, was M P for Carlisle 1626 and 1628-29, and was cr a Bart, as above, 29 March 1629 He adhered to the Royal cause with great fidelity and was severely wounded at the Battle of Marston Moor, 2 July 1644. He purchased the estate of Netherby and the Barony of Liddell, co Cumberland. He

---

(a) The name is frequently spelt "Grahme," and appears to have been so used by the earlier Baronets.

m, in or before 1624, Catharine, da of Thomas MUSGRAVE, of Cumcatch, co Cumberland, by Susanna, his wife She *d* 23 and was *bur* 27 March 1649, at Wath, co York, in her 48th year M I He *d* 28 Jan and was *bur* 11 Feb 1653/4, at Wath (a) Will dat 26 March 1653, and pr 30 Jan 1653/4

II 1654 SIR GEORGE GRAHAM, *or* GRAHME, Bart [1629], of Netherby aforesaid, s and h (b) *b* about 1624, *suc. to the Baronetcy* 28 Jan 1653/4 He *m* Mary, da of James (JOHNSTONE), 1st EARL OF HARTFELL [S], by his 1st wife, Margaret, 1st da of William (DOUGLAS), 1st EARL OF QUEENSBERRY [S] He *d* 19 March 1657/8, aged 33, and was *bur* at Arthuret, co Cumberland, M I Will dat 19 March 1657/8, pr 3 March 1658/9 His widow *m* Sir George FLETCHER, 2d Bart [1641], of Hutton, who *d* 23 July 1700, aged 67

III 1658, to 1690 SIR RICHARD GRAHAM, Bart. [1629], of Netherby aforesaid, s and h, *b* 24 Sep. 1648, at Netherby; *suc to the Baronetcy,* 19 March 1657/8, ed at Westm and at Ch. Ch, Oxford, matric. 20 June 1664, aged 15, M A 4 Feb 1666/7, admitted to the Inner Temple, 1664, was 16 years old at the Heralds' Visitation, 29 March 1665, M P for Cockermouth (4 Parls) 1675-81, and for co Cumberland, 1685-87, having meanwhile been *cr* a Scotch peer, 12 May 1681, as VISCOUNT PRESTON and LORD GRAHAM OF ESK [S] He *m*, 2 Aug 1670, Anne, 2d da of Charles (HOWARD), 1st EARL OF CARLISLE, by Anne da of Edward (HOWARD), BARON HOWARD OF ESCRICK. As an adherent of James II, he was found guilty of high treason and condemned to death by the English Parl, 17 Jan. 1689/90, under the designation of a Baronet, whereby the *Baronetcy* [E], and his English estates were *forfeited,* though "the attainder could not affect his Scottish peerage, as no act of forfeiture passed against him in Scotland"(c) He was, however, subsequently pardoned by Royal Sign Manual (d) dated June 1691 He *d* 22 Nov. 1695, and was *bur* at Nunnington, co York, aged 47 His widow living 5 Feb. 1706 See fuller particulars of him in *Peerage*

* * * * * *

[If the pardon granted to the 1st Viscount Preston had the effect of reversing the attainder of 1690, the Baronetcy would on his death, 22 Nov 1695, descend as below]

IV 1695 EDWARD (GRAHAM), 2d VISCOUNT PRESTON, [S], and a Bart.(e) [1629], 3d but 1st surv s and h, *b* 1679, *suc to the peerage,* 22 Nov 1695, *d* 1710

V 1710 CHARLES (GRAHAM), 3d VISCOUNT PRESTON, [S], and a Bart (e) [1629], s and h, *b* 25 March 1706, *suc to the peerage* in 1710, *d* s p 23 Feb 1738/9, when the *peerage* [S] became *extinct,* but the right to the Baronetcy, so far as it was not affected by the attainder of 1690, devolved as below (f)

[See fuller particulars in *Peerage*]

(a) See copious extracts from these registers, with notes by the Rev. John Ward, illustrating this family, in the *Top and Gen.,* vol iii, pp 414-436

(b) Richard Graham, the 2d s., *bap* 11 March 1635/6, at Wath, was *cr a Bart* 17 Nov 1662, as of Norton Conyers, co York, a dignity which still (1900) exists

(c) Wood's *Douglas's Peerage of Scotland*

(d) In an article by Peter Burke, Serjeant at Law [*Her. and Gen*, vol iv, p 369], it is stated that, before pronouncing positively as to whether this Baronetcy is affected or not by the attainder of 1690, "it will be necessary to find out whether the attainting judgment was of record and what was the exact nature of the pardon granted to Viscount Preston"

(e) On the assumption that the forfeiture of 1690 was invalid or had been reversed See note "d" above.

(f) The estate of Netherby and the other large estates of the family devolved on his lordship's aunts, the two daughters of the 1st Viscount Of these, Mary *d.* unm, 18 Oct 1753, and her surv sister, Catharine, Dowager Baroness Widdrington (who *d.* s p 1757) devised them to her cousin, Robert Graham, D D, 2d s. of William Graham, Dean of Wells, who was 4th s. of the 2d Bart, and consequently br. of the 1st Viscount. His s and h., James Graham, was *cr a Bart.* in 1782 as "of Netherby"

VI 1739. SIR WILLIAM GRAHAM, Bart (ª) [1629], cousin and h
male, being s and h of the Rev Charles GRAHAM, Rector of South-
church, Essex, by Priscilla, da of Case BILLINGSLEY, of Tottenham, Midx , merchant,
which Charles (d April 1734) was s and h of William Graham, D D , Dean of
Wells (d Feb 1711/2), yr br of Richard, 1st VISCOUNT PRESTON [S], both being sons
of the 2d Bart He was b 1730, at Tottenham aforesaid , and appears to have assumed,
23 Feb 1738/9, not *only the Baronetcy* [E] but also the *Viscountcy of Preston* [S] (ᵇ)
He is said to have been ed at St John's Coll , Cambridge, and was in Holy Orders
He m. 7 Nov 1761 at St. Botolph's, Aldgate, London, Susanna, widow of Richard
FRENCH, of Battle, Sussex, da of (—) REEVE, of Ashburnham, in that county He
d. 21 Sep 1774, aged 44, and was bur at Carmarthen (ᶜ) Admon (*query* at Carmarthen), Feb 1775 His widow d at Edinburgh, 1788, and was bur. there.

VII 1774 SIR CHARLES GRAHAM, Bart (ª) [1629], s and h *bap.* at
Battle aforesaid, 11 Nov. 1764, as "the Hon Charles Grayham, s of
the Rev William G., Lord Viscount Preston " He *suc to the Baronetcy*,(ª) 21 Sep.
1774 He d unm. 26 Nov 1795, and was bur at St. Martin's in the Fields

VIII 1795 SIR ROBERT GRAHAM, Bart (ª) [1629], of Dulwich and
Putney, Surrey, and afterwards of Dursley, co Gloucester, br and
h , *bap* 1 Nov 1769, at Battle aforesaid He *suc to the Baronetcy*,(ª) 26 Nov 1795.
He was one of the claimants of the EARLDOM OF ANNANDALE [S] as heir gen of Lady
Mary JOHNSTONE, eldest sister of James, 1st Earl, and wife of the 2d Bart. He m ,
25 April 1810, in Bloomsbury square, St Geo., Bloomsbury, Middlesex (by spec lic),
Elizabeth, only da. of John YOUNG, of Battle aforesaid, surgeon He d. 27 Jan
1852, at Dursley aforesaid, aged 82 Will pr Nov 1852 His widow d , 16 Dec.
1859, at Bayswater, aged 70

IX 1852 SIR EDWARD GRAHAM, Bart (ª) [1629], 4th but 1st surv
s and h , b. 1 and *bap.* 20 Jan 1820, at Dulwich aforesaid, regd at
St. Giles', Camberwell, *suc to the Baronetcy*,(ª) 27 Jan 1852; appointed 10 1855 to the
Turkish Contingent with local rank as Assistant Commissary of the 1st Class He
m firstly, 5 June 1841, (—) widow of Charles HENDERSON, of St. John's terrace,
Oxford, but by her had no issue He m secondly, 3 Aug 1841, Adelaide Elizabeth,
yst. da of James Dillon TULLY, M.D , Deputy Inspector-Gen of Army Hospitals in
Jamaica. She d 12 March 1852, from a fall downstairs, aged 30 He m thirdly,
20 Jan 1855, Amelia Ellen, da of William John AKERS He d 27 May 1864, at
Montreal, in Canada, aged 44 His widow m , 1870, James R JOHNSTON, and d.
April 1877

X. 1864. SIR ROBERT JAMES STUART GRAHAM, Bart.(ª) [1629],
s and h by 2d wife, b 2 Dec. 1845, in London, *suc to the Baronetcy*(ª)
27 May 1864 He m 1 Aug 1874, at New York, U.S A , Eliza Jane, da of Charles
BURNS, of Brooklyn

Family Estates —These were, in 1757, devised to the cadet line of the family of
Graham, afterwards, since 1783, Baronets, of Netherby. *Residence* —Brooklyn, New
York, U S A.

(ª) See p 70, note " e "
(ᵇ) " Neither as a Peer or a Baronet is the existence of this person or his posterity
admitted in Wood's edit (1813) of Douglas's *Peerage of Scotland*, nor is he inserted
[in Wotton's *Baronetage*, 1741] in Kimber and Johnson's *Baronetage*, 1771, either in
a distinct article or in the account of this family given in relation to the Norton
Conyers branch, which is also descended from the first Baronet of Esk. In the
Baronetage of 1819 an article for " Graham of Esk " is inserted, and thenceforward
the title [i e that Baronetcy] is recognised by all subsequent works of that class, but
we have failed to discover anywhere that the attainder of 1690 has actually been
reversed " [*Her. and Gen.*, vol iv., p. 278]
(ᵘ) In the *Gent Mag* for 1777 his death is thus recorded "Sep 21, at Mr Lewis',
in Carmarthen, the Rt Hon and Rev William Graham, Lord Viscount Preston,"
which notice is followed by an erroneous statement that he was son and successor of
the Viscount who died in 1739 That [erroneous] affiliation is, however, ascribed to
him in the old (1764) edit of *Douglas's Peerage of Scotland*, though not in the subsequent one of 1816.

TWISLETON :

cr 2 April 1629 ;

ex Oct 1635

I 1629, "GEORGE TWISLETON, of Barly, co York, Esq.," s and
to h of Christopher TWISLETON, of the same, by Alice, da of (—) HASEL-
1635 WOOD, of Maidwell, co Northampton , was aged 7 at the Visit. of
Yorkshire in 1612, and was *cr. a Bart*, as above, 2 April 1629 He
m Catharine, da of Henry STAPYLTON, of Wighill, co York, by Mary, illegit da of
Sir John FORSTER, of Alnwick He *d* s p Oct 1635 Will pr 1635, when the
Baronetcy became *extinct* ([a]) His widow *m* Sir Henry CHOLMELEY, of West Newton
She was *bur*, 14 June 1672 at Oswaldkirk

ACTON :

cr. 30 May 1629 ,

ex. 1651.

I 1629, "WILLIAM ACTON, of the city of London, Esq.," s and
to h of the same, citizen and mercer, by Margaret,
1651 da of (—) DANIEL, also of London, was apprenticed, 7 Sep. 1593, in
the Merchant Tailors Company , made free, 18 Jan 1601 , was on the
livery, 5 July 1616 , Alderman of Aldersgate, 12 Feb 1627/8 , Sheriff of London,
1628-29, and was, during office, *cr a Bart* ([c]) as above, 30 May 1629, being *knighted*
the subsequent day He was, subsequently, 1640, Lord Mayor of London, but
was discharged from his office, 6 Oct. 1640, (shortly after his election), as also
from being Alderman, by the House of Commons on account of his favouring
the party of the King He *m* firstly, Anne, da and h of James BILL, of
Astwell Herts He *m* secondly, Jane, widow of Sir William BIRD, D C L ,
Judge of the Admiralty Court (who *d* Aug 1624), da. of (—) JOHNSON.
She was *bur*, 1 March 1644/5, at St Peter's Cheap, London Her will dat.
3 Dec. 1640, pr 28 Feb 1644/5 He *d*. s p m.([d]) 22 Jan 1650/1, when the
Baronetcy became *extinct.* Will, in which he directs his burial to be at Edmonton,
dat 30 May 1650, pr 26 March 1651 and 5 Feb 1672/3

LE STRANGE, L'ESTRANGE, *or* STRANGE:

cr 1 June 1629 ,

ex 21 April 1762.

1. 1629 "NICHOLAS LE STRANGE, of Hunstanton, co. Norfolk,
Esq.," s and h ap.([c]) of Sir Hamon LE STRANGE, of Hunstanton
aforesaid, by Alice, da and coheir of Richard STUBBE, of Sedgeford, in that county,

---

([a]) The estates passed to his uncle, John Twisleton, of Drax, co York, ancestor,
in the male line, of the Lords Saye and Sele

([b]) This Richard was 2d s of William Acton, of Aldenham, Salop, ancestor of the
ACTONS, Barts , so *cr* 17 Jan 1643/4

([c]) This is the first Baronetcy conferred on a City dignitary, and it is to be noted
that the recipient, in this case, had not, as yet, attained the Mayoralty.

([d]) Elizabeth, his only da and h (by his 1st wife), *m* 16 April 1635, at Leyton,
co. Essex, Sir Thomas WHITMORE, Bart (so *cr* 1641), to whom she brought her
mother's estate of Astwell aforesaid

([e]) His younger br., Sir Roger Le Strange, *otherwise* LESTRANGE, attempted to reduce
Lynn for Charles I, but was taken prisoner and condemned to death He became,
subsequently, well known as a voluminous writer, and was "Licenser of the press."
He *d* 11 Dec. 1704, aged 87, and was *bur* at St Giles' in the Fields. M I.

was *bap* 27 March 1604, at Hunstanton, and was v.p, *or. a Baronet*,(a) as above, 1 June 1629 ,(a) suc. his father, 1654 He *m*, 26 Aug 1630, at St Stephen's Norwich, Ann, da. of Sir Edward LEWKENOR, of Denham, Suffolk, by Mary, da of Sir Henry NEVILL, of Billingbere, Berks. He *d* 24 July 1655 and was *bur* at Hunstanton, aged 52 M I Admon 15 May 1656 His widow *d* 15 July 1663, aged 51, and was *bur* at Hunstanton.

II. 1655 SIR HAMON LE STRANGE, Bart [1629], of Hunstanton aforesaid, s and h, *bap*. there 8 Dec 1631 , *suc to the Baronetcy*, 24 July 1655, but *d* s p., seven months afterwards, 15 Feb 1655/6 and was *bur*. at Hunstanton

III 1656 SIR NICHOLAS LE STRANGE, *otherwise* L'ESTRANGE, Bart. [1629], of Hunstanton aforesaid, br and h ; *bap*. there 17 Oct 1632 . *suc to the Baronetcy*, 15 Feb 1655/6 He *m* firstly, Mary, da of John COKE, of Holkham, Norfolk, by Muriel, da and h of Anthony WHEATLEY, Prothonotary of the Court of Common Pleas Her admon June 1662. He *m* secondly, 16 Oct. 1662, at Stowlangtoft, Elizabeth, da. of Sir Justinian ISHAM, 2d Bart [1627] by his 1st wife, Jane, da. of Sir John GARRARD, 1st Bart. [1622] He *d* 13 and was *bur*. 15 Dec. 1669, at Hunstanton. Admon. 17 June 1670 His widow, who was *b*. 22 Aug and *bap* 7 Sep 1636, at Lamport, co Northampton, was *bur*, 6 Aug 1689, in Westm Abbey Will dat 13 May and pr. 6 Aug 1689

IV. 1669. SIR NICHOLAS L'ESTRANGE, Bart. [1629], of Hunstanton aforesaid, s and h, by 1st wife, *b*. 2 Dec 1661, *suc to the Baronetcy*, 13 Dec 1669 ; matric at Oxford (Ch. Ch), 23 May 1677, aged 15 Col of the Yellow Regiment of Trained Bands, 1683 ; M.P for Castle Rising, 1685-87 He *m* , 2 Dec 1686, at St Giles' in the Fields (Lic Fac , he 25 and she 18), Anne, da of Sir Thomas WODEHOUSE, of Kimberley, Norfolk (s. and h ap of the 3d Bart), by Ann, da and coheir of Sir William ARMYNE, 2d Bart [1619] He *d*., 18 Dec 1724, at Gressenhall, co Norfolk Will dat. 8 March 1722, pr 14 May 1725 His widow *d* 1727. Will pr. 12 June 1727.

V 1724. SIR THOMAS L'ESTRANGE, Bart [1629], of Hunstanton aforesaid, eldest surv s and h,(b) *b*. 1689 ; *suc. to the Baronetcy*, 18 Dec 1724 He *m*., 27 July 1721, Anne, da and, at length, sole h. of Sir Christopher CALTHORPE, K.B , of East Barsham, Norfolk, by Dorothy, da. of Sir William SPRING, 1st Bart. [1641] She *d*. 1743 He *d* s p 8 and was *bur* 10 Nov 1751, at Hunstanton.

VI 1751. SIR HENRY L'ESTRANGE, Bart [1629], of Hunstanton aforesaid, and of Gressenhall, co Norfolk, br and h., *suc. to the Baronetcy* in 1751 He *m*. Mary, 3d da. of the Rt. Hon Roger NORTH, of Roughsm, Norfolk (s of Dudley, Lord North), by Mary, da. of Sir Robert GAYER, of Stoke Pogis. He *d* s p 2 Sep 1760,(c) and was *bur*. at Hunstanton. Admon 2 Oct. 1760, and, again, May 1826. The will of his widow was pr at Norwich, 19 Nov 1791.

(a) The patent was, in 1900, in the muniment room at Hunstanton. It has, at the foot, a quaint inscription in the handwriting of Sir Hamon le Strange, the father of the 1st Baronet, as follows.—"M⁴ that I, Hamon le Strange, Kn⁴, father of the within-named Sᵣ Nich⁸, was Knighted at the coronâcon of King James, ão 1604, and, because the dignitie of Baronet would give mee small exceedence, therefore I purchased the same for my sonn Nich⁸ and bestowed the same upon him ão 5° Caroli, wch. cost in money 300 li, and in charges 100 li ; all witnessed by this subscription of my name, under myne hande, Hamon le Strange" [*Ex inform* Hamon le Strange, Hunstanton Hall, Norfolk]

(b) Hamon, his elder br , *b* 1687 , *d*. unm and v p. in 1715, on his travels.

(c) Of his sisters and coheirs (1), Armyne, the eldest, *m* Nicholas STYLEMAN, of Snettisham, Norfolk, and their descendants (STYLEMAN-LE-STRANGE) inherit the estate of Hunstanton , (2), Lucy, the youngest, *m* Sir Jacob ASTLEY, 3d Bart. [1660], and their great grandson was, in 1841, as her representative, summoned to the House of Peers, in the BARONY OF HASTINGS, of which she and her elder sister abovenamed represented the junior coheir,

L

VII. 1760,   SIR ROGER L'ESTRANGE, Bart. [1629], cousin and h.
       to   male,(ᵃ) being only surv s of Roger L'ESTRANGE, of Hoe, near East
      1762.   Dereham, co Norfolk, by his 2d wife, Susan, da. and coheir of
                  Francis LANE, of Thuxton, which Roger last named (who d. 29 Oct
1706, aged 63) was a yr s of the 1st Bart. He was b 1682, and was living at
Harleston in 1703 He suc to the Baronetcy, but not to the family estate, 2 Sep.
1760, when nearly 80 He m firstly, Lettice, da. of Richard COGSDELL, of Harleston.
He m secondly, in 1713, Sarah NIXON, of Wymondham, co Norfolk, spinster He
m thirdly, in or before 1717, Elizabeth, da of Thomas REDE, of Weston, co Suffolk.
He d., s p m s, at Beccles, 21 and was bur 25 April 1762, at Weston, when the
Baronetcy became extinct. Will dat 26 Oct 1761, pr 1 June 1762, in Archdeaconry
of Suffolk His widow was bur 17 Nov 1779, at Weston.

HOLLAND :

cr. 15 June 1629 ;

ex. 17 Feb 1728/9.

I. 1629   "JOHN HOLLAND, of Quidenham, co. Norfolk, Esq," s
                and h of Sir Thomas HOLLAND of the same (living 1625), by Mary,
da. of Sir Thomas KNYVET, was b Oct. and bap Nov. 1603, and was cr a Baronet,
as above, 15 June 1629 ; was M P for Norfolk, April to May 1640, for Castle Rising,
Nov. 1640 till secluded in Dec 1648, and for Aldborough, 1661-79, was a Presbyterian and an energetic supporter of the Parl. measures, serving on many important
Committees, 1642-47, and being a Col. in the Parl army, was one of the New
Council of State, Feb to May 1660 He m, between Nov 1629 and Dec 1632,
Alathea, widow of William (SANDYS), LORD SANDYS OF THE VINE, 1st da. and testa-
mentary coheir of John PANTON, of Brynnelkib, in Henthlan, co. Denbigh, by
Helenor, da of Sir William BOOTH, of Dunham Massey, co Chester She d 22 May
1679 He d 19 Jan 1701, aged 98, and was bur. at Langley Will pr March 1705.

II. 1701.   SIR JOHN HOLLAND, Bart. [1629], of Quidenham afore-
                said, grandson and h, being son and h. of Col Thomas HOLLAND,
who d v p 28 Dec 1698, by Elizabeth, da. of Thomas MEADE, of Loftus, Essex He
suc to the Baronetcy, 19 Jan. 1701, was M P for Norfolk (four Parls.), 1701 10 ;
P.C, 2 June 1709, and Comptroller of the Household to Queen Anne, 1709-11.
He m, May 1699, Rebecca, 2d and yst. da and coheir of William (PASTON), 2d and
last EARL OF YARMOUTH, by his 1st wife, Charlotte Jemima Henrietta Maria BOYLE,
or FITZROY, illegit da. of King CHARLES II She was b 14 Jan. 1681 He d about
1724. Admon., as of Bury St. Edmunds, 22 July 1724, his widow being then alive

III. 1724 ?   SIR WILLIAM HOLLAND, Bart [1629], of Quidenham afore-
       to   said, s. and h., was b 17 April 1700, suc to the Baronetcy about
      1729.   1724. He m Mary, da of Arthur UPTON, merchant He d. s.p.
                  17 Feb 1728/9, when the Baronetcy became extinct Admon,
1 April 1729, to his widow, and, again, Feb. 1815. Her will pr May 1771

ALEYN, or ALLEN

cr. 24 June 1629 ,

ex. 15 Sep. 1759

I. 1629.   "EDWARD ALEYN, of Hatfield, co. Essex, Esq," s. and
                h. of Edmund ALEYN, of the same, by Martha, da and coheir of John
GLASCOCK, of Pewters Hall, in Witham, Essex, was b, about 1586 , suc his father,

---

(ᵃ) See ped by G. A. Carthew in the Visitation of Norfolk, 1553, vol. ı, pp. 444-
445, as published by the Norfolk Arch. Soc. See also Carthew's History of Laundith,
part ıı, pp 444-447.

12 Sep. 1616, being then aged 30 , and was *cr a Baronet*, as above, 24 June 1629 He was Sheriff for Essex, 1629-30. He *m.* Elizabeth, da and coheir of George SCOTT, of Little Leighs, Essex. He *d.* Nov. 1638 Will pr. 1638

II. 1638.   SIR EDMUND ALEYN, Bart. [1629], of Hatfield aforesaid, grandson and h , being s and h of Edmund ALEYN, by Mary, da of Nicholas MILLER, of Wrotham, Kent, which Edmund last-named, who *d v p* 1633, was 1st s of the late Bart He was aged about 2 years in 1634, and *suc. to the Baronetcy* in Nov 1638. He *m.*, 1 May 1651, at St Giles' in the Fields, Midx (marriage also reg at Birdbrook, Essex), Frances, only da and h of Thomas GENT, of Moynes in Steeple Bumpsted, Essex, and of Lincoln's Inn, Barrister at Law He *d s p m* 2 Nov 1656 His widow, who was *b* 1636 and who brought her husband an estate of about £600 a year, *d* 16 Jan 1657. Both *bur.* at Hatfield Church.(ª) Her will dat 15 Jan 1657, pr 1 Feb 1657/8

III. 1656   SIR EDMUND ALEYN, Bart. [1629], of Hatfield aforesaid, s and h., *suc. to the Baronetcy*, 2 Nov 1656 and *d.* soon afterwards, young and unm

IV. 1658 ?   SIR GEORGE ALEYN, Bart. [1629], of Little Leighs aforesaid, great uncle and h male, being br of the 2d and grandson of the 1st Bart , *suc to the Baronetcy* on the death of his nephew He *m.* firstly, Elizabeth, da of (—) HALL, of co Lincoln' She *d s p m* He *m* secondly, Martha, da. of Roger JONES, of co Monmouth. He *m* thirdly, (—) He *d.* 1664, and was *bur.* at Little Leighs

V 1664   SIR GEORGE ALEYN, Bart [1629], of Little Leighs aforesaid, s and h by 2d wife, *suc. to the Baronetcy* in 1664 He *m* Mercy, yst da of John CLOPTON, of Little Waltham, Essex. He *d* 1702 and was *bur.* at Little Leighs

VI 1702   SIR CLOPTON ALEYN, Bart. [1629], of Little Leighs afore said, s and h, *suc to the Baronetcy* in 1702. He *d* unm. 8 Sep. 1726 and was *bur* at Little Leighs (ᵇ)

VII 1726   SIR GEORGE ALEYN, Bart. [1629], of Little Leighs aforesaid, br. and h , *suc. to the Baronetcy* on the death of his brother. He *d.* unm about 1746 Will pr. 1746.

VIII 1746 ?   SIR EDMUND ALEYN, Bart. [1629], of Little Leighs aforeto   said, nephew and h , being s and h of Edward ALEYN, by Mary, da. of 1759.   the Rev. (—) TROTT, Vicar of Great Saling, Essex, which Edward was 3d s of the 5th Bart. He *suc to the Baronetcy* about 1746 and *suc* to the family estates in 1751 under the will of his cousin, the Hon Mrs. Howard(ᶜ): was Sheriff of Essex, 1752-53 He *d* unm 15 Sep. 1759, at Bath, co Somerset, when the *Baronetcy* became *extinct*. Will pr 1759.

(ª) Arabella, their only da., who was h to her br., the 3d Bart , eventually inherited their large estates She *m* firstly, Francis THOMPSON ; secondly, the Hon George HOWARD. Under her will, dat 20 June 1746, these estates passed in 1751 (after the death of Arthur Dobbs to whom she had conveyed them for life) to her cousin, Sir Edmund Aleyn, the 8th Bart

(ᵇ) Query if "*Sir Edmund Alen, Bart*," who was *bur.* "from Barnards Inn " 27 Dec 1726, at St. Andrew's, Holborn, may not have been next br. and successor to the 6th Bart

(ᶜ) See note "a" above. These estates passed on his death to his sister Arabella, wife of the Rev. James CHALMERS, M A., Vicar of Earls Colne and Rector of Little Waltham, Essex.

EARLE, or ERLE:

cr. 2 July 1629;

ex. 13 Aug 1697.

I. 1629.   "RICHARD ERLE, of Straglethorpe co Lincoln, Esq ," s
and h. ap. of Augustine ERLE, or EARLE, of the same, by Frances (m.
22 Jan 1599), sister of Sir Thomas CONY, of Bassingthorpe in that county, was
admitted to Gray's Inn 27 Jan 1626/7, and was, v.p., cr. a Baronet, as above, 2 July
1629 He suc his father in Nov. 1637[a]; was a prisoner of war to the King in
1645 ; one of the English hostages for the treaty with Scotland, 17 Dec 1646 ;
Sheriff of Lincolnshire, 1647-48   He m , in or before 1629, Frances, da. of Sir
Edward HARTOPP, 1st Bart {1619}, by Mary, da. of Sir Erasmus DRYDEN, 1st Bart
[1619]. He d 25 March 1667, aged 60, and was bur. at Straglethorpe   M.I   Will
dat 3 Oct 1665, pr. 14 May 1667. His widow, by whom he had 12 children, d.[b]
aged 80, and was bur. at Sturton, Notts.   M.I erected by her da Elizabeth, wife of
John Thornhagh.

II. 1667.   SIR RICHARD EARLE, or ERLE, Bart. [1629], of Straglethorpe aforesaid, grandson and h , being e. and h of Augustine
EARLE, by (—), da of (—) NODES, which Augustine (aged 5 years in 1634) was elder
s. of the late Bart., but d v p   He suc to the Baronetcy, 25 March 1667, but d
unm , of the small-pox, probably soon afterwards

III 1670 ?   SIR RICHARD EARLE, or ERLE, Bart. [1629], of Straglethorpe aforesaid, uncle and h , suc to the Baronetcy on his nephew's
death   He m., in or before 1673, Ellena, da. of William WELBY, of Denton, co
Lincoln , was Sheriff of Lincolnshire, 1675-76   He d about 1680   Will pr. 1680
His widow m Edward PAYNE, of Hough on the Hill, co Lincoln, who survived
her and was bur there 30 Dec. 1728   She d 2 and was bur. there, 10 March
1726/7.

IV. 1680 ?   SIR RICHARD EARLE, or ERLE, Bart. [1629], of Stragle-
to   thorpe aforesaid, s and h , b. about 1673, suc to the Baronetcy about
1697.   1680   He d. unm. at Kensington 13 Aug 1697, aged 24, and was
bur. at Straglethorpe, when the Baronetcy became extinct.[c]   M.I
there   Will dat. 9 Aug. 1697, pr 3 June 1699 [d]

(a) Among Sir Joseph Williamson's "Lincolnshire Families, temp Car. II," he is
noticed as "son of Anthony [should be " Augustine "] an Attorney, from an Attorney
at Stragglethorpe, near Newark ; £1,500 ; a retired man "   [Her and Gen., vol. ii,
p. 121].
(b) The date of her death, which had been inscribed on the monument, was
illegible when a copy, about 1870, of the inscription was made by Lord Hawkesbury
The parish register is, unfortunately, defective about that period
(c) The Rev W Earle, Curate of St. Clement Danes, Westm , was, in 1900, a
claimant of this Baronetcy.
(d) He " gave his estate to [his maternal cousin] William Welby, the younger, of
Denton, and in case of no issue to Thomas, yst s. of Edward Payne, on condition to
change the name to Earle." [Le Neve's Baronets]   The will was contested by
Elizabeth, wife of John Thornhagh, of Fenton in Sturton, and of Osberton, Notts
she being heir at law, as only da. of the 1st Bart. but a compromise was effected,
[Ex inform. Lord Hawkesbury.]

DUCIE : ?

cr 28 Nov. 1629;

sometime, 1661? to 1679, VISCOUNT DOWNE [I],

ex. May 1703.

I. 1629   " ROBERT DUCIE, Esq., Alderman of the city of London,"
1st surv s of Henry DUCIE, of London, and of Little Aston, co.
Stafford, merchant (d Nov, 1587), by Mary (m 2 July 1571, at St Lawrence Jewry),
da and eventually h of Robert HARDY, of London, was *bap*. 29 May 1575 at St
Lawrence Jewry, London, admitted Free of the Merchant Taylors' Company; Sheriff of
London, 1620 21, Alderman of Farringdon Without, 1620-25, of Billingsgate,
1625 27, and of Bassishaw, 1627 till death, being *cr. a Baronet*, as above, 28 May
1629. He was subsequently, 1630-31, Lord Mayor of London, and was *Knighted*,
during office, at Greenwich 5 June 1631. He is said to have been banker to
Charles I, and to have advanced to him £80,000, but to have been worth some
£400,000 notwithstanding He m, before 1609, Elizabeth, da of Richard PYOTT,
citizen and grocer of London, sometime, 1610-11, Sheriff of that city, by Margaret,
da. of Richard FLOYER, of Uttoxeter He d. 12 and was *bur*. 22 July 1634, at St.
Lawrence Jewry Inq p.m. 12 Aug 1634, at Tedbury Will pr 1634 His
widow was *bur* 9 Feb. 1635/6 at St. Lawrence aforesaid.

II. 1634   SIR RICHARD DUCIE, Bart [1629], of Tortworth, co.
Gloucester, 1st s and h, b about 1609, matric. at Oxford (Hart
Hall) 27 Jan 1625/6, aged 16, admitted to Middle Temple, 1627, aged 23 years and
more when he *suc to the Baronetcy*, 12 July 1634, Sheriff of Gloucestershire,
1636 37 In 1638 he was an inhabitant of St Michael's Bassishaw, London He
was a sufferer in the cause of Charles I, and was taken prisoner by Gen Waller;
sequestrated Oct. 1643, and fined £3,346 He d unm at his manor house at
Tortworth 7 March 1656/7, and was *bur* 10 April 1657 at Tortworth Admon
19 June 1657.

III. 1657   SIR WILLIAM DUCIE, Bart [1629], of Tortworth aforesaid, br and h, b about 1612; *suc. to the Baronetcy*, 7 March
1656/7, was Sheriff of Gloucestershire, 1660-61, made K B, at the coronation of
Charles II, 23 April 1661, and was, probably not long afterwards, *cr* (a) BARON
CLONEY and VISCOUNT DOWNE [I] He m (Lic Fac. 23 June 1662, he 40
and she 27), Frances, da. and coheir of Francis (SEYMOUR), 1st BARON SEYMOUR OF
TROWBRIDGE, by his 1st wife, Frances, da. and coheir of Sir Gilbert PRYNNE He
d s.p. 9 Sep. 1679, at Charlton, co Kent, and was *bur* at Tortworth, when the
peerage became *extinct* (b) Admon. 26 Sep. 1679. His widow, who was *bap* (at
the Lodge in the Great Park) at Great Bedwyn, Wilts, 27 April 1673, was *bur* there
20 Sep 1699.

IV 1679   SIR WILLIAM DUCIE, Bart [1629], of Islington, co
Midx, nephew and h. male, being s and h of Sir Hugh DUCIE, K B,
of Islington aforesaid, which Hugh, who d in or before March 1661/2, was yr s of
the 1st Bart He was a minor at his father's death, but was of full age on 1 June
1680, having *suc. to the Baronetcy*, 9 Sep 1679 He m Judith, da. of (---), of co
Hertford He d s p. in the Fleet prison, about 1691.

(a) Sir John Reresby, in his " *Memoirs*," states this creation to have been made at
the instance of Lord Halifax, who received on that account £25,000 from the grantee
(b) His estates devolved on his niece, Elizabeth, only da. and h. of his br, Robert
Ducie. She m. Edward MORETON, of Moreton, co. Stafford, and was mother of
Matthew Ducie Moreton, *cr*. 9 June 1720, LORD DUCIE, BARON OF MORETON, co.
Stafford.

V. 1691?   Sir Robert Ducie, Bart [1629], of Islington aforesaid,
    to   br and h ; suc to the Baronetcy about 1691. He d. unm May 1703,
    1703.   when the Baronetcy became extinct   Admon. 15 April 1704.

[After the date of the above creation, 28 Nov 1629, a very remarkable cessation
takes place in the creation of Baronetcies. In the space of somewhat more
than *eleven years*, that ensue therefrom, down to 1 Jan 1640/1, there are but *four
creations*, while during *seven years* of that period, 1632 to 1638 inclusive, there are
none]

GRENVILE, or GRANVILLE
cr. 9 April 1630 ;(ᵃ)
ex. 1658.

I. 1630,   "Richard Grenvile, of Killegarth, co. Cornwall, Knt
    to   and Colonel," 2d s of Sir Barnard Grenvile or Granville, of Stow,
    1658   in Kilkhampton, co Cornwall, by Elizabeth, da. and h of Philip
              Bevile, of Killegarth or Kellygarth aforesaid, was *bap* 26 June
1600, at Kilkhampton, being aged 20 at the Visit of Devon in 1620 ; was one of the
Captains in the expedition of the Duke of Buckingham , *Knighted,* 20 June 1627,
at Portsmouth , was M P for Fowey, 1628 29, and was *cr. a Baronet,* as above,
9 April 1630. He was thanked by the House of Commons, 30 Sep 1643, for his
services "against the Papist rebels in Ireland," but, soon afterwards, distinguished
himself as "the King's General in the West"(ᵃ) on the Royalist side, being
"excepted as to life and estate" in the propositions to the King, Sep 1644, Nov.
1645, and Nov 1648: was banished, and his estate confiscated, 16 March 1648/9   He
m , in Oct 1629, "a rich widow," viz , Mary, widow of Sir Charles Howard (4th s.
of the 1st Earl of Suffolk), formerly widow of the Hon Thomas Darcy, and,
before that, of Sir Allen Percy, K B , da of Sir John Fitz, of Fitzford, Devon, by
Bridget, da of Sir William Courtenay She, who was *bap.* 1 Aug. 1596, at Whitchurch, obtained a separation from him in Feb 1631 He d s p.m (ᵇ) 1658, at
Ghent, when the *Baronetcy* became *extinct.* His admon. as "late of Tavistock,
Devon, but died beyond the seas," 17 Aug. 1661   The admon. of his widow, 20 Oct.
1671, her will being subsequently pr. May 1672.

VAVASOUR, or VAVASOR:
cr 22 June 1631,
with a spec clause as to precedency ,(ᶜ)
ex Feb 1643/4.

I   1631,   "Charles Vavasor, of Killingthorpe, co. Lincoln, Esq.,"
    to   3d but 1st surv s and h. of Sir Thomas Vavasour, of Copmanthorpe,
    1644.   co York, by Mary, da. and h. of John Dodges, of Cope, co Suffolk,
              suc his father in Nov 1620, and was *cr a Baronet,* as above, 22 June
1631, "to take precedence(ᶜ) next after Thomas Mounson and next before George
Greisley, who were created Baronets in the year 1611," i e , 29 June 1611   He
attended the King at Oxford, where he d unm Feb and was *bur* 1 March 1643/4,
at St. Mary's, Oxford, when the *Baronetcy* became *extinct.* Admon April 1662 and
11 March 1664/5.

(ᵃ) These words are on his monument in Ghent. See *Nat Biogr ,* and see also a
letter of "W D. Pink" in *N and Q.,* 7th S , xi, 276
(ᵇ) Elizabeth, his da and h., *m.* Col William Lennard, and was administratrix to
her father, 17 Aug 1661.
(ᶜ) This clause was presumably invalid   It is certainly contrary to the Act of Parl.
31 Hen. VIII for settling the precedency *of Peers* "according to their ancienty and
times of creation." See also vol i, p. 40, note "a"

TYRRELL, or TIRRELL.

cr 9 Feb. 1638/9 ;

ex 20 Jan 1749

I. 1639.   "EDWARD TYRRELL, of Thorneton, co Bucks,
Knt," who had however, been cr a *Baronet* previously, viz,
on 31 Oct 1627, wishing to disinherit his eldest son, was, after, it is said, a
resignation(a) of the Baronetcy of 31 Oct 1627, cr *a Baronet*, as above,
9 Feb 1638/9, with, however, a spec rem, viz, "to hold the dignity for
life, with rem to his son Tobias Tyrell, Esq, in tail male, rem to Francis
Tyrell, another son in tail male ; rem. to the heirs male of the body of the
said Edward in tail male.   To take precedence of Baronets created since
31 Oct. [1627] 3 Chas I."(b)   He d. 2 July 1656

II 1656   SIR TOBY TYRRELL, Bart. [1627 and 1639], of Thornton
aforesaid, 2d but 1st surv. s. and h , *suc. to both Baronetcies*,
3 July 1656, his eldest br , Robert Tyrrell (who was the h. ap. to the Baronetcy
of 1627), having d v.p unm. 20 May 1644. Both Baronetcies, however,
became *extinct*, 20 Jan 1749.

(right margin, rotated:) See fuller particulars under "Tyrrell," Baronetcy cr. 31 Oct 1627

MOSLEY, or MOSELEY :

cr 10 July 1640 ;

ex 14 Oct 1665.

I. 1640.   "EDWARD MOSELEY, of Rowleston [i e, Rolleston], co
Stafford, Esq," s and h. of Rowland MOSELEY, or MOSLEY,(a) of the
Hough in that county (Sheriff thereof, 1615 16), by his 2d wife, Anne, sister and
coheir of Richard SUTTON, da. of Francis SUTTON, both of Sutton, co. Chester
(which Rowland was s. and h. of Sir Nicholas MOSLEY, sometime, 1599—1600, Lord
Mayor of London), was *bap.* at Didsbury, Sep 1616, inherited the manor of Manchester, on the death, 23 Feb 1616/7, of his father, and that of Rolleston on the
death, 1638, of his uncle (Sir Edward Mosley, Attorney Gen of the Duchy of Lancaster), and was cr. *a Baronet*, as above, 10 July 1640 , was Sheriff of Staffordshire,
1641-43 , was a zealous Royalist and was taken prisoner at Middlewich, 13 March
1642/3   He was fined £4,200, as also £64 a year , his estates were confiscated, but
restored on payment of £4,874, on 21 Sep. 1647   He was, subsequently, charged
with rape, but acquitted 28 Jan 1647/8 , lived many years in embarrassed circumstances   He m , 15 Nov. 1636, at Chorlton chapel, Mary, da of Sir Gervase
CUTLER, of Steinborough Hall, co York, and h of her mother, Elizabeth, da and h.
of Sir John BENTLEY, of Bradsal Park, co Derby. He was *bur* at Didsbury 4 Dec.
1657. Admon. 5 Nov. 1658 to principal creditor   The admon. of his widow as
"of St Martin's in the Fields, Midx," 15 Nov. 1658.

II. 1657,   SIR EDWARD MOSLEY, Bart. [1640], of Rolleston aforesaid,
to   s and h , matric at Oxford (Bras. Coll), 28 March 1655, and suc *to the*
1665   *Baronetcy* in Dec 1657   He was aged 25 at the Visit. of Lancashire in
1664 , was Sheriff of Lancashire, Nov. to Dec. 1660; M P. for
St. Michael's, 1661 till death ; purchased the estate of Hulme in 1661. He *m.*

(a) The resignation of this *Dignity* was, apparently, invalid. In the case of the
Viscountcy of Purbeck, 1678, it was laid down that "a dignity cannot be surrendered
to the Crown to the prejudice of the next heir, for it is annexed to the blood, and
nothing but a deficiency or corruption of the blood can hinder the descent." See
also p. 37, note "a," *sub* "Stonhouse.'
   (b) See p 78, note "c"
   (c) In Booker's "*Didsbury*" [Chetham Society, vol xlii] is a pedigree of the Mosley
family, copies of several of their wills, etc.

April 1665, Katharine, yr da. of William (GREY), 1st BARON GREY OF WERKE, by Priscilla, or Cecilia, da of Sir John WENTWORTH He *d.* s p. at Hough 14, and was *bur* 21 Oct 1665 at Didsbury, when the *Baronetcy* became *extinct* (a) His wills dat respectively 18 Dec. 1660, and 13 Oct. 1665, were disputed His widow, who enjoyed the estate of Rolleston in dower, *m.* (Lic Vic Gen , 6 April 1667, he about 25 and she about 23) Charles NORTH, who, presumably, in consequence of that alliance (though his wife was not heir or cohen to her father) was sum to Parl 24 Oct. 1673, as LORD GREY DE ROLLESTON, and who suc his father as LORD NORTH DE KIRTLING He *d* Jan 1690 in his 56th year, and was *bur.* at Kirtling She *m* thirdly (Lic Vic Gen , 30 April 1691, he above 30, she about 40), Col Francis RUSSELL, who *d* in Barbadoes about 1 Oct 1696 She *d* there before him in or before Jan 1694/5. Admon 18 June 1695.

LUMLEY, *or* LOMLEY :
cr. 8 Jan 1640/1 ,
ex 11 Dec. 1771

I 1641   "MARTIN LUMLEY,(b) of Bardfield Magna, co Essex, Esq ," s. and h. of Sir Martin LUMLEY, *or* LOMLEY, sometime, 1623-24, Lord Mayor of London, by his 1st wife, Mary, da and h. of Robert WITHORNE *or* WITHAM, of Yorkshire, Citizen and Upholsterer of London, was *b* about 1596, being aged 23 at the death of his mother in 1619 , was Sheriff of Essex, 1639-40 , suc. his father, 3 July 1634 , was M.P. for Essex in the Long Parliament,(c) Feb 1641, till secluded in Dec 1648, and was cr a *Baronet,* as above, 8 Jan 1640/1, being *Knighted* at Whitehall on the day following. He was a Presbyterian and a supporter of the Parl. measures, serving on several important committees, 1643-46. He *m.* firstly, 15 Jan 1620/1, at St. Andrew's Undershaft, London, Jane, da. and h. of John MEREDITH, of co Denbigh She was living 15 Oct 1624,(d) but *d* s p m within three years of that date. He *m* secondly, 29 May 1627, at St. Andrew's aforesaid, Mary, da of Edward ALLEN, of Finchley, Midx., Alderman and sometime, 1620 21, Sheriff of London, by his 1st wife, Judith, da of William BENNETT, of London He *d.* about 1651. Will pr. 1651. His widow was *bur.* 2 Oct. 1678, at Great Bardfield. Will pr 1678

II 1651?   SIR MARTIN LUMLEY, Bart [1641], of Great Bardfield aforesaid, s and h by 2d wife, aged 6 in 1634 ; *suc to the Baronetcy* about 1651 , Sheriff of Essex, 1662-63 He *m*, 16 July 1650, at St Helen's, Bishopsgate (Lic Fac she aged 18), Anne, da. of Sir John LANGHAM, 1st Bart [1660], by Mary, da. of James BUNCE, of London She was *bur* 20 Sep. 1692 at Great Bardfield He was *bur*, there 11 Sep 1702, aged 74

III. 1702   SIR MARTIN LUMLEY, Bart [1641], of Great Bardfield aforesaid, s and h. , *bap.* there 27 March 1662 , *suc to the Baronetcy* in Sep 1702 , Sheriff of Essex, Jan to Nov. 1710 He *m* firstly, 3 June 1683, at St Dionis Backchurch (Lic Fac , he 21 and she 15), Elizabeth, da. of Sir Jonathan

---

(a) The Lancashire estates devolved on his uncle, Sir Edward Mosley, of Hulme, co Lancaster, who *d* s.p m. 1695. The estate of Rolleston devolved, after his widow's death, on his 1st cousin, Oswald Mosley (son of his uncle, Nicholas Mosley), who eventually inherited the manor of Manchester, and who *d* 1726, being father of Oswald Mosley, cr a *Bart.* 18 June 1720 The nieces and heirs at law of the 2d Bart appear to have been passed over These were the two daughters and cohers of his sister, Mary, wife of Joseph Maynard, of whom (1) Elizabeth *m* Sir Henry Hobart, Bart [1611], and (2) Mary *m.* Henry (GREY), Earl of Stamford

(b) See pedigree in *Mis Gen. et Her.*, N.S., vol 1, p 474

(c) His name appears among "the members of the House of Commons that advanced horse, money, and plate for the defence of the Parl " June 1642 [*N and Q.* 1st S , xii, 358], to which object, also, he contributed four horses

(d) See funeral cert of her sister Prudence, whose heir she was,

DAWES, of Allhallows, Staining Alderman and sometime, 1671-72, Sheriff of London, by Anne, da of Sir Thomas BENDISHE, 2d Bart. [1611] She *d.* s p m s., and was *bur.* 21 Aug 1691, at Great Bardfield He *m.* secondly, 17 Jan 1695, at Great Bardfield, Elizabeth, da of Richard CHAMBERLAYNE, of Gray's Inn, Midx. She was *bur* 20 April 1704, at Great Bardfield He *m* thirdly, Elizabeth, da of Clement RAWLINSON, of Sanscute, co Lancaster, but by her had no issue He *d* 12 and was *bur.* 19 Jan. 1710/1, at Great Bardfield.

IV. 1711,   SIR JAMES LUMLEY, Bart. [1641], of Great Bardfield
to   aforesaid, only surv. s and b. by 2d wife, *b* about 1697, *suc to the*
1771.   *Baronetcy*, 12 Jan 1710/1, matric. at Oxford (Ch Ch), 15 March 1713/4, aged 17, was declared a lunatic, 29 June 1725 and that he had been one for four years, commission under the Great Seal granted, 17 July 1725, to Elizabeth NEVILLE, widow.[a] He *d* unm 11 Dec 1771, when the *Baronetage* became *extinct*

DALSTON

cr. 15 Feb. 1640/1 ;

ex. 7 March 1765.

I. 1641.   "WILLIAM DALSTON, of Dalston, co Cumberland, Esq,"
s and h. ap. of Sir George Dalston, of the same and of Heath Hall, near Wakefield, co York, (sometime M P and Sheriff for Cumberland), by Catharine, da. and coheir of John THORNWORTH, of Halsted, co Leicester, was admitted to Gray's Inn, 7 Dec. 1631, and was *cr. a Baronet*, as above, 15 Feb 1640/1, being *Knighted* at Whitehall, 31 July 1641, was M P for Carlisle, April to May 1640, and Nov 1640 till disabled in Jan. 1644 ; was Col. of Horse in the King's service During the rebellion both he and his father were great sufferers, paying as much as £3,700 to the sequestrators He suc his father in Sep. 1657 He *m* Anne, da. of Thomas BOLLES, of Osberton, Notts, by Mary, da of William WYTHAM, of Ledstone, co York, which Mary (after her husband's death) was cr a Baronetess [S.] in 1635, as "Dame Mary Bolles, widow" He *d.* 13 Jan. 1683.

II 1683.   SIR JOHN DALSTON, Bart [1641], of Dalston and Heath
Hall aforesaid, 1st surv. s and h male ; *Knighted* (with his 1st br., George Dalston) at Whitehall 16 Feb 1663/4, *suc to the Baronetcy*, 13 Jan 1683, Sheriff of Cumberland, 1686-87 He *m* Margaret, 2d da of Sir William RAMSDEN, of Byrom and Longley, co York, by Elizabeth, da and h. of George PALMES, of Naburn. She was *bap.* at Almondbury 9 Jan 1656 He *d* at Heath Hall, 1711.

III. 1711.   SIR CHARLES DALSTON, Bart [1641], of Dalston and
Heath Hall aforesaid, s and h, *suc. to the Baronetcy* in 1711 ; was Sheriff of Cumberland, 1712-13 He *m* firstly (—), da and coheir of Sir Francis BLAKE, of Whitney, Oxon. He *m.* secondly, in or after 1716, Anne, widow of Sir Lyon PILKINGTON, 4th Bart [S. 1635], da of Sir Michael WENTWORTH, of Woolley, co York, by Dorothy, da of Sir Godfrey Copley, 1st Bart. [1661] He *d.* 5 March 1723 His widow, who was *b.* 16 and *bap.* 18 March 1663, at Woolley (by whom he had no surv. issue), *m* for her 3d husband, 1 Dec. 1730, at Horbury, John MAUDE, of Alverthorpe Hall, and of Wakefield, co. York She *d.* at Chevet 15 Aug 1764, and was *bur.* at Wakefield.

IV 1723,   SIR GEORGE DALSTON, Bart. [1641], of Dalston and
to   Heath Hall aforesaid, only s and h, by 1st wife, *suc to the Baronetcy*
1765   5 March 1723 In 1740, being then unm, he was a volunteer on board Admiral Haddock's squadron ; Sheriff of Cumberland, 1752-53 ; Lieut.-Col. of the Yorkshire Militia, 1759 ; sold the estate of Dalston in 1761. He *m.* 28 Oct 1742, Anne, da of George HUXLEY He *d.* s p m.[b] 7 March 1765, when the *Baronetcy* became *extinct.* His widow *d.* 2 Nov 1776, at St. Omer's

---

(a) *Qy* if she was not his stepmother.
(b) His only da *m.* a French gentleman of the name of Dillon.

M

According however to Kimber's *Baronetage* [1771], the 4th Bart. left a son

V. 1765.   SIR WILLIAM DALSTON, " the present [1771]
        Bart " Of him, however, nothing is known, and it is conjectured that, if he ever existed, he probably was illegitimate (ª)

COLE :
cr 15 Feb 1640/1 ,
ex 25 March 1720

I. 1641   "NICHOLAS COLE, of Branspeth Castle, co pal of Durham, Knt," s. and h ap of Ralph COLE, of Newcastle on Tyne, merchant (Mayor, 1633, and the purchaser, in 1636, of Brancepeth Castle, who *d* Nov 1655), was thrice, 1640-42 and 1643-44, Mayor of Newcastle, and was, while such, *Knighted* at Whitehall 11 Feb 1640/1, and four days afterwards, *cr a Baronet*, as above 15 Feb 1640/1 Being a zealous Royalist, he was excepted from pardon in 1644 and 1645 and was fined £312 in June 1649 He *m*, in or before 1641, Mary, da of Sir Thomas LIDDELL, 1st Bart [1642], by Isabel, da of Henry ANDERSON He apparently was *bur* 12 Aug 1660 [1669 ?], at Brancepeth

II. 1660 ?   SIR RALPH COLE, Bart. [1641], of Brancepeth Castle aforesaid, s and h , *suc to the Baronetcy* on the death of his father , was M P. for Durham, March 1678 to Jan 1679, and March to July 1679 He *m* firstly, (—), da. of (—) WINDHAM He *m* secondly, Katharine, da of Sir Henry FOULIS, 2d Bart. [1620], of Ingleby, co York, by Mary, da. of Sir Thomas LAYTON. She was *bap.* at Ingleby, 23 Sep. 1637 He sold the Brancepeth estates on 19 April 1701,(ᵇ) for £16,800, with a life annuity of £500 and one for £200 for his wife if she survived him He *d* 9 Aug 1704 His widow *d* in Durham 29 Sep and was *bur* 2 Oct. 1704, at Brancepeth.

III. 1704.   SIR NICHOLAS COLE, Bart [1641], grandson and h., being s and h of Nicholas COLE, by Elizabeth, da of Sir Mark MILBANKE, 1st Bart [1661], which Nicholas last named was s. and h ap of the late Bart ,(ᶜ) but *d. v p* He was *bap* 9 June 1685, at St Nicholas', Newcastle, and *suc to the Baronetcy*, on the death of his grandfather, 9 Aug 1704 He *m.* firstly, Anne, da of Collier CAMPBELL. He *m.* secondly (Lic Fac 16 July 1705) Anne, sister of Sir George SAVILE, 7th Bart [1611], da. of Rev John SAVILE, by his second wife, Barbara, da and h of Thomas JENISON He *d* s p 1710/1 His widow *m.* a Belgian adventurer called " BARON DOGNYES."(ᵈ)

(ª) In the obituary of the *Annual Register* for 1771 there occurs the death, 1 Oct 1771, " at his seat at Acorn Bank in Westmoreland [*sic*] SIR WILLIAM DALTON [*sic*] Bart." [*sic*]. The family of *Dalston* of Acornbank, co *Cumberland*, recorded their pedigree in the Visitation of that County in 1664, being 6th in descent from Thomas Dalston, of Dalston, the lineal ancestor of the Baronets No member of the Acornbank branch of the family of Dalston and no one of the name of *Dalton* was apparently ever created a Baronet.

(ᵇ) Hutchinson's *Durham*

(ᶜ) Another son of the 2d Bart , *viz.,* " Ralph Cole, s. of Ralph, of Kepier, co Durham, Bart ," matric. at Oxford (Linc. Coll) 2 March 1679/80, aged 17, and became B A 1683 ; M A 1686.

(ᵈ) MS diary of Miss Gertrude Savile [*ex inform.* Lord Hawkesbury]

IV 1711,   SIR MARK COLE, Bart [1641], br and h. He was *bap*
to   8 Nov 1687, at St Nicholas', Newcastle ; *suc to the Baronetcy* in
1720   1711, but *d.* s p. and was *bur* 25 March 1720, at St Margaret's,
Durham, when the *Baronetcy* became *extinct*

FLETCHER.
cr. 19 Feb 1640/1 ,
ex 19 May 1712.

I 1641   "HENRY FLETCHER, of Hutton in le Forest, co. Cumberland, Esq ," only s and h of Sir Richard Fletcher, of the same,
formerly of Cockermouth in that county, merchant, by his 2d wife, Barbara, da of
Henry CRACKENTHORPE, of Newbiggen, *suc* his father between 1630 and 1637, and
was *cr. a Baronet*, as above, 19 Feb 1640/1 He was twice Sheriff for Cumberland,
1641 43 He raised a regiment for the Royal service at the head of which he fell at the
skirmish at Rowton Heath, near Chester, 24 Sep. 1645 He *m.*, about 1638, Catharine,
sister of Sir William DALSTON, 1st Bart [1641], da of Sir George DALSTON, of Dalston,
Cumberland, by Catharine, da. and coheir of John THORNWORTH He was slain as
above-mentioned in 1645 Admon. 27 May 1650 to his widow She, who endured,
with great spirit, sequestration, incarceration, etc., from the Parl , *m.* Thomas
SMITH, D D , BISHOP OF CARLISLE, 1684—1702, who *d* 12 April 1702, aged 88

II 1645   SIR GEORGE FLETCHER, Bart [1641], of Hutton aforesaid, only surv s and h , *b.* about 1633, *suc to the Baronetcy* 1645,
was fined in May 1647, for his father's delinquency, £2,200, afterwards reduced to
£714 , was Sheriff of Cumberland 1657-58 and 1679-80, M.P. thereof, 1661-79,
1681, 1689 90, 1690-95, 1695-98, and 1698-1700 He *m* firstly, 27 Feb. 1654/5,
at Totteridge, Herts, Alice, da of Hugh (HARE), 1st BARON COLERAINE [I], by
Lucy, da. of Henry (MONTAGU), 1st EARL OF MANCHESTER She, who was *bap*
20 Oct 1633, at Totteridge, was *bur* at Hutton He *m.* secondly, before 1665,
Mary, widow of Sir George GRAHAM, 2d Bart. [1629], da of James (JOHNSTONE,
1st EARL OF HARTFELL [S], by his 1st wife, Margaret, da. of William (DOUGLAS), 1st
EARL OF QUEENSBERRY [S]. He *d* 23 July 1700, and was *bur.* at Hutton, aged 67

III. 1700,   SIR HENRY FLETCHER, Bart [1641], of Hutton aforeto   said, s and h by 1st wife, *b* about 1661, being 3 years and 11 months
1712   old at the Visit. of Cumberland, 27 March 1665 , matric at Oxford
(Queen's Coll), 10 June 1678, aged 16 , M P for Cockermouth,
1689-90; *suc to the Baronetcy*, 23 July 1700 He settled his estate on his distant cousin,
Thomas Fletcher, of Moresby,[a] and retired into a monastery of English monks at
Douay, in France, where he *d* unm 19 May 1712, when the *Baronetcy* became
extinct. He was *bur* in a magnificent chapel at Douay, built at his own expense
Will pr May 1712.

PYE
cr 23 April 1641 ,
ex. 28 April 1673.

I 1641,   "EDMUND PYE, of Leckamsteed, co Bucks, Esq ," s and
to   h of Edmund PYE, of the same and of St Martin's, Ludgate, London,
1673?   scrivener, by Martha, "sister of Alderman ALLEN of London,"[b]
(both living May 1635) , was *b* about 1607, and was *cr a Baronet,*

(a) After much litigation it was arranged that, if this Thomas Fletcher *d* s.p
(which event took place), the estates should go to Henry VANE, 2d s of Lionel Vane,
by Catharine, one of the sisters (of the whole blood) and coheirs of the 3d Bart. This
Henry VANE, *suc* to the Hutton estate, took the additional name of Fletcher, and *d*
unm 1761. His br , Walter Vane, afterwards Walter Fletcher-Vane, then *suc* thereto,
and was father of Lionel Wright FLETCHER-VANE, *cr. a Bart* 1786

(b) See pedigree of Pye in *Visit. of London, 1634.*

as above, 23 April 1641, being *Knighted* at Whitehall four days later He was voted a delinquent by Parl and fined £3,065. He acquired the manor and estate of Bradenham, Bucks, where he chiefly resided ; was M P for High Wycombe, 1661 He *m.* (Lic Lond , 7 May 1635 he 28 and she 18), Catherine, sister of John, 1st BARON LUCAS OF SHERFIELD, da of Thomas LUCAS, of Colchester, by Elizabeth, da and h of John LEIGHTON He *d* *s p m* (a) and was *bur* 28 April 1673, at Braden-ham, about 1673 when the *Baronetcy* became *extinct*. Will pr. 1673. His widow *d.* 1701, aged 89. Will pr 1702.

Memorandum.—In au darter May 1641 down to the end of the reign of Charles I the enrolment of any patent was the exception Among the 116 Baronetcies that are given in the *Creations, 1483—1646* (ap 47th Rep D K Pub. Records) as having been created during that period, no patents, in as many as 85 cases, are enrolled, though, as to 67, the date of the signet bill, warrant, or privy seal is therein given as under, *viz.*, Every, 21 May 1641 , Napier, 23 June 1641 , Yelverton, 27 June 1641 , Cave, 28 June 1641 , Hatton, 2 July 1641 , Boteler, 3 July 1641 , Abdy, 5 July (Qy. June) 1641 , Cotton, 10 July 1641 , Bamfeild, 12 July 1641 , Thynne, Dewes, and Burgoyne, 13 July 1641 , Drake, 14 July 1641 , Rous, 16 July 1641 , Pratt, and Sydenham, 19 July 1641 , Norwich, and Nichols, 22 July 1641 ; Brownlow, 23 July 1641 , Hare, Northcote, and [another] Brownlow, 24 July 1641 , Strickland, 29 July 1641 , Windham, Maule-verer, Knatchbull, Chichester, and Boughton, 31 July 1641 , Wolryche, 2 Aug 1641, Pryce, and Carew, 5 Aug 1641 , Cholmeley, Spring, and Castleton, 7 Aug 1641 , Trevor, 11 Aug 1641 , Davie, 11 Aug 1641 ; Bindlosse, 13 Aug. 1611 ; Meux, 8 Dec 1641 , Willys, 13 Dec 1641 , Halford, 16 Dec 1641 , Cowper, and Thomas, 28 Feb 1641/2 , Dawney and Hamilton, 3 May 1642 , Morgan, Kemeys, and Williams, 11 May 1642 , Reresby, 14 May 1642 , Moore, 16 May 1642 , Hampson, 20 May 1642 , Hardres and Williamson, 22 May 1642 , Denny, 26 May 1642 , Aleton, 28 (?) May 1642 , Lowther, 31 May 1642 , Middleton, 10 June 1642 , Payler, 15 June 1642 , Corbett, [—] June 1642 , Rudston, 6 Aug 1642 ; Hungate, and Thorold, 10 Aug 1642 , Anderson 30 June 1643 , Jones, 24 July 1643 , Bate, 2 Nov. 1643 ; O'Neale, 9 Nov 1643 ; Hickman, 11 Nov. 1643, and Boteler, 30 Nov. 1643. To the above 67 Baronetcies must be added the 18 (with which the abovenamed list of *Creations, 1483—1646* concludes), of which neither patent, signet bill, warrant nor privy seal are enrolled, though the *docquet* of the creation is noticed in a publication generally known as *Black's Docquets* (b) These are as under, *viz* —Vavasour, 17 July 1643 , Waldegrave, 1 Aug 1643 ; Pate, 28 Oct. 1643 ; Acton, 17 Jan 1643/4 ; Hawley, 14 March 1643/4 , Preston, 1 April 1644 , Prestwich, 25 April 1644 ; Williams, 4 May 1644 , Thorold and Lucas, 14 June 1644 ; Bard, 8 Oct. 1644 ; Van Colster, 28 Feb. 1644/5 , De Boreel, 21 March 1644/5 , Carteret, 9 May 1645 , Windebanke, 25 Nov 1645 , Wright, 7 Feb 1645/6 , Charlton, 6 March 1645/6, and Willis, 11 June 1646.

"A CATALOGUE OF THE BARONETS OF ENGLAND" was (according to a statement made in Dugdale's *Ancient Usage of Arms*), "*published by authority* in 1667," being revised some "12 years and more" later [1681 ?]. This purports to be a "*catalogue* of such, touching whom the docquet books remaining with the Clerk of the Crown in Chancery do take notice."(c) In this *catalogue* there are

---

(a) Of his two daughters and coheirs, (1) Margaret *m* John (Lovelace), 3d Baron Lovelace of Hurley, and had issue, who inherited the Bradenham estate , (2) Eliza-beth, *m* the Hon Charles West, but *d. s p*

(b) "Docquets of letters patent and other instruments passed under the Great Seal of King Charles I, at Oxford in the years 1642, 1643, 1644, 1645 and 1646," edited by Mr. Black, an assistant keeper of the Public Records, from the original Crown office docquet book at that time preserved in the Ashmolean Museum, at Oxford

(c) It is as well, perhaps, to quote Dugdale's own words from his "Preface" to the said *catalogue*, as given in the edition [p. 67] of his *Ancient Usage of Arms*, edited by "T. C Banks, Esq," (folio 1812) —"Whereas in the year 1667, a catalogue of the Baronets of England was by authority published, to the end that such as had

as many as nineteen Baronetcies (whose existence for the most part has never been questioned) which are not named in the abovementioned list of the *Creations, 1483—1646* These are —Strutt, 5 March 1641/2 , St Quintin, 8 March 1641/2 , Kempe, 14 March 1641/2 ; Reade, 16 March 1641/2 , Enyon, 9 April 1642 , Williams, 19 April 1642 , Wintour, 29 April 1642 , Borlase, 4 May 1642 , Knollys, 6 May 1642 , Ingelby, 17 May 1642 , Widdrington [of Widdrington], 9 July 1642 ; Valckenburg and Constable, 20 July 1642 , Blakiston, or Blackstone, 30 July 1642 , Widdrington [of Cartington], 8 Aug 1642 , Markham and Lennard, 15 Aug 1642; Bland, 30 Aug. 1642, and Throckmorton, 1 Sep 1642. It is accordingly thought better, on and after the date of May 1641 when the enrolments are so very irregular, to follow this official (or semi official) *Catalogue* as given by Dugdale (referring to it as "*Dugdale's Catalogue*"), which includes the above-named nineteen Baronetcies, indispersed among those mentioned in the list of *Creations, 1483—1646.* There are, however, many other Baronetcies conferred during the Civil Wars which are *not* comprehended in this *Catalogue* (*e.g* , Bathurst, Cokayne, Courtenay, Haggerston, Lloyd, etc) which will be here dealt with at the end of those given by Dugdale.

EVERY ·

cr. 26 May 1641.(a)

I 1641. "SIMON EVERY, of Eggington, co Derby, Esq ," only s. and h of John EVERY, of Chardstock, co Somerset, and of Oxford, by Elizabeth, sister of William LAMBERT, of Oxford, was *b* about 1603, in Northamptonshire ; matric. at Oxford (Wadham Coll), 27 Nov 1618, aged 15 ; admitted to Middle Temple, 1620 ; pr. his father's will 29 Oct 1623, was M P for Leicester, April to May 1640, and, having been a great sufferer in the Royal cause and a steady adherent of Charles 1, was cr a Baronet, as above, 26 May 1641,(a) being *Knighted* at Whitehall 4 June following He was a Compounder. He *m* in or before 1629, Anne, 1st da and coheir, and eventually sole heir of Sir Henry LEIGH, of Eggington or Egginton aforesaid, by Catherine, da of (—) HORTON, of Catton in that county He *d* about 1647 Will pr 1649

II 1647? SIR HENRY EVERY, Bart [1641], of Egginton aforesaid, s. and h , *bap* there 15 Nov. 1629, *suc to the Baronetcy* about 1647 He, like his father, was a great sufferer for his loyalty to his King He *m* in or before 1653, Vere, 1st da of Sir Henry HERBERT, Master of the Revels to Charles I

---

obtained patents for that honour, which were not enrolled, should, by descerning an omission of their names therein, take care to supply that defect, so that upon a second impression thereof they might be inserted Now, whereas, after 12 years and more, no enrollments are yet to be found for sundry persons which have assumed this title, which causeth some to doubt whether they can make any justifiable claims thereto Whereas, therefore, no person [*sic*] whatsoever ought to take upon them [*sic*] this title of dignity, but such as have been really advanced thereto by letters patent under the Great Seal of England, it is thought fit by the Rt Hon Robert, Earl of Aylesbury, who, now excerciseth [*i e* as a Joint Commissioner, 30 June 1673] the office of Earl Marshall of England, that this present catalogue of such touching whom the Docquet books remaining with the Clerk of the Crown in Chancery do take notice, shall be published, to the end that those, of whom no memorial upon record is to be found to justifie their right to the title, may be known , and care henceforth taken in commissions of the peace and otherwise that it be not given unto them until they shall manifest the same unto the Lord Chancellor of England and have speciall order from his Lordship to enroll such patents where they pretend title to that dignity. As also that regard be had of giving credit to any other catalogues of the Baronets which are already publisht, or that shall be publisht, than what is taken from the authority of those Docquet books above mentioned or the enrollment of their patents "

(a) The patent is not enrolled. The date here given is that in Dugdale's *Catalogue,* See *Memorandum* on p. 84 The date of the signet bill is 21 May 1641.

and Charles II, by his 1st wife (—), da of)—) He *d* 29 Sep and was *bur* 3 Oct. 1700, at Egginton His widow, who was *b* 29 Aug 1627, was *bur* there 26 Feb. 1706/7

III. 1700. SIR HENRY EVERY, Bart. [1641], of Egginton aforesaid,
s and h, *b* about 1653, *suc. to the Baronetcy*, 29 Sep 1700 He *m* firstly, (Lic Vic. Gen , 30 April 1685, he about 30, she about 20), Mary, da of John (TRACY), 3d VISCOUNT TRACY OF RATHCOOLE [I], by Elizabeth, da of Thomas (LEIGH), 1st BARON LEIGH OF STONELEIGH She was *bur* at Egginton, 16 March 1692 He *m*. secondly, Anne, widow of Richard LYGON, of Madresfield Court, co. Worcester (*d.* s p 15 April 1687, aged 49), 1st da. and coheir of Sir Francis RUSSELL, 2d Bart. [1627] of Whitley and Strensham by Anne da. of Sir Rowland LYTTON He *d* s p Sep 1709, and was *bur* at Newton Solney, co Derby Will dat 14 May 1709, pr 10 March 1710 His widow *m* (as her 3d husband) Sir John GUISE, 3d Bart [1661], who *d* 16 Nov 1732 She *d.* 22 Feb. 1734/5

IV. 1709 SIR JOHN EVERY, Bart [1641], of Egginton aforesaid,
br and h., *b* about 1654 He was sometime Captain of the "Queen," man-of war, and served in the cause of William III, with some distinction , *suc to the Baronetcy* in Sep 1709, was Sheriff of Derbyshire, 1717-18 He *m* firstly, 28 April 1704, at Knightsbridge Chapel, Midx , Martha, da. of John (THOMPSON), 1st BARON HAVERSHAM, by Frances, da. of Arthur (ANNESLEY), 1st EARL OF ANGLESEY She *d* 9 and was *bur*. 14 Feb 1715, at Egginton. Her admon 10 July 1717 He *m* secondly, Dorothy, da of Godfrey MEYNELL, of Bradley, co Derby. He *d* s p. 1 and was *bur* 4 July 1729, at Egginton, aged 75 Will pr. 1730 His widow *d* 1749. Will pr. 1749

V 1729 SIR SIMON EVERY, Bart [1641], of Egginton aforesaid,
br. and h , *b* about 1658 , ed at Christ's Coll , Cambridge, of which he was sometime Fellow, B A , 1683 , M A , 1687 , in Holy Orders , Rector of Navenby, co Lincoln ; *suc to the Baronetcy* 1 July 1729 He *m* in or before 1708, Mary, da. of Rev. Joshua CLARKE, Rector of Somerby, co. Lincoln, and Prebendary of Lincoln. She *d.* 10 Aug 1723, aged 34 He *d.* 12 and was *bur* 17 Jan 1753, at Egginton aged 95.

VI. 1753 SIR HENRY EVERY, Bart [1641], of Egginton aforesaid,
1st s and h , *b* 25 Oct. 1708 , Sheriff of Derbyshire, 1749 50 , *suc to the Baronetcy* 12 Jan 1753 He *m* 1 July 1741, Frances, sister of Sir Henry IBBETSON, Bart. [1740], da of James IBBETSON, of Leeds, co York, by Elizabeth, da of John NICHOLSON, M D She *d* 21 Sep 1754 and was *bur* at Egginton, aged 52. He *d* s p 31 May and was *bur* 12 June 1755 at Egginton. Admon 20 Aug. 1755.

VII 1755 SIR JOHN EVERY, Bart [1641] of Egginton aforesaid,
br and h ; *b*. 17 Oct 1709 , ed at Christ's Coll , Cambridge , B A , 1729 , M A , 1733, in Holy Orders Rector of Waddington and Vicar of Bracebridge, both co Lincoln , *suc. to the Baronetcy*, 31 May 1755. He *m* , 1 Dec 1767, at Egginton, Dorothy PAKEMAN She was *bur* there 29 Aug 1769 He *d.* s p. 29 June and was *bur* 5 July 1779, at Egginton Admon 24 July 1779 to his cousin german and next of kin, Edward Every , further admon. Feb 1787.

VIII. 1779 SIR EDWARD EVERY, Bart [1641], of Egginton aforesaid,
cousin and h male, being only s and h. of John EVERY, of Derby, by Mary LUNN, his wife, which John (*bap* at All Saints', Derby, 20 Jan 1724/5, and *bur*. 1 April 1767 at Egginton) was 1st s of Henry EVERY, of St. Peter's, Derby (*bap*. 3 April 1701 and *bur* 15 March 1775 at All Saints' aforesaid), only s of John EVERY, of Castle Donington, co. Leicester and All Saints', Derby (*d.* 4 April 1746, aged 74), only s. of Francis EVERY, of Castle Donington aforesaid (*d.* Sep 1708), 3d s of the 1st Bart. He was *bap* 15 Aug. 1754, at All Saints', Derby *suc. to the Baronetcy*, as also to the family estate, 29 June 1779 , Sheriff of Derbyshire, 1783, and rebuilt

the mansion at Egginton He *m* 4 Sep. 1776, at St Alkmund's, Derby, Mary, widow of Joseph BIRD, of Loughborough, and formerly of William ELLIOT, of Derby, da of Edward MORLEY, of Horsley, co. Derby. He was *bur* 4 Jan 1786, at Egginton Will pr. 1786 His widow *m* (for her 4th husband) 10 March 1790, at Egginton, Ashton-Nicholas MOSLEY, of Park Hill, co. Derby (who *d.* 2 April 1830, aged 62), and *d.* 9 March 1826

IX 1786 SIR HENRY EVERY, Bart. [1641], of Egginton aforesaid, s and h. ; *b* 4 June and *bap.* 7 July 1777, at St. Alkmund's, Derby , *suc to the Baronetcy* in Jan 1786 , was Sheriff of Derbyshire, 1804-05. He *m* firstly, 22 Dec 1726, at Egginton, Penelope, 4th da of Sir John-Parker MOSLEY, 1st Bart [1781], by Elizabeth, da of James BAYLEY She (who was sister to her husband's step father abovenamed) *d* 30 Aug 1812 He *m* secondly, Elizabeth, da. of William SOAR, of Little Chester, near Derby, yeoman She *d.* s p s. a few months before him, and was *bur.* at Barrow upon Trent. He *d.* 28 Dec 1855, at Egginton Hall, in his 79th year. Will pr Feb 1856.

X. 1855 SIR HENRY FLOWER EVERY, Bart [1641], of Egginton Hall aforesaid, grandson and h., being s. and h of Henry EVERY, of Beaumont Lodge, near Windsor, Berks, sometime an officer in the Life Guards, by his 2d wife, Caroline, da. of Henry (FLOWER), 4th VISCOUNT ASHBROOK [I], which Henry Every was s. and h. ap. of the 9th Bart., but *d.* v p , 27 Feb. 1853, aged 53. He was *b* 25 Dec. 1830, in London , ed. at Cheltenham ; was sometime an officer in the 90th foot, *suc to the baronetcy*, 28 Dec 1855 ; Sheriff of Derbyshire, 1863 He *m.* firstly, 8 Feb 1855, Gertrude, 5th da of Hon and Rev Baptist-Wriothesley NOEL (yr br of Charles, 1st EARL OF GAINSBOROUGH), by Jane, da of Peter BAILLIE, of Dochfour. She *d* 26 Feb. 1858. He *m.* secondly, 12 Oct. 1859, Mary-Isabella, 1st da. of Rev. Edmund HOLLAND, of Benhall Lodge, near Saxmundham, Suffolk, by Isabella, 12th da of Sir John ROBINSON, 1st Bart [1819], of Rokeby Hall, co. Louth He *d* 26 Feb 1893, at Egginton Hall, aged 62. Will pr. at £14,678. His widow living 1900

XI. 1893 SIR EDWARD OSWALD EVERY, Bart. [1641], of Egginton Hall aforesaid, grandson and h., being 1st but only surv. s and h of Henry Edmund EVERY, Captain South Wales Borderers, by Leila Frances Harford, da of the Rev Henry Adderley BOX, which Henry was 1st s. and h ap of the late Bart. by his 2d wife, but *d* v.p. 1 Dec. 1892, aged 32. He was *b* 14 Jan 1886 and *suc to the Baronetcy*, 26 Feb. 1893

Family Estates.—These, in 1883, consisted of 2,231 acres in Derbyshire, worth £4,930 a year. *Principal seat* —Egginton Hall, near Burton on Trent, co. Derby.

LANGLEY :

cr. 29 May 1641

I. 1641. "WILLIAM LANGLEY, of Hygham Gobion, co Bedford, Esq ," as also of Stainton, co. York, s. and h of George LANGLEY, of Stainton aforesaid, by Jane, da. of John HALL, of Sherbourn, co. York, became possessed of the manor of Higham Gobion in 1639, and was *cr a Baronet*, as above, 29 May 1641 He *m.* Elizabeth, sister of Richard, 1st VISCOUNT LUMLEY OF WATERFORD [I.], da. of Roger LUMLEY, by Anne, da of (—) KURTWICH He *d* , at Mrs Eliz Threkill's house in High Holborn, 21 and was *bur.* 23 Aug 1653, at St Andrew's, Holborn Will p 1654 His widow *m.* before 24 March 1659, Roger GUNTER, of Isleworth, co. Midx. Her will, dat. 24 March 1659, pr. 7 Dec 1681, by her said husband.

II. 1653.   SIR ROGER LANGLEY, Bart [1641], of Sheriff Hutton
Park, co. York, s. and h, *b* about 1627 ; *suc to the Baronetcy*, 21 Aug.
1653 , was Sheriff of Yorkshire, 1663-64, and was aged 38 at the Visit. of Yorkshire in
1665   He sold the manor of Higham Gobion to Arabella, Countess of Kent   He was
Foreman of the Jury at the trial of the seven Bishops in 1688, and was a Commissioner
of the Prize Office, *temp* William III.   He *m* firstly (Lic. Fac , 26 April 1647, he being
then of Enfield, Midx , about 20 and she about 17), Mary, da of Thomas KEIGHLEY, of
Hertingfordbury, Herts.   He *m* secondly (Lic Fac , 10 April 1672), Barbara, widow of
(—) HOBSON, da and coheir of (—) CHAPMAN, of Foxton, co. Leicester, Serjeant at
Law. By her he had no issue. He had lic. to marry (Lic. London, 1 April 1684, being
then aged 58 and a widower) Mary REND, of St John's, Walbrook, widow, aged 34
He *m* shortly after that date (a da being *bap* Feb 1684/5, at St. Andrew's,
Holborn) Sarah, da of John NEALE, of Malden Ash, Essex   He was *bur* 4 Jan.
1698/9, at St Margaret's, Westminster   His will, dat 27 April 1697 and 17 Oct
1698, pr. 10 Jan. 1698/9 and again 4 Sep 1716   His widow was *bur* 4 Nov 1701,
at St Margaret's aforesaid   Will pr. June 1702

III   1699   SIR ROGER LANGLEY. Bart [1641], grandson and h ,
being s. and h of William LANGLEY, by Isabella, da of Sir John
Griffith, of Erith, Kent, which William (aged 18 in 1665) was s. and h. ap. of the
2d Bart , by his 1st wife, and *d*. v p 1689. He *suc* to the Baronetcy in Jan 1698/9
He *m* Mary, da of Stanislaus BROWNE, of Eastbourne, Sussex. He *d*. s p.s. 19 Sep.
1721   The will of his widow pr 1758

IV   1721   SIR THOMAS LANGLEY, Bart [1641], br and h , *suc to
the Baronetcy*, 19 Sep 1721   He *m*. (—), 2d da. of Capt. Robert
EDGWORTH, of Longwood, co Meath   He *d* s p m s , 1 and was *bur* 6 Dec. 1762,
with his parents at St. Margaret's, Westm., aged, it is said, 98 ([a])

V. 1762.   SIR HALDANBY LANGLEY, Bart [1641], nephew and h.
male, being 1st surv s. of Haldanby LANGLEY. by Mary, da. of
Charles PECK, of Gildersley, co Derby, which Haldanby lastnamed was yst br
of the 3d and 4th Barts , and *d* 30 May 1728   He *suc.* to the Baronetcy, 1 Dec
1762. The time of his death has not been ascertained, but he is stated to have left
a son and h , " but whether such were really the case has not been ascertained."([b])

VI ?   1770 ?   "SIR HENRY LANGLEY, Bart. [1641], called s. and
to   h ,"([b]) who, if so, would have *suc to the Baronetcy* on his
1820 ?   father's death. He, who was living 1818, "is presumed to
have *d* s p , *when the title became extinct*."([b])

PASTON.

cr. 7 June 1641([c]) ;

sometime, 1673-1732, VISCOUNTS YARMOUTH ,

and subsequently, 1679-1732, EARLS OF YARMOUTH ,

ex 25 Dec 1732

I. 1641.   " WILLIAM PASTON, of Oxnead, co. Norfolk, Esq.," s. and
h of Sir Edmund PASTON, of Paston and Oxnead, by Catharine, da.
of Sir Thomas KNEVITT, of Ashwelthorpe, all in co. Norfolk, was *b.* about 1610 ; suc.
his father (who *d.* aged 48) in 1632, was Sheriff of Norfolk, 1636-37, and was *cr a*

([a]) According, however, to the *Gent. Mag* , " Sir Thomas Langley, Bart., Uxbridge,"
died 1740, and another Sir Thomas Langley, Bart , aged 98, grandson of Sir Robert
[sic] of 1688 [sic] , " died in Westminster 1762."
   ([b]) Courthope's *Extinct Baronetage* [1835].
   ([c]) But, according to Dugdale's *Catalogue* (see *memorandum* on p 84) the patent
was dated *8* June 1641

Baronet, as above, 7 June 1641   He *m* firstly, in or before 1631, Catharine, 1st da of Robert (BERTIE), 1st EARL OF LINDSEY, by Elizabeth, da. of Edward (MONTAGU), 1st BARON MONTAGU OF BOUGHTON   She *d* 3 Jan 1636, and was *bur* at Oxnead.   He *m* secondly, Margaret, sister of Sir George HEWITT   He *d*. 22 Feb 1662/3.   Will pr. 1663   His widow *m* George STRODE   Her admon , as of St. Giles' in the Fields, Midx., 23 Dec. 1669, granted to her said husband

II 1663.   SIR ROBERT PASTON, Bart [1641], of Paston and Oxnead aforesaid, 1st s. and h by 1st wife, *b* 29 May 1631 , ed at Westm. School and at Trin Coll. Cambridge , *Knighted*, 26 May 1660 ; was M P. for Thetford, 1660, and for Castle Rising, 1661 73 ; *suc*. to the Baronetcy, 22 Feb. 1662/3 ; F R.S , 20 May 1663 ; a Gent of the Privy Chamber, 1666/7   He *m*., about 1650, Rebecca, 2d da of Sir Jasper CLAYTON, of St. Edmund the King, by Mary, da of William TOMSON, of Tinmouth Castle, Cumberland   She was living when he was *cr* , 19 Aug. 1673, VISCOUNT YARMOUTH, co. Norfolk, etc , and subsequently, 30 July, 1679, EARL OF YARMOUTH   In these peerages this Baronetcy thenceforth merged, till it and the other honours became *extinct*, 25 Dec. 1732, on the death of the 2d Earl and 3d Baronet

---

STONHOUSE, *or* STONEHOUSE

cr. 10 June 1641(a) ,

ex. 13 April 1695.

I. 1641.   "JAMES STONEHOUSE of Amerden Hall [in Debden] co. Essex, Esq ," s. and h of Sir James STONEHOUSE, of the same (who was the yst. br. of Sir William STONHOUSE, of Radley, 1st Bart [1628]), by his 2d wife, Anne, da of Sir Humphrey WELD, *suc* his father (who *d* aged 73) 1 Dec. 1638, and was *cr a Baronet*, as above, 10 June 1641 (a)   His estate was sequestrated in 1651 and he was fined £3,000 on 16 Sep 1652.   He *m* (—) (b)

II. 1652?   SIR JAMES STONEHOUSE, Bart [1641], of Amerden Hall aforesaid, s. and h.,(c) *suc to the Baronetcy* on the death of his father. He *m* Mary, d of (—) BLEWITT, of Holcombe, Devon.   His admon as "late of Amerden Hall, but decd at St Gregory's London," granted 2 May 1654, to his widow   She (who was living June 1669) *m* Sir John LENTHAL, of Besilden Lee, Berks, and was *bur* there

III. 1654?   SIR BLEWET STONEHOUSE, Bart [1641], of Amerden Hall aforesaid, s. and h., *suc to the Baronetcy* in his infancy about 1654 , matric at Oxford (Ch. Ch) 29 June 1669, aged 15 , *cr* M A 9 July following ; admitted to Lincoln's Inn, 1669.   He *d*. unm probably about 1670 (d)

IV. 1670?   SIR GEORGE STONEHOUSE, Bart. [1641], of Amerden Hall aforesaid, br and h , *suc to the Baronetcy* on his brother's death   He *m*. (—) da. of (—) HAMILTON (e)

(a) But, according to Dugdale's *Catalogue* (see *Memorandum* on p. 84), it was 8 June 1641.

(b) Neither his own burial nor that of any of his descendants took place apparently at Debden.—"Lady Stonhouse" [*Qy*. his wife or widow] is there buried 20 March 1651/2, and his father, Sir James, 3 Dec. 1638.   The will of " Dame Elizabeth Stonehouse " is pr 1655

(c) The statement of his succession is from Morant's *Essex*.   It is, however, possible that the 1st and 2d Baronets are in reality but one person.   The pedigree is very obscure and confused.

(d) In Morant's *Essex* the date of his death is given as 1693, but the date seems much too late.

(e) The will of " Dame Margaret Stonehouse," possibly being that of this lady, is pr. 1692

N

V. 1675?   SIR JOHN STONHOUSE, Bart [1641], of Amerden Hall
aforesaid, and of Bishops Itchington, co Warwick, s and h , *suc to
the Baronetcy* on the death of his father   He m Elizabeth, da of George COLE, of
Buckish, Devon, and of Enstone, Oxon   Will as " of the city of York, Bart.," dat
31 July 1681, pr. 12 Jan. 1681/2, by Elizabeth, the widow.

VI   1681,   SIR GEORGE STONHOUSE, Bart. [1641], of Amerden Hall
    to   aforesaid, s and h , *bap* 14 Jan. 1678/9, at Debden, *suc to the
    1695. Baronetcy* in 1681 ; matric at Oxford (Glouc Hall) 14 Feb 1693/4,
           aged 15   He *d* a minor and unm 13 April 1695, when the *Baronetcy*
became *extinct*.[a]

PALGRAVE

cr 24 June 1641 ;

ex 3 Nov 1732.

I   1641.   " JOHN PALGRAVE, of Norwood Barningham, co Norfolk,
Esq.," s and h of Sir Augustine PALGRAVE,[b] of the same (*d* Nov
1639, aged 72), by Elizabeth, sister of Sir Henry WILLOUGHBY, Bart [1611], 1st
da of Sir John Willoughby, of Risley, co. Derby, was *bap* 26 June 1605, at
Norwood Barningham, and was *cr a Baronet*, as above, 24 June 1641, being
Knighted at Whitehall four days later   He was M P for Norfolk, Nov. 1647,
till secluded in Dec 1648, and for Great Yarmouth, 1660, till void on 18 May ,
was a Colonel in the Parliamentary army , served on the Committee of Sequestrators for Norfolk, 1643, and of the " New Model," 1645   He *m*. firstly,
in or before 1629, Elizabeth, da of John JERMY, of Gunton, co Norfolk, Chancellor of Norwich, by his 1st wife, Mary, da. of Thomas MOULTON.   She was
bur. 19 Dec 1634, at Norwood Barningham   He *m*. secondly, at Merton, co.
Norfolk, Anne, widow of Cotton GASCOIGNE, of Illington, co Norfolk, da of Sir
William DE GREY, of Merton, co Norfolk, by Anne, da of Sir James CALTHORPE He
was *bur.* 26 April 1672, at Norwood Barningham   His widow *d* 25 Nov 1676, and
was *bur.* at St. Peter's, Hungate, Norwich   Will dat 15 Sep 1673, pr 2 Sep. 1678,
in Arch. Court, Norwich

II. 1672.   SIR AUGUSTINE PALGRAVE, Bart [1641], of Norwood
Barningham aforesaid, s and h by 1st wife ; *bap* 1 Dec 1629 , Gent.
of the Privy Chamber ; *suc to the Baronetcy* in April 1672 , was Sheriff of Norfolk,
1690 91 He *m* firstly, Barbara, da and h of the said Cotton GASCOIGNE and Anne, da
of Sir William DE GREY abovenamed   He *m* secondly (Lic. Vic Gen 13 Aug 1685,
he about 47 and she, therein called "Katharine LEMQUEL," about 37), Katharine, widow,
of Capt (—) LAWRENCE, of Brockdish, Herts, da. of Sir William SPRING, 1st Bart.
[1641], by Elizabeth, da. of Sir Hamon LE STRANGE She *d* 1 and was *bur* 6 Sep 1682,
at Norwood Barningham He *m* thirdly, 21 May 1686, at St. Martin's in the Fields
(Lic Fac. she about 30, spinster), Anne, da of Sir Richard Grubham HOWE, 2d Bart.
[1660], by Anne, da. of John KING, BISHOP OF LONDON   He *d* 13 March 1710/1, and
was *bur* at Norwood Barningham, aged 83   His widow *d*. 8 Aug 1714, and was *bur*
there, aged 69.

III 1711,   SIR RICHARD PALGRAVE, Bart. [1641], of Norwood
    to   Barningham aforesaid, only surv. s and h. by 3d wife , *bap* there
    1732. 6 Oct. 1688 ; *suc to the Baronetcy*, 13 March 1710/1   He *d* unm.
           in Norwich gaol 3 and was *bur.* 6 Nov. 1732, at Norwood Barning-
ham, aged 44, when the *Baronetcy* became *extinct*   Admon. 21 June 1735(c) to a
creditor.

(a) Elizabeth, his only sister, *m*. Thomas JERVOISE, of Herriard, Hants, who sold
the estate of Amerden Hall to Thomas Sclater BACON

(b) See a good pedigree in the *Visit. of Norfolk, 1563*, with copious additions, pub.
by the Norfolk Arch. Soc., vol. ii, pp. 23-34

(c) The estate was sold under a decree in Chancery (by his heirs (of the whole blood),
who were the four daughters of Samuel Smith of Colkirk, Norfolk, whose mother
Ursula, was da. of the 1st Bart. [*N and Q.*, 7th S , xii, 326]

NAPIER, or NAPER

cr. 25 June 1641(ª),

ex 25 Jan 1765.

I. 1641 "GERRARD NAPER [i e., NAPIER], of Middlemerth [i.e.,
Middlemarsh] Hall [near Sherbourne], co Dorset, Esq," s and h of
Sir Nathaniel NAPIER,(b) of the same, and of More Critchell in that county, sometime
Sheriff and M P for Dorset, by Elizabeth, da. and h of John GERARD, of Hyde,
in the Isle of Purbeck, was *bap.* 19 Oct 1606 at Steeple, was M P for Wareham,
1628-29, suc. his father in 1635, and was *cr a Baronet,* as above, 25 June 1641,(ª)
being *Knighted* at Whitehall four days later. He was afterwards, 1640, M.P. for
Meloomb Regis, till disabled in Jan. 1644/5, having sat in the King's Parl at Oxford,
though, on 20 Sep. 1644, he took the National Covenant. He was fined £3,514 on
19 Dec 1645, which was reduced, 21 June 1649, to £988, but his estates in Dorset
and Kent being sequestrated, his losses during the Civil Wars were estimated at
more than £10,000 He was Sheriff of Dorset, 1650-51 In 1665 he entertained
the King and Queen at More Critchell He m. Margaret, da. and coh of John COLLES,
of Barton, Somerset She d in 1660 Admon 19 June 1665 He d. 14 May 1673.
Both *bur* at Mintern Magna. M.I. His will dat. 12 Nov. 1667 to 9 May 1673, pr.
21 Oct 1673.

II 1673 SIR NATHANIEL NAPIER, Bart [1641], of Middlemarsh
Hall and of More Critchell aforesaid, only surv s and h., *b.* about
1638 ; matric. at Oxford (Oriel Coll.), 16 March 1653/4 ; *Knighted* 16 Jan 1661,
suc. to the Baronetcy, 14 May 1673 , was M.P for Dorset, April 1677, till void 21 May ;
for Corfe Castle (four Parls), 1679-81 and 1685-87 , for Poole (three Parls.) 1689-98,
and for Dorchester, Feb. to July 1702, and 1702-05 , elected Sheriff of Dorset (but
did not act), Nov. 1688 He was a good linguist and well versed in architecture
and painting, and wrote a journal of his travels He m firstly, 20 Dec 1657, at St
Bride's, Fleet Street, London, Blauche, da. and coh of Sir Hugh WYNDHAM, of
Sylton, co Dorset, Justice of the Court of Common Pleas, by his 1st wife, Jane, da.
of Sir Thomas WODEHOUSE, 2d Bart. [1611] She d in 1695 and was *bur* at Mintern
aforesaid. He m. secondly, 9 March 1696/7, at St. Dionis Backchurch, London (Lic.
Fac, he about 45, she about 21, with consent of her mother, Mrs Ann ARNOLD, widow),
Susanna, da of the Rev (—) GUISE, of co. Gloucester He d at Critchell
Jan 1708/9, aged 72, and was *bur* at Mintern aforesaid Will pr June 1709 The
will of his widow, by whom he had no issue, pr. Feb 1711.

III. 1709 SIR NATHANIEL NAPIER, Bart. [1641], of Middlemarsh
Hall and of More Critchell aforesaid, only surv. s and h , by 1st wife,
b about 1669 , admitted to Lincoln's Inn, 1683 ; matric at Oxford (Trin. Coll.)
10 April 1685, aged 16 ; M.P. for Dorchester (9 Parls), 1695—1708 and 1710-22 ,
suc. to the Baronetcy in Jan 1708/9 He m firstly, Jane, da of Sir Robert
WORSLEY, 3d Bart [1611], by Mary, da. of Hon James HERBERT, s of Philip, EARL
OF PEMBROKE She d s p., soon afterwards He m. secondly, 28 Aug 1694, at
Isleworth, Midx (Lic Fac, he about 25, bachelor [sic], she of Hammersmith,
spinster), Catharine, da of William ALINGTON, 1st BARON ALINGTON OF WYMONDLEY,
by his 3d wife Diana, da of William (RUSSELL), 1st DUKE OF BEDFORD She, who
was *b* 27 Sep 1677, and who was in Sep. 1691, coheir of her brother, the 2d Baron,
d 13 April 1724, and was *bur* at Mintern He *d* 24 Feb 1727/8. Will pr. 1728.

IV 1728 SIR WILLIAM NAPIER, Bart. [1641], of Middlemarsh
Hall and of More Crichell aforesaid, s and h , by 2d wife, *b* about
1696 ; *suc to the Baronetcy,* 24 Feb. 1727/8 , Sheriff of Dorset, 1732-33. He d.
unm 27 Jan. 1753 Will pr 1753.

(ª) The patent is not enrolled. The date here given is that in Dugdale's *Catalogue*
See *Memorandum* on p 84. The date of the signet bill is 23 June 1641.

(b) This Nathaniel was s. and h of Sir Robert Napier, who purchased Middlemarsh
in 1592, was Lord Chief Baron of the Exchequer of Ireland, 1593, and Sheriff of
Dorset, 1606 The said Robert was 3d s of James Napier, of Puncknoll, Dorset, 3d
s. of John Napier, of Swyre, in that county, who was a yr s. of Sir Alexander NAPIER,
of Merchistoun, in Scotland.

V. 1753   Sir Gerard Napier, Bart [1641], of Middlemarsh
             Hall and of More Critchell aforesaid, br and h, b about 1701;
matric. at Oxford (Ball Coll), 11 May 1719, aged 18, suc to the Baronetcy, 27 Jan
1753 He m, in or before 1740, Bridget, da of Edward Phelips, of Montacute,
Somerset She d. in 1758, aged 51. He d 23 Oct 1759, aged 59 Will pr. 1761.

VI. 1759,   Sir Gerard Napier, Bart [1641], of Middlemarsh Hall
    to   and of More Critchell aforesaid, only s and h., b about 1740; matric
    1765.   at Oxford (Trin Coll), 13 April 1758, aged 18, suc to the Baronetcy,
             23 Oct 1759, was M P for Bridport, 1761-65. He m Elizabeth,
da of Sir John Oglander, 4th Bart [1665], by Margaret, da. of John Coxe. He d
s p, 25 Jan 1765, aged 26, when the Baronetcy became extinct ([a]) Will pr Feb
1765 His widow m in 1779, James Webb, and d. 16 Oct. 1814 at Bath

---

WHITMORE
cr. 28 June 1641;
ex. March 1699.

I 1641   "Thomas Whitmore, of Apley, co. Salop, Esq.," 2d but
             1st surv. s and h ap of Sir William Whitmore, of the same (who
had purchased that estate and was Sheriff of Salop in 1620), by his second wife,
Dorothy, da of William Weld, of London, was b. 28 Nov. 1612, in London, matric.
at Oxford (Trin Coll), 29 Jan 1629/30, aged 17, B A, 10 May 1631, Barrister
(Mid Temple), 1639, M P for Bridgnorth, April to May 1640, and 1640 till disabled
in Feb 1644, and was cr a Baronet, as above, 28 June 1641, and Knighted the same
day at Whitehall He suc his father Dec 1648,([b]) was a Compounder in Jan
1648/9, fined £5,315 on 3 April 1649, reduced in May 1650 to £5,000 He m,
16 April 1635, at Leyton, co Essex, Elizabeth, da and h of Sir William Acton,
Bart (so cr 30 May 1629), Alderman and sometime [1640] Lord Mayor of London,
by his first wife Anne, da and h. of James Bill, of Astwell, Herts He d. 1653
Will pr 1664. His widow, who inherited her mother's estate of Astwell d 1666
Will pr. 1667.

II 1653,   Sir William Whitmore, Bart. [1641], of Apley aforesaid,
    to   s and h, b 8 April 1637; suc to the Baronetcy in 1653, was
    1699.   M P for Shropshire, 1660, for Bridgnorth (nine Parls), 1661, till
             decease. He m, about Aug 1658 Mary, da of Eliab Harvey, of
St Lawrence Pountney, London, Turkey Merchant, by Mary, da of Francis West, of
London.([c]) He d s p March 1699, and was bur at Stockton, Salop, when the
Baronetcy became extinct ([d]) Will dat. 12 Nov. 1695, pr 11 Nov 1700 His widow,
who was bap 15 Nov 1637, at St Lawrence's aforesaid, d 30 Jan. and was bur.
15 Feb 1710/1 (with her parents), at Hempstead, co. Essex Will dat. 1 May 1710,
pr. 21 Feb 1710/1

([a]) The estates devolved on his cousin and h, Humphrey Sturt, of Horton,
Dorset, only s. and h of Humphrey Sturt, of the same (who d. at Bath, 1 Feb
1739/40), by Diana, only da. of the 3d Bart
([b]) The admon. of this William was granted 11 Feb. 1658/9 to his grandson, "Sir
[—] Whitmore, Bart," the sons of the deceased, Richard Whitmore and George
Whitmore having renounced
([c]) See an elaborate ped. of Harvey in Mis. Gen. et Her., 2d S, vol iii, pp. 329,
362, and 381
([d]) The estate of Apley passed to his first cousin (once removed) and heir male,
William Whitmore, of Lower Slaughter, co. Glouc., whose descendants still hold it.

MAYNEY, *or* MAYNE:

cr 29 June 1641 ;

ex 1706

I   1641   "JOHN MAYNE [or MAYNEY], of Lynton, co Kent, Esq.,"
s and h of Walter MAYNEY, of Linton aforesaid, was b about 1608
and was cr. a *Baronet*, as above, 29 June 1641, being *Knighted* at Whitehall the
same day   He was a zealous Royalist, was fined £1,600 on 22 March 1648 and
£1,970 on 1 Aug 1649 , and, being eventually ruined in that cause, sold his
estate of Linton to Sir Francis Withens   He *m.*, before 1634, Mary, da. of Sir Peter
RICAUT, of AYLESFORD, co Kent and of London, merchant, by Mary, da of Roger
VERCOLCIA   He d about 1676, aged 68

II.   1676 ?   SIR ANTHONY MAYNEY, Bart [1611], s. and h. , *suc. to*
    to   *the Baronetcy* about 1676   He *d* unm. (his death said to have been
    1706.   caused by actual want([a])) in 1706, when the *Baronetcy* became
extinct

CAVE:

cr. 30 June 1641([b]) ;

sometime, in 1810, CAVE-BROWNE,

and afterwards, since 1810, CAVE-BROWNE-CAVE

I.   1641   "THOMAS CAVE, Junior, of Stanford, co Northampton,
Knt.," s and h ap of Sir Thomas CAVE, of Stanford on Avon aforesaid, by Elizabeth, da of Sir Herbert CROFT, of Croft Castle, co Hereford, was b
about 1622 , matric at Oxford (St John's Coll), 28 April 1637, aged 15 , *Knighted*
at Whitehall, 24 June 1641, and, a few days later, was *cr* a *Baronet*, as above, 30 June
1641.([b])   He, as well as his father, was a strenuous supporter of the cause of his King
He suc his father between June 1663 and Feb. 1666/7   He *m* firstly, Katharine,
da of Sir Anthony HASLEWOOD, of Maidwell, co Northampton, by Elizabeth, da of
Sir William WILLMER, of Sywell, in that county   She *d.* s p   He *m* secondly, in or
before 1651, Penelope, 2d da and cohen of Thomas (WENMAN), 2d VISCOUNT WENMAN
OF TUAM [I], by Margaret, da. and h. of Edmund HAMPDEN   Her will dat 2 Feb
1665, pr 27 March 1666   His will pr. Feb 1671

II.   1671 ?   SIR ROGER CAVE, Bart. [1641], of Stanford aforesaid, s
    and h., by 2d wife, b about 1651, *suc. to the Baronetcy* about 1671 ;
was Sheriff of Northants , 1679 80 ; M P for Coventry, 1685 87 and 1689-90   He
m firstly (Lic Vic Gen , 24 Feb. 1675/6, each aged about 21), Martha, da and h
of John BROWNE, of Eydon, co Northampton, Clerk of the Parliament, by Elizabeth,
1st da. of John PACKER, of Shillingford, Berks, one of the Clerks of the Privy
Seal.   She *d.* before 1691   He *m.* secondly, Mary, sister of William BROMLEY,
Speaker of the House of Commons, da. of Sir William BROMLEY, K B , of Bagington,
co Warwick   He *d.* 11 Oct. 1703, aged 49   His widow *d.* 22 Nov. 1721

III   1703   SIR THOMAS CAVE, Bart. [1641], of Stanford aforesaid,
    s and h., by 1st wife, b about 1682, matric. at Oxford (Ch Ch),
27 Jan 1698/9, aged 16 , *suc. to the Baronetcy* 11 Oct 1703 , M P for Leicestershire
(three Parls), 1711 till his death in 1719. He *m* 20 Feb. 1703, at St. Giles' in the Fields,
Margaret, sister of Ralph, 1st EARL VERNEY [I], da of John (VERNEY), 1st VISCOUNT

([a]) His brother, from a like cause, had previously, in 1694, committed suicide
([b]) The patent is not enrolled.   The date here given is that in Dugdale's *Catalogue*.
See *Memorandum* on p 84   The date of the signet bill is 28 June 1641

FERMANAGH [I], by his 1st wife, Elizabeth, da of Ralph PALMER   He d 21 April 1719, in his 39th year, and was *bur* at Stanford   M I.   Will dat. 20 Jan 1718-19, pr 23 July 1719. His widow (whose issue, in 1810, became heir to the family of Verney) d 17 May 1774   Her will pr May 1774.

IV. 1719   SIR VERNEY CAVE, Bart [1641], of Stanford aforesaid, s and h , *b* 4 and *bap* 18 Jan 1704/5, at St. Martin's in the Fields , *suc to the Baronetcy*, 21 April 1719 , matric at Oxford (Balliol Coll), 29 March 1722, aged 15   He d unm., 13 Sep 1734, aged 29, and was *bur* at Stanford. M.I Admon , 24 Oct. 1734, to br , Sir Thomas Cave, Bart.

V. 1734   SIR THOMAS CAVE, Bart. [1641], of Stanford aforesaid, br and h , *b* 27 May and *bap* 4 June 1712, at St Martin's in the Fields , matric at Oxford (Ball Coll), 3 Nov. 1729, aged 17 ; *suc to the Baronetcy*, 13 Sep 1734 , Barrister (Inner Temple), 1735 , M.P for Leicestershire, 1741-47, 1762-68 and 1768-74 ; *cr* D C L of Oxford, 7 April 1756.   He *m* , 1736, Elizabeth, da and sole surv issue of Griffith DAVIES, M D, of Theddingworth, co Leicester, and of Birmingham, co. Warwick, by Elizabeth, da of Sir John BURGOYNE, 3d Bart. [1641], of Sutton.   She d 15 May 1760.   He d 7 Aug 1778, aged 67.   Both *bur* at Stanford

VI 1778   SIR THOMAS CAVE, Bart [1641], of Stanford aforesaid, s and h., *b* 22 Aug 1737 , matric at Oxford (Balliol Coll), 1 April 1756, aged 18 , cr. D C L , 8 July 1773 , F.R S, F.S A , 1799 ; *suc to the Baronetcy*, 7 Aug. 1778 , Sheriff for Leicestershire, Feb. to June 1780.   He *m* in 1765 (it is said, at St Lawrence Jewry, London), Sarah, da and coh of John EDWARDS, merchant, of London and Bristol, by his wife, Sarah HOLFORD   He d. 31 May 1780, and was *bur* at Stanford   Will pr. July 1780   His widow d July 1819.   Will pr 1819

VII 1780   SIR THOMAS CAVE, Bart [1641], of Stanford aforesaid, only s and h., *b* 6 Oct. 1766 , matric at Oxford, 28 Oct. 1785, aged 19 ; *suc to the Baronetcy*, 31 May 1780 , M P for Leicestershire, 1790, till his death in 1792.   He *m*., 3 June 1791, Lucy, da. of Robert (SHERARD), 4th EARL OF HARBOROUGH, by his 2d wife, Jane, da. of William REEVE   He d s p 16 Jan. 1792, and was *bur* the 27th at Stanford.(ª)   Will pr Feb 1792.   His widow, who was *b*. 13 Oct. 1769, at Southwell, Notts, *m* 20 Aug. 1798, at St Geo Han sq , Hon Philip BOUVERIE, afterwards PUSEY, who d 14 April 1828, aged 81   She d. 27 March 1858, aged 89 (ᵇ)

VIII 1792   THE REV SIR CHARLES CAVE, Bart. [1641], uncle and h , being 2d and yst, s. of the 6th Bart, was *b* about 1747 , matric at Oxford (Balliol Coll] 7 March 1766, aged 19 , B A , 1769, M A (St. Mary Hall), 1772; in Holy Orders , Rector of Finedon, co Northampton, and Vicar of Theddingworth, co Leicester, F S A., 1781 ; *suc to the Baronetcy*, 16 Jan 1792.   He d. unm , 21 March 1810, and was *bur* at Stanford   Will pr May 1810.

(ª) The estate of Stanford, the paternal inheritance of the Cave family, devolved on his sister and heir, Sarah, *b* 2 July 1768   She *m* , 25 Feb. 1790, Henry Otway, of Castle Otway, co. Tipperary, who d. 13 Sep 1815, and, a quarter of a century after his death, obtained a peerage (not apparently for any services rendered by him, herself, or any of her family, but) as being the representative of one of six coheirs of a Barony (that of Braye) which had been in abeyance for about 300 years, and of which she did not inherit a single manor. See as to this pernicious practice (which prevailed during the earlier years of Queen Victoria's reign) the " *Complete Peerage*," by G E C., vol. i, p. 288, note " b," and p. 289, note " c," and, as to " BRAYE," vol ii, pp 11-13

(ᵇ) By her second husband she had nine children, of whom the second son was the well-known " Dr Pusey " [Edward Bouverie Pusey, D.D., Regius Professor of Hebrew and Canon of Christ Church, Oxford], who d 16 Sep 1882, aged 82

IX.   1810.   SIR WILLIAM CAVE-BROWNE, afterwards CAVE-BROWNE-
CAVE, Bart [1641], of Stretton Hall, in Stretton en-le-field, co Derby,
cousin and h, being s. and h of John CAVE-BROWNE, of Stretton Hall aforesaid,
by his second wife, Catherine, da. and h of Thomas ASTLEY, of Wood Eaton,
co. Stafford, and Asteley, co Salop, which John (who by Act of Parl, 1752, took the
name of *Browne*, as a final surname, on inheriting the Stretton estates from his
maternal grandfather, and who *d* 2 Oct 1798), was 2d s, but the only son
that had issue, of Roger CAVE, of Eydon, co Northampton, and Raunston, co
Leicester (by Catherine, da. and coheir of William BROWNE, of Stretton Hall aforesaid), which Roger (who *d* March 1741) was s of Sir Roger CAVE, 2d Bart by his
2d wife. He was *b* 19 Feb 1765 and *bap* 25 March, at Stretton aforesaid   He *suc*
to the Baronetcy, 21 March 1810, and soon afterwards assumed the name of CAVE
after that of CAVE-BROWNE, which surnames were confirmed to his issue male by
Royal Lic dat. 18 Jan 1839   He *m* firstly, 13 Oct 1788, at Croxall, co. Derby,
Sarah, da of Thomas PRINSEP, of Croxall   She *d* s p and was *bur* 21 June
1790, at Stretton aforesaid   He *m* secondly, 4 Jan 1793, at Stretton, Louisa,
4th da, of Sir Robert Meade WILMOT, 2d Bart [1759], of Chaddesden, by Mary, da
and h of William WOOLLETT   She, who was *b* 8 Feb 1771 and *bap*. at Chaddesden, *d* 23 and was *bur* 30 April 1824, at Stretton   He *d* 24 and was *bur* 29 Aug
1838, at Stretton, aged 73   Will pr. Nov 1838

X.   1838   SIR JOHN ROBERT CAVE-BROWNE-CAVE, Bart [1641], of
Stretton Hall aforesaid, s. and h, *b*. 4 March and *bap* 10 May 1798,
at Stretton ; *suc* *to the Baronetcy*, 24 Aug 1838; was confirmed in the surname
of *Cave-Browne-Cave* by Royal Lic. 18 Jan 1839, Sheriff of Derbyshire, 1844   He
m 22 Nov 1821, at Kenilworth, co Warwick, Catharine Penelope, yst. da. and
coheir of William MILLS, of Barlaston Hall, co Stafford   He *d* 11 Nov. 1855.   Will
pr. Jan 1856   His widow, who was *b*. 25 June and *bap*. 10 Oct 1799, at Basford,
co. Stafford, *d*. 13 March 1871, at Kenilworth, aged 71.

XI.   1855.   SIR MYLLES CAVE-BROWNE-CAVE, Bart [1641], of
Stretton Hall aforesaid, s and h, *b* 1 Aug. and *bap* 31 Nov 1822 at
Kenilworth, sometime an officer in the 11th Hussars ; *suc. to the Baronetcy* 11 Nov
1855   He *m* 15 May 1855, at Stretton en le field, Isabelle, yst. da of John TAYLOR,
of "The Newarke," Leicester.

Family Estates.—The estate of Stanford, co Northampton, passed away from the
family in 1792, see p. 94, note "a"   That now held by the Baronet, being at
Stretton en le field, co Derby, came into the family by the marriage, in 1721, of Roger
Cave (s of the 2d and grandfather of the 9th Bart.) with Catharine, da and coheir
of William Browne, of Stretton   This estate appears to have been in 1878 under
3,000 acres.   *Seat.*—Stretton Hall, near Ashby de la Zouche, co Derby.

<hr>

YELVERTON :

cr. 30 June 1641(ᵃ),

afterwards, 1676-1799, LORDS GREY DE RUTHIN,

subsequently, 1690-1799, VISCOUNTS LONGUEVILLE,

and *finally*, 1717-99, EARLS OF SUSSEX ;

ex. 22 APRIL 1799

I.   1641.   "CHRISTOPHER YELVERTON, of Easton Mauduyt [*i e*,
Mauduit], co. Northampton, Knt," s. and h of Sir Henry
YELVERTON,(ᵇ) of the same, one of the Judges of the Common Pleas (1625-30), by
Margaret, da of Robert BEALE, Clerk of the Council to Queen Elizabeth, was
admitted to Gray's Inn, 28 Feb 1606/7 ; was M P for Newport, 1626 and 1628-29,
for Bossiney, 1640 till secluded Dec. 1648, *Knighted*, 29 Jan 1629/30; suc. his father,

<hr>

(ᵃ) The patent is not enrolled.   The date here given is that in Dugdale's *Catalogue*.
See *Memorandum* on p. 84.   The date of the signet bill is 27 June 1641.

(ᵇ) This Henry was s. and h. of Sir Christopher Yelverton, a Judge of the King's
Bench, who purchased the estate of Easton Mauduit, and who *d* there, 1607.

in 1630 ; waa Sheriff of Northanta, 1639-40, and waa *cr*. a *Baronet*, aa above, 30 June 1641 (ᵃ) He *m* 20 April 1630, at St Giles', Cripplegate, Anne, yat. da of Sir William TWISDEN, 1st Bart. [1611], by Anne, da of Sir Moyle FINCH, 1st Bart [1611] He *d* 4 Dec 1654, and waa *bur* at Easton Mauduit M I Will pr. 1655 His widow *d* 3 Dec 1670, aged 67, and waa *bur* at Easton Mauduit. M I there and at East Peckham, co Kent Will pr. Nov. 1671.

II. 1654. SIR HENRY YELVERTON, Bart [1641], of Easton Mauduit aforesaid, only s and h , *bap* there 6 July 1633, matric at Oxford (Wad Coll), 12 Nov 1651 , *suc to the Baronetcy* 4 Dec. 1654 ; waa M.P for Northamptonshire, 1660, and March 1664, till his death He *m* in or before 1657, Susan, *suo jure* BARONESS GREY DE RUTHIN, da and h of Charles (LONGUEVILLE), LORD GREY DE RUTHIN, by Frances, da. and coheir of Edward NEVILL, of Keymer, co Sussex. He *d* 3 Oct 1670. Will pr. 1671. His widow *d* 28 Jan 1676 Both *bur* at Easton Mauduit

III 1670 SIR CHARLES YELVERTON, Bart. [1641], of Easton Mauduit aforesaid, 1st s and h , *b* there 21 Aug 1657, *suc to the Baronetcy* in Oct. 1670 ; matric at Oxford (Ch Ch), 1 July 1673, aged 16 By the death of his mother, 28 Jan 1676, he became LORD GREY DE RUTHIN, in which peerage this *Baronetcy* then *merged*. His br and h (the 4th Bart) waa *cr* 21 April 1690, VISCOUNT LONGUEVILLE, whose s and b (the 2d Viscount and 5th Bart) was *cr* 26 Sep 1717, EARL OF SUSSEX On the death s p m , 22 April 1799, of the 3d Earl, 4th Viscount, and 7th Baronet, *this Baronetcy*, as also the said Earldom and Viscountcy, became *extinct*, though the Barony devolved on the Earl's da. and h. general See *Peerage*, under "Grey de Ruthin."

BOTELER :

cr. 3 July 1641 ,(ᵇ)

ex 22 Jan 1772

I. 1641. "WILLIAM BOTELER, of Telton [*i.e.*, of Barham Court, in Teaton], co Kent, Esq ," 3d but only surv s and h. of Sir Oliver BOTELER, of the same aud of Shernbrooke, Beda, by Anne, da and b of Thomss BARHAM, of Barham Court aforesaid, was admitted to Gray's Inn, 22 May 1622 , suc. his father, 1632, and waa *cr* a *Baronet*, aa above, 3 July 1641 (ᵇ) He raised a regiment for the King, and waa slain, at the head of it, at the battle of Cropredy bridge, 29 June 1644 He *m* , 1 May 1631, Joan, sister of Thomas, 1st VISCOUNT FANSHAWE OF DROMORE [I], da of Sir HENRY FANSHAWE, of Ware Park, Herts, by Elizabeth, da of Thomas SMYTHE, of Ostenhanger, co. Kent. He *d*, aa aforesaid, 29 June and was *bur* 4 July 1644, at Oxford Will pr March 1645 His widow, who, in Dec 1647, was fined £2,782 for her late husband's delinquency, *m* , in 1646, Sir Philip WARWICK (who *d.* 15 Jan 1682, in his 74th year), and *d* before 5 June 1672, being *bur*. at Chislehurst, Kent M.I. Her admon 5 June 1672.

II. 1644. SIR OLIVER BOTELER, Bart. [1641], of Barham Court aforesaid, s and h , aged 10 in 1647 , *suc. to the Baronetcy*, 29 June 1644 He *m*. firstly, 1665,(ᶜ) Anne, da of Sir Robert AUSTEN, 1st Bart. [1660], of Bexley, by his 2d wife, Anne, da of Thomas MUNS. He *m*. secondly, Anne, da of Jacob UPHILL, of Dagenham, Essex, and Anne his wife He *d* about 1689. Admon. 21 Jan. 1689/90. His widow waa *bur*. 26 Jan 1712/3, at Dagenham M I Will dat 22 Dec. 1712, pr. 1 Feb 1713/4.

(ᵃ) *Vide* p 95, note "a "

(ᵇ) The patent is not enrolled. The date here given is that in Dugdale's *Catalogue*. See *Memorandum* on p. 84. The date of the signet bill is [the same date, *viz.*] 3 July 1641.

(ᶜ) There is a licence at the Fac. office, 12 March 1660/1, for Sir Edward Boteler, Knt and *Bart* , of St Paul's, Covent Garden, about 20, bachelor, son of Sir Allen Boteler, deceased, and Dame Katharine Boteler, to marry Jane Russell, about 21. a spinster. It is, however, difficult to identify the abovenamed Baronet. His father waa *Knighted* 16 Feb. 1645/6, at Oxford, aa "of Bucks."

III. 1689 ?   SIR PHILIP BOTELER, Ba'rt [1641], of Barham Court
aforessid, s. and h , b. about 1674 , suc to the Baronetcy about 1689 ,
M P. for Hythe (seven Parls), 1690—1708   He m. (Lic Vic Gen. 17 Dec 1690,
he about 26, she about 22) Anne, sister of Sir William Des Bouverie, 1st Bart [1714],
da of Sir Edward Des Bouverie, of Cheshunt, Herts, by Anne, da and coheir of
Jacob De la Forterie, of London, merchant   She d 1717, and was bur at Teston,
Admon 9 Oct 1717.   He d April 1719, and was bur at Teston aforesaid.   Will dat.
29 March 1708 [sic], pr 10 June 1719.

IV. 1719,   SIR PHILIP BOTELER, Bart. [1641], of Barham Court
to   aforesaid only s. and h , b about 1695 ; matric at Oxford (Ch Ch),
1772   10 Oct 1712, aged 17 ; suc to the Baronetcy in April 1719   He m.
May 1720, at St Anne's, Blackfriars, Elizabeth, da and h of Thomas
Williams, of Cabalva, co. Radnor   She d 8 Oct 1752, and was bur. at Teston.   He
d. s.p s 22 Jan. 1772, aged about 77, and was bur. at Teston aforesaid, when the
Baronetcy became extinct.   Will pr. Feb 1772 (a)

HATTON
cr 5 July 1641(b),
ex. 19 Sep. 1812

I 1641.   "THOMAS HATTON,(c) of Long Stanton, co. Cambridge,
Knt " 3d s of John HATTON, of the same, by Jane, da. of Robert
SHUTE, one of the Barons of the Exchequer, was b about 1583 ; admitted to Gray's
Inn, 2 Feb 1606/7 , Knighted, at Bletsho, 26 July 1616 , M.P. for Corfe Castle,
1621-22 , for Malmesbury, 1624-25 and 1625 , for Stamford, 1628-29, and April
to May 1640, and was cr a Baronet, as above, 5 July 1641 (b)   He m. Mary, 6th da.
of Sir Giles ALINGTON, of Horseheath, co Cambridge, by Dorothy, da. of Thomas
(CECIL), EARL OF EXETER   He d 23 Sep 1658, aged about 75   Will pr. 1659   His
widow, who was bap 19 Oct 1612, at Horseheath, was bur 27 Aug 1674 at Long
Stanton   Will dat. 3 Oct 1670, pr. 2 Sep 1674

II. 1658   SIR THOMAS HATTON, Bart. [1641], of Long Stanton
aforesaid, s and h , suc. to the Baronetcy, 23 Sep 1658 ; was Sheriff
of Cambridgeshire and Hunts, 1662-63   He m before 1660, Bridget, da of Sir
William GORING, 1st Bart [1621], of Burton, by Eleanor, da. and h of Sir Edward
FRANCIS.   He was bur. 19 April 1682, at Long Stanton   Admon. 24 April 1682 to
his widow.

III 1682.   SIR CHRISTOPHER HATTON, Bart. [1641], of Long Stanton
aforesaid, s. and h., suc. to the Baronetcy 19 April 1682 (d)   He d.
young and was bur. 26 Sep 1683, at Long Stanton.

(a) He devised one moiety of his real and personal estate to the Dow. Viscountess
Folkestone for her life, with rem. to her stepson, William, 1st Earl of Radnor, grandson and h. of his uncle, Sir William Des Bouverie, Bart, abovenamed , the other
moiety (in which was the manor of Teston) he devised to Elizabeth Des Bouverie, of
Chart Sutton, Kent, Spinster, da of another uncle, Sir Christopher des Bouverie

(b) The patent is not enrolled   The date here given is that in Dugdale's
Catalogue.   See Memorandum on p 84   The date of the signet bill is 2 July 1641.

(c) His eldest br , Sir Christopher HATTON, of Kirby, co. Northampton (bur
11 Sep 1619 at Westm. Abbey), inherited the great estates of the LORD CHANCELLOR
HATTON, whose h male he was   His son was cr BARON HATTON, 1643, and his grandson, VISCOUNT HATTON, 1706, titles which became extinct in 1762, the estates passing
to the family of FINCH, afterwards FINCH-HATTON, EARLS OF WINCHELSEA, the 6th
Earl of Winchilsea having m. the Hon Anne HATTON, sister and coheir of William, 2d
and last VISCOUNT HATTON.   These estates, including the magnificent but dilapidated
Hall at Kirby, were for sale in 1880.

(d) The marriage, 24 Dec. 1682, of "Sir John Hatton and Mary Hinton," at
Knightsbridge Chapel, does not, apparently, relate to any of these Baronets.

O

IV. 1683   SIR THOMAS HATTON, Bart. [1641], of Long Stanton aforesaid, br. and h., *suc to the Baronetcy* in Sep. 1683. He *d* young and was *bur* 15 March 1684/5 at Long Stanton.

V. 1685   SIR CHRISTOPHER HATTON, Bart [1641], of Long Stanton aforesaid, uncle and h male, *suc. to the Baronetcy*, 15 March 1684/5 He *m* 14 July 1674, at Westm. Abbey (Lic Vic Gen , he about 23 and of the Middle Temple, and she about 20), Elizabeth, da of Thomas BUCK, of Westwick, co Cambridge, by his 1st wife Rebecca, da of Thomas LOVERING, of Norwich. She *d.* July 1710 He *d.* Oct 1720

VI 1720.   SIR THOMAS HATTON, Bart [1641], of Long Stanton aforesaid, s and h , *suc to the Baronetcy* in Oct 1720 , was Sheriff of Cambridgeshire and Hunts, 1725-26 He *m* firstly, Elizabeth, da and h. of Cooper ORLEBAR, of Henwick, Beds. She *d* 5 May 1732, aged 44. He *m* secondly, Henrietta, da of Sir James ASTRY, of Woodend in Harlington, Beds, by Anne, 2d da of Sir Thomas PENYSTONE, 1st Bart [1611] He *d* s.p at Woodend aforesaid, 23 June 1733, and was *bur.* at Long Stanton M I Will pr. 1733

VII. 1733.   SIR JOHN HATTON, Bart [1641], of Melbourne, co Cambridge, br and h., *suc. to the Baronetcy*, 23 June 1733. He *m.* Mary, widow of William HITCH, da. of Thomas HAWKES He *d.* 1 July 1740 Will pr 1740. The will of Dame Mary Hatton pr. 1760

VIII 1740.   SIR THOMAS HATTON, Bart [1641], of Long Stanton aforesaid, s and h , b 14 Sep 1728, *suc. to the Baronetcy* 1 July 1740 He *m.* 26 April 1752, at Ely Chapel, Holborn (Lic Lond , he above 21 and she above 17), Harriet, da. of Dingley ASKHAM, of Connington, co. Cambridge. He *d.* 7 and was *bur* 14 Nov 1787, at Long Stanton, aged 59 Will pr. 1788. His widow *d.* 20 and was *bur.* 28 March 1795, aged 60, at Long Stanton. Will pr. April 1795

IX 1787.   SIR JOHN HATTON, Bart. [1641], of Long Stanton aforesaid, s and h , *suc. to the Baronetcy* 7 Nov. 1787. He *m.* in 1798 (—), da. of (—) BRIDGEMAN, an American refugee He *d* s p. 29 July 1811.

X. 1811,   SIR THOMAS DINGLEY HATTON, Bart. [1641], of Long
to   Stanton aforesaid, br. and h , b about 1771, *suc. to the Baronetcy*
1812   29 July 1811. He *d.* unm (in consequence of a fall from his curricle) 19 and was *bur* 29 Sep 1812, at Long Stanton, aged 41, when the *Baronetcy* became *extinct.* Admon May 1813.

ABDY:

cr. 14 July 1641 ;(ᵃ)

ex. 16 April 1868.

I 1641.   "THOMAS ABDY, of Felix Hall [in Kelvedon], co. Essex, Esq.," s. and h. of Anthony ABDY, of St Andrew Undershaft, Alderman and sometime, 1630-31, Sheriff of London, by Abigail, da of Sir Thomas CAMBELL, sometime, 1609-10, Lord Mayor of London, was *b.* about 1612 , admitted to Lincoln's Inn, 29 Jan 1631/2 , suc his father, 10 Sep 1640, and was *cr a Baronet,*(ᵇ) as above, 14 July 1641,(ᵃ) having, apparently, been previously, 8 July 1641, *Knighted.*(ᶜ) He *m* firstly, 1 Feb. 1637/8, at St. Peter le Poor, London (Lic. London, he 25, she

(ᵃ) The patent is not enrolled. The date here given is that in Dugdale's *Catalogue.* See *Memorandum* on p. 84 The date of the signet bill is 5 July 1641 ; the date of the Warrant [June ?] 1641

(ᵇ) He was one of three brothers, all of whom obtained Baronetcies, viz., (1) Thomas, 14 July 1641, *extinct* 16 April 1868 ; (2) Robert, 9 June 1660, *extinct* 2 April 1759 , and (3) John, 22 June 1660, *extinct* about 1662

ᶜ) He is, however, not designated a Knight in the patent of 14 July 1641.

21), Mary, 9th da and coheir of Lucas CORSELLIS, of London, merchant   She *d.*
s p m 6 April 1645, aged 27, and was *bur* at Kelvedon   M.I.   He *m* secondly,
16 Jan 1646/7, at St. Barth the Less, Anne, 1st da and coheir of Sir Thomas
SOAME, of Throcking, Herts, Alderman and sometime, 1635 36, Sheriff of London, by
Juane, da of William FREEMAN, of Aspeden, Herts.   She d 19 June 1679, aged 56
He *d* 14 Jan 1685/6, aged about 74   Both *bur* at Kelvedon.   M I.   His will dat.
15 Oct 1682, pr , with a codicil, 11 Feb 1685/6.

II   1686   SIR ANTHONY ABDY, Bart [1641], of Felix Hall afore-
               said, s and h. by 2d wife, *b.* about 1655 , *suc to the Baronetcy*,
14 Jan 1685/6.   He *m* , 10 or before 1690, Mary, only da and h of Richard MIL-
WARD, D D , Rector of Great Braxted, Essex, and Canon of Windsor, by Mary, da of
Sir Anthony THOMAS, of Chobham, Surrey, aunt and h. of Gainsford THOMAS, of
Chobham aforesaid He *d* 2 April 1704, aged about 49, and was *bur* at Kelvedon M I
Will pr 1704   His widow *d* 18 Aug 1744, aged 86, and was *bur* at Chobham.
M.I   Will dat. 2 April 1743 to 16 July 1744, pr 12 Oct. 1744

III   1704.   SIR ANTHONY-THOMAS ABDY, Bart. [1641], of Felix Hall
                 aforesaid, s. and h , *b.* about 1690 ; *suc to the Baronetcy*, 2 April
1704 , matric at Oxford (Trin. Coll), 19 April 1707, aged 17 ; admitted to Lincoln's
Inn, 1708   He *m* firstly, Mary, da and sole h of Hope GIFFORD, of Colchester,
Essex.   She *d.* s p. 1718   He *m.* secondly, in 1720, Charlotte, 3d da. and coheir of
Sir Thomas BARNADISTON, 3d Bart [1663], of Ketton, by Anne, da and coheir of Sir
Richard ROTHWELL, Bart., so cr in 1661   She *d.* s p m 19 Feb 1731   He *m.*
thirdly, Anne, da and h of Thomas WILLIAMS, of Tendring Hall, Suffolk, by
Elizabeth, da of Sir Thomas BARNADISTON, 1st Bart [1663], of Ketton   He *d.*
s p m.([a]) 11 June 1733, aged about 43   Will pr June 1733   His widow *d.* s.p
21 Sep. 1745, and was *bur* at Kelvedon   Will dat. 26 Dec. 1744, pr 7 Nov 1745

IV   1733   SIR WILLIAM ABDY, Bart. [1641] of Chobham Place,
               Surrey, and of Golden sq., St. James' Westm , br. and h male,
suc to the Baronetcy (but not to the Essex estates), 11 June 1733   He *m* about
1720, Mary, only da and h of Philip STOTHERD, of Terling, Essex.   She *d.* 6 April
1743   He *d* 18 Jan 1749/50.   Admon 5 Feb. 1749/50, and again 25 Feb 1777.

V   1750   SIR ANTHONY-THOMAS ABDY, Bart [1641], of Chobham
              Place aforesaid, 1st s and h , *b.* about 1720 , admitted to Lincoln's
Inn, 1738 , Barrister at Law (Lincoln's Inn), and finally King's Counsel ; *suc to the
Baronetcy*, 18 Jan 1749/50, suc , in 1759, to the estate of Albyns, in Stapleford
Abbots, Essex, under the will of Sir John Abdy, 4th and last Bart. [1660], of Albyns
aforesaid ; M P. for Knaresborough, 1763 till decease   He *m* 13 Aug 1747, at
St Paul's Cathedral, London, Catharine, da and coheir of William HAMILTON, of
Chancery Lane, London   He *d* s p 7 April 1775, aged about 55   Will pr. April
1775.   His widow *d* 1792.   Will pr. Oct. 1792.

VI.   1775   SIR WILLIAM ABDY, Bart [1641], of Chobham Place
                aforesaid, br and h , *b.* about 1732 , Captain, R N , *suc to the
Baronetcy*, 7 April 1775   He *m* 1771, Mary, only da. of James BREBNER-GORDON
(formerly James BREBNER), of More Place, Herts, by Ann LAVINGTON, his wife   He
d. 21 July 1803, aged 71, and was *bur.* at Chobham   M I   Will pr 1803 and again
Dec. 1835.   His widow, who was *b.* in Antigua, was aunt (her issue, in 1854, becoming
heir) to James-Adam GORDON, of Knockespock, co. Aberdeen, Naish House in
Wraxall, co. Somerset, and Stocks in Aldbury, Herts, who *d.* s.p March 1854, aged
63.   She *d.* 4 March 1829.   Will pr June 1829

VII   1803,   SIR WILLIAM ABDY, Bart [1641], of Chobham Place
      to   aforesaid (which he sold in 1809), s and h , *b.* at Marylebone, 1779 ;
      1868.   ed at Eton ; matric at Oxford (Ch Ch), 22 Jan 1796, aged 17 ,
                 suc to the Baronetcy, 21 July 1803   He *m* 3 July 1806, by spec lic ,

_____

([a]) Felix Hall went to his 1st da , who *m* in 1744 John Williams, by whom it was
rebuilt, but afterwards, in 1761, sold.

at Hyde Park Corner, Anne WELLESLEY, natural da of Richard (WELLESLEY), MARQUESS WELLESLEY [I], by Hyacinthe-Gabrielle ROLAND, spinster, da of Monsieur Pierre ROLAND. She was divorced by Act of Parliament, 25 June 1816 (ª) He d s p 16 April 1868, at 20 Hill street, Berkeley square, when the *Baronetcy* became *extinct*

COTTON:
cr. 14 July 1641 ,(ᵇ)
ex 25 Jan 1863.

I. 1641.   "JOHN COTTON, of Landwade, co. Cambridge, Knt.," s and h of Sir John COTTON, of the same, by his 3d wife, Anne, da. of Sir Richard HOGHTON, 1st Bart [1611], was b Sep 1615 , suc his father (when only five years old), 5 March 1620 , was *Knighted* at Whitehall, 26 June and was c) a Baronet, as above, 14 July 1641 (ᵇ) He was Sheriff of Cambridgeshire when the rebellion broke out, and proclaimed the Earl of Essex as a traitor in every market town in that county. He took up arms for the King, to whom, when at Oxford, he conveyed the plate sent by the University of Cambridge During the Usurpation he was forced to reside abroad. He m Jane, da and sole h of Edward HINDE, of Madingley Hall, co Cambridge, by (—), da and h. of Sir Thomas MAPLES, Bart [so c) 1627], of Stow, co Huntingdon She brought the Madingley estate to the Cotton family He d. in 1689,(ᶜ) aged about 74 Will pr. June 1689.

II 1689   SIR JOHN COTTON, Bart. [1641], of Madingley Hall aforesaid, s and h , suc to the Baronetcy in 1689 , Recorder of Cambridge and M P for that town (seven Parls), 1689-90, 1690-95, and Nov 1696 to 1708 He m 14 Jan. 1678/9, at Westm Abbey, Elizabeth, da. and coheir of Sir Joseph SHELDON, sometime, 1675-76, Lord Mayor of London, by his 1st wife, Elizabeth, daughter of William CLIFTON, of St Paul's, Covent Garden He d 20 and was bur 23 Jan 1712/3, at Landwade Admon 24 April 1716 His widow surv him, but d before 1716

III 1713.   SIR JOHN HINDE COTTON, Bart [1641], of Madingley Hall aforesaid, s and h , was c) M A. of Cambridge Univ [comitis regis], 1705 , suc to the Baronetcy, 20 Jan 1712/3, was M P for the town of Cambridge (four Parls.), 1708-22, for Cambridgeshire, 1722-27, for Cambridge, again (two Parls), 1727 41, and for Marlborough (two Parls), 1741 till decease One of the Lords Commissioners of trade and plantations, 1712, Treasurer of the Chamber, 1744 He m firstly, Lettice (portion £10,000), 2d da of Sir Ambrose CROWLEY, of Greenwich, Kent, sometime, 1706-07, Sheriff of London, by Mary, da of Charles OWEN, of Condover, Salop She d Aug 1718 He m secondly, Margaret, widow of Samuel TREFUSIS, 3d da of James CRAGGS, Joint Postmaster General, by (—), da. of "Brigadier" RICHARDS, of Westminster She d. s p 23 Aug 1734 Will pr 1737 He d 4 Feb 1752, in his 64th year, and was bur. at Landwade, with his two wives Will pr 1752.

IV. 1752.   SIR JOHN HINDE COTTON, Bart [1641], of Madingley Hall aforesaid, only surv s and h by 1st wife , M P for St Germains, 1741-47, for Marlborough (two Parls), 1752-61, and for Cambridgeshire (three Parls.), 1764 80 ; suc to the Baronetcy, 4 Feb 1752 ; cr. D.C L. of Oxford, 7 July 1763 He m Aug. 1754, his cousin Anne, 2d da of Humphrey PARSONS, of Reigate, Surrey, twice (1730-31 and 1740-41), Lord Mayor of London, by Sarah, 3d da of Sir Ambrose CROWLEY, abovenamed She d in or before 1769. Admon. 26 June 1769, under £1,000. He d 23 Jan 1795.

(ª) She m 16 July following, Lieut Col Lord William Charles-Augustus CAVENDISH-BENTINCK, being his 2d wife. He d 28 April 1826, aged 46, and she d. 19 March 1875.

(ᵇ) The patent is not enrolled The date here given is that in Dugdale's *Catalogue.* See *Memorandum* on p 84 The date of the signet bill is 10 July 1641.

(ᶜ) His son John, was returned as " Esq " to the Convention of 1689, but as "Baronet" to the Parl. of 1690.

V 1795.   Sir Charles Cotton, Bart. [1641], of Madingley Hall aforesaid, s and h, b about 1758, was Post Capt in the Royal Navy, 1779; was in command of the "Majestic" in the battle of 1 June 1794, *suc. to the Baronetcy*, 23 Jan. 1795, obtained a flag in 1797, serving in the Channel Fleet under Lord St Vincent, and, in 1807, in the expedition against Portugal; became Admiral in 1808 and Commander in Chief of the Channel Fleet   He m 27 Feb. 1798, Philadelphia, 1st da of Admiral Sir Joshua Rowley, 1st Bart. [1786], by Sarah, da. and h of Bartholomew Burton   He d. 24 Feb 1812, at Stoke, near Plymouth Will pr. 1812   His widow d. 5 April 1855, aged 92, at Madingley Hall aforesaid. Will pr. July 1855

VI 1812,   Sir St. Vincent Cotton, Bart [1641], of Madingley Hall
to   aforesaid, s and h., born there 6 Oct 1801, *suc to the Baronetcy*,
1863.   24 Feb. 1812; ed at Westm and at Ch Ch, Oxford; sometime an officer in the 10th Hussars, 1827 to 1830, when he retired on half pay, well-known in the hunting, racing, shooting, cricket and pugilistic world, and also as a celebrated "whip," driving, in 1836 and many years subsequently, the "Age" coach from Brighton to London, was also a great gambler and dissipated all his property   He m (by spec. lic.) in his own dwelling house, a few days before his death, Hephzibah, da of (—) Dimmick   He d. s p 25 Jan. 1863, at 5, Hyde Park terrace, Kensington Road, aged 61, when the *Baronetcy* became *extinct*.   His widow d. 12 May 1873, at Finborough Road, West Brompton.

BAMFYLDE, BAMFEILD, *or* BAMPFIELD
cr 14 July 1641 ;([a])
afterwards, since 1831, Barons Poltimore.

I 1641.   "John Bamfeild, Junior, of Poltimore, co Devon, Esq," s and h. ap of John Bampfield of the same (s and h. of Sir Amyas Bamfield, who d 9 Feb. 1625/6, aged 67), by Elizabeth, da of Thomas Drake, of Buckland, Devon, was b about 1610, matric at Oxford (Wadham Coll), 30 Oct 1629, aged 19; admitted to Middle Temple, 1630, was M P for Penrhyn, 1640 till decease, and was cr a Baronet, as above, 14 July 1641 ([a])   He, who was one of the "Extremists" or 'Independents," suc his father after Aug 1644   He m 3 May 1637, Gertrude, sister and coheir of John Coplestone, of Coplestone and Warleigh in Tamerton Foliot, Devon, 4th da of Amyas Coplestone, of the same, by Gertrude, da of Sir John Chichester. He d. April 1650, and was bur. at Poltimore M I His widow d. 1658.   Her will dat. 8 Nov 1657, pr. 29 Nov 1658

II 1650.   Sir Coplestone Bamfylde, Bart [1641], of Poltimore aforesaid, s. and h., was b. 1638, *suc to the Baronetcy* in April 1650, in his minority, matric. at Oxford (Corpus Coll), 20 March 1650/1, as a Gent Commoner, was an active Royalist, joining in a remonstrance to the "Rump" Parl., presented to Gen Monk a "petition of right" from the co. of Devon, for which he was imprisoned, was M P for Tiverton, 1659, Sheriff of Devon, 1660-61, and subsequently M.P., 1671 79 and 1685-87, for that county, Col of the Devon Militia   He m firstly, Margaret, da of Francis Bulkeley, of Burgate, in Fordingbridge, Hants   She was living Nov 1657.   He m secondly (Lic. Vic Gen 21 Oct. 1674, he about 30 and she about 20), Jane, da of Sir Courtenay Pole, 2d Bart [1628], of Shute, by Urith, da of Thomas Shapcote   He d. at Warleigh aforesaid, 9 Feb. 1691/2, aged 54, and was bur at Poltimore   Will, dat. 24 Aug 1691, pr. 2 May 1692   His widow, by whom he had no issue, m Edward Gibbons, of Whitechapel, Devon.   Her will, dat 2 Sep, pr. 5 Oct 1710 in the Cons. Court of Exeter.

([a]) The patent is not enrolled   The date here given is that in Dugdale's *Catalogue*. See *Memorandum*, on p. 84   The date of the signet bill is 12 July 1641.

III   1692   Sir Coplestone Warwick Bamfylde, Bart [1641], of
Poltimore aforesaid, grandson and h, being s and h. of Col Hugh
Bamfylde, of Wareley, Devon, by Mary, da. of James Clifford, of Kingsteignton in
that county, which Hugh, who was s and h ap of the last Bart by his 1st wife, d
v p 16 June 1691, aged 28   He was b about 1690, suc to the Baronetcy, 9 Feb 1691/2,
in his infancy; matric at Oxford (Ch Ch), 26 Jan 1707/8, aged 18, was M P for
Exeter, 1710-13, and subsequently, 1713 till his death, for Devon. He m, in or before
1718, Gertrude, widow of Godfrey Copley, 2d Bart [1661], da of Sir John Carew,
2d Bart. [1641], of Antony, by his 3d wife Mary, da of Sir William Morice, 1st Bart.
[1661]   He d 7 and was bur 14 Oct. 1727, at Poltimore   His widow d. 14 and was
bur 23 April 1736 with him   Will pr 1736

IV   1727   Sir Richard Warwick Bamfylde, Bart [1641], of Poltimore aforesaid, only s and h., bap. 21 Nov. 1722, at Poltimore, suc to
the Baronetcy, 7 Oct 1727, in his infancy, matric at Oxford (New Coll), 16 May 1739,
aged 17, cr M A . 4 July 1741, M P for Exeter, 1743-47, and for Devon (six Parls),
1747 till his death   He m 8 Aug 1742, at Somerset House chapel, Midx., Jane, da.
and h. of Col John Codrington, of Charlton House in Wraxall, Somerset, by Elizabeth, only da and h of Samuel Gorges, of Wraxall aforesaid   He d 15 and was
bur 25 July 1776, at Poltimore   Will pr Aug 1776, and at Dublin in 1807.   His
widow, who was b 14 Oct and bap 15 Nov. 1720, at Wraxall, d 15 and was bur.
there 24 Feb 1789   Admon. March 1789.

V   1776   Sir Charles Warwick Bamfylde, Bart [1641], of Poltimore aforesaid and of Hardington Park, Somerset, s and h., b and
bap 23 Jan. 1753, at St Augustine's, Bristol, matric at Oxford (New Coll), 6 Jan.
1770, aged 16, M P for Exeter in seven Parls, 1774-90 and 1796-1807, suc to the
Baronetcy, 15 Aug. 1776   He m 9 Feb 1776, at St. James', Westm, Catharine,
1st da. and coheir of Admiral Sir John Moore, Bart [cr 1766] and K B., by
Penelope, da. of Gen William Mathew   He d, in Montagu square, Midx, 19 April
1823, from a pistol shot received from one Morland (formerly his servant), on the 7th
and was bur the 25th, at Hardington   Will pr. 1823   His widow (from whom he
had been separated for many years) d 20 March 1832, aged 75, at Egham, Surrey
Will pr April 1832

VI   1823   Sir George Warwick Bamfylde, Bart [1641], of
Poltimore, etc, aforesaid, only s and h   b 23 March and bap
20 April 1786, at St James', Westm, matric at Oxford (Bras Coll), 10 Oct. 1804,
aged 18 ; suc. to the Baronetcy, 19 April 1823   H m firstly, 2 May 1809, at St Geo,
Han sq, his cousin, Penelope, 3d da of the Rev Ralph Sneyd, Chaplain to Geo IV,
by Penelope, 2d da and coheir of Admiral Sir John Moore, Bart, and K B abovenamed   She, who d s p m, was living when he was cr, 10 Sep. 1831,(a) BARON
POLTIMORE of Poltimore, co Devon   In that peerage this Baronetcy then became
merged, and still so continues.   See Peerage

THYNNE
cr 15 July 1641(b),

afterwards, since 1682, Viscounts Weymouth,

and *subsequently*, since 1789, Marquesses of Bath

I   1641   "Henry-Frederick Thynne, of Course [i e, Caus]
Castle, co Salop, Esq," being also of Kempsford, co Gloucester, 4th
s of Sir Thomas Thynne, of Longleate, Wilts, being his 1st s, hy Catharine his 2d

---

(a) This was a coronation peerage   The Annual Register of 1858 (in his obituary)
speaks of it as given "for zealous services rendered in the cause of Reform"—but
though the zeal might have been great, the actual service of a man who was never
in Parliament and never held any public office must have been somewhat small.

(b) The patent is not enrolled.   The date here given is that in Dugdale's *Catalogue.*
See *Memorandum* on p 84.   The date of "warrant for granting receipt for £1,095
to Henry Frederick Thynne of Course Castle co Salop, Esq., on his creation as
Baronet" is 13 July 1641

wife, da. and coheir of Hon. Charles LYTE-HOWARD, (yr s of Thomas, 1st VISCOUNT
HOWARD OF BINDON,) was *b.* 1 March 1615 (the Queen-Consort being his godmother,
who gave him the additional name of "Frederick," being that of her father, the King
of Denmark); matric. at Oxford (Ex. Coll.), 13 Nov 1632, aged 17; admitted to
Lincoln's Inn, 1634, and was *cr a Baronet*, as above, 15 July 1641 [a]. He *m* Mary, da.
of Thomas (COVENTRY), 1st BARON COVENTRY OF AYLESBOROUGH, sometime Lord
Keeper of the Great Seal, by Elizabeth, his 2d wife, da of John ALDERSEY. He *d* at
Oxford 6 March 1680, aged 66 years and 5 days, and was *bur.* at Kemsford. M I
Will pr 1680.

II 1680. SIR THOMAS THYNNE, Bart [1641], of Drayton, Salop,
and afterwards, 1682, of Longleate, Wilts, s. and h, *b* about 1640,
matric at Oxford (Ch Ch), 21 April 1657, having the famous Dr John Fell for his
tutor, F R S 23 Nov 1664, M.P. for Oxford University, 1674-79, and for Tamworth (three Parls), 1679-81; *suc to the Baronetcy*, 6 March 1680, was High Steward
of Tamworth, 1681. By the death of his 1st cousin, Thomas THYNNE, of Longleate,
who was murdered in his coach in Pall Mall, 12 Feb 1681/2, and the consequent extinction of all elder issue male of his grandfather, he *suc* to that estate and became the
representative of his family. He *m* in or before 1675, Frances, 1st da of Heneage
(FINCH), 2d EARL OF WINCHILSEA, by his 2d wife, Mary, da. of William (SEYMOUR),
2d DUKE OF SOMERSET. She was living when he was *cr.* 11 Dec 1682, VISCOUNT
WEYMOUTH, co Dorset, etc, with a *spec rem*, failing his issue male, to his two
yr brothers and the heirs male of their bodies respectively. In that peerage this
Baronetcy then merged and so continues, the 3d Viscount Weymouth being *cr.*
18 Aug. 1789, MARQUESS OF BATH. See *Peerage* under those titles

---

D'EWES:

cr. 15 July 1641, [b]

ex 21 April 1731.

I. 1641. "SIMON [*i.e.*, SIMONDS] D'EWES, of Stow Hall [in Stow-
langtoft], co Suffolk, Knt," s. & h. of Paul D'EWES, of the same,
by Cecilia, only da and h of Richard SIMONDS, or SYMONDS, of Coxden, co Dorset,
was *b.* 18 Dec. 1602, at Coxden, was a student of St John's Coll, Cambridge;
Barrister (Middle Temple), 27 June 1623, was *Knighted* at Whitehall, 6 Dec. 1626, suc.
his father, 14 March 1630/31, was Sheriff of Suffolk, 1639-40, M P for Sudbury,
1640, till secluded Dec. 1648, and was *cr a Baronet*, as above, 15 July 1641 [b]. He
gave £100 to aid the Earl of Essex, 11 Oct 1642, and served in the "New Model"
Feb 1645. His knowledge of history and antiquity was very great. He was the
author of "*The Journals of all the Parliaments, temp. Eliz*," and other valuable
works [c]. He *m* firstly, 24 Oct 1626, at St Anne's, Blackfriars, London, Anne, da
and eventually h of Sir William CLOPTON, of Kentwell, Suffolk, by his 1st wife,
Anne, da of Sir Thomas BARNADISTON, of Clare, Suffolk. She, who was *bap* at
Clare, 2 March 1612, *d* s p m in 1641. He m. secondly, Elizabeth, 5th and yst
da and coh of Sir Henry WILLOUGHBY, Bart. (so *cr* 1611), of Risley, by his 2d wife,
Lettice, da and coheir of Sir Francis DARCY. He *d.* 18 April and was *bur.* 7 June
1650, at Stowlangtoft, aged 48. Will pr. 1650 and 1652. His widow *m.* about
1654, as his 1st wife, John WRAY, of Glentworth, co. Lincoln (who shortly after her
death became 3d Bart [1611]), and was *bur* 3 Nov. 1655, at Glentworth aforesaid.
Her admon 7 Feb 1655/6 to her said husband.

---

[a] *Vide* note "b," p. 102.
[b] The patent is not enrolled. The date here given is that in Dugdale's *Catalogue*.
See *Memorandum*, on p 84. The date of the signet bill is 13 July 1641
[c] The "*Autobiography of Sir Simonds D'Ewes*" was edited by J. O Halliwell,
2 vols, 1845. Extracts from the registers of Stowlangtoft, relating to the family of
D'Ewes, are in *N. and Q.*, 3d series. ix, 294 and x, 33.

II 1650.   SIR WILLOUGHBY D'EWES, Bart [1641], of Stowlangtoft
Hall aforesaid, only s and h. by 2d wife ; b about 1650 , suc to the
Baronetcy, 18 April 1650, when an infant , matric at Oxford (Ch. Ch), 23 April 1664,
aged 14 , Sheriff of Suffolk, 1677-78   He m Priscilla, da of Francis CLINTON, otherwise FIENNES, of Stourton Parva, co Lincoln, by Priscilla, da. of John HILL   He d
at Stow Hall, 13 and was bur 16 June 1685, at Stowlangtoft   Admon 14 July 1685,
to the widow   She d 1719. Her will, dat 6 Feb 1718/9, pr 31 Aug 1719.

III 1685.   SIR SIMONDS D'EWES, Bart [1641], of Stowlangtoft
Hall aforesaid, s and h , b. about 1670 ; suc to the Baronetcy,
13 June 1685.   He m firstly, in or before 1687, Delariviere, 5th da and coheir of
Thomas (JERMYN), 2d BARON JERMYN OF ST EDMUNDSBURY, by Mary, da of Henry
MERRY.   She d at St. Anne's, Westm , and was bur 12 Feb 1708/9, at Stowlangtoft
Admon 19 Dec 1709 to her husband   He m secondly, 21 March 1709/10, at St.
Bride's, London (Lic Vic Gen., he about 41 and she about 24), Elizabeth KIEFE, of
St Margaret's, Westm., spinster   He d in May 1722.   Will pr. 1722

IV 1722,   SIR JERMYN D'EWES, Bart [1641], of Stowlangtoft
to   Hall aforesaid, 1st s and h , by 1st wife ; bap 2 April 1688, at
1731   Stowlangtoft, suc to the Baronetcy in May 1722   He d unm
21 April 1731, when the Baronetcy became extinct.[a]   Will pr. 1732

BURGOYNE·
cr 15 July 1641 ([b])

I. 1641.   "JOHN BURGOYNE, of Sutton, co Bedford, Esq ," as also
of Wroxhall and Honiley, co. Warwick, s and h of Roger BURGOYNE,
of the same, by his 1st wife, Margaret, da of Thomas WENDY, of Hashngfield, co
Cambridge, was bap. at Hashngfield, 29 Jan 1591 , suc his father, 28 June 1636 ,
was Sheriff of Beds, 1640-41 , M P. for Warwickshire, Oct. 1645, till secluded Dec
1648, and was cr a Baronet, as above, 15 July 1641 ([b])   He served on several
important Committees, on the side of the Parl , 1643-47   He m about 1617, Jane,
da. and h. of William KEMPE, of Spain's Hall in Finchinfield, co Essex, by Philippa,
da and coheir of Francis GUNTER, of Aldbury, Herts   He was bur at Sutton
9 Oct. 1657   Admon 25 May 1663 to his son.

II. 1657   SIR ROGER BURGOYNE, Bart [1641], of Sutton and
Wroxhall aforesaid, s. and h , bap 10 March 1618 at Wroxall ;
admitted to Lincoln's Inn, 11 Nov 1637, Knighted, v p 14 July 1641, at Whitehall ;
M P. for Bedfordshire, April to May 1640, and Jan 1641 till secluded in Dec 1648 ,
for Warwickshire, 1656-58.   He (like his father) served on several important Com-
mittees on the side of the Parl , 1643-45 , suc to the Baronetcy in Oct 1657 ; was
Sheriff of Beds, 1661-62   He m firstly, about 1650, Anne, da and h of Charles
SNELLING, of London   She was bur at Sutton 1658   He m secondly, Anne, da of
John ROBINSON, of Dighton, co. York, by Elizabeth, da of Sir Thomas HUTTON, of
Poppleton   He d 16 and was bur 21 Sep 1677 at Sutton aforesaid, aged 59   M.I.
Will dat. 13 Sep. and pr. 26 Nov. 1677.   His widow d. s p.m s, 5 Feb. 1693/4, aged
51, and was bur. at Wroxall.   M I   Will pr 1694.

III. 1677.   SIR JOHN BURGOYNE, Bart [1641], of Sutton Park and
Wroxhall aforesaid, only s and h , by 1st wife, suc to the Baronetcy,
16 Sep 1677.   He m. (Lic Fac., 18 July, and Lic Vic Gen , 4 Nov. 1677, he about
25 and she about 19) Constance, da of Richard LUCY, of Charlecote, co Warwick, by
Elizabeth, da and h of John URRY, of Thorley, in the Isle of Wight   He d. 9 and
was bur. 16 April 1709 in his 58th year at Sutton.   Will dat. 29 Jan 1705, pr 4 July
1709   His widow d. 22 and was bur 30 April 1711, aged 52, also at Sutton   M I.

([a]) See the names and alliances of his four sisters and coheirs in Burke's " Extinct
Baronetage "
([b]) The patent is not enrolled.   The date here given is that in Dugdale's Catalogue.
See Memorandum on p. 84.   The date of the signet bill is 13 July 1641.

IV. 1709.   SIR ROGER BURGOYNE, Bart. [1641], of Sutton Park and Wroxhall aforesaid, s and h, ed at Rugby 1695, *suc to the Baronetcy*, 9 April 1709. He *m*. 22 June 1703, at St Andrew's, Holborn (Lic Lon; 21 and settl. 10 June 1703) Constance, da of Sir Thomas MIDDLETON, of Stansted Mountfichet, co Essex, by Mary, da and h of Sir Stephen LANGHAM, of Quentin, co. Northampton. He *d* 1716   His will dat 2 Nov 1710, pr. 29 March 1716.   His widow *m* 8 March 1715, at Cople, Beds, Christopher WREN, afterwards of Wroxhall aforesaid (s. of the celebrated Sir Christopher Wren), and *d*. 23 May 1734

V. 1716   SIR JOHN BURGOYNE, Bart [1641], of Sutton Park aforesaid, 1st s and h, *b*. about 1705, *suc to the Baronetcy* in 1716.   He *d*. young and unm only six months after his father

VI. 1716   SIR ROGER BURGOYNE, Bart [1641], of Sutton Park aforesaid br. and h, *b*. about 1710, *suc to the Baronetcy* in 1716; M P for Beds, 1734-41 and 1741-47. He *m* Jan 1738/9, Frances, 1st da of George (MONTAGU), 1st EARL OF HALIFAX, by his 2d wife, Mary, da of Richard (LUMLEY), EARL OF SCARBROUGH   He *d* 31 Dec 1780 aged 70   Will dat 19 Feb 1755, pr. (with five codicils) 22 Jan 1781   His widow *d* in Harley street, Marylebone, 24 July 1788. Will dat. 31 Jan. 1784, pr. 5 Aug 1788

VII. 1780   SIR JOHN BURGOYNE, Bart [1641], of Sutton Park aforesaid, s and h, *b* 21 Sep 1739, entered the army, becoming finally Lieut.-Gen, was Col of the 58th Foot and of the 19th Light Dragoons, having *suc. to the Baronetcy*, 31 Dec 1780   He *m* 13 July 1772, Charlotte Frances, 1st da. of (—) JOHNSTONE, of Overstone, co. Northampton, General in the Army.   He *d* 23 Sep 1785, in the East Indies   Will pr 1787   His widow *m* Lieut.-Gen. Eyre Power FRENCH, and *d*. 14 April 1820   Her admon dat. 26 May 1820

VIII 1785   SIR MONTAGU ROGER BURGOYNE, Bart [1641], of Sutton Park aforesaid, s and h., *b* 2 May 1773, *suc to the Baronetcy*, 23 Sep 1785. He entered the army, becoming finally Major-Gen   He *m*. 1 Nov 1794 (by spec lic.), at Bramshill, Catherine, da of John BURTON, of High House in Sheffield, and of Bramley Hall, in Harasworth, co. York   He *d* 11 Nov. 1817, at his mother's residence in Oxford   Will, dat 13 Oct 1810, pr. 6 Nov 1817   His widow, who was *b* 25 Feb. 1773, at Bramley Hall aforesaid, *d* in Eaton square 1 May 1855, aged 82.   Will pr. June 1855

IX. 1817   SIR JOHN MONTAGU BURGOYNE, Bart [1641], of Sutton Park aforesaid, s. and h, *b* there 17 Oct. 1796, *suc to the Baronetcy*, 11 Nov 1817, entered the army, becoming, finally, Col in the Grenadier Guards, 1846, but retired 1848, Sheriff of Bedfordshire, 1820, but did not act, and again 1852.   He *m*, 20 Dec 1831, Mary Harriet, 1st da of William GORE-LANGTON, *formerly* GORE, of Newton Park, co Somerset, by Bridget, da. and h of Joseph LANGTON, of Newton Park aforesaid   He *d* 17 March 1858, aged 61   His widow *d*. 1 April 180, aged 84, at 9 Eaton place.

X. 1858.   SIR JOHN MONTAGU BURGOYNE, Bart. [1641], of Sutton Park aforesaid, only s and h, *b* 23 Oct 1832, in London; ed. at Eton, entered the army 1850, being severely wounded at the Alma in the Crimean War, Lieut.-Col Grenadier Guards, 1860, but retired in 1861, having *suc to the Baronetcy*, 17 March 1858; Sheriff of Beds, 1868   He *m* 10 Nov. 1858, Amy, only da. of Henry Nealson SMITH, Capt Royal Engineers   She *d*. 12 Oct. 1895, at Cowes, Isle of Wight.

Family Estates—These, in 1883, consisted of 2,375 acres in Bedfordshire, worth £3,547 a year   *Residence*—Sutton Park, near Biggleswade, Beds.

P

NORTHCOTE:

cr. 16 July 1641 ;([a])

afterwards, since 1885, EARLS OF IDDESLEIGH

I 1641   "JOHN NORTHCOTE, of Haine [*i e*, Hayne, in Newton
St Cyres], co Devon, Esq," 1st surv s and h of John Northcote,
of Upton, in that county, by his 2d wife, Susanna, da of Sir Hugh POLLARD, of
Kingsnympton, Devon, was *b* about 1600, matric at Oxford (Exeter Coll), 9 May
1617, aged 16; admitted to Middle Temple 1618, is stated to have been 21 in 1620
(Visit of Devon), was Sheriff of Devon, 1626-27, suc his father in Dec 1632, was
M.P for Ashburton, 1640, till secluded in Dec 1648; for Devon, 1654-55, 1656-58,
1659 and 1660, and for Barnstaple, 1667 till his death, having been *cr. a Baronet*, as
above, 16 July 1641 ([a]) He was an active Parliamentarian, was Col of a Reg. of
1,200 men in Sep 1643, was excepted from pardon by the King but joined in the
Restoration([b]) He *m*, in or before 1627, Grace,([c]) da and coheir of Hugh HALSE-
WELL, of Halsewell, co Somerset, by Elizabeth, da of Sir William BROUNKARD
She, who was aged 14 in 1623 (Visit of Somerset), was *bur.* 19 July 1675, at Newton
St Cyres. He was *bur.* there 24 June 1676, aged 77 Will pr 2 Dec 1676

II. 1676.   SIR ARTHUR NORTHCOTE, Bart [1641], of Kingsnympton aforesaid, s. and h, *bap* 25 March 1628, at Newton St
Cyres, *suc to the Baronetcy* in June 1676 He *m.* firstly, Elizabeth, da and h of
James WELSH, of Alverdiscott She *d* s p He *m.* secondly probably in or before
1650, Elizabeth, 1st da of Sir Francis GODOLPHIN, K B, of Godolphin, co Cornwall,
by Dorothy, da of Sir Henry BERKELEY, of Yarlington, co Somerset He *d.* in or
before July 1688 Will pr July 1689 His widow, who was *bap* 8 Feb. 1635 at
Breage, *d* in or before 1707 Admon 30 Oct 1707

III. 1688   SIR FRANCIS NORTHCOTE, Bart. [1641], of Kingsnympton
aforesaid 1st surv s and h, by 2d wife, *b* about 1659, *suc to the
Baronetcy* in or before July 1688 He *m* 26 July 1688, at St Bennet Fink, London
(Lic Vic Gen, he about 29, and she 22) Anne, da of Sir Christopher WREY, 3d
Bart [1628], of Trebitch, by Anne. COUNTESS DOWAGER OF MIDDLESEX, 3d da. and
coheir of Edward (BOURCHIER), EARL OF BATH He *d.* s p 1709 Admon 25 May
1711 to a creditor, his widow, Anne, renouncing Her will pr 1730

IV. 1709   SIR HENRY NORTHCOTE, Bart [1641], of Corfe, near
Barnstaple, Devon, br and h, *b* about 1667, matric at Oxford
(Exeter Coll), 7 March 1686/7, aged 19; Fellow, 1689-1704, B A 1693, M A 1695,
B Med 1697, D Med 1701; *suc to the Baronetcy* in 1709. He *m* in or before
1711, Penelope, da. and coheir of Robert LOVETT, of Liscombe, Bucks, and of Corfe
aforesaid, by his 2d wife, Joan, da and h of James HEARLE, of Tawstock, Devon.
He *d.* at Corfe aforesaid, Feb 1729-30 Will pr. 1730 That of his widow pr 1732

V. 1730   SIR HENRY NORTHCOTE, Bart. [1641], of Pynes, in
Upton Pyne, near Exeter, Devon, only s. and h, *bap* at Tawstock,
1710; matric at Oxford 23 April 1729, aged 18; *suc to the Baronetcy*, Feb 1729/30,
M P for Exeter, 1735, till his death He *m* 16 Aug 1732 at Uffculme, Bridget
Maria, only surv da. and h of Hugh STAFFORD, of Pynes aforesaid, by Bridget, da
of John KELLAND, of Painsford He was *bur* 28 May 1743 at Newton St. Cyres
His widow, who was *b* 21 Jan and *bap* 5 Feb. 1711/12 at Upton Pyne, *m* there
11 Sep. 1754, Richard MADDON, of Exeter, and *d.* 15 being *bur* 19 Aug 1773, at
Newton St. Cyres Her will pr Aug 1773

([a]) The patent is not enrolled The date here given is that in Dugdale's *Catalogue.*
See *Memorandum* on p 84. The date of the signet bill is 24 [*sic*] July 1641, which
possibly is a mistake, but more probably the error is in the date of the patent
That date, however, is also assigned to it in Wotton's *Baronetage*, where it is placed
between Burgoyne, 15 July, and Haie, 23 July 1641.

([b]) The proof of his authorship of the well known "Note Book," attributed to him
is doubtful See a note of W D Pink, in *N. and Q.*

([c]) Her sister Jane *m* John TYNTE, of Chelvey, Somerset, and had a son and h.,
Halsewell TYNTE, who suc. to the estate of Halsewell and was *cr. a Bart* 1674.

VI. 1743   SIR STAFFORD NORTHCOTE, Bart. [1641], of Pynes aforesaid, s. and h., *bap* 6 May 1736, at Upton Pyne, *suc. to the Baronetcy* in May 1743 He *m* 17 Oct. 1761, Catharine, da of Rev. George BRADFORD, M A , Rector of Talaton, Devon. He *d.* 11 and was *bur* 12 March 1770, at Newton St. Cyres His widow *d.* Jan 1802. Will pr 1802.

VII 1770.   SIR STAFFORD HENRY NORTHCOTE, Bart. [1641], of Pynes aforesaid, s. and h , *b* 6 Oct 1762, *suc to the Baronetcy,* 11 March 1770 ; Sheriff of Devon, 1803 04 He *m.* 6 May 1791, Jacquetta, da of Charles BARING, of Larkbear, Devon, by Margaret, da and h of William Drake GOULD, of Lew Trenchard in that county, which Charles was br. to Francis BARING, *cr. a Bart* in 1793 She, who was *b.* 3 June 1768, *d* 22 Jan 1841 at Newton St. Cyres He *d.* 17 March 1851, aged 89. Will pr May 1851

VIII 1851.   SIR STAFFORD HENRY NORTHCOTE, Bart [1641], of Pynes aforesaid, grandson and h , being s and h of Henry Stafford NORTHCOTE, by his 1st wife, Agnes Mary, only da of Thomas COCKBURN (East India Company's service), of Portland place, Marylebone, which Henry was s. and h ap of the 7th Bart, but *d v p*, 22 Feb 1850, aged 57. He was *b.* in Portland place aforesaid, 27 Oct 1818, and *bap* at Upton Pyne the year following , ed at Eton and at Balliol Coll Oxford , matric 3 March 1836, aged 17 , Scholar, 1836-42 , B A. (1st Class classics and 3d mathematics), 1839 , M A 1842, Private Sec to Pres of the Board of Trade (W E Gladstone), 1843-45 ; Barrister (Inner Temple), 1847 , *suc. to the Baronetcy*, 17 March 1851 ; C B , 1851. M P. for Dudley, 1855-1857 , for Stamford, 1858-1866 , and for North Devon, 1866, till created a Peer He was Financial Sec to the Treasury, Jan to June 1859 , *cr.* D C L of Oxford, 27 June 1863 , P C 1866 ; President of the Board of Trade, 1866-67 , Sec of State for India and President of the Council for India, 1867-68 ; a member of the High Joint Commission at Washington, Feb 1871 ; Chancellor of the Exchequer and *Leader of the House of Commons*, 1874-1880 , G C B , 20 April 1880 , FIRST LORD OF THE TREASURY, June 1885 to Feb 1886, during which period he was created a Peer, as stated below He *m.* 5 Aug 1853, at Trinity Church, Marylebone, Cecilia Frances, sister of Thomas, 1st BARON FARRER OF ABINGER, da of Thomas FARRER, of Lincoln's Inn Fields, solicitor, by Cecilia, da of Richard WILLIS, of Halsnead, co Lancaster She was living when he was raised to the peerage, being *cr*, 3 July 1885, EARL OF IDDESLEIGH, etc In that peerage this *Baronetcy* then *merged*, and so continues See "*Peerage.*"

DRAKE:

cr 17 July 1641 ;(ᵃ)

ex. 28 Aug. 1669.

I. 1641,   "WILLIAM DRAKE, of Sherdelowes, co. Bucks, Knt.,"
to   s. and h. of Francis Drake, of Esher, co Surrey, one of the Gentle-
1669   men of the Privy Chamber, by Joan, 1st da and coheir of William TOTHILL, of Shardeloes aforesaid, was *bap.* 28 Sep 1606 ; suc. his father, 17 March 1633 , was Chirograhper to the Court of Common Pleas; was *Knighted* at Whitehall, 14 and was *cr a Baronet*, as above, 17 July 1641 (ᵃ) He was M P. for

---

(ᵃ) The patent is not enrolled The date here given is that in Dugdale's *Chronicle.* See *Memorandum* on p. 84 The date of the signet bill is 14 July 1641.

Amersham, April to May 1640, 1640 till secluded Dec 1648, and 1661 till his death ; was *cr.* M A of Oxford, 15 July 1669 He *d* unm. 28 Aug and was *bur* 29 Sep 1669, at Amersham, aged 63, when the *Baronetcy* became *extinct.*(a) Will pr. 8 Sep 1669.

ROUS, *or* ROUSE:

cr. 23 July 1641 ;(b)

ex. 29 Dec. 1721

I. 1641 "THOMAS ROUS, of Rouslench, co. Worcester, Esq.," s. and h. ap. of Sir John ROUS of the same, by Esther, da of Sir Thomas TEMPLE, of co Warwick, was *b* 1608 , matric. at Oxford (Bras Coll), 20 Oct 1626, aged 18 , B A. (Corpus Coll.), 31 Jan 1627/8 , admitted to Middle Temple, 1628 , was *cr* a Baronet, as above, 23 July 1641,(b) but was, notwithstanding, a great opponent of the Royal cause He suc his father, 1645 , was Sheriff of Worcestershire, 1647 48 , M P thereof 1654 55, 1656-58 , and for Evesham, 1660 , Sheriff of Warwickshire, 1667-68 He *m* firstly, Jane, da of Sir John FERRERS, of Tamworth Castle, by Dorothy, da of Sir John PUCKERING, L Keeper of the Great Seal. He *m.* secondly, Frances, da of David MURRAY. He *m* thirdly, Anne, da of (—) He *d.* 27 May 1676, aged 68 Will pr 1679

II 1676. SIR EDWARD ROUSE, Bart [1641], of Rouselench aforesaid, s and h , by 1st wife , matric at Oxford (Trin. Coll), 12 Dec 1654 ; admitted to Inner Temple, 1656 , *suc to the Baronetcy*, 27 May 1676 He *m* Elizabeth, da of John LISLEY, of Moxhall, co Warwick. He *d* s p. 5 Nov 1677 Will pr 1678. That of his widow pr 1692.

III 1677 SIR FRANCIS ROUSE, Bart [1641], of Rouselench aforesaid, br of the half blood and h., being s. of the 1st Bart by his 2d wife, *suc to the Baronetcy*, 5 Nov 1677. He *m.* (Lic Worc , 7 Aug 1682) Frances, da. of Thomas ARCHER, of Umberslade, co. Warwick by Anne, his wife. He *d.* s p , 31 July 1687 His widow *m* John CHAPLIN, of Tashwell, co. Lincoln, who *d.* before June 1715. Her will dat. 25 June 1715, pr. 2 June 1719

IV 1687, SIR THOMAS ROUSE, Bart. [1641], of Rouselench aforeto said, br. of the full blood and h , *b.* 1664 , *suc to the Baronetcy*, 1721. 31 July 1687. He *m* Anne, da. of Charles HOOKER He *d* s.p s., 29 Dec 1721, aged 57, when the *Baronetcy* became *extinct* (c) Will pr. 1722.

(a) The estates devolved on his nephew and h., Sir William Drake (s and h. of Francis Drake, of Walton upon Thames, Surrey), ancestor of the family of TYRWHITT-DRAKE, of Shardeloes aforesaid.

(b) The patent is not enrolled The date here given is that in Dugdale's *Chronicle* See *Memorandum* on p 84 The date of the signet bill is 16 July 1641

(c) The estate passed to his sister Elizabeth, who *d* unm. 1729, when Thomas Philipps succeeded to them and took the name of Rouse only, being Sheriff of Worcestershire, 1733. He was grandson of Elizabeth Philips, by Mary, da of Sir Thomas Rouse, 1st Bart., by his 1st wife He *d.* unm 30 Dec 1768, leaving the estate to Charles William Boughton, who also took the name of Rouse, and was *cr* a Baronet in 1791, succeeding, however, in 1794 (as 9th Baronet) to the Baronetcy *cr* in 1641 This Charles was 2d son of Shuckburgh Boughton, by Mary (*d* 1786, aged 72), da of the Hon. Algernon Greville and Catharine, da of Lord Arthur Somerset, by Mary, da. of Sir William Russell, Bart. [*cr.* 1660], and Hester, his wife, da of Sir Thomas Rouse, 1st Bart , by his 1st wife See "Boughton," Baronetcy, *cr.* 4 Aug. 1641.

HARE·

cr. 23 July 1641 ,(ᵃ)

ex. 18 March 1764.

I   1641   "RALPH HARE, of Stow Bardolf, co Norfolk, Esq.,"
s and h. of Sir John HARE, of the same, by Margaret, da of Thomas
(COVENTRY), 1st BARON COVENTRY OF AYLESBOROUGH sometime L. Keeper of the Great
Seal, was b about 1614, matric at Oxford (Mag Coll), 14 Sep 1638, aged 14 , suc his
father, in or shortly before 1638, and was cr a Baronet, as above, 23 July 1641 (ᵃ)
He was Sheriff of Norfolk 1650-51 , M P thereof 1654-55, 1656-58 , for King's Lynn,
1660, and for Norfolk, again, 1661 till his death He m firstly (Lic Fac, 26 Oct
1647, he about 23 and she about 18), Mary, 1st da and coheir of Sir Robert CRANE,
Bart. [so cr. 1626], of Chilton, co Suffolk, by his 2d wife, Susan, da of Sir GILES
ALINGTON She was b and bap. 19 March 1628, at Chilton He m secondly, 30 Aug.
1660, at St. Christ le Stocks, London (Lic Vic Gen , he about 34, she about 19) Vere,
sister of Horatio, 1st VISCOUNT TOWNSHEND OF RAYNHAM, da of Sir Roger TOWNSHEND,
1st Bart [1617], by Mary, 2d da and coheir of Horatio (DE VERE), BARON VERE OF
TILBURY She d s p He m thirdly (Lic Vic Gen , 12 July 1671, he about 47,
widower, she of Westm , about 31, spinster), Elizabeth, da of (—) CHAPMAN, of
Suffolk, by Mary, his wife He d Feb. 1671/2. Will pr 1674 The will of his
widow, dat 19 Feb 1680, was pr 11 April 1684 by Mary Chapman, her mother.

II   1672.   SIR THOMAS HARE, Bart. [1641], of Stow Bardolph
aforesaid, s and h, by 1st wife, b about 1658, suc to the Baronetcy in
Feb 1671/2 ; was M.P. for Norfolk (soon after he came of age), 1685-87. He m
Elizabeth, sister of Sir Robert DASHWOOD, 1st Bart [1684], da. of George DASHWOOD,
Alderman of London, by Margaret, da of William PERRY, of Thorpe, co Surrey.
He d 1 Jan. 1693, aged 35, and was bur at Stow Bardolph. M I His widow
d at Bush Common, Essex, 1750, aged 90. Will pr 1750

III   1693   SIR RALPH HARE, Bart. [1641], of Stow Bardolph aforesaid, s and h , suc to the Baronetcy, 1 Jan 1693. He m. Susan, da.
and coheir of Walter NORBONNE, of Calue, Wilts She was bur. 15 July 1730, at St.
James' Westm. Admon 21 Nov 1730 to her husband He d. s.p. 22 Sep 1732,
aged 51. Will pr. 1734

IV   1732   SIR THOMAS HARE, Bart. [1641], of Stow Bardolph
aforesaid, br and h , b about 1688 , matric. at Oxford (Oriel Coll),
18 March 1702/3, aged 15 , suc to the Baronetcy, 22 Sep 1732 He m Rosamond,
da of Charles NEWBY, of Hooton, co York He d s p m 21 Feb. 1760, aged about
72 (ᵇ) Will pr. 1760. His widow d 1773. Will pr 1773

V   1760,   SIR GEORGE HARE, Bart. [1641], of Stow Bardolph aforeto   said, br. and h, b. about 1701 ; a Major of Dragoons ; suc. to the
1764.   Baronetcy, 21 Feb 1760 He d unm 18 March 1764, aged 63, when
the Baronetcy became extinct. Will pr. 1764

(ᵃ) The patent is not enrolled The date here given is that in Dugdale's Chronicle.
See Memorandum, on p 84 The date of the signet bill is 24 [suc] July (i.e , the
day after the patent), so that there is, apparently, an error in the date of one of them
(ᵇ) Of his children, two daughters were living 1741, viz , Elizabeth, who is
supposed to have d. unm , and Mary, who m Sir Thomas HARRIS, sometime [1764-65],
Sheriff of London, who d. 15 June, 1782 She, apparently, inherited Stow Bardolph
in 1760, on the death of her uncle, the 5th and last Bart She d. a widow at Finchley,
Midx , at a great age, on 24 March 1791. On her death the estates went to Thomas
LEIGH, grandson and h of Thomas LEIGH, of London, Turkey merchant, by Mary,
the only da. that left issue, of Sir Thomas HARE, 2d Bart This Thomas Leigh took
the name of Hare and was cr a Baronet, in 1818.

NORWICH

cr. 24 July 1641(a),

ex, presumably, Jan. 1741/2.

I 1641.   "JOHN NORWICH, of Brampton, co. Northampton, Knt," s and h. of Sir Simon NORWICH, of the same, by his 1st wife, Ann, da of Sir William WILLOUGHBY, of Marlow, Bucks, was *bap* 19 Sep. 1613 at Great Marlow, ed at Oundle School, *suc* his father, 10 Feb 1624 ; was *Knighted* 19 July 1641, at Whitehall, and was cr a Baronet, as above, 24 July 1641 (a) He was a Parliamentarian and served on several Committees, 1643-45 ; was Sheriff of Northants, 1645 46 ; M P thereof 1654-55, and for Northampton 1660 and 1661, till void 22 May 1661 He *m* firstly in or before 1636, Anne, da of Sir Roger SMITH, of Edmundthorpe, co Leicester, by his 2d wife, Anna, da of Thomas GOODMAN, of London She was *bur* 23 July 1650 at Brampton He *m* secondly, Mary, sister of Sir Richard ATKINS, 1st [Bart. 1660], da of Sir Henry ATKINS, of Cheshunt, Herts, by Annabella, da. of John HAWKINS, of Chiddingstone, Kent He was *bur* 19 Oct 1661, at Brampton Will pr 1661 That of his widow pr 1693.

II 1661   SIR ROGER NORWICH, Bart [1641], of Brampton aforesaid, s and h, by 1st wife, *bap.* 29 Sep 1636 at Brampton, *suc. to the Baronetcy* in Oct. 1661, M.P for Northamptonshire, 1679 and 1685-87. Verderer of the Forest of Rockingham, but resigned that post, *temp* James II, with whose measures he disagreed In July 1666 he obtained the royal pardon for having slain one Roger Halford He *m*. 12 May 1663, at Brampton, Catharine, widow of Sir John SHUCK-BURGH, Bart. [1660], da. of Sir Hatton FERMOR, of Easton Neston, co. Northampton, by Anne, da. of Sir William COKAYNE, of Rushton in that county, sometime, 1619-20, Lord Mayor of London She *d.* in St. Paul's, Covent Garden, and was *bur* 28 May 1681 at Brampton Admon. 16 March 1681/2 He was *bur* at Brampton 24 Sep 1691 Admon 14 Aug. 1693 and 31 Jan 1693/4.

III 1691   SIR ERASMUS NORWICH, Bart [1641], of Brampton aforesaid, s and h He was *b* and *bap* 24 July 1668, at Brampton, *suc to the Baronetcy* in Sep 1691, Sheriff of Northants, 1704-05 He *m* firstly, Annabella, yst da of Thomas (SAVAGE), EARL RIVERS, by Elizabeth, da. and coheir of Thomas (DARCY), 3d BARON DARCY OF CHICHE She *d.* s p and was *bur* 3 Feb. 1702/3, at Brampton. Admon 1 June 1703 He *m* secondly (Lic Fac, 6 April 1704), Jane,(b) da and h of William ADAMS, of Sprowston Hall, Norfolk (s. and h ap. of Sir William ADAMS, 2d Bart [1660]), by Mary, relict of Francis BULLER, da. and sole heir of Sir John MAYNARD, of Isleham, co Cambridge. He *d.* Aug. 1720, and was *bur*. at Brampton Will pr Sep 1720

IV. 1720,   SIR WILLIAM NORWICH, Bart. [1641], of Brampton
    to   aforesaid, only surv s. and h, by 2d wife. He was *b.* and *bap.*
    1742.   11 Nov 1711 at St. Anne's, Westm, though registered at Brampton. He *suc.* to the Baronetcy, Aug. 1720, but is said to have ruined the family by gambling, and to have sold the family estates. He *d* unm Jan 1741/2, at Market Harboro', when the Baronetcy is presumed to have become *extinct*,(c) unless any issue male of the younger sons of the 1st Bart was still in existence (d) Admon April 1742 to his sister and next of kin, Arabella Catharine, wife of " Henry Barwell, Esq "

(a) The patent is not enrolled The date here given is that in Dugdale's *Catalogue*. See *Memorandum* on p 84. The date of " warrant for granting receipt for £1,095 to John Norwich, of Brampton, co Northampton, Knt, on his creation as Baronet " is 22 July 1641.

(b) On the death of her uncle, Sir Charles ADAMS, 3d Bart [1660], who *d.* s p. 12 Aug 1716, she inherited Sprowston Hall and other estates in Norfolk.

(c) He had three sisters, (1) Arabella Catharine, *m* in 1738, Henry BARWELL, of Marston, Trussell, co Northampton (2) Annabella, unm in 1741. (3) Jane, *m.* (—) NICHOLS, of Hiltoft, near Edgworth Midx.

(d) The will of " Sir Erasmus Norwich," proved 1750, seems to indicate a successor of that name to the Baronetcy.

The title seems to have been assumed as under —

V 1742. "SIR JOHN NORWICH, Bart.," said to have been br.
and h of the late Bart He was a pensioner of the Dukes of
Montagu (ª)

VI. 1780? "SIR JOHN NORWICH, Bart.," s and h He d in
the Workhouse at Kettering, co Northampton

VII 1820? "SIR SAMUEL NORWICH, Bart." s and h He was
a sawyer, at Kettering aforesaid His widow "very poor and
very ignorant "(ᵇ) d. there 21 June 1860 (ª)

VIII 1850? "SIR WILLIAM NORWICH, Bart" [Qy s and h of
above], "the present [1863] heir of the family now in
America (ᵇ)

BROWNLOW, or BROWNLOWE
cr. 26 July 1641(ᶜ),
ex 23 Nov. 1679.

I 1641,
to
1679
"JOHN BROWNLOWE of Belton, near Grantham, co.
Lincoln, Esq," s. and h of Richard BROWNLOW, of Kirby Underwood in that county, chief Prothonotary of the Court of Common
Pleas, by Katharine, da of John PAGE, of Wembly, co Midx, a
Master in Chancery, was b. about 1594, matric at Oxford (St Mary Hall) 26 June
1607, aged 13; B A. (Univ Coll), 28 April 1610, admitted to Inner Temple, 1608, suc
his father in 1638, was Sheriff of Lincolnshire, 1639 40, and again (but did not act)
1665, and was cr. a Baronet, as above, 26 July 1641 (ᶜ) He was indicted at Grantham
for high treason April 1643 He m Alice, 2d da but eventually h of Sir John
PULTENEY, of Misterton, co Leic. He d s p 23 Nov. 1679,(ᵈ) when the Baronetcy
became extinct Will pr 1680

BROWNLOW, or BROWNLOWE
cr. 27 July 1641(ᵉ),
sometime, 1718-54, VISCOUNT TYRCONNEL [I],
ex. 27 Feb. 1754

I 1641. "WILLIAM BROWNLOWE, of Humby, co Lincoln, Esq,"
yr br of Sir John Brownlow, Bart [1641], next abovenamed, was
b about 1595, matric at Oxford (St Mary Hall), 26 June 1607 (the same day as

---

(ª) Sir Bernard Burke's Vicissitudes of Families," 3d series [1863], pp 13-16.
(ᵇ) Northampton Herald, (—) Nov 1862.
(ᶜ) The patent is not enrolled The date here given, as also the description of the
grantee, is that in Dugdale's Catalogue See Memorandum on p 84 The date of
the "warrant for granting receipt for money paid on creation, filed on the same
bundle of signet bills," is 23 July 1641, but the christian name of "William" is
erroneously given for that of "John."
(ᵈ) In Sir J. Wilhamson's "Notes on Lincolnshire Families," temp. Car II [Her
and Gen, vol ii, p 120] he and his estates are thus mentioned, "At Belton, near
Grantham, at Runxton, near Bourne; Snarford, near Lincoln, £8,000 per annum,
rich, about £20,000 in purse; beares 10 horses in ye militia."
(ᵉ) The patent is not enrolled. The date here given is that in Dugdale's Catalogue.
See Memorandum on p. 84. The date of the signet bill is 24 July 1641

his elder brother), aged 12 , B A. (Univ Coll), 28 Jan. 1610/1 , Barrister (Inner Temple), 1617 ; and was cr a Baronet, as above, 27 July 1641(a), on the day following the creation of his brother, as a Baronet. He was a Parliamentarian, serving on several committees, 1643-45 , was M P for Lincolnshire, 1653 (b) He m , in or before 1624, Elizabeth, da and coheir of William DUNCOMBE, of London, Haberdasher, by Agnes, da. of Sir Thomas BENNET, sometime, 1603-04, L. Mayor of London. He d. 1666   Will pr 1668

II. 1666   SIR RICHARD BROWNLOW, Bart. [1641], of Humby aforesaid and of Rippingale, co Lincoln, s and h , admitted to Gray's Inn, 21 Jan 1645/6 , suc to the Baronetcy in 1666 He m Elizabeth, da of John FREKE, of Ewern Courtney, Dorset, by his 2d wife, Jane, da. and coheir of Sir John SHIRLEY, of Ifield, co Sussex He d. 30 Aug and was bur 5 Sep. 1668 at Rippingale, co Lincoln, in his 40th year. Admon 24 Oct. 1668   His widow d 2 Feb 1683/4 and was bur. at Somerby, co Lincoln, in her 51st year.   M I

III 1668   SIR JOHN BROWNLOW, Bart. [1641], of Humby aforesaid, s and h , b. 26 June and bap 6 July 1659 at Rippingale aforesaid , suc to the Baronetcy, 30 Aug 1668 On 23 Nov 1679, by the death of his great uncle, Sir John Brownlow, Bart [cr 25 July 1641], of Belton, he suc to Belton and the other family estates in co Lincoln , was Sheriff of Lincolnshire, 1688-89 , M P. for Grantham, 1689-90, 1690-95, and 1695 till death. He m (at the age of 16) 27 March 1676, at Westm Abbey (lic Dean of Westm), Alice, sister to Sir John Sherard, 1st Bart [1674], 1st da of Richard SHERARD, of Lobthorpe, co. Lincoln, by Margaret, da. of Lumley DEWE, of Upton Bishop, co. Hereford He d s p.m 16 July 1697, and was bur at Belton Will, as "of Belton," dat. 29 July 1689, pr 2 Sep 1697 (c) His widow d. 27 June 1721 Will pr 1721.

IV. 1697   SIR WILLIAM BROWNLOW, Bart [1641], of Belton and Humby aforesaid, br and h male, b 5 and bap 10 Nov 1665 at Rippingale aforesaid , suc to the Baronetcy, 16 July 1697, was M P. for Peterborough, 1689-90, 1690 95, and 1695 98 , for Bishops Castle 1698 till unseated 4 Feb 1700 He m firstly, Dorothy (aged 3 in 1668), 1st da and coheir of Sir Richard MASON, of Sutton, Surrey, Clerk of the Green Cloth, by Anne Margaret, da of Sir James LONG, of Draycott, Wilts. Her will pr May 1700. He m secondly, Henrietta He d at St Martin's in the Fields, 6 March 1700/1 Admon 20 March 1700/1, and again 16 Sep 1714 His widow living March 1700/1.

V 1701,   SIR JOHN BROWNLOW, Bart. [1641], of Belton and
to   Humby aforesaid, s and h by 1st wife ; suc. to the Baronetcy,
1754.   6 March 1700/1 ; was of full age in Sep. 1714 ; M P for Grantham 1713-15 , for Lincolnshire, 1715-22, and for Grantham again (3 parls.) 1722-41 , was cr 23 June 1718, BARON CHARLEVILLE, co Cork, and VISCOUNT TYRCONNEL [I], was made K B on the revival of that order, 27 May 1725 He m firstly, Eleanor, 4th da and coheir of his uncle Sir John BROWNLOW, 3d Bart [1641] by Alice, da. of Richard SHERARD, all abovenamed. She d s p 11 Sep 1730 He m. secondly, 24 Jan 1731/2, at Marnham, Notts, Elizabeth, da. of William Cartwright, of Marnham aforesaid He d s p 27 Feb 1754, at Belton aforesaid, when all his honours became extinct.(d) Admon 1 Feb 1755. His widow d at Buxton, 17 July 1780

(a) See p 111, note " e "
(b) His estate was "At Humby, near Grantham ; £1,600 " [i.e , a year]   See Williamson's notes, as on p 111, note " b."
(c) All of his four daughters and coheirs m noblemen, viz, (1) Jane, m Peregrine (Bertie), 2d Duke of Ancaster ; (2) Elizabeth, m John (Cecil), 6th Earl of Exeter ; (3) Alicia, m Francis (North), 2d Baron Guilford , and (4) Elizabeth, m her cousin, John (Brownlow), Viscount Tyrconnel [I], and 5th Bart [1641], as mentioned in the text
(d) His sister, Ann, m Sir Richard Cust, 2d Bart [1677], and their son, Sir John Cust, 3d Bart. Speaker of the House of Commons, inherited the estate of Belton. Sir John's s and h. was (for his father's services) in commemoration of his descent from the Brownlow family, cr. BARON BROWNLOW OF BELTON in 1776, and left a son who, in 1815, was cr. EARL BROWNLOW.

SYDENHAM
cr. 28 July 1641(ᵃ);

ex 10 Oct 1739

I   1641   "JOHN SYDENHAM, of Brimpton, co Somerset, Esq," s and h of John SYDENHAM, of the same, by Alice, sister and heir of Sir William HOBY, da of William HOBY, of Hales, co. Glouc, was *b.* about 1620 ; suc his father, 10 March 1626 , and was *cr a Baronet,* as above, 28 July 1641 (ᵃ)   He *m* in 1638, Anne, sister of Sir Ralph HARE, 1st Bart. [1641], 2d da of Sir John HARE, of Stow Bardolph, co Norfolk, by Elizabeth, da of Thomas (COVENTRY), 1st BARON COVENTRY OF AYLESBOROUGH   He *d.* 1643, and was *bur.* at Stow Bardolph Will pr 1643

II.   1643.   SIR JOHN SYDENHAM, Bart. [1641], of Brimpton aforesaid, posthumous s. and h , *b* 1643, and *suc to the Baronetcy* on his birth , was M P for Somerset, Nov 1665, till void 9 Nov. 1666, again, Nov 1669 to 1679, and 1679   He *m* firstly, Elizabeth, da of John (POULETT), 2d BARON POULETT OF HINTON ST GEORGE, by his 1st wife, Catherine, da. of Horatio (DE VERE), BARON VERE OF TILBURY   She *d s p s* and was *bur* at Brimpton in 1669   M I   He *m* secondly, Mary, 2d da of Philip (HERBERT), 5th EARL OF PEMBROKE, by Penelope, da and h of Sir Robert NAUNTON.   She, who was *bap.* 7 May 1650, *d.* 1686, and was *bur* at Brimpton   M I   He *d* 1696 in his 54th year   Admon. 18 Jan 1696/7 and 4 March 1697/8.

III   1696,   SIR PHILIP SYDENHAM, Bart. [1641], of Brimpton aforeto   said, 2d but 1st surv s and h , was *b.* about 1676 *suc to the Baronetcy*
1739   in 1696 , was of full age in March 1697/8   He, who was sometime M P. for Helston, 1700-01 ; for Somerset, 1701-02 and 1702-05 ; wasted an estate of £4,000 a year, and sold Brimpton to his cousin, Humphrey Sydenham   He *d* unm 10 and was *bur.* 25 Oct 1739, at Barnes, co Surrey, aged about 63, when the *Baronetcy* became *extinct*

PRATT :
cr 28 July 1641(ᵇ);

ex 17 Jan. 1673/4

I.   1641   "HENRY PRATT, of Coleshull, co Berks, Esq," s of Henry PRATT, of Cirencester, Clothier, was *b.* about 1573 ; apprenticed, 8 Dec 1587, in the Company of Merchant Taylors , was on the Livery, 16 July 1610 , 3d Warden, 17 July 1627 , 2d Warden, 13 July 1630 , Master, 4 Aug. 1630 , Alderman of Bridge Ward, 4 July 1633 to March 1641(ᶜ) , Sheriff of London, 1631-32, purchased, in 1626, the estate of Coleshill, Berks, and was *cr a Baronet,* as above, 28 July 1641, being *Knighted* subsequently at Whitehall, 26 [*sic.* but query] July 1641 (ᵇ)   He *m* , in or before 1605, Mary, da of Thomas ADAMS, of Wisbeach, co. Cambridge   He *d* 6 April, and was *bur* 9 May 1647 at Coleshill, aged 75.   M I. Will, dat 2 July 1645, pr. 16 April 1649   His widow *d* before 6 April 1672

(ᵃ) The patent is not enrolled   The date here given is that in Dugdale's *Catalogue.* See *Memorandum* on p. 84.   The date of the signet bill is 19 July 1641

(ᵇ) The patent is not enrolled   The date of Baronetcy here given is that in Dugdale's *Catalogue* (see *Memorandum* on p 84), and also in the Visit. of Berks, 1664, but as the Grantee was Knighted, *as a Baronet,* two days previously, there is, apparently, some mistake.   The date of the signet bill is 19 July 1641.

(ᶜ) Clode's *London during the Great Rebellion,* p. 28.

Q

II. 1647.   SIR GEORGE PRATT, Bart [1641], of Coleshill aforesaid,([a]) s and h , b. about 1605 , matric at Oxford (Mag. Hall),
27 June 1623, aged 18 , admitted to Gray's Inn, 1626 ; *suc. to the Baronetcy*, 6 April
1647, was Sheriff of Berks, 1654-55   He entered his pedigree in the Visit of Berks,
1665, being then aged 58   He *m*, in or before 1650, Margaret, da of Sir Humphrey
FORSTER, 1st Bart [1620], of Aldermaston, Berks, by Anne, da of Sir William
KINGSMILL.   He was *bur* 11 May 1673 at Coleshill   Will dat 6 April 1672, pr.
21 June 1673.   His widow was *bur* there 24 March 1698/9

III. 1673,   SIR HENRY PRATT, Bart. [1641], of Coleshill aforeto   said, only s and h., *b* about 1650 , matric. at Oxford (Trin Coll),
1674   15 July 1665, aged 15 , admitted to Inner Temple, 1667 ; *suc. to the
Baronetcy* in May 1673.   He *d*. s p , probably unm., and was *bur.*
17 Jan. 1673/4, at Coleshill, when *the Baronetcy* became *extinct* ([b])   Will pr 1674

NICHOLS, *or* NICOLLS:
cr. 28 July 1641 ;([c])
ex 1717

I   1641.   "FRANCIS NICHOLS, of Hardwick, co. Northampton, Esq.,"
s. and h of Francis NICHOLS, of the same, Gov of Tilbury Fort,
1588, by Anne, da of David SEYMOUR, being nephew of Sir Augustine
NICOLLS, *or* NICHOLS, of Faxton, co Northampton, one of the Judges of the Court of
Common Pleas, was *b* about 1587 , matric at Oxford (Bras Coll), 15 Oct. 1602, aged
15 ; admitted to Middle Temple, 1602, suc. his father, 1 April 1604, and suc his
said uncle (in the estate of Faxton), 3 Aug. 1616 ; was M P for Bishop's Castle,
1621-22, and for Northamptonshire, 1628-29 , Sheriff thereof, 1630-31 , Sec to
the Elector Palatine in 1640 , and was *cr. a Baronet*, as above, 28 July 1641 ([c])   He
m. in or before 1618, Mary, da of Edward BAGSHAW, of London   She *d* 10 July
1634, in her 47th year, and was *bur.* at Faxton. M I.   He *d* 4 March 1641/2, and
was *bur* at Hardwick   M.I.

II.   1642   SIR EDWARD NICHOLS, *or* NICOLLS, Bart. [1641], of Faxton
aforesaid, only s and h ; *b* about 1619 , matric at Oxford (Linc
Coll.), 8 May 1635, aged 15 , admitted to Middle Temple, 1637 , *suc to the Baronetcy*,
4 March 1641/2, was on the Northants Committee, Aug 1644 , Sheriff of that
county, 1657-58   He *m*. firstly, Judith, da of the Hon Sir Rowland ST. JOHN, K B.,
by Sibylla, da of John VAUGHAN.   She, by whom he had seven daughters, was *bur*.
15 June 1663, at St Leonard's Shoreditch   He *m* secondly, 20 Feb 1664/5, at
St Margaret's, Westm (Lic Dean and Chapter of Westm)   Jane, sister of Sir
Peter SOAME, 2d Bart [1685], 8th da. of Sir Stephen SOAME, of Heydon, Essex, by
Elizabeth, da of Sir Thomas PLAYTERS, 1st Bart. [1623]   He *d* 28 Feb 1682/3, aged
63 years and 4 months, and was *bur* at Faxton.   M.I   His widow resided at Old,
co. Northampton   Her admon 19 June 1707, 4 May 1719, and 10 Dec 1720.

III.   1683,   SIR EDWARD NICHOLS *or* NICOLLS, Bart [1641], of Faxton
to   aforesaid, only s and h, by 2d wife, *suc to the Baronetcy*, 20 Feb.
1717   1682/3.   He *d*. s.p. 1717, when the *Baronetcy* became *extinct.*   Will
pr. 1717

([a]) The house at Coleshill was rebuilt in 1650, the well known Inigo Jones being
the architect.

([b]) His only sister, Mary, *m.* 16 Feb 1666/7, at Coleshill, Thomas Pleydell, of
Shrivenham, and their great grandson, Mark Stuart Pleydell, of Coleshill, was *cr. a
Baronet* in 1732

([c]) The patent is not enrolled.   The date here given is that in Dugdale's *Catalogue.*
See *Memorandum* on p. 84.   The date of the signet bill is 22 July 1641.

STRICKLAND :
cr. 30 July 1641(ª),
sometime, 1865-74, CHOLMLEY.

I 1641. " WILLIAM STRICKLAND, of Boynton, co. York, Knt ,"
s and h of Walter STRICKLAND, of the same, by Frances, da. of
Peter WENTWORTH, of Lillingston Dayrell, Bucks, was *b* about 1596, being aged 16
in 1612 (Visit of Yorkshire); admitted to Gray's Inn, 21 May 1617, *Knighted,* 24 June
1630 ; suc his father in 1635, and was *cr. a Baronet,* as above, 30 July 1641.(ª) He
was a vehement Parliamentarian, serving on nearly every important Committee,
1641-59, save that of the king's trial, and being in command at Hull in July 1643
He was M P for Hedon 1640-53, and for the East Riding of Yorkshire, 1654-55 and
1656, and was summoned by Cromwell to "*the other house*" (as it was then called)
under the designation of LORD STRICKLAND (ᵇ); was P C. (to Richard Cromwell)
1659 He was, however, unmolested at and after the Restoration He *m* firstly,
18 June 1622, at St Leonard's, Shoreditch (Lic London, he 23 and she 18),
Margaret, da. of Sir Richard CHOLMLEY, of Whitby, co York, by his 1st wife,
Susanna da of John LEGARD She *d* s p m 1629, and was *bur* at Whitby He
m secondly, 3 May 1631, at St George's, Canterbury, Frances, 1st da of Thomas
(FINCH), 1st EARL OF WINCHELSEA, by Cicely, da. of John WENTWORTH He *d* 1673.

II. 1673. SIR THOMAS STRICKLAND, Bart [1641], of Boynton
aforesaid, only s and h , by 2d wife, *b* about 1639, was M P. for
Beverley, 1659 , aged 26 in 1665 (Visit of Yorkshire) , *suc to the Baronetcy* in 1673.
He *m* 19 Nov 1659 at Kensington, Elizabeth, 2d da. and coheir of Sir Francis
PILE, 2d Bart. [1620], by his 2d wife, Jane,(ᶜ) said to be yet da of John STILL,
Bishop of Bath and Wells He *d.* 20 Nov 1684

III 1684 SIR WILLIAM STRICKLAND, Bart [1641], of Boynton
aforesaid, s and h , *b* March 1665, matric. at Oxford (Ex Coll),
12 Nov 1680, aged 15 , *suc. to the Baronetcy* in 1684 ; was M P. for Malton (in seven
Parls , 1689-98, 1700 08, and 1722-24 , for Yorkshire, 1708-10, and for Old Sarum,
1716-22 Commissary General of the Musters to George I He *m* 28 Aug 1684,
at St Michael's, Malton, Elizabeth, da and eventually sole h of William PALMES, of
Malton aforesaid, and of Lindley, co York, by Mary, da. and coheir of Col. the Hon
Sir William EURE, yr. s of William, 4th BARON EURE He *d* 12 May 1724, aged 59.
The will of his widow was pr 1740

IV. 1724. SIR WILLIAM STRICKLAND, Bart. [1641], of Boynton
aforesaid, s and h was a Commissioner of the Revenue [I], 1709 ,
M P for Malton (three Parls), 1708-15 ; for Carlisle, 1715-22, and for Scarborough
(three Parls.), 1722 till death *suc to the Baronetcy,* 12 May 1724, was one of the
Lords of the Treasury, 1725-27 ; Treasurer to the Queen's household , Secretary at
War, 1730-35 ; P.C, 11 June 1730 He *m*. Catharine, da of Sir Jeremy SAMBROOKE,
of Gobions, Herts, by Judith, da of Nicholas VANACKER, of London, Merchant. He
d., at Boynton, 1 Sep 1735 Will pr 1736 The will of his widow pr. Feb 1767.

V 1735 SIR GEORGE STRICKLAND, Bart. [1641], of Boynton
aforesaid, s. and h , *b* March 1729, *suc to the Baronetcy,* 1 Sep 1735 ;
Sheriff of Yorkshire, 1768-69 He *m* 25 Nov 1751, at Wragby, Elizabeth Lætitia,
5th da of Sir Rowland WINN, 4th Bart [1660], of Nostell, co York, by Susanna, da
of Edward HENSHAW, of Eltham, co Kent. He *d.* 13 Jan 1808 Will pr 1809
His widow *d* at Hildenley Hall, co York, 1813, aged 79 Will pr. 1813.

(ª) The patent is not enrolled. The date here given is that in Dugdale's *Catalogue.*
See *Memorandum* on p 84 The date of the signet bill is 29 July 1641
(ᵇ) His 2d br , Walter, was, also, one of Cromwell's Lords, under the designation of
" LORD WALTER STRICKLAND " He, like his brother, was unmolested at and after
the Restoration,
(ᶜ) See p. 57, notes " a " and " b," *sub* " PILE."

VI 1808.   SIR WILLIAM STRICKLAND, Bart [1641], of Boynton
aforesaid, s and h., b 12 March 1753 ; suc to the Baronetcy, 13 Jan
1808   He m. 15 April 1778, Henrietta, 3d da and coheir of Nathaniel CHOLMLEY
of Whitby Abbey and of Howsham, co. York, by his 2d wife, Henrietta-Catharine
da of Stephen CROFT, of Stillington   She, who was b 28 Aug 1760 at Howsham
d. 26 March 1827   He d 8 Jan. 1834 at Boynton, in his 81st year   Will pr. 1834.

VII 1834   SIR GEORGE STRICKLAND, afterwards (1865-74), CHOLMLEY
Bart [1641], of Boynton and Hildenley Hall aforesaid, and of
Hildenby Hall, co. York, s and h ; b 26 Nov. 1782, at Welburn, Kirby Moorside, co
York , Barrister (Lincoln's Inn), 1810 ; M P for Yorkshire, 1831 , for West Division
of Yorkshire, 1832-41, and for Preston, 1841-57 ; suc to the Baronetcy, 8 Jan
1834.   By royal lic , 17 March 1865, he took the name of CHOLMLEY, in lieu of that
of STRICKLAND   He m firstly, 30 March 1818, at Sigglesthorne, Mary, only child of
Rev Charles CONSTABLE, of Wassand, co Lincoln   She d 10 Jan 1865, at Walcot, co
Lincoln, aged 67.   He m secondly, 25 May 1867 (being then aged 85), at St Martin's
in the Fields, Jane, 1st da. of Thomas LEAVENS, of Norton's Villas, Yorkshire.   He
d. 23 Dec 1874, in his 92d year, at Newton Hall, Boynton   His widow d. 19 Oct.
1898, in her 89th year, at 139 North Marine Road, Scarborough   Will pr at £95,811
the net personalty being £52,364

VIII 1874.   SIR CHARLES WILLIAM STRICKLAND, Bart. [1641], of
Boynton and of Hildenley Hall aforesaid, s. and h , by 1st wife ,
b. at Hildenley Hall, 6 Feb 1819 , ed at Rugby . B A , Cambridge (Trin Coll),
1842 , M A , 1847 , Barrister (Lincoln's Inn and Middle Temple), 1847 , suc. to the
Baronetcy, 23 Dec 1874 , Sheriff of the North Riding of Yorkshire, 1880   He m.
firstly, 19 Feb 1850, Georgina Selina Septima, da of Sir William Mordaunt Stuart
MILNER, 4th Bart. [1717], by his 2d wife, Harriet Elizabeth. da. of Lord Edward
Charles CAVENDISH BENTINCK   She d 13 June 1864,.   He m secondly, 22 May 1866,
at Thorney, Notts, Anne Elizabeth, yst da of Rev. Christopher NEVILE, of Thorney
aforesaid   She d. 7 April 1886, aged 42, at Hildenley

Family Estates —These, in 1883, consisted of 16,000 acres in the North, East, and
West Ridings of Yorkshire, worth 17,000 a year   *Principal Seats* —Hildenley Hall,
near Malton ; Boynton, near Bridlington ; Whitby Abbey and Howsham, all in
co York

WINDHAM, or WYNDHAM
cr. 4 Aug. 1641.(a)
ex 1663.

I. 1641,   "HUGH WINDHAM, of Pilsden Court, co. Dorset, Esq ,"
to   4th surv s of Edmond WINDHAM, of Kentsford, in St Decumans,
1663   Somerset (2d s of Sir John WYNDHAM, of Orchard Wyndham), by
Margaret, da. and eventually coheir of Richard CHAMBERLAIN,
Alderman of London, was living at Aldermanbury, London, as a merchant in 1626 ,
entered and signed his pedigree in the Visit. of London, 1634, and was cr. a Baronet,
as above, 4 Aug 1641,(a) being Knighted the 10th following , was a Compounder (with
his father) in 1645, being, in Nov. 1651, fined £692 , was Sheriff of Dorset, 1651-52 ,
He m , in or before 1625, Mary, da. of Christopher ALANSON, of London   She d.
before Sep 1661   He d. s.p.m.s., in 1663,(b) when the Baronetcy became extinct.
Will dat. 17 Sep. 1661, pr 18 July 1663, directing his burial to be at Pilsden.

(a) The patent is not enrolled   The date here given is that in Dugdale's *Catalogue*
See *Memorandum* on p 84   The date of the signet bill is 31 July 1641.
(b) The Sir Hugh Windham, who was M.P. for Minehead, 1661, till his death in
1671, was his great nephew, being s and h. ap. of Sir Edmund Windham (who
survived his said son), s. and h. of Sir Thomas Windham, all of Kentsford aforesaid.

MAULEVERER :

cr 4 Aug 1641([a]) ;

ex. 27 March 1713.

I 1641.   "THOMAS MAULEVERER, of Allerton Maulever [*sic*] co
York, Esq," s and h of Sir Richard MAULEVERER, of the same, by
his 2d wife, Katherine, da of Sir Ralph BOURCHIER, was *bap* 9 April 1599 , admitted
to Gray's Inn, 22 Oct 1617 , was M P for Boroughbridge, 1640-53 and, though he
had opposed the King's party, was *cr. a Baronet*, as above, 4 Aug 1641 ([a]) He shortly
afterwards raised two regiments of foot and a troop of horse for the Parl , fought at
the battle of Atherton in 1643 , served on several important Committees, 1643-46 ,
was one of the Regicide Judges, attending every day and signing the death warrant.
He *m* firstly, Mary, da of Sir Richard HUTTON, Chief Justice of the Common Pleas,
but by her had no issue. He *m* secondly, about 1622, Elizabeth, da of Thomas
WILBRAHAM, of Woodhey, Cheshire, by his 2d wife, Mary, da. of Peter WARBURTON,
of Arley, in that county She was *bur*. 10 March 1652/3 in Westm Abbey ([b]) He
d about June 1655 Admon. 9 June 1655 and 13 Feb 1656/7 He, though
dead, was, after the Restoration, excepted out of the bill of pardon.

II. 1655.   SIR RICHARD MAULEVERER, Bart [1641], of Allerton
Mauleverer aforesaid, s and h , by 2d wife, *b* about 1623, was, in
opposition to his father, a zealous loyalist . was admitted to Gray's Inn, 12 July 1641,
and was *Knighted* v p at Christ Church, Oxford, 27 March 1645 , was fined £3,287
by Parl in 1649, his estate sequestered, 1650, and declared an outlaw in 1654 He
suc to the Baronetcy about June 1655 , was in Lord Wilmot's rising, 1655, and was
taken prisoner to Chester, 1655, but escaped thence to the Hague; returned to London,
1659, and was again imprisoned for some months , was confirmed in title and estate
by Charles II, and made Gent. of the Privy Chamber and Captain of Horse in 1660 ,
M P for Boroughbridge, 1661, till death ; was a Commissioner for licensing hackney
coaches, 1665 , Sheriff of Yorkshire, 1667 68 He *m* 10 Aug 1642, at St Giles' in
the Fields (Lic Lond , he about 19, and she about 20), Anne, da of Sir Robert
CLERKE,([c]) of Pleshey, Essex, by Judith, da. of Sir William DANIEL, of London
He was *bur*. 25 July 1675 in Westm Abbey

III. 1675.   SIR THOMAS MAULEVERER, Bart [1641], of Allerton
Mauleverer aforesaid, 1st s and h , *b* about 1643 , *suc. to the
Baronetcy* in July, 1675 ; was M.P (four Parls) for Boroughbridge, 1679, till death ,
held a command, 1685, against the rebels under the Duke of Monmouth, sold " Armley
Hall " and other Yorkshire estates He *m* Katherine, da and h of Sir Miles STAPLETON,
of Wighill, co. York, by Mary, da of Sir Ingram HOPTON. He *d. s p legit* ([d]) and
was *bur* 13 Aug 1687, in Westm Abbey Will dat 10 June, pr 16 Aug 1687, by
Richard, his br and universal legatee His widow, with whom he had lived
unhappily, *m* her cousin, John HOPTON, of Ingersgill, and *d* s p and intestate,
31 Jan. 1703/4, being *bur* at Nether Poppleton.

IV. 1687.   SIR RICHARD MAULEVERER, Bart. [1641], of Allerton
Mauleverer aforesaid br and h., *suc to the Baronetcy* in Aug 1687
He *m* (Lic Vic Gen , 10 April 1688, he 22 [*sic*, but query if not 42] and she 19) Barbara, da. of Sir Thomas SLINGSBY, 2d Bart [S. 1635], of Scriven, co York, by Dorothy,
da and coheir of George CRADOCK He was *bur* 11 May 1689 in Westm Abbey. Will
dat 15 Oct 1688, pr 13 June 1689 His widow *m* (as 2d wife) 14 Feb 1692/3, at
Allhallows', Staining, London (Lic Vic Gen., she about 25), John (ARUNDELL), 2d
BARON ARUNDELL OF TRERICE, who was *bur* 23 June 1698 at St James', Westm ,
aged 49. She *m* (for her 3d husband and his 2d wife) 21 Sep 1708, at St James'

([a]) *Vide* p 116, note " a."
([b]) See note in Col. Chester's *Registers of Westm Abbey*, as to her being generally
called " Mary "—also as to her husband's intended marriage, July 1659, with
Susanna Raylton, of Fulham, widow.
([c]) See Col. Chester's *Westm. Abbey Registers*, p. 186, note 11, as to the error in
calling her da. of " Sir *Henry* Clerke, *Bart.*"
([d]) His illegit. son, Thomas Newsham, *otherwise* Mauleverer, was well provided for
under the will of the 4th Bart

aforesaid, Thomas (HERBERT), 3d EARL OF PEMBROKE, who *d* 22 Jan. 1732/3 She *d*, and was *bur.* 9 Aug 1721, in Salisbury Cathedral. Admon 8 May 1733 and 30 April 1759

V 1689,
to
1713

SIR RICHARD MAULEVERER, Bart [1641], of Allerton Mauleverer aforesaid, only *s* and *h*, *b.* 18 and *bap* 25 March 1689 at St Martin's in the Fields, *suc to the Baronetcy* a few months later, in May 1689. He *d* unm of the small pox, at the Earl of Pembroke's house, and was *bur* 27 March 1713, in Westm Abbey, aged 24, when the *Baronetcy* became *extinct*.

KNATCHBULL ·

cr 4 Aug. 1641 (ª);

sometime, 1746-63, KNATCHBULL-WYNDHAM

I 1641

"NORTON KNATCHBULL, of Mersham Hatch,(ᵇ) co. Kent, Esq," *s* and *h* of Thomas Knatchbull, of the same, by Eleanor, da and eventually coheir of John ASTLEY, of Maidstone (by Margaret, da and h. of Lord Thomas GREY, br of Henry, DUKE OF SUFFOLK), which Thomas was br and h to Sir Norton KNATCHBULL, of Mersham Hatch, was *b* about 1602, at Mersham, suc his father, 1623, and was *cr a Baronet*, as above, 4 Aug 1641 (ª) He was M P for Kent, April to May 1640, for New Romney, 1640 till secluded in Dec 1648, and again 1660 and 1661-77, was somewhat inclined to the Parl. side, though sequestrated in 1643, and fined 1,000 marks; was esteemed a person of great learning He *m* firstly (Lic at Canterbury, 22 Oct. 1630, he aged 23), Dorothy, da. of Thomas WESTROW, Alderman and sometime (1625) Sheriff of London by Mary (who subsequently *m* the abovementioned Sir Norton KNATCHBULL), da. of, John ALDERSEA, of Spurgrove, co. Chester By her he had thirteen children He *m* secondly, 27 Nov. 1662, at St Martin's in the Fields (Lic Vic Gen. he about 50 and she about 40), Dorothy, widow of Sir Edward STEWARD, da of Sir Robert HONYWOOD, of Pett, in Charing, Kent, by Alice da of Sir Martin BARNHAM, of Hollingbourne He *d* 5 Feb 1684/5, aged about 83, and was *bur.* at Mersham. M I Will dat. 30 June 1682, pr 7 Aug 1685. His widow, who was *b* 30 Aug and *bap* 8 Sep 1611, at Charing, and by whom he had no issue, was *bur* 2 May 1694, at Mersham

II 1685

SIR JOHN KNATCHBULL, Bart [1641], of Mersham Hatch aforesaid, *s* and *h.*, by 1st wife, was a Commissioner for the office of Lord Privy Seal, 1650 51, M P. for New Romney, 1660, for Kent (three Parls), 1685-95, *suc to the Baronetcy*, 5 Feb 1684/5 He *m* 17 Jan 1659, Jane, da of Sir Edward MONINS, 2d Bart [1611], by Elizabeth, da of Sir Thomas STYLE, 1st Bart [1627], of Wateringbury He *d* *s p m s*, 15 Dec. 1696, aged 60 His widow *d* 7 June 1699, aged 59 Both *bur* at Mersham. M I

III. 1696.

SIR THOMAS KNATCHBULL, Bart [1641], of Mersham aforesaid, br and h, *suc to the Baronetcy*, 15 Dec 1696 He *m*. Mary, da of Sir Edward DERING, 2d Bart [1627], by Mary, da of Daniel HARVEY, of Coombe, co Surrey He *d* about 1712 Will dat. 12 Dec 1711 His widow was living 1724

IV. 1712?

SIR EDWARD KNATCHBULL, Bart [1641], of Mersham Hatch aforesaid, *s* and *h*, *suc to the Baronetcy*, on the death of his father, was M P for Rochester, 1702-05, for Kent, 1713-15 and 1722-27, and for Lostwithiel, 1728 till death He *m* about 1698, Alice, sister of Thomas, BARON WYNDHAM OF FINGLASS [I], sometime [1726-39] Lord Chancellor of Ireland, 1st da. of Col John WYNDHAM,(ᶜ) of Norrington, Wilts, by Alice, da of Thomas FOWNES. She, who was *b.* 11 April 1676, *d* 15 and was *bur* 16 April 1723, at Mersham He *d* in Golden square, Midx 3 April 1730 Will pr. 1730

(ª) *Vide* p. 116, note "a"

(ᵇ) Mersham Hatch was purchased by Richard Knatchbull in 1485, and has ever since remained with his descendants

(ᶜ) See *Mis. Gen. et Her*, 2d series, vol. IV, for many interesting particulars of the Wyndham family, together with some of that of Knatchbull as connected therewith.

V. 1730   SIR WYNDHAM KNATCHBULL, *afterwards* (1746 49), KNATCHBULL-WYNDHAM, Bart [1641], of Mersham Hatch aforesaid, s and h , *suc to the Baronetcy*, 3 April 1730 ; was Sheriff of Kent, June to Dec. 1733 , took the addit. name of *Wyndham*, by act of Parl. 1746 He m , 23 June 1730, Catharine, da. of James HARRIS, of Salisbury, only child of his 1st wife, Catherine, da of Charles COOKS, of Worcester. She *d* 6 Jan 1740/1, at St James', Westm Admon 27 June 1751 He *d*. 3 July 1749. Will pr 1749

VI. 1749   SIR WYNDHAM KNATCHBULL-WYNDHAM, Bart [1641], formerly (1737-46), KNATCHBULL, of Mersham Hatch aforesaid, s. and h., *b* in Golden square, 16 Feb 1737 , *suc. to the Baronetcy*, 3 July 1749 ; was M P. for Kent, 1760-61, and 1761 till death He *d* unm , 26 Sep 1763 Will pr. 1763.

VII 1763.   SIR EDWARD KNATCHBULL, Bart. [1641], of Mersham Hatch aforesaid, uncle and h , *b* 12 Dec. 1704, or 17 Dec 1705 , was M P. [I] for Armagh, 1727-60) *suc to the Baronetcy*, 26 Sep 1763 He m. Grace, 2d da. of William LEGGE, of Salisbury Her admon April 1788. He *d*. 21 Nov. 1789, aged 85. Will pr. 1789.

VIII 1789.   SIR EDWARD KNATCHBULL, Bart [1641], of Mersham Hatch aforesaid, only surv s and h , *b* about 1760, matric. at Oxford (Ch Ch), 25 Jan 1777, aged 17 , Sheriff of Kent, 1785 , *suc to the Baronetcy*, 21 Nov 1789 , M.P for Kent in six Parls , 1785-86, 1790-1802, and 1806 till his death , was a zealous supporter of Pitt's administration ; *cr* D C L of Oxford, 6 July 1810 He m. firstly, July 1780, Mary, da and one of the two coheirs of William Western HUGESSEN, of Provenders, near Faversham, co Kent, by Thomazine, da of Sir John HONYWOOD, 3d Bart [1660] She *d* 24 May 1784 He m secondly, 4 June 1785, Frances, da of John GRAHAM, Lieut. Governor of Georgia. She *d* 23 Nov 1799 He m. thirdly, 13 April 1801, at St Geo Han sq , Mary, da and coheir of Thomas HAWKINS, of Nash Court, in Boughton under Blean, Kent, by Mary Theresa only da. of John BRADSHAW, of Stretton, Cheshire He *d* 21 Sep 1819, in his 61st year Will pr 1819 His widow *d*. 19 Dec. 1850, at Dover. Will pr Jan. 1851

IX. 1819.   SIR EDWARD KNATCHBULL, Bart. [1641], of Mersham Hatch aforesaid, s and h by 1st wife, *b.* 20 Dec. 1781 ; matric at Oxford (Ch. Ch) 5 Feb. 1800, aged 18 , admitted to Lincoln's Inn, 1803 , *suc to the Baronetcy*, 21 Sep 1819 , M P for East Kent, 1833-45, P C 16 Dec 1834 , Paymaster General of the Forces, 1834-35 and 1841-45 He m firstly, 25 Aug 1806, Annabella Christiana, 2d da. of Sir John HONYWOOD, 4th Bart [1660], by Frances, da of William (COURTENAY), 2d VISCOUNT COURTENAY. She *d* 4 April 1814. He m secondly, 24 Oct 1820, Fanny Catherine, 1st da of Edward KNIGHT, *formerly* AUSTEN, of Godmersham Park, Kent, by Elizabeth, da. of Sir Brook BRIDGES, 3d Bart [1718]. He *d*. 24 May 1849,(a) at Mersham Hatch, aged 67 Will pr July 1849 His widow *d*. 24 Dec. 1882, at Provenders, in her 90th year

X 1849.   SIR NORTON JOSEPH KNATCHBULL, Bart [1641], of Mersham Hatch aforesaid, s and h by 1st marriage, *b.* 10 July 1808, at Provenders aforesaid ; ed at Winchester and at Christ Church, Oxford ; matric. 20 Nov. 1826, aged 18 ; *suc. to the Baronetcy*, 24 May 1849 He m 31 May 1831, Mary, 1st da of Jesse WATTS-RUSSELL, *formerly* RUSSELL, of Ilam Hall, co. Stafford, and of Biggin, co Northampton, by Mary, da and h of David Pike WATTS, of Portland Place, Marylebone. He *d*. 2 Feb. 1868, at 3 Chesham place. His widow *d*. 3 Sep 1874, at Maidstone

---

(a) His sixth son (the 1st son by his 2d wife), Edward Hugessen Knatchbull, *afterwards* (1849), Knatchbull-Hugessen, who inherited the Hugessen estates belonging to his grandmother's family, was *cr* 26 May 1880, BARON BRABOURNE of Brabourne, co. Kent.

XI   1868.   SIR EDWARD KNATCHBULL, Bart. [1641], of Mersham
Hatch aforesaid, 1st s. and h , *b* 26 April 1838 ; Barrister at Law ,
suc to the Baronetcy 2 Feb. 1868   He *d* unm. 30 May 1871, at Mersham Hatch,
aged 33

XII   1871   SIR WYNDHAM KNATCHBULL, Bart [1641], of Mersham
Hatch aforesaid, only br and h , *b.* 9 Aug. 1844 , ed at Eton ;
Barrister at Law , somctime a Civil servant in the Gen. Post Office , *suc to the
Baronetcy,* 30 May 1871 ; M P for East Kent, 1875-76

*Family Estates —*These, in 1883, consisted of 4,638 acres in Kent, valued at £7,224
a year, besides 483 acres (let at £930), belonging to the Dowager Lady Knatchbull.
*Seat —*Mersham Hatch, near Ashford, Kent.

CHICHESTER ·
cr 4 Aug 1641 (ª)

I   1641   "JOHN CHICHESTER, of Raleigh [in Pilton] co Devon,
Esq ," s and h of Sir Robert Chichester,(ᵇ) K B , of Raleigh afore-
said, by his 2d wife, Mary, da of Robert HILL, of Shilston, in that county, was *b*
23 April 1623, suc his father, 24 April 1624, and was *cr a Baronet*, as above, 4 Aug
1641 ,(ª) was M P for Barnstaple 1661 till death   He *m* firstly, Elizabeth, da of
Sir John RAYNEY, 1st Bart [1642], by his 1st wife, Catharine, da of Thomas STYLE.
She *d* 1654   He *m* secondly, 18 July 1655, at St Anne's, Blackfriars, Mary
WARCUP, widow, of that parish   He *d.* 1667

II   1667   SIR JOHN CHICHESTER, Bart [1641], of Raleigh aforesaid, and of Youlston, near Barnstaple, co Devon, 2d but 1st surv.
s and h , *b.* about 1658, matric at Oxford (Ex Coll), 8 May 1675, aged 17 , *suc to
the Baronetcy* in 1677 ; admitted to Inner Temple, 1679   He *m.* (Lic Vic Gen ,
4 Nov 1679) Elizabeth, 1st da of Sir Charles BICKERSTAFFE, of the Wilderness in
the parish of Sele, co. Kent, by Elizabeth, his wife   They *d* s p , both being taken ill
the same day, and *bur* 16 Sep 1680, at Sele aforesaid, he aged 22 years and
3 months and she aged 21 years and 3 months   M I.   His will dat 6 and pr. 11 Sep.
1680.

III   1680.   SIR ARTHUR CHICHESTER, Bart. [1641], of Youlston
aforesaid, br and h , *suc to the Baronetcy* in Sep. 1680 , M P for
Barnstaple, 1685-87, 1689-90, 1713-15, and 1715 till death   He *m* Elizabeth, da. of
Thomas DREWE, of the Grange, Devon   He *d* 3 Feb 1717/8

IV.   1718   SIR JOHN CHICHESTER, Bart [1641], of Youlston aforesaid, s and h , *bap.* 2 Jan 1688/9 , *suc. to the Baronetcy*, 3 Feb.
1717/8 , M P for Barnstaple, 1734 till death   He *m* firstly, in or before 1718,
Anne, da. of John LEIGH, of Newport, in the Isle of Wight   She was *bur* 16 July
1623, at Sherwell, co Devon, aged 28   M I   He *m* secondly, Frances, who
survived him   He *d* 2 and was *bur* 10 Sept 1740, at Sherwell   Will dat 4 Feb
1736, pr 22 Nov 1740

V.   1740.   SIR JOHN CHICHESTER, Bart [1641], of Youlston aforesaid, s and h by 1st wife, *bap* 26 March 1721 at Sherwell ; matric.
at Oxford (Balliol Coll) 13 April 1739, aged 18 , *suc to the Baronetcy*, 2 Aug. 1740 ;
Sheriff of Devon, 1753-54   He *m.*, in or before 1752, Frances, 2d da. and coh of Sir
George CHUDLEIGH, 4th Bart [1622], by Frances, da and coh of Sir William DAVIE,
4th Bart. [1641]   Her admon , 14 March 1752, to her said husband   He *d.* in
London 18 and was *bur* 30 Dec 1784, at Ashton, near Exeter   Admon Feb 1785.

(ª) *Vide* p 116, note "a."
(ᵇ) This Robert was s and h of Sir John Chichester, yr. br of (1) Arthur
Chichester, Lord Deputy of Ireland, 1603, who was *cr* BARON BELFAST [I], 1612
(which Barony became *ex.* in 1624), and (2) of Edward Chichester, *cr* VISCOUNT
CHICHESTER [I.], who was ancestor of the EARLS AND MARQUESSES OF DONEGALL [I.]

VI. 1784. SIR JOHN CHICHESTER, Bart [1641], of Youlston aforesaid, only s aud h, b about 1752, matric. at Oxford (Mag Coll), 29 March 1771, aged 19; suc to the Baronetcy, 18 Dec 1784, Sheriff of Devon, 1788 89 He d unm, at Wickham, co Kent, 30 Sep. and was bur. 16 Oct 1808, at Ashton aforesaid. Will pr 1809.

VII. 1808. SIR ARTHUR CHICHESTER, Bart [1641], of Youlston aforesaid, cousin and h male, being s and h. of John CHICHESTER, of Hart. (d 1 Aug 1800, aged 48), by Elizabeth, da of (—) CORY, of Newton, which John was only s of the Rev. William CHICHESTER, Rector of Georgeham and Sherwell, both co Devon (d Sep 1770, aged 48), who was 2d and yst s of the 4th Bart, was b 25 April 1790, suc to the Baronetcy, 30 Sep. 1808, Sheriff of Devon, 1816-17. He m 8 Sep 1819, at Clovelly, Charlotte, youngest da of Sir James HAMLYN-WILLIAMS, 2d Bart [1795], by Diana Anne, da of Abraham WHITAKER She d 18 and was bur 25 Aug 1834, at Sherwell, aged 36 M I He d at Youlston 30 May, and was bur 6 June 1842 at Sherwell, aged 52 Will pr. Aug. 1842 and Oct 1843.

VIII 1842. SIR ARTHUR CHICHESTER, Bart. [1641], of Youlston aforesaid, s and h, b there 4 Oct 1822; ed at Eton, suc to the Baronetcy, 30 May 1842, Capt., 7th Dragoons, 1847, Lieut. Col of North Devon Yeomanry Cavalry, 1862 He m firstly, 20 Nov 1847, Mary, 1st da of John NICHOLETTS, of South Petherton, Somerset She d 28 June 1879 at Youlston He m secondly, 23 Jan 1883, Rosalie, widow of Sir Alexander Palmer Bruce CHICHESTER, 2d Bart [1840], of Arlington, Devon, da of Thomas CHAMBERLAYNE, of Cranbury Park, Hants He d 13 July 1898 at Youlston, aged 75. Will pr at £106,673 gross, and £4,831 net personalty. His widow living 1900

IX 1898 SIR EDWARD CHICHESTER, Bart. [1641], of Youlston aforesaid, 2d but 1st surv s. and h., b. 20 Nov 1849 and bap. 24 Jan 1850 at Sherwell, entered the royal navy, served in the Egyptian campaign in 1882 (medal and bronze star); Capt, R N, being transport officer in Natal, 1899, suc to the Baronetcy, 13 July 1898; C M G, 1899, aide-de-camp to Queen Victoria, 1899 He m. 12 Oct 1880, Catharine Emma, 1st da of Robert Charles WHYTE, of Instow, Devon, Commander, R.N

Family Estates —These, in 1883, consisted of 7,022 acres in Devon, worth £6,051 a year Residence —Youlston, near Barnstaple, Devon.

BOUGHTON.

cr 4 Aug 1641 ;(ᵃ)

afterwards, since 1794, ROUSE-BOUGHTON.

I. 1641. "WILLIAM BOUGHTON of Lawford Parva, co. Warwick, Esq," s. and h of Edward Boughton, of the same, and of Hillmorton and Bilton in the same county, by Elizabeth, da. and h of Edward CATESBY, of Lapworth Hall, co Warwick, was b. about 1600, matric at Oxford (Queen's Coll), 28 April 1615, aged 15, admitted to Mid. Temple, 1617; suc his father 9 Aug 1625; was Sheriff of Warwickshire, 1633, and was cr a Baronet, as above, 4 Aug 1641 (ᵃ) He m Abigail, 1st da and coheir of Henry BAKER, of South Shoebury, Essex. She d 21 Feb 1634/5 and was bur. at Newbold upon Avon M I He d in 1656, and was bur there, aged about 56 Will dat 30 Aug 1655, pr. 4 Dec. 1656

II. 1656 SIR EDWARD BOUGHTON, Bart. [1641], of Lawford Hall in Lawford Parva aforesaid, s. and h, b about 1628, suc to the Baronetcy in 1656, was Sheriff of Warwickshire, 1660-61, M P thereof, 1678/9 and 1679 till death He m. firstly, Mary, da. of Thomas (POPE), 3d EARL OF DOWNE [I.], by Beata, da. of Sir Henry Poole She d. s p He m secondly, Anne, da of Sir John HEYDON, Governor of the Bermudas He d. s p. 1680, aged about 52. Will pr. Feb 1681

(ᵃ) Vide p 116, note "a."

R

III. 1680.   SIR WILLIAM BOUGHTON, Bart [1641], of Lawford Hall
aforesaid, br and h , *b* about 1632, *suc to the Baronetcy* in 1680, was
aged about 50 at the Visit of Warwickshire in 1682 He *m* Mary, da of
Hastings INGRAM, of Little Woolford, co Warwick He *d.* 12 Aug 1683, aged 53,
and was *bur* at Newbold Will pr Aug 1683. His widow *d* 24 Feb 1693 and
was *bur.* there. M I Will pr 1693

IV   1683   SIR WILLIAM BOUGHTON, Bart. [1641], of Lawford Hall
aforesaid, s and h , *b* about 1663 , matric at Oxford (Mag Coll),
1 Dec. 1681, aged 17 , *suc. to the Baronetcy*, 12 Aug. 1683; nom Sheriff of Warwickshire, Nov 1688, but did not act till April (to Nov) 1689 , M P , for that county,
1712-13 , is said to have declined being raised to the Peerage He *m.* firstly (Lic. Vic.
Gen , 28 Feb 1684/5, he about 22, she about 16 and au orphan), Mary, da. of John
RAMSEY, Alderman of London. She *d* in or before July 1694 , admon. 7 July 1694
He *m.* secondly, Catharine, da of Sir Charles SHUCKBURGH, 2d Bart [1660], by his
1st wife, Catharine, da of Sir Hugh STEWELEY, or STUKELEY, 2d Bart [1627] He
d 22 July 1716, aged 53, and was *bur* at Newbold aforesaid M I. Will pr Aug
1716 His widow *d.* about 1725. Will pr 1725

V.   1716   SIR EDWARD BOUGHTON, Bart. [1641], of Lawford Hall
aforesaid, s and h., by 1st wife, *b* about 1689, *suc to the Baronetcy* 22
July 1716 , Sheriff of Warwickshire, 1720 21 He *m* about 1718, Grace, 1st da. of
Sir John SHUCKBURGH, 3d Bart [1660] (br of the whole blood to his step-mother), by
Abigail, da. of George GOODWIN. He *d* 12 Feb. 1721/2, aged 33. Will pr 1722
His widow *m.*, in or before 1723, Matthew LISTER, of Burwell, co Lincoln She *d*
before him, Feb and was *bur.* 4 March 1779, at Burwell, aged 77

VI   1722.   SIR EDWARD BOUGHTON, Bart [1641], of Lawford Hall
aforesaid, s and h , *b* about 1719, *suc to the Baronetcy*, 12 Feb.
1721/2 ; matric. at Oxford (Mag Coll.), 22 July 1736, aged 17 , Sheriff for Warwickshire, 1748-49 He *m* firstly, after 1741, (—), da of (—) BRIDGES, of co Somerset.
She *d.* s p. He *m* secondly, in or before 1760, Anna Maria, da and coheir of John
BEAUCHAMP, of co Warwick He *d* suddenly 3 March 1772 and was *bur* at Newbold Will dat 3 May 1759, pr 22 May 1772 His widow, who was living 1781,
d at Bath in or before 1787 Admon. Sep 1787.

VII. 1772   SIR THEODOSIUS EDWARD ALLESLEY BOUGHTON, Bart
[1641], of Lawford Hall aforesaid, s and h , by 2d wife, *b* Aug. 1760,
suc. to the Baronetcy, 3 March 1772 He *d* a minor and unm , 29 Aug 1780, aged
20, at Lawford Hall, having been poisoned by "laurel water," administered to him
by his sister's husband, Capt. John Donellan.[a] He was *bur.* in the family vault at
Newbold. Will pr 1780.

VIII 1780   SIR EDWARD BOUGHTON, Bart [1641], of Lawford Hall
aforesaid, and of Poston Court, co Hereford cousin and h. male,
being s and h. of Shuckburgh BOUGHTON, of Poston Court aforesaid, by Mary, da of
the Hon Algernon GREVILLE, 2d s of Fulke, 5th BARON BROOKE OF BEAUCHAMP'S
COURT, which Shuckburgh Boughton (who *d* 1763, aged 60) was s of the 4th Bart.,
by his 2d wife, Catherine, da of Sir Charles SHUCKBURGH, 2d Bart. [1660] He was *b.*
about 1742 ; *suc. to the Baronetcy*, 29 Aug. 1780, pulled down Lawford Hall and sold
most of the estates in Warwickshire and Leicestershire to enlarge those at Poston Court,

---

(a) Donellan was executed for murder, at Warwick, 2 April 1781, the trial having
caused the greatest sensation He had *m* , in June 1777, Theodosia Beauchamp, only
sister and (by this murder) sole heir of the unfortunate Baronet, by whom he had a
son and a daughter, both of whom took the name of Beauchamp (being that of their
maternal grandmother, Lady Boughton) in lieu of Donellan, and died unm (See
order of the Lord Chancellor, 21 Nov. 1816, in "Hume v King *et al* ") The widow
m. secondly, Sir Egerton Leigh, 2d Bart [1772]. She *m* thirdly, 10 Feb 1823,
Barry E. O'Meara, surgeon R.N. (the attendant of Napoleon at St. Helena), who
survived her She *d* 14 Jan 1830.

etc., in Herefordshire, which had been purchased by his father   He was Sheriff for Herefordshire, 1786-87   He *d* unm s p legit (*a*) 26 Feb 1794, in his 53d year and was *bur* in Vow church, co Hereford   Will pr. April 1794

IX. 1794.   SIR CHARLES WILLIAM ROUSE-BOUGHTON, Bart   [1641]
I   1791   *formerly* BOUGHTON-ROUSE, Bart [1791], of Rouse Lench, near
Evesham, co Worcester, and of Downton Hall, near Ludlow, Salop,
br   and h, was *b* in the parish of St. Nicholas, Worcester
In 1765 he went to India in the Bengal Civil Service, and was a Judge in several Courts there   In 1769 he took the name of ROUSE after that of BOUGHTON on succeeding to the estates of the Rouse family at Rouse Lench abovenamed (*b*)   M P for Evesham, 1780-84, and 1784-90, and for Bramber, 1796-99   Secretary to the Board of Control for Indian Affairs, 1784 to 1791   On 13 May 1791 he obtained a Royal lic to use the name of Rouse either *before* or *after* that of Boughton, and a few days afterwards, 28 July 1791, was *cr a Baronet* under the surname of BOUGHTON-ROUSE (the mode in which, since 1769, the names had been used), and the description " of Rouse Lench, co Worcester, and Downton Hall, co Salop"   When, however, on 26 Feb 1794, he *suc to the* more ancient (1641) *Baronetcy* of Boughton (though to none of the family estates), he transposed the order of these names to ROUSE BOUGHTON In 1799 he was one of the Commissioners for auditing public accounts   He was also Commander of the Chiswick Volunteers   He *m* 3 June 1782, at St James', Westm , Catharine, da and h of William PEARCE, *otherwise* HALL, of Downton Hall aforesaid, which estate she inherited   She *d* 14 Aug 1808   He *d* 26 Feb 1821, in Devonshire place, Marylebone   Will pr March 1821   Both were *bur.* at Rouse Lench.

X and II 1821   SIR WILLIAM EDWARD ROUSE-BOUGHTON, Bart
[1641 and 1791], of Rouse Lench and of Downton Hall aforesaid, only s. and h , *b* 14 Sep 1788, in Lower Grosvenor street , matric at Oxford (Ch Ch), 21 Jan 1806, aged 17 , B A , 1808, M P for Evesham, 1818-19 and 1820-26 , *suc to the Baronetcies*, 26 Feb 1821 , F R S   He *m* 24 March 1824, at St Marylebone, Charlotte yst. of the three daughters and coheirs of Thomas Andrew KNIGHT, of Downton Castle, co Hereford (*d* 11 May 1838, in his 80th year), by Frances, da of H FELTON   She *d* 14 May 1842, aged 41, at Downton Hall.   He *d* 22 May 1856, aged 67   Will pr. Aug 1856   Both were *bur* at Rouse Lench

XI and III 1856.   SIR CHARLES HENRY ROUSE-BOUGHTON, Bart
[1641 and 1791], of Downton Hall aforesaid, s and h , *b* 16 Jan 1825, at Henley Hall, near Ludlow, and *bap* at Bitterley, Salop , ed. at Harrow , an officer in the 52d foot, 1843-50 ; *suc to the Baronetcies*, 22 May 1856 , Capt 10th Shropshire Rifle Volunteers, 1860 , Sheriff for Salop, 1860   He *m* 23 Aug. 1852, at Thenford, co. Northampton, Mary Caroline, 2d da of John Michael SEVERNE, of Thenford aforesaid and of Wallop Hall, Salop, by Anna Maria, da of Edmund Meysey WIGLEY, of Shakenhurst, co Worcester   She was *b* 12 Dec 1832

Family Estates —These, in 1883, consisted of 5,456 acres in Shropshire, valued at £7,645 a year ; in 1878 the amount was 4,891 acres in Shropshire, and 14 (valued at £58 a year) in Herefordshire, it being added that " the return mentions some property in Worcestershire, since sold," the total, at that date, being 4,905 acres, valued at £6,000 a year , in 1876 the amount stands as 4,891 acres in Shropshire, 2,325 (valued at £3,170) in Worcestershire, and 14 in Herefordshire, the total (at that date) being 7,230 acres, valued at £9,170 a year   *Residence.*—Downton Hall, near Ludlow, Salop

---

(*a*) His illegit da , Eliza, *m* Sir George Charles Braithwaite, 2d Bart [1802], who took the name of Boughton.
(*b*) These estates came to him, 30 Dec. 1768, under the will of his cousin, Thomas Phillips-Rouse (formerly Thomas Phillips) of Rouse Lench aforesaid ; see p 108, note " c."

WOLRYCHE.
cr. 4 Aug 1641(ᵃ),
ex. 25 June 1723

I   1641   " THOMAS WOLRYCHE, of Dudmaston, co Salop, Knt ,"
s and h of Francis WOLRYCHE, of the same, by Margaret, da of
George BROMLEY, of Hatton, in the said county, was *b* at Worfield in 1598 , suc.
his father in 1614 , ed at Cambridge Univ , admitted to Inner Temple, 11 Oct
1615 , M P for Wenlock, 1621-22, 1624-25 and 1625 , was Col in the Royal Army,
during the Civil Wars , a zealous supporter of the King by whom he was made
Governor of Bridgnorth , was *Knighted* at Whitehall, 22 July 1641, and *cr* a *Baronet,*
as above, 4 Aug 1641   He was twice sequestered, once imprisoned and was, 11 March
1647, fined £730   He *m*, in or before 1628, Ursula, da of Thomas OTLEY, of Pich-
ford, Salop by Mary, da of Roger GIFFORD, M D , Physician to Queen Elizabeth
He *d* 4 and was *bur* 9 July 1668 at St Chad's, Shrewsbury, in his 71st year.   M I
at Quatt, co Salop   Will dat. 21 Dec. 1662 to 2 Feb 1662/3, pr. 7 Nov 1668, by
Ursula, his widow

II   1668   SIR FRANCIS WOLRYCHE, Bart [1641], of Dudmaston
aforesaid, s and h., *b.* about 1627, was aged 35 in 1663 [*Visit of Salop*],
suc to the Baronetcy, 4 July 1668   He *m* Elizabeth, 1st da of Sir Walter
WROTTESLEY, 1st Bart. [1642], by Mary, da of Ambrose GREY, of Enville, co Stafford
He *d* s p m. 12 and was *bur* 15 June 1688 at Quatt, in his 62d year   M.I.   Admon.
3 Sep 1689   The will of his widow dat 7 April 1711, pr 2 May 1713

III.   1688   SIR THOMAS WOLRYCHE, Bart [1642], of Dudmaston
aforesaid nephew and h male, being 1st s and h of John WOLRYCHE,
of Dudmaston, by Mary, da of the Rev. Matthew GRIFFITH, D D , Chaplain to
Charles I, which John (who was *cr.* D.C.L of Oxford 1670, and who *d* before June
1688, his admon being dat 8 April 1690) was yr s of the 1st Bart.   He was *bap.*
14 April 1672, at Quatt and *suc to the Baronetcy,* 12 June 1688   He *m* 26 Nov 1689,
Elizabeth, 1st da of George WELD, of Willey, Salop, Lieut. of the Tower, by Mary,
da of Sir Peter PINDAR, 1st Bart [1662]   He *d.* 3 and was *bur* 6 May 1701, at Quatt,
aged 29   M I   His widow (who survived him 64 years) *d* 1 and was *bur* 5 April
1765, at Quatt, aged 93   M I   Will dat. 12 June 1753, pr 26 April 1765

IV.   1701,   SIR JOHN WOLRYCHE, Bart [1641], of Dudmaston aforeto   said, only s and h , *b* about 1691, *suc to the Baronetcy,* 3 May 1701
1723.   Sheriff of Salop, 1715-16   He *d* unm , being drowned in the Severn
while endeavouring to cross it on horseback, 25 and was *bur* 26 June
1723, at Quatt, aged 32, when the *Baronetcy* became *extinct*   M I.   Will dat
15 Aug 1722, pr 26 July 1723 (ᵇ)

PRYSE, *or* PRICE:
cr 9 Aug 1641 ;(ᶜ)
ex. 1694

I.   1641.   " RICHARD PRYSE, of Gogarthan [*i e*, Gogerddan], co
Cardigan, Knt ," s and h of Sir John PRYSE, of the same, by Mary,
da. of Sir Henry BROMLEY, of Shawardine Castle, co Salop, was, having previously
(after 1639) been *Knighted, cr* a *Baronet,* as above, 9 Aug 1641 (ᵉ)   He was

---

(ᵃ) The patent is not enrolled. The date here given is that in Dugdale's *Catalogue*
See *Memorandum* on p 84   The date of the signet bill is 2 August 1641.

(ᵇ) The Dudmaston estates were held by his mother and sisters till the death of
the survivor of the latter, Mary Wolryche, spinster, 21 June 1771, in her 78th year,
under whose will they devolved for 4 years on Lieut. Col Thomas Weld, and, at his
death in 1774, on William Whitmore, great grandson of Richard Whitmore, of
Slaughter, co Gloucester, by Anne, sister of George Weld, her maternal grandfather
In that family (which has no descent from that of Wolryche) they still remain

(ᶜ) The patent is not enrolled   The date here given is that in Dugdale's *Catalogue*
See *Memorandum* on p 84   The date of the signet bill is 5 August 1641.

Sheriff of Cardiganshire, 1639-40 ; was M.P thereof, Aug 1646, till secluded in Dec. 1648. He *m.* firstly, Hester, 5th da of the well known Sir Hugh MIDDLETON, 1st Bart [1622], by his 2d wife, Elizabeth, da and coheir of John OLMSTEAD She was *bap.* 10 Jan. 1612/3, at St. Matthew's, Friday street, London He *m* secondly, Mary, widow of Sir Anthony VANDYKE (the famous painter, who *d* Dec. 1641), da of the Hon. Patrick RUTHVEN, yr s of William, 1st EARL OF GOWRIE [S]. She *d* before him Her admon 8 May 1651 and 12 Jan 1651/2 He was *bur.* 21 Oct. 1651 in Westm Abbey Admon 27 Nov. 1651

II. 1651.   SIR RICHARD PRYSE, Bart [1641], of Gogerddan afore-
            said, 1st s and h. by 1st wife , *suc to the Baronetry* in Oct 1651,
was Sheriff of Cardiganshire, 1656 57 He *d.* s p and probably unm

III 1680?   SIR THOMAS PRYSE, Bart [1641], of Gogerddan aforesaid,
            br of the whole blood and h was Sheriff of Cardiganshire (as
" Esq ") 1675 76 , *suc to the Baronetcy* on the death of his brother. He *d* s.p., probably unm , in May 1682 Will pr. 1682

IV. 1682,   SIR CARBERY PRYSE, Bart [1641] of Gogerddan aforeto   said, nephew and h , being only s and h of Carbery PRYSE, by
1694.   Hester, da of Sir Bulstrode WHITLOCK, which Carbery last named
            was yr br., of the whole blood, to the 3d and 2d Barts , *suc. to the*
Baronetcy in May 1682 In 1690, mines of immense value were discovered on his estate, as to the working of which he obtained two acts of Parl He *d* s p, probably unm., in 1694, when the *Baronetcy* became *extinct* (a). Will pr. Jan 1694 [1694/5 ?], revoked and admon granted, 8 Aug 1696, to his mother, Hester SCAWEN, *alias* PRYSE

CAREW

cr. 9 Aug 1641(b),

ex , presumably, 24 March 1748 ,

but *assumed* after that date

I 1641.   " RICHARD CAREW, of Antony, co Cornwall, Esq ," s.
            and h of Richard CAREW, of the same (the celebrated antiquary and
the author of the ' Survey of Cornwall ") by Julian, da of John ARUNDELL, of Trerice, co Cornwall, was *b* about 1580; matric at Oxford (Merton Coll.), 20 Oct 1594, aged 14 , admitted to Middle Temple, 1597 , suc his father, 6 Nov 1620 , was M P for Cornwall, 1614, and for St Michael's, 1621-22, and was *cr* a Baronet, as above, 9 Aug 1641 (b) He *m* firstly, in or before 1609, Bridget, da of John CHUDLEIGH, of Ashton, Devon, by Elizabeth, da of Sir George SPEKE He *m* secondly, 18 Aug 1621, at Petrockstowe, Grace, da of Robert ROLLE, of Heanton, Devon, by Joane, da of Thomas HELE, of Fleet, in that county He was *bur* 14 March 1642/3 [presumably] at Antony aforesaid

II. 1643   SIR ALEXANDER CAREW, Bart. [1641], of Antony afore-
            said, s and h by 1st wife, *b* 30 Aug and *bap* 1 Sep 1609 at Antony,
being aged 10 at the Visit. of Devon, 1620 , M P for Cornwall, 1640, till disabled 4 Sep. 1643, and, at that time, a great supporter of the Parl measures , *suc to the Baronetcy*, 14 March 1642/3 He agreed to surrender the isle of St Nicholas, near Plymouth, to the royal forces, but was discovered, committed to the Tower of London, 5 Dec. 1643, and condemned " for adhering to the King and betraying his trust " and was executed on Tower Hill, 23 Dec. 1644, being *bur.* the same day at Hackney, aged 35. His estate was freed from sequestration, 27 Nov 1645 Will dat

(a) The estates passed eventually to his kinsmen of the name of Pryse, of whom Lewis Pryse *d* s p m s 12 March 1798, leaving Pryse Loveden (son of his da. Margaret) as his grandson and heir who assumed the surname of Pryse, and whose grandson was *cr. a Baronet* in 1866

(b) See p 124, note " c," *sub* " Pryse "

20 to 22 and pr 28 Dec 1644 He had *m.*, 17 Dec 1631 at Petrockstowe (Lic
Exeter), Jane, sister of Grace Rolle abovenamed, being da of Robert ROLLE, by
Joan, da of Thomas HELE, all abovenamed   His widow, who was *bap* 25 Jan
1605/6, at Petrockstowe, was *bur* 28 April 1679 at Antony   Will dat 18 Nov.
1678, pr 3 Nov 1679

III   1644   SIR JOHN CAREW, Bart [1641] of Antony aforesaid, s.
and h , *b* about 1633, *suc to the Baronetcy*, 23 Dec 1644, M P for
Cornwall, 1660, for Bodmin, 1661-79, for Lostwithiel, 1679, 1679 81 and 1681 ; for
Cornwall, again, 1689-90, and for Saltash, 1690 till death , el Sheriff of Cornwall,
Nov 1688, but did not act   He *m* firstly, before 8 Aug 1664, Sarah, da
of Anthony HUNGERFORD, of Farley Castle, Wilts   She who was living at that
date, *d* s p.m (a) He *m* secondly, Elizabeth, 1st da of Richard NORTON, of Southwick,
Hants   She, who *d* s p, was *bur*. 14 Aug. 1679 at Antony   He *m* thirdly, in or
before 1682, Mary, da. of Sir William MORICE, 1st Bart [1661], of Werrington, by
Gertrude, da of Sir John BAMFYLDE, 1st Bart [1641]   He was *bur* 6 Aug 1692, at
Antony   Will dat 29 Oct 1691, pr 7 Dec 1692   His widow was *bur* there,
8 June 1698

IV   1692   SIR RICHARD CAREW, Bart [1641], of Antony aforesaid,
s and h , by 3d wife, *bap* 2 March 1683, at Antony, *suc to the
Baronetcy* 10 Aug 1692   He *d* uom in 1703 or 1704   Will dat. 24 June, 1703, pr.
9 May 1704

V   1704 ?   SIR WILLIAM CAREW, Bart. [1641], of Antony aforesaid,
br of the whole blood and h , *b*. about 1689, matric at Oxford (Ex
Coll) 4 Sep 1707, aged 18, having previously *suc. to the Baronetcy*, was M P for Saltash
1711 13, and for Cornwall (six Parls) 1713 till death , was *cr* D C L of Oxford,
22 May 1736   He *m* (Lic. Worc , 31 Dec 1713, he 24 and she 18) Anne only da
and h of Gilbert (COVENTRY), 4th EARL OF COVENTRY, by his 1st wife, Dorothy, da
of Sir William KEYT, 2d Bart [1660]   She *d* before him   He *d* 8 March 1743/4
Admon 27 April 1744, 11 Aug 1750, and 22 Dec 1762.

VI   1744,   SIR COVENTRY CAREW, Bart [1641], of Antony aforesaid,
to   only s and h , *b*. about 1717, matric at Oxford (Balliol Coll) 21 Feb.
1748.   1734/5, aged 18 , *suc to the Baronetcy*, 8 March 1743/4, was M P for
Cornwall 1744 till death   He *m*. 1 July 1738 at St George the
Martyr, Queen Square, Midx , his cousin, Mary, only da of Sir Coplestone Warwick
BAMFYLDE, 2d Bart , [1641] by Gertrude, sister of the whole blood of Sir William
CAREW, 5th Bart , abovenamed   He *d*. s p 24 March 1748, when the *Baronetcy*
probably became *extinct*   Will pr 1748   His widow *m* before 1750 Francis BULLER,
of Morval, Cornwall (who *d* s p. 1766) and *d* before Dec 1762   Will pr 1763

According to Burke's *Extinct Baronetage*, on the death, in 1748, of the
6th Bart the Baronetcy reverted to his kinsman

SIR ALEXANDER CAREW, (who was "in Holy Orders") in right of his descent
from " Thomas CAREW, of Harrowbear, 2d s of Sir Alexander, the 2d Bart.,"
and that at his death without issue it became extinct.
This, apparently, is a mistake. Thomas Carew, abovenamed, had, by Wilmot
his wife, two sons, of whom the yr son, John Carew, living 1691, *d* s p ,
while the elder son, Alexander, living 1678 and 1691, who was in Holy Orders
and Vicar of St. Wenn, *d* (also) s p in 1709 (b)   This Alexander appears to
be the person presumed (erroneously) to be living in 1748, and consequently
then entitled to the Baronetcy   Sir Thomas Carew, co Bailey of Bailey, co Devon (a
yr s of the 1st Bart by his 2d wife), had by Elizabeth, da of John Cooper,
several children, on some of whose descendants, if such there were, the
Baronetcy is more likely to have devolved

(a) Jane, her eldest da., *m* Jonathan Rashleigh, whose da and h , Sarah, *m* the Rev
Carolus Pole and was grandmother of Reginald Pole who, after the death, s p m, of
John Carew, of Camerton, inherited the estate of Antony and took the name of Carew
(under the will of the 6th Bart.), being ancestor of the family of Pole-Carew
(b) Vivian's *Visitations of Cornwall*.

CASTLETON.
cr 9 Aug 1641 , (ᵃ)
ex 17 Nov 1810.

I   1641.   "WILLIAM CASTLETON, of St Edmondsbury, co Suffolk, Esq," s and h of William CASTLETON, of the same and of Clopton Hall in Woolpit and Rattlesden in that co , by Anne, da of William HILL, of St. Edmundsbury aforesaid, was b about 1590 ; suc his father 24 May 1616, being then aged 26, and was cr a Baronet, as above, 9 Aug 1641 ,(ᵃ) Sheriff of Suffolk, 1641-42 He m (—), widow of (—) BACON, of Hesset, co. Suffolk da of (—) MASSAM of the said county He d about 1643.

II   1643?   SIR JOHN CASTLETON, Bart [1641], of Shipdam co Norfolk, and of Sturston, co Suffolk, s and h , suc to the Baronetcy about 1643 , Sheriff of Suffolk, 1660 61 He m 26 April 1642, at Sturston,(ᵇ) Margaret, da and h of Robert MORSE, of Hoo Margarets in Sturston aforesaid, by Margaret, da of Henry BEDINGFIELD He was bur 20 Nov. 1677 at Sturston His widow was bur there 12 Aug. 1702

III   1677.   SIR JOHN CASTLETON, Bart [1641], of Sturston Hall, in Sturston aforesaid, s and h ; bap 4 Aug. 1644, at Sturston ; ed at Botesdale and Eye schools; admitted to Caius Coll , Cambridge, as Fellow Commoner, 29 June 1661, aged 16 ; admitted to Gray's Inn, 2 May 1662 ; suc. to the Baronetcy in Nov 1677 , el Sheriff of Suffolk, in Nov 1686, but did not act He m. 8 Nov. 1677, at Bardwell, Suffolk, Bridget, sister of Sir Charles CROFTS READ, of Bardwell, da. of Thomas READ, of Wrangle, co Lincoln, by Bridget, da. of Sir Charles CROFTS, of Bardwell aforesaid He d s p. and was bur 14 June 1705, at Sturston Will pr March 1706 His widow, who was bap at Bardwell, 3 Jan 1649/50, was bur 24 March 1726, at Sturston aforesaid

IV.   1705   SIR ROBERT CASTLETON, Bart [1641], of Sturston Hall aforesaid, br and h , bap. 6 Nov. 1659, at Sturston , suc to the Baronetcy in June 1705 He d unm

V.   1710?   SIR PHILIP CASTLETON, Bart [1641], of Sturston Hall aforesaid, br and h ; bap. 26 July 1663, at Sturston , suc to the Baronetcy on the death of his brother. He m 6 May 1708, at Sturston, Elizabeth, da of Osborn CLARKE, of that place He d s p s and was bur 1 Aug 1724, at Sturston, aged 61. His widow was bur there 13 Nov. 1748.

VI   1724.   SIR CHARLES CASTLETON, Bart [1641], Rector of Gillingham, Norfolk, cousin and h , being surv s and h. of William CASTLETON, of Oakley, co Suffolk, by Sarah, da. of (—) SIDNEY, or SYDNOR,(ᶜ) which William was 2d s of the 1st Bart He was bap at Sturston, 4 Sep 1659 , ed at Thetford and Bury schools ; admitted to Caius Coll , Cambridge, as sizar, 16 April 1678, aged 18 , scholar, 1678-83, B.A., 1682 , M A , 1685 ; took Holy Orders , Rector of Gillingham aforesaid, 1692-1745 , suc to the Baronetcy, 1 Aug 1724 He m in 1693, Elizabeth, 2d da of Edward TAVERNER, of St Olave's Abbey, in Heringfleet, Suffolk He d. Sep. 1745, aged 86.

VII.   1745   SIR CHARLES CASTLETON, Bart. [1641], s. and h , suc to the Baronetcy in Sep 1745 and d unm 22 Oct. 1749

(ᵃ) The patent is not enrolled The date here given is that in Dugdale's *Catalogue.* See *Memorandum* on p 84 The date of the signet bill is 7 August 1641

(ᵇ) There are copious extracts from the Parish Register of Sturston in the *East Anglian,* vol iii, which illustrate this pedigree.

(ᶜ) They were m 7 Aug 1655, at Sturston

VIII 1749   SIR JOHN CASTLETON, Bart. [1641], Vicar of Gorleston and Hopton, Suffolk, br and h ; *b*. about 1698, at Gillingham, ed at Woodbridge school, admitted, as sizar, to Caius Coll., Cambridge, Oct. 1715, aged 18 ; scholar, 1715 20 , B A 1720 In Holy Orders , Vicar of Gorleston, Suffolk, 1722 77 , Vicar of Hopton in said county, 1725 77 : *suc to the Baronetcy*, 22 Oct 1749 He *m* but *d* s p , 7 Nov 1777 M I at Gorleston to him and his wife

IX 1777,   SIR WILLIAM CASTLETON, Bart [1641], br and h., *b* about 1701, *suc to the Baronetcy*, 7 Nov 1777 He *m*. (—) He *d*. at Hingham, Norfolk, 16 Jan 1788, aged 87.

X 1788,   SIR JOHN CASTLETON, Bart. [1641], only s and h., *suc.*
Jan   *to the Baronetcy*, 16 Jan 1788, and *d* s p a few months later, 11 June 1788

XI 1788   SIR EDWARD CASTLETON, Bart [1641], Rector of Thorn-
June.   ham cum Holme, Norfolk, uncle and h , *b* about 1706 at Gillingham, ed at Beccles and Woodbridge schools, admitted as Sizar to Caius Coll., Cambridge 1725, aged 18 , B A , 1729 , in Holy Orders , Rector of Thornham aforesaid, 1761-94 , *suc to the Baronetcy*, 11 June 1788 He *m* (—) He *d* 15 Oct 1794 in his 89th year. M I at Ringstead

XII. 1794,   SIR EDWARD CASTLETON, Bart [1641], of Lynn, Norfolk,
to   s and h , *suc to the Baronetcy*, 15 Oct 1794, but being in reduced
1810   circumstances, did not for some time assume the title. He *d* s.p. 17 Nov 1810, aged 58, when the *Baronetcy* became *extinct*. Will pr

1810.

CHOLMLEY, *or* CHOLMELEY
cr 10 Aug. 1641([a]),
ex 9 Jan 1688/9

I. 1641   " HUGH CHOLMELEY, of Whitby, co York, Knt ," s and h of Sir Richard CHOLMELEY, *or* CHOLMLEY, of the same ([b]) by his 1st wife Susanna, da. of John LEGARD, of Ganton, co York, was *b* 22 July 1600, at Roxby, near Thornton ; *Knighted* at Whitehall, 29 May 1626 , *suc* his father (who *d* aged 51), 3 Sept. 1631 , was M P for Scarborough, 1624-25, 1625, 1626, April to May 1640, and 1640 till disabled in April 1643, and was *cr* a *Baronet*, as above, 10 Aug. 1641 ([a]) He was, in 1643, "for the public liberties," and fought against the Royalists at Malton and Gainsborough, but in that year declared for the King, by whom he was made General of the Northern parts of England and Governor of Scarborough Castle, which he held for more than a year and only surrendered on highly honourable terms in 1645 His estate was sequestrated and he went into exile until he compounded for £850 on 27 June 1649 ([c]) He *m* 10 Dec 1622, at St Mary Magdalen, Milk Street, London, Elizabeth, 1st da. of Sir William TWYSDEN, 1st Bart. [1611], of Peckham, by Anne, da of Sir Moyle FINCH, 1st Bart [1611] She, with whom he had £3,000 portion, was *b*. 18 Aug 1600, *d* 17 April 1655, in Bedford Street, Covent Garden in her 55th year He *d* 20 Nov 1657 in his 58th year Both were *bur* at East Peckham, co Kent M I His will pr Nov 1660

II 1657   SIR WILLIAM CHOLMLEY, *or* CHOLMELEY, Bart [1641], of Whitby Abbey in Whitby aforesaid, s and h , *b* Dec 1625 and *bap.* at East Peckham, Kent, *suc to the Baronetcy*, 20 Nov 1657 He *m* firstly, 17 Aug 1654, Katharine, yst. da of Sir John HOTHAM, 1st Bart. [1622], by his 5th wife, Sarah, da of Thomas ANLABY, of Etton, co York She *d* s p s in childbed, 15 June

---

([a]) The patent is not enrolled. The date here given is that in Dugdale's *Catalogue* See *Memorandum* on p. 84. The date of the signet bill is 7 Aug 1641

([b]) In *Mis Gen et Her*, Orig. Series, vol ii, p 218, is a good account of this family.

([c]) One hundred copies of his life and adventures, with particulars of his family (from a MS. in his handwriting, in possession of Nathaniel Cholmley, of Whitby and Howsham, in 1787) were printed in 1870.

1655 and was *bur* at Whitby   He *m* secondly, April 1657, Katharine, da. of John SAVILE, of Methley, co. York, by his 2d wife, Margaret, da. of Sir Henry GARRAWAY, Alderman, and sometime 1639-40, Lord Mayor of London   He *d* at Mitcham, co. Surrey, 11 Oct 1663, and was *bur* at East Peckham aforesaid   M I   Nunc. will dat 11 Oct, pr. 13 Nov. 1663.   His widow *m* after July 1665, Sir Nicholas STRODE, of Cnipsted House, Kent, and *d.* in 1710

III. 1663.   SIR HUGH CHOLMLEY, Bart. [1641], of Whitby Abbey
aforesaid, only s and h., *suc to the Baronetcy*, 11 Oct 1663   He *d* in infancy at Mitcham, Surrey, 2 July 1665, aged 3 years, and was *bur* at East Peckham aforesaid.   M.I   Admon 28 July 1665'

IV. 1665,   SIR HUGH CHOLMLEY, Bart [1641], of Whitby Abbey
to   aforesaid, uncle and h., *b* 2? July 1632 at Fyling Hall, co. York, *suc*
1689   *to the Baronetcy*, 2 July 1665.   In 1665 he was Governor of Tangier, in Morocco, where he resided many years and directed the building of the mole there , was M.P for Northampton, 1679, for Thirsk, 1685-87.   He *m* 19 Feb 1665/6, at Hamerton, co Hunt, Anne, 1st da. of Spencer (COMPTON), 2d EARL OF NORTHAMPTON, by Mary, da of Sir Francis BEAUMONT   He *d.* s.p.m (a) at Whitby 9 Jan 1688/9, aged 56, when the *Baronetcy* became *extinct*   His widow *d* there 26 May 1705, aged 68   Both were *bur* in Whitby Church.

SPRING.

cr. 11 August 1641(b),

ex. 17 August 1769.

I 1641   "WILLIAM SPRING, of Pakenham, co. Suffolk, Esq," 2d
but only surv s and h of Sir William SPRING,(c) of the same, by Elizabeth, sister of Sir Thomas SMITH, 1st Bart. [1661] of Hill Hall, da. of Sir William SMITH, of Theydon, co. Essex, was *bap* 13 March 1613, at Stanton All Saints, suc his father, 1638 · was Sheriff of Suffolk, 1640-41, and was *cr* a *Baronet*, as above, 11 Aug 1641.(h)   He was a Parliamentarian, serving on several important committees, 1643-46 ; was M P for Bury St Edmunds 1646 till secluded, Dec. 1648, for Suffolk, 1654 till death in that year   He *m*, in or before 1642, Elizabeth, sister of Sir Nicholas L'ESTRANGE, 1st Bart [1629], da of Sir Hamon L'ESTRANGE, of Hunstanton, co Norfolk, by Alice, da and coheir of Richard STUBBS.   He *d* 17 Dec 1654, and was *bur* at Pakenham   Will dat 18 Oct. 1653, pr 1655.   His widow, who was *b.* 10 March 1613, *d* 21 March 1678, and was *bur* there

II 1654.   SIR WILLIAM SPRING Bart. [1641], of Pakenham afore-
said, 1st and only surv s and h , *b* May 1642 , *suc. to the Baronetcy*, 17 Dec 1654   Sheriff of Suffolk, 1674-75 ; M P. thereof, 1679-81 and 1681.   He *m.* firstly (Lic Fac., 11 Oct 1661 both aged 21), Mary, da of Dudley (NORTH), 4th LORD NORTH DE KIRTLING, by Anne, da. of Sir Charles MONTAGU.   She *d.*, in childbirth, 23 Oct 1662 and was *bur* at Pakenham.   He *m* secondly, in or before 1670, Sarah, da of Sir Robert CORDELL, 1st Bart [1660], by Margaret, da. and coheir of Sir Edmund WRIGHT   He *d.* 30 April and was *bur* 3 May 1684, at Pakenham   Will pr 1684   His widow *d* 2 Aug 1689 and was *bur* there

---

(a) Mary, the only child that survived infancy, *b* 21 Sep 1667, *m* , for her first husband, 16 Oct 1683, at Whitby, her cousin, Nathaniel Cholmley, of London, merchant, who *d.* 20 April 1687 (in her father's lifetime), by whom she was ancestress of the family of Cholmley, of Whitby and Howsham, co. York, extinct in the male line, March 1791

(b) The patent is not enrolled   The date here given is that in Dugdale's *Catalogue*. See *Memorandum* on p 84.   The date of the signet bill is 7 Aug 1641.

(c) In J. J. Howard's *Visitations of the County of Suffolk* (vol. i, pp 166-206) is a good account of this family.

S

III 1684. SIR THOMAS SPRING, Bart. [1641], of Pakenham aforesaid, 1st surv s and h , by 2d wife, *b.* 1 and *bap.* 12 Dec 1672, at
Pakenham, *suc to the Baronetcy*, 30 April 1684 He *m.* 28 May 1691, at Rushbrooke,
co Suffolk, Merolina, 5th da and coheir of Thomas (JERMYN), 2d BARON JERMYN OF
ST EDMUNDSBURY, by Mary, da of Henry MERRY He *d* 5 and was *bur* 6 April
1704, at Pakenham, aged 31. Admon 20 Sep 1710 and 28 Nov 1727 His widow
m as his 2d wife, Sir William GAGE, 2d Bart [1662] of Hengrave, co Suffolk, who *d*
8 Feb. 1726/7 She *d* at Hengrave and was *bur* 5 Sep 1727, at Pakenham Admon
28 Nov. 1727

IV. 1704. SIR WILLIAM SPRING, Bart [1641], of Pakenham afore-
said, only surv. s and h , *bap* Jan 1696/7, at Pakenham, *suc. to the
Baronetcy*, 5 April 1704. He *d* unm and was *bur* 22 March 1735/6, at Pakenham
Admon. 9 April 1737 and Oct 1811 (ª)

V. 1736. SIR JOHN SPRING, Bart. [1641], of Coney Weston, co.
Suffolk, uncle and h male, *b* 14 and *bap* 15 Jan 1673/4, at Pakenham,
suc to the Baronetcy in March 1736 He *m* 24 June 1704, at Gazeley, co Suffolk,
Mary [or Elizabeth], da of Joseph NIGHTINGALE, of Cambridge He was *bur.* 30 May
1740 at Pakenham, aged 66

VI. 1740, SIR JOHN SPRING, Bart [1641], s. and h , *suc to the*
to *Baronetcy* in May 1740, resided in Bolton street, Piccadilly He *m*
1769 Anne, da of Charles Barlow, of Worksop, Notts He *d.* s p in Vere
street, 17 and was *bur* 25 Aug 1769, at St Marylebone, when the
Baronetcy became *extinct* Will pr 1769 His widow was *bur.* there 5 Jan. 1776
Will pr. Jan. 1776

TREVOR·
cr. 11 Aug 1641(ᵇ) ,
ex 5 Feb 1676.

I. 1641, " THOMAS TREVOR, of Enfield, co Middlesex, Esq ," only
to s. and h ap of Sir Thomas TREVOR, one of the Barons of the Court
1676 of Exchequer (1625-49), by his 1st wife, Prudence (*d* 1614), da of
Henry BUTLER, was *b.* about 1612 , was M.P. for Monmouth, 1640
till void, 29 Nov 1644 , for Tregony, Feb. 1647 till excluded, Dec 1648, and was *cr*
a Baronet, as above, 11 Aug 1641(ᵇ), was *Knighted* at Whitehall 12 Dec following ,
was Auditor of the Duchy of Lancaster, and suc his father, 21 Dec 1656 At the
coronation of Charles II, 23 April 1661, he was made K B He *m* firstly (Lic. Lond ,
15 May 1632, he 20 and she 15), Anne, da of Robert JENNER, of St. Leonard's, Foster
Lane, London He *m* secondly (Lic Fac 16 July 1647, he 35 and she 24), Mary,
da of Samuel FORTREY of Kew, co Surrey, by Catherine, da of John DE LATFEUR,
of Heynalt. He *d.* s p 5 Feb. 1676, when the *Baronetcy* became *extinct* (ᶜ) Will pr
1677. His widow *m* (as the 2d of his three wives) Lieut -Gen the Hon Sir Francis
COMPTON, of Hamerton, co Huntingdon, who *d.* 20 Dec 1716, aged 87, and was *bur*
at Fulham. She *d* between June 1694 and April 1696 Her will, in which she directs
to be *bur.* at Leamington-Hastings, co. Warwick, dat. 1 June 1694 pr. 20 Jan 1698/9

(ª) The estates devolved on his sisters and coheirs, of whom (1) Merolina, *m.*
Thomas Disciphne and had issue, and (2) Mary *m* Rev. John Symonds, D.D., and had
issue.

(ᵇ) The patent is not enrolled The date here given is that in Dugdale's *Catalogue.*
See *Memorandum* on p 84 The date of the signet bill is *also* 11 Aug 1641

(ᶜ) He settled the inheritance of the estate of Leamington-Hastings, co Warwick
(which had been purchased by his father) on his cousin, Sir Charles Wheler, 2d Bart.
[1660], who was s. and h. of William Wheler, by Eleanor, da. and h. of Edward
Puleston and Winifred his wife, only sister of Sir Thomas Trevor, his father, which
Eleanor (who *d.* 1 June 1678, aged 85) survived the testator by a few years.

OWEN :
cr. 11 Aug 1641(ᵃ),
afterwards, 1844-51, OWEN-BARLOW,
ex. 25 Feb. 1851.

I. 1641. "HUGH OWEN, of Orielton, co. Pembroke, Esq.," s
and h of John OWEN, of the same, who was yr s of Sir Hugh OWEN,
of Bodowen, co. Anglesey and of Orielton aforesaid, by Elizabeth, da. and h. of George
WYRRIOT, of Orielton, was M P for Pembroke, 1626 and 1628-29, for Haverfordwest,
April to May 1640; for Pembroke (again), Nov 1640 till secluded in Dec 1648, and
for Pembrokeshire, 1660 He was Sheriff of Pembrokeshire, 1633-34, 1653-54, and
1663 64, and was *cr. a Baronet,* as above, 11 Aug 1641,(ᵃ) having apparently being
Knighted (as a Baronet) the day before His estate was sequestrated 6 May 1651
He m firstly, Frances, da of Sir John PHILIPPS, 1st Bart [1621], of Picton, by Anne,
da and coheir of Sir John PERROT, Lord Deputy of Ireland He m secondly,
Catharine, widow of John LEWIS, of Prescoed, da of Evan LLOYD, of Yale, co-
Denbigh He d 1670 Will pr June 1671

II 1670 SIR HUGH OWEN, Bart. [1641], of Orielton aforesaid, 1st
surv. s and h, by 2d wife, was b about 1645, matric. at Oxford (Ch
Ch), 7 Dec. 1660, aged 15; admitted to Inner Temple 1672, *suc to the Baronetcy* in
1670. M P for Pembroke, 1676-79, for Pembrokeshire (four Parls), 1679-81 and
1689-95, Sheriff of Anglesey, 1688, but did not act. He m. firstly, Anne, da.
and sole h. of his paternal uncle, Henry OWEN, of Bodowen aforesaid He m
secondly, Catharine, widow of Lewis AMWELL, of Park, da of William GRIFFITH,
of Len, but by her he had no issue He d. 1698/9 Will pr 1699. The admon.
of his widow, as of "Long Shipping, co Pembroke," 9 June 1699, was granted to
her son "William Lewis Amwell, Esq"

III. 1699 SIR ARTHUR OWEN, Bart [1641], of Orielton and Bodowen
aforesaid, and of Llansillin, co Denbigh, s and h by 1st wife, *suc.*
to the Baronetcy in 1699; was M P for Pembrokeshire (five Parls), 1695—1705, for
Pembroke, 1708-10 and 1710 till unseated in 1712, for Pembrokeshire, again, 1715-22
and 1722-27 Lord Lieutenant of Pembrokeshire He voted for the Hanoverian
succession, thereby making the number equal, which, by the vote of Mr Rice (M P. for
Carmarthenshire), was turned into a majority He is said to have been offered a Peerage
by George I He m Emma, only da of Sir William WILLIAMS, 1st Bart [1688], of
Anglesey, sometime Speaker of the House of Commons, by Margaret, da and coheir
of Watkin KYFFIN, of Glascoed, co Denbigh He d 6 June 1753 Will pr 1754

IV 1753. SIR WILLIAM OWEN, Bart. [1641], of Orielton and Bodowen aforesaid, s and h, b about 1697, matric at Oxford (New
Coll) 16 June 1713, aged 16 M P for Pembroke, 1722-47, for Pembrokeshire,
1747 61, and for Pembroke again 1761 74; *suc to the Baronetcy,* 6 June 1753;
Lord Lieutenant of Pembrokeshire He m firstly, Elizabeth, da and sole h. of
Thomas LLOYD, of Grove, co Pembroke She d s p m He m secondly, Elizabeth,
da of John WILLIAMS, of Chester He d 7 May 1781 Will pr June 1781.

V. 1781. SIR HUGH OWEN, Bart [1641], of Orielton and Bodowen
aforesaid, s and h, by 2d wife, *suc to the Baronetcy,* 7 May 1781, was
M P for Pembrokeshire (four Parls), 1770 till death, being sometime Lord Lieutenant
of that county He m 1775, Anne, da of John COLBY He d 16 Jan. 1786 Will
pr Jan 1786. Will of Dame Anne Owen pr 1823

VI. 1786 SIR HUGH OWEN, Bart [1641], of Orielton and Bodowen
aforesaid, only child and h., b 12 Sep. 1782, ed at Eton, *suc. to the*
Baronetcy, 16 Jan. 1786, matric at Oxford (Ch Ch.) 28 Jan 1801, aged 18; Sheriff
of Pembrokeshire, 1804-05; M P. for Pembroke, 1809, till his death in that year.
He d. unm. 8 Aug. 1809 Will pr. 1809 (ᵇ)

(ᵃ) This patent, unlike many of the preceding ones (including all those in the month
of July) is enrolled, as are also many more in and after the month of Aug 1641

(ᵇ) He devised Orielton and other family estates to his second cousin, John LORD,
who took the name of OWEN, and was *cr. a Baronet,* 1813. This John was s and h
of Joseph Lord, by Corbetta, sister of Sir Arthur Owen, 7th Bart., da of Lieut

VII 1809   Sir Arthur Owen, Bart [1641], cousin and h male, being s and h. of Lieut General John Owen, by Anne, his cousin, da of Charles Owen, of Nash, which John, who d Jan 1776, was 2d s. of the 3d Bart. He, who was a Colonel in the army and sometime Adjutant General in the East Indies, *suc. to the Baronetcy*, 8 Aug 1809 He d. unm. 4 Jan 1817, in his 77th year.

VIII 1817,   Sir William Owen, *afterwards* (1844-51) Owen- to Barlow, Bart [1641], of Lawrenny, co. Pembroke, nephew 1851 and h , being s and h of Brig -Gen William Owen, by Ann, da of John Tripp, Barrister, which William (who d 1795) was next br. to the late Bart. He was b 11 April 1775 ; was Barrister (1799) and subsequently Bencher of the Middle Temple, Attorney-General of the Carmarthen circuit, and "Postman" of the Court of Exchequer He *suc. to the Baronetcy* (but to none of the Owen estates) 4 Jan 1817 By royal lic., Aug 1844, he took the name of Barlow after that of Owen on succeeding, for life, to th- estate of Lawrenny, on the death of his aunt, Emma Anne, widow of Hugh Barlow, of Lawrenny aforesaid He d. unm 25 Feb 1851, at his chambers in Fig Tree Court, Temple (where he lived more than half-a-century), and was *bur* 1 March, in the Middle Temple vault, Temple church, London, aged 76, when the *Baronetcy*, presumably, became *extinct* (a) Will pr March 1851

CURZON

cr 11 Aug 1641(b) ;

having been previously, 18 June 1636, *cr.* a Baronet [S.],

afterwards, since 1761, Barons Scarsdale

I. 1641   "John Curzon, of Kedleston, co Derby, Baronet of Scotland," 1st s and h of John Curzon, of Kedleston aforesaid, by Millicent, da of Sir Ralph Sacheverell, of Stanton, co. Derby, was b about 1599, matric.

General John Owen (d Jan 1776), a yr s of the 3d Bart. Inasmuch, however, as the said Corbetta had a brother, Brigadier General William Owen (d. 1795), who was father not only of the 8th Bart (who d unm), but of Frances, who m Rev Charles Tripp and had issue, the family of Tripp (and not that of Lord) represented these Baronets

(a) A petition was presented, soon after 1851, to the Crown, by the Rev Henry Tripp, M A , Fellow of Worcester College, Oxford, eldest s of Charles Tripp, D D , Rector of Silverton, Devon, by Frances, sister and coheir (being the only sister who left issue) of Sir William Owen-Barlow, 8th and last Bart [1641], praying that the dignity of a Baronet should be conferred on him "in consideration of his being the heir-in-blood of the ancient Baronets [of Owen] of Orielton," adding that this had been recently done in the cases of Pakington [cr 1846], Barker-Mill [cr 1836], and Mackenzie, afterwards Douglas of Glenbervie [cr. 1831] To this the petitioner thought fit to add several very irrelevant statements, e.g , that his grandfather, the Rev John Tripp, Rector of Spofforth, Yorkshire, was a friend of George (O'Brien), Earl of Egremont, and was the son of Dr Tripp, Barrister at Law, Deputy Recorder of Taunton, the family being traditionally descended "from a scion of the illustrious house of Norfolk, whose arms they bear in addition to the scaling ladder which was substituted for their bend by Henry V, when their name was changed from Howard to Tripp" The ridiculous statements thus set forth by the petitioner failed, naturally enough, to gain him his object. His eldest son, however, Owen Howard Tripp, took by royal licence in 1898 the name of Owen, though he inherited none of the estates of that family, which had been devised to the family of Lord. In the *Times* of (22 or 23 ?) August 1900 he advertised his *intention to assume this Baronetcy* of 1641 [one, it is to be observed, limited to heirs *male* of the body of the grantee] as being grandson of Frances, *sister* of the late Baronet, and consequently his heir, not however stating that, though (through this *female* descent) he was heir *general*, he was *not* the heir *male*, to whom only the succession was limited.

(b) See p. 131, note "a," under "Owen"

at Oxford (Mag Coll), 12 June 1618, aged 18, admitted to Middle Temple, 1620, M.P
for Brackley, 1623-29, for Derbyshire, April to May 1640, and 1640 till secluded in
1648, Sheriff of Derbyshire, 1637-38, having been cr a Baronet of Nova Scotia,
18 June 1636, and subsequently, 11 Aug 1641,(a) a Baronet of England as aforesaid,
after having been Knighted at Whitehall three days previously He was a Parliamentarian, and served on several important committees, 1643-46 He m Patience,
sister of John, 1st BARON CREWE OF STENE, da. of Sir Thomas CREWE, of Stene, co.
Northampton, by Temperance, da and coh of Reginald BRAY, of Stene aforesaid.
She d 30 March 1642 He d. 13 Dec 1686 in his 89th year Will pr Feb 1687,
Both were bur. at Kedleston M I

II   1686   SIR NATHANIEL CURZON, Bart. [E 1641 and S 1636], of
Kedleston aforesaid, only surviving s and h, b about 1640, was a
merchant of London in 1671, suc. to the Baronetcies, 13 Dec 1686 Sheriff of Derbyshire, 1691-92 He m (Lic Vic Gen, 5 July 1671, he about 30 and she about 16)
Sarah, da of William PENN, of Penn, Bucks. He d 4 March 1718/9 Will pr March
1719. His widow d. 4 June 1727/8. Will pr 1728 Both were bur at Kedleston M I

III.   1719.   SIR JOHN CURZON, Bart [E 1641 and S 1636], of Kedleston
aforesaid, s and h, b about 1674; matric. at Oxford (Trin Coll.),
18 July 1690, aged 16; B A 1693, admitted to Inner Temple, 1692, M P for Derbyshire (eight Parls.), 1701-27, suc to the Baronetcies, 4 March 1718/9. He d unm.
6 Aug 1727 and was bur at Kedleston Will dat 10 May 1725, pr 13 Sep. 1727.

IV.   1727   SIR NATHANIEL CURZON, Bart [E 1641 and S 1636], of
Kedleston aforesaid, br. and h, b about 1676, matric. at Oxford
(Trin Coll), 2 July 1692, aged 16, Barrister (Inner Temple), 1700; M P. for Derby,
1713-15, for Clitheroe, 1722-27, and for Derbyshire (four Parls.), 1721-54, suc. to the
Baronetcies, 6 Aug 1727. He m Mary, da and coh of Sir Ralph ASSHETON, 2d Bart
[1660], of Middleton, co Lancaster, by his 1st wife, Mary, da and h of Thomas
VAVASOUR With her he acquired the estate of Whalley Abbey, co Lanc (b) He
d 18 Nov 1758 Admon 5 Dec 1758 and Jan 1789. His widow d 18 March
1776, aged 81, and was bur at Kedleston Her will pr. May 1776

V.   1758   SIR NATHANIEL CURZON, Bart [E 1641 and S 1636], of
Kedleston aforesaid, surviving s and h, b in Queen Square, and bap
19 Jan. 1726/7, at St Geo the Martyr, Midx, matric at Oxford (Ch Ch), 14 Feb
1744/5, and was cr. D C L 14 April 1749, was M P for Clitheroe 1748-54, and for
Derbyshire 1754-61, suc to the Baronetcies, 18 Nov. 1758 He m 27 Oct. 1750 at St.
Geo Han sq., Caroline, 1st da of Charles (COLYEAR), 2d EARL OF PORTMORE [S], by
Juliana, Dow DUCHESS OF LEEDS, da and cohen of Roger HALE. She was living
when he was cr 9 April 1761 BARON SCARSDALE, co. Derby, in which peerage
these Baronetcies then merged and still so continue. See Peerage.

SANDFORD:

cr. 11 Aug 1641(c),

ex 2 April 1723

I   1641.   "THOMAS SANDFORD, of Howgill Castle, co Westmorland, Esq," s and h ap of Sir Richard SANDFORD, of the same
(whose will, dat 2 Oct 1660, was pr 25 Aug 1663), by Anne, da. of Henry
CRACKENTHORPE, of Newbiggin, was v p cr a Baronet, as above, 11 Aug 1641 (c)

(a) See p. 131, note "a," under "Owen"
(b) This estate passed to their 3d and youngest s Assheton Curzon, b 2 Feb 1733,
cr BARON CURZON OF PENN, in 1794 and VISCOUNT CURZON OF PENN, in 1802 He d.
1820 and was suc. by his grandson, Richard William Penn CURZON HOWE, b 11 Dec
1796, cr EARL HOWE, in 1821, who sold the property.
(c) See p 131, note "a" under "Owen" The date of the patent in this instance
is given as 12 Aug but in the Creations, 1483-1646 [ap 47th Rep. D.K Pub.
Records] it is given as 11 Aug 1641

He was M P for Cockermouth, April 1642 till disabled in 1644 ; was a Col in the Royalist Army ; was sequestrated and fined £600, on 18 Jan 1649. He m. Bridget, da of Sir George DALSTON, of Dalston, co Cumberland, by Catherine, da. and coheir of John THORNWORTH, of Halsted, co Leicester. He d v p before 2 Oct 1660. His widow living 25 Aug 1663

II 1655? SIR RICHARD SANDFORD, Bart [1641], of Howgill Castle aforesaid, s and h ; suc. to the Baronetcy on the death of his father He m. Mary (aged 15 in 1666), da. of Sir Francis BOWES, of Thornton, co. Durham, by his third wife, Margaret, da and coheir of Robert DELAVAL He was murdered(a) in Whitefriars 8 and was bur 11 Sep 1675 in the Temple church, London The admon of his widow, as ' of St. George the Martyr, Midx ," is dated 22 June 1734

III. 1675, SIR RICHARD SANDFORD, Bart [1641], of Howgill Castle
to aforesaid, only s and h , b 8 Sep. 1675, said to have been at the hour
1724 of his father's death , suc. to the Baronetcy at his birth; ed at
Christ's College, Cambridge; was M P for Westmorland (three Parls.),
1695-1700 ; for Morpeth, 1701 , for Westmorland, again, 1701-02 , for Morpeth, again
(three Parls), 1705-13, and for Appleby (three Parls), 1713 till death He d unm.
2 April 1723, when the Baronetcy became extinct.(b) Admon. 19 May 1724.

BRIGGES

cr. 12 Aug. 1641 ,(c)

ex , presumably, 27 Oct 1767 ,

but assumed till 1816 or later

I 1641 "MORTON BRIGGES, of Haughton [in Shiffnal], co. Salop,
Esq ," s. and h of Humphrey BRIGGES, of Ernestry Park, near
Ludlow, in that co (Sheriff, 1605), by Anne, 1st da and coheir of Robert MORETON,
of Haughton aforesaid, was b about 1587 , matric. at Oxford (Exeter Coll),
18 March 1602/3, aged 16 , B A, 23 Oct 1605 , admitted to Lincoln's Inn, 1606 ,
and was cr a Baronet, as above, 12 Aug 1641 (c) He m , about 1610, Chrisogena, da
of Edward GREY (living 1601), of Buildwas, Salop She d. aged 97 (d)

II 1650? SIR HUMPHREY BRIGGES, Bart [1641], of Haughton afore-
said, s and h , b about 1615 , admitted to Lincoln's Inn, 1 Nov 1631 , said to have
been Knighted, v p , suc. to the Baronetcy on his father's death between 1641 and
1665 , M P for Wenlock, July 1646 till secluded in Dec. 1648. Sheriff of Salop,
1665-66 He m four times, viz., firstly, about 1630, Elizabeth, da. of Sir Philip Carey,
of Aldenham, Herts (br to Henry, 1st Viscount FALKLAND [S]), by Elizabeth, da.
of Richard BLAND, of Carlton, co. York She was bap 1 Sep 1611, at Great Berkhampstead, Herts. He m secondly, about 1648, Elizabeth, yst da of Sir Richard
WILBRAHAM, 1st Bart [1621], by Grace, da. of Thomas (SAVAGE), 1st VISCOUNT
SAVAGE OF ROCKSAVAGE He m. thirdly (Lic. Fac., 30 June 1665, he 50 and she 47),
Anne, widow of Richard MORETON, of co Montgomery, but by her had no issue He
m fourthly, Magdalen, da of Sir John CORBET, 1st Bart [1627], of Stoke, by Ann,
da of Sir George MAINWARING, but by her, also, he had no issue He was bur
at Shrewsbury, 21 May 1691 Admon 16 June 1691, and 13 Jan 1709/10. His
widow living June 1691, but dead before 1693 Will pr. 10 Nov. 1693

(a) The assassins, Henry Symbal and William Jones, suffered death soon afterwards.
(b) The estates devolved on his only sister, Mary, who had m , between 1694 and
1696, Robert Honywood, of Markshall, Essex, Col of a Reg. of Foot, who was bur.
there 26 Jan 1734/5. She, also, was bur. there 11 Aug. 1745, leaving issue, which
became extinct on the death of her 5th and yst. son, Philip Honywood, 20 Feb 1785,
aged 73
(c) See p. 131, note " a," under " Owen '
(d) Note to Visit. of Salop 1628, pub by the Harleian Society.

III   1691   SIR HUMPHREY BRIGGES, Bart. [1641], of Haughton afore-said, only surv s and h by 2d wife, *b* about 1650 , admitted to Lincoln's Inn, 25 Nov 1687 ; *suc. to the Baronetcy*, 21 May 1691. He *m* Barbara, da. of Sir Wadham WYNDHAM, of Norrington, Wilts, one of the Justices of the Court of King's Bench, by Barbara, da. of Sir George CLARKE, of Watford, co Northampton She, who was *b* 7 Nov 1649,(a) *d* before him He *d* 1699, aged 49 Admon 6 May 1700

IV.   1699   SIR HUMPHREY BRIGGES, Bart. [1641], of Haughton afore-said, s. and h , *b* about 1670 , matric at Oxford (Wadham Coll), 3 July 1687, aged 17, admitted to Lincoln's Inn, 1687, *suc. to the Baronetcy* in 1699 , M P for Salop, 1700-01 ; for Bridgnorth, 1702-10, and for Wenlock, 1716-27 He *d* unm 8 Dec 1734, at Haughton Will pr. Feb 1735

V.   1734,   SIR HUGH BRIGGES, Bart. [1641], of Haughton aforesaid, to   br and h , *b* about 1684 , matric at Oxford (Wadham Coll.), 17 Dec 1767   1708, aged 16 ; *suc. to the Baronetcy*, 8 Dec 1734 , Sheriff for Salop, 1747-48 He *d.* unm 27 Oct 1767, when the *Baronetcy* became *extinct* (b) Will pr. Nov 1767.

The title, however, was assumed as under

VI.   1767.   SIR JONATHAN BRIGGS, styling himself " Baronet," as being descended from a younger branch of the family He was Surveyor of Excise at Milford Haven He *d* 3 Dec 1774.

VII.   1774,   SIR JOHN BRIGGS, styling himself " Baronet," s. to   and h. of above He was of Blackbrook, co. Monmouth ; was 1816.   plaintiff in a cause tried at Hereford in 1795 He *d* in Dublin, 3 Oct. 1816. Doubtless the will of " Sir John Briggs, Bart ," pr 1819, refers to him (c)

HEYMAN.

cr 12 Aug 1641(d) ,

ex. 20 Nov 1808.

I   1641.   " HENRY HEYMAN, of Somerfeilde [in Sellinge], co Kent , Knt.," s and h. of Sir Peter HEYMAN, of the same (sometime M.P. for Hythe), being only s by his 1st wife, Sarah, da and coheir of Peter COLLET, of London, merchant, was *b.* 20 Nov 1610, at Sellog ; suc. his father in or before March 1640/1 , was M P. for Hythe, April to May 1640, and 1640-53 , was a pro-nounced Parliamentarian, serving on several important committees, 1642-49 , was *Knighted*, 7 July 1641, at Whitehall, and, a few weeks later, was *cr a Baronet*, as above, 12 Aug. 1641.(d) He *m.* Mary, da and h of Daniel HOLFORD, of West Thurrock, co Essex She *d* before him He *d.* at Grays, co. Essex, 1658, and was *bur.* at Sellinge (e) Admon 7 Dec. 1658

(a) *Mis Gen et Her.*, 2d S , vol iv, p. 55, where an interesting account of this branch of the Wyndham family is given.

(b) The estates passed to the descendants of his three sisters ; that of Houghton de-volving on those of Elizabeth, who *m.* Leigh Brooke, of Blacklands, co. Stafford By act of Parl, 1800, a more regular partition of these estates was made

(c) The will of " Sir John Briggs, Bart., Guernsey," proved April 1842, and the admon. of " Dame Tamar Priscilla Briggs, Guernsey," May 1827, doubtless refer to other persons who assumed this Baronetcy.

(d) See p. 131, note " a," under " Owen."

(e) Philipot, in his *History of Kent*, speaks of his great obligations to him.

II   1658   SIR PETER HEYMAN, Bart [1641], of Somerfield afore-
                 said, s and h, b 10 and bap 21 July 1642, at St. Anne's, Black-
friars, London ; suc to the Baronetcy in 1658   He dissipated all the family inheritance   He m Mary, da of (—) RICH, of Clapham, Surrey   The will of ' Dame Mary
Hayman, Surrey " was pr June 1711   He d at Canterbury, 5 Oct 1723, and was
bur. (as was his wife) at St Alphage's, in that city

III 1723.   SIR BARTHOLOMEW HEYMAN, Bart. [1641], s and h,
                 b about 1690, suc to the Baronetcy, 5 Oct 1723   His eyesight,
having been impaired in his youth by gunpowder, rendered him unfit for military
service   He was one of the Poor Knights at Windsor, Berks   He m, about 1720,
Elizabeth, da of Thomas NELSON, of Sandwich, Kent, merchant.   He d. 9 June 1742,
and was bur in St George's chapel Windsor, aged 52   M I.

IV   1742   SIR PETER HEYMAN, Bart [1641], of Windsor aforesaid,
                 only s and h, b about 1720, and suc. to the Baronetcy, 9 June 1742.
He was an officer in the army   He m, when aged only 17, in 1737, (—), only child
of (—) KEMPE, of Plymouth   He d, a widower, s p s, July 1790, aged 70 (a)

V   1790,   SIR HENRY PIX HEYMAN, Bart [1641], cousin and h
     to   male, being s and h of Henry HEYMAN, of Stroud, by Elizabeth, da
     1808.   of Hatch UNDERWOOD, which Henry last named was s and h of
                 the Rev Peter HEYMAN, Rector of Headcorn, Kent, 2d s of the 2d
Bart, was ed at Emmanuel Coll Cambridge, of which he was sometime Fellow ;
B A, 1784, M A., 1787; B D, 1794; suc to the Baronetcy, in July 1790: was
Rector of Fressingfield, Suffolk, 1797.   He d. s p. 20 Nov. 1808, when the
Baronetcy became extinct

GOODRICK, or GOODRICKE
cr 14 Aug 1641(b),
ex. 9 March 1839.

I.   1641   " JOHN GOODRICK, of Ribston, co York, Esq ," s and h
                 of Sir Henry GOODRICK, of the same,(c) by Jane, da. of Sir John SAVILE,
of Methley, one of the Barons of the Exchequer, is said to have been b 20 April 1617
and bap. 31 Aug. 1620, at St Mary's, York, suc. his father, 22 July 1641, and was,
the next month, cr a Baronet, as above, 14 Aug 1641 (b)   During the Civil Wars he
was a great sufferer in the Royal cause, and was imprisoned at Manchester and
afterwards in the Tower of London, being fined £1,508, (or £1,200, with £40 a
year,) on 23 Nov 1646   He was aged 48 at the Visit of Yorkshire in 1665, and
was M P for Yorkshire, 1661 till death   He m firstly, 7 Oct 1641, at Trinity,
Micklegate, York, Katharine, da and coheir of Stephen NORCLIFFE, of York, by (—),
da of (—) UDALL   She was bap 31 Aug 1620, at St Mary's Castlegate, York   He
m secondly, before 1665, Elizabeth, Dow VISCOUNTESS FAIRFAX OF ELMLEY [I], da.
of Alexander SMITH, of Stutton, co Suffolk   He d Nov 1670   Will dat 19 Sep.
1669, pr. at York 25 Nov 1670   The will of his widow dat 4, pr 15 June 1692,
in London and 13 Sep following at York

II   1670.   SIR HENRY GOODRICK, or GOODRICKE, Bart [1641], of
                 Ribston aforesaid, s and h by 1st wife, b 24 Oct 1642, aged 22 at
the Visit of Yorkshire in 1665; suc. to the Baronetcy, Nov 1670, was M P for
Boroughbridge (ten Parls), Nov 1673 to 1705; was Envoy Extraordinary, from
Charles I, to Charles II, King of Spain, Lieut. Gen. of the Ordnance, 1668-1702, and

---

(a) He was in such reduced circumstances that, in 1783, a concert was got up for
his benefit   See an interesting account of this in Burke's Extinct Baronets, edit 1841.
(b) See p 131, note " a," under " Owen "
(c) See an account of this family in Dugdale's Visitation of Yorkshire, 1665, as
edited by J. W Clay, F S.A., with copious additions.

CREATIONS [E] BY CHARLES I.

P.C. 13 Feb. 1689/90, to William III. He *m* Mary, sister of George, 1st BARON DART-MOUTH, da. of Col. William LEGGE, by Elizabeth, da. of Sir William WASHINGTON He *d* s p, at Brentford, Midx., 5 March 1704/5, and was *bur.* at Ribston Will dat. 2, pr 24 March 1704/5 His widow *d* aged 70, and was *bur.* (with her father) at Trinity Minories, London. Her will dat. 13 Feb 1714/5, was pr. 9 April 1715, at the Archdeaconry of Midx.

III. 1705   SIR JOHN GOODRICKE, Bart [1641], of Ribston aforesaid, br. of the half blood and h, being s of the 1st Bart by his 2d wife, *b* 16 Oct 1654; aged 10 at the Visit of Yorkshire, 1665, *suc to the Baronetcy,* 5 March 1704/5 He *m* Sarah, da. of Sir Richard HOPKINS, of Coventry, Serjeant at Law He *d* 10 Dec 1705. Will dat 21 Nov 1705, pr. at York 22 Sep 1706 The will of his widow dat 24 Feb. 1731, pr. at York 5 March 1732

IV. 1705.   SIR HENRY GOODRICKE, Bart [1641], of Ribston aforesaid, s and h, *b* 8 Sep. 1677; *suc to the Baronetcy,* 10 Dec 1705 He *m* 26 April 1707, at York Minster, Mary, only da and h. of Tobias JENKINS, of Grimston, co York, by his 1st wife, Mary, da of Charles (PAULET or POWLETT) 1st DUKE OF BOLTON. He *d* 21 July 1738, and was *bur.* at Ribston Will dat 11 Feb 1737/8, pr at York 31 July 1738

V. 1738   SIR JOHN GOODRICKE, Bart [1641], of Ribston aforesaid, s. and h, *b* 20 May 1708 at Ribston; *suc to the Baronetcy,* 21 July 1738. P.C. 1 Sep. 1773, M P for Pontefract, 1774 80 and for Ripon, Dec. 1787 till death, Comiss Board of Trade, Aug 1788, Envoy Extraordinary to Stockholm, where he chiefly resided He m. 28 Sep. 1731, at Hendon, Mary JOHNSON, *afterwards* BENSON, spinster, illegitimate da. of Robert (BENSON) BARON BINGLEY, by (——), da of James SILL, of Wakefield, mercer. He *d* 3 Aug 1789, and was *bur.* at Hunsingore Will dat 20 May 1788, pr at York 29 Aug. 1789.

VI. 1789.   SIR HENRY GOODRICKE, Bart [1641], of Ribston aforesaid, grandson and h, being 2d but only surv. s and h of Henry GOODRICKE, of Groningen, in Holland, by Levina Benjamina, da. of Peter SESSTER, of Namur,[a] which Henry was only s and h ap of the late Baronet, but *d* v p 9 July 1784 He was *b* 12 Oct 1765, at Groningen, was M P for Lymington, Dec 1778 to 1780, *suc to the Baronetcy,* 3 Aug 1789. He m., 30 Nov 1796, at Mold, Charlotte, sister to William Charles, 2d VISCOUNT CLERMONT [I], 2d da of Rt Hon. James FORTESCUE, of Ravensdale park, co Louth, by Henrietta, da. of Thomas Orby HUNTER, of Croyland, co. Lincoln He *d* 23 March 1802, and was *bur* at Hunsingore. Will dat 9 Dec 1801, pr at York 31 July 1802 His widow *d* 10 Aug 1842. Will pr. Oct. 1842

VII. 1802.   SIR HENRY-JAMES GOODRICKE, Bart. [1641], of Ribston aforesaid, only s. and h, *b* 26 Sep at Dublin and *bap.* 23 Oct 1797 at St. Thomas', in that city; *suc to the Baronetcy,* 23 March 1802, at the age of 4 years, ed at Rugby, matric at Oxford (Ch Ch), 19 Oct 1816, aged 19 In March 1829 he suc. to the vast estates in Ireland of his maternal uncle, above-named, the 2d and last VISCOUNT CLERMONT [I] His income is said to have been £40,000 a year; was Sheriff of Yorkshire, 1831-32 "Sir Harry" was well known in the sporting world, and was, from 1831 till his death in 1833, Master of the Quorn Hunt, the whole expenses of which he defrayed. He *d.* unm., after an illness of forty-eight hours, at Ravensdale park, co Louth, in his 36th year, 22 Aug. 1833, and was *bur* at Hunsingore Will dat. 25 July, and pr 27 Oct 1833, devising Ribston Hall and his other English estates to Francis Lyttleton HOLYOAKE,[b] one of his sporting friends, who was, however, in no way connected with the family, thereby excluding his three aunts, who were his coheirs, as well as his heir male

----

(a) They were married in, or shortly before, 1764, at Woldhuysen, in East Friesland.

(b) He took the additional name of GOODRICKE, after that of HOLYOAKE, and was cr a Baronet, 31 March 1835 (some few years before the extinction of the old Baronetcy of that name) as "of Ribston, co York," etc., a title which became extinct on the death of his son, the 3d Bart., 11 Aug. 1888.

T

VIII. 1833,   SIR THOMAS FRANCIS HENRY GOODRICKE, Bart. [1641],
to   cousin and h male, being 2d but last surv. s. of Lieut Col
1839. Thomas GOODRICKE, 25th Regt., by Elizabeth, da. of James BUTTON,
of Rochester, which Thomas last named (who was b 12 March
1711/2) was 2d surv. s of the 4th Bart He was b 24 Sep 1762, at Rochester,
suc to the Baronetcy (but to none of the estates), 22 Aug 1833 He m. April 1794,
at Hunsingore, his cousin Harriet. sister of the 6th Bart., 1st da of Henry GOOD-
RICKE, of Groningen, by Levina Benjamina, da of Peter SESSTER, all abovenamed
She was b 20 Oct. 1767, at Hunsingore He d s p in London 9 March 1839, and
was bur at Kensal Green, aged 76, when the Baronetcy became extinct Will dat
8, and pr 23 March 1839

POTTS :

cr. 14 Aug. 1641 ;

ex 14 Jan. 1731/2.

I. 1641   "JOHN POTTS, of Mannington, co. Norfolk, Knt.,"
s. and h of John POTTS, of Lincoln's Inn, London, by Anne, da
and coheir of John DODGE, of Mannington aforesaid, was admitted to Gray's Inn,
10 Oct 1634, was M.P for Norfolk, 1640, till secluded in Dec. 1648, and for Great
Yarmouth 1660, was Knighted, 9 Aug 1641, at Whitehall, being, a few days later
cr a Baronet, as above, 14 Aug. 1641, was a Parliamentarian, serving on several
important Committees, 1643-48, and was on the Council of State, Feb to April 1660.
He m firstly, apparently when a minor,(a) (—), da of (—) GOODSILL She d. s p m.
He m secondly, Ursula, widow of (—) SPELMAN, da of Sir Henry WILLOUGHBY, of
Risley, co. Derby Banns of marriage were pub May 1654, between him (then a
widower) and "Mrs. Mary HANGER, of Enfield, Midx, widow" He d 1673. Admon.
19 Nov. 1673 to a creditor

II. 1673.   SIR JOHN POTTS, Bart. [1641], of Mannington aforesaid,
s and h by 2d wife, was admitted to Gray's Inn, 10 Oct. 1624,
suc. to the Baronetcy in 1673 He m firstly, in or before 1640, Susan, da of Sir John
HEVENINGHAM, of Heveningham, Norfolk He m secondly, Elizabeth, da. of Sir
Samuel BROWNE, of Arlesley, Beds, one of the Justices of the Common Pleas,
(1660-68), by Elizabeth, da of John MEADE, of Finchingfield, Essex. She survived
him many years.

III. 1690 ?   SIR ROGER POTTS, Bart [1641], of Mannington afore-
said, only s. and h., b. about 1641, aged 23 in 1664, suc to the
Baronetcy on the death of his father He m, in or before 1675, Mary, da and h. of
William DAVY, of Great Ellingham, Norfolk, by Margaret, da of Thomas GOURNAY,
of West Barsham She d 8 March 1701/2 (the same day and hour as King
William III), and was bur. at Ellingham He d 14 Oct 1711, aged 70

IV 1711   SIR ALGERNON POTTS, Bart [1641], of Mannington
aforesaid, 1st s. and h., b. in or before 1675, suc. to the Baronetcy, 14 Oct.
1711 He m Frances, widow of Thomas CRANE, of Norwich, merchant, da and coheir
of (—) CALIBUT, of Saham Toney He d. s p, 17 Sep. 1716 His widow d. Nov 1717.

V 1716,   SIR CHARLES POTTS, Bart. [1641], of Mannington aforeto   said, br and h., b 1676; was a Citizen and Merchant Taylor, and some-
1732 time a merchant in London, suc. to the Baronetcy, 17 Sep. 1716 He
m firstly, Elizabeth, only sister of William or Thomas NEWMAN, of
Baconsthorpe, Norfolk She d at Kensington, 21 Sep 1706, and was bur. at Great
Ellingham. He m. secondly Mary, da. of Thomas SMITH, of London, merchant He
d s p 14 Jan. 1731/2, aged 56, and was bur. at Mannington, when the Baronetcy
became extinct.(b) Will pr 1732. His widow, who had the estate of Mannington for
her life, d. 7 Feb. 1735/6 and was bur. at Mannington Admon. 21 Feb 1735/6

(a) An old writer in the time of the Court of Wards says that "He was obliged
to marry a da. of (—) Goodsill, Esq., a favourite at Court, with a small fortune."
[Burke's Extinct Baronetcies.]

(b) There is, however, the will of a "Sir Roger Potts," proved in 1751, which
possibly may be that of some one who (rightly or wrongly) assumed this Baronetcy.

RODES

cr 14 Aug. 1641;

ex presumably, Oct 1743

I. 1641   "FRANCIS RODES,(*) of Balbrough [Barlborough], co. Derby, Knt ," 2d s but h. (by entail) of Sir John RODES,(b) of the same, being his 1st s by his 3d wife Frances, da of Marmaduke CONSTABLE, of Holderness, was *b* about 1595, admitted to Gray's Inn, 21 May 1617, suc. his father in his estates Sep 1639, was *Knighted* at Whitehall, 9 Aug 1641, and a few days afterwards was *cr a Baronet*, as above, 14 Aug 1641. He *m.* Elizabeth, da and h of Sir George LASCELLES, of Sturton and Gateford, Notts He *d* 8 Feb 1645/6 Admon 27 May 1646 His widow, who was aged 19 in 1614, *m.* Allan LOCKHART. She *d* 5 and was *bur* 6 Dec. 1666 at Barlborough

II. 1646   SIR FRANCIS RODES, Bart [1641], of Barlborough aforesaid, 2d but 1st surv s. and h ; *suc. to the Baronetcy*, 8 Feb 1645/6 Was fined, as a Royalist, £500 on 25 March 1650 He *m* Ann, da. of Sir Gervase CLIFTON, 1st Bart [1611], by his 2d wife, Frances da. of Francis (CLIFFORD), EARL OF CUMBERLAND He *d*. 3 May 1651 Admon 10 June 1651.

III 1651.   SIR FRANCIS RODES, Bart [1641], of Barlborough Hall aforesaid, only s and h ; *suc to the Baronetcy*, 3 May 1651, aged 14 at the Visit. of Derby, 1662, Sheriff of Notts, 1670-71 He *m* (Lic Fac. 1 May 1665, each being about 20), Martha, da. of (his guardian), William THORNTON, of Grantham, co Lincoln He *d* 14 March 1675, in his 28th year His widow *d*. 25 Oct. 1719, in her 77th year Both *bur*. at Barlborough M I

IV 1675,   SIR JOHN RODES, Bart [1641], of Barlborough Hall aforeto   said, only s and h , *b* about 1670, being aged 25 on 28 July 1695, 1743   having *suc to the Baronetcy*, 14 March 1675 He *d*. unm Oct 1743, when, presumably, the *Baronetcy* became *extinct* Will dat 12 March 1731,(c) pr 1744

SPRIGNELL:

cr. 14 Aug 1641;

ex Aug. 1691.

I 1641.   "RICHARD SPRIGNELL, of Coppenthorp, in the county of the city of York, Esq ," only s and h of Robert SPRIGNELL,(d) of Hornsey, co Midx (lessee of the Rectory of Copmanthorpe aforesaid), by Susan his

---

(a) Pedigree in Glover's *Derbyshire*, vol. ii, p 83.

(b) This John was s and h of the learned Francis RODES, one of the Justices of the Common Pleas, *temp* Eliz , by whom the stately Elizabethan mansion of Barlborough Hall was erected in 1583

(c) In this he entails the estates, on failure of issue male of his sister, Frances HEATHCOTE (which issue, however, inherited the estates and took the name of RODES), to his cousin, John RODES, of Northgate in Horbury This John RODES (if no nearer heir existed) would have been, if alive in 1743, entitled to the Baronetcy He was s of William RODES (aged 6 in Feb 1694/5), who was the only s. (that survived infancy) of John RODES, of Cornhill, London, linen draper (living 1695), the s. and h of John RODES, of Sturton, Notts, 4th s. of the 1st Bart. Of the two other (younger) sons of the said John RODES, of Sturton, Francis RODES emigrated to Maryland, *m.* twice, and had issue living 1695, and Charles RODES also *m.*, having emigrated to Virginia See MS notes by Brooke (*Somerset Herald*) in his own copy of Wotton's *Baronetage*

(d) This Robert was only s of Richard Sprignell, Citizen and Barber Surgeon of London, whose curious will (apologising for his last marriage) is dat. 12 and pr. 27 Feb 1602/3.

wife, suc. his father between 1618 and 1624; matric at Oxford (Bras. Coll), 28 Jan 1619/20, aged 20 , B A 28 Feb. 1621/2, and was *cr a Baronet*, as above, 14 Aug 1641 He *m* Anne, only da of Gideon DE LAUNE, of Sharsted, co Kent, and of London, apothecary, by Judith, da of Henry CHAMBERLAINE, of London He resided at Highgate, co Midx , and was *bur* there, 19 Jan 1658/9 Will dat. 13 Aug 1656, pr. 12 Feb 1658/9 His widow was *bur* at Highgate, 9 May 1661

II 1659.   SIR ROBERT SPRIGNELL, Bart. [1641], of Coppenthorp aforesaid, 1st s and h , *suc to the Baronetcy* 10 Jan 1658/9. He *m* Anne, da of Sir Michael LIVESEY, Bart [1627], the regicide. He *d*. s p before Nov 1688.

III. 1680 ?   SIR WILLIAM SPRIGNELL, Bart [1641], of London, br.
to   and h , *suc to the Baronetcy* on the death of his brother. He *d.*
1691.   unm and was *bur* 6 Sep 1691, at Highgate, when the *Baronetcy* became *extinct* Will dat 12 Nov 1688, pr. 3 Sep 1691 in the Commissary Court of London.

BINDLOSSE:

cr 16 Aug 1641 ,(a)

ex Nov 1688

I. 1641,   "ROBERT BINDLOSSE, of Borwick, co Lancaster, Esq,"
to   s and h of Sir Francis BINDLOSSE (only s and h ap of Sir Robert
1688.   BINDLOSSE, of the same,) by his 2d wife, Cecilia, da of Thomas
          (WEST), LORD DELAWARR, was *bap*. 8 May 1624 , suc his father
(who *d.* v p aged 26) 25 July 1629, and was *cr a Baronet*, as above, 16 Aug 1641 (a)
He was M P for Lancaster, 1646, till secluded in Dec 1648 and for Lancashire, 1660 ,
Sheriff of that county, 1657-58, 1671-72, and 1672-73. He *m* Rebecca, 3d and yst.
da and coheir of Hugh PERRY, Alderman and sometime [1632-33] Sheriff of London,
by Catharine, da of Richard FENNE, of London, merchant He *d* s p m (b) and was
bur. 15 Nov. 1688, at Wharton, co Lancaster, when the *Baronetcy* became *extinct*.(c)
His widow was *bur* 17 June 1708, at Wharton aforesaid.

> The dignity was, however, assumed many years afterwards (on what grounds is unknown) by EDWARD BINDLOSSE, who was a J P for Westminster He *d* s p m or before 1789. The will of ' Sir Edward Bindlosse, Bart , Midx ," is proved May 1789

LAWLEY.

cr 16 Aug 1641;

sometime, 1831-32, BARON WENLOCK;

afterwards, since 1851, BARONS WENLOCK

I 1641   "THOMAS LAWLEY, of St. Poonell [*i e.*, Spoonhill], co Salop, Esq ," 2d s. of Francis LAWLEY, of the same, by Elizabeth, da and h of Sir Richard NEWPORT, of High Ercall, Salop suc his eldest br, Richard LAWLEY, of Spoonhill aforesaid, in 1623, and was *cr a Baronet*, as above,

---

(a) The patent is not enrolled The date here given is that in Dugdale's *Catalogue* See *Memorandum* on p 84 The date of the " privy seals and signed bills, Chancery," is 13 Aug 1641.
(b) Cecilia, his da and h., *m* William Standish, of Standish, co. Lancaster (who *d.* 8 June 1705), and *d* 19 Jan 1729/30, leaving issue.
(c) The will of a " Sir Robert Bindlosse " is proved 1655.

16 Aug 1641   He was M P for Wenlock, 1625, 1626 and 1628-29.   He *m.* Anne, da and coheir of John MANNING, of Hackney, Midx , and of Cralle, Sussex   He *d* 19 Oct. 1646.   Will, without date, pr 16 Dec. 1646.   His widow *m* (for his 2d wife) Sir John GLYNNE, Lord Chief Justice of the Upper Bench, 1655, who *d* 15 Nov. 1666   Her will, directing her burial to be with her parents at St Andrew's, Undershaft, London, dat 23 Jan 1666, pr 19 Dec 1668.

II. 1646   SIR FRANCIS LAWLEY, Bart [1641], of Spoonhill aforesaid,

s and h , *suc to the Baronetcy*, 19 Oct 1646 ; was M P for Wenlock, 1659 and 1660 and for Salop 1661-79 , Gent of the Privy Chamber, 1660 ; a Comis of Customs, 1675-79 , el Sheriff of Staffordshire, 1688, but did not serve He purchased Canwell Priory, co. Stafford   He *m* , about 1650, Anne, 1st da of Sir Thomas WHITMORE, 1st Bart [1641], by Elizabeth, da and h of Sir William ACTON, Bart [1629]   He *d* Oct. 1696   Will dat 15 May 1693 to 31 July 1696, pr 28 Oct 1696   The will of his widow dat. 29 June 1713 to 25 Oct 1715, pr 18 Dec 1718

III. 1696.   SIR THOMAS LAWLEY, Bart [1641], of Canwell Priory

and Spoonhill aforesaid, s and h , *b* about 1650 , was M P for Wenlock, 1685-87 , *suc to the Baronetcy* in Oct. 1696   He *m.* firstly, Rebecca, 2d da and coheir of Sir Humphrey WINCH, Bart [1660], by Rebecca, da. of Martin BROWNE, Alderman of London   By her he had fourteen children   He *m* secondly, 3 March 1711/2, at St Paul's Cathedral, London, Elizabeth, widow of (—) PERKINS   He *d* 30 Sep 1729, aged about 80   Will dat 6 Dec 1727/8 to 22 Oct. 1729, pr 31 Dec. 1729.   His widow *m* 22 Feb 1730, in Somerset House Chapel, Mark HALFPENN, and *d* 28 Jan 1739/40   Will dat 27 May 1739, pr 17 May 1740

IV   1729   SIR ROBERT LAWLEY, Bart. [1641], of Canwell Priory

aforesaid, s and h by 1st wife ; *suc to the Baronetcy*, 30 Sep 1729 Sheriff of Staffordshire, 1743-44   He *m* in 1726, Elizabeth, 1st da of Sir Lambert BLACKWELL, 1st Bart. [1718], by Elizabeth, da. of Sir Joseph HERNE   She *d* 21 March 1774   Her will dat 17 Nov. 1770, pr 6 April 1774   He *d* 28 Nov 1779 Will dat. 15 March 1776, pr 19 Jan 1780

V. 1779.   SIR ROBERT LAWLEY, Bart [1641], of Canwell Priory,

etc , aforesaid, only surv s and h , *bap.* 22 March 1735/6 , *suc to the Baronetcy*, 28 Nov 1779 , M P for Warwickshire, 1780 93   He *m.* 11 Aug 1764, Jane, only da. (whose issue became sole heir) of Beilby THOMPSON, of Esrick, co York, by Janet, relict of Sir Darcy DAWES, 5th Bart [1663] , da and coheir of Richard ROUNDELL, of Hutton Wansley, co York   He *d* 11 March 1793. Will dat. 10 Feb 1792, pr 28 March 1793   His widow *d* Nov 1816   Will pr 1816

VI. 1793.   SIR ROBERT LAWLEY, Bart [1641], of Canwell Priory,

etc , aforesaid, *b* 1768 , *suc to the Baronetcy*, 11 March 1793 ; was an officer in the Guards , Equerry to H.R H. the Duke of Cumberland , Sheriff of Staffordshire, 1797-98 , was M P for Newcastle under Lyne, 1802-06 , and was, 10 Sep 1831, *cr* a Peer as BARON WENLOCK of Wenlock, co Salop, it being one of the " Coronation " Peerages of William IV   He *m* 16 Sep 1793, at Seamer, co York, Anna Maria, da. of Joseph DENISON, of Denbies, co. Surrey, and of St Mary's Axe, London, Banker, by his 2d wife, Elizabeth, da of William BUTLER, of Lisbon, merchant   He *d*. s p, at his villa near Florence, 10 April, and was *bur* 19 Aug 1834, at Hints, co Stafford, aged 66, when the *Peerage* became *extinct*   Will pr June 1834.   His widow *d* 20 Aug 1850, in Carlton house terrace   Will pr Oct 1850.

VII. 1834.   SIR FRANCIS LAWLEY, Bart [1641], of Middleton Hall,

co Warwick, br and h , *b* about 1782 , matric at Oxford (Ch Ch), 20 Oct 1800, aged 18 ; Fellow of All Souls' College, Oxford, till 1815 ; B.C L , 1808 , D C L. 1813 ; M P for Warwickshire, 1820-32 ; *suc to the Baronetcy*, 10 April 1834 , sometime Lieut. Col of the Warwickshire Yeomanry Cavalry, resigning in 1848 He *m.* 18 May 1815, Mary Anne, 1st da and coheir of George TALBOT, of TempleGuiting, co Gloucester, by Charlotte Elizabeth, da and coheir of Rev Thomas DRAKE, D D , of Amersham, Bucks.   He *d* s p , 30 Jan 1851, at Middleton Hall aforesaid, aged 68.   Will pr. June 1851.   His widow *d* 21 Dec. 1878, at 10 Chichester terrace, Kemp town, Brighton.

VIII. 1851   PAUL BEILBY (LAWLEY-THOMPSON), 1st BARON WEN-
           LOCK [1839] and 8th Bart. [1641], br and h , was, in his elder
brother's lifetime, *cr.*, 13 May 1839, BARON WENLOCK of Wenlock. co Surrey,
and, afterwards, *suc to the Baronetcy*, 30 Jan 1851, which thenceforth became
merged in that peerage. See *Peerage.*

WALTER

cr 16 Aug 1641 ,

ex. 20 Nov. 1731.

I   1641.   "WILLIAM WALTER, of Larsdenn [*i.e*, Sarsden], co.
           Oxford, Esq.," s and h of Sir John WALTER, of Wolvercot, Oxon,
Lord Chief Baron of the Exchequer (1625-30), by his 1st wife, Margaret, da of
William OFFLEY, of London, was *b* about 1604 , matric at Oxford (Ch. Ch),
16 March 1620/1, aged 17 , Barrister (Inner Temple), 1630 , suc his father, 18 Nov
1630, and was *cr* a Baronet, as above, 20 Nov 1641   He was *cr* D C.L of Oxford,
2 Nov. 1642, was M P. for Weobley, 1628-29 and for Oxfordshire, April 1663 till
declared void , was a Compounder and was fined £1,430 in Aug 1646 , Sheriff of Oxon,
1656-57   He *m* (Lic Lond 20 Dec. 1632, he said to be 23 and she 20), Elizabeth,
sister of John, 1st BARON LUCAS OF SHENFIELD da of Thomas LUCAS, of St John's,
near Colchester, by Elizabeth, da and h of John LEIGHTON   He *d* 23 and was *bur*
27 March 1675, at Sarsden   Admon 24 Nov 1675 to his widow   She was *bur*.
12 May 1691, at Sarsden   Her admon 6 July 1691, registered in Oxford Act book

II   1675   SIR WILLIAM WALTER, Bart [1641], of Sarsden aforesaid,
           s and h , *b* probably about 1635 , matric at Oxford (Queen's Coll.),
2 Oct. 1652, being, presumably, *cr* M A , 28 Sep 1663 , admitted to Inner Temple,
1649 , *suc to the Baronetcy*, 23 March 1674-5   Sheriff of Oxon, 1688-89.   He *m*.
firstly, in or before 1671, Mary, da. of John (TUFTON), 2d EARL OF THANET, by
Margaret, da. and coheir of Richard (SACKVILLE), EARL OF DORSET   She was *bur*
7 Feb. 1673/4, at Sarsden. He *m*. secondly (settlement 22 March 1677/8), Mary, 4th
da of Robert (BRUCE), 2d EARL OF ELGIN [S] and 1st EARL OF AILESBURY, by Diana,
da of Henry (GREY), 1st EARL OF STAMFORD   He *d* 5 and was *bur* 8 March 1693/4,
at Sarsden. Will dat 5 May 1692, pr. 14 Feb. 1697/8. His widow, who was *b.*
31 Dec 1657, was *bur* 15 May 1711, at Sarsden.

III   1694.   SIR JOHN WALTER, Bart. [1641], of Sarsden aforesaid,
           2d but 1st surv. s. and h by 1st wife, *b.* about 1673 ,[a] matric.
at Oxford (Queen's Coll), 21 Aug 1691, and was *cr* D C.L., 27 Aug. 1702, having
suc to the Baronetcy, 5 March 1693/4   He was M P for Appleby, 1694 95 and
1697-1700 , for Oxford (six Parls.), 1706 till death   Clerk of the Green Cloth
He *m* Elizabeth, da of Sir Thomas VERNON, of Twickenham park, Midx   He *d*
s p 11 and was *bur*. 16 June 1722, at Sarsden. His widow *m* 30 Sep 1724, in
Oxfordshire (as his 3d wife), Simon (HARCOURT), 1st VISCOUNT HARCOURT OF
STANTON HARCOURT, who *d* 28 July 1727, aged 66   She *d*. 12 July 1748 and was
bur. at Sarsden. Will dat. 13 Feb. 1747, pr 22 July 1748

IV   1722,   SIR ROBERT WALTER, Bart [1641], of Sarsden aforesaid,
    to   br of the half blood and h male, being s of the 2d Bart by his 2d
1731.   wife, was *b* 29 Aug and *bap* 3 Sep 1680, at Ampthill, Beds; matric
at Oxford (New Coll), 15 Sep 1693, aged 13 ; admitted to the Inner
Temple, 1695 , *suc to the Baronetcy*, 11 June 1722   He *m* Elizabeth Louisa, 1st da.
of the Hon Henry BRYDGES, D D , Archdeacon of Rochester (br of James, 1st DUKE
OF CHANDOS), by Annabella, da. of Henry ATKINS   He *d*. s p 20 Nov 1731, and was
bur. at Churchill, Oxon, when the *Baronetcy* became *extinct.*   Will dat 7 Oct and
pr 6 Dec. 1731 and 22 June 1748   His widow *m*. John BARNEVAL, " Esq ," and *d*
in or near Paris. 1740   Admon 21 May 1746, her said husband being then alive.

---

[a] His elder br , William, who *d.* v p and unm , was *b*. 1671.

FERMOR, FARMOR, or FARMER

cr. 6 Sep 1641 ;

subsequently, 1692-1867, BARONS LEOMINSTER, *or* LEMPSTER ,

afterwards, 1721-1867, EARLS OF POMFRET, *or* PONTEFRACT ,

ex 8 June 1867

I. 1641   " WILLIAM FARMER, of Easton Neston, co Northampton, Esq ," 1st s and h of Sir Hatton FARMER, *or* FERMOR, of the same, by Anne, sister of Charles, 1st VISCOUNT CULLEN [I], da of Sir William COKAYNE, of Rushton, co Northampton, sometime (1618 19) Lord Mayor of London, was *b.* at Cokayne House, Broad street, and *bap* 7 Nov 1621, at St. Peter le Poor, London , matric. at Oxford (Ex. Coll), 1 June 1636, aged 14 , suc his father (who had distinguished himself in the royal cause) 28 Oct 1640 ; and was, a few months later, *cr. a Baronet,* as above, 6 Sep 1641 Col of Horse for the King , a Compounder and was fined £1,400 in Aprıll 1645 He was made K B. at the Coronation of Charles II, in 1661 , was M P for Brackley, 1661, till void 18 July , P C 1660 He *m.* 8 Sep. 1646, at North Luffenham, Rutland, Mary, widow of the Hon Henry NOEL (who *d* s p), da and coheir of Hugh PERRY, Alderman and sometime (1632-33) Sheriff of London, by Catharına, da of Richard FENNE, of London, merchant He *d* of the small pox, " at the house of Mr Hill, a tailor, at the 'Sign of the Lyon's Head,' in Covent Garden," 14 and was *bur* 22 May 1661, at Easton Neston Nunc will, dat 14, pr 21 May 1661 and 3 June 1673 His widow *d* in London 18 July, and was *bur.* 5 Aug 1670, at Easton aforesaid Will dat. 9 July 1670, pr 1 Aug 1671

II. 1661.   SIR WILLIAM FERMOR, *or* FARMOR, Bart [1641], 2d but 1st surv s and h , *b* 3 and *bap* 18 Aug 1648 at Easton Neston, *suc to the Baronetcy,* 14 May 1661 , matric at Oxford (Mag Coll), 20 June 1664, aged 15, and was *cr.* M A , 17 April 1667 ; was M P for Northampton, 1670-79 and 1678-79 He *m* firstly, in London (Lıc Vıc Gen , 21 Dec 1671), Jane, da of Andrew BARKER, of Fairford, co Glouc., by Elizabeth, da of William ROBINSON, of Cheshunt, Herts She *d.* s p m 10 and was *bur* 12 Aug 1673, at Easton Neston He *m.* secondly, June 1682, Catherine, 1st da of John (POULETT), 3d BARON POULETT OF HINTON ST GEORGE, by his 1st wife, Essex, da of Alexander POPHAM She, who was *b* 9 and *bap* 15 March 1664, at Hinton St George, co Somerset, *d* also s p m He *m* thirdly, 5 March 1691/2 (Lıc Vıc Gen , 8 Feb.), his 2d cousın, Sophia, widow of Donough O'BRIEN, *styled* LORD O'BRIEN, 6th da of Thomas (OSBORNE), 1st DUKE OF LEEDS, by Bridget, da. of Montagu (BERTIE), 2d EARL OF LINDSEY She was living when he was *cr* , 12 April 1692, BARON LEOMINSTER, co Hereford. In that peerage this *Baronetcy* then *merged,* the second Baron being *cr* , 27 Dec 1721, EARL OF POMFRET, *or* PONTEFRACT, but *all these honours* became *extinct,* 8 June 1867, on the death of the 5th Earl, 6th Baron, and 7th Baronet

---

DAVIE.

cr. 9 Sept 1641 ,(ᵃ)

ex 12 Jan 1846

I. 1641.   " JOHN DAVIE, of Creedie [in Sampford and of Crediton], co Devon, Esq," s and h of John DAVIE, of the same, by Margaret, da of George SOUTHCOTE, of Calverley, Devon, was *b.* about 1589 , matric at Oxford (Ex Coll), 22 Feb 1604/5, aged 16, as an " Esq " ; was living with four children, 1620 (Visit. of Devon, 1620), was M P. for Tiverton 1621-22 , Sheriff of Devon, 1629 30 , and was *cr a Baronet,* as above, 2 Sep 1641 (ᵃ) He *m.* firstly, Juliana, 5th da of Sir William STRODE, of Newnham, co Devon, by his 1st wife, Mary, da. of Thomas SOUTHCOTE, of Bovey Tracey She *d* 14 and was *bur.* 25 May, 1627, at Sandford He *m.* secondly, Isabel, da of (—) HELE, of Gnaton, Devon. He was *bur* 13 Oct. 1654, at Sandford His widow, who *d.* a p m was *bur* there 28 Oct. 1656.

(ᵃ) The patent is not enrolled The date here given is that in Dugdale's *Catalogue* See *Memorandum* on p. 84. The date of the " privy seals and signed bills chancery " is 11 Aug 1641.

II 1654.   SIR JOHN DAVIE, Bart. [1641], of Creedie aforesaid, s.
and h by 1st wife; *bap* 6 Dec. 1612, at Sandford, aged 8 at the
Visit of Devon, 1620; matric at Oxford (Ex Coll), 2 Dec. 1631, aged 19, *suc to
the Baronetcy* in Oct 1654, was M P. for Tavistock, May to Dec 1661, Sheriff of
Devon, 1670 71 [a] He *m* firstly Eleanor, da of Sir John ACLAND, 1st Bart. [1644], by
Elizabeth, da of Sir Francis VINCENT, 1st Bart. [1620] She *d* s p He *m* secondly,
in or before 1645, Triphena, da. and coheir of Richard REYNELL, of Lower Creedy,
Devon, by Margaret, da. and coheir of John PERYAM She was *bur* 1 Feb 1658/9,
at Sandford He *m* thirdly, Amy, da of Edmund PARKER, of Burrington, Devon
She, by whom he had no issue, was *bur* 25 April 1670, at Sandford. He *d* s p s [b]
and was *bur.* there 31 July 1678 Will pr. 1678.

III 1678.   SIR JOHN DAVIE, Bart. [1641], of Creedie aforesaid,
nephew and h male, being s and h of William DAVIE, of Dura,
co Devon, Barrister at Law, by Margaret, da of Sir Francis CLARKE, of Putney,
Surrey, which William, (who was *bur* 28 Nov. 1663, at Sandford, aged
49), was 2nd s of the 1st Bart. He was *b* 1660, matric. at Oxford (Ex. Coll), 21
March 1677/8, aged 17; *suc to the Baronetcy* in July 1678, was M P for Saltash
1679-81 and 1681; el Sheriff of Devon 1689, but did not serve He *d* unm.
30 Sep, and was *bur* 1 Oct 1692, at Sandford, aged 32 M I Will pr. 1693

IV 1692   SIR WILLIAM DAVIE, Bart [1641], of Creedie aforesaid,
br and h, *bap* 1 July 1662, at Sandford, matric at Oxford (Ex.
Coll), 30 March 1680, aged 17, *suc to the Baronetcy*, 30 Sep 1692. Sheriff of Devon,
1697-98 He *m*. firstly, in or before 1688, Mary, da and h of (—) STEDMAN, of
Downside, Somerset She was *bur* 4 March 1690/1, at Sandford He *m*. secondly,
in or before 1694, Abigail, da of John POLLEXFEN, of Wembury, Devon. He *d* s p m.
and was *bur* 24 March 1706/7, at Sandford, aged 44 M I. Will pr. May 1707.
The will of his widow pr April 1725

V. 1707.   SIR JOHN DAVIE, Bart [1641], of Creedie aforesaid,
cousin and h male, being s and h of Humphrey DAVIE, formerly of
London, but afterwards (about 1662) of New England, merchant by Mary, sister of
Edmund WHITE, of Clapham, Surrey, merchant, which Humphrey (who was *bap.*
24 Aug 1625, at Sandford) was yst s of the 1st Bart He was B A. of the
University of Cambridge in New England, and was a merchant there till he *suc. to
the Baronetcy* in March 1706/7, as well as to the family estates. He is said to have
been much respected for his piety and generosity He *m*. in or before 1700, "Mrs.
Elizabeth RICHARDS," of New England She was *bur* 3 Dec 1713, at Sandford.
He was *bur* there 29 Dec. 1727 Will dat 25 April 1727, pr 13 July 1728

VI. 1727.   SIR JOHN DAVIE, Bart [1641], of Creedie aforesaid,
s and h, *b* 1700: *suc to the Baronetcy* in Dec. 1727 He *m* 3 May
1726, at Broad Clyst, Devon, Elizabeth, da. of John ACLAND, of Kelleton, by
Elizabeth, da of Richard ACLAND, of Barnstaple He was *bur* 3 Sep. 1737, at
Sandford Admon 8 May 1738 and 7 April 1744 to the curators of his four minor
children His widow was *bur* 25 March 1738, at Sandford. Will pr 1738.

VII. 1737.   SIR JOHN DAVIE, Bart [1641], of Creedie aforesaid,
s and h, *bap* 4 Aug. 1734, at Sandford; *suc. to the Baronetcy*, in
his infancy, in Sep 1737, matric at Oxford (Mag Coll), 9 April 1750, aged 18; *cr*
M.A., 21 Nov 1754, Sheriff of Devon, 1761-62. He *m*, in or before 1764, Catherine,
da of John STOKES, of Rill, co Devon She was *bur.* 24 Dec. 1776, at Sandford.
Will pr 1790. He was *bur* 26 Sep 1792, at Sandford, aged 58 Admon July
1797, March 1815, and March 1840.

VIII. 1792.   SIR JOHN DAVIE, Bart [1641], of Creedie aforesaid,
2d but 1st surv s and h, *bap.* 9 April 1772, at Sandford, matric
at Oxford (Mag Coll), 20 Feb. 1790, aged 18, *suc to the Baronetcy* in Sep 1792.
Sheriff of Devon, 1802-03. He *m* 6 Sep 1796, Anne, 1st da of Sir William LEMON,
1st Bart [1774], by Jane, da of James BULLER, of Morval, co. Cornwall He was
bur 16 May 1803, at Sandford, aged 31 Will pr. 1803. His widow was *bur.* there
12 Dec 1812, aged 46

---

[a] He is, however, described only as an "Esq" on the list
[b] John Davie, his only son (by 2d wife), matric. at Oxford (Ex Coll.), 3 June
1663, aged 18, *d* v.p and unm. and was *bur.* 11 Jan 1667/8, at Sandford.

IX. 1803.   SIR JOHN DAVIE, Bart [1641], of Creedie aforesaid,
s and h, *bap* (with his twin brother) 28 March 1798, at Sandford,
suc. to the Baronetcy, 16 May 1803, matric at Oxford (Ex. Coll), 26 Jan 1818, aged
19 He *d.* unm 18 Sep 1824 (a) Will pr 1824

X   1824,   SIR HUMPHREY PHINEAS DAVIE, Bart. [1641], of Creedie
to   aforesaid uncle and h male, *b* 12 Jan and *bap* 5 April 1775, at
1846.   Sandford, matric. at Oxford (Ch Ch), 1 Feb 1793, aged 18, Colonel
in the army, *suc to the Baronetcy*, 18 Sep 1824. He *d* unm 12
Jan 1846, at Sandford, aged exactly 71, when the *Baronetcy* became *extinct*. M I.
Will pr Feb 1846.

PETTUS :
cr 23 Sep. 1641,
ex 31 July 1772

I 1641   "THOMAS PETTUS, of Rackheath, co Norfolk, Esq," s
and h of Sir Augustine PETTUS,(b) of the same, by his 1st wife,
Mary, da. of Henry VYLETT. of Lynn, was *cr a Baronet*, as above, 23 Sep 1641.
He was a zealous Loyalist. He *m* firstly, Elizabeth, da of Sir Thomas
KNYVETT. of Ashwelthorpe, Norfolk. She *d.* 1653 He *m* secondly, Anne, da. of
Arthur EVERARD, of Stow Park, Suffolk. He *d.* 21 Nov 1654 His widow *m* 18
Feb 1657/8, at St. Dionis Backchurch, London (Banns pub at St. Paul's, Covent
Garden), Francis WARNER, of Parham, Suffolk She *d* 1662

II 1654   SIR THOMAS PETTUS, Bart [1641], of Rackheath aforesaid, s and h, by 1st wife, *suc to the Baronetcy*, 21 Nov. 1654;
Sheriff of Norfolk, 1664-65 He *m*, in or before 1640, Elizabeth, da of William
OVERBURY, of Barton, co Warwick He *d* s p m s, 1671 Admon 9 May 1672, to
Elizabeth, the relict Will pr Nov 1673, but subsequently revoked and admon
granted 7 March 1676/7, and 6 Nov 1684 His widow *m* (—) PODE Her admon
as of St. Mary's Savoy, widow, 25 June 1687.

III 1671   SIR JOHN PETTUS, Bart. [1641], of Rackheath aforesaid,
br of the whole blood, and h. male, *b.* about 1640, *suc. to the
Baronetcy* in 1671. He was Cup bearer to Charles II, James II, and William III, and
one of the Commissioners of Appeal. F R S (c) He *m* (Lic. Vic. Gen., 27 May 1670,
he about 30 and she about 20), Mary, da and cohen of Nicholas BURWELL, of Gray's
Inn, Midx., brother of Sir Geoffrey BURWELL, of Rougham, Suffolk He *d.* 29 Oct
1698, aged 58

IV. 1698   SIR HORATIO PETTUS, Bart. [1641], of Rackheath aforesaid, s and h, *b* about 1672; *suc to the Baronetcy*, 29 Oct. 1698
He *m* (Lic. Fac., 1 May 1701, he about 29 and she about 21), Elizabeth, yst. da.
of Sir Thomas MEERS, of Kirton, co Lincoln He *d* 9 March 1730/1, aged 63 The
will of his widow dat. 22 Sep 1744, pr 17 Aug. 1746, and 4 Jan. 1768

V 1731   SIR JOHN PETTUS, Bart [1641], of Rackheath aforesaid,
1st surv. s and h, *suc to the Baronetcy*, 9 March 1730/1 His
mother, in her will, mentions having paid £5,500 for his debts and those of his
father He *m* 4 Dec 1744, Rebecca, da. of Edmund PRIDEAUX, of Padstow, Cornwall, by Hannah, da. of Sir Benjamin WRENCH, of Norwich. He *d.* s p m May
1743. His widow *d* 17 Nov 1780, aged 50, and was *bur* at Rackheath.

(a) Frances Juliana, his only surv sister and h, *m* 20 March 1823, Henry
Robert FERGUSON, and suc to the family estates, on her uncle's death, in Jan 1846.
Her husband took the name of DAVIE after that of FERGUSON, and was *cr. a Baronet*,
9 Jan. 1847.

(b) There was a "Thomas Pettus, s of Sir John, Knt of Norwich," admitted,
29 May 1609, to Lincoln's Inn, also a "John Pettus, 2d s. of Sir Augustine, Knt
of Rackheath, co Norfolk, Knt, deceased," who was so admitted 13 May 1635
This John, who was Knighted, 21 Nov 1641, was M.P for Droitwich, 1670, was of
Chesterton Hall, Suffolk, and *d* s p.m about 1690 He is often confused with the 3d
Baronet, and *he* possibly (and not that Baronet, as stated in the text) was "F.R.S."

(c) See note "b" above, *ad finem*.

U

VI 1743,   SIR HORATIO PETTUS, Bart. [1741], br and h. male ,
to   *suc. to the Baronetcy* in May 1743 , was Sheriff of Norfolk, 1746-47
1772.   He *d* s p. 31 July 1772, when the *Baronetcy* became *extinct*.
Admon Dec. 1808

MEUX:

cr 11 Dec 1641 ;([a])

ex. 6 March 1705/6

I   1641   "JOHN MEUX, of the Isle of Wight, co Southampton,
Esq.," only s. and h of Sir William MEUX, of Kingston, in that
island, by his 1st wife, Winifred, da of Sir Francis BARRINGTON, 1st Bart. [1611]
was admitted to Gray's Inn, 11 Feb 1629/30, and was *cr a Baronet*, as above, 11 Dec.
1641 ([a]) M P for Newtown (Isle of Wight) April to May 1640 and Nov 1640 till
disabled, 5 Feb 1643/4 , was a Compounder, April 1646, and fined £375 in Oct 1646
He *m* Elizabeth, da of Sir Richard WORSLEY, 1st Bart. [1611], by Frances, da of Sir
Henry NEVILLE She was *bur* 28 Dec 1652, at Kingston aforesaid He was *bur*
there 12 Feb. 1657.

II. 1657.   SIR WILLIAM MEUX, Bart [1641], of Kingston aforesaid,
1st s and h., *suc to the Baronetcy* in Feb. 1657. He *m* firstly
(Banns pub 1657, at Kingston), Mabel, sister of Sir Robert DILLINGTON 2d Bart
[1628], da of Robert DILLINGTON, of Knighton, in the Isle of Wight She *d*
s p m s. and was *bur* 19 Sep 1670, at Kingston. He *m* secondly, in or before 1681,
Elizabeth, da of George BROWNE, of Buckland, co Surrey He *d* about 1697 Will
dat 24 June 1693, pr 11 May 1697 His widow was *bur* 29 Jan 1731/2, at St
Margaret's, Westm. Will dat 31 Aug 1730, pr. 9 June 1732.

III   1697 ?   SIR WILLIAM MEUX, Bart [1641], of Kingston aforesaid,
to   1st surv s and h , by 2d wife, *bap* 25 June 1683, at St. Paul's,
1706   Covent Garden , *suc to the Baronetcy* about 1697 He *d* unm 6 and
was *bur* 13 March 1705/6, at Kingston, aged 22, when the *Baronetcy*
became *extinct* ([b])

ANDREWE, *or* ANDREWS

cr. 11 Dec. 1641.

ex. 1804

I.   1641   "WILLIAM ANDREWE, of Denton, *alias* Little Dodding-
ton, co Northampton, Esq ," was *cr a Baronet*, as above, 11 Dec. 1641;
was a Royalist, and a Compounder, Feb 1648 He *m* (—) da of (—) PARIS, of
Linton, co Cambridge By her he had five sons, of whom three fell at the battle
of Worcester, fighting for their King He *d* of the gout, in or before Jan 1649,
and was *bur* at Bury St Edmunds, Suffolk Will pr 1649

II.   1649 ?   SIR JOHN ANDREWE, Bart [1641], of Denton *otherwise*
Denton aforesaid, s and h , *suc. to the Baronetcy* in or before 1649.
He *d* s.p m ([c])

([a]) The patent is not enrolled The date here given is that in Dugdale's *Catalogue*.
See *Memorandum* on p 84 The date of the signet bill is 8 Dec. 1641.

([b]) His sister Elizabeth, the only one that was married, was *bap* 19 July 1677, at
Kingston ; *m* 2 May 1710, at St. Dunstan's in the West, London, Sir John Miller,
2d Bart [1705], and had issue Another Baronetcy was conferred, 30 Sep 1831, on
Henry Meux, of Theobald's Park, Herts (a descendant of Bartholomew Meux, br. of
the 1st Bart), but this, in Jan 1900, became, also, extinct

([c]) His only da died unm.

III 1665? SIR WILLIAM ANDREWE, or ANDREWS, Bart [1641], of
Denton aforesaid, br and h , *suc to the Baronetcy* on his brother's
death. He *m* Eleanor, da and h of Edward ATSLOW, of Downham Hall, Essex
(aged 30 in the Visit of Essex of 1634, and unm), by (—), da. of (—) PARIS. He
d 15 Aug 1684, and was *bur.* at Downham aforesaid. Will pr 1684

IV 1684. SIR FRANCIS ANDREWS, Bart. [1641], of Denton and
Downham aforesaid, s. and h , *suc to the Baronetcy*, 15 Aug 1684
He sold the estate of Downham under an Act of Parl dat 1698   He *m* Bridget, da
and coheir of Sir Thomas CLIFTON, Bart. [1660], of Clifton, co. Lancaster, by his 2d
wife, Bridget, da of Sir Edward HUSSEY   He *d* at Chelsea, Middlesex, 3 April
1759

V. 1759, SIR WILLIAMS ANDREWS, Bart [1641], only s and h. ,
to *suc to the Baronetcy*, 3 April 1759   He *d* s.p in 1804, when the
1804 *Baronetcy* became *extinct.*

GURNEY, *or* GOURNEY

cr 14 Dec. 1641 ,

ex. 6 Oct 1647

I. 1641, "RICHARD GOURNEY, Knt., now Mayor of the City of
to London," 2d s of Bryan GOURNARDS,[a] GOURNEY, *or* GURNEY, of
1647. Croydon, Surrey (*bur* there 24 Aug 1602), by Magdalen (*m* 27 April
1567, at Croydon), da of (—) HEWET, was *bap* 8 March 1577/8,
at Croydon ,[b] was apprenticed to R. Coleby, a silk mercer in Cheapside, who left
him his shop and £6,000 ; became Free of the Clothworkers' Company , was Sheriff
of London, 1633-34, in which year he entered and signed (as " Richard Gurney ")
his pedigree in the *Heralds' Visit* of that city , was Alderman of Bishopsgate,
1634-37, and of Dowgate, 1637 till ejected, 11 Aug 1642 , was (after a severe contest,
he being a sturdy Loyalist) Lord Mayor, 1641-42 (though ejected by Parl., 11 Aug
1642), being, during office, *Knighted*, 25 Nov 1641, at Kingsland, near Shoreditch,
on the King's return from Scotland, whom, next day, he entertained at Guildhall,
and was *cr a Baronet*, as above, a few weeks later, 14 Dec 1641   He was, by the
Commons, committed to the Tower (where he remained upwards of five years),
11 July 1642, and ejected from office 11 Aug following   On 6 March 1644/5 he was
fined £5,000   He *m* firstly, probably before 1620, Elizabeth, da of Henry SANDFORD,
of Birchington, in the Isle of Thanet, co Kent   He *m* secondly, in Oct 1632, Elizabeth, widow of Robert SOUTH, da of Richard GOSSON, of Odiham, Hants, and of
London, goldsmith. He *d. s p m s* ,[c] 6 and was *bur* 8 Oct 1647, at St Olave's,
Jewry, aged about 70, when the *Baronetcy* became *extinct*   Will pr. 1647. His
widow, by whom he had no issue, was *b.* at Odiham aforesaid, and living 1652, at
Pointer's Grove, in Totteridge, Herts

---

[a] See pedigree in *Visit. of London, 1634,* amplified by G S Steinman, in *Coll
Top. et Gen* , vol. iv, p. 91, and see copy of the donation of land at Fulham, Midx ,
18 Feb 1633, by Elizabeth, his wife, to the poor of Odiham, Hants, in vol viii,
p 233

[b] In Steinman's pedigree (see note " a " above) he is said to have been " born at
Croydon, 17 April 1577 ; *bap.* there 8 March 1578," but query the authority for his
birth nearly a year before his own baptism, and but four months after the baptism
of his brother John

[c] Richard Gurney, only s. and h. ap. by 1st wife, was living 1633, but *d.* v p
and s.p.

WILLIS, *or* WILLYS:
cr. 15 Dec 1641 ,(ª)
ex. 14 April 1732.

I   1641.   "THOMAS WILLYS, of 'Fenn Ditton, co. Cambridge, Esq," s. and h of Richard WILLYS, of the same, and of Exhall and Horningsey, in the same county, by Jane, da and h of William HENMARSH, of Balls, in Ware, co. Herts, was *b* about 1614, (being aged about 72 at the *Het. Visit of Cambridgeshire, 1684*) ; suc. his father, 16 Oct 1628 , and was *cr. a Baronet*, as above, 15 Dec 1641 (ª), M P for Cambridgeshire, 1659 ; for Cambridge, 1660 ; Sheriff of Cambridgeshire and Hunts , 1665-66   He *m* , about 1633, Anne, 1st da and coheir of Sir John WYLD, of Mystole and of St Martin's, Canterbury, Kent, by Anne, da of Robert HONYWOOD, of Charing, in that county   She, who was *b* at her maternal grandfather's house, at Markshall, co Essex, *d* 20 Oct 1685, aged 75. He *d* 17 Nov 1701, aged 87. Will dat. 13 and pr 25 Nov. 1701.

II   1701   SIR JOHN WILLYS, Bart [1641], of Fen Ditton aforesaid, 2d but 1st surv s. and h. *b* about 1635 (aged 49 in 1684) , suc. *to the Baronetcy*, 17 Nov 1701   He *m* Mary, da of Thomas SAVAGE of Elmley Court, co Worcester, by Mary, da of Sir John HARE, of Norfolk   He was *bur* 9 Aug 1704, aged 68, at Fen Ditton   Will dat 28 Oct 1701 to 14 Oct 1703, pr 4 Oct 1704   His widow *d.* 1709   Her will dat. 26 Oct. 1708, pr 5 April 1709.

III. 1704.   SIR THOMAS WILLYS, Bart. [1641], of Fen Ditton aforesaid, s and h , *b* there about 1674 (aged 9 years in 1684) ; suc *to the Baronetcy* in Aug 1704   He *m* , in or before 1704, Frances, da of (—) RIX. He *d.*, of the small pox, 17 June 1705   Admon 25 July 1705   His widow *m* the Rev. Matthew BAINES, and was living, as his wife, in 1724.

IV. 1705.   SIR THOMAS WILLYS, Bart [1641], of Fen Ditton aforesaid and of St Mary's, Islington, Midx , only surv s and h , *b.* about 1704, and *suc. to the Baronetcy* in his infancy, 17 June 1705   He *d.* unm. about 1724, aged 20   Admon. 14 April 1724, granted to his mother

V   1724?   SIR THOMAS WILLYS, Bart. [1641], of Fen Ditton aforesaid and of Hackney, Midx , cousin and h male, being s and h of William WILLYS, of Austin Friars, London, Hamburg merchant, by his 2d wife, Catharine, da of Robert GORE, of London, merchant, which Thomas (who was *bur* at Fen Ditton 9 Aug 1696, aged about 66) was 3d s of the 1st Bart   He was *b* about 1680, and *suc to the Baronetcy* about 1724   He *d* unm. 17 July 1726, aged 46, and was *bur.* at Nackington, Kent   Will dat 13 April 1713 pr 5 Aug. 1726 and 9 Feb 1732

VI   1726,   SIR WILLIAM WILLYS, Bart [1641], of Fen Ditton aforeto   said, only br and h. , *b* about 1685 , *suc. to the Baronetcy*, 17 July
1732.   1726   M P for Newport (Isle of Wight) Jan to July 1727, and for Great Bedwyn, 1727 till death   He *d.* unm. 14 April 1732, when the *Baronetcy* became *extinct* (ᵇ)   Will pr. 1732

(ª) The patent is not enrolled   The date here given is that in Dugdale's *Catalogue.* See *Memorandum* on p. 84   The date of the signet bill is 13 Dec. 1641

(ᵇ) The estate of Fen Ditton was purchased in 1733 from his six sisters and coheirs by Sarah, the famous DUCHESS OF MARLBOROUGH, for her grand-daughter, Lady Mary GODOLPHIN, whose husband, the DUKE OF LEEDS, sold it, in 1749, to Thomas PANTON, of Newmarket

ARMYTAGE
cr 15 Dec 1641,
ex. 12 Oct. 1737.

I. 1641.   "FRANCIS ARMYTAGE,(ª) of Kirklees [in the parish of
Hartshead], co York, Esq," 2d but 1st surv s. and h ap of John
ARMYTAGE,(ᵇ) of the same (Sheriff of Yorkshire, 1615), by Winifred, da and
h of Henry KNIGHT, of Knighthill and Brockholes, in Lambeth, co. Surrey,
was *b* about 1600, was Bow Bearer of the Free Chase of Mashamshire, 1632, and
was v p, *cr a Baronet*, as above, 15 Dec 1641 He suc his father, in July 1650
He *m*, in 1629, Catherine, da of Christopher DANBY, of Farnley, near Leeds, and of
Thorpe Perrow, co York, by Frances, da of Edward (PARKER), LORD MORLEY.
He *d* v p, and was *bur* 12 June 1644, in York Minster His widow, who was *bap.*
at Leeds, 29 Feb 1611/2, was *bur* 13 Jan. 1666, at Wakefield.

II. 1644.   SIR JOHN ARMYTAGE Bart [1641], of Kirklees aforesaid,
s and h, *bap* 15 Dec 1629, at Hartshead, *suc to the Baronetcy* in
June 1644, and to the estates (on the death of his grandfather), in July 1650, aged
38 at the *Heralds' Visitation of Yorkshire, 1666*; Sheriff of Yorkshire, 1668-69,
Capt of a Troop of Volunteer Horse He *m* in or before 1651, Margaret,
2d da. of Thomas THORNHILL, of Fixby, co York, by Ann, da. and coheir
of Thomas TRIGOT By her he had eight sons and five daughters He was *bur.*
9 March 1676/7, at Hartshead His widow, who was *bap* 1 Feb 1633/4, at Elland,
was *bur* 10 Feb 1695, at Hartshead

III. 1677.   SIR THOMAS ARMYTAGE, Bart [1641], of Kirklees aforesaid, s and h, *bap* 10 May 1652, at Hartshead, *suc to the
Baronetcy* in March 1676/7; matric at Oxford (Univ Coll), 19 Dec 1668, aged 16
He *d* unm between Feb and May 1694. Will dat 23 Feb 1693/4, pr at York,
26 May 1694

IV. 1694   SIR JOHN ARMYTAGE, Bart [1641], of Kirklees aforesaid, br and h, *bap* 14 April 1653, at Hartshead; *sur. to the
Baronetcy* in 1694 He *d* unm 2, and was *bur* 7 Dec 1732, at Hartshead, aged
about 80 Will dat 17 April 1732, pr at York, 22 March 1732/3 (ᶜ)

V 1732.   SIR GEORGE ARMYTAGE, Bart [1641], of Kirklees aforesaid, and of Mirfield br. and h, being 7th and only surv s of the
2d Bart, *bap* 23 Aug 1660, at Hartshead, *suc to the Baronetcy*, 2 Dec 1732
He *d.* unm and was *bur* 24 April 1736, at Hartshead,(ᵇ) aged 75.

VI. 1736,   SIR THOMAS ARMYTAGE, Bart. [1641], of South Kirkby,
to   co York, cousin and h male, being only surv. s and h. of Francis
1737.   ARMYTAGE, of South Kirkby aforesaid, by Mary, da of Robert
TRAPPES, of Nidd, in that county, which Francis (who was *bap* 3
Jan 1631/2, at Hartshead, and who d. between Nov. 1695 and Oct 1728) was 2d s
of the 1st Bart He, who was *bap* 31 July 1673, at South Kirkby, *suc to the
Baronetcy*, 24 April 1736 He *d* unm 12 Oct 1737, aged 64, and was *bur* at
South Kirkby, when the *Baronetcy* became *extinct*. M I. at South Kirkby

---

(ª) Though the name is apparently enrolled as "Armitage" it is spelt
"Armytage" in the patent (which is now in possession of Sir G J Armytage, 6th
Bart. [1738]), and is so signed by the grantee and all his successors.
(ᵇ) See *Mis. Gen. et Her*, orig. series, vol ii, pp 87-94, as to this family.
(ᶜ) He left Kirklees and other estates after the death of his br, George, to his
cousin Samuel Armytage, who was *cr. a Baronet*, 4 July 1738, and whose descendants
still enjoy that estate and title

HALFORD

cr 18 Dec 1641,([a])

ex 21 July 1780

I 1641   "RICHARD HALFORD, of Wistowe, co. Leicester, Esq ,"
s and h of Edward HALFORD, of Langham, co Rutland, by Dionysia,
da of (—) BURY, of co Rutland, was *b* about 1580 , was Sheriff of Rutland, 1619-20 ,
of Leicestershire, 1621-22, and of Rutland (again), 1631-32, *greatly distinguished,*
in the time of the Civil Wars, for his loyalty to the King, whom he entertained
at his house of Wistow, and by whom he was *cr a Baronet,* as above, 18 Dec
1641,([a]) being subsequently *Knighted,* 8 Jan 1641/2, at Whitehall. He was very
heavily fined, viz , £5 000 on 27 July 1644, and £2,000 on 16 Aug 1645.
He *m* firstly, *circa* 1602, Isabel, da of George BOWMAN, of Medbourne,
co Leicester He *m* secondly, Joan, widow of Thomas ADAMS and formerly of
(—) LEAVER, da. of (—) ARCHER He *d* 1658, aged 78, *bur* at Wistow Will dat.
4 June 1657, pr. 17 Nov 1658, and again 1698. His widow, by whom he had no
issue, *d* 1665 Will, as "of Sheavesby, co. Leicester, widow," dat 2 Oct. 1664,
pr 16 Jan 1665

II 1658   SIR THOMAS HALFORD, Bart. [1641], of Wistow aforesaid, grandson and h , being s and h of Andrew HALFORD, by his
1st wife Elizabeth, da of Sir George TURPIN, of Knaptoft, co. Leicester, which
Andrew was s and h ap. of the 1st Bart. (by his 1st wife) but *d* v p 1657, aged
54([b]) He *suc to the Baronetcy* in 1658. He *m* Selina, 1st da of William WELBY,
of Denton, co Lincoln, by whom he had 22 children He *d* 1679, and was *bur* at
Wistow. Admon 4 July 1679 That of his widow 1st April 1698

III 1679.   SIR THOMAS HALFORD, Bart [1641], of Wistow aforesaid,
s and h , *suc to the Baronetcy* in 1679 ; M P. for Leicestershire,
1689 90 He *d* unm 1690, and was *bur* at Wistow Will dat. 5 Feb 1689, pr
30 May 1690

IV 1690   SIR WILLIAM HALFORD, Bart. [1641], of Wistow afore
said, br and h, *suc to the Baronetcy* in 1690, being then under 21
He *m* Judith, da of Thomas BOOTHBY, of Tooley Park, co Leicester He *d* s p
1695, and was *bur* at Wistow Will dat. 18 May 1695, proved by his br Richard
the same year

V. 1695.   SIR RICHARD HALFORD, Bart. [1641], of Wistow aforesaid, br and h : was probably B A of Cambridge (Queen's Coll)
1700, and M A , 1704 ; was in Holy Orders. He *suc. to the Baronetcy* in 1695, and
purchased the Manor of Kibworth Harcourt in Leicestershire He *m* Mary, da of
Rev William COTTON, Rector of Broughton Astley, Leicestershire He *d* 5 Sep
1727, and was *bur* at Wistow

VI. 1727.   SIR WILLIAM HALFORD, Bart [1641], of Wistow aforesaid, s and h , *b* 1709 ; matric at Oxford (Lincoln Coll), 10 May
1723, aged 14 , B.A 26 Jan. 1726/7 ; M A 1730, having *suc to the Baronetcy,* 5 Sep
1727 At the coronation of George II he claimed the office of "Great Pannater"
Sheriff of Leicestershire, 1760-61. He *d* unm 1768 Will pr May 1768.

VII 1768,   SIR CHARLES HALFORD, BART [1641], of Wistow aforeto   said, nephew and h , being 4th but 1st surv s. and h. of Thomas
1780   HALFORD, by Elizabeth, da of Thomas PALMER, of Leicester, which
Thomas was 2d s of the 5th Bart. He *suc to the Baronetcy*
in 1768 ; was Sheriff of Leicestershire, 1769-70 He *m* Sarah, yst da. of Edward
FARNHAM, of Quorndon House, co Leicester He *d* s.p 21 July 1780, when

---

([a]) The patent is not enrolled. The date here given is that in Dugdale's *Catalogue*
See *Memorandum* on p 84 The date of the signet bill is 16 Dec 1641

([b]) It is said that this Andrew was condemned to death by Cromwell, for having
hanged a party of rebels against the King, but that his life was spared for a bribe
of £30,000

the *Baronetcy* is presumed to have become *extinct*([a]). He was *bur.* at Wistow Will. dat. 13 Sep 1777 ; pr 13 Dec 1780. His widow *m.* 21 July 1783, at Wistow (as his 2d wife), Basil (FEILDING), 6th EARL OF DENBIGH, who *d* 14 July 1800 She, who was *b.* 25 Oct 1741, *d* s.p 2 Oct 1814, at Brighton, and was *bur* at Wistow([b]) Will pr 1815

TUFTON :

cr 24 Dec 1641 ,

ex. 14 Oct. 1685

I 1641. "HUMFREY TUFTON, of Le Mote, in the parish of Maidstone, co Kent, Knt." being also of Bobbing Court in that county, yr br to Nicholas, 1st EARL OF THANET, and to Sir William TUFTON, 1st Bart. [I 1622], being 3d s of Sir John TUFTON, 1st Bart. [1611], of Hothfield, in that county, by his 2d wife Christian, da and coheir of Sir Humphrey BROWN, was *b.* 1584 , matric at Oxford (Univ Coll), 30 June 1598, aged 14 , admitted to the Inner Temple, 1601 , *Knighted*, 18 Jan 1613/4 , was M P. for Maidstone in the long Parl 1640, till secluded Dec 1648 , and was *cr. a Baronet*, as above, 24 Dec 1641 He was a Parliamentarian, serving on several important Committees, 1642-45 , was Sheriff of Kent, 1654-55 He *m.* Margaret,([c]) 1st da and coheir of Herbert MORLEY, of Glynd, co Sussex, a Colonel in the Parliament Service, by Anne, da of Sampson LENNARD, and Margaret, (*suo jure*) BARONESS DACRE. He *d* at Bobbing Court, Oct. 1659, aged 76, and was *bur.* at Bobbing. Admon 8 Oct 1659 The will of his widow pr 1667

II 1659, SIR JOHN TUFTON, Bart [1641], of the Mote and of
to Bobbing Court aforesaid, 2d but eldest surv. s. and h , *b* 1623 ,
1685 matric at Oxford (Univ. Coll), 29 April 1636, aged 13 ; *Knighted*, 21 Dec. 1641, at Whitehall , *suc to the Baronetcy*, Oct 1659 He *m* firstly, Margaret, 3d da. and coheir of Thomas (WOTTON), 2d BARON WOTTON OF MARLEY, by Mary, da. and coheir of Sir Arthur THROCKMORTON He *m.* secondly, Mary, da and coheir of Sir James ALTHAM, of Marks Hall, in Latton, co Essex, by Alice, da. and h of Sir John SPENCER, Bart [1626], of Offley, Herts He *d* s p 11 Oct 1685, aged 62, and was *bur* in Maidstone Church, when the *Baronetcy* became *extinct*([d]) Will pr. June 1686

COKE ·

cr 30 Dec. 1641 ;

ex. 26 Aug. 1727.

I. 1641 "EDWARD COKE, of Langford, co Derby, Esq." s and h of Clement COKE, by Sarah, da and h of Alexander REDDISH, of Reddish, co Lancaster, and of Langford aforesaid (which Clement was 7th and

---

([a]) See *N and Q.*, 6th S vii , 387, for some conjectures as to this not being the case
([b]) On her death, the Halford estates passed under the will of her late husband, the last Baronet, to his great nephew Sir Henry HALFORD, Bart, formerly Henry VAUGHAN, M D. See the Baronetcy of Halford, *cr.* 27 Sep 1809
([c]) See a curious account of her intimacy (Platonic, or otherwise) with the Hon Sir Christopher NEVILL (s of LORD ABERGAVENNY) in Pocock's Memorials of the family of Tufton—small 8vo , Greenwich, 1800 , p 34, etc.
([d]) He directed Bobbing Court to be sold for payment of his debts, but left "The Mote" (which had been purchased by his father of Thomas CÆSAR) to his niece Tufton, da. of Sir William Wray, 1st Bart [1660], of Ashby, by his sister Olympia, whose issue became sole heir of her family She *m.* Sir James MONTAGU, Lord Chief Baron of the Exchequer, and sold that estate to Sir John MARSHAM Bart., ancestor of the EARLS OF ROMNEY, who resided there till the 4th Earl sold it, May 1897, to Alderman Samuel

yet s of the celebrated Lord Chief Justice Sir Edward Coke), suc. his father, 23 May 1629, and was *cr a Baronet*, as above, 30 Dec 1641 He was Sheriff of Derbyshire Jan to Dec 1646   He *m* in or before 1645, Catherine, da and coheir of Sir William DYER, of Great Stoughton, co Huntingdon His will pr 1669

II   1669 ?   SIR ROBERT COKE, Bart [1641], of Langford aforesaid,
            s and h , *bap.* 29 April 1645, at Langford. Sheriff of Derbyshire, 1671-72 , M P thereof, 1685-87 , *suc to the Baronetcy* about 1669   He *m* Sarah, da and coheir of (—) BARKER, of Abrighlee, Salop   She was *bur* 13 Feb 1685, at Langford. He *d*. s p and was *bur* there 15 Jan. 1687/8   Will pr July 1689.

III. 1688,   SIR EDWARD COKE, Bart [1641], of Langford aforesaid,
    to   br and h , *bap* 6 Oct 1648, at Langford , matric at Oxford (Lincoln
    1727   Coll), 13 July 1666, aged 17 ; Barrister (Middle Temple) 1675 , *suc.
            to the Baronetcy*, 15 Jan 1687/8   He *m* in or before 1684, Catharine
She was *bur* 13 Dec 1688, at Langford   He *d* s p. 26 Aug 1727, when the *Baronetcy* became *extinct*   Will pr Dec 1727

Memorandum —ALL BARONETCIES CONFERRED by Charles I, AFTER 4 JAN 1641/2,[a] WERE (until the Restoration) DISALLOWED under the act of [the Rump] Parl dated 4 Feb 1651/2, whereby " all and every honours, titles, dignities and precedences whatsoever granted, confirmed and given by the late King since 4 Jan 1641 " were made " null and void " ; no one, after 25 March 1652, being allowed to assume them , each Peer so doing to forfeit £100, each Baronet or Knight to forfeit £40 , all such patents to be brought into the Court of Chancery so that they might be cancelled
All Royalist Baronetcies conferred after 22 May 1642[a] had previously been so disallowed by Parl, 11 Nov 1643, under the act which made void " all grants since 22 May 1642 of any honours, dignities, baronies, hereditaments or other thing whatsoever to any person or persons which have voluntarily contributed, or shall voluntarily contribute any aid or assistance to the maintenance of the unnatural war raised against the Parliament "   The new Great Seal " already made and provided [i.e , on 28 Sep 1643] was then placed in the hands of six Commissioners for use   Thus, for nearly three years there were *two* (rival) Great Seals of England, until, on 11 Aug. 1646, the *King's* Great Seal (which was taken at Oxford) was broken to pieces with great solemnity in the presence of both houses of Parl.   After that date this seal of 1643 would, presumably, be, even after the Restoration of the Monarchy, considered as the legitimate Great Seal of the realm, but it seems a moot point how far the Parliamentary Great Seal, when for nearly three years (1643—1646) it ran concurrently with, and often in opposition to, that of the King, would be thus acknowledged. On 9 Jan 1648/9, a new Great Seal was ordered [*Ex inform* W D Pink].

(a) There is some reason for the selection of the date of 22 May 1642, but there is none for that of the earlier date of 4 Jan. 1641/2   " By no manner of reasoning could it be pretended that Grants and Patents which had passed the (one) Great Seal between Jan and May 1642, when that Seal *was* in actual attendance upon Parl could be illegal "   The date of 4 Jan 1641/2, however, appears to have been chosen as being that on which the King attempted the arrest of the five members of the House of Commons, and so to have been looked on as the *date of the commencement of the Civil War*, after which everything done by the King alone was considered illegal   The fixing of this early date (4 Jan. 1641/2) was an afterthought, enacted nine years after the later date, 22 May 1642, had been fixed upon on the much more intelligible ground, as being that on which the Great Seal was held to have deserted the Parl on its having been delivered by Lord Keeper Lyttelton to the King at York. [*Ex inform* W. D. Pink]

CUNNINGHAM, *or* CUNYNGHAME:

cr. 21 Jan. 1641/2([a]).

I 1642, "DAVID CUNNINGHAM, of the city of London, Knt. and
to Bart of Scotland," s of Patrick CUNNINGHAM, of Kirkland, was
1659. Master of the Works to James VI [S], whom he accompanied
into England, being made Cofferer to Charles, Prince of Wales, bought
Balgray in the parish of Irvine, 1630, had crown charter of Auchenharvie in the
parish of Stewarton, co Ayr, 19 Feb 1631; had charter of the Barony of
Auchenharvie in Cape Breton, 23 Dec 1633, of Bohnshaw, 25 July 1634; and of
Drumilling, Feb 1636([b]); was cr a Baronet [S] about 1626, though the patent, said to
be one with rem. to heirs male whatsoever, was not sealed till 22 April 1634, and was
cr. a Baronet [E], as above, 21 Jan 1641/2 ([a]) He appears to have d unm ,([c]) at all
events s p, and was bur 7 Feb. 1658/9, at Charlton co. Kent, when the Baronetcy [E]
became extinct and the Baronetcy [S] became dormant. Will as "of Covent Garden,
Midx," dat 15 Dec 1647, to 18 Jan 1658/9 (leaving his "honoured kinsman, Sir
David Cuningham. of Robertland, Knt. and Bart," his universal legatee), pr
26 Aug. 1659, and 4 March 1674/5.

ASTLEY

cr. 21 Jan. 1641/2 ,([a])

ex 7 Dec 1659

I 1642, "ISAAC ASTLEY, of Melton Constable, co. Norfolk, Esq,"
to as also of Hill Morton, co Warwick, 2d s of Thomas ASTLEY, of the
1659 same, by Frances, da and coheir of George DEANE, of Tilney, co
Norfolk, and his eldest br, Sir Frances Astley, in 1635, and was
cr a Baronet, as above, 21 Jan. 1641/2,([a]) being Knighted the same day([d]) at
Whitehall He was Sheriff of Warwickshire, 1641-42, and of Norfolk, 1645-46
He m. firstly, Rachael, da. of Augustine MESSENGER, of Hackford, Norfolk He m
secondly, Bridget, widow of Edward DOYLEY, of Shottisham, Norfolk, da of John
COKE He d s p 7 Sep 1659, and was bur at Melton Constable, when the Baronetcy
became extinct ([e]) M I His widow d Oct. 1700

RAYNEY ·

cr. 22 Jan 1641/2([a]);

ex. 1721

I 1642. "JOHN RAYNEY, of Wrotham, co. Kent, Baronet of
Scotland," s and h of John RAYNEY, of the same, and of West
Malling in that county (who was fined for declining the post of Alderman, and who
was bur. at St Benet's Gracechurch, London, 25 April 1633), by Susan, da. of Walter
MANN, of Kingston, was bap. 5 April 1601, at St Leonard's, Eastcheap, was cr a

---

([a]) Disallowed 4 Feb 1651/2 by Parl till the Restoration; see *Memorandum* as to
creations after 4 Jan 1641/2, on p 152

([b]) *Ex inform*, R. R Stodart, Lyon Depute

([c]) There is a marriage licence 3 June 1637 (Bishop of London's office), for Sir
David Cunynghame, Knt. and Bart., of St Martin's in the Fields, bachelor, aged 29,"
with Elizabeth Harriott, of the same parish, widow of James Harriott, Esq, aged 28
This, presumably, must refer to Sir David Cuningham, Bart. [S 1630], of Robertland, and in the *History of Heriots Hospital* it is so assigned The age, unless grossly
misstated, militates against its referring to this Sir David.

([d]) The Isaac Astley who was Knighted 23 Feb. 1642/3 (afterwards the 2d Baron
Astley of Reading), is, in Metcalfe's "List of Knights," called *rightly* ' son of Sir
Jacob," as also, but *wrongly*, is this one

([e]) His estates devolved on his nephew and h, Jacob Astley, who was *cr.* a Baronet
1660.

V

Baronet [S.], 13 Sep 1636, with rem. to heirs male whatsoever, and was subsequently *cr. a Baronet* [E.], as above, 22 Jan 1641/2([a]), having been *Knighted* at Windsor, the day before, 21 Jan 1641/2 He was Sheriff of Kent 1644-45. He *m.* firstly, in or before 1627, Catherine, da of Thomas STYLE, of St. Dionis Backchurch, London, by his 2d wife, Elizabeth, da. of John WOODWARD, of London. She, by whom he had seven children, was *bap.* 8 Sep. 1605, at St. Dionis Backchurch, and was *bur.* there 28 Sep. 1637 He *m* secondly, 3 Oct 1639, at Eltham, Kent, Frances, da of Edward GIBBES, of Watergall, co Warwick, by Margaret, da. of William WILKES He *d.* at Wrotham, 3 and was *bur.* thence 9 March, 1660/1, at St. Benet's Gracechurch Will dat 22 Oct 1660, pr 2 April 1661 His widow *d.* in St Bride's, London, and was *bur.* 28 Aug. 1690, at St Benet's aforesaid M I Admon. 21 Nov. 1690.

II. 1661.   SIR JOHN RAYNEY, Bart [E 1642 and S. 1636], of Wrotham, and West Malling aforesaid, 1st s and h , by 1st wife, was *b* about 1627 , *suc to the Baronetcies*, 3 March 1660/1 He *m* firstly, Susan, or Mary, da of Jeremy BLACKMAN, of Southwark, Merchant, of London He *m.* secondly, Ellen, da. of William SHORT, of co Midx He *d.* 1680, aged 53 Admon. 9 July 1680

III 1680.   SIR JOHN RAYNEY, Bart [E 1642, and S. 1636], of Wrotham aforesaid, s and h. by, apparently, his 1st wife, *b* 1660 ; *suc to the Baronetcies* in 1680, when a minor He *m.* firstly, Vere, da. and coheir of Sir Thomas BEAUMONT, 3d Bart [1627], of Grace Dieu, by Vere, da. of Sir William TUFTON, Bart [I 1622] She *d.* 7 Dec. 1697, and was *bur* at Wrotham. M I He *m.* secondly, 29 Dec 1698, at St. Bride's, London, (Lic Vic -Gen , she about 30), Jane, 1st da. and coheir of Thomas MANLEY, of Rochester. She *d.* 14 Feb. 1700, and was *bur.* at Wrotham M I. Admon 16 Feb 1703/4 He *m.* thirdly, Jane, da. of Sir Demetrius JAMES, of Ightham, co. Kent, by Anne, da of George BATE, M D He *d* Feb. 1704/5, and was *bur* at Wrotham. M I Will pr. 21 March 1704/5 His widow *d.* 27 Feb 1714/5, aged 52, and was *bur.* at Wrotham. M.I. Will dat. 10 April 1711, pr. 9 March 1714/5.

IV 1705.   SIR JOHN BEAUMONT RAYNEY, Bart [E 1642 and S 1636], of Wrotham aforesaid, s. and h , by 1st wife, *b.* about 1688 , *suc to the Baronetcies* in Feb. 1704/5, shortly after which he sold the estate of Wrotham Place, in Wrotham aforesaid. He was Lieut Col in the army. He *d.* in 1716. Admon. 7 Aug. 1716.

V. 1716,   SIR THOMAS RAYNEY, Bart. [E 1642 and S 1636], br.
to   of the whole blood and h , *b.* 1690 ; *suc to the Baronetcies* in 1716.
1721.   He *d* unm 1721, aged 31, when the *Baronetcy* [E.] became
to Mary RAYNEY, his sister.   *extinct*, and the *Baronetcy* [S] *dormant* Admon 5 Oct. 1721,

---

ELDRED.

cr. 29 Jan. 1641/2([a]) ;

ex. 1652 or 1653.

I 1642,   "REVETT ELDRED, of Great Saxham, co. Suffolk, Esq.,"
to   s. and h., of John ELDRED, of the same, by (—) da. of Reginald
1653?   BROOKE, of Aspall, in that county, and of St. Michael's Bassishaw,
London, was *cr. a Baronet*, as above, 29 Jan 1641/2([a]) ; was Sheriff of Suffolk, 20 Nov 1645, but excused 6 Dec He *m.*, before 4 June 1638, Anne, da and coheir of John BLAKEY, or BLACKWELL, of co. Salop He *d* s p. about 1653 Will dat. 21 May 1652, pr 3 May 1653, when the *Baronetcy* became *extinct*. His widow *m* (—) ARNOLD, of London, fined for declining the post of Alderman. Her will pr. June 1671

([a]) Disallowed 4 Feb. 1651/2 by Parl. till the Restoration , see *Memorandum* as to creations after 4 Jan. 1641/2, on p. 152.

GELL·

cr. 29 Jan 1641/2([a]);

ex. 14 July 1719

I. 1642. "JOHN GELL, of Hopton, co. Derby, Esq.," s. and h. of
Thomas([b]) GELL, of the same, by Millicent, da. of Ralph
SACHEVERELL, of Stanton-by-Bridge, in that county, was *b* 22 June 1592, at
Carsington, co Derby, suc his father in his infancy, before 1595, and was brought
up at Kedleston, in the house of John Curzon, his step-father; matric. at Oxford
(Mag Coll.), 16 June 1610, aged 16, was Sheriff of Derbyshire, 1634 35, and was
cr a *Baronet*, as above, 29 Jan 1641/2([a]). He, however, in Oct 1642, raised a
regiment of Foot for the service of Parl., occupied Derby, and was appointed Gov. of
that town by the Earl of Essex, 5 Jan 1643, which he held against the King
throughout the Civil War, in which he was one of the most active commanders, taking
a share in the capture of Lichfield, the battle of Hopton Heath, etc.([c]) He was,
however, subsequently found guilty of plotting against the Commonwealth, 27 Sep
1650, his estate sequestrated, March 1651, and himself imprisoned till April 1653,
when he obtained a full pardon. On 4 June 1660, he claimed the benefit of the
King's Act of Indemnity. He m. firstly, 22 Jan 1609 (when only 16), Elizabeth,
da. of Sir Perceval WILLOUGHBY, of Wollaton, Notts, by Bridget, da. and coheir
of Francis WILLOUGHBY, of Wollaton aforesaid He m secondly, Mary, widow of
Sir John STANHOPE, of Elvaston, da of Sir Francis RADCLIFFE, of Ordsall, co.
Lancaster, by Alice, da of Sir John BYRON, of Newstead, Notts. She, by whom he
had no issue, appears to have d before him He d. 26 Oct 1671, at his house in
St Martin's Lane, London, aged 79 years, and was *bur.* at Wirksworth, co Derby.
M I. Will dat. 24 May to 31 July, pr 11 Nov. 1671.

II. 1671 SIR JOHN GELL, Bart [1642], of Hopton aforesaid, s and
h, by 1st wife, *bap.* at Kedleston, Oct 1613, matric. at Oxford (Mag
Coll), 23 Nov 1632, aged 17, M P for Derbyshire (three Parls), 1654-59, and Jan
to Feb 1688/9, *suc to the Baronetcy*, 26 Oct. 1671, Sheriff of Derbyshire, 1672-73.
He m, in or before 1648, Katharine, da of John PACKER, of Donington Castle, Berks
She apparently d before him. He d. 8 Feb. 1688/9, aged 75. Will dat. 18 Aug.
1687, pr. 14 May 1689

III 1689, SIR PHILIP GELL, Bart [1642], of Hopton aforesaid, 1st
to surv s and h([d]), *b*, probably about 1655, was M P for Steyning,
1719. 1679-81, and for Derbyshire, 1689-90; *suc. to the Baronetcy*, 8
Feb. 1688/9. He m, Elizabeth, one of the sixteen children of Sir
John FAGG, 1st Bart [1660], of Wiston, co. Sussex, by Mary, da. of Robert MOBLE,
of Glynd, in that county He d. s.p 14 July 1719, when the *Baronetcy* became
extinct([e]) Will pr. 1721

([a]) See p 154, note "a"

([b]) See *N and Q* 8th S., xii 401, correcting the article in the *Nat. Biogr.*, where
(as elsewhere) the father's name is erroneously given as "John."

([c]) He left a MS account of his military services to vindicate certain charges
brought against him by the Independents Lord Clarendon says that the whole of
Derbyshire was under the power of Sir John Gell, there being no visible party in it
for the King

([d]) John Gell, the 1st s. and h ap, said to be aged 15 in 1662 (Visit. of Derbyshire); matric at Oxford (St Edm Hall), 26 July, 1666, when he is said to be
aged 16, Barrister (Gray's Inn), 1674, d s.p and v p.

([e]) His nephew, John Eyre (2d s of his sister Catharine, by William Eyre, of
Highlow, co Derby), inherited the Hopton estate, and took the name of Gell, being
grandfather of the well-known classical antiquary, Sir William Gell, who d. 4 Feb.
1838, aged 59.

CORBET ·

cr 29 Jan 1641/2(ª),

ex. July or Aug 1688

I. 1642   "VINCENT CORBET, of Morton Corbet, co Salop, Knt ,"
s and h of Sir Andrew CORBET, of the same, by Elizabeth, da of
Wilham BOOTBBY, was b 13 June and bap there 13 July 1617 , matric at Oxford
(Queen's Coll) 24 Oct. 1634, aged 17 , admitted to Lincoln's Inn, 11 Nov 1637 , suc
his father, 7 May 1637 , was M P for Salop, April to May 1640, was Knighted, 29 June
1641, at Whitehall, and was cr a Baronet, as above, 29 Jan 1641/2(ª)   He was an
active supporter of the Royal cause, and was fined £2,022 on 3 Dec 1646, which was
reduced to £433. He m (b) Sarah, 4th da and coheu of Sir Robert Monson,
of North Carlton co Lincoln, which Robert was bur there 15 Sep 1638. He
d. at St Clement Danes, Midx , 28 Dec 1656, aged 40   Admon 1 June 1657, and 11
July 1676   His widow, on account of her husband's services on behalf of the late
King, was cr. 23 Oct 1679, a Peeress for life as VISCOUNTESS CORBET OF
LINCHLADE, co Buckingham   She m (two months later), 18 Dec. 1679, at Stoke
Newington, Midx , as his 4th and last wife (Lic Vic Gen , he aged 58), Sir Charles LEE,
of Billesley, co Warwick and of Edmonton, Midx , who was bur at Edmonton, 18
Dec 1700   She d 5 and was bur there 10 June 1682, when the life peerage became
extinct   Admon 30 June and 11 July 1682, and 7 Nov 1709

II. 1656.   SIR VINCENT CORBETT, Bart [1642], of Moreton Corbet
aforesaid and Acton Reynold, co Salop, 2d but 1st surv s and h ,(c)
b about 1642 , suc to the Baronetcy, 28 Dec 1656 , was M P. for Salop 1678/9 and
1679 till death   He m in or before 1670, Elizabeth, da and coheir of Francis
THORNES, of Shelvock, Salop. He d of the small pox, 4 Feb 1680, aged about 37.
Admon 14 May 1681, and 8 March 1705/6   His widow, living Sep 1688, d about
1702   Will pr Feb 1702/3.

III 1680,   SIR VINCENT CORBET, Bart [1642], of Moreton Corbet
to   and Acton Reynold aforesaid, only s and h , b 22 May 1670, suc
1688   to the Baronetcy, 4 Feb 1680, matric at Oxford (Ch. Ch), 4 May
     1686, aged 15   He d unm, in College, 22 July or 6 Aug 1688,
when the Baronetcy became extinct(d).   Admon 5 Sep 1688

KAYE .

cr. 4 Feb 1641/2(ª);

ex 25 Dec 1809.

I. 1642   "JOHN KAYE, of Woodsome [in Almondbury], co York,
Knt ," only s and h of Sir John KAYE, of the same (M P for Eye,
1610-11), by Anne, da of Sir John FERNE, secretary to the Council of the North, was
bap 15 Aug 1616, at Almondbury ; suc his father, 9 March 1640/1, was Knighted
24 May 1641, at Whitehall, and was cr a Baronet, as above, 4 Feb 1641/2(c).   He
was Colonel of a Regiment of Horse in the King's Service, and was a compounder
18 Feb 1644/5, and was on 22 March fined £500   He m firstly, 27 April 1637, at
Kirkby Wharf, Margaret, da and coheir of Thomas MOSELEY, of Northcroft, sometime Mayor of York, by Elizabeth, da and coheir of Thomas TRIGET, or TRIGOTT, of
South Kirkby, Yorkshire   He m secondly, before 1619, Elizabeth, widow of Thomas

---

(ª) Disallowed 4 Feb 1651/2 by Parl. till the Restoration ; see Memorandum as to
creations after 4 Jan 1641/2, on p 152

(b) The " Vincent Corbett, Esq , of the Inner Temple, Bachr , aged 26," on 15 July
1642, when he had lic (London) to marry Jane Acton, Spinster, was, though exactly
contemporary, probably the " Vincent Corbet " of Ynysmaengwyn, co Merioneth (s
and h of Robert Corbet)," who was admitted to Inner Temple in Nov 1639.

(c) Andrew Corbet, the 1st son, was bur 6 Sep 1645, at Moreton Corbet

(d) Beatrice, his only sister and h , b 1669, m before March 1705/6, John KYNASTON,
by whom (besides a da., Beatrice, who d unm), she had a son, Corbet KYNASTON,
sometime M P for Salop, who d unm 1741. The estate of Moreton Corbet, however,
passed to his great uncle and h. male, Richard Corbet, ancestor of the Corbet,
Baronets, so cr. 1808

BURDETT, of Birthwaite, co. York, da and h of Sir Ferdinando LEIGH, of Middleton, near Leeds She (by whom he had nine children, all of whom *d* s p) was *bur* 9 Sep 1658, at Almondbury He *m* thirdly, 12 Feb 1660, at Almondbury, Catharine, widow of Michael WENTWORTH, of Woolley, co York, da of Sir William ST QUENTIN, 1st Bart. [1642], by Mary, da and cohen of John LACY By her he had no issue He *d.* 25 and was *bur* 26 July 1662, at Almondbury His widow *m.* Henry SANDYS, of Down, co Kent She subsequently *m* (for her 4th husband and his 2d wife), Alexander (MONTGOMERIE), 8th EARL OF EGLINTOUN [S], who *d.* 1701 She was *bur.*, with her 3d husband, 6 Aug 1700, at Down aforesaid Admon 4 Feb 1700/1

II 1662.   SIR JOHN KAYE, Bart. [1642], of Woodsome aforesaid, s. and h by 1st wife, *b.* 1641 , *suc to the Baronetcy,* 25 July 1662, and was aged 25 at the Visit of Yorkshire, 1665 , M P for Yorkshire (four Parls), 1685-98 and 1701, till death He *m*, in or before 1663, Ann, da of William LISTER, of Thornton in Craven,[a] by Catherine, da and h of Sir Richard HAWKSWORTH, of Hawksworth. She was *bur* June 1702, at Almondbury He *d* 8 and was *bur* there 14 Aug 1706, aged 65 Will dat 21 June, pr 26 Nov 1706, at York

III. 1706   SIR ARTHUR KAYE, Bart [1642], of Woodsome aforesaid, s and h *b* 1660 matric at Oxford (Ch Ch), 2 March 1685/6, aged 15 , *suc to the Baronetcy,* 8 Aug 1706 , M P. for Yorkshire (four Parls), 1710 till his death He *m* (lic at York, 22 July 1690), Anne, 1st da and cohen of Sir Samuel MAROW, Bart [1679], of Berkswell, co Warwick, by Mary, da and h of Sir Arthur CAYLY, of Newland, in that county He *d* s p m [b] in London 10 and was *bur* 24 July 1726, at Almondbury. Will pr 1726 His widow was *bur* there 25 Aug 1740 Will pr 1740

IV. 1726   SIR JOHN LISTER KAYE, Bart [1642], of Denby Grange, in Kirkheaton, near Wakefield, co York, nephew and h male, being s. and h of George KAYE, of the same, by Dorothy, da and h of Robert SAVILE, of Bryan Royd, near Eland, co York, which George (who was *bur.* 4 April 1710, at Almondbury) was 3d s. of the 2d Bart He was *bap* 4 Sep 1697, at Almondbury, matric at Oxford (Ch. Ch), 24 May 1715, aged 18 *suc. to the Baronetcy,* 10 July 1726, and suc. to the Lister estates[a] in 1745, on the death of his paternal uncle, Thomas Lister, *formerly* Kaye He was M.P. for the city of York, 1734-40 , Alderman of that city, 1735, and Lord Mayor, 1737 He *m* firstly, before 1745, at Huddersfield, Ellen, da. of John WILKINSON, of Greenhead, co. York. She *d.* 29 Jan. 1729 He *m.* secondly, 29 July 1730, at Wibsey, Dorothy, da of Richard RICHARDSON, M.D , of North Bierley, in the West Riding of York, by Dorothy, da of Henry CURRER, of Kildwick. He *d.* 5 April 1752, and was *bur* at Flockton Will dat 8 Oct. 1751. His widow, who was *b* 16 June 1712, *d* 24 Aug 1772, at Gainford

V. 1752.   SIR JOHN LISTER Kaye, Bart [1642], of Denby Grange aforesaid, s and h by 1st wife, *b* 26 June 1725, probably at Huddersfield , matric at Oxford (Lincoln Coll), 28 Feb 1743/4, aged 18 , *suc. to the Baronetcy,* 5 April 1752 , Sheriff of Yorkshire, 1761-62. He *d.* unm , 27 Dec 1789 [c]

VI 1789,   SIR RICHARD KAYE, Bart. [1642], Dean of Lincoln, etc ,
     to   *br* of the half blood and h , being yst s. of the 4th Bart , by his 2d
     1809. wife, was *b* 11 Aug and *bap* 8 Sep 1736, at Kirkheaton , matric. at
            Oxford (Bras Coll.), 27 March 1754, aged 17 , Vinerian Scholar of
Laws at Oxford, 1758, being the first so elected , B C L , 1761 , D C L , 1770 ; was

[a] Christopher Lister, of Thornton aforesaid, only s and h of another Christopher Lister, of the same, *d* unm Nov 1701, having devised his estates to his cousin Thomas Kaye, 2d surv s of the 2d Bart He took the name of Lister, but *d* unm 1745, in his 70th year, when the estates devolved on his nephew, the 4th Bart , whose s and h the 5th Bart devised them as in note "c" next below

[b] Elizabeth, his only da and h , who inherited the family estate of Woodsome, *m* firstly, William LEGGE, *styled* VISCOUNT LEWISHAM, by whom she was mother of William, 2d EARL OF DARTMOUTH She *m* secondly, Francis (NORTH), 3d LORD GUILFORD (*cr* in 1752, after her death, EARL OF GUILFORD), by whom she also had issue She *d* 21 April 1745

[c] He devised his estates, being principally those inherited from the family of Lister, to his illegitimate son, John, who, as John LISTER KAYE, was *cr* a *Baronet,* 1812

in Holy Orders , chaplain to the King, 1766 ; sometime Rector of Kirkby Clayworth, Notts , Preb of York, 1768-88 , of Southwell, 1774-80 and 1783—1809 ; of Durham, 1777-84 , Archdeacon of Notts, 1780—1809 , Preb and Dean of Lincoln, 1783-1809 , Rector of Marylebone, Midx , 1788-1809 , F R S and F S A , *suc to the Baronetcy*, 27 Dec 1789 He *m.*, 29 Aug 1791, Helen, widow of Thomas MAINWARING, of Goltho', co Lincoln, da of William FENTON, of Glasshouse, near Leeds, co. York   He *d* s p m (a) 25 Dec 1809, aged 73, and was *bur.* in Lincoln Cathedral, when the *Baronetcy* became *extinct*   Will pr. 1810. His widow *d* 14 July 1841, at Coleby. near Lincoln, aged 96   Will pr. 1842

TROLLOPE, *or* TROLLOP·
cr 5 Feb. 1641/2(b) ;
afterwards, BARONS KESTEVEN OF CASEWICK.

I. 1642.   "THOMAS TROLLOP, of Casewicke, [in Uffington], co Lincoln, Esq ," s and h of William TROLLOPE, of Casewicke, and of Bourne and Thurlby, in the said county, by Alice, da. of William SHARPE, of Bourne aforesaid, suc his father, 8 June 1638 , was Sheriff of Lincolnshire 1641-42, and was cr a Baronet, as above, 5 Feb 1641/2 (b)   He m. firstly, in or before 1620, Hester, da of Nicholas STREET, or STURT, of Hadley,Suffolk   He m secondly, 16 Nov 1635, Mary, da of Sir Christopher CLITHEROE, Lord Mayor of London, 1635-36, by his 2d wife, Mary, da of Sir Thomas CAMBELL, Lord Mayor of London, 1609-10. He d. about 1654. Will dat 20 March 1651/2 pr 7 March 1654/5   His widow, who was b 10 Aug 1608, was bur 16 June 1688, at Uffington.

II 1654 ?   SIR WILLIAM TROLLOPE, Bart [1642], of Casewick House, in Casewick aforesaid, s and h by 1st wife, b. 3 Jan 1621 ; suc to the Baronetcy about 1654 , Sheriff of Lincolnshire, 1659 60   He m Elizabeth, widow of William THOROLD, of Marston co Lincoln, da of Sir Robert CARR, 3d Bart. [1611], Chancellor of the Exchequer   She was bur 27 Feb. 1661, at Uffington. He d s p m , 16 May 1678   Will dat. 21 Feb. 1669, pr 1678.

III 1678.   SIR THOMAS TROLLOPE, Bart. [1642], of Casewick House, aforesaid, nephew, of the half blood, and h male, being s. and h. of Thomas TROLLOPE, of Barham, co Lincoln, by Anne, da of Anthony COLLINS, of Whitton, Midx , which Thomas, last named, was s by his 2d wife, of the 1st Bart , was b about 1667 , suc. to the Baronetcy, 16 May 1678 ; matric at Oxford (Trin Coll.), 31 March 1682, aged 15 , was Sheriff of Lincolnshire, 1703-04. He m in or before 1690, Susanna 2d da and coheir of Sir John CLOBERY(c), of Bradstone, Devon, by his 2d wife, Anne, sister and coheir of Sir William CRANMER, da. of George CRANMER(d), of Canterbury   She d. 2 and was bur. 5 June 1724/5, at Uffington He d at Casewick House, 22 and was bur. 25 Nov 1729, at Uffington. Will pr. 1729.

IV. 1729   SIR THOMAS TROLLOPE, Bart. [1642], of Casewick House aforesaid, 1st surv s and h , bap 21 Dec 1691, at Uffington , admitted to Lincoln's Inn, 15 Nov 1716 , suc to the Baronetcy, 22 Nov 1729   He m , in or before 1721, Diana, da and coheir of Thomas MIDDLETON, of Stanstead, Essex, by Mary, da of Sir Richard ONSLOW, 1st Bart [1660] He d. 7 Oct. 1784, aged 93 Will pr Nov 1784

(a) Dorothy, *bap* 31 March 1741, at Kirkheaton, wife of Robert Chaloner, of Bishop's Auckland, was the only child that married.
(b) Disallowed 4 Feb 1651/2 by Parl till the Restoration ; see *Memorandum* as to creations after 4 Jan 1641/2, on p. 152
(c) A good account of the family of Clobery, and of the life of this Sir John, is given in Wotton's *Baronetage*. Edit 1741
(d) See full account of the family of Cranmer in R E Chester Waters' *History of the family of Chester, of Chicheley*

V. 1784.   SIR THOMAS-WILLIAM TROLLOPE, Bart [1642], of Casewick House aforesaid, grandson and h , being s. and h. of Thomas-
Middleton TROLLOPE (by Isabella, 1st da of Sir John THOROLD, 8th Bart. [1642], of
Marston, which Thomas last named (who d v.p. 27 April 1779, aged 58) was s. of
the 4th Bart (ª) He was b about 1762 , was ed at St John's Coll Cambridge ,
M.A., 1785, having suc to the Baronetcy, 7 Oct. 1784 He d unm , 13 May 1789,
aged 27. Will pr. 1789

VI. 1789   SIR JOHN TROLLOPE, Bart. [1642], of Casewick House
aforesaid, br and h , b about 1766 , suc. to the Baronetcy, 13 May
1789 ; Sheriff of Lincolnshire, 1811-12 He m 24 March 1798, at St Margaret's,
Lincoln, Anne, da of Henry THOROLD, of Cuxwold, co Lincoln. He d. 28 April
1820, aged 54 Will pr 1820. His widow d. 23 Dec 1855, at Casewick Will pr
Jan 1856.

VII. 1820.   SIR JOHN TROLLOPE, Bart [1642], of Casewick House
aforesaid, s. and h , b. there 5 May 1800 ; suc to the Baronetcy,
28 April 1820 , Sheriff of Lincolnshire, 1825-26 , M P. for South Lincolnshire, 1841-68 ,
Chief Commissioner of the Poor Law Board, Feb to Dec 1852 , P.C , 1852 He
m 26 Oct 1847, at St Marylebone, Julia Maria, 1st da of Sir Robert SHEFFIELD,
4th Bart [1756], by Julia Brigida, da of Sir John NEWBOLD, Ch Justice of Madras
She was living when, on 15 April 1868, he was cr a Peer, as BARON KESTEVEN
OF CASEWICK, co Lincoln, in which peerage this Baronetcy became henceforth
merged. See Peerage.

THOMAS :

cr 3 March 1641/2(ᵇ) ;

ex about 1690.

I. 1642   " EDWARD THOMAS, of Michael's Ville, anglice Michael's
town, co Glamorgan, Esq.," otherwise described as of Bettws in
Tir-y-jarll, and of Llanvihangell, both in that county, s. and h of Thomas AP
GWILLIM AP Howell GOCH, of Bettws aforesaid, Barrister, by Ann, da and h
of entail of Robert THOMAS, of Llanvihangell aforesaid(ᶜ), was Sheriff of Glamorganshire, 1633-34, and was cr a Baronet, as above, 3 March, 1641/2(ᵇ) He m Susan, da.
of Sir Thomas MORGAN, of Ruperra In or about 1650, he sold his estates to
Humphrey Edwin He d. at Windsor, Berks, 1673. Will pr 1673.

(ª) " Middleton Trollope [b. 31 July 1721], eldest son of Sir Thomas Trollope, died
at Devizes." see burial entry, 27 April 1779, at Uffington The 5th and yst. son of
the 4th Bart , the Rev Anthony Trollope. Rector of Cotterel, Herts (d. 3 June 1806,
aged 71), was father of Thomas Anthony Trollope, Barrister (d 26 Oct 1835, aged
61), who by Frances, da. of Rev. William Milton, Vicar of Heckfield, Hants (she,
well-known as a writer of fiction, d 6 Oct 1863, aged 83), had two sons, viz :
Thomas Adolphus Trollope. who d. 11 Nov 1892, aged 82, and Anthony Trollope,
who d 6 Dec. 1882, aged 67, both of whom were also novelists, the younger being
the most distinguished
(ᵇ) Disallowed 4 Feb 1651/2 by Parl. till the Restoration , see Memorandum as to
creations after 4 Jan 1641/2, on p. 152 The patent is not enrolled The date here
given is that in Dugdale's Catalogue See Memorandum on p. 84 The date of the
signet bill is 28 Feb 1641/2
(ᶜ) " Edward Thomas, s and h ap of William [sic] Thomas, of Llanyhangell co
Glamorgan, Esq., Bencher," was admitted to Lincoln's Inn, 9 March 1619/20.

II. 1673,   SIR ROBERT THOMAS, BART. [1642], s. and h ; Gent of
   to   the Privy Chamber, 1660 ; M P. for Cardiff (three Parls), 1661 81 ;
  1690 ?   *suc to the Baronetcy* in 1678   He *m.*, in or before 1654, Mary, 2d da.
           of David JENKINS, of Hensol   He *d.* s p m s (a), at some date after
1681, when the *Baronetcy*, presumably became *extinct.*

COWPER.

cr 4 March 1641/2 ;(b)

afterwards, since 1706, BARONS COWPER OF WINGHAM,

and subsequently, since 1718, EARLS COWPER

I   1642   " WILLIAM COWPER, of Ratlinge Court [in Nonington],
           co Kent, Baronet of Scotland," 2d s , but eventually h, of John
COWPER, of St Michael's Cornhill, Alderman of London, and sometime, 1551-52,
Sheriff of that city, by Elizabeth, da of John IRONSIDE, of co Lincoln, was *b*
7 March 1582, suc his father, 3 June 1609, was Collector of the imposts in the
port of London, was *cr a Baronet* [S], between 1625 and 1641, and was *cr a
Baronet* [E], as above, 4 March 1641/2(b), being *Knighted* at Theobald's, 1 March
following 1642/3   He and his eldest son, John COWPER, were, in Feb 1642/3, imprisoned at Ely House, London, for their exertions on behalf of the King. On his
release he resided at his Castle in Hertford   He was famed for his charity, hospitality,
etc   He *m*, 26 Sep 1611, at Ospringe, Kent, Martha(c), sister of Sir Edward MASTER,
da of James MASTER, of East Langdon Court, in that county, by his 1st wife
Martha, da of (—) NORTON, of London   She was *bur* 25 Nov 1659, at St
Michael's, Cornhill. He *d* 20, and was *bur* there 23 Dec. 1664, aged 82.   Will pr 1664

II. 1664   SIR WILLIAM COWPER, Bart [E 1642, S. 1640 ?], of Ratling
           Court and Hertford Castle aforesaid, grandson and h , being s and h
of John Cowper, of Lincoln's Inn, London (adm⁴ 20 Jan. 1631/2), by Martha, da of
George HEWKLEY, of London, merchant, which John was s and h. ap of the 1st
Bart, but *d* v p. when in confinement at Ely house aforesaid, in Sep.
1643 (d)   He *suc.* to the *Baronetcies*, 20 Dec. 1664.   He was M P for Hertford in
six Parls , 1679-1700 , was an active Whig, and joined with the Earl of Shaftesbury, etc , in presenting, in 1680, an indictment against James, Duke of
York, for non-attendance at church : was clerk of the Parliaments   He *m* (Lic.
Fac , 8 April 1663, she about 20 parents decd) Sarah, da of Samuel HOLLED, of St.
Clement's, Eastcheap, London, merchant, by Anne his wife.   He *d* 26 Nov. and was
bur 2 Dec 1706, at St Michael's, Cornhill   Will pr Jan 1707   She *d* 3 and
was *bur.* 10 Feb. 1719, at Hertingfordbury, Herts, aged 76

III. 1706   SIR WILLIAM COWPER, Bart. [E. 1642 and S 1640 ?], of
           Ratling Court, and Hertford Castle aforesaid, s and h (e), is said to
have been *b* at Hertford Castle, about 1665 , ed at St Albans' School ; admitted to
Middle Temple, 8 March 1681/2 , Barrister, 25 May 1688 ; took an active part in assist-

---

(a) He is incorrectly called " Edward " in Burke's and in Courthope's *Extinct
Baronetages*   His son, Robert Thomas, matric at Oxford (Jesus Coll), 14 Dec. 1671,
aged 17 , B A 1675 , M.A. 1678, having been admitted to Lincoln's Inn, 1676, as 2d
s of Sir Robert Thomas, Bart.   The last named Robert is presumed to have *d* v p
and s p m   Susanna, said to have been the only surv. child of the 2d Bart , *m*
Robert SAVOURS, of Bresch, and *d.* s.p. 2 Feb. 1747   Her portrait was at Llanvihangel
in 1865

(b) See p 159, note " b "

(c) See a good account of the family of Master by Rev George Streynsham Master,
M A , of which only 105 copies were privately printed, 1874 , large 8vo, pages 104.

(d) This John was the " Mr John Copper, out of Show lane," who was *bur*
25 Sep 1643, at St Michael's, Cornhill

(e) His next br , Spencer Cowper, one of the Justices of the Court of Common
Pleas, 1727-28 (*d* 10 Dec 1728, aged 59), was father of the Rev John Cowper, D.D ,
Rector of Berkhampstead, Herts (*d* 10 July 1756, aged 62), who was father of
William Cowper, the well-known Poet, *b* 15 Nov. 1731 ; *d.* unm. 25 April 1800.

ing the Dutch invasion of England ; King's Counsel 1694, Recorder of Colchester,
M.P. for Hertford (two Parls), 1695-1700, and for Beeralston 1901 02; was made P C
and Lord Keeper of the Great Seal 11 Oct. 1705, a Commissioner for the treaty of
the Union with Scotland 10 April 1706 ; *suc to the Baronetcies*, 26 Nov 1706, being
a few weeks later *raised to the Peerage* as stated below He *m* firstly, about 1686,
Judith, da and h of Sir Robert BOOTH, of Wallbrook, London, merchant She *d.*
s p 2 April 1705 He *m* secondly, "privately," bringing her home, 25 Feb 1706/7,[a]
Mary, da of John CLAVERING, of Chopwell, co Durham She was living when he,
being then L KEEPER OF THE GREAT SEAL, was *cr* a peer 9 Nov or 14 Dec 1706,
as BARON COWPER OF WINGHAM, co Kent, and, subsequently when (for the
2d time) L Chancellor, he was *cr.* 18 March 1717/8, EARL COWPER, etc. In
that peerage this *Baronetcy* then *merged* and still so continues See *Peerage*

STRUTT
cr. 5 March 1641/2 ;[b]

ex. Sep. 1661.

I   1642,   "DENNER STRUTT, of Little Warley Hall, co Essex,
to   Esq.," only s of John STRUTT, of Toppesfield Hall in Hadley, co
1661   Suffolk,[c] by Elizabeth, da and h of Edward DENNER, of Little
Warley aforesaid, was admitted to Gray's Inn, 6 March 1627/8, and was
cr a Baronet, as above, 5 March 1641/2 [b] He adhered loyally to the Royal cause,
was distinguished in the defence of Colchester, Aug 1648, was a Compounder,
30 Nov 1648, being, 11 Dec 1648, fined £1,350 He *m* firstly, Dorothy, da
of Francis STASMORE, of Forlesworth, co Leicester, sometime M P. She *d* s p
17 Aug 1641 He *m* secondly, Elizabeth, 4th da. of Sir Thomas WODEHOUSE,
2d Bart [1611], by Blanche da of John (CAREY), 3d BARON HUNSDON He *m*
thirdly, Mary, da and h. of Thomas CHAPMAN, of St. Leonard's, Foster Lane,
citizen and leatherseller of London She *d.* s p 4 Aug. 1658, aged 32 Will dat
2 Jan 1655/6, pr. 7 Sep 1658 He *m* fourthly, Elizabeth, da. of (—) CUSS, of co
Somerset He *d* s p m s[d] Sep. 1661, and was *bur* at Little Warley, when the
Baronetcy became *extinct* M I Will dat 6 and pr 19 Sep 1661. His widow *m*,
as his 3d wife, William WARD, of Little Houghton, co Northampton, who was *bur*
13 Jan 1672/3, at St Martin's in the Fields She was *bur.* there 27 March 1675.
Will dat. 18 Feb. 1674/5 pr. 1 Dec. 1675

ST. QUINTIN:
cr. 8 March 1641/2[b] ;

ex 22 July 1795.

I   1642   "WILLIAM ST. QUINTIN, of Harpham, co York, Esq,"
s and h of George St. QUINTIN, of the same, by Agnes, da of William
CREYKE, of Cottingham, in that county, was *b* 1579, and was *cr a Baronet*, as above,

---

(a) Luttrell's *Diary*.

(b) Disallowed by Parl, 4 Feb. 1651/2 till the Restoration ; see *Memorandum* on
p. 152 as to creations after 4 Jan, 1641/2 No patent is enrolled The date, as
well as the description of the party, here given is that in Dugdale's *Catalogue*
See *Memorandum* on p 84 It is to be observed that the creations of (1) Strutt ;
(2) St Quintin ; (3) Kemp, (4) Reade ; (5) Enyon ; (6) Williams, (7) Wintour ;
(8) Borlase ; (9) Knollys, and (10) Ingilby, are omitted in the *List of Creations,
1483—1646*" (ap 47th Rep D K. Pub Records), in which the date of the
warrant or Signet bill (failing that of the patent) for most of the Baronetcies down
to Feb 1644/5 is given

(c) This John suc. his elder br, Nicholas Strutt, clothier, in that estate, both being
sons of Nicholas Strutt, of the same, an opulent clothier, whose will dat. 23 Oct.
1601, is pr 21 Feb 1602 [*N and Q*, 4th S., vi, p 180, and Essex *Arch Assoc*,
Vol v, p 147

(d) Thomas Strutt, his son (by 2d wife), was living 2 Jan 1655/6.

X

8 March 1641/2(ᵃ)   He was Sheriff of Yorkshire 1648/49. He *m*, in or before 1605, Mary, sister and coheir of John LACY, 1st da of Robert LACY, both of Foulkton, co York She *d*. at St. Mary's, Beverley, 4 May 1649   He *d* there a few months later, in his 70th year, and was *bur* 8 Oct 1649, at Harpham M I to both of them at Harpham Will pr 1651

II. 1649   SIR HENRY ST QUINTIN, Bart [1642], of Harpham aforesaid, s and h aged 7 in 1612, and aged 59 in 1665 [Visit of Yorkshire] ; *suc to the Baronetcy* in Oct 1649 He *m* Mary, 2d da of Henry STAPLETON, of Wighill, co York, by Mary, illegit da of Sir John FORSTER, of Alnwicke. He *d* in, or shortly after, Nov 1695, at a great age.

III 1695?   SIR WILLIAM ST QUINTIN, Bart [1642], of Harpham, aforesaid, grandson and h, being 1st surv. s and h (ᵇ) of William ST. QUINTIN, by Elizabeth, da. of Sir William STRICKLAND, 1st Bart [1641], which William St Quintin, was s and h ap. of the 1st Bart, and *d*. v p, being *bur*. at Harpham, 6 Nov 1695, aged 63 He was aged 3 in 1665 ; *suc. to the Baronetcy* in, or shortly after, 1695, was M P for Hull (in eleven Parls), 1695 till his death, a Commissioner of the Customs, 1698-1701, of the Revenue [1], 1706-13, one of the Lords of the Treasury, 1714 17, and Vice Treasurer and Receiver General of Ireland, 1720 till his death He *d*. unm, "universally lamented by all who knew him for his great abilities," 30 June, and was *bur* 15 July 1723, at Harpham, in his 63d year. M I. Will pr. 1723

IV. 1723   SIR WILLIAM ST QUINTIN, Bart. [1642], of Harpham aforesaid, and of Scampston, co. York, nephew and h., being s and h of Hugh ST QUINTIN, by Catherine, 1st da of Matthew CHITTY, which Hugh (who *d*. 6 Dec 1702, aged 31), was yst. br. of the 3d Bart He was *b*. about 1700, *suc to the Baronetcy*, 30 June 1723, was M P for Thirsk, 1722 27, Sheriff of Yorkshire, 1729-30 He *m* 11 June 1724, at Somerset House Chapel, Rebecca, da. and h of Sir John THOMPSON, Lord Mayor of London, 1736-37, by his 1st wife. She *d*. Oct 1757, and was *bur* at Harpham M I. Admon. as "of Scampston, co. York," 20 Oct 1757. He *d*. 9 May 1770, at Bath Will pr. May 1770

V. 1770,   SIR WILLIAM ST. QUINTIN, Bart [1642], of Harpham
    to   and Scampston aforesaid, only surv. s and h, *bap* 4 July 1729, at
    1795   Rillington, *suc to the Baronetcy*, 9 May 1770 ; Sheriff of Yorkshire, 1772-73 He *m*. 14 May 1758, at St James' Westm, Charlotte, da of Henry FANE, of Wormsley, Oxon., M D (br. of Thomas, 8th EARL OF WESTMORLAND), and only child of his 1st wife, Charlotte, da of Nicholas ROWE, the Poet She *d*. 17 and was *bur* 24 April 1762, at Harpham M I He *d*. s p 22 and was *bur*. 31 July, 1795, at Harpham, when the *Baronetcy* became *extinct*(ᶜ) M I. Will pr Dec. 1797

KEMP, *or* KEMPE :
cr. 14 March, 1641/2(ᵃ).

I. 1642.   "SIR ROBERT KEMPE, of Gissing(ᵈ), co Norfolk, Knt.", s and h of Robert KEMPE, of the same, by Dorothy, da and sole h. of Arthur HERRIS, of Crixeth Essex, was admitted to Gray's Inn, 26 Feb.

(ᵃ) See p 161, note "b," *sub* Strutt.
(ᵇ) Henry, aged 11 at the Visit. of 1665, (being eight years his senior,) was the eldest son.
(ᶜ) The estate of Scampston, co. York, went to his Nephew, William Thomas DARBY, of Sunbury, Midx., s of George DARBY, of Newton, Hants, by Mary, the only one of his sisters who had issue He, in 1795, took the surname of ST QUINTIN, and *d*. 18 Jan. 1805, aged 35, leaving issue
(ᵈ) This manor came into the family as early as 1324, by the marriage of Alan *Kemp*, with Isabel, da. of Sir Philip HASTINGS, of Gissing aforesaid.

1604/5 ; *suc* his father 24 April 1614, was Gentleman of the Bed Chamber to Charles I, in 1631, and, being distinguished for his loyalty to that King, was *Knighted,* 7 Aug 1641, at Whitehall, and was cr a *Baronet,* as above, 14 March 1641/2(a), all the fines and fees of passing the patent thereof being remitted He m Jane, da of Sir Matthew BROWNE, of Beechworth Castle, Surrey, by Jane, da of Sir Thomas VINCENT, of Stoke Dabernon He d 20 Aug 1647. Will pr. in Consistory Court of Norwich, 1647

II 1647. SIR ROBERT KEMPE, *or* KEMP, Bart [1642], of Gissing aforesaid, s and h b. 2 Feb 1627, at Walsingham Abbey, Norfolk, *suc. to the Baronetcy,* 20 Aug 1647, M P for Norfolk, May 1675 to 1679, for Dunwich 1679-81 and 1681 He m firstly, 15 July 1650, at St Barth the Less, London, Mary, da of Thomas KERRIDGE, of Shelley Hall, Suffolk, by Susan, his wife She was b Feb 1631, and d s p June 1655. He m. secondly, 20 Nov 1657, Mary, da and sole h of John SONE, of Ubberston, Suffolk, by Mary, da of William DADE, of the same county She, who was b 6 April 1637, d at Ubberston, 29 July, and was *bur* 2 Aug 1705, at Gissing He d 26 Sep 1710, aged 83, and was *bur* at Gissing M I Will pr 1710, in Archdeaconry of Suffolk

III 1710. SIR ROBERT KEMP, Bart [1642], of Gissing and Ubberston aforesaid, s and h by 2d wife, bap 25 June 1667, at Ubberston, *suc to the Baronetcy,* 26 Sep 1710, was several times M P for Dunwich, 1701-09 (four Parls) and 1713-15; for Suffolk, Feb 1732 to 1734, and 1734 till death He m. firstly, Letitia, widow of Sir Robert KEMPE, of Finchingfield, Essex, da of Robert KING, of Great Thurlow, by Elizabeth, da of Thomas STEWARD, of Barton Mills. She d s p m He m. secondly, in or before 1699, Elizabeth, da. and h of John BRAND, of Edwardston, Suffolk She d 1709 He m thirdly, Martha, da of William BLACKWELL, of Mortlake, Surrey She d 1727. He m fourthly, 9 July 1723, Amy, widow of John BURROUGH, of Ipswich, da of Richard PHILLIPS, of Edwardston aforesaid, but by her had no issue He d 18 Dec 1734, aged 68, at Ufford, Suffolk. Will pr 1735 His widow d 1745 Her will pr 1746

IV 1734 SIR ROBERT KEMP, Bart [1642], of Gissing aforesaid, s and h by 2d wife, b 9 Nov 1699, *suc to the Baronetcy,* 18 Dec. 1734, was M P for Orford, Feb. 1730 to 1734 He d unm 15 Feb 1752.

V 1752. SIR JOHN KEMP, Bart. [1642], of Gissing aforesaid, br., of the whole blood, and h, b 19 Dec 1700, was sometime a merchant in London, *suc to the Baronetcy,* 15 Feb 1752 He m Elizabeth, widow of Isaac Brand COLT, of Brightlingsea, co Essex, da of Thomas MANN He d. s p 25 Nov 1761. Will pr 1761 The will of his widow pr. March 1768.

VI 1761. SIR JOHN KEMP, Bart [1642], of Gissing aforesaid, nephew and h, being s and h of Rev Thomas KEMP, Rector of Gissing and Flordon, Norfolk, afterwards of Penryn, Cornwall, by Priscilla (who, in May 1771, was wife of Andrew Merry), which Thomas (who d 1761, aged 65) was br. of the whole blood to the 4th and 5th Baronets He was b 1754, *suc to the Baronetcy,* 25 Nov 1761, was ed at Westminster School, but d, a minor, and unm, 16 Jan. 1771. Admon. 16 May 1771.

VII 1771. SIR BENJAMIN KEMP, Bart. [1642], of Gissing aforesaid, uncle and h., being br, of the whole blood, of the 4th and 5th Baronets; b 29 Dec 1708, ed at Caius Coll, Cambridge, of which he was Fellow, 1733 till death; B A., 1731, M A, 1735; was a Physician; *suc to the Baronetcy,* 16 Jan. 1771 He m. Elizabeth, widow of John COLT, of Tooting, co Surrey He d s p. 25 Jan 1777, at Coln St Denis, co Glouc M I there. Will pr 1777 That of his widow (as of Tooting, Surrey) pr 1790 in the Prerog Court [I]

(a) See p 161, note "b" *sub* Strutt

VIII. 1777　　Sir William Kemp, Bart [1642], of Gissing aforesaid,
　　　　　　　cousin and h male, being s and h of William Kemp, of Antingham,
Norfolk, by Elizabeth, only da and h of Henry Shardelow, Alderman of Norwich,
which William, last named, was younger s of the 2d Baronet, by his 2d wife He was
b. 31 Dec 1717, suc to the Baronetcy 25 Jan 1777　He m Mary, da of (—)
Ives, of Colts Hall　She was bur 22 Nov. 1751　He d 5 Nov 1799

IX. 1799　　Sir William Robert Kemp, Bart [1642], of Gissing
　　　　　　　aforesaid, s and h, bap 18 May 1744 ; suc to the Baronetcy 5 Nov.
1799　He m, 9 Dec 1788, Sarah, da and h. of Thomas Adcock, of Carleton, Norfolk　He d. 11 Oct 1804.　His wife survived him

X. 1804.　　Sir William Robert Kemp, Bart [1642], of Gissing
　　　　　　　aforesaid, s and h, b 14 Nov 1791, suc to the Baronetcy 11 Oct
1804, ed at Christ's Coll, Cambridge, M A 1813, was in Holy Orders, Rector of
Gissing and Flordon, co Norfolk, 1816 till his death　He m, 10 March 1859, Mary,
5th da of Charles Saunders, of Camberwell, Surrey, and of Gissing aforesaid　She
d. Jan 1866　He d 29 May 1874, at Gissing Hall, in Gissing, in his 83d year.

XI. 1874,　　Sir Thomas John Kemp, Bart. [1642], of Gissing Hall,
　　　May　　aforesaid, br and h, b 14 Oct 1793, suc. to the Baronetcy, 29 May
　　　　　　　1874, but d. unm, a few months later, 7 Aug. 1874, at Long
Stratton, in his 81st year

XII. 1874,　　Sir Kenneth Hagar Kemp, Bart [1642], of Gissing
　　　Aug　　Hall aforesaid, cousin and h male, being only surv s and h. of the
　　　　　　　Rev Nunn Robert Pretyman Kemp, of Erpingham, Norfolk, by Mary
Harriet, da of Rev Thomas Hagar, of Lonmay, co. Aberdeen, which Nunn (who d
v p 25 Aug. 1859, aged 45,) was 1st s of the Rev Thomas Cooke Kemp, Vicar of East
Meon, Hants (d. 17 Oct 1867, aged 79), s and h of Thomas Benjamin Kemp, of
Swafield, co Norfolk (d 24 June 1838), who was br to the 9th and s of the 8th Baronet.
He was b April 1853, at Erpingham aforesaid, ed at Jesus Coll, Cambridge, B A,
1874, suc to the Baronetcy, 7 Aug 1874　Barrister (Inner Temple), 1880, Major
3d Batt Norfolk Reg (Militia), partner in the banking firm of "Lacon, Youells and
Kemp," at Yarmouth and Norwich. He m., 30 Aug 1876, at Chilham, co Kent,
Henrietta Maria Eva, 1st da of Henry Hamilton, of Chilham aforesaid, formerly
of Blackrock, co Leitrim.

Family Estates.—These, in 1883, consisted of 2,133 acres in Norfolk, worth £3,163
a year.　*Principal Residences* —Gissing Hall, near Diss, and Mergate Hall, near
Braconash, co. Norfolk

READE:

cr. 16 March 1641/2 ,(a)

ex. 22 Feb. 1711/2 ;

but assumed since 1810

I. 1642　　"John Reade,(b) of Brockett Hall [in Hatfield], co
　　　　　　　Herts, Esq," 4th but 2d surv s(c) of Sir Thomas Reade, of
Dunstew, Oxon (bur there 20 Dec. 1650), by Mary, 5th da and coheir of Sir John

---

(a) See p 161, note "b," *sub* "Strutt"
(b) See "A record of the Redes," by Compton Reade, 4to, 1899
(c) He is called "second son" in his admittance to Linc Inn in 1632, as also in a
deed made by his father 2 Jan 1639　Of his three elder brothers (1), Walter Reade,
d. unm v p and was bur 9 Sep 1625, at St Nicholas', Abingdon, aged 24,
(2) Thomas Reade, b at Barton Court, and bap 12 Feb 1606/7, at St Helen's,
Abingdon, m 8 Sep 1624, without his father's consent, and d v p Sep 1634, leaving

BROCKET, of Brocket Hall aforesaid, was *b* about 1616 ; admitted to Lincoln's Inn, 7 June 1632 , was *Knighted* at Newmarket, 12 March 1641/2, and was, four days later (tho' apparently only under the designation of an "Esq") *or a Baronet*, v.p , as above, 16 March 1641/2 (a)   He was assessed at £600 for the war expenses, but was respited (b)   During the Usurpation he was Commissioner for Herts, Nov. 1650 , Sheriff of Herts, 1655-56 ; and (the honours conferred on him by Charles I(a) not being recognised) was base enough to accept *a fresh Baronetcy*, dated 25 June 1656, *from the Protector* for himself and "his heirs," being the first hereditary honour granted by Cromwell.   At the Restoration he obtained a pardon, 7 June 1660, for all offences during the Civil War and the Commonwealth   He was again Sheriff of Herts, 1673-74, and was also elected as such Nov 1671, Nov 1676, and Nov 1677, but did not act   On 20 Jan 1679, he purchased the estate of Calthorp, co Oxon   He *m.* firstly, 2 Jan. 1640, Susanna, 2d da. of Sir Thomas STYLE, 1st Bart [1627], of Wateringbury, by Elizabeth, da and h of Robert FOULKES. She was *bur.* 18 May 1657 in the Brocket chapel at Hatfield M.I   He *m* secondly, 15 Jan 1662/3, at St Nicholas Acons, London (Lic. Lond 13, he aged 46, she of Hatton Garden aged 40), "Lady Alismon" widow of the Hon Francis PIERREPONT   They were, however, separated in about three and a half years' time,(c) and she was living 6 May 1682   He was *bur* 6 Feb 1693/4 in the Brocket chapel aforesaid   Admon 26 Feb 1693/4, as also in the Prerog. Court of Dublin

II. 1694.   SIR JAMES READE, Bart [1642], of Brocket Hall and Dunstew aforesaid, 4th but only surv s. and h by 1st wife, *bap.* 10 March 1654/5, at Hatfield , matric at Oxford (Trin Coll.), 14 May 1675, and then called 17 , Sheriff of Herts, 1693 94 , *suc to the Baronetcy* Feb. 1693/4 , Sheriff of Oxon, 1700-01. He *m* 26 Jan 1689/90, at Mercers' chapel, Cornhill, London (Lic Vic Gen 24, he about 30 and she about 25), Love, 2d da and coheir of Robert DRING, of Isleworth, Midx , Alderman of London (*d* about 1697), by Dorothy his wife   He *d* of a fever 16 and was bur 21 Oct. 1701, in the Brocket chapel aforesaid, aged 46 years, 7 months and 11 days M I   Admon 10 Dec 1701   His widow, whose dowry was £10,000, *d* 9 and was *bur* , with her husband, 18 Nov. 1731, aged 76 M I   Will dat 23 July 1729, pr 26 Nov 1731

III. 1701,   SIR JOHN READE, Bart [1642], of Brocket Hall and **to**   Dunstew aforesaid, only s and h , *b* 1691 , *suc to the Baronetcy*, 16 **1712.**   Oct 1701 , ed at Eton , matric at Oxford (Wadham Coll), 7 Nov 1705, aged 14 , became a Jacobite,(d) and *d. unm* , of the small pox, at Rome, 22 Feb , being *bur.* 11 June 1712, in the Brocket chapel aforesaid, aged 21, when the *Baronetcy* became *extinct*.(e)   Admon 24 March 1711/2.

---

issue. of whom Compton Reade, of Shipton Court, Oxon, was cr *a Baronet*, 4 March 1660/1, and (3) Richard Reade, *b* 12 June 1610, living in 1623, sometimes thought to be ancestor of the family of Reade, of Rossenara in Ireland, but who more probably *d* v p and s p

(a) See p. 161, note "b" *sub.* "Strutt"

(b) "Though a Baronet, he is a very poor one . has a poor stock and only a little money, which his father send [*sic*] him " See p 164, note "b."

(c) "He kept a mistress in his house and encouraged her to insult his wife   He padlocked her into her room," etc. See p 164, note "b"

(d) His uncle, Almericus (de Courcy) Baron Kingsale (I), who had married his mother's sister, held a post in the court of the titular James III

(e) Of his five sisters and coheirs, two *d unm* and two *d* without issue, one of which last, Love, inherited the Brocket Hall estate, and *m.*, 6 Aug 1719, Thomas Winnington, who by his will, pr 2 May 1746, left it to his own collateral relations, by whom it was sold to Matthew Lambe, and became the seat of Viscount Melbourne [I.], Prime Minister, 1834 and 1835-39, and subsequently of Viscount Palmerston [I], Prime Minister, 1855 58 and 1859-65   Dorothy, the eldest sister, and the only one who had issue, *m.* Robert Dashwood, and was mother of Sir James Dashwood, 2d Bart [1684], who is called in the will (dat 7 Aug 1752, and pr 7 Aug. 1754) of his maternal aunt, Mary Reade, spinster, "the only living branch of the coheirs of Sir John Reade, Bart "   This Dorothy inherited the estate of Dunstew, as also that of Minsden (in Hitchin), Herts, which had been inherited by the Reades, thro' the families of Brocket and Lytton.

This Baronetcy was assumed in April 1810 by the Rev William Reade, who at first alleged himself to be descended from a younger son of the 1st Bart., whom, at that date, he stated to be Major John Reade (ᵃ) The name of this younger son he subsequently, however, altered to Matthew, and a statement was added that this Matthew, whose very existence is questionable, succeeded to the Baronetcy in 1712   As to the fact that Matthew, or any of the persons undermentioned, were, until 1810, ever known as "Baronets," it seems more than doubtful   The pedigree, as finally alleged, is as under (ᵇ)

IV.   1712   "SIR MATTHEW READE, Bart" [1642], of Kileavy, co Clare, stated to have been uncle and h male of the 3d, and younger s of the 1st Bart   and to have *suc to the Baronetcy*, 22 Feb 1711/2. He *m* Anne, da of Sir Edward DOWDALE, of Drogheda, by Anne, da of ' the Right Hon THE EARL OF DESMOND" He *d* June 1721   The will of " Sir Matthew Reade, of Kileavy, co Clare," dat 15 June 1721 (in which, most aptly for proving the pedigree, be mentions his son John Reade his father, Sir John Reade, Bart, deceased, and his brother, Sir James Reade, Bart, deceased) proved to be a forged one (written on modern paper), brought into the Prerog. Office [I] for proof, by the claimant's son, 18 April 1710, about 90 years after the death of the alleged testator

V   1721   "SIR JOHN READE, Bart." [1641], of Kileavy aforesaid, only s and h   He *m* Anastacia, da and h of Michael NICHILL, of Glascongue, co. Clare, and of Pennywell (or Rennywell), co Limerick   No date of death is given (ᵇ)

VI   1750 ?   "SIR WILLIAM READE, Bart." [1641], of Ballymacranen, co. Clare, only s and h   He was M P [I] for Dublin till his death. He *m* Sarah, da and h of Thomas LUCAS, of Ballingaddy, co Clare, niece to Charles LUCAS, M.D   He *d* 12 Aug 1787.

VII.   1787.   "SIR WILLIAM READE, Bart ' [1641], of Moynoe House, co Clare, 1st s and h (ᶜ) of six sons , *b* 1762; was in Holy Orders, being sometime Rector and Preb of Tomgraney, co Clare ; was a Magistrate for co. Clare in 1791, but not described as a Baronet, though that date was four years after his father's death   He took an active part against the Irish rebels of 1798.   In 1810, however, he *assumed the style of a Baronet*(ᵃ) as above mentioned   He *m*, in or before 1788, Alicia, da. of Anthony BRADY, of Kielty, co Clare   He was living 1811, in his 50th year.

VIII   1820 ?   "SIR JOHN READE, Bart " [1642], of Moynoe House aforesaid, only s. and h, *b* 3 Aug. 1788   He, having presented himself for Knighthood as the eldest son of a Baronet,(ᵈ) at the Court of the

(ᵃ) In a "letter from Sir William Betham to George Nayler, Esq.," dat 31 March 1814, the writer states that, in 1809, the Rev William Read said he had a claim to an English Baronetcy, through his ancestor, Major John [*sic*] Read, 2d son of the 1st Bart , but that sometime afterwards he produced a copy of the will of Sir Matthew Read, "making out a very different case to that originally stated to me " This was printed in 1832, as also were copies of all papers in the Heralds' College connected with this claim

(ᵇ) The pedigree, as in the text, deducing the "Sir William," of 1810, from the "Sir Matthew," of 1712, is printed in (that most uncritical work) Playfair's *Baronetage*, 1811.   It was doubtless furnished by Sir William himself, together with a laudatory account of his own exploits against the Irish rebels

(ᶜ) Two *elder* brothers, the Rev John Reade and Charles Reade, are, however, stated to have been living in 1810.

(ᵈ) This misrepresentation was apparently the cause of the omission of the clause enforcing such Knightage in the patents of Baronetage   It would have been a more desirable result had it lead to the granting such Knighthood, in the cases only where *proof* of the father's Baronetcy had been furnished.

Viceroy [I] (the Duke of Richmond) was *Knighted* accordingly 18 June 1811. He was a Magistrate for co. Clare, 1814 , took Holy Orders, and subsequently became blind. He *m* , 4 Nov 1810, Urania Maria, da. and coheir of Edward VERO,[a] of Dublin, and or Lough Raer, co Galway, by Mary, da. and h of Jervis HBRIDE, of Aunadonn, co Galway She *d* in 1842 [b] He was *bur.* 14 Dec. 1842, at St Anne's, Soho

IX 1842. "SIR JOHN CECIL READE. Bart." [1644], 1st surv. s and h , was Governor of Darlinghurst gaol, Sydney, New South Wales. He *m* 28 Nov. 1838, Ann, 1st da. of Michael EAGAN, of Dublin He *d* March 1899 His widow living 1900, at Arawa Bronte, Waverley, in New South Wales [b]

X 1899. "SIR WILLIAM VERO READE, Bart " [1644], 1st s. and h , *b* 22 Sep 1839 , was, as early as 1855, in the employ-ment of the Railway Department in New South Wales, and for many years chief traffic manager He *m* , in 1867, Emily Anne, 5th da of William TINDALE, of Hornsey Wood, Penrith, New South Wales, and has issue, William John Cecil Read, being his eldest son [b]

ENYON

cr. 9 April 1642[c] ,

ex the same year

I 1642. "JAMES ENYON, of Flowre [*i e*, Flore], co Northampton, Esq , only s and h of James Enyon, of the same, by Dorothy, da of Thomas COXE, of Bishop's Itchington, co Warwick (which James last named, was s and h. of James Enyon, of Whitechapel, Brewer, who purchased the manor of Flore, and *d*. in 1623,) was *b* about 1587 , matric. at Oxford (Ch Ch), 30 March 1604, aged 17 , adm to Gray's Inn, 17 March 1602/3, being then of St Mary's White-chapel, late of Barnard's Inn, and was *cr. a Baronet*, as above, 9 April 1642 [c] He *m* Jane, da of Sir Adam NEWTON 1st Bart [1620], of Charlton, by Dorothy, da. of Sir John PUCKERING, sometime Lord Keeper of the Great Seal He was killed in a duel at the quarters of the Royalist army at Gloucester, a few months after his creation, by his friend, Sir Nicholas Crispe, who ever afterwards wore mourning for him He *d*. s p m [d] when the *Baronetcy* became *extinct* His admon (as " Sir James Onion ") 19 May 1648, to a creditor The will of his widow was pr 1664

(a) A correspondent writes that "in the old Dublin almanacs, I find, 1798—1819, an Edward Vero, a tailor, but he may not be the father [of Urania] however *Si non e Vero, e ben trovato* "
(b) The information as to this family, since 1811, is kindly furnished by C. M. Tenison, of Hobart, in Tasmania
(c) See p 161, note " b," *sub* " Strutt."
(d) The estate of Flore went to his three daughters and coheirs [Baker's *North-amptonshire*, vol i, p 153]

WILLIAMS·

cr. 19 April 1642(a);

ex 14 Nov. 1680.

I 1642   "EDMUND WILLIAMS, of Marnhull, co Dorset, Knt.,"
s and h of John WILLIAMS of Marnhull aforesaid, and of St Peter's
Eastcheap, London, citizen and goldsmith, by Joan, sister of Edward ALLEN, Alderman and sometime (1620 21) Sheriff of London, 3rd da of Thomas ALLEN, citizen
and haberdasher of London, by his 1st wife Joan, da of Edward WOODGATE, of Kent ;
suc. his father, 14 Sep 1637, was one of the Gentlemen of the Privy Chamber ;
was *Knighted*, as "of London," 8 Jan 1638/9, at Whitehall, and was cr a *Baronet*,
as above, 19 April 1642 (a) He m May, 4th da of Sir John BEAUMONT, 1st Bart
[1627], of Gracedieu, by Elizabeth, da. of John FORTESCUE He d early in 1644.
Will, in which he directs to be *bur* with his father, at St Peter's, in Cheapside,
dat 15 to 20 Dec 1643, pr 10 April 1644 (b) His widow, who was b 7 July 1617,
m before 1647, John TASBURGH, and had issue Her admon. 18 Jan. 1650/1, to her
said husband.

II. 1644,   SIR JOHN WILLIAMS, Bart [1642], only s and h. ; *bap*
to   11 Sep 1642, at St. Andrew's, Holborn , suc *to the Baronetcy* (when
1680   an infant) in 1644 , matric at Oxford (St John's Coll) 26 Oct. 1660,
and was cr M A , 9 Sep 1661. He suc to the estate of Minster
Court, co Kent, on the death, 26 March 1669, of his uncle, Sir John Williams, Bart
[so cr 22 April 1642], of the same He m , 30 April 1673, at Westm Abbey, Susan,
da of Sir Thomas SKIPWITH, 1st Bart [1678], of Metheringham, by his 1st wife
Elizabeth, da and h of Ralph LATHAM He d s.p m ,(c) in St. Martin's in the
Fields, and was *bur* 14 Nov 1680, in the Temple Church, London, when the
Baronetcy became *extinct* Admon 22 Nov. 1680 His widow was *bur* 26 Sep
1689, at Westm Abbey. Her will dat 15 Sep 1689, pr 13 Jan 1689/90, and Jan
1692/3

WILLIAMS:

cr. 22 April 1642(a) ,

ex 26 March 1669.

I. 1642,   "JOHN WILLIAMS, of Minster in the Isle of Thanet, co.
to   Kent,"(d) yr br of Sir Edmund WILLIAMS, 1st Bart. [1642], of Marn
1669   hull, Dorset, being 4th s of John WILLIAMS, of Marnhull aforesaid,
by Joan, da of Thomas ALLEN, was b about 1609 ; matric at Oxford
(Oriel Coll), 8 July 1625, aged 16 , Barrister (Inner Temple), 1637, and was cr. a
Baronet, as above, 22 April 1642(a) He was Sheriff of Kent, 1667-68 He d. unm
in the Inner Temple, 27 Feb , and was *bur* 26 March 1669, in the Temple church,
when the *Baronetcy* became *extinct* M.I Admon 26 March 1669, to his nephew
and next of kin, Sir John WILLIAMS, 2d Bart. [1642] next above mentioned ; again,
7 May 1681 and 16 Dec 1689.

(a) See p 161, note "b," *sub* "Strutt."
(b) He directed the estate of Marnhull to be sold, which was effected before 1657
(c) Of his two daughters and coheirs (1) Mary m. (for her 2d husband) Lieut
Gen Henry CONYNGHAM, by whom she was ancestress of Henry, MARQUESS CONYNG-
HAM [1], who was cr , in 1821, BARON MINSTER of Minster Abbey, co Kent, having
inherited that estate   (2) Susanna, m Henry CORNWALL, of Bradwardine Castle
co Hereford, and had issue
(d) No description of the grantee (as "Knight, "Esq," or "Gent ") is given in
Dugdale's *List*.

WINTOUR:

cr. 29 April 1642(a),

ex. 4 June 1658.

I 1642, "GEORGE WINTOUR, of Huddington, co. Worcester, Esq.,"
to was cr a Baronet, as above, 29 April 1642 (a) He *m.* firstly, Frances,
1658. 1st da of John (TALBOT), 10th EARL OF SHREWSBURY, by his 1st wife,
Mary, da. of Sir Francis FORTESCUE He *m* secondly (Lic Worcester,
4 July 1642), Mary, da of Charles (SMITH), 1st VISCOUNT CARRINGTON OF BURFORD
[I], by Elizabeth, da of Sir John CARYLL He *m* thirdly, Mary da and coheir of
Sir George KEMPE, Bart. [*cr* 1627], of Pentlow, co Essex, by Thomazine, da of (—)
BROOKE. He *d* s.p 4 June 1658, when the *Baronetcy* became *extinct* He devised
his estate to the Talbot family

BORLASE

cr. 4 May 1642(a);

ex. 1 Feb. 1688/9.

I. 1642 "JOHN BORLASE, of Bockmer [in Medmenham], co
Bucks, Esq.," and of Stratton Audley, co. Oxon, 1st s and h of Sir
William BORLASE,(b) of the same (*d.* 10 Dec 1629), by Amy, da of Sir Francis
POPHAM, of Littlecote, Wilts, was *b* at Littlecote, 21 Aug 1619 (reg at Medmenham,
Bucks), matric. at Oxford (Mag Hall), 30 April 1625, aged 16; admitted to the Inner
Temple, 27 Jan 1636/7, was a staunch Royalist, was M P for Great Marlow, April
to Nov. 1640, for Corfe Castle, from Jan 1641 till disabled, 4 March 1643/4 (being one
of 118 members who attended the King's summons to Oxford), and for Wycombe, 1661
till his death, and was *cr a Baronet,* as above, 4 May 1642 (a) He was fined £6,800,
on 10 Jan 1645/6, as a delinquent, and was imprisoned by the Puritan party.(c) He
m 4 Dec 1637, at St Giles' in the Fields, Alice, 1st s of Sir John BANCKS, Lord
Chief Justice of the Common Pleas, 1641-44, by Mary,(d) da. of Ralph HAWTREY, of
Ruislip, Midx. He *d.* at Bockmer, 8 and was *bur.* 12 Aug 1672, at Little Marlow,
aged 53. Will dat 7 and pr 19 Aug 1672 His widow, who, at the age of 57,
adopted the Roman Catholic faith while staying at Bourbon in France, *d.* in Paris
16 Nov 1683, and was *bur* "among the poor, whose nurse she was, in the churchyard of St Jaques, in this city." M.I.(e) Will dat 8 Jan. 1679, pr. 31 Jan. 1683/4 (f)

II. 1672, SIR JOHN BORLASE, Bart. [1642], of Bockmer and
to Stratton Audley, aforesaid, 1st s and h, *b* about 1640, at Bockmer,
1689 matric. at Oxford (Oriel Coll), as "John Borlase, Esq," 31 July
1658; *suc* to the *Baronetcy,* 8 Aug 1672, was M P for Wycombe

(a) See p. 161, note " b," *sub* " Strutt "
(b) See family of *Borlase, of Borlase,* by W O Copeland Borlase, 8vo., 1888.
(c) He is constantly confused with his cousin and contemporary, Sir John Borlase,
"Knt.," master of the ordnance, and subsequently, 1643, one of the Chief Governors
of Ireland, under the title of Lord Chief Justice That John Borlase (*Knighted* at
Greenwich, 13 July 1606), *m* 1 Oct 1610, at Stoke Newington, Midx, Alice, widow of
Thomas Ravis, Bishop of London, 1607-1609, and *d* 15 March 1647, in his 72d year, at
St Barth the Great, London, leaving, among other issue, Sir John Borlase, junior
(*Knighted* at Dublin, 1 Nov. 1641), who *d* 15 Feb. 1675, and was *bur* at St. Patrick's,
Dublin
(d) This Mary was the celebrated Lady Banks who so successfully defended Corfe
Castle against the rebels
(e) This curious inscription is printed in Borlase's " *Borlase Family,*" p. 59. See
note " b " above.
(f) Portraits by Vandyke of herself and her husband are at Kingston Lacy, Dorset,
the seat, after the destruction of Corfe Castle, of the family of Banks.

(four Parks) 1673-81, and for Marlow 1685 till death   He *d* unm 1 Feb 1688/9, and was *bur* at Stratton Audley, aged 48, when the *Baronetcy* became *extinct*   M I   Will dat. 7 Jan. 1683, pr 8 Nov. 1689 ([a])

KNOLLYS

cr 6 May 1642 ,([b])

ex July 1648.

I   1642,   " HENRY KNOLLYS, of Grove Place, [in Nursling], co.
to   Southampton, Esq ," 1st s and h of Sir Henry KNOLLYS,([c]) of the
1648   same, Comptroller of the Household to Charles I, by Catherine, only
da. of Sir Thomas CORNWALLIS, Groom Porter to James I, was *b*
about 1611, was, probably, the " Henry Knowles, Esq " admitted to Gray's Inn, 5 March
1630/1 , was aged 22 in Jan 1633/4 ; suc his father, 9 Oct 1638, and was *cr* a
Baronet, as above, 6 May 1642 ([b])   He was a Royalist, and was fined £1,250 on
7 March 1646.   He *d* unm at Bowcombe, in the Isle of Wight, July 1648. when
the *Baronetcy* became *extinct*   Will, directing his burial to be at Carisbrooke, dat
22 May, and pr 29 July 1648 ([d])

HAMILTON.

cr. 11 May 1642 ,([e])

ex. probably about 1670

I.   1642,   " JOHN HAMILTON, of London, Esq ," was *cr* a *Baronet*,
to   as above, 11 May 1642,([e]) but nothing further has been ascertained
1670?   about him   The *Baronetcy* became *extinct* presumably at his death,
say about 1670, but certainly before 1727.([f])

([a]) Of his six sisters (1) Amy or Ann, was *bap* 11 and *bur* 12 April 1640, at Little Marlow.   (2) Mary, *m* 1 March 1663/4, at Medmenham, Sir Humphrey Miller, 1st Bart [1660], and had issue, but *d* before 1683.   (3) Frances, *bap* 25 July 1647, at Medmenham, *m* (Lic Fac. 6 Feb 1667/8), Joseph Langton, of Newton St Loe, co. Somerset, and was living 1683   She had issue, of which, in 1900, Earl Temple is the representative.   (4) Katherine, *m* John Webb, of Mussenden, Bucks, Lieut. General in the army, and *d* before 1683, leaving issue, her husband being then living.   (5) Amie, who *d* unm. Nov or Dec. 1673   (6) Anne, *bap*. 12 March 1656/7, at Medmenham ; *m* 26 June 1676, at St Barth the Less, London, Arthur Warren, of Stapleford Hall, Notts, Sheriff of Notts, 1685   She, who *d* a widow in Aug 1703, inherited the whole of the estates of the Borlase family, which passed to her great grandson Admiral Sir John Borlase Warren, Bart., so *cr*. 1 June 1775, and were (save as to the estate of Stratton Audley) alienated by him

([b]) See p 161, note " b," *sub* " Strutt "

([c]) See pedigree by B. W. Greenfield in *"the Hampshire Field Club Papers,"* 1895

([d]) He was suc in his estates by his brother, Thomas Knollys, M.P. for Southampton, 1659, Oct. 1670 to 1679, and March to July 1679, whose male issue became extinct 8 Dec 1752, when they passed to the family of Mill, Baronets (a creation of 1619) till that title became extinct in Feb 1835

([e]) Disallowed 17 Feb 1651/2 by Parl , till the Restoration.   See *Memorandum* as to creations after 4 Jan 1641/2 on p 152   No patent is enrolled   The date here given is that in Dugdale's *Catalogue*   See *Memorandum* on p. 84.   The date of the signet bill is 3 May 1642.

([f]) It is omitted accordingly in Wotton's [*existing*] Baronetage of England, published in 1727.

MORGAN:

cr. 12 May 1642,(ª)

ex between 1715 and 1727

I. 1642 "EDWARD MORGAN, of Llanternam, co Monmouth, Esq," s and h of William MORGAN, of the same (admon 24 March 1639), by Frances, da of Edward (SOMERSET), 4th EARL OF WORCESTER, was *b* about 1604 ; matric at Oxford (Jesus Coll), 3 May 1616, aged 14 , B A , July 1619 ; Sheriff of Monmouthshire, 1624-25 and 1640-41 ; and *ci a Baronet*, as above, 12 May 1642 (ª) He was a Royalist, and his estate was sequestrated in 1645, but discharged in 1653 He *m* Mary, da of Sir Francis ENGLEFIELD, 1st Bart [1611], by Jane, sister of Anthony Mary, 2d VISCOUNT MONTAGU, da of the Hon Anthony BROWNE He *d* 24 June 1653. aged 48. Will dat. 20 July 1650, pr. 30 March 1654, by his widow and executrix

II ‑ 1653 SIR EDWARD MORGAN, Bart. [1642], of Llanternam aforesaid, s and h , *suc. to the Baronetcy*, 24 June 1653,(ª) being then under age He *m* before 4 Nov 1661, Frances, widow of (—) LEWIS, of Llandewy Court, co Monmouth, da. of Thomas MORGAN,(ᵇ) of Maughan, in that county, by his 2d wife, Elizabeth, da and h of Francis WINDHAM He was living 13 March 1664/5 and probably survived his wife, who was *bur* Dec 1669, at Llanternam.

III 1675 ? SIR EDWARD MORGAN, Bart. [1642], of Llanternam aforesaid, s and h , *suc to the Baronetcy* on the death of his father ; was M P for Monmouthshire, Nov 1680 to 1681, and 1681 till death He *m* Mary, da and coheir of Humphrey BASKERVILLE, of Pontrilas, co Hereford He *d s p m* (ᶜ) at an early age, in 1682 Will dat 22 Jan 1680/1, pr. 4 July 1682 His widow *m* John Grubham HOWE, of Stowell, co. Gloucester (who *d.* 1721), and was mother of the 1st BARON CHEDWORTH

IV 1682, SIR JAMES MORGAN, Bart [1642], of Abergavenny, uncle
to and h male, being 3d s of the 1st Bart., *suc to the Baronetcy* in
1720 ? 1682, was "an English Catholic nonjuror" in 1693 and 1715 Estate, co Monmouth, valued at £158 rental He *m.* Alice (a "Protestant"), widow of Nicholas JONES (whom she *m* 17 April 1683), da of Sir Edward HOPTON, of Canon Froome, by Deborah, da of Robert HATTON. He *d.*, presumably s p m s., between 1715 and 1727,(ᵇ) when the *Baronetcy* appears to have become *extinct* (ᵈ)

KEMEYS, *or* KEMEYES

cr 13 May 1642,(ª)

ex 29 Jan. 1734/5.

I 1642 "NICHOLAS KEMEYES, *or* KEMEYS, of Keven Mabley [Cefn Mabley], co Glamorgan, Knt," 2d s of Rhys KEMEYS, of Llanfair Castle, co Monmouth, by Wilsophet, da of Rev. William AUBREY, D.C.L,

(ª) Disallowed 17 Feb 1651/2 by Parl , till the Restoration See *Memorandum* on p 152 No patent is enrolled The date here given is that in Dugdale's *Catalogue* See *Memorandum* on p 84. The date of the signet bill is 11 May 1642

(ᵇ) He (in his will, dat 4 Nov. 1661, pi. 2 Dec. 1664), and his widow (in her will, dat 13 March 1664/5, pr 11 May 1666) mention their da., "Dame Frances Morgan."

(ᶜ) Of his two daughters and coheirs (1) Anne *d* unm. ; (2) Frances *m.* Edmund Braye, being, by her da Mary, who *m* John Blewitt, ancestress of the family of Blewitt, who inherited the Llantarnam estate

(ᵈ) An apparently groundless claim to this title was made through Robert Morgan, said to have been a yr s of the 1st Bart , and to have settled in Ireland. There appear, however, to have been but four sons, of whom Edward and James inherited the Baronetcy , Henry, the yst , *d.* before 1693, and William, the 2d son, before 1688, his admon being dat. 7 Feb. 1687/8.

of Brecknock ; was M.P. for Monmouthshire, 1628-29 , inherited the estate
of Cefn Mabley, on the death of his great niece, 31 June 1637 ; was Sheriff of
Glamorganshire, 1638-39 , was Colonel of a Regiment of Horse in the army of
the King, was *Knighted*, 31 May 1641, at Whitehall, and was *cr. a Baronet*, as
above, 13 May 1642 [a] He was imprisoned Jan 1646 to Sep 1647 , was Governor
of Chepstow Castle which he held for a long time against Cromwell's forces, but, a
breach having been effected, he was, with forty of his men, slain at its capture
His estate was valued at £1,800 a year He was a man of gigantic stature and
strength He *m* firstly, Jane, da of Sir Rowland WILLIAMS, of Llangibby, co
Monmouth, by Jane, da of Sir Edward MANSEL, of Margam, co Glamorgan He
m secondly, in 1644, Jane, widow of William HERBERT, of Cogan Pill, da of Sir
Raleigh BUSSEY. He *d* as aforesaid, 25 May 1648 Admon 3 July 1652 [b] and
22 Feb 1660/1

II 1648.   SIR CHARLES KEMEYS, Bart [1642], of Cefn Mabley
            aforesaid, s and h , *b.* about 1614 , matric at Oxford (Jesus Coll),
3 Feb 1631/2, aged 17 , admitted to Gray's Inn, 1634 , *Knighted* at Oxford, 13 June
1643 , served in the Royal forces, and was with his father during the siege of
Chepstow Castle. Sheriff of Glamorganshire, 1643 45 , *suc to the Baronetcy*,
25 May 1648 [a] , was fined, for his father's delinquency, £5,262 He *m* firstly,
Blanche, ds. of Sir Lewis MANSEL, 2d Bart [1611], of Margam, by his 2d wife
Katharine, da of Sir Edward LEWIS, of Van, co Glamorgan She *d* s p. Admon
30 April 1651 He *m.* secondly, in or before 1651, Margaret, da of Sir George
WHITMORE, sometime, 1631-32, Lord Mayor of London, by Mary, da and h of
Reginald COPCOTT. He *d* 1658. Will dat 15 May, and pr. 2 July 1658, that of his
widow, dat 20 May 1682, pr 25 June 1684.

III 1658.   SIR CHARLES KEMEYS, Bart. [1642], of Cefn Mabley afore-
            said, s. and h. by 2d wife , *b* at Balmes House, 18 and *bap* 29 May
1651, at Hackney, Midx , *suc to the Baronetcy* in 1658, matric at Oxford (Wad
Coll), 26 May 1669, aged 18 , *cr* M A 9 July following ; was M P for Monmouthshire,
1685 87 , for Monmouth, 1690 95, and for Monmouthshire (again) 1695-98 , elected
Sheriff of Glamorganshire, 1689, but did not act   He *m* firstly, in 1678,
Mary, widow of Edward THOMAS, of Wenvoe, co Glamorgan, sister of Thomas
(WHARTON), 1st MARQUESS OF WHARTON, da of Philip, 4th BARON WHARTON, by
his 2d wife, Jane, da. and h of Arthur GOODWIN   Her will (during coverture)
dat 27 March, and pr 16 May 1699. He *m* secondly, in 1701, Mary, widow of Sir
John AUBREY, 2d Bart [1660], and formerly, 1691, of William JEPHSON, 1st da and
coheir of William LEWIS, by Margaret, da and h. of Laurence BANISTER, both of
Boarstall, Bucks He was *bur* 22 Dec 1702 (with his ancestors) at Michaelstown
Will dat 8 June 1702, pr 5 May 1703 and 7 July 1710 His widow *m* 10 Aug
1703, at Boarstall (for her 4th husband), William AUBREY, B C.L (Oxford), and *d*
s.p. 1717, being *bur.* at Boarstall

IV. 1702,   SIR CHARLES KEMEYS, Bart. [1642], of Cefn Mabley
      to   aforesaid, only s and h , *b.* 23 Nov. and *bap* 8 Dec 1688, at
    1735.   Ruperra ; *suc. to the Baronetcy* in Dec. 1702 ; Sheriff of Glamorgan-
            shire, 1712-13 ; was M P. for Monmouthshire (thirteen Parls) 1718-15
and Feb 1716 to 1734. He was a Jacobite and a staunch adherent to the exiled
Royal Family He *d* unm 29 Jan 1734/5, when the *Baronetcy* became *extinct* [c]
Admon. 8 March 1734/5 to his sister, Dame Jane Tynte, widow

(a) See p 171, note "a," *sub* " Morgan "
(b) In this he is described as " Knight," and his eldest son. Charles, as " Esq.," the
Baronetcy not being at that date recognised See *Memorandum* on p. 152.
(c) The estates devolved on his nephew, Charles Kemeys TYNTE, youngest son of
his only sister Jane, by Sir John Tynte, 2d Bart. [1673]. He, on the death of his
two brothers, became, in 1740, the 5th Bart., but *d. s.p.* 1785, when that Baronetcy
became extinct.

WILLIAMS:

cr. 14 May 1642 ,(ᵃ)

ex. Dec. 1758.

I. 1642 "TREVOR WILLIAMS, of Llangibbie, co. Monmouth, Esq ," s and h. of Sir Charles WILLIAMS, of the same, (*d.* March 1641/2, aged 52), by his 2d wife, Anne, da. of Sir John TREVOR, of Plas Têg, co. Flint (which Charles was s and h of Sir Rowland WILLIAMS, also of the same, Sheriff of Monmouthshire, 1604-05), was *b* about 1622 . admitted to Gray's Inn, 3 March 1633/4, and, having suc. his father in March 1641/2, was, *cr a Baronet*, as above, 14 May 1642 (ᵃ) He was Gov. of Moumouth, for the King, on its capture in Oct. 1645 ; was M P for Moumouth, 1660 , for Moomouthshire, Nov. 1667 to 1679 ; for Monmouth (again), March to July 1679 , and for Monmouthshire (again, in three Parls), 1679 90. He *m* Elizabeth, da and h of Thomas MORGAN, of Machen and Tredegar, co Monmouth, by his 1st wife, Rachel, sister and coheir of Ralph (HOPTON), BARON HOPTON OF STRATTON, da of Robert HOPTON, of Wytham, co Somerset, by Jane, da. of Rowland KEMEYS. He *d* Dec. 1692, aged 69

II. 1692. SIR JOHN WILLIAMS, Bart [1642], of Llangibby Castle aforesaid, and Pontrylas, co Hereford, 1st surv s and h ,(ᵇ) *b.* about 1651 ; matric. at Oxford (Jesus Coll), 28 May 1666, aged 15 ; admitted to Gray's Inn, 21 March 1667/8, being, presumably, Barrister thereof, 1680 , was M P for Monmouth, Feb 1688/9 to Feb 1689/90 ; for Monmouthshire (four Parls), 1698 till death , *suc to the Baronetcy* in Dec 1692 ; was Lord of the manors of Ewyas Lacy, Waterslow, and Trescaillou, co. Hereford, and of that of Cairwent, co Monmouth, which last he sold, under an act of Parl., to pay debts contracted in the public service He *m* firstly, Anne, da. and coheir of Humphrey BASKERVILLE, of Pontrylas aforesaid He *m* secondly, Catharine (*b* 9 and *bap* 10 June 1654, at St. Bennets', Paul's Wharf, London), 2d da of Philip (HERBERT), 5th EARL OF PEMBROKE, by his 2d wife, Catharine, da of Sir William VILLIERS, 1st Bart. [1619] He *d* s.p. Nov 1704 Will dat 31 Oct 1704, (his wife Catherine being then living), pr Feb 1704/5

III. 1704 SIR HOPTON WILLIAMS, Bart. [1642], of Llangibby Castle aforesaid, br and h , aged 20 in 1683 [*Visit of Monmouthshire*], *suc to the Baronetcy* in Nov 1704, was M P. for Monmouthshire, 1705-08 He *m* Mary, da of [—].(ᶜ) He *d* s p m s , at Llangibby, 25 Nov 1722, aged 60.

IV. 1722 SIR JOHN WILLIAMS, Bart [1642], of Llangibby Castle, aforesaid, nephew and h , being s. and h of Thomas WILLIAMS, by his 1st wife, Dela'riviere (relict of Thomas LEWIS, of St. Pierre), da of Gen. Sir Thomas MORGAN, which Thomas Williams (aged 18 in 1683), was yst. s. of the 1st Bart He *suc to the Baronetcy*, 25 Nov 1722 , was Sheriff of Monmouthshire, 1725-26. He *m* Temperance, widow of [—] WILLIAMS, of co. Monmouth, and da. of [—] RAMSEY He *d* s p m ,(ᵈ) 11 March 1738/9. Will dat 13 Jan 1735 to 14 Feb. 1738, pr. 18 June 1739. The will of his widow as " of Bristol," dat. 2 Sept. 1773, pr 28 July 1774.

V 1739, to 1758 SIR LEONARD WILLIAMS, Bart [1642], br. of the half blood and h. male, being s of Thomas WILLIAMS abovenamed (the yst s of the 1st Bart), by [—], his 2d wife He *d.* s.p at Usk, co. Monmouth, Dec. 1758, when the *Baronetcy* became *extinct.*

(ᵃ) See p 171, note " a," *sub* " Morgan "

(ᵇ) Trevor Williams, his eldest br. was aged 34, and married in 1683 [*Visit. of Monmouthshire*], but *d* s p. and v p.

(ᶜ) She is said by Le Neve to have been " a servant maid." Le Neve assigns two sons to her, Thomas and John, both of whom presumably died s p m s and v p.

(ᵈ) Ellen, his 1st da , *m* William ADDAMS, and was mother of William ADDAMS-WILLIAMS, of Llangibby Castle aforesaid.

RERESBY

cr. 16 May 1642 ;(ᵃ)

ex 11 Aug 1748.

I   1642   "JOHN RERESBY, of Thribergh, co. York, Esq.," s and
h of Sir George RERESBY, of the same, by Elizabeth, da and coheir
of John TAMWORTH, of Sherville Court, Hants, was *bap* 11 April 1611, at Thribergh,
suc his father 3 Feb 1628, took the Royalist side in the Civil War, though never
accepting any command, and was cr a *Baronet*, as above, 16 May 1642 (ᵃ) He *m.*,
21 April 1638, at Thribergh, Frances, da of Edmund YARBURGH, of Balne Hall, near
Snaith, co York, by Sarah, da and coheir of Thomas WORMELEY, of Hatfield, in that
county He *d* April 1646 at Thribergh, where he had for two years been a prisoner
His widow *m* 12 Jan 1650, at Beverley, James MOYSER, of Beverley, where she *d.*
She was *bur*. 7 Sep. 1669, at Thribergh.

II   1646   SIR JOHN RERESBY, Bart [1642]. of Thribergh aforesaid,
s and h, *b.* there 14, and *bap* 21 April 1634, *suc.* to *the Baronetcy*
in April 1646(ᵃ), Sheriff of York, 1666-67, Governor of Bridlington, 1678, M P.
for Aldborough, Nov 1373 to 1679, April 1679 till void, and 1681, and for York
1685-87, Governor of York, 1682, is the author of an interesting autobiography,
the *Memoirs of Sir John Reresby*, 1634-89 He *m* 9 March 1664/5, at St. Dunstan's
in the West, London, (Lic 4, at Vic. Gen, she 23, of St. Mary's Savoy, parents
dead,) Frances, da. of William BROWNE, of York, Barrister He *d* 12 and was
bur. 28 May 1689, at Thribergh M.I Will dat. 15 May 1688, pr at York His
widow *d* 11, and was *bur* 16 May 1699, at Thribergh Will. as "of Doncaster,"
dat 17 July 1697 pr at York 25 Oct. 1699.

III   1689   SIR WILLIAM RERESBY, Bart. [1642], of Thirbergh aforesaid, s and h, *bap* 19 Jan 1668/9, at Thriberg; *suc* to *the
Baronetcy*, 1689 He wasted all his estate by gambling and every other kind of
debauchery, and is said to have staked and lost the estate of Denuaby on a single
main In 1705 he sold Thriberg to John SAVILE, of Methley, co. York, and was
eventually reduced to great poverty, being, at one time, Tapster of the Fleet
Prison.(ᵇ) He *d* s p m s. and presumably unm., between 1727 and 1741 (ᶜ).

IV   1735?   SIR LEONARD RERESBY, Bart. [1642], br and h, being
to   5th and yst. s of the 2d Bart, *bap* 23 Oct 1679, at Thriberg,
1748   *suc.* to *the Baronetcy* between 1727 and 1741 (ᵈ) He *d.* unm, at his
chambers in the King's Bench Walk, Temple, London, 14 and was
bur 27 Aug 1748, at Thriberg, aged 69, when the *Baronetcy* became *extinct*. M.I.
Will dat 27 Feb. 1745/6, to 23 Nov 1746, in which he leaves the Foundling Hospital
as his residuary legatee, pr. 17 Nov 1748

INGLEBY :

cr. 17 May 1642,(ᵈ)

ex 14 July 1772.

I   1642.   "WILLIAM INGLEBY, of Ripley, co York, Esq.," s and
h of Sampson INGLEBY, of Spofforth manor, Steward to the Earl of
Northumberland, by Jane da of [—] LAMBERT, of Killinghall, which Sampson (who

(ᵃ) The Baronetcy was disallowed, 4 Feb. 1651/2, by Parl till the Restoration
See *Memorandum* as to creations after 4 Jan 1641/2, on p. 152. No patent is
enrolled The date here given is that in Dugdale's *Catalogue.* See *Memorandum*
on p 84 The date of the signet bill is 14 May 1642.
(ᵇ) Thoresby, in his *History of Leeds*, says that though he had "an estate of £1,700
a year, and £4,000 in monies left him by his father," he has not £100 a year left.
(ᶜ) Wotton's [existing] *Baronetages* of those dates
(ᵈ) See p 161, note "h," *sub* "Strutt."

d 18 July 1604) was 4th s (his issue becoming heir male) of Sir William INGLEBY, of Ripley (*d* Feb 1578/9, aged 60) ; was *b* about 1603, being nine years old in 1612 , suc his father, 18 July 1604; admitted to Gray's Inn, as "heir of Sir William Ingleby, of Ripley Knt," 20 Nov 1611 whom he suc 5 Jan 1617, and was *cr a Baronet*, as above, 17 May 1642 (ª) He served as a Volunteer, on behalf of the King, at the battle of Marston Moor in 1644, and was fined £718 for delinquency He *m* Ann, da of Sir James BELLINGHAM, of Levens, Westmoreland. She *d* 1640. He *d.* 22 Jan 1652, and was *bur* at Ripley.

II. 1658. SIR WILLIAM INGLEBY, Bart. [1642], of Ripley aforesaid, s and h ; *bap* 13 March 1620/1, at Ripley, matric at Oxford (Mag Coll), 14 Sep 1638, aged 16 , admitted to Gray's Inn, 2 Nov 1639 , *suc to the Baronetcy*, 22 Jan 1652 (ª) He *m* Margaret, 1st da. of John SAVILE, of Methley, co York, by his 2d wife, Margaret, da of Sir Henry GARRAWAY, sometime (1639-40) Lord Mayor of London He *d* 6 Nov 1682, aged 61 His widow *d* 9 Nov 1697, and was *bur.* at Ripley

III. 1682 SIR JOHN INGLEBY, Bart [1642], of Ripley aforesaid, only s and h , *bap* 9 Oct 1664, at Ripley , *suc to the Baronetcy*, 6 Nov 1682 He *m* Mary, da of (—) JOHNSON She was *bur* 14 July 1733, at Ripley, aged 64 He *d* 21 Jan and was *bur.* 6 Feb 1741/2, at Ripley

IV. 1742, SIR JOHN INGLEBY, Bart [1642], of Ripley aforesaid,
to   only surv s and h , *b* about 1705 ; *suc. to the Baronetcy*, 21 Jan
1772.   1741/2. He *d* s.p. 14 July, and was *bur.* 20 Aug 1772, when the *Baronetcy* became *extinct* (ʰ) Will dat. 11 June 1770

MOORE, *or* MORE
cr. 18 May 1642 ;(ᶜ)
ex. 24 July 1684

I. 1642 "POYNINGS MOORE [*or* MORE], of Loseley [near Guildford], co. Surrey, Esq," s and h of Sir Robert MORE, of Loseley aforesaid, by Frances, da of Sampson LENNARD and Margaret *suo jure* BARONESS DACRE, was *b* 13 Feb. 1605/6, suc his father, 2 Feb 1625/6, and his grandfather, Sir George MORE, 16 Oct. 1632 , was M.P for Haslemere, 1624-25, 1625 and 1626, and for Guildford, 1628-29, and for Haslemere (again), Nov. to Dec 1640 , and was *cr. a Baronet*, as above, 18 May 1642 (ᶜ) He *m* in or before 1644, Elizabeth, widow of Christopher ROUS, of Henham, co. Suffolk, da. of Sir John FYTCHE, of Woodham Walter, co Essex, by Dorothy, da of Sir Charles CORNWALLIS He *d* at Loseley, 11 April 1649, and was *bur* in the Loseley chapel, at St Nicholas, Guildford, aged 43 years, 1 month, and 27 days. M I Admon 23 April 1649 His widow *d* at Loseley 13 Sep. 1666, and was *bur* with him Admon 14 Nov 1666

II 1649, SIR WILLIAM MORE, Bart [1642], of Loseley aforesaid,
to   2d but 1st s and h , *b.* 1644 , *suc. to the Baronetcy*, 11 April 1649(ª) ,
1684   was admitted to Gray's Inn, 3 July 1661 , elected Sheriff of Surrey, 1668, but did not act , was M P for Haslemere June 1675 to 1679,
April to July 1679, Oct 1679 till void in Nov , and 1681 , Sheriff of Sussex, 1670

(ª) The Baronetcy was disallowed, 4 Feb 1651/2, by Parl. till the Restoration. See *Memorandum* on p. 152

(ᵇ) John INGILBY (*b* 1757), his illegitimate son (by Mary Wright), inherited Ripley, and was *cr a Baronet*, 6 June 1781 That Baronetcy, however, became extinct on the death of (the grantee's son), the 2d Bart , 14 May 1854, who devised the estates to his cousin, John Henry Ingleby, s and h of the Rev Henry Ingleby (*d* 4 Sep 1833, aged 72), who was another illegit son of the 4th Bart. [1642] This John Henry Ingilby, being then of Ripley, was *cr. a Baronet*, 26 July 1866.

(ᶜ) Disallowed, 4 Feb 1651/2, by Parl till the Restoration See *Memorandum* as to creations after 4 Jan 1641/2, on p 152 No patent is enrolled The date here given is that in Dugdale's *Catalogue*. See *Memorandum* on p 84 The date of the signet bill is 16 May 1642

He *m.* 18 Feb. 1663, Mary, da and h. of Sir Walter HENDLEY, Bart. [*cr* 1661], by Frances, da and coheir of Sir Thomas SPRINGETT, of Broyle Place, Sussex He *d.* s p 24 July 1684, in his 41st year, when the *Baronetcy* became *extinct* (ᵃ) Will pr Feb. 1684/5 His widow *m* in 1685, William CLARK, of Gray's Inn, Barrister, and was living in 1691, when she sold her father's estate at Cuckfield, co Sussex

---

A Baronetcy was assumed by William Moore, as early or earlier than 1701, but whether it was in right of any presumed claim for *this* Baronetcy, or for any other, is not known

" SIR WILLIAM MOORE, Knt and Bart , of St Margaret's, Westm , Bachr , aged 27," had lic. (Bp of London) 16 Sep 1701, to marry " Abigail SNELLGROVE, of St Mary, Whitechapel, spr , aged 16, with her parents consent." It appears from Peter Le Neve's notes [*Top. and Gen.*, iii. 47] that in 1703, she being then aged 17 (her father being described as " of Deptford, Kent ") eloped from her husband " Sir William Moor, of York place, Surrey, Bart " The death of William Moore, of South Lambeth," occurs in 1732, and the will of " Sir William Moore, Midx ," is pr July 1738

DAWNAY, or DAWNEY
cr 19 May 1642 (ᵇ),
ex. probably in 1657.

I 1642   " CHRISTOPHER DAWNEY, of Cowick, co York, Esq.,"
2d s of John DAWNEY, or DAWNAY, of Wormsley in that county (*d* v.p 15 March 1629/30, aged 36), by Elizabeth, da. of Sir Richard HUTTON, of Goldesborough, one of the Justices of the Court of Common Pleas, was *b* about 1620 ,(ᶜ) was admitted to Gray's Inn, 2 Nov 1639, suc. his grandfather, Sir Thomas DAWNAY, of Sessay and Cowick aforesaid, in May 1642, and was, within a few days thereof, *cr. a Baronet*, as above, 19 May 1642(ᵇ). He *m.* Jane, da. and h of John MOSELEY, of Uskelfe, co York. He *d.* 13 and was *bur* 25 July 1644, at Snaith   Inq p.m. at York, 17 Oct. 1644   His widow was then living

II. 1644,   SIR THOMAS DAWNAY, Bart. [1642], of Cowick aforesaid,
to   only surv s. and h. ; aged 3 months at his father's death, when he
1657 ?   *suc to the Baronetcy*,(ᵇ) 13 July 1644   He *d* unm and presumably
in his infancy, though sometimes said to be aged 13.(ᵈ) [*Qy* in 1644, or 1657], when *the Baronetcy* became *extinct*(ᵉ).

(ᵃ) The Loseley estate reverted to his uncle and h. male, the Rev. Nicholas More, Rector of Fetcham, who *d* a few months later, 22 Dec 1684, and was suc by his son, Robert More, of Loseley, who *d. s p.* 1689   His sister Margaret, wife of Sir Thomas Molyneux, became eventually his sole heir and on her death 14 Sep 1704, it passed to her son and heir, Sir More Molyneux

(ᵇ) Disallowed 4 Feb 1651/2 by Parl. till the Restoration   See *Memorandum* as to creations after 4 Jan. 1641/2, on p 152   No patent is enrolled. The date here given is that in Dugdale's *Catalogue*, see *Memorandum* on p. 84. The date of the signet bill is as early as 3 May 1642

(ᶜ) His eldest br. Thomas Dawnay, *d* unm , and was *bur* 19 April 1639, aged 22

(ᵈ) The age of 13 is given in Foster's *Yorkshire pedigrees*, but the date of death there given is 1644, when it is certain he was only 3 months old

(ᵉ) It has often been supposed that Sir John Dawnay, of Cowick, who suc to the estates, being br. of the 1st and uncle of the last Bart , suc also to the Baronetcy There is, however, no evidence of any spec rem having been in the grant of that dignity, and this John Dawnay was, when returned M.P. in April 1660, designated an " Esq ", was *Knighted* 2 June following, and was, as a " Knight," not as a Baronet," *cr.* 19 Feb. 1680, VISCOUNT DOWNE [I.]

HAMPSON
cr. 3 June 1642 ;(ª)

I. 1642   "THOMAS HAMPSON, of Taplow, co. Bucks, Esq," 2d
s of Sir Robert HAMPSON, Alderman and, sometime [1598-99], Sheriff
of London (d. 2 May 1607, in his 70th year), by Katharine, da of John GOOD,
Citizen and Merchant Tailor of London, was b. about 1589, matric at Oxford (Oriel
Coll) 21 Nov 1606, aged 17, admitted to Gray's Inn, 1609, becoming an Ancient
thereof in 1632, was Master of the Statute office ; suc his eldest br. Nicholas
HAMPSON (who d aged 59), 6 Oct 1637, and was cr a Baronet, as aforesaid, 3 June
1642(ª) He, presumably, though possibly it was his son, is the "William Hampson,
of Taplow, Esq.,"(ª) who was Sheriff of Bucks, 1653-54 He m Ann, 1st da. and
cohen of William DUNCOMBE, of London, and of Ivinghoe, Bucks, by Anne, da
of Sir Thomas BENNET, sometime [1603-4], Lord Mayor of London She d. 2 Feb
1643, aged 47 He d. 14 Aug 1655 Both were bur at Taplow

II. 1655.   SIR THOMAS HAMPSON, Bart.(ª) [1642], of Taplow aforesaid, s and h, b about 1626 ; matric at Oxford (Oriel Coll), 4 June
1641, aged 15 ; admitted to Middle Temple, 1644, suc to the Baronetcy, 21 Aug
1655(ª) He m. (Lic Fac 28 Dec 1650, he aged 24), Mary, 1st da. and cohen of Sir
Anthony DENNIS, of Buckland and Orleigh, Devon, by his 2d wife, Gertrude, da. or
Sir Bernard GRANVILLE, of Stow, co. Cornwall He d at St George's, Southwark,
[Qy in the King's Bench prison] 22 and was bur 23 March 1670, at Taplow Admon
31 May 1671. His widow was bur. 7 July 1694, at Taplow, aforesaid Will pr 1694.

III 1670   SIR DENNIS HAMPSON, Bart [1642], of Taplow, aforesaid, s and h, suc to Baronetcy, 22 May 1670 being then under age.
Sheriff of Bucks, 1680 (but did not act), and again, 1683-84, M P for Wycombe.
1685-87 He d unm, and was bur at St. Sepulchre's, London, 10 April 1719
Admon 29 April 1719, to a creditor.

IV 1719   SIR GEORGE HAMPSON, Bart. [1642], of St. Michael's,
Gloucester, cousin and h male, being s and h of George HAMPSON,
M D, by Grace, da of Edward HOLTE, and sister of Sir Robert HOLTE of Aston, 2d
Bart [1611] which George (who d before Nov 1677), was 4th s of the 1st Bart He
who was a minor in 1677 and was subsequently a Physician at Gloucester, suc to the
Baronetcy, in April 1719 He m Mary, da of John COGHILL, of Blechington, Oxon
He d 9 Sep 1724 and was bur at St Michael's, Gloucester Admon. 12 Nov 1729,
his widow being then living

V. 1724   SIR GEORGE HAMPSON, Bart. [1642], of the island of
Jamaica, s and h, suc to the Baronetcy, 9 Sep 1724 He m. firstly
Sarah, da of Thomas SEROCOLD, of London She d. s p 1 Jan 1737/8, at Hackney,
...... Middlesex, aged 39. Admon. 3 Jan. 1737/8 He m secondly, at Plobsheim, in
Alsace, 16 Feb 1738, Jane da of (—) STILL, or SILL, of Halifax, co York. He d
in 1754, in Jamaica

VI 1754   SIR GEORGE FRANCIS HAMPSON, Bart. [1642], of
Jamaica, aforesaid, only surv s and h by 2d wife,(b) b 10 Nov.
1738, at Plobsheim aforesaid, suc to the Baronetcy in 1754 He m in 1759, Mary,
1st da. of Thomas PINNOCK, of Pinnock, in St Andrew's, Jamaica. She d there
Jan. 1772, aged 35. He d 25 Dec. 1774 Will pr Jan 1776.

(ª) The Baronetcy was disallowed 11 Nov. 1643, by Parl till the Restoration See
Memorandum as to creations after 4 Jan. 1641/2, and 22 May 1642 (this being,
apparently, the first Baronetcy created after the latter date), on p 152 No patent
is enrolled The date here given is that in Dugdale's *Catalogue*, see *Memorandum*
on p 84 The date of the signet bill is 20 May 1642.
(b) Kimber, in his *Baronetage* of 1771, states this title to be *extinct*. He must
either have been unaware of the birth of this Baronet, or have considered him to
have been illegitimate

VII 1774. SIR THOMAS PHILIP HAMPSON, Bart [1642], s and h,
b. Oct 1765; suc to the Baronetcy, 25 Dec 1774, admitted to
Lincoln's Inn, 23 Jan 1783, matric at Oxford (Univ Coll), 28 Feb 1783, aged 18,
B A. 1787. He m 25 June 1788, at St. Geo Han Sq, Jane, 1st da and eventually
coheir of Peter HODGSON, of London, and of Buck, co Cumberland. She d. 6 May
1791. Admon Nov 1840 He d. in Manchester sq, Marylebone, 22 Feb. 1820.
Will pr 1820, and again, Oct 1840.

VIII 1820 SIR GEORGE FRANCIS HAMPSON, Bart [1642], only surv
child and h., b. 22 Oct 1788; ed at Eton, admitted to Lincoln's
Inn, 1 Nov 1806, aged 18, Barrister, suc. to the Baronetcy, 22 Feb 1820 He m.
25 Aug 1822, Mary Foreman, 1st da. of Rear Admiral William BROWN He d
8 May 1833, in Bolton street, Piccadilly. Will pr June 1833

IX 1833 SIR GEORGE FRANCIS HAMPSON, Bart. [1642], of Thurnham
Court, near Hollingbourne Kent, s and h, b 28 Sep 1823, in Hertford
street, Mayfair, suc to the Baronetcy, 8 May 1833, ed at Eton; Captain 2d
Dragoons, 1847-58, and served in the Crimean campaign of 1855, at the battle of
Tchernaya and at the fall of Sebastopol He m 12 July 1854, Ann, only child of
Thomas Hastings ENGLAND, of Snitterfield, co Warwick She d 4 May 1893 He
d s p, 21 July 1896, at Thurnham Court, aged 73. Will pr at £3,658 personalty

X 1896. SIR GEORGE FRANCIS HAMPSON, Bart [1642], nephew
and h male, being s and h of the Rev William Seymour HAMPSON,
M A, Rector of Stubton, co Lincoln, by Julia Jane, da. of Charles FRANKS, which
William (who d. 8 June 1868, aged 37), was 2d s of the 9th Bart He was b 14 Jun
1860, was ed. at Charterhouse School and Exeter College, Oxford, matric, 13 Oct.
1877, B A 1880, suc to the Baronetcy, 21 July 1896 He m. 1 June 1893, Minnie
Francia, 1st da. of Col Clark KENNEDY, C B, of Knockgray, co Kirkcudbright

---

HARDRES :

cr 3 June 1642(ᵃ),

ex. 31 Aug 1764.

I. 1642. " RICHARD HARDRES, of Hardres Court [in Upper
Hardres], co Kent, Esq," s and h of Sir Thomas HARDRES, of the
same, by Eleanor, da and h of Henry THORESBY, of Thoresby, co. York, was bap.
23 April 1606, at Upper Hardres, admitted to Gray's Inn, 3 Feb 1625/6, suc. his
father, 29 March 1628, and was cr. a Baronet, as above, 3 June 1642(ᵃ) He was one
of the Sequestration Committee for Kent, 1643 He m Anne, sister of Sir Thomas
GODFREY, da. of Thomas GODFREY, of Lydd, Kent, by Dorothy, da of Thomas
WILDE, of Canterbury He was bur 25 Oct. 1669, at Upper Hardres. Will dat.
12 Nov 1668, but not pr till 1 Feb 1681/2 . His widow d at Hammersmith, Midx,
and was bur 3 Jan 1679/80, at Upper Hardres. Admon. 24 Jan 1679/80

II 1669. SIR PETER HARDRES, Bart. [1642], of Hardres Court
aforesaid, s and h, bap. 15 Feb 1635, at St Giles, Cripplegate,
London, reg. at Upper Hardres, admitted to Gray's Inn, 28 June 1651, suc to the
Baronetcy, in Oct 1669 He m Phœbe, da. of Edward BERRY, of Lydd, Kent. He
was bur. 6 March 1673 at Upper Hardres Admon. 22 July 1675. His widow was
bur there 30 Oct 1724, aged 88.

(ᵃ) Disallowed by Parl 11 Nov 1643, till the Restoration. See *Memorandum* as to
creations after 4 Jan 1641/2 and 22 May 1642, on p 152 No patent is enrolled.
The date here given is that in Dugdale's *Catalogue*; see *Memorandum* on p. 84
The date of the signet bill is 22 May 1642.

III. 1673   SIR THOMAS HARDRES, Bart [1642], of Hardres Court
aforesaid, s. and h, b 6 and bap 21 Dec 1660 at Hinxhill, registered
at Upper Hardres, suc to the Baronetcy, 6 March 1673 He m Ursula, da of Sir
William ROOKE, of Horton, co Kent, by Jane, da and coheir of Thomas FINCH, of
Coptree He d 23 and was bur 26 Feb 1688, aged 28, at Upper Hardres His
widow was bur there 10 Jan 1707

IV. 1688   SIR WILLIAM HARDRES, Bart. [1642], of Hardres Court
aforesaid, s and h, b 25 July and bap 5 Aug 1686, at St. Laurence,
near Canterbury, registered at Great Hardres, suc to the Baronetcy, 23 Feb. 1688,
M P. for Kent, June 1711 to 1713, for Dover, 1713-15, for Canterbury, 1727 34
and 1784 till unseated, in April 1735 He m Elizabeth, widow of William DISHER,
of London, merchant, da of Richard THOMAS, of Lamberhurst, Kent He d at
Hardres Court, 8 July 1736, and was bur. at Upper Hardres His widow was bur
there 22 June 1755 Her admon, as "of East Malling, Kent," 11 Nov 1755

V 1736,   SIR WILLIAM HARDRES, Bart [1642], of Hardres Court
   to   aforesaid, only s. and h, bap 12 June 1718, at Great Hardres, suc
   1764.   to the Baronetcy, 8 July 1736 He m Frances, da of John CORBET,
LL D, of Bourne Place, Kent, by Elizabeth, da of Sir Anthony
AUCHER, 1st Bart [1666] He d s p, 31 Aug., and was bur 7 Sep 1764, at Upper
Hardres, aged 46, when the Baronetcy became extinct Will pr 1764 His widow,
to whom he had devised all his estates in fee, d intestate,(a) 23 Feb 1783, at
Walmer, aged 66, and was bur at Upper Hardres Admon. April 1783

WILLIAMSON.

cr 3 June 1642 (b)

I 1642   "THOMAS WILLIAMSON, of East Markham, co Notts,
Esq.," s and h of Robert WILLIAMSON, of the same, by Faith, 5th
da of Sir Edward AYSCOUGH, of South Kelsey, co Lincoln, was bap 14 May 1609, at
East Markham, suc his father, 28 Jan 1632/3; was Sheriff of Notts, 1639-40, and,
for his fidelity to the King during the Civil Wars, was cr a Baronet, as above, 3 June
1642(b) He had to pay £3,400 to the sequestrators of estates, and lost £30,000
for the royal cause, thereby ruining his estate He m firstly, 27 Aug 1633,
at Honington, co Lincoln, Jane, 1st surv. da of Sir Edward HUSSEY, 1st Bart
[1611], by Elizabeth, da of George ANTON She, who was bap 27 Jan 1611/2 at
Honington, was bur 22 Aug 1642/3 at East Markham. He m secondly, 5 May
1647, at St Barth the Less, London, Dionysia(c) (b. 1611), da of William HALE,
of King's Walden, Herts, by Rose, da of Sir George BOND, sometime (1587-88) Lord
Mayor of London He d 14 and was bur 16 Oct 1657, at East Markham Will
pr Nov 1657 His widow, who was b. 17 and bap. 31 March 1611, at King's Walden,
d s p 1684 Will pr Feb 1685.

(a) The estates consequently devolved on her heirs, i e, her four sisters or their
descendants These are set forth in Burke's Extinct Baronets [edit 1841, p 243]

(b) Disallowed by Parl. 11 Nov. 1643, till the Restoration See Memorandum as to
creations after 4 Jan 1641/2 and 22 May 1642, on p 152. No patent is enrolled
The date here given is that in Dugdale's Catalogue; see Memorandum on p. 84
The date of the signet bill is 22 May 1642

(c) She contributed £4,000 towards the rebuilding, after the great fire, of the
church of St. Dunstan's in the East, London, where there is a monument to her
grandfather, Richard Hale, who d. 1620

II 1657   Sir Thomas Williamson, Bart [1642], of East Mark-
            ham aforesaid, s aud h by 1st wife, *bap.* there 10 May 1636, *suc*
to the Baronetcy, 14 Oct. 1657 (ᵃ) He *m.* Dorothy yst da and coheir of George
Fenwick, of Brinkburne, Northumberland, and of Monk Wearmouth Hall,(ᵇ) near
Sunderland, co Durham, a Col in the Parl army, by Alice, sister and h of Edward
Apsley, da. of Sir Edward Apsley, of Thakeham, co Sussex She *d* 4 Nov 1699,
being her birthday of 53 He *d* s p. 23 April 1703 Both *bur*. at Monk Wearmouth. M I

III. 1703.   Sir Robert Williamson, Bart [1642], of Monk Wear-
               mouth Hall aforesaid, br of the whole blood, and h *suc to the
Baronetcy*, 23 April 1703 He *m* in or before 1681, Rebecca, da. of John Burrows,
merchant of London. He was *bur* 25 May 1707 Will pr. April 1708.

IV 1707.   Sir William Williamson, Bart [1642], of Monk Wear-
             mouth Hall aforesaid, only surv s and h, *bap* 9 Oct 1681, *suc. to
the Baronetcy* in 1708, Sheriff of co Durham, 1723 till death. He *m.* firstly,
1703, Elizabeth, yst da. and coheir of John Hedworth, of Harraton, co Durham
She *d* 1736, by her he had twelve children He *m* secondly, before 1741,
Mary, widow of Thomas Wilkinson, of Durham, da and eventually h of William
Featherstonhaugh, of Brancepath and Stanley, co Durham. By her he had no
issue He *d.* April 1747 His widow *d* s p 17 April 1752.

V 1747.   Sir Hedworth Williamson, Bart. [1642], of Monk
            Wearmouth Hall aforesaid, 2d but 1st surv s and h,(ᶜ) by 1st wife,
b about 1710, *suc to the Baronetcy* in April 1747, Sheriff of co Durham, 1747 till
death He *m* 1748, Elizabeth, 1st da. and coheir of William Hudleston, of Millom
Castle, Cumberland, by Gertrude, da of Sir William Meredith, of Henbury, in
Cheshire He *d.* 9 Jan. 1788. His widow *d* 10 Oct 1793

VI 1788   Sir Hedworth Williamson, Bart [1642], of Whitburn
            Hall, co Durham, and Millom Castle aforesaid, s and h., *b.* 1751;
matric at Oxford (Line Coll), 13 March 1769, aged 18, B A and M A, 1778; *suc
to the Baronetcy*, 13 Jan 1788; Sheriff of co Durham, 1788 till death He *m.*
23 Oct 1794, Maria, da of Sir James Hamilton, of co Monaghan He *d.* 14 March
1810. Will pr. 1810 His widow *d* 10 Jan 1848 Will pr March 1848

VII. 1810   Sir Hedworth Williamson, Bart [1642], of Whitburn
              Hall aforesaid, s and h, *b* there 1 Nov 1797, *suc to the Baronetcy*,
14 March 1810, ed at St John's Coll, Cambridge, M A, 1819, M.P for co.
Durham, 1831-32; for North Durham, 1832 37, and for Sunderland, Dec 1847 to
1852, Mayor of Sunderland, 1841 42, and 1847-48 He *m* 18 April 1826, Anne
Elizabeth, 3d da. of Thomas-Henry (Liddell), 1st Baron Ravensworth, by Maria
Susanna, da. of John Simpson He *d* 24 April 1861, at Whitburn Hall, aged 63
His widow *d.* 4 Nov. 1878, aged 77, at 32 Lower Belgrave street.

VIII. 1861   Sir Hedworth Williamson, Bart. [1642], of Whitburn
               Hall aforesaid, s and h, *b.* 25 March 1827, at Florence, ed at Eton
and at Christ Church, Oxford, matric. 15 May 1845, aged 18, Attaché at
St. Petersburgh, 1848, and at Paris, 1850 to 1854; *suc. to the Baronetcy*, 24 April
1861, M P in the Liberal interest for North Durham, 1864-74; Sheriff of co
Durham, 1877, Provincial Grand Master of the Durham Freemasons, 1885. He *m*
3 Feb 1863, his cousin, Elizabeth, 4th da. of Henry Thomas (Liddell), 1st Earl of
Ravensworth, by Isabella Horatia da. of Lord George Seymour He *d* at Whitburn Hall, 26 and was *bur* 30 Aug 1900, at Whitburn, aged 73. Will pr at
£302,136, the net personalty being £250,626 His widow, who was *b.* 20 March
1831, living 1900

_____

(ᵃ) The Baronetcy was disallowed till the Restoration. See p. 179, note "b."
(ᵇ) This estate, which she left to her husband, became, subsequently, the principal
seat of his family, their paternal estates in Notts having been much incumbered.
(ᶜ) His elder br., Fenwick Williamson, matric at Oxford (Merton College), 5 March
1724/5, aged 17; was an Ensign in the Guards, and *d.* unm, v p., in 1737.

IX 1900   SIR HEDWORTH WILLIAMSON, Bart [1642], of Whitburn Hall aforesaid, 1st s. and h., b. 23 May 1867, ed. at Eton and at Christ Church, Oxford; matric. 16 April 1886, aged 18, *suc. to the Baronetcy*, 26 Aug 1900

DENNY.

cr. 3 June 1642, (a)

ex. 19 June 1676

I. 1642,   "WILLIAM DENNY, of Gillingham, co Norfolk, Esq.,"
to   said(b) to be s. of "Sir William DENNY, Serjeant at Law, by (—), da.
1676.   of (—) KNEVITT" (being, presumably, the "William, son of William
Denny, of Bockells, Suffolk, Esq.," who was admitted to Gray's Inn,
2 Nov 1621), was cr. a *Baronet*, as of Gillingham abovenamed, 3 June 1642 (a)
He m. Catharine, da. of (—) YOUNG. He d. s.p. of fever, in extreme indigence, and
was *bur.* 19 June 1676, at St Giles', Cripplegate, London, when the *Baronetcy* became
extinct. In the same register there is, 9 Dec. 1682, recorded the burial "at
Tindalls," of "Jane, the reliqus of Sir William Denny, Knt decd," possibly a second
wife of this Baronet

LOWTHER.

cr. 11 June 1643, (c)

ex. 2 Jan. 1755

I 1642   "CHRISTOPHER LOWTHER, of Whitehaven, co Cumberland, Esq.," 2d s of Sir John LOWTHER, of Lowther, co Westmorland, by Eleanor, da. of William FLEMING, of Rydal in that county, was Sheriff of
Cumberland, 1640, and was cr. a *Baronet*, as above, 11 June 1642(c) He m.
Frances, da. and h. of Christopher LANCASTER, of Stockbridge, Westmorland. He
d. 1644, and was *bur.* at St Bees, Cumberland Admon. 14 March 1653/4 His
widow m. John LAMPLUGH, of Lamplugh, co Westmorland

II 1644.   SIR JOHN LOWTHER, Bart. [1642], of Stockbridge, co
Westmorland, only s. and h., *bap.* 20 Nov 1642, at St Bees, *suc. to the
Baronetcy*,(c) when an infant, in 1644, matric at Oxford (Balliol Coll), 29 Oct 1657;
was M P for Cumberland (nine Parls), 1665-81, 1685-87, and 1689-1700; one of the
Commissioners of the Admiralty, 1689-96. He m. Jane, da. of Woolley LEIGH, of
Addington, co Surrey, by Elizabeth, da. of Sir John HARE, of Stow Bardolph She
probably d. before Oct 1705 He was *bur.* 17 Jan 1705/6, at St Bees aforesaid
Will dat. 8 Oct. to 26 Dec 1705, pr. 22 April 1706

(a) The Baronetcy was disallowed by Parl 11 Nov 1643, till the Restoration See
Memorandum as to creations after 4 Jan. 1641/2 and 22 May 1642, on p 152. No
patent is enrolled The date here given is that in Dugdale's *Catalogue*, see
Memorandum on p 84 The date of the signet bill is 26 May 1642

(b) Le Neve's *Baronetage* William Denny, of Norwich, King's Councillor, was
Knighted, at Norfolk, 31 Oct. 1627, and, when a widower and about 50, had lic.
(Fac. office), 18 Feb 1632/3, to marry Dorothy Kempe. He, possibly, was the
William Denny, then of Thavies Inn, admitted to Lincoln's Inn, 8 Aug 1612,
as "son of Thomas Denny, of Thuilton, co Norfolk, Gent"

(c) See note "a" above save that, in this case, the date of the signet bill is
29 May 1642.

III   1705.   SIR CHRISTOPHER LOWTHER, Bart [1642], 1st s and h ,
b. about 1666 , matric at Oxford (Queen's Coll), 3 Nov. 1685, aged
19 , was a Barrister (Middle Temple), 1690 , *suc to the Baronetcy*, Jan 1705/6, but
was disinherited by his father save as to a weekly allowance. He *m.* firstly, Jane, da
of the Rev P NANSON, Rector of Newnham, Hants   He *m* secondly, Hannah [*Qy*
Hannah TAYLOR, spinster]   He *d s p*, in Brook street, Holborn, 2 and was *bur.*
7 Oct. 1731, at St Andrew's, Holborn.   Admon. 2 Dec. 1731, to the widow   She *d*
in or before 1753   Her admon , as "Dame Hannah Lowther, *alias* Taylor, of
St James', Clerkenwell, widow," granted, 13 April 1753, to a creditor

IV.   1731,   SIR JAMES LOWTHER, Bart [1642], of Whitehaven aforeto   said, br and h , *b* about 1673 , matric at Oxford (Queen's Coll),
1755   17 Dec 1688, aged 15 , Barrister (Middle Temple), 1712 , Bencher,
1714 ; M P for Carlisle (five Parls), 1694-1702 ; for Appleby,
1723-27 , for Cumberland (nine Parls), 1708-22, and 1727 till death , F S A , etc. ;
suc to the Baronetcy, 2 Oct 1731   He *d* unm 2 Jan 1755, when the *Baronetcy*
became *extinct.*   Will pr 1755   His fortune, said to be £2,000,000, devolved on his
cousin, James Lowther, afterwards (1784), 1st Earl of Lonsdale.

ALSTON

cr 13 June 1642(ª) ,

ex 29 June 1791 ,

but assumed till 1853

I   1642   "THOMAS ALSTON, of Odell, co. Bedford, Knt.," 2d s.
of Thomas ALSTON(ᵇ), of Polstead and Asin, co Suffolk, by Frances,
da of Simon BLUNDEVILL, *otherwise* BLOMFIELD, of Monks Illey in that county, was *b.*
about 1609 ; matric at Oxford (St John's Coll) 8 July 1625, aged 16 , was of the
Inner Temple before 1634 (Visit of Beds, 1634) , Barrister, 1639, having suc his
eldest br , William ALSTON, 16 March 1636/7 , was Sheriff of Beds, 1641-42, and,
having been *Knighted* before 1641, was *cr a Baronet*, as above, 13 June 1642(ª)
He was an Assessment Commissioner for Beds, 1643 and 1660   He was aged 60 in
1669, when he entered and signed his pedigree in the Visit of Bedfordshire.   He *m.*
in or before 1650, Elizabeth, sister of Sir Oliver ST JOHN, 1st Bart [1660], da. of
Sir Rowland ST JOHN, K B , by Sybella, da of John VAUGHAN.   She *d.* 8 and was
bur 10 Sep 1677, at Odell, otherwise Woodhall   He was *bur* there 11 July 1678
M I.   His will dat. 25 April, pr 19 July 1678.

II   1678   SIR ROWLAND ALSTON, Bart. [1642], of Odell aforesaid,
2d but 1st surv s and h ,(ᶜ) *b.* about 1654, being aged 17 in
1669 , *suc. to the Baronetcy* in July 1678   He *m.* in or before 1676,
Temperance, 2d da and coheir of Thomas (CREWE), 2d BARON CREWE OF STENE, by
his first wife, Mary, da of Sir Roger TOWNSHEND, 1st Bart [1617]   He was *bur*
24 Sep. 1697, at Odell, in his 47th year.   M I.   Will dat 23 Dec 1686, pr. 6 April
1698   His widow, who was *bap.* 8 May 1656, at Flore, co Northampton, *m* 7 Feb
1699, at Allhallows, Bread street, London (as his second wife), Sir John WOLSTEN-
HOLME, 3d Bart [1665], who was *bur* 6 Feb. 1708/9, at Enfield.   She *d.* 18 Oct.
1728, and was *bur*. at Odell   M I   Will pr. 1728.

(ª) Disallowed by Parl. 11 Nov. 1643, till the Restoration.   See *Memorandum* as to
creations after 4 Jan. 1641/2 and 22 May 1642, on p 152   No patent is enrolled.
The date here given is that in Dugdale's *Catalogue* , see *Memorandum* on p 84.
There is also no signet bill, but the warrant for granting the receipt for money paid
on creation (filed on the bundle of signet bills) is dated 28 May 1642.

(ᵇ) The editor is indebted to Lionel Cresswell, of Wood Hall, Calverley, Yorkshire,
for much information as to this family.

(ᶜ) His eldest br , Thomas Alston, matric. at Oxford (St. Edm. Hall), 9 Nov 1666,
aged 18, and *d.* unm and v.p at Oxford, 2 June 1668.

III 1697.   SIR THOMAS ALSTON, Bart. [1642], of Odell aforesaid,
s and h, b about 1676, suc. to the Baronetcy, Sep. 1697, M P for
Bedford, 1698 1700   He is said(ᵃ) to have wasted his estate, and to have lived in the
Fleet prison   He d unm Dec. 1714   Will dat 9 Dec 1714, pr 3 March 1714/5.

IV. 1714   SIR ROWLAND ALSTON, Bart [1642], of Odell aforesaid,
br and h ; suc to the Baronetcy, Dec 1714, M P. for Bedfordshire
(three Parls), 1722-41.   He m., after 1714, Elizabeth, da and h of Capt. Thomas
REYNES   She d. 12 Aug 1742, aged 44, and was bur at Odell   M I   Admon.
1 Dec 1742   He d at St Marylebone, Midx, 2 Jan. 1759, aged 80, and was bur
at Odell   M I   Will dat 27 May 1758, pr. 15 Jan 1759, and again, 16 July 1766

V 1759.   SIR THOMAS ALSTON, Bart [1642], of Odell aforesaid,
s and h ; M P. for Bedfordshire, 1747, and for Bedford in 1760 ;
suc to the Baronetcy, 2 Jan 1759   He m 30 Aug 1750, at Longstow, co Cambridge,
Catharine DAVIS BOVIE spinster, da of (—) DAVIS and heir of the Rev (—) BOVEY,
D D, Rector of Longstow aforesaid   They were separated some two years after
marriage by mutual consent.   He d s p leg (ᵇ) and was bur. at Odell, 18 July 1774
Limited admon. 14 Feb 1776, reciting that Dame Catharine, his relict, was surviving, as also his br., Sir Rowland ALSTON, Bart, and his sister, Ann, wife of
Robert PYE LL D, they being his only next of kin   Will dat 6 Sep 1766, and
pr. 21 Nov 1776, by Margaret LEE, of Great James street, St. Margaret's, Westm.,
spinster, extrix and universal legatee of all real and personal estate   His widow
was bur. at Longstow.

VI 1774,   SIR ROWLAND ALSTON, Bart [1642], br and h , Colonel
to   of the 1st Regiment of Foot Guards , suc to the Baronetcy, 18 July
1791   1774   Sheriff of Beds, 1779 80   He m. Gertrude, sister of Stilling-
fleet DURNFORD, of the Tower of London, da of the Rev (—)
DURNFORD, D D   He d s p, 29 June 1791, when the Baronetcy became extinct
Will dat 22 March 1790, pr. 13 July 1791 by his widow and universal legatee.
She d. 13 March 1807, in Harley street, Midx , aged 76.   Will dat 10 Jan 1792,
pr April 1807.

VII   1791 ?   "SIR JOHN ALSTON, Bart" [1642], formerly JOHN
WASSE s. of Catherine, the wife of the 5th Bart , by John
WASSE, of Stafford (said to have been a Horse Dealer), was b at Gayton, in
1763, some years after his mother's separation (1752) from her husband, and
was bap under the name of Wasse   He assumed the name of Alston, and, many
years after the death (1774) of his mother's husband, styled himself a Baronet
He m in or before 1789, Elizabeth, da of Charles WASSE   He d. s.p.m s
20 Feb 1807, in his 45th year.   Will pr 1807   The will of "Dame Elizabeth Alston," was pr in 1808, and that of "Dame Elizabeth Alston, co.
Huntingdon," in Sep 1852.

VIII. 1807,   "SIR CHARLES ALSTON, Bart" [1642], formerly
to   CHARLES WASSE, own br of the above b 17 Dec 1769
1853. assumed the title of Baronet at his brother's death   He m.
28 Sep 1807, at Bath, Mary, widow of Col Pigot, da of
John WILLIAMSON, and niece of General JOHNSON.   He d. s p m s(ᶜ) 1853
Admon. April 1853, as "Sir Charles Alston, Bart., Midx"

(ᵃ) Le Neve's Baronetage
(ᵇ) His illeg. son (by Margaret Lee), Thomas Alston, inherited, under his will, the
family estates, and was ancestor of the present (1900) owner, Sir Francis Beilby
Alston, K C. M G
(ᶜ) Charles Twisleton, student of Corpus Christi, who died 16 Jan 1834, aged 22,
"was his only son" [Ex inform L. Cresswell , see p. 182, note "b."]

CORBET, or CORBETT.

cr 20 June 1642([a]);

ex probably 25 Sep 1774;

but assumed 1774 to 1808.

I 1642   EDWARD CORBETT, of Leighton, co Montgomery, Esq," s of Sir Thomas Corbet, of the same by (—), da and coheir of (—) MORETON, was *cr a Baronet* as above, 20 June, 1642([a]) He was Sheriff of Salop, 1650-51, and of Montgomeryshire, 1651-52 He *m* Margaret, da and h of Edward WAITESS, of Leighton aforesaid, and of Burway, Salop. He was living in May 1653, but *d* before July 1658

II. 1655 ?   SIR RICHARD CORBET, Bart [1642], of Leighton, aforesaid, and of Longnor, Salop. grandson and h, being s and h of Edward Corbet, by Anne, da of Richard (NEWPORT), 1st BARON NEWPORT OF HIGH ERCALL, which Edward (*b* 1620, matric at Oxford, 1638), was s and h ap of the 1st Bart, but *d v p*, 30 May, 1653 He was *b*. 1640, matric. at Oxford (Ch. Ch), 31 July 1658, having *suc to the Baronetcy*,([a]) on the death of his grandfather, before that date; was M P for Shrewsbury (four Parls), 1677-81, Chairman of the Committee of Elections, *temp* Charles II He *m* (Lic Fac 5 Jan 1661/2, he 23 and she 21) Victoria, 1st da and coheir of Sir William UVEDALE of Wickham, Hants, by Victoria, then wife of Bartholomew PRICE, "Esq." She *d* 1679 He *d* 1 and was *bur* 3 Aug. 1683, at St. Margaret's, Westm, in his 43d year. M I. Will pr. Aug. 1683.

III 1683   SIR UVEDALE CORBET, Bart [1641], of Condover, co Salop, and of Leighton and Longnor aforesaid, only s and h, *b* about 1668, *suc to the Baronetcy*, 1 Aug 1683, matric at Oxford (Christ Church), 10 April 1685, aged 17 Sheriff of Montgomeryshire, 1699-1700 He *m*. (Lic Fac. 14 Aug 1693, he 21 and she 18) Mildred, 5th da of James (CECIL), 3d EARL OF SALISBURY, by Margaret, da. of John (MANNERS), EARL OF RUTLAND He *d*. 15 Oct 1701 Will pr March 1702 His widow *m* after Oct 1707 (as his 2d wife), Sir Charles HOTHAM, 4th Bart [1622], who *d* 8 Jan 1722/3 She *d* 18 and was *bur* 26 Jan. 1726/7, at St Margaret's, Westm M I.

IV 1701,   SIR RICHARD CORBET, Bart. [1642], of Leighton and
to   Longnor aforesaid, s and h, *b* 1696, *suc. to the Baronetcy*, 15 Oct
1774.   1701; matric. at Oxford (New Coll), 30 June 1713, aged 17; M P
for Shrewsbury (four Parls), 1723-27 and 1734-54. He *d*. unm, 25 Sep 1774, aged 78, when the *Baronetcy* probably became *extinct* Will dat. 19 Nov. 1764 to 7 June 1771, pr Nov 1774

The *Baronetcy* was *assumed*, possibly rightfully, as under.

V 1774   "SIR CHARLES CORBET, Bart" [1642], said to be cousin and h male, being s and h of Charles CORBET, of London, bookseller, by Ann, da of Nathan HORSBY, of Norfolk, which Charles (*b* 16 Feb. 1709/10, at St Mary's Hill, London, and *d* 1752) was s of Thomas CORBET, of St Dunstan's in the West (*d*. 5 Aug. 1741, aged 58), who is stated to have been s of Waitess CORBET, of Elton, co. Hereford, s of (another) Waitess CORBET, by Margaret, da of (—) WEAVER, of Elton aforesaid, which last named Waitess Corbet (*d* 20 Feb. 1689) was yst. s. of the 1st Bart He was *b*. 1734, at St. Clement Danes; was a clerk in a lottery office in

---

([a]) The Baronetcy was disallowed by Parl. 11 Nov. 1643, till the Restoration See *Memorandum* as to creations after 4 Jan 1641/2, and 22 May 1642, on p 152. No patent is enrolled. The date here given is that in Dugdale's *Catalogue*, see *Memorandum* on p. 84. The date of the signet bill is (—) June 1642

London, and *assumed* the *Baronetcy* in Sep. 1774 He *m* Elizabeth, da. of Thomas ROBBINS, of Barbadoes. She was *bur* at Clerkenwell He *d* in much reduced circumstances, in Compton street, 15 and was *bur* 26 May 1808, at St. Anne's, Soho, on the same day as his son, Thomas Corbet, who had married, but who *d s p* seven days after his father, at the same place, and who, as well as his father, is styled "Baronet" in the burial register.

VI, or VII. 1808 RICHARD CORBET, last surv. s of the above-named Charles, was *b* at St Dunstan's in the West, and appears never to have assumed the title He was in the East India Company's service, and was living in 1811, but of him nothing further is known

---

MIDDLETON ·

cr 24 June 1642(ᵃ),

ex 27 Feb. 1673.

I 1642, " GEORGE MIDDLETON, of Leighton, co Lancaster,
to   Knt," s and h of Thomas MIDDLETON. of Leighton Hall, in
1673   Leighton aforesaid, by Katharine, sister of Sir Richard HOGHTON, 1st Bart [1611], da of Thomas HOGHTON, of Hoghton Tower, co Lanc, was *b*. 1600, *Knighted* at York, 26 [16?] June 1642, and was *cr* a *Baronet*, as above, 24 June 1642(ᵃ). He was a zealous adherent of the King, during the Civil War, in whose army he was Colonel, and was accordingly fined £855 on 9 Nov 1648, subsequently increased to £1,015 He was Sheriff of Lancashire, 1660-62 He *m* firstly, Frances, da and h of Richard RIOG, of Little Strickland He *m* secondly, Anne, da of George PRESTON, of Holker Hall, co Lancaster. He *d s* p.m s , 27 Feb 1673, aged 73, and was *bur*. at Warton, when *the Baronetcy became extinct.* His widow was *bur* there 12 April 1705.

PAYLER :

cr 28 June 1642 ;(ᵇ)

ex 30 Sep 1705

I 1642 " EDWARD PAYLER, of Thorraldby [*i e.*, Thoroby] co.
York, Esq " (whose parentage is not given in the Visit of Yorkshire of 1666) was, probably, the " Edward Payler, of York, gent , son of William Payler, Esq," admitted to Gray's Inn, 5 June 1592, and was *cr* a *Baronet*, as above, 28 June 1642.(ᵇ) He *m* Anne, da of William WATKINSON. He *d*. about 1642 Will pr. 1649.

(ᵃ) Disallowed by Parl. 11 Nov 1643 till the Restoration See *Memorandum* as to creations after 4 Jan 1641/2 and 22 May 1642, on p 152 No patent is enrolled The date here given (24 June 1642) is that in Dugdale's *Catalogue* See p 84. The date of the signet bill is 10 June 1642 The date of *Knighthood* is said to have been *26* June 1642, but he is, however, styled a "Knight" when, on *24* June 1642, he was *cr* a *Baronet*
(ᵇ) Disallowed by Parl 11 Nov 1643 till the Restoration See *Memorandum* as to creations after 4 Jan. 1641/2, and 22 May 1642, on p. 152 No patent is enrolled The date here given is that in Dugdale's *Catalogue*, see *Memorandum* on p. 84. The date of the signet bill is 15 June 1642

2 A

II. 1642?
to
1705

SIR WATKINSON PAYLER, Bart [1642], of Thoroby afore-said, grandson and h, being s and h Watkinson PAYLER, by Margaret, da. of Thomas (FAIRFAX), 1st VISCOUNT FAIRFAX OF EMLEY [I], which Watkinson (who was admitted to Gray's Inn, 10 Aug 1616), was s and h ap of the late Bart, but d v p. He *suc to the Baronetcy*([a]) on his grandfather's death, was admitted to Gray's Inn ([a]) 23 March 1651/2, and entered his pedigree in the Visit of Yorkshire, 1666, was M P for Malton, 1678/9, 1678-81 and 1681. He *m* in or before 1664, Alathea, da of Sir Thomas NORCLIFFE, of Langton, co York, by his maternal aunt, Dorothy, da of Thomas (FAIRFAX), 1st VISCOUNT FAIRFAX OF EMLEY [I], abovenamed. He *d*, s p m s,([b]) and was *bur*. 30 Sep. 1705, from St Anne's, Soho, when the *Baronetcy* became *extinct*. Will pr May 1707.

WIDDRINGTON

cr 9 July 1642([c]);

afterwards, 2 Nov. 1643, BARONS WIDDRINGTON OF BLANKNEY,

forfeited 31 May 1716

I. 1642. "WILLIAM WIDDRINGTON, of Widdrington, co Northumberland, Knt," s and h of Sir Henry WIDDRINGTON, of the same, by Mary, da of Sir Henry CURWEN, of Workington, co Cumberland, was aged 4 in 1615, suc. his father, 4 Sep 1623, was *Knighted*, 18 March 1631/2; was Sheriff of Northumberland, 1636-37, M P for that County, April to May 1640, and Nov 1640 till disabled in Aug. 1642; was one of the most zealous of the King's supporters, and was *cr a Baronet*, as above, 9 July 1642 ([c]). He *m*., in 1629, Mary, da and h. of Sir Anthony THOROLD of Blankney, co Lincoln, by Elizabeth, da of Thomas MOLYNEUX, of Haughton. She was living when he was *cr*, 2 Nov 1643, BARON WIDDRINGTON OF BLANKNEY, co Lincoln. In that peerage this *Baronetcy* then *merged*, and so continued, till by the attainder, 31 May 1716, of the 4th Baron and Baronet, it and all other his honours became *forfeited*. See *Peerage*.

VALKENBURG, *or* VAN VALKENBURG

cr. 20 July 1642([c]);

ex, presumably, 1 Sep. 1679

I. 1642. "MATTHEW VALKENBURG [*or* VAN VALKENBURG], of Middleing, co York Esq," br of "Mark VAN VALKENBURG,([d]) Esq." (living May 1643), was apparently a member of the East India Company in Holland, and was *cr a Baronet*, as above, 20 July 1642 ([c]). He *m* Isabella, da. of (—). He *d*. in or before 1649. Will dat. 1 May 1643, pr 3 Jan 1649/50, and 7 July 1664. His widow, living 1649/50, *d* before 1664.

([a]) The admission to Gray's Inn, 23 March 1651/2, of "Watkinson Payler, of Thoraldby, co. York, Esq.," can only refer to him, and is to be accounted for by the non-recognition of the Baronetcy at that period, see *Memorandum* on p 152

([b]) His son, Watkinson Payler, *b* 1668, *d v p*. He had Lic. (Fac) 30 May 1693 (being then 25), to marry Dame Mary Stoughton, widow, which he accordingly did on 1 June, following, at St. Mary Mag, Old Fish street, London

([c]) See p. 161, note "b," *sub* "Strutt."

([d]) Cornelia, da of Marcus Van Valkinburgh, of Valkinburgh in Holland, *m* in or before 1656, Roger Tocketts, of Tocketts, co York, and was living as mother of six children in 1666 [Visit. of Yorkshire, 1666]

II.   1649 ?   Sir John Anthony Van Valkenburg, Bart [1642], s
to   and h., *suc to the Baronetcy*, in or before 1649; was a minor in
1679.   1650, but of full age in July 1664   He *d*, apparently, s p.m s, and
was *bur* 1 Sep 1679, at St. Margaret's in the Close, Lincoln, when
the *Baronetcy*, presumably, became *extinct*

CONSTABLE
cr 20 July 1642(ᵃ);
ex. July 1746

I   1642   "Philip Constable, of Everingham, co York, Esq," s
and h of Marmaduke Constable, of the same, by Jane, da of Thomas
Metham, of Metham, co York (which Marmaduke was s and h of Sir Robert
Constable, of Everingham aforesaid), was *b* about 1595, being aged 17 in 1612; suc
his father, 3 April 1632, and was *cr.* a *Baronet*, as above, 20 July 1642(ᵃ) He was a
great sufferer in the Royal cause, his estate being included in the bill for the sale
of forfeited estates, 2 July 1652 and 28 Oct 1655, but he apparently was let off
with a fine of £758. He *m.*, in or before 1618, Anne (*b* 28 April 1587), only da of
Sir William Roper, of Well hall in Eltham, Kent, by his 1st wife, Katharine, da. and
cohen of Sir Humphrey Browne, one of the Justices of the Court of Common Pleas.
He *d* 25 Feb 1664, and was *bur* at Steeple Barton, Oxon M I.

II.   1664.   Sir Marmaduke Constable, Bart [1642], of Everingham
aforesaid, s and h, *b* 22 April 1619, *suc* to the *Baronetcy*, 25 Feb.
1664, aged 45 at the Visit of Yorkshire in 1665   He *m*, in or before 1650, Anne,
da of Richard Sherborne, of Stonyhurst, co Lancaster, by his 2d wife, Elizabeth,
da. of Thomas Walmesley, of Dunkenhalgh. She was *bur.* 5 June 1679, at St
Martin's, Coney street, York

III   1680 ?   Sir Philip Mark Constable, Bart. [1642], of Everingham aforesaid, only s and h, *b* 25 April 1651, *suc* to the *Baronetcy*
on his father's death; was committed to the Tower 26 April 1696.(ᵇ)   He *m*
Margaret, da. of Francis (Radcliffe), 1st Earl of Derwentwater, by Katharine,
da and h of Sir William Fenwick, of Meldon, co. Northumberland. She was *bur.*
19 Aug. 1688, at Everingham.

IV.   1710 ?   Sir Marmaduke Constable, Bart. [1642], of Everingham
to   aforesaid, s and h, *bap.* 7 Aug. 1682, at Everingham; *suc.* to the
1746.   *Baronetcy* on his father's death   He *d* abroad and unm July 1746,
when the *Baronetcy* became *extinct* (ᶜ)   Will pr. 1747

BLAKISTON, *or* BLACKSTONE ·
cr. 30 July 1642 (ᵃ),
ex 8 Oct. 1713.

I.   1642   "Ralph Blackstone [*or* Blakiston], of Gibside [in
Whickham], in the Bishopric of Durham, Esq," s and h. of Sir
William Blakiston, of the same (*Knighted*, 24 April 1617), by Jane, da of Robert
Lambton, of Lambton, was *b* about 1589, admitted to Gray's Inn, 3 May 1608;
aged 26 in 1615 [Visit. of Durham]; *suc.* his father, 18 Oct 1641; and was *cr.* a
Baronet, as above, 30 July 1642 (ᵃ)   He *m.* firstly, Margaret, da. of Sir William

---

(ᵃ) See p 161, note "b," *sub* "Strutt."
(ᵇ) Luttrell's *Diary*
(ᶜ) The estates passed to his great nephew William Haggerston, 2d s of Sir
Carnaby Haggerston, 3d Bart. [1643], who was s. and h of William Haggerston, by
Anne, sister of the said Sir Marmaduke Constable   He assumed the name of
Constable in addition to his own, and was grandfather of William Constable-
Maxwell, who in right of his grandmother, Lady Winifred Maxwell, was declared
in 1858 to be Lord Herries [S]

FENWICK, of Wallington, co Northumberland He m. secondly, Frances, da of Sir Charles WREN, of Bincheste, Durham, by whom he had no issue. He was bur 20 Dec. 1650, at Whickham aforesaid. Admon 14 Feb 1650/1, to a creditor

II 1650.   SIR WILLIAM BLAKISTON, Bart. [1642], of Gibside aforesaid, s and h, by 1st wife, admitted to Gray's Inn, 10 Feb 1640/1, and *suc to the Baronetcy*, 20 Dec 1650 He m Mary, da of Cecil (CALVERT), 2d BARON BALTIMORE [I], by Anne, da of Thomas (ARUNDELL), 1st BARON ARUNDELL OF WARDOUR He d s p s, and was bur. 26 Feb 1692, at Whickham aforesaid

III. 1692,   SIR FRANCIS BLAKISTON, Bart [1642], of Gibside afore
  to   said, br (of the whole blood) and h, *suc to the Baronetcy*, 26 Feb
  1713   1692 He m Anne, da. of Sir George Bowes, of Bradley, co Durham She was bur. 26 Jan. 1700/1, at Whickham He d s p m (a) s and was bur. there 11 Oct 1713, when the *Baronetcy* became *extinct*.

WIDDRINGTON:
cr. 8 Aug 1642(b);
ex 13 July 1671.

I 1642,   "SIR EDWARD WIDDRINGTON, of Cartington, co North-
  to   umberland, Baronet of Scotland," s and h. of Roger WIDDRINGTON,
  1671   of Cartington aforesaid, by Mary, da of Francis RADCLYFFE, of Derwentwater, was aged 1 year in 1615 was cr a Baronet [S], 26 Sep 1635 with rem to "heirs male," and was cr a Baronet [E], as above, 8 Aug 1642 (b) He was a devoted Royalist, and his estate was included in the bill of sale by the Treason trustees He m "Christiana STUART," grand-daughter [*neptem*] of the EARL OF BOTHWELL [S], presumably, da of the Hon John STEWART, Commendator of Coldingham, 2d s of Francis, 1st Earl (c) He d s p m.s (d) 13 July 1671, in his 57th year, and was bur in the Convent of Capuchin Monks, at Bruges, when the *Baronetcy* [E.], became *extinct*, and the *Baronetcy* [S.], *dormant*, or *extinct* M I (b)

MARKHAM
cr 15 Aug 1642(b),
ex 1779

I. 1642   "ROBERT MARKHAM, of Sedgebrooke, co Lincoln, Esq,"
      2d s, but eventually h of Sir Anthony MARKHAM, of the same (who d Dec 1604), by Bridget da of Sir James HARINGTON, 1st Bart. [1611], was b 1597, admitted to Gray's Inn, 11 May 1621, and cr. a Baronet, as above, 15 Aug. 1642 (b) He was a Royalist, and fought at the siege of Newark, 1644, and was fined £1,000 on 5 June 1646 He m firstly, Barbara, da. of Edward EYRE, of Derby.(e)

(a) Elizabeth, his da and h. m Aug 1693, Sir William Bowes, of Streatlam Castle See Surtees' *Durham*, vol ii, p. 255
(b) See p 161, note "b," *sub* "Strutt."
(c) *Top and Gen.*, vol. ii, p 491
(d) Roger, his s and h ap, b. about 1641, was living 1652, but d v p and s.p Mary, his 1st da. and coheir, m. Sir Edward Charleton, Bart [so cr 1645] of Hesleyside, who d. s p m
(e) Wotton's *Baronetage*, and *Her and Gen*, vol vii, p 401, but see p. 189 of this work, note "a," as to his 1st wife being "a Nevill" In Markham's *Markham Family* [1854, 8vo] only one wife (Rebecca Hussey), is assigned to him

She *d* s.p 1641 He *m* secondly, 21 April 1642, at Honington, co Lincoln, Rebecca, da. of Sir Edward HUSSEY, 1st Bart , by Elizabeth, da of George AUTON She, who was *bap.* there, 16 Oct. 1622, *d* June 1664 He *d* on Candlemas day [2 Feb], 1667 ([a])

II. 1667.   SIR ROBERT MARKHAM, Bart [1642], of Sedgebrooke aforesaid, s and h by 2d wife, *b* 1644 , matric at Oxford (Wad Coll), 6 June 1660 , *suc to the Baronetcy*, 2 Feb 1667 , M P for Grantham, March 1678 to Jan 1679 ; for Newark upon Trent (three Parls) 1679 81 He *m*, 31 Aug 1665, at York, Mary, 3d da and coheir of Sir Thomas WIDDRINGTON, of Chesbourne, co Northumberland, and of Shirburne Grange, Durham, Serjeant at Law, by Frances, da of Ferdinando (FAIRFAX), 2d LORD FAIRFAX OF CAMERON [S] She was *b.* 19 Jan 1644, and *d.* in childbirth 7 and was *bur* 13 April 1683 (in great state), at Sedgebrooke ([b]) He *d* 27 Oct 1690, and was *bur* at Sedgebrooke .Will, dat 25 Aug 1690, pr 6 March 1690/1

III. 1690   SIR GEORGE MARKHAM, Bart [1642], of Sedgebrooke aforesaid, s and h, *b* 27 May 1666, at Sedgebrooke , *suc to the Baronetcy*, 27 Oct 1690 ; was F.R S He *d.* unm , at Bath, 9 June 1736, and was *bur.* at Sedgebrooke.([c]) Will pr. 1736.

IV   1736,   SIR JAMES JOHN MARKHAM, Bart [1642], cousin and h
    to   male, being s and h of Thomas MARKHAM, by Frances, da of
    1779.   Andrew COVENANT, M.D , which Thomas was only s. of Anthony MARKHAM, Colonel in the Guards (*b* March 1646), who was 2d s of the 1st Bart He was *b* 1698, and *suc to the Baronetcy* (but to none of the estates) 9 June 1736 He *m* 29 Aug 1755, Sarah, sister of Robert, 1st BARON CLIVE OF PLASSEY [I], 2d da of Richard CLIVE, of Styche, co Salop, by Rebecca, da. of Nathaniel GASKELL He *d* s p 1779, aged 81, when the *Baronetcy* became *extinct* Will pr Jan 1779 His widow, who was *b* 20 April 1737, *d* 2 Feb 1828. Will pr. March 1828 and Nov 1844

HUNGATE :

cr. 15 Aug 1642([d]) ;

ex 3 Dec 1749

I   1642   "PHILIP HUNGATE, of Saxton, co. York, Esq.," 2d s. of William HUNGATE, of the same, by Margaret, da and h of Roger SOTHEBY, of Pocklington, co York , *suc* his elder br , Sir William HUNGATE, of Saxton aforesaid, Dec 1634, and was *cr a Baronet*, as above, 15 Aug 1642 ([d]) He *m* Dorothy, widow of Andrew YOUNG, of Bourne, in Brayton, co. York, da. of Roger LEIGH, *or* LEE, M D , of York and Hatfield, in that county. He was *bur* 20 Dec. 1655, at Hatfield.

([a]) "MARKHAM ; at Sedgebrooke, neare Grantham, about £1,600 per ann The present son is a hopefull yong man ; is to marry the da and h of Sir Tho Widdrington They descend lineally from Judge Markham in Hen VI time, and possess the same estate. Sir Robert is the present chiefe , bred a soldier, being a second brother , married a Hussey, by whom he hath his children. His 1st wife was a Nevill The Judge settled first at Sedgebrook. He was of Markham, Notts, which is nere Sir T. Williamson's " [Sir Joseph Williamson's *Lincolnshire Families, temp. Car II.* See *Her and Gen* , vol ii, p 123]

([b]) An account of her funeral is in *N & Q*, 2d S, xi, 263

([c]) He devised his estates to the Rev Bernard WILSON, D D , Prebendary of Worcester and Rector of Newark-upon-Trent.

([d]) Disallowed, 11 Nov 1643, by Parl till the Restoration See *Memorandum* as to creations after 4 Jan. 1641/2, and 22 May 1642, on p. 152 No patent is enrolled The date here given is that in Dugdale's *Catalogue*, see *Memorandum* on p. 84. The date of the warrant for granting receipt for £1,095 on the creation is 10 August 1642.

II   1655   Sir Francis Hungate, Bart [1642], of Saxton aforesaid,
grandson and h being 1st s. and h of Francis Hungate, a Colonel in
the Royalist army, by Joan, da of Robert, and sister and coheir of Francis Middleton,
of Leighton, co Lancaster, which Francis Hungate last named was only s. and h ap.
of the late Bart but d. v p, being slain at Chester, 1645   He was b 1643, *suc. to the
Baronetcy*,(a) 20 Dec 1655, and was aged 23 at the Visit of Yorkshire, 1666.   He m,
in or before 1661, Margaret, 4th da of Charles (Smith), 1st Viscount Carrington of
Barreford [I], by Anne, da of Sir John Caryll   She was *bur.* 28 Feb 1674/5,
at Saxton   M I   He d intestate, at St Paul's, Covent Garden, Westm.   Admon
23 Oct 1682, at York

III   1682?   Sir Philip Hungate, Bart [1642], of Saxton aforesaid,
1st s and h, b 1661, being aged 5 in 1666, *suc to the Baronetcy*,
on the death of his father   He m Elizabeth, da of William (Monson), Viscount
Monson of Castlemaine [I], being the only child of his third wife, Elizabeth, da of
Sir George Reresby   He d 10 April 1690, and was *bur* at Saxton   M I   Will dat.
9 April, pr May 1690   His widow m Lewis Smith, of Wotton Wawen, co Warwick,
both being living, 1712

IV   1690   Sir Francis Hungate, Bart [1642], of Saxton aforesaid,
s and h, b 1683; *suc to the Baronetcy*, 10 April 1690, cut off the
entail of the estates   He m., 22 Dec 1707, Elizabeth, widow of Nicholas Fairfax, of
Gilling, co York, only da of William Weld, of Lulworth Castle, Dorset, by Elizabeth,
da of Richard Sherburne, of Stonyhurst, co Lancaster   He d s p m, 26 July
1710,(b) at York, aged 27   Admon. there 29 July 1710.   His widow d 1 July 1740
Will dat 10 June 1736, pr 18 Dec 1740, at York

V.   1710   Sir Philip Hungate, Bart [1642], br and h. male,
b about 1685   He was in the army, and was, in Sept 1707, Lieut
Col of the Earl of Essex's Dragoons, having in 1706 conformed to the Church of
England   He *suc to the Baronetcy*, 26 July 1710   He m Elizabeth, da. of (—)
Cotton   He d s p s, before 1741 (c)

VI   1740?   Sir Charles Carrington Hungate, Bart. [1642], br. and
to   h male, b 1686, was a Capt. of Marines, *suc to the Baronetcy*, on
1749.   the death of his brother   He d. a lunatic 3 and was *bur* 8 Nov
1749, at Saxton, aged 63, when the *Baronetcy* became *extinct*   M I.(d)

> The Baronetcy was, however, subsequently assumed.   It was
> before 1835, "the subject of claim by a Lieut. Hungate, who entirely failed
> in establishing his right to the dignity"(e)   Admon of the goods of "Sir
> William Anning Hungate, *Bart.*, co. York and Surrey," was granted Oct. 1852.
> He, possibly, was the "Lieut Hungate," abovenamed.   "William Anning
> Hungate" was (according to Foster's *Yorkshire Pedigrees*), son of William
> Hungate, son of John Hungate of London (b. 1712), who was a descendant of
> Robert Hungate, of Saxton, co. York, great uncle of the 1st Bart.

(a) The title was, however, disallowed by Parl. till the Restoration.   See p. 189,
note "d"
(b) Mary, his only surv. da. and h, b 10 Aug 1709, m firstly, 26 Nov 1726, at
Saxton, Sir Edward Gascoigne, 5th Bart [S. 1635], who d at Cambray, in Flanders,
May 1750.   She m. secondly, 15 Nov. 1753, Gerard Strickland (who d. 1 Sep 1791),
and d Jan 1764.
(c) Wotton's *Baronetage*, 1741.
(d) He is there called "the last male heir of that ancient family," and was, doubtless, the last male descendant of the 1st Baronet.
(e) Courthope's *Extinct Baronetage*, 1835.

LENNARD :

cr 15 Aug. 1642(ᵃ),

ex 8 Oct. 1727.

I 1642   "STEPHEN LENNARD, of West Wickham, co Kent,
Esq.," s and h of Sir Samuel LENNARD, or the same, by Elizabeth
da of Sir Stephen SLANY, sometime [1595 96], L Mayor of London (which Stephen,
was 3d s. of John LENNARD, of Chevening, co Kent), was b about 1604 , suc his
father, 16 April 1618 ; was admitted to Gray's Inn, 15 May 1622 and was cr a
Baronet, as above 15 Aug. 1642.(ᵃ)   He m firstly, in or before 1626, Catherine, da.
of Richard HALE, of Clatry, co Essex   She d s p m   He m. secondly, 24 Nov 1631,
at St Peter le Poor, London (Lic Lond , he 27 and she 17) Anne, da of Sir Multon
LAMBARD, of Westcombe, Kent, by Jane, da of Sir Thomas LOWE, sometime [1604-05]
Lord Mayor of London.   She, who was b 13 Oct 1614, d 15 and was bur. 26 Feb.
1633, at West Wickham   He m thirdly, in or before 1635, Anna, sister of Sir
William OGLANDER, 1st Bart [1665], 1st da of Sir John OGLANDER, of Nunwell,
Hants, by Frances, da of Sir George MORE, of Loseley, Surrey.   He was bur " in
woollen " 29 Jan 1679/80, from Addington, at West Wickham.

II 1680   SIR STEPHEN LENNARD, Bart. [1642], of West Wickham
aforesaid, 3d but 1st surv s. and h ,(ᵇ) by third wife, was bap. there
2 March 1636/7 ; suc to the Baronetcy, 29 Jan 1679/80, was M P for Winchelsea,
1681 , for Kent, 1698-1700, and 1708 till death   He m (settlement 30 Dec 1671)
Elizabeth, widow of John ROY of Woodlands, da and h of Delalynd HUSSEY, of
Tomson and Shapwick, by Elizabeth, da of James HANHAM, of Holwell, all in co
Dorset.   He d 15 and was bur 23 Dec 1709, at West Wickham.   Will dat 5 Jan
1705, pr 23 May 1710   His widow was bur. there 14 June 1732   Will pr 1732

III 1709,   SIR SAMUEL, *erroneously* SAMPSON(ᶜ) LENNARD, Bart
   to   [1642], of West Wickham aforesaid, only s and h , was b there
   1727   2 and bap 3 Oct 1672 , admitted to Middle Temple, 1689 , matric
at Oxford (Trin Coll), 4 April 1690, aged 16 , suc to the Baronetcy,
15 Dec. 1709   was Lieut Col 2d troop of Horse Guards , M P for Hythe (three
Parls) 1715 till his death   He d unm. and s p legit (ᵈ) at St Martin's in the Fields,
8, and was bur 25 Oct 1727, " in linnen," at West Wickham, when the *Baronetcy* became *extinct*   Will dat. 16 Dec 1726 pr 29 Oct. 1727, 7 June 1809, and 25 June 1734

(ᵃ) See p 161, note " b," *sub* " Strutt "
(ᵇ) His eldest br (of the half blood) Samuel Lennard, was b 15 and bap 29 Jan
1632, at West Wickham, and was bur there 11 Aug. 1638   while another elder br
(of the whole blood) John Lennard, was bap. 23 Feb 1635, and bur 2 Dec 1638,
both at West Wickham.
(ᶜ) The will is that of Sir *Sampson* Lennard, but it is manifest that this must
be a clerical error   In the pedigree entered at the College of Arms he is called
" Samuel ", the baptism, the entrance to the Temple, the matric at Oxford, the
return to Parl , etc , all refer to " Samuel ", the will of " Sir *Sampson*," directs his
burial to be at West Wickham, where, accordingly (two days before its proof) " Sir
Samuel Lennard, Bart ," is buried   The name of " *Sampson* Lennard" does not occur
either among the burials or anywhere else, in the parish register of West Wickham.
(See *Mis Gen et Her* , 2d Series, vol iv, p 394), where, from 1672 to 1686, seven
of the children of the 2d Bart are baptized
(ᵈ) He had two bastard sons by Mary Johnson , the elder of whom, Stephen
Lennard, suc to the estate of West Wickham, and was bur there 15 March 1755,
aged 31, leaving by Jane, his wife, a da and h., Mary, b 19 Jan and bap 14 Feb.
1750, at West Wickham, who m Sir John Farnaby, 4th Bart. [1726], and had issue

THOROLD
cr. 24 Aug 1642 (ª)

I. 1642.   "WILLIAM THOROLD, of Marston, co Lincoln, Knt," 2d
s of William THOROLD, by Frances, da of Sir Robert TYRWHITT, of
Kettleby, in that county, which William, who *d* v p, was yr br of Thomas THOROLD,
who also *d* v.p and s p m , both being sons of Sir Anthony THOROLD, of Marston aforesaid (who *d* , at a great age, 26 June 1594), was *b* about 1591 (being in his 3d year at
his grandfather's death), was admitted to Gray's Inn, 19 Aug. 1610 , *Knighted*,(ᵇ)
presumably 3 Aug 1617 , suc his elder br , Anthony THOROLD (who was Sheriff of
Lincolnshire, 1617-18, but who *d* s p m), as heir male, was Sheriff of Lincolnshire,
1632-33, and was *cr* a *Baronet*, as above, 24 Aug. 1642 (ª)   He was a great sufferer
for the Royal cause, his estate being sequestrated 15 March 1643 and himself fined
£4,160, on 1 Dec 1646. He was M P. for Grantham 1661 till death.(ᶜ)   He *m*
Anne, da of John BLYTHE, of Stroxton, near Grantham, co Lincoln. He *d.* 1677
The will of Dame Anne Thorold, co Lincoln, is pr Feb 1683

II 1677.   SIR WILLIAM THOROLD, Bart [1642], of Marston aforesaid, and of Cranwell, near Sleaford, co Lincoln, grandson and h ,
being s and h of Anthony THOROLD, by Grisel (*m* 19 Dec. 1654, at Glentworth, co.
Lincoln), da of Sir John WRAY, 2d Bart. [1611], which Anthony, who was 2d s , but
eventually h ap. of the late Bart., *d.* v p   He, who was *b.* about 1659, *suc to the
Baronetcy*, in 1677   He *m* 11 March 1679/80, at St Benet's Fink, London (Lic.
Fac , he 20, Baronet, she 17), Rebecca, da of (—) GARRETT, of St Matthew, Friday
street, London (then decd), by Mary, his wife   He *d.* s p in or before 1681.
Will pr 1681

III. 1681 ?   SIR ANTHONY THOROLD, Bart [1642], of Marston and
Cranwell aforesaid, br and h , *b* about 1663 ; *suc to the Baronetcy*
in or before 1681   He *m* 20 Aug 1683, at St Giles' in the Fields (Lic Fac on 17th,
he about 20 and a Baronet, and she about 19), Anna Maria, only da of Thomas
HARRINGTON, of Boothby Pannell, co Lincoln   He *d.* a.p. between April and
Dec 1685, in France   Admon. 19 Dec 1685 to his relict   His widow *m.* John
Lewis MORDAUNT. Her admon , as " of Boothby, co Lincoln," granted 21 Nov 1689
to him

IV 1685   SIR JOHN THOROLD, Bart. [1642], of Marston and Cranwell aforesaid, br and h ; *suc to the Baronetcy* in 1685   He was
M P. for Grantham 1685-87, and Dec 1697 to 1700 ; for Lincolnshire, 1701-08,
and for Grantham, again, Jan 1711 to 1715 , was one of the most accomplished
gentlemen of his time.   He *m* 7 Aug. 1701, at Westm Abbey, Margaret,
widow of the Hon. Francis COVENTRY (who *d* 16 Nov. 1699, aged 86), da of
(—) WATERER, and sometime, 9 Feb 1687/8, a maidservant to her first husband's

---

(ª) See p 189, note " d," *sub* " Hungate "
(ᵇ) William Thorold, of " co York," was *Knighted* 3 Aug 1617, at Brougham
Castle. This description can be explained by his not having as yet succeeded
his brother Anthony in the *Lincolnshire* estates. It is hardly probable that the
William Thorold of Lincolnshire, who was knighted 15 March 1603/4, can
refer to him, as he was then but a younger son, aged about 13   This last-named
William was probably of the Harmeston branch
(ᶜ) He and his then eldest surv. s , Anthony, are thus mentioned in Sir Joseph
Williamson's *Lincolnshire Families, temp. Car II*
" THOROLD   There are three familyes of them, all [descended] from an Atturney
at Comon law by about 3 or 4 descents "
" Sir Wilham, Bart , of Maston, neare £2,500 [a year], a Dep Lieut. His eld. son
is Mr Anthony, a hopefull young man, married Sir Jo Wray's daughter. His elder
son [William], dead, who *m* Sir Robert Carre's daughter, yᵉ now Lady Trollop "
" Sir Robert, Bart , at yᵉ Heath House, near Grantham, a Papist, not more than
£600 a year   In yᵉ Fleet now "
" Sir Wilham, Knt, of Hough on the Hill , a Papist about £800 [a year]; a very
spreading family of this county   Many Papists and severall under branches of £300
and £400 per an " [*Her and Gen.*, vol ii, p. 125]

first wife (ª) He *d* s p. 14 Jan. 1716/7, aged 54, and was *bur.* at Syston, co. Lincoln. M.I. Will dat 12 Dec. 1712, pr. 15 Jan 1716/7. His widow *d* 23 and was *bur.* 29 Jan 1732/3, with her first husband, at Mortlake, co. Surrey, aged about 81. Will dat. 23 July to 30 Oct. 1732, pr. 29 Jan. 1732/3.

V 1717.   SIR WILLIAM THOROLD, Bart [1642], of Cranwell aforesaid, cousin and h male, being s and h of John THOROLD, by Elizabeth,(ᵇ) his 1st wife, da. of Sir William TREDWAY, which John was 3d s of the 1st Bart. He *suc. to the Baronetcy,* 14 Jan 1716/7

VI 1720?   SIR ANTHONY THOROLD, Bart [1642], of Cranwell aforesaid, s and h, *b* about 1710 ; *suc to the Baronetcy* on the death of his father He *d* at school, in his 12th year, 25 and was *bur.* 30 Aug 1721, at Hough-on-the-hill, co. Lincoln

VII 1721   SIR JOHN THOROLD, Bart. [1642], of Cranwell aforesaid and of Syston Park, near Grantham, co Lincoln, uncle of the half blood and h male, being s of John THOROLD abovenamed (3d s of the 1st Bart), by Elizabeth, his 2d wife,(ᶜ) relict of Thomas SAUNDERSON, M D He was *bap* 8 Dec. 1675, at Grantham , *suc to the Baronetcy* in Aug 1721 ; Sheriff of Lincolnshire, 1722-23 He *m.* firstly, in or before 1703, Alice, only da. and h of William SAMPSON, of Gainsborough He *m* secondly, Shortcliff, da of William LANGLEY He *d* Jan 1748. His widow *d* at Bath, 1789. Admon. May 1789

VIII 1748.   SIR JOHN THOROLD, Bart. [1642], of Cranwell and of Syston Park aforesaid, s and h, by 1st wife, *b* 1703 ; matric. at Oxford (Lincoln Coll.), 10 Oct 1721, aged 18 ; B.A , 1724 , *suc to the Baronetcy* in Jan 1748. Sheriff of Lincolnshire, 1751-52. He *m* 6 Aug 1730, at Gray's Inn Chapel, Midx , Elizabeth, da. and coheir of Samuel AYTON, of West Herrington, co Durham. He *d* 5 June 1775, on his return journey from Bath, aged 72, and was *bur* at Marston. M.I Admon 22 March 1775. Will pr March 1776. The will of his widow pr May 1779

IX 1775.   SIR JOHN THOROLD, Bart. [1642], of Syston Park aforesaid, s and h , *b* 18 Dec. 1734, and *bap* 5 Jan 1734/5, at St. James', Westm , matric at Oxford (Hertford Coll), 24 Nov 1752, aged 18 ; *suc. to the Baronetcy,* 5 June, 1775 , was Sheriff of Lincolnshire, 1751-52 ; M.P thereof (four Parls), Dec. 1779 to 1796 He *m* 18 March 1771, at St. Marylebone, Jane, only da. and h. of Millington HAYFORD, of Oxton Hall, Notts and of Millington, co Chester She *d* March 1807. Will pr 1807 He *d* 25 Feb. 1815 aged 81. Will pr. April 1815, and July 1842.

X 1815.   SIR JOHN-HAYFORD THOROLD, Bart [1642], of Syston Park aforesaid, s and h , *b* 30 March 1773 , *suc to the Baronetcy,* 25 Feb 1815 He *m.* firstly, 1 Oct 1811, Mary, sister, whose issue (in 1848) became coheirs, to Sir Charles William EGLETON-KENT, 2d Bart [1782], 1st da of Sir Charles KENT, 1st Bart [1782], by Mary, da of Josias WORDSWORTH. She *d* Dec 1829 Will pr Jan 1830 He *m* secondly, 12 July 1830, Mary-Anne, widow of John DALTON, of Turnham Hall, co Lancaster, da. of George CARY, of Tor Abbey, Devon, by his 2d wife, Frances, da of Thomas STONOR He *d* 7 July 1831. Will pr Aug 1831 His widow *m* 10 April 1834, as his 3d wife, and her 3d husband, Admiral Sir Charles OGLE, 2d Bart [1816], who *d* 16 June, 1858, aged 83, at Tunbridge Wells. She *d* s p in Belgium, 4 Feb 1842

(ª) The conjecture in the note by Col Chester to this marriage in his *Westm. Abbey Registers,* is confirmed by his subsequent MS. addition thereto, viz , that in the will of Dame Eliz Hoskins (1st wife of the said Francis Coventry), dat 9 Feb. 1687/8 and pr 2 Oct. 1688 (in the Surrey Archdeaconry Court) legacies are left to her maid, " Margaret Waters " [*sic*], who, however, twice signs herself therein (as witness) " Margaret Waterer "
 .(ᵇ) They were *m.* 3 Aug. 1665, at Grantham, co. Lincoln.
  (ᶜ) They were *m.* 8 Oct. 1674, at Grantham.

2 B

XI 1831. SIR JOHN CHARLES THOROLD, Bart [1642], of Syston Park aforesaid, s and h. by 1st wife, b 26 June 1816, at Gipple House, near Grantham, ed at Eton, suc to the Baronetcy, 7 July 1831; matric. at Oxford (Ch Ch), 15 May 1834, aged 16; Sheriff of Lincolnshire, 1841. He m, 17 March 1841, Elizabeth Frances, da of Col Thomas Blackborne THOROTON-HILDYARD, of Flintham Hall, Notts. He d 26 April 1866, in his 50th year, at Syston Park Will pr. at Lincoln His widow d 3 April 1894, at 64 Rutland Gate

XII. 1866. SIR JOHN-HENRY THOROLD, Bart. [1642], of Syston Park aforesaid, s and h, b 9 March 1842, in Eaton square, ed at Eton; entered the army, 1859, Lieut 17th Foot, 1862; M P for Grantham, 1865-68; suc to the Baronetcy, 26 April 1866, Sheriff of Lincolnshire, 1876, LL D. of Cambridge, 1894 He m. 3 Feb 1869, at Wollaton, Notts, Henrietta-Alexandrina-Matilda, 1st da. of Henry (WILLOUGHBY), 8th BARON MIDDLETON, by Julia Louisa, da of Alexander William Robert BOSVILLE She was b 6 Oct. 1845

Family Estates.—These, in 1883, consisted of 12,533 acres in Lincolnshire, worth £17,652 a year. *Principal Seat.*—Syston Park, near Grantham, co Lincoln

---

RUDSTON :

cr 29 Aug. 1642 ;([a])

ex, probably, about 1700.

I 1642 "WALTER RUDSTON, of Hayton, co. York, Esq.," s. and h of Walter RUDSTON, of the same, by Frances, sister of Sir Philip CONSTABLE, 1st Bart [1642], da of Marmaduke CONSTABLE, of Everingham, was b about 1597, being aged 15 in 1612 [Visit of Yorks], was cr. a Baronet, as aforesaid, 29 Aug 1642 ([a]) He was a zealous Royalist, and entertained the King at Hayton when on his road to demand possession of Hull His estates were accordingly confiscated. He m firstly (—), da of (—) RAMSDEN. She d. s p He m. secondly, at Snaith, co York, 9 May 1631, Margaret (bap. at Snaith 11 Nov 1595), da of Sir Thomas DAWNAY, of Sessay and Cowick in that county, by Faith, da. of Richard LEGARD He d. between 20 Sep. 1650 and 20 Feb 1651 ([b]) Admon 7 March 1654/5 to Margaret, his widow

II. 1650? SIR THOMAS RUDSTON, Bart. [1642], of Hayton aforesaid, s. and h, bap. there 8 Aug 1639; suc to the Baronetcy, about 1650, and was fined £878, on behalf of his late father, matric at Oxford (Ch. Ch.), 29 Oct 1657. He m Katharine, da and h of George MOUNTAYNE, of Westow, co York, and was living 1682

III. 1690? SIR THOMAS RUDSTON, Bart. [1642], of Hayton aforesaid, to s and h, suc to the Baronetcy on the death of his father. He d 1700? s p, probably about 1700, when the Baronetcy became extinct ([c])

([a]) Disallowed by Parl. 11 Nov. 1643 till the Restoration See *Memorandum* as to creations after 4 Jan 1641/2 and 22 May 1642 on p 152 No patent is enrolled. The date here given is that in Dugdale's *Catalogue* See *Memorandum* on p. 84. The date of the signet bill is 6 Aug. 1642.

([b]) The respective dates of his own petition and that of his s. and h., Sir Thomas, to compound

([c]) The estates devolved on his sister Elizabeth, who m Henry Cutler, and d a widow and s p., devising them to her heir at law Rudston Calverley, great grandson of William Calverley, by Hester, da of William Rudston, yr. br of the 1st Baronet. He, consequently, took the name of Rudston.

WROTTESLEY, WROTESLY, or DE WROTESLEY :
cr. 30 Aug. 1642(ª) ;
afterwards, since 1838, BARONS WROTTESLEY

I. 1642.   "WALTER WROTESLY, *or* DE WROTESLEY [*or* Wrottesley], of Wrotesley [Wrottesley], co Stafford, Esq.," s and h of Sir Hugh Wrottesley,(ᵇ) of Wrottesley aforesaid, by Mary, sister of Walter, 5th VISCOUNT HEREFORD, da of the Hon Sir Edward DEVEREUX, 1st Bart. [1611], was *bap* 6 May 1606, at Castle Bromwich (registered at Aston, near Birmingham), was eight years old in 1614 , suc. his father in 1633, and was *cr a Baronet*, as above, 30 Aug 1642.(ª) He was a zealous Royalist, his house being converted into a garrison for the King's soldiers, and he himself fined £1,332 He *m* in or before 1632, Mary or Margaret, da. of the Hon Ambrose GREY, of Enville co. Stafford, by his 1st wife, Margaret, da. of Richard PRINCE He *d* 6 Nov. 1659 The will of Dame Mary Wrottesley pr. 1665.

II. 1659   SIR WALTER WROTTESLEY, Bart. [1642], of Wrottesley aforesaid, s. and h , b about 1632, being aged 32 at the Visit. of Staffordshire in April 1663 . admitted to Lincoln's Inn, 11 May 1646 , *suc to the Baronetcy*, 6 Nov. 1659 Sheriff of Staffordshire, 1666-67 He *m.* in or before 1658, Elizabeth, da of Sir Thomas WOLRYCH, 1st Bart [1641], by Ursula, da of Thomas OTELEY, of Pitchford, Salop. He *d* in or before 1686. Will pr June 1686

III. 1686 ?   SIR WALTER WROTTESLEY, Bart. [1642], of Wrottesley aforesaid, s and h , aged 5 years in April 1663 , matric. at Oxford (Mag. Hall), 18 March 1675/6, aged 17 ; *suc to the Baronetcy* in or before 1686 Sheriff of Staffordshire, 1686-87. He pulled down the old mansion, and in 1696 erected the more stately one called Wrottesley Hall. He *m* firstly (Lic. Vic. Gen , 27 June 1678, he aged 20 and she 18), Eleanor, da of Sir John ARCHER, of Coopersale, in Theydon Garnon, Essex, Justice of the Common Pleas (1663-81), by Eleanor, da. of Sir John CURZON, Kedleston, co Derby He *m* secondly, Anne, of da of (—), BURTON, of Longnor, Salop He *d* 1712 Will pr March 1713 The will of Dame Anne Wrottesley, pr 1732

IV 1712   SIR JOHN WROTTESLEY, Bart [1642], of Wrottesley Hall aforesaid, 1st surv. s and h. by 1st wife , M P for Staffordshire, 1700-10 ; *suc to the Baronetage* in 1712 He *m* in or before 1708, Frances, sister of Harry, 3d EARL OF STAMFORD, da of Hon John GREY, of Enville aforesaid, 3d s. of Henry, 1st EARL OF STAMFORD, by his 2d wife, Katharine, da of Edward (WARD), LORD DUDLEY and BARON WARD OF BIRMINGHAM He *d* Oct 1726, and was *bur* at Tetnal. Will dat 12 March 1725, pr. 1 Feb. 1726/7 by his widow Her will pr 1769

V 1726   SIR HUGH WROTTESLEY, Bart [1642], of Wrottesley Hall aforesaid, 1st surv s and h , *suc. to the Baronetcy* in Oct 1726 He *d. a* minor and unm , 1729. Admon 18 Nov 1729

VI. 1729.   SIR WALTER WROTTESLEY, Bart [1642], of Wrottesley Hall aforesaid, br. and h. ; *suc. to the Baronetcy* in 1729. He *d. a* minor and unm., Feb 1731 Will pr 1732

(ª) Disallowed by Parl. 11 Nov 1643, till the Restoration See *Memorandum* as to creations after 4 Jan 1641/2, and 22 May 1642, on p 152 The patent of this creation and of many others in the later months of 1642, as also in Feb. and March 1642/3, is enrolled, though those in the earlier months of that year (between 28 Feb 1641/2, and 10 Aug 1642) are not.

(ᵇ) This Hugh was 8th in descent and heir male of Sir Hugh de Wrottesley, one of the Founders of the most noble Order of the Garter.

VII   1731.   SIR RICHARD WROTTESLEY, Bart [1642], of Wrottesley
            Hall aforesaid, br. and h , b about 1721 ; *suc. to the Baronetcy* in
Feb 1731 ; ed. at Winchester School, 1736 , matric. at Oxford (St John's Coll),
31 Aug 1739, aged 18, was M P for Tavistock, Dec 1747 to 1754 ; one of the
principal Clerks of the Board of Green Cloth, June 1749   He afterwards took Holy
Orders, and became Chaplain to the King, 1763 ; Dean of Worcester, 1765 till death
He *m.* in or before 1744, Mary, da of John (LEVESON-GOWER), 1st EARL GOWER, by
his 1st wife, Evelyn, da of Evelyn (PIERREPONT) DUKE OF KINGSTON   He *d.*
29 July 1769   Will pr. 1769   His widow *d* 30 April 1778.

VIII   1769   SIR JOHN WROTTESLEY, Bart [1642], of Wrottesley Hall
            aforesaid, only s and h , b 1744 ; entered the Army, becoming
eventually, in 1782, Major-Gen ; Col of the 45th Foot ; Master of the Horse to H R.H.
the Duke of York.   M P for Newcastle under Lyne, March to June 1768, and for
Staffordshire (fourteen Parls), July 1768 till death, having *suc to the Baronetcy*, 29
July 1769 , cr D C L of Oxford 8 July 1773   He *m* 17 June 1770, at St. James',
Westminster, Frances, 1st da of William (COURTENAY), 1st VISCOUNT COURTENAY OF
POWDERHAM, by Frances, da of Heneage (FINCH), 2d EARL OF AILESFORD   He *d*
23 April 1787. Will pr. June 1787   His widow, who was *b* March 1746/7, and
who was sometime Maid of Honour to Charlotte, the Queen Consort, *d.* 24 Feb
1828.   Will pr March 1828

IX   1787   SIR JOHN WROTTESLEY, Bart. [1642], of Wrottesley Hall
            aforesaid, s and h , b. 24 Oct 1771 , *suc to the Baronetcy*, 23 April
1787 , sometime an officer in the 13th Lancers, serving in Holland and France ;
M P (in the whig interest) for Lichfield, March 1799 to 1806 , for Staffordshire,
1823 32 and for South Staffordshire, 1832-37 . F S A ; Lieut Col of the West
Staffordshire Militia   He *m* firstly, 23 June 1795, Caroline, 1st da of Charles (BENNET),
4th EARL OF TANKERVILLE, by Emma, 2d da and coheir of Sir James COLEBROOKE,
Bart [1759]   She, who was *b* 22 Oct. 1722, *d* 7 March 1818   Will pr 1823   He *m*
secondly, 19 May 1819, Julia, widow of (his 1st wife's brother), Hon John Astley
BENNET, Capt R N , da of John CONYERS, of Copthall, Essex   She was living when
he was cr , 11 July 1838, BARON WROTTESLEY, of Wrottesley, co Stafford   In
that peerage *this Baronetcy* thenceforward *merged*, and so continues   See *Peerage.*

BLAND :
cr 30 Aug 1642 ,(a)
ex. 16 Oct 1756.

I.   1642.   "THOMAS BLAND, of Kippax Park [near Ferrybridge],
            co. York, Esq ," s and h ap of Sir Thomas BLAND,(b) of the same, by
Katherine, sister of Thomas, 1st EARL OF SUSSEX, da of John (SAVILE), 1st BARON
SAVILE OF POMFRET, was *b* about 1614, served in the Royal army, and was, in
consideration of his father's and his own services to the King, *cr* a Baronet, as
above, 30 Aug 1642 (a)   He was fined £405, on 24 March 1648, and his estates
sequestrated, though he obtained some relief by pleading that he had never been in
Parl., was not a Popish recusant, was £1,500 in debt, had "a wife and five small
children," etc   He *m* in or before 1642, Rosamond, 2d da of Francis NEVILE, of
Chevet, co. York, by his 1st wife, Rosamond, da of Cyril ARTHINGTON   He was *bur.*
24 Oct 1657, at Kippax   M I   Admon 10 Feb 1657/8, to his widow. She, who was
b 1617, *m.* Walter WALSH, of Houghton, and was *bur* 6 Oct. 1669, at Castleford.

II.   1657.   SIR FRANCIS BLAND, Bart [1642], of Kippax Park afore-
            said, 1st s and h , b about 1642 , *suc. to the Baronetcy*, Oct 1657.
He *m* Jane, da of Sir William LOWTHER, of Great Preston, co. York, by Jane, da of
William BUSFIELD, of Leeds. He *d* 14 Nov. 1663, aged 21, and was *bur* at Kippax
M I   His widow, who outlived him fifty years, *d.* 7 and was *bur* 10 April 1713, at
Norton, co. Durham, aged 72. M I.

(a) See p. 161, note "b," under "Strutt."
(b) See Nicholas Carlisle's *History of the Family of Bland*   London, 4to, 1826.

III   1663.   SIR THOMAS BLAND, Bart [1642], of Kippax Park aforesaid, 1st s. and h, b 21 Dec 1662 ; suc to the Baronetcy, 14 Nov.
1663. He d. in childhood, 14 Dec 1668, and was bur. at Kippax   M I.

IV   1668.   SIR JOHN BLAND, Bart [1642], of Kippax Park aforesaid,
only br and h, b 2 Nov 1663, suc to the Baronetcy 14 Dec 1668,
matric at Oxford (Un.v. Coll), 14 Nov 1670, aged 16 , was M P for Appleby (when
under age) 1681, and for Pontefract (eight Parls.),1690—1713, was a Commiss of
the Revenue [I], 1704-06.   He m 31 March 1685, at Chorlton Chapel, Manchester
(Lic Fac , he about 22 and she about 23), Anne, da and h of Sir Edward MOSELEY,
of Hulme, in Manchester, by Jane Merial, da of Richard SALTONSTALL   He d.,
on his journey from Bath to Yorkshire, 25 and was bur 29 Oct 1715, at Didsbury,
in Manchester, aged 52   M I   Will dat 24 Dec 1712, pr 7 May 1716   His widow
d 26 July and was bur 3 Aug 1734, at Didsbury.   Will dat 20 June 1721.

V.   1716.   SIR JOHN BLAND, Bart. [1642], of Kippax Park and
Hulme aforesaid, only sm v s and h b about 1691, matric. at
Oxford (Ch. Ch), 10 Oct 1707, aged 16 ; M P for Lancashire (three Parls), 1713-27,
suc to the Baronetcy, 25 Oct 1715, in which year he was committed to custody on
suspicion of high treason.   He m. 16 Oct 1716, Frances (£8,000 portion), 5th da of
Heneage (FINCH), 1st EARL OF AYLESFORD, by Elizabeth, da. and cohen of Sir John
BANKS, Bart [c] 1661].   He d 9 April 1743, at Bath, and was bur at Kippax.   M I
Will dat 6 Jan. 1741, pr 1744.   His widow resided at St Geo Han. sq , Midx.   Her
will dat 4 Aug. 1758, pr 21 March 1759

VI   1743.   SIR JOHN BLAND, Bart [1642], of Kippax Park and
Hulme aforesaid, 1st s. and h , b. about 1722, matric at Oxford
(St John's Coll.), 28 Jan 1739/40, aged 18 , suc to the Baronetcy, 14 April 1743,
was M P for Ludgershall, 1754 till death   " By his wild dissipation and his
unconquerable disposition to play, he squandered immense estates—the whole of
Manchester and its environs—and left little more at his death than the family
patrimony at Kippax "(a)   He d unm , near Calais in France, 3 Sep 1735   Admon
1 Oct. 1755 and 12 Jan. 1757.

VII   1755,   SIR HUNGERFORD BLAND, Bart [1642], of Kippax Park
to   aforesaid, only br and b , b. about 1726, Lieut 3d Reg of Foot
1756.   Guards, 1753, and afterwards Capt in the Horse Guards Blue, suc.
to the Baronetcy, 3 Sep 1755   He d unm , 16 Oct 1756, aged 30,
at Kippax Park, and was bur. at Kippax, when the Baronetcy became extinct.(a)   M I
Admon. 12 Jan 1757.

THROCKMORTON, or THROGMORTON :
cr. 1 Sep 1642([b]),
sometime, 1819-26, COURTENAY-THROCKMORTON.

I.   1642   " ROBERT THROCKMORTON, of Coughton, co Warwick,
Esq " being also described(c) as " of Weston Underwood, Bucks,
Knt.," s and h of John THROCKMORTON, by Agnes, da. of Thomas WILFORD, of
Newman Hall, in Quendon, Essex, which John was s and h ap of Thomas THROCK-
MORTON, of Coughton and Weston aforesaid, suc his said grandfather 13 March 1614,
and was cr a Baronet, as above, 1 Sep 1642 (b)   He kept a bountiful house at

---

(a) The Kippax estate passed firstly to his two sisters, Elizabeth and Anne, who
both d. unm, the yst and survivor on 20 Jan. 1786, when they went to her cousin,
Thomas Davison, who thereupon took the name of Bland after his patronymic   He
was s and h of Thomas Davison, of Blakiston manor, co Durham (d 5 April 1756,
aged 43), who was s. and h. of Thomas Davison, of the same, by Anne, 1st da of Sir
John Bland, 4th Bart.
(b) See p 161, note "b," under " Strutt "
(c) On the M I to his first wife who died in 1617

Weston till his estates were sequestrated in the time of the Civil War, his house at
Coughton being turned into a garrison for the parliament forces, and he himself
obliged to retire to Worcester for security   He *m* firstly, Dorothy, da of Sir John
FORTESCUE, **K B.**, of Salden, Bucks   She *d* ap 4 Nov 1617, and was *bur* at
Coughton.   M I   He *m* secondly, Mary, sister of Charles, 1st VISCOUNT CARRINGTON
OF BARREFORE [I], da. of Sir Francis SMITH, of Ashby Folville, co Leicester, by
Anne, da of Sir Thomas MARKHAM   He *d* 16 Jan 1650, and was *bur.* at Coughton.
M I   The will of Dame Mary Throckmorton pr 1663

II   1650.   SIR FRANCIS THROCKMORTON, Bart [1642], of Coughton
          Court in Coughton and of Weston Underwood aforesaid, s and h by
2d wife, *suc to the Baronetcy*, 16 Jan 1650   He rebuilt the house at Coughton,
where he exercised great hospitality after the Restoration   He *m* Anne, da. and sole
h of John MONSON, of Kinnersley, Surrey   He *d* 7 Nov 1680, aged 40, and was
bur at Weston   M I   Will pr 1681.   The will of Dame Anne Throckmorton, pr 1728
1728

III.   1680.   SIR ROBERT THROCKMORTON, Bart. [1642], of Coughton
          Court and of Weston Underwood aforesaid, 1st surv s and h, *b*
10 Jan 1662, at Moorhall, co Warwick , *suc to the Baronetcy*, 7 Nov. 1680, and was
admitted to Gray's Inn, 15 Jan. 1682/3   He partially re-built the mansion at
Weston, and was a great benefactor to that parish and that of Coughton.   He *m*
Mary, sister and h. (1690) of Sir John YATE, 4th Bart [1622], da of Sir Charles
YATE, 3d Bart , by Frances, da of Sir Thomas GAGE, 2d Bart. [1622], of Firle,
co. Sussex   By her he acquired the estate of Buckland, near Farringdon, Berks   He,
who was one of the " Catholic nonjurors," *d* 8 and was *bur* 15 March 1720/1, aged
58, at Weston   Will pr 1721.   His widow was *bur.* there 12 May 1722

IV.   1721.   SIR ROBERT THROCKMORTON, Bart [1642], of Coughton
          Court, Weston Underwood and Buckland aforesaid, only surv s.
and h , *b* 21 and *bap* 22 Aug 1702, at Weston ; *suc to the Baronetcy*, 8 March
1720/1   He *m* firstly, Theresa, 5th da of William (HERBERT), 2d MARQUESS OF
POWIS, by Mary, da. and coheir of Sir Thomas PRESTON, 3d Bart. [1644]   She *d.*
17 and was *bur.* 22 June 1723, at Weston aforesaid   He *m* secondly, Jan 1737/8,
Catharine, da. of George COLLINGWOOD, of Elsington, Northumberland.   She *d*
ap m   He *m.* thirdly, in 1763, Lucy, da of James HEYWOOD, of Mornston, Devon,
but by her had no issue   He *d* 3 Dec 1791, and was *bur.* at Coughton.   Will pr
Feb. 1792.   The will of his widow pr Dec 1795

V.   1791.   SIR JOHN COURTENAY THROCKMORTON, Bart. [1642], of
          Coughton Court, Weston Underwood and Buckland aforesaid, grand-
son and h , being s and h. of George THROCKMORTON, by Anna Maria, only da of
William PASTON, of Horton, co Gloucester (by Mary, his wife, only child that had
issue of John COURTENAY, of Molland, Devon), which George was s and h. ap of
the 4th Bart , but *d* v p. 30 Aug. 1767   He was *b.* 27 July 1753 ; *suc to the
Baronetcy*, 8 Dec 1791, and was *cr* D C L of Oxford, 15 June 1796   He *m.*
19 Aug 1782, Maria Catharine, da of Thomas GIFFARD, of Chillington, co. Stafford,[a]
by his 1st wife, Barbara, da of Robert James (PETRE), 8th BARON PETRE OF
WRITTLE   He *d* ap, 3 Jan 1819   Will pr 1819.   His widow *d* 7 Jan 1821, in
her 59th year, at Hengrave Hall, Suffolk.   Will pr. 1821

VI   1819.   SIR GEORGE COURTENEY-THROCKMORTON, Bart. [1642], of
          Coughton Court, Weston Underwood, and Buckland aforesaid, and of
Molland, co. Devon , br. and h , *b.* 15 Sep. 1754   In 1792 he took the name of
COURTENAY before that of THROCKMORTON, having inherited, through his mother, the
estate of Molland, formerly that of the Courtenay family   He *suc to the Baronetcy*,
3 Jan 1819   He *m.* 29 June 1792, Catharine, only da of Thomas STAPLETON, of
Carleton, co York, by his 1st wife, Catherine, da of Henry WITHAM, of Cliffe.   He
d ap , 16 July 1826, aged 72, at Weston , *bur* there.   M.I.   Will pr. Sep. 1826.
His widow *d.* 22 Jan 1839   Will pr March 1839.

(a) She was a friend of the poet COWPER.

VII 1826. Sir Charles Throckmorton, Bart [1642], of Coughton Court, Weston Underwood, and Bockland aforesaid, br and h, b. 2 Nov. 1757, and bap at Weston aforesaid ; suc to the Baronetcy, 16 July 1826 He m 28 Dec 1787, Mary Margaretta, da. of Edmund Plowden, of Plowden, Salop, by Elizabeth, da and coheir of Sir Berkeley Lucy, 3d Bart [1618] He d. s p., 3 Dec. 1840. Will pr Feb. 1841

VIII. 1840 Sir Robert-George Throckmorton, Bart. [1642], of Coughton Court, Weston Underwood, and Buckland aforesaid, nephew and h, being s. and h. of William Throckmorton, by Frances, only da of Thomas Giffard, of Chillington, co Stafford, which William was br. to the 5th, 6th and 7th Barts., and d 31 March 1819, aged 56 He was b 5 Dec 1800, in Queen street, Mayfair, Middlesex, M P for Berks, 1831 1835, Sheriff of that county, 1843 suc. to the Baronetcy, 3 Dec 1840 He m 16 July 1829, Elizabeth, only da of Sir John-Francis-Edward Acton, 6th Bart [1644], by (his niece) Mary Anne, 1st da of (his brother) Gen Joseph Edward Acton She d 4 April 1850 He d 28 June 1862, in Hereford street, Park lane, aged 61

IX 1862 Sir Nicholas-William-George Throckmorton, Bart [1642], of Coughton Court, Weston Underwood and Buckland aforesaid, 1st surv. s. and h, b 26 April 1838, at Buckland aforesaid, suc to the Baronetcy, 28 June 1862, Sheriff of Berks, 1872.

Family Estates—These, in 1883, consisted of 7,618 acres in Warwickshire (worth £9,918 a year) ; 6,589 in Devon ; 3,618 in Worcestershire ; 3,008 in Berks, and 1,552 in Bucks *Total*, 22,385 acres, worth £27,092 a year. *Principal Seat.*—Coughton Court, co Warwick.

HALTON:
cr. 10 Sep. 1642(a),
ex. 9 Feb. 1823.

I 1642 "William Halton, of Samford(b) [or Little Sandford], co. Essex, Esq," 3d s of Robert Halton, of Sawbridgeworth, Herts, by his 1st wife, Heather, da. of William Booth, of co Lincoln, was b about 1620, was executor and testamentary heir of his uncle Sir William Halton, of Great Abington, Cambridgeshire (who d 20 Nov 1639, aged nearly 70), and was cr. a Baronet, as above, 10 Sep 1642(a) He m firstly, Mary, da of Sir Edward Altham, of Marks Hall, in Latton, Essex, by Joan, da of Sir John Leventhorpe, 1st Bart. [1622] She d 29 Dec. 1644, aged 26, and was bur. at Little Sandford He m. secondly, 12 June 1649, at St James', Clerkenwell (Lic. Fac, 11th, he about 28), Ursula, da (whose issue became heir), of Sir Thomas Fisher, 1st Bart. [1627], by Sarah, da and coheir of Sir Thomas Fowler, Bart (cr 1628), of Islington, co Midx He was bur. 29 Oct. 1662, at St Leonard's, Shoreditch Admon Oct. 1662 His widow m Matthew Meriton, of London, merchant

II. 1662 Sir William Halton, Bart [1642], of Little Sandford aforesaid, s. and h by 1st wife, suc to the Baronetcy, Oct. 1662. He sold the estate of Little Sandford in 1670 to Edward Peck He d. unm, 4 March 1675/6 at Salisbury, and was bur. at Latton, Essex. Admon 12 June 1676. Will pr Dec following.

III 1676. Sir Thomas Halton, Bart [1642], of Barnsbury in Islington, co. Midx. (which he inherited from his mother's family), half br. and h., being s. of the 1st Bart by his 2d wife, suc to the Baronetcy,

(a) See p 195, note " s," under " Wrottesley."
(b) He had recently purchased this estate from Sir Edward Green, Bart [cr. 1660], paying his fine for ingress, in 1640

4 March 1675/6 He *m.* Elizabeth, da of John CRESSENER, of London. She *d* 26 Aug 1716. He *d* 6 Sep 1726, both were *bur.* at Islington. His admon. 26 Sep 1726 and 7 July 1756.

IV. 1726. SIR WILLIAM HALTON, Bart [1642], of Barnsbury aforesaid and of Turnham Green, Midx, only surv s and h ; *suc to the Baronetcy,* 6 Sep 1726. He *m* Frances, widow of John JERMY, of Sturton, Suffolk, da and h of Sir George DALSTON (s. and h. ap of Sir William DALSTON, 1st Bart [1641]), by Brown, da of Sir William RAMSDEN, of Byrom, co. York. He *d.* s.p, 12 Feb 1754, having devised the valuable manor of Barnsbury to the family of TUFNELL. Will pr 1754

V 1754 SIR THOMAS HALTON, Bart [1642], cousin and h. male, being s and h of George HALTON, by Hannah, 1st da of Fenwick LAMBERT, of London, which George (who *d.* 7 May 1729), was s. and h of Richard HALTON (*d* 1703), youngest s of the 1st Bart. by his 2d wife, *suc. to the Baronetcy,* 12 Feb 1754 He *m* Mary, da of (—) BURTON, of London He went abroad about 1762, and *d.* 1766

VI. 1766, SIR WILLIAM HALTON, Bart. [1642], s. and h, *b.* about
to   1751 ; *suc to the Baronetcy* in 1766 He *m* in or before 1771, in
1823   which year he was about 20, Mary, da of Michael GARNER, of Kings Ripon, co. Huntingdon. He *d.* s.p.m ,[a] 9 Feb 1823, when the *Baronetcy* became *extinct.*

SPENCER.

cr 26 Sep. 1642 ,[b]

ex. 16 Nov. 1712.

I. 1642 "BROCKETT SPENCER, of Offley, co. Hertford, Esq ," only br. and h male of Sir John SPENCER of the same, Bart (so *cr* 1627), was *b.* about 1605, suc his said brother in the family estate, Sep 1633, and was *cr a Baronet,* as above, 26 Sep 1642 [b] He *m* in or before 1646, Susan, da of Sir Nicholas CAREW, formerly THROCKMORTON, of Beddington, Surrey, by his 2d wife, Susan, da. or (—) BRIGHT He *d.* 3 and was *bur.* 5 July 1668, at Offley, aged 63. His widow, who was *bap* 8 July 1619, at Beddington, *d.* 9 and was *bur* 12 May 1692, at Offley, aged 72 Will pr. 1692.

II. 1668. SIR RICHARD SPENCER, Bart. [1642], of Offley aforesaid, s. and h., *b* about 1647 ; *suc to the Baronetcy,* 3 July 1668. He *m* 23 July 1672, at Hornsey, Midx (Lic Lond. 18th, he 24 and she 19), Mary, da of Sir John MUSTERS, of Colwick, Notts, by Anne, da. of Sir John MAYNARD He *d.* 21 and was *bur.* 23 Feb. 1687/8, at Offley, aged 41 Will pr. 1688. His widow *m* (settlement 22 April 1691), Sir Ralph RADCLIFFE, of Hitchin, Herts, whose will, dat. 3 Feb 1713/4. was pr 29 July 1720. Her will, dat 19 May 1719 (in his lifetime), was pr 18 Sep. following

III. 1688. SIR JOHN SPENCER, Bart. [1642], of Offley aforesaid, only surv. s and h., *bap.* 27 Feb 1677/8, at Offley , *suc to the Baronetcy,* 21 Feb. 1687/8 He *d,* unm. 6 and was *bur.* 12 Aug 1699, at Offley. Admon. 21 Aug 1699.

---

[a] Mary, his only da. and h , *m.* John Haughton JAMES, of Haughton Hall, in Jamaica, and had a numerous family.

[b] See p. 195, note " a," under " Wrottesley "

IV 1699, SIR JOHN SPENCER, Bart. [1642], of Offley aforesaid,
to uncle and h, b about 1650, matric at Oxford 12 July 1667, aged
1712 17, Barrister (Inner Temple), 1675, *suc. to the Baronetcy*, 6 Aug
1699 He d s p, 16 Nov, and was *bur.* 1 Dec 1712, at Offley,
when the *Baronetcy* became *extinct* (ª) Will pr 1712

GOLDING

cr. 27 Sep. 1642(ᵇ),

ex Dec 1715

I 1642 " EDWARD GOLDING, of Colston Bassett, co Nottingham,
Esq.," s and h of Edward GOLDINO,(ᶜ) of Eye, co. Suffolk, by Mary,
da of Richard GODFREY of Hendringham, co. Norfolk, was cr a Baronet, as above,
27 Sep 1642 (ᵇ) He m in or before 1610, Ellinor, sister of Sir Robert THROCK-
MORTON, 1st Bart. [1642], da. of John THROCKMORTON, of Coughton, co. Warwick,
by Agnes, da of Thomas WILFORD She was *bur.* 22 Sep 1652, at Colston (ᵈ)
He was living Jan 1655/6, and became eventually a Capuchin Friar He d at
Rouen, in Normandy

II 1656? SIR CHARLES GOLDING, Bart. [1642], of Colston Bassett
aforesaid, 2d s and h ,(ᵈ) b about 1624, *suc. to the Baronetcy*, on the
death of his father, in or after 1656 He m 9 Jan. 1655/6, at St Paul's, Covent
Garden, Mary, da. of James RAVENSCROFT, of Alkmondbury, co Huntingdon He
d. 28 and was *bur* 30 Sep. 1661, at Colston, aged 37 His widow was *bur* there
15 Feb 1688/9, aged 53

III 1661, SIR EDWARD GOLDING, Bart [1642], of Colston Bassett
to aforesaid, s and h , *suc to the Baronetcy*, in 1667 He m Winifred,
1715. da. and h of John WYLDMAN, of co Leicester He d s p m, and
was *bur* 8 Dec 1715, at Colston, when the *Baronetcy* became *extinct*
Admon 30 April 1716, to Winifred, the relict

SMITH, *or* SMITHE ·

cr 27 Sep 1642(ᵇ),

ex in or before 1661

I 1642, " WILLIAM SMITHE, of Crautock, co Cornwall, Esq ,"
to presumably a descendant of the family of SMITH, of Tregonnack, in
1661? that county, was a merchant in London, and was cr a Baronet, as
above, 27 Sep 1642 (ᵇ) He m (—), but d. s.p.m in or before 1661,
when the *Baronetcy* became *extinct* Will pr. 1661

(ª) The Offley estate became vested in his four sisters, all of whom d s p.
excepting Elizabeth, who m 2 Nov. 1677, Sir Humphrey GORE, of Gilston, Herts
Their only da. and h , Elizabeth, m 1714, Sir Henry PENRICE, LL D , whose only
da. and h , Anna Maria, m Sir Thomas SALISBURY, LL D , and conveyed the estate
and manor to him She d s p , 7 March 1759. See Clutterbuck's *Herts*, vol iii, p. 97
(ᵇ) See p. 195, note " a," under " Wrottesley "
(ᶜ) " Edward Golding, of Eye, co. Suffolk," was admitted, 16 Oct 1588, to Gray's
Inn
(ᵈ) *Genealogist*, vol. ii , 99, where extracts from this parish register are given
(ᵉ) John Golding, the 1st s., b before 1614, became a Capuchin Friar at Rouen. It
is possible that, though passed over as succeeding to the Baronetcy, he may have
survived his father, in which case the burial, 15 April 1689, of " John, son of Sir
Edward Golding, Baronet," may refer to him, and not to some (infant) son of the
3d Baronet

2 C

HENN, or HENE ·
cr 1 Oct 1642,(ᵃ)
ex about 1710.

I. 1642   "HENRY HENN, of Wingfeild [ɪ e , Winkfield], co Berks,
Esq ," 2d s of William HENE, of Dorking, co Surrey, by Anne (m at
Dorking, 2 Sep 1565), da of (—) BIRCH, of Birches in Coleshill, was b about 1577, and,
having acquired the manor of Folijohn, in Winkfield, Berks, in 1630, was cr a
Baronet, as above, 1 Oct 1642(ᵃ) He m Dorothy, da of Henry STAPLEFORD, of
Pauls Walden, Herts   He was living 28 March 1665 (Visit of Berks), aged 88, and
d in or before 1668. Will pr 1668

II 1668?   SIR HENRY HENE, Bart [1642], of Winkfield aforesaid,
s and h , b about 1632 , matric at Oxford (Christ Church), 17 May
1647 , aged 31 in 1665 , suc. to the Baronetcy in or before 1668   He m. in or before
1652,(ᵇ) Muriel, da of Sir John CORBET, 1st Bart [1627], of Stoke, by Ann, da of
Sir George MANWARING

III 1675?   SIR HENRY HENE, Bart [1642], of Winkfield aforesaid,
1st s and h ; bap 14 Oct 1651; was aged 13 in 1665 ; suc to the
Baronetcy on the death of his father He m (—) He d 16 Jan 1705

IV 1705,   SIR RICHARD HENE, Bart [1642], of Winkfield aforesaid,
   to   only surv s and h , b about 1675 , was an idiot in 1697 ; but was
   1710?   m in or before 1702 He suc to the Baronetcy between 1702 and
1708, but d s p m (ᶜ) about 1710, when the Baronetcy became extinct
The will of "Dame Ann Hene, Berks," was pr. Nov 1716

BLUNT, or BLOUNT :
cr. 6 Oct 1642(ᵃ)

I 1642   "WALTER BLUNT, of Sillington [ɪ e , Sodington], co
Worcester, Esq ," s and h of Sir George BLOUNT, or BLUNT,(ᵈ), of
the same, by Eleanor, da of William NORWOOD, of Leckhampton, co Gloucester, was
b about 1594 , matric at Oxford (Ball Coll), 12 Oct 1610, aged 16 , admitted to
Inner Temple, 1611 , Sheriff of Worcestershire, 1619-20 , M P for Droitwich, 1624-25 ;
and was cr a Baronet, as above, 6 Oct 1642 (ᵃ) He was taken prisoner at Hereford
in December 1645 ; was a great sufferer for the King in the Civil War, and was
imprisoned at Oxford and afterwards in the Tower of London (ᵉ) His house at
Sodington was burnt by Cromwell's soldiers, and his estates confiscated, 2 Nov 1652,
and sold in 1655 He m (when very young) Elizabeth, da. of George WYLDE, of
Droitwich, Serjeant at Law, by Frances, da of Sir Edmond HUDLESTON, of Sawston,
co Cambridge He d at Blagdon, co Devon, 27 and was bur. 29 Aug 1654, at
Paignton, in that county M I His widow d at Mawley Hall, 23 and was bur 25
April 1656, at Mamble, co Worcester M I.

II 1654.   SIR GEORGE BLOUNT, or BLUNT, Bart [1642], of Sodington
aforesaid, and of Mawley Hall, co Worcester, s and h , suc to the
Baronetcy, 27 Aug 1654 He m Mary, d and h of Richard KIRKHAM (s and h of Sir

---

(ᵃ) See p. 195, note "a," under "Wriottesley "
(ᵇ) In the Visit of Berks for 1665 he had six children, of whom the two sons were
(1) Henry, aged 13, and Corbett This Corbett Hene, who was a Col in the Army,
m (Lic Fac 30 Sep 1686, aged 32), Dame Mary Beckford, widow, and d Sep 1693,
in Golden square Will pr 1693
(ᶜ) Of his two daughters (1) Ann was bap. 17 Feb 1702/3 (when he was Esq), and
(2) Arabella, 8 April 1708 (when he was a Baronet), at Clewer, Berks. According to
Lysons' Berks, the estate of Folijohn was inherited by his two daughters.
(ᵈ) See "Croke family, originally named Le Blount," by Sir Alexander Croke,
D C L and F S A., 2 vols 4to, Oxford, 1823
(ᵉ) His four surviving sons, his three brothers, as also he himself, bore arms
for the Royal cause

William KIRKHAM), of Blagdon aforesaid, by his 2d wife, Mary, da of Sir Henry TICHBORNE, 3d s of the 1st Bart. [1611]   He d. 12 Nov 1667, at Mawley Hall, and was *bur* at Mamble aforesaid.   M 1   Admon 10 Feb 1667/8, to his relict

III   1667   SIR WALTER KIRKHAM BLOUNT, Bart. [1642], of Sodington aforesaid, s and h ; *suc to the Baronetcy*, 12 Nov. 1667 , was Sheriff of Worcestershire, 1687-88   He was an author, translating *The Office of the Holy Week*, printed at Paris in 1670   He m firstly, Alicia, da of Sir Thomas STRICKLAND, of Sizeig, co Westmorland, by his 1st wife, Jane, da of John MOSELEY   She d 1 Dec 1680   He m secondly, Mary, da of Sir Cæsar CRANMER, *otherwise* WOOD, of Astwoodbury, Bucks, by Lehs, da of Charles PELLIOTT, Sieur de la Garde, of Paris   She was living 11 Nov 1690 (ᵃ)   He d s.p , at Ghent, in Flanders, 12 May 1717   Will pr. 17 Oct 1717

IV.   1717   SIR EDWARD BLOUNT, Bart [1642], of Sodington and Mawley Hall aforesaid, nephew and h , being s and h of George BLOUNT, of Mawley Hall aforesaid, by Constantia, his 2d wife, da of Sir George CAREY, of Tori Abbey, Devon, which George BLOUNT was 2d s of the 2d Bart , and d 20 May 1702   He *suc to the Baronetcy*, 12 May 1717   He m (Lic Worcester, 11 Aug. 1722, each above 21), Apollonia, da. of Sir Robert THROCKMORTON, 3d Bart [1642], of Coughton, by Mary, da of Sir Charles YATE, 3d Bart [1622]   She d at Mawley 19 Jan. 1749   He d. there 16 Feb 1758.   Both *bur* at Mamble   M I   His will pr 1758

V   1758   SIR EDWARD BLOUNT, Bart [1642], of Sodington and Mawley Hall aforesaid, s and h , b about 1724 , *suc to the Baronetcy*, 16 Feb 1758   He m 1752, Frances, da and h of William MOLYNEUX, of Mosborough, co Lancaster.   He d at Bath, s.p s , 19 Oct 1765, aged 41, and was *bur* at Mamble   M I   Admon 31 Dec. 1765   His widow d 18 Dec 1787.   Will pr 1788.

VI   1765   SIR WALTER BLOUNT, Bart [1642], of Sodington and Mawley Hall aforesaid, br and h ; ed at Donay College , *suc to the Baronetcy*, 19 Oct 1765   He m 21 Sep 1766, at Worksop Manor, Notts, Mary, 1st da and coheir of James (ASTON), 5th LORD ASTON [S], by Barbara, da of George (TALBOT), EARL OF SHREWSBURY   He d at Lisle, in Flanders, 5 Oct 1785   Will pr March 1806   His widow d 31 Jan 1805   Will pr 1805

VII.   1785.   SIR WALTER BLOUNT, Bart [1642], of Sodington, and Mawley Hall aforesaid, s and h , b 3 Sep 1768, *suc to the Baronetcy*, 5 Oct 1785, was *cr* D C L of Oxford, 4 July 1793   He m. 25 Nov 1792, Anne, yst da. of Thomas RIDDELL, of Felton Park and Swinburne Castle, both co Northumberland, by Elizabeth, da and h of Edward Horsley WEDDRINGTON, of Felton aforesaid   He d. at Laycock Abbey, Wilts, and was *bur* 31 Oct 1803, at Bath Abbey, aged 35   Admon Nov 1803   His widow d. 15 Feb 1823   Will pr 1823

VIII.   1803   SIR EDWARD BLOUNT, Bart [1642], of Sodington and Mawley Hall aforesaid, only surv s and h , b. 3 March 1795, at Mawley Hall , *suc to the Baronetcy*, Oct 1803 , Sheriff of Worcestershire, 1835   He m 14 Sep 1830, at St Mary's, Bryanstone square, Marylebone, Mary Frances, sister of Walter Aston Edward BLOUNT, Clarenceux King of Arms [d. 9 Feb 1894, aged 87] 1st da of Edward BLOUNT, of Shablington, Bucks, sometime M P for Steyning, by Frances, da and cohen of Francis WRIOHT, which Edward was next br of the late Baronet. He d 28 May 1881, at Mawley Hall, and was *bur* at Mamble aforesaid, aged 86   His widow, who was b 28 April 1804, at Mapledurham, Oxon, d. at Mawley Hall, 26 May 1893, in her 90th year.

IX   1881   SIR WALTER DE SODINGTON BLOUNT, Bart. [1642], of Sodington and Mawley Hall aforesaid, 1st s and h b 19 Dec. 1833, in Great Cumberland street, and *bap* at St James' Catholic chapel, Spanish place ,

---

(ᵃ) Will of that date of Thomas Wood, Bishop of Coventry and Lichfield

ed at Oscott College , sometime Capt Worcester Yeomanry Cavalry; *suc. to the Baronetcy*, 28 April 1881 He *m.* in 1874, Elizabeth Anne Mould, da of James Zacharies WILLIAMS, of Cader Idris.

Family Estates —These, in 1883, consisted of 2,861 acres in Salop, and 2,622 in Worcestershire Total, 5,483 acres, worth £5,069 a year *Principal* ·eats.—Soding ton Court and Mawley Hall, near Bewdley, co. Worcester.

LITTLETON

cr. 14 Oct 1642 ;(a)

afterwards POYNTZ, *otherwise* LITTLETON ,

ex. 1 Jan 1709/10

I 1642   " ADAM LITTLETON, of Stoke Milburge, co Salop, Esq ," s and h of Thomas LITTLETON,(b) of the same by Frances, da of Adam LUTLEY, of Bronscroft Castle, in that county ; suc his father, 1621, and was *cr a Baronet*, as above, 14 Oct 1642 (a) By the death of his wife's cousin, Richard POYNTZ, *otherwise* MAURICE, on 15 Aug 1643, he suc. to the estates of that family at North Ockendon, co Essex He *m* Etheldred, 1st da and coheir, but eventually sole h , of Thomas POYNTZ, of North Ockendon aforesaid, by Jane, da and coheir of Sir William PERIAM, Lord Chief Baron of the Exchequer He was *bur* 6 Sep 1647, at North Ockendon His widow *bur* there 25 May 1648 Her will dat 10 March 1647/8, pr 27 Oct 1648.

II 1647.   SIR THOMAS LITTLETON, *otherwise* POYNTZ, Bart [1642], of North Ockendon and Stoke Milburgh aforesaid, s. and h , b about 1622 ; matric at Oxford (Jesus Coll), 15 June, 1638, aged 16 , Barrister (Inner Temple), 1642 , *suc to the Baronetcy*, Sep 1647 , was M P for Much Wenlock, April to May 1640, and Nov. 1640 till disabled, Feb 1643/4 , re-elected 1661-78 , M P. for East Grinstead, April to July 1679 , and for Yarmouth (Isle of Wight), Feb 1681 till death , was a Compounder "on his own discovery," 4 May 1649 , fined £220 on 9 Aug 1649, afterwards raised to £295 ; was a Lord of the Admiralty, Feb. 1679/80 till his death He *m* (Lic Lond , 6 Oct 1637, he stated to be 17 and she 12), his cousin Anne da and h of Edward (LITTLETON), BARON LYTTELTON OF MOUNSLOW (so cr 18 Feb 1640/1), sometime Lord Keeper of the Great Seal, by Ann, da. of John LITTLETON, of Frankley, co Worcester. He *d* 12 and was *bur*. 16 April 1681, at North Ockendon, aged 57 Will dat 2 Dec 1665, to 11 April 1681, pr 18 June 1681 His widow, who was *b* 21 Aug 1623, *d* 27 Nov and was *bur* 4 Dec 1705, at North Ockendon, aged 82 Admon as ' of St. Giles' in the Fields, Midx ," 8 Dec 1705

III 1681,   SIR THOMAS LITTLETON, *otherwise* POYNTZ, Bart [1642], to   of North Ockendon and Stoke Milburgh aforesaid, *b* 3 April 1647 , 1710.   matric at Oxford (St Edm Hall), 21 April 1665, aged 18 ; Barrister (Inner Temple), 1671 , *suc to the Baronetcy*, 12 April 1681 , M.P for New Woodstock (six Parls), 1689—1702 , for Castle Rising, 1702 05 , for Chichester, 1705 08 , and for Portsmouth, 1708 till death , was one of the Lords of the Treasury, 1696 99 , Privy Councillor , SPEAKER OF THE HOUSE OF COMMONS, 6 Dec 1698 to 1700 ; Treasurer of the Navy, 1699 till death He *m* Ann, da of Benjamin BAUN, or BARON, of Weston, co Gloucester. He *d* s p, 1 Jan 1709/10, and was *bur* at North Ockendon, M I , when the *Baronetcy* became *extinct* Will dat 19 to 23 Sep 1709, pr. 21 Jan 1709/10 His widow *d* 21 July 1714, and was *bur* at North Ockendon. Will dat 13 Feb 1713, pr. 11 Aug 1714.

(a) See p 195, note "a," under "Wrottesley."

(b) This Thomas was descended, as also Sir Edward LITTLETON, Lord Keeper of the Great Seal, 1640-1645 (cr BARON LYTTELTON OF MOUNSLOW, in 1640), from Thomas LITTLETON, of Spechley, co Worcester, 3d s of Sir Thomas LITTLETON, K.B , of Frankley, in that county, the celebrated Judge.

LIDDELL.

cr. 2 Nov 1642 ,(a)

sometime, 1747-84, BARON RAVENSWORTH,

subsequently, since 1821, BARONS RAVENSWORTH;

and, since 1874, EARLS OF RAVENSWORTH.

I   **1642**   "THOMAS LIDDELL, of Ravensholme [i e, Ravensworth] Castle, co pal Durham, Esq," s and h. of Thomas LIDDELL, of the same, by Margaret, da. of John WATSON, suc. his father in 1615; was admitted to Gray's Inn, 15 March 1619/20, and was *cr a Baronet*, as above, 2 Nov 1642 He was a zealous Royalist, and gallantly defended Newcastle against the Scots He was fined £4,000 as "a delinquent." He m Isabel, da. of Henry ANDERSON, by (—), da and coheir of (—) MORLAND He d 1650 Will pr. 1652

II.   **1650**   SIR THOMAS LIDDELL, Bart [1642], of Ravensworth Castle aforesaid, grandson and h, being s and h of Sir Thomas LIDDELL (by Bridget, da of Edward WOODWARD, of Lee, Bucks), which Thomas was s and h ap. of the 1st Bart, and d. v p 1627 He *suc to the Baronetcy*, 1650 He m Anne, da. of Sir Henry VANE, of Raby Castle, Durham, by Frances, da and coheir of Thomas DARCY, of Tolleshunt Darcy, Essex He d. 1697

III   **1697**   SIR HENRY LIDDELL, Bart. [1642], of Ravensworth Castle aforesaid, s and h, M P for Durham city, 1689 98, for Newcastle, 1700 05 and Jan 1706 to 1710, *suc. to the Baronetcy* in 1697. He m in or before 1670, Catharine, only surv da and h of Sir John BRIGHT, Bart (so cr 1660), of Badsworth, co York, and Carbrook, co Derby, by his 1st wife, Catharine, da of Sir Richard HAWKSWORTH She was *bur.* 24 Feb. 1703, at Kensington He d 1 Sep. 1723 Will dat 17 July 1722 and 19 Aug 1723, pr 2 Nov 1723

IV   **1723.**   SIR HENRY LIDDELL, Bart. [1642], of Ravensworth Castle aforesaid, grandson and h, being s and h of Thomas LIDDELL, by Jane (m 12 Oct 1707), da of James CLAVERING, of Greencroft, co Durham, which Thomas (who d v p 3 June 1715, aged 34), was s and h. ap of the late Baronet. He was *b.* 1708; *suc to the Baronetcy*, 1 Sep 1723, was M P for Morpeth, 1734 47, being, on 29 June 1747, *cr* a Peer, as LORD RAVENS-WORTH, BARON OF RAVENSWORTH, co. Durham He m, 27 April 1735, Ann, only da of Sir Peter DELME,(b) Lord Mayor of London [1723-24], by his 1st wife Anne, da of Cornelius MACHAM, of Southampton He d s p m,(c) 30 Jan, and was *bur* 8 Feb 1784, at Lamersley, co Durham, when the *Peerage* became *extinct* Will pr March 1784 His widow, who was b 5 and bap 11 June 1712, at St Gabriel's Fenchurch, London, d. 12 June 1794, in St James' square, aged 82 Will pr June 1794

V   **1784**   SIR HENRY GEORGE LIDDELL, Bart [1642], of Ravensworth Castle aforesaid, nephew and h male, being s and h of Thomas LIDDELL, by Margaret, da of Sir William BOWES, of Gibside, which Thomas was next br to the 4th Bart He was b 25 Nov 1749, and *suc to the Baronetcy*, on the death of Lord Ravensworth, 30 Jan 1784. He m April 1773, Elizabeth, da. of Thomas STEELE, of Hampsnett, Sussex He d 26 Nov 1791 Will pr Feb 1792

(a) See p. 195, note "a," under 'Wrottesley'

(b) An interesting account of the Delmé family, by the Rev G W Minns, LL B, is in the Hampshire Field Club Papers, 1895, with an engraving of the beautiful picture of "Lady Betty Delmé and two children," by Sir Joshua Reynolds, which picture, in 1895, sold for 11 000 guineas, the estate and mansion of Cams Hall, near Fareham, Hants (from whence it was taken), realising but £10,250 !

(c) Anne, his only da. and h, became Duchess of Grafton, and, subsequently, having been divorced, in 1769, Countess of Upper Ossory [I]

(d) He is said to have had "a warm generous, but somewhat romantic disposition" His excursion in Lapland (for a wager) is described in Consett's "Tour through Sweden"

VI. 1791   SIR THOMAS HENRY LIDDELL, Bart [1642], of Ravens-
            worth Castle aforesaid, s and h, b 8 Feb 1775, at Newton Hall,
co. Durham, suc. to the Baronetcy, 26 Nov 1791; ed at Trin Coll, Cambridge;
M A, 1795, was M P for co Durham, 1806-07   He m. 26 March 1796, at her
mother's house, in Upper Harley Street, Marylebone, Maria Susanna, da of John
SIMPSON, of Bradley, co Durham, by Anne, da of Thomas (LYON), EARL OF
STRATHMORE AND KINGHORN [S.]   She was living when he was cr 17 July 1821,
BARON RAVENSWORTH of Ravensworth Castle, co. Durham   In that title this
Baronetcy then merged, and still so continues, the 2d Baron being cr 2 April 1874,
EARL OF RAVENSWORTH   See Peerage.

LAWDAY, or LAWDEY ·

cr 9 Nov. 1642 ,(ᵃ)

ex 1648

I. 1642,   " RICHARD LAWDEY, of Exeter co Devon, Esq," whose
   to   only connection with that county was through his marriage(ᵇ), was
  1648   cr a Baronet, as above, 9 Nov 1642 (ᵃ)   He was a Colonel in the
            King's service   He m (—), widow of Nicholas MARTIN, of Exeter,
da of (—) SHEERS, with whom he had £3,000 or £4,000   He d., s p m, being slain
while in arms under the Earl of Worcester in Wales, in or shortly before Oct 1648,
when the Baronetcy presumably became extinct (ᶜ)   A sum of £800 together with his
estate was sequestrated 1 Nov 1648 for his delinquency   Will pr 1648

CHAMBERLAYNE or CHAMBERLYNE ·

cr. 4 Feb. 1642/3(ᵃ) .

ex 25 Jan 1776

I   1643   " THOMAS CHAMBERLYNE, of Wickham, co Oxford, Esq,'
            s and h of Sir Thomas CHAMBERLAYNE, one of the Justices of the
Court of King's Bench, by his first wife Elizabeth, da of Sir George FERMOR, of
Easton Neston, Northants, suc his father in Sep 1625; was a Royalist, and was
cr a Baronet, as above, 4 Feb 1642/3(ᵃ), Sheriff of Oxfordshire, 1643.   He m firstly,
(—), da of (—) ACLAND   He m secondly, Anne, da of Richard CHAMBERLAYNS, of
Temple House, co Warwick, and of the Court of Wards   He d. (during his Shrievalty
and a few months after receiving his Baronetcy) 6 Oct 1643

II   1643   SIR THOMAS CHAMBERLAYNE, Bart [1643], of Wickham
            aforesaid, and of Northbrooke, Oxon, 1st s and h, b probably about
1635, suc. to the Baronetcy, 6 Oct 1643, but the title (one conferred after 4 Jan.
1641/2) being void under the Act of Parl (4 Feb 1651/2) then in force, he accepted
another Baronetcy from " the Lord Protector," being by him cr a Baronet, 6 Oct
1657, under the designation of " Thomas Chamberlayne, of Wickham, Esquire "
This creation became, of course, invalid after the Restoration   He m (under the
designation of " Sir Thomas,") 8 April 1657, at St Dionis, Backchurch, London

---

(ᵃ) See p. 195, note " a," under " Wrottesley "
(ᵇ) Le Neve's MS Baronetage
(ᶜ) " Mr William Lawday, sometime of Bath, in Somersetshire, living in 1822,
claimed to be the immediate representative of the Baronet, but the title has lain
dormant (if it did not then become extinct) since the decease of Sir Richard "
[Burke's Extinct Baronetage]

(Banns pub at St. Dunstan's in the West), Margaret, da of Edmund PRIDEAUX, of Ford Abbey, Devon, sometime (1649) Attorney General, by his second wife Margaret, da. of William IVERY, of Cotthay, Somerset He *d* s p m (a) 1682 Will dat 16 Sep 1681, pr. 23 Nov 1682

III. 1682 SIR JAMES CHAMBERLAYNE, Bart [1643], of Dunstew, Oxon, br aud h male, *b* probably about 1640, matric at Oxford (Queen's Coll.), 15 June 1657, *suc. to the Baronetcy,* in 1682 He *m* Margaret, da of (—) GOODWIN, of Bodicote, Oxon He *d* Oct 1694 Will pr. 1694

IV. 1694 SIR JAMES CHAMBERLAYNE, Bart. [1643], of Dunstew aforesaid, s and h., *suc to the Baronetcy,* in Oct 1694, was sometime Lieut.-Col in the Horse Guards He *m* 15 June 1725, at St Paul's, Covent Garden, 'Betty Clarke WALKER, of Little London, in Hillingdon, Midx, spinster," da of (—) WALKER Clerk to the House of Commons She *d* before him He *d* s.p m, 23 Dec 1767, and was *bur* at Dunstew Admon 29 Jan 1768, to his three daughters, and only issue

V 1767, SIR HENRY CHAMBERLAYNE, Bart. [1643], br and h to male; *suc. to the Baronetcy,* 23 Dec 1767 He *d* s p 25 Jan 1776 1776, and was *bur* at Dunstew, when the *Baronetcy* became *extinct* (b) Will pr Feb. 1776.

HUNLOKE

cr 28 Feb 1642/3 ;(c)

ex. 22 June 1856

I 1643. "HENRY HUNLOKE, of Wingerworth, co Derby, Esq," s and h. of Henry HUNLOKE,(d) of the same, Sheriff of Derbyshire, 1624 (who *d.* when in office, 14 Aug 1624), by his 2d wife, Anne, da and h. of Richard ALVEY, of Corber, co Derby, was *bap* 28 Oct. 1618, at Wingerworth ; admitted to Gray s Inn, 14 May 1636, suc his father, 14 Aug. 1642, was in his 23d year, at the battle of Edgehill, 23 Oct. 1642, where he was severely wounded, and was *cr a Baronet,* as above, 28 Feb 1642/3,(c) being subsequently *Knighted* at Oxford, 2 March 1642/3 (e) He had levied a troop of horse for the King at his own expense whereof he was Colonel. His estates were sequestrated 18 Aug 1646, and himself fined £1,458, and his house at Wingerworth was made into a garrison for the Parl. troops He *m* June 1644, at Worcester, Marina, sister of Thomas (WINDSOR, *formerly* HICKMAN), 1st EARL OF PLYMOUTH, da of Dixie HICKMAN, of Kew, co Surrey, by Elizabeth, da of Henry (WINDSOR), LORD WINDSOR He *d* 13 and was *bur* 14 Jan 1647/8, at Wingerworth Will pr 15 Dec 1648 and 30 May 1649 His widow *m.* 25 May 1653, at St. Andrew's Wardrobe, London, Col William MICHELL, one of Cromwell's officers (through whose influence much of the Hunloke estate was spared from forfeiture), who was, in 1662, Dep Gov of Jamaica. She was *bur* at Worcester, 7 Feb 1669/70, aged 50 Will dat 29 Jan 1669, pr. 8 June, 1671

(a) Of his two daughters and coheirs (1) Katharine, who inherited the estate of Wickham, became Viscountess Wenman [I], and, subsequently, Countess of Abingdon, (2) Penelope, who inherited the estate of Northbrooke, *m* Robert Dashwood, who was *cr a Baronet,* in 1684, as "of Northbrooke."

(b) There was, however, a younger brother Thomas Chamberlayne who is sometimes conjectured (though apparently, in error), to have left male issue

(c) See p 195, note "a," under "Wrottesley"

(d) In J. J Howard's *Catholic Families of England,* is a well worked up pedigree of Hunloke, from which this account is, mostly, compiled

(e) The tradition that he was Knighted by the King on the battlefield of Edgehill, 22 Oct. 1642, seems groundless

II. 1648.   SIR HENRY HUNLOKE, Bart [1643], of Wingerworth
aforesaid (which estate he enjoyed 67 years), s and h , b 20 and bap
21 Nov 1645, at St Michael's, Bedwardine, Worcester ; suc to the Baronetcy, when
an infant, 13 Jan 1647/8 admitted to Gray's Inn, 16 Dec 1654, at 9 years of age ;
elected Sheriff of Derbyshire, Dec 1687, but did not act   He m 28 (settlement 27
Jan 1673/4), Catharine, only da. and h of Francis TYRWHITT, of Kettleby, co
Lincoln, by Elizabeth, da and h. of Robert LLOYD, M D   She was b at Kettleby,
13 May 1657   He d 3 and was bur 5 Jan 1714/5, at Wingerworth, in his 70th
year   Will dat 5 July 1711, pr. 8 Nov 1715

III 1715.   SIR THOMAS WINDSOR HUNLOKE, Bart. [1643], of Wingerworth aforesaid, only surv s and h , b and bap 10 Nov 1684, at
Wingerworth , suc to the Baronetcy, 3 Jan 1714/5. He pulled down the old mansion
at Wingerworth and erected a more stately one, on a hill adjoining, 1726 30   He
m 2 May (settlement 12 April) 1720, at Weston Underwood, Bucks, Charlotte, 5th
da of Sir Robert THROCKMORTON, 3d Bart [1642], of Coughton, by Mary, da of
Sir Charles YATE, 3d Bart [1622]   She d at Wingerworth, 31 Dec 1738, and was
bur there, 3 Jan 1738/9, aged 38   He d there 30 Jan and was bur 4 Feb 1752, at
Wingerworth, aged 68.   Will dat 13 March 1744, pr 24 April 1752

IV 1752.   SIR HENRY HUNLOKE, Bart [1643], of Wingerworth
aforesaid, s and h., b and bap there, 25 March 1724 ; suc. to the
Baronetcy, 30 Jan 1752   He m 21 Dec 1769 (reg at Holkham, co Norfolk, and at
Langford, co Derby), Margaret, sister of Thomas William, 1st EARL OF LEICESTER,
1st da of Wenman COKE, formerly ROBERTS, of Holkham and Langford aforesaid,
by Elizabeth, da and sole h. of George DENTON, formerly CHAMBERLAYNE, of Hillesden, Bucks, and of Wardington, Oxon. He d 15 and was bur. 21 Nov. 1804, at
Wingerworth, aged 81   Will dat 6 Sep 1799, pr 28 July 1805   His widow d.
22 Jan and was bur 2 Feb. 1824, at Wingerworth, aged 69   Will pr Nov 1825

V 1804   SIR THOMAS WINDSOR HUNLOKE, Bart [1643], of Wingerworth aforesaid, 1st s and h., b. there 2 and bap. 3 March 1773 ;
suc. to the Baronetcy, 15 Nov 1804   He m 18 Oct. 1807, Anne, sister and eventually
coheir of Charles SCARISBRICK, formerly ECCLESTON, 1st da. of Thomas ECCLESTON, of
Scarisbrick Hall, co Lancaster, by Eleanor, da of Thomas CLIFTON, of Lytham, in
that county   He d 19 Jan 1816, of fever, at Paris, aged 42, and was bur in the
Eastern Cemetery there   Will dat. 16 Jan 1816, pr 18 July 1817   His widow,
who was b 15 March 1788, and who, by Royal lic in 1860, took the name of Scarisbrick in lieu of Hunloke, d. at Scarisbrick Hall 6 and was bur 13 March 1872, at
Wingerworth, aged 83   Will dat 4 June 1828

VI 1816.   SIR HENRY JOHN JOSEPH HUNLOKE, Bart. [1643], of Wingerworth aforesaid, only s and h , b there 29 and bap. 30 Sep
1812 , suc to the Baronetcy, 19 Jan. 1816.   He d unm,(a) in Grafton street, 8 and
was bur 16 Feb 1856, at Wingerworth, aged 43   Will pr March 1856.

VII. 1856,   SIR JAMES HUNLOKE, Bart [1643], of Birdholme, co
Feb   Derby, uncle and h. male, being 3d s of the 4th Bart. , b and bap
to   5 July 1784, at Wingerworth , suc to the Baronetcy, 8 Feb 1856.
June   He d. unm a few months later, at Birdholme, 22 and was bur.
27 June 1856, at Wingerworth, aged 72, when the Baronetcy became
extinct.(b) Will pr Aug 1856

(a) Of his two sisters and coheirs (1) Charlotte d unm 16 May 1857, and
(2) Eliza Margaret m Leon BIODOS, MARQUESS DE CASTEJA
(b) The estates were inherited by the descendants of his sister Harriet, being the
only one of the eight daughters of the 4th Baronet who left issue.   She m. 29 April
1799, at Wingerworth, John Shelley-Sidney, and d. 5 Feb 1811 aged 28, being
mother of Philip Charles, 1st Baron De L'Isle and Dudley, so cr 13 Jan. 1835.

BADD:

cr. 28 Feb. 1642/3 ;(ᵃ)

ex. 10 June 1683.

I. 1643,
to
1683.
"THOMAS BADD, of Cames Oyselle, co. Southampton, Esq," son of "Emmanuel Bad, Esq," who d 18 Aug 1632 and was *bur* at Fareham, Hants, was *b.* about 1607, and was cr *a Baronet*, as above, 28 Feb. 1642/3 (ᵃ) He was subsequently *Knighted* at Oxford, 5 March 1642/3 ; was a Royalist, and was fined £470 in Dec. 1647, being then styled "of Fareham" He *m* in or before 1658 (—), possibly indeed he had previously married, before 1632, a wife, named Elizabeth (who was *bur* at Fareham 11 Dec 1634), and another wife before 1638 (ᵇ) He *d.* s.p s , 10 June 1683, aged 76, and was *bur.* at Fareham, Hants, when the *Baronetcy* became *extinct* His widow was *bur.* 2 June 1688, at Fareham aforesaid.

CRANE:

cr. 20 March 1642/3 ;(ᵃ)

ex. March 1644/5.

I 1643,
to
1645.
"RICHARD CRANE, of Woodrising, co. Norfolk, Esq., one of the Gentlemen of the Privy Chamber," br. and h of Sir Francis CRANE, Chancellor of the Order of the Garter, and Director of the Tapestry Works, at Mortlake, Surrey ; suc. his said brother in the estate of Woodrising aforesaid, and in that of Stoke Nash, in Stoke Bruen, co. Northampton,(ᶜ) in June or July 1636, being then a Captain and a Gentleman of the Privy Chamber, and was cr *a Baronet*, as above, 20 March 1642/3 (ᵃ) He *m* firstly, Mary, da. of William (WIDDRINGTON), 1st BARON WIDDRINGTON OF BLANKNEY, by Marr, da. and h of Sir Anthony THOROLD, of Blankney aforesaid She *d* s p He *m* secondly, in 1639, Jane, widow of Jacob JAMES He *d* s p at Cardiff, March 1644/5, when the *Baronetcy* became *extinct.* Admon 17 May 1648, and 10 March 1653/4, the will, dat 20 Sep. 1643, being pr. 12 March 1655/6 (probably a mistake for 1654/5). The will of his widow, as "of Woodrising, Norfolk, dat. 9 March 1646/7, pr. 25 Feb 1651/2.

DANVERS:

cr. 21 March 1642/3 ;(ᵃ)

ex. 20 Aug. 1776.

I. 1643
"SAMUEL DANVERS, of Culworth, co. Northampton, Esq.," 2d but 1st surv. s and h of Sir John DANVERS, of the same, by Dorothy, da. of Gabriel PULTENEY, of Misterton, co Leicester, was *bap.* 29 Oct.

(ᵃ) See p. 195, note " a, ' under " Wrottesley "

(ᵇ) There are baptisms at Fareham, 8 April 1632, to 11 Aug 1633, and again from 27 Dec. 1638, to 21 Aug 1643, of children of "Mr Thomas Badde," or "Thomas Badd, Esq," and there is the burial, 11 Dec 1634, of "Elizabeth, wife of Thomas Badde, Esq," and, on 20 Oct. 1658, the baptism of Margaret, da. of "*Sir* Thomas Badd "

(ᶜ) See pedigree in Baker's *Northamptonshire*, vol ii, p 243

(ᵈ) There is a good pedigree of the Culworth branch of the Danvers family in Baker's *Northamptonshire*, vol. i, p. 605 See also F. N. Macnamara's *Danvers Family, of Dauntsey and Culworth.* London, 8vo, 1895.

2 D

1611, at Culworth; suc his father (who *d* aged 63), 17 Feb 1641/2. and was *cr. a Baronet*, as above, 21 March 1642/3 (ª)   On 27 June 1644, the King slept at his house at Culworth, before the battle of Cropredy Bridge.   He was Sheriff of Northamptonshire, 1648-49, the year the King was murdered, and appeared at the assizes with all his retinue clothed in black   He was a great sufferer during the Rebellion   He *m.* in 1634 (Lic. Oxford, she aged 18 and he 23), Anne, sister of Thomas, 2d EARL OF DOWNE [I.], da. of the Hon Sir William POPE, of Wroxton, Oxon, by Elizabeth, da. of Sir Thomas WATSON, of Halstead, Kent.   She was *bur* 22 March 1677/8, at Culworth. He *d.* 27 and was *bur.* there 30 Jan. 1682/3, aged 73   M I   Admon 27 April 1683

II. 1683.   SIR POPE DANVERS, Bart. [1643], of Culworth aforesaid, 3d but only surv. s. and h., *bap.* 12 Dec. 1644, at Culworth; matric at Oxford (Trin. Coll), 12 Dec. 1661, aged 17, admitted to Middle Temple, 1664; *suc to the Baronetcy*, 27 Jan 1682/3. He *m* Anne, da and coheir of William BARKER, of Sunning, Berks, by Mary, da of William BRIDEN, of Ipswich, merchant   He *d.* 4 and was *bur.* 6 May 1712, at Culworth, aged 68. M.I   Will pr. June 1712   His widow *d.* 16 and was *bur.* 18 May 1718, also at Culworth   Her will pr 1718.

III 1712.   SIR JOHN DANVERS, Bart. [1643], of Culworth aforesaid, 3d but 1st surv. s and h., *b.* at Sunning, Berks, 10 July 1673; birth reg at Culworth, matric at Oxford (St John's Coll.), 23 Jan. 1691/2, aged 17; *suc to the Baronetcy*, 4 May 1712   He *m.* firstly, Muriel, da. of Sir Robert LEYCESTER, 2d Bart [1660] of Tabley, by Muriel, da and h of Francis WATSON, of Church Aston, Salop   She *d* in childbirth, 22 Dec. 1701, aged 29, at Tabley aforesaid. He *m.* secondly, Susannah, eldest sister and coheir of Sir Edward NICHOLS, 3d Bart, da. of Sir Edward NICHOLS, 2d Bart. [1660], of Hardwick, by his 2d wife Jane, da. of Sir Stephen SOAME   This marriage was an unhappy one, and they were separated   She *d s p* 17 June 1730, and was *bur* at Faxton, co. Northampton.   Will, leaving her estates to her nephew, John Nichols RAYNSFORD, pr. 1730.   He *m.* thirdly, in or before 1731, Mary, da of the Rev John HUTCHINS, Rector of Eydon, co North ampton (1692-1729)   He *d* 26 and was *bur.* 29 Sep. 1744, aged 71, at Culworth. M I   Will dat 1740, pr 5 Oct. 1745, at Northampton, by the widow.   She, who is said to have *m.* soon afterwards "a villager of humble station," *d.* 4 Dec 1784, aged 75, and was *bur.* at Culworth.

IV. 1744.   SIR HENRY DANVERS, Bart. [1643], of Culworth aforesaid, s. and h by 3d wife, *b* 30 April and *bap* 20 May 1731, at Culworth; ed at Abingdon School; *suc to the Baronetcy*, 26 Sep. 1744; matric at Oxford (Linc. Coll), 16 July 1748, aged 17.   He *d.* unm 10 and was *bur* 13 Aug. 1753, at Culworth, aged 22   M.I.

V 1753,   SIR MICHAEL DANVERS, Bart. [1643], of Culworth aforeto   said, br and h, *b* 29 Sep. and *bap* 22 Oct. 1738, at Culworth, ed.
1776.   at Abingdon School; *suc to the Baronetcy*, 10 Aug 1753; matric at Oxford (Linc. Coll.), 17 May 1757, aged 18, Sheriff of Northamptonshire, 1763-64.   He *d.* unm 20 and was *bur.* 26 Aug 1776, at Culworth, when the *Baronetcy* became *extinct.*   Will pr. 8 Feb. 1777 (ᵇ)

(ª) See p 195, note " a," under " Wrottesley."
(ᵇ) The estate passed to his sister, Meriel, who *d.* unm. 5 Nov. 1794, aged 60, having devised it to her two cousins, Martha and Frances, daughters and coheirs of Daniel RICH, by Martha, da and coheir of her uncle Daniel Danvers, of Eydon.   See Baker's *Northamptonshire*, vol. 1, p 605.

ANDERSON :
cr. 3 July 1643 ;(ª)

ex 16 Aug. 1699 ;

assumed from 1699 to 1741, or later.

I 1643   " HENRY ANDERSON, of Penley [in the parish of Tring],
co Herts, Esq ," s. and h of Sir Richard ANDERSON,(ᵇ) of the same,
by Mary, da of Robert (SPENCER), 1st BARON SPENCER OF WORMLEIGHTON, was *b.*
about 1608 , admitted to Lincoln's Inn, 18 Nov 1628 , suc. his father, 3 Aug 1630,
and was *cr. a Baronet,* as above, 3 July 1643 (ª) He was a devoted Royalist,(ᶜ) and,
as such, had to pay £2,810 to the sequestrators, besides other fines He *m* firstly
(Lic Fac. 18 Dec 1632, he about 23), Jacomina, da of Sir Charles CÆSAR, of Benington, Herts, Master of the Rolls, by his 1st wife, Anne, da of Sir Peter VANLORE.
She, who was *bap.* 10 Dec. 1615, at Benington, *d* Oct. 1639, and was *bur.* at Tring.
M I. He *m.* secondly, Mary, said to be a da of Sir William LYTTON. He *d.* 7 July
1653, aged 45, and was *bur.* at Tring   M I. Will pr. 1659. His 2d wife survived
him.

II. 1653,   SIR RICHARD ANDERSON, Bart. [1643], of Penley aforesaid,
    to   s. and h by 1st wife, *b.* about 1635 , *suc to the Baronetcy,* 7 July
    1699   1653 He was a benefactor to the church of Tring. He *m.* firstly,
           Elizabeth, sister of the whole blood and coheir of George, VISCOUNT
HEWETT OF GOWRAN [I], da. of Sir William HEWETT, 1st Bart [1660], of Pishiobury,
Herts by his 2d wife, Margaret, da of Sir William LYTTON, of Knebworth She *d*
25 Dec. 1698, and was *bur.* at Albury, Herts   M I. Will pi 1698 He *m* secondly,
Mary, widow of Humphrey SIMPSON, da of the Right Hon John METHUEN, sometime
Lord Chancellor of Ireland and Ambassador to Portugal, by Mary, da of Seacole
CHEVERS, of Comerford, Wilts. He *d. s p m s* ,(ᵈ) 16 and was *bur.* 20 Aug. 1699, at
Albury aforesaid, aged 64, when the *Baronetcy* became *extinct*   M I Admon. 1 Jan.
1699/700. Will dated 25 July 1699, pi 5 March following   His widow *m.* Sir
Brownlow SHERARD, 3d Bart. [1674], of Lopthorpe, co. Lincoln, who *d.* 30 Jan.
1736, aged 60

> III. 1699.   " SIR RICHARD ANDERSON, Bart " [1643], of East
>   Meon, Hants, calling himself " nephew to the said Sir Richard
> and grandson to Sir Henry, who was cr. a Baronet,"(ᵉ) is stated to have
> *suc. to " the title* but not to the estate "(ᵉ) His parentage is unknown. He
> *m.* Anne, da of (—) ALDERSEY, of Faversham, Kent   He *d.* 1724.(ᵉ)

(ª) Disallowed by Parl , 11 Nov 1643, till the Restoration   See *Memorandum* as to
creations after 4 Jan 1641/2 and 22 May 1642, on p. 152   The patent is not enrolled
The date here given is that in Dugdale's *Catalogue.*   See *Memorandum* on p 84
The date of the " warrant for granting receipt for £1,095 to Henry Anderson, of
Penley, co. Herts, Esq , on his creation, as Baronet " (Signet Bills) is 30 June 1643.

(ᵇ) This Richard was only surv s and h of Sir Henry Anderson, of St Olave's,
Jewry, Alderman and sometime (1601-02), Sheriff of London, who *d.* 13 April 1605.
See pedigree in Clutterbuck's *Herts*, vol 1, p 285

(ᶜ) On his monument it is tastefully said of him that he was " Regi dilectus,
quem non, vel desertum, deseruit "

(ᵈ) Richard Anderson, his 2d s but eventually (1677) h ap , who was admitted to
Lincoln's Inn, 10 Feb. 1675/6 , was M P. for Aylesbury, 1685-87 , married, but *d* v p
and s.p., 1695. Elizabeth, his only da by his 1st wife, *m.* (Lic Fac 3 Jan.
1677/8), Simon HARCOURT, Clerk of the Crown, by whom she had a son, Henry
Harcourt, who inherited the Penley estate

(ᵉ) See Wotton's *Baronetage* (1741), where the authority is given as " *Ex inform.*
Dum Ric Anderson, Bar., 1724," to which, however, Wotton appends the following
note —" I don't yet find that Sir Richard [the 2d Baronet] above mentioned ever
had a brother. Indeed, his father, Sir Henry [the 1st Baronet] had a brother

IV. 1724.   "SIR KENDRICH ANDERSON, Bart." [1643], s. and
                     h.,(ᵃ) *bap.* 5 July 1705, at Stifford, Essex. He *d* unm.
10 Nov. 1735 (ᵃ)

V. 1735.   "SIR RICHARD ANDERSON, Bart." [1643], br and
                     h He d s p, "at the Black Horse Alehouse, Southwark,"(ᵇ)
18 Sep 1738 (ᵃ) Will pr 1739

VI. 1738,   "SIR FRANCIS ANDERSON, Bart" [1643], called, in
      to   1741, "the present Baronet,"(ᵃ) br. and h, who "was in
    1760 ?   foreign parts when his br died."(ᵇ) After his death, at some
                     date, presumably, before 1771, the *assumption of the Baronetcy*
was, apparently, discontinued.(ᶜ)

VAVASOUR, *or* VAVASOR:

cr. 17 July 1643 ;(ᵈ)

ex. 18 Feb. 1659

I 1643,   "WILLIAM VAVASOR, of Yorkshire, Esq," *i e*, of Cop-
    to   manthorpe in that county, br. of Sir Charles VAVASOUR, Bart (so
  1659.   cr 22 June 1631), both being sons of Sir Thomas VAVASOUR, of
                     Copmanthorpe aforesaid (*d* Nov. 1620), by Mary, da and h of
John DODGES, of Cope, co York, was cr a Baronet, as above, 17 July 1643 (ᵈ) He, who
was a Royalist and banished from England in Dec 1645, was a Major Gen in the
service of the King of Sweden He *m* firstly a Dutch lady He *m* secondly, in or
before 1654, Olive, da of Brian STAPLETON, *or* STAPYLTON, of Myton, co. York, by
Frances, da of Sir Henry SLINGSBY, of Scriven He *d*. s.p m ,(ᵉ) 18 Feb 1658/9,
when the *Baronetcy* became *extinct* Admon 11 March 1658/9, as "late of Medring-
ham, co Lincoln, but deceased at the siege of Copenhagen," to his widow.
She, who was *b* at Lacock Abbey, Wilts, 1620, *m*. Richard TOPHAM, of Westminster,
and was *bur.* 26 Nov. 1714, at Chelsea

Robert, of Chichester, from whence some have imagined *this* Sir Richard descended,
but then he could not be a Baronet, unless [there was] a particular limitation in the
patent," but as Sir Richard, of East Meon, and his sons have been deemed Baronets,
and as I know nothing certain to the contrary, I have inserted the account of them."
There is, however, no reason to suppose that there was any special limitation in this
creation.

(ᵃ) See p 211, note "e"

(ᵇ) MSS. additions [*Qy.* in Brooke's writing ?] to the copy of Wotton's *Baronetage*, in
the Editor's possession.

(ᶜ) No mention is made of this Baronetcy in Kimber's *Baronetage* (1771).

(ᵈ) Disallowed by Parl, till the Restoration. See *Memorandum* as to creations
after 4 Jan 1641/2 and 22 May 1642 on p 152   No patent is enrolled The
date of "July 1643" (between 3 and 25 July) is in Dugdale's *Catalogue*, and
the date "17 July 1643" is that of the docquet in Black's *Docquets.* See *Memorandum* on p. 84

(ᵉ) Frances, his only da and h (by 2d wife), *b*. 26 Oct. 1654 in Drury Lane, *m.*
firstly, Sir Thomas Norcliffe, and secondly, Moses Goodyere, and was *bur.* at Chelsea,
16 Dec. 1731, leaving issue.

JONES

cr. 25 July 1643 ,(ᵃ)

ex. in or before May 1644.

I 1643,   "HENRY JONES, of Abermarles, co. Caermarthen, Knt ,"
to   only s aud h of Sir Henry(ᵇ) JONES, of the same, by his 1st wife,
1644?   Elizabeth, sister of Edward, 1st BARON HERBERT OF CHERBURY, da
of Richard HERBERT, of Montgonery, was Sheriff of Carmarthenshire,
1638-39 , suc his father in or shortly before 1641 , was *Knighted* 7 Sep 1642, at
Caermarthen, and was *cr a Baronet*, as above, 25 July 1643 (ᵃ)   He m Margaret,
da of Sir Henry WILLIAMS, of Gwernevet, co Brecon, by Eleanor (living Aug. 1642),
da of Eustace WHITNEY   He *d.* s p.m.,(ᶜ) in or before May 1644, when the
Baronetcy became *extinct*   Will dat 15 Aug 1642, desiring to be *bur* at
Llansadorn, or at Aberllyney, co Brecon . Inventory of goods dat. 31 May 1644
Probate renounced by the widow 29 July, and will pr. 6 Dec 1644 at Carmarthen.

WALDEGRAVE :

cr. 1 Aug 1643 ,(ᵈ)

afterwards, since 1686, BARONS WALDEGRAVE OF CHEWTON ,

and subsequently, since 1729, EARLS WALDEGRAVE

I. 1643   "EDWARD WALDEGRAVE, of Hever Castle, co. Kent, Knt ,"
being also of Staininghall, co Norfolk, and of Chewton, co Somerset, s.
and h of Charles WALDEGRAVE, of Staininghall and Chewton aforesaid, by Jeronyma,
da. of Sir Henry JERNINGHAM, of Cossey Hall, co Norfolk, was *b* about 1568 , was,
possibly, M P for Sudbury, 1584 85 , was *Knighted*, 19 July 1607, at Greenwich, and
was *cr a Baronet*, as above, 1 Aug. 1643 (ᵈ)   Though aged above 70 at the breaking
out of the Civil War, he commanded a Regiment of Horse, with which he did great
service against the Parliamentary troops in Cornwall and elsewhere   He lost two sons
in the Royal cause, is said to have lost £50,000 therein, and was, 7 Sep 1647, named
by the Parliamentary party among those to be removed from the King's Council
and to be made incapable of any appointment.   He *m.* in or before 1598,
Eleanor, sister and heir of Sir Francis LOVELL, da. of Sir Thomas LOVELL, both of
Harling, co Norfolk.   She *d.* 12 Dec 1604   He survived her more than 43 years

II. 1650?   SIR HENRY WALDEGRAVE, Bart [1643], of Staininghall
and Chewton aforesaid, s and h , *b* 1598; *suc to the Baronetcy,* on
the death of his father   He m firstly Anne, da. of Edward PASTON, of Appleton,
and by her had eleven children   He m. secondly, Catharine, da of Richard BACON,
and by her had twelve more children   He *d* 10 Oct 1658, aged 60, and was *bur*
in Cossey church, co Norfolk   M.I   The will of his widow pr 1695

(ᵃ) Disallowed by Parl till the Restoration   See *Memorandum* as to creations
after 4 Jan 1641/2, and 22 May 1642, on p. 152   No patent is enrolled.   The date
here given is that in Dugdale's *Catalogue.* See *Memorandum,* on p 84   The date of
the signet bill is 24 July 1643

(ᵇ) This Henry, who matric at Oxford (Jesus Coll), 28 April 1598, aged 16 , was
admitted to Lincoln's Inn, 28 Oct 1599, became a Barrister in 1605, and whose will
was proved at Carmarthen 1640-41, was s and h. of Sir Thomas JONES, of Abermarles
(*d* 1604) by Jane, da of Rowland PULESTON, of Carnarvon   [*Ex inform* W D. Pink,
who has supplied many other particulars in the above account, correcting that generally received, as also the suggestion (*N and Q*, 1st S , xi, 38) that there were two
Baronets, each named Henry]

(ᶜ) Elizabeth, his 2d and yst da , and eventually sole heir (a minor in 1642), *m* , in
1665, Sir Francis Cornwallis, who thus became of Abermarles   He was *bur* 4 Sep
1675, at St. Giles' in the Fields, leaving issue

(ᵈ) Disallowed by Parl , till the Restoration   See *Memorandum* as to creations after
4 Jan 1641/2 and 22 May 1642 on p 152.   No patent is enrolled.   The date here
given for the patent is that in Dugdale's *Catalogue,* but (oddly enough) the *same*
date is assigned to the docquet in Black's *Docquets* See *Memorandum* on p. 84.

III. 1658.   SIR CHARLES WALDEGRAVE, Bart. [1643], s and h.; *suc.*
to the Baronetcy, 10 Oct 1658 (ª)   He *m.* Helen, da of Sir Francis
ENGLEFIELD, 2d Bart [1611], by Winifred, da. and coheir of William BROOKSBY.
He *d.* in or before 1684. Will pr 1684.

IV. 1684?   SIR HENRY WALDEGRAVE, Bart [1643], of Chewton,
Navestock, and Staininghall aforesaid, 1st s and h; *suc to the*
Baronetcy, about 1684. Having *m*, 29 Nov. 1683, Henrietta FITZJAMES, spinster, illegit.
da. of James II, by Arabella CHURCHILL, spinster (sister of John, the famous DUKE
OF MARLBOROUGH), he was, by that King (in his said wife's lifetime), *cr* 20 Jan.
1685/6, BARON WALDEGRAVE OF CHEWTON, co. Somerset, in which peerage
this *Baronetcy* then *merged* and so continues, the 2d Baron and 5th Baronet being
cr., 13 Sep 1729 EARL WALDEGRAVE See *Peerage.*

PATE:

cr. 28 Oct 1643 ;(ᵇ)

ex. 5 Sep. 1659.

I. 1643,   "JOHN PATE, of Sysonby, co. Leicester, Esq.," 2d s. of
to   Edward PATE, of Eye Kettleby, was Sheriff of Leicestershire, 1640-41,
1659.   and was *cr* a *Baronet*, as above, 28 Oct. 1643 (ᵇ)   He was a zealous
Royalist and was fined £523 in Oct. 1649, increased to £4,316 but
reduced, in 1651, to £1,520. He *m.* firstly, Elizabeth, da of Sir William SKIPWITH,
of Cotes, co Leicester She *d* 17 Aug 1628, aged 37. He *m* secondly, Lettice,
widow of Francis BRADSHAW, of Derbyshire, 1st da of Sir Thomas DILKE, of
Maxstoke Castle, co Warwick She *d* before him Admon. as "of Ham, co.
Surrey," 15 Jan 1658/9 He *d.* s p m, and was *bur.* from St. Martin's in the Fields,
at St Giles' in the Fields, 5 Sep. 1659, when the *Baronetcy* became *extinct.* Admon.,
as of Ham aforesaid, 20 Sep 1659, to his daughters Abigail Smyth and Frances
Carrington, *alias* Smyth.

BALE.

cr 9 Nov 1643 ;(ᶜ)

ex. shortly before 1654

I 1643,   "JOHN BALE, of Carlton Curlieu, co Leicester, Esq,"
to   s and h ap of Sir John BALE, of the same, and of Sadington in that
1653?   county (Sheriff of Leicestershire, 1624, living 1652), by his 1st wife,
Emma, da of William HALFORD, of Welham, co Leicester, was *b.*
about 1617, was a stedfast Royalist, his house at Carlton being made a garrison for
that cause, was one of the King's Commissioners of Array in June 1642, and was
cr. a *Baronet*, as above, 9 Nov 1643 (ᶜ) He is said to have been heavily fined He
m. in or shortly after 1651, Jane,(ᵈ) last surv .child of Sir Thomas PUCKERING, Bart.

(ª) Imhoff (*Genealogy of Great Britain*, 1690, p 234), speaking of the Peerage conferred on his son, writes, "Pate natus est Medico Primario Regis Jacobi II," etc
The person, however, here alluded to was not this Sir *Charles* Waldegrave, but Sir
William Waldegrave, probably a son of Philip Waldegrave, of Borley, co Essex. He
was a doctor of medicine at Padua 12 March 1659, and was, by James II, constituted,
in 1686, a Fellow of the Coll of Physicians of London. His will was pr. June 1702.

(ᵇ) See p. 213, note "c," under "WALDEGRAVE."

(ᶜ) Disallowed by Parl. 11 Nov 1643 (being only two days after its creation)
till the Restoration See *Memorandum* as to creations after 4 Jan 1641/2, and
22 May 1642, on p. 152 No patent is enrolled The date here given is that in
Dugdale's *Catalogue.* See *Memorandum*, on p. 84 The date of the signet bill is
2 Nov. 1643

(ᵈ) She had previously been abducted, 26 Sep. 1649, from Greenwich, and married
under compulsion at Dunkirk, but this marriage was set aside in 1651. [Drake's
Hasted's Kent, vol. i, p. 121].

[so. cr 1611], by Elizabeth, da. of Sir John MORLEY. She d. in childbirth, 27 Jan 1651/2 aged about 24 Admon , as of St Martin's in the Fields, 10 Feb 1651/2, to her husband. He d shortly afterwards, before 1654,([a]) when the *Baronetcy* became *extinct.*

O'NEILL, *or* O'NEALE
cr ([b]) 13 Nov. 1643 ,([c])
dormant, since 1799

I 1643.   "BRIAN O'NEALE, of Dublin, Esq.," s of Owen O'NEIL([d]) (who was 5th in descent from Henry Caoch O'NEIL, 2d s of Murtagh Ceanfadda, Chief of the Claneboys) served in Holland, under the Prince of Orange, serving afterwards in England on the Royalist side ; was taken prisoner by the Scots at Newburn, and was, in consideration of his gallant services to the Royal side at the battle of Edgehill, *cr a Baronet,*([b]) as above, 13 Nov 1643 ([c]) He m firstly, Jane, da of (—) FINCH He m secondly, Sarah, 1st da of Patrick SAVAGE, of Portaferry, co. Down, by Jeane, da. of Hugh (MONTGOMERY), 1st VISCOUNT MONT-GOMERY OF THE GREAT ARDS [I] His will as "of Backerstown, co. Dublin, Knt. and Bart.," dat 8 Oct 1670, pr the same year in Prerog Court [I.]. His widow m (Lic Dublin, 1 Dec 1671), Richard RICH.

II 1670.   SIR BRIAN O'NEALE, *or* O'NEILL, Bart. [1643], of Backers-town aforesaid, s an h, by 1st wife; admitted to Gray's Inn, 30 June 1664 ; *suc. to the Baronetcy,* 1670 ; was one of the Justices of the Court of King's Bench in Ireland, 26 Jan. 1686/7, to 3 Nov 1690. He was an adherent of James II, and, as such, suffered great loss of estate He m , in or before 1674, Mary, widow of James WOLVERSTON, of Stillorgan, co. Dublin, sister to Christopher, BARON DUNSANY [I], da of Hon Edward PLUNKETT, by Catharine, da of Randal (McDONNELL), 1st EARL OF ANTRIM [I.]. He d 1694 The will of his widow pr. 1699 in Prerog. Court [I]

III 1694.   SIR HENRY O'NEILL, Bart. [1643], of Kellystown, near Drogheda, co Meath, s and h , b. about 1674 ; *suc to the Baronetcy,* in 1694. He m. firstly, Mary, da of Mark BAGOT, of Mount Arran, co Carlow, by [presumably] Mary, relict of Sir Daniell O'NEILL, 3d Bart [I 1666], 1st da. of Sir Gregory BYRNE, 1st Bart. [I. 1671], by Margaret, da and coheir of Col Christopher COPLEY, of Wadworth, co York She d. intestate. Admon 12 April 1715, in Prerog. Court [I]. He m secondly, Rose (b 23 Aug. 1688), 2d da. of Capt. James BRABAZON,([e]) by Mary, da of Dudley COLLEY, of Castle Carbery, co. Kildare. He d. 1 Nov 1759, "near Drogheda," aged 85, and was bur in the old church at Mount Newton Will dat. 22 Dec 1755 (codicil unproved dat. 11 June 1756), pr 31 Oct. 1760, in the diocese of Meath, by Rose O'Neill, the widow.

IV. 1759   SIR BRIAN O'NEILL, Bart. [1643], of Kellystown afore-said, 1st surv. s. and h.,([f]) by first wife; *suc. to the Baronetcy,* 1 Nov 1759 He d s p m.

([a]) In 1654 his estates were purchased by Sir Geoffrey Palmer, 1st Bart. [1660].

([b]) This creation is *subsequent* to the Act of Parl , 11 Nov 1643, by which all creations conferred by the King after 22 May 1642 were disallowed See *Memorandum* as to creations after 4 Jan. 1641/2, and 22 May 1642, on p. 152

([c]) No patent is enrolled. The date here given is that in Dugdale's *Catalogue* as to which see the *Memorandum* on p. 84. The date of the warrant is 9 Nov. 1643

([d]) The principal information as to this family has been kindly furnished by G. D. Burtchaell, of the Office of Arms, Dublin. In Burke's *Vicissitudes of Families* (1st series, pp. 149-161), is an account of these Baronets, brought down, presumably, to the date (1859) of that work The exact date could, probably, be ascertained, as it is therein mentioned that Sergeant-Major Bryan O'Neill (youngest son of "Sir Francis O'Neill the 6th [sic] Baronet") was "now in his 75th year"

([e]) This James was 6th s. of James Brabazon, 2d s of the Hon Sir Anthony Brabazon, the 3d s of Edward, 1st Baron Brabazon of Ardee [I]

([f]) The sole authority for the existence and succession of this Brian is a pedigree in Ulster Office. No such son, however, is mentioned in the third Baronet's will, and it has been conjectured that, even if he ever existed, he d. v.p. and s.p.

V. 1765 ?   SIR RANDALL O'NEILL, Bart [1643], of Kellystown aforesaid, br of the whole blood and h.(ᵃ) ; *suc. to the Baronetcy*, about
1765 , was a Surveyor of Excise at Rush, co. Dublin, and is called(ᵇ) "M.D"
He *m* about 1750, "Margaret THOMPKIMS, a lady of English extraction "(ᵃ) He *d* at
Rush, June 1779

VI. 1779   SIR WILLIAM O'NEILL, Bart [1643], of Kellystown aforesaid, only s and h ; *b*. about 1754 ,(ᵃ) *suc to the Baronetcy*, in June
1779 He *d* s p m at Rush, March 1784

VII 1784,   SIR FRANCIS O'NEILL, Bart [1643], of Kellystown aforeto   said, uncle (of the half blood) and h. male, being 6th and yst s of
1799   the 3d Bart by his 2d wife He was *b*. probably about 1730,
and *suc. to the Baronetcy* in March 1784. He was ejected from
his property under the *Popery Acts*, and after renting two small farms near
Kellystown, kept "a small huckster's shop and dairy " at Slane (ᶜ) He *m*. (—), da. of
(—) FLEMING, of co Louth, by whom he had fourteen or fifteen children He was in
possession of the patent of Baronetcy in 1798, but *d* 1799, being *bur*. (with his father)
at Mount Newton. His widow *d*. eighteen months later Since his death the
Baronetcy has remained *dormant*.(ᵈ)

HICKMAN
cr 16 Nov. 1643 ,(ᶜ)
ex March 1781.

I 1643   " WILLOUGHBY HICKMAN, of Gaynsborough, co Lincoln,
Esq.," s and h of Sir William HICKMAN, of the same, by his 2d wife
Elizabeth, sister of William, 3d BARON WILLOUGHBY OF PARHAM, da. of Hon William
WILLOUGHBY, by Elizabeth, da and h of Sir Christopher HILDYARD, was *b* 25 May
and *bap* 3 June 1604, at Gaynsborough ; suc his father, 25 Sep. 1625, and, in
consideration of his fidelity to Charles I, was *cr. a Baronet*, as above, 16 Nov 1643 (ᵉ)
He was fined £1,100 in March 1646 He *m*. in or before 1628, Bridget, 1st da. of Sir
John THORNHAUGH, of Fenton, Notts, by (—), da of Francis RODES, of Staveley
Woodthorpe, Notts, Justice of the Common Pleas. He *d* 28 May 1650 His widow
d. 14 March 1682/3, in her 77th year Both were *bur*. at Gaynsborough M.I

II. 1650   SIR WILLIAM HICKMAN, Bart [1643], of Gaynsborough
aforesaid, only s and h, *bap*. there 8 Jan 1628/9, *suc to the
Baronetcy*, 28 May 1650 He was Sheriff of Notts, 1653-54 , M P for East Retford
(five Parls), 1660-81 He *m* , about 1652, Elizabeth, da and h. of John NEVILE,
of Mattersly, Notts He was *bur* 10 Feb. 1681/2,(ᶠ) and his widow 24 Nov. 1691,
at Gaynsborough His will pr. 1682

(ᵃ) Kimber's *Baronetage* [1771]
(ᵇ) "The Freeman's Journal" [June 1779]
(ᶜ) The information about this Baronet and his issue is entirely from Burke's
Vicissitudes [1859] See p 215, note "d."
(ᵈ) The eldest son, Henry, was last heard of in 1798, being then in a Spanish
Regiment Francis O'Neill, 1st s of John, the second son, was [1859 ?] a working
millwright in Drogheda James, another son of Sir Francis, was a working baker in
Dublin, and *d* about 1800 Bryan, the yst. and only surv son, was *b*. in Kellystown ; was Sergeant Major in the Army, 1813 1830, and Chief Officer of the
Newgate Guards, Dublin, 1830 1836 ; was living [1859 ?] at the age of 75 in Dublin,
with his eldest son, Francis O'Neill, a coffin maker In Burke's *Extinct Baronetage*
[1844], it is said that " One of the sons of Sir Francis was employed about twenty-
five years ago at a small Inn near Duleek in the capacity of boots and ostler."
(ᵉ) See p 215, note "b," under O'NEILL No patent is enrolled The date here
given is that in Dugdale's *Catalogue*, as to which see *Memorandum* on p 84. The
date of the warrant is 11 Nov. 1643
(ᶠ) In Sir Joseph Williamson's *Lincolnshire Families, temp. Charles II*, he is thus
noticed " Sir Wm. Hickman, of Gaynsborough, yᵉ best of his estate [is] in his dues
upon yᵉ faires kept there , about £800 per annum, not more ; but a late family."
[*Her. and Gen* , vol. ii, p. 122].

III   1682.   SIR WILLOUGHBY HICKMAN, Bart [1643], of Gainsborough
aforesaid, 1st surv. s and h., bap there 29 Aug 1659, was M.P for
Kingston-on-Hull, 1685-87, for East Retford (three Parls.), 1698-1705, and for
Lincolnshire (two Parls), 1713 till death, suc. to the Baronetcy, 10 Feb 1681/2.
He m. (Lic Vic Gen , 8 Sep 1683, he 24 and she 17), Anne, da of Sir Stephen
ANDERSON, 1st Bart [1664] of Eyworth, Beds, by his 1st wife Mary, da of Sir John
GLYNNE. She was bur 15 May 1701, at Gainsborough. He d 28 and was bur
31 Oct 1720, also at Gainsborough Will pr. 1721

IV.   1720   SIR NEVILE HICKMAN, Bart [1643], of Gainsborough
aforesaid, 1st surv. s. and h., bap there 13 May 1701; suc. to the
Baronetcy, 31 Oct. 1720 He m about 1722, Frances, da of Edward HALL, said to
be one of the family of HALL, of Gretfold, co Lincoln He d June 1733 His
widow m. Feb 1737, as his 2d wife, Sir Francis WHICHCOTE, 3d Bart [1660], who
d at Grantham, 27 Oct 1775.

V   1733,   SIR NEVILE GEORGE HICKMAN, Bart. [1643], of Thonock
     to   Grove, near Gainsborough, only surv a and h , suc to the Baronetcy
     1781.   when a minor, June 1733. He m 13 Sep 1746, Frances Elizabeth,
               da. of Christopher TOWER of co Essex Her admon. 17 Dec 1772.
He d. s.p m., March 1781, when the Baronetcy became extinct Will pr May 1781.

BOTELER ·

cr. 7 Dec 1643 ,(ª)

ex 25 June 1657.

I   1643,   "GEORGE BOTELER, of Bromfeild [i e, Brantfield], co.
     to   Hertford, Esq," yr. br of the half blood to John, 1st BARON
     1657   BOTELER OF BRANTFIELD, being 5th s of Sir Henry BOTELER,
               of Hatfield Woodhall, Herts, and of Brantfield aforesaid, and 4th s.
by the 2d wife, Alice, da of Edward PULTER, was b about 1583; and was cr a
Baronet, as above 7 Dec 1643(ª), was a Royalist, and was fined £569 on 13 June
1648, being then "of Ellerton, co York" He m Jane, widow of Sir Hugh
BETHELL, of Ellerton aforesaid (d 1611), da of Thomas YOUNG, Archbishop of
York He d s p and was bur 25 June 1657, at Tewin, Herts, aged 74, when
the Baronetcy became extinct Will pr 1657.

ACTON.

cr 17 Jan 1643/4 ;(ᵇ)

afterwards, since 1833, DALBERG-ACTON,

subsequently, since 1869, BARONS ACTON OF ALDENHAM

I   1644   "EDWARD ACTON, of Aldenham [i e., Aldenham Hall, in
             Morville], co. Salop, Esq," being also of Acton Scott, in that county,
s. and h. of Walter ACTON, of Aldenham Hall aforesaid, by Frances, da. and h of
Edward ACTON, of Acton Scott abovenamed, was bap 20 July 1600; was M.P. for
Bridgnorth, April to May 1640 and Nov 1640 till disabled, 5 Feb 1643/4; sat in the
Oxford Parl , and, on account of his loyal service to his King, was cr a Baronet, as
above, 17 Jan 1643/4 (ᵇ) He was fined £5,242 in Feb 1647, reduced to £2,000 in

---

(ª) See p. 215, note "b," under O'NEILL No patent is enrolled The date here
given is that in Dugdale's Catalogue (as to which, see Memorandum on p 84), where,
however, the grantee is erroneously called "John [sic] Butler." The date of the
warrant is 30 Nov. 1643.

(ᵇ) See p 215, note "b," under O'NEILL. No patent is enrolled The date
(presumably that of the patent) here given is that in Dugdale's Catalogue, but the
same date is assigned to the docquet in Black's Docquets. See Memorandum on
p. 54.

2 E

July 1649 He *m* Sarah, da. of Richard MYTTON, of Halston, Salop, by Margaret, da
of Thomas OWEN, one of the Justices of the King's Bench. He was *bur* 29 June
1659, aged 59. Will dat. 20 March 1651, pr 20 Dec 1659, by his widow She *d*
13 Sep 1677.

II 1659   SIR WALTER ACTON, Bart. [1644], of Aldenham Hall and
              Acton Scott aforesaid, s and h, *b* about 1620 ; *suc to the Baronetcy*,
29 June 1659 , M P for Bridgnorth, 1660 He *m* Catharine, da of Richard
CRESCETT,(ᵃ) of Upton Crescett and Cound, Salop He *d* 1665, aged 44 The will
of his widow pr Dec 1691

III 1665.   SIR EDWARD ACTON, Bart [1644], of Aldenham Hall and
               Acton Scott aforesaid, s and h, *b* about 1650(ᵇ) ; *suc to the
Baronetcy*, 1665 , matric. at Oxford (Queen's Coll), 4 May 1666, aged 16 , *cr* M A ,
23 April 1667 , Sheriff of Salop, 1684-85 , M P , for Bridgnorth (seven Parls), 1698-
1705 , Recorder of Bridgnorth, 1701 He *m* Mary, da and h. of (—) WALTER, of
Somerset He *d*. 28 Sep 1716, aged 66, and was *bur* (as was his wife) at Morville.
Will dat 28 Sep 1714, pr 31 Oct 1716.

IV 1716   SIR WHITMORE ACTON, Bart [1644], of Aldenham Hall
              and Acton Scott aforesaid, s. and h, *b*. about 1674 ; matric at
Oxford (St Edmund's Hall), 14 Feb 1694/5, aged 17 , admitted to Middle Temple,
1698 , M P for Bridgnorth, *v p*, 1710 13 ; *suc to the Baronetcy*, 28 Sep 1716 ;
Sheriff of Salop, 1727-28 He *m* Elizabeth, da of Matthew GIBBON, of Westcliffe,
Kent, and of Putney, Surrey, by Hester, his wife. He *d*. 8 Jan. 1731/2, aged 56,
and was *bur* at Morville Will dat 19 Dec 1731, pr 27 March 1732 His wife, who
was *bap*. 2 Jan 1680, at St Andrew's Undershaft, London, survived him

V. 1732.   SIR RICHARD ACTON, Bart [1644], of Aldenham Hall
              and Acton aforesaid, s and h , *b* 1 Jan 1711/2 ; *suc. to the
Baronetcy*, 8 Jan 1731/2 , Sheriff of Salop, 1751-52 He *m*. 21 Sep 1744, Anne, da of
Henry (GREY), 3d EARL OF STAMFORD, by Dorothy, da. of Sir Nathan WRIGHT, Lord
Keeper of the Great Seal She *d* at Worcester, and was *bur*. at Acton He *d*. at
Aldenham, s p m ,(ᶜ) 20 Nov. 1791, and was *bur*. at Acton Will pr May 1792

VI. 1791.   SIR JOHN-FRANCIS-EDWARD ACTON, Bart [1644], cousin
              and h. male, being s and h of Edward ACTON, of Besançon, in
Burgundy, by Catharine, da of Francis-Loris DE GREY, also of Burgundy, which
Edward was s and h of Edward ACTON, of Birchin lane, London, goldsmith and
banker, s. and h of Walter ACTON, of London, goldsmith and mercer, who was 2d s
of the 2d Bart He was *bap* 3 June 1736, and served under the King of the Two
Sicilies, being Commander-in-Chief of the Land and Sea Forces of Naples, and for
several years Prime Minister there He *suc. to the Baronetcy*, 20 Nov. 1791, and
after the death of his cousin, Mrs Langdale, the da and h of the late Baronet
(under his will) to the whole of the family estates, of which (under the said will) he
had obtained a portion in her lifetime. In 1796 or 1800, at the mature of age of 60

(ᵃ) Richard Crescett, aged 52 in the Visit. of co Stafford in 1663, is there stated
to have *m*. Jane, da of John HUXLEY, and to have had two sons No daughters,
however, are mentioned
(ᵇ) He and his six brothers averaged 6 feet 2 inches each in height. He rebuilt,
with stone, the family mansion at Aldenham, which is said in Wotton's *Baronetage*
(1741) to be " perhaps the best house in the county " [of Shropshire], and " with a
fine park adjoining."
(ᶜ) He devised his estates after the death without issue of his only surv child
Elizabeth, wife of Philip LANGDALE, to his cousin and successor in the Baronetcy, in
tail male, who inherited accordingly.

or 64, having procured a dispensation from the Pope, the marriage ceremony[a] was performed between him and one of his nieces, then aged 14 or 18, viz , Mary-Anne, 1st da. of his br. Joseph Edward ACTON, Lieut. Gen in the service of the said King of the Two Sicilies, by Eleanora, COUNTESS BERO DE TRIPS of Dusseldorf, in Germany.   He *d* at Palermo, 12 Aug 1811, aged 75.   Will pr. 1811   His widow *d* (sixty-two years afterwards) 18 March 1873 [b]

VII. 1811.   SIR FERDINAND-RICHARD-EDWARD ACTON, *afterwards*, (since 1833), DALBERG ACTON, Bart [1644], of Aldenham Hall and Acton aforesaid, s and h , *b* 24 July 1801, and *suc to the Baronetcy*, 12 Aug 1811. He, having *m*. at Paris, 9 July 1832, Marie Louise Pelline, only da and h of Emeric-Joseph, DUKE OF DALBERG, in France, took by royal lic , 20 Dec 1833, the surname of DALBERG before that of ACTON.   He *d* 31 Jan 1837   His widow *m* , at the Spanish chapel and afterwards in Devonshire House, Piccadilly (as his first wife), 25 July 1840, George Granville (LEVESON GOWER), 2d EARL GRANVILLE, who *d* 31 March 1891, aged 75   She *d* 14 March 1860, aged 48, at Brighton

VIII   1837   SIR JOHN-EMERICH-EDWARD DALBERG-ACTON, Bart. [1644], of Aldenham Park and Acton aforesaid, only s and h , *b*. 10 Jan 1834, at Naples ; *suc to the Baronetcy*, 31 Jan 1837 , ed at the Roman Catholic Coll at Oscott ; M P for Carlow, 1859-65, and for Bridgnorth, 1865-66   He *m*. 1 Aug 1865, the COUNTESS MARIE ARCO-VALLEY, da. of Maximilian ARCO-VALLEY, of Austria and Bavaria, by Anne (*née*) COUNTESS MARESCALCHI   She was living when he was *cr* , 11 Dec 1869, BARON ACTON OF ALDENHAM, co. Salop.   In that title this *Baronetcy* then *merged*, and so continues   See *Peerage*

HAWLEY :
cr. 14 March 1643/4 ;[c]
afterwards, 1645-1790, BARONS HAWLEY OF DONAMORE [I.],
ex. 19 Dec. 1790,

I   1644.   " FRANCIS HAWLEY, of Buckland, co Somerset, Knt ," 2d s of Sir Henry HAWLEY, of Wivelscombe, in that county, by Elizabeth, da of Sir Anthony PAULETT, was *b* about 1608 : distinguished himself in the Royal cause, for which he raised a troop of horse in 1642, and, having been *Knighted*,[d] was *cr* a Baronet, as above, 14 March 1643/4 [c]   He *m* Jane, da of Sir Ralph GIBBES, of Honington, co Warwick, by Gertrude, da. of Sir Thomas WROUGHTON   She *d* before him, possibly before he was *cr*. 8 July 1645, LORD HAWLEY, BARON OF DONAMORE, co Meath [I]   In that peerage this *Baronetcy* then *merged*, till both became *extinct*, by the death of the 4th Baron and Baronet, 19 Dec. 1790   See *Peerage*

(a) This marriage, which was "*voidable*," became eventually valid (having never been set aside by the Ecclesiastical Court of England, during the lifetime of both the parties), under (Lord Lyndhurst's) Act of Parliament, which confirmed all marriages, incestuous or otherwise, made before 31 Aug 1835, where one, or both of the parties, were dead before that date   See " Hubback's Evidence of Succession," edit 1844

(b) Their 2d s , Charles-Januarius-Edward ACTON, *b*. 6 March 1803, became a Cardinal, 24 Jan 1842, and *d* 27 June 1847

(c) See p 217, note " b," under " ACTON."

(d) His Knighthood was recognised by Parl when he "compounded " in 1645, and so was probably (not, however, certainly) conferred before the Civil War.

PRESTON
cr. 1 April 1644 ,(ª)
ex 27 May 1709.

I   1644.   "JOHN PRESTON, of the manor of Furnese, co Lancaster,
Esq ," being also of Preston Patrick and Under Levins, co West-
morland, 2d but only surv. s. and h of John PRESTON, of the same (admitted to
Gray's Inn, 2 Feb 1590/1), by Elizabeth, da and coheir of Richard HOLLAND, of
Denton, co Lancaster, was *b* 1617 , suc his father in or shortly after Sep 1642,
and, having distinguished himself in the Royal cause, was *cr a Baronet*, as above,
1 April 1644 (ª) His estates were forfeited, as "a Papist in arms," and given to
John Pym's children. He *m.* in or before 1640, Jane da and cohen of Thomas
MORGAN, of Weston-sub Weathley, co Warwick, and of Heyford Hall, co. Northamp-
ton (slain at Newbury, 20 Sep 1643), by Jane, da of Sir Richard FERMOR, of
Somerton, Oxon He was mortally wounded, at Furness, in 1645 at the head of a
regiment he had raised

II   1645.   SIR JOHN PRESTON, Bart [1644] of Furness Manor,
Preston Patrick, Under Levins and Heyford aforesaid, s and h ,
suc to the Baronetcy in 1645 He *d*. unm April 1663 Will pr 1663

III.   1663,   SIR THOMAS PRESTON, Bart [1644] of Furness Manor,
to   Preston Patrick, Under Levins and Heyford aforesaid, br and h , *b*
1709.   about 1641, being aged 21 in 1664, having *suc to the Baronetcy*, in
April 1663 He *m* firstly, Elizabeth (a French lady), da. of Peter
DE PLAUZE She *d* s p a few weeks later He *m* secondly, Mary, da. of Caryll
(MOLYNEUX), 3d VISCOUNT MOLYNEUX OF MARYBOROUGH [I], by Mary, da of Sir
Alexander BARLOW She *d* at Furness, 6 June 1673, and was *bur* at Heversham,
co Westmorland He entered the society of Jesuits, 28 June 1674 (aged 31), and
d s p m s.,(ᵇ) at Watten, in France, 27 May 1709, when the *Baronetcy* became *extinct*

WEBB ·
cr. 2 April 1644 ,(ᶜ)
ex 19 Aug. 1874

I.   1644   "JOHN WEBB, of Odstock, *otherwise* Oadstock, co Wilts,
Esq ," s and h of Sir John WEBB of the same, and of Great
Canford, Dorset, by his 2d wife Catharine, da of Sir Thomas TRESHAM, of Rushton,
co Northampton was admitted to Gray's Inn, 11 Aug. 1619, and (apparently),
again, 10 Feb 1622/3, suc his father in or before Feb 1626, and was, as a reward
for the loyalty of his family, *cr a Baronet*, as above, 2 April 1644.(ᶜ) In 1646, his
lands in Wilts, worth £300 a year, were sequestrated He *m* Mary. da of Sir John
CARYL, of Harting, Sussex, by Mary, da. of Robert (DORMER), 1st BARON DORMER OF
WING. She *d* 1661 He *d*. 1680, and was *bur*. at Odstock Will pr 1681.

(ª) See p 217, note "b," under "ACTON." The original patent of this creation
was at Ugbrook, Devon, in 1830, in the possession of Lord Clifford, of Chudleigh,
a descendant of the grantee
(ᵇ) Francis, his only son, *d* young, 18 Sep 1672 Of his two daughters and
coheirs (1) Mary, Marchioness of Powis, inherited the Northamptonshire estates, and
Anne, Baroness Clifford of Chudleigh, inherited those in Westmorland The manor
of Furness he devised to the society of the Jesuits, which devise, however, was
declared to be illegal
(ᶜ) See p. 215, note "b," under O'NEILL The patent is enrolled, being the first
that was so for the space of more than a year (viz after that of Danvers, 21 March
1642/3), and being the penultimate one so enrolled of the Baronetcies [E.] conferred
by Charles I , that of Vyvyan, 12 Feb. 1644/5, being the last.

II. 1680.   SIR JOHN WEBB, Bart [1644], of Odstock and Great
           Canford aforesaid, s. and h , *suc to the Baronetcy* in 1660   He *m.*
Mary, the childless widow of Richard DRAYCOT, only da. of William BLOMER, of
Hatherop, co Gloucester, by Frances, da of Anthony (BROWNE), 2d VISCOUNT
MONTAGU   He *d* 29 Oct 1700, and was *bur* at Odstock   Will pr Nov 1700   His
widow *d* 29 March 1709, and was *bur* at Hatherop   Will pr June 1709

III. 1700.   SIR JOHN WEBB, Bart [1644], of Odstock, Great Canford
           and Hatherop aforesaid, only s and h., *suc to the Baronetcy*, 29 Oct.
1700   He *m.* firstly, in or before 1700, Barbara, da and coheir of John (BELASYSE),
BARON BELASYSE OF WORLABY, by his 3d wife, Anne, da of John (PAULET), 5th
MARQUESS OF WINCHESTER   She *d.* 28 March 1740   Will pr 1740   He *m* secondly,
Helen, da of Sir Richard MOORE, 3d Bart. [1627], of Fawley, Herts, by Anastacia,
da. of John AYLWARD.   He *d* at Aix la Chapelle, in France, Oct 1745   Will pr 1745

IV 1745   SIR THOMAS WEBB, Bart [1644], of Odstock, Great
           Canford and Hatherop aforesaid, 1st surv s and h male([a]), *suc to*
Baronetcy, Oct. 1745   He *m*, about 1738, Anne, da and coheir of William GIBSON,
of Welford, co Northampton   He *d* 29 June 1763, and was *bur*. at St Pancras,
Midx   Will pr 1763   His widow *d.* 7 Oct 1777, and was *bur* at St Pancras   Will
pr. 1777.

V. 1763.   SIR JOHN WEBB, Bart [1644], of Odstock, Great Canford
           and Hatherop aforesaid, s and h ; *suc to the Baronetcy*, 29 June
1763   He *m* in or before 1760, Mary, 1st da of Thomas SALVIN, of Easingwold, co
York, by Mary TALBOT, his wife   She *d* 1782, and was *bur* at Louvaine.   He *d.*
s.p m , April 1797, and was *bur* at St Pancras   Will pr 1797 ([b])

VI 1797   SIR THOMAS WEBB, Bart [1644], nephew and h male,
           being s and h of Joseph WEBB, of Welford aforesaid, by Mary, da
of John WHITE, of Canford, which Joseph was 2d s. of the 4th Bart.   He *suc to the*
Baronetcy in April 1797.   He *m* firstly, 14 March 1799, at St Geo. Han sq , Frances
Charlotte, da. of Charles (DILLON), 12th VISCOUNT DILLON OF COSTELLO GALLEN [I],
by his 1st wife, Henrietta Maria, da of Constantine (PHIPPS), 1st BARON MULGRAVE
[I]   She, who was *b* 17 Feb 1780, *d* 17 April 1819   He *m* secondly, 11 July 1822,
at the British Embassy, Paris, Martha Matilda, Dow. VISCOUNTESS BOYNE [I.], da of
Sir Quayle SOMERVILLE, 2d Bart. [I 1748], by his 2d wife, Mary, da of Thomas
TOWERS   He *d* 26 March 1823, at Grillon's Hotel, Albemarle street, aged 48
Will pr. 1823   His widow, by whom he had no issue, *d* 16 Sep 1826

VII. 1823,   SIR HENRY WEBB, Bart [1644], only s and h by 1st
       to   wife, *b* 27 April 1806, at Lyons, in France , *suc to the Baronetcy*,
     1874   26 March 1823   He *d* unm 19 Aug 1874, at Esslingen, Wurthem-
berg, when the *Baronetcy* became *extinct*   Will pr. 9 Nov. 1874.

([a]) John Webb, his elder br., *m.* twice, but *d* v p and s p m 9 March 1744/5, aged
44, leaving an only da Barbara, who *m* Sir Edward Hales, 5th Bart [1611].
([b]) "He left the manor of Great Canford to Edmond Arrowsmith, Esq , upon
certain trusts and uses, by a will almost as extraordinary as Mr Theilusson's "
[Hutchins's *Dorset*]   Barbara, Countess of Shaftesbury (*b* 1762), his only surv child
and sole heir, left an only child, Barbara, who *m* in 1814 the Hon. William Francis
Ponsonby   He, in 1838, was *cr.* BARON DE MAULEY, his wife being (through her
mother's mother, Mary Salvin, abovementioned) a coheir of the old Barony of De
Mauley.

PRESTWICH :

cr 25 April 1644 ,(ᵃ)

ex Sep. 1676 ,

assumed 1787 ? to 1795

I   1644.   " THOMAS PRESTWICH, of Holme [*i e.*, Hulme, in Manchester], co Lancaster, Esq ," 2d but 1st surv s and h of Edmund PRESTWICH, of the same (who entered and signed his pedigree in the Visit. of Lancashire, 1613, and who was *bur* 17 Feb. 1628/9, in the Coll. Church of Manchester), by Margaret, da of Edward BRERETON, was *bap* there 6 Dec 1604(ᵇ) · matric at Oxford (Bras Coll), 2 Nov 1621, aged 18 , B A , 1626 ; M A , 1629, being incorporated at Cambridge, 1632 , admitted to Gray's Inn, 15 June 1624 , was found by the Court-leet to be heir to his father, 21 April 1629 , was a Commissioner of Array, 1642 , served in Cheshire in 1644, and elsewhere, on behalf of the King, and was *cr a Baronet*, as above, 25 April 1644 (ᵃ) In the same year, after having been taken prisoner, 20 Aug 1644, at the battle of Ormskirk, he was 1 Sep 1644, *Knighted* on the field of battle, during the pursuit of Essex's army, whereby he is often considered a *Knight Banneret*. He was a compounder, and was, 30 March 1647, fined £925, reduced to £443, which was paid 2 Nov 1649 In July 1648, he was a prisoner for being within the lines of communication In 1660, he alienated the Hulme estate to Sir Edward Mosley, the sale being confirmed by Act of Parliament in 1673 He *m* in or before 1625, Elizabeth. He was *bur*. in the church of St. Martin's in the Fields, Midx , 3 Jan 1673/4

II   1674,   SIR THOMAS PRESTWICH, Bart. [1644], s and h , *b*. about
to   1625, admitted 20 March 1649/50, to Gray's Inn , *suc. to the*
1676   *Baronetcy*, in Jan 1673/4 He *m* 29 Nov 1649, at Mortlake, Surrey (Lic Fac., same day, he 24 and she 13), Mary, da of " Edward HUNT, Esq , deceased," and grandchild of Elizabeth CHILD, widow. He *d s p m s*, and was *bur* , with his father, 20 Sep 1676, when the *Baronetcy* became *extinct* Admon 4 June 1689, to a creditor, his daughters(ᶜ) having been cited

From information kindly supplied by G. D. Burtchaell [Office of Arms, Dublin], it appears that in 1775 a pedigree of PRESTWICH, of Holme in Lancashire, was registered in Ulster's office, verified 10 Jan 1775 (1) by the joint certificate of George Evans PARKER and of George Purdon DREW, one of the six clerks in Chancery [I], the latter being s of Francis DREW, of Drew's Court, co Limerick, by the eldest da. of John RINGROSE, who was s of Richard RINGROSE of Minoe, co Clare, by Margaret, 3d da of Sir Thomas PRESTWICH, of Holme in Lancashire, Bart , which Margaret " came over to Ireland to her brother Elias, the s of Sir Thomas PRESTWICH, who resided at Balliculline in co Limerick " , and (2) by the affidavit

(ᵃ) See p 217, note " b," under " ACTON "

(ᵇ) This fact and many others in this article have been kindly supplied by Ernest Axon

(ᶜ) In the admon of 1689, they are called *Isabella* Prestwich and *Priscilla* Prestwich Their real names appear to have been *Arabella*, who, 23 June 1692, was wife of Matthew Moreton, afterwards 1st Baron Ducie, and who *d* 14 March 1749/50, aged 90, and *Penelope*, who was unm. at the said date of 23 June 1692. See a deed of that date in the *Mis Gen. et Her* , new series, vol. i, p. 14. In that deed they call themselves heirs to John Prestwich, late of All Souls' College, Oxford, the brother of Sir Thomas, their grandfather The printed continuation of the pedigree in the Visit of Lancashire, 1613 [*Chetham Soc* , vol 82, p 41], accords therewith, and states that the said John (who *d*. 30 July 1672, aged 72), gave a legacy of £20 in his will, proved 1680, to his cousin Elias Prestwich, of Ballacullom, near Limerick, in Ireland It appears also that Arms to be used at the funeral, at Mortlake, 6 July 1655, of another sister, Mary, were ordered [Harl MS. 1372] In Burke's *Extinct Baronetage* yet another sister is mentioned, who does not elsewhere appear, viz., Margaret, wife of Richard Ringrose, of Moynoe, co Clare, Col. in the Army, whose issue is there set out, but the existence of this Margaret seems doubtful

sworn 16 Feb. 1775, of " Elias PRESTWICH, of the city of Dublin, gent," stating that he is the true and lawful son and heir of Richard PRESTWICH, who was the s and h. of Elias PRESTWICH, who was the s. and h. of Thomas PRESTWICH, of Holme, in Lancashire, Bart

In the following year (1776) there is registered the "Genealogy of John PRESTWICH, Esq , only s. of Sir Elias PRESTWICH, Bart " This second pedigree gives more details, but they are practically the same so far as the descent and marriages of the male line are concerned. John PRESTWICH was not married at the time the first pedigree was entered According to the second pedigree, it was Margaret, yst (not eldest) da of John RINGROSE, who m Francis DREW

The daughters of Sir Thomas PRESTWICH are stated to be Arabella (eldest da.) m Matthew DUCIE, Lord Morton, " Precelia, her name supposed to be, 2d da , m (—), merchant of London, d without issue," and Margaret, 3d da , m Richard RINGROSE, of Barraboy, near Moynoe, co Clare.

Elias PRESTWICH is mentioned as 'brother-in-law" by Captain William GOUGH, of Dunass, co Clare, who m Mercy, da of George PARKER, of Dunkip, in his will dat. 14 Sept 1664 , and also as " brother-in-law " by William CARPENTER, of Limerick, gent , in his will dat 27 March 1684 He (Carpenter) presumably m another da of George PARKER, of Dunkip

The Pedigrees registered in Ulster Office state that—

THOMAS PRESTWICH, of Holme, in Lancashire, Esq , or a Baronet, 25 April 1644, had two sons. John, the eldest, d unm. in England, and

ELIAS PRESTWICH, 2d son, who was in the Army, and who came over to Ireland in the Army, under the command of Oliver Cromwell, settling at Ballaculice, co. Limerick He m Anne, da of George PARKER, of Dunkip, co. Limerick, Esq , and had

RICHARD PRESTWICH, who was a minor about eight years old at his father's death His house and effects were burned by the Irish, but he was preserved and secreted by his nurse (an Irish Roman Catholic), during the late wars in Ireland He m Elizabeth, eldest da of John LOMBARD, of White Church, co Cork, and had

ELIAS PRESTWICH, about sixteen years old at the death of his father. He m Catherine, da of John LANDER, of the City of Cork, merchant, and had an only son,

JOHN PRESTWICH, "now [i e, 1775] living in London," b 29 Jan 1744/5, or (according to second pedigree) " January the 30th 1744/5, o s , at six o'clock in the evening " He m in April 1776, at London, Margaret, da of Joseph HALL, Alderman of Dublin, by Ruth, 2d da of Francis DREW, of Drew's Court, co Limerick.

These two pedigrees do not give the title of " Sir " or the style of " Baronet " to any of the above, and in some particulars differ from the one in the Visit of Lancashire, as printed in the *Chetham Society* They both ignore Thomas PRESTWICH, the 2d Baronet, who undoubtedly was the first surviving son [and successor] of Sir Thomas, the 1st Bart

---

The title is stated by Courthope, in his *Extinct Baronetage* [1833] to have been "assumed and borne for several generations by the possessors of Holm " It certainly was assumed, late in the eighteenth century by the John PRESTWICH, last abovenamed. who signs himself as " Baronet " in his preface, dated " Bath, 5 April 1787," to his ' *Respublica*," and whose arms, surmounted with the badge of Baronetcy, appear on the title page thereto His descent (indicated on p 152 therein) is set forth fully in a pedigree (apparently composed by himself), which is printed as an addition to the Visit of Lancashire, 1613 [*Chetham Society*, vol lxxxii, p. 41] This makes his father, "Sir Elias PRESTWICH, now [1787] living in London," to be s of "Sir Richard PRESTWICH," who was s of " Sir Elias PRESTWICH," s of " Thomas PRESTWICH, of Hulme, co Lancaster, Bart., cousin to Sir Thomas PRESTWICH, Banneret " He d. in Dublin, 15 Aug 1795

WILLIAMS.

cr. 4 May 1644 ,(ᵃ)

ex in 1694 or 1695 ;

but assumed from about 1740, to 21 Jan 1798

I 1644 " HENRY WILLIAMS, of Gwernevet, co Brecon, Esq ," s.
and h. of Sir Henry WILLIAMS,(ᵇ) of the same, by Eleanor, da. of
Eustace WHITNEY, of Whitney, co Hereford, was b about 1607 , matric at Oxford
(St John's Coll), 24 Oct. 1623, aged 16 , admitted to the Middle Temple, 1621 ,
was M P for Breconshire, 1628-29 , suc. his father 21 Oct 1636, and was *cr a
Baronet*, as above, 4 May 1644 (ᵃ) He was a Royalist, and entertained Charles I, at
Gwernevet, after the defeat at Naseby. in June 1645, being in that year a Commissioner of Array for Breconshire His estates were, apparently, confiscated and
mostly sold He *m* (post nuptial settl) 25 Aug 1631) Anne, da of Sir Walter PYE,
of the Mynde co Hereford, by his 1st wife, Joine, da. of William RUDHALL, of
Rudhall, in that county He was living 10 Feb 1649, but *d* in or before 1652.
Admon 8 May 1652, to a creditor, and probably again in April 1666. The will
of his widow, then of " Hereford," dat. 4 March 1685, pr 1 July 1689.

II. 1652? SIR HENRY WILLIAMS, Bart. [1644], of Gwernevet aforesaid, s and h , b about 1635 , matric. at Oxford (Queen's Coll),
10 Nov. 1651, *suc to the Baronetcy* in or before 1652, was M P for Brecknock,
1660 and 1661 till void, 25 July 1661. He *m* Jan 1657/8, at St Dunstans in
the West, London, Abigail, da of Samuel WIGHTWICK, of St Margaret's, Westm ,
Prothonotary of the King's Bench He *d* s p m (ᶜ) before 22 March 1665/6, when his
widow was sued (Brecon Plea Rolls) as his executrix. Possibly it is his admon that
was granted (C P C) April 1666 His widow *m* (Lic. Vic. Gen '26 Aug. 1667, being
then about 26) " Thomas Lane, Esq ," of Bentley, co. Stafford, who *d* 1715. She
was living 9 July 1675

III. 1665? SIR WALTER WILLIAMS, Bart [1644], of Ludlow, co Salop,
 to br. and h male, *b.* about 1636 ; matric at Oxford (Ball Coll.),
1695? 27 June 1652 , admitted to Middle Temple, 1656 , *suc. to the
Baronetcy* before 22 March 1665/6 He *d.* s p in or before 1695, when
the *Baronetcy* became *extinct* Will, directing his burial to be at Ludlow, dat
24 May 1694, pr 11 Feb 1694/5 (ᵈ)

(ᵃ) See p 217, note " b," under " ACTON."

(ᵇ) This Sir Henry was eldest of the nine sons of Sir David Williams, of
Gwernevet, one of the Justices of the King's Bench, 1604-13, who *d.* 22 Jan
1612/3 He matric at Oxford (St. John's Coll), 16 April 1594, aged 15, and is
often (erroneously) called the 1st Baronet, but was dead eight years before the
creation of that dignity, as he *d.* at Gwernevet, 21 Oct 1636, and was *bur* at
Aberllynfri, co Brecon Funeral certificate in Coll. of Arms Will dat 12 Sep. 1633,
pr. 11 Feb 1636/7

(ᶜ) Elizabeth, the first of his three daughters and coheirs, was *bap* 19 May 1662,
at Glasbury, co Brecon, *m* (Lic Vic Gen , 9 July 1675 she about 13, with consent
of her mother, Abigail Lane), Sir Edward Williams, who (to the great confusion of
the Williams pedigree) thus became of Gwernevet. She was *bur* at Glasbury,
27 Jan 1705, and he 28 July 1721 He was a younger son of Sir Thomas Williams,
1st Baronet [1674] of Elham, and was father of Sir David Williams, 3d Baronet
[1674], who inherited the estate of Gwernevet.

(ᵈ) In this will he leaves the £1,000 charged on the Gwernevet estate to his
nephew [i e , great nephew] Henry Williams, 1st s. of Sir Edward Williams and
Elizabeth [i e , Elizabeth, da. of testator's brother , see note " c " above] He leaves
his watch to his cousin " David Williams, of Herts, minister," but devises the
bulk of his property to a family named Wigmore

After a lapse of above forty years, the title was assumed by the Rev Gilbert Williams, whose relation to the previous Baronets was as under.

I, or VIII?(a) *1740?* GILBERT WILLIAMS, *called* SIR GILBERT WILLIAMS, Bart [1644], s and h of Matthew WILLIAMS, citizen and mercer of London by Elizabeth, only child that had issue of Robert GILBERT, of Goldington in Sarratt, Herts, citizen and mercer of London, which Matthew (who d 8 July 1737, aged 76) was br. and h of Carew WILLIAMS (d. s p 1722, aged 59), br and h. of David WILLIAMS, M D (d s.p. 27 Nov 1709, aged 58), all three being sons of David WILLIAMS, of Corneden in Winchcombe, co Gloucester (d 18 Jan 1698, aged 85), s and h of Thomas WILLIAMS, of Corneden aforesaid (d May 1636, aged 64), who was a yr br. of Sir Henry WILLIAMS, of Gwernevet abovementioned, the father of the 1st Baronet, both being sons of Sir David WILLIAMS, the Judge (b) He was b about 1692; matric at Oxford (Trin. Coll), 22 Oct 1709, aged 17 , B A , 1713 ; M A , 1719, took Holy Orders , was Vicar of Sarratt, Herts, 1725 ; Rector of Hinxworth, Herts, 1728 39 , Vicar of Islington, Midx , 1740-68 , suc. his father 8 July 1737, becoming then of Clifford's Court, co Hereford, and of Goldington aforesaid, shortly after which date, certainly before 1741(c) he "under an erroneous impression as to his descent, some years after the death of Sir Walter WILLIAMS of Gwernevet, Bart , in 1698 [*sic*, but query 1695] assumed the title which was in error continued by his son and grandson"(d) He m 5 Feb 1724, Dorothy, widow of Thomas DAY, of Rickmansworth, Herts, da. of William WANKFORD, of the same. He was bur at Sarrett 9 April 1768, aged 75 Will dat 14 July 1763, pr. 31 May 1768 His widow was bur. 20 Sep. 1773 at Sarrett aforesaid.

II or IX (a) *1768.* DAVID WILLIAMS, *called* SIR DAVID WILLIAMS, Bart [1644], of Clifford's Court and Coldington aforesaid, s and h., b 13 May and bap 13 June 1726 at Sarratt ; matric at Oxford (Trin. Coll), 16 June 1742, aged 16 , B.A , 1748 , M.A., 1751 ;

(a) To the succession to the Baronetcy after the death of Sir Walter in 1695 there were at least four more persons entitled prior to himself, viz, his father, two of his father's elder brothers, and his grandfather. This, too, is exclusive of any issue male of the numerous *brothers* of the 1st Baronet, one of whom, Thomas Williams, of London (1653), had a son, David Williams, of Stapleford, Herts, whose will dat. 16 Jan. 1712/3 to 26 Oct 1715, was pr 3 Sep 1717. [*Ex inform* H J. T Wood] The claimant's ancestor was but an *uncle* of the grantee.

(b) The pedigree in Clutterbuck's *Herts* (vol iii , p 224) is wrong in making David Williams, of Corneden, the grandfather of "Sir Gilbert" to be son of Henry Williams, of Gwernevet and Eleanor (Whitney), and in making the said Henry (instead of his son) to be the 1st Bart The information supplied by "Sir Gilbert" to Wotton for his *Baronetage* of 1741 (who is careful to quote him as his sole authority) as to his descent from the 1st Baronet is false and must apparently have been known so to be by the informant, who speaks of himself as "successor to his cousin, Sir Walter" [who died in or before 1695], but styles his father, through whom he derived his claim, and who did not die till 1737 as "Matthew Williams, Esq ," and makes no mention of any of his uncles, the elder brothers (living long after Sir Walter's death) of the said Matthew, having either assumed or even laid claim to the title The descent of "Sir Gilbert" from Sir David Williams, the Judge, as given in the text, is from the pedigree recorded in the College of Arms [*Norfolk*, vol vii] in 1836

(c) Wotton's *Baronetage* of that date. The "Sir David Williams, Bart , Guernever [*sic*] and Langoyd Castle, Breconshire," who died 1740, and the "Sir Henry Williams, Bart , Guernevel [*sic*], Breconshire, aged 18," who died 1741, were of the family of Williams, Baronets (so cr 1674) See p 224, note "c"

(d) Pedigree registered in College of Arms See note "b" above

2 F

suc his father in April 1768   He m 19 Aug 1762 at Aylesbury, Rebecca, da. of Thomas Harding ROWLAND, of that town, by Martha, sister and coheir of George ROWLAND, of the same   He d 9 and was bur 15 Dec 1792, at Sarratt   His widow d 3 and was bur 11 Jan 1819 at Sarratt   Will, as of Aston Clinton, Bucks, dat 8 Dec. 1818, pr 1819

III or X (ᵃ) *1792,*   DAVID WILLIAMS, *called* SIR DAVID
      to   WILLIAMS, Bart [1644], of Clifford's Court and
     1798.   Goldington aforesaid, s and h, *bap* 27 April
             1765, at Sarratt , suc his father in Dec 1792
He m 10 June 1794, at Chenies, Bucks, Sarah Sophia, 1st da and coheir of the Rev John Fleming STANLEY, Rector of Warehouse, Kent, by Elizabeth, his wife. He d. s p m (ᵇ) 21 and was bur 29 Jan. 1798 at Clifford, co Hereford, when the male issue of his grandfather became extinct, and the *assumption of this Baronetcy* came to an end   Admon. 12 March 1798.   His widow m 7 Sep 1798, Bigoe ARMSTRONG who d at Boulogne 24 March 1825. She m. thirdly, 27 July 1832, at Shoreditch, James Deacon GIBBON, and was living 1836

LUCAS :

cr 20 May 1644 ,(ᶜ)

ex. in or before 1668

I. 1644,   "GERVASE LUCAS, of Ferton *alias* Fenton, co Lincoln,
   to   Esq ," s of Anthony LUCAS, of the same, was *bap.* there 28 July
 1668 ?   1611, suc his father, 25 May 1613, was a zealous Royalist, was
            Gov. of Belvoir Castle for the King, and was *cr* a *Baronet,* as above,
20 May 1644.(ᶜ)   He d. unm (ᵈ) at Bombay, in the East Indies, in or before 1668, when the *Baronetcy* became *extinct*   Admon 10 Feb 1668/9, and 29 April 1674

THOROLD :

cr 14 June 1644 ,(ᵉ)

ex. 30 Nov. 1706

I 1644.   "ROBERT THOROLD, of Hawley [*i e,* the Haugh], co
          Lincoln, Knt," s and h. of Anthony THOROLD, of the same, by
Catharine, da of Edward HASELWOOD, of Maidwell, co. Northampton, was admitted to Gray's Inn, 9 Feb 1589/90 ; *Knighted* at Whitehall, 1 June 1641, and was *cr.* a *Baronet,* as above, 14 June 1644 (ᵉ)   He was a Royalist, was fined £1,300 on 5 June 1646, being then of Harrowby, co Lincoln, and was assessed at £800 in May 1650   He m firstly, Anne, sister to Sir Henry CARVIL, of St Mary's in Marshland,

---

(ᵃ) See p. 225, note "a "

(ᵇ) Sophia Charlotte, only da. and h (*b.* 11 June 1795), who inherited the estate of Rose Hall in Sarratt, Herts m. Thomas Tyringham Bernard, of Winchinden, Bucks, and d. 15 May 1837.

(ᶜ) See p 215, note "a," under ' O'NEILL "   No patent is enrolled   The date here given as that of the patent (20 May 1644) is that in Dugdale's *Catalogue,* but a subsequent date, 14 June 1644, is given to the Docquet in Black's *Docquets,* being the same as that of Thorold   See *Memorandum* on p 84   There is therefore some error.

(ᵈ) There is, however, a marriage lic (London) 11 Feb 1641/2, of " Jervas Lucas, of London, gent., aged 28, bachelor," with " Experientia White, aged 28, spinster "

(ᵉ) See p. 217, note "b," under " ACTON."

Norfolk, da. of Henry CARVIL. She d s p He m secondly, about 1630 (after 1622) Katharine, da of Christopher (ROPER), 2d BARON TEYNHAM, by Katharine, da. of John SEBORNE. She was living (probably as a widow) 1662

II. 1660? SIR ROBERT THOROLD, Bart [1644], of the Haugh afore-said, s and b, by 2nd wife He suc to the Baronetcy on the death of his father, and is, presumably, the " Sir Robert Thorold, Baronet, at yᵉ Heath House, near Grantham, a Papist; not more than £600 per annum, in the Fleet now,"(ᵃ) who was living temp. Car II (ᵇ) He was committed to the Tower for high treason in May 1692. He m in or before 1653, Katharine (aged 5 in Jan 1633/4), da of Sir Henry KNOLLYS, of Grove Place, in Nursling, Hants, Comptroller of the Household to Charles I, by Katharine, da of Sir Thomas CORNWALLIS, groom porter to James I He d in or before 1695. Will pr. 1695.

III 1695? SIR ROBERT THOROLD, Bart. [1644], s and h, said to
to   have been "a gentleman of very solid judgment much improved by
1706   learning," suc to the Baronetcy in or before 1695 He d. s p at St James' Place, 30 Nov and was bur. 1 Dec 1706, at St James', Westminster, at night (being a "Papist,") when the Baronetcy became extinct Will pr Dec 1706.

SCUDAMORE

cr 23 June 1644 ,(ᶜ)

ex between 1718 and 1727.

I 1644 "JOHN SCUDAMORE, of Ballingham, co Hereford, Esq,"
1st s of William SCUDAMORE,(ᶜ) of the same, by Sarah, da and h of Anthony KYRLE, surveyor of York, was b. 2 Aug 1600, and was cr a Baronet, as above, 23 June 1644 (ᵈ) He m, in 1625, Penelope, da of Sir James SCUDAMORE, of Holme Lacy, co. Hereford. He d before 1649 The will of his widow pr 1658.

II. 1649? SIR JOHN SCUDAMORE, Bart [1644], of Ballingham afore-said, 1st s and h, b 30 July 1630, matric at Oxford (Ch Ch), 17 May 1647, aged 17, admitted to Middle Temple, 1648, suc to the Baronetcy before 1649, and was K B, 23 April 1661, at the Coronation of Charles II He m Margaret, da of Sir George GRYMES, otherwise CRIMES, of Peckham, Surrey, by Alice, da. and coheir of Charles LOVELL, of West Harling, Norfolk He d s p m., and was bur 22 Aug 1684 Admon 24 Oct. 1684, to Margaret, the relict, and again 10 Feb 1684/5, to Barnaby, the brother. His widow, who was bap. 1 May 1640, at Camber-well, was bur. 20 Dec 1715.

III. 1684, SIR BARNABY SCUDAMORE, Bart [1644], br. and h male;
to   suc to the Baronetcy 22 Aug. 1684, was a citizen and mercer of
1720?   London (voting as such 1710), being also Collector of Customs at Liverpool He m Sarah, widow of William HARRIS, of London, da. of John Row, merchant of Bristol. She was bur 31 Dec. 1710 He d s p s, between 1718 and 1727, when the Baronetcy became extinct.

(ᵃ) There is a burial at St Bride's, Fleet Street, of a "William Thorold, aged, from the Fleet," 27 Oct. 1692
(ᵇ) See p 192, note "c," under ' THOROLD," Baronetcy cr 1642.
(ᶜ) See pedigree in J C Robinson's Mansions of Herefordshire
(ᵈ) See p. 215, note "b," under "O'NEILL" No patent is enrolled, and no signet bill or docquet exists The date and description, as above, is as given in Dugdale's Catalogue See Memorandum on p 84

BARD·

cr 8 Oct 1644 ;([a])

afterwards, 1645—1660, VISCOUNT BELLOMONT [I],

ex 1660

I. 1645,   "SIR HENRY BARD, of Staines, co Midx, Knt.,
to   Commander in the King's army," 2d and yet s of the
1660   Rev George BARD,([b]) Vicar of Staines aforesaid (*d* 1616), by
Susan, da of John DUDLEY ; was ed at Eton, admitted to King's
Coll, Cambridge, 1631, distinguished himself as a linguist, and was a great
traveller in the East and elsewhere ; was a zealous Royalist; *cr* D C L of
Oxford, 1643 ; *Knighted*, 22 Nov. 1643 ; lost his arm at the battle of Cheriton
Down, was Governor of Campden House, co Gloucester, and subsequently of
Worcester, and was cr a *Baronet,* as above, 8 Oct. 1644 ([a]) He was at the
taking of Leicester in May 1645, and was in command at Naseby the month
following He was cr, 18 July 1645, BARON BARD OF DROMBOY, co
Meath, and VISCOUNT BELLOMONT [I] He accompanied Charles II to
the Hague, and was by him sent, in 1656, on an embassy to the Shah of
Persia([c]) He *m*, in 1645, Anne, da of Sir William GARDINER, of Peckham, co
Surrey, by Frances, da of Christopher GARDINER, of Bermondsey. He *d* 8 p.m,([d])
1660, in Arabia (being choked by sand in a whirlwind in the desert),
when *all his titles* became *extinct* His widow, who applied for relief to King's
Coll, Cambridge, *d* in or before 1668, at St Martin's in the Fields, Midx.
Admon as "Lady Ann Bard, widow," 13 July 1668

VYVYAN *or* VIVIAN

cr 12 Feb 1644/5 ([e])

I. 1645   "RICHARD VYVYAN, of Trelewaren [*i e*, Trelowarren,
near Helston], co Cornwall, Knt," s and h of Sir Francis
VYVYAN, of the same (Sheriff of Cornwall, 1617-18), by Loveday, da of John
CONNOCK, of Treworgy, in St. Cleere, co Cornwall, was *b* about 1613, matric
at Oxford (Ex Coll) 20 June 1631, aged 18, being made B A the same
day, admitted to the Middle Temple, 1631, suc his father, 11 June 1635,
was *Knighted*, 1 March 1635/6 ; was M P for Penryn, April to May 1640,
for Tregony, 1640 till disabled Jan 1644, for St Mawes, 1661 and March
1663 till death, having been cr D C L of Oxford, 19 Feb 1643/4, and cr
a *Baronet,* as above, 12 Feb 1643/4 ([e]) He was a zealous Royalist, and during
the Civil Wars was Master of the Mint at Exeter He sat in the Oxford Parl
Jan 1644, was fined £600, in Oct. 1646, by the sequestrators of the estates,

---

([a]) See p 217, note "b," under "ACTON"

([b]) A good pedigree of the family is in *Coll. Top. et Gen*, vol IV, pp 59-61,
and vol III, pp 15 and 18 See also *Mis Gen et Top*, 2d series, vol V,
pp 64 and 80, but the statement therein "that the first Viscount Bellomont
had a son, Charles, 2d Viscount, slain 1685" seems a confusion for the death
of Charles, *Earl* of Bellomont, who died 1683, and who was of a totally different
family

([c]) Anthony a Wood (*Fasti Oxon.*) describes him as "a compact body of
vanity and ambition, yet robust and comely." He is also ill-spoken of. in
Clarendon's *Rebellion*

([d]) Of his daughters (1) Ann was living unm in July 1668, (2) Frances
was mistress to Prince Rupert, and mother by him of Dudley Bard, otherwise
Rupert Dudley, who was slain at the siege of Buda, 1686, aged about 20,
in her lifetime, (3) Persiana, *m* her cousin, Nathaniel Bard, of Caversfield, and
died 1739, leaving issue

([e]) See p 215, note "b," under "O'NEILL" The patent is enrolled, and is the
last patent of any Baronetcy created by Charles I that is so

having previously lost nearly £1,000 in the King's service. He *m* (Lic. Exeter, 24 Sep. 1636), Mary, da. of James BULTEEL, of Barnstaple, Devon He *d* 3 and was *bur*. 10 Oct 1665, at Mawgan in Meneage Will dat. 1 Aug 1665, pr 1 Nov. 1666 His widow living 1665.

II 1665.   SIR VYELL VYVIAN, BART [1645], of Trelowarren aforesaid, 1st s and h, *bap* 20 May 1639 at Mawgan aforesaid; *suc. to the Baronetcy*, 8 Oct. 1665, was *Knighted* before 29 Oct 1657, when he matric at Oxford (St John's Coll), M P. for St Mawes, Dec. 1665 till void, for Helston, 1679-81; Sheriff of Cornwall, 1682-83 He *m* firstly, 30 June 1671, at Constantine, Thomazine, da and coheir of James ROBYNS, of Glasney and Penrhyn, co Cornwall, Attorney at Law She *d s p* He *m* secondly, 24 Feb 1683/4, at Mawgan aforesaid, Jane, widow of Michael COADE, da of Thomas MELHUISH, of Penrhyn. He *d s p s*, 24 and was *bur* 27 Feb 1696/7. at Mawgan. Will dat 5 Sep 1696, pr 23 April 1697 His 2d wife, Jane, survived him

III. 1697.   SIR RICHARD VYVIAN, Bart [1645], of Trelowarren aforesaid, nephew and h, being 1st s and h of Charles VYVIAN, of Merthen, Cornwall, by Mary, 1st da. and coheir of Richard ERISYE, of Trevaona, in that county, which Charles (who was *bur* 12 Nov 1687, at Constantine) was 2d s. of the 1st Bart. He was *b*. about 1677, matric. at Oxford (Ex Coll.), 7 July 1694, aged 17, being Fellow, 1696-97; admitted to Middle Temple, 1694; *suc to the Baronetcy*, 24 Feb 1696/7; was M.P. for St. Michael's, 1700/1, and 1701-02, for Cornwall, 1703-10 and 1712-13, was suspected of being a Jacobite, and, accordingly, imprisoned in the Tower, 1717. He *m*, 9 Nov 1697, at St Eval, Mary, only da. and h of Francis VIVIAN, of Cosworth, by Anne, da. and h of Henry MAYNARD, of Cosworth, his wife, da. and h of Sir Samuel COSWORTH, of Cosworth aforesaid He *d* 9 May or 12 Oct 1724. Will dat. 27 Oct 1712 to 28 Oct 1721, pr 1724, in Archdeaconry Court of Cornwall His widow, who was *bap*. 28 Sep 1681, at Colan, was *bur* 3 Dec. 1736, at Mawgan.

IV. 1724.   SIR FRANCIS VYVIAN, Bart [1645], of Trelowarren aforesaid, 1st s. and h, *bap* 29 Sep. 1698, at Mawgan, matric at Oxford (Ex Coll), 17 Dec 1718, aged (it is said) 15, *suc to the Baronetcy*, 12 Oct 1724; Sheriff of Cornwall, 1739 He *m* 30 May 1730, Grace only da. and h of Rev Carew HOBLYN,(a) of Georgeham, Devon. She *d* 3 and was *bur* 11 Nov 1740, at Mawgan He was *bur* there 29 Dec. 1745.

V 1745.   SIR RICHARD VYVIAN, Bart. [1645], of Trelowarren aforesaid, 1st s and h, *b* 11 and *bap* 12 May 1731, at Mawgan, *suc to the Baronetcy*, 29 Dec. 1745, matric. at Oxford (Oriel Coll), 27 Nov 1749, aged 17 He *m* 6 Dec. 1754, Jane, da of Christopher HAWKINS, of Trewinnard, Cornwall He *d s p*. 13 or 20 Oct 1781. Will pr Dec 1781 The will of his widow pr Feb 1787

VI 1781   SIR CAREW VYVIAN, Bart. [1645] of Trelowarren aforesaid, br. and h, *bap* 11 Jan 1736/7, at Mawgan; matric at Oxford (Oriel Coll), 4 April 1754, aged 17; B A, 1757, M A, 1762; was in Holy Orders, *suc to the Baronetcy*, 20 Oct. 1781. He *d s p*, 4 Oct 1814. Admon Nov 1814

VII 1814   SIR VYELL VYVYAN, Bart. [1645], of Trelowarren aforesaid and of Tresmarrow, Cornwall, cousin and h male, being s and h of Philip VYVIAN of Tresmarrow aforesaid, by Mary, da and h. of Sheldon WALTER, of Tremeal, Cornwall, which Philip (who *d* March 1791, aged 59), was s

(a) He was s. of Robert Hoblyn, by Grace, 1st da and coheir of John CAREW, of Penwharne, Cornwall.

and h of Richard VYVYAN, of Tresmarrow,([a]) Barrister, Recorder of Launceston (*d.* 14 Jan 1771, aged 70), who was 2d s of the 3d Bart He was *b.* 12 July 1767; matric at Oxford (Trin. Coll), 10 Oct 1785, aged 18 , *suc. to the Baronetcy,* 4 Oct 1814; Sheriff of Cornwall, 1815-16 He *m.* 14 Aug. 1799, Mary, only da of Thomas-Hutton RAWLINSON, of Lancaster She *d.* 5 Sep 1812. He *d.* 27 Jan 1820 Will pr. 1820

VIII 1820 SIR RICHARD-RAWLINSON VYVYAN, Bart [1645], of Trelo-
        warren aforesaid, s. and h , *b* there 6 June 1800 , educated at
Harrow ; matric at Oxford (Ch Ch), 22 May 1818, aged 18 , *suc to the Baronetcy,* 27 Jan 1820 , was M P for Cornwall, 1825 31 , for Okehampton, 1831-32 , for Bristol, 1832 37, and for Helston, 1841-57 Sheriff of Cornwall, 1840. He *d* unm , 15 Aug. 1879, at Trelowarren, aged 79.

IX 1879. SIR VYELL-DONNITHORNE VYVYAN, Bart [1645], of Trelo-
        warren aforesaid nephew and h., being s and h of Rev Vyell-Francis
VYVYAN, Rector of Withiel, co Cornwall, by Anna, yst da of John-Vych-Rhys TAYLOR, of Southgate, Middlesex, which Vyell Francis (who *d* 30 Jan 1877, aged 75), was next br. of the late Baronet He was *b* 16 Aug 1826, was ed at St Aidan's College and at St John's College, Cambridge , took Holy Orders, 1854 , Rector of Winterbourne Monkton, Dorset, 1856-66 , Vicar of Broad Hinton, Wilts, 1866 77 ; Rector of Withiel aforesaid, 1877 79 , *suc to the Baronetcy,* 15 Aug 1879 He *m* 16 April 1857, Louisa Mary-Frederica, 3d da of Richard BOURCHIER, of Brook Lodge, Dorset.

Family Estates —These, in 1883, consisted of 9,738 acres in Cornwall, worth £13,147 a year *Principal Seat* —Trelowarren, near Helston, and Trewan, near St Colomb, both co. Cornwall.

VAN COLSTER:
cr 28 Feb 1644/5 ,([b])
ex , apparently in or before 1665.

I 1645, "WILLIAM [but apparently should be JOSEPH] VAN
   to   COLSTER,([c]) of Amsterdam, in Holland," was *cr a Baronet,* as above,
1665?   28 Feb 1644/5,([b]) being apparently the first foreigner on whom
        that distinction was conferred He *m* (—) He *d*, it is said, s p m ([d]) in or before April 1665, when, apparently, the *Baronetcy* became *extinct.* The admon of " Sir *Joseph* Van Colster, of Fulham, co Midx , Knt. and Bart.," granted 22 April 1665, to a creditor ([e])

([a]) The wife of this Richard (*m* 16 Jan 1728) was Philippa, 1st da and h of Philip PYPER, of Tresmarrow aforesaid
([b]) See p 217, note " b," under " ACTON "
([c]) The Christian name is " William " in Black's *Docquets* and in Dugdale's *Catalogue* [See *Memorandum* on p 84], but it is given as " Joseph " in most accounts, which name is borne out by the admon of 1665 See also note " d " next below.
([d]) " Henrietta Maria, da. of Sir Joseph [*sic*] Van Colster, of Colster, in Germany, Bart ," was mother by " Henry Stanihurst, Esq., of Godoff, in Ireland," of Cecilia Stanihurst, one of the English Ladies of Pontoise, who died 1746, aged 73 [*Her. and Gen* , vol. iii, p 415].
([e]) BARONETCIES CONFERRED ON FOREIGNERS
The following account of these creations seems worth reproducing from Wotton's *Extinct Baronetage,* edit 1741, vol iv, p 268 —
' A list of those Baronets who were foreigners at the time of creation, and still [1741] continue so if in being, whereof no certain information can be had to be depended on , with the dates of their several creations and the order they stood in

BOREEL, *or* DE BOREEL
cr 21 March 1644/5 (ᵃ)

I   1645   "WILLIAM DE BOREEL, of Amsterdam, in Holland,"(ᵇ)
2d s of Sir James BOREEL,(ᶜ) of Middleburgh, Envoy from the States
Gen to England, by his 2d wife, Mary GRIMMINCK, was *b* 24 March 1591 ; Envoy to
England, where it is said he was *Knighted* by James I, about 1619 ; Pensionary of
Amsterdam, 1628 ; Ambassador to Venice, 1636 ; to Sweden, 1640 ; to England
(again) 1642, being *cr. a Baronet*, as above, 21 March 1644/5 (ᵃ) He was again, in
1648, Ambassador to Venice He is said to have had a Royal warrant from
Charles II in exile, 28 June 1653, to create him a Baron He *m* 22 Sep 1626,
Jacoba CARELS She *d* in Paris 17 June 1657 He *d* there 29 Sep 1668

II   1668.   SIR JOHN BOREEL, *or* DE BOREEL, Bart [1645], s and h,
b 29 Oct 1627, *suc to the Baronetcy*, 29 Sep 1668 He was Marshal
at the Court of the Prince of Orange (afterwards William III), and a Lieut.-Col. in
the Dutch Service He *m* 7 Nov. 1666, Amarantha VAN VREDENBURGH He *d.*
29 March 1691 His widow *d.* 27 July 1715

III   1691   SIR WILLIAM BOREEL, Bart. [1645], s. and h, *b.* 4 Oct.
1672 ; *suc to the Baronetcy*, 29 March 1691 , was a Capt. in the
Dutch Service. He *d.* unm 23 Sep. 1710.

IV.   1710.   SIR ADRIAN BOREEL, Bart. [1645], br and h, *b* 9 Dec
1674 , *suc to the Baronetcy*, 23 Sep 1710 , Lieut.-Col in the Dutch
Army, and a Capt in the Dutch Navy , Chief D'Escadra, and Contra Admiral in
Portugal He *m* Margaret VAN DEN-BOSCH He *d* 8 p m. 15 July 1723. His
widow *d.* 14 April 1726

[By] King Charles I
1644 [*i e*, 1644/5] Feb 28. VAN-COLSTER, of Amersterdam.
"   "   March 21   DE BOREEL, of Amsterdam

[By] King Charles II
1652   April 2   CURTIUS, Resident to the King of Sweden
1658   Aug [—]   CARPENTIER, of Brussels
1660   April [—] DE MEROES, of France
"   May 30   DE RAED, of Holland
"   Nov. 16.   MOTTET, of Liege
1661   Oct. 4.   VAN-FREISENDORF, of Herdick, Sweden.
1674   March 25. TRUMP, Vice-Admiral of Holland.
1675   April 23   TULPE, of Amsterdam
1680   Oct 22.   SAS-VAN-BOSCH, servant to the Prince of Orange, Holland.
1682   June 29.   GANS, of the Netherlands.

[By] King James II
1686   Sep. 9   SPEELMAN, of Holland

[By] King William III.
1699   June 9.   VANDERBRANDE.

[By] Queen Anne
1709 [*i e*, 1708/9] NEUFVILLE, of Franckfort, Germany "

(ᵃ) See p 217, note "b," under "ACTON." Arms were granted to him by a
docquet of the King, 22 Aug following
(ᵇ) See p 230, note "e," as to Baronetcies conferred on Foreigners
(ᶜ) Nearly all the particulars of this family are from Burke's *Baronetage*, 1875,
nothing, apparently, having previously been known about them in this country, till
Sir J Bernard Burke, Ulster King of Arms, obtained an elaborate pedigree of Boreel
from Amsterdam, which he printed in the above stated work.

V   1723   SIR BALTHASAR BOREEL, Bart [1645], cousin and h male,
being surv. s and h of James BOREEL, Ambassador from the United
Provinces to France, by Isabella COYMANS, his wife, which James (who d 21 Aug
1697, aged 67), was 2d s of the 1st Bart   He was b 21 May 1673; was Counsellor
Deputy of Holland, and *suc to the Baronetcy*, 14 April 1723   He *m* 17 Dec 1720,
Apollonia RENDORP   He *d* s p 28 June 1744   His widow *d* 28 Oct 1757

VI   1744.   SIR WILLIAM BOREEL, Bart [1645], nephew and h, being
1st surv s. and h of James BOREEL, Commissary of the Post, by Sarah
SAMAER, his wife, which James (who *d* 28 March 1736, aged 57) was br to the 5th
Bart and grandson to the grantee   He was *b* 1712, was Master of the Vendution [?]
at Amsterdam, and *suc to the Baronetcy*, 28 June 1744   He *d*. unm 14 Feb. 1787.
Will pr. Sep 1787

VII   1787   SIR WILLIAM BOREEL, Bart. [1645], cousin and h, being
surv s and h of James BOREEL, Ambassador from the United
Provinces to England, by Agnes Margarette MUNTER, his wife, which James (who
d 4 April 1778, aged 67) was s. and h of John Hieronymus BOREEL, Echevin of
Amsterdam (*d* 9 Sep. 1738, aged 53), who was 5th s of James BOREEL (father of the
5th and grandfather of the 6th Bart.) abovenamed, the 2d s of the 1st Bart   He
was *b* 20 June 1744, was Echevin of Amsterdam, Deputy to the States General, and
suc to the Baronetcy, 14 Feb 1787.   He *m* 30 Dec 1766, Mary TRIP   He *d* 31 July
1796   His widow *d* 28 Jan 1813

VIII   1796   SIR JAMES BOREEL, Bart [1645], s and h., *b* 25 Oct.
1768, Member of the Equestrian Order of the States of Holland ;
suc to the Baronetcy, 31 July 1796   He *m* 21 Aug 1791, Jane Margaret, da of
William MUNTER, Echevin of Amsterdam   He *d* at the Hague, 12 April 1821   Will
pr Oct 1821   His widow *d* there 1 Nov. 1846

IX.   1821.   SIR WILLIAM BOREEL, Bart. [1645], s and h, *b* 23 March
1800, at Velsen, *suc to the Baronetcy*, 12 April 1821, Member of
the Upper House of the Netherlands, Minister of State, and several times Governor
of North Holland.   He *m* 24 July 1833, Margaret Jaqueline Mary Pauline, da of
his paternal uncle, Lieut Gen William Francis BOREEL, by Catharine Anne, da of
Francis FAGEL, Greffier of the States General.   She was sometime Dame-du-Palais
to the Queen of Holland.   He *d*. in 1883.   His widow *d* about 1893.

X.   1883   SIR JACOB WILLIAM GUSTAVUS BOREEL, Bart [1645], of
Meervliet, Velsen, in North Holland, s and h, *b* 10 Sep 1852, of
Velsen ; ed at Leyden Univ ; Gent. of the Privy Chamber to the King of the
Netherlands, and *suc. to the Baronetcy* in 1883   He *m* 14 March 1878, Maria
Cornelia, da. of the BARON SCHIMMELPENNICK VANDEROYE, Grand Master of the
Ceremonies to the King of the Netherlands   She *d*. Nov 1891

CARTERET, *or* DE CARTERETT
cr. 9 May 1645 ;(ª)
afterwards, 1681—1776, BARONS CARTERET OF HAWNES ;
and subsequently, 1744—1776, EARLS GRANVILLE ,
ex 13 Feb 1776.

I.   1645.   "GEORGE DE CARTERETT, of Metesches, in Jersey, Esq,"
s and h. of Helier DE CARTERET, of the same, Deputy Governor of
Jersey (who was 2d s of Sir Philip DE CARTERET, Seignior of St Owen in that
island), by Elizabeth DUMASQUE (*m*. 1608), his wife, was *b*. between 1609 and 1617 ,
entered the naval service and was Lieut in 1632 , Capt. in 1633, being second in
command in the expedition, 1637, to Sallee, and being in 1639 Comptroller of the
Navy , was Bailiff of Jersey, 1643, and an active supporter of the King, by whom

(ª) See p. 217, note " b," under " ACTON."

he was made Lieut.-Gov of that island. He is stated to have been *Knighted*[a]
21 Jan 1644 [1644/5?] and was *cr. a Baronet*, as above, 9 May 1645 [b] In 1646 he
received Prince Charles in Jersey, and again after that Prince was King, 17 Sep
1649 to 13 Feb 1650, when he received the grant of several Seigneuries, as also
of the island of New Jersey, in America. He was, however, finally compelled to
surrender Jersey, 12 Dec. 1651, to the Parliament, though when Castle Elizabeth
lowered the Royal Standard, it was the last fortress in the kingdom that surrendered
He joined the exiles in France, but was expelled therefrom in 1657 After the
Restoration he was made P C, 11 July 1660; was Treasurer of the Navy (1660 67);
Vice-Chamberlain of the Household (to which post he is said to have been appointed
as early as 1647), 1660-70, Vice-Treasurer [I], 1667 73, Commissioner of the Board
of Trade, 1668-72, and a Lord of the Admiralty, 1673-79 He was M.P for
Portsmouth, 1661-79 He acquired au enormous fortune [c] He *m* Elizabeth,
da. of his paternal uncle, Sir Philip CARTERET, of St Owen in Jersey, by Anne, da
of Sir Francis DOWSE He *d.* 14 Jan. 1679/80, aged about 70 Will pr 1700 His
widow is said to have been granted by warrant,[d] 14 Feb 1680, the precedence of a
peer's widow, in consequence of a peerage about to have been conferred on her
husband Her will pr. Feb 1700

II 1680   SIR GEORGE CARTERET, Bart [1645], grandson and h.,
being s. and h of Sir Philip CARTERET, Governor of Mount Orgueil,
by Jemima (mar. lic 29 July 1665 Fac Office), da of Edward (MONTAGU), 1st EARL OF
SANDWICH, which Philip *d v p*, being blown up at sea (together with the said Earl,
his wife's father) in the fight off Solebay, 28 May 1672 He was *b* about 1667,
and was *m* through his grandfather's influence (Lic Fac, 15 March 1674/5) when but
a boy, to Grace, yst da. of John (GRANVILLE), 1st EARL OF BATH He *suc* to the
Baronetcy, on his grandfather's death, 14 Jan. 1679/80, and shortly afterwards was
cr, 19 Oct. 1681, in his said wife's lifetime,[e] BARON CARTERET OF HAWNES,
co Bedford In that Peerage this *Baronetcy* then *merged*, the 2d Baron succeeding
his mother, 27 Oct 1744, as EARL GRANVILLE It continued thus merged till,
on the death of Robert, EARL GRANVILLE, 3d BARON CARTERET OF HAWNES, and
4th Baronet, 13 Feb, 1776, it and all other his honours became *extinct* See *Peerage*.

WINDEBANKE:
cr. 25 Nov 1645 ,[b]
ex, presumably, 23 Sep 1719.

I. 1645.   "THOMAS WINDEBANKE, of Haynes Hill [in Hurst], co.
Wilts [should be Berks], Esq.," 1st s and h ap of Sir Francis
WINDEBANKE, of the same, the well known Sec of State to Charles I (*d* 1 Sep 1646,
in Paris, aged 64), by (—) his wife, was *b*. about 1612; was a Gent. of the Privy
Chamber, 1627; matric at Oxford (St John's Coll), 13 Nov 1629, aged 17, was
admitted to Lincoln's Inn, 19 March 1632/3; was Clerk of the Signet about 1636;
M.P for Wootton Basset, April to May 1640; was a Royalist, and was *cr a Baronet*,
as above, 25 Nov 1645 [b] He was a Compounder in Aug 1646, being fined £810.
He took out admon to his father, 16 Oct. 1650 He *m*, in or before 1646, Anne,
da of John GRYMES, of Bury St Edmunds, by Susan, da of Ambrose JERMYN, of
Stanton, co Suffolk [f] He was living 1655, but *d*. before July 1669 [f]

---

[a] He was, however, apparently called " Esq " in his creation as a Baronet a few
months later
[b] See p. 217, note " b," under " ACTON "
[c] The *Flagellum Parl* accuses him of having robbed the King of £300,000.
[d] *Dict. Nat Biogr*, where it is stated that this warrant is quoted by Chalmers
[e] She, survived him, and was, after his death, *cr*, 1 Jan 1714/5, Countess
Granville, with rem of that Earldom to her issue male.
[f] *Coll. Top et Gen*, vol. iii, p. 157 It is presumed that he was the father of
" Frances Windebanck of St Paul's, Covent Garden, spinster, about 23, parents dead,"
12 July 1669, when she had licence (Vic Gen) to marry Sir Edward Hales, 3d Bart.
[1611] The father of this lady, however, is usually called " Sir Francis [*sic*] Windebank, of Oxford," but if she was, as is possible, the da. of the Secretary of State, she
must have been born the year of her father's death (1646), when he was 64. See,
however, W. D Pink's " Notes on the Windebank Family " in *N. & Q*, 8th S, I, 23

2 G

II. 1660? SIR FRANCIS WINDEBANK, Bart [1645], s. and h., b about
   to   1656, was apparently suspected as a Jacobite, being "taken into
  1719   custody" 14 May 1692, and "committed to a messenger" 9 April
         1696 (a) He m. 4 May 1686, at Lee, co. Kent (Lic Fac, 28 April,
he "of the Tower of London, Bart, aged 30, bachelor"), Elizabeth PARKHURST,
about 20, spinster, da of Frances Parkhurst, widow. He d in Eagle street,
apparently s.p m, and was bur. 23 Sep 1719 at St. Andrew's, Holborn, when the
Baronetcy presumably became extinct Will dat 3 Feb. 1715/6, pr 8 Oct 1719,
leaving all to his wife, Elizabeth. Her will pr. 1730.

WRIGHT:

cr. 7 Feb. 1645/6 ;(b)

but "suspended by the King's warrant";

ex on death of grantee

I 1646,   "BENJAMIN WRIGHT, of Dennington, co Suffolk, Esq.," yr
   to   br. of Nathan Wright, of London, the father of Sir Benjamin Wright,
  1670? 1st Bart [1661], both being sons of the Rev. Robert WRIGHT, D D.,
         Rector of Dennington aforesaid (d 1624), by Jane, sister of Sir
Oliver and da. of John BUTLER, of Sheby, co. Essex, was a merchant of London,
and was cr a Baronet, as above, 7 Feb 1645/6, the patent, however, being
"suspended" by the King's warrant He m (—) He d. s p.m. in Spain, when the
Baronetcy became extinct.

CHARLTON, or CHARLETON.

cr 6 March 1645/6 ,(c)

ex. on death of grantee.

I. 1646,   "EDWARD CHARLTON, of Hesleyside, co. Northumber-
   to   land, Gent.," s and h of William CHARLTON, or CHARLETON, of the
  1670? same, was cr a Baronet, as above, 6 March 1645/6 (c) He m Mary,
         da and coheir of Sir Edward WIDDRINGTON, Bart [1642], of Carting-
ton, co Northumberland, by Christiana STUART, his wife. He d s p m (d) when the
Baronetcy became extinct.

WILLIS, or WILLYS:

cr 11 June 1646 ,(e)

but suspended;

ex. 1701.

I 1646.   "RICHARD WILLYS, of Ditton, co Cambridge, Knt.,"
         next br to Sir Richard WILLYS, 1st Bart. [1641], both being sons of
Richard WILLYS, of Fen Ditton and Horningsey, co Cambridge, by Jane, da and h
of William HENMARSH, of Balls, in Ware, co Herts, was b. about 1615, was a

---

(a) In 1692, however, he is called [erroneously] Sir Thomas, though [correctly]
in 1696, Sir Francis Windebank [Luttrell's Diary]

(b) See p 217, note "b," under "ACTON." In a marginal note to the docquet
is written "Suspended per warrant Regis."

(c) See p 217, note "b," under "ACTON"

(d) Of his three daughters and coheirs, one m her first cousin, William Charleton,
who, by purchase and otherwise, acquired the whole of the estate of Hesleyside, and
is ancestor of the family there seated.

(e) See p 217, note "b," under "ACTON." In a marginal note to the docquet
is written "suspended," but whether by order of the King (as in the case of Wright,
7 Feb 1645/6), or of Parl., is not stated.

Royalist, being, eventually, Colonel of a Regiment of Horse, Colonel General of the counties of Lincoln, Notts, and Rutland, and Governor of Newark for the King, by whom he was *Knighted*, 1 Oct. 1642, at Shrewsbury, and was cr a *Baronet*, as above, 11 June 1646 (ᵃ) He m , in or before 1659, Alice, da and sole h of Thomas Fox, M D , of Warlies, in Waltham Holy Cross, Essex [bur there 26 Nov 1662], and of Shipton, Oxon, by Anne, da of Robert HONYWOOD, of Pett, in Charing Kent. Her will, dat. 27 Oct. 1684 pr 28 March 1688   He was *bur*. 9 Dec 1690, at Fen Ditton. His will dat. 16 to 20 May, and pr. 10 Dec 1690

II. 1690,   SIR THOMAS FOX WILLYS, Bart [1646], of Warlies aforeto   said, s and h , *b*. 30 June 1661, and *bap* at Waltham aforesaid , *suc*
1701   *to the Baronetcy*, 9 Dec 1690   He, who was "bereft of his wits," d
unm. 1701, aged 59, when the *Baronetcy* became *extinct* (ᵇ)   Will pr.
Nov 1701

Memorandum —On 11 Aug 1646, the Great Seal of Charles I was broken to pieces in the presence of both houses of Parliament   See *Memorandum* on p 152.

(ᵃ) See p 234, note "e"
(ᵇ) Anne Fox Willys, *bap* 21 Feb 1659/60, at Waltham, his only surv. sister and heir, *m.* Christopher Davenport, and had issue, living 1690.

Baronetcies [E.] not on record,

1640—1648,

ARRANGED ALPHABETICALLY.

Memorandum.—There are some Baronetcies conferred shortly before or during the *Civil War*, of which not only the patents (which possibly in many cases had never passed the Seals), but not even the docquets or warrants were enrolled and which are not mentioned in Dugdale's carefully compiled CATALOGUE OF THE BARONETS OF ENGLAND, as to which see *Memorandum* on p 84   A complete, or even approximately complete, list of these is unattainable, but there seems reason to believe that the following persons obtained, or at all events had the Royal warrant for, Baronetcies   The unlawful assumption of titles, which was so common in the nineteenth and even in the eighteenth century, was not usual in the seventeenth , and it will be observed that the position of the parties who thus styled themselves, and were recognised as, Baronets, was such as to render it unlikely that they would expose themselves to the ridicule and contempt attending such assumption   At the same time it is evident that in the cases of some of them (*e g*, in those of Acland, Boothby, and Edwards, where a patent *de novo* was granted with a clause giving the precedency of the former creation), the grant of the dignity by Charles I was not held to be sufficient , while on the contrary, the sufficiency of the creation of others has been generally acknowledged   Each case therefore should be judged separately. The dates of these Baronetcies, not being in many cases ascertainable, the names are here given in alphabetical order

---

ACLAND :
cr (ª) 24 June 1644 ,(ᵇ)
cr , de novo, 21 Jan. 1677/8.

I　1644　　JOHN ACLAND, of Columb-John, in Broadclyst, Devon, Esq , s. and h of Sir Arthur ACLAND, of the same, by Elizabeth, da. and h of Robert MALLET, of Woolley, Devon, was b about 1591 , suc his father, 26 Dec 1610 , was aged 29 at the Visitation of Devon in 1620 , Sheriff of Devon, 1641, and, having distinguished himself in the cause of his King, was cr a Baronet,(ª) 24 June 1644 (ᵇ)   He maintained a garrison at Columb-John, which at one time was the only force for the King that remained in the county   The house was afterwards plundered, and he himself fined £1,800   He m before 1635, Elizabeth, da of Sir Francis VINCENT, 1st Bart., [1620], by his 1st wife, Sarah, da. of Sir Amyas PAULET He d. 24 Aug 1647, and was bur at Stoke D'Abernon, Surrey   M 1   Will, in which he describes himself as ' Baronet," dat. 1 Dec 1646, pr 30 Nov 1648, 19 Feb 1650, 25 June 1670, and 5 July 1671   His widow d in or before 1650 ; her admon. 25 Jan. 1650/1, 25 June 1670, and 6 July 1671

II.　1647　　SIR FRANCIS ACLAND, Bart [1644] of Columb-John and Killerton, in Broadclyst aforesaid, s and h , suc to the Baronetcy, 24 Aug 1647　He d unm and a minor, 1649, and was bur at Stoke D'Abernon

---

(ª) See p 215, note " b," under " O'NEILL."   No patent, docquet, or sign manual is enrolled , nor is the creation given in Dugdale's *Catalogue*; see *Memorandum* in text above.

(ᵇ) The date of the creation, as in the text, is that given in Wotton's *Baronetage* (edit 1741)

III. 1649. SIR JOHN ACLAND, Bart [1644], of Columb John and
Killerton aforesaid, br and h, b about 1636, *suc ta the Baronetcy* in
1649 He *m* about 1654, Margaret, da and coheir of Denms ROLLE, of Stevenstone,
Devon, by Margaret, da of John (POULETT), 1st BARON POULETT OF HINTON ST.
GEORGE He *d.*, under age, in 1655 His widow *m.* Henry AYSHFORD She *d* about
1673 Admon. 25 Nov. 1673, to her da Margaret Acland.(a)

IV. 1655. SIR ARTHUR ACLAND, Bart [1644], of Columb John and
Killerton aforesaid, only s. and h, b about 1655, *suc. ta the Baronetcy*
in his infancy, 1655; matric at Oxford (Ex Coll), 27 July 1669, aged 14, subscribing
himself as a Baronet. He *d* a minor and unm, 1672.

V. 1672. SIR HUGH ACLAND, Bart. [1644], of Columb John and
Killerton aforesaid, uncle and heir male, was *b* about 1639, matric.
at Oxford (Ex Coll), 27 Nov 1652, B A, 22 June 1655; *suc.*, by the death of his
nephew in 1672 *to the Baronetcy* conferred, 24 June 1644 on his father, and, though
styled "Baronet" in his marriage license (Vic Gen), 19 March 1673/4, was nevertheless *cr a Baronet* [*de novo*] 21 Jan. 1677/8, it being stated(b) that "amidst the
confusion of those Civil Wars, the letters patents [24 June 1644] were destroyed,
and new letters patents not being granted till the year 1677 (by reason of a long
minority in this family), there was in them inserted a special clause of precedency
from the date of the first, viz, 24 June 1644 "(c) See "ACLAND" Baronetcy, *cr.*
21 Jan 1677/8

BATHURST:

cr 15 Dec. 1643,(d)

ex, or *dormant*, about 1780;

but *assumed* subsequently

I. 1643. EDWARD BATHURST, of Lechlade, co Glouc, and of Farring-
ton, co Oxon, Esq, 2d s of Robert BATHURST, of the same, by
Elizabeth, relict of Sir John LAURENCE, da of Ralph WALLER, was *b* about 1603, *suc*
his elder br., Robert Bathurst, in 1628, being then aged 13, distinguished himself in
the cause of the King in the Civil War, and was *cr. a Baronet*, 15 Dec. 1643,(d)
being subsequently(e) *Knighted*. He was a Royalist, and was fined £720 by the

(a) This Margaret, who was h to her br, the 4th Bart., *m.* John (Arundell), 2d
Baron Arundell of Trerice Under the will of her grandson, the 4th Baron, the
Acland family inherited Trerice and other of the Arundell estates.

(b) Wotton's *Baronetage*, edit 1741.

(c) The previous creation of Boothby, 13 July 1660, was practically a similar case,
and that of Edwards, 22 April, 1678 (the next creation following this one) was
precisely similar

(d) See p 236, notes "a" and "b" In this case, however, there is said to
have been a warrant for its creation under the Privy Seal at Oxford, dat 15 Dec.
1641. If the creation was before 4 Jan 1641/2, it would not be affected by the
disallowing acts of Parl (see *Memorandum* on p 152). Unlike many other un-
recorded creations of this period, this particular one appears to have been considered
fictitious by (Dugdale) Garter, as also by (St George) Clarenceux, and four other
Heralds, 3 Sep 1679 and 19 May (1681), 33 Car II See "1 L 2," (p. 156b, 145)
in the College of Arms, London It was, however, recognised in the Visitation of
Gloucestershire in 1682, and is said [but *Query*] to have been exemplified under the
Great Seal by Car. II, 18 Jan (1682/3), 34 Car II

(e) In the Cal Com. for advance of money, p 824, it is stated, under 28 May 1647,
"that he was made a Baronet by the King since the war began; gave £170 to
Richard Lloyd to be a Baronet, and *afterwards* £20 to be made a Knight", again,
under 6 and 7 Sep 1648, "Information that he is a delinquent, and was at Oxford
when it was the King's garrison Depositions to prove that when at Oxford he paid
£160 for a blank warrant for a Baronetcy, which was filled in with his name." [*Ex
inform*, W D Pink]

sequestrators He *m.* firstly, in or before 1634, Anne, da. of Thomas MORRIS, of
Great Coxwell, Berks He *m.* secondly, in or before 1654, Susan, widow of Thomas
COOK, da. of Thomas RICH, of North Cerney, co Glouc He *m* thirdly, Dorothy, da.
of (—) NASH, of Worcestershire He *d* 6 Aug 1674, aged 61, at Lechlade M I
His widow, by whom he had no issue, *d* 18 March 1683/4, and was *bur.* at Spelsbury,
co. Oxford M I Will pr 1684

II 1674   SIR EDWARD BATHURST, Bart [1643], of Lechlade afore-
            said, grandson and h , being s and h of Laurence BATHURST, by
Susan, da. of the abovenamed Thomas COOK, of Stanton, co Worcester, which
Laurence (who was admitted to Gray's Inn, 10 Feb 1657/8), was s. and h ap. of the
late Baronet, by his 1st wife, but *d* v p , 15 Sep 1671 He, who was *b* about 1665,
suc to the Baronetcy, 6 Aug 1674, and *d* unm. 21 March 1677, aged 12 ([a])

III 1677   SIR EDWARD BATHURST, Bart , [1643], of Lechlade afore-
            said, uncle and heir male, being 2d s of the 1st Bart by his 1st wife,
and *b* about 1635, *suc to the Baronetcy,* 21 March 1677 , entered his pedigree at the
Heralds' Visitation of co Glouc in 1682, being then aged 47, in which his own, his
nephew's, and his father's Baronetcy are all recognised He *m* in or before 1672,
Mary, da of Francis PEACOCK, of Chawley, Oxon , she was living 1682

IV 1688?   SIR EDWARD BATHURST, Bart [1643], s and h , said
            to be aged about 10 in the Visitation of 1682, was a scholar at
Winchester College, 1686 (then said to be 12) to 1688, when, apparently (1688) as
"Dominus Bathurst" he became a commoner of that School,([b]) having previously
suc. to the Baronetcy on his father's death He *d.* unm.

V. 1690?   SIR FRANCIS BATHURST, Bart [1643], br and h , aged
            about 6 in 1682, *suc. to the Baronetcy* on his brother's death He *m*
Frances, da of the Rev. (—) PEACOCK He, with his wife and part of his family,
embarked (with Gen Oglethorpe) for New Georgia, where his wife *d* Jan. 1736/7,
and he himself, shortly afterwards, about 1738.

VI 1738?   SIR LAURENCE BATHURST, Bart [1643], 1st and only
    to   surv s and h ,([c]) *suc to the Baronetcy* about 1738, and was
    1780?   residing in Georgia, 1741 and 1771 ([d]) He *d* there s p , prob-
            ably about 1780, at whose decease the *Baronetcy* is said([e]) to have
become *extinct,* though it is stated([f]) " by other accounts to be vested in a gentleman
still([g]) [1841] resident in America," possibly a descendant of Lancelot Bathurst, 5th
s. of the 1st Bart , aged 36 in 1682, and then living in Virginia with issue.

([a]) The manor of Lechlade devolved on his two sisters and coheirs, passing finally
to Thomas Coxeter, s and h of one, and nephew and h of the other.
    ([b]) See *N. & Q.,* 1st S , iv, 345
    ([c]) Robert, his only br , was killed in Georgia by the Indians, before 1741.
    ([d]) See note " b," p 237
    ([e]) Courthope's *Extinct Baronetage*
    ([f]) Burke's *Extinct Baronetage* [1841]
    ([g]) It seems extremely probable that there may be heirs to this Baronetcy among
the issue of two of the 4 younger sons (by the 2d wife) of the 1st Baronet Of these
two (I), Robert Bathurst, of Lechlade, was living 1682, aged 38, having had several
sons, of whom Robert (aged 14), Charles (aged 8), Edmond (aged 2), and Laurence
(aged 9 months), were then alive , (II) Lancelot Bathurst, of Virginia, was living
there, 1682 aged 36, with issue In the additions made by Sir Thomas Phillipps to
the Visitation of Gloucestershire of 1682 (printed by the Harleian Society), the abovenamed Robert Bathurst, s. of Robert, is said to have died 1726, aged 59, having had
two sons (1), Robert, who *d* 1765, aged 67, and (2), Edward, who *m* Barbara
Coxeter, and *d* 1762, aged 57

"H H" [*Genealogist*, vol iv, p 58], states that he is "credibly informed that the title actually expired as under " —

VII. 1780? SIR ROBERT BATHURST, "7th and last Bart ' [1643], who *suc to the Baronetcy* about 1780, being s. of Robert Bathurst [aged 5 in 1682], yr br of the 4th and 5th Barts , all three being sons of the 3d Bart.

Besides the above-named Robert, there was also (see *N. & Q*, 7th S , ix, 377, 1st S., xii, 379 and 357) .—

CHARLES BATHURST, *b* 15 and *bap* 18 Nov. 1711, at St. Martin's in the Fields (being s of John Bathurst, *bur.* there 11 Dec. 1719), who was "generally reputed a Baronet [Bathurst of Lechlade, *cr* 15 Dec 1643], though he did not choose to assert his title " It is not, indeed, by any means clear how (if, indeed, anyhow) he descended from the grantee He was a Bookseller, opposite St Dunstan's Church, in Fleet street, and suc his partner (brother-in-law to his wife) therein, 12 March 1738 He *m* firstly, a da of the Rev Thomas BRIAN, Head Master of Harrow School, by whom he had one son, Charles Bathurst, who *d* v p and s p 1763, and was *bur.* at Harrow. He *m.* secondly, at Kelmscott, Oxon, Elizabeth CARTER, spinster, and *d* s.p m s 21 July 1786, aged 77

BOOTHBY :
cr.(ᵃ) 5 Nov 1644 ,(ᵇ)
cr., de novo, 13 July 1660.

I. 1644. HENRY BOOTHBY, of Clater Clote, co. Oxford, Esq , 3d s but eventually (23 Aug 1623) heir of William BOOTHBY, citizen and haberdasher of London, by Judith (afterwards wife of Sir Richard CORBET, K B , of Moreton Corbet, Salop), da of Thomas AUSTEN, of Oxley, co. Stafford, was *b* about 1592, suc his mother, 21 March 1637, in the estate of Clater Clote aforesaid, Croperdy, co Oxford, Boddington, co. Northampton, Broadlow Ash, in Ashbourne, co Derby, and others, which she had acquired since the death of her first husband, and was *cr a Baronet*,(ᵃ) 5 Nov 1644,(ᵇ) such Baronetcy being recognised in the Heraldic Visitations of Derbyshire, 1662, and of Staffordshire in 1663, as also on his monumental inscription (ᶜ) He was a Royalist, and compounded in 1646 for £2,500, having, as early as Oct 1643, been assessed at £1,000 He *m*, in or before 1638, Mary, one of the twenty children of Sir Thomas HAYES, sometime, 1614-15, Lord Mayor of London, being, presumably, a da by his [4th?] wife, Mary (*m* 26 Sep. 1609), da. of Humphrey MILWARD, of London, merchant He *d* 3 Sep 1648, aged 56, and was *bur* (with his eldest br William Boothby, who *d* 23 Aug 1623) at Boddington aforesaid M I (ᵇ) Will dat 2 Sep. 1648, pr 6 Jan. 1648/9 His widow, who was *bap* 5 May 1613, at St Mary Aldermanbury, London, was living 1649.

II. 1648. SIR WILLIAM BOOTHBY, Bart. [1644], of Broadlow Ash, Croperdy, etc , aforesaid, only s and h , *b* about 1638, and *suc to the Baronetcy*, 3 Sep. 1648, but was, nevertheless, *cr a Baronet [de novo]*, 13 July 1660,

---

(ᵃ) See p 236, note " a "
(ᵇ) "Created Baronet by letters patent, 5 Nov. 1644, signed by His Majesty's sign manual , but the Civil Wars prevented its passing the seals " [Wotton's *Baronetage*, 1741]
(ᶜ) " Sir Henry Boothby, Baronet, the first Baronet of that family, sonne to Dame Lady Judith Corbet " etc

it being stated([a]) ["*ex inform dom Will Boothby, Bar*"] that "at the Restoration, the King was pleased to renew his patent gratis([b]) by the name of SIR WILLIAM BOOTHBY, OF BROADLOW ASH, the former patent being OF CLATER-COTE." See "BOOTHBY" Baronetcy, *cr.* 13 July 1660

COKAYNE, *or* COKAINE
cr. about 10 Jan. 1641/2 ,([c])
ex 13 Feb. 1683/4.

I. 1642,   ASTON COKAYNE, *or* COKAINE, of Ashbourne Hall, co.
to   Derby, and of Pooley, in Polesworth, co Warwick, Esq , 1st s and h.
1684   of Thomas COKAYNE (s and h. of Sir Edward COKAYNE), of the same,
by Anne, sister (of the half-blood) to Philip, 1st EARL OF CHESTER-
FIELD, da. (by 2d wife) of Sir John STANHOPE, of Shelford and Elvaston, co Derby, was *b* at Elvaston and *bap* 20 Dec 1608, at Ashbourne, was ed (as a Fellow Commoner) at Trin Coll, Cambridge , suc his father, 26 Jan 1638/9, and was *cr a Baronet* about 10 Jan 1641/2,([c]) such Baronetcy being acknowledged in the Heralds' Visitation of Derbyshire, 1662, and in that of Hampshire, 1686 (under "LACY"), as also in his will, burial register, etc. He was *cr* M A of Oxford, 21 Feb 1642/3 A zealous Royalist and "a Popish delinquent," he was assessed (with his mother) 17 Dec 1646, at £1,500, his estate being sequestrated for non-payment, 8 March 1648 ; was fined £356, and finally suffered such heavy losses that in 1671 he sold the long-inherited estate of Ashbourne, and in 1683 that of his "beloved Pooley"([d]) He *m* in or before 1635, Mary, da. of Sir Gilbert KNIVETON, 2d Bart [1611], of Mercaston, co. Derby, by his 1st wife, Mary, da of Andrew GREY She *d* shortly before him, and was *bur* 14 May 1683, at Polesworth He *d* s p m s ([e]) at Derby, "at the breaking up of the great frost," and was *bur* 18 Feb 1683/4, at Polesworth, aged 75, when the *Baronetcy* became *extinct* Will (signed "Aston Cokaine") dat 6 Feb. 1683/4, pr. 24 March([f]) following at Lichfield.

([a]) Wotton's *Baronetage* [edit. 1741], where it is also said that he "was Knighted by King Charles II in the field," which, considering that he was but 13 at the battle of Worcester (which, presumably, is the "field" alluded to) seems improbable

([b]) The creations, *de novo*, of Acland, 21 Jan 1677/8, and of Edwards, 22 April 1678, are, practically, similar cases

([c]) If the creation was *before* 4 Jan 1641/2 it would not be affected, but if *later* it would have been disallowed by Parliament till the Restoration See *Memorandum* as to creations after 4 Jan 1641/2 and 22 May 1642, on p. 152. No patent, docquet, or sign manual is enrolled, nor is the creation given in Dugdale's *Catalogue*, (see *Memorandum* on p. 236), but its existence is acknowledged (as stated in the text) in the Heralds' Visitations and elsewhere The date of creation is indicated in Lodge's *Peerage of Ireland* (edit 1789, vol. IV, p 328), as "created, after the King had by violence been compelled to leave the Parliament, about 10 Jan 1641"

([d]) See his Poems. Anthony a Wood says that he "was esteemed by many an ingenious gentleman, a good poet and a great lover of learning, yet by others a perfect boon fellow, by which means he wasted all he had." He was a friend and cousin of Charles Cotton (well known as an angler and poet), who, in his poems, praises him highly for his "Tragedy of Ovid "

([e]) Thomas Cokayne, his only s., *b* 8 May 1636, *m.*, 14 Jan. 1657/8, at St Peter's, Paul's wharf, London, Rachel, da and coheir of Carew STURRY, of Rossall, co. Salop, and *d* v p and s p about 1680, his widow dying before 1 Dec. 1686, when admon was granted to her sister, wife of Sir Thomas Kniveton, 4th Bart. [1611]

([f]) This is the date on the endorsement That in the body is "24 *April*, 1683," which, as the date of the will is 6 Feb, and the inventory 27 Feb. 1683 [*i e.*, 1683/4], is clearly a clerical error See a facsimile of his signature thereto and other particulars about him in the *Mis. Gen. et Her*, 3d S., vol. IV.

CROKE, or CROOKE·

cr in or soon after 1642 ,([a])

ex 16 Jan 1728

I. 1642 ?   JOHN CROKE, of Chilton, Bucks, Esq., s. and h. of Sir John
CROKE of the same (*d* 10 April 1640, aged 54), by Rachael, da and
h. of Sir. William WEBB, of Motcombe, Dorset, was *b*. probably about 1610, suc his
father, 10 April 1640, and having raised for the King in the Civil War a troop of
horse, of which he was Colonel, was *cr* a Baronet in or soon after 1642 ([a]) He was
removed from his office of Justice for his conduct as to a charge of felony (1668)
against the Incumbent of Chilton, whom he undertook to "hang at the next assizes."
He *m.* firstly, Jane, da. of Moses TRYON, of Harringworth, co Northampton She *d*
s p m., in childbirth, 9 May 1636, aged 20, and was *bur.* at Chilton. M I. He *m*
secondly, Sarah (—), in or before 1644 She was living 14 Jan 1672 [MS deed], but
was dead in May 1676 He alienated the family estates, and *d* a prisoner in the Fleet,
being *bur.* 14 March 1678/9, at St Bride's, Fleet street, London Will, in which he
makes no mention of his son, dat 4 Oct. 1678, pr 11 July 1682, by Mary HIDE,
widow, da and extrix

II. 1679,   SIR DODSWORTH CROKE, Bart. [1642 ?], only s. and h., by
to   2d wife, *b* about 1644, *suc to the Baronetcy* in March 1678/9 He
1728.   *d* unm. and in obscurity,([b]) 16 Jan 1728, aged 84, and was *bur* at
Chilton, when the *Baronetcy* became *extinct*.

COURTENAY.

cr Feb. 1644 ,([c])

afterwards, 1762—1835, VISCOUNTS COURTENAY ;

and, since 1831, EARLS OF DEVON.

I. 1644.   WILLIAM COURTENAY, of Powderham Castle, co. Devon,
Esq , s and h of Francis COURTENAY (s and h of Sir William
COURTENAY), of the same, by his 2d wife, Elizabeth, da of Sir Edward SEYMOUR, 3d
Bart. [1611], was *bap* 7 Sep 1628 ; suc his father, 5 June 1638, and was, at the age
of 16, *cr a Baronet*, by Privy Seal,([d]) in Feb. 1644,([c]) such Baronetcy being
recognised in the pedigree recorded in the College of Arms He was fined under the
Oxford Articles, April 1649 , was instrumental in promoting the Restoration, raising
a troop in co Devon for that purpose, was nominated a Knight of the intended

---

([a]) See p. 236, note "a." In a deed dat 20 Jan 1664, the grantee, as "Sir John
Croke, *Bart*, with "Dame Sarah, his wife," and "Dodsworth Croke, Esq.," his son,
and others, conveyed Whitsand Leas, in Chilton, to Martha Lloyd He is also
described as a Baronet in the relation (entitled "The Perjured Phanatick," etc ")
of the trial against him, in 1668, also on the margin of his will, etc. Neither he
nor his son were apparently Knighted. See Lipscomb's *Bucks*, vol i, pp. 132-148,
for an account of this family, where (p 140) is given in full and interesting account
of the above mentioned trial.

([b]) Nothing seems known of him save that in the trial of 1668 (see note "a"
above), he swears that "the ring stolen had been *pawned* by himself" to the plaintiff.

([c]) See p. 236, note "a." The date here given is that of the Privy Seal See
note "d" below

([d]) Notice of this Privy Seal is recorded in College of Arms (Norfolk, iv, 210), in
which the grantee and his successors are styled Baronets. Le Neve (in his MS
Baronetage, vol. ii, 230) states that "Sir William Courtenay had a like patent
[of Baronetcy] with Acland in 1644, but never passed the patent " In Collins'
Peerage (vol. vi, 259, edit 1779) it is said that "some time before the Restoration he
was *cr a Baronet*, but not affecting that title, as much greater he thought of right
appertained to his family, never took out his patent, and therefore was not inserted

2 H

order of " The Royal Oak " (estate valued at £3,000 a year) ; was Sheriff of Devon, 1664-65 , M.P for Ashburton, 1668, and for Devon (three Parls), 1677-81. He *m.* about 1643, Margaret, da of Sir William WALLER, the well-known Parliamentary General, by his 1st wife, Jane (of whom she was only child), da. of Sir Richard REYNELL, of Wolborough, Devon, their united ages being, it is said, under 30, when their first child was born She was *bur* 9 Jan 1693/4, at Wolborough. He *d.* of palsy, 4 Aug. 1702, and was *bur.* with her, aged 74 Will dat 28 July 1702.

II 1702. SIR WILLIAM COURTENAY, Bart [1644], of Powderham Castle aforesaid, grandson and h., being s and h. of Francis COURTENAY, by Mary (*m* Nov 1670), da. of William BOEVEY, of Flaxley Abbey, co Glouc., and of St. Dunstan's in the East, London, merchant, which Francis, who *d.* v.p. and was *bur.* 12 May 1699, at Chelsea, aged 47, was 1st s and h ap. of the late Baronet. He was *b* 11 March 1675/6 , was M P for Devon (eleven Parls), 1701-10, and June 1712 till death ; *suc to the Baronetcy*, 4 Aug. 1702; was L.-Lieut. of Devon, 1715. He *m* 20 July 1704, Anne, 2d da. of James (BERTIE), 1st EARL OF ABINGDON, by his 1st wife, Eleanor, da and coheir of Sir Henry LEE, 3d Bart [1611]. She *d.* 31 Oct 1728, and was *bur.* at Powderham. Admon 26 March 1734, granted to her husband, " Sir William Courtenay, *Baronet.*" He *d* 6 and was *bur.* 11 Oct. 1735, at Powderham Will dat 19 Sep. 1734, as " Sir William Courtenay, Baronet," pr. 15 Jan 1735/6, by ' Sir William Courtenay, Baronet," the son.

III 1735. SIR WILLIAM COURTENAY, Bart. [1644], of Powderham Castle aforesaid, 3d but 1st surv s and h , *b.* 11 and *bap.* 15 Feb 1709/10, at St. Martin's in the fields, matric at Oxford (Mag Coll), 4 June 1729 (as son of a Baronet), aged 19 , *cr* M A 28 Jan 1730/1, and D.C.L. (as a " Baronet") 26 May 1739, having *suc to the Baronetcy* 6 Oct. 1735. He was M.P. for Honiton, 1734-41, and for Devon, 1741-62, and was *cr*, 6 May 1762, VISCOUNT COURTENAY OF POWDERHAM CASTLE, co. Devon (a) He *m.* (Lic., 2 April 1741, to marry at Duke street Chapel, Westm) Frances, 4th da. of Heneage (FINCH), 2d EARL OF AYLESFORD, by Mary, da and h of Sir Clement FISHER, 3d Bart. [1622]. She, who was *b* 4 and *bap* 21 Feb 1720/1, *d* at Bath, 19 and was *bur.* 31 Dec 1761, at Powderham He *d* in London (ten days after his elevation to the peerage), 16 and was *bur.* 31 May 1762, at Powderham Will pr June 1762.

IV. 1762. WILLIAM (COURTENAY), 2d VISCOUNT COURTENAY OF POWDERHAM and 4th Baronet [1644], only s and h , *b.* 30 and *bap.* 31 Oct 1742, at St James', Westm , matric. at Oxford (Mag Coll), 21 March 1761, aged 18 ; *suc to his father's titles*, 16 May 1762. He *m* , at Edinburgh, 7 May 1762, and, again subsequently, 19 Dec 1763, at Powderham, Frances, da. of Thomas CLACK, of Wallingford, Berks She *d.* in Grosvenor square 25 March, and was *bur* 5 April 1782, at Powderham. He *d.* in Grosvenor square, 14 Dec 1788, and was *bur.* at Powderham Will pr Dec 1788.

V. 1788. WILLIAM (COURTENAY), 3d VISCOUNT COURTENAY OF POWDERHAM and 5th Baronet [1644], only s. and h , *b.* 30 July and *bap.* 30 Aug 1768, at Powderham , *suc to his father's titles*, 14 Dec 1788 He was by an extraordinary decision of the House of Lords, confirmed 15 May 1831, declared EARL OF DEVON, under the remainder in the creation of that dignity, 3 Sep 1553, to the " heirs male " of the grantee, he being, indeed, collaterally heir male to the Earl thus created (who *d.* unm., 1556, three years after such creation), inasmuch as his grandfather's grandfather's grandfather, Sir William Courtenay, who *d* 1557 (though he and his abovenamed descendants were all unconscious of any right to such Earldom), was, though a very distant cousin, collaterally heir male of the grantee of 1553, whose ancestor in the seventh degree (a man who *d.* in 1377),

---

in the list of Baronets , but he was always styled Baronet in the Commissions sent him by the King." This, however (as also the motive thus strangely attributed to him) is incorrect, for both he and his two successors manifestly *did* " affect " the title till 1762, when it became merged in the Peerage See also *Herald and Genealogist*, iv, 279.

(a) As " Sir William Courtenay, *Baronet*," he kissed the King's hand at St. James', 28 April 1762, on being created an English Peer [*Ann. Reg* , 1762].

was the said Sir William's grandfather's grandfather's grandfather's grandfather In the Earldom of Devon this *Baronetcy* then (1831) *merged*, and still so continues, though on the death of this Earl, 26 May 1835, the *Viscountcy of Courtenay* became *extinct* See *Peerage*.

EDWARDS, *or* EDWARDES:
cr 21 March 1644/5 ,([a])

cr., *de novo*, 22 April 1678 ,

ex. 24 Aug 1900.

I. 1645   THOMAS EDWARDS, of Grete and of the College, Shrewsbury, co Salop, Esq , 2d s of Thomas EDWARDS of the same (who was Sheriff of Salop 1622, and *d.* 19 March 1634, aged 79, being *bur.* at St Chad's, Shrewsbury), by Anne, relict of Stephen DUCKET, da. and coheir of Humphrey BASKERVILLE, Alderman and sometime (1561-62) Sheriff of London, was possibly the "Thomas Edwards of Salop, son of an Esq," who matric at Oxford (Ex Coll), 31 May 1616, aged 16, being B A 13 June 1616 He, who was probably the King's Sheriff of Salop 1644, was *cr.* a Baronet, 21 March 1644/5. He was assessed, 11 May 1647 at £500, as "Thomas, or Sir Thomas, Edwards, of Creet," but let off, in 1651, on the ground of having compounded. He is styled "Knt. and Bart." in the admission of his 2d son to Gray's Inn, 1 July 1665. He *m.*, after 1623,([b]) Anne, da of Bonham NORTON, of Stretton, Salop, the King's printer She *d* s p m He *m* secondly, before 1645, Cicely, da of Edward BROOKES, of Stretton aforesaid. He *d.* and was *bur* 27 April 1660, at Shrewsbury. Admon. 10 Aug. 1660 His widow was *bur.* there 28 Dec. 1677 Her will pr. 1678

II. 1660.   SIR FRANCIS EDWARDS, Bart. [1644], of Grete and of Shrewsbury aforesaid, 1st s and h , being one of six sons by 2d wife , *b.* probably about 1645 ; *suc. to the Baronetcy*, 27 April 1660, and matric., *as a Baronet*, at Oxford (Ball Coll), 26 Oct. 1660, but was, nevertheless, *cr. a Baronet, de novo*, 22 April 1678, it being stated([c]) that "in the Civil Wars 'tis supposed the Baronet's patent [of 1644] was lost, for in April 1678, a new one was granted([d]) to Francis (then Sir Francis) Edwards of Shrewsbury, and to the heirs male of his body, with remainder to [his brothers] Thomas, Benjamin, Herbert, and Jonathan, and the heirs male of their bodies, etc , with a special clause for precedency before all Baronets, created after the year 1644, viz , according to the former patent." See "EDWARDS" Baronetcy, *cr.* 22 April 1678.

GREAVES, *or* GRAVES.
cr 4 May 1645 ,([e])

ex 11 Nov. 1680.

I   1645,   EDWARD GREAVES, *or* GRAVES, of St. Leonard's Forest, to   Sussex, Doctor of Medicine, yr br. of John GREAVES, Savilian Pro-1680   fessor of Astronomy at Oxford and Gresham Professor of Geometry, both being sons of the Rev James GREAVES, Rector of Colemore, Hants, was *b* at Croydon, 1608 , ed at Merton Coll , Oxford ; B.A. 23 Oct. 1633 ;

([a]) See p. 236, note "a." The date of the *year* of the creation "1644," is given in Wotton's *Baronetage* (1741), but the exact date, 21 March 1644/5, is given in Burke's *Baronetage* (1900) and elsewhere.

([b]) Visit. of Salop, 1623.

([c]) Wotton's *Baronetage* (1741).

([d]) The previous creation, that of the Baronetcy of Acland, 21 Jan. 1677/8, is a precisely similar case, as also practically was that of Boothby, 13 July 1660

([e]) See p 236, note "a " This Baronetcy is omitted in all the printed lists of Baronets, except in the 5th edit [1679] of Guillim's *Heraldry*, where it is placed

Fellow of All Souls' Coll , 1634 ; M A., 13 July 1637 ; B Med , 18 July 1640 ; D. Med , 8 July 1641 ; Senior Linacre Lecturer of Physic, 1643 , travelling physician to Charles, Prince of Wales (afterwards Charles II), and was *cr a Baronet,* 4 May 1645 (a) Admitted to Coll of Physicians, 4 April 1653 ; Fellow, 1 Oct 1657 ; Hervelan Orator, 1661 , one of the Physicians in Ordinary to Charles II, and for many years a resident in Bath   He *m* firstly (Lic. Fac 20 Jan. 1663/4), Hester, da. of Thomas TYTHER, of Northaw, Herts, citizen and draper, of London.   She was living Dec. 1664, and was *bur* at Northaw aforesaid.   Admon 21 March 1665/6, to her husband, "Sir Edward Greaves, Bart "   He *m* secondly, 27 Feb 1667/8 (Lic. Fac., he said to be aged 45 and she 35), Alice, widow of Peter CALFE (*bur* 5 Dec. 1667), of Tottenham, Midx. He *d* s p m in his house in Henrietta street, and was *bur* 11 Nov 1680, at St Paul's, Covent Garden, when the *Baronetcy* became *extinct* (b)   Will, as a "Baronet," dat. 25 March 1679, pr 23 Nov. 1680, by da , Mary Greaves   His widow was *bur* (with her two husbands) 15 Jan. 1683/4.   Will dat 22 July 1683, pr. 3 Nov. 1684, by her son, "Peter Calfe, Esq "

HAGGERSTON :
cr 15 Aug 1642.(c)

I   1642.   THOMAS HAGGERSTON, of Haggerston Castle, co Northumberland, Esq , s and h of William HAGGERSTON of the same, by Margaret, da of Henry BUTLER, of Rowcliffe, co Lancaster, having distinguished himself in the Civil Wars, where he was Colonel of a regiment on behalf of the King, was *cr a Baronet,* 15 Aug 1642 (c)   He *m* Alice, da. and h of Henry BANASTER, of Bank, co Lancaster, by (—), da and h of (—) CUERDON, of Cuerdon, in that county   She was *bur.* 10 April 1673   He *d* at a great age, and was *bur.* 7 March 1673/4.

II   1674.   SIR THOMAS HAGGERSTON, Bart. [1642], of Haggerston Castle aforesaid, 2d but yst surviving s and h ,(d) *suc to the Baronetcy,* 7 March 1673/4   He was Governor of Berwick Castle, his house there being burnt down 19 Feb. 1687 and the damage sustained being above £6,000   He *m.*

---

as the 450th, between Boreel and Carteret.   Anthony a Wood indeed speaks (*more suo*) of Dr. Greaves as a "Pretended Baronet," but Dr Munk, in his "Roll of the Royal College of Physicians," aptly remarks, "I am disposed to believe, despite Wood's sneer, that he was really entitled to that dignity   I find him so characterised in the *Annals* ; he styles himself Baronet on the title page of his Hervelan Oration   .   Thomas Guidott, M B , of Bath, writing of him in 1676 says, 'he is full of honour, wealth, and years, being a Baronet, a Fellow of the College of Physicians in London, and Physician in Ordinary to His Majesty," and in the official list of the Fellows of the College prefixed to the *Pharmacopœia Londinensis* of 1677, his Baronetcy is acknowledged, and he appears as *Edvardus Greaves Baronettus*   The point is of some interest, as this is the first instance of an English Physician being honoured with an hereditary title."   The original patent of creation is said to be "in the family of one Mr. Calfe, of St Leonard's Forest, Sussex " [probably descendants of his 2d wife], and a letter of Le Neve, Norroy, says that "he was apt to think " that "as the patent was dated at Oxford, 4 May 1645, there was no enrollment thereof, which was the case of several persons of honour passed about that time, the Rolls being taken into the possession of Parliament."

(a) See p 243, note "e."
(b) The burial at Christ Church, London, 19 Nov 1669, of "Sir Thomas Graves, *Barronet,* from Newgate," may possibly, if not an erroneous designation, relate to this creation
(c) See p 236, note "a "   Le Neve in his MS *Baronetage* (vol ii, p 217) writes, "Sir Thomas Haggerton in his letter to me, dated 12 July 1696, saith his patent is dated 15 Oct. 1642," but the date usually [though apparently incorrectly] given to it is a year later, *viz,* 15 Oct. 1643, between Waldegrave (1 Aug. 1643) and Pate (28 Oct 1643).
(d) John Haggerston, his elder br., *d.* s p. and v p , being slain Oct. 1644 at Ormskirk fight.

firstly, Margaret, da. of Sir Francis HOWARD, of Corby Castle, co Cumberland, by his 2d wife Mary, da of Sir Henry WIDDRINGTON. She, by whom he had nine sons, *d* in childbirth. He *m* secondly, Jane, da and coheir of Sir William CARNABY, of Farnham, Northumberland, but by her had no issue

III. 1710?   SIR CARNABY HAGGERSTON, Bart [1642], of Haggerston
              Castle aforesaid, grandson and h, being s and h. of William
HAGGERSTON, by Ann, da. of Sir Philip Mark CONSTABLE, 3d Bart. [1642], of
Everingham, co York, sister and h. of the 4th Bart, which William, who was 2d
s. of the 2d Bart by his 1st wife, *d v.p* He, who was probably *b* about 1700,
suc. to the Baronetcy on the death of his grandfather   He *m.*, 20 Nov. 1721, Elizabeth,
sister and coheir of William MIDLETON, of Kilvington and Stockeld, co. York, da. of
Peter MIDLETON, of Stockeld aforesaid. He was *bur.* 20 July 1756   His widow *d.*
at York, Dec. 1769.

IV. 1756.   SIR THOMAS HAGGERSTON, Bart. [1642], of Haggerston
              Castle aforesaid, s. and h, *bap.* 11 Sep 1722, *suc to the Baronetcy*,
20 July 1756. He *m* 1754, Mary, da of George SILVERTOP, of Minster Acres, co.
Northumberland. She *d* 22 May 1773, on her journey from Bath to London   He
d. 1 Nov. 1777.

V. 1777.   SIR CARNABY HAGGERSTON, Bart. [1642], of Haggerston
              Castle aforesaid, s and h., *b* May 1756, *suc to the Baronetcy* 1 Nov
1777   He *m.* Frances,[a] 2d da of Walter SMYTHE (2d s of Sir John SMYTHE, 3d
Bart [1661], of Eshe), by Mary, da of John ERRINGTON. He *d.* s p m [b] at Haggerston Castle, 3 Dec. 1831, aged 75   Will pr May 1844   His widow *d.* 1836   Will
pr. May 1844.

VI 1831   SIR THOMAS HAGGERSTON, Bart. [1642], of Ellingham,
              co. Northumberland, nephew and h male, being s and h. of Thomas
HAGGERSTON, of Sandoe, co. Northumberland, by Winifred, da of Edward CHARLTON,
which Thomas was 2d s. of the 4th Bart, and *d* 1829. He was *b* 13 July 1785,
and *suc. to the Baronetcy* 3 Dec 1831   He *m* 24 Jan 1815, Margaret, only da of
William ROBERTSON, of Ladykirk, co Berwick. She *d* 26 Oct 1823. He *d* s.p.m,
11 Dec 1842

VII. 1842   SIR EDWARD HAGGERSTON, Bart [1642], of Ellingham
              aforesaid, br and h male, *b* about 1797, *suc to the Baronetcy* 11 Dec
1842. He *d.* s.p. 6 May 1857, at Ellingham, aged 59   Will pr Sep 1857.

VIII. 1857.   SIR JOHN HAGGERSTON, Bart [1642], of Ellingham afore-
              said, br. and h male, *b* 18 Aug 1798, sometime Captain in the 80th
Foot, *suc. to the Baronetcy* 6 May 1857. He *m* 5 Aug 1851, Sarah Anne, da of
Henry KNIGHT, of Terrace Lodge, Axminster, Devon   He *d* 8 March 1858, aged 59.
His widow *d* 24 March 1883, aged 65, at Cathcart House, South Kensington.

IX. 1858   SIR JOHN DE MARIE HAGGERSTON, Bart [1642], of Elling-
              ham aforesaid, s. and h, *b.* 27 Nov 1852 at Furzebrooke House,
Axminster, *suc to the Baronetcy* 8 March 1858, ed. at Ushaw College, Durham   He
m 11 Jan 1887, at the Servite Fathers' (Roman Catholic) Church, St. Mary's Priory,
Fulham, his cousin, Marguerite, 2d da of Lewis EYRE, of 78 Redcliffe Gardens,
South Kensington.

Family Estates—These, in 1883, consisted of 14,285 acres in Northumberland,
worth £8,623 a year   *Principal Seat.*—Ellingham Hall near Alnwick, co. Northumberland.

———————

(a) Her sister, Mrs. FITZHERBERT, who *d.* 27 March 1827, was well known for her
connection with the Prince Regent, afterwards George IV.
(b) Mary, his only da and h., *m.*, 1805, Sir Thomas STANLEY, 9th Bart. [1661], of
Hooton, and *d.* 20 Aug. 1857, leaving issue.

I'ANSON

Warrant for Baronetcy given by Charles I,
probably between 1642 and 1644,(ᵃ)
recognised to the grantee by Charles II.
Baronetcy cr. (de novo) 28 Dec 1651 ;
See Creations of Baronetcies [E.]
under that date.

LLOYD.

cr 21 June 1647 .(ᵇ)

ex 1 April 1700

I. 1647.   EVAN LLOYD, of Yale, co Denbigh, Esq, s. and h of
John LLOYD, of the same, by his 1st wife, Margaret, da of Sir Bevis
THELWALL, which John was s and h of Evan LLOYD, of Yale (d 17 April 1637, being
bur. at Llanarmon), was b. about 1622 ; matric at Oxford (Ch Ch) 12 Sep 1640,
aged 18 , was a Royalist ; was fined £1,000 on 16 June 1646 , and was cr a Baronet,
21 June 1647 (ᵇ)   He m in or before 1654, Anne, sister of Sir Trevor WILLIAMS,
1st Bart [1642], da of Sir Charles WILLIAMS, of Llangibby, co. Monmouth, by
Anne, da of Sir John TREVOR.   He d. Oct. 1663   Will pr 1664.

II. 1663,   SIR EVAN LLOYD, Bart. [1646], of Yale aforesaid, s and
to   h., b about 1654, suc to the Baronetcy, Oct 1663   He m (Lic. Fac,
1700.   17 March 1674/5, he 20 [sic], and she 30 [sic], spinster, parents
deceased) Mary, da. and coheir of Rice TANNAT, of Abertanat, Salop.
He d. s p m.(ᶜ) 6 April 1700, when the Baronetcy became extinct

---

NEALE :

cr 26 Feb 1645/6 ;(ᵈ)

ex , presumably, 28 March 1691.

I. 1646,   SIR WILLIAM NEALE, of Wollaston, co. Northampton,
to   Knt., probably the 3d s. of John NEALE, of the same, by his
1691.   2nd wife, Elizabeth, da. of Sir Richard CONQUEST (which John
entered his pedigree in the Visit of Northamptonshire in 1618, .
having then three sons, Edward, aged 18, John, and William) ; was "Scout
Master General " in the Civil Wars to the forces of the King, by whom he was

---

(ᵃ) The creations after 4 Jan. 1641/2 were disallowed till the Restoration, under
an Act of Parl , 4 Feb 1651/2, and those after 22 May 1642 were so disallowed,
11 Nov. 1643. See Memorandum on p 152
(ᵇ) See p 236, note " a "   No date is assigned to this creation in the list of
Baronetcies in Kimber's Baronetage [1771], but the date of " 21 June 1647 " is given,
both by Courthope and Burke, in their respective Extinct Baronetages.   It is, however, to be observed that this date is after the King's Great Seal had been broken
up, at Oxford, 11 Aug. 1646.
(ᶜ) Margaret, his da and h , m. Richard VAUGHAN, of Corsygedol, and was mother
of Catherine, who m Rev. Hugh WYNN, D.D., Prebendary of Salisbury   Their da.,
Margaret, was h. to her uncle, William Vaughan, and m. Sir Roger MOSTYN, 5th Bart.
[1660], of Mostyn.
(ᵈ) See p. 236, note " a "

Knighted at Oxford, 3 Feb 1642/3, and was, by warrant,(a) dat. at Oxford, 26 Feb. 1645/6,(b) *or. a Baronet*, as above He, as "Sir William NEALE, Baronet," was Capt of a troop of horse in Ireland, 1666.(c) He *d* apparently s.p.m., and was *bur* 28 March 1691, at St Paul's, Covent Garden (from St Andrew's, Holborn), when, presumably, the *Baronetcy* became *extinct*.(d)

PETRE

cr, probably between 1642 and 1644;

ex., presumably, 22 Feb 1722

I 1642? FRANCIS PETRE, of Cranham Hall, co. Essex, s and h. of the Hon. Thomas PETRE, of the same, by Elizabeth, 2d da and coheir of William BASKERVILLE, of Wanborough, Wilts (which Thomas, who was 3d s of John, 1st BARON PETRE OF WRITTLE, *d* 3 Oct 1625, aged 40), was *b* about 1605, and was, apparently, *cr a Baronet* by Charles I, probably between 1642 and 1644 He sold the estate of Cranham He *m*, probably about 1628, Elizabeth, 2d da. of Sir John GAGE, 1st Bart [1611] of Firle, by Penelope, da of Thomas (DARCY), EARL RIVERS. She *d* before 14 March 1655, and was *bur* at Hengrave, Suffolk His will, as a Baronet, dat 14 March 1655, pr. 26 July 1660, 28 Nov 1670, and 22 Feb. 1697.

II 1660? SIR FRANCIS PETRE, Bart. [1642?] of London, s. and h., *b*. about 1630; *suc to the Baronetcy* between 1655 and 1660: living 18 Nov 1670, but *d* unm before 12 Jan. 1679. Will as ' of St. Bride's, London," pr 28 Nov 1681, and 19 Nov 1698 (f)

III. 1679? SIR EDWARD PETRE, Bart. [1642], br. and h, *b* about 1632, in London, ed at St Omer's College, 1649, and at the Society of Jesuits at Watten, 1652; becoming "professed" in 1671, *suc. to the Baronetcy* in or before 1679, was Vice-Provincial of the Jesuits of England, 1680, Clerk of the Royal Closet, P C. [11 Nov 1687], and Chief Almoner to James II, on whose expulsion he also quitted England and became, in 1693, Rector of St Omer's College. He, well known as "Father Petre" *d* unm at Watten, near Flanders, 15 May 1699, aged 68 Admon as a ' Baronet," 17 May 1699, to his sister Mary Petre.

IV 1699. SIR THOMAS PETRE, Bart. [1642], next br and h., *b*. 1640, ed at St Omer's College; *suc. to the Baronetcy*, 15 May 1699, but it is uncertain if he ever assumed it. He was living at Rome 1712, but is presumed to have *d*. unm. before 1722

V. 1715? SIR WILLIAM PETRE, Bart. [1642], br and h., being yst.
to   of six brothers, *b* 1650 He joined the Society of the Jesuits in
1722.   1670, becoming "professed" in 1687, and, presumably, at some
          date after 1712, *suc. to the Baronetcy* on his brother's death He *d* unm, 22 Feb. 1722, at Ghent, when, unless the elder br Thomas abovementioned was still surviving, the issue male of the grantee and the *Baronetcy* became *extinct*.

(a) Copy of this warrant is in *The Genealogist* [O.S], vol vi, p. 211, but the date of 3 Feb 1642/3 is sometimes given [W. D Pink]

(b) See p 236, note "a"

(c) Hist. MSS com, 14th Rep, Ormonde MSS, vol. i, p. 347

(d) Of this family was "Edmund Neale, of Wollaston," who *d* 21 Sep. 1671, aged 73, and was *bur* there M I. [Bridges's *Northamptonshire*] As also "Sir Charles Neale, of Woolaston, co Northampton, Knt., aged 28, and a bachelor," 27 Feb. 1678/9, when he had lic (Fac Office) to marry Frances Clerke, spinster.

(e) See p 246, note "a" It is possible, however, that the creation of the Baronetcy of Petre may have been by Charles II, during his exile, in which case it would, of course, not be recognised by Parl till the *de facto* accession of that King in 1660

(f) Statement in the elaborate pedigree in J. J. Howard's *Catholic Families*, from which this article is chiefly compiled.

WARD.

HUMBLE WARD, of Himley, co Stafford, whow as *cr*, 23 March 1643/4, BARON WARD OF BIRMINGHAM, had previously [1643 ?] received the *promise of a Baronetcy*,(a) of which, however, no official record seems extant. For particulars of him see *Peerage*.

(a) Deposition, 15 May 1646, of William Ward, of Himley, co Stafford, that he is the reputed owner of Himley, Dudley, and other manors, co. Stafford, which cost him £30,000 , that he and his son [Humble Ward] lent the King £400 or £500, and that he *gave £500 to have his son made a Baronet*, and £1,500 to have him made a Peer of Parliament. [*Ex inform*, W D Pink]

Baronetcies of Ireland,[a]

1619—1800.

SECOND PART,

VIZ.

CREATIONS BY CHARLES I,

27 March 1625 to 30 Jan 1648/9

BARRET ·

"SIR JAMES BARRET, Knight and Baronet," is so described in a funeral entry, 1626, in the Office of Arms, Dublin He was *Knighted* 7 Feb 1621/2, in Dublin, but there is no record of his having been *cr a Baronet* He *m* Janet, da of Dominick (SARSFIELD), 1st VISCOUNT SARSFIELD OF KILMALLOCK [I.], in whose funeral entry, 1637, he is described only as a "Knight," so that the previous one is probably erroneous He *d.* 30 June 1629 Inq p m , wherein, also, he is described as "Miles" [only]. His grandson, William Barret, was *cr* a Baronet [I], 4 June 1665

MAC DONELL, *or* MACDONNELL.

cr. 30 Nov. 1627 ;[b]

forfeited 1690

I. 1627   "ALEXANDER MAC-DONELL, Esq , of Moye [or Moyane], co Antrim," ' natural "[c] s of Sir James MAC-SORLEY-BOYE-MACDONNEL, of Dunluce, in said county (bi of Randal, EARL OF ANTRIM [I]), by Mary, da of Hugh MAC PHELIMY O'NEILL, of Claneboye, was, by patent dat. at Dublin, 30 Nov 1627 (Privy Seal dat at Southwick 20 June previous), *cr a Baronet* [I] as above,[b] being subsequently *Knighted* in Ireland, 21 May 1628 He was Sheriff of co Antrim, 1629 He *m* Evelyn, da of Arthur (MAGENNIS), 1st VISCOUNT MAGENNIS OF IVEAGH [I], by Sarah, da of Hugh (O'NEILL) EARL OF TYRONE [I] He *d* 10 May 1634, at Moyane, and was *bur.* in the abbey of Bonamargy. Funeral certificate

---

(a) See vol. i, p 223, note "a," for acknowledgment of the kind assistance of Sir Arthur Vicars, Ulster, and others, and more especially of the copious and invaluable information given by G. D Burtchaell (of the Office of Arms, Dublin), as to the Irish Baronetcies

(b) See vol. i, p 223, note "b," as to the description and dates of these Irish Baronetcies

(c) Funeral certificate in Ulster's Office.

II   1634   SIR JAMES MACDONNELL, Baronet(^a) [I 1627], of Bally-
bannagh, co Antrim, s and h , *suc to the Baronetcy*, 10 May 1634.
He *m* Mary, da of Donal O'BRIEN, of Dough, co Clare, by Ellis, da of Edmund
FITZGERALD, called the " Knight of Glyn." He was living 1678 , *attainted*, after
death, 10 July 1691

III [1680 ?   SIR RANDAL MACDONNELL, Baronet [I. 1627], of Moye
    to   aforesaid, 2d and yst but only surv s and h ,(^b) *suc to the*
    1691 ?   *Baronetcy* on the death of his father , was Captain of a ship of war
to Charles II in the action of Mamora against the Moors, and,
subsequently, served in the Army of James II to whom he remained faithful, and
whom he accompanied into exile, being, consequently, attainted, 10 July 1691, when
the *Baronetcy* became *forfeited*, his estates being granted in 1696 in trust for his
wife and children He *m* , Jan 1686, Hannah, da of Edward ROCHE, of Ballinard,
co Tipperary, by Joanna, da of Richard BUTLER, of Killenault, in that county. He
d about 1697 Will pr 1697. His widow *d* 26 Dec 1628, and was *bur* at St
James' Church, Dublin Will pr 1728 in the Prerog. Court [I]

The right to the Baronetcy, subject to the attainder, appears to have been
as under —

IV.   1710   " SIR JAMES MACDONNELL, Baronet " [I 1627], 1st
s and h. He *d.* unm. 24 May 1728, and was *bur.* in St.
James Churchyard, Dublin

V   1728   " SIR RANDAL MACDONNELL, Baronet " [I 1627],
of Cross, co Antrim, br and h , assumed the style and title
of a Baronet on the death of his br He was a Captain in the French service,
and *d* unm 1740 Will pr 1741, in the Prerog Court [I]

VI   1740   JOHN RICHARD MACDONNELL, yst and only surv
br and h , of whom and whose successors, if any, nothing
further is known

(^a) The words " Baronet " [in full] and " Bt." [when abbreviated], are henceforth
used in this work instead of the word " Bart," which familiar abbreviation appears
to have recently [1900] become odious to several existing Baronets, indeed, in *The
Athenæum* of 1 Sep 1900, the reviewer of Pixley's *History of the Baronetage* speaks
of this usage as being, in that work, indicated to be " one of the worst wrongs
inflicted on the long-suffering degree." According to the statement of a certain
Baronet (10 Sep. 1900), " the words *Bart* and *Barts.* cannot be recognised as
anything but very impure English," but, as he also states in the previous sentence
that they " do not exist," his sense of impurity seems supernatural The compiler of the present work is no philologist, and consequently is not deeply moved
in the matter, but for the sake of courtesy he is willing to comply with the
suggestion as under, made to him, 19 Sep 1900, by the author of the abovenamed
valuable work, " Francis W Pixley, F S A , Registrar to the Honourable Society of
the Baronetage " —" It would be gratifying to this Representative Society if you
would instruct your printers and publishers to refrain throughout the work from
printing the abbreviation *Bart* for Baronet, and to substitute *Bt* in cases where
it is desired not to print the title at full length "

(^b) The eldest son, Alexander Macdonell, was killed in a duel, 1677, having had
an only son, Randal, who *d.* young This Alexander is sometimes mistaken for his
namesake, generally known as " Coll. Kittagh," who was killed at the battle of
Knockranos, 13 Nov 1647 [O'Donovan's *Annals of the Four Masters*]

STAPLES

cr 18 July 1628 (ᵃ)

I   1628   " THOMAS STAPLES, Esq , of Lisson [*i e*, LISSANE], co
Tyrone,"(ᵃ) and of Faughanvale, co Londonderry, 5th s of Alexander
STAPLES, of Yate Court, co Gloucester, was by patent dat 18 July 1628, at Dublin
(the Privy Seal being dat 4 June previous, at Westm.) *cr a Baronet* [I], as above,(ᵃ)
being *Knighted* 6 Aug following , was of the Middle Temple , Sheriff of co Tyrone,
1640   He *m.* before Sep 1623, Charity, only da. and h of Sir Baptist JONES, of
Vintnerstown, co. Londonderry, by Elizabeth, da of Robert LEE, of Dublin   He *d*
31 May 1653.   Inq p m

II   1653.   SIR BAPTIST STAPLES, Baronet [I 1628], of Lissane
and Faughanvale aforesaid, s and h , *suc to the Baronetcy* in 1653.
He *d.* s p (probably unm), June 1672   Will dat 30 May 1672, pr 19 March 1673/4,
at Derry

III   1672   SIR ALEXANDER STAPLES, Baronet [I 1628], of Lissane
and Faughanvale aforesaid, br and h , Sheriff of co Tyrone, 1661 ,
M P [I] for Strabane, 1661, till expelled, 14 Nov 1665, for the plot against the Duke
of Ormond, the then Viceroy [I]   He *suc. to the Baronetcy*, June 1672, and enjoyed
it only a few months   He *m.* Elizabeth   He *d.* s p m   Will dat 26 May 1665, pr
5 March 1672/3, in Prerog Court [I], that of his widow was pr there 1681

IV.   1673?   SIR ROBERT STAPLES, Baronet [I 1628], of Lissane aforesaid, br. and h , *suc to the Baronetcy* about 1673 ; M P [I] for
Dungannon, 1692 95, and for Clogher, 1695-99 ; Sheriff of co Tyrone, 1703   He *m* ,
in or before 1684, Mary, 1st da. of John VESEY, Archbishop of Tuam [1678—1716],
by his 1st wife, Rebecca.   He *d* 21 Nov 1714   Will pr 1714, in Prerog Court. [I].

V.   1714   SIR JOHN STAPLES, Baronet [I 1628], of Lissane aforesaid, *b* 22 Sep 1684, ed at Trin Coll , Dublin : B A , 1706 , M A ,
1709 ; *suc to the Baronetcy*, 21 Nov. 1714 , in Holy Orders , Preb of Cloneamery,
in diocese of Ossory, 1728 30   He *m* Mary, widow of Josias HAYDOCK, of Kilkenny,
da of (—) GOSLIN   He *d.* s p m. in 1730.   Admon , 1 Oct 1730, in Prerog Court
[I]   The will of his widow was pr 1748, in the Prerog Court [I]

VI   1730   SIR ALEXANDER STAPLES, Baronet [I 1628], of Dublin,
next surv. br. and h male, being 4th s of the 4th Bt , *b* 11 June
1693 ; ed at Trin Coll , Dublin , B A., 1714 , *suc. to the Baronetcy* in 1730   He *m*
(Lic., Dublin, Sep 1735) Abigail, da and h of Thomas TOWNLEY, of co Cavan
He *d* 6 July 1741, and was bur. at St. Mary's, Dublin.   His will pr 1741, in Prerog
Court [I]   That of his widow was pr there 1748

VII   1741.   SIR ROBERT STAPLES, Baronet [I. 1628], of Dunmore,
Queens County, only s and h , *b* 1 Aug 1740 , *suc to the Baronetcy*
in his 1st year ; was B A , Dublin, 1761 , was Sheriff of co Tyrone, 1763, and of
Queens County, 1776   He *m* firstly (Lic 6 Oct. 1761), Alicia, da of Rev Thomas
STAPLES, of Lissane (3d s of the 1st Baronet), by Grace, da of John HOUSTON, of
Castle Stewart, co. Tyrone.   She *d* s p m   He *m* secondly, in or before 1771, Mary,
widow of Chambre Brabazon PONSONBY, 1st da. of Sir William BARKER, 3d Baronet
[1676], of Kilcooley Abbey, co Tipperary, by Mary, da. of Valentine QUIN.   She *d.*
in 1773.   He *m.* thirdly, 29 Feb 1776, Jane, 3d da of John Denny (VESEY), 1st
BARON KNAPTON [I], by Elizabeth, da. of William BROWNLOW, of Lurgan.   He *d*
1816   His widow *d.* 1822.

(ᵃ) See p 249, notes " a " and " b "   G. D Burtchaell (see vol i, p. 223, note " a ")
supplies the succession of the 2d and 3d Baronets, (omitted in the Baronetages of
Playfair, etc., and, till supplied as above in 1900, in that of Burke), and many other
particulars as to this family

VIII. 1816   SIR ROBERT STAPLES, Baronet [I 1628], of Dunmore,
aforesaid, 2d but only surv s and h ,(a) by 2d wife, b 13 Feb 1772,
suc. to the Baronetcy, 1816 ; Sheriff of Queens County, 1819   He d unm 24 June
1832.

IX. 1832.   SIR THOMAS STAPLES, Baronet [I 1628], of Lissane
aforesaid, cousin and h male, being 1st s and h of the Rt Hon John
STAPLES (many years M P [I] for co. Antrim), by his 2d wife, Henrietta, da of
Richard (MOLESWORTH), 3d VISCOUNT MOLESWORTH OF SWORDS [I], which John (who
d 22 Dec 1820, aged 86) was s and h of the Rev Thomas STAPLES, Rector of
Derryloran (d. Aug 1762, aged 60), br of the 5th and 6th Baronets, and 5th s of the
4th Baronet   He was b 31 July 1775, in Palace row, Rutland sq , Dublin , was ed
at Eton and Trin Coll , Dublin , B A , 1796 ; LL B and LL D , 1807 , M P [I] for
Knocktopher, co. Kilkenny, 1799-1800 ,(b) Barrister, Dublin, 1802 , King's Counsel,
1822, and King's Advocate in the Admiralty Court [I] till his death ; *suc. to the
Baronetcy*, 24 June 1832 , Bencher of King's Inns, Dublin, 1833   He m 27 Oct.
1813, Catherine, da of Rev John HAWKINS, 1st s of James HAWKINS, Bishop of Raphoe,
by Anne, sister of Sir Henry Conyngham MONTGOMERY, 1st Baronet [1808], da of
Alexander MONTGOMERY, of the Hall, co Donegal   He d. s.p 14 May 1865, at 11
Merrion square, Dublin, in his 90th year.   His widow d 20 Jan 1872

X   1865.   SIR NATHANIEL ALEXANDER STAPLES, Baronet [I 1628],
of Lissane aforesaid, nephew and h , being 2d but 1st surv s and
h of the Rev John Molesworth STAPLES, Rector of Lissane and Upper Melville by
Annie, da. of Nathaniel ALEXANDER, Bishop of Meath, which John (who d 4 April
1859, aged 82), was next br to the late Baronet   He was b 1 May 1817, at Lissane ,
was ed at Addiscombe College , was sometime 1834-54, in the Bengal Artillery,
retiring as Captain , *suc to the Baronetcy*, 14 May 1865   He m , 27 Oct 1844,
Elizabeth Lindsay, only da and h of James HEAD, Capt in East Indian Service, by
Cecilia Maria, da of the Hon Robert LINDSAY, 2d s of James, 5th EARL OF
BALCARRES [S]   He d 12 March 1899, at Lissane aforesaid, in his 82d year

XI   1899.   SIR JOHN MOLESWORTH STAPLES, Baronet [I 1628], of
Lissane aforesaid, 1st s and h , b 29 Dec 1848, at Dumdum, in
the East Indies ; *suc. to the Baronetcy*, 12 March 1899

Family Estates.—These, in 1883, consisted of 3,078 acres in co Tyrone, 1,457
in co Dublin, and 990 in co Londonderry   *Total*, 5,525 acres, worth £4,018 a year
Principal Seat —Lissane, near Cookstown, co Tyrone

BOURKE, *or* BURKE
cr 2 Aug 1628 (c)

I.   1628   " ULICK BOURKE, Esq, of Glinsk, co Galway," s
and h of Edmund BOURKE, of Imlaghvodagh, co Roscommon, by
Ellis, 1st da of Iriel O'FERRALL BOY, of Mornine, co Longford, which Edmund was
s and h ap of Sir Hubert BOURKE, of Glinsk aforesaid, suc his said grandfather in
1598, when aged 4 years (though deprived of part of his estate by his uncle, Festus
BOURKE), and was cr. a Baronet, as above, by patent dat at Dublin, 2 Aug 1628, the
Privy Seal being dat. at Westm 27 June previous (c)   He was M.P [I.] for co.
Galway, 1639-48   He, in 1660, though apparently then dead, was restored to his
estate as an " Ensignman " by the Act of Settlement   He m firstly Katharine,
6th da of Theobald (DILLON), 1st Viscount DILLON OF COSTELLO GALLEN [I], by
Eleanor, da. of William TUITE, of Tuitestown, co Westmeath.   He m. secondly,
Jennet, da of (—) BROWNE   She, who survived him, d s p.   Her Admon., 1 July
1679, in Prerog Court [I]

(a) William the 1st s , b 1 Feb. 1771 , d 9 June 1773
(b) At his death in 1865 he was the last surviving of the members of the last Irish
Parliament
(c) See p 249, notes " a " and " b."

II.   1660 ?   SIR EDMUND BOURKE, *or* BURKE, Baronet [I 1628], of
Glinsk aforesaid, and of Garvagh, co Galway, s and h, *suc. to the*
Baronetcy on the death of his father   He was restored to his estate, as a
" Nominee," by the Act of Explanation   He *m.* firstly (—), da of (—) FLEMING, of
Slane   He *m* secondly, Honora, da of Col John KELLY, of Skreen   He *m* thirdly,
April 1674, Mary, 2d da of Nicholas NETTERVILLE, of Lecarrow, co Galway, by
Cecilia, da of Sir Redmond BURKE.   His will dat 20 Aug 1676, pr 5 Feb 1686/7
in Prerog Court [I]   His widow *m* Roger O'SHAGNESSY, of Castlegar, co Galway

III.   1686 ?   SIR ULICK BURKE, Baronet [I 1628], of Glinsk aforesaid,
only s and h by 1st wife, *suc to the Baronetcy* on the death of his
father   He was M P. [I] for co. Galway, in the Parl of James II, in 1689 (whose
cause he espoused), and was included in the articles of Limerick   He *m* Ismay,
4th da of the abovenamed Col John KELLY, of Skreen, by Ismay, da of Sir William
HILL, of Allenstown, co Meath.   He *d. s p* 1708

IV.   1708   SIR JOHN BURKE, Baronet [I 1628], of Milford, co
Galway and of Glinsk aforesaid, br. of the half blood and h, being
only s of the 2d Baronet by his 2d wife , *suc to the Baronetcy* in 1708   He *m* Jane,
da of Theobald (DILLON), 7th VISCOUNT DILLON OF COSTELLO GALLEN [I], by
Mary, da of Sir Henry TALBOT, of Templeoge, co Dublin   His will dat. June
1721, pr. 1724, in the Prerog. Court [I]

V.   1722 ?   SIR FESTUS [FEIAGH] BURKE, Baronet [I 1628], of
Glinsk aforesaid, 1st s and h., *suc. to the Baronetcy* between 1721
and 1724   He *m* (settl 23 Nov 1708) Lætitia, 1st da of John (DE BURGH), 9th
EARL OF CLANRICARDE [I], by Bridget, da of James TALBOT, of Temple Oge, co
Dublin   He *d s p*   His widow *d.* 29 June 1740   Will pr 1743, in Prerog Court [I]

VI   1730 ?   SIR THEOBALD BURKE, Baronet [I. 1628], of Glinsk aforesaid, br and h , *suc to the Baronetcy* on the death of his brother
He was found to be a lunatic   He *d* unm.

VII.   1740 ?   SIR HENRY BURKE, Baronet [I 1628], of Glinsk aforesaid,
br and h., *suc to the Baronetcy* on the death of his brother.   He *m*
Cicely, 1st da of Patrick NETTERVILLE, of Longford, co. Galway, by Margaret, sister
of James FERRALL, of Kilmore, co Roscommon   He *d* 15 March 1747/8.   Will
dat 25 May 1747, pr 17 July 1756, in Prerog Court [I]

VIII.   1748.   SIR ULICK BURKE, Baronet [I 1628], of Glinsk aforesaid,
s. and h , *suc to the Baronetcy*, 15 March 1747/8.   He *m* , May 1753,
Elizabeth, da. of Remigius O'CARROLL, of Ardagh, co Galway, by Susanna, da of
Robert CARROLL, of Emmett, co Tipperary   He *d* 11 April 1759   His widow *m*
her husband's first cousin, Sir John BURKE,[a] afterwards of Glinsk, Knight of St
Jago in Spain (who *d.* 1781), by whom she was grandmother of the 10th and
11th Baronets.

IX   1759.   SIR HENRY JOHN BURKE, Baronet [I. 1628], of Glinsk
aforesaid, only s. and h , *suc to the Baronetcy* on his father's death
He was declared an idiot, and his estate was settled by Act of Parl. on the next heir
male, viz., Sir John BURKE, his stepfather, abovenamed   He *d* unm in April 1814.

X.   1814   SIR JOHN IGNATIUS BURKE, Baronet [I 1628], of Glinsk
aforesaid, cousin and h male, being s and h of Rickard BURKE, of
Keelogues, co Galway, and Glinsk, by Joanna Harriet, 1st da of Joseph BLAKE, of
Ardfry, co Galway, which Rickard (who *d* in or before Dec. 1791), was s and h of
Sir John BURKE,[a] of Glinsk, Knight of St Jago in Spain, abovementioned (*d* 1781),
who was s and h of Rickard BURKE, yr. br of the 5th, 6th, and 7th Baronets, and
4th s. of the 4th Baronet.   He was *b* 19 March 1784, suc his father in the Glinsk
estate, when a minor, and *suc to the Baronetcy* in 1814.   He *m* firstly, 26 Oct 1816,
at the British Embassy at Paris, Sydney, sister to Hughes BALL.   She *d* 1830
He *m.* secondly, April 1834, Sophia, 1st da of William DAWSON, of Settle, co York,
and of St Leonard's Hill, Berks   He *d s p m* , 1845   His widow *d s p*, 6 May 1862

(a) This Sir John Burke appears to have considered his stepson, the 9th Baronet,
as legally defunct, and to have accordingly assumed that Baronetcy   In his mar. lic.
[I.], 1 Dec 1780, he is called " Baronet," as also elsewhere.

XI 1845   Sir Joseph Burke, Baronet [I 1628], of Glinsk aforesaid, br and h, b 31 Jan. 1786, at Ardfry, *suc to the Baronetcy* in
1845. He m, 9 Aug 1816, Louisa, 1st da. of Sir William Manners, *afterwards*
Talmash, 1st Baronet [1793], *styled* Lord Huntingtower (s and h ap. of Louisa, *suo
jure* Countess of Disart [S]), by Catherine Rebecca, da of Francis Grey, of
Lehena co. Cork   She, who was b 1791, d 18 April 1830   He d. at Nice, 30 Oct.
1865.

XII 1865.   Sir John Lionel Burke, Baronet [I 1628], of Glinsk
aforesaid, only s. and h   b 26 Nov. 1818 at Glinsk, *suc. to the
Baronetcy*, 30 Oct. 1865   He d unm, 21 July 1884, aged 65

XIII 1884.   Sir Theobald Hubert Burke, Baronet [I 1628], of
Glinsk aforesaid, cousin and h male, being the 4th but 1st surv. of the
seven sons[a] of William Burke, of Knocknagur, co Galway, by Fanny Xaveria, only
da of Thomas Tucker, of Brook Lodge, Sussex, which William (who d 1877, aged
83) was s and h of Rickard Burke, of Keelogues, co Galway (d. Aug. 1819), s and
h of William Burke, of Keelogues aforesaid, the yst. br [b] of Rickard Burke, abovementioned, of Glinsk, father of the 10th and 11th Baronets   He was b 25 March
1833, was sometime an officer in the 18th Regiment, serving in the Crimean War
and Indian Mutiny, retiring as Lieut. Col., *suc to the Baronetcy*, 21 July 1884.

COLCLOUGH, *or* COCKLEY:

cr. 21 July 1628 ,[c]

ex 22 Sep 1687 ,

but *assumed* from about 1790 to 1794

I. 1628.   "Adam Cockley [i e, Colclough], Esq., of Tinterne
[Abbey], co Wexford," s and h. of Sir Thomas Colclough, of Tintern
Abbey aforesaid, by his 1st wife, Martha, 4th da. of Adam Loftus, Archbishop
of Dublin, was b probably about 1590, suc his father (who d, aged 60) 23 Aug.
1624, and was cr a Baronet [I], as above, by Privy Seal dat at Westm, 21 July
1628, no patent being enrolled [c]   He m in or before 1624, Alice, da of Sir Robert
Rich, a Master in Chancery, in London   He d. 4 April, and was bur. 1 June 1637
in the Church of Tintern.   Funeral certif [I]   Will dat 4 April, pr. 3 May 1637
in Prerog. Court [I]

II 1637   Sir Cæsar Colclough, Baronet [I 1628], of Tintern
Abbey aforesaid, only s and h, b 1624, *suc to the Baronetcy* in 1637,
was M P for Newcastle under Lyne, 1661-79   He m, 5 June 1647, at St Bartholo-
mew the Less, London, Frances, da of Sir Francis Clerke, of Weston, and Tame,
Oxon.   She d before him   He d. 22 June 1684, at Tintern and was bur. there
Will pr. 1684 in Prerog Court [I].

III 1684,   Sir Cæsar Colclough, Baronet [I 1628], of Tintern
to   Abbey aforesaid, only s and h, b. about 1650, matric at Oxford
1687.   (Ch Ch) 5 Aug 1668, aged 18   He d unm 22 Sep. 1687 at
Tintern, and was bur there, when the *Baronetcy* became *extinct*.[d]

---

[a] The second of these sons, Thomas Henry Burke, Under Secretary of State for
Ireland, was barbarously murdered in Phœnix Park, Dublin, 6 May 1882, aged 52,
being at that date heir presumptive to this Baronetcy
[b] There was, however, an intermediate brother, Michael Burke, who had two
sons, James and William, whose issue male, if any, would come before that of this
William.
[c] See p. 249, notes "a" and "b"
[d] The estates devolved on his sister, Margaret, who m twice, but d. s p. 1722,
when they devolved on Col Cæsar Colclough, descended from a br of the 1st
Baronet, whose grandson *assumed* the Baronetcy, as stated in the text.

1766?
to
1794.
"SIR VESEY COLCLOUGH, Baronet" [I 1628], of Tintern Abbey aforesaid, *assumed this Baronetcy* (on a supposed right), probably on or soon after 15 April 1766, at which date he suc his grandfather, Col Cæsar COLCLOUGH, on whom that estate had devolved in 1722,(a) and who was great grandson and heir of Sir Dudley COLCLOUGH, a younger br. of the 1st Baronet. He was M P [I] for co Wexford, 1766 90, and is described as a "Baronet" in the Commons Journals [I] 1783 90, but only as "Esquire" when M P [I] for Enniscorthy, 1790-94 He *d.* 8 July 1794, aged 49. His will, as "Baronet," dat 12 June 1794, pr 3 March 1798, in Prerog. Court [I] After his death, however, though he left male issue (*extinct* 23 Aug 1842), the assumption of this Baronetcy appears to have ceased

---

ESMOND, *or* ESMONDE:
cr 28 Jan. 1628/9 (b)

I. 1629   "THOMAS ESMOND, Esq, afterwards Knt, of Clonegall, co Wexford," illegit s (c) of Laurence (ESMOND), BARON ESMOND of Limerick [I], by (—), sister of (—) O'FLAHERTY, of Connaught, was cr a *Baronet*, as above, by patent dat at Dublin, 28 Jan 1628/9, the Privy Seal being dat. 13 Aug. previous at Southwicke, Hants,(h) where (three days later), 16 Aug 1628, he had been *Knighted* He was M P. [I] for Enniscorthy 1641, till expelled, 22 June 1642 He was a Royalist and was General of Horse in the service of Charles I On the death of his father, 26 March 1645, he is said to have succeeded to a considerable estate He *m* firstly (pardon, 19 March 1629), Ellice, DOWAGER BARONESS CAHER [I], da of Sir John FITZGERALD, of Dromana, co Waterford She *d* 16 Jan 1644 Funeral entry [I] He *m* secondly, Joane, widow of Theobald PURCELL, of Loughmoe, co. Tipperary, formerly wife of George BAGENAL, of Dunleckney, co Carlow (who *d* 17 Sep 1625), 5th da of Walter (BUTLER), EARL OF ORMONDE AND OSSORY [I], by Helena, da of Edmund (BUTLER), 2d VISCOUNT MOUNTGARRET [I] She was living when he, she, and his son, Laurence, were "transplanted," 22 Aug. 1656. He was restored to his estate, as a "Nominee," by the Act of Explanation, and was living, 1664, at Dunleckney aforesaid

II. 1665?   SIR LAURENCE ESMONDE, Baronet [I 1629], of Huntington Castle, co Carlow (which he built), 1st s and h by 1st wife, *suc to the Baronetcy* on the death of his father, was Sheriff of co Carlow, 1687. He *m* firstly Lucia, 1st da of Col. Richard BUTLER, of Kilcash, co Tipperary (br of James, 1st DUKE OF ORMONDE), by Frances, da of Mervyn (TOUCHET), 1st EARL OF CASTLEHAVEN [I] She *d* at Clonegal 17 and was bur 21 April 1685 at Limbrick Funeral entry [I] He *m* secondly, Lucy, da of Charles KAVANAGH, of Carrickduff, co Carlow, by Mary, da of Brian KAVANAGH, of Borris, in the same county He *d* 1688 Admon. 22 Oct. 1688 to his widow She *m*, about 1691, Col. the Hon Richard BUTLER, 2d s of Edward, 2d VISCOUNT GALMOY [I.].

(a) See p 254, note "d"
(b) See p 249, notes "a" and "b"
(c) As "Sir Thomas Esmonde, of Faralstown, co Wexford, *Knt and Baronet*, sonne to the said Lord Esmond," he signs the funeral certificate of the latter, whose wife is therein stated to have been Ellis, da of Walter Butler, of Nodstone co. Tipperary, by whom he had no issue [Original certificate in Ulster's office] The contemporary author of "An Aphorismical Discovery of Treasonable Faction" refers to him as "a spurious son of Lord Esmond," whose widow also refers, 19 June 1645, to her late husband's "illegitimate son" The extinction of the peerage, as also the admon to his father's estate which was granted to a nephew, 6 April 1646, militates against there having been a *lawful* son. [*Ex inform.* G. D Burtchaell]

III. 1688   SIR LAURENCE ESMONDE, Baronet [I 1629], of Huntington Castle aforesaid, 1st s and h by 1st wife , was a Privy Councillor [I] to James II ; *suc to the Buronetcy* in 1688   He *m.*, in 1703, Jane, da.
of Matthew FORDE, of Coolgreany, co Wexford, by Margaret, da of Sir George
HAMILTON, 1st Baronet [I. 1662], of Donalong, co Tyrone. His admon. 20 June 1717
in Prerog Court [I.].

IV.   1717?   SIR LAURENCE ESMONDE, Baronet [I 1629], of Huntington Castle aforesaid, only s and h , *suc. to the Baronetcy* on the death
of his father   He *d* unm 1738   Admon 26 Feb 1739, in Prerog Court [I]

V   1738   SIR JOHN ESMONDE, Baronet [I 1629], of Huntington
Castle aforesaid, uncle and h , *suc to the Baronetcy* in 1738. He *m.*
(Lic Cork, 22 Oct. 1742) Helen, da of William GALWEY, of Lota, co Cork, by Mary,
da. of John BUTLER, of Westcourt, co Kilkenny   He *d* s.p.m , 30 June 1758.   Will
pr 1760, in Prerog Court [I.]

VI.   1758.   SIR WALTER ESMONDE, Baronet [I 1629], of Creggi, co
Tipperary, only surv br and h male, *suc to the Baronetcy*, 30 June
1758   He *m.*, after Jan 1722, Joanna, widow of James BUTLER, of Caherbane, co
Clare, 2d da of Theobald (BUTLER), 7th BARON CAHIR [I], by his 1st wife, Mary, 1st
da of Sir Redmond EVERARD, 2d Baronet [I 1622]   He *d* s p m , Feb. 1766, at
Creggi, and was *bur* at Limbrick   Will pr. 1769, in Prerog Court [I]

VII.   1766   SIR JAMES ESMONDE, Baronet [I 1629], of Ballynastragh,
co Wexford, cousin and h male, being s and h of Laurence
ESMONDE, of the same, by Elizabeth, da of Henry BROWNRIGG, of Wingfield, co.
Wexford, which Laurence (who *d* from a fall, when out hunting, aged 84), was s
and h of James ESMONDE of Ballynastragh aforesaid, 4th s. of the 1st Baronet.   He
was *b* 23 April 1701, and was, when young, an officer in the French service   He *m*
Ellice, da. and h of Thomas WHITE, of Pembrokestown, co Waterford, by Catharine,
da of Arthur DUIGNAN   He *suc to the Baronetcy* in Feb 1766, but *d.* two days
afterwards, and was *bur* the same day as his predecessor, at Limbrick   Admon.,
wherein he is styled "James Esmonde, *Esq*," 22 July 1767, to his widow.

VIII.   1766.   SIR THOMAS ESMONDE, Baronet [I 1629], of Ballynastragh
aforesaid, 1st s and h , *suc to the Baronetcy* in Feb 1766   He *m.*
firstly, in March 1776, at Arran Chapel, co. Dublin, Catherine Mary, da and h of
Myles DOWDALL, of Clown, co Meath   He *m* secondly, Lætitia, da of (—) HILL,
niece and h of Nicholas DEVEREUX, of Ringville, co. Kilkenny   He *d* s p , in
London, 19 Dec 1803   Will pr 1805

IX   1803   SIR THOMAS ESMONDE, Baronet [I. 1629], of Ballynastragh, aforesaid, nephew and h , being s and h. of John ESMONDE,
by Helen, da and coheir of Bartholomew CALLAN, or O'CALLAN, of Osberstown
House, co Kildare, which John, who was slain in the Irish Rebellion of 1798, was 2d
s of the 7th Baronet.   He was *b* 10 Dec 1786 , suc. to the Baronetcy in 1803 ; was
M P for Wexford, 1841 47 , P C. [I.], 1847   He *m* firstly, Mary, only da of
E PAYNE   She *d.* 7 March 1840   He *m.* secondly, 16 April 1856, Sophia Maria,
widow of Hamilton Knox Grogan MORGAN, of Johnstown Castle, co Wexford, da of
Ebenezer Radford ROWE, of Ballyharty, co. Wexford.   She *d* 22 Nov 1867, at
Johnstown Castle, in her 62d year   He *d* s p 31 Dec 1868, at Johnstown Castle,
aged 82, and was *bur* 5 Jan 1869 in the cemetery in Marlborough street, Dublin.

X. 1868.   SIR JOHN ESMONDE, Baronet [I 1629], of Ballynastragh, aforesaid, nephew and h , being s. and h. of James ESMONDE, of Pembrokestown, co Waterford, Lieut. R.N , by Anna Maria, da. of James MURPHY, of Ringmahon castle, co. Cork, which James ESMONDE, who d. 4 Oct 1842, was yr. br. of the late Baronet. He was b 16 May 1826 , ed at Trin. Coll , Dublin , B A., 1848 , admitted to Lincoln's Inn, 6 May 1848, aged 22; Barrister (King's Inns, Dublin), 1850 , was M P. for co Waterford, 1852-76 , Sheriff of co. Wexford, 1866 ; one of the Lords of the Treasury for a few weeks (2 June to 12 July) in 1866 , *suc to the Baronetcy*, 31 Dec 1868 , was Sheriff of co Wicklow, 1875 ; sometime Lieut. Col. of the Waterford Artillery Militia, 1875. He m 11 April 1861, Louisa, 4th da. and coheir of Henry GRATTAN, of Tinnehinch, co. Wicklow (s. of the Rt. Hon. Henry GRATTAN), by Mary O'Kelly, da and h of Philip Whitfield HARVEY, of Grove House, co. Dublin He d, 9 Dec. 1876, at Ballynastragh His widow d. 31 Jan. 1880, of bronchitis, at Kensington.

XI 1876   SIR THOMAS HENRY GRATTAN ESMONDE, Baronet [I. 1629], of Ballynastragh aforesaid, 1st s and h , b. 21 Sep. 1862, at Pau, in France ; ed at Oscott College , *suc to the Baronetcy*, 9 Dec. 1876 , M P for South div. of co Dublin, 1885-92, and for West Kerry since 1892 , Sheriff for co Waterford, 1887, being, however, immediately superseded , Chairman of the co Wexford County Council ; Chamberlain to the Pope at Rome. He m , 21 July 1891, Alice Barbara, da. of Patrick DONOVAN, of Frogmore, near Tralee, co. Kerry, br. of Sir Henry DONOVAN.

Family Estates—These, in 1883, consisted of 3,533 acres in co. Wexford ; 2,088 in co Wicklow , 717 in co Tipperary , 701 in co. Waterford ; 629 in co. Kilkenny, and 389 in King's County   *Total*, 8,057 acres, worth £4,563 a year, besides a rental of £264 in co Longford, shared into two others   *Principal Seats*—Ballynastragh, near Gorey, co Wexford, and Glenwood, near Rathdrum, co. Wicklow.

MAC MAHON :
cr 15 Aug 1628 ,(ª)
ex , presumably, about 1680.

I. 1628.   " TIEGE MAC-MAHON, Esq ," s. and h. of Terence, *otherwise* Tirlagh roe MAC MAHON, of Clondirrala, co Clare (Sheriff of that county, 1609), by his 1st wife, Any, da of Sir Donal O'BRIEN, of Duagh, co. Clare, had livery of his estate, 24 March 1629, for a fine of £72 10s Irish ; was cr a *Baronet* [I], as above,(ª) by Privy Seal dat at Southwick, Hants, 15 Aug 1628,(ª) no patent being enrolled,(ᵇ) and was *Knighted* 14 Dec. following (ᶜ) He m. Mary, 3d da. of Dermot O'RYAN

II. 1650 ?   SIR TURLOGH MAC-MAHON, Baronet [I 1628], s. and h.,
   to   *suc to the Baronetcy* on the death of his father. He m Elinor, 1st
  1680 ?   da of Col the Hon. Garret FITZMAURICE (2d s of Thomas, LORD KERRY [I]), by Lucia, relict of John ANKETILL, of Newmarket, co. Cork, da of Mervyn (TOUCHET), 2d EARL OF CASTLEHAVEN [I.] She d s p On his death [Qy. about 1680 ?] the *Baronetcy* is presumed to have become *extinct*

(ª) See p. 249, notes " a " and " b "
(ᵇ) The patent of Esmond, of which the date of the Privy Seal was 13 Aug 1628 (2 days before this date), was dated 28 Jan 1628/9, and that of Magrath, of which the Privy Seal was 18 Aug 1628 (3 days after this date), was 5 June 1629. The date of the Privy Seal for Mac-Mahon was, however, 25 (not 15) Aug. 1628, according to the Calendar of State Papers [I.], *temp* Car. I.
(ᶜ) The pedigree was, in 1625, registered in Ulster's office, at which date the father of the 1st Baronet was living.

2 K

BUTLER :
cr 16 Aug. 1628 (ᵃ)

I. 1628.   "THOMAS BUTLER, of Cloughgrenan, co. Carlow, Esq.,"
an illegit s (ᵇ) of Sir Edmund BUTLER, of Cloughgrenan aforesaid,
and of Roscrea, co Tipperary (who was 2d s of James, 9th EARL OF ORMOND [I] ;
was Sheriff of co Carlow, 1612 and 1622, and was cr. a Baronet [I], as above, the
Privy Seal being dat. at Southwick, 16 Aug. 1628,(ᵃ) but the date of the patent,
which was not enrolled, being unknown   He was M P [I] for co. Carlow, 1634-35
and 1639 till his death. He m (settlmt. 3 July 1618) Anne, widow of Nicholas
BAGENAL, da of Sir Thomas COLCLOUGH, of Tyntern Abbey, co. Wexford, by
Martha, da. of Adam LOFTUS, Archbishop of Dublin. He was living 1639.

II. 1640?   SIR EDMUND BUTLER, Baronet [L 1628], of Cloughgrenan
aforesaid, and of Ballybar, co Carlow, s. and h., admitted to Lincoln's
Inn, 5 June 1637, after which date he suc to the Baronetcy on the death of his father
He m Juliana, da of Barnard HYDE, of Shinfield, Berks   He was bur at Cloydagh (ᶜ)
Admon 1653 to his widow. She d at Ballybar 1 and was bur 4 Jan 1683, at
Cloydagh aforesaid   Funeral certificate in Ulster's office   Will dat. 10 July 1683,
pr 10 Jan 1683/4, at Leighlin.

III. 1650?   SIR THOMAS BUTLER, Baronet [L 1628], of Garryhunden,
co. Carlow, s and h., suc to the Baronetcy on the death of his father.
He was Sheriff of co Carlow, 1670 and 1691 ; M P [I] thereof, 1692-95, 1695-99, and
1703 till death. He m firstly, Jane, da of Richard BOYLE, Bishop of Ferns and
Leighlin [1666-82], by Abigail, da of (—) WORTH   He m. secondly, July 1700, Jane,
widow of John REYNOLDS, da of Capt. Edward POTTINGER. He d Jan or Feb 1703.
Admon , 21 July 1705 in Prerog. Court [I] to his brother, James   His widow, by
whom he had no issue, m Agmondisham VESEY, of Lucan, co. Dublin.

IV. 1703   SIR PIERCE BUTLER, Baronet [I 1628], of Garryhunden
aforesaid, s and h by 1st wife : admitted to Lincoln's Inn, 14 Jan
1691/2 , suc to the Baronetcy in Jan or Feb 1703   He was M P [I] for co. Carlow
(two Parls), 1703-14 ; P C [I], 7 June 1712   He m (settl 8 Dec. 1697), Anne, da
of Joshua GALLIARD, of Edmonton, co Midx , by Anne, da of William WAKEFIELD.
His will dat 10 Nov. 1731, pr 1732, in Prerog Court [I.]

V. 1732?   SIR RICHARD BUTLER, Baronet [I. 1628], of Garryhunden
aforesaid, nephew and h , being s and h of James BUTLER, by his 1st
wife, Frances, relict of Sir John PARKER, of Fermoyle, co Longford, da. of Sir
Edward ABNEY, which James (whose will, dat. 23 Aug 1720, was pr. 14 March 1723,
in the Prerog Court [I]) was next br. of the late Baronet   He was b. 1699, and suc
to the Baronetcy about 1732. He was M P [I] for co. Carlow, 1729 60   He m in
1728, Henrietta, da. and coheir of Henry PERCY, of Seskin, co Wicklow (s of Sir
Anthony PERCY, Lord Mayor of Dublin, 1699), by Eliza, da and h. of William PAUL,
of Moyle, co. Carlow. She d. a widow 14 Jan 1794.

(ᵃ) See page 249, notes "a " and " b."
(ᵇ) Since the publication, in 1880, of the Calendar of the State Papers, Ireland,
1615-25, his parentage has ceased to be a matter of conjecture   There was considerable litigation between him and the representatives of his legitimate brother,
Theobald, Viscount Butler of Tulleophelim [I], who d s p. in Jan. 1613. Tulleophelim is part of the estate of these Baronets, and the bordure that surrounds their
arms is an indication of their illegitimacy.
(ᶜ) He, probably, is not identical with Sir Edmund Butler, Knight (in no place
called Baronet), who was killed, 4 Oct. 1649, at the taking of Wexford by Cromwell
That Edmund, who possibly was the " Sir (—) Butler, Irish," Knighted at Oxford,
15 July 1640, was a Roman Catholic, whereas the Cloughgrenan family, from the 1st
to the present Baronet, have always been Protestants   [Ex inform. G. D Burtchaell]

VI 1768?   SIR THOMAS BUTLER, Baronet [I 1628], of Garryhunden
aforesaid, s and h, *suc. to the Baronetcy* on the death of his father.
He was M.P [I] for co Carlow, 1761-68, and for Portarlington, 1771-72. He *m.*
(settl 19 June 1759), Dorothea, only child of Edward BAYLY, D D, Archdeacon of
Ardfert and Dean of St Patrick's, Dublin (2d s of Sir Edward BAYLY, 1st Baronet
[I 1730]), by Catharine, da and coheir of James PRICE, of Hollymount, co. Down
He *d* 7 Oct 1772   Will pr 1772 in Prerog Court [I.]   She *d.* a widow, at Bath,
1824, aged 81, and was *bur.* at Walcot, Somerset. Will pr 1824.

VII. 1772.   SIR RICHARD BUTLER, Baronet [I 1628], of Garryhunden
aforesaid, s and h, *b* 14 July 1761, *suc. to the Baronetcy* on the
death of his father   He was M P. [I and UK] for co Carlow, 1783-90, 1796-97,
1798-1800, and 1801-02, Sheriff of that county, 1784   He *m* 23 Aug. 1782, Sarah
Maria, only da of Thomas Worth NEWENHAM, of Coolmore, co. Cork, by Elizabeth,
da of William DAWSON, of Castle Dawson, co. Londonderry. He *d* 16 Jan 1817

VIII. 1817.   SIR THOMAS BUTLER, Baronet [I 1628], of Garryhunden
and of Ballintemple, co Carlow, s and h, *b.* 23 Oct. 1783, sometime
Capt in 6th Dragoon Guards, *suc. to the Baronetcy*, 16 Jan 1817; Sheriff of co
Carlow, 1818. He *m* 30 Jan. 1812, Frances, 4th da. of John Graham CLARKE, of
Fenham, co Northumberland, and Sutton, co York, by Arabella, da. and coheir of
Roger ALTHAM, of Mark Hall, Essex. He *d.* 9 Nov 1861, and was *bur* at Clonmulsh,
aged 78.   M I.   His widow *d.* 30 Aug 1868, at Westwood Park, aged 78.

IX. 1861.   SIR RICHARD PIERCE BUTLER, Baronet [I 1628], of
Ballintemple and Garryhunden aforesaid, s and h, *b* 4 March 1813,
suc. to the Baronetcy, 9 Nov 1861, Sheriff of co Carlow, 1836   He *m.* 28 May 1835,
Matilda, 2d da. of Thomas COOKSON, of Hermitage, co Durham, by Elizabeth, da and
eventually h of Charles Edward SELBY, of Earle, co Northumberland   He *d.*
21 Nov. 1862, in his 49th year, and was *bur.* at Clonmulsh   She *d.* 18 Sept 1893,
and was *bur.* at Clonmulsh

X. 1862.   SIR THOMAS PIERCE BUTLER, Baronet [I 1628], of
Ballintemple and Garryhuudon aforesaid, s and h, *b* 16 Dec 1836,
ed. at Cheltenham Coll., sometime an officer in the 24th Foot, and served as Lieut
in 56th Foot in the Crimean War, but resigned in 1858, *suc. to the Baronetcy*, 21 Nov
1862, was Sheriff of co Carlow, 1866   He *m* 8 Sep 1864, at Castle Bellingham
church, Hester Elizabeth, 1st da. of Sir Alan Edward BELLINGHAM, 3d Baronet [1796],
by Elizabeth, da and h of Henry CLARKE, of Boston, co Lincoln

Family Estates.—These, in 1883, consisted of 6,455 acres in co Carlow, valued at
£4,130 a year   *Principal Seat*.—Ballintemple, near Tullow, co. Carlow.

MAGRATH :

cr 5 June 1629 ;(a)

ex, presumably, about 1670.

I. 1629.   " JOHN MAGRATH, Esq., of Allevollan, co Tipperary," s.
and h of Terence, *otherwise* Terlogh MAGRATH, of Allevolan (who was
s and h of Meiler MAGRATH, Archbishop of Cashel, 1570—1622), suc his father in
1627, and was by patent, dat at Dublin, 5 June 1629, the Privy Seal being dat
at Southwick, 18 Aug. 1628, was *cr a Baronet* [I], as above (a)   He was Sheriff of
co Tipperary, 1641, and was excepted from pardon of life and estate, 1652   He *m*
Ellen, 1st da of Sir Edward FITZHARRIS, 1st Baronet [I. 1622], by Gyles, da and h.
of John ROCHE

(a) See p. 249, notes " a " and ' b "   The King, in consequence of a petition in 1628
of Sir Frederic Hamilton ' of the Boyne family," granted to him by Privy Seal the
creation of two Irish Baronets, and in consequence accepted his nomination, 20 May
1629, of Magrath and Wilson to that dignity.

II. 1652?   SIR TERENCE *or* TERLOGH MAGRATH, Baronet [I. 1629],
           s. and h., *suc to the Baronetcy* on the death of his father   He *m*
firstly, Catherine, 3d da of Sir Valentine BROWNE, 1st Baronet [I 1622], by his 1st
wife, Ellis, da. of Gerald (FITZGERALD), EARL OF DESMOND [I]   He *m.* secondly,
Mary, da of (—) MAC I BRIEN ARA.   She *d.* s.p.

III. 1660?   SIR JOHN MAGRATH, Baronet [I 1629],(ᵃ) s. and h   He
   to   *m.* Ellen, sister of Patrick and Almericus, successively BARONS
1670?   KINGSALE [I.], da of John (DE COURCY), BARON KINGSALE [I.], by
           Ellen, da. of Charles MAC CARTHY REAGH.   He *d.* apparently s.p m ,
when the *Baronetcy*, presumably, became *extinct*.

WILSON .

cr. 2 July 1629 ;(ᵇ)
ex. 16 April 1636.

I   1629,   " JOHN WILSON, Esq [Knight ?], of Killenure, co
   to   Donegal," s. and h of William WILSON, of Aghagalla, in that county,
1636.   was by patent, dat. at Dublin, 2 July 1629, the Privy Seal being dat.
           at Southwick, 18 Aug. 1628, cr. *a Baronet* [I.], as above (ᵇ) having
been *Knighted* in Ireland 28 June previous.   His estates were, by patent dat. 24 Feb.
1629/30, erected into the manor of Wilson's Fort   He m Martha, 1st da of Sir
Thomas BUTLER, 1st Baronet [I 1628], of Cloughgrenan, by Ann, da of Sir Thomas
COLCLOUGH, of Tintern.   She *d* 28 Sep., and was *bur* 5 Oct. 1634, at Claudy.
Funeral Certif. [I]   He *d.* s p m (ᶜ) at Lifford, 16 April 1636, and was *bur.* at the
Cathedral of Raphos, when the *Baronetcy* became *extinct*.   Funeral Certif [I.]
Will as " of Wilson's Fort, co. Donegal," pr. 1636(ᵈ) in Prerog. Court [I]

OSBORNE :

cr 15 Oct 1629 (ᵉ)

I. 1629.   " RICHARD OSBORNE, Esq., of Ballintaylor, co. Tipper-
           ary " [should be " co Waterford"], whose parentage is unknown,(ᶠ)
was, together with Henry OSBORNE, appointed, 4 Oct. 1616, Joint Clerk of the King's
Courts, Prothonotary, Clerk of the Crown and Clerk of the Assizes to the counties
of Limerick and Tipperary, offices which they surrendered 26 Jan. 1628/9, the said
Richard being shortly afterwards cr *a Baronet* [I], as above, by patent dat. at
Dublin, 15 Oct 1629, the Privy Seal bearing date, at Whitehall, 27 March 1628 (ᵉ)
He was also of Ballymelon, co Waterford.   He, in the Civil Wars, took the side
of Parl , but had to surrender his castle of Knockmoane, near Ballintaylor, after a
long siege in 1645, and with difficulty obtained the benefit of the " Cessation."
He was M P [I] for co. Waterford, 1639-49 and 1661-66.   He is said(ᵍ) to have

---

(ᵃ) There is a draft pedigree of these three Baronets in Ulster's Office.
  (ᵇ) See p. 259, note " a," under " Magrath."
  (ᶜ) Anne, his only da and h , *d* Aug. 1639, aged 5.   Inq. p m.
  (ᵈ) See vol 1, p 223, note " a "
  (ᵉ) See p 249, notes " a " and " b "
  (ᶠ) ' The origin of the family has been obscured by Betham having attributed to
them the arms of a totally different family, that of Osborne of Dublin, which arms
now appear in all the Baronetages.   The arms, however, used by them on seals,
certainly as old as the Baronetcy, are .—Quarterly, *Argent* and *azure* a cross,
engrailed *or* ; in the 1st and 4th quarters an ermine spot." [G. D Burtchaell]
  (ᵍ) *N & Q* , 5th S. II, 494, where it is said, by " Y.S M." (following Betham's
unsupported statement), that the 1st Baronet died in 1638, and the 6th Baronet on
13 May (not 13 Jan) 1718.   The returns to Parl. [I] of the father and son in 1639, in
which the latter is called " Esq ," and the fact that both " Sir Richard Osborne " and
" Mr Richard Osborne " are named on a Committee, 28 July 1641, and the former
on one, I Aug 1642, disprove the first statement, and the careful and accurate
Lodge gives 1667 and 13 *Jan.* 1718 as the date of the respective deaths.

m. "Mary, 2d da. of Sir George CAREW, Lord Deputy" [*Qy* Sir George CAREY, L. Deputy of Ireland, 1603-04, but no such da is attributed him]. He, presumably, *m* (—), da. of Roger DALTON, of Knockmoan, co Waterford.(a) He *d* in or before 1667. Admon, at Waterford, 1667.

II. 1667 ?   SIR RICHARD OSBORNE, Baronet [I. 1629], of Ballintaylor aforesaid, s and h, was M P. [I.] for Dungarvan, 1639-48 He *suc. to the Baronetcy* about 1667, was Sheriff of co Waterford, 1671 He *m.*, in or before 1645, Elizabeth (—), who survived him He *d.* 2 March 1684/5. Will dat. 20 Nov. 1684, pr. at Waterford, 12 March 1684/5.

III. 1685.   SIR JOHN OSBORNE, Baronet [I. 1629], of Taylorstown or Ballintaylor aforesaid, 1st s and h, *b* about 1645, *suc. to the Baronetcy*, 2 March 1685. He *m.* in 1669, Elizabeth, 4th da. of Col Thomas WALSINGHAM (*d.* 22 Nov. 1691), of Scadbury, co Kent, by Ann, da of Theophilus (HOWARD), 2d EARL OF SUFFOLK He *s* p., 4 April 1713, in his 69th year Will dat 18 April 1695, pr 17 Feb. 1713/4, in Prerog. Court [I.]. His widow *d.* 22 Feb 1733, aged 86 M I. at Saffron Walden.

IV   1713.   SIR RICHARD OSBORNE, Baronet [I. 1629], of Ballintaylor aforesaid, br. and h, *suc to the Baronetcy* in April 1713. He, who was a lunatic, *d* unm probably a few months later, in or before 1714

V. 1714 ?   SIR THOMAS OSBORNE, Baronet [I. 1629], of Tickencor, co Waterford, cousin and h male, being s. and h of Nicholas OSBORNE, of Cappagh, Clerk of the Crown, 2d s. of the 2d Baronet, was Sheriff of co. Waterford, 1672, was *Knighted*, v.p, 5 Nov. 1679, in the Presence Chamber, Dublin Castle. He, probably not long before his death, *suc. to the Baronetcy* about 1714. He *m* firstly (—) He *m.* secondly, in 1704, his cousin, Anne, yst da of Beverley USHER, of Kilmeadon, by Grace, da. of Sir Richard OSBORNE, 1st Baronet [I. 1629] Will, in which he is described as 'Knight," dat 16 Oct. 1713, pr 1717 in Prerog Court [I.] He was living 25 Dec 1714. His widow *m* Aug 1717, Francis SKIDDY, of Dublin.

VI   1715 ?   SIR NICHOLAS OSBORNE, Baronet [I 1629], of Tickencor aforesaid, grandson and h., being s. and h of Nicholas OSBORNE, by Anne, da of Sir Laurence PARSONS, 1st Baronet [I 1677], which Nicholas, last-named, was only s. and h. ap. of the late Baronet, but *d* v p 25 Dec 1714, his will being pr at Waterford, 9 May 1715. He was *b* in or soon after 1685, and *suc to the Baronetcy*, probably about 1715. He *m.* in or before 1709, Mary, da. of Thomas SMITH, D D, Bishop of Limerick (1695-1725), by Dorothea, da of Ulysses BURGH, Bishop of Ardagh (1692) He *d. s p m*, 13 Jan 1718/9 Will dat 1 April 1718, pr. 17 Feb 1718/9 in Prerog Court [I] His widow *m.* Col. John RAMSAY, and *d.* at Clontarf, 9 Feb 1762

VII. 1719   SIR JOHN OSBORNE, Baronet [I. 1629], of Newtown, *otherwise* Newtown-Anner, co Tipperary, br and h. male, *b* about 1697, *suc to the Baronetcy*, 13 Jan 1718/9, admitted to Trin. Coll, Dublin, 8 Oct 1713, aged 16, and to the Middle Temple, London, 13 Jan 1714, and to King's Inns, Dublin, 1726, Barrister-at-Law; was M P [I] for Lismore, 1719-27, and for co Waterford, 1727-43 He *m.* Editha, only da of William PROBY, Gov. of Fort St George, in India, by Henrietta, da. of Robert CORNWALL, of Berington, co. Hereford. He *d.* 11 April 1743. Admon, 20 June 1745, to a creditor His widow *d.* 19 Jan. 1745.

(a) This Roger Dalton *d.* 25 Dec 1620, leaving Richard his heir. The manor of Knockmoan was granted to Sir Richard Osborne, "Knt and Bt.," 13 May 1639, who calls his 3d son "Roger," a name which bears out the suggested marriage [*Ex inform.* G D. Burtchaell]

VIII 1743.   Sir William Osborne, Baronet [I. 1629], of Newtown
            aforesaid, 1st s and h, *suc to the Baronetcy*, 11 April 1743, was
Sheriff of co Waterford, 1750, M P. [I.] for Carysfort, 1761-68, for Dungarvan (two
Parls), 1768-83, and for Carysfort (again), Oct 1783, till death; P.C. [I], 7 May
1770   He *m*. (Lic dat 20 March 1749), Elizabeth, 1st da. of Thomas Christmas, of
Whitfield, co Waterford, by Elizabeth, da. of Robert Marshall.   He *d*. Nov. 1783,
Will pr. 1794, in Prerog Court [I].   The will of his widow pr. there 1793.

IX. 1783.   Sir Thomas Osborne, Baronet [I 1629], of Newtown
            aforesaid, 1st s. and h., *b*. 1757; *suc to the Baronetcy*, Nov 1783,
was M.P [I.] for Carysfort (three Parls), 1776-97, Sheriff of co Waterford, 1795
He *m*. 6 April 1816, Catherine Rebecca, 1st da of Robert Smith, Major, Royal
Engineers   He *d* 3 June 1821   His widow *d* 10 Oct. 1856, at Newtown aforesaid

X 1821.   Sir William Osborne, Baronet [I 1629], of Newtown
            aforesaid, only s and h., *b* 1817, *suc. to the Baronetcy*, 3 June 1821,
and *d* in boyhood, 23 May 1824(a)

XI. 1824.   Sir Henry Osborne, Baronet [I 1629], of Beechwood,
            co. Tipperary, uncle and h. male,(b) being 4th s of the 8th
Baronet, *suc. to the Baronetcy*, 23 May 1824.   He was M P. [I.] for Carysfort,
1798-99, and for Enniskillen, 1800, Sheriff of co. Tipperary, 1804.   He *m* firstly, in
or before 1783, Harriet, 1st da and coheir of Daniel Toler, of Beechwood aforesaid
(br to John, 1st Earl of Norbury [I]), by Rebecca, da of Paul Minchin   He
m secondly,(c) 12 June 1813, Elizabeth, da. of William Harding, of Ballyduff, co.
Tipperary.   He *d*. 27 Oct. 1837.   His widow *d* 9 Jan 1864, at Walham Green,
Fulham, Midx.

XII. 1837.   Sir Daniel Toler Osborne, Baronet [I 1629], of Beech-
            wood, aforesaid, 1st s and h., by 1st wife; *b* 10 Dec. 1783 *suc*.
to the Baronetcy, 27 Oct 1837   He *m*. Jan 1805, Harriet, da of William Power
Keating (Le Poer Trench), 1st Earl of Clancarty [I], by Anne, da of the Rt Hon
Charles Gardiner   He *d* 25 March 1853, at Rathmines, near Dublin, aged 70   His
widow who was *b*. Sep 1785, *d*. 17 Nov 1855, at the house of her son-in-law (then)
Lieut. Col Wynne

XIII 1853.   Sir William Osborne, Baronet [I 1629], of Beechwood,
            aforesaid, 1st s and h, *b* 16 Oct 1805, *suc to the Baronetcy*,
25 March 1853, was Sheriff of co Tipperary, 1861.   He *m* 22 July 1842, Maria,
only da of William Thompson, of Clonfin, co Longford, by Mary, da. of John
Garnet, of Hollywoodrath, co. Dublin   He *d* s.p, 2 July 1875, in his 70th year, at
Dunleckney Manor, Bagnalstown.   His widow *d*, shortly afterwards, 25 Oct. 1875.

XIV. 1875.   Sir Charles Stanley Osborne, Baronet [I. 1629], of
            Beechwood, aforesaid, br. and h, being 5th and yst s of the 12th
Baronet, *b* 30 June 1825: *suc to the Baronetcy*, 2 July 1875   He *m*. firstly, 13 July
1846, Emilie, da of Geantz De Reuilly, of Ardenues, in France. She *d* 20 Dec.
1869   He *m*. secondly, 8 July 1873, Emma, da. of Charles Webb, of Clapham

---

(a) The estates, above 13,000 acres in the counties of Waterford and Tipperary,
devolved on his only sister, Catherine Isabella, who *m*. 20 Aug. 1844, Ralph Bernal,
afterwards Bernal-Osborne, of Newtown Anner aforesaid, and *d* s p m 21 June 1880.

(b) According to some pedigrees, the Rt Hon. Charles Osborne (*d*. 5 Sep 1817) was
older than Henry, the 11th Baronet   This Charles left an only son, William Osborne,
Major 71st Foot, who in the supposed case would, in 1824, have been entitled to the
Baronetcy, but who *d*. s p 13 July 1867, aged 73.   According, however, to the will
of the 8th Baronet, the order of his sons was (1) Thomas, (2) John Proby, (3) William,
(4) *Henry*, (5) *Charles*, and (6) Robert

(c) In Foster's *Baronetage* (1883) "the evidences" of this marriage are cited in
full as if there was some question of its validity, of which, however, the proofs seem
conclusive.

Common, Surrey He *d* s p , 16 July 1879, aged 54, at St. Stephen's Green, Dublin (ᵃ)
His widow living 1900

XV. 1879.   SIR FRANCIS OSBORNE, Baronet [I 1629], of the Grange,
             Framfield, Sussex ; cousin and h male, being 1st s. and h. of Charles
OSBORNE, of the Audit Office, Somerset House, by Ann, da of Stephen GEARY, of
Euston Place, Architect, which Charles (*b* 14 July 1816, and *d* 15 June 1871) was
s of Sir Henry, the 11th Baronet, being his 1st s by his 2d wife   He was *b* 1 Nov.
1856, ed at Lancing College ; *suc. to the Baronetcy*, 16 July 1879   He *m*. 1 July
1890, Kathleen Eliza, da of George WHITFIELD, of Modreeny, co Tipperary, and of
Cornwall Gardens, London.

HERBERT, *or* HARBERTT
cr. 4 Dec 1630(ᵇ);
ex Dec 1712

I. 1630   "SIR GEORGE HARBERTT [*i e*, Herbert] late Esq., now
            Knight, of Dorrowe [*i e.* Durrow], King's County,"(ᵇ) s and h. of Sir
Edward HERBERT, of the same, by Elizabeth, da. of Patrick FINGLASS, of Westpalstown,
co Dublin , was Sheriff of King's county 1614, and 1624 , suc his father, 3 Oct 1629,
was *Knighted*, 21 March 1629/30, at Whitehall, and was *cr. a Baronet* [I], as above,
by patent dat. at Dublin, 4 Dec. 1630, the Privy Seal being dat at Westm 31 March
1630(ᵇ)   He *m* , in or before 1620, Frances, da of Sir Edward FITZGERALD, of
Tecroghan, co Kildare, by Alison, da of Sir Christopher BARNEWALL, of Turvey, co.
Dublin

II 1650?   SIR EDWARD HERBERT, Baronet [I 1630], of Durrow,
             aforesaid, s and h , *b.* about 1620 , entered Trin. Coll., Dublin, 1 June
1638, aged 18 , *suc. to the Baronetcy* on the death of his father   He *m* 8 May 1662
Hester, da of Charles (LAMBART), 1st EARL OF CAVAN [I], by Jane, da of Richard
(ROBARTES), 1st BARON ROBARTES OF TRURO   He *d* May 1677   Will dat 3 May
1677, pr. 19 May 1713 in Prerog Court [I]   His widow *m* 19 Nov. 1679, Lieut. Col.
Simon FINCH, of Kilcolman, co Tipperary.

III 1677,   SIR GEORGE HERBERT, Baronet [I. 1630], of Durrow, afore
     to   said, only s and h., *b* about 1673 ; *suc. to the Baronetcy* in May
    1713.   1677. He *m* (Lic. Fac , 20 Oct 1697, he about 24 and she about 22)
             Jane, da and coheir of Sir John KNATCHBULL, 2d Baronet [1641], by
Jane, da and coheir of Sir Edward MONINS, 2d Baronet [1611]   He *d* s p , Dec.
1712, when *the Baronetcy* became *extinct* (ᶜ)   Admon 12 Sep 1714, in Prerog Court
[I]   His widow *m* Richard WHITSHED, of Dublin

(ᵃ) His estates in 1876, consisted of 940 acres, co Tipperary, and 492 co Westmeath. *Total*, 1,432 acres valued at £909 a year. His name was on the list of those
returned to serve as Sheriff for co Tipperary in 1878, and retained in 1879 and 1880
notwithstanding his death, and it is even stated that a warrant so appointing him
was made out in Jan. 1881. [*Ex inform.* G D Burtchaell]
   (ᵇ) See p. 249, notes "a " and "b."
   (ᶜ) The estates of Durrow passed to his sisters Rose, Frances, and Elizabeth, of
whom two *d. unm* , but the other, Frances, *m* , before Sep 1714, Major Patrick Fox,
and *d. s p.* in 1740, being *bur.* at Durrow.

MORRES

*c*₁ 28 March, 1631 ;(ᵃ)

afterwards, since 1795, VISCOUNTS MOUNTMORRES [I].

I   1631   "JOHN MORRES, Esq, of Knockagh, co Tipperary "(ᵃ),
s. and h of Redmond MORRES, of the same (*d* 31 Aug 1624, aged 72),
by his 1st wife, Elinor, da of (—) CANTWELL, of Lahagres, co Tipperary, was *b*
probably about 1573, and, having suc his father, 31 Aug. 1624, was *ei. a Baronet* [I],
as above, by patent dat at Dublin, 28 March 1631, the Privy Seal being dat at Westm
30 April 1630 (ᵃ)   He *m.* before 1601, Catherine, da. of Sir Edmond WALSHE, of
Owney Abbey, *otherwise* Abington, co. Limerick, and of Grange, co. Kilkenny, by
Ellis, da. of (—) GRACE.   He *d.* 1647/8, aged 75.   Will dat 29 Jan 1647/8, pr at
Prerog Court [I]

II   1648   SIR REDMOND MORRES, Baronet [I. 1631], of Knockagh,
aforesaid, 1st s and h ; *b* probably about 1595, *suc to the Baronetcy,*
1647/8.   He *m.* in or before 1620, Ellice, da. of Garret WALL, of Coolnamucky Castle,
co Waterford.   He *d* in or before 1656, in which year his widow was, on account of
her great age, exempted by Cromwell's Commissioners from transplantation into
Connaught.

III.   1655?   SIR JOHN MORRES, Baronet [I. 1631], of Knockagh, aforesaid, 1st s and h , *b* 29 Aug 1620 , *suc to the Baronetcy* in or before
1656, was known for his wit and eccentricities and was also a poet   He *m* probably
about 1665, Ellin, (*b.* 11 Feb 1638), da of Thomas (BUTLER), 3d BARON CAHER [I],
by Elinor his wife   He *d* 26 Oct 1720, and was *bur* at Lateragh, co Tipperary,
aged 100   M.I   Will dat 11 July 1719, pr. in Prerog Court [I] 12 Dec 1720.   His
widow *d* 27 May 1721, aged 83.

IV.   1720.   SIR JOHN MORRES, Baronet [I 1631], of Knockagh and
Lateragh, aforesaid, grandson and h , being 1st s and h. of Redmond
MORRES, a Colonel in the French service, by Mary da of (—) TRACY, a Merchant in
France, which Redmond, *d* v p in London in 1704, being *bur* at St. Mary's in that city,
his heart being sent to Drom, near Knockagh   He was a minor at his father's death
in 1704, and *suc to the Baronetcy,* 26 Oct. 1720   He *m* , in or before 1717, Margaret,
da of Edmund O'SHEE, of Cloran, co Tipperary, by Catherine, da of (—) O'DWYER.
He *d* 1723.   Will dat. 4 Feb. 1723, pr at Cashel

V.   1723.   SIR REDMOND MORRES, Baronet [I. 1631], of Knockagh
and Lateragh, aforesaid, 1st s and h.,(ᵇ) *b.* probably about 1717,
suc to the Baronetcy in 1723.   He conformed to the established religion , enclosed
the deer park at Lateragh with a wall, and, having quarrelled with his uncle,
devised all the family estates to his cousin Hervey Morres, afterwards 1st Viscount
Mountmorres of Castle Morres [I.].(ᶜ)   He *d* unm. of the small 'pox at Carlow,
11 Oct 1740, and was *bur.* at Lateragh.   Will pr 1740 in Prerog. Court [I]

VI.   1740   SIR SIMON MORRES, Baronet [I. 1631], uncle and h.
male, *suc to the Baronetcy,* but to none of the estates, 11 Oct. 1740
He *m.* Jane, da of the Rev. (—) GREGORY.   He was living 5 July 1747 when he
took out admon to his sister

(ᵃ) See p 249, notes "a " and "b"
(ᵇ) Edmond Morres his only br., who was living 25 Nov 1725, *d* unm before him
(ᶜ) He, according to Playfair's *Irish Baronetage,* " sold the Lordships and Castles
of Knockagh, Lateragh, and Castle Lyny, which for upwards of 600 years [*sic*] had
been in possession of the Montmorency-Morres [*sic*] family "

VII 1750?   SIR GEORGE MORRES, Baronet [I 1631], of Maine, co
     Louth, only s and h , *suc to the Baronetcy* on the death of his father
He *m* (—), who *d* 24 April 1758, only two days before him. He *d* s.p. 26 April
1758, at Maine aforesaid Admon. 7 Dec 1758 at Prerog Court [I], to his sister
Mary Cockhill, *otherwise* Morris, widow.

VIII. 1758   SIR RICHARD MORRES, Baronet [I. 1631], cousin and h.
     male, being 3d(a) but only surv s of Nicholas MORRES, of Seafield, near
Malahide, co Dublin, by Susanna, da of Richard TALBOT, of Malahide aforesaid,
which Nicholas (who *d* 23 March 1742, aged 66, was 3d s of Sir John MORRES, 3d
Baronet [I]. He was a Col in the French Service He *suc to the Baronetcy*, 26 April
1758, though he does not appear to have assumed the title He resided in France
He *d* unm , being killed, 1774, by the fall of a scaffold at the coronation of Louis XVI
of France

IX 1774   SIR NICHOLAS MORRES, Baronet [I 1631], cousin and h.
     male, being 2d(b) but only surv s of James MORRES, of Rosetown, co
Tipperary, by Anne, da of Edward MORRES, which James (who *d* 1718) was 4th s of
Sir John MORRES, the 3d Baronet. He was *b*., probably, about 1710 ; was a Col. in
the French Service and a Knight of St Louis of France He *suc to the Baronetcy* in
1774, though he does not appear to have assumed the title He *m.* Isabel, 1st da.
of Donald CAMERON, of Lochiel, by Anne, da of Sir James CAMPBELL, 5th Baronet
[S. 1628] of Anchinbreck in Scotland He *d* s p 1795

X. 1795   HERVEY REDMOND (MORRES), VISCOUNT MOUNTMORRES
     OF CASTLE MORRES [I], and 10th Baronet [I 1631], cousin and h.
male, being s and h of Hervey, 1st VISCOUNT MOUNTMORRES OF CASTLEMORRES [I.]
(so cr 29 June 1763), by his 1st wife, Letitia, da of Brabazon (PONSONBY), 1st EARL
OF BESSBOROUGH [I], which Hervey, who *d* 6 April 1766, was s. and h of Francis
MORRES, of Castle Morres, co Kilkenny, who was s and b of Hervey MORRES, of the
same (*d* 1722/3), 2d s of Sir John MORRES, 2d Baronet [I. 1731], abovenamed He
was *b* about 1743 , *suc to the Peerage* [I], as above, as second Viscount, on the death
of his father, 6 April 1766, and *suc to the Baronetcy*, on the death of his cousin, the
9th Baronet, in 1795. In that peerage this *Baronetcy* then *merged*, and still so
continues. See *Peerage.*

BARRET
cr. possibly in 1631

"ANDREW BARRET, of Inniscarry, co. Cork," is given as the
14th Baronet [I],(c) cr by Charles I, in Beatson's *Political Index* [1806], but
not, apparently, elsewhere He was s and h. of Sir James BARRET, was M P
[I] for co Cork, 1613-15 (as " Esq.") and for Cork city (as a " Knight "),
1639 48, having been *Knighted*, 7 July 1639, at Dublin. He was father of
William BARRET, cr a Baronet [I.] by Privy Seal, 4 July 1665.

(a) The 1st s , John Morres, *d* unm Will pr 1744 in Prerog Court [I] The 2d
s , Nicholas Morres, who was a Brigadier Gen. in the French Service and a Knight of
St. Louis of France, *m* (—), da. of (—) Fraser, but *d* 1745 s p , at Amboise, in France
This Nicholas is, in Playfair's *Irish Baronetage*, erroneously made to succeed the 7th
Baronet in the title (whereas he died thirteen years before him) and is confused
with Nicholas, the 9th Baronet, who was also a Knight of St Louis.
   (b) John Morres, his elder br., *d.* unm
   (c) Of the 13 previous Baronetcies [I] 11 (viz , Macdonnel, Staples, Bourke, Butler,
Colclough, Esmond, Magrath, Wilson, Osborne, Herbert and Morris are the same as
in the text above (Mac Mahon being omitted) , the 12th and 13th are ' John Talbot, of
Cartown, co. Kildare (Lord Tyrconnel), 1631," and "William Dungan, of Castletown,
co Kildare (Earl of Limerick), 1631," of which two, however, (1) Talbot, a creation
of 4 Feb. 1622/3, and (2) Dungan, one of 23 Oct. 1623, belong to the previous reign.

FITZGERALD ·(ᵃ)

cr. 8 Feb 1643/4 ,(ᵇ)

attainted 1691 ,

assumed 1780 to 1894 ,

being from 1861 to 1894, DALTON-FITZGERALD

I 1644   " SIR EDMOND FITZGERALD, Knt, of Clenlish, co Limerick " s and h of Thomas FITZGERALD, of the same, by Mary, da of Cormac MacDermot MACCARTHY, of Muskerry, co. Cork, suc. his father (who d in London), Dec 1635, and was cr a Baronet [I], as above, by patent dat at Dublin, 8 Feb 1643/4, the Privy Seal being dat at Oxford, 23 April 1643 He is said(ᶜ) to have raised a regiment of horse for the Royal cause during the great rebellion, and to have burnt his castle of Clenlish to prevent it falling into the enemy's hands He suffered great losses, and was one of the persons named in 1662, by Charles II, in ' the Act of Explanation," to be restored as far as possible to his former possession, but he d before Feb 1670, and before such restoration (ᵈ)

II 1665?   SIR JOHN FITZGERALD, Baronet [I 1644], of Gortnatub-
to   brid, co Limerick, s and h., suc to the Baronetcy on his father's
1691.   death , was restored to a portion of his father's estate (of which Gortnatubbrid was part) by decree enrolled in Chancery [I] 16 Feb 1670 (ᵉ) . was M P [I] for co Limerick, 1689, in the Parl of James II He m in 1674 Ellen, da of (—), on which occasion he settles his estates with a remainder to his brothers, Maurice, Richard, Thomas and Edmund Adhering to James II, he was attainted in 1691, when the Baronetcy became forfeited He d abroad, being, it is said,(ᶠ) killed at the battle of Oudenarde, 11 July 1708 His wife, or widow, was living 21 June 1703, when his estates, subject to her interest, were sold to the family of FitzMaurice

> For nearly 100 years no trace appears of this Baronetcy, but on 18 Nov 1780, Sir William Hawkins, Ulster King of Arms, certified, at the end of a pedigree recorded by him in the College of Arms, Dublin, " that Sir Richard FitzGerald, of Castle Ishen, in the county of Cork Baronet, is lawfully descended in a direct line from Sir Edmund FitzGerald, of Clulish, in the

---

(ᵃ) Between the creations of Morres and FitzGerald the following creation is inserted in the Liber Munerum Hibernicæ

"SIR PIERCE CROSBIE, Knt , of Queen's County Neither King's letter nor patent is enrolled, but I suppose him, says Lodge, to have been created about this time He is a Baronet of Nova Scotia." [He was so created in July 1630 See those creations]

(ᵇ) Disallowed by Parl , 11 Nov 1643, till the Restoration See Memorandum on p 152 as to all Baronetcies cr after 4 Jan 1641/2, and 22 May 1642. See p 249, notes " a " and " b "

(ᶜ) Playfair's Baronetage of Ireland

(ᵈ) This Edmond seems often confused with another Sir Edmond FitzGerald of Cloyne, co Cork, who m., in or after 1589, Honora, widow of John FitzGerald, Seneschal of Imokilly, da. of James FitzGerald, of Desmond, and who d 10 March 1611 By her (according to a pedigree entered 1684 in Ulster's office) he had four sons of whom the youngest, Maurice, was of Castlelisheen, sometimes (incorrectly) called Castle Ishen, co. Cork This Honora FitzGerald, widow, in her will, pr 1628 in Prerog Court [I], mentions her sons, John and Maurice Of these two sons John, who was b 1594, was Knighted 17 April 1617, and d 2 Jan 1640/1, leaving male issue, and mentioning in his will, dat 1 Sep 1640, his brother Maurice Fitz-Gerald, of Castlelisheen. This, apparently, is the same Maurice who, in a pedigree certified, 19 Nov 1780, by Hawkins, Ulster King of Arms, is (incorrectly) made to be a son of Sir Edmond FitzGerald, the Baronet (of Clenlish), and whose descendant, in right of such descent, assumed that Baronetcy, as stated in the text below.

(ᵉ) Deed " recited in a decree, dat. Dec 1701 " (No. 1564, Trustee Collection, P R O , Ireland)

(ᶠ) Dalton's King James' Irish Army List (vol ii, p. 423), but see also O'Callaghan's Irish Brigades, pp 116, 119, 120.

county of Limerick, Knt, who was *cr a Baronet* the 8 Feb 1644,"[a] a state-
ment which (coupled with the title of " Baronet " having been given to the said
Richard), presumably, implied that he was *heir male of the body* of the said
grantee, and, as such, was *entitled to the Baronetcy of the abovenamed date.*
The pedigree as given by Hawkins, the parts within brackets being however
supplied from elsewhere, is below —" Sir Richard Fitzgerald, of Castle
Ishin, co Cork, Baronet, son of Maurice Fitzgerald, by Helen, da of Walter
Butler (1st son of Richard Butler, Esq , of Kilcash), which Maurice [who d ,
presumably v.p., 16 Sep 1726, being *bur* at Buttevant Abbey, and called on
the M I there ' of Castle Ishin, of the house of Desmond '] was a [and h] of
James Fitz-Gerald (living Jan 1753), by [his 1st wife] Amy, da of Thomas
Fitzgerald, Knight of Kerry, which James was [a younger] son[b] of Garret
Fitzgerald, by [his 2d wife] Catherine, da of Charles O'Brien, commonly
called Lord Viscount Clare [I], which Garret was son of Maurice Fitz
Gerald, of Castle Ishin [will dat 20 March 1678/9 as ' of Castlehsahyne,
co Cork, Esq,' pr 7 June 1679 in Prerog Court of Ireland], by Lady
Honora [Maccarthy], da of [Donogh] Earl of Clancarty [I], which Maurice
was [according to this pedigree, see, however, p 266, note " d "] son of Sir
Edmund Fitzgerald, of Clonlish, co Limerick, Knt, who was *cr a Baronet*
[I], 8 Feb 1644 "

VIII?[c] 1780   ' Sir Richard Fitzgerald, Baronet" [I 1644], of
        Castle Ishen, co Cork, whose parentage and alleged ancestry
have been above stated   He apparently was *b* between 1710 and 1721,[d] and
having suc his father, 16 Sep. 1726, obtained, 18 Nov 1780, the certificate
from Ulster King of Arms mentioned above styling him a Baronet, and
implying that he was entitled to the Baronetcy [I] conferred 6 Feb. 1643/4 [e]
He *m.* Joanna Maria, da and h of James Trant, of Dingle, co. Kerry   He *d.*
about 1787.   Will pr 1787 in Prerog Court [I]

(a) Foster's *Baronetage* for 1883, p 698 (being in the part of that work called
" Chaos "), where a full account of this assumption is given, from which the one in
the text is mainly derived

(b) An elder br of this James is said to have been Maurice FitzGerald ' of Castle
Ishen," who *d* s p Feb. 1750, but the date of the will of the said James, also of
Castle Ishen, dat. 19 Jan 1753, and pr 27 Nov 1768, is hardly consistent with his
son and his son's wife (the continuators of the line), having *d.* in 1726 and 1721
respectively

(c) This number is purely conjectural   " Sir Richard " is stated in Playfair's
Baronetage to have been ' the second of this family who bore that title, but the 6th
in descent from the 1st Baronet "   The *second* Baronet was, however, s and h. of
the first, and was not (even according to Hawkins' pedigree) one of " Sir Richard's "
lineal ancestors.   " Sir Richard's " grandfather had an elder brother, Maurice,
who *d.* s p Feb. 1750 (see note " b " above), and who may, apparently, be reckoned,
equally with himself, as entitled to this dignity, thereby rendering ' Sir Richard "
the 7th in succession

(d) His sister Mary, who *m* 29 Nov. 1731, the Earl of Fingall [I], was probably
b about 1710 ; their mother *d* in 1721

(e) ' There can be no doubt that the claim of the Castle Ishen (properly Castle-
lishen) family to the title was devoid of foundation   It was not acknowledged by Sir
W Betham, Ulster King of Arms   The fact that Maurice Fitzgerald, late of
Castlehsheen, Esq, was 4th and yst. s of Sir Edmund FitzGerald, of Cloyne (by
Honora, widow of John FitzGerald, of Ballymarter, commonly called the Seneschal
of Imokilly, da of James FitzGerald, of Desmond) appears from a pedigree of the
Desmond family in Ulster's office in the year 1684, as also that Katharine, 2d da of
Conor O'Bryen, 2d Lord Clare, married Garrott FitzGerald, surv s of Maurice, of
Castlehsheen " [G. D. Burtchaell]

VIII ?(ᵃ) 1787?   " SIR JAMES TRANT FITZGERALD, Baronet "
[I   1644], of Castle Ishen aforesaid, only s. and h , suc his
father in 1787   He m 1 Oct. 1786, Bridget Anne, da. of Robert DALTON, of
Thurnham Hall, co Lancaster, by his 3d wife, Bridget, da (whose issue
became eventually sole h) of Thomas MORE, of Barnborough, co York   He d.
July 1824   Will pr. 1825   His widow d abroad.   Will pr. Aug 1835.

IX ?(ᵃ) 1824   " SIR JAMES FITZGERALD, Baronet" [I. 1644], of
Castle Ishen aforesaid, and of Wolseley Hall, co Stafford,
only s. and h , b. 22 Aug 1791 , suc his father in July 1824   He m 27 Sep
1826, at Swanbourne Bucks, Augusta Henrietta, sister of the 1st BARON
COTTESLOE, 2d da of Vice Admiral Sir Thomas Francis FREMANTLE, G.C B.,
by Elizabeth, da. of Richard WYNNE, of Falkingham, co Lincoln.   He d
25 Sep 1839, at Chalons-sur-Saone, near Nice   Will pr Oct. 1839   His
widow d. 11 June 1863, at the Convent, Roehampton, Surrey, aged 60

X ?(ᵃ) 1839   " SIR JAMES GEORGE FITZGERALD, afterwards
(1861) DALTON FITZGERALD, Baronet " [I 1644], of Castle
Ishen aforesaid, 1st s and h., b. 6 Jan 1831 , suc. his father, 25 Sep 1839.
He took, by royal lic 31 May 1861, the name of Dalton before that of
Fitzgerald, on succeeding to the estate of Thurnham Hall aforesaid, formerly
the possession of the Dalton family.   He m 26 June 1856, Blanche Mary, 3d
da. of the Hon Philip Henry Joseph STOURTON, of Holme Hall, co. York (3d s.
of Charles Philip, BARON STOURTON), by Catherine, da of Henry HOWARD, of
Corby   He d. s p 16 Jan 1867, aged 36   His widow, who took the veil, d
7 June 1875, at the Convent of the Sisters of Charity, Harold's Cross, Dublin

XI ?(ᵃ) 1867,   " SIR GERALD RICHARD FITZGERALD. afterwards
to   (March 1867) DALTON FITZGERALD, Baronet " [I 1644], of
1894   Castle Ishen and Thurnham Hall aforesaid, br. and h., b
21 Aug 1832 , suc his brother 16 Jan. 1867, and shortly
afterwards took, by royal lic 23 March 1867, the name of Dalton before
that of FitzGerald   He m 15 Jan 1861, Agnes Georgiana, 2d da. of George
WILDES, of Manchester. He d s p at 36 Lowndes sq , 22 Feb 1894, and was
bur. at Thurnham aforesaid, aged 61, when the issue male of Richard FitzGerald,
who in 1760 assumed this Baronetcy, became extinct.   His widow living 1900

BUTLER.

cr. 8 July 1645 ;(ᵇ)

ex. or *dormant,* 1762

I.   1645   " WALTER BUTLER, Esq, of Poulstoun [Polestown], co.
Kilkenny,"(ᵇ), s and h of Edmund BUTLER,(ᶜ) of the same (M P [I.]
for co Kilkenny, 1634-35), by Ellice (d 1651), 6th da. of Nicholas SHORTALL, of
Upper Claragh, co. Kilkenny, suc his father, 21 April 1636, and was cr a Baronet [I],
as above, by patent dat at Dublin, 8 July 1645, the Privy Seal being dat at

(ᵃ) See p 267, note " c."
(ᵇ) See p 266, note " b," under " FITZGERALD "
(ᶜ) This Edmund, was s and h. of Sir Richard Butler (Knighted 21 April 1605), s.
and h of Walter Butler, s and h. of Edmund Butler, s and h. of Richard, s and h
of (another) Walter Butler, 2d s of (another) Edmund Butler, all of Polestown
aforesaid, which Edmund last named, was 3d s. of James, 3d Earl of Ormonde [I.]
[Pedigree in Ulster's office, 23 July 1636]

Oxford, 19 April 1643 (ᵃ)   He was Gov of Kilkenny, when it surrendered, 28 March 1650, to Cromwell (ᵇ)   He *m* Elizabeth, 1st da of Richard (BUTLER), 3d VISCOUNT MOUNTGARRET [I] by his 1st wife, Margaret, da or Hugh (O'NEILL), EARL OF TYRONE [I]   He, having with his troop quitted Kilkenny after its surrender, *d.* soon afterwards at Polestown, about May 1650 (ᶜ)   His widow was living 1683, as party to a Chancery suit on behalf of her grandson   She, presumably, *d* 31 Aug. 1686 (ᵈ)

II. 1650   SIR RICHARD BUTLER, Baronet [I. 1645], of Polestown, aforesaid, only s and h , *suc to the Baronetcy* about May 1650   He *m* before 1675, Elizabeth (ᵉ)   He *d* in Germany 1679 or 1680   Will dat 16 Nov 1678 ["now going into Germany"], pr 20 Jan 1680 in Ireland   His widow *m* about 1684, Theobald DENN, of Grenan, co. Kilkenny.

III. 1679 ?   SIR WALTER BUTLER, Baronet [I 1645], of Polestown aforesaid, only s and h , *b* about 1678, being directed in his father's will "to be called by the name of Edmond, and Walter when the Bishop shall confirm him ", *suc to the Baronetcy* in 1679 or 1680 , was a dissolute spendthrift and drunkard, and was, before 1706 "delirious and of non sane memory "   He *m* firstly, April 1697, Lucy, 3d da. or Walter BUTLER, of Garryicken, co Kilkenny, by Mary, da. of Christopher (PLUNKETT), EARL OF FINGALL [I]   She *d* 1703   He *m* secondly, in or before 1706 (—), " with whom he had no fortune," and who subsequently left him and went to live in London   He *d* 8 Oct. 1723.   Admon 14 March 1723/4, in Ireland, to a creditor.

IV. 1723,   SIR EDMUND BUTLER, Baronet [I. 1645], 2d but only
    to   surv s and h , being only s by 2d wife(ᶠ), *b* about 1708 , *suc.*
    1762   *to the Baronetcy,* 8 Oct. 1723, and filed a bill in the Exchequer [I] 29 March 1732 to recover the family estates, but no decree was made thereon   He was a Col. in the French Service   He *d.* presumably s p m in Paris, in Sep or Oct 1762, aged 54(ᵍ) when *the Baronetcy* became *extinct* or *dormant.*

BORROWES, *or* BURROWES ·
cr 14 Feb. 1645/6 (ᵃ)

I 1646   "ERASMUS BORROWES, Esq , of Grangemellon, co Kildare," s and h of Henry BORROWES (who emigrated from Devonshire into Ireland) by (as stated in the registered pedigree) his 2d wife, Jane, da. of Sir Arthur SAVAGE, of Rheban, co. Kildare, but more probably by his 1st wife, Cathanne,

(ᵃ) See p 266, note " b," under " FITZGERALD "
(ᵇ) This and almost all the other particulars in this article are supplied by G D Burtchaell.   See vol 1, p 223, note " a "
(ᶜ) Petition to the Court of Claims by his daughter, who adds, that " he died in His Majesty's service in opposition to the late Usurper "
(ᵈ) Lodge [*Irish Peerage,* 1st edit., vol 11, p 14] says, "1636," presumably an error for 1686
(ᵉ) " I suspect a sister of Edmond Blanchfield or Blanchville, who, with her, is made one of the Executors of Sir Richard's will   If so, she was da of Capt Garret Blanchville, who *d* v p 21 Feb 1646, being eldest s. and heir ap of Sir Edmond Blanchville, of Blanchevillestown, co Kilkenny, by Elizabeth, sister of Sir Edward Butler, *cr* Viscount Galmoy [I] in 1646.   Lodge states that Sir Edmond Blanchville married Elizabeth, da of Walter (Butler), 11th Earl of Ormond [I], but this is utterly wrong , there is abundant proof that his wife was the lady stated above   She was living as his widow in 1664 "   [G. D. Burtchaell]
(ᶠ) By the first wife were two children, viz , Richard, who *d* v p , and a daughter
(ᵍ) " The Dublin newspapers of 2 Oct. 1762, contain notice of this death, viz , " At the beginning of this month, at Paris, aged 54, Sir Edmund Butler, of Polestown, Baronet, Colonel of Horse in the French Service' "   [G D. Burtchaell.]

da of Alexander EUSTACE, of Grangemore, co Kildare, suc. his father, 20 March 1614 ; was of Gilltown, co. Kildare ; Sheriff for that county, 1641-42, at the breaking out of the Irish Rebellion, in the course of which he lost in goods, corn, and cattle, at his several houses of Grangemellon, Gilltown, and Corbally, £9,396 , in debts, £11,932, besides an annual income of about £1,200, and, having suffered much in the Royal cause, was cr. a Baronet [I], as above, by patent dat. at Dublin, 14 Feb 1645/6, the Privy Seal being dat at Ragland, 7 July 1644 (a) He m firstly, about 1620, Sarah, 1st da of Walter WELDON, of Athy, by Jane, da of John RYDER, Bishop of Killaloe (1612 32). He m secondly (Lic 13 Dec 1632), Martha, widow of Barnabas HANCOCK, afterwards TOTTENHAM, of Ballyduffe, co Waterford, formerly widow of (—) HOUMAN, da of John SALISBURY He m thirdly (Lic. 11 Jan 1644), Rebecca, widow of Sir Nathaniel CATELYN, Speaker of the House of Commons [I 1634-35], 3d da of William THIMBLEBY, of Dublin, by Alice, da of Richard CLARK, of Chimpton Hall, co Suffolk. He d probably about 1650 The will of his widow dat 1 July 1681, pr. 1682 in the Prerog Court [I]

II 1650 ?   SIR WALTER BORROWES, Baronet [I 1646], of Gilltown aforesaid, s and h , b. about 1620 ,(b) suc to the Baronetcy on the death of his father , Sheriff of co Kildare, 1673 He m. firstly, 16 Feb 1656, in great state, before the Lord Mayor of Dublin, Eleanor, 3d da. of George (FITZ-GERALD), EARL OF KILDARE [I], by Joan, da of Richard (BOYLE), 1st EARL OF CORK [I]. She d 3 Aug 1681, and was bur at Gilltown He m secondly, Margaret, 5th da of the Rt Hon Sir Adam LOFTUS, of Rathfarnam, by Jane, da of Walter VAUGHAN, of Golden Grove, King's County, but by her had no issue. He d 1685, and was bur. at Gilltown. Will pr 1691, in Prerog Court [I] That of his widow pr there 1698

III 1685   SIR KILDARE BORROWES [I 1646], of Gilltown aforesaid, s. and h , by 1st wife, b about 1660 ; suc to the Baronetcy in 1685 , was Sheriff of co Kildare, 1697 and 1707 , M P [I.] thereof, 1703, till death He m. Elizabeth, sister and coheir of Robert DIXON, of Colverstown, co Kildare, da. of Sir Richard DIXON, by Mary, da of William EUSTACE, of Blackrath He d in or shortly before May 1709, and was bur. at Gilltown. Will pr 1709, in Prerog Court [I] His widow d. 11 March 1745.

IV. 1709.   SIR WALTER DIXON BORROWES, Baronet [I 1646], of Gilltown aforesaid, s and h , suc to the Baronetcy in 1709 He was M P. [I] for Harristown, 1721-27, and for Athy, 1727 41 On 5 March 1725, he inherited the estate of Colverstown aforesaid, on the death of his maternal uncle Robert DIXON abovenamed. He m. 18 March 1720, Mary, da and coheir of Capt Edward POTTINGER, of Belfast. He d 9 June 1741, at Colverstown. Admon 19 Jan 1742 in Prerog Court [I] His widow d 28 Sep 1763 Her will, as " of Dublin," pr 1764, in Prerog Court [I]

V 1741   SIR KILDARE DIXON BORROWES, Baronet [I 1646], of Gilltown and of Colverstown aforesaid, s and h. ; suc to the Baronetcy, 9 June 1741; was M P [I] for co Kildare, 1745-76 , Sheriff of that county, 1751 He m. firstly, Feb 1759, Elizabeth, da. and h. of John SHORT, of Grange, in Queen's County, by Elizabeth, da. of Sir Kildare BORROWES [I 1646] She d 23 Aug 1766 He m secondly, 10 May 1769, Jane, da of Joseph HIGGINSON, of Mount Ophaley, co. Kildare, by Bridget, da of James MOTTLEY, of Tullow, co Carlow He d 22 June 1790, aged 69, and was bur. at Gilltown Will pr 1790, in Prerog Court [I] His widow d Sep. 1793.

(a) See p 266, note " b," under " FITZGERALD."
(b) His yr br. Wingfield Burrowes matric at Oxford (Linc Coll), 12 Sep 1640, aged 15.

VI   1790   SIR ERASMUS DIXON BURROWES, Baronet [I 1646], of Colverstown aforesaid, of Lauragh [near Portarlington], in Queen's County and of Barretstown, co Kildare, s. and h., by 1st wife, *b* 20 Dec. 1759 , *suc to the Baronetcy*, 22 June 1790 , was Sheriff of Queen's County, 1800, and of co Kildare, 1809   He *m* 1783, Henrietta de Robillard (sister of the Countess of Uxbridge), yst da of the Very Rev Arthur CHAMPAGNÉ, Dean of Clonmacnoise, by Marianne, da of Col Isaac HAMON. She *d.* 11 June 1807   He *d.* 19 Sep 1814

VII.   1814.   SIR WALTER DIXON BORROWES, Baronet [I 1646], of Lauragh and of Barretstown Castle aforesaid, s and h, *b* 21 Sep 1789 , *suc. to the Baronetcy*, 19 Sep. 1814 ; Sheriff of Queen's County, 1817, and of co Kildare, 1829.   He *d* unm , 7 March 1834

VIII   1834   SIR ERASMUS DIXON BORROWES, Baronet [I 1646], of Lauragh and of Barretstown Castle aforesaid, only surv br and h , *b* 21 Sep. 1799, at Portarlington, Queen's County, *suc to the Baronetcy*, 7 March 1834 , was in Holy Orders , Rector of Ballyroan, in Queen's County   He *m* , March 1825, Harriett, 4th da of Henry HAMILTON, of Ballymacoll, co Meath (niece of Hans HAMILTON, thirty years M P for co Dublin) by Mary, da of John WETHERALL, of Dublin   He *d* 27 May 1866, at Lauragh aforesaid in his 67th year His widow *d* in or before 1880

IX   1866   SIR ERASMUS DIXON BORROWES, Baronet [I 1646], of Barretstown Castle aforesaid, 2d but 1st surv s and h. , *b* 19 Dec 1831, in Dublin ; ed at Cheltenham College, Ensign 80th Foot, 1852 ; Capt 1859 , Major (13th Foot), 1867, had medal for service in the Burmese War, 1853, and in the Indian Mutiny where he was wounded , *suc to the Baronetcy*, 27 May 1866 ; Sheriff for co Kildare, 1873, and for Queen's County, 1880   He *m* firstly, 14 Aug 1851, Frederica Esten, 1st da of Brig. Gen George HUTCHESON, Col 97th Foot   She *d.* 17 Aug 1886, at Barretstown Castle aforesaid   He *m* secondly, 5 Oct. 1887, Florence Elizabeth, da of William RUXTON, of Ardee House, Ardee. He *d.* Oct 1898. Will pr at £4,179   His widow living 1900.

X   1898   SIR KILDARE BORROWES, Baronet [I 1646], of Barretstown Castle aforesaid, 1st s and h , *b* 21 Sep 1852, ed. at Cheltenham College , sometime Capt 11th Hussars, retiring as Lieut Col ; was A D C to the Viceroy of Ireland , *suc to the Baronetcy* in Oct 1898, served in the Imperial Yeomanry in the Transvaal War, 1900   He *m* 31 March 1886, at St Paul's, Knightsbridge, Julia Aline, yst da of William HOLDEN, of Palace House, co. Lancaster, by Blanche, da of J PAULET, of Seaforth House, in that county.

Family Estates —These, in 1883, consisted of 5,065 acres in co Kildare, Queen's County and co. Meath, worth £2,774 a year.

Baronetcies [I.] not on record,

1640—1648;

ARRANGED ALPHABETICALLY.

Memorandum —As in England (see *Memorandum* on p 236), so in Ireland there were apparently some Baronetcies conferred during the Civil Wars, of which no patent, nor even docquet or warrant was enrolled A complete list of these is unattainable, but the following persons, herein arranged alphabetically, seem to have been among them

BOURKE
cr about 1645 ;
ex or *dormant* about 1700

I 1645   DAVID BOURKE, of Kilpeacon, co Limerick, Esq.. s and
h of Oliver Bourke, of Limerick, merchant (Sheriff, 1585, and Mayor, 1591, of that city) was *b* 1588 , was in ward to Thomas Ashe, 10 May 1597; had livery, 12 June 1611, of the estate of his br , Edmund BOURKE , was one of the Sheriffs of the city of Limerick, 1613 and again 1614, and was *cr* a *Baronet* [I] by the Earl of Ormonde, according to the direction of the King, "during the time of the cessation after the beginning of the Rebellion "(ª) [*i e*, the Ulster Civil War, which began Oct 1641], but no patent or Privy Seal is enrolled He was transplanted to Clare in 1653, being then aged 65, and was living at Monanoe in that county in 1661 (ᵇ) He *m* in or before 1615, Catherine, widow of (—) BLAKE, da. of (—) COMYN, of Limerick. He *d*. 1661 Will dat. 8 July 1660, pr. 1661 in Prerog Court [I]

II 1661   SIR OLIVER BOURKE, Baronet [I 1645 ?], s. and h., *b*
about 1615 ; was (with his parents and brother) transplanted in 1653 , *suc to the Baronetcy* in 1661 He, with Mary his wife, formerly wife of Pierce CREAGH, claimed in 1676, lands set out to his father, " Sir David BOURKE, Baronet," and to the said Pierce CREAGH, both of whom being " transplanted Papists " In his will, dat 29 April 1695, pr at Killaloe 2 Feb. 1696, he mentions his nephew James, son of his br David, as his heir

III 1696,   SIR JAMES BOURKE, Baronet [I 1645 ?] nephew and h ,
to   being s of David BOURKE, 4th s of the 1st Baronet ; *suc to the*
1700 ?   *Baronetcy* An undated petition from him, " to be placed on the establishment," is among the Ormonde MSS. The *Baronetcy* at his death became *extinct* or *dormant* (ᶜ)

(ª) The name of " James Bourke, of co Limerick," occurs, as the recipient of a Baronetcy, in a list in the Office of Arms [I.] of " all the honours granted by the Earl of Ormond by direction of the late King during the time of the cessation after the beginning of the Rebellion," but this seems to be a mistake for ' David." [G D Burtchaell.]

(ᵇ) *Ex inform* C M Tenison.

(ᶜ) Sir David Bourke, the 1st Baronet, had three younger sons, viz., Edmund, Patrick, and David Of these, Edmund and Patrick appear to have died s.p.

HORSFALL :

possibly, 1642 ? to 1693.

"SIR CIPRIAN HORSFALL," only s and h of John HORSFALL, Bishop of Ossory, 1586-1609 , was *Knighted* in Ireland, 6 Aug 1628 , Sheriff of co Kilkenny, 1641, and is sometimes stated to have been *cr a Baronet*(a) by Charles I [1642 ?] He m firstly, 15 July 1601, at Knockmoan, co Waterford, Jane, da of Roger DALTON, of Knockmoan aforesaid, and Kirkbynsperton, co York He m secondly, before July 1606, Margaret, 1st da. of David CLERE, Dean of Ossory, 1582-1602 He d s p m.(b) in or before 1693 when the *Baronetcy*, if indeed it ever existed, became *extinct*. His admon, in which, however, he is styled a "Knight," 31 Oct 1693, in Prerog Court [I], to his next of kin

---

HURLY ·(c)

cr. about 1645 ,

attained 1691 ;

assumed till 1714, or later.

I   1645?   THOMAS HURLY, of Knocklong, co Limerick, s. and h of Maurice HURLY, of the same (who d. 3 June 1637), by his 1st wife, 'Grania, da of Ogan O'HOGAN, of Ardcrony, co Tipperary ; suc his father in June 1637 , was Sheriff of co Limerick, 1639, and is said to have been cr. a Baronet [I] by Charles I, presumably about 1645 He m , before June 1637, Lettice, da of Lucas SHEE, of Kilkenny,(d) by Ellen, da. of Edmund (BUTLER), 2d VISCOUNT MOUNTGARRET [I] He d. before 1653. His widow, Lettice, was transplanted, in 1653 to Connaught, being then aged 60

II.   1647?   SIR MAURICE HURLY, Baronet [I 1645?] of Knocklong aforesaid, of Kilduff, co Limerick, and afterwards of Doone, co Galway, s and h ; suc to the Baronetcy on the death of his father, and was one of the supreme council at Kilkenny in 1647. He (with his mother) was transplanted, in 1653, into Connaught, and his estates forfeited He m Margaret, da of (—) O'DWYER. His will, as of "Doone, co Galway, Baronet," dat 1683, pr 1684, in Prerog. Court [I.].

(a) Iu three copies of lists of Baronets of Ireland in Ulster's office, in the handwriting of Thomas Preston, Ulster, the name of Horsfall, but with a query, is placed between those of MacMahon and Esmond , but in these lists the names of Bourke, Colclough, Butler, Wilson, Osborne, and Harbert are omitted, and those of Barnewall, MacBrian, Magrath, and Morres are (also) queried In a revised list, dat 7 March 1639, Horsfall is omitted, but so also are Colclough and Butler

(b) Joan, his only child, m Oliver Grace, of Courtstown, co Kilkenny

(c) Most of the particulars in this article have been supplied by G. D Burtchaell and C M Tenison See vol 1, p 223, note " a " There is an account of this family, by Richard Caulfield and John B'Alton, in the *Top and Gen.*, vol. iii, pp. 462-467.

(d) Lettice Shee, who survived him, is the only wife assigned to him, when he entered and signed his father's funeral certificate in June 1637. A previous wife (unsupported, however, by the O'Ryan pedigree) is sometimes given to him, *viz* , Joanna, da of John BROWN, of Camus, co Tipperary, by Catherine, da of Dermot O'RYAN, of Solloghod, in that county

2 M

III 1684? SIR WILLIAM HURLY, Baronet [I 1645?] s and h, *suc*
to   *to the Baronetcy* on the death of his father, was M P [I] for Kill-
1691   mallock, 1689, in the Parl of James II, for whom he was in
          command of a troop, near Cashel, in 1690, where he received wounds,
of which he probably died. He *m* Mary, da of Col. BLOUNT, by (—), da. of Walter
BOURKE, of the Devil's Bit, co Tipperary He *d* 1691, and was attainted, whereby
his estate and *Baronetcy* became *forfeited* His widow *m* BRIAN O'BRYAN.

IV 1691 "SIR JOHN HURLY, Baronet" [I 1645?] s and h,
          who, notwithstanding the attainder, assumed the title on his
father's death He was arrested in Dublin, about 1714, for trying to raise
forces for the titular King James III

V. 1720? "SIR JOHN HURLY, Baronet" [I 1645?], said to be
          s and h of the above, and to have also assumed the title. Of
him, however, if he ever existed, nothing further is known, and there is no
mention of him in the pedigree entered in Ulster's office.

WALSH .(a)

cr. July 1645,

ex. about 1690?

I. 1645 "JAMES WALSH, of Little Island, co Waterford, Esq,"
          and of Ballygoner, co Waterford, 1st s and h of Robert WALSH,
of the same, sometime (1601 and 1602) Mayor of Waterford, by Beale, da. of
James WHITE, of Kells, co Kilkenny, was *b* about 1580, suc his father, 3 Jan
1603, was M P [I] for co Waterford, 1634-35, and was *cr a Baronet* [I], the
Privy Seal being dat at Oxford, 23 Jan 1644/5, and "Fiant" at Dublin, 9 July [1645]
21 Car I, no patent being enrolled He *m*. firstly, Katherine, da of (—) SHERLOCK
He *m* secondly, in 1603, Katherine, da. of Piers BUTLER, of Callan, co Kilkenny,
by his 1st wife, Jenet, da of Edward WHITE, of Ballinderry, co Roscommon He *d.*
about 1650.

II 1650? SIR ROBERT WALSH, Baronet [I 1645] of Ballygoner
to   aforesaid, s and h,(b) by (—) wife. He was *Knighted*, v p, 24 Oct.
1690?   1642, at Edgehill, by Charles I, and *suc to the Baronetcy* about 1650
          He *m*. before July 1629, Mary, 2d da of Sir George SHERLOCK,(c) of
Leitrim, co Cork, by Anstace, da of (—) WYSE, of Waterford He and his son Pierce
were living 1663, claiming as "Innocents" and again 22 Dec 1680 as defendants in a
Chancery suit. He *d.* s p m s,(d) probably about 1690, when the *Baronetcy* became
extinct.

(a) See p. 248, note "a" "It is given to few mortals to comprehend even super
ficially the mysteries of the maze of Irish political movements, 1641 1651, but the
Cessation, 15 Sep 1643, and the Peace, 30 July 1646, are well marked points in
connection with dealing out honours to the Catholic Loyalists who were against the
Government Several privy seals were issued, while these negotiations were proceeding, some of which were afterwards enrolled, some suggested titles appear never
to have reached a privy seal, and so were not assumed, e g, the Earldom of Wexford
for Viscount Mountgarret, and the Viscounty of Newry for Walter Bagenal, of
Dunleckney The privy seal for Walsh is set out in full in the *Fiant* I think the
same year may be assigned to Bourke and Hurly "[G D Burtchaell].
(b) He had two brothers, neither of whom left male issue
(c) Knighted 28 Nov 1606.
(d) His son, Pierce, who was living 1663 and 1666 [5th Rep D K R Ireland, p. 69,
and 19th Report, p 70], as well as in Dec 1680, *m*. Henrietta Maria de Mouzan, of
Lorraine, and *d* v p and s p m.

Baronetcies of Scotland, or Nova Scotia,[a]

1625—1707.

Memorandum.—The province of Nova Scotia in North America was annexed to the Kingdom of Scotland, and granted, under the Great Seal, 10 [not 29] Sep 1621, to Sir William Alexander, of Menstrie (subsequently EARL OF STIRLING [S.]) as a foreign plantation "The personal influence of Sir William with the King [James I] caused him to approve of the scheme of creating in Scotland an hereditary dignity under the titles of Knights Baronets of Nova Scotia, by means of a scheme similar to that which had proved successful for colonising the districts in the province of Ulster "[b] He accordingly informed the Privy Council of Scotland of his design, 18 Oct 1624, who, on 30 Nov following, issued a proclamation announcing the King's intention of creating 100 such Baronets on 1 April next Before that date was reached, viz on 27 March 1625, King James died, but the grant of 1621 was confirmed in a *novodamus*, 12 July 1625 by Charles I, who, however (six weeks before), on 28 May 1625, had already nominated the premier Baronet, Gordon, as also, then, or a few days later, some others Pixley [*History of Baronetage*, p 160], states that *ten* Baronetcies had been created between 28 May and 19 July 1625, viz , Gordon, Strachan, Keith, Campbell, Innes, Wemyss, Livingston, Douglas, Macdonald and Murray This statement is probably correct, but it is added that, on the said 19 July, the King acquainted the Lords of the Privy Council [S], "that he *had created the above* [ten] *Baronets,*" whereas in his letter of that date, he makes no mention of the names or number of such his creations, but merely says that " we have preferred *some* to be Knight Baronetts " The Royal charter of 28 May 1625 (given in full in Pixley's work, pp 59-89), "which was twice ratified and confirmed by acts of the Parl of Scotland, viz , 31 July 1630 and 28 June 1633 was made, by subsequent instruments under the Great Seal, the regulating charter for the Baronets of Scotland and Nova Scotia "[b] Each Baronet received, on the resignation of Sir William Alexander, above-named "a grant of 16,000 [or more in some cases, as in that of Keith] acres of land in the Royal Province of Nova Scotia (which, as anciently bounded, comprehended Nova Scotia proper, Cape Breton, Anticosti, Gaspe, Prince Edward's Island and New Brunswick), to be incorporated into a full entire and free Barony and Regality for ever to be held of the Kingdom of Scotland[b] The number of persons when this order was instituted in 1625 was not to exceed 150, and Nova Scotia was nominally divided into so many Baronies. The sum payable by each was 3,000 merks (the equivalent to £166 13s 4d sterling) of which one-third was to go into [Sir W] Alexander's pocket, he engaging that the other two-thirds should be expended in setting forth the plantation. During the first four years the applicants who received patents were only about 60 , during the next 10 years about 50 more, and thus the object remained unaccomplished during the reign of Charles although its original sphere was so enlarged as to render persons not connected with Scotland admissible to this dignity "[b] During the entire reign of Charles I "122 Baronets [S] appear to have

---

(a) The Editor is deeply indebted to Sir James Balfour Paul, Lyon King of Arms, for numerous and most valuable additions (of which the most important only are specifically acknowledged) to the account here given of these dignities. The reader, however, must not imagine that (unless expressly so stated) this account has the official, or even the practical *imprimatur* of "Lyon," but must consider it merely as the one which seems to be the most correct, or at least the most probable, to the compiler Robert Riddle Stodart, Lyon Clerk Depute (1863-86), kindly gave, from his own genealogical collection, much information as to some of these Baronetcies.

(b) *History of the Baronetage*, by Francis W Pixley, 1900

been created, of whom about 111 had grants of 16,000 acres each,"[a] but such giants ceased altogether after 1638 [b]

The somewhat complicated history of Nova Scotia as respects its alternate possession by England or France, and the sale, or alleged sale, in 1630, by Sir W. Alexander of all "his title to the whole of Nova Scotia, with the exception of Port Royal," are set forth in Laing's *New Scotland Tracts* [c]

"It is no easy matter to prepare a very accurate or satisfactory LIST OF THESE KNIGHT BARONETS [S]   The earliest list I have met with is contained in *A catalogue of the Dukes, etc. of England, Scotland, and Ireland*, etc., collected by T W [i.e, Thomas Walkeley] London, 1640, 12mo   At p 21 [pp 117-120 of the edit pub in 1642] *the names of Knight Baronets of Scotland*, amounting in all to 95, including Sir Henry Gib (of St Martin's) but the dates of the patents are not given   Of this catalogue by T W, or Thomas Walkeley, Lowndes quotes several editions."[c]   This catalogue ends about 1638, with the names of Sir John Lowther, Sir Gilbert Pickering, Sir Edward Longevile, Sir Thomas Perse [i e, Piers], Sir Edward Musgrave, and Sir William Witherington, all six stated to be English

Another list (containing, however, but 70 Baronets) ending about the same date, with the name of Sir Henry Bingham [cr 30 June 1634], and signed "T P, Ulster" [i.e., Thomas Preston, Ulster King of arms, 1633-1642], is now remaining in Ulster's office   A copy of this has courteously been sent to the Editor by G D Burtchaell, with the kind permission of Sir Arthur Vicars, Ulster King of arms

The "ROLL OF BARONETS OF NOVA SCOTIA who had territorial grants from Sir William Alexander Earl of Stirling," is printed in Laing's *New Scotland Tracts* [c]   The grantees there given are 114 in number and it is stated that 'the Precepts are entered" in a volume at the General Register House, Edinburgh, entitled "*Regist Precep Cart pro Baronettis Nov Scotiæ*, 1625 1630"   The reference to the pages in that volume, which refers to 94 of these Baronetcies, are set out, it being (somewhat perplexingly) added, that as to the remaining 20, "the names having no references are given on the authority of former lists"   The date presumably that of the creation of the dignity is affixed to all but these three, viz —No 41, "James Campbell of Aberuchill," placed between 13 Dec 1627 and 1 Jan following, No 63, "Edward Barrett, Lord of Newburgh," placed between 2 Oct 1628, and 26 June following, and No 93 "Sir John Gascoigne" placed next, after 6 Jan 1634/5, to whom however the date *in brackets* of "8 June" is affixed   At the end of this list, which concludes with No 114, Sir Edward Longueville, 17 Dec 1638, is added.   "Two blank precepts, names and dates not supplied   Several of the above are included in the Register of the Great Seal, and also at great length in the *Register of Signatouris in the office of Comptrollerie*, but others, probably from not having paid the fees, seem not to have been registered."[c]   This chronologically arranged list is the one chiefly followed, as to the placing of these Baronetcies, by the editor of this present work

By far the most valuable list of these Baronets is that by Robert Milne, printed from a MS. in the Advocates' Library, Edinburgh, supposed to have been taken from a list or book of accounts in the Exchequer which was destroyed by a fire that occurred in that office.   This list has been printed (with various additions) by Joseph Foster in his *Baronetage* for 1883, and (unlike the lists abovenamed) extends beyond the reign

(a) See p 275 note "b."

(b) The following interesting and contemporary account of this institution is given by the first member thereof, Sir Robert Gordon, in his *History of the Earldom of Sutherland*.   "This year of God 1625, King Charles created and instituted the order of *Knights-Baronets in Old Scotland*, for the furtherance of the plantation of *New Scotland* in America, being the true mean or honor betuen a Barone of Parliament and a Knight, a purpose intended by his father of worthie memorie, bot perfyted by his Majestie.   Sir Robert Gordoun, tutor of Southerland, wes maid *the first Baronet of the Kingdome of Old Scotland* and called *Baronet Gordoun*, which dignitie wes by his Majestie's lettres patent under his Great Seale granted to him and to his heyrs-maill whatsoever.   The Lairds of Cluny and Lesmoir, both of the surname of Gordoun, were also this yeir created Baronets.   James Gourdoun, the Laird of Lesmoir's eldest sone, wes knighted, according to the tennor of his father's patent, wherby the Baronet's eldest sones are to be knighted at the aige of 21 years, iff ther fathers bee then alive"

(c) "Royal Letters, Charters and Tracts relating to the colonization of New Scotland, and the institution of the order of Knight-Baronets of Nova Scotia, 1621—1638," by David Laing, published by the Bannatyne Club, Edinburgh, 1867.

of Charles I, down to the end of these creations in 1707, being the date of the Union with Scotland

Another list, extending also through the whole period (1625—1707), but in which no date save that of the year is given to the various creations, is in Beatson's *Political Index* (1806), vol III, pp 70-77   In this work 141 creations are assigned to Charles II, 89 to Charles II, 17 to James II, 23 to William III and 27 to Queen Anne, in all 297 creations

Besides the above, there is in Banks's *Baronia Anglica concentrata* (1843, 4to, vol II, pp 210-248), an account of the institution and continuance of this degree   The author of that work styles himself "Sir T C Banks, Bart, N S," but though his claim to that dignity was very absurd, the work itself has considerable merit.   In it is a "List of Baronets, who had sasine of their Baronies in Nova Scotia taken from the minute book of general register of sasines at Edinburgh"   This list commences with Sir Alexander STRACHAN, July 1625, and ends with Sir Andrew KER Dec 1637, and Sir Robert CAMPBELL, Nov 1640   It contains 73 names in all, out of which three seem to relate to the same Baronetcy   There is also another list, viz, of "The persons [who] obtained charters of lands in Nova Scotia, which do *not* appear to have been followed by seisin"   The number of these is 41

These lists, when referred to, will be styled *Milne's List, Laing's List, Walkeley's List, Ulster's List, Beatson's List,* and *Banks's Lists,* which last refer as well to the Baronets who *did,* as to those who *did not* obtain seizin of the Nova Scotia territory

"After the restoration of King Charles II, the description of *Nova Scotia* was omitted ; so that the Baronets thus created cannot be considered as coming under the conditions of the original foundation of that order   The following patents *de titulo Militis Baronetti in Scotland* are given as a few examples [from the] Index to [the] Register of the Great Seal of Scotland   *Diploma* to Sir Andrew Gilmour, 16 Aug. 1661, to Sir John Foulis, of Ravelston, 15 Oct 1661 ; to Sir George Ogilvy, of Barras, 5 March 1661/2, to Sir David Carnegy, 20 Feb 1663, to Sir Thomas Hay, of Park, 23 Aug 1663, to Sir George Mowat, of Inghston, 2 June 1664, to Sir James Brown, of Barbadoes, 17 Feb 1664, to Sir James Murray, of Stanhope, 13 Feb 1664 ; to Sir John Henderson, of Fordel, 16 July 1664 [and] to Sir John Kilcaldie, of Grange, 14 May 1664." [Banks's *Baronia Anglica concentrata* above mentioned]

GORDON

(Premier Baronetcy of Scotland) ·
cr 28 May and sealed 23 July 1625[a],
dormant, 1795—1806,
re-assumed, since 1806

I 1625   THE HONBLE SIR ROBERT GORDON, Knt., 4th but 2d
                surv s[b] of Alexander (GORDON), EARL OF SUTHERLAND [S], by his 2d wife, Jean da of George (GORDON), 4th EARL OF HUNTLY [S], was *b* 14 May 1580, at Dunrobin Castle, co Sutherland ; ed at the Univ of St Andrew's and, 1598, at that of Edinburgh, was in 1606 a Gent. of the Privy Chamber to King James, and subsequently, 1625, to Charles I, was *cr* M A of the Univ of Cambridge, March 1614/5, and, having been *Knighted,* was *cr* a Baronet "with precedence of all the rest by particular clause in his patent,"[a] 28 May 1625, "sealed 23 July 1625" with rem to heirs male whatsoever[a] and with a grant of 16,000 acres in

---

(a) Milne's List and Laing's List   A copy *in extenso* of the lengthy patent of this Baronetcy is printed in Douglas' *Baronage of Scotland* [1798], pp 2-13, under "Gordon, of Gordonstoun," as also (31 pages, close print, 4to) in Pixley's *History of the Baronage,* pp 59-89

(b) He was one of five brothers, of whom the 2d and 3d died in infancy, the issue male of the first brother, John, Earl of Sutherland [S], became extinct, 16 June 1766, on the death of William, the 17th Earl.   The 5th and yst. br, was the Hon Sir Alexander Gordon, of Navidale.   He was *b* 5 March 1585, emigrated with his family to Ireland in 1631, and had five sons (born 1614 to 1627), all of whom apparently died without issue.   Had any male issue been existing in 1795 the heir to the Baronetcy would, presumably, have been among such issue.

Nova Scotia, forming the Barony and Regality of Gordon, of which, however, no seizin appears to have followed (ᵃ) He was Sheriff of Invernesshire 1629, and M P [S] thereof 1630, was guardian to his nephew, the Earl of Sutherland [S], 1615-30; Vice-Chamberlain of Scotland, 1630, and P C [S], 1634 He was the author of the well known *History of the Earldom of Sutherland*, which was, however, not printed (though written nearly 200 years before) till 1813 Having bought the estate of Plewlands, co Moray, it and others were by charter, 20 June 1642, erected into *the Barony of Gordonstoun*. He *m* 16 Feb 1612/3, in London, Louisa, da and h of John GORDON, of Glenluce, co Wigtoun and of Longormes in France, Dean of Salisbury, 1602 19 (son of Alexander Gordon, Bishop of Galloway, 1568-83), by his 2d wife Genevieve(ᵇ), da of Gideon PÉTAU, Seigneur de Moylett, President of the Parl of Brittany He *d* March 1656, aged 76 Will dat. 11 July 1654 His widow, who was *b*. 20 Dec 1597, *d* Sep 1680, aged 83

II 1656   SIR LUDOVICK GORDON, Baronet [S 1625], of Gordonstoun aforesaid, s and h, *b* 15 Oct 1624, at Salisbury,(ᶜ) M P [S] for Elgin and Forresshire, 1649, *suc to the Baronetcy* in March 1656, suffered severely during the Civil War, his losses amounting to £10,000, and was fined £3,600 in 1667. In or about 1688 he registered in Lyon's office, his arms and supporters as *Premier Baronet of Scotland* He *m*. firstly, 2 Jan 1644, at Aberdeen, Elizabeth, da. and coheir of Sir Robert FARQUHAR, of Menie in Daviot, co Aberdeen She *d* Nov 1661, age 38 He *m* secondly (contract 6 March 1669) Jean, da of John STEWART, of Ladywell He *d* in or before 1688, possibly in Sep 1685

III 1685 ?   SIR ROBERT GORDON, Baronet, [S. 1625], of Gordonstoun aforesaid 1st s and h by 1st wife, *b* 7 March 1647, at Gordonstoun, was M P [S] for co. Sutherland, 1672-74, 1678, 1681 82 and 1685-86, for Elgin and Forresshire, 1696, till void 1 Oct 1696, said to have been *Knighted* about 1683(ᵈ), *suc to the Baronetcy* in or before 1688, possibly in Sep 1685, F R S, 3 Feb 1686, being a scientific mechanist and inventor of machinery, was served heir general to his father, 21 Sep 1688, was a gent of the household to James II He executed an entail of the Gordonstoun estate in 1697, and obtained a "Novodamus" thereof, 27 June 1698 He *m* firstly, 23 Feb 1676, Margaret, Dow BARONESS DUFFUS [S], da of William (FORBES), LORD FORBES [S], by his 1st wife, Jean, da of Sir John CAMPBELL. She *d* s.p.m 13 April 1677. He *m* secondly, in 1691, Elizabeth, da and h of Sir William DUNBAR, 1st Baronet [S 1700], of Hempriggs, by Margaret, da of Alexander SINCLAIR, of Lathron He *d* 5 Sep. or Oct 1704 M I at Ogston His widow *m* Hon James SUTHERLAND, afterwards DUNBAR, who inherited the estate of Hempriggs, and was cr a Baronet S] 10 Dec. 1706, whom see.

IV 1704   SIR ROBERT GORDON, Baronet [S 1625], of Gordonstoun aforesaid, s and h by 2nd wife, *b* 1696, *suc to the Baronetcy*, 5 Oct 1704, served heir general of his father, 12 July 1705, was M P for Caithness, 1715 22, was out in the rising of 1715, but soon afterwards conformed to Government. In 1766 he claimed the EARLDOM OF SUTHERLAND [S] as heir *male*, but without success, against the heir *general*. On 11 May 1767, he entailed various lands in Morayshire He *m* 26 May 1734, Agnes, 1st da of Sir William MAXWELL, 3d Baronet [S. 1627] of Calderwood, by Christian, da of Alexander STEWART, of Torrence He *d*. 8 Jan 1772. Will pr Dec 1773 His widow *d* 11 March 1808, aged 89, at Lossiemouth

V. 1772   SIR ROBERT GORDON, Baronet [S 1625], of Gordonstoun aforesaid, s and h, *b* about 1738, *suc to the Baronetcy*, 8 Jan 1772, and was, on 30 April 1774, served h of provision general to his father. He *d*. unm 2 June 1776 in his 39th year

(ᵃ) Banks' Lists
(ᵇ) She *d* at Gordonstoun, 6 Dec. 1643, in her 83d year
(ᶜ) James, Duke of Lennox, and George, Lord Gordon, were his godfathers, and Frances, Duchess of Richmond and Lennox, was his godmother, by whose direction he was called Ludovick, after the late Duke
(ᵈ) He is called a Knight in 1685, but not in 1682, possibly, however, the word "Knight" may be used for ' Baronet '

VI. 1776,   SIR WILLIAM GORDON, Baronet [S 1625], of Gordonstoun([a])
to   aforesaid, only br and h ; *suc. to the Baronetcy*, 2 June 1776, and was,
1795.   on 20 Dec 1776, served h of proximon general to his br. He *d*
unm in the Canongate of Edinburgh (Thursday) 5 and was *bur*
11 March 1795 in the Chapel Royal of Holyroodhouse, aged 56,([b]) when the issue
male of the grantee became, presumably, *extinct* ([c])

[The Baronetcy remained dormant for about 10 years after the death
in 1795 of the 6th Baronet, at which date the collateral heir male of the grantee is
supposed to have been among the descendants of one of the two younger brothers of
his grandfather's grandfather, Adam Gordon, of Aboyne, *jure mariti* Earl of Sutherland
[S], the 2d son of George, 2d Earl of Huntly [S] Sir William Gordon, of Gight,
co Aberdeen (who was killed at Flodden 9 Sep 1513) was the elder of these two,
but his male issue is supposed to have become *extinct* on the death of Sir George
Gordon, the 8th of Gight The younger brother (4th and yst s of the said Earl of
Huntly) was Sir James Gordon of Letterfourie, co Banff, Admiral of the Fleet [S],
1513, whose descendant assumed the Baronetcy in 1806, as below]

VII. *1795.*   ALEXANDER GORDON, of Letterfourie, co. Banff, was
(according to the Scotch service, obtained in 1806 by his son) cousin
and h male of the late Baronet and, as such, would have been, after 5 March 1795,
entitled to the Baronetcy, which, however, he never assumed. He was 4th and yst
s of James GORDON of Letterfourie aforesaid, by Glicerie, da of Sir William DUNBAR,
1st Baronet [S 1698], of Durn, which James (who *m.* 1695, and *d* aged 87,) was s.
and h of John GORDON, of the same (*b* 1627, and *d* 1721), s and h of James
GORDON of Letterfourie, 1633 and 1649, who, according to the service of 1806, was
s of another James GORDON,([d]) the s. and h of James GORDON, Admiral of the
Fleet [S] 1513, the first of Letterfourie, who was youngest br of Adam (GORDON),
EARL OF SUTHERLAND [S], the great great grandfather of the 1st Baronet He
was *b* 1715 , was in the rising of 1745, soon after which he joined his br , James
GORDON, a wine merchant in Madeira. On 12 July 1791 he was served heir general
or his father and of his said br He *m* , 1778, Heleo, da of Alexander RUSSELL, of
Moncoffer, co Banff He *d* 16 Jan 1797, in his 83d year.

VIII. *1797*   JAMES GORDON, *afterwards* (according to the service
to   of 22 April 1806) SIR JAMES GORDON, Baronet [S 1625], of Letter-
1806   fourie aforesaid, s and h , *b* 1779 On 11 Nov 1797 was served
heir special of his father in estates at Durn, etc., co Banff On
3 May 1804 was served heir male and heir of line general to his great great great

---

([a]) Gordonstoun is called in Douglas' *Baronage* [S], 1798, "a noble house with fine
gardens," and together with "Drainy and Dollas all in the county of Murray," is
said to be among "the chief seats" of the family.

([b]) He had an illegitimate son, William GORDON, of Halmyre, co Peebles, who had
issue The estates, after a law suit between the descendants (heirs of line) of Lucy,
wife of David SCOTT, of Scotstarvit, da. of the 3d Baronet, and Alexander Peurose
CUMMING, of Altyre (great great grandson of Lucy, da of the 2d Baronet by her 1st
husband, Robert CUMMING, of Altyre), went to the latter (presumably under some
entail), who took the name of GORDON, and was cr a Baronet in 1804

([c]) The issue male of Robert Gordon, of Pulrossie, co Sutherland, the only one of
the younger sons of the 1st Baronet who had issue, had apparently failed He bought
the estate of Cluny, co Aberdeen, from Sir John Gordon, 2d Baronet [S 1625] of
Cluny, and was ancestor of Robert Gordon, of Cluny, living in Oct 1745 but "past
the age of action in the field," who however had then a son described as "a very fine
young gentleman and may be of great use," which son, however, presumably died
s p before the death of the 6th Baronet in 1795

([d]) No evidence appears to exist for this part of the pedigree It is to be noted
that there are only 7 generations in more than 300 years The 1st Laird of Letterfourie was *b* probably about 1460, while Sir James GORDON, who assumed the
Baronetcy in 1806, and who was 7th in descent from him, was *b* 1779 There is
evidence also of a William GORDON, of Letterfourie in 1572, and of a Patrick
GORDON, of Letterfourie in 1592 and in 1625.

great grandfather, Sir James GORDON, the first of Letterfourie   On 22 April 1806 he was served heir male general to his cousin, Sir William GORDON, 6th Baronet [S 1625] of Gordonstoun, after which date he *assumed the Baronetcy*. He *m* in 1801 Mary, 1st da. and coheir of William GLENDONWYN, of Parton, co Kircudbright. He *d* 24 Dec 1843 at Letterfourie   His widow *d* 18 May 1845, aged 62

IX   1843   SIR WILLIAM GORDON, Baronet [S 1625],(a) of Letterfourie aforesaid, s and h., *b* 26 Dec 1803   Major, 66th Regiment, Lieut Col in the army, *suc to the Baronetcy*,(a) 24 Dec 1843   He *d* unm. 5 Dec. 1861, aged 58, at Letterfourie.

X   1861   SIR ROBERT GLENDONWYN GORDON, Baronet [S 1625],(a) of Letterfourie aforesaid, youngest br and h, *b* 1824   Deputy Lieut for Banffshire, *suc to the Baronetcy*,(a) 5 Dec 1861

Family estates —These, in 1883, consisted of 2,331 acres, in the counties of Banff, Dumfries and Kirkcudbright   *Principal Seat* —Letterfourie, near Buckie, co Banff.

KEITH,

EARL MARISCHAL [S]

cr 28 May 1625,

forfeited, 1716.

I   1625   WILLIAM (KEITH), EARL MARISCHAL [S.], who had succeeded to that dignity on the death of his father, 2 April 1623, was *cr* a *Baronet* [S.], 28 May 1625,(b) with rem. to heirs male whatsoever, and with a grant of no less than 48,000 acres (three times the usual amount) in Nova Scotia, of which however he appears never to have had seizin (c) By another charter of the same date he gets the ratification of a grant by Sir William Alexander "de officio Admiralitatis" of the said lands, and of coining money in Nova Scotia, for nineteen years after the date of 23 May 1625, and the ratification of a contract made between them "apud Strand" on the date last named. The patent is not in the Great Seal Register [S] This Baronetcy devolved with the peerage, till *forfeited* therewith in 1716 See *Peerage*

INNES

cr 28 May 1625, but not sealed till 2 April 1628,(d)

afterwards, 1769—1807, INNES-NORCLIFFE,

subsequently, since 1807, INNES-KER,

and, since 1812 (*de jure* since 1805), DUKES OF ROXBURGHE [S].

I   1625   SIR ROBERT INNES, of that ilk, in Urquhart, co Elgin, s and h. of Robert INNES, of the same (M P [S] for Elgin, 1612), by Elizabeth, da. of Robert (ELPHINSTONE), 3d LORD ELPHINSTONE [S], was *cr* a *Baronet* [S], 20 May 1625,(d) sealed 2 April 1628, but not recorded in the Great Seal Register, with rem to heirs male whatsoever and with a grant of presumably 16,000

(a) According to the service of 22 April 1806, whereby his lineal ancestor was served heir male general to the 6th Baronet

(b) Laing's List, not, however, in Milne's List nor in the Great Seal Register.

(c) Ranks's Lists

(d) Milne's List, where the date is given as 28, and Laing's list, where it is given as 29 May 1625 This Baronetcy is called in Douglas' *Baronage* [S] the second [i e, second according to order of *creation*, not of precedency] in the order of Baronets [then] existing in Scotland   Douglas apparently reckons this Baronetcy next to that of Gordon

acres in Nova Scotia, of which he had seizin in May 1628 (a) Was M P. [S] for Elgin, 1639-41 and 1648 ; had charters of the lands and barony of Delny, 12 Feb 1631, and of those of Newton, Banscoul, etc , 25 July 1636 He was made by the Parl one of the committee of estates and a P C [S], yet in 1649 appears to have been considered a Royalist He m Grizel, da of James (STEWART), EARL OF MORAY [S], by Elizabeth, 1st da and heir of line of James (STEWART), EARL OF MORAY [S], sometime Regent [S] He d between 1649 and 1660

II. 1655 ?   SIR ROBERT INNES, Baronet [S 1625], of that ilk, 1st s and h. ; *suc to the Baronetcy* on his father's death, and had (being then a Baronet) charter of his lands, 15 July 1661 , was M P [S] for Elgin, 1661-63 and 1678 He m Jean, da of James (ROSS), 6th LORD ROSS OF HALKHEAD [S], by Margaret, da. of Walter (SCOTT), 1st LORD SCOTT OF BUCCLEUCH [S] She was served, 6 Feb 1649, coheir to her brother, and again 19 Oct 1653, coheir to her mother (b)

III   1690 ?   SIR JAMES INNES, Baronet [S 1625], of that ilk, 1st s. and h ; *suc to the Baronetcy* on his father's death He m (contract 18 July 1666) Margaret, 3d da and coheir of Harry KER, *styled* LORD KER, by Margaret, da. of William (HAY), EARL OF ERROLL [S], which Harry was only surv. s and h ap of Robert (KER), 1st EARL OF ROXBURGH [S], but d v p and s p m Feb 1642/3 She d before 25 Feb 1691

IV   1700 ?   SIR HARRY INNES, Baronet [S 1625], of that ilk, 2d but 1st surv s and h (c), b about 1670 , M P [S] for Elgin and Forres shire, 1704-07 . *suc to the Baronetcy* on his father's death, before 1704 He m (contract 3 and 4 Sep 1694) Jean, da of Duncan FORBES, of Culloden He d. 12 Nov. 1721

V   1721   SIR HARRY INNES, Baronet [S 1625], of that ilk, 2d but 1st surv s and h.(d), *suc to the Baronetcy,* 12 Nov 1721, and was served heir male to his father 29 June 1723 , Inspector of Seizures [S], March 1748 He m. (contract 9 Oct 1727) Anne, 2d da of Sir James GRANT, *formerly* COLQUHOUN, 6th Baronet [S. 1625], by Anne, da. and h of Sir Humphrey COLQUHOUN, 5th Baronet [S 1625] He d 31 Oct 1762. His widow d at Elgin 9 Feb. 1771.

VI   1762.   SIR JAMES INNES, *afterwards,* [1769-1807], INNES-NOR-CLIFFE, *and subsequently* INNES-KER, Baronet [S. 1625], sometime of Innes aforesaid, 2d but 1st surv s and h (e); b 10 Jan 1736 at Innes House, in Innes ; ed at Leyden Univ , Capt 88th Foot 1759, 58th Foot 1779 , *suc to the Baronetcy,* 31 Oct 1762, being served heir, 7 Feb 1764 , sold the ancient family estate of Innes in 1767 to James (DUFF), Earl Fife [I] He m. firstly, 19 April 1769, at St James' Westm , Mary, 1st sister and coheir (10 Jan 1805) of Sir Cecil WRAY, 12th Baronet [1611], da of Sir John WRAY, 11th Baronet, by Frances, da. and h of Fairfax NORCLIFFE of Langton, in the East Riding of Yorkshire She inherited her mother's estates, whereupon he, by royal lic , 31 May 1769, took the name of *Norcliffe* after that of *Innes,* but, on losing the Langton estate by her death, s p , 20 July 1807, he dropped the name of Norcliffe and took that of *Ker* in addition to *Innes* He m secondly (8 days after his 1st wife's death) 28 July 1807, at Kensington, Harriet, da of Benjamin CHARLEWOOD, of Windlesham, Surrey. She was living when, by a decision in the House of Lords, 11 May 1812, he was declared

(a) Banks's Lists.
(b) In the first of these services she is called " Domina Jeanna Ross, Domina Innes, sponsa Roberti Innes, Junioris, de eodem," and in the second one " Jean Ross, Lady Innes." It seems clear that her husband being called *" Junior "* in 1649 had not at that date succeeded to his father's title It is just possible that the word " Domina " in 1649 (as also, perhaps, " Lady " in 1653) was applied to her as being the daughter of a Peer
(c) Robert Innes, the 1st s , d. in France v p and unm.
(d) Robert Innes, the 1st son, capt in the army, d v.p. and unm
(e) Harry Innes, the 1st son, d. v.p. and unm

to have succeeded as DUKE AND EARL OF ROXBURGHE, etc. [S], after the death of the late Duke, 22 Oct 1805, and when, accordingly (not having done so before), he assumed that title(a) in which this *Baronetcy* then *merged* and so continues See *Peerage*.

WEMYSS, *or* WEEMS
cr 29 May 1625, sealed 30 Sep 1626(b),
afterwards, 1628-1679, LORD WEMYSS OF ELCHO [S];
and subsequently, 1633-1679, EARLS OF WEMYSS [S],
dormant, June 1679.

I 1625   SIR JOHN WEEMS [*or* WEMYSS], of that ilk, co Fife, 2d s of Sir John WEMYSS, of the same, by his 2d wife, Mary [not Anne], sister of James, EARL OF MORAY [S], da. of James (STEWART), 1st LORD DOUNE [S], was served heir, 17 April 1610, to his elder br, David WEMYSS (who *d.* v p in Aug. 1608, having, however, been enfeft of the property), was M P [S] for Fifeshire, 1617, suc his father after Aug 1620, and was cr. a Baronet [S.], 29 May 1625,(b) sealed 30 Sep 1626 with rem to heirs male whatsoever, and with a grant of, presumably, 16,000 acres in Nova Scotia, entitled the Regality of New Wemyss, of which he had seizin Nov 1626 (c) He *m*, 1610, Jean, 1st da of Patrick (GRAY) LORD GRAY [S], by his 2d wife, Mary, da of Robert (STEWART), 1st EARL OF ORKNEY [S] She was living when he was cr 1 April 1628, LORD WEMYSS OF ELCHO [S], and, subsequently, 25 June 1633, EARL OF WEMYSS [S] In those peerages this *Baronetcy* then *merged*, till on the death of his son, the 2d EARL OF WEMYSS [S], s p m s. June 1679, the peerage titles devolved in the female line (see *Peerage*), but the *Baronetcy*, to which the heir male of the grantee was entitled, became *dormant*, and so continues

---

CAMPBELL :
cr 29 May 1625, but not sealed till 30 June 1627 ,(b)
sometime, 1677-81, EARL OF CAITHNESS [S],
afterwards, since 1681, EARLS OF BREADALBANE AND HOLLAND [S.],
and sometime, 1831-62, and since 1885, MARQUESSES OF BREADALBANE.

I 1625   SIR DUNCAN CAMPBELL, of Glenurchie, *otherwise* Glenorchy, co Perth, s and h of Sir Colin CAMPBELL, of the same, by Catherine, da of William (RUTHVEN), 2d LORD RUTHVEN [S], was *b* about 1550; suc his father, 11 April 1583, was one of the Barons to attend at the Coronation of Anne, Queen Consort of James VI [S], 18 May 1590, when he was *Knighted*, was a minor Baron [S] 1592 and again Dec 1599, was M P [S] for Argyllshire, 1593 and was cr a Baronet [S.], 29 May 1625,(b) sealed 30 June 1627, but not recorded in the Great Seal Register, with rem to heirs male whatsoever and with a grant of, presumably, 16,000 acres in Nova Scotia, of which both he (July 1627) as also his son (Sep 1631) had seizin (d) He was made, by Charles I, Hereditary Sheriff of Perthshire for life. He was known as "Black Duncan," and was a great planter

---

(a) This Dukedom had been conferred, 25 April 1707, on the 5th Earl of Roxburghe [S], with the same remainder as that of the Earldom Sir James was neither *heir male* nor even *heir of line* of the 1st Earl, though he was a descendant of him through his yst. grand-daughter He, in fact, inherited the Peerage under a nomination in 1648 of the Roxburghe dignities.

(b) Milne's List and Laing's List

(c) Banks's Lists.

(d) Banks's Lists The seizin of Sir Colin in Sep 1631 is spoken of as that "of the Barony of Glenurquhy Campbell in Nova Scotia and haill iron and gold mines within the same, and privilege of transporting all gold affecting mines thereto "

and builder, as well as a great traveller He *m* firstly, in 1574, Jean, 4th da. of
John STEWART), 4th EARL OF ATHOLL [S], Lord Chancellor [S] 1577-79, being his
2d da by his 2d wife, Margaret, da of Malcolm (FLEMING), 3d LORD FLEMING [S]
Her will confirmed 25 July 1595   He *m.* secondly, Elizabeth, da of Henry
(SINCLAIR), LORD SINCLAIR [S], by his 2d wife, Elizabeth, da. of William (FORBES),
7th LORD FORBES [S]   He *d* 23 June 1631, aged 81, and was *bur.* at Finlarig,
near Loch Tay

II   1631   SIR COLIN CAMPBELL, Baronet [S 1625], of Glenorchy
                  aforesaid, 1st s. and h , by 1st wife. *b* about 1577 , *suc. to the
Baronetcy*, June 1631   He, 10 Sep. 1631, had seizin of the lands in Nova Scotia (a)
He *m.* about 1600, Juliana, 1st da of Hugh (CAMPBELL), 1st LORD LOUDOUN [S], by
his 1st wife, Margaret, da of Sir John GORDON, of Lochinvar.   She, who was 52 in
1633, was living 1648   He *d. s p* , 6 Sep 1640, aged 63

III   1640.   SIR ROBERT CAMPBELL, Baronet [S. 1625], of Glenorchy
                  aforesaid, br and h , *b* about 1580 , was sometime of Glenfalloch ,
suc to the Baronetcy, 6 Sep and was served heir to his brother, 27 Oct. 1640 , M P.
[S] for Argyllshire, 1639-41, 1643 44, and 1644 49   He *m.* about 1610 (before Nov
1620), Isabel, da of Lachlan MACINTOSH, of Torcastle, Captain of the clan Chattan.
He was living 1647

IV.   1650 ?   SIR JOHN CAMPBELL, Baronet [S. 1625], of Glenorchy,
                  1st s. and h , *b* about 1615 ; *suc to the Baronetcy* after 1647   He
was M.P [S.] for Argyllshire, 1661 63   He *m* firstly, in or before 1635, Mary, 1st
da. of William (GRAHAM), EARL OF AIRTH AND MENTEITH [S], by Agnes, da of
Patrick (GRAY), LORD GRAY [S]   He *m* secondly, Christian, da. of John MUSCHET,
of Craighead, in Menteith   He *d* before June 1677

V.   1670 ?   SIR JOHN CAMPBELL, Baronet [S 1625], of Glenorchy
                  aforesaid, only s and h , by 1st wife, *b* about 1635, took an active
part in the rising [S] for Charles II, which was suppressed in 1654   He, or
his father, was M P [S] for Argyllshire 1669-74   He *m.* firstly, 17 Dec 1657,
at St Andrew's Wardrobe, London, Mary, da of Henry (RICH), 1st EARL OF
HOLLAND, by Isabel, da and h of Sir Walter COPE, of Kensington   She *d* 8 Feb.
1666   He, before his 2d marriage (7 April 1678) with Mary, DOW COUNTESS OF
CAITHNESS, was, under the style of " Sir John Campbell, of Glenorchy, Baronet,"(b)
cr. 28 June 1677, EARL OF CAITHNESS, etc [S], which dignity, however, he
resigned in 1681, when he was *cr* , 13 Aug 1681, EARL OF BREADALBANE AND
HOLLAND [S], with the precedency of 28 June 1677   In these Earldoms this
Baronetcy then *merged*, and in the title of Breadalbane has so continued, save that on
the death of the 1st Earl, 19 March 1717, it should, apparently, have passed to his
1st s and h., Duncan, *styled* LORD ORMELIE, who, on account of his incapacity, was
passed over in the succession to the Earldom, and who *d s p* in 1727, aged 67,
when the said Baronetcy vested in the next brother the 2d Earl, the heir male of
the grantee   See *Peerage*

DOUGLAS

cr. 28 May,(c) and sealed 18 Aug 1625 ,(c)

dormant since 28 Nov 1812

I.   1625   SIR WILLIAM DOUGLAS of Glenbervie, co. Kincardine,
                  s and h of the Hon Sir Robert DOUGLAS, of the same, by Elizabeth,
da of Sir George AUCHINLECK, of Balmanno, which Robert (living July 1592, was 2d

(a) See p 282, note " d "
(b) Wood's *Douglas' Baronage* [S], vol 11, p 688 [appendix]
(c) The date of 30 May 1625 is that assigned both in Milne's List and Laing's List,
but it is stated (Macfarlane's *Genealogical Collections*, vol 11, p. 272) that "the patent
itself is of the date 28 May 1625." This Baronetcy is in Douglas' *Baronage* called

s. of William, 9th EARL OF ANGUS [S], had charter of the Barony of Glenbervie
3 Dec. 1622, and was *cr* a *Baronet* [S] 28 May,[a] sealed 18 Aug 1625, with rem
to heirs male whatsoever, and with a grant of, presumably, 16,000 acres of land called
the Barony of Douglas in Nova Scotia, of which he had seizin in the said month of
Aug (b) Living 25 March 1653 He *m.* before 1624, Jauet, 3d da of Alexander
IRVINE, of Drum.

II. 1660 ?   SIR WILLIAM DOUGLAS, Baronet [S. 1625] of Glenbervie
aforesaid, only s and h , *suc to the Baronetcy* on the death of his
father He *m.* in 1642, Anne, only da and h of James DOUGLAS, of Stoneypath
and Ardit, with whom he had a great estate He *d* before 1688, probably before
1685 Will confirmed at Brechin, 11 Jan 1688

III. 1680 ?   SIR ROBERT DOUGLAS, Baronet [S 1625], of Glenbervie
aforesaid, only s and h , *suc to the Baronetcy* on the death of his
father. He was a general officer in the army, Col of the Scotch Greys, which
he commanded at the battle of Steinkirk, where he was slain He *m* Jane He *d.*
s p m 24 July 1692 (c) Admon 15 Dec 1692 to a creditor "Jane, relict of Sir
Robert DOUGLAS of Glenberry," *i e* "Glenbervie," *d.* Dec 1735 Will pr 1735 in
Prerog. Court [I]

IV 1692   SIR ROBERT DOUGLAS, Baronet [S. 1625], of Ardit,
afterwards called Glenbervie, co Fife, cousin and heir male collateral,
being only s and h. of William DOUGLAS, of the same, by Agnes, da of Patrick and
sister of Sir John SCOTT, 1st Baronet [S 1671] of Ancrum, which William was s and
h of the Rev George DOUGLAS, D D , Rector of Stepney, Midx (1634-41), which
George DOUGLAS was next br to Sir William DOUGLAS, 1st Baronet He was *b.*
about 1662, and *suc to the Baronetcy*, 24 July 1692 He *m* firstly in or before
1690, Mary, 1st da of Sii William RUTHVEN, of Duoglass, by Katharine, da.
of William (DOUGLAS), MARQUESS OF DOUGLAS [S] He *m.* secondly in or before
1694, Janet PATERSON, heiress of Dunmure He *d* 27 Jan 1748, in his 87th year (d)
His widow, who was *b* 2 Feb 1655, *d* 9 Feb 1750, aged 95, having had 60
descendants, of whom 41 were then living.

V. 1750.   SIR WILLIAM DOUGLAS, Baronet [S 1625], of Ardit,
otherwise Glenbervie aforesaid, s and h by 1st wife , *b* about 1690 ,
was an Advocate of some eminence, and from 1726 to 1745 was annually chosen as
Provost of the city of St Andrew's ; was Inspector of the Customs on Tobacco in
Scotland He *suc to the Baronetcy*, Feb 1748 He *m* , about 1718, Elizabeth, da.
of John DOUGLAS, of Garvald, by Elizabeth, da of William and Isabel DOUGLAS
He *d.* s p 23 July 1764, in his 75th year His widow *d* 11 May 1777

VI. 1764.   SIR ROBERT DOUGLAS, Baronet [S. 1625] of Ardit,
otherwise Glenbervie aforesaid br of the half-blood and h being
s of the 4th Baronet by his 2d wife , was *b* 1694, and when, nearly 70, *suc to the
Baronetcy*, 23 July 1764. He was the author (1764) of the well known *Peerage of
Scotland*,[e] as also of a posthumous work (1798) called *The Baronage of Scotland*,
of which, however, but one vol. was published Both these works have been the

"the third" of the order of Baronets or Knights of Nova Scotia now [1798] sub
sisting in Scotland according to the dates of their patents" ; the Baronetcy of Innes
being therein called the second, and that of Gordon the first
    (a) See p 283, note " c."
    (b) Banks's Lists
    (c) The standard of his regiment having been captured he "jumped over a hedge
into the midst of the enemy, seized it from the officer in whose charge it was, threw
it back to his own men and fell pierced with wounds, unmarried" [Wood's *Douglas'
Peerage of Scotland*, vol. i, p. 440]
    (d) Douglas' *Baronage* [S] states " died *anno* 1750, in the 85th year of his age."
    (e) A second edit , 2 vols , folio, ed by J P Wood, was issued in 1813.

text for all succeeding genealogical writers on Scotch families. He *m* firstly, Dorothea, da. and coheir of Anthony CHESTER, Attorney General of Barbadoes, said(ᵃ) to be "2d s of Sir Anthony CHESTER, Baronet" She *d.* s p He *m* secondly, before 1738, Margaret, 1st da. of Sir James MACDONALD, 6th Baronet [S 1625] of Macdonald, by Janet da of Alexander MACLEOD, of Grishairnish He *m* thirdly, Anne da. of Alexander HAY, of Huntingdon, Advocate He *d* at Edinburgh 24 April 1770, in his 77th year

VII	1770,	SIR ALEXANDER DOUGLAS, Baronet [S 1625], of Ardit
	to	otherwise Glenbervie aforesaid, only surv s and h, by 2d wife;
	1812	*b* 1738, studied medicine at Leyden 1759, M D of St Andrew's

College, 1760; *suc to the Baronetcy,* 20 April 1770; Fellow of the Coll of Physicians at Edinburgh, where he practised for more than 50 years, being founder, in 1781, of the Dispensary for the Poor there, physician to the King's forces in Scotland, licentiate of the Royal College of London, 1796 He *m*, 1778, Barbara, da of James CARNEGIE, of Finhaven, "a lady of great beauty and accomplishments "(ᵇ) He *d* s p m s.(ᶜ) 28 Nov. 1812, since which time *the Baronetcy* has remained *dormant* Will pr 1813 The admon. of his widow granted Feb 1816

STRACHAN, *or* STRAQUHAN

cr 28 May, and sealed 24 June 1625(ᵈ),

dormant, since 1659,

but assumed till 1854

I	1625,	SIR ALEXANDER STRAQUHAN(ᵉ) *or* STRACHAN, of Thornton,
	to	co Kincardine, s and h. of Robert STRACHAN, by Sarah (*m* 5 April
	1659	1586), 4th da of William (Douglas) 9th EARL OF ANGUS [S], the

said Robert (who *d* v p, before March 1597) being s and h ap of Alexander STRACHAN, of Thornton was *b* about 1587, suc his grandfather, the said Alexander STRACHAN in May 1601, being, 30 Sep 1606, served his heir male, was M.P [S.] for Kincardineshire, 1617 and 1630, and possibly, 1650, and was cr a *Baronet* [S], 28 May 1625,(ᵈ) sealed 24 June following, with rem to heirs male whatsoever, and with a grant of, presumably, 16,000 acres in Nova Scotia, of which seizin

---

(ᵃ) Douglas' *Baronage* [S], but not according to Chester Waters's *Family of Chester of Chicheley.*

(ᵇ) Playfair's *Baronetage* [S]

(ᶜ) His only son, Robert Douglas, *d* 1780, in infancy

(ᵈ) Milne's List as also Laing's List, in which last, however, the creation is stated to be "given on the authority of former lists." In Macfarlane's *Genealogical Collections* (vol ii, p 272) there is given ' a demonstrative proof that the patent was the next immediately following [that of] Sir William Douglas, which from the patent itself is of the date 18 May 1626," and it is also stated, that this date is "marked" for it in the *minute book* of David Sibbald, Dep Keeper of the Great Seal [S], the writer adding that "I know none [that] has precedency of the heir male of the house of Thornton, but Sir William Gordon and Sir Robert Douglas" Playfair in his *Baronetage* [S.] states the grantee to have been "the third Baronet [S] created," and designates the then [1811] Baronet as "Premier Baronet" [S], considering the Baronetcy of Gordon (which, however, he, subsequently, acknowledges in the appendix as being then dormant, and placing "Strachan" above Innes, Leslie, Livingston, and Douglas, which last (at all events) should (as above stated) rightly precede it.

(ᵉ) See *Memorials of the families of Strachan and Wise,* by Rev Charles Rogers, LL D [1873, 2d edit, 1877), and *Her. and Gen,* viii, pp 302-307 where it is (not very favourably) reviewed See also Macfarlane's *Genealogical Collections,* vol ii, pp 270-273, also *N & Q* 8th iv, 242-243, and 323-325 The account here given, down to the date of 1686 has been kindly revised by Sir J Balfour Paul (see p 275, note " a ") with the result of making it a very different one from any previously given

was subsequently made in July following (ᵃ) He was a Commissioner of the Exchequer in 1630, and subsequently, of the Treasury, being allowed £3 000 in 1631 for the surrender of some of his offices   He *m* firstly (contract 19 Jan 1605), Margaret, 3d da of John LINDSAY, of Balcarres, a Lord of Session [S], under the style of Lord Menmuir, (s of David, EARL OF CRAWFORD [S]), by Margaret, da of Alexander GUTHRIE, of Edinburgh   He *m* secondly, after April 1623, Margaret, Dow COUNTESS MARISCHAL [S], da of James (OGILVY) LORD OGILVY OF AIRLIE [S] by Jean, da of William (FORBES), LORD FORBES [S]   He, and his then only son and h ap Alexander, were living 1 Aug 1635 but he appears to have wasted his estates, "lived long in France" with his 2d wife and *d* in exile at Bruges about 1659, s p m s. Will dat 15 May 1657, confirmed 24 Jan 1662 at Edinburgh (ᵇ)

[ALEXANDER STRACHAN, *b* probably about 1608, yr of the two sons of the 1st Baronet (both being by his 1st wife), is generally said to have *suc.* him *as 2d Baronet*, but there is no record of his having done so. His elder br. John is spoken of as " Fiar of Thornton " in Aug 1626, but must have died before 1 Aug 1635, when this Alexander is described as " only lawful son of Sir Alexander Strachan " and as being married to Elizabeth DOUGLAS   He, presumably (and not his father) was M P for Kincardineshire, 1650   There is no mention of him in his father's will, dat 15 May 1657, and he probably was then dead without issue]

> The title was assumed as under by a descendant " from a remote ancestor of the 1st Baronet "(ᶜ) The relationship, however, is so distant, and the pedigree so uncertain that the right of such assumption seems extremely doubtful
>
> II. 1659   SIR JAMES STRACHAN, Baronet [S 1625],(ᵈ) of Thorn-
> ton aforesaid, of Inchtuthill, in the parish of Delvine, co Perth, of Fettercairn and Monboddo, s and h of James Strachan, of Inchtuthill (ᵉ) Fettercairn, and Monboddo, an opulent Burgess of Edinburgh, by Mary, da of David RAMSAY, of Balmaine, which James (who *d* 6 Jan 1651), was s and h of (—) Strachan, the 1st s and h ap of James Strachan, of Monboddo aforesaid (*d* 10 July 1614) and was heir to the said James, his grandfather, who was the s and h of Sir William Strachan, of Monboddo, " third son of John Strachan, of Thornton, great great grand-uncle of the first Baronet "(ᶜ) He had acquired lands at Thornton, is called the " Laird of Thornton " as early as 1658   By him, also, Thornton Castle was subsequently enlarged   On the death of the 1st Baronet in 1659 he appears to have *assumed the Baronetcy*, and as " Sir James Strachan, of Thornton, Knight Baronet,"(ᶠ) sold the estate of Inchtuthill, 20 April 1661   He *m* 24 Jan 1654, at Ellon, his cousin, Elizabeth 3d da of Thomas FORBES, of Waterton, by Jean, da of David RAMSAY, of Balmain   She *d* 10 Jan. 1661 in her 25th year, and was bur at Marykirk   M I   After her death he " involved his estate and impoverished his fortune,"(ᶜ) and (with James his s and h ap) sold the lands of Thornton, 28 March 1683, for £13,924   He *m.* secondly (—) by whom he had no male issue   He *d* 1686
>
> [JAMES STRACHAN, only s. and h ap. of the above, *b.* probably about 1656, entered King's College, Aberdeen, 1670   He *m* when young (contract 9 June 1669, registered 16 Nov. 1670), Barbara, 3d da. of Robert FORBES,

(ᵃ) Banks's Lists.
(ᵇ) He, who was probably a Royalist, is often confused with Col Archibald Strachan, a Parliamentarian, as to whom see *Her. and Gen*, viii, 302
(ᶜ) Rogers's *Strachan Family*, see p 285, note " c "
(ᵈ) According to the assumption of that dignity.
(ᵉ) The estate of Inchtuthill was purchased by him 29 May 1650, and sold by his son, 20 April 1661   It has sometimes, in error, been attributed to Thomas Strachan, who was *cr. a Baronet* [S], 8 May 1685.
(ᶠ) In the M.I erected to his wife in 1661, he, however, describes himself (only) as " *Eques auratus* "

of Newtoun, with a dowry of 8,000 merks. They were both living 28 March 1683, but he *d v p* before 1686, leaving a son James, who, according to one account, " died in infancy,"(a) but according to another account " was alive in 1710, probably then being about 40 years of age, '(b) but who apparently never assumed the Baronetcy]

* * * *

III   1686   SIR JAMES STRACHAN, Baronet [S 1625],(c) of Pittendreich (part of the Thornton estate), said to be "probably a nephew,"(a) but who more likely was a cousin of the late Baronet,(c) was *b* about 1640 , ed at King's College, Aberdeen , M.A, 28 March 1660 , took Holy Orders and was Minister of Keith, 1665 till deprived in Nov 1689 for nonconformity , *assumed the Baronetcy* in 1686 (d)   He *m* about 1680. Katherine Ross. She, by whom he had six sons, *d* 8 April 1689, and was *bur* at Keith M I. He *d.* at Inverness, 1715, aged 75.

IV. 1715   SIR WILLIAM STRACHAN, Baronet [S 1625],('), 1st surv. s. and h , *suc to the Baronetcy*(c) in 1715 He is named *Sir William Strachan of Thorntoun* in the parish register of Marykirk, where William, his natural son was baptized, 21 July 1715

V. 1725?   SIR FRANCIS STRACHAN, Baronet [S 1625],(c) br. and h. male , *suc. to the Baronetcy*(°) on the death of his brother. He lived at Paris, took Holy Orders in the Church of Rome, became a Jesuit, and was Rector of the College at Douay, 1734 He *d.* unm , having, it is said, previously resigned the title to the next presumptive heir, John STRACHAN, of Sweden (e)

VI 1753?   SIR JOHN STRACHAN, Baronet [S. 1625],(e) cousin and h male, stated to be grandson of a brother of the grandfather of the late Baronet.(e) He, presumably, is the " John Strachan, born in London and made [*sic*, but *query* if not tantamount to "inherited as "] a Baronet of Nova Scotia in 1753," being s of " John STRACHAN, of Sweden, by Margaret, da of Peter BOMGREEN, also of Sweden "(f) He having, presumably, inherited the Baronetcy(c) in 1753, *d* s p.m in about 1765   Will of " Sir John Strachan, Midx.," pr. Aug 1769.

* * * * *

VII 1765?   SIR JOHN STRACHAN, Baronet [S 1625],(c) apparently nephew and h , being 1st surv s and h of Patrick STRACHAN, Surgeon and Elizabeth (*m* in or before 1718), da of Edward GREGORY, Capt.

(a) Rogers's *Strachan Family*, see p 285, note " c "
(b) Statement of R R Stodart, Lyon Clerk Depute (1863-86) as furnished by Sir J Balfour Paul, Lyon King of Arms
(c) According to the assumption of that dignity
(d) " In the records of the Synod of Moray in 1687, he is styled *Mr. James Strachan* , and in the baptismal register of Keith, he is, on 6 Jan 1687, described as " *Sir James Strachan*, of Thornton, Minister " See note " a " above In his wife's M I., erected in 1689 at Keith, he describes himself as ' *D Jac. Strachanus de Thornt hujus ecclesiæ Pastor*
(e) In Macfarlane's *Genealogical Collections* it is said that Francis (the 5th Baronet) " has now the matter, though perhaps not with all the formalitys requisite, resigned the title of the Baronetship of the family of Thornton to another gentleman, John Strachan, who resides in Sweden and designs himself by the title of Thornton, as the heir male of the family, and in one of his letters he acknowledges that his own grandfather and this gentleman's grandfather were two brothers."
(f) Burke's " *Commoners* " (1837), vol ii, p 405, foot note

R.N., which Patrick([a]) who was *bur.* at Greenwich, 10 Sep. 1749, was, presumably, yr. br. of the late Baronet. He was *bap.* 10 March 1728/9 at Greenwich; was Lieut. R.N. Jan. 1746/7; captured, when in command, 8 July 1757, of a French privateer of 20 guns off Alicante; was attached to the fleet under Hawke, 1759-69, and under Harland, to the East Indies, 1770-72, having *suc.* to the Baronetcy([b]) about 1765. He *m.* Elizabeth, da. of Robert LOVELACE, of Battersea Rise, co. Surrey. He *d.* s.p.m., 26 Dec. 1777, at Bath. Will pr. 1778. His widow *m.* Lieut.-Col. Joseph WALTON. The will of "Dame Elizabeth Strachan, Midx.," was pr. April 1833.

VIII. 1777,   SIR RICHARD JOHN STRACHAN, Baronet([b]) [S. 1625],
to   nephew and h. male, being 1st s. and h.([c]) of Patrick
1828. STRACHAN, Lieut. R.N., by Caroline (*m.* 1759), da. of John
PITMAN, Capt. R.N., which Patrick (*bap.* 10 Sep. 1733, at Greenwich) was yst. br. of the late Baronet and *d.* in New York, 1776. He was *b.* 27 Oct. 1760, at Plymouth; *suc. to the Baronetcy*,([b]) 26 Dec. 1777, when aged 17, and, having entered the navy in 1772, became Lieut. 1779; Capt. 1783; captured four French ships off Cape Finisterre, 4 Nov. 1805, that had escaped from Trafalgar, receiving the thanks of both houses, with an annual pension of £1,000; Rear-Admiral, 1805; **K.B.**, 29 Jan. 1806, becoming afterwards (1815) **G.C.B.** Had the naval command of the disastrous expedition against Walcheren in 1808, the Earl of Chatham being in command of the military([d]); became Vice-Admiral, 1810; and Admiral, 1821. He *m.*, April 1812, Louisa DILLON, spinster. He *d.* s.p.m.s.([e]) at his house in Bryanston sq.,

([a]) This Patrick (called "Doctor Patrick Strachan" and "Patrick, M.D., Physician to Greenwich Hospital") is stated in the *second* edit. (differing entirely from the account of his descent given in the *first* edit.) of Rogers's "Families of Strachan," etc. [see p. 285 note "e"], to have been a yr. br. of Sir Thomas Strachan, who was *cr. a Baronet* [S.], 8 May 1685, and to have assumed that Baronetcy on the death, s.p., of his said brother. This statement is said to be, "according to a family pedigree deposited in the College of Arms, by Admiral Sir Richard Strachan," grandson of the said Patrick. No such pedigree, however, is recorded either in the College of Arms, London, or in the Lyon office, Edinburgh, and the statement is at variance with all other accounts of the family. The burial at Greenwich of the said Patrick Strachan (the Surgeon), 10 Sep. 1749 (64 years after the said Sir Thomas, his alleged brother, had been created a Baronet), does not describe him as a Baronet; there is no proof that the said Sir Thomas (whose parentage is unknown) ever had any brothers; and, finally, the creation of the Baronetcy of 8 May 1685 was to the heirs male *of the body* of the grantee, and consequently could not have passed, after his death without such issue, to a younger brother, but must have become *extinct*.

([b]) According to the assumption of that dignity.

([c]) His only br., Jervis Henry Strachan, an officer in the marines, *d.* unm. being slain in 1780, during a sea fight.

([d]) The recriminations of the two commanders as to their respective dilatoriness gave rise to the well known epigram, quoted thus in the *Dict. Nat. Biogr.*, under "Pitt," John, 2d Earl of Chatham :—

> "Great Chatham, with his sabre drawn,
> Stood *waiting* for Sir Richard Strachan;
> Sir Richard, longing to be at 'em,
> Stood *waiting* for the Earl of Chatham.

According, however, to a writer in the *Athenæum* (27 April 1701), quoting "the late Mr. Carrick Moore, whose reminiscences, through his father, Dr. Moore, and his uncle, Sir John, reach back to the date of Walcheren," the first line was—

> "Chatham, impatient for the dawn."

This seems the more appropriate version, as being in allusion "to the combined action by the land and sea forces *intended* to take place at daybreak." Another version, given in the *Morning Chronicle* of 6 Feb. 1810, is quoted in G.E.C.'s *Complete Peerage* (vol. ii, p. 213), under "Chatham."

([e]) He left three daughters, all married to foreigners.

3 Feb 1828, after a short illness, aged 67, when *the Baronetcy* became *dormant* Will dat 12 Feb 1816 to 31 Jan 1828, pr Feb 1828 His widow *m* (—) PICALILLO, an Italian She resided at Naples, and was by the King thereof *cr* MARCHESA DI SALZA (a) She *d.* there in 1868, at an advanced age

* * * * *

[Notwithstanding the resignation of the Baronetcy to "the heir male" expectant, by Sir Francis STRACHAN, the 5th Baronet,(b) the title was, after his death, assumed as under]

VI bis 1753? SIR ALEXANDER STRACHAN, Baronet(b) [S. 1625], called "the 6th Baronet of Nova Scotia," conjectured to be grandson of the Rev Sir James STRACHAN, Baronet abovenamed. He *m* before 1736, "Jane BREMNER, of Atterbury "(c)

VII bis 1760? SIR ALEXANDER STRACHAN, Baronet(b) [S. 1625], s. and h , "*suc to the title*, with its slender income, on the death of his father " He was a Jesuit Priest, and having travelled much, *d.* unm in his old age, 3 Jan. 1793, at the English College at Liege.(c)

VIII bis 1793, ROBERT STRACHAN, *or* SIR ROBERT STRACHAN,
to Baronet(b) [S 1625], br and h , *b* about 1737 He was a
1826 clerk in Gaudolfe's Bank, Exeter He *suc to the Baronetcy*, 3 Jan 1793, but possibly never assumed the title He *d* unm at Exeter, 3 April 1826, aged 89, and was *bur* at St Nicholas in that city.(c)

* * * * *

The title was also assumed as under.

"About 12 years after the death of Admiral Sir Richard Strachan, Mr John Strachan, of Cliffden, Teignmouth, Devonshire, preferred a claim to the representation of the house of Thornton and passed through a form of service before the *Bailies of Canongate* In his claim, or brief Mr Strachan sought to instruct his descent from Roger Strachan, of Glichno, brother of John Strachan, of Thornton, great grandfather of the 1st Baronet Roger Strachan was set forth as father of Dr. Robert Strachan, Physician in Montrose [*d.* between 1656 and 1659], whose son, John was Minister of Strachan [and *d* Feb 1701] George [said, in a sasine of 8 June 1696, to be] a son of the Minister, was represented as a Merchant in Montrose, and father of James Strachan, Lieut. R N , father of the claimant This statement of pedigrees, unsupported by evidence and in entire variance with chronological requirements, being accepted by a friendly jury and certified by the Canongate Bailies, formed the basis of a retour in Chancery, bearing date 8 Nov. 1841 " [Rogers's *Memorials of the Strachans* as quoted in *Her. and Gen*, viii, p 306]

IX 1841 "SIR JOHN STRACHAN, Baronet,"(d) [S 1625], of Cliffden, Teignmouth, Devon, only s of James STRACHAN, Lieut. R.N (*d* 9 Sep 1794, aged 93, *bur* at Montrose), by Catherine, da of James DONALDSON, of Montrose, was *b* 22 March 1751, and *assumed the style of a Baronet* after the abovementioned retour of 8 Nov 1841, as heir male collateral of the grantee He was a magistrate for Stirlingshire He *m.* Elizabeth, da of David HUNTER, of Blackness, co Forfar He *d.* 9 June 1844, aged 93, at Cliffden aforesaid Will pr. Aug. 1844

(a) She is said to have purchased that title with a legacy left to her, in 1842, by the Marquess of Hertford
(b) According to the assumption of that dignity
(c) Rogers's *Strachan Family*, see p 285, note "e "
(d) According to the assumption of the title, in consequence of the retour of 8 Nov. 1841.

X 1844,   "SIR JOHN STRACHAN, Baronet "(a) [S 1625], of
    to   Cliffden aforesaid, 1st and only surv. s and h , b at Montrose ,
1854   was, presumably, ed at Winchester School 1799 , suc to the
    Baronetcy,(a) 9 June 1844 He m. Mary Anne, da of Isaac
ELTON, of Whitestanton, co Somerset, and Stapleton House, co Gloucester.
He d s p 28 Jan 1854, at Cliffden aforesaid when the assumption of the
Baronetcy ceased He was bur at East Teignmouth M I (b) Will dat
29 June 1848, pr March 1854. His widow m in 1855, John Chappell
TOZER, of Teignmouth and d apparently in 1857.

LIVINGSTONE, or LIVINGSTOUN.

cr 30 May 1625(c);

dormant, since about 1634

I 1625,   SIR DAVID LIVINGSTOUN, of Dunipace, co Stirling, 2d s
   to   of John Livingstoun, or LIVINGSTONE, who was s and h apparent of
1631?   another John LIVINGSTONE, of the same, was served heir general of
his said grandfather, as also of his elder br , John LIVINGSTONE, of
Dunipace, 22 Jan 1620, inheriting thereby an immense estate, and was cr a
Baronet [S], 30 May, sealed 20 Aug 1625,(c) with rem to heirs male whatever and
with a grant of, presumably, 16 000 acres in Nova Scotia, being the Barony of
Livingstone-Dunipace of which he had seizin, July 1625 (d) He, being then "heir
ap of Dunipace," m. before 3 May 1609, Barbara FORRESTER, probably da or Sir
James FORRESTER, of Garden He was living 1631, but d , having apparently,
dissipated all his property(e), before 25 Feb 1634, leaving male issue, but after his
death the *Baronetcy* appears to have become *dormant* (f)

(a) See p 289, note " d "
(b) See p 289, note ' c '
(c) Milne's List and Laing's List The creation is between that of Strachan
and Macdonald , see p 291, line 8, and p 285, note " d " A Baronetcy
[S] of this same date (30 May 1625) is sometimes said to have been conferred
on Sir George Livingstone of Ogleface, co Linlithgow, a yr br of Alexander,
1st Earl of Linlithgow [S], but this is an error That creation is, however, indicated (though not actually asserted) in Playfair's Baronetage [S], and has
been adopted in some more modern Baronetages.
(d) Banks's Lists
(e) Dunipace was in the hands of the Earl of Callender (S) before 1646 In 1649
Margaret, da of the Baronet, had a decree for £500 for parts of the land of
Dunipace The Livingstones of Balrourie, 1600 to 1729, descend from Patrick
Livingstone, of the same, uncle of the Baronet , there appear also to have been other
branches of the Dunipace family, all of whom would be within the limitation of the
Baronetcy. Alexander Livingstone, the founder of the family of Dunipace (beheaded
1446), was a bastard br of the 1st Lord Livingstone (S) [Ex inform R R Stodart.
Lyon Clerk Depute, 1863-86]
(f) His son, John Livingstone, living as "heir ap. of Dunipace," 9 Aug 1630,
11 June and 9 July 1631, survived him, and was living 25 Feb 1634, when he had
protection from the creditors of his deceased father, but, having inherited nothing
from him, he apparently *never assumed the Baronetcy*, and nothing more is known of
him There were two sisters of the first Baronet, one of whom m , about 1590,
James Arbuthnott, and was mother of Sir Robert Arbuthnott of that ilk, while
the other, Jean, known as "Lady Warriston," m John Kincaird, of Warriston,
near Edinburgh, and was executed 5 July 1600 for his murder. See an interesting
article thereon in the *Scottish Record*, for Oct 1850

MACDONALD.

cr 14 July 1625(ᵃ);

afterwards, since 1776, BARONS MACDONALD OF SLATE [I]

I 1625   DONALD MACDONALD, *formerly* GORME, of Slate, in the
Isle of Skye, co. Inverness, s. and h of Archibald MACDONALD, of the
same, by Margaret, or Mary, da of Angus MACDONALD, of Duniveg and Glennis,
suc his uncle Donald MACDONALD, *otherwise* GORME, of Slate, in 1616 and was *cr
a Baronet* [S], 14 July 1625, with rem to heirs male whatever, and with precedency over Douglas, Strachan, and Livingstone, the three creations next above
him,(ᵃ) and with the grant of. presumably, 16,000 acres in Nova Scotia, of which,
however he never had seizin (ᵇ) The patent is not in the Great Seal Register,
but "only in one old list."(ᵃ) He supported Charles I in the Civil Wars He *m.*
Janet, sister of Colin, 1st EARL OF SEAFORTH [S], 2d da of Kenneth (MACKENZIE),
1st LORD MACKENZIE OF KINTAIL [S] by his 1st wife Anne, da of George ROSS, of
Balnagowan He *d* Oct 1643.

II 1643   SIR JAMES MACDONALD, Baronet [S 1625], of Slate aforesaid, s. and h , *suc to the Baronetcy* in Oct 1643 and was served heir
to his father, 20 Feb 1644. He supported the Royal Cause in 1645, again in 1651,
and quelled a disturbance in the Highlands in 1664   He *m.* firstly (contract 23 Feb
1633), Margaret, aunt of George, 1st EARL OF CROMARTY [S], da of Sir Roderick
MACKENZIE, of Lorgeach, by Margaret, da. and h of Torquil MACLEOD, of Lewes. He
m secondly, Mary, da. of John MACLEOD, of Macleod, by Sybella, da of Kenneth
(MACKENZIE), 1st LORD MACKENZIE OF KINTAIL [S]   He *d* 8 Dec 1678

III. 1678.   SIR DONALD MACDONALD, Baronet [S 1625], of Slate aforesaid, s and h by 1st wife, *suc to the Baronetcy*, 8 Dec 1678   In 1684
he was ' sued as unfaithful."(ᶜ) He *m* , 24 July 1662, at Perth, Mary, 2d yst
da of Robert (DOUGLAS) EARL OF MORTON [S], by Elizabeth, da of Sir Edward
VILLIERS. She, in 1681, became coheir to her br., Robert, EARL OF MORTON [S] He
d 5 Feb 1695.

IV 1695.   SIR DONALD MACDONALD, Baronet [S. 1625], of Slate
aforesaid, and of Duntulm, in the Isle of Skye, s and h , *suc to the
Baronetcy*, 5 Feb. 1695   He engaged in the rebellion of 1715 and is said to have been
attainted, but no forfeiture of the title, apparently, followed He *m.* Mary, da. of
Donald MACDONALD, of Castleton. He *d.* 1718

V 1718.   SIR DONALD MACDONALD, Baronet [S. 1625], only s. and h ,
b about 1697 , mat at Oxford (Ch Ch), 7 Nov 1712, aged 15 ; *suc
to the Baronetcy*, in 1718. He *d* unm. 1720.

VI 1720   SIR JAMES MACDONALD, Baronet [S 1625], of Slate aforesaid, and of Oransay, uncle and h male , *suc to the Baronetcy* in 1720
He *m.* firstly, Janet, widow of John MACLEOD, of Talisker, da and h of Alexander
MACLEOD of Grishernish, in Skye   He *m* secondly, Margaret, da of John MACDONALD,
of Castleton, by whom he had no issue (ᶜ) He *d* 1723, at Forres.

VII. 1723   SIR ALEXANDER MACDONALD, Baronet [S 1625], of Slate
aforesaid, s and h. by 1st wife, *b.* 1711 ; *suc. to the Baronetcy* in 1723
He was almost the only person of consideration in that district, who, in 1745, sup-
ported the Government, and was consequently in great favour with the Duke of
Cumberland. He *m* firstly, 5 April 1733, Anne, widow of James OGILVY, *styled* LORD
OGILVY OF AIRLIE da of David ERSKINE of Dun, co Forfar, a Lord of Session [S]

(ᵃ) Milne's List and Laing's List.
(ᵇ) Banks's Lists
(ᶜ) Alexander Sinclair's *Macdonalds of the Isles*

She *d* at Edinburgh, 27 Nov 1785, in her 27th year. He *m* secondly, 24 April 1739, at St. Paul's, Edinburgh, Margaret, 9th da of Alexander (MONTGOMERIE), 9th Earl of Eglington [S] being his 4th da. by his 3d wife Susanna, da of Sir Archibald KENNEDY, 1st Baronet [S 1681], of Culzean   He *d.*, suddenly at Bernera (on his way to London) 23 Nov 1746, aged 35   His widow, who was a distinguished partisan of the exiled house of Stuart, *d.* 30 March 1799 in Welbeck Street, Marylebone   Will pr April 1799.

VIII. 1746   SIR JAMES MACDONALD, Baronet [S 1625], of Slate afore-
              said, s. and h by 2d wife, *b* at Edinburgh about 1742 , matric at
Oxford (Ch Ch), 9 May 1759, aged 17 , was an accomplished scholar and mathe-
matician, being considered " The Marcellus of the North " , *suc to the Baronetcy* in
Nov 1746   He *d.* unm , at Rome, 26 July 1766, aged 24, and, though a protestant,
had, by leave of Pope Clement XIII, a public funeral   M I at Slate

IX 1766   SIR ALEXANDER MACDONALD, Baronet [S 1625], of Slate
              aforesaid, br and h ,[a] *b* about 1745 , was, sometime about 1761-66,
an officer in the Coldstream Guards , *suc to the Baronetcy*, 26 July 1766.   He *m*
3 May 1768, at St. Giles' in the Fields, Elizabeth Diana, 1st da of (whose issue in
1813 became coheir to) Godfrey BOSVILLE, of Gunthwaite, co. York, by Diana, da. of
Sir William WENTWORTH, 4th Baronet [1664], of Bretton   She, who was *bap*
25 July 1748, was living when he was raised to the peerage, being *cr* 17 July 1776,
BARON MACDONALD OF SLATE, CO ANTRIM [I][b]   In that peerage this
Baronetcy then merged and still so continues

MURRAY :

cr 19 July 1625[c],

subsequently, 1636-58, EARLS OF ANNANDALE [S.],

dormant, since 1658.

I 1625   SIR RICHARD MURRAY, of Cockpool, 6th s of Sir Charles
              MURRAY, of the same, by Margaret, da of Hugh (SOMERVILLE) LORD
SOMERVILLE [S], suc , in 1620 his elder br Sir James Murray in that estate, and was
cr. a *Baronet* [S], 19 July 1625, sealed 20 Oct 1625,[c] with rem to heirs male whatsoever, and a grant of, presumably 16,000 acres in Nova Scotia, entitled the Barony
of Cockpool, of which he had sasine in Oct following[d]   In 1635 he had sasine of
the lands of Lockerbie, Hutton, Hoddam, etc He *d. s p* , probably unm , in 1636

II 1636.   JOHN (MURRAY) EARL OF ANNANDALE [S] (so *cr*
              13 March 1624/5), only surv br. and h male, being 8th and yst s. of
Sir Charles MURRAY abovenamed, *suc to the Baronetcy* as heir male collateral in 1636,
when *the Baronetcy merged* in this peerage till its extinction (*See* " Peerage "), on the
death of the 2d Earl, 28 Dec 1658, on which date the *Baronetcy* became *dormant,*
the issue male of the grantee as well as of his father being *extinct*

------

[a] Archibald Macdonald, the 3d and yst br , was L Ch. Baron of the Exchequer, 1793-1813, and was *cr* a *Baronet*, 27 Nov 1813.

[b] " Slate, co Antrim in Ireland," is non-existent, the place referred to being Slate or Sleat *in the island of Skye, in Scotland.*   Such fictions, however, were not unusual when Scotsmen were (after the union with Scotland) raised to the peerage   Such *e g* , was the elevation to the Irish peerage of William Duff, in 1735, as Baron Kilbryde, co *Cavan,* and in 1759 as Earl Fife, *in Ireland.*

[c] Milne's List and Laing's List.

[d] Banks's Lists, where it is added " Represented by the Earl of Mansfield," which representation, however, is only in right of female descent through the families of Scott and Grierson, from the 1st da and heir of line to Sir James Murray, of Cock-pool, elder br. of the first Baronet.

ALEXANDER

cr., 12 July 1625(ª);

afterwards, 1630—1739, VISCOUNTS STIRLING [S];

and subsequently, 1633—1739, EARLS OF STIRLING [S],

dormant, since 4 Dec 1739

I 1625   SIR WILLIAM ALEXANDER, of Menstre, in Logie, co.
Clackmannan, afterwards, 1630, VISCOUNT, and subsequently, in 1633,
EARL OF STIRLING [S.] (for whom see fuller accounts in *Peerage*), was *b* about 1567,
Sec. of State and P C [S], 1626, *Knighted* at Whitehall, 2 March 1626/7, had a
grant from Charles, 10 Sep 1621, of the vast territory of Nova Scotia, with permission
(for the purpose of Colonization) to divide the same into 100 tracks of 16,000 acres and
dispose of each, *together with the rank of Baronet* This grant was, however, not
acted upon, until it was confirmed by Charles I (the number of 100 being changed
to 150), by Charter, 12 July 1625, sealed 9 Sep. following,(ª) on which date the
grantee himself is said(ª) to have been *cr a Baronet* [S], with rem to his heirs male
whatever,(ᵇ) He had seizin "of one part of the continent of Nova Scotia" in the
same month of Sep 1625 (ᶜ) As late, however, as 30 Nov 1629 he styles himself
[only] "Knight"(ᵈ) On 2 Feb 1628 he had charters of the Lordship of Canada
He was *cr* 4 Sep 1630, VISCOUNT STIRLING, etc [S], and subsequently, 14 June
1633, EARL OF STIRLING, VISCOUNT CANADA, etc [S], with rem in both
cases to his heirs male of the name of Alexander In these peerages *this Baronetcy*
then *merged*, and so continued till, on the death of his great grandson the 5th Earl,
4 Dec 1739, it, and the said Peerage dignities became *dormant* See *Peerage*

COLQUHOUN,

cr. 30 Aug 1625(ᵉ),

regranted, with a different remainder, 29 April 1704;

afterwards, 1719—1811, GRANT,

and finally, since 1811, EARLS OF SEAFIELD [S]

This Baronetcy was (erroneously) assumed

by the heir male,

1718—1838

I 1625.   JOHN COLQUHOUN, of Luss and Tilliquhoun, co Dumbarton, s and h of Alexander COLQUHOUN, of the same, by Helen,
da. of Sir George BUCHANAN, of Buchanan, suc his father, 23 May 1617, was M P [S]

(ª) Milne's List This creation does not appear in Laing's List, nor is it registered
in the great Seal Register, though apparently it is in the *Registrum Preceptorum
Cartarum pro Baronettis Novæ Scotiæ, 1625-30*

(ᵇ) It seems curious that, as he had all the land of which a grant of but 16,000
acres constituted a Baronetcy, he should not if he accepted of a Baronetcy have had
one of the earliest date. In Beatson's list of these (edit 1806) he is placed but 13th,
those of Gordon of Gordonstoun, Wemyss, Innes, Strachan, Douglas, Colquhoun,
Livingstone, Murray, Gordon or Cluny, Leslie, Campbell of Glenorchy, and Gordon
of Lesmore, being placed above him Most unquestionably the premier Baronetcy
was Gordon of Gordonstoun, but it must be born in mind that by the charter of 1625
the said "Sir William Alexander and his Leirs male descending of his body as
Lieutenants aforesaid [i e., of Nova Scotia] shall * * * take * * * precedence as well
before all Esquires Lairds, and Gentlemen of our said kingdom of Scotland as
before all the aforesaid Knight Baronets of our said Kingdom" [Banks's *Baronia
Anglica Concentrata*, vol. ii, p 213]

(ᶜ) Banks's List.

(ᵈ) The use, however, of the word "Knight" for "Baronet" was not uncommon
in the early days of the Baronetcy

(ᵉ) Milne's List and Laing's List.

for Dumbartonshire, 1621, and was cr a Baronet [S], 30 Aug 1625, sealed 20 Oct following,(a) with rem. to heirs male whatsoever, and with a grant of, apparently, 16,000 acres in Nova Scotia, afterwards called Tilliquhoun, of which seizin was made in the said month of October (b) He was ' fugitated and excommunicated," and deprived of the life rent of his estates, as the result of a criminal suit in 1632 for his seduction of his wife's sister, Lady Katherine Graham He m (contract 30 June and 6 July 1620) Lilias, 1st da of John (GRAHAM), 4th EARL OF MONTROSE [S], by Margaret, da of William (RUTHVEN), 1st EARL OF GOWRIE [S] He d about 1650

II 1650 ? SIR JOHN COLQUHOUN, Baronet [S. 1625], of Luss afore-said, 1st s and h , b about 1622 , suc to the family estates in 1647 (which had been preserved to the family by his uncle, Sir Humphrey Colquhoun, of Balvie, who was M P [S], for Dumbartonshire, 1643-49) ; suc. to the Baronetcy about 1650 He purchased the estate of Balloch in 1652, and acquired that of Lochend, co Haddington (which, however, he sold in 1678) by marriage , was M P [S] for Dumbartonshire 1650, 1661-63, 1665, 1667, and 1669-74. He m (contract, 17 Feb 1636) Margaret, da and h of Sir Gideon BAILLIE, Baronet [S 1636], by Magdalen, da and coheir of David CARNEGIE, styled LORD CARNEGIE. He d 11 April 1676. Will pr. 27 Feb 1677 His widow m 1 April 1677, Archibald STIRLING, of Garden, and d 20 July 1679

III 1676 SIR JAMES COLQUHOUN, Baronet [S. 1625] of Luss afore-said, 2d but only surv s and h , suc to the Baronetcy, 11 April 1676 He d unm 1680 (c)

IV. 1680. SIR JAMES COLQUHOUN, Baronet [S 1625], of Luss afore-said, uncle and h male, formerly of Corcagh, co Donegal , suc to the Baronetcy in 1680 He m , before Nov. 1669, being then of Corcagh aforesaid, Penuel, coheir of her brothers John and Robert Cunningham, of Ballyachen, co Donegal, yst da of James(d) CUNNINGHAM of the same (d) He d 1688

V 1688 SIR HUMPHREY COLQUHOUN, Baronet [S. 1625], of Luss aforesaid, only s and h , suc to the Baronetcy in 1688 , was M P [S] for Dumbartonshire, 1703 07, voting on all occasions against the Scotch union , was a Commissioner of Supply , Lieut -Col of the Militia of the Counties of Argyll, Dumbarton, and Bute He m (contract 1 and 4 April 1684) Margaret, 1st da. of Sir Patrick HODSTON, 1st Baronet [S 1668] by Anne, da of John (HAMILTON), 1st LORD BARGENY [S] He, having no male issue, resigned his Baronetcy, 30 March 1704, into the hands of the Crown, and obtained a new grant (novodamus) thereof, with the former precedence, to himself and the heirs male of his body, whom failing, to (his son-in-law) JAMES GRANT, of Pluscardine, and the heirs male begotten between the said James, by Anne, his wife, only da of the said Humphrey, with rem to heirs male of the body of the said Anne, rem to the other heirs of entail of the said Humphrey.(e)

(a) Milne's List and Laing's List
(b) Banks's Lists
(c) He had several sisters, who or whose issue became the heirs general of the 1st Baronet
(d) Not "William" as stated in Fraser's Chiefs of Colquhoun (vol 1, p 294) See will of James Cunningham, of "Ballyachen, co. Donegall, Esq ," dated 7 May 1664, and pr. 11 March 1667 Admon of John Cunningham, 13 Nov 1669 (to Robert Sanderson, Esq , and Katherine his wife, and James Colquhoun and Penuel his wife, sisters of the deceased) and of Robert Cunningham, 22 Dec 1682 There are also several Chancery bills, concerning the Cunningham estate, to which Sir James was a party, further bearing out the connection [Ex. inform , G D Burtchaell]
(e) By the Scotch law which prevailed before the union [S] there is no doubt that this surrender and re-grant (unlike the law in England) was valid

He also executed an entail of the Colquhoun estates, with a proviso that they should never be held with those of the family of Grant. He d. s.p m., 1718, when, according to the *novodamus* of 1704, the Baronetcy of 1625 devolved as under.

VI. 1718. SIR JAMES COLQUHOUN, *subsequently* (after 1719) GRANT, Baronet [S 1625], formerly JAMES GRANT, of Pluscardine, 2d s of Ludovic GRANT, of Grant (d 1717), by his 1st wife, Janet, da and h. of Alexander BRODIE, of Lethen. He was b 28 July 1679, and, having m 29 Jan. 1702, Anne (b 1685), only child of Sir Humphrey COLQUHOUN, the last Baronet, by Margaret his wife, both abovenamed, *suc to that Baronetcy* on the death of his said father-in-law, in 1718 (by virtue of the spec rem in the *novodamus* of that dignity), and to the estate of Luss, by virtue of the entail thereof, on which occasion he took the name of COLQUHOUN. The next year, however, he suc on the death, in 1719, s p s, of his elder brother, Brig.-Gen. Alexander Grant, to the paternal estate of Grant, and re-assumed his patronymic of GRANT. He was M P for Inverness-shire (three Parls), 1722-41, and for the Elgin burghs, 1741-47. His wife d 25 June 1724, aged 39. He d. 16 Jan. 1746/7.

VII. 1747. SIR LUDOVIC GRANT, Baronet [S 1645], of Grant, *formerly* (1719-32) LUDOVIC COLQUHOUN, of Luss, 2d but 1st surv s and h, b 13 Jan 1707, received from his father, in 1719, the Colquhoun estates, and accordingly continued to bear the name of Colquhoun. These he endeavoured, unsuccessfully, to retain[a] after the fee expectant of the Grant estates had, in 1735, been made over to him on the death of his elder brother, Humphry Grant, who d. s p and unm in 1732. He thereupon took the name of GRANT, was M P for Elgin and Forres shire (three Parls), 1741-61, and suc. to the Baronetcy, 16 Jan 1746/7. He m firstly, Marion, 2d da of the Hon Sir Hew DALRYMPLE, 1st Baronet [S 1698], by Marion, da of Sir Robert HAMILTON. She, who was b 6 July 1686, d. s p m. He m secondly, Nov 1735, Margaret, eldest of the two daughters of James (OGILVY), 5th EARL OF FINDLATER [S], and 2d EARL OF SEAFIELD [S], by Elizabeth, da of Thomas (HAY), 6th EARL OF KINNOUL [S]. She d. 20 Feb. 1757. He d 18 March 1773.

VIII. 1773. SIR JAMES GRANT, Baronet [S 1625], of Grant, only s and h by 2d wife, b 19 May 1738, was M P for Elgin and Forres-shire, 1761-68, and for Banffshire, 1790, suc to the Baronetcy, 18 March 1773, served heir to his father, 14 May 1773, raised the 1st Reg of Fencible Infantry in 1793, and the 97th Reg in 1794, was Receiver and Cashier [S], 1790-95, Receiver of Excise [S], 1795, L Lieut. of Inverness-shire, 1794-1809. He m 4 Jan 1763, Jean, only da of Alexander DUFF, of Hatton, co Aberdeen, by Anne, 1st da of William (DUFF), 1st EARL FIFE [I]. She d. 15 Feb 1805. He d. 18 Feb 1811.

IX. 1811. SIR LEWIS-ALEXANDER GRANT, Baronet [S. 1625], of Grant aforesaid, s and h., b 22 March 1767, admitted to Lincoln's Inn, 1788, was an Advocate [S], 1789, M P for Elginshire, 1790-96, suc to the Baronetcy, 18 Feb 1811, and, eight months later, suc, 5 Oct 1811, as EARL OF SEAFIELD, etc [S], on the death of his father's 2d cousin, James (OGILVY), EARL OF FINDLATER and EARL OF SEAFIELD [S.], when he assumed the name of OGILVY after that of GRANT, and registered arms at the Lyon office, with the badge thereon of a Baronet of Nova Scotia. In the Earldom of Seafield this *Baronetcy* then *merged*, and still so continues. See *Peerage*.

---

[a] Luss and the other Colquhoun estates were confirmed by a legal decision in 1738, to his younger brother, James Grant, who accordingly took the name of Colquhoun, and was cr a Baronet, as 'Colquhoun of Luss," 27 June 1786.

The Baronetcy was (erroneously) assumed in 1710, as under, by the *heir male* (to whom it had, in the original patent, been limited), notwithstanding the surrender by the 5th Baronet, and the *novodamus* thereof, in 1704, which had altered the line of its descent.

VI   1718   SIR JOHN COLQUHOUN, Baronet [S. 1625],(a) of Tillyquhoun, *otherwise* Tillychewan, co Dumbarton, s and h of Alexander COLQUHOUN, of the same, by Annabella, da. of George STEWART, of Scotstoun, the said Alexander being 3d and yst. s of the 1st Baronet and br of the 2d and 4th Baronets, suc his father before 1718, in which year he became heir male to his cousin, the 5th Baronet, and, as such, *assumed the Baronetcy* He *m.* Elizabeth, da. of Andrew ANDERSON, King's Printer for Scotland

VII.   1720?   SIR HUMPHREY COLQUHOUN, Baronet [S 1625],(a) only s and h *suc to the Baronetcy*(a) on his father's death, shortly after which he sold the estate of Tillyquhoun to the widow of his uncle, Captain James Colquhoun, hereafter mentioned He *d* unm 19 Aug. 1722, 'by cutting his own throat with a penknife at the 'Katherine Wheel,' without Bishopsgate "(b)

VIII.   1722   SIR GEORGE COLQUHOUN, Baronet [S 1625],(a) of Tillyquhoun aforesaid, cousin and h male, being s. and h of Capt James COLQUHOUN, 3d Foot Guards, by Elizabeth, da of John COLQUHOUN, of Auchintarlie, which James was br. of the 6th Baronet.(a) He was *b* 1708, and *suc to the Baronetcy*(a) in 1722, and to the estate of Tillyquhoun on the death of his mother, who had purchased the same as above-stated. He was a Col. in the service of the States General He *m* firstly, 7 Jan 1751, Rebecca, only da of William JONES, Collector of the Stamp Duties [S] She *d* s p m He *m* secondly, in 1777 (being then in his 70th year), Charlotte, da. of David BARCLAY He *d* at Edinburgh, 1785 Will pr. June 1787 His widow *d* 10 Feb 1816, also at Edinburgh

IX   1785   SIR JAMES COLQUHOUN, Baronet [S 1625],(a) of Tillyquhoun aforesaid, 1st s and h by 2d wife, *suc to the Baronetcy*,(a) when a child, in 1785 He was Lieut in the 19th Foot, and *d* unm, on the march to Seringapatam in the East Indies 1799 Will pr 1807.

X   1799   SIR GEORGE WILLIAM ORANGE COLQUHOUN, Baronet [S 1625],(a) of Tillyquhoun aforesaid, next br and h., was Capt in the 2d Royals, *suc to the Baronetcy*,(a) in 1799. He *d* unm, being slain at the battle of Salamanca, 22 July 1812 Admon March 1813 and June 1816

XI.   1812,   SIR ROBERT DAVID COLQUHOUN, Baronet [S 1625](a)
to   only suiv br and h , *b* (posthumous) 1786 , *suc to the*
1838   *Baronetcy*,(a) 22 July 1812 , was Brevet Major in the Bengal army He *m* Feb 1822, at Calcutta, Anna Maria, 2d da of James COLVIN, of Calcutta He *d* s p at sea, on his passage to India, 2 June 1838, aged 52, when the *issue male of the 1st Baronet* became *extinct*, and the *assumption of the Baronetcy* ceased

---

(a) According to the assumption of the title by the heir male, notwithstanding the *novodamus* of 1704, whereby the right of such heir thereto was barred.
(b) Mawson's Obits.

GORDON.

cr 31 Aug. and sealed 20 Oct. 1625 ;([a])

dormant, before 1668.

I   1625.   SIR ALEXANDER GORDON, of Cluny, co. Aberdeen,([b]) s. and h. of Sir Thomas GORDON ([c]) of the same, by Grizel, da. of James (STEWART) LORD INNERMEATH [S], had spec service to his father, 11 July 1607, was M P [S.] for Aberdeenshire, 1612-1617, *Knighted* (*Qy* at Lanark ?), May 1617, and was cr a *Baronet* [S], 31 Aug , sealed, 20 Oct 1625, with rem to heirs male whatsoever, and with a grant of presumably, 16,000 acres in Nova Scotia. entitled the Barony of New Cluny, of which he had seizin in the same month of Oct ([d]) His affairs soon became involved, and in 1630 he was a prisoner for debt in the Tolbooth in Edinburgh In 1632 he sold his estate of Tillyfour, etc In 1639 he was Lieut of the North in 1644 he was adjudged a prisoner till payment was made of 1,100 marks, due to Sir Thomas NICOLSON. He m firstly, Elizabeth, da. of William (DOUGLAS), 9th EARL OF ANGUS [S], by Egidia, da of Sir Robert GRAHAM He m secondly, Violet, da of John URQUHART, of Craighntry, co Aberdeen He m thirdly, 22 June 1641, a few months after her husband's death, Elspeth, widow of Sir John LESLIE, 1st Baronet [S 1625], of Wardes, da. of John GORDON, of Newton. She had previously intrigued with him, and had caused her then husband to make over to him his heavily burdened estates in co Aberdeen She d at Durham 2 Dec 1642. He d before 1650

II   1648 ?   SIR JOHN GORDON, Baronet [S 1625], of Cluny aforesaid, to   s and h He, who about 1622, had become a Roman Catholic, *suc* 1665 ?   *to the Baronetcy* before 1650. In 1650 he wadset the estate of Cluny to the abovenamed Sir Thomas Nicholson, from whom it passed by apprising sale to Robert GORDON, of Pulrossie. He m. Elizabeth, da of the abovenamed Sir John LESLIE, 1st Baronet [S], of Wardes, by his step mother Elspeth, da of John GORDON, of Newton. He d. before 1668, when the *Baronetcy* became *dormant*.([e]) His widow m. Colonel Sir George CURRIER.

LESLIE

cr. 1 Sep 1625 , sealed 5 April 1626 ,([a])

dormant after about 1660 ,

but assumed since about 1800

I   1625.   JOHN LESLIE, of Wardis, co. Aberdeen, 1st s and h of John LESLIE, of the same, by Jane, da. of Sir James CRICHTON, of Freudraught, suc his father about 1620, and was cr a *Baronet* [S], 1 Sep 1625, sealed 5 April 1626, with rem to heirs male whatsoever and with a grant of,

---

([a]) Milne's List , Laing's List

([b]) The Editor is indebted to R R Stodart *Lyon Clerk Depute* (1868-86), for most of the information in this article

([c]) This Thomas was s and h. of John Gordon, of Cluny aforesaid, who was s and h of the Hon Alexander Gordon, of Strathdon, co Aberdeen, 3d s of Alexander, 3d Earl of Huntly [S].

([d]) Banks's Lists

([e]) His brother german, William Gordon, of Cotton, near Aberdeen, had, by Marion, da of Patrick GORDON, of Gordonsmilne, two sons of whom (1) John Gordon, a Capt in the Swedish service, d at Cracow, about 1664 ; and (2) William Gordon (then late Bailie of Old Aberdeen) had a birthbrief, 4 June 1668, to prove him heir to his said brother All of these that survived the 2d Baronet would, in their turn, have been entitled to the Baronetcy If the issue male of all the younger sons of the 3d Earl of Huntly [S] has failed, the MARQUESS OF HUNTLY [S] would be entitled to the Baronetcy, and to him, accordingly, it is assigned in Broun's *Baronetage*.

2 P

presumably, 16,000 acres in Nova Scotia, entitled the Barony of Wardes and Findrassie, of which he had seizin in June 1626 (ᵃ)   He had charter, 30 July 1629, of lands of Balcomie, co Fife   He *m* Elspeth, da of John GORDON, of Newton   He *d* 1640   His widow *m* (as his 3d wife), 24 June 1641, Sir Alexander GORDON, 1st Baronet [S 1625] of Cluny, who *d* before 1650   She *d* at Durham 2 Dec 1642.

II   1640.   SIR JOHN LESLIE, Baronet [S 1625], of Wardis aforesaid, 1st but only surv. son,(ᵇ) *suc. to the Baronetcy*, in 1640, and *d.* unm. 1645.

III.   1645,   SIR WILLIAM LESLIE, Baronet [S 1625], uncle and h
to   male being next br to the 1st Baronet and consequently *entitled*
1660 ?   *to the Baronetcy* in 1645, under the term to heirs male whatsoever
He " is the last we find designed by this title "(ᶜ) and, not having inherited the family estates, it is doubtful whether he ever assumed it. He *m* Helen, da of George GORDON, of Newton, by whom he had four sons, John, William, Patrick, and Alexander, " but there is no male succession to any of them."(ᶜ)

WILLIAM LESLIE, of Aberdeen, s and h of Patrick LESLIE, of New Rame (who in 1700 sold that estate), s and h of John LESLIE, of New Rame, s and h of Norman LESLIE, yst br of the 1st Baronet, is said to have had " undoubtedly a title to the Baronetcy, as he appears to be the male representative of the family."(ᶜ)   He is also said(ᵈ) to have had an only s William, who *d.* s p.

JOHN LESLIE, though not mentioned in Douglas' *Baronage*,(ᶜ) is said(ᵈ) to have been a brother of William Leslie, of Aberdeen, and a yr s of the said Patrick, and to have left issue, as under

IV ?(ᵉ)   1800 (ᶠ)   SIR JOHN LESLIE, Baronet [S. 1625],(ᵍ) of Findrassie, co Moray, s and h of John LESLIE, next abovenamed, *b* about 1750 , was Writer to the Signet, 10 Nov 1784, *assumed the Baronetcy*, probably about 1800 (ᶠ)   He *m* , 15 July 1794, Caroline Jemima, da and h , of Abraham LESLIE, of Findrassie aforesaid   She *d* 1810.   He *d* at Edinburgh, 30 Sep 1825, aged 75.

V ?(ᵉ)   1825   SIR CHARLES ABRAHAM LESLIE, Baronet [S. 1625],(ᵍ)
of Findrassie aforesaid, 1st s and h, *b* 4 July 1796 , *suc. to the Baronetcy*,(ᵍ) 30 Sep. 1825.   He *m* , in or before 1822, Anne, da of Adam WALKER   He, who is said to have dissipated all his fortune, *d* 1 March 1847, in Edinburgh, aged 50.   His widow *d.* 7 Oct. 1868, at Mellenden lodge, Wanstead, Essex

---

(ᵃ) Banks's Lists.
(ᵇ) His younger brothers, Francis and Alexander, both *d.* unm , being killed in the German Wars
(ᶜ) Douglas' *Baronage* [S], 1798
(ᵈ) Burke's *Baronetage* 1901 states him positively to be a yr s of Patrick   Playfair's *Baronetage* [S], published in 1811, where this John first appears, states that Patrick " we have *reason to believe*, had two sons William and John "
(ᵉ) This is the enumeration given in Burke's *Baronetage*, but it is evident that there must have been many who should have been reckoned as *entitled* to the Baronetage after the death of the 3d Baronet, before those who are here set out.
(ᶠ) " It is said that this Baronetcy was claimed and assumed without even the customary service of a Jury   No date given " [Foster's *Baronetage* 1883 in " Chaos "].
Playfair's *Baronetage* [S], published in 1811, states that " within these few years only it has been claimed."
(ᵍ) According to the assumption of the Baronetcy in or about 1800

VI ?(ᵃ) 1847. SIR NORMAN ROBERT LESLIE, Baronet(ᵇ) [S 1625], 1st s and h ; b 10 Dec. 1822 ; suc to the Baronetcy(ᵇ) 1 March 1847(ᶜ) , was Lieut , 5th Irregular Bengal Cavalry He m, 17 Dec. 1846, Jessie Elizabeth, 3d da of Robert Wood SMITH, Major 6th Bengal Light Cavalry He was murdered at Rohnee, in India, 12 June 1857, during the Sepoy mutiny, aged 34 His widow d 1 July 1876, at Lucknow

VII ?(ᵃ) 1857. SIR CHARLES HENRY LESLIE, Baronet(ᵇ) [S 1625], only s and h., b 27 Nov 1848, at Lahore, in Bengal, suc to the Baronetcy(ᵇ), 12 June 1857 , ed at Grange School, Edinburgh, and at Sandwich , an officer, 107th Foot, 1867 , Major, 1887 ; Col , Bengal Staff Corps , served in the Chin Lushai, Manipur, Chitral, and Tirah campaigns, 1895-98. C.B , 1896 He m, 7 Jan 1879, Emma May, da of R M. EDWARDS, of the Bengal Civil Service.

Residence.—Rakloh, Punjab.

GORDON ·
cr. 2 Sep. 1625 , sealed 6 April 1626 ,(ᵈ)
dormant since 9 Nov. 1839.

I. 1625 JAMES GORDON,(ᵉ) of Lesmoir, co Aberdeen, s and h. of Alexander GORDON,(ᶠ) of the same, by Marion, da of Alexander FORBES, of Pitsligo, co Aberdeen, had, on 18 March 1592, a remission for his complicity in the slaughter of the Regent [S], the Earl of MORAY [S], suc his father in 1609, to whom, on 10 April 1610, he had spec. service in lands at Balmad, etc , and was cr a Baronet [S.], 2 Sep 1625, sealed 6 April 1626 with rem to heirs male whatsoever,(ᵈ) and with a grant of, presumably, 16,000 acres in Nova Scotia, entitled the barony of New Lesmoir, of which he had seizin in June 1626 (ᵍ) He m firstly, Anna MERCER, who was living 1605 He m secondly, Rebecca, da of William KEITH, of Ravenscraig, co. Aberdeen He was alive 1637, but d. in or before 1641

II 1640 ? SIR JAMES GORDON, Baronet [S. 1625], of Lesmoir aforesaid, great grandson and h , being only s and h of James GORDON (by (—), da of (—) MENZIES, of Pitfoddels, co Kincardine), which James (who d. July 1634), was only s and h of James GORDON, M.P [S], for Aberdeenshire, 1625, who was 1st s and h. ap of the late Baronet, but who d v p in France, 5 Sep. 1633 He suc his father in July 1634, being served his heir general 15 Dec 1637. He suc. to the Baronetcy in or before 1641, and on 9 June 1641, was served heir general of his said great grandfather, and, on 24 April 1642, his heir special in the Barony of Newton of Garioch with the privilege of Free Royalty He d. s.p before 1648

(ᵃ) See p 298 note " e."
(ᵇ) According to the assumption of the Baronetcy in or about 1800
(ᶜ) The date of his succession to the title is given in Dod's *Baronetage* and elsewhere as 1833 The Hon. Sir Charles Leslie, 2d Baronet [1784], died 4 Feb 1833, and it is probable that the two Baronets of the same name have been confounded
(ᵈ) Milne's List , Laing's List
(ᵉ) The Editor is indebted to R R Stodart (*Lyon Clerk Depute*, 1863-86) for most of the information in this article
(ᶠ) This Alexander was s and h. of George, the s and h. ap of James Gordon the first owner of Lesmoir, and suc. his grandfather in that estate before 25 Sep 1607. This family is one of the illegitimate branches of the race of Gordon.
(ᵍ) Banks's Lists.

III. 1647 ?   SIR WILLIAM GORDON, Baronet [S 1625], of Lesmoir aforesaid, great-uncle and h. male, being 2d and yst. s of the 1st Baronet   He *suc to the Baronetcy* about 1647, and had spec service on 19 Jan. 1648, to his grand-nephew in the Barony of Newton aforesaid, and also as heir male general of his said father. He *m* Christian WALKER, whose father was probably of Peterhead. He is also said to have *m* Isabella, da of Sir Patrick LESLIE, of Iden, co Aberdeen, Provost of Aberdeen. He *d* before 1672

IV. 1671 ?   SIR WILLIAM GORDON, Baronet [1625], of Lesmoir aforesaid, s. and h. by Christian WALKER aforesaid; *suc to the Baronetcy* about 1671, and on 9 Oct 1672 was served heir general of his cousin german, James GORDON, "Fiar of Lesmoir," and heir spec of his grandfather, the 1st Baronet, in lands at Essie, etc   He registered arms, about 1672, in the Lyon office. He *m* Margaret, da of Sir James LEARMONTH, of Balcomie, co Fife, a Senator of the College of Justice [S], 1627-57   He was alive 1683, but *d*. in or before 1685

V. 1684 ?   SIR JAMES GORDON, Baronet [S 1625], of Lesmoir afore-said, s and h, who, in 1681, had, v p, been enfeoffed in the said Barony of Newton, *suc to the Baronetcy*, about 1684   He *m*, about 1680, Jean, only child of Sir John GORDON, 2d Baronet [S 1642], of Haddo, by Mary, da. of Alexander (FORBES) 1st LORD FORBES OF PITSLIGO [S]   He was living 1696

VI. 1710 ?   SIR WILLIAM GORDON, Baronet [S 1625], of Lesmoir aforesaid, grandson and h, being only s and h. of William GORDON, by Margaret, da of William DUFF, of Drummuir, co Banff, which William GORDON last named was s and h. ap of the late Baronet, but *d* v.p. He *suc to the Baronetcy* about 1710   He *m* Lilias, da. of James GORDON, of Carnousie, co. Banff. He *d*. s.p, 15 Sep 1750, leaving very little property

VII. 1758.   SIR ALEXANDER GORDON, Baronet [S 1625], of Lesmoir aforesaid, cousin and h., being s. and h. of Alexander GORDON, Collector of Customs at Aberdeen, by Isabel, da. of James GORDON, merchant of Holland, which Alexander was 3d s of the 5th Baronet   He *suc. to the Baronetcy* 15 Sep 1750   He *m*, 5 April or 2 May 1759, Margaret, 1st da of Robert SCOTT, of Dunmald, co Forfar, by Anne, da. of George MIDDLETON, of Seaton, co Aberdeen. He *d* 25 March 1782

VIII. 1782,   SIR FRANCIS GORDON, Baronet [S. 1625], 3d but 1st surv.
to   s. and h, *b* about 1764, *suc. to the Baronetcy* in 1782   He was in
1839   the service of the Hon East India Company, had a severe sunstroke when young, from which he never altogether rallied, returned home in 1800, and lived many years in Yorkshire. He *d* s.p, presumably unm, 9 Nov 1839, aged 75, when the *Baronetcy* became *dormant*

(a) The cadets of this family were numerous and founded several families, which lasted for generations, so that it is unlikely that the title is extinct. A caveat was lodged, 23 Oct 1871, by Hugh GORDON, then in India   John Gordon, of Kinneller, co. Aberdeen, 4th of the five sons of Sir James Gordon, the 5th Baronet, had four sons, whose male issue, if any, would probably be entitled.   In Aug. 1887 Herbert Spence-Compton Gordon, Capt of the Princess Louise's Argyll and Sutherland Highlanders, s and h of John Henry Gordon (by Amelia, da. of Sir Herbert Compton, Chief Justice of Bombay) and nephew and h of Edward Gordon, who *d* s p, claimed the Baronetcy, on the ground that his said uncle, Edward Gordon, was, on the death of Sir Francis Gordon in 1839, the *de jure* Baronet, being s. and h of Edward GORDON (*d* 1832), who was s and h of Edward GORDON (*d*. 1802), who was the 1st s that left male issue of John GORDON (*d*. 18 Nov. 1728), which last named John, who left Scotland for India, was supposed to be s and h of Alexander Gordon, of Gerry, the yr s of the 1st Baronet. This supposition, however, is, by a comparison of the dates, very unlikely

RAMSAY

cr. 3 Sep. and sealed 2 Nov. 1625 ,([a])

sometime, 1754—1806, RAMSAY-IRVINE ,

dormant, 11 Feb. 1806 ;

but assumed, till 1830.

I   1625.   GILBERT RAMSAY, of Balmain, co Kincardine, s. and h ,
ap. of David RAMSAY, of the same, sometime (1612, 1625, and 1630)
M.P. [S.] for Kincardineshire (who *d.* 1636), by Margaret, da of Sir Gilbert OGILVIE, of
Ogilvie, was *cr.* a *Baronet* [S.] as " of Balmaine," 3 Sep , sealed 2 Nov. 1625,([a]) with
rem to heirs male whatsoever, and with a grant of, presumably, 16,000 acres in Nova
Scotia, of which he had seizin in the said month of Nov ([b]) He took part with the
Covenanters in 1636 , was M.P. [S] for Kincardineshire, 1639-41, 1645-46, and
1661-63 ; was one of the committee appointed by Parl. [S] in 1641 to collect the
English supply ; one of the Committee of Parl [S.], July 1644 : a Commissioner of
Excise, etc., 1646   He is said([c]) to have *m* Elizabeth, da of George AUCHINLECK, of
Balmanno   He undoubtedly([d]) *m* " Grizel DURHAM," *i e*, Grizel, widow of Sir
Alexander FOTHERINGHAM, da of James, and sister of Sir Alexander DURHAM, of
Pitkerrow   He was living July 1639, and some years afterwards,([e]) probably as late
as 1663.   His widow *m.*, as his 1st wife, John (MIDDLETON), 1st EARL OF MIDDLETON
[S], who *d* , 1673, at Tangiers.   She *d* Sep. 1666, at Cranstoun.

II   1663?   SIR DAVID RAMSAY, Baronet [S 1625], of Balmain aforesaid, only s. and h , *suc. to the Baronetcy* on the death of his father.
He had charter *de novo* of his lands and Barony, 12 Aug 1670.   He is said([e]) to have
m firstly, Margaret, da of Sir James CARNEGIE, of Balnamoon ([f])   He was M P [S]
for Kincardineshire, 1672, till his death   He *m* secondly, in or after 1663, Elizabeth,
widow of Sir Alexander BURNETT, 2d Baronet [S 1626], da of (—) COUTTS, of
Auchtercoull.   He *d.* Sep 1673, being killed by a fall from his horse.

III.   1673.   SIR CHARLES RAMSAY, Baronet [S. 1625], of Balmain
aforesaid, only s and h. by 1st wife, *suc to the Baronetcy* in 1673.
He *m* firstly, about 1673, Margaret, 1st da. of Sir John CARNEGIE, of Boysack.   She
d. s p   He *m* secondly, Elizabeth, only da of Sir Alexander FALCONER, of Glenfar-
quhar.   He *d* 1695.

IV   1695   SIR DAVID RAMSAY, Baronet [S. 1625], of Balmain
aforesaid, 1st s. and h. ; *suc. to the Baronetcy* in 1695 ; was
M P [S] for Kincardineshire 1705-07, and again [G.B], 1707-08 and 1708-10
He *d s p*, probably unm , Sep 1710

V.   1710.   SIR ALEXANDER RAMSAY, Baronet, [S 1625], of Balmain
aforesaid, next br and h , Advocate [S.] 1705 , *suc to the Baronetcy*
in Sep 1710; was M.P. for Kincardineshire 1710-13 , when he retired to improve
his estate by better methods of agriculture   He *d.* unm 27 Jan 1754

VI.   1754,   SIR ALEXANDER RAMSAY-IRVINE, Baronet [S. 1625] of
to   Balmain aforesaid, nephew and h , being only s. and h of Charles
1806.   RAMSAY, by Catherine, da of James MILL, of Balweylo, sometime
Provost of Montrose, which Charles, who *d* in 1727, was br of the
late two baronets, being 3d and yst s of the 3d Baronet   He, being then Alexander

---

([a]) Milne's List ; Laing's List.

([b]) Banks's Lists.

([c]) Playfair's *Baronetage* [S.]

([d]) See a Charter, dat 31 July 1632, in the Laing Charters, no. 2114

([e]) *Ex inform* , Sir J Balfour Paul, Lyon King of Arms.

([f]) No such " Sir James " is mentioned, and no such alliance is given in Lord
Southesk's *History of the Carnegie Family*

RAMSAY, took the name of IRVINE after that of RAMSAY, *suc to the Baronetcy*, 27 Jan 1754, was M P for Kincardineshire 1765-68 He *d* unm 11 Feb. 1806, when the issue male of the grantee was apparently extinct and the *Baronetcy* became *dormant* (a)

The title was, however, assumed as under :—

VII 1806. JAMES RAMSAY, sometime resident in Barbadoes, whose parentage and descent is unknown "in the year 1806, served himself [*sic*] heir to the 1st Baronet,'(b) becoming thus "SIR JAMES RAMSAY, Baronet" (b) [S. 1625] He *d* s p 1807 Will as "Baronet," pr. 1808.

VIII 1807, "SIR THOMAS RAMSAY, Baronet "(c) [S. 1625], only
to surv br and h, *b* about 1765, was in the East India Com-
1830. pany's service, *suc to the Baronetcy*(c) in 1807, but returned to the East Indies in 1809 to resume his situation as Captain.(b) He, being then "of Edinburgh," *m* firstly, 29 June 1809, at St James', Westminster, "Anne STEELE," then of St James's Street, spinster, da of the Rev Dr STEELE, late of Jamaica, deceased He *m* secondly, in 1819, Elizabeth, widow of William CHISHOLM, of Chisholm, 2d da. of Duncan MACDONNELL, of Glengarry, by Margery, da. of Sir Ludovick GRANT, 6th Baronet [S. 1688], of Dalvey He *d*, abroad, s p m, in 1830, when the assumption of this Baronetcy ceased. Will pr. June 1832 His widow *d* 7 Oct 1859, at Thorn Faulcon, co Somerset, aged 82.

GRAHAM, *or* GRÆME ·

cr 28 Sep 1625, sealed 23 Jan 1630 ,(d)

dormant, since, apparently, about 1700.

I　1625　　THE HON SIR WILLIAM GRAHAM, of Braco, in the parish of Muthill co Perth, 2d s of John (GRAHAM), 3d EARL OF MONTROSE (S), by Jean, da of David (DRUMMOND), LORD DRUMMOND (S) had in 1614 a wadset from his wife's father of his whole estate redeemable on payment of 80,000 marks, had sasine of the Barony of Braco in Anti Costi, 28 Dec. 1625, and was *cr* a Baronet [S], as "Sir William Græme, of Bracco," 28 Sep. 1625, sealed 23 Jan 1630,(d) but not recorded in the *Registrum Praeceptorum Cartarum pro Baronettis Novæ Scotiæ*, with rem to heirs male whatsoever, and with a grant of, presumably, 16,000 acres in Nova Scotia, called the Barony of New Braco, of which he had seizin in Jan 1630 (e) He *m* Mary, widow of John CUNNINGHAM, of Cunninghamhead, co Ayr, da of Sir James EDMONSTONE, of Duntreath, co. Stirling He *d* before 1636

(a) He devised his estates to his nephew Alexander Burnett, 2d s. of his sister Catherine, by Sir Thomas Burnett, 6th Baronet [S 1626], which Alexander accordingly took the name of Ramsay, and was *cr* a Baronet as "of Balmain, co. Kincardine," 13 May 1806

(b) Playfair's *Baronetage* [S.] where it is added that "Sir Thomas is also the representative collateral descendant of the family of Ramsay, of Abbotshall, in Fife, an old family in which there was also a Baronetage [*cr* 1669], which is now extinct or dormant."

(c) According to the service of 1806 abovementioned

(d) Milne's List the date, however, of the creation in Laing's List is "28 *Dec* 1625," and there placed between the creations of "Erskine" and "Hume," both of the same date, all three being after that of "Forrester," 17 Nov. 1625.

(e) Banks's Lists.

II. 1635?   Sir John Graham, Baronet [S 1625], of Braco aforesaid,
s. and h, *suc.* to *the Baronetcy* about 1635 and was served heir gen
of his father, 23 Jan 1636, was a Royalist and was imprisoned for aiding his cousin
the gallant Marquis of Montrose [S], but released 8 March 1645 on paying 2,000 merks,
etc. He m Margaret, da. of Sir Dugald Campbell, 1st Baronet [S 1628], of Auchinbreck, by his 1st wife, Mary, da. of Sir Alexander Erskine, of Gogar. He d. before
1647.

III. 1646?   Sir William Graham, Baronet [S 1625], of Braco aforesaid, s and h, *suc.* to *the Baronetcy* about 1646 and was, on 9 Oct
1647 served heir spec. in Braco, etc, co Perth. and in the Barony of Aithray,
co. Stirling   He registered arms about 1672 in the Lyon office. He m. Mary,[a]
da. of John Cowan, of Tulzartoun, co Stirling, by Katherine, da. of Patrick
Smith, of Braco, in the parish of Redgorton, co Perth   He d before 1685.

IV. 1684?   Sir James Graham, Baronet [S 1625], of Braco aforesaid,
to   s and h, *suc to the Baronetcy* about 1684, under 25 years of age in
1700?   1685, being then next agnate, on the father's side, to James, 4th
Marquess of Montrose [S]   He d unm but the date, however, is
not given in his funeral escutcheon   At his death *the Baronetcy* became *dormant*, the
issue male of the grantee and that of his only yr br (Sir Robert Graham, of Scotstoun,
who d s p in or before Oct 1617), being, apparently, extinct. In that case the title
would vest in the Dukes of Montrose [S], the heirs male of the body of the grantee's
eldest brother, John, 4th Earl of Montrose [S]

FORRESTER :

cr. 17 Nov 1625,[b] sealed 4 Dec. 1630,[c]

afterwards, 1633-54, Lord Forrester of Corstorphine [S],

dormant, since 1654

I. 1625,   "Sir George Forrester, Knt,"[b] of Corstophine co
to   Edinburgh, s and h of Henry Forrester, ot the same, by Helen, da
1654   of (—) Preston, of the house of Craigmiller, was served heir to his
uncle Sir James Forrester, of Corstorphine aforesaid (who d s p June
1589) 17 May 1622, and was *cr. a Baronet* [S] 17 Nov 1624,[b] sealed 4 Dec 1630,[c]
but not registered in the Great Seal register with rem to heirs male whatsoever, and
with a grant of, presumably, 16,000 acres, entitled the Barony of Corstorphine in Nova
Scotia, of which he had seizin in Jan 1630/1 [d]   He was M P [S] for Edinburgh-
shire, 1625 and 1628-33   He m, before 15 Nov 1607, Christian, da of Sir
William Livingstone, of Kilsyth   He was cr, 22 July 1633, LORD FORRESTER
OF CORSTORPHINE [S]   Having no male issue then living,[e] he resigned
his peerage and obtained a regrant thereof 5 July 1651 with a spec rem in favour
of James Baillie his son-in-law, etc   He d. s p m s,[e] 1654, when the peerage
devolved according to the spec rem, and the *Baronetcy* became *dormant*   See *Peerage*.

---

[a] So called in her son's funeral escutcheon, though called "Katherine," in
Douglas' *Peerage* [S]
[b] Laing's List, the date of the creation in Milne's List (in which the Knighthood
is not mentioned) is "17 *March* 1625"
[c] Milne's List.
[d] Banks's Lists.
[e] His s and h., ap "the master of Corstorphine," m in 1634 the widow of
Alexander Keith, but d v p and s p.

NICOLSON :

creation, " sealed 17 Dec 1625 ,"(a)

but nothing more is known.

I. 1625.   " MR. JAMES NICOLSON, of Cockburnspeth," 1st s. of
Thomas NICOLSON, Advocate [S], Commissary of Aberdeenshire, by
his wife, Margaret SCOTT, was *cr a Baronet* [S], as above, with rem to heirs male
whatsoever, such creation being "sealed 17 Dec 1625,"(a) but not recorded in
the Great Seal Register [S] Nothing more is known of this creation or of the
grantee,(b) and no grant or seizin of lands in Nova Scotia is recorded.

ERSKINE .

cr., 28 Dec. 1625 ,(c)

but nothing more is known

I. 1625.   " [—] ERSKINE " is said(c) to have been *cr a Baronet*
[S], 28 Dec 1625, but no particulars are known of him, and, though
he, apparently, obtained a grant of, presumably, 16,000 acres in Nova Scotia, no seizin
thereof is recorded (d)

HUME, *or* HOME :

cr 28 Dec. 1625 ;(e)

afterwards, 1690—1794, LORDS POLWARTH [S],

and 1697—1794, EARLS OF MARCHMONT [S];

dormant, since 10 Jan. 1794.

I. 1625   PATRICK HUME *or* HOME, of Polwarth, s. and h of Sir
Patrick HOME, of the same, by Janet (afterwards COUNTESS OF
HADDINGTON [S]), da of Sir Thomas KERR, of Fernihirst, suc. his father, 10 June 1609
to whom he was returned heir special, 1 Feb 1611, and was *cr a Baronet* [S] as " of
Polwart," 28 Dec 1625.(e) The usual grant of lands in Nova Scotia was, presumably,
made to him, but no seizin is recorded thereof (d) He was M P [S] for Berwickshire,
1630. He *m,* in or before 1640, Christian, da of Sir Alexander HAMILTON, of
Innerwick, by (—). He *d* April 1648. His widow *m* Robert (Kerr), 4th LORD
JEDBURGH [S.], who *d. s p* 4 Aug 1692.

II. 1648.   SIR PATRICK HUME, *or* HOME, Baronet [S. 1625], of
Polwarth aforesaid, 1st s and h, *b* 13 Jan 1641 , *suc to the
Baronetcy* in April 1648 ; was M P. [S] for Berwickshire, 1665, 1667, 1669-74, and
1689-90 , took part against the Government and was imprisoned, 1675 79   He joined
in Argyll's invasion of Scotland, 1685 , was, accordingly, *attainted,* and fled to Utrecht ;
but was, however, restored 1689, having come over with William, Prince of Orange,

---

(a) Milne's List ; no such creation, however, is in Laing's List, Walkley's List, etc.

(b) The estate of Lasswade was acquired by John Nicolson, Advocate [S.],
Commissary of Edinburgh, who was an uncle of this James   Of this John's sons (1)
John Nicolson was *cr a Baronet* [S], 27 July 1629, and (2) Thomas Nicolson was of
Cockburnspath.

(c) Laing's List (though stated therein to be "given on the authority of former lists; ')
not, however, in Milne's List nor in the *Registrum Preceptorum Cartarum pro Baronettis
Novæ Scotiæ*

(d) Banks's Lists

(e) Laing's List (though stated therein to be " given on the authority of former
lists "), as also, though without any date, in Milne's List, where it is added—" In one
old list, and so designed in his patent when nobilitate " It is not, however, in the
Registrum Preceptorum Cartarum pro Baronettis Novæ Scotiæ.

afterwards **William III**, with whom he was in the greatest favour He *m*, in or before 1665, Grizel, da of Sir Thomas KER, or CARRE, of Cavers She was living when he was raised to the peerage, being cr 26 Dec 1690, LORD POLWARTH [S] with a spec rem., and subsequently, 23 April 1697, EARL OF MARCHMONT, etc. [S], with rem to heirs male whatsoever. In these peerages this *Baronetcy* then merged, and so continued till the death, s p m s, of the 3d Earl and 4th Baronet, when, the issue male of the grantee apparently failed and both dignities became *dormant* The Barony of Polwarth [S.], however, was in 1835 allowed to the grandson and heir general of the last Earl. See *Peerage*.

FORBES
cr, 30 March, and sealed, 2 May 1626 ,([a])
sometime, 1864-66, HEPBURN-STUART-FORBES

I 1626. WILLIAM FORBES, of Monymusk, co Aberdeen, s and h. of William FORBES, of the same, by Margaret, da. of William (DOUGLAS), EARL OF ANGUS [S], suc his father between 1608 and 1618, and was cr a *Baronet* [S] as " of Monymusk," 30 March, sealed 2 May 1626,([a]) with rem. to heirs male whatsoever, and with a grant of, presumably, 16,000 acres in Nova Scotia, called the Barony of Forbes, of which he had seizin in the said month of May 1626 ([b]) He *m.* Elizabeth, da of (—) WISHART, of Pittarrow He *d.* before July 1661

II 1650 ? SIR WILLIAM FORBES, Baronet [S 1626], of Monymusk aforesaid, 1st s and h · *suc to the Baronetcy* before 22 July 1661, when he obtained a charter under the great seal He *m* Jane, da of Sir Thomas BURNETT, 1st Baronet [S 1626], of Leys, by his first wife, Margaret, da of Sir Robert DOUGLAS, of Glenbervie

III. 1680 ? SIR JOHN FORBES, Baronet [S 1626], of Monymusk aforesaid, only s. and h ; *suc to the Baronetcy* on the death of his father He *m* firstly, Margaret, da of Robert (ARBUTHNOTT), 1st VISCOUNT ARBUTHNOTT [S], by his first wife, Marjory, da of David (CARNEGIE) 1st EARL OF SOUTHESK [S] He *m.* secondly, 21 Feb 1673, Barbara, da. of John DELMAHOY, by Rachel WILBRAHAM, his wife, which John was 2d son of Sir John DALMAHOY, of Dalmahoy He *d.* before 1713.

IV 1700 ? SIR WILLIAM FORBES, Baronet [S 1626], of Monymusk aforesaid, 1st s and h by first wife, *suc to the Baronetcy* before 1713, in which year he sold the estate of Monymusk to Sir Francis Grant, a Lord of Session [S]. He *m.* Jean, 1st da of John (KEITH), 1st EARL OF KINTORE [S], by Margaret, da of Thomas (HAMILTON), 2d EARL OF HADDINGTON [S.]

V. 1720 ? SIR WILLIAM FORBES, Baronet [S 1626], of Edinburgh, grandson and h , being 1st s and h. of John FORBES, by Mary, da [whose issue, in 1781, became heir of line] of Alexander (FORBES), 3d LORD FORBES OF PITSLIGO [S] He was an Advocate [S], 6 Jan 1728 He *m* in 1730 Christian, da of John FORBES, of Boyndlie, by his 1st wife, Susan, da. of George MORISON, of Bognie, which John was a yr s , by the 2nd wife, of the 3d Baronet He *d.* 12 May 1743 His widow *d.* 1789.

VI 1743 SIR WILLIAM FORBES, Baronet [S. 1626], of Edinburgh and afterwards of Pitsligo, co Aberdeen, 2d but 1st surv s and h., *b* in Edinburgh, 5 April 1739 , *suc to the Baronetcy* in 1743; was apprenticed to Messrs Coutts & Co, Bankers Edinburgh, in 1754, becoming a partner in 1760 That firm in 1773 was known as " Forbes, Hunter and Co," and began to issue notes in 1783 He is said to have been frequently consulted in financial matters, and to have declined in 1799 an Irish Peerage He was well known for his literary taste, was author of a life of the poet Beattie, etc. He acquired, both by purchase and by the devise of the attainted heir (who *d.* 1781), much of the estate of Pitsligo, co Aberdeen

---

([a]) Milne's List; Laing's List. The date is given as 2 April 1626 in Douglas' *Baronage* [S.], followed by Playfair's *Baronetage* [S]
([b]) Banks's Lists.

2 Q

(the inheritance of the family of his paternal grandmother abovementioned), which he greatly improved (ª) He *m* 20 Sep 1770, Elizabeth [" the beautiful and truly amiable Miss Hay "(ª)] 1st da of Sir James HAY, 4th Baronet [S. 1635], of Haystoun, by Dornel, da. and coheir of Daniel CAMPBELL, of Greenyards She, who was *b* 1 Feb 1753, *d.* 1802 He *d.* 12 Nov. 1806 Will pr 1808 .

VII. 1806. SIR WILLIAM FORBES, Baronet [S 1626], of Pitsligo, co Aberdeen, 1st s and h.,(ᵇ) *b.* 21 Dec 1773, *suc to the Baronetcy*, 12 Nov 1806, and was head of the Banking house abovenamed , F S A He *m* , 19 Jan. 1797, Williamina, only child of Sir John STUART [previously (1777-97) Sir John BELSHES WISHART, and before that, John BELSHES], 3d Baronet(ᶜ) [S 1707], of Fettercairn, co Kincardine, one of the Barons of the Exchequer [S.], by Jane, da. of David (LESLIE), 6th EARL OF LEVEN [S] She *d.* v.p 5 Dec 1810 He *d.* at Edinburgh, 24 Oct 1828

VIII 1828   SIR JOHN STUART FORBES, *afterwards* (1864 66), HEP-BURN STUART-FORBES, Baronet [S 1626], of Fettercairn and Pitsligo aforesaid, and *afterwards* (1864) of Invermay and Balmanno, both in co. Perth, 2d but 1st surv s and h ,(ᵈ) *b* 25 Sep 1804, at Dean House, near Edinburgh ; was an Advocate [S] 8 July 1826 , *suc to the Baronetcy*, 24 Oct 1828 On the death, in 1864, of his cousin, Alexander HEPBURN-MURRAY-BELSHES, he inherited the estate of Invermay as heir of entail, and that of Balmanno (both abovenamed) as heir at law when he assumed the additional surname of HEPBURN He *m.*, 14 June 1834, Harriet Louisa Anne, 3d da of William (KERR), 6th MARQUESS OF LOTHIAN [S], by his second wife Harriet, da of Henry (SCOTT), DUKE OF BUCCLEUCH [S.] He *d* s p m ,(ᶜ) 27 May 1866, in Wimpole Street, aged 61 His widow, who was *b.* 19 Oct 1808, *d* 26 April 1884, at 67 Princes Gate, Hyde Park.

IX 1866   SIR WILLIAM FORBES, Baronet [S 1626], nephew and h. male, being s and h of Charles FORBES, of Canaan park, co Edinburgh, by Jemima Rebecca, da of Alexander Ranaldson MACDONNELL, of Glengarry, which Charles, who *d* 5 Nov 1859, aged 53, was next br to the late Baronet He was *b* 16 June 1835 and *suc to the Baronetcy*, but presumably to none of the family estates, 27 May 1866 He *m* , 1 July 1865, Marion, 3d da. of J. WATTS, of Bridgend, Nelson, in New Zealand, Civil Engineer. She *d* 1890

Family Estates —Those assigned to the 9th Baronet in Bateman's *Great Land-owners* (1883), consist of 5,007 acres, co Kincardine, valued at £4,056 a year, being, apparently, the Stuart property at Fettercairn. These 5,007 acres of the value of £4,056 appear, however, also in the same work as assigned to Lord Clinton, to whom (with the other estates) it is believed they went At all events, in more recently dated Baronetages, no such property is attributed to the 9th Baronet, whose residence is given as "Carterton, Wellington, New Zealand, ' and whose estates, if any, are not mentioned

(ª) Playfair's *Baronetage* [S.], where there is a flaming account both of his improvements of the Pitsligo estate, and of other of his " patriotic labours "

(ᵇ) The second son John Hay Forbes, of Medwyn, co Peebles, was a Lord of Session [S], as Lord Medwyn (1825-54), and *d* 25 July 1854, aged 77.

(ᶜ) In 1797 his right to the Baronetcy [S], of Wishart, was confirmed by the Lyon Court This Baronetcy was cr 17 June 1706, with a spec rem , failing heirs male of the body, to " heirs whomsoever and their heirs male for ever." The grantee *d* s p m , between 1718 and 1722, and the title was assumed by his grandson William Stuart, of Colinton co Edinburgh whose mother, Margaret, was 1st da and heir of line of the grantee He *d* s p. Dec 1777. It was then assumed by the Grantee's great nephew, John Belshes (mentioned in the text), s and h. of William Belshes, by Emilia Stuart, only child of her mother Mary, 1st surv. sister of the late Baronet. [*Ex inform* , R. R Stodart, Lyon Clerk Depute, 1863-86]

(ᵈ) William Forbes, Capt in the army, the eldest son, *d.* unm and v p., 16 Sep 1826, at Malta

(ᶜ) His estates (Invermay, Balmanno, Pitsligo, and, presumably, Fettercairn, or a part thereof) passed to his only child, Harriet Williamina, Baroness Clinton, first wife of Charles Henry Rolle (Trefusis, *afterwards* Hepburn Stuart-Forbes-Trefusis) Lord Clinton. She died 4 July 1869, aged 34.

JOHNSTON :

cr 31 March, and sealed 23 May 1626 ;([a])

I. 1626   GEORGE JOHNSTON, of Caskieben, co. Aberdeen, s. and h of John JOHNSTON, of the same (who had sold the fee of Johnston in 1595, though retaining the superiority) by his 1st wife Janet, da. of (—) TURING, of Foveran, co Aberdeen, suc his father, 4 Feb 1613/4, and had spec. service to him in the Barony of Johnston, etc , 3 May 1614, and was cr a *Baronet* [S] 31 March, sealed 23 May 1626, as " of Caskieben," with rem to heirs male whatsoever, and with a grant of, presumably, 16,000 acres in Nova Scotia entitled the Barony of Johnston, of which he had seizin in the said month of May, and again in Nov 1626,([b]) was Sheriff of co Aberdeen, 1630-31 In 1641 he and his son were cited before Parliament as incendiaries He *m* Elizabeth, da of William FORBES, or Tolquhoun, co Aberdeen

II. 1650?   SIR GEORGE JOHNSTON, Baronet [S 1626], of Caskieben aforesaid, s. and h. ; *suc. to the Baronetcy* on the death of his father. In 1660 he sold Caskieben to Sir John Keith, who changed its name to Keith Hall He *m.*, in or before 1648, (—), da. of Sir William LESLIE, 3d Baronet [S 1625], of Wardes, by Helen, da of George GORDON, of Newton He *d* before 10 June 1695

III. 1680?   SIR JOHN JOHNSTON, Baronet [S. 1626], only s and h , *b* about 1648 , *suc to the Baronetcy* on the death of his father , was a Capt in the army and served at the battle of the Boyne, on behalf of King William In Nov 1690, having aided in the abduction, by Capt. the Hon James([c]) CAMPBELL, of Mary Whalton, a rich heiress aged 13, he (though Campbell escaped) was hanged at Tyburn, 23 Dec. 1690, aged 42. He *d.* unm

IV. 1690   SIR JOHN JOHNSTON, Baronet [S, 1626], of New Place, near Aberdeen, cousin and h male, being s. and h of John JOHNSTON, or New Place aforesaid, by his cousin, (—), da of Thomas JOHNSTON, of Craig, in the parish of Dyce, which John last named was 2d and yst. s of the first Baronet He *suc to the Baronetcy*, 23 Dec 1690, but did not assume the title till 10 years later He entailed the estate of Craig, 18 Dec 1699 (which he had purchased), and bought part of the estate of Cordyce, changing its name to "Caskieben" He was in the rising in 1715, his only son, John, being slain (at his side) at Sheriffmuir, aged 25 He *m* , April 1683, Janet, da of Thomas MITCHELL, Bailie of Aberdeen He *d.* s p m s , at Edinburgh, Nov. 1724. His widow *d.* Sep. 1725

V. 1724.   SIR WILLIAM JOHNSTON, Baronet [S 1626], of Craig aforesaid, cousin and h male, being s and h of John JOHNSTON, of Bishopstown, by Margaret (*m.* Nov 1672), da and coheir of John ALEXANDER, which John JOHNSTON (who *d* 1716, aged 67) was 3d s of Thomas JOHNSTON, of Craig aforesaid (*d* Aug. 1656), yr br , of the half-blood, to the 1st Baronet, being s of John JOHNSTON, of that ilk, by his 2d wife, Katherine, da of William LUNDIE He was *b* about 1675 ; was an Advocate in Aberdeen , *suc. to the Baronetcy* in Nov 1724, but became insolvent in 1725, when his property was soon afterwards sold He *m* (contract 8 Jan 1704) Jean, sister of Alexander SANDILANDS, M.D , 1st da of James SANDILANDS, of Craibston. near Aberdeen, by his 2d wife, Elizabeth, da of (—) DONALDSON, of Hilton She *d* June 1744. He *d.* 18 March 1750

VI 1750   SIR WILLIAM JOHNSTON, Baronet [S 1626], of Hilton, in the parish of Old Machar, co Aberdeen, s. and h , *b.* Nov. 1714 , Lieut R N., 1741 , Commander, 1750 , *suc to the Baronetcy* in March 1750. He purchased the estate of Hilton aforesaid with his prize money and entailed it, 21 Feb 1784 He *m* firstly, Sarah, da of Thomas KIRBY, of London, merchant, a West Indian proprietor. She *d* s.p m s He *m.* secondly, March 1757, Elizabeth,

---

([a]) Milne's List ; Laing's List
([b]) Banks's Lists
([c]) This Capt James Campbell was yst s of Archibald, 9th Earl, and br. of Archibald, 1st Duke of Argyll [S] In Anderson's *Scottish Nation* the young lady's consent to the proposed marriage is alleged, and the hard fate of Johnston is attributed " to the bitter animosity then entertained by the English against the Scotch "

da of William CLELAND, of that ilk, co. Lanark, Capt. R N , by whom he had six sons and five daughters. She d 25 Aug. 1772, aged 41 He m thirdly, Amy, widow of John PUDSEY, da. of Newman FRENCH, of Belchamp, co Essex He d at Brompton Row, Midx , 19 March 1794, in his 81st year Admon. Oct. 1794.

VII. 1794 SIR WILLIAM JOHNSTON, Baronet [S 1626], of Hilton aforesaid, s and h , by 2d wife, b Aug 1760 at Hilton He served against the French in India in seven actions on the coast of Malabar *suc to the Baronetcy*, 19 March 1794. In 1798 he raised a regiment of Fencibles, which was disbanded in 1802 , was a Colonel in the army ; was M P. for New Windsor, 1801-02; was subsequently insolvent and consequently lived within the precincts of Holyrood Abbey He m. firstly, 24 Feb 1783 or 1784, Mary, da. of John BACON, of Shrubland Hall, Suffolk. She, who was 34 years older than her husband, d. s p , July 1802, in Gloucester Place He m secondly, Dec. 1802, Maria da. of John BACON, of Fryern House, Midx., and of the First Fruits Office. He d at the Hague, 13 Jan 1844 Will pr June 1844. His widow d at Ramsgate, 27 Oct. 1847. Admon April 1849

VIII. 1844. SIR WILLIAM BACON JOHNSTON, Baronet [S. 1626], of Hilton aforesaid, s and h by 2d wife, b. 17 March 1806 was an officer in the First Royals , *suc to the Baronetcy*, 13 Jan 1844 In July 1852 he disentailed the estate of Hilton (describing himself as unmarried), and paid his brother and cousins for their consent thereto He m at St. Pancras, Midx , 11 Sep 1855,[a] Mary Ann, da. of William TYE, of Medlesham, Suffolk, shoemaker, by Susan HOWLETT, his wife. He d 3 Aug 1865, at Hilton House aforesaid, aged 59. His widow living 1901

IX. 1865. SIR WILLIAM JOHNSTON, Baronet [S. 1626], only s and h , b 31 July 1849 at Hawley Road, Kentish town, before his parents' marriage, but legitimated thereby 11 Sep. 1855, according to the law of Scotland , *suc. to the Baronetcy*, 3 Aug 1865, and was in 1867, during his absence in China, served h gen to his father by the Court of Chancery in Scotland ; is Secretary to the Travancore plantation Tea Company

Family Estates.—These appear to have been alienated by the late Baronet The *Residence* of the present (1901) Baronet and of his mother is given as " The Ranche, Buckhurst Hill, Essex "

BURNET, *or* BURNETT

cr. 21 April, and sealed 12 June 1626 [b]

I. 1626. SIR THOMAS BURNET, of Leys, co. Kincardine, 1st surv s. and h of Alexander BURNET, of the same, M P. [S] for Kincardineshire, 1621, by Katharine, da of Alexander GORDON, of Lesmoir, co Aberdeen, suc his father in 1619 , was *Knighted* before 6 Aug 1621, and was cr a *Baronet* [S] as "of Leys," 21 April, sealed 12 June 1626, with rem to heirs male whatsoever and a grant of, presumably, 16,000 acres in Nova Scotia, of which he had seizin in the said month of June [c] He was, however, an active Covenanter. He endowed three Bursaries in the University of Aberdeen. He m firstly, Margaret, da. of Sir Robert DOUGLAS, 1st Baronet [S 1625], of Glenbervie, by Elizabeth, da of Sir George AUCHINLECK He m. secondly, 1621, Jane, widow of Sir Simon FRASER, of Inverallochy, da of Sir John MONCREIFF, 1st Baronet [S. 1626], of Moncreiff, by Mary, da. of William (MURRAY), 2d EARL OF TULLIBARDINE [S]. He d 1653 [d]

---

[a] " We have heard there were two marriages, the first private, the second by special licence in England " [See *Doubtful Baronetcies* in the *Herald and Genealogist*, vol v, pp. 89 and 186]

[b] Milne's List , Laing's List

[c] Banks's Lists

[d] Gilbert Burnett, the celebrated Bishop of Salisbury (1689—1716), author of the *History of His own Time*, etc , was nephew of the 1st Baronet being s of his yr br Robert Burnett, who was a Lord of Session [S] under the name of Lord Crimond.

II. 1653.   Sir Alexander Burnett, Baronet [S 1626], of Leys aforesaid, grandson and h., being s and h of Alexander Burnett, by Jane (m 1633), da. of Sir Robert Arbuthnott, of Arbuthnott, which Alexander was s. and h ap. of the 1st Baronet, by his 1st wife, but d v p   He suc to the Baronetcy in 1653.   He m. Elizabeth, da of (—) Coutts, of Auchtercoull   He d. 1663.   His widow m   Sir David Ramsay, 2d Baronet [S. 1625], of Balmain, who d 1673.

III. 1663.   Sir Thomas Burnett, Baronet [S 1626], of Leys aforesaid, s and h, suc to the Baronetcy in 1663, M.P. [S] for co Kincardine 1689—1707 (three Parls.), and [G B] 1707 08, being a zealous opponent of the Scotch Union.   He m in 1677, Margaret, da of Robert (Arbuthnot), 2d Viscount Arbuthnot [S], by Elizabeth, da of William (Keith), 7th Earl Marischal [S]   He d. 1714

IV. 1714   Sir Alexander Burnett, Baronet [S 1626], of Leys aforesaid, s and h, suc to the Baronetcy in 1714   He m Helen, 1st da of Robert Burnett, of Muchalls.   He d. 1758.

V 1758.   Sir Robert Burnett, Baronet [S. 1626], of Leys aforesaid, 3d and yst but only surv s and h, suc to the Baronetcy in 1758   He d unm 1759.

VI. 1759.   Sir Thomas Burnett, Baronet [S 1626], of Crathes Castle, co Kincardine, cousin and h male, being s and h of William Burnett, of Criggie, by Jean, da of Robert Burnett, of Muchalls, which William (who d 1747, aged 64) was 2d s. of the 3d Baronet   He suc to the Baronetcy in 1759   He m in or before 1755, Catherine, sister, whose issue became heir (11 Feb. 1806) to Sir Alexander Ramsay, 6th Baronet [S 1626], of Balmain, 4th da. of Charles Ramsay, by Catherine, da of James Mill, Provost of Montrose   He d May 1783. His widow d 10 Dec 1798.

VII. 1783.   Sir Robert Burnett, Baronet [S. 1626], of Crathes Castle aforesaid, s. and h, b 20 Dec 1755, was an officer in the Royal Scots Fusileers, serving in the first American War, and being taken prisoner in 1777 at Saratoga ; suc to the Baronetcy in May 1783   He m 16 Sep 1785, Margaret, 4th da. of General Robert Dalrymple-Horn-Elphinstone (formerly Dalrymple), of Logie Elphinstone, co. Aberdeen, by Mary, da and h of Sir James Elphinstone, of Logie aforesaid   He d 5 Jan. 1837   Will pr April 1838   His widow d 18 March 1849, at Logie Elphinstone, aged 84.

VIII 1837.   Sir Thomas Burnett, Baronet [S. 1626], of Crathes Castle aforesaid, s and h, b 22 Aug. 1778, suc to the Baronetcy, 5 Jan 1837 ; Lieut and Sheriff Principal of Kincardineshire, 1847   He d unm. 16 Feb. 1849, at Crathes aforesaid, aged 60.

IX. 1849.   Sir Alexander Burnett, Baronet [S. 1626], of Crathes Castle aforesaid, br and h, b 1789 at Crathes aforesaid, was an officer in the East India Company's service ; suc to the Baronetcy, 16 Feb 1849   He d. unm 20 March 1856.

X 1856.   Sir James Horn Burnett, Baronet [S 1626], of Crathes Castle aforesaid, br and h, being 5th and yst s. of the 7th Baronet, b 22 June 1801 at Crathes Castle, Writer to the Signet [S.], 1824, suc to the Baronetcy, 20 March 1856, Lord Lieut of Kincardineshire, 1863   He m. firstly, 3 Feb 1831, Caroline Margaret, da. of Charles Spearman, of Thornley Hall, co Durham, by Sarah, da and coheir of Samuel Brooke, of Birchington, co. Kent   She d 22 March 1836.   He m secondly, 12 July 1837, Lauderdale, widow of David Duncan, of Rosemount, co. Forfar, da of Sir Alexander Ramsay, 1st Baronet [1806], of Balmain (formerly Alexander Burnett), by Elizabeth, da and coheir of Sir Alexander Bannerman, 4th Baronet [S. 1682]   He d 17 Sep 1876, at Crathes Castle, aged 75   His widow d 4 Nov. 1888, at 47 Heriot Row, Edinburgh

XI. 1876.   SIR ROBERT BURNETT, Baronet [S. 1626], of Crathes
Castle aforesaid, s and h, b at Edinburgh, 28 Aug 1833, matric at
Oxford (Ch Ch), 22 Oct 1851, aged 18, B A, 1856 ; suc to the Baronetcy 17 Sep.
1876   He m 23 May 1864, Matilda Josephine, da of James MURPHY, of New York
She d 25 April 1888   He d s p m s (a) 15 Jan 1894, at Crossburn House, East
Wemyss, aged 60.   Personalty sworn at £47,799

XII. 1894.   SIR THOMAS BURNETT, Baronet [S 1626], of Crathes
Castle aforesaid, br of the half-blood and h, being 2d s, 1st by the
2d wife, of the 10th Baronet, b. 27 Nov. 1840, sometime in the Royal Horse
Artillery . Lieut.-Col, 1885 , Col, 1890 , suc. to the Baronetcy, 15 Jan 1894   He m,
2 June 1875, Mary, 1st da of James CUMINE, of Rattray, co Aberdeen

Family Estates —These, in 1883, consisted of 12,025 acres in Kincardineshire, and
84 in Aberdeenshire   *Total*, 12,109 acres, worth £5 114 a year   *Principal Seat.—*
Crathes Castle, co Kincardine.

MONCREIFF ·

cr 22 April and sealed 22 June 1626(b),

dormant in 1744, *but assumed* since about 1750 ;

afterwards, 1767—1827, MONCREIFF-WELLWOOD ;

subsequently, 1827—1883, WELLWOOD-MONCREIFF ,

and finally, since 1883, BARONS MONCREIFF

I. 1626.   JOHN MONCREIFF, of Moncreiff, co Perth, 2d but 1st
surv s and h of William MONCREIFF, of the same (who sat as a
minor Baron [S] 1579), by Anne, da of Robert MURRAY, of Abercairnie, sat (as
" Laird of Easter Moncreiff") as a minor Baron [S] 1605, and was cr. a Baronet [S] as
" of Moncreiff," 22 April, sealed 22 June 1626,(b) with rem to heirs male whatsoever,
and with a grant of, presumably, 16,000 acres in Nova Scotia, entitled the Barony of
Moncreiff, of which he had seizin in the said month of June(c), was M P [S] for
Perthshire, 1639-41   He m firstly Anne, da of David BEATON, of Creich.   He m
secondly, in or before 1635, Mary,(d) da of William (MURRAY), 2d EARL OF TULLI-
BARDINE [S], by his 2d wife, Dorothea, da of John (STEWART), 5th EARL OF ATHOLL
[S].   She d. Dec 1650 " att Moncrefe in Stratherne," and he d shortly afterwards.

II. 1651 ?   SIR JOHN MONCREIFF, Baronet [S 1626], of Moncreiff
aforesaid, 2d but 1st surv s and h., being 1st s by the 2d wife, b
1635 , suc. to the Baronetcy on the death of his father about 1651   His estates being
greatly encumbered, he, in 1657, sold his lands of Carnbee, co Fife, and in 1663 sold
the Barony of Moncreiff to his cousin, Thomas Moncreiff one of the Clerks of the
Exchequer.(e)   He d unm at Edinburgh, 1674.

III. 1674   SIR DAVID MONCREIFF, Baronet [S. 1626], next br and
h , suc. to the Baronetcy on the death of his brother.   He d unm

IV. 1690 ?   SIR JAMES MONCREIFF, Baronet [S 1626], only surv. br.
and h., was an officer in the army, becoming eventually a Colonel
He suc to the Baronetcy on the death of his brother   He d. s.p 1698, when the issue
male of the 1st Baronet became *extinct*

(a) James Lauderdale Burnett, his only s , d in childhood, 1874.
(b) Milne's List , Laing's List
(c) Banke's Lists
(d) " By mistake called *Anne* in the peerage " (Douglas's *Baronage* [S]).
(e) He accordingly was cr a Baronet [S] 30 Nov 1685, as " of Moncreiff "

V. 1698   SIR JOHN MONCREIFF, Baronet [S 1626], of Tippermalloch,
or Tippermalach, cousin and h male, being only s and h of Hugh
MONCREIFF (living 12 Oct 1666), by Isabel, da. of (—) HAY of Megginch, co Perth,
which Hugh MONCREIFF was next br to the 1st Baronet. He was b about 1628;
suc. to the Baronetcy in 1698   He was a physician   He m. about 1680, Nicholas,
da of (—) MONCREIFF, of Easter Moncreiff   Was living 1709, having then relin-
quished his estates to his son. He d 27 April 1714, aged 86.

VI 1714   SIR HUGH MONCREIFF, Baronet [S 1626], only surv s
and h., *suc to the Baronetcy* 27 April 1714, and d unm 1744 (a)

[The Baronetcy was apparently *dormant* for some years(b) but
was assumed ' after 1744, without service or proof of pedigree " as under]

VII. *1744.*   SIR WILLIAM MONCREIFF, Baronet(c) [S 1626], cousin
and h male (d) being s and h (one of sixteen children) of the Rev.
1750? Archibald MONCREIFF, Minister of Blackford [1697—1739], by
Catherine, da. of John HALLIDAY, of Tullibole, or Tulliebole Castle,(e)
co Kinross, which Archibald (who d. 1739) was s and h of the Rev William MON-
CREIFF, Minister of Moonzie, co Fife (d about 1711), who was s and h. of the Rev
George MONCREIFF, Minister of Arngask (d before 1665), who was 2d s of the Rev
Archibald MONCREIFF, of Balgony (which he purchased before 1611), Minister of
Abernethy (1580) and Commendator of the Monastery of Elcho (1601), who was yr
br of William MONCREIFF (d. v p 26 Nov 1570), the father of the 1st Baronet, both
being sons of William MONCREIFF of that ilk, who d. between 1573 and 1575   He
was in Holy Orders and was Minister of Blackford aforesaid   His right to the
Baronetcy is supposed to have accrued on the death of the 6th Baronet, in 1744, and,
some years later (1750?) he accordingly assumed that dignity   He m. in or before
1749, Catherine, niece of Henry WELLWOOD, of Garvock, co Kinross, and of Tullibole
Castle abovenamed, 1st da of Robert WELLWOOD, of Garvock aforesaid   He d 9 Dec.
1767.

VIII. 1767   SIR HENRY MONCREIFF-WELLWOOD, Baronet(e) [S 1626],
of Tullibole Castle aforesaid, formerly Henry MONCREIFF, 1st s and

---

(a) The estate of Tippermalloch devolved on his nephew, John Moncreiff, s and h.
of his sister, Bethia, by the Rev William Moncreiff, Minister of Methven

(b) In Douglas' *Baronage* [S] it is stated that "the Baronetcy appears to have
devolved upon Sir William [Moncreiff, 4th Baronet of the creation of 1685], of
Moncrieff, as next heir male, being lineally descended from John, the 3d son of Sir
John Moncreiff," who was great great grandfather of the 1st Baronet   This Sir
William Moncreiff is accordingly designated therein as ' the 4th Baronet [1685] of
this branch, the 6th [should be 7th] Baronet [1626] of the house of Moncreiff "

(c) According to the assumption of the Baronetcy, in, or about, 1750

(d) Foster's *Baronetage* for 1883, under "Chaos," p 703, where it is added that
William Moncreiff, Minister of Blackford, who assumed the Baronetcy, "was 4th in
descent from Archibald, Minister of Abernethy, Perthshire   *   *   *   The pedigree in
Douglas's *Baronage* [S] only mentions William and David as brothers of [which two
brothers] William [was] father of the 1st Baronet, though a note is appended that he
[the said William] is said to have had another brother, Archibald, Minister of
Abernethy   The pedigree in Playfair's *Baronetage* [S] gives six brothers [i e ,
William, Archibald, Hugh, David, John, and James] and four sisters, but unaccom-
panied by any evidence to prove that Archibald was the *next* brother of William
father of the 1st Baronet "

(e) The estate of Tullibole (a picturesque though not large castle, erected about
1608) was sold in 1749 by the creditors of Robert Halliday, grandson of John
Halliday, the *maternal* grandfather of Sir William Moncreiff. It was purchased by
Henry Wellwood, of Garvock, who, three years later, conveyed it to Henry Moncreiff,
afterwards the 8th Baronet, 1st s and h of his niece, Catharine (da of his yr br ,
Robert Wellwood), by her husband, Sir William Moncreiff, the 7th Baronet, on
condition of his taking the name of Wellwood.

b., *b* 7 Feb 1750 at Blackford, inherited in infancy the Tullibole estate(ᵃ) from his maternal uncle, Henry Wellwood abovenamed, when he took accordingly the additional name of WELLWOOD; was ed at Glasgow College, *suc to the Baronetcy*(ᵇ) 9 Dec 1767   He was in Holy Orders, and was in 1771 Minister of Blackford (ᶜ) and of St. Cuthbert's, Edinburgh, 1775 , Moderator of the Gen. Assembly of the Church of Scotland, Chaplain to the Prince of Wales, and D D. of the Univ of Glasgow, all in 1785   In 1772 he obtained a Crown charter for the Tullibole estate.(ᵈ) He *m.* 16 Nov 1772, Susan Robertson, 1st da of James Robertson BARCLAY, of Keavil, co Fife. She *d* 1826   He *d* 9 Aug 1827, in Edinburgh.

IX. 1827.   SIR JAMES MONCREIFF, *otherwise* WELLWOOD-MONCREIFF, Baronet(ᵇ) [S 1626] of Tullibole Castle aforesaid, 2d but 1st surv. s and h (ᵉ), *b* about 1776 , matric at Oxford (Ball Coll), 30 Nov. 1793, aged 17 ; B C L , 1800, Advocate [S], 1799 ; *suc. to the Baronetcy*(ᵇ) 9 Aug 1827 , was a Lord of Session [S.] 1829 51, with the courtesy title of *Lord Moncreiff*   He *m* 19 June 1808, Anne, da of George ROBERTSON, Lieut R N   She *d* 28 May 1843, in Brompton Square, Midx   He *d* 4 April 1851, at Moray Place, Edinburgh, in his 75th year

X   1851   SIR HENRY MONCREIFF, *otherwise* WELLWOOD-MONCREIFF, Baronet(ᵇ) [S 1626], of Tullibole Castle aforesaid, 1st s and h , *b.* in Edinburgh, 12 May 1809 , ed. at the High School and at the Univ there; matric (as Gent Commoner) at Oxford (New Coll), 5 May 1827, aged 17 , B A , 1831 , 3d class classics and math , was in Holy Orders, Minister (in the Established Church) of Baldernock, co Stirling, 1836-37 , of East Kilbride co Lanark, 1837 43, and subsequently of the Free Church there, and after that, 1852-83, of St. Cuthbert's, Edinburgh ; *suc to the Baronetcy,*(ᵇ) 10 April 1851 , D D (Edinburgh), Prin Clerk of the Free Church General Assembly and Moderator, 1861. He *m* firstly, 8 March 1838, Alexina Mary, da of George BELL, of Edinburgh She *d.* 12 April 1874, at 3 Bruntsfield Terrace, Edinburgh   He *m* secondly, 19 Aug 1875, at Stenton, co. Perth, Lucretia, yst da of Andrew MURRAY, of Murraysball, co. Perth, sometime Sheriff of Aberdeenshire   He *d* s p , 3 Nov 1883, at Morningside Crescent, Edinburgh, in the 75th year of his age and the 48th of his ministry   His widow *d* 10 Sep. 1885, at 4, Lynedoch Place, Edinburgh.

XI   1883.   JAMES (MONCREIFF), 1st BARON MONCRIEFF OF TULLIE- BOLE, br and h , *b* 29 Nov 1811 at Edinburgh   He, who had been *cr. a Baronet,* as " of Kilduff, co Kinross," 23 May 1871, and raised to the peerage, as above, 9 Jan 1874, *suc to the Baronetcy*(ᵇ) [S 1626], 3 Nov 1883, which then became *merged* in that peerage, and still so remains. See *Peerage.*

(ᵃ) See p 311, note "c"
(ᵇ) According to the assumption of the Baronetcy, in, or about, 1750.
(ᶜ) He was the 6th in lineal succession of a line of officiating Clergymen of the Church of Scotland.
(ᵈ) It was granted to him, as under   "Reverendo Domino Henrico Moncreiff Wellwood, Baronetto, de Denham Tullibole, Ministro Evangelii apud Blackford, filio legitimo natu maximo demortui Domini Gulielmi Moncreiff, Baronetti, nuper Ministri evangelii apud Blackford "   The designation of the estate as " *Denham's* Tullibole" was in compliance of the wish of Henry Wellwood (the Baronet's uncle), whose mother, Catherine, was 6th da of John *Denham,* of Muirhouse and West Shields   As a matter of fact, however, this designation was never used
(ᵉ) The eldest br William Wellwood-Moncreiff, matric at Oxford (Ball Coll) 20 March 1793, aged 17 ; B A , 1797 ; M A , 1799 , B C.L and D C.L 1803 , Barrister (Mid Temple), 1800 Fellow of the Coll of Advocates, London, 21 Nov. 1807 ; King's Advocate in the Admiralty Court, Isle of Malta ; *d.* unm., 5 Sep. 1813, aged 38.

OGILVY, or OGILVIE:

cr 24 April and sealed 22 June 1626 ,(ᵃ)

succession unknown till about 1800;

dormant since 20 Feb 1861

I. 1626.   GEORGE OGILVIE, of Carnousie, co. Banff, s. and h. of
George OGILVIE,(ᵇ) of the same, M P [S] for Banffshire, 1621, by
Margaret his wife, suc his father, 1 Feb. 1625, being served heir to him 10 May
following, and was *cr. a Baronet* [S] 24 April, sealed 22 June 1626 as "of Carnousie," with rem to heirs male whatsoever, and with a grant of, presumably,
16,000 acres in Nova Scotia, called the Barony of "New Carnousie," of which, however, he appears never to have had seizin (ᶜ) He *m* Jean, da of Sir Thomas
GORDON, of Cluny (*Reg Mag Sig*).(ᵈ) He was alive in 1668, but there is no
record of his having had any issue (ᵈ)

*   *   *   *   *

> The succession to this Baronetcy is unknown, but it was
> borne early in the nineteenth century as below, by, presumably, the
> collateral heir male, possibly a descendant of a br. of the grantee.(ᵉ)
>
> VIII 1800?   SIR WILLIAM OGILVIE, Baronet [S. 1625] He *m*
>   Christian, da. of the Rev John PATTISON, of Edinburgh He
> *d* 1824 Will pr 1824
>
> IX 1824,   SIR WILLIAM OGILVIE, Baronet [S 1625], s and h.,
>   to   *b* 1810, *suc* to the Baronetcy, 1824, is called ' the 9th
> 1861.   Baronet", was a claimant of the Barony of Banff [S] as heir
>   male collateral. He *m* 1838, Augusta Porter, da of James
> GRANGE, of the Treasury He *d* s p m. at Christchurch, New Zealand,
> 20 Feb 1861, when the *Baronetcy* became *dormant.* His widow was apparently
> living in 1893 (ᶠ)

(ᵃ) Milne's List, Laing's List
(ᵇ) This George was yr. br of Sir Walter Ogilvy, of Banff and Dunlugus, father of
George, *cr* 31 Aug 1642, Lord Banff [S]
(ᶜ) Banks's Lists
(ᵈ) *Ex inform.*, Sir J. Balfour Paul, Lyon, who states that there is absolutely
nothing to be found about the succeeding Baronets, and that there are no services of
heirs in the family It appears that "Capt. Gordon, son of Edinglassie, had a charter
of Carnousie, in 1695, the lands having fallen under recognition, owing to alienation
made thereof by the deceased Sir George" Ogilvy, but "the decreet of recognition
which would no doubt give the names of Sir George's heir or heirs" cannot be found.
(ᵉ) George Ogilvy, the grantee's father, *m.* twice By his 1st wife he had (besides
two daughters Elspeth and Helen) three sons, viz. · (1), George, the Baronet , (2),
John Ogilvy, of Burns, of whose posterity, if any, nothing is known , (3), Thomas, of
whom nothing is known By his 2d wife, Barbara, da. of Sir Alexander Fraser, of
Philorth, he appears to have had (4), Alexander No Alexander is mentioned in
Margaret Ogilvy's testament dative, *Ogilvie of Carnousie*, but John Ogilvy of Burns is
called cousin german both of Sir George and of Alexander. Alexander Ogilvy was
of Knock and had at least three sons, viz (1), James, his s and h., who *m* Christian
Stewart, and sold Knock in 1659 ; (2), Alexander, (3), Patrick   [*Ex inform.*
J. Maitland Thomson, communicated by Sir J Balfour Paul, Lyon.]
(ᶠ) She appears in Dod's *Baronetage* for 1893, but not in that for 1894

2 R

GORDON :

cr. 1 May 1626 ([a]) ;

afterwards, 1633-1716 and 1824-47, VISCOUNTS KENMURE [S] ,

attainted, 1716-1824 ,

dormant, since 1 Sep. 1847.

I. 1626. SIR ROBERT GORDON, of Lochinvar, co Kirkcudbright, and of Stichill, co Roxburgh, s and b of Sir John
GORDON, of the same, by his 2d wife, Elizabeth, da of John (MAXWELL)
LORD HERRIES [S], was *b.* about 1565 was one of the Gentlemen of the
Bedchamber , suc his father, 23 Aug 1604 , was M P. [S] for Kirkcudbright
1612, had a grant of the Barony of Galloway in Nova Scotia, 8 Nov 1621,
and a charter of the Barony and Lordship of Charles' island 1 May 1626, with,
(as is sometimes, though, probably erroneously, conjectured) the *grant of a
Baronetcy*([a]) [S] He appears to have been Governor of Nova Scotia ([a]) He
m Isabel, da. of William (RUTHVEN), 1st EARL OF GOWRIE [S], by Dorothea,
da of Henry (STEWART), LORD METHVEN [S] She was divorced from him,
and *m.,* as the second of his three wives, Hugh (CAMPBELL), 1st LORD CAMPBELL
OF LOUDOUN [S], who *d.* 15 Dec 1622 He *d* Nov 1628

II. 1628. SIR JOHN GORDON, Baronet ([b]) [S 1626], of Lochinvar aforesaid, 1st s and b , *b* about 1600 , suc his father
Nov. 1628, and was served heir 20 March 1628-9, shortly after which date he
sold the Barony of Stichill He *m* in 1628, Jean, 3d da of Archibald
(CAMPBELL), 7th EARL OF ARGYLL [S.], by his 1st wife, Anne, da of William
(DOUGLAS), 1st EARL OF MORTON [S] She was living when he (having
attended the King's coronation in Scotland), was cr (about 16 months before his
death) 8 May 1633, VISCOUNT KENMURE and LORD LOCHINVAR [S],
with rem to heirs male whatsoever In that peerage this *Baronetcy* then
merged, and followed the fortunes thereof. See *Peerage*

MURRAY .([c])

cr. 1 June 1625; *sealed* 14 July following .([d])

dormant about 1700

I. 1626 SIR WILLIAM MURRAY, of Clermont, co Fife, 1st s. of
Sir Mungo MURRAY of Feddalls, Dinoch and Clermont, by Margaret,
relict of Sir Andrew MURRAY, of Balvaird da. of (—) CRICHTON, was (having pre-

---

([a]) Milne's List, where it is added " He was made Governour of Nova Scotia, but
his patent does not invest him [in the] tytle [of] Baronet, bot he hes power to create
Judges, Generals, Archbishops, Bishops, etc " The patent is not recorded in the
" Registrum Preceptorum Cartarum pro Baronettis Novæ Scotiæ " The creation is
in Laing's List, it being, however, stated that it is " given on the authority of
former lists "

([b]) According to the (probably erroneous) conjecture stated in the text above

([c]) Nearly all the information in this article has been furnished by Sir J Balfour
Paul, Lyon King of Arms.

([d]) *Precept curt pro Baronnettis Novæ Scotiæ,* 1625, folio. 27 The date of the
sealing is that given in Milne's List, where the date of creation is given as 1 *July*
1625. In Laing's List, however, the date is correctly given as 1 *June* 1626.

viously been knighted)(a) cr a Baronet [S], 1 June 1626, the patent being sealed 14 July following(b) with rem to heirs male whatsoever, and with a grant of, presumably, 16,000 acres in Nova Scotia, called the Barony of Clermont of Hillhead,(c) of which he had seizin in the said month of July 1626 (c) He was served heir to his father 27 July 1630 : and had seizin of the lands of Blebo, 31 Jan 1634. on the ratification of John Traill, of Blebo He m Euphemia Ogilvy. He d between 1643 and 1648

II 1645 ? Sir Mungo Murray, Baronet [S 1626] of Blebo aforesaid, s and h, suc. to the Baronetcy, 1643-48 , had Crown charter of lands of Westertown of Airtbrey to himself and "Lady Anne Graham, his spouse," 24 May 1648 , made a renunciation of Blebo to Sir William Bruce, of Balcaskie, 19 July 1666

*   *   *   *   *

III. 1670 ? Sir Mungo Murray, Baronet [S 1626], of Blebo aforeto said, presumed to be s and h of the above and to have suc him to 1700 ? the Baronetcy He m Christian Hamilton He appears to have died s p m, as, after his death, the Baronetcy became dormant. His widow d Feb 1709/10, her will being recorded 15 June 1710 in the Commissariat Court of Edinburgh.

BLACKADER or BLACCADER:

cr 28 July 1626, sealed 3 Feb 1627 ;(d)

dormant about 1670 ;

but assumed, wrongfully, 1734-36

I 1626, John Blaccader [i e., Blackader], of Tulliallan, co to Perth, s and h of James Blackader, of the same, by Elizabeth, da. 1670 ? of (—) Bruce (probably Archibald Bruce of Powfoulis, otherwise Batfoulis), was b. the Sunday after Easter, 1596, and bap. June following(e) , suc his father at the age of 14, in 1610, and was cr a Baronet [S], as " of Tulliallan,' 28 July 1626, the patent being sealed 3 Feb 1627, with rem to heirs male whatsoever, and with a grant of, presumably, 16,000 acres in Nova Scotia, of which he had seizin in Feb 1627 (f) He was one of the captains in the Scotch regiment levied for the King of France in 1642 He m Christian, da of John (Graham), Earl of Menteith [S], by Mary, da of Sir Colin Campbell, of Glenorchy " By his foolish generosity, whoredom, and every other unfortunate way, together with the prodigality and pride of his Lady he squandered away an honourable and ancient estate of 3,600 marks or £2,000 sterling yearly "(e) He was living 1666 and d before 1675 leaving male issue, but after his death the Baronetcy became dormant.

(a) He is called a knight in Laing's List.
(b) See p 314, note " d."
(c) Banks's Lists.
(d) Milne's List , Laing's List.
(e) MS. relating to the Blackader family belonging to R. R Stodart, Lyon Clerk Depute [1863 86], to whom the Editor is indebted for most of the information in this article The estate of Tulliallan was acquired in 1486 by the marriage of Cuthbert Blackader, of Blackader, co Berwick, with Elizabeth, da and h. of Sir James Edmonstone, of Tulliallan
(f) Banks's Lists.

JAMES BLACKADER, 1st s., joined as heir ap. with his father, 20 Feb. 1644, in a deed of sale He never assumed the title, and *d.* before 1675, possibly in his father's lifetime

ARCHIBALD BLACKADER, s and h of the above James; was living in 1675 and 1676 as a merchant factor at Cadiz, and was at that time anxious to redeem the estate of Tulliallan, which had been sold to Col John Erskine. He, however, never assumed the title

> JOHN BLACKADER, a tailor of Edinburgh, s of John, who was s of Patrick BLACKADER, a bastard uncle of the 1st Baronet, was served heir, 10 April 1734, to the 1st Baronet, who was stated in that service to be his grandfather. He, accordingly, *assumed the Baronetcy,* and for two years was called "SIR JOHN BLACKADER, Baronet," [S. 1626] In Jan 1736, however, his pedigree was disproved, and on 8 Jan 1737 he was sentenced to have his ear nailed to the post for perjury.

OGILVY

cr 29 Sep 1626, sealed 30 June 1627 (ᵃ)

I 1626 JOHN OGILVY, of Inverquharity, in the parish of Kirriemuir, co Forfar, s and h of Sir John OGILVY, of the same (*d.* about 1624), by Matilda, da of Thomas FOTHERINGHAM, of Powrie, co Forfar, was *b* about 1587 and was *cr a Baronet* [S], 29 Sep. 1626, the patent being sealed 30 June 1627, but not recorded in the Great Seal register, with rem to heirs male whatsoever, and with a grant of, presumably, 16,000 acres in Nova Scotia, of which he had sasine in July 1627 (ᵇ) He *m*, covenant 16 Sep 1622, Anne, da. of Sir Alexander IRVINE, of Drum, co. Aberdeen, by Marion, da. of Robert (DOUGLAS) EARL OF BUCHAN [S] He, who was a zealous royalist, was living in 1647, when he had a remission on payment of a fine, but *d.* before 1663

II 1660? SIR DAVID OGILVY, Baronet [S 1626], of Inverquharity aforesaid, 3d but 1st surv. s. and h.,(ᶜ) *b* about 1630, *suc. to the Baronetcy* on the death of his father, M P [S] for co. Angus, 1665 and 1678. He *m.*, 1662, Margaret, da of Sir John ERSKINE, of Dun, co Forfar. He *d.* in or before 1679

III. 1679? SIR JOHN OGILVY, Baronet [S 1626], of Inverquharity aforesaid, s and h , *suc to the Baronetcy* on the death of his father He *m.* 1697, Margaret, 1st da. of James OGILVY, of Cluny. He *d* in or before 1735.

IV 1735? SIR JOHN OGILVY, Baronet [S 1626], of Inverquharity aforesaid, s and h , *suc to the Baronetcy* before 23 June 1735, when he had general service to his father He *m.* firstly, 1720, Helen, 2d da. and coheir of Sir Laurence MERCER, of Aldie, Melgins and Lethendy, co. Perth. He *m* secondly, Anne, 1st da and coheir of James CARNEGIE, of Finhaven, co. Forfar, by Margaret, da of Sir William BENNETT, Baronet [S 1670], of Grubbet He *d* at Kinnordy, Feb. 1748. His widow *d* at Inverquharity, 1 Dec. 1750

(ᵃ) Milne's List, Laing's List.
(ᵇ) Banks's Lists.
(ᶜ) Alexander Ogilvy, the 1st s , fought under Montrose, was taken prisoner at Philiphaugh, and executed, v.p., 23 Oct. 1646, aged 18.

V. 1748.   SIR JOHN OGILVY, Baronet [S 1626], of Inverquharity
aforesaid, s. and h., by 1st wife, b. about 1732, suc. to the Baronetcy
in Feb 1748 In 1781 he was served h gen. of his father and of his paternal
great great grandfather, and in 1798 h of his maternal uncles, Charles and Robert
MERCER, in Lethendy, co Perth, and other lands About 1790 he sold the estate of
Inverquharity.(a) He m , 1754, Charlotte, 1st da. and coheir of Walter TULLIEDEPH,
of Tullhedeph (formerly Bank), in Strathmartine, co Forfar, sometime a physician
in the island of Antigua. She (by whom he had nine sons) inherited this estate,
and d there aged 70, being bur at Strathmartine He d 15 March 1802, and was
bur in St. Cuthbert's churchyard, Edinburgh. Will pr 1802.

VI 1802   SIR WALTER OGILVY, Baronet [S 1626], of Baldovan,
formerly Tullhedeph aforesaid, s and h ; suc to the Baronetcy,
1 March 1802 ; had spec. service on 2 May 1806, to his granduncle Robert MERCER
in parts of Lethendy and Pittendreich ; and on 27 March 1807, to his father, in
Baldovan and Lethendy He appears to have sold the estate of Lethendy. He
d. unm 21 Aug 1808

VII. 1808.   SIR JOHN OGILVY, Baronet [S 1626], of Baldovan
aforesaid, br and h , suc to the Baronetcy 21 Aug 1803 , on 16 Oct
1809, had spec service to his br in the lands of Baldovan, etc He d unm
1819.

VIII. 1819.   SIR WILLIAM OGILVY, Baronet [S 1626], of Baldovan
aforesaid, br. and h, b about 1765 , served in the Royal Navy,
becoming eventually Rear-Admiral , suc. to the Baronetcy in 1819 He m in
1802, Sarah, da of James MORLEY, of Kempshot, Hants, an officer in the Bombay
civil service He d. 1823 His widow d. 26 May 1854 Admon Sep 1854

IX. 1823.   SIR JOHN OGILVY, Baronet [S. 1626], of Baldovan, aforesaid, s and h , b in Edinburgh, 17 March 1803 , matric at Oxford
(Ch. Ch), 5 Nov 1811, aged 18 , suc. to the Baronetcy, 1823 , Convener of co Forfar,
1855, Hon Col. of Dundee R.V , 1865 M P for Dundee (four Parls) 1857-74, Major-
Gen of the "Royal Company of Archers," i.e , the Royal Body Guard He m
firstly, 7 July 1831, at St Geo , Han sq , Juliana Barbara, yst da. of Lord
Henry HOWARD-MOLYNEUX HOWARD (br to the Duke of Norfolk), by Elizabeth, da
of Edward LONG, Chief Judge of the Vice-Admiralty Court in Jamaica She, who
was b 31 March 1812, d. 27 Dec 1833. Will pr. Aug. 1835 He m. secondly,
5 April 1836, at Charlton, Wilts, Jane Elizabeth, 3d da of Thomas (HOWARD), 16th
EARL OF SUFFOLK, by Elizabeth Jane, da of James (DUTTON), 1st BARON SHERBORNE
She, who was b 25 July 1809, d 28 July 1861 at Baldovan House. He d 29 March
1890, in his 88th year, at Archerfield, East Lothian

X 1890.   SIR REGINALD HOWARD ALEXANDER OGILVY, Baronet
[S 1626], of Baldovan aforesaid, 1st s and h , being only s by 1st
wife ; b 29 May 1832 at Edinburgh , matric. at Oxford (Oriel Coll), 5 Dec 1850,
aged 18 , B A , 1854, admitted to Inner Temple, 1860 , Hon Col Forfar and Kincardine Artillery , Aide-de-camp to Queen Victoria , suc. to the Baronetcy, 29 March
1890 He m 27 July 1859, Olivia Barbara, only da and h of George William Fox
(KINNAIRD), 9th LORD KINNAIRD, by Frances Anne Georgiana, da of William Francis
(PONSONBY), 1st BARON DE MAULEY She, who was b 22 Jan. 1839, d 6 Aug 1871

Family Estates —These, in 1883, appear to have been under 2,000 acres *Principal
Residence* —Baldovan House, near Strathmartine, Forfarshire

(a) He reserved, however, the Castle (now a ruin) and a piece of land round it, but
without any right of access The estate is said to have been in the family for
fourteen generations.

NAPIER:

cr 2 March, or 2 May 1627, sealed 9 June 1627 ,(ᵃ)
sometime, 4 May 1627 to 1683, LORDS NAPIER OF MERCHISTOUN [S],
dormant, 1683—1817 ,
assumed since 1817
being then named MILLIKEN-NAPIER

I. 1627 SIR ARCHIBALD NAPIER, of Merchistoun, co Midlothian, s. and
h of John NAPIER, of the same (distinguished for his learning and for
the invention of logarithms), by his 1st wife, Elizabeth, da of Sir James STIRLING, of
Keir, was *b* about 1575 , matric at Glasgow Univ , March 1593 , was Gent of the
Privy Chamber to James VI [S], whom he accompanied to England on his accession
to that kingdom , P C , 1615 ; was *Knighted* at Royston, 28 July 1616 , suc his
father 3 April 1617 , Treasurer Depute [S], 1622 31 , Lord Justice Clerk [S],
1623 24 , a Lord of Session [S], 1623-25 , extra Lord of Session 1616, and was *cr*
a Baronet [S] 2 March or 2 May 1627(ᵃ), the patent being sealed 9 June 1627,
but not entered in the Great Seal register, with rem. to heirs male whatsoever,
and with a grant of, presumably, 16,000 acres in Nova Scotia, called the Barony
of Nepar (being on the north side of Aiguilis bay), of which, however, he
apparently never had seizin (ᵇ) He *m.* (contract 15 April 1619) Margaret, 2d da
of John GRAHAM, 4th EARL OF MONTROSE [S], by Margaret, da of William (RUTHVEN),
1st EARL OF GOWRIE She, who was living 15 Dec 1626, was presumably alive
when on 4 May 1627, he was *cr* LORD NAPIER OF MERCHISTOUN [S].
For particulars of his after career see *Peerage*. He *d* Nov. 1645, aged about 70.

II 1645 ARCHIBALD (NAPIER), LORD NAPIER OF MERCHIS-
TOUN [S], and a Baronet [S 1627], 2d but only surv s and
h , *b* about 1625 , suc. to his father's honours, Nov. 1645 He *d.* 1660

III 1660, ARCHIBALD (NAPIER), LORD NAPIER OF MERCHIS-
to TOUN [S.], and a Baronet [S 1627], s and h , suc. to his
1683. father's honours in 1660, when under age He resigned his
peerage, 20 Nov 1676, and received a new grant thereof
17 Feb. 1677 in favour of his sisters and their issue He *d* unm , Aug 1683,
when the peerage devolved on his sister's son, but the *Baronetage* became
dormant, and so continued for 134 years, not being noticed in Douglas'
Baronage [S] or in Playfair's *Baronetage* [S.], till assumed in 1817, as
under.

For further particulars see Peerage

*   *   *   *   *   *

VIII (ᶜ) 1817 SIR WILLIAM JOHN MILLIKEN-NAPIER, Baronet(ᵈ) [S 1627],
of Milliken, co Renfrew, heir male collateral of the grantee(ᵈ),
being s and h of Col Robert John MILLIKEN-NAPIER, *formerly* NAPIER, of Cul
creuch, co Stirling, and of Milliken aforesaid, by Anne, da of Robert CAMPBELL,
of Downie, co Argyll, which Robert John (who was *b.* 1765 , who was in command
at the siege of Mangalore in the East Indies ; and who assumed the additional name
of MILLIKEN on inheriting the estates of his maternal grandfather, and who *d* 1803,
having previously sold the estate of Culcreuch), was only s of William NAPIER, of
Culcreuch, by Jean, 1st da of James MILLIKEN, of Milliken aforesaid, the said
William Napier (who was under age in 1735) being only s of John NAPIER, of
Culcreuch (*b* 1686, *d* 1735), s and h of Alexander NAPIER (*d.* 1702), of

(ᵃ) 2 March 1627 in Milne's List, but 2 May 1627 in Laing's List
(ᵇ) Banks's Lists, and Banks's *Bar Ang Conc*, vol ii, p 241.
(ᶜ) This is the numbering given in Burke's *Baronetage* of 1901, reckoning
apparently Alexander, John, William, and Robert, the four immediate ancestors of
the "8th Baronet" to have been the 4th, 5th, 6th, and 7th Baronets
(ᵈ) According to the service of 17 March 1817.

Culcreuch (by purchase from his elder brother), who was 4th s of Robert NAPIER, of Drumbony, 1628, and afterwards of Culcreuch aforesaid (d before June 1655), who was younger br., of the half blood, of Archibald the 1st Baronet, and the 1st LORD NAPIER OF MERCHISTOUN [S] (ᵃ) He was b. 1783 at Milliken House, suc his father in 1808, and was, on 17 March 1817, served heir male general of Archibald (NAPIER), 3d LORD NAPIER OF MERCHISTOUN [S], and 3d Baronet [S 1627], when he consequently *assumed that Baronetcy.* He was Convener of co Renfrew He m, 11 Nov 1815, Eliza Christian, 5th and yst da of John STIRLING, of Kippendavie, co Perth He d 4 Feb 1852, at Milliken house aforesaid, aged 63 His widow d 3 March 1860, at Pau in France

IX.(ᵇ) 1852. SIR ROBERT JOHN MILLIKEN-NAPIER, Baronet(ᶜ) [S 1627], of Milliken aforesaid, 1st s and h, b. 7 Nov 1818 at Milliken house, entered the army 1835, Capt 79th Foot, 1844, *suc. to the Baronetcy*(ᶜ) 4 Feb 1852, Lieut.-Col. Renfrewshire Militia, 1854, Convener of that County, 1859, Hon Col 4th Batt. Sutherland and Argyll Highlanders He m, 4 April 1850, at Pitfour Castle, co Perth, Anne Salisbury Meliora, only suiv da of John Ladeveze ADLERCRON, of Moyglare, co Meath He d. 4 Dec. 1884, at Edinburgh, aged 66. His widow living 1901

X (ᵇ) 1884. SIR ARCHIBALD LENNOX MILLIKEN-NAPIER, Baronet(ᶜ) [S. 1627], of Westfield, North Berwick, 1st s and h, b in Moray place, Edinburgh, 2 Nov. 1855; *sometime* Lieut Grenadier Guaras, *suc to the Baronetcy*(ᶜ) 4 Dec 1884 He m, 16 Dec 1880, at St Paul's, Knightsbridge, Mary Allison Dorothy, 4th and yst da of Sir Thomas FAIRBAIRN, 2d Baronet [1869], by Allison, da of Thomas CALLAWAY, of Chiselhurst, Kent

---

MACKAY

cr. 28 March 1627, sealed 2 Nov 1628 ,(ᵈ)

afterwards, since 1628, LORDS REAY [S].

I. 1627. SIR DONALD MACKAY, of Far, Tongue, and Strath-naver, s and h of Hugh MACKAY, of the same, by his 2d wife, Jean, da of Alexander (GORDON), 11th EARL OF SUTHERLAND [S], was b. Feb 1590/1; suc his father 11 Sep 1614; was Coroner of North Kintyre, 1615; *Knighted* about 1616; raised 3,000 men in 1626 to assist Count Mansfeld in Germany, and was *cr a Baronet* [S] 28 March 1627, as "of Stranaver," sealed 2 Nov 1628,(ᵈ) but not recorded

(ᵃ) The pedigree, as above given, is that in Burke's *Baronetage* of 1901, where it is stated that the issue of the elder brothers [two of whom undoubtedly left issue] of Alexander Napier, who purchased Culcreuch, is now extinct In Foster's *Baronetage* for 1883, p 704, under "Chaos"] three different descents are given of this family from Robert Napier, the yr br. of the 1st Baronet and Peer, viz [1] "in Burke's *Peerage*, edit. 1837-41," wherein William John Millikin Napier (b 1788, who obtained the service of 17 March 1817) "is said to be third in descent from this Robert, viz, son of Robert John, son of Alexander, son of Robert, of Culcreuch aforesaid; [2] In the editions of the same work, 1846 52, Robert, of Culcreuch, is said to be ancestor of William, father of Robert John aforesaid (Alexander being omitted), and [3] since 1853 the descent has been published in the same work as follows —William Millikin, b 1788, son of Robert John, b 1765, son of William, b 1712, son of John, b 1665 [sic, but in the edit of 1901 the date is 1686] son of Alexander, b 1621, son Robert, of Culcreuch aforesaid It would be interesting to know which of these three descents was under consideration, when, after a lapse of 134 years, William Millikin Napier was served heir male general of Archibald, 3d Baron Napier, on 17 March 1817"
(ᵇ) See p 318, note "c"
(ᶜ) See p 318, note "d'
(ᵈ) Laing's List in which the creation is given as 18 March 1627, and Milne's List in which it is given as 28 March 1627.

in the Great Seal Register [S], with rem to heirs male whatsoever, and with a grant of, presumably, 16,000 acres in Nova Scotia, of which he had seizin in Nov. 1628 (ª) He *m.* firstly, Aug 1610, Barbara, 1st da of Kenneth (MACKENZIE), 1st LORD MACKENZIE OF KINTAIL [S], by Anne, da of George Ross, of Balnagowan She was living 9 Jan. 1517, but possibly was dead before he was *cr* , 20 June 1628, LORD REAY [S] In that peerage this *Baronetcy* then *merged*, and still so continues. See *Peerage*

MAXWELL:
cr. 18 or 28 March 1627 ; sealed 17 Sep 1630 ;(ᵇ)
afterwards, since 1885, BARONS FARNHAM [I.]

I 1627   SIR JAMES MAXWELL. of Calderwood, co Lanark, 2d but 1st surv s and h of Sir James MAXWELL, of the same, by his 2d wife, Isabel, da of Sir Alexander HAMILTON, of Innerwick, suc his father in 1622, and was *cr* a *Baronet* [S], 18 or 28 March 1627, sealed 17 Sep 1630,(ᵇ) but not entered in the Great Seal Register [S] till (as late as) 1830, as "of Calderwood," with rem to heirs male whatsoever, and with a grant of, presumably, 16,000 acres in Nova Scotia, called the Barony of Mauldslie, of which he had seizin in April 1631 (ᶜ) On the death, s p in 1647, of his cousin, Sir John Maxwell, of Pollock, he unsuccessfully claimed that estate under a deed, dat 18 Dec 1400, whereby two brothers, John Maxwell, of Pollock, and Robert Maxwell, of Calderwood, the respective lineal ancestors of the said John and of himself, had agreed that, failing male issue of the one, the male issue of the other should inherit both estates. He *m* firstly, Jean, da of Sir James HAMILTON, of Evandale, by Margaret, da. of James (CONYNGHAM), 7th EARL OF GLENCAIRN [S]. She *d s p m* He *m* secondly (contract, 1 July 1637), Mary, da. of James COUTTES, of Edinburgh He was living, "old and blind," 1670, but *d* soon afterwards.

II 1670 ?   SIR WILLIAM MAXWELL, Baronet [S. 1627], of Calderwood aforesaid, only s and h, by 2d wife, *b.* about 1640, *suc to the Baronetcy* about 1670 He continued, but also unsuccessfully, in 1695, his father's claim to the Pollock estates He *m* , before 9 Nov 1666, Jean, da of his paternal uncle, Sir Alexander MAXWELL, of Saughton Hall, by Janet, da and h. of Thomas MOODIE, of Saughton Hall aforesaid. He *d s p s* (ᵈ), 30 April 1703.

III. 1703.   SIR WILLIAM MAXWELL, Baronet [S. 1627], of Calderwood aforesaid, formerly of Abington, cousin and heir, being only s and h of Col John MAXWELL, by Elizabeth, da of Sir James ELPHINSTONE, of Blythswood, which John (who was slain on the King's side at the battle of Dunbar, 1650) was yr br (of the half blood) to the 1st Baronet, being s of Sir James MAXWELL, of Calderwood, by his 3d wife, Margaret, (*m.* 8 Sep 1610, she being then the widow of Sir James HAMILTON), da of James (CONYNGHAM), 7th EARL OF GLENCAIRN [S], all abovenamed. He *suc. to the Baronetcy,* as h male collateral of the grantee, 30 April 1703, but did not assume the title (ᵉ) He *m* Margaret, da of Capt. WOOD, of Culter He *d* before 23 March 1716 His widow living 1729.

IV. 1715 ?   SIR WILLIAM MAXWELL, Baronet [S. 1627], of Calderwood aforesaid, only surv s. and h. , *suc to the Baronetcy* on the death of his father He *m* Christian, da of Alexander STEWART, of Torrance, by Isabel, da. of Sir Patrick NISBET, of Deen He *d* 1750.

(ª) Banks's Lists.

(ᵇ) Milne's List, in which the creation is given as 18, and Laing's List, in which it is given as 28 March 1627.

(ᶜ) Banks's Lists

(ᵈ) His son, Alexander Maxwell, *m.* Margaret, da of Sir George Maxwell, of Pollock, but *d s p* and *v.p.*

(ᵉ) *Ex inform.* Sir J Balfour Paul, Lyon King of Arms, by whom many of the statements in this article have been supplied

V. 1750.   SIR WILLIAM MAXWELL, Baronet [S. 1627], of CALDERWOOD aforesaid, 1st s and h , *suc. to the Baronetcy* in 1750 He m , in or before 1747, Grizel, da. of James PEADIE, of Roughill. He d 2 Jan 1789

VI 1789.   SIR WILLIAM MAXWELL, Baronet [S 1627], of Calderwood aforesaid, only surv. s and h , *b* 7 Jan 1748 , *suc. to the Baronetcy* 2 June 1789 He m , 5 May 1807, Hannah Leonora, yst. da of Robert PASLEY, of Mount Annan, co. Dumfries. He d s p 12 Aug 1829 Will pr Nov 1829

VII 1829   SIR WILLIAM MAXWELL, Baronet [S. 1627], of Calderwood aforesaid, cousin and h , being s and h of Alexander MAXWELL, of Leith, merchant, by Mary, da of Hugh CLERK, of Edinburgh, merchant, which Alexander was 8d and yst s of the 4th Baronet He was *b* 4 Dec 1754 , was an officer in the army , served in the American War ; was taken prisoner at Saratoga, 1777, and at Yorktown, 1781, becoming a full General, 1812 He *suc to the Baronetcy* 12 Aug. 1829 He m , 2 July 1792, Isabella, da and h of Henry WILSON, of Newbottle, co Durham. She *d* 1 Oct 1829. Admon Nov. 1829 He *d* 16 March 1837, at Edinburgh, aged 82 Will pr. June 1837

VIII 1837   SIR WILLIAM ALEXANDER MAXWELL, Baronet [S 1627], of Calderwood aforesaid, 1st s and h , *b.* in Edinburgh, 30 April 1793 , sometime an officer in the 1st Dragoons, becoming Colonel in 1851, but retiring in 1853 , *suc to the Baronetcy* 16 March 1837 He m , 15 June 1847, "at St Mary's, Grosvenor Square," Catherine Cameron, widow of Henry Paget GILL, Capt 50th Foot, 5th da. of Walter LOGAN, of Fingalton, co Lanark He *d.* s p , 4 April 1865, at 27 Adelaide Crescent, Brighton His widow *d* there 13 Oct. 1866

IX 1865.   SIR HUGH BATES MAXWELL, Baronet [S 1627], of Calderwood aforesaid, only surv br and h , *b* 14 Feb 1797, at Parkhill, co Stirling ; admitted an Advocate [S], 1818 , *suc to the Baronetcy* 4 April 1865 He m , 1 May 1827, Mary Anne Barbara, only surv da of John HUNTER, of Lisburne, co Antrim He *d* 9 Feb 1870, at Edinburgh. His widow *d* 18 July 1875, at Gilsland, co. Cumberland

X. 1870.   SIR WILLIAM MAXWELL, Baronet [S. 1627], of Calderwood aforesaid, only s and h , *b* 11 Aug 1828, *suc to the Baronetcy,* 9 Feb 1870 He m 20 April 1880, at 20 Belhaven terrace, Glasgow, Jane, yst da. of Frank BAIRD, of Glasgow He *d.* s p 4 Dec. 1885, aged 56, at Calderwood Castle, co Lanark, when the issue male of the father of the grantee is presumed to have become extinct His widow m in 1887, George Leader OWEN, of Withybush, co. Pembroke, and was living 1901

XI 1885   JAMES PIERCE (MAXWELL), 9th BARON FARNHAM [I 1756], cousin and h male collateral, *b* 1813 , *suc to the Peerage* on the death of his brother, 4 June 1884, and *suc to the Baronetcy* on the death of his distant cousin, the 10th Baronet, 4 Dec 1885, proving his right thereto in the Lyon Court, in 1900 His lineal ancestor, Robert MAXWELL, Dean of Armagh, was yr br of Sir James MAXWELL, of Calderwood, the father of the 1st Baronet, both being sons of Sir John MAXWELL, of Calderwood aforesaid The said Dean of Armagh (who *d* March 1625), was suc by his eldest s , Robert MAXWELL, Bishop of Kilmore and Ardagh (*d* 7 Nov 1672), whose s , Henry MAXWELL, Rector of Derrynoose, co Armagh (*d* 1703), was father of John MAXWELL, of Farnham, co Cavan, who became in 1737 the representative of his great grandfather, and who was cr 6 May 1756, BARON FARNHAM [I], being great grandfather of James Pierce (MAXWELL), 9th Baron Farnham [I. 1756], and 11th Baronet [S 1627] abovenamed See *Peerage.*

2 s

HAMILTON:

cr. in 1627

dormant or *extinct* about 1670.

I. 1627
to
1670 ?
WILLIAM HAMILTON, called " 3d brother to the EARL OF ABERCORN " [S](ᵃ), was *cr* a *Baronet* [S], presumably " as of Westport," in 1627, apparently before 28 March 1627(ᵃ), but no record is entered in the Great Seal Register, and no grant, or seizin of lands in Nova Scotia, is recorded   In Burke's *Extinct Baronetage,* however, " SIR JAMES [*sic*] HAMILTON, of Preston, sprung from Alexander, son to the LORD HAMILTON " is said to have been thus created in 1627   The grantee was probably the HON WILLIAM HAMILTON, yr br of James, 2d EARL OF ABERCORN [S], being 3d s of James, the 1st Earl, by Marion, da of Thomas (BOYD), LORD BOYD [S]   He was *b* about 1605 , was Resident in Rome, about 1660, on behalf of the Queen Dow of Charles I   He *m* , after 1645, Jean, Dow BARONESS CATHCART [S], widow of Sir Duncan CAMPBELL, 2d Baronet [S 1628], of Auchinbreck, who was slain in 1645   He *d* s p. (*Qy* about 1670 ?) when the *Baronetry* became *dormant* or *extinct.*

STEWART, *or* STUART.

cr 28 March 1627 , sealed 28 April 1632(ᵇ) ;

afterwards, since 1703, EARLS OF BUTE [S] ,

and, since 1796, MARQUESSES OF BUTE

I 1627
JAMES STEWART, of the isle of Bute, Hereditary Sheriff of Buteshire, s and h of Sir John STEWART, of the same (living Aug 1615), by Elizabeth, 1st da and coheir of Robert HEPBURN, of Foord, co Edinburgh, was *cr* a Baronet [S] as " of Bute " 28 March 1627, sealed 28 April 1632(ᵇ), but not recorded in the Great Seal Register [S], with rem to heirs male whatsoever, but no grant, or seizin of lands in Nova Scotia, is recorded   He was retoured heir of all his ancestors, 1630 , was M P [S] for Buteshire, 1644-45 , was a zealous Royalist, being the King's Lieutenant over the West of Scotland , was fined 5,000 marks by the Parl of 1646, his estate being sequestrated   He *m* Isabella, 1st da of Sir Duncan CAMPBELL, 2d Baronet [S 1628], of Auchinbreck, by Mary, da of Sir Alexander ERSKINE, of Gogar   He *d* in London, 1662, and was *bur* in Westm Abbey (ᶜ)

II 1662
SIR DUGALD STEWART, Baronet [S 1627], of Bute aforesaid, Hereditary Sheriff of Buteshire, 1st s and h. ; *suc to the Baronetcy* in 1662, was M P [S] for Buteshire, 1661-63, 1665 and 1669-70 , was made Baillie of the regality of Glasgow, 2 Sep. 1671. He *m* Elizabeth, da. of Sir John RUTHVEN, of Dunglass, by Barbara, da. of Alexander (LESLIE), 1st EARL OF LEVEN [S]. He *d* 1672

III 1672
SIR JAMES STEWART *or* STUART, Baronet [S 1627], of Bute aforesaid, Hereditary Sheriff of Buteshire, 1st s and h., *suc. to the Baronetcy* in 1672, at an early age , was Sheriff of Tarbet, 1684 , of Argyllshire, 1685 , admitted as an Advocate, 1685 , was M P [S] for co Bute, 1685-86, 1689,

---

(ᵃ) Milne's List, in which, however, no date is given.   This Baronetcy is not given in Laing's or Walkeley's Lists, but in Beatson's List the creation of " Hamilton, of Westport," is placed between " Maxwell ' and " Stuart," which indicates the date (given in Burke's *Extinct Baronetage*) of 1627   In Ulster's List [ending 1642] " Sir William Hamilton, br of the Earl of Abercorn " occurs

(ᵇ) Milne's List ; not, however, in Laing's List.

(ᶜ) Douglas' *Peerage* [S]   No such burial, however, is recorded in the Register of Westm Abbey, edited by Col Chester

1689-93 (when unseated for not having taken the oath of allegiance) and 1702-03 , P C to Queen Anne, a Commissioner for a proposed union with Scotland, 1702 He *m*, firstly, Agnes, 1st da of Sir George MACKENZIE, of Rosehaugh, King's Advocate [S], by his first wife, Elizabeth, da of John DICKSON, of Hartree, a Lord of Session [S] She, who was *b*. 2 Jan 1663, was living 28 Nov 1692. He *m*, secondly, Christian, da and coheir of William DUNCAN, of Kincavel, Advocate [S] She was living when he was *cr* 14 April 1703, EARL OF BUTE, etc. [S] In that peerage this *Baronetcy* then *merged* and still continues, the 4th Earl being *cr*, 21 March 1796, MARQUESS OF BUTE.

STEWART ·

cr. 18 April 1627(a) ;

afterwards, since 1649, EARLS OF GALLOWAY [S].

I 1627.   THE HON JAMES STEWART, of Corsewall, 2d and yst s of Alexander, 1st EARL OF GALLOWAY [S], by Grizel, da. of Sir John GORDON, of Lochinvar, was *b*. about 1604, and was v p *cr a Baronet* [S], 18 April 1627(a), as " of Corsewall," with rem to heirs male, and with, presumably, a grant of 16,000 acres in Nova Scotia, of which, however, he never appears to have had seizin(b) He was served heir, 5 Sep 1643, to his elder br , Alexander Stewart, *styled* LORD GARLIES, being, after that date, himself *styled* LORD GARLIES He was constant to the Royal cause, and was accordingly fined £4,000 under Cromwell's " Act of Grace " in 1654 He *m* in 1642, Nicola,(c) da of Sir Robert GRIERSON, of Lag, co Dumfries She, presumably, was living when, in 1649, he suc his father as EARL OF GALLOWAY [S] In that peerage this *Baronetcy* then *merged*, and still so continues

---

LIVINGSTONE, *or* LEVINGSTON :

cr 29 June and sealed 17 July 1627(d) ;

afterwards, 1647-94, VISCOUNTS NEWBURGH [S] ;

and subsequently, 1660-94, EARLS OF NEWBURGH [S] ;

dormant, since 6 April 1694.

I 1627   SIR JOHN LIVINGSTONE, of Kinnaird, in Gowrie, co. Perth, was Groom of the Bedchamber to James I before 1612 ; was *Knighted* before 1617 ; acquired the Barony of Kinnaird, from John Kinnaird, of that ilk, and had charter thereof 26 March 1618, ratified by Crown charter 6 Dec. 1618, and by Parl [S], in 1621 , was *cr a Baronet* [S.] 29 June, sealed 17 July 1627(d), but not entered in the Great Seal register, with rem to heirs male whatsoever, and with a grant of, presumably, 16,000 acres at Anti Costi, in Nova Scotia, of which he had seizin in July 1627.(b) He *m* Janet, da of (—) THOXTON He *d*. March 1628 His widow *m* 1645, as his 2d wife, Edward (GORGES), 1st BARON GORGES OF DUNDALK [I], who *d* before 16 April 1652 She was *bur.* from Lincoln's Inn Fields, 15 May 1666, at St Margaret's, Westm. Admon 11 July 1665, to her son James, Earl of Newburgh [S]

(a) Laing's List
(b) Banks's Lists
(c) As to his alleged marriage with Catherine, da. of Sir Robert Hoghton, 1st Baronet [1611], see *Northern Notes and Queries* (*Scottish Antiquary*), vol. IV, p 42.
(d) Milne's List. In Laing's List the creation is dated 25 June 1627.

II 1628   SIR JAMES LIVINGSTONE, Baronet [S 1627], of Kinnaird
            aforesaid, s. and h , *suc to the Baronetcy* March 1628, being then
under age, but obtaining his majority in 1640. His uncle, James Livingstone, was
served tutor to him 22 Dec 1628, and he was served heir to his father in the Barony
of Kinnaird, &c., 19 March 1629   He was one of the Gentlemen of the Bedchamber
to Charles I   He *m* after 23 Oct 1642, Catherine, widow of Lord George STUART,
da of Theophilus (HOWARD), 2d EARL OF SUFFOLK, by Elizabeth, da of George
(HOME), EARL OF DUNBAR [S]. She was living, though possibly not then as his wife,
13 Sep 1647, when he was *cr* VISCOUNT NEWBURGH [S], being subsequently
cr , 31 Dec 1660, EARL OF NEWBURGH, &c. [S.] In these peerages this
Baronetcy then *merged*, and so continued, till on the death s p m , 6 April 1694, of
his son, Charles, the 2d Earl, the issue male of the grantee became extinct, and the
Baronetcy became *dormant*([a]).

LIVINGSTONE, *or* LEVINGSTONE

cr. 29 June 1627 ,([b])

sometime, 1696—1711, VISCOUNT TEVIOT [S.] ;

dormant since 1718

I 1627   THOMAS LIVINGSTONE, of Newbigging, co Lanark, 2d s
            of Mungo LIVINGSTONE,([c]) of the same, by Jean, da of John LINDSAY,
of Covington in that county, was a Colonel in the service of the States General of
Holland, and was *cr a Baronet* [S], 29 June 1627,([b]) with a grant of, presumably,
16,000 acres in Nova Scotia, of which he had seizin in March 1629 ([d])   He acquired a
large fortune by his marriage with (—), da and h of Col EDMOND, an officer in the
service of the said States, the son of a baker in Stirling.

II 1660 ?   SIR THOMAS LIVINGSTONE, Baronet [S. 1627], s and h ,
            b about 1650 in Holland , *suc to the Baronetcy* on his father's
death , was a Colonel in the service of the States General , accompanied the Prince
of Orange, afterwards William III, to England, serving in several of his campaigns ;
Col 2d Reg of Dragoons, 1688 , Com. in chief of the forces in Scotland . Major
General, 1696, and finally, 1704, Lieut General. He *m* Macktellina WALRAVE, a
native of Nimeguen, who was living when he was *cr* 4 Dec 1696, VISCOUNT
TEVIOT, etc [S.] In that peerage this *Baronetcy* then *merged*, till on his death,
s p. 14 Jan. 1710/1, in his 60th year, his peerage honours became *extinct*. For fuller
account of him after 1696, see *Peerage*

III. 1711,   SIR ALEXANDER LIVINGSTONE, Baronet [S 1627], only br
   to   and h. He was a Col. of Foot in the service of the States General,
   1718.   and was afterwards, in the English service, Col of the Scots
            Cameronian Regiment   He *suc to the Baronetcy*, 14 Jan 1710/1,

---

([a]) The heir male to the Earldom (which was, however, limited to heirs *general*),
and, consequently, to the Baronetcy was James Livingston, s and h of John Livingston, Capt of Dragoons, by Eliz , da of Sir Robert Hamilton, of Silverhill.
Possibly he was a grandson of James Livingston (br. of the 1st Baronet), who
was served tutor to his nephew, the 2d Baronet, 22 Dec. 1628, as above stated

([b]) Wood's *Douglas' Peerage*, vol II, p 590   The date is the same as the creation
of the Baronetcy of Livingstone of Kinnaird, and possibly is confused therewith.
This creation is not mentioned in Milne's List or Laing's List, but it is stated in
Banks's Lists that "Sir James [*sic*] Livingstoun, of Newbigging, represented by
Viscount Teviot," had seizin of lands in Nova Scotia in March 1629, so that the date
cannot be very far wrong.

([c]) This Mungo was a yr s of William Livingstone, of Jerviswood, co. Lanark,
whose grandson and heir sold that estate about 1644 to George Baillie, and died soon
afterwards s.p. [*Ex inform* R R. Stodart, Lyon Clerk Depute, 1863-86, as also
is much else in this article.]

([d]) Banks's Lists.

and was served heir to his brother, 8 May 1711, in the estates of Waughton, co. Haddington, Abbotshall, co. Fife, etc. He *m* Sarah TIELLEUS, da of a Burgomaster of Amsterdam. He *d* s p m.(ᵃ) in Holland in 1718, when the *Baronetcy* became *dormant*. Will pr. Dec 1718.

CUNINGHAM, CUNINGHAME, *or* CONYNHAM,

cr. 4 July 1627, and sealed 26 July 1627(ᵇ);

sometime, April to Oct. 1722, RUTHVEN,

dormant, since Oct 1732.

I. 1627.   WILLIAM CUNINGHAM, of Cuninghamhead, in the parish of Dreghorn, co Ayr, s and h of John CUNINGHAM, of the same, by Mary, 1st da of Sir James EDMONSTONE, of Duntreath, co Stirling, was *b* 24 Nov 1601, was heir general of his Father, 24 Oct. 1610; was heir general of his father, 24 Oct 1610, was *cr. a Baronet* [S] 4, sealed 26 July 1627,(ᵇ) but not recorded in the Great Seal register [S], with rem. to heirs male whatsoever, and with a grant of, presumably, 16,000 acres, called the Barony of Cuningham in Anti Costi, Nova Scotia, of which he had seizin July 1627 (ᶜ) He was M.P [S] for co Ayr, 1628 33 and 1639-40. He *m*. firstly, in 1619, Elizabeth, da of Thomas NICOLSON, Commissary of Aberdeen. He *m* secondly, Margaret, da of Hugh (CAMPBELL), 1st LORD CAMPBELL OF LOUDOUN [S], by Elizabeth, da of William (RUTHVEN), 1st EARL OF GOWRIE [S]. He *d* June 1640.

II. 1640.   SIR WILLIAM CUNINGHAME, Baronet [S 1625], of Cuninghamhead aforesaid, only s. and h by 1st wife; *suc. to the Baronetcy* June 1640, and had the gift, *gratis*, of his own ward and marriage, on account of his father's death in service of the State On 12 May 1642, he had spec service to his father, was Colonel and a member of the Committee of Estates, 1649 He was M P. [S] for Ayrshire, 1648-49 and 1650, was a great Anti-Episcopalian, and in 1661 was fined £4,800, committed to prison in Sep 1662, and was not finally discharged till 1669 He *m* in Aug 1661, Anne, 1st da. of Thomas (RUTHVEN), 1st LORD RUTHVEN OF FREELAND [S.], by Isabel, da of Robert (BALFOUR *formerly* ARNOT), 2d LORD BALFOUR OF BURLEIGH [S]. He *d* 1670. His widow *m*. William CONINGHAME, of Craigends, and *d* about 1689, when her son was served her heir

III. 1670,   SIR WILLIAM CUNINGHAME, *afterwards* (April to Oct
    to   1722) SIR WILLIAM RUTHVEN, Baronet [S 1627], of Cuninghamhead(ᵈ)
    1722   and of Freeland, co Perth, only s and h, was *b*. about 1665, *suc to the Baronetcy* in 1670, and had spec. service to his father, 29 Aug. 1672, heir general of his mother, 21 May 1689. On the death, s p, of his maternal uncle, David (RUTHVEN), 2d LORD RUTHVEN [S], in April 1701, he became heir(ᵉ)

(ᵃ) Catherine Elizabeth, his da and h, *m* Matthew le Stevenson Van Barkenrode, Burgomaster of Amsterdam, and their son entered his pedigree in the Lyon office, Edinburgh, 20 Aug 1764

(ᵇ) Milne's List, Laing's List.

(ᶜ) Banks's Lists

(ᵈ) The estate of Cuninghamhead was sold 28 Jan. 1728, for £23,309 to John Snodgrass.

(ᵉ) The Barony of Ruthven of Freeland [S] was cr about Jan. 1651, with a limitation (according to the Macfarlane MS in the Advocates library) to heirs *male* No patent, however, was ever enrolled, and since 1701 it has been irregularly assumed in right of *female* descent, and that too not always (even) by the heir of line.

of line to his maternal grandfather, Thomas (RUTHVEN), LORD RUTHVEN OF FREE-LAND [S], but did not take that title which was arbitrarily assumed by his aunt Jean, the yst. of the three sisters and coheirs of the late Lord, on whose death the said Jean had, under a deed of entail, 26 April 1674, suc to the family estate of Freeland. This, on her death unm in April 1722, devolved on him (six months before his death) when he assumed the name of RUTHVEN. He *m.* Ann, da of Sir Archibald STEWART, 1st Baronet [S 1668] of Castlemilk, by Mary, da of William CARMICHAEL, s and h ap of James, 1st LORD CARMICHAEL [S]   He *d s p* Oct 1722, when the *Baronetcy* became *dormant*. Will "given up" 28 March 1723

CARMICHAEL ·

cr. 17 July 1627(ᵃ),

subsequently, 1647—1817, LORD CARMICHAEL [S];

and, 1701—1817, EARLS OF HYNDFORD [S],

dormant since 18 April 1817.

I   1627.   SIR JAMES CARMICHAEL, of Westraw and Hyndford, both in co Lanark, s and h of Walter CARMICHAEL, of Hyndford aforesaid, by Grizel, da of Sir John CARMICHAEL, of Meadow Flat, in that county, Captain of the Castle of Crawfurd, suc his Father in 1616 , was Cupbearer, Carver and Chamberlain [S] to James I, and was cr a Baronet [S], 17 July 1627,(ᵃ) as "of Westraw," being designed "the King's servant," with rem to heirs male whatsoever, and with, presumably, a grant of 16,000 acres, called the Barony and Regality of Carmichael, in Nova Scotia, of which he had seizin in Jan. 1633, "with power to dig for searching of gold mines, and for that effect to transport thither all gold affecting mines "(ᵇ) Having, on the death of his cousin, Sir John Carmichael, of Carmichael, co Lanark (living 9 Feb 1619), suc to that estate, he was thenceforth designated "of Carmichael," was Sheriff of Lanarkshire, 1632; Lord Justice Clerk, 1634-36, and again 1649 , Treasurer Depute 1636 , P.C. [S] for life (by Parl), 1641.   He *m* Agnes, sister of John WILKIE of Foulden, co. Berwick, da of William WILKIE. She, presumably, was living when, for his services to the King, he was cr , 27 Dec 1647, LORD CARMICHAEL [S.], with rem to heirs male whatsoever. He, however, did not assume that title till the patent was ratified, 3 Jan 1651   Between these dates, 10 March 1649, he was deprived of all his offices for his part in "the engagement "   In that peerage this *Baronetcy*, accordingly, *merged*, the 2d Baron being cr , 25 July 1701, EARL OF HYNDFORD [S], and so continued till, on the death, unm., 18 April 1817, of the 6th Earl, 7th Baron, and 7th Baronet, it became *dormant*.

MACGILL:

cr 19 July and sealed 3 Dec 1627(ᶜ),

afterwards, 1661-1706, VISCOUNTS OXFURD [S];

dormant since 8 Dec 1706.

I.   1627   JAMES MACGILL, of Cranston-Riddell, co. Midlothian, 2d s of David MACGILL of the same, by Mary, da of Sir William SINCLAIR, of Herdmanstoun, suc his elder br , David MACGILL, 15 May 1619, and was *cr* a *Baronet* [S.] 19 July, sealed 3 Dec 1627(ᶜ), but not recorded in the Great Seal register, with rem to heirs male whatsoever, and with the grant of, presumably,

(ᵃ) Milne's List.
(ᵇ) Banks's Lists
(ᶜ) Milne's List and Laing's List, in which last the grantee is called " Master James Makgill, of Cranstounriddell."

16,000 acres in Nova Scotia, of which he had seizin, Dec. 1627(a) He was a Lord of Session [S], 3 Nov. 1629, and was again so appointed by Parl 14 Nov 1641, by which also he was made, 1 Feb 1643, a Commissioner, was M P [S] for co Edinburgh, 1630 He m firstly, before 1630, Catharine, da of Sir John COCKBURN, of Ormston He m. secondly, about 1645, Christian, da of Sir William LIVINGSIONE, of Kilsyth She, presumably, was living when he was cr , 19 April 1661, VISCOUNT OXFORD, &c [S.]. In that peerage this *Baronetcy* then *merged*, and so continued till the death s.p m s 8 Dec. 1706, of the 2d Viscount and Baronet, when both titles became *dormant*

OGILVY

cr 30 July, sealed 4 Aug 1627(b) ,

afterwards, 1642-1803, LORDS BANFF [S] ;

dormant, since 4 June 1803.

I 1627   SIR GEORGE OGILVY, of Banff, s and h of Sir Walter OGILVY, of Dunlugus, co Banff, by Helen, da of Walter URQUHART, of Cromarty, suc. his father soon after 1625, and was cr a Baronet [S], 30 July, the patent being sealed 4 Aug 1627,(b) but not recorded in the Great Seal Register, with rem to heirs male whatsoever, and with a grant of, presumably, 16,000 acres in Nova Scotia, of which apparently (though the name is given, probably, in error, as "Sir *James* Ogilvy, of Banff"), he had seizin in Aug 1627 (a) He is styled "*Dominus Georgius Ogilvy, Baronettus,*" in a charter to him, 28 Jan. 1628/9, of the Barony of Banff He m firstly, before 9 March 1610/1, Margaret, da of Sir Alexander IRVINE, of Drum She d s p m He m secondly, Mary SUTHERLAND, of Duffus She, presumably, was living as his wife, when (after having distinguished himself in an engagement against the Covenanters at the bridge of Dee, 19 June 1639), he was cr , 31 Aug 1642, LORD BANFF [S] In that peerage, this *Baronetcy* then *merged* till on the death, 4 June 1803, of the 8th Lord and 8th Baronet, both became *dormant*

COCKBURN (c)

cr 22 Nov 1627, sealed 16 April 1629(d) ;

dormant, since 20 Nov 1880

I 1627   WILLIAM COCKBURN, of Langton, co. Berwick, Heretable Usher [S,], s and h of William COCKBURN,(e) of Langton aforesaid, by Janet, da of (—) HOME, of Wedderburn , suc his father 15 Feb 1587 , was M.P [S] for Berwickshire, 1612, and was cr a *Baronet* [S.], 22 Nov 1627 , the

(a) Banks's Lists.

(b) Milne's List, in which, however, the Christian name is left blank ; in Laing's List the date is 20 July 1627 , in Beatson's List the creation is called "Ogilvie, of Forglen, now Lord Banff"

(c) The pedigrees of Cockburn are most contradictory (1) The most reliable, and the one that is here followed, appears to be a tabular one in MS compiled by Sir Edward Cludde Cockburn, and lent by him, 10 July 1901, to Sir James Balfour Paul, Lyon King of Arms (2) An extensive pedigree, compiled by Sir William Betham, Ulster King of Arms [1820 53] for "Sir William Cockburn, Baronet" [see the 7th Baronet under "Cockburn" Baronetcy [S] said to have been cr in 1628], which pedigree is now among the Betham MSS in Ulster's Office (3) The very confused account given in Playfair's *Baronetage* [S], published in 1811 , and (4) *The House of Cockburn of that ilk*, by T H C Hood, Edinburgh, published in 1888

(d) Milne's List , Laing's List, where however, the date is given as 21 Nov. 1627

(e) This William was s of James and grandson of Alexander, both of Langton aforesaid, the said Alexander, who was slain with his father at the battle of Flodden, 9 Sep 1513, being one of the three sons of Sir William Cockburn, of that ilk, by Anne, da. of Alexander (Home) Lord Home [S] Of the two other sons (1) William Cockburn, was father of William, father of Alexander, father of William, father of

patent being sealed 16 April 1629,(ª) but not entered in the Great Seal Register, with rem to heirs male whatsoever, and with a grant of, presumably, 16,000 acres in Nova Scotia, of which his son had seizin in April 1629(ᵇ). He *m.*, about 1600, Helen 4th da of Alexander (ELPHINSTONE), 4th LORD ELPHINSTONE [S.], by Jean, da of William (LIVINGSTONE), LORD LIVINGSTONE [S]. He *d.* in or about Dec. 1628. His widow *m* Henry ROLLO, of Woodside.

II. 1628 ?   SIR WILLIAM COCKBURN, Baronet [S 1627], of Langton aforesaid, 1st s. and h , *suc to the Baronetcy*, on the death of his father, to whom he was retoured heir 21 May 1629 M P [S] for Berwickshire, 1640-41 In 1641, while the question of Usher was being discussed, he seized the rod and took his place, for which conduct he was, by the King's order, imprisoned, but was released after a few days on the remonstrance of the House He subsequently alienated a moiety of his office He *m.* Margaret, da of Sir Archibald ACHESON, 1st Baronet [S. 1628] by his 1st wife, Agnes, da. of (—) VERNOR

III. 1650 ?   SIR WILLIAM COCKBURN, Baronet [S. 1627], of Langton aforesaid, 1st s and h , *suc to the Baronetcy* on the death of his father He *d* s p., probably unm , before Dec. 1657

IV. 1657 ?   SIR ARCHIBALD COCKBURN, Baronet [S 1627], of Langton aforesaid, s and h , *suc. to the Baronetcy* in or before 1657, being retoured heir to his brother, William, 10 Dec. 1657 In 1674, he by purchase and grant obtained the moiety of the office of Usher, which his father had alienated, together with a salary of £250 , Heretable Sheriff of Berwickshire, 1686 , M.P [S.] thereof 1678, 1685 86, 1689, and 1689-1702 He *m* firstly, Marion, da of John SINCLAIR, the younger, of Stevenson He *m* secondly, Anna, da. of Sir Thomas STEWART, of Cultness, by Margaret ELLIOT, his wife. He was *bur* 28 June 1705, at Langton.

V. 1705.   SIR ARCHIBALD COCKBURN, Baronet [S. 1627], of Langton aforesaid, grandson and h , being surviving s. and h of Archibald COCKBURN, Advocate [S] 1686, and M P [S.] for Berwickshire, 1685-86, by Elizabeth, da of Sir George MACKENZIE, of Rosehaugh, which Archibald was s and h. ap of the last Baronet, by his 1st wife, but *d.* v p., 22 and was *bur* 26 Aug. 1702, at Langton, aged about 42 He was *b* 16 Nov 1687 ; *suc to the Baronetcy*, 20 June 1705 ; was Lieutenant in the regiment of the Earl of Orkney [S.] He *d.* unm and was *bur* 18 Feb 1709/10, at St. Martin's in the Fields. Admon. 27 April 1711, to a creditor.

VI 1710.   SIR ALEXANDER COCKBURN, Baronet [S 1672], of Langton aforesaid uncle and h , *suc. to the Baronetcy* in Feb. 1709/10, and was retoured heir to his br. Archibald COCKBURN, abovenamed, 11 Feb 1711. He *m.* Mary, da of William ANCRUM, of Duns. He *d* May 1739.

VII 1739.   SIR ALEXANDER COCKBURN, Baronet [S 1627], of Langton aforesaid, grandson and h , being s. and h. of Archibald COCKBURN, by Mary (*m.* 11 April 1719), da of John (CAMPBELL), 1st EARL OF BREADALBANE [S],

---

another William, father of John, all of that ilk, which John was father of James Cockburn, *cr. a Baronet* [S] as of that ilk, 24 May 1671 The remaining son (2) Christopher Cockburn, was father of William, father of James, all of Choushe, which James was father of James Cockburn, of Ryslaw, said to be *cr. a Baronet* [S] in 1628, whose representative, Sir Edward Cludde Cockburn, claims (1) not only that Baronetcy, but, (2) the Baronetcy (of that ilk) of 1671, as well as (3) that (of Langton) of 1627. [See Sir E C Cockburn's MS pedigree, mentioned on p 327, note "c."

(ª) That he and not his son (as generally stated) was the 1st Baronet, is shewn by a deed dat 21 July 1631, to "John Cockburn, lawful son of umquhile Sir William Cockburn, of Langton, Knt. and Baronet" This John, who was an advocate [S.] 7 June 1642, and who *d.* 1666, is not to be confused with his nephew, John (son of Sir William, the 2d Baronet), who, being a minor in 1656, was not born till many years after 1631.

(ᵇ) Banks's Lists.

which Archibald, who was admitted an advocate, 18 June 1715, was s and h ap of the last Baronet, but *d* v p Jan 1735 He *suc to the Baronetcy* on the death of his grandfather, was an officer in the Guards, and *d* unm, being slain 30 April 1745, at the battle of Fontenoy Will pr. 1745

VIII. 1745   SIR JAMES COCKBURN, Baronet [S. 1627], of Eyemouth, co Berwick, cousin and h being 2d(ᵃ) but 1st surv s of William COCKBURN, of Eyemouth aforesaid, merchant, by Frances, da. of James COCKBURN, of Jamaica, which William (whose will was pr 5 Oct 1731), was 2d s of Alexander, the 6th Baronet. He was *b* about 1729, *suc to the Baronetcy*, but to none of the family estates,(ᵇ) 30 April 1745, being retoured heir, 3 Jan 1749, to his cousin Alexander, the late Baronet He was M P for Linlithgow Burghs (three Parls) 1772-84 He *m* firstly, 31 March 1755, Mary said to be di of Henry DOUGLAS, of London, merchant, br of Sir James DOUGLAS, 1st Baronet [1786] She *d* at Bristol, Hotwells, 5 April 1766. He *m* secondly, 10 July 1769, Augusta Anne, da of Francis AYSCOUGH, D.D, Dean of Bristol, by Anne, da of Sir Thomas LYTTELTON, 4th Baronet [1618] He *d* 22 or 26 July 1804, aged 75 His widow *d* 14 Nov 1837, aged 88, and was *bur.* in Kensal Green Cemetery. Will pr Jan 1838.

IX. 1804   SIR JAMES COCKBURN, Baronet [S 1627], s and h, by 2d wife, *b* 21 March, 1771, *suc. to the Baronetcy*, July 1804, Major General in the Army, 1831, Under Secretary of State for War and Colonies, 1806 07, Governor and Commander in Chief of Curaçoa, 1807-11 Governor of the Bermudas, 1811-19, G C H ; LL D.; Sheriff of Carmarthenshire, 1847. He *m* 14 Oct 1801, Mariana, 1st da of George (DEVEREUX), 13th VISCOUNT HEREFORD, by Mariana, only da and h of George DEVEREUX, of Tregoyd, co Brecon She *d* 9 Dec 1817 He *d*, s p m, 26 Feb 1852, in Portman sq, and was *bur* in Kensal Green Cemetery Will pr. March 1852.

X. 1852   SIR GEORGE COCKBURN, Baronet [S 1627], br and h, *b*. 22 April 1772, in London, entered the Navy as Captain's servant, 13 March 1781, becoming, subsequently, Captain, in 1794, Commander-in-Chief at St Helena 1815 16, and in North America and West India Station, 1832-36, Admiral, 1837, Rear Admiral 1847, and, finally, 1851 till death, Admiral of the Fleet, Major General of Marines, 1821, M P for Portsmouth, 1818 20, for Weobley, 1820 28, for Plymouth (three Parls) 1828 32, and for Ripon, 1841 47 One of the Lords of the Admiralty, 1818 to 1830, and 1841 to 1846, K C B, 2 Jan 1815, G C B, 20 Feb. 1818, F R S, 1820; P C, 30 April 1827, *suc to the Baronetcy*, 26 Feb 1852 He *m* 23 Nov. 1809, Mary, yst da and eventually cohen of Thomas COCKBURN, of Jamaica, by Mary, da of (—) AYLWARD He *d*, s p m, 19 Aug 1853, at Leamington Will pr Oct 1853 His widow *d* 20 Jan. 1859, at Highbeech, Essex Both were *bur* in Kensal Green Cemetery.

XI 1853   SIR WILLIAM COCKBURN, Baronet [S 1627], br and h, *b* 2 June 1773, ed at St John's Coll, Cambridge, B A and 12th Wrangler, 1795, M A, 1798, B D and D D, 1832; Fellow, 1796-1806, Christian

(ᵃ) His elder br, Alexander Cockburn, survived their father, and was retoured his heir, 22 July 1732. He *d* unm, being then an officer of H M.S "Medway," apparently before April 1745 Admon 1747 He is said in Hood's *House of Cockburn* (p. 102), to have died on his way to India a few months *after* the battle of Fontenoy (30 April 1745), aged 17 In that case he would have been entitled to the Baronetcy for a short time. This account, however, is disbelieved in Sir E C Cockburn's MS. pedigree [see p. 327, note " c "], and he is not described as a Baronet in his admon

(ᵇ) The Langton estates and the office of Usher had been disponed 6 May 1690, by the 4th Baronet, the then possessor, to his cousin, Sir James Cockburn, 1st Baronet [S 1671] of that ilk, and the amount charged on them appears in 1745 to have exceeded their value Sir James Cockburn, 3d Baronet [S. 1671] of that ilk, was, 25 Nov. 1754, retoured heir special of his father in Langton and in the office of Usher. These possessions, however, were finally sold by auction at Edinburgh, 15 Dec 1757, being set up at about 23 years' purchase The Barony of Langton set up at £26,500, sold for £50,000 or £60,000 ; the estate of Simprim, set up at £6,784, sold for £12,200, and the office of Heritable Usher of Scotland (salary £250), set up at £5,166, sold for £6,500, the purchaser of the latter being Alexander Coutts, of London.

2 T

Advocate to Univ of Cambridge, 1803-10 , Dean of York, 1822-58 ; Rector of Kelston, co Somerset, 1832-58 , *suc to the Baronetcy*, 19 Aug 1853   He *m* firstly, 30 Dec. 1805, Elizabeth, 2d da of Sir Robert PEEL, 1st Baronet [1800], by his 1st wife, Ellen, da of William YATES   She *d* 16 June 1828.   He *m*. secondly, 14 Sep 1830, Emma, da. of (—) PEARSE, of Hatley St George. co. Cambridge, Lieut -Col. 15th Foot   He *d* , s p m s , 30 April 1858, at Kelston Rectory, aged 84   His widow *m* 5 July 1859, at Weaverham, Cheshire, the Rev Thomas William WHALE, Rector of Dolton, North Devon   She *d* there 24 Aug 1876

XII 1858,   SIR ALEXANDER JAMES EDMUND COCKBURN, Baronet
     to   [S 1627], nephew and h, being only s and h of Alexander
  1880   COCKBURN, sometime 1820-23, Envoy Extraordinary to the Court
            of Stuttgart, and, subsequently, 1826-29, to Columbia, by Yolande,
da of VISCOMTE DE VIGNIER, of St. Domingo, which Alexander (who *d* 14 Oct. 1852, aged 76), was 4th s of the 6th Baronet   He was *b* 24 Dec 1802, ed at Trin Hall, Cambridge , Fellow Commoner, 1825 , Fellow, 1829 , LL B , 1829 , Hon D C L of Oxford, 22 June 1870 , Hon LL D of Cambridge, 1874 , Student at the Middle Temple, Nov 1825 , Barrister, Feb 1829, and a member of the Western Circuit. One of the Municipal Corporation Commissioners ; Recorder of Southampton, 1840-46 , Q C , 1841 , Bencher of the Middle Temple , M P., for Southampton, 1847 to 1856 , Solicitor General, Aug 1850 to March 1851 , being *Knighted*, 14 Aug. 1850 , Attorney General, March 1851 to Feb 1852, and again Dec. 1852 to Nov 1856, conducting the prosecution of Palmer, the Rugeley poisoner, who was hanged 14 June 1856 , Recorder of Bristol, 1854-56 ; LORD CHIEF JUSTICE OF THE COMMON PLEAS, Nov 1856 to June 1859 , Privy Councillor, 2 Feb 1857 , LORD CHIEF JUSTICE OF THE QUEEN'S BENCH,(a) June 1859, till his death , one of the Arbitrators, under the treaty of Washington, respecting the Alabama claim, 1871-72 , G C B (extra) 12 Feb 1873, having declined a peerage.   He presided, 1873-74, at the trial of the Tichborne case, (188 days), which was the last important incident of his brilliant professional career, one that was throughout conducted with the strictest regard to the rules of honour and integrity.   He *d* unm in Hertford Street, Mayfair, late at night, 20 Nov 1880, having been presiding in his Court that afternoon   *Bur* in Kensal Green Cemetery   At his death the *Baronetcy* became *dormant* (b)

COCKBURN :

said to have been cr in 1628 (c)

I   1628   JAMES(d) COCKBURN, of Ryslaw, co Berwick, s
(apparently 2d s) of James COCKBURN, of Choushe (*d*. 22 July 1586), by Marion, da of John DOUGLAS,(e) was *b* about 1576 , was M P [S]

(a) Strictly speaking he was Chief Justice of *the Queen's Bench Division of the High Court of Chancery* from and after 2 Nov 1875, when the Judicature Act of 1873 came into operation, by which the *old* Court of Queen's Bench was extinguished.

(b) The following advertisement appeared in *The Times* newspaper for 10 May 1881 —"The relatives of the widow and three children of the late George Henry Cockburn, eldest son of the late George Henry Cockburn, Admiral of the British Navy, and nephew of the late Sir Alexander Cockburn, Lord Chief Justice of England, can be heard of at the Cottage of Content, Mary Street, Waterloo, near Sydney, New South Wales "

(c) This creation does not appear in Milne's, Laing's, Walkley's, or Ulster's Lists of Scotch Baronets, nor even in that of Beatson (1810), but it is stated in Playfair's *Baronetage* [S], pub in 1811 that "Sir James Cockburn, of Ryslaw, Baronet was so created in 1628," and the descent of that title is deduced therefrom to William, the then Baronet   There is, however, no record of any grant of land in Nova Scotia to any such person

(d) He is called "John" (not "James") in Burke's *Baronetage* of 1871 while in the more recent editions of that work the Baronetcy itself is altogether ignored

(e) The pedigree of Cockburn here followed, unless otherwise stated, is the carefully compiled one in MS. of Sir E C Cockburn   See p 327, note "c."

for Berwickshire, 1625, and is said to have been e. a Baronet [S.] in 1628 ([a])
A letter from Charles II, dated Oct 1653, at Chantilly, and addressed to *Sir
James Cockburn*, of Ryslaw, *Knight Baronet of Nova Scotia*, is, if correctly
inscribed, confirmatory thereof. He m. Mary, da of Sir Andrew EDMONSTONE,
of that ilk, by Mary GORDON, his wife ([b]) He d in 1643

II. 1643 SIR JAMES COCKBURN, Baronet [S. 1628] ([c]) of Ryslaw
aforesaid, nephew and b male,([d]) being s of William
COCKBURN, of Choushe, by Sybilla, da of Matthew SINCLAIR, of Longformacus,
which William, who d. 1628, was elder br of the 1st Baronet He *suc to the
Baronetcy*([c]) in 1643, and is said to have been in command on the King's side
at Edgehill and Worcester He entered his Arms in the Lyon Office, about
1670, as "*Sir James Cockburn, of Ryslaw*," without, however, the style of
"Baronet," and with no indication of his parentage He m firstly, Jean, da.
of Alexander SWINTON, of Swinton, co Berwick, by Margaret, da. of James
HOME, of Frampath. He m. secondly, Jane, da. of Andrew KER, of Lintoun,
co Roxburgh. He d. in or before April 1666

III. 1666? SIR JAMES([e]) COCKBURN, Baronet([c]) [S 1628], of
Ryslaw aforesaid, s. and b, by 1st wife, b about 1646, *suc. to
the Baronetcy*([c]) in or before 1666, being retoured heir to his father ; was, as
' Sir Jas Cockburne, Knt," Lieut in the Royal Reg of Foot, 1689 ; Capt. in
or before July 1693; wounded at Landen; left the regiment in May 1694, Capt.
in Lord Lindsay's reg of Foot, April 1696 He m firstly, Alison, 2d da of
Sir Robert SINCLAIR, 1st Baronet [S 1664], of Longformacus, by Elizabeth,
da of Sir Robert DOUGLAS, of Blackerstoun She was bur 14 Feb 1669, at
Holyrood ([b]) He m secondly,([f]) about 1675, (—) He d 1711.([b])

([a]) See p 330, note " c "
([b]) See p. 330, note " e "
([c]) Presuming that a Baronetcy [S] with rem to heirs male whatsoever was
conferred on James Cockburn of Ryslaw in 1628.
([d]) This is the parentage assigned to him in Sir E C Cockburn's pedigree (see
p 327, note " c ") and to his brother, Christopher Cockburn, of Choushe (b about
1647. inherited the family estate, and d about 1653), whose male issue continued
for three generations, when (writes Sir Edward) "the *elder* line became extinct "
But if Christopher was (as would thus appear) elder br to James, the latter could
not have succeeded their uncle as h male This difficulty, however, is solved by
considering James, the 2d Baronet, to have been son (not nephew) of the 1st Baronet,
as is done by Betham, by Playfair, and by most others
([e]) The succession in Betham's pedigree (see p 327, note " c ") is entirely different
The 3d Baronet is therein called WILLIAM (not James), and is said to have " lived in
England," to have m (—), da. of (—) Douglas of Blackerstoun, in Berwick, and to
have died in 1680 To him three sons are assigned, viz (1), James, the 4th Baronet,
father of William. the 5th Baronet, as in the text ; (2), Charles, a General under
the Duke of Marlborough, whose male issue failed with his two sons, Charles and
George, both Captains in the army , (3), William Cockburn, M D , Physician to the
army, who m. Margaret, da of John Maitland, and who d at Kilkenny in 1730,
leaving two sons, the elder of whom William Cockburn, M D, of Dublin, d s p.m ,
while the younger [therein, erroneously, called], James [not John, as in the text]
Cockburn, of Kilkenny (d 1758), was father of James, the 6th Baronet (on the death,
in 1782, of his cousin, William, the 5th Baronet), who was father of Sir William, the
7th and then existing Baronet
The succession given by Playfair differs from the above in making William, the
then Baronet (and not his father, James) succeed to the Baronetcy, and in making
this William's great grandfather, William Cockburn, M D , abovenamed, to be a son
of the 1st [!] Baronet instead of a son of the 3rd
([f]) Presuming the date [1669] of the burial of Alison Sinclair, wife of the 3d
Baronet, and that [1677] of the birth of his s , the 4th Baronet, to be correctly given
in Sir E C Cockburn's pedigree, it is manifest that the 4th Baronet must be the s
of a subsequent, presumably a second, wife

IV. 1711.   SIR JAMES COCKBURN, Baronet [S. 1628],(a) 1st s.
and h., *b* 27 March 1677, and *bap* at Edinburgh,(b) *suc. to the
Baronetcy*(a) in 1711 ; was a Colonel in the service of the States of Holland.(c)
He *m* Catherine da of (— VAN OFFLE, of Friesland. He *d* at the Hague
1720 (c)

V 1720.   SIR WILLIAM COCKBURN, Baronet [S 1628] (a) 1st s
and h , *b* in Holland, *suc to the Baronetcy*(a) in 1720 ; was
Lieut. Col. in the service of the States of Holland He *m* (—), da of
(—) VON AKERSDYCK, of the province of Utrecht He *d* s p 1782, at the
Hague

VI 1782.   SIR JAMES COCKBURN, Baronet [S. 1628] (a) cousin
and h male, being yr. br. of William COCKBURN, Archdeacon
of Ossory (1762), who *d* s p m , at Bath, 7 June 1776 both being sons of
John COCKBURN, Surgeon, of Kilkenny, by Martha, da. of (—) RICH, of
Kilkenny, which John (*b* 12 Nov. 1683, at Fogo, *d.* 12 Dec 1758, at Kilkenny)
was yr br. of James, 4th Baronet,(a) both being sons of the 3d Baronet (a)
He was *b* 1723 , was Lieut Colonel in the 35th Regt , Brigadier General
and Quartermaster General in North America He *suc to the Baronetcy*(a)
in 1782, but it is doubtful if he ever assumed the title (d) He *is said*(e) *to
have suc ,* as h male collateral, on the death, 9 Jan 1800, of Sir William
James COCKBURN, 4th Baronet [S 1671], *to that Baronetcy* (cr. 24 May
1671), of which, however, the limitation is not known. He *m* in or before
1770, Lætitia, da and coheir of Luke LITTLE, of Carlow, an officer of Cavalry,
by Jane, da of Col John RUSSELL, of the Guards (c) He *d* at Stapleton,
near Bristol, 1801 (b) His widow *d* 11 Nov 1804, at her son's house at
Weston, near Bath.

VII 1801   SIR WILLIAM COCKBURN, Baronet [S 1628,(a) and
possibly(f) 1671] s and h , *b* 26 Jan 1771, at Winchester,(c)
suc. to the Baronetcy(a) *or Baronetcies* on the death of his father, was

---

(a) See p 331, note " c "

(b) See p 330, note " e "

(c) Betham's pedigree : see p 327, note " c."

(d) The account given of this family in Playfair's *Baronetage* [S] in 1811, seems to
have been furnished by " Sir William " the then Baronet. The elaborate and *nihil
ad rem* narrative therein set forth of the families of Rossiter and Devereux (from
whom his mother Lætitia Little was descended), as also of that of Creutzer (being
that of his wife), could hardly have come from another source Yet, not only is
Sir William's father (the date of whose death is not given) spoken of merely as
" Esq ," but it is also stated that " *Sir William Cockburn,* only son of James, is *the
present Baronet,* having *succeeded to the title* [not on the death of his father, but]
on the branch of Sir James the 4th [sic] *Baronet becoming extinct."* The subsequent
discovery of Betham that the then Baronet's *father,* James, had himself been a
Baronet, and had in 1782 suc his cousin as such, was in 1811 apparently unknown to
(Sir William) his son and successor ! The account in Playfair is more in harmony with
Sir William having assumed the Baronetcy [S 1671] of Cockburn of Cockburn soon
after the death (9 Jan 1800) of the 4th Baronet of *that* creation, which death took
place not long before the death of his own father, who probably never assumed it

(e) " Sir William James Cockburn [4th] Baronet [S 1671] .. died 9 Jan 1800
. was suc in the title by his kinsman, Col James Cockburn, who had previously
[1782 ?] inherited the Ryslaw Baronetcy, who dying in 1801 was suc by his only son,
William Cockburn," who came home from India in that year [MS account of the
Baronetcy of Cockburn, of Cockburn, written by Sir Edward Cludde Cockburn,
and lent by him to Sir J Balfour Paul, Lyon, in July, 1901.]

(f) In Broun's *Baronetage* for 1844, the Baronetcy assigned to this family is the one
created in 1671, of which creation the then holder is called the *sixth* Baronet, no mention
being made of the creation of 1628 , but, on the other hand, *that* creation (and not
the one of 1671) is the one attributed to these Baronets by Playfair in 1811, and by
Burke till (at some date after 1871) he *dis*continued to include them among existing
Baronets

an officer in the Army, sometime Major in the 73d Foot, becoming eventually (1821) Lieut General, was, *cr* D C L of Oxford, 26 June 1816 He *m* firstly, 1 Jan 1791, at Madras, Elizabeth Anne, widow of Thomas DAVIS, M D., and previously of Charles CLIFTON, Major R.A, sister and h of Henry Jacob CREUTZER, da of Col. Henry Frederick CREUTZER, of Manheim in Germany, by Elizabeth, da of Lieut Col Alexander JACOB She *d*. 30 June 1829, at Wrockwardine, Salop, and was *bur* there He *m* secondly, 2 July 1834, at Swainswick, Martha Honora Georgina widow of Osborne MARKHAM, 1st da and coh. of William Henry RICKETTS-JERVIS, of Longwood, Hants, Capt R N, by Elizabeth Jane, da of Richard (LAMBART), 6th EARL OF CAVAN [I] He *d* at Lansdowne Crescent, Bath, 19 March, and was *bur*. 3 April 1835, at Wrockwardine, aged 67 M I in Bath Abbey Will pr May 1835. His widow, who after her marriage, assumed the name of JERVIS only, *d* 26 Feb 1865, at Batheaston, Somerset, in her 71st year

VIII. 1835. SIR WILLIAM SARSFIELD ROSSITER COCKBURN, Baronet, [S. 1628(ᵃ) and possibly 1671], of Downton, near Kington, co. Hereford, only s and h , *b*. 11 June 1796, at Bath, matric at Oxford (Ex Coll) 22 March 1818, aged 18 , B.A , 1819 , M A , 1823 , *suc to the Baronetcy*(ᵃ) *or Baronetcies* 19 March 1835 He was author of a work called " The Massacre of St Bartholomew," and of other publications. He *m* 15 Oct 1823, at Gardesley, co Hereford, Anne, 1st da. of the Rev. Francis COKE, of Lower Moor, co Hereford, Preb of Hereford, by Anne, da cf Robert WHITCOMBE, of Kington He *d* suddenly, 12 April 1858, at Downton aforesaid His widow *d* 12 April 1879.

IX 1858. SIR EDWARD CLUDDE COCKBURN, Baronet [S 1628(ᵃ) and possibly 1671], of Pennockstone, co Hereford, and of Downton aforesaid, 2d but 1st surv. s and h ,(ᵇ) *b* 10 June 1834, at Downton, matric at Oxford (Ex Coll), 18 May 1853, aged 18 , entered the army 1854 , Capt. 11th Hussars, 1858 , *suc to the Baronetcy*(ᵃ) *or Baronetcies* 12 April 1858 , Sheriff for Herefordshire, 1866 He *m* in 1859, Mary Anne Frances, da of Robert Keri ELLIOT, of Harwood Park and Clifton, co Roxburgh (ᶜ)

CAMPBELL.
cr. 13 Dec. 1627 ,(ᵈ)
dormant in or before 1696.

I. 1627 SIR COLIN CAMPBELL, of Lundy in Angus, co Forfar(ᵉ) being s. and h of the Hon COLIN CAMPBELL, of Lundy aforesaid, which Colin was 2d s of Colin 6th EARL OF ARGYLL [S] was served heir gen of his father, 15 May 1619, and was *cr* a *Baronet* [S], 13 Dec. 1627, such creation not, however, being recorded in the Great Seal register, with rem to heirs male what-

(ᵃ) See p 331, note " c "
(ᵇ) His elder br. Devereux Cockburn, an officer in the Scots Greys, *d* unm and v p at Rome, 3 May 1850, in his 22d year
(ᶜ) After the death, 20 Nov 1880, of Lord Chief Justice Cockburn, the 12th Baronet [S.] of the creation, 22 Nov. 1627, of Cockburn, of Langton, it seems not impossible that this dignity as well as the Baronetcy [S. 1671] (see note " " above) may have devolved on Sir E C Cockburn, and he indeed in his MS pedigree (see note " c " above) as " 9th Baronet of Ryslaw, 7th of that ilk, and 13th of Langton "
(ᵈ) Laing's List ; in Milne's List this entry is given as " 28 May 1625 (—) Campbell, of Lundie, wes nixt Straquhan, of Thorntoun in Denmill's List, bot is extinct " The date and place thus assigned to this creation seem clearly erroneous
(ᵉ) He is, erroneously, designated in Ulster's List as " brother to the Earl of Argyll," as also in Wood's Douglas' Peerage [S.]

soever, and with a grant of, presumably, 16,000 acres in Nova Scotia, of which he had seizin in May 1628 (a) He is styled Baronet in a spec service to his father, 22 May 1630, and elsewhere He appears to have sold Lundie, before 1648, to a person of his own surname (b)

II   1650 ?   SIR COLIN CAMPBELL, Baronet [S 1627], s. or grandson
      to   and heir appears to have *suc to the Baronetcy* and to have *d* s p.m (c)
      1696 ?   before 1696, when it became *dormant*, and the issue male of the
                  grantee became probably extinct, in which case the title vested and
still vests in the EARLS (now DUKES) OF ARGYLL [S.].(b)

*   *   *   *   *

ACHESON, or ATCHISON

cr 1 Jan 1628, *sealed* 8 Aug 1631 ;(d)

afterwards, since 1776, BARONS GOSFORD [I];

since 1785, VISCOUNTS GOSFORD [I];

and since 1806, EARLS OF GOSFORD [I]

I. 1628.   SIR ARCHIBALD ATCHISON [*or* ACHESON], of Market Hill,
                  in Clonekearney, or Glencairny, co. Armagh, "Secretaire," some-
time styled " of Monteagle," eldest s of Captain Patrick ACHESON, a cadet of the family of Acheson, of East Lothian,(e) was *b* in Edinburgh, but having settled in Ireland, as early as 1610, was (with his son, Patrick), made a denizen of Ireland, 12 Feb 1618. Being a zealous supporter of the Protestant interest there, he obtained large grants of land in Armagh and Cavan, acquiring others by purchase from his br Sir Henry ACHESON, of Dromleck, co Armagh He was made a Master in Chancery [I] 27 June 1621 (being admitted to King's Inn, Dublin, 16 Nov following), which post he resigned when made a Lord of Session [S] in 1627. He was for many years Secretary of State for Scotland, which office he held till his death He was *Knighted* at Theobald's, 1 April 1620, was M P [S] for Haddington Constabulary, 1625, and was *cr a Baronet* [S.], 1 Jan. 1628, sealed 8 Aug. 1631,(d) but not recorded in the Great Seal Register, with rem to heirs male whatsoever, and with a grant of, presumably, 16,000 acres in Nova Scotia, of which, apparently, he never had seizin.(f) He *m* firstly, in or before 1610, Agnes VERNOR, of Edinburgh He *m.* secondly, 1622, Margaret, da and h of the Hon. Sir John [not(e) George] HAMILTON (2d s. of Claude, 1st LORD PAISLEY [S.], by Johanna (afterwards BARONESS SEMPILL [S]), da. of Levinus EVERARD, of Mechlin, Counsellor of State She was living Aug 1629   He *d* at the house of Sir William Sempill, at Letterkenny, co. Donegal, 9 Sep. and was *bur* 8 Oct. 1634, at Mullaghbracke, co. Armagh Funeral cert. [I.], 4 June 1635 Admon [I.], 1634

II. 1634   SIR PATRICK ACHESON, Baronet [S 1628], of Market Hill
                  aforesaid, s and h by 1st wife, was (with his father) made a
denizen of Ireland, 12 Feb 1628 ; *suc to the Baronetcy*, Oct 1634 He *m* in 1634

(a) Banks's Lists.

(b) Much of the information in this article was supplied by R R. Stodart, Lyon Clerk Depute (1863-86).

(c) Katherine, his 1st da and coheir, *m* in 1696, Alexander Russell, of Moncoffer

(d) Milne's List, Laing's List. In the "Lords' Entries," at the Office of Arms, Ireland, the grantee is spoken of as having been " created Baronet by Privy Seal in the year 1620, and in the year 1628 created Knight and Baronet of Nova Scotia," and the Arms of the 1st Lord Gosford are depicted as surrounded by the ribbon and badge of a Baronet of Nova Scotia, *and charged* [also] *with the hand of Ulster,* thus implying that the grantee had a Baronetcy [E or I and S] before the creation of 1628

(e) This and much else of the information in this article has been kindly given by G D Burtchaell, of the Office of Arms, Dublin

(f Banks's Lists.

Martha, only child of William [not John] MOORE, *or* MORE, of Loudon, one of the Clerks of the Signet in ordinary. He *d* *s p m* 6 Oct 1638, in his 28th year, and was *bur* 24th at St. Martin's in the Fields, Middlesex Funeral certificate Admon 26 June 1639 granted to a creditor His widow *d.* at St Margaret's, Westm , and was *bur* 21 Feb. 1674/5, at St Martin's aforesaid Admon 6 March 1694/5, to George More, cousin and next of kin.

III 1685 SIR GEORGE ACHESON, Baronet [S 1628], of Market Hill aforesaid, br of the half-blood and h., being s of the 1st Baronet by his 2d wife ; *bap* 4 Aug 1629, at Edinburgh ,(a) *suc to the Baronetcy*, 6 Oct 1638 ; Sheriff for counties of Armagh and Tyrone, 1657 He *m* firstly, (—) sister of Jane, Countess of Mountrath [I], da of Sir Robert HANNAY, 1st Baronet [S 1629], of Mochrum, by (—), da. of (—) STEWART He *m* secondly, 3 Nov. 1659, Margaret, 3d da of William (CAULFEILD), 2d BARON CHARLEMONT [I], by Mary da. of Sir John KING He *d* 1685 Will dat. 10 March 1684, pr 17 Nov. 1685 [I], directing his burial to be at Mullaghbracke.

IV 1685. SIR NICHOLAS ACHESON, Baronet [S 1628], of Market Hill aforesaid, s and h by 1st wife , *suc to the Baronetcy*, 1685 , Sheriff of co Armagh 1695 , M P. [I.] for the same, 1695-99. He *m* 1686, Anne, sister of Sir Thomas TAYLOR, 1st Baronet [I 1704], only da of Thomas TAYLOR, of Kells, co Meath, by Anne, da. of William AXTELL, of Berkhampstead, Herts He *d* 1701 Will dat 8 Nov. 1701, pr 1702 [I] The will of his widow dat 23 June 1739, pr 1743 [I.].

V. 1701. SIR ARTHUR ACHESON, Baronet [S 1628], of Market Hill aforesaid, s and h , *b* 26 Jan 1688 , *suc to the Baronetcy*, 1701 , entered Trin Coll, Dublin, 25 May 1705, aged 17 , B A 1707 , M P [I] for Mullingar, 1727, till death , Sheriff of co Armagh, 1728 He *m* 1715, Anne, only da and h of the Rt. Hon Philip SAVAGE, Chancellor of the Exchequer in Ireland, by Mary, his wife She was *bur* 1 Nov 1737, at St. Audoen's, Dublin He *d* 8 Feb 1748/9, and was *bur* in the family vault at Mullaghbracke, co Armagh M l. Will dat 23 Nov 1748, pr. 1749 [I.]

VI 1749. SIR ARCHIBALD ACHESON, Baronet [S 1628], of Market Hill aforesaid, 3d but 1st surv. s and h ,(b) *b* 1 and *bap* 29 Sep 1718 , *suc to the Baronetcy*, 8 Feb 1748/9 , was (previously) M P [I] for the Univ of Dublin, 1741 60, for co Armagh, 1761 and 1768, and for co Enniskillen (for a few months), in 1776 , Sheriff of co Armagh, 1751 , of co Cavan, 1761 , Dep. Gov of co Armagh, 1756-61 , P C [I], 7 May 1770 He *m* in 1740, Mary, da of John RICHARDSON, of Rich Hill, co Armagh, by Anne da of William BECKETT, 2d Serjeant at Law [I.] She was living when he was *cr* 20 July 1776, BARON GOSFORD(c) OF MARKET HILL, co Armagh [I], and subsequently, 20 June 1785, VISCOUNT GOSFORD OF MARKET HILL, co Armagh In this peerage this *Baronetcy* then merged, and still so continues, the 2d Viscount being *cr*. 4 Feb 1806, EARL OF GOSFORD [I] See *Peerage*.

(a) Bap. as son of Sir Archibald Acheson, and Margaret HAMILTON
(b) His two elder brothers, Nicholas and Philip, *d* young, and were *bur* 12 Jan 1716/7, and 22 May 1727, at St Audoen's, Dublin
(c) In the "Lords' Entries" (see p 334, note "d "), the 1st Baronet is called " of Gosford in Scotland " The estate of Gosford in East Lothian was for about 65 years possessed by a branch of the family of Acheson of Prestoupans, who were, however, not the lineal ancestors of Sir Archibald, and who, about 150 years before the Barony was created, had alienated the property [*N. & Q* , 2d S x, 99]

MONTGOMERY, *or* MONTGUMRY ·

cr 1 or 10 Jan, sealed 22 Dec 1628 ,(ᵃ)

dormant, since 14 Jan 1735

I　1628　　Sɪʀ Rᴏʙᴇʀᴛ Mᴏɴᴛɢᴏᴍᴇʀʏ, *or* Mᴏɴᴛɢᴜᴍʀʏ, of Skelmoihe,
s. of Rᴏʙᴇʀᴛ Mᴏɴᴛɢᴏᴍᴇʀʏ, of the same, by Dorothy, da of Robeit
(Sᴇᴍᴘɪʟʟ), 3d Lᴏʀᴅ Sᴇᴍᴘɪɪʟ [S], was 5th in male descent from Geoige Mᴏɴᴛɢᴏᴍᴇʀʏ,
of Skelmoihe (d 1505), 2d s of Alexander, 1st Lᴏʀᴅ Mᴏɴᴛɢᴏᴍᴇʀʏ [S], suc his father
in 1583, was *Knighted* by James I, and *ci a Baronet* [S] 10 or 1 Jan , sealed 22 Dec
1628,(ᵃ) the patent being not recorded in the Great Seal Registei, with rem to heirs
male whatsoevei, and with a grant of, presumably, 16,000 acres in Nova Scotia, of
which he had seizin in Dec 1628 (ᵇ) He was M P [S] for Buteshire, 1644 He *m*
Margaret, 1st da of Sir William Dᴏᴜɢʟᴀs, of Drumlannig, by Margaret, da of Sir
James Gᴏʀᴅᴏɴ, of Lochinvar She *d* 1624 He *d*. Nov 1651, having had 67 years'
tenure of the family estate

II.　1651　　Sɪʀ Rᴏʙᴇʀᴛ Mᴏɴᴛɢᴏᴍᴇʀʏ, Baronet [S 1628], s. and h ,
suc to the Baronetcy in Nov 1651 He *m* Mary, 4th da of
Archibald (Cᴀᴍᴘʙᴇʟʟ), 7th Eᴀʀʟ ᴏғ Aʀɢʏɪʟ [S], by his 1st wife, Anne, da of William
(Dᴏᴜɢʟᴀs', Eᴀʀʟ ᴏғ Mᴏʀᴛᴏɴ [S.]. He *d*. befoie 22 May 1654 (ᶜ)

III　1654.　　Sɪʀ Rᴏʙᴇʀᴛ Mᴏɴᴛɢᴏᴍᴇʀʏ, Baronet [S 1628], of Skelmorlie aforesaid, s and h , *suc to the Baronetcy* in or before May
1654 He *m* Anna, da and coheii of Sir James Scott, of Rossie, co Fife, by
Antonia Wɪʟʟᴏʙɪᴇ, his wife He *d* 7 Feb 1684 (ᵈ)

IV.　1684　　Sɪʀ Jᴀᴍᴇs Mᴏɴᴛɢᴏᴍᴇʀʏ, Baionet [S 1628] of Skelmorlie
aforesaid, 1st s and h , *suc to the Baronetcy*, 7 Feb 1684 , was M P
[S] foi Ayrshire, 1689-93 (till unseated 28 April 1693 for not signing the assurance),
being one of the Deputies from the Parl. [S] to present the Crown to William and
Maiy He, howevei, afterwards, though a Protestant, joined the Court of the exiled
James II at St Germains He *m* (contract 14 Sep 1678) Margaret, 2d da of James
(Jᴏʜɴsᴛᴏɴᴇ) Eᴀʀʟ ᴏғ Aɴɴᴀɴᴅᴀɪᴇ [S], by Harriet, da of William (Dᴏᴜɢʟᴀs), 1st
Mᴀʀǫᴜᴇss ᴏғ Dᴏᴜɢʟᴀs [S] He *d* in London, Sep 1694.

V　1694　　Sɪʀ Rᴏʙᴇʀᴛ Mᴏɴᴛɢᴏᴍᴇʀʏ, Baronet [S 1628], of Skelmorlie
aforesaid, s and h ; *suc. to the Baronetcy*, Sep 1694 : was Gov of a
garrison in Ireland He *m* Fiances, 1st da. of Col Francis Sᴛɪʀʟɪɴɢ,(ᵉ) by
Agnes, da of Robeit Mᴜʀʀᴀʏ, of Blackbarony He *d* s p m (ᶠ) 15 Aug 1731, at
Limeiick His widow *d* at Skelmorlie 9 June 1759

(ᵃ) Miloe's List ; Laing's List, in which last the date is given as the 10th.

(ᵇ) Banks's Lists

(ᶜ) At that date a commission issued for seiving his son Robert as heii to the
deceased's father, Sir Robert, the elder This was done, 26 July 1654, as to the
small property of Oimshench, to which probably the 2d Baronet nevei made up his
title. There are no seivices to the property of Skelmoiie *Ex infoim* , Sii J Balfour
Paul, Lyon, who refers to Fraser's *Memoir s of the Montgomei ies*, vol i, p. 161

(ᵈ) "Was a gentleman of an exceeding fair reputation foi honoui, virtue and
integrity " [Wood's *Douglas Peeraqe of Scotland*]

(ᵉ) This Francis was 2d s of James, who was grandson of Sir Archibald Stirling,
of Keir

(ᶠ) Lilias, 1st of his three daughters and coheirs became, eventually, the heir to the
consideiable estates of her great uncle, the 5th Baronet She was seived his heir, of
tailhe, 28 Aug 1735. She *m* , 11 June 1735, her cousin, Alexandei Montgomeiy, of
Coylsfield, co Ayr, great grandson of Alexander, 6th Earl of Egliuton [S] She
obtained an Act of Parl. in 1759 to enable her to sell her estates, co Reiifrew, and
purchase lands near hei husband's estates co Ayr She *d* 18 Nov , her husband
dying 28 Dec 1783 Their s and h , Hugh, on 30 Oct. 1796, became Earl of
Eglinton [S.]

'I. 1731,   SIR HUGH MONTGOMERY, Baronet [S 1628], of Skelmorlie
    to   aforesaid (which he had purchased from his nephew), uncle and h.
   1735.   male, being 3d s of the 3d Baronet, was a merchant at Glasgow,
               and sometime Provost of that city, M.P. thereof [S], 1702-07, and
G B.] 1707-08, being one of the Commissioners for the treaty of the Union [S];
tector of the Univ. of Glasgow, 1724, *suc to the Baronetcy* in Aug. 1731 He *m.*
contract 26 Aug 1687) Lilias, da of Peter GEMMEL, Merchant and Baillie of
Glasgow, by Christian, da of William BOYD, of Portincross He *d s p.* 14 Jan.
735, "at his house," when the *Baronetcy* became *dormant*, but the estates devolved,
under an entail made in 1728, on his great niece and heir of line, Lilias, 1st da. of
he 5th Baronet (ª)

SANDILANDS

cr. 10 Jan 1628 ,(ᵇ)

dormant or *extinct* soon afterwards

A *Baronetcy* [S.] is said to have been conferred 10 Jan 1628(ᵇ) on
'(—) SANDILANDS," but no further particulars are known No grant or seizin of
ands in Nova Scotia is recorded.(ᶜ)

HALYBURTON:

cr. 10 Jan. 1628 ;(ᵇ)

dormant or *extinct* soon afterwards.

[. 1628,   JAMES HALYBURTON, of Pitcur, co Forfar, s. of (—)
    to   HALYBURTON, of the same, a descendant of Walter HALYBURTON
  1660?   (2d s. of Walter, 1st LORD HALYBURTON OF DIRLETOUN [S]), who
               acquired Pitcur 1432, by marriage with Cathaiine, da and coheir of
Alexander CHISHOLM, of Pitcur, was *cr. a Baronet* [S], 10 Jan 1628,(ᵇ) but no
seizin of any lands in Nova Scotia is recorded.(ᶜ) The *Baronetcy*, presumably,
became *dormant* or *extinct* at or soon after the death of the grantee.(ᵈ)

INNES:

cr. 12 Jan. 1628 ,(ᵉ)

dormant in 1817;

but assumed since that date

1628   ROBERT INNES, of Balveny, co. Banff, and of Innermarkie,
          s and h. of Robert INNES, of Innermarkie aforesaid, by Margaret, da
f William INNES, of Innes, co Moray, suc his father, 1584, and, having acquired

---

(ª) See p 336, note " f."
(ᵇ) Laing's List (where it is " given on the authority of former Lists "), but not in
Milne's List, nor in the *Registrum Preceptorum Cartarum pro Baronettis Novœ Scotiœ.*
(ᶜ) Banks's Lists.
(ᵈ) James Halyburton, of Pitcur, M P for Forfarshire [S.], 1702-07 and [G.B]
707-08, who was, presumably, the representative of the family, was not a Baronet
Agatha, da. and h of James Halyburton, of Pitcur, *m* (as his 1st wife) in or before
731, James (Douglas), Earl of Morton [S.], and *d* 12 Dec 1748, being ancestress
f the succeeding Earls
(ᵉ) Milne's List, where it is added " not recordit [i e, not in the Great Seal Register]
ut is in Denmill's List " The date of the creation as given in Playfair's
Baronetage [S] is 12 Feb. 1631, but on what authority is unknown

in 1615 the Barony of Balveny, got a charter of the same under the great seal, and was *cr* a *Baronet* [S] as "of Balveny," 12 Jan 1628,(ª) with rem. to heirs male whatsoever,(ᵇ) such creation, however, not being recorded in the Great Seal Register [S]

II.   1650?   SIR WALTER INNES, Baronet [S 1628] of Balveny, s
                    and h , *suc to the Baronetcy* on the death of his father   He *m*
Lilias, da of Sir John GRANT, of Grant, by Mary, da of Walter (OGILVY), LORD
OGILVY OF DESKFORD [S]   Being a zealous Royalist, he so encumbered his estate
that he had to join with his son in selling the estate of Balveny soon after the
Restoration

III   1670?   SIR ROBERT INNES, Baronet [S 1628], s and h , who
                    jointly with his father sold the estate of Balveny, on whose death
he *suc to the Baronetcy*   He *d* unm

IV.   1680?   SIR GEORGE INNES, Baronet [S 1628], of Denoon, cousin
                    and h. male, being s and h of Col James INNES, a yr s of
the 1st Baronet, was in Holy Orders of the Church of Rome, and *suc. to the
Baronetcy* on the death of his cousin   He *d* unm

V.   1690?   SIR JAMES INNES, Baronet [S 1628], of Ortoun, cousin
                    and h male (grand-nephew of the 1st Baronet), being s and h of
Walter INNES, of Ortoun, by Margaret, da of Sir James HAMILTON, of Elstou,
which Walter was s and h of William Innes of Kinnermony, yr br of the 1st
Baronet, *suc to the Baronetcy* about 1690   He *m* in or before 1703, Margaret, da
of Thomas FRASER, of Cairnbuddy   He *d* 1722

VI   1722   SIR ROBERT INNES Baronet [S 1628], s, and h , *b.*
                    about 1703, *suc to the Baronetcy* in 1722   He was sometime a
private soldier, but afterwards an officer in a regiment of Dragoons (ᵈ)   He *m*
Margaret, da of Col (—) WINRAM   He *d* s p m ,(ᶜ) 31 Aug 1758, at Elgin,
aged 55   His widow *d* 30 Sep 1765

VII.   1758   SIR CHARLES INNES, Baronet [S 1628], br and h male,
                    b about 1704, sometime Capt 71st Foot , *suc to the Baronetcy* in
1758   He *m* Isabel da and h of (—) PATON, of Kinnaldie   He *d* s p m s (ᵈ)
8 April 1768, aged 64, and was *bur* at St Marylebone, M I   Will pr April
1768 (ᵉ)

VIII   1768,   SIR WILLIAM INNES, Baronet [S 1628], br and h. male,
        to   sometime Capt in the 2d Regt of Light Dragoons, *suc to the
        1817   Baronetcy*, 8 April 1768   He *m* firstly, Sarah, da and h of Thomas
                    HODGES, of Ipswich   She *d* at Ipswich, s p m , 15 May 1770   He
m secondly, 22 March 1774, Mary Maria, da and h of Major (—) PARSONS, of the
city of York, by whom he had no issue   He *d* s p m 1817, when the issue male
of the grantee appears to have become extinct and the *Baronetcy dormant*   Will
pr 1817   The admon of his widow (as of "Nottingham") May 1819

(ª) See p 337, note " e "
(ᵇ) There is no notice in Banks's Lists of any grant or seizin of land in Nova Scotia
to this grantee
(ᶜ) Catharine, his only da and h , *m* James (Forbes) 17th Lord Forbes [S],
and *d* 16 April 1805
(ᵈ) See an account of his romantic career in Anderson's *Scottish Nation*
(ᵉ) His only son John *d* unm before him
(ᶠ) The admon 2 Nov 1769 of " Dame Isabel Innes, of Killswell, co Aberdeen,
widow," may possibly apply to her, but more probably is that of a widow of " Sir
John Innes, Baronet," who *d* at Aberdeen in Nov 1768   It was granted to
" Sir Alexander Gordon, Baronet, now residing in Aberdeen, cousin german and
next of kin "

The Baronetcy was assumed as under.

IX   1817.   SIR JOHN INNES, Baronet [S 1628],(a) of Edengight, co Banff, said to be heir male of the grantee, being, presumably, s and h of John Innes, of Edengight (d 6 June 1796), and stated to be a lineal descendant of John INNES, of Edengight, said to have been a great uncle of the 1st Baronet (b)   He was b 23 June 1757, and *assumed the Baronetcy* apparently without service or proof of pedigree, in 1817   He m 1796 Barbara, 3d da of George FORBES, son of Sir John FORBES of Monymusk   He d 23 March 1829 at Aberdeen, aged 71

X   1829.   SIR JOHN INNES, Baronet [S 1628],(c) of Edengight aforesaid, s and h, b about 1801, *suc to the Baronetcy*(a) 23 March 1829   He d s p 2 Dec 1838, aged 37

XI   1838   SIR JAMES MILNE INNES, Baronet [S 1628],(a) of Edengight aforesaid, hr and h, b there 24 Feb 1808, *suc to the Baronetcy*(a) 2 Dec 1838 (c)   He m 4 April 1837, Elizabeth, da of Alexander THURBURN, of Keith   He d 11 May 1878 at Edengight house, aged 70   His widow d 29 April 1899

XII   1878   SIR JOHN INNES, Baronet [S 1628],(a) of Edengight aforesaid, s and h, b 25 Nov 1840, was a magistrate at Christchurch, New Zealand, where he engaged in sheep farming, *suc to the Baronetcy*(a) 11 May 1878, Vice-Lieut of Banffshire

CAMPBELL.

cr. 12 or 24 Jan, and sealed 23 Dec 1628 ;(d)

dormant, apparently, in 1812,

but assumed in or before 1828, and again since 1841

I   1628.   SIR DUGALD CAMPBELL, of Auchinbreck, s and h of Duncan CAMPBELL, of Auchinbreck and Castlewenc, by Mary (m 1567), da and h. of William MACLEOD, of Dunvegan, was b about 1570, *Knighted* by James I, and was cr a Baronet 12 or 24 Jan, sealed 23 Dec 1628,(d) but not entered in the Great Seal Register [S], with rem to heirs male whatsover, and with a grant of, presumably, 16,000 acres in Nova Scotia, of which he had seizin in Dec 1628 (e)   He was a Royalist   He m firstly, Mary, sister of Thomas, 1st VISCOUNT FENTOUN [S], 3d and yst da of the Hon Sir Alexander ERSKINE, of Gogar, by his first wife Margaret, da of George (HOME), LORD HOME [S]   He m secondly, Isabel BOYD   He d, at an advanced age, 1641

(a) According to the assumption in 1817

(b) No such person, however, is mentioned in Douglas' *Baronage*.

(c) In the Baronetage given in Lodge's *Peerage*, 1845, there is this note to "Innes of Balvenie" [1628], ' The name of the Baronet of Balvenie is not inserted because the gentleman who at present bears the title does not appear to be the nearest male heir of the first Baronet "

(d) Milnes' List, Laing's List, in which latter the date is 12, though it is given as 24 Jan 1628 in the former, where, however, it is added that "Denmill sayes 12 Jan 1628 "

(e) Banks's Lists.

II. 1641.   SIR DUNCAN CAMPBELL, Baronet [S. 1628], of Auchin-
                breck aforesaid, 2d but 1st surv. *s.* and h. by first wife; was
M.P. [S.] for Argyllshire 1628-33, 1639-41, and 1643, taking part with the Parl.
against the King; serving on a Committee of Supply 1641, in which year he *suc.*
to the Baronetcy; was in command of a Regiment in Ireland. He *m.* firstly,
Margaret, da. of Brice BLAIR, of Blair. She *d. s.p.* He *m.* secondly (—) da. of
(—) MAXWELL, of Newark. He *m.* thirdly, after Aug. 1628, Jean, Dow. BARONESS
CATHCART [S.], da. of Sir Alexander COLQUHOUN, of Luss, by Helen, da. of Sir
George BUCHANAN. He was slain in 1645 fighting against Montrose's army, at
Inverlochy. His widow *m.* the Hon. Sir William HAMILTON, Resident in Rome
for the Queen Dow., Henrietta Maria.

III. 1645.   SIR DUGALD CAMPBELL, Baronet [S. 1628], of Auchin-
                breck aforesaid, s. and h. by second wife; *suc. to the Baronetcy* in
1645, as also to the command of his father's regiment in Ireland, receiving 10,000
marks in recognition of his late father's service. He, however, resigned his command and declared for the King. He was M.P. [S.] for Argyllshire, 1649. He *d.*
unm. soon after the Restoration.

IV. 1661?   SIR DUNCAN CAMPBELL, Baronet [S. 1628], of Auchin-
                breck aforesaid, nephew and h., being 1st s. and h. of Alexander
CAMPBELL, of Knockemelie, by (—), da. of Colin CAMPBELL, of Calder, which
Archibald was br. of the half blood to the late Baronet, being s. of the 2d
Baronet by his 3d wife. He *suc. to the Baronetcy* about 1661. He was forfeited
in 1686, but restored shortly afterwards; was M.P. [S.] for Argyllshire 1689 till,
probably, his death, having, however, in 1698, become a Roman Catholic. He *m.*
in or before 1679, Harriet, 3d da. of Alexander (LINDSAY), 1st EARL OF
BALCARRES [S.], by Anne da. and coheir of Colin (MACKENZIE), 1st EARL OF
SEAFORTH [S.]. He *d.* in or before 1700.

V. 1700?   SIR JAMES CAMPBELL, Baronet [S. 1628], of Auchin-
                breck aforesaid, s. and h., b. about 1679; *suc. to the Baronetcy* in
or before 1700; was M.P. [S.] for Argyllshire 1702-07 and [G.B.] 1707-08. He
m firstly, Janet, 2d da. of John MACLEOD, of Macleod, by Florence, da. of Sir
James MACDONALD, 2d Baronet [S. 1625], of Slate. He *m.* secondly, Susanna,
da. of Sir Archibald CAMPBELL, of Calder. He *m.* thirdly, Margaret, da. of
(—) CAMPBELL, of Carradale. He *d.* at Lochgair, co. Argyll, 14 Oct. 1756, aged 77.

VI. 1756,   SIR JAMES CAMPBELL, Baronet [S. 1628], of Auchin-
to   breck aforesaid, grandson and h., being only s. and h. of Duncan
1812.   CAMPBELL, by Jean, da. of Alexander CLERK, of Glendoik, which
                Duncan was 1st s. and h. by the 1st wife of the late Baronet,
but *d. v.p.* He *suc. to the Baronetcy* 14 Oct. 1756; was sometime Capt. 49th Foot.
He *d. s.p.* 1812, when, apparently, the Baronetcy became *dormant.*

VII. 1820?   SIR THOMAS CAMPBELL, Baronet([a]) [S. 1628],
                whose parentage is unknown, assumed the title on the
death of Sir James,([b]) and was apparently living 1828.([b])

                *   *   *   *   *

VIII.([c]) 1841.   SIR JOHN EYTON CAMPBELL, Baronet,([a]) [S. 1628],
                of Kildalloig, near Campbelltown, co. Argyll, "*assumed*
the title in 1841,"([d]) having "caused legal proceedings to be taken and proofs
made out showing himself to be heir male general of the Auchinbreck

([a]) According to the assumption of that title.
([b]) Burke's "Peerage" of 1828, as quoted in Foster's *Baronetage* (*Chaos,*
p. 694), where it is added that "in the edition [thereof] of 1841 the 7th Baronet is
omitted, and in 1846 the pedigree also, which, however, re-appears in 1856."
([c]) This numbering is according to the assumption of the title in 1841, in
which the then Baronet's father, Dugald Campbell, would have been the *de jure*
7th Baronet, 1812-34.
([d]) Burke's *Baronetage* for 1901.

family, and he accordingly as such took up the title."(ª)   He was s. and h.
of Dugald CAMPBELL, of Kildalloig aforesaid, Deputy Keeper of the Privy
Seal of Ireland, by Catharine KINGSLEY (d. 29 Dec. 1832) his wife, which
Dugald (b. in or before 1780 and d. April 1834, having, apparently, declined
to assume the Baronetcy which would have devolved on him in 1812 on
the death of the 6th Baronet, said to be his father's first cousin) was s.
and h. of John CAMPBELL, of Kildalloig, said to be s. of Dugald CAMPBELL,
the 2d s. (by 1st wife) of the 5th Baronet.(ᵇ)   He was b. 22 May 1809,
Advocate [S.] 11 March 1831, and by the death of his father in April 1834,
suc. to such right as his father had to the Baronetcy, but (as above stated)
did not assume the title till 1841.   He m. 29 April 1841, Charlotte, yr. da.
of Louis Henry FERRIER, of Belsyde, co. Linlithgow.   He d. 9 Dec. 1853,
at Gibraltar, aged 44.   His widow, m. 16 Oct. 1855, James GARDINER, of
Haughhead, Sheriff substitute of Argyllshire (who d. 8 Dec. 1879), and
was living 1901.

IX.(ᶜ)   1853.   SIR LOUIS HENRY DUGALD CAMPBELL, Baronet,(ª)
            [S. 1628], of Kildalloig aforesaid, 1st s. and h., b. 2 March
1844, suc. to the Baronetcy(ᵈ); was an officer in the Royal Navy.   He m.
3 Aug. 1870, at Canterbury Cathedral, Mary Ellen Edith (then aged 20),
da. of Harry George AUSTIN, of the Archbishop's Palace, Canterbury.
He d. s.p. 18 June 1875, at Kildalloig.   His widow d. there 26 Sep. 1879,
aged 30.

X.   1875.(ᶜ)   SIR NORMAN MONTGOMERY ABERCROMBY CAMP-
            BELL, Baronet(ᵈ) [S. 1628], of Nelson, in New Zealand,
br. and h., b. 2 March 1846; suc. to the Baronetcy,(ᵈ) 18 June 1875.   He m.
19 May 1886, Isabella Sara, widow of George COTTERELL, da. of Jerome
CARANDINI, MARQUIS DI SARZANO.

CAMPBELL :

cr. 15 Jan., and sealed 23 Dec. 1628 ;(ᵉ)

extinct 1651 ;

but *assumed*, since 1804.(ᶠ)

I.   1628,   SIR DONALD CAMPBELL, of Ardnamurchan, co. Argyll,
     to   and also, by purchase, of Airds in that county, illegit. s. of Sir
     1651.   John CAMPBELL, of Calder, " being a man of considerable power
            and consequence, and the terror of the district in which he lived ;"(ᶠ)
was cr. a Baronet [S.] 15 Jan., sealed 23 Dec. 1628, but not recorded in the
Great Seal Register [S.], with rem. to heirs male whatsoever, and with a grant of,
presumably, 16,000 acres in Nova Scotia, of which he had seizin in Dec. 1628.(ᵍ)

(ª) Burke's *Baronetage* for 1871.   It is not, however, stated therein whether
any legal *decision* on these " proceedings " was given.
    (ᵇ) The 5th Baronet (who d. 1756 aged 77) had no less than eight sons, *viz.*,
Duncan (whose male issue was extinct in 1812) and Dugald, by his 1st wife ;
James, Gilbert, Alexander, and William, by his 2d wife ; and James and Donald
by his 3d wife.   No dates of death, marriage or other particulars appear to be
known of any of them save the eldest.
    (ᶜ) See p. 340, note "c."
    (ᵈ) See p. 340, note " a."
    (ᵉ) Milne's List.
    (ᶠ) Playfair's *Baronetage* [S.], where, however, the date of creation is given as
14 June 1628.
    (ᵍ) Banks's Lists.

He obtained a new enfeoffment of Airds and other his estates, 28 Aug. 1643, with rem. to George CAMPBELL, s. of Sir John CAMPBELL, of Calder, the legit. s. of his [the Baronet's] father. He m. firstly, Jane, da. of Colin (CAMPBELL), 6th EARL OF ARGYLL [S.], by, presumably, his 2d wife, Agnes, da. of William (KEITH), EARL MARISCHAL [S.]. He m. secondly, Anne CAMPBELL, illegit. da. of the said Earl. He d. s.p.m.s., 1651, when the *Baronetcy* became *extinct*, and the estate of Ardnamurchan passed to the Earls of Argyll [S.], but that of Airds devolved, under the entail of 1643, to the abovenamed George CAMPBELL.

After the lapse of 150 years this Baronetcy was assumed, as below, on the ground that, together with the settlement of the Airds estate, 28 Aug. 1644, there had been a regrant of the Baronetcy with a similar remainder.

VII.([a]) 1804.   SIR JOHN CAMPBELL, Baronet([b]) [S. 1628], who assumed that dignity in 1804, was only s. and h. of John CAMPBELL, of Aird saforesaid, sometime an officer in the Scots Greys, by Jane, da. of Archibald CAMPBELL, of Storesfield, which John (who obtained a charter in 1791 as heir to his deceased father), was 1st s. and h. of Donald CAMPBELL, of Airds (1734), s. and h. of Alexander CAMPBELL, of Airds (1711), s. and h. of John CAMPBELL, of Airds, sometime a Capt. in the army (d. before 1711), s. and h. of George CAMPBELL abovementioned, who inherited the estate of Airds, under the settlement of 1643, (on the death, in 1651, of the 1st Baronet), and who obtained in 1652 a confirmation thereof from the Marquess of Argyll [S.] to him and his heirs male.([c]) He was b. 15 March 1767, was in 1804 served heir male([d]) to Sir Donald CAMPBELL, the 1st Baronet, of Ardnamurchan, and, accordingly, then *assumed the Baronetage*.([c]) He was Lieut. Col. of the Argyllshire and Bute Militia. He m. 27 July 1803, Margaret Maxwell, 6th da. of John CAMPBELL, of Lochend. He d. 7 Nov. 1834. His widow d. 19 Aug. 1865 at Woolwich in her 89th year.

VIII.([a]) 1834.   SIR JOHN CAMPBELL, Baronet([b]) [S. 1628], of Airds aforesaid, only s. and h., b. 27 Nov. 1807; Advocate [S.], 1831; *suc. to the Baronetcy*,([b]) 7 Nov. 1834; Lieut. Gov. of St. Vincent's, 1845, till his death in 1853. He m. 21 Nov. 1833, Hannah Elizabeth, da. of James MACLEOD, of Rasay. He d. 18 Jan. 1853 at Kingstown, in St. Vincent's. Will pr. Aug. 1855. His widow m. Henry MAULE, of Twickenham, who survived her, and d. 4 Nov. 1873.

IX.([a]) 1853.   SIR JOHN WILLIAM CAMPBELL, Baronet([b]) [S. 1628], of Airds aforesaid, b. 3 March 1836; *suc. to the Baronetcy*([b]) 18 Jan. 1853; served in the Crimean campaign, 1854-55, serving in the trenches before Sebastopol; in the China war, 1860; in Afghanistan, 1878-80; and the Zhob Valley Expedition, 1884; was 2d Capt. in the Artillery, 1861, becoming finally, 1885, Col. and Hon. Major; C.B., 1888. He m., 24 July 1867, at Stoke Damarel, Devon, Catherine Lyona Sophia, only da. of W. Woolby CAVIE, of Harwood House in Tamerton Foliott, near Plymouth.

([a]) This is according to the numbering that would have been if his five immediate ancestors (as given in the text) had *suc. to the Baronetcy* on the death of the grantee in 1651, when the first of them suc. to his estate of Airds.

([b]) According to the assumption of that dignity in 1804.

([c]) Playfair's *Baronetage* [S.], where there is the advantage of a few dates to elucidate this descent, such being wholly wanting in the descent (at variance herewith) given in Burke's *Baronetage* of 1901. In that work Sir John is made s. and h. of Donald, s. of Alexander, s. of John, s. of George Campbell, all of Airds aforesaid, the said George being the successor of the 1st Baronet in that estate.

([d]) This service, accordingly, implies that there can be a lawful heir to a bastard, other than one of his own descendants.

HOPE

cr. 19 Feb and sealed 3 May 1628 ;([a])

sometime, 1730 ? to 1766, BRUCE-HOPE.

I. 1628   THOMAS HOPE, of Craighall, co Fife, one of the sons of Henry HOPE, of Edinburgh, merchant to France and Holland, by Jacquehne DE TOI, a native of France, was admitted Advocate [S] 1605, and, having greatly distinguished himself the next year by his able defence of the six Ministers impeached for treason, obtained a very lucrative practice and purchased estates in the counties of Fife, Stirling, Midlothian, Haddington, and Berwick, was, in May 1626, joint, and in April 1628 sole Lord Advocate [S], and was *cr a Baronet* [S] 19 Feb, sealed 3 May 1628,([a]) with rem to heirs male whatsoever, and with a grant of, presumably, 16,000 acres in Nova Scotia, of which he had seizin in May 1628 ([b]) He held office till his death, contriving to avoid any serious rupture with either King or Parl He was P C [S] 1641, and was Lord High Commissioner at the meeting of the General Assembly of the Church [S], 2 Aug 1643, being the only Commoner that was ever so appointed He *m* in or before 1605, Elizabeth, da of John BINNING, of Wallyford, co Haddington, by whom he had fourteen children She was living April 1625 He *d* 1 October 1646.

II. 1646.   SIR JOHN HOPE, Baronet [S 1628], of Craighall aforesaid, *b* about 1605 ,([c]) was M A of Edinburgh Univ, 14 July 1621, incorp at Oxford, 3 July 1622, and at Cambridge, 1623, was *Knighted* 1632 when made a Lord of Session [S], under the designation of *Lord Craighall*, was one of the Committee of 1640 to oppose the King's measures, was P C [S] 1645, *suc to the Baronetcy,* 1 Oct 1646, was, in May 1652, one of Cromwell's Committee of Justice, and sometime President thereof, M P in "Barebone's Parl.," 1653 He *m*, in or before 1632, Margaret, 1st da of Sir Archibald MURRAY, 1st Baronet [S 1628] of Blackbarony, by Margaret, da of (—) MAULE He *d* 28 April 1654, at Edinburgh

III. 1654   SIR THOMAS HOPE, Baronet [S 1628], of Craighall aforesaid, 1st s and h, *b* 11 Feb 1633, *suc to the Baronetcy* 28 April 1654 He *m* Elizabeth, da of Sir John AYTOUN, of Aytoun, co Fife He *d* before 26 March 1663, on which date his widow *m* John GIBSON, of Durie, co Fife, sometimes, erroneously, considered a Baronet [S 1628]

IV. 1660 ?   SIR THOMAS HOPE, Baronet [S 1628], of Craighall aforesaid, s and h, *suc to the Baronetcy* on the death of his father He *m* Anne, sister and (after 1687) heir of Sir John BRUCE, 2d Baronet [S 1668] of Kinross, only da of Sir William BRUCE, 1st Baronet [S 1668] of Balcaskie, co Fife, by his 1st wife Mary, da of Sir James HALKETT, of Pitfirran His will is recorded 22 Sep 1686, at St Andrews' Commissariat She survived him, and *m* Sir John CARSTAIRS, of Kilconquhar.

V. 1686 ?   SIR WILLIAM HOPE, Baronet [S 1628], of Craighall aforesaid, 1st s and h, *suc to the Baronetcy* on the death of his father He *d* unm. in the lifetime of his mother His will is recorded 7 April 1707, as above.

([a]) Milne's List and Laing's List These agree as to dates, but in the former the grantee is incorrectly called " Sir James," and in the latter "Master *Thomas* Hope, of Craighall, King's Advocate

([b]) Banks's Lists

([c]) He was eldest of three brothers, all of whom were Lords of Session [S]. Of the two younger (1) Sir Thomas Hope, of Kerse, Col in the army of the Covenanters and a Lord of Session [S], was ancestor of the Baronets [S 1672] of Kerse, and (2) Sir James Hope, also a Lord of Session [S], was ancestor of the Baronets [S. 1698] of Kirkliston and of the Earls of Hopetoun [S. 1703]

VI. 1707 ?   SIR WILLIAM HOPE, *afterwards* BRUCE-HOPE, Baronet
[S 1628], of Craighall aforesaid, br and h , *suc to the Baronetcy*
on the death of his brother, and, subsequently, to the estate of Kinross on the
death of his mother, when he took the name of BRUCE before that of HOPE
He sold the estate of Craighall in 1729 to the Earl of Hopetoun [S] He *d*
unm between 1734 and 1741

VII   1740 ?   SIR JOHN BRUCE HOPE, Baronet [S 1628], of Kinross
aforesaid, formerly JOHN HOPE, br and h , was an officer in the
Army and sometimes in command of a regiment of Foot, becoming, eventually,
1758, Lieut -General, was Governor of Bermuda, 1721-27, M P for Kinross-
shire, 1727-34 (being then " of Culdraines "), and subsequently 1741-47, *suc to*
the Baronetcy about 1740, when he took the name of BRUCE, before that of HOPE
He *m* firstly, Charlotte, 6th da of Sir Charles HALKETT, 1st Baronet [S 1662]
of Pitfirran, by Janet, da. of Sir Patrick MURRAY, of Pitdennis He *m* secondly,
in 1706, Marianne, da of the Rev William DENUNE, of Pencaitland, East
Lothian   He *d* s p m s (a) 5 June 1766

VIII   1766.   SIR THOMAS HOPE, Baronet [S. 1628], of Rankeillor,
cousin and h male, being 2d but 1st surv s and h of Sir
Archibald HOPE, of Rankeillor aforesaid, by Margaret, da of Sir John AYTOUN,
of Aytoun, which Archibald, who was a Lord of Session [S], 1689, under the
designation of *Lord Rankeillor*, and who *d* 10 Oct 1706, aged 67, was yr s of
the 2d Baronet   He was admitted Advocate [S], 8 July 1701 , was M P [S] for
Fifeshire 1706-07, *suc to the Baronetcy*, when very old, 5 June 1766   He was a
great agriculturist and in his honour *Hope Park*, near Edinburgh, was so named
He *m* 16 March 1702, Margaret, 1st da of James LOWIS, of Merchiston   He *d*
17 April 1771

IX. 1771.   SIR ARCHIBALD HOPE, Baronet [S 1628], of Rankeillor
aforesaid, grandson and h , being only surv s and h of Archibald
HOPE " the younger, of Rankeillor," by Catherine, 1st da of Hugh TOD, D D ,
Dean of Carlisle, which Archibald, who *d* v p , was s and h ap of the late
Baronet   He was *b* 1735 , was Sec to the Board of Police [S] for life, *suc to the*
Baronetcy, 17 April 1771, purchased in 1778 the estate of Pinkie, in Midlothian,
from the Marquess of Tweeddale [S]   He *m* firstly, in 1757, Elizabeth, da of
William MACDOWALL, of Castle Sempill   She *d* 12 Oct 1778   He *m* secondly, in
1779, Elizabeth, da of John PATOUN, of Inveresk, by Jean, da of George DOUGLAS,
of Friarshaw   He *d* 10 June 1794   His widow *d* 1818

X. 1794   SIR THOMAS HOPE, Baronet [S 1628], of Pinkie aforesaid, 1st surv s and h by 1st wife, *b* 1768, *suc to the Baronetcy*,
10 June 1794   He *m* 1792 Hester, da of (—) PIERCE   He *d* s p , 1801

XI   1801   SIR JOHN HOPE, Baronet [S 1628], of Pinkie aforesaid, br of the half blood and h being s of the 9th Baronet, by
his 2d wife   He was *b* 13 April 1781 at Pinkie house , *suc to the Baronetcy* in
1801, Lieut Col Commandant of the Midlothian Yeomanry Cavalry, 1843   M P for
Edinburgh (three Parls) 1845 till death   Vice Lieut and Convenor of that county
He *m* 17 June 1805, at Ballindean, co Perth, Anne, da of " Sir " John WEDDER-
BURN, who, save for the attainder of 1736 would have been 6th Baronet [S 1704],
by his 2d wife Alicia, da of James DUNDAS, of Dundas   He *d* 5 June 1853 in
his 73d year, in Gloucester terrace, Hyde Park   His widow *d* 17 March 1867, at
67 Cadogan place.

XII. 1853   SIR ARCHIBALD HOPE, Baronet [S 1628], of Pinkie
aforesaid, 1st s and h , *b* 28 Feb 1808 at Pinkie house , admitted
Advocate [S] 1829, *suc to the Baronetcy*, 5 June 1853, Lieut Col of the

—————————————————————

(a) Anne, his only surv child (by his 2d wife) the heir of line of the family of
Bruce of Kinross, did not inherit the estates of that family which passed to that
of Carstairs, the heirs *male* of the body of Dame Anne Hope (the heiress of
the Bruce family) by her 2d husband, Sir John Carstairs

Midlothian Militia, 1856-77 He *m* 17 July 1862 at St Peter's, Pimlico, Aldina, 1st da. of Henry Robert KINGSCOTE, of Eaton Place He *d* *s p* 24 Jan 1883 in his 75th year, at Pinkie house Will pr July 1883 over £13,000 His widow living 1901

XIII. 1883 SIR JOHN DAVID HOPE, Baronet [S 1628], of Pinkie aforesaid, br and h, *b* 27 April 1809 at Pinkie house, *d* there unm, 14 July 1892, aged 83

XIV. 1892 SIR WILLIAM HOPE, Baronet [S 1628], of Pinkie aforesaid, br and h, *b* 12 July 1819, entered the army, 1835, serving with the 71st Highlanders in the Crimea, 1855-56 (receiving the Order of the Medjidie), and in Central India, 1858, commanding the 71st foot in 1863 at Ensofyzie, becoming eventually, 1881, Lieut General and General (retired), **C B**, 1859, *suc to the Baronetcy* 14 July 1892, **K C B**, 1897 He *m* 22 Jan 1862 at Keith house, East Lothian, Alicia Henrietta, 1st da of Sir John WEDDERBURN, 2d Baronet [1803], by Henrietta Louisa, da of William MILBURN, of Bombay He *d* *s p* 5 April 1898 at Pinkie house aforesaid in his 80th year His widow *d* 19 June 1901, at 9 Albert Hall Mansions, S W Will pr at £13,498 personalty

XV. 1898 SIR ALEXANDER HOPE, Baronet [S 1628], of Pinkie aforesaid, br and h, being 7th s of the 11th Baronet, *b* 22 Oct 1824, served in the Bengal Civil Service, 1845-75, *suc to the Baronetcy,* 5 April 1898

SKENE

cr 22 Feb 1628, [a]

extinct, or *dormant*, since about 1680

I. 1628 SIR JAMES SKENE, of Curriehill, President of the College of Justice [S], s and h of Sir John SKENE, of the same, Lord Clerk Register [S], by Helen, da of Sir John SOMERVILLE, of Carnnethan, suc his father in 1617, and was *cr a Baronet* [S], 22 Feb 1628, [a] the "patent, which is not dated," being recorded in the Register of Signatures, 16 Jan 1630 [b] No grant or seizin of lands in Nova Scotia is recorded [c] He *m* 7 Dec 1603, Janet, da of Sir John JOHNSTON, of Hilton He *d* at Edinburgh, 10 Oct 1633, and was *bur* at the Grey Friars there

II 1633, SIR JOHN SKENE, Baronet [S 1628], of Curriehill afore-
to said, only s and h, *suc to the Baronetcy* 20 Oct 1633 He, in
1680? 1637, sold the estate of Curriehill and levied a regiment, which he commanded in the Imperial service He *d* apparently s p in Germany, when the *Baronetcy* (of which the limitation is unknown) became *extinct* or *dormant* [d]

---

[a] Laing's List (where it is "given on the authority of former lists"), but not in Milne's List, or in the *Registrum Preceptorum Cartarum pro Baronettis Novæ Scotiæ*

[b] Burke's *Extinct Baronetage*

[c] Banks's Lists

[d] "Sir John Skeane, of Greenock, Baronet," died at Edinburgh 16 and was *bur* 28 April 1693, in the King's Chapel of Holyrood house [Funeral entries at Lyon office] Possibly this was a successor (perhaps, indeed, a son) of the 2d Baronet Gilbert Skene, of Pollerton, co Aberdeen, Professor of Medicine in King's College, Aberdeen (who was living 1597, and who was yr br of Sir John Skene, father of the grantee), left a large family, among whose issue the heir male of the Baronetcy probably exists, the issue male of the two yr brothers of the 1st Baronet being extinct [Burke's *Commoners*, vol iv, 476]

2 v

PRESTON

cr 22 Feb 1628,(ª)

dormant since 1791 or 1792.

I 1628   JOHN PRESTON, of Airdrie, in the parish of Crail, co Fife, and of Penicuik, co Edinburgh, s and h of John PRESTON,(ᵇ) of Penicuik aforesaid, sometime Lord President [S], by the last of his many wives, "Margaret Collace, Lady Muretoun," relict of Walter REID, Abbot of Kinross, da of (—) COLLACE,(ᶜ) suc his father, 24 June 1616, was Solicitor Gen [S], 1621 and was *cr a Baronet* [S], 22 Feb 1628,(ª) as "of Airdrie," with rem to heirs male whatsoever, such creation, however, not being entered in the Great Seal Register [S] No grant or seizin of lands in Nova Scotia is recorded (d) He sold the estate of Penicuik He m before 1613, Elizabeth, only da and h of William TURNBULL, of Airdrie aforesaid and of Thomastoun She was served heir to her father in 1614 and d 1623 He m secondly, Agnes, da of John LUNDIN, of that ilk, by Margaret DURIS He was living 1652 His widow d 1668

II 1655?   SIR JOHN PRESTON, Baronet [S 1628], of Airdrie aforesaid, s and h by his last wife, had spec service to his mother and her father, 15 July 1640, in various lands, co Fife, and, subsequently, *suc to the Baronetcy* on the death of his father He m (see a charter in Great Seal Register) Christina AYTOUN He is also said to have m Susanna, da or sister of Ninian MACMARRAN of Newhall He also m , 29 April 1652 (contract 26 March 1652), Margery, widow of Sir James SCOTT, of Scotstarvit, da of John (CARNEGIE), 1st EARL OF NORTHESK [S], by his 1st wife, Magdalen, da of Sir James HALYBURTON He d at Cupar, 10 June 1660 The will of "Sir John PRESTON, Baronet," is pr 1663

III. 1660   SIR JOHN PRESTON, Baronet [S 1628], of Airdrie aforesaid, s and h , *suc to the Baronetcy*, 10 June 1660, and had spec service to his father, 3 March 1663, in the Barony of Airdrie, etc That estate, however, he sold in 1673 He m 20 Nov 1670, Jean, 1st da of Sir James LUMSDEN, of Innergallie, co Fife, with 12,000 merks as her tocher He d March 1675 The will of "Dame Elizabeth PRESTON" is pr 1698

IV. 1675   SIR JOHN PRESTON, Baronet [S 1628], of Prestonhall (a mansion on the estate of Thomastoun abovenamed), co Fife, s and h , *suc to the Baronetcy* in March 1675, and had spec service to his father, 30 Jan and 25 March 1701 in Thomastoun, Castlefield, etc He m 16 Feb 1692, Margaret, da of John (ELPHINSTONE), 4th LORD BALMERINO [S], by his 1st wife, Christian, da of Hugh (MONTGOMERY), EARL OF EGLINTON [S]

*   *   *   *   *   *   *

The holding of this Baronetcy from 1701 to 1784 is uncertain

V? 1784, to 1791, or 1792   SIR ROBERT PRESTON, Baronet(ᵉ) [S 1628], presumably son or nephew of the above, was b about 1706, was a graduate at the Univ of St Andrew's 1724, Minister of Arbirot, 1731, of Cupar, 1758 , was served in 1784 "heir male and of line general to his grandfather, Sir John PRESTON, Baronet, of Airdrie," and, accordingly, then *assumed the Baronetcy* He m firstly, (—),

(ª) Laing's List, Milns's List in which it is remarked "no document but Denmill's List "

(b) Much of the information in this article was supplied by R R Stodart, Lyon Clerk Depute [1863-86], and Francis J Grant, Rothesay Herald

(ᶜ) She survived him, but d 25 Sep 1617 Another wife was Elizabeth Hawsyde, who d 1 Oct 1583, another is said to have been (—) Scott, and another Lilias Gilbert

(d) Banks's Lists

(ᵉ) According to the service of 1784

he *m.* secondly, Margaret, da. and eventually coheir of Robert SPEID, of Ardovie, co. Forfar. He *d.* in his 86th year (being then "Father of the Church of Scotland"), 1 May, or Sep. 1791 or 19 Oct. 1792. His widow *d.* at Dundee Aug. 1,794. He had two sons, George and Alexander, but whether they survived him is unknown. After his death the *Baronetcy,* presumably, became *dormant.*

GIBSON :
said (apparently in error) to have been cr. 22 Feb. 1628.([a])

I. 1628.   ALEXANDER GIBSON, of Durie co. Fife, s. and h. of George GIBSON, of Goldingstones, Clerk of Session [S.], by Elizabeth, da. of (—) AIRTH, was himself made Clerk of Session [S.] 14 Dec. 1594; purchased the estate of Grantoun, co. Edinburgh, 1603, and subsequently the fine estate of Durie, including the town and harbour of Leven, in 1614, and other lands, all erected into the Free Barony of Durie; and was a Senator of the College of Justice [S.], 10 July 1621, being designated "LORD DURIE," and was L. President of the Court of Session [S.], 1642. On 22 Feb. 1628, he had sasine from Sir William Alexander of the Barony of Durie in Anticosti, Canada,([b]) perhaps *with a view to being created a Baronet,* but, apparently, no such creation followed. Lord Durie's "Practicks" or decisions, 1621-1642, were published in 1690. He *m.,* 14 Jan. 1596, Margaret, da. of Sir Thomas CRAIG, of Riccarton, co. Edinburgh, a celebrated feudal lawyer. He *d.* at Durie 10 June 1644, and was *bur.* 24 July, at Scoonie.

II. 1644.   SIR ALEXANDER GIBSON, sometimes considered a Baronet([a]) [S. 1628], of Durie aforesaid, s. and h.; was Clerk of Session [S.], 25 July 1632; *Knighted* 15 March 1641. Lord Clerk Register [S.], 13 Nov. 1641; had spec. service to his father, 26 Sep. 1644. Senator of the College of Justice [S.], 2 July 1646, but deprived 13 Feb. 1649. Was a strong anti-covenant man. He *m.* in 1625, Cecilia, da. of Thomas FOTHERINGHAM, of Powrie, co Forfar. He *d.* June 1656.

III. 1656.   SIR ALEXANDER GIBSON, sometimes considered a Baronet([a]) [S. 1628], of Durie aforesaid, s. and h.; M.P. 1659 for the shires of Fife and Kinross [S.], 1661 till death; P.C. [S.] April 1661. He *m.,* 10 June 1651, Marjory, da. of Andrew (MURRAY), 1st Lord BALVAIRD [S.], by Elizabeth, da. of David (CARNEGIE), 1st EARL OF SOUTHESK [S.] He *d* s.p.m.,([c]) of fever, at Durie, 6 Aug. 1661, in his 32d year. His widow *d.,* also of fever, at Perth, 10 Aug. 1667.

IV. 1661.   JOHN GIBSON, sometimes considered a Baronet([a]) [S. 1628], of Durie aforesaid, br. and h., was served 5 Aug. 1662, br. and h. male general and of entail to Sir Alexander GIBSON, *Knight,* in the Baronies of Durie, Largo, etc. In May 1662 he sold Largo to Sir

---

([a]) This creation is omitted in Milne's List, though inserted in Laing's List as "given on the authority of former lists." No such creation, however, is entered in the *Registrum Preceptorum Cartarum pro Baronettis Novæ Scotiæ,* and it is remarked by R. R. Stodart [Lyon Clerk Depute, 1863-86] that the long line of Knights and the grant in 1628 of land in Nova Scotia led to the error of *supposing a creation of Baronetcy* in that year, but that, in point of fact, the only Baronetcy [S.] granted to the name of Gibson is the one cr. 31 Dec. 1702.
([b]) No seizin of this territory is recorded in Banks's Lists.
([c]) Anne, his only da. and h., *m.* John Murray, of Touch Adam, co Stirling, and *d.* 1720, leaving issue.

Alexander Durham, for 85 000 marks   About 1673, he reg arms in the Lyon Office, *not*, however, assuming the title of "Sir," and *without* the Baronet's badge   He *m* 26 March 1663, Elizabeth, widow of Sir Thomas HOPE, 3d Baronet [S 1628], of Craighall, da of Sir John AYTOUN, of that ilk, co Fife   He *d* before 1698

V   1697 ?   ALEXANDER   GIBSON, sometimes considered a Baronet(ᵃ) [S 1628], of Durie aforesaid, s and h   Had general service to his father (neither of them being therein styled "Sir"), 26 April 1698   He *m* (—) da of John MURRAY, of Polmaise and Touch Adam, co Stirling   He *d* s p , at Edinburgh, 30 Jan 1699   Will pr 14 April 1699 [S]

VI   1699   SIR   JOHN   GIBSON, sometimes considered a Baronet(ᵃ) [S 1628], of Pentland, co Edinburgh, cousin and h male, being s and h of Sir Alexander Gibson, of Pentland aforesaid, a Principal Clerk of Session [S], by Helen, da of Sir James FLEMING, of Rathobyres, which Alexander (who *d* 1693) was s and h of Sir John GIBSON, of Pentland aforesaid, also a Clerk of the Session [S], who was 2d s of Sir Alexander GIBSON, of Durie who (as above stated) was supposed to have been *cr a Baronet* [S] in 1628   He was *Knighted* in or before 1690, was Depute Clerk Register [S], 1696 to 1700   On 7 Sep 1693 he was served heir spec of his father in the Barony of Lamerton, etc, co Berwick , on 16 March 1696, served his heir general, and on 4 April 1699, served heir male of entail in Durie, and of provision general and special to his cousins, John Gibson and Alexander Gibson, both of Durie   He sold the estate of Durie(ᵇ) about 1700   He *m* 3 Nov 1687, Elizabeth, da of Lewis CRAIG, of Riccarton   He *d* 13 May 1704

VII   1704   ALEXANDER   GIBSON, sometimes considered a Baronet(ᵃ) [S 1628], of Pentland aforesaid, s and h , suc his father 13 May 1704, when a minor, and was served heir gen to him 4 April 1705, and heir special in Pentland, Boghall, and Alderston, co Edinburgh   By the death, 2 June 1727, of his cousin, Sir Edward Gibson, 2d Baronet [S 1702], he *suc to the Baronetcy* [S] which had been conferred on his great uncle, Thomas GIBSON, of Keirhill, co Edinburgh, 31 Dec 1702   See that dignity

---

FRASER, *or* FRAZER
cr on or before 15 March 1628 ,(ᶜ)
afterwards, since 1669, LORDS SALTOUN [S.]

I. 1628.   "ALEXANDER   FRAZER, of Philorth, is *designated* Baronet [S], 15 March 1628, but [in] no other document,"(ᶜ) and no such creation is in the Great Seal Register, and no grant or seizin of lands in Nova Scotia is recorded (ᵈ)   He was s and h of Sir Alexander FRASER, of Philorth aforesaid (who succeeded thereto 17 Dec

---

(ᵃ) See p 347, note "a "
(ᵇ) The purchaser was his br Alexander Gibson, Principal Clerk of Session [S], who *d* 1 March 1729, leaving John Gibson his s and h , who built the present (1901) house at Durie, and *d* 18 Jan 1787, leaving two sons · (1), Alexander Gibson, of Durie, who *d* 13 May 1785 (when that estate was sold), leaving a s and h , John GIBSON-CARMICHAEL, who *suc*, as 6th Baronet, *to the Baronetcy* [S] of Gibson, *cr* 31 Dec 1702 [see that dignity], and (2), William Gibson, Merchant of Edinburgh, whose 2nd s , James GIBSON-CRAIG, of Riccarton, co Midlothian, was *cr a Baronet*, 30 Sep 1831
(ᶜ) Milne's List   No such Baronetcy is given in Laing's List.
(ᵈ) Banks's Lists

1624) by his 1st wife Margaret, da of George (ABERNETHY), LORD SALTOUN [S] was b March 1604, suc his grandfather in certain lands (under some special trust), of which he was enfeoffed in 1628, was in command of a regiment raised to rescue Charles I in 1648, advanced large sums to Charles II when in Scotland, and fought and was wounded on his side at the battle of Worcester, in 1651, was M P [S] for Aberdeenshire, 1643, 1648, and 1661-63 He m firstly, Isabel, da of William FORBES, of Tolquhoun She d s p m He m secondly, Elizabeth, da and h of Alexander SETON, of Meldrum She, presumably, was living, when, soon after the death s p of his maternal cousin Alexander (ABERNETHY), LORD SALTOUN [S], in 1669, he was served heir of line to his maternal grandfather abovenamed and the said peerage being confirmed to him by patent dat 11, ratified by Parl [S] 21 July 1670, he became LORD SALTOUN [S], in which peerage all right to this *Baronetcy* then *merged*, and still so continues

---

STEWART

cr, apparently, in or before March 1628 ,([a])

afterwards, 1628-1861, LORDS STEWART OF TRAQUAIR [S],

and *subsequently*, 1633-1861, EARLS OF TRAQUAIR [S],

dormant 2 August 1861

I   1628?   SIR JOHN STEWART, of Traquair, co. Peebles, s and h. of John STEWART (who d v p), by Margaret, da of Alexander STEWART, Master of Ochiltree suc his grandfather, James STEWART, of Traquair, 9 May 1606, was M P [S] for Peebles, 1621-25, being *Knighted* about the same date, and was *cr a Baronet* [S], apparently in or before March 1628 ([a]) He was *cr*, 19 April 1628, LORD STEWART OF TRAQUAIR [S] and, subsequently, 23 June 1633, EARL OF TRAQUAIR [S] In those peerages this *Baronetcy* then *merged*, till on the death, 2 Aug 1861, of the 8th Earl, all his dignities became *dormant*

CRAWFURD, *or* CRAUFORD ;

cr 14 May 1628([b]) ,

dormant from 1662 to 1765 ,

sometime, 1820-85, CRAWFURD-POLLOK ,

again dormant since 1885

I   1638   JOHN CRAWFURD, of Kilbirnie, co Ayr, 1st s and
to   h of John CRAWFURD of the same, by Mary da of James (CUN-
1662 ;   INGHAM), 7th EARL OF GLENCAIRN [S], was cr a Baronet [S], 14
         May 1628([b]) with, presumably, rem to heirs male whatsoever([c]),
but the creation is not in the Great Seal Register or in the *Registrum Preceptorum*

([a]) The creation, without date, is given in Milne's List, "Sir John Steuart of Traquair, no document thairfoir, bott ditto Balfour," not in the Great Seal Register It is also in Beatson's List, where the date given is 1629 No grant or seizin of land in Nova Scotia is recorded

([b]) This date is given in Laing's List " on the authority of former lists " The creation, *without date*, is given in Milne's List, where it is added that " Mr Crawfurd in his *history of Renfrew* sayes he was made a Barronet in anno 1642 and he is so designed in the Lyon office "

([c]) The devolution of the title, according to service of 1765, assumes such a limitation.

Cartarum pro Baronettis Noæe Scotæ, neither is there record of any grant or seizin of lands in Nova Scotia(ᵃ)   He commanded a Regiment of Foot on behalf of the King during the Civil War, but lived in retirement during the Commonwealth was M P [S] for Ayrshire, 1644 and (being then designated as a *Knight*) 1661 till his death   He *m* firstly Margaret, 2d da of Margaret, *suo jure* BARONESS BALFOUR OF BURLEIGH [S], by Robert ARNOT, *afterwards* BURLEIGH, LORD BALFOUR OF BURLEIGH [S]   She *d s p*   He *m* secondly Magdalen, widow of Sir Gideon BAILLIE of Lochend, 1st da and coheir of David CARNEGY, *styled* LORD CARNEGY (s and h ap of David, 1st EARL OF SOUTHESK [S]) by Margaret, da of Thomas (HAMILTON), 1st EARL OF HADDINGTON [S]   He *d s p m*,(ᵇ) in 1662, having by deed dat 31 July 1662 settled his estate on Margaret, his 2d and yst. da and coheir and her issue   On his death the *Baronetcy* became *dormant*

*   *   *   *   *   *   *

The Baronetcy continued dormant for above a hundred years when it was assumed as under

II.(ᶜ) 1765   SIR HEW CRAWFURD, Baronet(ᶜ) [S 1628], of Jordanhill co Renfrew, s and h of Hew CRAWFURD, of the same, by Mary, da of the Rev James GREENSHIELDS, Rector of Finnough, co Tipperary, which Hew (who *d* 8 Feb 1756) was s and h of James CRAWFURD, Sheriff Depute of Renfrewshire (*d* 1695), 2d s of Hew CRAWFURD, s and h ap (*d v p*) of Cornelius CRAWFURD of Jordanhill aforesaid (*d* 1687), s and h of Hew CRAWFURD, of the same (1586-1621), 2d s of Thomas CRAWFURD, also of Jordanhill (*d* 1603), who was yr br of Hugh CRAWFURD, of Kilbirnie, ancestor of the 1st Baronet, both being sons of Laurence CRAWFURD, of Kilbirnie, who *d* 1547, aged 41   He suc his father 8 Feb 1756, and was served his heir 8 Dec 1756   On 19 July 1765, he was served, by the Sheriff of Edinburgh and a special jury, heir male of the 1st Baronet, and, consequently, *assumed the Baronetcy*   He *m* Robina, only da and h of Capt John POLLOK, of Balgray, by Ann, da of John LOCKHART, of Lee, which John Pollok was 3d s of Sir Robert POLLOK, 1st Baronet [S 1703], of Nether Pollok, co Renfrew   He *d* 1 July 1794   His widow, who, on the death of Jean POLLOK, spinster in 1807, inherited the estates of the Pollok family, took the name of *Pollok*, and *d* 1820   Her admon, as "of York," Aug 1828

III (ᶜ) 1794   SIR ROBERT CRAWFURD, *afterwards* CRAWFURD-POLLOK Baronet(ᶜ) [S 1628], of Pollok Castle, co Renfrew, s and h, *b* 1762, sometime Capt in the army, *suc to the Baronetcy*(ᶜ) 1 July 1794   On the death of his mother (to whose estates he *suc*) in 1820, he took the name of *Pollok*, in addition to that of *Crawfurd*   He *m*, before 1810, (—), only da of (—), MUSHET, M D, of York, Physician Gen to the army in Germany   He *d s p*, 7 Aug. 1845, at Edinburgh   Will pr Dec 1845

IV (ᶜ) 1845   SIR HEW CRAWFURD-POLLOK Baronet(ᶜ) [S 1628], of Pollok Castle aforesaid, nephew and h, being s and h of Hew CRAWFURD, a Capt in the army, by Jane, da of William JOHNSTONE, of Headfort, co Leitrim which Hew (who *d* 25 Dec 1831) was next br of the late Baronet He was *b* 1794 at Taunton, Somerset, *suc to the Baronetcy*(ᶜ) 7 Aug 1845, when he assumed the name POLLOK after that of CRAWFURD   He *m* 1839, Elizabeth Oswald, da of Matthew DUNLOP   He *d* 5 March 1867, in his 73d year, at Pollok Castle   His widow living 1900(ᵈ)

(ᵃ) Banks's Lists
(ᵇ) He had two daughters (1) Ann, *m* Sir Archibald Stewart, 1st Baronet [S 1667] of Blackhall, co Renfrew, and had issue (2) Margaret, *m* 27 Dec 1664 the Hon Patrick Lindsay, *afterwards* Crawfurd, who inherited the Kilbirnie estate, and *d* 1680, his son John being cr 26 Nov 1705 Viscount Garnock and Lord Kilbirnie [S]
(ᶜ) According to the service of 19 July 1765, the numeration, however, here given does not include the persons who would thereunder have been entitled to the Baronetcy between 1662 and 1765
(ᵈ) Dod's *Baronetage*, 1900, omitted in that for 1901.

V.(ᵃ) 1867,   SIR HEW CRAWFURD-POLLOK, Baronet(ᵃ) [S 1628], of
       to   Pollok Castle aforesaid, only s and h , b there 1843, sometime
       1885   Captain in the Renfrew Militia , suc to the Baronetcy(ᵃ) 5 March
                 1867   He m 8 June 1871, Annie Elizabeth GREEN, of Hull, co
York, spinster   He d s p , suddenly, in the coffee room of an hotel at Dover,
14 Dec 1885, when the Baronetcy became dormant   His widow living 1901

RIDDELL

cr 14 May 1628 , sealed 16 Feb 1629(ᵇ),

I   1628   SIR JOHN RIDDELL, of Riddell, co Roxburghe, s and
                 h of Andrew RIDDELL, "Laird of Riddell," M P [S] for Rox-
burghshire, 1617 and 1621, by Violet, da of William DOUGLAS, of Pumpherston,
was, after having been Knighted at an early age, cr a Baronet [S], 14 May 1628,
sealed 15 Feb 1629,(ᵇ) but not recorded in the Great Seal Register, with rem to
his heirs male whatsoever and with a grant of, presumably, 16,000 acres in Nova
Scotia, of which he had seizin, Feb 1629 (ᶜ)   He m firstly, before 30 Sep 1602,
Agnes, 2d da of Sir John MURRAY, of Blackbarony, by his 1st wife, Margaret, da
of Sir Alexander HAMILTON, of Innerwick   He m secondly, before July 1630,
Jane, widow of the Hon James DOUGLAS, Commendator of Montrose (yr s of
William, EARL OF MORTON [S]), da of Sir James ANSTRUTHER, of Anstruther, by
Jean, da of Thomas SCOT, of Abbotshall   By her he had no male issue   Both
were living July 1630, but he d March 1632   Funeral entry in Lyon office

II   1632   SIR WALTER RIDDELL Baronet [S 1628], of Riddell
                 aforesaid, 1st s and h by 1st wife , was M P [S] for Roxburgh-
shire, 1628-33, 1646-47, and 1650 , was Knighted v p before July 1630, suc to the
Baronetcy in March 1632   He m , before July 1630, Jane, da of William RIGGE,
of Althenrie, or Aithernie (near Edinburgh, but in), co Fife, a great supporter
of the Presbyterian Clergy   He d about 1669

III 1669?   SIR JOHN RIDDELL, Baronet [S 1628], of Riddell
                 aforesaid, 1st s and h , suc to the Baronetcy on his father's death ,
was M P [S] for Roxburghshire, 1690 till death   He, m 1687, got a remission
for treason from James 11   He m firstly, 1 Dec 1659, Agnes, sister of Walter,
EARL OF TARRAS [S], 1st da of Sir Gideon SCOTT, of Highchester, by Margaret,
da of Sir Thomas HAMILTON, of Preston   She d s p   He m secondly, Nov 1661,
Helen, da of Sir Alexander MORISON, of Preston Grange, by Jean, da of Robert
(BOYD) 6th LORD BOYD [S]   He m thirdly, Oct 1669, Margaret, da of Sir John
SWINTON, of Swinton   She d at Edinburgh 4 and was bur 6 March 1699, in the
Grey Friars   Funeral entry, displaying her seize quartiers, in Lyon office   He
d at Edinburgh 1 April 1700

IV   1700   SIR WALTER RIDDELL, Baronet [S 1628], of Riddell
                 aforesaid, 2d but 1st surv s and h by 2d wife, b 1664 , suc to the
Baronetcy 1 April 1700   He m , 18 April 1692, Margaret, da of Adam WATT, of
Rosehill, near Edinburgh   He d 27 April 1747

V   1747   SIR WALTER RIDDELL, Baronet [S 1628], of Riddell
                 aforesaid, 1st s and h , b 1695 , suc to the Baronetcy, 27 April
1747   He m , 1724/5, Jane, da of John TURNBULL, of Houndwood   She d before
1744   He d 13 May 1765

(ᵃ) See p 350, note " c "
(ᵇ) Milne's List and Laing's List
(ᶜ) Banks's List

VI 1765 SIR JOHN RIDDELL, Baronet [S 1628], of Riddell aforesaid, 2d but 1st surv s and h, b 1726, *suc to the Baronetcy* 13 May 1765 He *m*, in 1762, Jane, sister and, in 1772, heir to Archibald BUCHANAN, of Sundon, Beds, 1st da of James BUCHANAN, of Sundon aforesaid, Merchant and Banker of London He *d* 16 April 1768 at Hampstead Will pr Aug 1768 His widow *d* 24 Feb 1798

VII 1768 SIR WALTER BUCHANAN RIDDELL, Baronet [S 1628], of Riddell aforesaid, 1st s and h, b 1763, *suc to the Baronetcy*, 16 April 1768 He *d* unm 16 Jan or 7 Feb 1784, at Launestoun Admon July 1789

VIII 1784 SIR JAMES BUCHANAN RIDDELL, Baronet [S 1628], of Riddell aforesaid, br and h, b 1765, was Lieut in the 1st Foot Guards, *suc to the Baronetcy* early in 1784, matric arms in the Lyon office, 20 March 1784, and *d* unm, a few months afterwards, 4 Sep 1784, at Brunswick, being drowned while bathing Admon July 1789

IX. 1784 SIR JOHN BUCHANAN RIDDELL, Baronet [S 1628], of Riddell aforesaid, br and h b 1768, adm to Lincoln's Inn, 27 May 1784, *suc to the Baronetcy* 4 Sep 1784, was M P for Linlithgow burghs (two Parls) 1812 till his death He *m* 17 Aug 1805, Frances, 1st da of Charles (MARSHAM), 1st EARL OF ROMNEY, by Frances, da of Charles (WYNDHAM), 2d EARL OF EGREMONT He *d* 26 April 1819, aged 50 His widow, who was *b* 26 Oct 1778, *d* 30 June 1868, in her 90th year, at the Palace Maidstone

X 1819 SIR WALTER BUCHANAN RIDDELL, Baronet [S 1628], of Hepple, near Rothbury, co Northumberland, 1st s and h, b 8 Aug 1810, at Ramsgate, *suc to the Baronetcy* 26 April 1819, ed at Eton, matric at Oxford (Ch Ch) 14 June 1828, aged 17, B A 1831, M A 1834; Barrister (Lincoln's Inn) 1834, Recorder of Maidstone 1846-68, Judge of the County Courts of North Staffordshire, 1859-62, and of the Whitechapel County Court, 1862-80 He *m* 18 Aug 1859, at St James, Westm, Alicia da of William RIPLEY, Lieut 52d Light Infantry He *d* s p 27 Aug 1892, at Henham Hall, Suffolk His widow living 1901

XI. 1892 SIR JOHN WALTER BUCHANAN RIDDELL, Baronet [S 1628], of Hepple aforesaid, nephew and h, being 1st s and h of the Rev John Charles RIDDELL, M A, Rector of Harrietsham, co Kent, and Hon Canon of Canterbury, by Frances Sophia, da of George James CHOLMONDELEY, Receiver Gen of Excise, which John, who *d* 2 March 1879, aged 64, was next br to the late Baronet He was *b* 14 March 1849, at Harrietsham, ed at Eton, matric at Oxford (Ch Ch) 12 June 1867, aged 18, B A 1872, M A 1899, Barrister (Inner Temple) 1874, *suc to the Baronetcy*, 27 Aug 1892 Sheriff of co Northumberland, 1897, and County Councillor for the Harbottle division He *m* 4 Aug 1874, Sarah Isabella, da of Robert WHARTON, Barrister

Family Estates —These, in 1883, appear to have been under 2,000 acres *Principal Residence* —Hepple, near Rothbury, co Northumberland

---

MURRAY ·

cr 15 May, and sealed 25 Aug 1628 ([a])

I 1628 SIR ARCHIBALD MURRAY, of Blackbarony, co Peebles, 2d but 1st surv s and h of the seven sons of Sir John MURRAY, of the same, M P [S] for Peebles-shire, 1608 and 1609, by his 1st wife Margaret, da of Sir Alexander HAMILTON, of Innerwick, had charter of lands, v p, 13 Aug 1607 and 21 Dec 1613, being then "of Darnhall", was *Knighted* by James I when young, was M P [S] for Peebles-shire, 1617 and 1625, and was *cr a Baronet* [S] 15 May, sealed 25 Aug 1628,([a]) but not recorded in the Great Seal

([a]) Laing's List. Milne's List, in which last it is stated that "Denmill says 19 May 1628"

Register, as " of Blackbarony," with rem to heirs male whatsoever, and with a grant of, presumably, 16,000 acres in Nova Scotia, of which he had seizin in Oct 1628 (a) He m before 1617, Margaret MAULE He d before 1 March 1634

II. 1634? SIR ALEXANDER MURRAY, Baronet [S 1628], of Blackbarony aforesaid, 1st s and h, suc to the Baronetcy before 1 March 1634, was M P [S] for Peebles-shire, 1639-41, being then called "Knight", was fined by Parl 13 April 1646, for services done to the King, but was appointed by Cromwell, Sheriff of co Peebles, 1 Aug 1657 He m firstly, Margaret, da of Sir Richard COCKBURN, of Clerkington He m secondly, Margaret, sister of Sir David MURRAY, of Stanhope, yst da of John MURRAY, of Halymyre, and previously of London, Merchant, by Jonet HOWIESON,(b) of the family of Braehead He d between 1667 and 1669

III 1668? SIR ARCHIBALD MURRAY, Baronet [S 1628], of Blackbarony aforesaid, 1st s and h, was M P for the Sheriffdom of Selkirk and Peebles, 1659, and [S] for Peebles-shire, 1661-63, 1665, 1667 (being then called "the younger"), 1669-74 (being then a Baronet), 1678, 1681-82, 1685-86 and 1689 till death, having suc to the Baronetcy about 1668, was Lieut Col of the Linlithgow and Peebles Militia, 1669, and Master of the Works, etc [S], 1689 He m Mary, widow of Sir James HOPE, of Hopetoun (d 1661), 1st da and coheir of William (KEITH), 7th EARL MARISCHAL [S], by Elizabeth, da of George (SETON), 3d EARL OF WINTON [S] He d shortly before 28 May 1700

IV. 1700? SIR ALEXANDER MURRAY, Baronet [S 1628], of Blackbarony aforesaid, suc to the Baronetcy in or shortly before May 1700, was M P [S] for Peebles-shire, 1700-02, Sheriff Depute of that county, 1732 He m 28 July 1687, Margaret, da of William WALLACE, of Helington Having no issue he, in 1741, entailed the Blackbarony estate on Margaret,(c) the da of his brother, Archibald MURRAY, and, failing her issue, on the family of Murray of Elibank He d s p, 31 Dec 1741 The will of "Dame Margaret Murray, Midx," was pr Sep 1779

V. 1741. SIR WILLIAM MURRAY, Baronet [S 1628], cousin and h male, being s and h of Richard MURRAY, of Spittlehaugh, Lieut Col of the Linlithgow and Peebles Militia, by his 2nd wife, Jean, da of James DAVIDSON, of Edinburgh, which Richard was br of the 3d and 2d s of the 2d Baronet He suc his father in the estate of Spittlehaugh, which he sold in 1738, and subsequently suc to the Baronetcy, 31 Dec 1741 He m in or before 1722 Jane, da of James ALLAN, of Saughlan, co Edinburgh

VI 1760? SIR RICHARD MURRAY, Baronet [S 1628], 1st s. and h, suc to the Baronetcy on the death of his father He d unm 4 Oct 1781

VII 1781 SIR ARCHIBALD MURRAY, Baronet [S 1628], br and h., being 4th and yst s of the 5th Baronet, b about 1726, suc to the Baronetcy, 4 Oct 1781 He m firstly, 4 May 1760, Mary MOORHEAD She d 8 Dec 1779 He m secondly, 27 May 1784, (—), widow of (—) BARRY, of London. He d 23 June 1794, in his 68th year Will pr Aug 1794

(a) Banks's Lists
(b) See *Genealogist*, N S, vol xv, p 198, under "Murray, of Romanno"
(c) This Margaret m John Stewart, of Ascog, who took the name of Murray on inheriting the estate of Blackbarony, but d s p 5 April 1771, when it devolved on the Murrays of Elibank, and was in possession of Alexander Murray, M P for Peebles-shire, 1783-84, who, on 12 Nov 1785, became 7th Lord Elibank [S]

VIII 1794   Sir John Murray, Baronet [S 1628], 2nd but 1st surv.
s and h , by 1st wife, b 27 Jan 1766, sometime an officer in the
46th Foot *suc to the Baronetcy*, 23 June 1794   He *m* 3 Nov 1791, Anne, da of
John Digby, of Sandy lane, co Limerick, by Mary, da and h of R Thompson, of
Cork   He *d* 30 Aug 1809, in London   His widow *d* there 31 May 1818   Will
pr 1818

IX 1809   Sir Archibald John Murray Baronet [S 1628], s and
h b 3 Aug 1792, *suc to the Baronetcy*, 30 Aug 1809, sometime
Lieut Col Scots Fusileer Guards   He *m* 6 Nov 1856, at Cheddon Fitzpaine,
Somerset, Eliza Hope only da of Samuel Unwin, of Manchester   He *d* s p
22 May 1860   His widow *d* 26 Oct 1899 at Arundel Gardens, Kensington park,
aged 83   Will pr at £16,547 personalty

X 1860.   Sir John Digby Murray, Baronet [S 1628] br and
h , b 17 April 1798 , served sometime in the Scots Fusileer Guards,
and was sometime Lieut Col in the army , *suc to the Baronetcy*, 22 May 1860
He *m* firstly, 1 April 1823, Susanna, da of John, or James, Cuthbert   She *d*
3 Dec following   He *m* secondly, 14 June 1827, Frances, 3d da and coheir of
Peter Patten-Bold, *formerly* Patten, of Bold Hall, Lancashire, by Mary, da of
the Rev John Parker, of Astle, co Chester   He *d* 8 May 1881 at Florence, aged
83   His widow *d* there 17 June 1885, in her 86th year

XI 1881   Sir Digby Murray, Baronet [S 1628], 2d but 1st
surv s and h , being 1st s by 2d wife, b 31 Oct 1829 in Hill
street, London , sometime, 1844-49 in the Royal navy, professional member of the
marine department of the Board of Trade, 1873-96 , *suc to the Baronetcy*, 8 May
1881   He *m* 7 May 1861, Helen Cornelia, da of Gerry Sanger, of Utica, U S A
She *d* 8 Aug 1888 at 34, Colville road, W

———

MURRAY

cr 16 May 1628 and sealed 28 Sep. 1630 ,(a)

afterwards, since 1643, Lords Elibank [S]

I 1628   Patrick Murray, of Elibank, co Selkirk, s and h. of
Sir Gideon Murray,(b) of the same, who acquired that estate in
1595, and who was one of the Lords of Session [S] under the style of *Lord
Elibank*, 1613-21, by Margaret Pentland, his wife, was made keeper of the Castle
of Caerlaverock, 27 June 1611, suc his father, 28 June 1621, was M P [S]
for Haddington Constabulary, 1628-33, and 1640-41 , and was *cr a Baronet*
[S], 26 May 1628, sealed 28 Sep 1630, but not recorded in the Great Seal
Register [S], with rem to heirs male whatsoever, and with a grant of, presumably, 16,000 acres in Nova Scotia, of which he had seizin Oct 1630 (c)   He *m*
firstly, in or before 1612, Margaret Hamilton   He *m* secondly, Elizabeth, da of
Sir James Dundas, of Arniston   He *m* thirdly, Agnes Nicholson, who *d* 7 Dec
1637, being (*more Scotiæ*) called *Lady Elibank* in her funeral entry in Lyon's
office   He *m* fourthly, Helen, da of Sir James Lindsay, Gentleman of the Bedchamber   She, presumably, was living when he was *cr*, 18 March 1642/3, Lord
Elibank [S], with rem to his heirs male whatsoever   In that peerage this
Baronetcy then *merged*, and still so continues

———

(a) Laing's List , Milne's List
(b) This Gideon was a yr br of Sir John Murray, of Blackbarony, father of
Archibald, *cr a Baronet* [S] 15 May 1628, whose descendant, the 4th Baronet,
devised that estate to the Elibank family
(c) Banks's Lists.

CADELL

cr. 21 May 1628(ᵃ),

dormant soon afterwards

"[—] CADELL" is said to have been *cr a Baronet* [S], 21 May 1628,(ᵃ) but no further particulars are known of him, and no seizin of land in Nova Scotia is recorded (ᵇ)

MACKENZIE

cr 21 May 1628, sealed 2 Jan 1630,(ᶜ)

sometime 1685-1704, VISCOUNT TARBAT [S.],

and *afterwards*, 1703-04, EARL OF CROMARTY [S]

I   1628   SIR JOHN MACKENZIE, of Tarbat, co Ross, s and h. of Sir Roderick MACKENZIE,(ᵈ) of Cogeach, co Cromarty, and of Tarbat aforesaid, by Margaret, da and heir of Torquil MACLEOD, of Lewis, suc his father in Sep 1626, was, apparently, *Knighted* before 1628, M P [S] for Inverness-shire, 1628-33 and 1639-40, and was *cr a Baronet* [S], 21 May 1628, sealed 2 Jan 1630(ᶜ) but not recorded in the Great Seal Register [S], with rem to heirs male whatsoever, and with a grant of, presumably, 16,000 acres in Nova Scotia, of which he had seizin in March 1630 (ᵇ) He, in 1649, purchased the extensive estate of Cromarty from Sir Robert Innes He *m* in or before 1630, Margaret, da and coheir of Sir George ERSKINE, of Innerteil, co Fife, a Lord of Session [S] under the style of *Lord Innerteil* (1617-46), which George was a yr br of Thomas, 1st VISCOUNT FENTOUN [S] He *d* 10 Sep 1654 His widow *m* Sir James FOULIS, 2d Baronet [S 1634] of Colinton, a Lord of Session and Lord Justice Clerk [S] till his death, 19 Jan 1688

II.   1654   SIR GEORGE MACKENZIE, Baronet [S 1628], of Tarbat and Cromarty aforesaid, 1st s and h, *b* 1630 at Innerteil aforesaid; ed at the Univ of St Andrew's and at King's Coll, Aberdeen, where he graduated, 1646 joined, in 1653, Glencairn's expedition on behalf of Charles II, on defeat of which, 26 July 1654 he fled to the continent, *suc to the Baronetcy*, 10 Sep 1654, was, after the Revolution, the chief confidant of the Earl of Middleton [S], who had the management of Scotch affairs, was M P [S] for Ross-shire, 1661-63, 1678, and 1681-82, was a Lord of Session [S], 1661-64, under the style of *Lord Tarbat*, Lord Justice General [S], 1678-81, and Lord Clerk Register [S], 1681-88 and 1692-96 From 1682 to 1688 he was Chief Director of Affairs for Scotland He, having previously *m* in 1654 (as his 1st wife) Ann, da of Sir James SINCLAIR, Baronet [S 1631], of Canisbay, by Elizabeth, da of Patrick (LESLIE), 1st LORD LINDORES [S], was *cr* by James II, 15 April 1685, VISCOUNT TARBAT, etc [S], being subsequently *cr*, 1 Jan 1702/3, EARL OF CROMARTY [S] In those peerages this *Baronetcy* then *merged* till 1704, when he *resigned the Baronetcy* in favour of his 2d son He *d* 17 Aug 1714, in his 84th year See fuller particulars of him after 1685 in the *Peerage* under "Cromarty"

(ᵃ) Laing's List (where it is "given on the authority of former lists"), but not in Milne's List, neither is the creation enrolled in the *Registrum Preceptorum Cartarum pro Baronettis Novæ Scotiæ*

(ᵇ) Banks's Lists

(ᶜ) Laing's List, Milne's List He is called "Dominus Johannes McKeinzie de Tarbat" in the diploma dat at Whitehall 21 May 1628, as recited in the Diploma of 29 April 1704

(ᵈ) He was yr br of Kenneth, 1st Lord Mackenzie of Kintail [S.], both being sons of Sir Colin Mackenzie, of Kintail

III. 1704   THE HON SIR KENNETH MACKENZIE, Baronet [S 1628], of Cromarty aforesaid and of Grandvale, 2d s (by 1st wife) to whom his father in 1695 had made over the estate of Cromarty He was M P [S] for Cromartyshire (two Parls), 1693-1707 and [G B] 1707-08, 1710-13 and 1727 till death, having been a supporter of the treaty of Union [S] By patent 29 April 1704 he was *cr a Baronet* [S], with rem to heirs male whatsoever, " on his father's resignation(a) as air to Sir John McKenzie, of Tarbet, *with his precedency which is 21 May 1628*,"(b) thus becoming the 3d Baronet of that creation He *m* in 1701, Ann CAMPBELL He *d* 13 Sep 1728

IV 1728   SIR GEORGE MACKENZIE, Baronet [S 1628], of Cromarty and Grandvale aforesaid, s and h, was M P [S] for Ross-shire, 1704-7, and [G B] for Inverness burghs, 1710-13, and for Cromartyshire, 1729-34, was (as "Master George Mackenzie of Inchculter") Provost of Fortrose, *suc to the Baronetcy*, 13 Sep 1728 He became bankrupt, and, consequently, the estate of Cromarty was sold in 1741 to William URQUHART He *m* Elizabeth REID, sister of Capt John REID, of Greenwich He *d* s p, 20 May 1748 His widow *d* 24 Aug 1807, aged 84

V 1748,   SIR KENNETH MACKENZIE, Baronet [S 1628], br and
to   h, *suc to the Baronetcy* in 1748 He *d* s p 14 Sep 1763 Will
1763   pr 1763 On his death the issue male of his grandfather, the 3d Baronet (who obtained the *novodamus* of the Baronetcy 29 April 1704), became extinct, and the *Baronetcy fell under attainder*, inasmuch as the right thereto devolved on the *attainted* heir male of the body of the elder brother(c) of the 1st Baronet That heir was GEORGE MACKENZIE, sometime (1731-46) EARL OF CROMARTY [S], who suc his father, John, the 2d Earl, in that title, 20 Feb 1731, which John was s and h of George, the 1st Earl and 2d Baronet [S 1628] This George was engaged in the Rising of 1745, and sentenced to death for high treason, 1 Aug 1746, whereby his peerage honours were forfeited in that year, and the *Baronetcy* when, in 1763, it devolved upon him, became likewise *forfeited* (d)

(a) See p 294, note "e," under "Colquhoun," shewing the validity, before the Scotch Union, of such resignation and regrant

(b) Milne's List He is styled in the diploma, dat 29 April 1704 at Kensington, as " Magister Kennett McKeinzie filius legitimus natu secundus Georgii Comitis de Cromartii et nepos prædicti quondam domini Johannis McKeinzii de Tarbat, ejus avi," and it is expressly stated that he is to have the same precedency as if he, instead of his said grandfather, had been *cr a Baronet* on 21 May 1628

(c) According to Scotch law the next *junior* brother is heir *before* the elder, but the only junior brother, Sir James Mackenzie, Baronet [S 1704], had died previously, s p m s, 9 Nov 1744

(d) In 1796 the issue male, if any such remained, of Roderick Mackenzie, of Prestonhall (one of the Lords of Session [S] under the title of Lord Prestonhall), who was 2d and yst s of the 1st Baronet, and who *d* 4 Jan 1712, would, barring the attainder, have been entitled to this Baronetcy, after the extinction of the issue male of the Earls of Cromarty, which happened on 4 Nov 1796 Alexander Mackenzie, s and h of the said Roderick, *m*, in 1702, Amelia, 1st da and h of hne of Hugh (Fraser), Lord Lovat [S], and claimed that peerage He changed his name to Fraser, and was of Fraserdale, but was attainted for taking part in the Rising of 1715 Failing such issue, the representation would devolve on the issue male of Kenneth Mackenzie of Scattwell, co Ross, next yr *brother* of the 1st Baronet, whose son Kenneth was *cr a Baronet* [S], 22 Feb 1703 The 6th Baronet of that line is said to have suc to this Baronetcy "in 1882" (Debrett's *Baronetage*), but no reversal of the attainder of 1746 has, apparently, ever taken place so as to enable him to do so.

ELPHINSTONE·

cr 20 June 1628(ᵃ) , sealed 20 Jan 1630(ᵇ) ;

dormant after Dec 1645 ,

but assumed since 1877.

I   1628,
to
1645

"MASTER WILLIAM ELPHINSTONE, Cupbearer to His Majesty,"(ᵃ) called also "the King's servant, brother to Woodhead,"(ᵇ) was yst br to Sir George ELPHINSTONE, Lord Justice Clerk [S], both being sons of George ELPHINSTONE, of Blythswood, co Lanark, was Cupbearer to Charles I, and was *cr a Baronet* [S], 20 June 1628,(ᵛ) being then apparently of Glasgow, with rem to heirs male whatsoever (the patent being sealed 20 Jan 1630(ᵇ) but not recorded in the Great Seal Register) with a grant of, presumably, 16,000 acres in Nova Scotia entitled the Barony of New Glasgow, of which he had seizin Jan 1630 (ᶜ)   He was a Lord of Session [S] in 1637, and shortly afterwards Lord Justice General [S], but was apparently displaced in 1641   He was *Knighted*, at Whitehall, 3 Feb 1636/7   He *d s p*, probably unm, and was *bur* (under the name of "Elveston") 10 Dec 1645, in Westm Abbey, when the *Baronetcy* became *dormant*   Will, in which (ignoring the Baronetcy) he describes himself merely as "Knight, Justice General, and one of the Senators of the College of Justice" [S], dat at Westm 26 Nov 1639 and proved by Sir David CUNNINGHAM, Baronet [S], the universal legatee save as to £100 bequeathed to testator's "nephew, William ELPHINSTONE, son of James ELPHINSTONE, of Woodside

---

The Baronetcy, after the space of more than 230 ¹ years, "was assumed in 1877,"(ᵈ) as under—

X (ᵉ) 1877

SIR NICHOLAI WILLIAM ELPHINSTONE, Baronet(ᶠ) [S 1628], next br to (ᵍ) to John ELPHINSTONE, Major Gen in the East India service (who *d s p m s* 15 Sep 1877, aged 53), both being sons of Alexander Francis ELPHINSTONE, of Livonia, in Devonshire, Capt in the navy and said to be a noble in the province of Livonia, in Russia, by Amelia Ann (*m* 5 May 1819), da of A LOBACH, of Cumenhoff, near Riga, which Alexander (who *d* 24 Sep 1865, aged 76) was 1st s of Samuel William ELPHINSTONE,(ʰ) Capt in the Russian navy (*d* 1789), yr br of John ELPHINSTONE, also a Capt in the navy (who, surviving him, *d* 1801), both being sons(ⁱ) of John ELPHINSTONE, a Capt in the British navy and

---

(ᵃ) Laing's List
(ᵇ) Milne's List
(ᵛ) Banks's Lists, in which also he is entitled "His Majesty's Cupbearer"
(ᵈ) Lodge's *Baronetage*, 1897, and Debrett's *Baronetage*, 1900
(ᵉ) This numbering is the one given in Dod's *Baronetage*, 1901, where it is added that "the 6th and 7th Baronets were in the military service of Russia
(ᶠ) According to the assumption of the title in 1877
(ᵍ) The 4th and yst br was Major Gen Sir Howard Craufurd Elphinstone, K C B, etc, who received the Victoria Cross for his services in the Crimea, and who *d s p m*, 8 March 1890, aged 60, being drowned off Teneriffe
(ʰ) In Foster's *Baronetage*, 1883 (p 209), the Baronetcy is spoken of as having been assumed by him, but, as he died before his *elder* brother, such assumption, if indeed it ever was made, would have been absurd
(ⁱ) The 6th and yst s, Howard Elphinstone, was *cr a Baronet* 25 May 1816, for his services in the Peninsular War.

an Admiral in that of Russia, who *d* 28 Feb 1785, aged 63 (ª)   He was *b*
16 Dec 1825, said to be a Noble in the province of Livonia, entered
the army in 1845, retiring in 1865 as Lieut Col, was sometime Deputy
Commissioner of the Punjaub, a Chevalier of the Legion of Honour in
France, *assumed the Baronetcy* on the death of his brother, 15 Sep 1877,
"as representative of the 1st Baronet"   He *m* 20 Jan 1860, at the
Cathedral in Calcutta, Georgina Henrietta Elliot, 3d and yst da of Lieut
Gen the Rt Hon Sir George ARTHUR, 1st Baronet [1841], K C H, by
Eliza Ord Ussher, da of Lieut Gen Sir John Frederick SMITH, K C B

BRUCE

cr 26 June or 29 Sep 1628, sealed 10 Aug 1629 (ᵇ)

I   1628   "WILLIAM BRUCE, of Stenhouse" [co. Stirling], 2d s
            of William BRUCE, by Jean, da of John (FLEMING), 5th LORD
FLEMING [S], having received, previous to 1603, from his grandfather, Sir
Alexander BRUCE, of Airth (his father having *d* v p), the lands of Stenhouse, to
"remain with him and his heirs", was *cr* a Baronet [S], 26 June or 29 Sep
1628, sealed 10 Aug 1629,(ᵇ) but not recorded in the Great Seal Register [S],
with rem to heirs male whatsoever, and with a grant of, presumably, 16,000 acres
in Nova Scotia, of which he had seizin, Aug 1629 (ᶜ)   He *m* firstly, (—), da
and h of Gen MIDDLETON, of Lethem   She *d* s p m   He *m* secondly, before
1621, Rachel, widow of John JACKSON, of Edinburgh, merchant, da of Joseph
JOHNSTON, of Hilltoun, co Berwick   He *d* Feb 1630   Funeral entry in Lyon
office

II.   1630   SIR WILLIAM BRUCE, Baronet [S 1628], of Stenhouse
            aforesaid, s and h by 2d wife, *b* 19 Aug 1621, *suc to the*
Baronetcy on the death of his father   He *m* Helen, da of Sir William DOUGLAS,
of Cavers, Heritable Sheriff of Tiviotdale   He was on the Parl side during
the Civil Wars, and joined Argyll's party against the Duke of Hamilton's
"engagement"   In 1649 he was one of the "Colonels" for the county of Stirling

III   1660?   SIR WILLIAM BRUCE, Baronet [S 1628], of Stenhouse
            aforesaid, only s and b, *suc to the Baronetcy* on the death of his
father   He *m* firstly, 16 Sep 1665, Jean FORTUNE   He *m* secondly, 17 April
1679, Alison TURNBULL, "Lady Kirkland"   He *d* March 1682

IV   1682   SIR WILLIAM BRUCE, Baronet [S 1628], of Stenhouse
            aforesaid, s (or possibly grandson, see service 23 April 1714) and
h, *suc to the Baronetcy* in 1682   He *m* Margaret, da of John BOYD, of
Trochrigg   He *d* March 1721

(ª) According to the pedigree in Burke's *Baronetage* of 1901, Admiral Elphinstone was son of "John Elphinstone of the Royal Navy," son of another "John
Elphinstone," who was son of "John Elphinstone, of Lopness-Waas," only son of
"Robert Elphinstone, Page to Prince Henry, eldest son of James VI," one of the
two sons of "Ronald Elphinstone, who settled at Orkney," who was son of John
Elphinstone, of Baberton, 3d son of Robert, 3d Lord Elphinstone [S] and yr
br of James, 1st Lord Balmerino [S]   No such John, however, appears as a
younger br to the said Lord Balmerino in Wood's *Douglas' Peerage* [S], but, even
if the pedigree as above is correct, it seems to have no bearing on the heirship
to this *Baronetcy*, but only to that of the attainted Barony of Balmerino [S.].

(ᵇ) In Laing's List the creation is given as 26 June 1629, but in Milne's List as
29 Sep. 1628, sealed 10 Aug 1629.

(ᶜ) Banks's Lists.

V. 1721   SIR ROBERT BRUCE, Baronet [S 1628], of Stenhouse
aforesaid, 2d but 1st surv s and h , *suc to the Baronetcy* on the
death of his father   He *d.* unm

VI. 1760 ?   SIR MICHAEL BRUCE, Baronet [S 1628], of Stenhouse
aforesaid, br and h , *suc to the Baronetcy* on the death of his
brother   He *m* May, 1st da of General Sir Andrew AGNEW, 5th Baronet
[S 1629], by Eleanor, da of Thomas AGNEW   He *d* 1 Nov 1795

VII. 1795   SIR WILLIAM BRUCE, Baronet [S 1628], of Stenhouse
aforesaid, 3d but 1st surv s and h ([a]) ; was sometime in Jamaica,
suc to the Baronetcy, 1 Nov 1795   He *m* June 1795, Anne Colquhoun, 3d da of
Sir William CUNINGHAM (afterwards CUNINGHAM FAIRLIE), 5th Baronet [S 1630],
by Anne, da of Robert COLQUHOUN, of the island of St Christopher   He *d*
17 Nov 1827

VIII 1827   SIR MICHAEL BRUCE, Baronet [S 1628], of Stenhouse
aforesaid, s and h, *b* 31 March 1798, *suc to the Baronetcy*,
17 Nov 1827   He *m* 10 June 1822, Isabella, da and h of Alexander MOIR, of
Scotstoun, co Aberdeen, by Margaret, da of James GORDON, of co Banff   He *d*
s p 14 Dec 1862   His widow *d* 19 Nov 1867

IX 1862   SIR WILLIAM CUNINGHAM BRUCE, Baronet [S 1628],
nephew and h, being s and h of William Cuningham BRUCE, of
the Bombay Civil Service, by Jane Catherine, da of William CLARK, of London,
which William Cuningham BRUCE (who *d* 11 Nov 1842, aged 44) was 2d s of
the 7th Baronet   He was *b* 20 Sep 1825, at Bombay, was sometime Capt
74th Highlanders, *suc to the Baronetcy*, 14 Dec 1862   He *m* 21 Aug 1850,
at Monkstown, co Dublin, Charlotte Isabella, 3d da of the Hon Walter O'GRADY
(2d s of Standish, 1st VISCOUNT GUILLAMORE [1]), by Grace Elizabeth, da of
Hugh (MASSY), 3d BARON MASSY [1]   She *d* 16 Oct 1873

BRUCE:

Qy if not *cr* about 1628, and
dormant or *extinct* soon afterwards

I   1628 ?   "SIR JOHN BRUCE, of Clackmannan," is said([b]) " in
ane old list " to have been *cr* a Baronet [S]   His identity is not
certain   His name, as above, occurs in a list of the Nova Scotia Baronets com-
piled before 1643,([c]) but no such person in or near that date appears among the
Clackmannan family   It is not improbable that the elder br of Sir William
BRUCE, of Stenhouse, *cr* a Baronet [S] in 1628, is meant, viz, SIR JOHN BRUCE
OF AIRTH, co Stirling, grandson and h to Sir Alexander BRUCE, of Airth and
Stenhouse   This Sir John, who had a charter, 1610, as Dominus Johannes Bruce de
Airth, *m* in 1601, Margaret, da of Alexander ELPHINSTONE, 4th LORD ELPHINSTONE
[S], and was father of ALEXANDER BRUCE, of Airth aforesaid, who was father of
SIR ALEXANDER BRUCE, of Airth aforesaid, who *d* s p m, when the issue male of
his grandfather became *extinct*

([a]) Andrew Bruce, the 2d son and h ap, sometime a Capt in the 38th Foot,
became Col in the Army and Brig General in the American War   He *d.* v p
and s p, at Naples, in 1791

([b]) Milne's List, where however no date is given   In Laing's List there is no
notice of the creation, neither is there in Banks's Lists any record of grant or
seizin of lands in Nova Scotia

([c]) Ulster's List

BARR

cr. 29 Sep 1628 ,(a)

dormant, soon afterwards

ROBERT BARR, a Burgess of Glasgow, is said to have been *cr* a *Baronet* 29 Sep 1628,(a) but no further particulars are known of him and no seizin of lands in Nova Scotia is recorded (b)

FORBES.

cr 29 Sep , and sealed 10 Oct 1628 ,(c)

afterwards, since 1675, VISCOUNTS GRANARD [I] ,

and subsequently, since 1684, EARLS OF GRANARD [I]

I. 1628   "CAPT ARTHUR FORBES, of Castle Forbes," in the parish of Clongish, co Longford, 6th s of William FORBES, of Corsse, by Elizabeth, da of (—) STRACHAN, of Thornton, settled in Ireland in 1620, and was made a free denizen thereof. 1 April 1622, received lands, in the counties of Leitrim and Longford, erected into the manor of Castle Forbes, and was *cr* a *Baronet* [S], 29 Sep , sealed 10 Oct 1628,(c) with rem to heirs male whatsoever, and with a grant of, presumably, 16,000 acres in Nova Scotia, of which he had seizin in Nov 1628 (b) He was Col of a regiment in the service of Gustavus Adolphus, King of Sweden He *m*, between 12 Feb 1618 and 1623, Jane, widow of Sir Claud HAMILTON, of Clonyn, co Cavan, da of Robert LAUDER, of the Bass [S] He *d* 14 April 1632, being slain in a duel at Hamburgh His widow suffered greatly in the Civil Wars, and was besieged for many months at Castle Forbes till forced to surrender in Aug 1642

II 1632   SIR ARTHUR FORBES, Baronet [S 1628], of Castle Forbes aforesaid, 1st s and h , b about 1625, being aged 7 when he *suc to the Baronetcy,* 24 April 1632, was in command in Scotland for the Royal cause in 1655, was a Commissioner of the Court of Claims [I] in 1661, and Capt of a troop of horse , M P [I] for co Tyrone, 1661-66 , P C [I], Marshal of the army [I], 1670, and one of the Lord Justices [I], 1671, 1678 and 1681 He *m* about 1655, Catharine, widow of Sir Alexander STEWART, 2d Baronet [I 1623], da of Sir Robert NEWCOMEN, 4th Baronet [I 1625], by his 1st wife Anne, da of [—] BOLEYN She was living when he was *cr* 22 Nov 1675, VISCOUNT GRANARD, co Longford [I], being subsequently *cr* , 30 Dec 1684, EARL OF GRANARD [I] In these peerages this *Baronetcy* then *merged,* and still so continues

---

HAMILTON.

cr 29 Sep , sealed 10 Oct 1628 ,(c)

dormant 4 Feb 1713/4

I 1628   FRANCIS HAMILTON of Killaugh, co Down, was 1st s and h of Sir Claud HAMILTON, of Clonyn, *otherwise* Tagleagh, co Cavan (patent 23 June 1610), by Jane, da of Robert LAUDER, of the Bass [S],

---

(a) Laing's List (where it is given "on the authority of former lists"), but not in Milne's List, nor in the *Registrum Preceptorum Cartarum pro Baronettis Nova Scotiæ*

(b) Banks's Lists.

(c) Laing's List , Milne's List

which Claud (who *d v p* before Feb 1618) was 2d s of Sir Alexander HAMILTON of Enderwick, in Scotland, and (patent 23 June 1610) of Clonkine and Carrotubber co Cavan (ᵃ) He and his widowed mother were made denizens of Ireland by patent 12 Feb 1618 (ᵇ) He received from his said grandfather, 20 July 1621, the Cavan estates, was P C [I] as one of the Council of Munster to James I, and was *cr a Baronet* [S], 29 Sep, sealed 10 Oct 1628,(ᶜ) with rem to heirs male whatsoever, and with a grant of, presumably, 16,000 acres in Nova Scotia of which he had seizin in Nov 1628 (ᵈ) The three estates of Clonkine, Carrotubber and Clonyn were (patent 17 June 1631) formed into the manor of Castle Killagh afterwards called Castle Hamilton), co Cavan He was M P [I] for Jamestown, 1639-48, and for co Cavan, 1661-66, was Custos Rot for that county, and a Commissioner for the Act of Settlement, 1661 He *m* firstly Laetitia, or Nicola, da of Sir Charles COOTE, 1st Baronet [I 1620], by Dorothea, da and coheir of Hugh CUFFE, of Cuffeswood, co Cork He *m* secondly, Elizabeth, widow (his 3d wife) of Sir Francis WILLOUGHBY, Dep Lieut Gov of Galway (who *d* 19 Feb 1658/9, aged 84), formerly widow of William HAY, of Castlebarne, co Longford (who *d* March 1634/5), only da of Randall BARLOW, Archbishop of Tuam [1629-38], by his 1st wife Elizabeth, da of Jonas WHEELER, Bishop of Ossory [1613-40] She *d s p* 19 May, and was *bur*, 1 June 1664, in Christ Church, Dublin Will pr. 4 Jan 1664/5 in Prerog Court [I] He *d* 1673 Funeral entry in Ulster's office His will, as of "Castle Hamilton," pr 1674 in Prerog Court [I]

II 1673   SIR CHARLES HAMILTON, Baronet [S 1628], of Castle Hamilton aforesaid, s and h by 1st wife, *Knighted* at Whitehall, 13 Feb 1661, M P [I] for co Donegal, 1661-66, *suc to the Baronetcy* in 1673, and was Custos Rot for co Cavan, 12 Feb 1673/4 He *m* firstly, Catherine (or Francescina(ᵉ)), da and h of Sir William SEMPILL, of Lettenkenny, co Donegal, by Anne, da of Sir William STEWART, 1st Baronet [I 1623] He *m* secondly (mar lic at Hereford, 12 Dec 1685, he being then "of St Martin's in the Fields, wid"), Penelope, widow of Nicholas PHILPOTT, of Poston, co Hereford (who *d* 1683, aged 40), da of James HAWARD, of Fletherhill, co Pembroke He *d* before 9 May 1689, the date of his admon in the Prerog Ct [I] His widow *d* between 1689 and 1693 (ᶠ)

III 1689?   SIR FRANCIS HAMILTON, Baronet [S 1628], of Castle
to   Hamilton aforesaid, s and h by 1st wife, *suc to the Baronetcy* in
1714   or before 1689, in which year he was attainted by the Parl of
James II, was M P [I] for co Cavan, 1692-93, 1695-99, and 1703-13, Sheriff of co Donegal, 1694 He *m* firstly, about 1685, Catherine, 1st da of Hugh (MONTGOMERY), 1st EARL OF MOUNT ALEXANDER [I], by his 2d wife, Catherine, da of Arthur (JONES), 2d VISCOUNT RANELAGH [I] She *d* 6 Jan 1692, aged 29 M I at Killeshandra He *m* secondly, 26 March 1695 Anne, da and h of Claud HAMILTON(ᵍ), by Anne, da of William HAMILTON, of Hamilton's Bawn, co Cavan He *d s p s*(ʰ) 4, and was *bur* 9 Feb 1713/4, at Killeshandra, when the *Baronetcy* became *dormant* M I Funeral entry in

(ᵃ) Much of the information in this article has been kindly supplied by G D Burtchaell, of the Office of Arms, Dublin There is a confused account of this family (containing, however, some useful notices as to collaterals) in Archdall's *Lodge's Irish Peerage* (1789, vol vi, p 97), under "Southwell"

(ᵇ) 'Jane Locher, otherwise Hambleton of Castle Kelagh, and Francis Hambleton of the same," naturalised in the same patent of denization as that of Archibald Acheson

(ᶜ) Milne's List and Laing's List

(ᵈ) Banks's Lists

(ᵉ) So called in the M I at Killeshandra

(ᶠ) Manor Rolls of Merton, co Surrey, where Sir Charles (whose death is reported as before 1689) is called 'of the Kingdom of Ireland"

(ᵍ) This Claud was possibly br of the 1st Baronet, and a gr s of Sir Claud Hamilton, of Clonyn His da Anne, is spoken of, on the monument of her husband, as being "patruelem suam"

(ʰ) He had an illegit da called Frances Tweedy

2 Y

Ulster's Office. Will dat. 19 Jan. 1713/4, pr. 24 Feb. 1717/8 in Prerog. Court [I.]. His widow *m.* (as the 2d or 3d(a) of his many wives) Lord Archibald HAMILTON (yr. br. of James, DUKE OF HAMILTON [S.]), who *d.* 5 Dec. 1753, aged 80. She *d.* (shortly after her marriage) 29 March, and was *bur.* 4 April 1719 in Westm. Abbey.

STEWART:

cr. 2 Oct. 1628 ;(b)

afterwards, since 1629, BARONS CASTLE-STEWART [I.];

since 1793, VISCOUNTS CASTLE-STEWART [I.],

and, since 1800, EARLS CASTLE-STEWART [I.].

I. 1628.　　THE HON. ANDREW STEWART, 1st s. and h. ap. of Andrew (STEWART), 1st BARON CASTLE STEWART [I.], formerly LORD OCHILTREE [S.], by Margaret, da. of Sir John KENNEDY, of Blairquhan, was *b.* about 1600, and was v.p. *cr.* a Baronet [S.], 2 Oct. 1628,(b) though not recorded in the *Registrum Preceptorum Cartarum pro Baronettis Novæ Scotiæ.* The limitation is unknown, and no grant or seizin of lands in Nova Scotia is recorded.(c) He *m.,* 4th da. and coheir of John (STEWART), 5th EARL OF ATHOLL [S.], by Mary, da. of William (RUTHVEN), EARL OF GOWRIE [S.]. She, presumably, was living when, on the death of his father, he became BARON CASTLE STEWART, co. Tyrone [I.], a dignity *cr.* 7 Nov. 1619. In that peerage this *Baronetcy* then *merged,* and still so continues, the 9th Baron and 8th Baronet being *cr.* 20 Dec. 1793 VISCOUNT CASTLE STEWART, co. Tyrone [I.], and subsequently, 29 Dec. 1800, EARL CASTLE STEWART, co. Tyrone [I.].

BARRETT:

LORD BARRETT OF NEWBURGH [S.];

cr. on, or soon after, 2 Oct. 1628 ;(d)

dormant, or *extinct,* 2 Jan. 1644/5.

I. 1628,　　EDWARD (BARRETT), LORD BARRETT OF NEWBURGH, CO.
to　　　　Fife [S.], who had been so *cr.* 17 Oct. 1627, was, about a year later,
1645.　　*cr.* a Baronet [S.], on,(d) or soon after, 2 Oct. 1628,(d) such creation, however, not being in the Great Seal Register [S.], receiving a grant of, presumably, 16,000 acres in Nova Scotia, of which he had seizin in Jan. 1629.(c) He *d.* s.p. and was *bur.* 2 Jan. 1644/5, at Aveley, co. Essex, when the peerage became extinct, and the *Baronetcy* (the limitations of which are not known) either *extinct* or *dormant.* See fuller particulars of him in the *Peerage.*

(a) The marriage (by Licence) at St. Martin's in the Fields, 5 Oct. 1693, of "Capt. Archibald Hamilton and Anne Pennington of St. James' Westm.," probably refers to a first marriage, though none such seems to have ever been attributed to him. In that same year, 1693, he obtained his Captain's commission in the navy.

(b) Laing's List, being therein stated to be "on the authority of former lists." It is not in Milne's List.

(c) Banks's Lists.

(d) Laing's List, where the creation is placed next after 2 Oct. 1628, being that of Andrew Stewart.

JOHNSTON

cr 18 Oct., and sealed 21 Nov 1628 ([1])

dormant about 1700

I 1628   SAMUEL JOHNSTON, of Elphinstone,([b]) in the parish of Tranent, co Haddington s, and h of Patrick JOHNSTON, of the same, by Elizabeth, da of George DUNDAS, of Dundas, was b about 1600, and was *cr* a *Baronet*, 18 Oct, sealed 21 Nov 1628,([a]) but not recorded in the Great Seal Register [S], with rem to heirs male whatsoever, and with a grant of, presumably, 16,000 acres in Nova Scotia, being the Barony of Elphinstone in New Brunswick, of which he had seizin 18 Oct 1628 ([c]) He m Joan da of Archibald DOUGLAS, of Spot, co Haddington, by Jean, da and h of Robert HOME, of Spot aforesaid He d in or before 1644

II 1644 ?   SIR JOHN JOHNSTONE, Baronet [S 1628], of Elphinstone aforesaid, s and h, *suc to the Baronetcy* in or before 1644 and on 20 Feb 1645 had spec service to his father in Leuchie, co Haddington, was member of the Committee of War, etc, 1644 to 1649 He m Margaret, da and cohen of Robert KEITH of Benholme He d in or before 1666

III 1666 ?   SIR JAMES JOHNSTONE, Baronet [S 1628], of Elphinstone
to   aforesaid, s and h, *suc to the Baronetcy* on the death of his
1700 ?   father and was, on 5 May 1666, served h gen to his grandfather, and on 2 June 1673 h spec of his father, in Leuchie Of him, however, or his descendants nothing further is known Cadets of the family settled in Edinburgh as merchants, Burgesses, etc and in the records are styled as "of Elphinstone"

NICOLSON

cr 27 July, and sealed 31 Dec 1629 ,([d])

dormant, apparently, 1713-1826 ,

assumed since 1826

I 1629   JOHN NICOLSON, of Lasswade, co Midlothian, s and h of John NICOLSON, of the same, Advocate [S] and Commissary of Edinburgh (who had acquired that estate([e]) in 1590), by Elizabeth, da of Edward HENDERSON, was *cr* a *Baronet* [S] 27 July, the patent being sealed 31 Dec 1629([d]) with rem to heirs male whatsoever and with a grant of, presumably, 16,000 acres in Nova Scotia, of which he had seizin in Feb 1630 ([f]) He m Magdalen, da of David PRESTON, of Craigmillar He d May 1651

II 1651   SIR JOHN NICOLSON, Baronet [S 1629] of Lasswade aforesaid, grandson and h, being s and h of John NICOLSON of Pilton (who d v p 1648), by (—), da of (—) He *suc to the Baronetcy* on the death of his grandfather He was M P [S] for co Edinburgh, 1672-74 He m Elizabeth da of Sir William DICK, of Braid

---

([a]) Milne's List, but in Laing's List the date of creation is assigned to the previous year, viz, as being on 18 Oct *1627*

([b]) This estate was acquired, about 1472, by the marriage of Gilbert Johnston with Agnes Elphinstone, the heiress thereof

([c]) *Ex inform* of R Stodart (Lyon Clerk Depute, 1863-86) See also Banks's Lists

([d]) Milne's List, Laing's List

([e]) See p 304, note "b," and corrigenda thereto

([f]) Banks's Lists

III 1680 ? SIR JOHN NICOLSON, Baronet [S 1629] of Lasswade
aforesaid s and h , *suc to the Baronetcy* on the death of his
father He *d s p* May 1681 probably unm

IV 1681 SIR WILLIAM NICOLSON, Baronet [S 1629], of Lasswade aforesaid, br and h , *suc to the Baronetcy* on the death
of his brother, to whom he was served heir 21 Sep 1681 He *m* Elizabeth, da
of John TROTTER, of Mortonhall He was *bur* 29 Jan 1687 at Lasswade His
widow *d* 28 March 1723

V 1687 SIR JOHN NICOLSON, Baronet [S 1629], of Lasswade
aforesaid, s and h , *suc to the Baronetcy* Jan 1687 He *d s p m*,
presumably unm , and was *bur* in Greyfriars churchyard, 30 Oct 1689

VI 1689 SIR THOMAS NICOLSON, Baronet [S 1629], br and h ,
suc to the Baronetcy, 30 Oct 1689 , *d s p m*, presumably unm
and was *bur* in Greyfriars churchyard, 8 April 1693

VII 1693, SIR JAMES NICOLSON, Baronet [S 1629], br and h ,
to   *suc to the Baronetcy* in April 1693 He *m* firstly, 16 Dec 1721,
1743   Isabel, da of Henry SIMPSON, factor, at Eishington, co Northumberland He *m* secondly, Elizabeth, daughter of James
CARNEGIE, of Craigs He *d s p* May 1743, after which the *Baronetcy* appears
to have remained *dormant* for some 80 years His widow was living 1764 [a]

*   *   *   *   *   *   *

The title was assumed in 1826 as under

VIII [b] 1826 SIR ARTHUR NICOLSON, Baronet[c] [S 1629], of Brough
Lodge, Fetlar, in Shetland, cousin and h male,[c] being s
and h of Arthur NICOLSON, of Lochend, in Shetland aforesaid by Mary da of
Alexander INNES, Commissary Clerk of Aberdeen, which Arthur last named (who
d May 1796, aged 39, was s and h of another Arthur NICOLSON, also of Lochend
(*d* 1793), s of John NICOLSON, of Gilsbreck (*d* 1728), 2d s of Rev James
NICOLSON, Minister of Tingwall in Shetland, 1660 (*d* before 1675), s of James
NICOLSON Advocate [S] and Commissary of Brechin (*d* before 1685), s of
James NICOLSON, Bishop of Dunkeld, 1606-07, who was yr br [d] to John NICOLSON,
of Lasswade, the father of the 1st Baronet He was *b* 1794, and was *in 1826*
served heir male to the 1st Baronet, and thereupon *assumed the Baronetcy* He
m 27 April 1821, Eliza Jane, da of the Rev William JACK, D D , Principal of King's
College, Aberdeen He *d s p* 16 Sep 1863 at Norwood, co Surrey, aged 69
His widow *d* 26 March 1891, at Hayden Court, Cheltenham, aged 91

---

[a] The information respecting him and the earlier Baronets has been kindly
supplied by Sir J Balfour Paul, Lyon King of Arms
[b] This numbering is exclusive of any Baronets who may have succeeded, or
have been entitled, to that dignity, between the death of his 7th Baronet in 1743
and the date of the service in 1826.
[c] According to the service in 1826
[d] If, as is believed to be the case, Thomas Nicolson of Carnock, *cr a Baronet*
[S], 16 Jan 1636/7, was *brother* of the grantee of 1629, the heir to the Baronetcy
of 1629 would be the (now existing) Baronet of 1637 in preference to the
descendant of an *uncle* See p 304, note " b," and the *corrigenda* thereto

IX (ª) 1863   SIR ARTHUR BOLT NICOLSON, Baronet(ᵇ) [S 1629], of
                Melbourne, in Australia, cousin and h male, being 1st surv s
of James NICOLSON, of Aith, Capt R N by Katharine Anne, sister of Alexander
Maxwell BENNETT, Major in the army, da of Thomas BENNETT, which James, who
d 1827, was uncle of the late Baronet   He was b 6 March 1811, served as an
officer in the 4th Foot, in New South Wales, in 1831, was again in New South
Wales, in 1853, being sometime Sub-Commissioner of Goldfields in Victoria, suc
to the Baronetcy,(ᵇ) 16 Sep 1863, and was served heir male to his cousin in Nov
1866   He m in 1839, Margaret, da of the Rev George BISSET, of Udny, co
Aberdeen   She d at Melbourne aforesaid, in 1869   He d 14 July 1879 in
Portland street, Richmond, Melbourne

X (ª) 1879   SIR ARTHUR THOMAS BENNETT ROBERT NICOLSON,
                Baronet(ᵇ) [S 1629], of Melbourne aforesaid, only s and h,
b at Morphett Vale, Adelaide, South Australia 1842, ed at Melbourne College,
suc to the Baronetcy,(ᵇ) 14 July 1879   He m 14 July 1881, at St Peter, Windermere, Annie, 1st da of John RUTHERFORD, of Bruntsfield place, Edinburgh
formerly of Illilawa, New South Wales

ARNOT, or ARNOTT

cr 27 July 1629, sealed 3 July 1630 ,(ᶜ)

succession doubtful after 1711

assumed till 1782 or possibly till about 1840

I   1629   MICHAEL ARNOT, "fiar of Arnot,"(ᵈ) co Fife, s. and
                h ap of Walter ARNOT of the same, by Mary, sister of Michael,
1st LORD BALFOUR OF BURLEIGH [S], da of Sir James BALFOUR, was cr a
Baronet [S], 27 July 1629, the patent being sealed 3 July 1630,(ᶜ) but not recorded
in the Great Seal Register [S], with rem to heirs male whatsoever, and with
a grant of, presumably, 16,000 acres in Nova Scotia, of which he had seizin in
July 1630 (ᵉ)   He m April 1612, Anne, eldest of the three das and coheirs of Robert
BROWNE, of Balquharne, co Clackmannan, Finderlie, co Kinross, and of Auchin
gowrie co Perth, Gentleman of the Wine Cellar to King James, by Katharine
DOUGLAS, his wife   He was alive in 1670, but d before 1685

II   1680 ?   SIR DAVID ARNOT, Baronet [S 1629], of Arnot afore-
     to   said, grandson and h being s and h of Col Charles ARNOT,
     1711   by Helen, da of James REID of Pitlethie (by Margaret BRUCE,
his wife), which Charles was 1st s of the 1st Baronet, but d
v p before 1652   He was served h to his father, 1670, *suc to the Baronetcy* on
his grandfather's death and was served heir to him, 1685, was M P [S] for
Kinross, 1689 1702   He, who appears to have sold the estate of Arnot, d s p
1 Jan 1711 (ᶠ)

(ª) See p 364, note "b"
(ᵇ) According to the service in 1826
(ᶜ) Milne's List and Laing's List
(ᵈ) Laing's List
(ᵉ) Banks's Lists
(ᶠ) Helen, his sister, widow of James LIVINGSTONE, was in 1729 served his
heir special in lands of Balrowme, Ballichill, etc, co Forfar   In Playfair's
Baronetage [S] he is said to be father of two sons, John and William, of whom
the eldest is said to have been the 3d Baronet, who d July 1782 and who is
conjectured to be father of John, the 4th Baronet, father of William, the 5th
Baronet, father of William, the 6th and then (1811) existing Baronet   Thus
the Sir William, who d July 1782, is made the 3d, instead of the 7th Baronet, as
in the text above

III. 1711?   SIR JOHN ARNOTT, Baronet(ª) [S. 1629], of
            Abbotshall (near Kircaldy), co. Fife, the name of which he
changed to "Arnott," and afterwards of York, whose relationship to the
grantee is unknown; *assumed the Baronetcy*, probably in or about 1711.
He was Adj. Gen. of Scotland, 1727; Brig. Gen., 1735; Major Gen. 1739,
and afterwards Lieut. Gen. in the army. By deed, dat. 16 Feb. 1749/50,
he disponed his Barony of Arnot in trust for his two sons and three
daughters. He *m.* Mary, da. of (—). She was *bur.* 11 Oct. 1745 at
Trinity in Micklegate, York. He *d.* 4 and was *bur.* there 6 June 1750.
Will dat. 17 Feb. 1749 50, pr. 20 June 1750.

IV. 1750.   SIR JOHN ARNOTT, Baronet(ª) [S. 1629], 1st s.
            and h., sometime Capt. in Col. La Torrey's regiment of
marines; *suc. to the Baronetcy*,(ª) 4 June 1750. He *m.* Eleanor, da. of
(—). He *d.* s.p.m., about 1762. Will (in which he leaves all to his wife
for life, with rem. to his da., Anne Arnott) dat. 17 March 1762, but not
proved till 19 March 1774, his widow (the extrix.) being then living.

          *   *   *   *   *   *   *

V. 1762?   SIR JOHN ARNOTT, Baronet(ª) [S. 1629], of the
            island of Jersey, whose relationship to the grantee is un-
known(ᵇ); was sometime (1750) a Capt. in Foulis' regiment; and *assumed
the Baronetcy* probably about 1762. He *d.* a widower and s.p. probably
about 1765, although the admon. to his effects was dated as late as 10 Aug.
1781, when it was granted to "Matthew Robert ARNOTT, Esq.," a creditor,
Mary ARNOTT, spinster, sister and only next of kin, having renounced.

          *   *   *   *   *   *   *

VI. 1765?   SIR ROBERT ARNOT, Baronet(ª) [S. 1629], of Dal-
            ginch, co. Fife, s. and h. of Major William ARNOT, of the
same, and formerly of Auchmuir, but whose relationship to the grantee
is unknown; suc. his father 6 Oct. 1735, being served his heir special,
1736; and *assumed the Baronetcy* probably about 1765. He *d.* s.p. at
Dalginch aforesaid 3 June 1767.

VII. 1767,   SIR WILLIAM ARNOT, Baronet(ª) [S. 1629], of
  to   Dalginch aforesaid, br. and h.; Lieut. Col. of the 2d
 1782.   (Queen's) Dragoon Guards; entered the army 1735, and
            sold out in 1779. He *suc. to the Baronetcy*,(ª) 5 June
1767. He *m.* Mary, 3d da. of Richard NASH, of St. Peter's, Droitwich,
co. Worcester, by Elizabeth, da. of George TREADWAY, Turkey merchant
(sister to Dr. Treadway NASH, the Historian of Worcestershire). He *d.*
s.p. 19 July 1782, at Powick, co. Worcester, and was *bur.* there. Will
dat. 25 Feb. 1780, proved 28 Sep. 1782. His widow, who was *b.* 19 Feb.
1716/7, *d.* 6 March 1783, and was *bur.* at Powick aforesaid. By her will,
dat. 13 July 1782, in her husband's lifetime, she left her estate of Orleton,
co. Worcester, to her brother, Dr. NASH abovenamed.

          *   *   *   *   *   *   *

(ª) According to the assumption of that dignity.
(ᵇ) He, certainly, was not a son of William Arnot, Col. of the 53d Regt., only br.
of the last Baronet, as that William *d.* s.p. before 1762, when his sisters were
served his coheirs of provision general.

VIII. 1782?   MATTHEW ROBERT ARNOTT,(ᵃ) Clerk of the Private Committees of the House of Commons, Usher of the Green Rod, etc., was (according to a statement said to be in the "Scottish Nation") a *de jure* Baronet, presumably as succeeding to this Baronetcy [S. 1629] in July 1782. He was s. and h. of the Rev. George ARNOT, Vicar of Wakefield, co. York, 1728 to 1750, but his relationship to the grantee is unknown. He *d.* s p. 1801, his sister's son, George ROBINSON, Capt. R.N., being, it is believed, his heir.

*   *   *   *   *   *   *

IX. 1801?   SIR WILLIAM ARNOT, Baronet(ᵉ) [S. 1629], is
to   given in Playfair's *Baronetage* [S.], 1811, and in Burke's
1840?   *Baronetage*, 1837 to 1840, as the then existing Baronet of
            this creation, but of him (if, indeed, he ever existed)
nothing is known.

OLIPHANT:

cr. 28 July, and sealed 24 Aug. 1629 ;(ᵇ)

dormant probably soon after 1691.

I. 1629.   SIR JAMES OLIPHANT, of Newtoun, formerly of Muir-house, a Lord of Session [S.], s. and h.(ᶜ) of Sir William OLIPHANT(ᵈ) of Newtoun aforesaid, Lord Advocate [S.] by Katherine BLAIR, his wife, suc. his father (who *d.* aged 77) 13 April 1623 and was *cr.* a *Baronet* [S.] 28 July, the patent being sealed 24 Aug. 1629, but not recorded in the Great Seal Register [S.], with rem. to heirs male whatsoever and with a grant of, presumably, 16,000 acres in Nova Scotia, of which he had seizin in Aug. 1629.(ᵉ) He resigned his seat as a Lord of Session [S.] before 27 July 1632.(ᶠ) He *m.* firstly, Marjory, da. of Patrick GRAEME, of Inchbrackie. He *m.* secondly, Geilis, apparently widow of the Rev. James BENNET, Minister of Auchtermuchtie (in which case the date must have been after 1640), da. of (——) MONCRIEFF. He *d.* 1648.

(ᵃ) Doubtless the person who, as creditor, was the administrator to "Sir John Arnott, Baronet," 10 Aug. 1781.

(ᵇ) Milne's List, where, however, the word *Ogilvie* is by error put for *Oliphant*. The same date of creation is given in Laing's List, but the grantee is there called "Master *John* Oliphant of Newtoun."

(ᶜ) He had three yr. brothers: [i], William Oliphant, of Kirkhill, Advocate [S.], who *m.* Janet, da. of William Maule, Burgess of Edinburgh, and had two sons, of whom the yr., William Oliphant, *d.* s.p. before 1652, when his br. Patrick was served his heir. This Patrick Oliphant, *bap.* 2 Aug. 1618, Advocate [S.] 1649, was for many years the possessor of the Newtoun estate in virtue of a royal gift of the escheat of the 2d Baronet. He *m.* Isobel, widow of Sir William Douglas, da. of (——) Hay, and *d.* s.p.m., leaving two daughters; [ii], John Oliphant, portioner of Broughton, Advocate [S.] and King's Solicitor (S.), who *m.* Elizabeth Winram; [iii], Laurence Oliphant, of Fordun, Advocate [S.].

(ᵈ) This William was yr. br. to Laurence Oliphant, of Williamston, afterwards of Forgandenny, who was ancestor of the Oliphants of Bachilton, and whose male line failed in 1770, the heir of line being Lord Elibank [S.]. They were sons of Thomas Oliphant, of Freeland, afterwards of Williamston aforesaid [1546-77], by Isabel Gibb, which Thomas is the first on record of the family, being traditionally said to have been descended from Lawrence, Abbot of Machaffray, who fell at Flodden.

(ᵉ) Banks's Lists.

(ᶠ) The cause, according to the *Staggering State* (p. 139), by Scot of Scotstarvet, was that he had "shot his gardener dead with a hagbut."

II. 1648   SIR JAMES OLIPHANT, Baronet [S 1629], s and h by 1st wife, who, having stabbed his mother, fled the country, and when by his father's death he *suc to the Baronetcy*, probably never assumed that dignity (ᵃ) He d s p 1659

III 1659,   SIR GEORGE OLIPHANT, Baronet [S 1629], of Newtoun
     to   aforesaid, br and h, *suc to the Baronetcy* in 1659 on the death of
     1695?   his br, to whom he was served h in 1674 (ᵇ) He, in 1691, sold the estate of Newtoun He *m* firstly Margaret, da of (—) DRUMMOND, of Invermay Ho *m* secondly, Margaret, 1st da of James (ROLLO), 1st LORD ROLLO [S], by his 2d wife, Mary, da of Archibald (CAMPBELL), 7th EARL OF ARGYLL [S] He *d s p*, probably not long after 1691 when the *Baronetcy* became dormant (ᶜ)

AGNEW(ᵈ) .

cr 28 July 1629 ,

sealed 22 Feb 1630(ᵉ)

I 1629   SIR PATRICK AGNEW, of Lochnaw, co Wigtown 8th Hereditary Sheriff of Galloway, s and h of Sir Andrew AGNEW, of the same 7th Hereditary Sheriff as aforesaid by Agnes, da of Sir Alexander STEWART, of Garlies, was *b* about 1578 suc his father in 1616 being served h to him 17 Jan 1617, and having been *Knighted* was cr *a Baronet* [S] 28 Feb 1629, the patent being sealed 22 Feb 1630(ᵉ) with rem to heirs male whatsoever, and with a grant of presumably, 16,000 acres in Nova Scotia, which were erected into the Barony of Agnew of which he actually got enfeoffment on the Castle Hill, Edinburgh(ᶠ) He was M P [S] for Wigtownshire, 1628-33, 1643 1644, and 1645 47 He acted as Sheriff of Galloway for thirty-three years, but resigned that office in 1649 to his son He *m* about 1598 Margaret 1st da of the Hon Sir Thomas KENNEDY of Culzean (s of Gilbert 3d EARL OF CASSILIS [S]) by Elizabeth, da of David McGILL of Cranstoun Riddel He *d* at Lochnaw, at a good old age, in the autumn of 1661 and was *bur* with his wife, in the old church of Leswalt, M I

II 1661   SIR ANDREW AGNEW, Baronet [S 1629], of Lochnaw aforesaid, 9th Hereditary Sheriff of Galloway, s and h, *suc to the Baronetcy* in 1661, and was served h to his father 29 Oct 1661 He had been previously *Knighted*, was five times M P [S] for Wigtownshire, 1644, 1648-49, 1665, 1667, and 1669-72, was one of the Commissioners for Scotland, during the interregnum after the execution of Charles I In 1656 he was *appointed* Sheriff of *all* Galloway, which included Kircudbrightshire In 1661 he was *restored* to

---

(ᵃ) He was, apparently, landless, the estate of Newtoun had been granted to his cousin. Patrick Oliphant See p 367, note "c"

(ᵇ) Neither he nor his elder brother are styled Baronets in this retour, but in the disposition of 1691 he is styled ' Sir George "

(ᶜ) He had two yr brothers, viz [1], William Oliphant, mentioned in 1641. and [II], John Oliphant, *bap* 13 Oct 1626 No heir male, however, of the family is now [1901] known to exist [*Ex inform* Sir J Balfour Paul, Lyon King of Arms, chiefly from notes supplied by J Maitland Thomson, Curator of the Scottish Historical dept , from which source, also, almost all the information in this article is taken]

(ᵈ) See "The Agnews of Lochnaw, Hereditary Sheriffs of Galloway" by Sir Andrew Agnew, Baronet, M P Edinburgh, 1st edit 1864, 2d edit (2 vols) 1893

(ᵉ) Milne's List, Laing's List

(ᶠ) See note "d" above, but, according to Banks's *List*, no seisin appears to have followed the grant

his ancient *Hereditary* Shrievalty   He *m* (contract 22 March 1625) Anne, da of Alexander STEWART, 1st EARL OF GALLOWAY [S], by Grisel, da of Sir John GORDON, of Lochinvar   He *d* 1671   Will dat at Lochnaw, 15 Feb 1668

III   1671   SIR ANDREW AGNEW, Baronet [S 1629], of Lochnaw aforesaid, 10th Hereditary Sheriff of Galloway, s and h, *suc to the Baronetcy* in 1671, and was enfeoffed in his father's estates, 2 Oct. 1671   In 1682 he was superseded as Sheriff(a) for refusing to take the test act, but was restored, 25 April 1689, by the Grand Convention of Estates, of which he was a member He was M P [S] for Wigtownshire, 1685, and 1689 till his death   He *m* (covenant dat 24 Oct 1656) Jane, da of Sir Thomas HAY, of Park, 1st Baronet [S 1663], by Marion HAMILTON, an illegit da of James, DUKE OF HAMILTON [S] He was *bur* 9 June 1702

IV   1702   SIR JAMES AGNEW, Baronet [S 1629], of Lochnaw aforesaid, 11th Hereditary Sheriff of Galloway, s and h, *suc to the Baronetcy* in June 1702   In 1708 he sold the Irish estates of the family (which had been long in their possession) to his agent, Patrick Agnew   In 1724 he resigned the Sheriffdom to his son   He *m* (covenant dat 22 June 1683) Mary da of Alexander MONTGOMERIE, 8th EARL OF EGLINTON [S] by his 1st wife, Elizabeth, 1st da of William (CRICHTON), 2d EARL OF DUMFRIES [S]   By her he had a large family   He *d* aged 75 and upwards, at Edinburgh, 9 March 1735 His widow *d* April 1742, aged 90   Both *bur* in the Abbey of Holyrood

V   1735   SIR ANDREW AGNEW, Baronet [S 1629], of Lochnaw aforesaid, 12th Hereditary Sheriff of Galloway, s and h, *b* 21 Dec 1687 *suc to the Baronetcy*, 9 March 1735   Having entered the army, he was in command of the Government troops at Blair Castle in 1745 against the young Chevalier   He was made Governor of Tinmouth Castle, becoming finally, 1759, Lieut Gen in the Army   In 1747, on the final abolition of all Hereditary jurisdictions in Scotland, he received £4,000 as compensation for his Hereditary Shrievalty, or the county of Wigtown(c)   He *m* 12 May 1714, at St Benet's Paul's wharf, London, his cousin, Eleanor, only da, and eventually sole h of Thomas AGNEW, of Creoch and of Richmond, co Surrey, sometime a Captain in the Scotch Greys by (—), da of John DUNBAR of Mochrum   It was a runaway match, the bride being only 15, and the post-nuptial settlement was dated 22 April 1719   By her he had 7 sons and 11 daughters   He *d* 14 or 21 Aug 1771, aged 84   His widow *d* 29 May 1785

VI   1771   SIR STAIR AGNEW, Baronet [S 1629] of Lochnaw aforesaid, 15th child and 5th but 1st surv s and h *b* 9 Oct 1734, sometime a merchant, and, as such, had been to Virginia, *suc to the Baronetcy* in Aug 1771   He *m* firstly, Marie, da of Thomas BAILLIE, of Polkemmet   She *d* Nov 1769   He *m* secondly, 11 April 1775, Margaret da of Thomas NASMYTH, of Dunblan   He *d* 28 June 1809   His widow *d* 30 May 1811

VII   1809   SIR ANDREW AGNEW, Baronet [S 1629], of Lochnaw aforesaid, grandson and h, being posthumous s and h of Andrew AGNEW, an officer in the army, by Martha, da of John (DE COURCY) LORD KINGSALE [I], which Andrew was 1st s and h ap of the late Baronet, but *d v p* 11 Sep 1792   He was *b* 21 March 1793, *suc to the Baronetcy*, 28 June 1809, M P for Wigtownshire, 1830-37, and was well-known for his endeavours to enforce a stricter observance of Sunday   He *m* 11 June 1816 Madeline, yst da of Sir David CARNEGIE, of Southesk, 5th Baronet [S 1663], by Agnes-Murray, da of Andrew ELLIOT   He *d* 12 April 1849 at his house, Rutland sq, Edinburgh, aged 56   His widow *d* 21 Jan 1858, at Edinburgh, aged 62

(a) John Graham, of Claverhouse, was appointed in his room

(b) In only four families was, after 1567, the Shrievalty of their respective counties continuous, viz (1) the Campbells, Earls and afterwards Dukes of Argyll [S], for co Argyll and co Tarbert, (2) the Leslies, Earls of Rothes [S], for co Fife, the Murrays of Philiphaugh for co Selkirk, and (4) the Agnews for Galloway

2 Z

VIII. 1849   SIR ANDREW AGNEW, Baronet [S 1629], of Lochnaw
                aforesaid s and h, b 2 Jan 1818 at Edinburgh, ed at Harrow,
entered the army 1835, sometime an officer of the 93rd Foot, serving during the
rebellion in Canada, 1838, but retired when Captain in the 4th Light Dragoons,
suc to the Baronetcy 12 April 1849, was M P for Wigtownshire, 1856-68, Vice-
Lieut, 1852   He *m* 20 Aug 1846, Mary Arabella Louisa, 1st da of Charles
(NOEL), 1st EARL OF GAINSBOROUGH, by his 3d wife, Arabella, da of Sir James
WILLIAMS, *formerly* HAMLYN, 2d Baronet [1795]   She who was b 16 March 1822,
d 27 June 1883, aged 61, at Lochnaw Castle   He *d* there 25 March 1892, aged 74

IX.   1892   SIR ANDREW NOEL AGNEW, Baronet [S 1629] of Loch-
                naw aforesaid, 1st s and h, b 14 Aug 1850 at Exton Park co
Rutland, ed at Harrow and at Trin Coll, Cambridge, LL B 1871, Barrister
(Inner Temple), 1874, M P for South Edinburgh since 1900, *suc to the Baronetcy*,
25 March 1892   He *m*, 15 Oct 1889, at St Peter's, Eaton sq, Pimlico, Gertrude,
3d and yst da and coheir of the Hon Gowran Charles VERNON (yr s of the
1st BARON LYVEDEN), by Caroline, da of John Nicholas FAZAKERLEY, of Burwood,
Surrey   She was b 16 June 1860

Family Estates —These, in 1883, consisted of 6 777 acres in Wigtownshire worth
£11,100 a year   *Principal Seat* —Lochnaw Castle, near Stranraer, co Wigtown

---

KEITH

cr 28 July 1629,

sealed 8 May 1630(ᵃ),

dormant, apparently, after 14 Feb 1771

I   1628   SIR WILLIAM KEITH, of Ludquhairn, only s and h of
                Sir William KEITH, of the same, by Margaret sister of George,
5th EARL MARISCHAL [S], da of William KEITH, *styled* LORD KEITH, suc his
father before 1625 and was cr a Baronet [S] 28 July 1629, the patent being sealed
8 May 1630(ᵃ) with rem to heirs male whatsoever, no grant or seizin of lands in
Nova Scotia however being recorded   He was a Royalist and was Col of horse
in Hamilton's "engagement"   He *m* (—)   He *d* before 1660

II   1655?   SIR ALEXANDER KEITH, Baronet [S 1629] of Ludquhairn
                aforesaid, 2d but only surv s and h (ᶜ) *suc to the Baronetcy* on the
death of his father   He *m* Margaret, da of Alexander BANNERMAN of Elsick,
co Kincardine

III 1680?   SIR WILLIAM KEITH, Baronet [S 1629], of Ludquhairn
                aforesaid, s and h, *suc to the Baronetcy* on the death of his father
He *m* (—), da and coheir of George SMITH, of Rapness in the Orkneys, by
Anne, da of Patrick GRAHAM, of Inchbraikie   He *d* before her   His widow *m*
Sir Robert MURRAY, of Abercairny

IV   1700?   SIR WILLIAM KEITH, Baronet [S 1629], of Ludquhairn
                aforesaid, s and h, b about 1669, *suc to the Baronetcy* on the
death of his father, was, from 1716 to 1726, Governor of Pennsylvania in
North America   He *m* (—), da of (—) NEWBERRY   He *d* 18 Nov 1749, aged
80

(ᵃ) Milne's List, and Laing's List, in which last he is called "Knight"   The
creation is sometimes given as 28 *June*

(ᵇ) This William was 6th in descent from John Keith, of Innerugy, 2d son of
Sir Edward Keith, Marischal of Scotland

(ᶜ) His eldest son, Sir William Keith, was much in favour with Charles I, by
whom he was, though a young man, made Knight Marischal [S]   He *d s p*
and *v p*

V. 1749, SIR ROBERT KEITH, Baronet [S. 1629], s. and h., *suc. to*
to *the Baronetcy*, 18 Nov. 1749. He served in the Prussian
1771. service, under his cousin, the well-known Field-Marshal Keith,
in Russia, Poland, Germany, Turkey, and Sweden, becoming a
Lieut.-Colonel, and was subsequently (after the Marshal's death in 1758) in the
Danish service, in which he became Major-General, and Commandant of Hamburg.
He *m.* in or before 1751, Margaret Albertina Conradina, only da. of Ulrich
Frederich VON SUCHIN, Envoy from the King of Poland (Elector of Saxony) to
the court of Russia, by Elizabeth, da. of Peter VON LITH, Envoy from the Czar
of Russia to the Court of Prussia. He *d.* 14 Feb. 1771, when the *Baronetcy*
became *dormant*.(ª)

SAINT ETIENNE, *or* DE LA TOUR :
cr. 30 Nov. 1629 (ᵇ)
dormant or *extinct* probably about 1660.

I. 1629. "SIR CLAUDE SAINT ETIENNE, Knight, Seigneur de la
Tour and Uuarse" sometimes spoken of as "CLAUDE DE LA TOUR,"
a native of France, who had rendered Sir William Alexander, great assistance
in the settlement of the colony of Nova Scotia, was *cr. a Baronet* [S.] by patent,
dat. at Whitehall, 30 Nov. 1629, with rem. to the heirs male of his body(ᵇ), the
said patent, however, not being recorded in the *Registrum Preceptorum cartarum
pro Baronettis Novæ Scotiæ*, or in the Great Seal Register [S.]. He, together with
his son Charles (who was similarly created 12 May 1630) received, 30 April 1630,
a grant of lands, presumably 16,000 acres each, in Nova Scotia, entitled respectively
the Barony of St. Etienne and the Barony of De la Tour(ᶜ), on condition that
they, their heirs and successors should be "good and faithful vassels" of the
King of Scotland. This condition he ceased to fulfil (thereby apparently, forfeiting the said grant) when he took part with the French, on their entry into Nova
Scotia after the treaty of St. Germain (29 March 1632) by whom he was made
Gov.-Gen. of the province, another Frenchman, named D'Aulney, being subsequently added as a co-partner with him. He apparently was dead before 13 May
1649, when Charles, his son and successor (see next below) is called "Lord of De
la Tour in France."

II. 1645? SIR CHARLES SAINT ETIENNE, Baronet [S. 1629], s. and h.,
to who, v.p., as "CHARLES SAINT ETIENNE, Esquire, Seigneur de St.
1660? Denniscourt and Baigneux" had already been *cr. a Baronet* [S.]
by patent dat. at Whitehall, 12 May 1630,(ᵇ) in like manner as
his father, with whom he received grant of lands in Nova Scotia, as above stated(ᶜ).
He *suc. to the Baronetcy* conferred on his father, apparently before 13 May 1649,
when as "Lord of De la Tour in France and Knight Baronet of Scotland" he, for
£2,084 to be redeemed 20 Feb. 1652, mortgages the Fort La Tour and plantation
near the mouth of the St. John's river, as the same was purchased, 30 April 1630, by
Sir Claude St. Etienne, of Sir William Alexander. This fort he had held for many
years against the French, when they, according to their construction [or miscon-
struction] of the treaty of St. Germain (29 March 1632) invaded Nova Scotia.
He made good his title to these premises when in England in 1656. On his death,
both of his *Baronetcies* appear to have become *dormant* or *extinct*.

(ª) He had two sons : (1), Frederick William Keith, *b.* 7 Oct. 1751, Lieut. in
the Danish Guards ; (2), Robert George Keith, *b.* 6 Oct. 1752. Of these,
however, nothing more is known. They possibly *d.* unm. and before their father.

(ᵇ) The patent of 30 Nov. 1629; an abstract of that of the Baronetcy [S.],
12 May 1630 and the grant of lands,. dat. 30 April 1630 are given in Banks's
account of Nova Scotia Baronets [*Baronia Anglica concentrata*, vol. ii, pp. 210-248]
from which work the description of these grantees and the particulars of their
career are also taken. The same dates of creation are given in Laing's List,
"on the authority of former lists."

(ᶜ) No Seizin of these lands is recorded in Banks's Lists.

HANNAY, or AHANNAY

cr 31 March 1630, (^a)

dormant, 1689—1783, and again since 1842

I. 1630   ROBERT HANNAY, *or* AHANNAY, of Mochrum, co Kirk-
                cudbright, " Knight,"(^a) whose parentage is unknown, was
appointed Clerk of the Nichells [1] by Privy Seal, 19 Oct 1629 (patent 11 Dec
1631), which office he surrendered 30 May 1639, and was *cr a Baronet* [S]
31 March 1630,(^a) the patent, however, not being in the Great Seal Register, [S]
with rem to heirs male whatsoever, and with a grant of, presumably, 16,000
acres in Nova Scotia, of which he does not appears to have had seizin (^b)   He
m (—), da of (−) STEWART   He *d* 8 and was *bur* 24 Jan 1657/8 in Dublin
Funeral entry [1] Admon 29 Nov 1658 [I] to his s, Sir Robert Hannay   His
widow *d* 22 March and was *bur* 27 March 1662 in Christ Church, Dublin
Funeral entry [I]

II. 1658   SIR ROBERT HANNAY, Baronet [S 1630], s and h, *suc*
     to   *to the Baronetcy* 8 Jan 1657/8, was a Captain of Foot [I] 1661
     1689   He *d s p*,(^c) presumably unm,(^d) and was *bur* at St Michan's,
                Dublin, 30 April 1689,(^e) when the *Baronetcy* appears to have
remained *dormant* for nearly 100 years

        *   *   *   *   *   *   *

III 1783   SIR SAMUEL HANNAY, Baronet(^f) [S 1630] of Kirkdale,
                co Galloway was served and retoured heir male of the 1st
Baronet, 26 Sep 1783, and *assumed the Baronetcy* accordingly   He was s and h of
William HANNAY, of Kirkdale aforesaid, by Margaret da of the Rev Patrick John-
STON, of Girthon, which William is said to have been(^g) s of Samuel, s of William, s
of Patrick, s of another Patrick, s of John s of Alexander HANNAY, who purchased
Kirkdale, in 1532, and who was uncle to Patrick HANNAY, of Sorbie, ancestor of
the first Baronet   He *m* in 1768, Mary, da of Robert MEAD   He *d* 11 Dec
1790 Admon Jan 1791   Admon of his widow, March 1800

IV   1790,   SIR SAMUEL HANNAY, Baronet(^f) [S 1630], s and h, *b*
     to   12 Aug 1772, *suc to the Baronetcy,*(^f) 11 Dec 1790, was in the
     1842.   service of the Emperor of Austria, holding an official post at
                Vienna, where he *d s p m* (presumably unm) 1 Jan 1842,
when the *Baronetcy* became *dormant*

(^a) Laing's List, in which he is called " Knight," though in Milne's List, where
no date of creation is given, he is called " Esquire of the body "

(^b) Banks's Lists

(^c) Of his two sisters and coheirs one *m*, as his 1st wife, Sir George Acheson,
3d Baronet [S 1628], who *d* 1685, aged 55, while the other, Jane, *m* firstly,
before May 1645, Charles (Coote), 1st Earl of Mountrath [I] secondly, Sir
Robert Reading, Baronet [I], and *d* Nov 1684

(^d) " The Lady Elinor Hanna " *bur* 4 Jan 1673 at St Mary's, Reading, may
possibly have been his wife

(^e) G D Burtchaell, of Ulster's office, Dublin, has kindly supplied most of the
information in this article.

(^f) According to the retour of 1783

(^g) Playfair's *Baronetage* [S] but the number of generations in 200 years
[1581 1783] seems excessive

STEWART

cr. 18 April 1630(ª)

cancelled 7 June 1632.

I 1630,   JAMES (STEWART), LORD STEWART OF OCHILTREE [S.],
to   who had been so *cr* 9 June 1615 was *cr* a *Baronet* [S] 18 April
1632.   1630,(ª) but being shortly afterwards "under a criminal processe " (ᵇ)
the patent was cancelled, 7 June 1632, before it passed the Great
Seal Register [S] There is no record of any grant or seizin of lands in Nova
Scotia For further particulars of him, see *Peerage*

FORBES ·

cr. 20 April 1630.(ᶜ)

I 1630   WILLIAM FORBES, of Craigievar and Fintray, co. Aber
deen, 1st s and h of William FORBES, of the same, Merchant,
(who had purchased Craigievar in 1610, and who finished building the Castle
there), by Margaret, da of Nicol UDWARD, Provost of Edinburgh, suc his father
in Dec 1627, and was *cr* a *Baronet* [S] 20 April 1630,(ᶜ) the patent, however
not being recorded in the Great Seal Register [S], with rem to heirs male whatsoever, and with a grant of, presumably, 16,000 acres in Nova Scotia, of which he
does not appear to have had seizin(ᵈ) He was M P [S] for Aberdeenshire,
1639-41 , 1644, and 1645-46, was Sheriff of Aberdeen, 1647, commanded a troop
of horse in the Parliamentary service and held various public offices for that
party during the Civil War He *m*, in or before 1636, Bethia, 2d da of Sir
Archibald MURRAY, 1st Baronet [S 1628], by Margaret, da of (—) MAULE. He
d 1648 His widow *m* Sir Alexander FORBES of Tolquhoun

II 1648.   SIR JOHN FORBES, Baronet [S 1630], of Craigievar and
Fintray aforesaid, 1st s and h , *b* 1636, *suc* to the *Baronetcy* in
1648, was known as "Red Sir John " and as a man of great energy He was
M P [S] for Aberdeenshire, 1689, and 1689-1702 He *m* in or before 1659,
Margaret, da of (—) YOUNG of Auldbar He *d* 1703

III 1703.   SIR WILLIAM FORBES, Baronet [S 1630], of Craigievar
and Fintray aforesaid, 1st s and h , *b* 1660, *suc* to the *Baronetcy*
in 1703 He *m* 16 Oct 1684, Margaret, 1st da of Hugh ROSE, of Kilravock, by
Margaret, da of Sir Robert INNES, of Innes

IV 1730 ?   SIR ARTHUR FORBES, Baronet [S 1630], of Craigievar
and Fintray aforesaid, 6th but 1st surv s and h (ᵉ), *b* 1709, *suc*
to the *Baronetcy* on the death of his father, was M P for Aberdeenshire, 1732-47
He *m* firstly, in 1729, Christian, 1st da of (—) Ross, of Arnage, Provost of
Aberdeen She *d* s p m He *m* secondly, in 1750, Margaret, widow of John
BURNETT, of Elrick, co Aberdeen, da of (—) STRACHAN, of Balgall He *d* 1 Jan
1773

(ª) Laing's List, where it is stated to be "given on the authority of former
lists "

(ᵇ) Laing's List, as in note "a" above In 1631 he was imprisoned for having
made, but failed to establish, a charge of high treason against the Marquess
of Hamilton [S]

(ᶜ) Laing's List, Milne's List, in which last these words are added " No
document before bot ane old list "

(ᵈ) Banks's Lists

(ᵉ) One of his elder brothers, Hugh Forbes, the 2d s and for a long time the
heir ap of his father, *m* Jane, da of James (Ogilvy), Earl of Finlater [S], but
d s p. and v.p before 1722

V. 1773   SIR WILLIAM FORBES, Baronet [S 1630], of Craigievar and Fintray aforesaid, 2d but 1st surv s and h, by 2d wife, b 1755, suc to the Baronetcy 1 Jan 1773 He m 7 June 1780, at Sempill house, Sarah, 1st da of John (SEMPILL), 13th LORD SEMPILL [S], by Janet, da of Hugh DUNLOP, of Bishoptoun She d 8 Dec 1799 at Fintray House He d 15 Feb 1816 in his 68th year

VI 1816   SIR ARTHUR FORBES, Baronet [S 1630], of Craigievar and Fintray 1st s and h, b 1784, sometime an officer in the 7th Hussars, suc to the Baronetcy, 15 Feb 1816 He d unm 1823

VII 1823.   SIR JOHN FORBES, Baronet [S 1630], of Craigievar and Fintray aforesaid, br and h, b 2 July 1785, was sometime a Judge in the East India Company's service, suc to the Baronetcy, 1823 He m 24 May 1824, Charlotte Elizabeth, 3d da of James Ochoncar (FORBES), 17th LORD FORBES [S], by Elizabeth, da and h of Walter HUNTER, of Polmood He d 16 Feb 1846 at Fintray House, aged 60 His widow d 5 Feb 1883, in her 83d year, at 26 Albyn place, Aberdeen

VIII 1846   SIR WILLIAM FORBES, Baronet [S 1620], of Craigievar and Fintray aforesaid, 1st s and h, b at Fintray House, 20 May 1836, suc to the Baronetcy, 16 Feb 1846, ed at Eton, sometime, 1854-57, Lieut Coldstream Guards, serving in the Crimean campaign, Capt 9th Aberdeenshire Rifle Volunteers, 1859-61 and subsequently Hon Col thereof He m firstly, 23 June 1858, at Clapham, Surrey, Caroline Louisa only da of Sir Charles FORBES, 3d Baronet [1873] of Newe, by Caroline, da of George BATTYE She was divorced in Dec 1861(a) He m secondly, 18 Nov 1862, at St James' Westm, Frances Emily, 7th and yst da of Sir Robert John ABERCROMBY, 5th Baronet [S 1636], by Elizabeth Stephenson da of Samuel DOUGLAS, of Netherlaw She was living when he suc to the Peerage as LORD SEMPILL [S] on the death, 5 Sep 1884, of his cousin, Mary Jane, suo jure BARONESS SEMPILL [S] In that Peerage this Baronetcy then merged and still so continues, see Peerage

---

MURRAY ·

cr 20 April or 2 Oct., and sealed 4 Dec. 1630 ,(b)

sometimes, 1794—1811, MURRAY-PULTENEY.

I 1630   WILLIAM MURRAY, of Dalzene, i e, Dunerne, co Fife, s and h ap of William MURRAY, of Dunerne aforesaid, by his 1st wi e, Marjorie SCHAW (which William, last named, was 4th and yst s of Andrew MURRAY, of Blackbarony) was cr a Baronet [S], 20 April or 2 Oct, the patent being sealed 4 Dec 1630(b), but not recorded in the Great Seal Register [S], with a grant of, presumably, 16,000 acres in Nova Scotia, called the Barony of New Dunearn, of which he had seizin in the said month of Dec 1630 (c) He, who had suc his father, 25 Dec 1628, purchased the lands and Barony of Newton, in Midlothian He m 27 July 1620 at Kensington, Mary, 2d da of William (ALEXANDER), 1st EARL OF STIRLING [S], by Janet, da and coheir of Sir William ERSKINE He d in or before 1641 Will cont 4 March 1641

(a) She m 19 June 1862, Septimus E Carlisle, and d 11 Dec 1872

(b) "No charter of this Baronetcy is known to be on record, except in an instrument of sasine, where a charter of creation is narrated, the date of which is 20 April 1630" [Burke's *Baronetage,* 1901] The date of the creation is 2 Oct and that of the sealing, 4 Dec 1630, in Milne's List In Laing's List the date is also 2 Oct 1630, it being there stated to be given "on the authority of former lists"

(c) Banks's Lists

II 1641 ? SIR WILLIAM MURRAY, Baronet [S 1630], of Newton aforesaid, 1st s and h , *suc to the Baronetcy* on the death of his father He m (contract 3 Feb 1644) Jane, da of Patrick (MURRAY), 1st LORD ELIBANK [S], by his 4th wife, Helen, da of Sir James LINDSAY

III 1670 ? SIR WILLIAM MURRAY, Baronet [S 1630], of Newton aforesaid, 1st s and h , *suc to the Baronetcy* on the death of his father He m (--) Marion CRICHTON

IV. 1700 ? SIR WILLIAM MURRAY, Baronet [S 1630], of Newton aforesaid, only s and h , *suc to the Baronetcy* on the death of his father He d s p s

V 1730 ? SIR JAMES MURRAY, Baronet [S 1630], of Hilhead, cousin and h male, being 2d s of James MURRAY, of Outerston, by Magdalen, da and h of John JOHNSTON of Polton, which James last named was 4th and yst s of the 1st Baronet He who was Receiver General of the Customs [S], *suc to the Baronetcy* on the death of his cousin He m Marian, da of James NAIRN He d s p at Edinburgh, 14 Feb 1769

VI 1769 SIR ROBERT MURRAY, Baronet [S 1630], nephew and h male, being only s of Colonel William MURRAY, by Anne, da of Hosea NEWMAN, which William was yr br of the late Baronet, being 3d and yst s of James MURRAY, of Polton abovenamed He was Receiver Gen of the Customs [S], by resignation of his uncle, on whose death in 1769 he *suc to the Baronetcy* He is said to to have m firstly, 22 June 1750, Janet, 4th da of Alexander (MURRAY) 4th LORD ELIBANK [S], by Elizabeth, da of George STIRLING, of Edinburgh She d 9 Aug 1759 He m secondly, Susan, da of John RENTON, of Lamerton, by Susan, da of Alexander (MONTGOMERIE), EARL OF EGLINGTON [S] He d 21 Sep 1771

VII 1771 SIR JAMES MURRAY, *afterwards* (1794 1811) MURRAY-PULTENEY, Baronet [S 1630], 1st s and h by 1st wife b about 1755, *suc to the Baronetcy* 21 Sep 1771, having entered the army that year, served in America, 1775, was at the capture of St Lucia, 1778, Adjutant-General to the troops in Flanders, 1793-94, Col of the 18th Foot, 1794, becoming finally Lieut -General, 1799 He was M P for Weymouth, 1790 till his death, was P C 30 March, 1807 and Secretary at War, 1807-09 Having m , 23 July 1794 Henrietta Laura, *suo jure* BARONESS BATH, *afterwards* COUNTESS OF BATH, only da and h of Sir William JOHNSTONE, *afterwards* PULTENEY 5th Baronet [S 1700], by his 1st wife, Frances, da and eventually sole heir of Daniel PULTENEY, he assumed the name of PULTENEY, his wife having inherited the vast estates, formerly belonging to William (PULTENEY) EARL OF BATH She, who was b 6 Dec 1766, and who was cr a Baroness 23 July 1792 and a Countess 26 Oct 1803, d at Brighton 14 and was bur 23 July 1808 (with her parents) from Bath House, Picadilly, in Westm Abbey, aged 41 Will pr Aug 1808 He d s p , 26 April 1811, from the bursting of a powder flask at Buckenham, co Norfolk Will pr 1811, and again May 1825 (a)

VIII 1811. SIR JOHN MURRAY, Baronet [S 1630], br of the half-blood and h , being s of the 6th Baronet by his 2d wife He was b about 1768, entered the army, 1788, served in Flanders, 1793-94, was in command in India, 1800-05, was tried, Jan 1815 by court-martial for his conduct at Tarragona, in May 1813, but acquitted of all but "error in judgment," and

(a) He is said to have left £600,000 to his brother of the half-blood, John Murray, afterwards the 8th Baronet and £200,000 to William Murray, another such brother, afterwards the 9th Baronet The Pulteney estates which he enjoyed seventeen years (for he held them for life after his wife's death) were valued at £40,000 a year

became Col of the 56th Foot in 1818, and a full General in 1825   He was M P
for Wootton Bassett, 1807-11, and for Weymouth, 1811-18   He *suc to the
Baronetcy*, and to a fortune of above half-a-million, on the death of his br , 26
April 1811, was **G.C H** , and had the orders of the Red Eagle of Prussia and of
St Januarius of Naples   He *m* 25 Aug 1807, Anne Elizabeth, only da and h of
Constantine John (PHIPPS), 2d BARON MULGRAVE [I], by Anne Elizabeth, da and
coheir of Nathaniel CHOLMLEY, of Whitby Abbey and Howsham, co York   He
d s p 15 Oct 1827, at Frankfort-on-Maine   Will pr Jan 1828   His widow *d* at
Turin, 10 April 1848 aged 50   Will pr Oct 1848

IX   1827   SIR WILLIAM MURRAY, Baronet [S 1630], next br and
               h , *b* in Edinburgh about 1769, ed at Westminster, matric at
Oxford (Ch Ch) 14 June 1786, aged 17, B A , 1790, M A , 1793, was in Holy
Orders, Rector of Lavington, Wilts, 1795, Rector of Lofthouse, co York, 1802-42,
suc to the Baronetcy, 15 Oct 1827   He *m* in 1809, Esther Jane, da of (—) GAYTON
He *d* 14 May 1842   Will pr Sep 1842   His widow *d* 6 Feb 1875, at 52 Elgin
terrace Notting Hill, Midx , aged 83

X   1842   SIR JAMES PULTENEY MURRAY, Baronet [S 1630], of
               Englefield Green, Berks, 1st s and h , *b* about 1814, *suc to the
Baronetcy*, 14 May 1842   He *d unm* 20 Feb 1843, in his 30th year   Will pr
July 1843

XI   1843   SIR ROBERT MURRAY, Baronet [S 1630], br and h , *b*
               1 Feb 1815, in London, *suc to the Baronetcy*, 20 Feb 1843   He *m*
firstly 21 Aug 1839, at St Geo Han sq , Susan Catherine Saunders, widow of
Adolphus COTTIN-MURRAY, 2d da and coheir of John MURRAY, of Ardeley Bury,
Herts, Commissary Gen in the Peninsular War   She *d* 31 April 1860   He *m*
secondly 1 Dec 1868, at Walcot, near Bath, Laura, widow of the Rev William
Henry CRAWFORD of Haughley park, Suffolk, yst da of the Rev Charles TAYLOR,
Rector of Biddesham, Somerset   She *d* 5 March 1893   He *d* , at 21 Brunswick sq ,
Brighton, 15 April 1894, aged 79   Both were bur at Brighton   His will pr
28 Nov 1894, at £5,156

XII   1894   SIR WILLIAM ROBERT MURRAY, Baronet [S 1630] of
               Ashenden Lodge, in Buntingford, Herts, only s and h , by 1st wife,
b 19 Oct 1840, at Ardeley Bury aforesaid, *suc to the Baronetcy*, 15 April 1894
He *m* firstly, in 1868, Lastania, da of J FONTANILLA, of La Plata   She *d s p m*
in 1873   He *m* secondly, in 1874, Esther Elizabeth, widow of John RICKARD, of
London, da of P BODY, of co Sussex   She *d* 1884   He *m* thirdly, 22 Sep 1885,
Magdalene Agnes, da of Gerard GANDY, of Oaklands, Windermere

CROSBIE, or CROSBY
c 24 April 1630 ,([a])
dormant in 1646 or 1647.

I.   1630,   "SIR PIERS CROSBIE, Knt , Privy Councellor of Ire-
     to   land"([a]) of Maryborough, in Queen's County, only s and h of
     1646 ?   Patrick CROSBIE, or CROSBY,([b]) of Maryborough aforesaid, (who *d*
22 March 1610, being older br of John CROSBIE, Bishop of Ardfert,
1600-21) by (—) da of (—),([c]) was *Knighted* at Theobalds, 17 July 1616, served

([a]) Laing's List
([b]) Most of the information in this and the following article has been supplied
by G D Burtchaell, of Ulster's office, Dublin
([c]) This Patrick, in his will, calls Sir Thomas Roper (afterwards, 1627, 1st
Viscount Baltinglass [I]), his brother, so possibly he *m* Roper's sister   Roper's
wife, Ann, was a da of Sir Henry Harington

at the relief of Rochelle, 1627, and also, as Colonel, under Gustavus Adolphus, King of Sweden, was a Gent of the Privy Chamber to Charles I, P C [I] and was cr a Baronet [S] 24 April 1630(a) (being the same date as the creation of his cousin, Walter Crosbie), the patent, however, not being recorded in the Great Seal Register [S], with rem to heirs male and with a grant of, presumably, 16,000 acres in Nova Scotia, of which he appears never to have had seizin (b) He was M P [I] for Queen's County, 1634-35, and for Gowran, 1641-46, opposing the Irish policy of the Earl of Strafford, for which conduct he was condemned by the Star Chamber and confined in the Fleet prison By patent 4 April 1637, his lands in Queen's County were erected into the Manor of Ballyfin, and those in co Kerry into the Manor of Odorney He m firstly, after 1610, Sarah, 3d da of Sir Patrick Barnewall, of Gracedieu and Turvey, co Dublin, by Mary, da of Sir Nicholas Bagenall, Marshall of the Army [I] She d s p m (c) 10 March 1617/8 Funeral certificate [I] He m secondly, 6 March 1618/9, at St Bride's, London, Elizabeth, Dow Countess of Castlehaven [I], sister of Edward, 2d Viscount Campden, da of Sir Andrew Noel, of Dalby, co Leicester, by Mabel, da of Sir James Harington She was living 8 Dec 1644 He d s p s between Nov 1646 and Nov 1647, when the Baronetcy became dormant Will in which he directs his burial to be at St Patrick's, Dublin, or in the Franciscan Monastery of Kildare, and in which he devises all his estate to "his lawful heir," Sir John Crosbie, Baronet [S 1630] dat 17 Nov 1646, pr by the said Sir John, 12 Nov 1647 at Leighlin and again in the Prerog Court [I] 28 Oct 1663

CROSBIE, or CROSBY
cr 24 April 1630(a)

I 1630 WALTER CROSBIE, of Maryborough, 1st s and h (d) of John Crosbie, Bishop of Aldfert, 1600-21, suc his father in Sept 1621 was Sheriff of Queen's County, 1626-27, and was cr a Baronet [S] 24 April 1630(a) (being the same date as the creation of his cousin, Piers Crosbie), the patent, however, not being recorded in the Great Seal Register [S], with rem to heirs male and with a grant of, presumably, 16,000 acres in Nova Scotia, of which he appears never to have had seizin (b) He was M P [I] for Maryborough 1634-35 He m firstly. Mabel, sister of Sir Valentine Browne, 1st Baronet [I 1622], 4th da of Sir Nicholas Browne, of Molahiffe, co Kerry, by Sheela, da of O'Sullivan Beare He m secondly Anne, widow of Capt Richard Christy, da of John Tendall, of Dickleborough, Norfolk He d at Ballybrittas, Queen's county, 4 and was bur 6 Aug 1638, in Maryborough Church Funeral certificate [I] Will dat 21 April 1630, pr 1 Sept 1638 [I] Inq p m 17 Jan 1668 His widow m in 1662, Walter Furlong Will dat 31 Dec 1662, pr 4 Jan 1662/3 [I]

(a) Laing's List
(b) Banks's Lists
(c) Elizabeth, her only da, d unm 11 Jan 1625 Funeral certificate
(d) The 2d son, David Crosbie, of Ardfert, was ancestor of the Barons Brandon [I] 1758-1832, who were Earls of Glandore [I] from 1776 to 1815, the 3d son (who is often ignored and who is not to be confounded with his nephew, Sir John Crosbie, the 2d Baronet) was Sir John Crosbie, or Crosby, of Tullyglass, co Down, Knighted at Southwick, 16 Aug 1628, who m 23 July 1638, at St Werburgh's, Dublin, Mary, widow of Richard Fowler, of Bedfordshire, sister of Elizabeth, Countess of Devonshire, both being daughters of Edward Boughton, of Causton, co Warwick He d s p 14 and was bur 16 Jan 1639/40, in Dromore Cathedral Funeral Certificate [I] The will of his widow was pr 1658 in Prerog Court [I] The 4th son of the Bishop was Patrick Crosbie, admitted to Gray's Inn, 7 May 1619, who is also generally ignored [See p 376, note "b"]

3 A

II 1638   SIR JOHN CROSBY, or CROSBIE, Baronet [S 1630], of
               Ballyfin, Queen's County and of Waterstown, co Kildare, 3d but
1st surv s and h ,(ª) by 1st wife, *suc to the Baronetcy* 4 Aug 1638, was indicted
for high treason, 1642, and his estates forfeited during the Commonwealth He
m after Oct 1638, Elizabeth FITZGERALD (ᵇ) He was living 1688

III 1695 ?   SIR WARREN CROSBIE, Baronet [S 1630], of Crosbie
               Park co Wicklow grandson and h , being s and h of Maurice
CROSBIE, of Knockmoy, Queen's County, by Dorothea da of John ANNESLEY, of
Ballysonan, co Kildare, which Maurice was attainted in 1688 and *d v p* (ᶜ) He
suc to the Baronetcy on the death of his grandfather He was Capt in Gen
Sutton's Reg of foot He *m* Dorothy, da of Charles HOWARD, of Haverares, co
Northumberland She *d* 29 Oct 1748, being drowned in the Slaney, while
passing the ford, co Carlow He *d* at Crosbie park 30 Jan 1759 Will dat
3 June 1757, pr 21 Feb 1759 [I]

IV 1759   SIR PAUL CROSBIE, Baronet [S 1630], of Crosbie Park
               aforesaid, s and h , *suc to the Baronetcy* 30 Jan 1759 He *m* Mary,
da of Edward DANIEL of Freadsom, Cheshire He *d* in Jarvis street, Dublin,
Nov 1773 Admon [I] 7 Dec 1773 to his brother, Edward CROSBIE

V 1773   SIR EDWARD WILLIAM CROSBIE, Baronet [S 1630], of
               Crosbie Park aforesaid, and of Viewmount, co Carlow, s and h ,
suc to the Baronetcy in Nov 1773, was B A (Trin Coll) Dublin, 1774 He
registered his pedigree in Ulster's office, 14 Feb 1776 He *m* by spec lic 14 Dec
1790 in Granby Row, Dublin, Castiliana, widow of Capt Henry DODD, of the 14th
Dragoons, 1st da of Warner WESTENRA, of Rossmore park, co Monaghan, by
Hester, da of Richard (LAMBART) 4th EARL OF CAVAN [I] He *d* 5 June 1798,
being executed at Carlow for alleged complicity with the Irish rebels Will pr
[I] 1804, that of his widow pr [I] 1806

VI 1798   SIR WILLIAM CROSBIE, Baronet [S 1630], of Bray, co
               Wicklow, only s and h , *b* 18 May 1794 at Viewmount aforesaid,
suc to the Baronetcy 5 June 1798 He *m* 30 March 1830, his cousin, Dorothea
Alicia, da of John WALSH, of Dublin, by Henrietta, 3d da of Sir Paul CROSBIE,
4th Baronet abovenamed He *d s p*, 3 Oct 1860, at Bray Will pr [I] 25 April
1861, by his widow She *d* 11 Feb 1880 Her will pr [I] 7 April 1880

VII 1860   SIR WILLIAM RICHARD CROSBIE, Baronet [S 1638], of
               Bedford, Beds , cousin and h male, being only s and h of Edward
CROSBIE, by Jane, yst da of James HENRY, of co Kildare, which Edward (who *d*
25 June 1834) was only s and h of Richard CROSBIE (*m* 1780), who was 2d son
of Sir Paul CROSBIE, 4th Baronet abovenamed He was *b* 30 Sep 1820, and *s*
to the Baronetcy 3 Oct 1860 He *m* 11 April 1854, Catherine, only da of the
Rev Samuel MADDEN, of Kells Grange, co Kilkenny, by Thomasine, only child of
Thomas DUCKET, of Graignasmutton, Queen's County He *d* 6 May 1877, at
Bedford, aged 56 His widow *d* 5 Dec 1882

(ª) Of his elder brothers (1) John *d* an infant, and (2) Maurice *d* 18 and was
bur 20 April 1633 at St Audeen's, Dublin, being then the heir apparent Funeral
certificate [I] [See p 376, note "b"]

(ᵇ) She is said (by James McCullagh, Ulster King of Arms, 1759-65) to have
been a da of Thomas, Earl of Kildare [I], but this is impossible Possibly she
may have been sister to George, 16th Earl of Kildare [I], and yst da of Thomas
Fitzgerald, by Frances, da of Thomas Randolph She is *not*, however, named in
the pedigree registered in Ulster's office [See p 376, note "b"]

(ᶜ) Admon [I.] 16 Jan 1716/7, to his son

VIII 1877 SIR WILLIAM EDWARD DOUGLAS CROSBIE, Baronet
[S 1630], 1st s and h, b 13 Oct 1855, sometime Lieut in
the Bedfordshire Militia, suc to the Baronetcy 6 May 1877 He m, 21 June, 1893,
Georgina Mary, 1st da of Thomas Edward Milles MARSH, of 34 Grosvenor Place,
Bath

SAINT ETIENNE
cr 12 May 1630,
dormant, or extinct, probably about 1660

I 1630,   "CHARLES SAINT ETIENNE, Esquire, Seigneur de St
to   Denniscourt and Baigueux," s and h ap of Sir Claude SAINT
1660?   ETIENNE, Baronet [S], so cr 30 Nov 1629 with rem to the heirs
male of his body, was himself cr a Baronet [S] 12 May 1630, with
like remainder receiving, 30 April 1630, a grant of land in Nova Scotia together
with his father, to whose Baronetcy he succeeded apparently before 13 May 1649
See fuller particulars, p 371, under the creation of 30 Nov 1629 On his death
[Qy about 1660?] both these Baronetcies appear to have become dormant or
extinct

SIBBALD
cr 24 July 1630; (a) sealed 31 Dec 1630,
dormant 1680? to 1833, and since 1846

I 1630   JAMES SIBBALD, of Rankeillour, in the parish of Moni-
mail, co Fife, 1st s and h (b) of Andrew SIBBALD, of the same,
by Margaret, da of George LEARMOUTH of Balcomie, co Fife, was cr a Baronet
[S] 24 July 1630(a) the patent being sealed 30 Dec following (but not entered in
the Reg Precept Curt pro Baronettis Novæ Scotiæ) with rem to heirs male whatsoever, with a grant of, presumably, 16,000 acres in Nova Scotia, entitled the
Barony of Rankeillour-Sibbald in Anti Costi, having on the 28th, a Crown Charter
of the same as a Regality, and having seizin thereof 3 Feb 1631 (c) He m in
1606, Margaret, 1st da of David BARCLAY, of Cullernv He d at his house at
Cupar, 21 May 1650, and was bur at Cupar (d)

II. 1650,   SIR DAVID SIBBALD, Baronet [S 1630], of Rankeillour
to   aforesaid s and h Knighted, 22 June 1633, at Holyrood, suc to
1680?   the Baronetcy, 21 May 1650 He sold Rankeillour to Sir Archibald HOPE On 9 Dec 1673 he was served heir to his uncle,
George SIBBALD MD, of Gibliston, co Fife He m (contract 12 Nov 1625)
Anna, da of Sir Henry WARDLAW, of Pitreavie, by whom he had several sons, (c)
who all d s p and possibly v p (d), on his death the Baronetcy became dormant
and remained so more than one hundred and fifty years

*   *   *   *   *   *   *

(a) Laing's List
(b) His yst br, David Sibbald, was father of Sir Robert Sibbald, MD, author
of several antiquarian works, who died Aug 1722, aged 81
(c) Banks's Lists, see also Banks's Bar Angl Conc, vol ii, p 241
(d) Ex inform R R Stodart, Lyon clerk depute (1863-86)
(e) James, probably the 1st son, was b 4 Nov 1627, the 2d son, Henry
Sibbald of Gibliston abovenamed, was living 1674 and soon afterwards sold
that estate The youngest son, George d s p, his brother, John Sibbald, being
served, 27 May 1678 his heir general

III. 1833,   SIR WILLIAM SIBBALD, Baronet(a) [S. 1630], of
   to   Edinburgh, sometime a sailor at South Shields, was only
   1846.   s. of James SIBBALD, master mariner at South Shields,
            2d s. of James SIBBALD, desk and trunk maker at South
Shields, 3d s. of David SIBBALD, a sailor, Portioner of Canongate (who, on
28 July 1694, was served heir general of his grandfather), s. of George
SIBBALD, of Canongate, only s. of George SIBBALD, of the same, formerly
of Uthrogall, near Rankeillour aforesaid, who was 2d of the 1st Baronet.
He, on 31 May 1831, was served heir male of Henry SIBBALD, 2d s. of the
2d Baronet, and on 18 Nov. 1833 was served heir male special to the
1st Baronet in the Barony and Regality of Rankeillour-Sibbald in Nova
Scotia, whereupon he *assumed the Baronetcy.* He, on 13 May 1834 (as a
Baronet) was served heir to his great grandfather,(b) David SIBBALD. In
1846, however, these services were reduced before the Court of Session
at the instance of the Lord Advocate, though it has been remarked thereon
(by Maidment) that the evidence in *Sir* William's case was better than
that produced by many wealthy persons left to enjoy their assumed
honours without challenge.(c)

RICHARDSON :

cr. 13 Nov. 1630 ; sealed 31 Jan. 1631(d) ;

dormant 1640, or 1642, to 1678? ; 1752 to 1783? and 1821 to 1837.

I. 1630.   ROBERT RICHARDSON, of Pencaitland, co. Haddington,
            younger s. of James RICHARDSON, of Smeaton in that county and
of Pencaitland aforesaid, by Elizabeth DOUGLAS, his wife; was M.P. [S.] for co.
Haddington 1630, and was *cr. a Baronet* [S.] 13 Nov. 1630, the patent being sealed
13 Jan. 1631,(a) but not recorded in the Great Seal Register [S.], with apparently
rem. to heirs male whatsoever, and with a grant of, presumably, 16,000 acres in
Nova Scotia, entitled the Barony of Pencaitland in New Brunswick, of which
he had seizin in Feb. 1631.(e) He *m.* 4 Jan. 1610, Euphan, da. of Sir John
SKENE, of Currichill, Lord Clerk Register [S.] 1594-1612. In 1634 he was old
and in bad health, and, being offended with his eldest son, sold his estate to
John SINCLAIR, but *d.* April 1635, within a year of this transaction, when his son
reduced the sale(f).

II. 1635,   SIR ROBERT RICHARDSON, Baronet [S. 1630], of Pencait-
   to   land aforesaid, 1st s. and h., *b.* 24 Jan. 1613, *suc. to the Baronetcy*
   1640 ?   in April 1635, and was on 30 of that month served heir general of
            his father, and on 30 Sep. following, heir special. He sold his
estate of Pencaitland to James MACGILL, of Cranstoun Riddell. He *d. s.p.,*(g)

(a) According to the service of 18 Nov. 1833.

(b) In both cases it was before a respectable jury. In 1833 one of the jury was
a writer to the Signet and the trial was held before George Tait, Sheriff
Substitute of Edinburgh. In 1834, one of the jurors was John Melville, afterwards Knighted and sometime Lord Provost of Edinburgh.

(c) See p. 379, note " d."

(d) Laing's List; as also in Milne's List, where the date of the sealing is added,
and the description given as " of Eister Pentland."

(e) Banks's Lists.

(f) *Ex inform.* R. R. Stodart, Lyon clerk depute (1863-86), as also is much else
contained in this article.

(g) His only br., Alexander Richardson had *d.* the year before him, presumably, s.p.m.

being then an "indweller in Smeaton" in 1640, or 1642 when the *Baronetcy* became *dormant* and remained so for nearly forty years

*   *   *   *   *   *   *

III   1678 ?   SIR JAMES RICHARDSON, Baronet [S 1630,] of Smeaton
aforesaid, cousin and h male, being s and h of James RICHARDSON,
of the same (d 11 June 1634), by Rachel WARDLAW, which James, was s and h
of Sir James RICHARDSON, of Smeaton aforesaid (d 25 Dec 16**), elder br of the
1st Baronet   He, however, did not assume the Baronetcy till long after the death
of the 2d Baronet, though they both were actually residents in the same parish
He was *Knighted* by Charles II, at Scone, 2 Jan 1651, and was served heir
general of his grandfather, 30 June 1656   On 25 May 1672 the testament of his
1st wife is recorded as ' spouse of Sir James Richardson of Smeaton, *Knight*"
Before the end of 1678, however, he *assumed the Baronetcy*, and recorded his
arms as ' *Knight Baronet*," though (oddly enough) the badge of Nova Scotia was
omitted   He m firstly, before 1649, Anne McGILL, whose will is recorded 25 May
1672   He m secondly, Helen, widow of Sir John HAMILTON, of Redhouse co
Haddington, formerly Helen RICHARDSON, spinster, probably one of the two
sisters and coheirs of the 2d Baronet (ᵃ)   He d 1680   His widow d 1688

IV   1680   SIR JAMES RICHARDSON, Baronet [S 1630,] of Smeaton
aforesaid, s and h by 1st wife, *suc to the Baronetcy*, 1680   In
1707 he petitioned Parliament for protection from arrest   In 1708 he sold the
estate of Smeaton   He m in 1666, Margaret, 6th da of William (KERR), EARL OF
LOTHIAN [S], by Ann, *suo jure* COUNTESS OF LOTHIAN [S]   He d 28 May 1717,
at Holyrood   His widow was confirmed as his sole executrix on 29 Nov following

V   1717   SIR JAMES RICHARDSON, Baronet [S 1630], s. and h ;
sometime Captain in the Scots Foot Guards, *suc to the Baronetcy*,
28 May 1717   He d s p 13 April 1731   Will pr 1731

VI   1731   SIR WILLIAM RICHARDSON, Baronet [S 1630], br and
h , sometime Lieut in Col Kerr's Dragoons, *suc to the Baronetcy*,
13 April 1731   He m Eleanor, 1st da of Robert HILTON, of Bishop's Auckland,
by Elizabeth, da of George CROZIER, of Newbiggin   He d in England, 4 April
1747 (ᵇ)

VII   1747,   SIR ROBERT RICHARDSON, Baronet [S 1640], s and h ,
to   sometime Captain in the Royal Artillery, *suc to the Baronetcy*, 4
1752   April 1747   He d s p, 1752,(ᶜ) when the *Baronetcy* again became
dormant, and so remained for about thirty years

*   *   *   *   *   *   *

VIII   1783 ?   SIR JAMES RICHARDSON, Baronet,(ᵈ) [S 1630,] having
assumed the title without a service, registered arms in the Lyon
office [S], 8 Feb 1783, as "*Sir James Richardson*, of Bellmount, in Hanover
parish, Jamaica, *Baronet*, heir male of the families of Smeatoun and Pencaitland "
In 1768, however, no such Baronetcy is mentioned in the registration of arms
(10 May 1768) to his yr br George RICHARDSON, who is merely described as
"descended of a younger son of the family of Richardson of Smeaton "   He was

---

(ᵃ) This match may have been the cause of his (tardy) assumption of the
Baronetcy, but it is, however, *just possible* that the heir male from 1640 to 1678
might be a son or grandson of Alexander Richardson next elder br of the 1st
Baronet, though no such descendant can be found in any of the family pedigrees
     (ᵇ) The will of "Sir William Richardson" is proved 1769, being, however,
apparently that of a "Knight," who died at Bermondsey, 16 March 1769
     (ᶜ) His uncle, George Richardson, Captain in Col Handysides' Reg of Foot,
had d s p 1748
     (ᵈ) According to the registration of 8 Feb 1783

s. and h. of George RICHARDSON,(ᵃ) Writer [S.], by Jean, da. of James WATSON, of Woodend, co. Stirling, which George was s. and h. of James RICHARDSON, Burgh Clerk of Perth (d. 1723), s. of James RICHARDSON, said to have been Notary Public at Forgandenny,(ᵇ) co. Perth (but more probably at Forgan, co. Fife), who is said to have been a legitimate s. of Robert RICHARDSON, who was (undoubtedly) 2d s. of Sir James RICHARDSON, of Smeaton, Knt., br. of the 1st Baronet. He d. unm., 24 Nov. 1788, at Paradise, Savannah-le-Mar, Jamaica.

IX. 1788.   SIR GEORGE RICHARDSON, Baronet(ᶜ) [S. 1630], of Abingdon street, Westminster, br. and h.; sometime a naval officer in the East India Company's service, and Capt. of the ship "Pigott," when he registered arms, 10 May 1768, in the Lyon office [S.]. Was Commander of the "Ganges"; suc. to the Baronetcy,(ᶜ) 24 Nov. 1788. He m. at Freeland, co. Perth (at some date subsequent to the birth of their sons, who, of course were legitimated [S.] thereby), Mary, da. of David COOPER, R.N. He d. 11 and was bur. 20 Dec. 1791, at St. Margaret's Westm. Will pr. Jan. 1792. His widow was bur. there (from Marylebone) 15 Jan. 1828, aged 76. Will pr. Feb. 1828.

> IX. bis. 1791,   SIR JOHN RICHARDSON, Baronet(ᵈ) [S. 1630], br.;
> to   who, denying the legitimacy of his nephews, assumed the
> 1801.   Baronetcy(ᶜ) in 1791. He was a Barrister at Law of the
>   Middle Temple, London. He d. s.p. at Calcutta, 1801.
> Will pr. 1804.

X. 1791.   SIR GEORGE PRESTON RICHARDSON, Baronet(ᶜ) [S. 1630], s. and h. of Sir George abovenamed, suc. to the Baronetcy,(ᶜ) 11 Dec. 1791; was a Major in the 64th Foot. He was mortally wounded at the taking of St. Lucia, 22 June 1803 and d. unm. 21 Oct. following in his 26th year at Barbadoes. Admon. Jan. 1805.

XI. 1803.   SIR JAMES RICHARDSON, Baronet(ᶜ) [S. 1630], br. and h.; Lieut. 17th Native Infantry. He suc. to the Baronetcy,(ᶜ) 22 June 1803. He d. unm. in India, 8 Nov. 1804, of wounds received in Lord Lake's action. Admon. March 1808.

XII. 1804,   SIR JOHN CHARLES RICHARDSON, Baronet(ᶜ) [S. 1630], to   br. and h.; b. about 1785; sometime Commander in the Royal 1821.   Navy; suc. to the Baronetcy,(ᶜ) 8 Nov. 1804, and entered and signed his pedigree at the Heralds' College, London, 15 June 1807. He d. s.p., in Marylebone, 12 and was bur. 19 April 1821, at St. Margaret's Westm., aged 36, when the Baronetcy became again dormant, and so remained for sixteen years. Will pr. 1823.

*   *   *   *   *   *   *

(ᵃ) This George is styled " Sir George Richardson, Baronet" in the service of 9 Jan. 1837, mentioned in the text below, but if he had been a Baronet, or had even so styled himself, surely his son George would not (as abovestated) have been described in 1768 as " descended of a younger son, etc."

(ᵇ) In a service dated 26 Jan. 1693, of James Richardson, the Burgh Clerk of Perth to (his maternal grandmother) Janet JOHNSTON, (mother of his mother, Margaret MILLER) of Forgan, he is stated to be son of James Richardson, Notary Public in Forgan, not Forganderry, which last is a small village in Perthshire.

(ᶜ) According to the registration of 8 Feb. 1783.

(ᵈ) According to his own view of his heirship to the person registered as a Baronet in 1783.

XIII.   1837   SIR JOHN STEWART-RICHARDSON, Baronet(a) [S 1630],
of Pitfour, co Perth, cousin and h male, being s and h of James
RICHARDSON, of Pitfour aforesaid, by Elizabeth, 1st da and coheir of James
STEWART, of Urrard, co Perth, which James RICHARDSON (who d 26 July 1823,
having assumed the supporters granted to the Baronetcy, though, apparently, not
the Baronetcy itself, on the death, 12 April 1821, of the 12th Baronet), was s
and h of John RICHARDSON, of Pitfour (who purchased that estate and d 1821),
who was s of Thomas RICHARDSON of Perth, a Baker, and 'Deacon of the
Bakers" of that burgh (b) who was s of William RICHARDSON, of Forgandenny,
co Perth, who is stated (in the service of 1837) to have been younger s of
James RICHARDSON,(c) Notary Public (see p 382, line 3), to have been a legitimate
s of Robert RICHARDSON, who was (undoubtedly) 2d s of Sir James RICHARDSON,
of Smeaton, Knt, br of the 1st Baronet   He was b 1 Sep 1797, was an
Advocate [S] 1 July 1820   He, on inheriting one-third of the estate of Urrard,
being that of his maternal grandfather, assumed the name of *Stewart* before
that of *Richardson*   He was served 9 Jan 1837 heir male of Sir John Charles
RICHARDSON the 12th Baronet and of that Baronet's father, Sir George, the
10th Baronet, and on the 27 May 1837 *was entered* in Lyon's office [S] *as a
Baronet*, was Secretary to the order of the Thistle, 1843-75, was Major-Gen of
"the Royal Company of Archers" [S] *re* the Queen's body-guard   He m 20
Dec 1826, Mary da of James HAY, of Colliepriest, Devon   He d 1 Dec 1881, at
Edinburgh, aged 84   His widow d there 21 July 1886 in her 79th year

XIV   1881.   SIR JAMES THOMAS STEWART-RICHARDSON, Baronet(a)
[S 1630], of Pitfour aforesaid, 1st s and h, b 24 Dec 1840,
sometime Captain in the 78th Highlanders, Hon Colonel 3d Vol Batt of the
Black Watch, Secretary to the Order of the Thistle (on the resignation of his
father) 1875-95, *suc to the Baronetcy*,(a) 1 Dec 1881   He m 20 Oct 1868, Harriett
Georgina Alice, 2d surv da of Rupert John COCHRANE, of Halifax, Nova Scotia
He d 14 Feb 1895, at Pitfour Castle, aged 54   His widow living 1901

XV   1895   SIR EDWARD AUSTIN STEWART-RICHARDSON, Baronet(a)
[S 1630], 1st s and h, b 24 July 1872, Lieut 3d Batt Black
Watch, *suc to the Baronetcy*,(a) 14 Feb 1895, aide-de-camp to the Gov -Gen of
Queensland
Seat —Pitfour Castle, co Perth

MAXWELL
cr 25 Nov 1630 ,(d)
ex or *dormant* 1 Nov 1647

I   1630,   SIR JOHN MAXWELL, of Pollok, co Renfrew, only
to   s and h of Sir John MAXWELL, of Pollok aforesaid, by his 1st
1647   wife, Margaret (m 1569), da of William CUNNINGHAM, of Caprington, was b about 1583, suc his father (who was killed at the
battle of Lockerby), 7 Dec 1593, and was cr a Baronet [S], 25 Nov 1630 (d) there

---

(a) According to the entry in the Lyon office [S] of 27 May 1837   As to this
entry, R R Stodart (see p 380, note 'f") remarks —" On which assumption [i e,
that of the Baronetcy of Richardson] much has been and is said, but Sir John is
as safe as anyone in such a false position can be, having had every sort of
recognition "

(b) Thomas, s of William Richardson bap at Forgandenny, 23 Feb 1696, was
probably this Thomas   It is difficult to see how any satisfactory proof was
afforded of the parentage of the said William   There are other Richardsons in
these Registers, all of them apparently obscure people

(c) In the pedigree lodged with his petition, this James, the "notary," is left out,
and James Richardson, the town clerk (ancestor of the 8th and 9th Baronets),
and William Richardson, of Forgandenny, are put as *sons* (not as grandsons) of
Robert, the 2d s of Sir James

(d) Laing's List, where however it is stated to be "given on the authority of
former lists

being however no record of the same in the *Reg Precept Cart pro Baronettis Novæ Scotiæ*, with rem apparently to the heirs male of his body(ᵃ) and with a grant of presumably, 16,000 acres in Nova Scotia of which, however, he appears never to have had sasine (ᵇ) He *m* firstly, before he was twelve years of age(ᶜ) (contract 21 Aug 1593), Isobel, 2d da of Hugh (CAMPBELL), 1st LORD CAMPBELL or LOUDOUN [S], by his 1st wife, Margaret, da of Sir John GORDON, of Lochinvar. She *d* 1612 He *m* secondly, before 1615, Grizel, widow of David BLAIR, of Adamton, da of John BLAIR, of Blair, by Grizel, da of Robert (SEMPILL), LORD SEMPILL [S] He *d* s p m 1 Nov 1647, when the *Baronetcy* became extinct(ᵛ) or dormant (ˡ)

CUNINGHAM

cr 25 Nov. 1630, sealed 8 June 1631(ᶜ),

sometime, 1811-81, CUNINGHAM-FAIRLIE,

and, since 1881, FAIRLIE-CUNINGHAME

I 1630 DAVID CUNINGHAM, of Robertland, in the parish of Stewarton, co Ayr, s and h of David CUNINGHAM,(ᶠ) of the same, by Margaret, da of Patrick FLEMING, of Barochan, co Renfrew, suc his father in April 1619, being in Nov following served his heir general and, in Oct 1628, his heir special in Robertland and was cr a Baronet [S], 25 Nov 1630, sealed 8 June 1631,(ᶜ) but not recorded in the Great Seal Register [S], with rem to heirs male whatsoever, and with a grant of, presumably 16,000 acres in Nova Scotia, entitled the Barony of New Robertland, of which, however, he appears never to have had seizin (ᵍ) He was, as "my honoured kinsman, Sir David Cuningham, of Robertland, Knt and Baronet," appointed universal legatee and executor in the will, dated 15 Dec 1647, of "Sir David Cuningham, of Covent Garden, co Midx, Knt and Baronet,"(ʰ) which he accordingly proved 26 Aug 1659 He was a Commissioner of Supply [S] in 1661 He, apparently, is the "SIR DAVID CUNYNGHAME, KNI AND BARONET of St Martin's in the Fields, Bachelor, aged 29," who had lic (London), 8 June 1637, to marry at St Faith's, "Elizabeth HARRIOTT, of the same parish widow, aged 28, widow of James HARRIOTT, Esq," i e, widow of James HERIOT, Jeweller to the King, da of Robert JOYCE, Keeper of the Robes (ⁱ) He, possibly (though more probably it was his son) *m*, as a 2d wife, Eva,(ᵏ) sister of James, 1st EARL OF KILMARNOCK [S] da of James (BOYD), 8th LORD BOYD [S], by Catharine, da of Robert CREYKE He *d* between Oct 1661 and Nov 1671 His will, unless, indeed, it is that of his son and successor, styling himself as "of

---

(ᵃ) In the petition for the grant of the Baronetcy [S] of Maxwell, of Pollok, cr 25 May 1682, it was asked (though not granted) that "the title might be revived and a patent granted bearing precedence from the date of the former"

(ᵇ) Banks's Lists

(ᶜ) Fraser's *Maxwell of Pollok*, vol 1, p 44

(ᵈ) He left his estate to his distant cousin, possibly his heir male, George Maxwell, of Auldhouse, a descendant of Thomas Maxwell, of Pollok living 1440, from whom testator was 6th in descent This George was father of John Maxwell, of Pollok cr a Baronet [S], 25 May 1682

(ᵉ) Laing's List, Milne's List

(ᶠ) This David, who *d* in April 1619, was s and h of Sir David Cuningham (living 1597, being ancestor of the 5th and succeeding Baronets), s of David, s of another David, who was the 1st of Robertland, 1530, and who is said to have been a yr s of William Cuningham, of Craigends

(ᵍ) Banks's Lists

(ʰ) See page 153 *sub* "Cuningham"

(ⁱ) See the *History of Heriots hospital*, where this Baronet is assigned as husband to this lady

(ᵏ) As her father was b about 1600 (his elder brother, the 6th Lord was b Nov 1595), the marriage is more likely to belong to the 2d than the 1st Baronet

Scotland, Knt and Baronet," is dat 8 Oct 1661 In it he directs his burial
to be at Kilmaurs, with his predecessors, stating his "great debts, burthens, etc,
and not mentioning any wife or child other than his "son and heir" David,
who is said (possibly by mistake),(a) to have pr the same 2 Nov 1671

II. 1665?   Sir David Cuningham, Baronet [S 1630], of Robertland
             aforesaid, only s and h , *suc to the Baronetcy* on the death of his
father   He presumably (and not his father), m Eva,(b) sister of James, 1st
Earl of Kilmarnock [S], da of James (Boyd), 8th Lord Boyd [S], by Catharine,
da. of Robert Creyke   She d. 6 May 1665 (c)   Will confirmed 20 May 1667 in
the Glasgow Com Court   He d s p (d) before 2 Nov 1671, when admon was
granted, he being therein styled as "Knight and Baronet of Robertland in
Scotland" to "Sir James Cunningham, Knight and Baronet [*sic*](e) uncle by
the father's side and next of kin "

III 1671?   Sir Alexander Cuningham, Baronet [S 1630], of
             Robertland aforesaid, uncle and h male *suc to the Baronetcy* in or
before 1671.   Had spec service, in Kirkland of Kilmaurs, to his nephew David,
29 Feb. 1672, and to his brother, David, in Robertland, 21 July 1692   He was
much in debt and disponed Robertland to Sir David Cuningham, 1st Baronet [S.
1702] of Milncraig.   He m Elizabeth, da and coheir of the Hon John Cuningham,
of Cambuskeith, a yr s of James, 7th Earl of Glencairn [S]   He was dead
in 1696.

IV 1690?   Sir David Cuningham, Baronet [S 1630], s. and h. *suc.*
    to   *to the Baronetcy* on the death of his father   He was insolvent and
    1708? was a prisoner in the Tolbooth of Ayr   In 1696 was released by
           Parliament and had authority to dispose of all his estates for his
creditors   Was accused of many frauds, as also of an endeavour to murder his
father   He m Elizabeth, widow of James Cuningham, *styled* Lord Kilmaurs, 2d
da and coheir of William (Hamilton), 2d Duke of Hamilton [S], by Elizabeth,
da and coheir of James (Maxwell), Earl of Dirleton [S]   He was living,
Aug 1705, but d s p m ,(f) probably soon afterwards when *the Baronetcy* became
dormant for about 70 years

                *   *   *   *   *   *   *

V 1778.   Sir William Cuningham, Baronet(g) [S 1630], of
            Auchinskeith in Riccarton, cousin and h male, being s and h of
William Cuningham, of Auchinskeith aforesaid, by (—), da of (—) Macilvein,
of Grimmet, co Ayr, which William, who d June 1727, was s and h of John

(a) This date of probate (2 Nov 1671) is also that of the admon of " Sir David
Cunningham, Baronet, of Robertland," i e (presumably) the *second* Baronet [S]
The admon *de bonis non* to the will of Sir David Cunningham, the English
Baronet [1642], pr 26 Aug 1659 by Sir David Cunningham, the 1st Baronet [S]
of Robertland, is granted 4 March 1674/5, "to Sir James Cunningham, Knight,
administrator of Sir David Cunningham, of Robertland in Scotland, Knight and
Baronet deceased, son of David Cunningham, of Robertland aforesaid, who was exor
and principal legatee of Sir David Cunningham, of Auchinharvey " The administration thus mentioned can apparently be no other than that of 2 Nov 1671,
i e , that of the 2d Baronet, as assigned to him in the text
    (b) See p. 384, note " k."
    (c) Burke's Baronetage for 1901
    (d) Euphemia, his only sister m James (Livingstone), 1st Viscount Kilsyth[S],
who d 7 Sep 1661.
    (e) The word "Baronet " is probably a mistake, and he is not so designated,
4 March 1674/5, see note "a." above   This James was a yr. br. of Alexander, who
(as in the text) suc their nephew as the 3d Baronet
    (f) Diana, his da and h m Thomas Cochrane, of Polkelly, co. Ayr, who d. s p
1694
    (g) According to the service of 3 Aug 1778.

    3 B

CUNINGHAM, of Wattieston, who was s and h of Christierne CUNINGHAM, yr br to Sir David CUNINGHAM, of Robertland, father of the 1st Baronet, to whom and to whose brothers the said Christierne, in 1619, was "Tutor" He suc his father in June 1727, to whom he was served h general, 19 March 1734, had sasine of Inchbean and other lands, 12 Oct 1764, and was served heir male of his great great grandfather, Sir David CUNINGHAM, of Robertland, 3 Aug 1778, when he *assumed the Baronetcy*, as consin and h male of the 1st Baronet, grandson of Sir David last named He m in 1741, Margaret, da of William FAIRLIE, of Fairlie, co Ayr He d 25 Oct 1781 His widow subsequently, in 1803, suc her br, Alexander FAIRLIE, in the family estates, and became heir-of-line of the family of MURE, of Rowallan She d 1811

VI   1781   SIR WILLIAM CUNINGHAM, afterwards (on his mother's death), CUNINGHAM-FAIRLIE, Baronet(ᵃ) [S 1630], of Fairlie aforesaid, s and h *suc to the Baronetcy*,(ᵃ) 25 Oct 1781 He m firstly, Anne, da of Robert COLQUHOUN, of the Island of St Christopher's He m secondly, Marianne, da of Sir James CAMPBELL, 3d Baronet [S 1668], of Aberuchill, by his 2d wife, Mary Anne, da of Joseph BURN He d at Fairlie House, 15 Oct 1811 His widow m James HATHORN and d s p

VII   1811   SIR WILLIAM CUNINGHAM-FAIRLIE, Baronet(ᵃ) [S 1630], of Fairlie House aforesaid, s and h, *suc to the Baronetcy*,(ᵃ) 15 Oct 1811 He m 21 May 1818, Anne, da of Robert COOPER, of Woodbridge co Suffolk He d s p, 1 Feb 1837 His widow d 21 Dec 1873

VIII 1837   SIR JOHN CUNINGHAM-FAIRLIE, Baronet(ᵃ) [S 1630], of Fairlie House aforesaid, br and h b 29 July 1779 He *suc to the Baronetcy*,(ᵃ) 1 Feb 1837, and registered arms as a Baronet in the Lyon office, 13 Dec 1837 He m 8 Aug 1808, Janet Lucretia, da of John WALLACE, of Cessnock and Kelly, co Renfrew He d s p 28 Feb 1852, at Fairlie House, in his 73d year His widow, who, after his death, resumed her patronymic of WALLACE, d 25 June 1877, at Mabie House, co Kirkcudbright, aged 95

IX.   1852   SIR CHARLES CUNINGHAM-FAIRLIE, Baronet(ᵃ) [S 1630], of Fairlie House aforesaid, br and h, b 22 Sep 1780 in Scotland, sometime in the East India Company's service He *suc to the Baronetcy* 28 Feb 1852 (ᵃ) He m 10 June 1806, Frances, 3d da of Sir John CALL, 1st Baronet [1791], by Philadelphia, 3d da and coheir of William BATTY, M D She d at Pisa, 12 May 1848 He d 1 June 1859, at 34, Thurloe Square, Brompton, Midx, aged 78

X   1859   SIR ARTHUR PERCY CUNINGHAM-FAIRLIE, Baronet(ᵃ) [S 1630], of Fairlie House aforesaid, s and h, b 22 Oct 1815, at Forston House, Dorset, *suc to the Baronetcy*,(ᵃ) 1 June 1859 About 1870 he sold the estate of Fairlie He m 5 Feb 1839, Maria Antonia, 6th da of William Bowman FELTON, of Sherbrook, Canada East, a member of Parliament in Quebec He d at Monaco, in the Riviera, 21 Sep 1881, aged 65 His widow, who was b 23 March 1820, d 9 Jan 1897, aged 76, at 8 Grosvenor street

XI   1881.   SIR CHARLES ARTHUR FAIRLIE-CUNINGHAME, Baronet(ᵃ) [S 1630], of Garnock House, Ryde, in the Isle of Wight, 1st s and h, b 2 Jan 1846, at Dieppe, educated at Cheltenham College and Trinity College, Cambridge, Lieutenant in the Ayrshire Yeomanry, 1865-75, *suc to the Baronetcy*,(ᵃ) 21 Sep 1881, when (the estate of Fairlie having been sold) he assumed the name of FAIRLIE-CUNINGHAME in lieu of that of CUNINGHAM-FAIRLIE He m 7 Nov. 1867, Caroline Madelina, 2d da of William Fordyce BLAIR, of Blair Dalry, co Ayr, Capt R N, by Caroline Isabella, da of John SPROT He d s p m 27 Dec 1897 in his 52d year, at the Hotel Victoria, Northumberland Avenue, Strand His widow living 1901

(ᵃ) See p. 385, note "g"

XII 1897   SIR ALFRED EDWARD FAIRLIE-CUNINGHAME, Baronet([a])
[S 1630], of Dawlish, co Devon, br and h, b 20 April 1852, at
Dieppe, assumed (like his brother) in 1881, the name of FAIRLIE-CUNINGHAME in
lieu of that CUNINGHAM-FAIRLIE, *suc to the Baronetcy*,([a]) 27 Dec 1897 He *m*
12 Nov. 1885, Arabella Annie, only da of Frederick CHURCH, an officer R N, by
Emma, da of the Rev Theobald WALSH, of Grimblethorpe Hall, co Lincoln, and
of Bridge House, Dawlish, co Devon

CUNINGHAM

supposed to have been cr. about 1630,

ex or *dormant* about 1670

I   1630?   "SIR WILLIAM CUNINGHAM, of Capringtoun" [i e,
to   Caprington in the parish of Riccarton, co Ayr], appears in
1670?   Milne's List of Scotch Baronets without any date and
with the remark that the creation is ' only in ane old list "([b])
No record thereof is in the Great Seal Register [S], and no grant of lands
in Nova Scotia is known, and the probability is it never existed The
person indicated was, doubtless, SIR WILLIAM CUNINGHAM, of Capringtoun,
or Caprington, s and h of William CUNINGHAM, of the same, by Agnes, da of
Sir Hugh CAMPBELL, of Loudoun He suc his father, between 1602 and
1618, was *Knighted* before 31 July 1618 He had several charters of lands
under the Great Seal, 1619-37, and was, according to the above account cr
a Baronet [S] probably about 1630 He was at first on the side of the
Parliament and was one of their Commissioners in 1640 and 1641, but subsequently joined Montrose, was fined £1,500 and imprisoned in Edinburgh Castle in 1646 to 1647 By these fines and by his own extravagance
he ruined his estate, from which he was finally evicted by his creditors,
who sold the same He *m* Margaret, 2d da of James (HAMILTON), 1st
EARL OF ABERCORN [S] by Marion, da of Thomas (BOYD), 5th LORD BOYD
[S] Her will as that of ' Dame Isabel Hamilton, spouse to Sir William
Cuningham, Knight," pr at Edinburgh, 4 May 1642 He *d* s p m and
probably s p, when the *Baronetcy* (if indeed it ever existed) became *extinct*
or *dormant*

WARDLAW.

cr. 5 March 1630/1, sealed 14 April 1631([c]).

I   1631   SIR HENRY WARDLAW, of Pitreavie, co. Fife, s and
h of Cuthbert WARDLAW, of Balmule, was *b* 1565, suc his
father in or before 1596; was Chamberlain to Anne, the Queen Consort [S],
acquired the estate of Pitreavie in 1606, which was erected into a Barony in 1627,
was *Knighted* 23 Oct 1613, at Royston and was *cr a Baronet* [S], 5 March 1630/1,
sealed 14 April 1631([c]), but not recorded in the Great Seal Register [S], with
rem to heirs male whatsover and with a grant of, presumably, 16,000 acres in

(a) See p 385, note "g"
(b) No such creation is mentioned in Laing's List where there are very many
creations given "on the Authority of former lists."
(c) Milne's List, Laing's List,

Nova Scotia, called the Barony of Wardlaw, of which he had seizin in April 1631 (ᵃ) He *m* Elizabeth, da. of (—) HUTTON (ᵇ) He *d.* 5 April 1637 Will pr at Edinburgh Commissariat, 8 Feb 1638

II 1637 SIR HENRY WARDLAW, Baronet [S 1631], of Pitreavie aforesaid, s and h, *suc to the Baronetcy*, 5 April 1637, and in July 1637 had seizin of the lands in Nova Scotia (ᵃ) He *m* Margaret, da. of DAVID BETHUNE of Balfour (ᶜ) He *d* 2 March 1653 Will at St Andrew's Commissariat, 26 April 1653

III 1653. SIR HENRY WARDLAW, Baronet [S 1631], of Pitreavie aforesaid, s and h, *bap* 24 March 1618, at Edinburgh, *suc to the Baronetcy*, 2 March 1653, was M P [S] for Fifeshire, 1661-63 He *m* 24 April 1672, Elizabeth, da of John SKENE, of Hallyards Will at St Andrew's Commissariat, 16 May 1683

IV 1683? SIR HENRY WARDLAW, Baronet [S 1631], of Pitreavie aforesaid, 1st s and h, *b* 1674, *suc to the Baronetcy* on the death of his father He *m* 13 June 1696, at Edinburgh, Elizabeth,(ᵈ) 2d da of Sir Charles HALKETT, 1st Baronet [S 1662], of Pitfirrane, by Janet, da of Sir Patrick MURRAY, of Pitdonnis Will pr at St Andrew's Commissariat, 5 Oct 1709, at Edinburgh, 19 March 1714

V 1709? SIR HENRY WARDLAW, Baronet [S 1631], of Pitreavie aforesaid, only s and h., *b* 1705, *suc to the Baronetcy* on the death of his father He *d s p*

VI. 1720? SIR GEORGE WARDLAW, Baronet [S 1631], uncle and h. male, being 2d s of the 3d Baronet, *b* 1675, *suc to the Baronetcy* on the death of his nephew. He *m* (—) da of (—) OLIPHANT

VII. 1730? SIR HENRY WARDLAW, Baronet [S 1631], only s and h. *suc to the Baronetcy* on the death of his father He was "a private soldier in the 3d Reg of the 2d Foot Guards," and, as such, made his will, 20 June, proved at St Andrew's, 15 July 1739. He *d* unm between those dates

VIII. 1739. SIR DAVID WARDLAW, Baronet [S 1631], of Craighouse, uncle and h male, being 4th s. of the 3d Baronet, *b* 1678, *suc to the Baronetcy* in 1739 He *m* firstly, Jean, da and h of (—) ROLLAND, of Craighouse aforesaid, and of Drumcaple, by Christian, da of (—) HUTTON He *m* secondly, Jean, da of (—) MERCER, of Aldie. but by her had no issue.

IX. 1750? SIR HENRY WARDLAW, Baronet [S. 1631], of Craighouse aforesaid, only s and h by 1st wife, *suc to the Baronetcy* on the death of his father He *m* Janet, da of (—) TAYLOR He *d* Feb 1782

(ᵃ) Banks's Lists
(ᵇ) Chalmers' *History of Dunfermline* Her father was possibly of Edinburgh, merchant, as she is elsewhere called "da of (—) Wilson [sic], of Edinburgh, merchant."
(ᶜ) Sir Henry Wardlaw, Baronet, is sometimes said to have *m* in 1653, as a 2d wife, Margaret, da of Sir John Henderson, of Fordell, by whom he had a da, Elizabeth This said Margaret is also said to have secondly married (—) Hay, of Naughton
(ᵈ) She was a Poetess and the author of the well known Scotch poem called *Hardy Knute*

X. 1782.   SIR DAVID WARDLAW, Baronet [S 1631], s. and h., *suc. to the Baronetcy* in Feb. 1782   He *m.* Margaret, da of Andrew SIMSON, of Broomhead, Town Clerk of Dunfermline   He *d* 13 April 1793.

XI. 1793   SIR JOHN WARDLAW, Baronet [S 1631], 5th and yst. but only surv s and h,[a] *suc to the Baronetcy*, 13 April 1793 He was an officer in the army, becoming finally Lieut Col in the 64th Reg.   He *m* Jean, sister of Admiral Sir Andrew MITCHELL, 2d da of Charles MITCHELL, of Piteadie and Baldridge, by Margaret, da of William FORBES, writer to the Signet She *d* at his house in Gayfield place, Edinburgh, 16 Feb 1800, and was *bur* in the family vault at Dunfermline   He *d* s p m s, 1 Jan 1823

XII 1823   SIR WILLIAM WARDLAW, Baronet [S 1631], cousin and h male, being 1st s and h of Alexander WARDLAW, an officer of Excise, by Margaret, da of (—) CAMPBELL, of Burnside, which Alexander was s of William WARDLAW[b] (*b* 1680), yr br of the 4th, 6th, and 8th Baronets, and 5th s of the 3d Baronet   He was *b* 1794, and *suc to the Baronetcy*, 1 Jan 1823   He *m* 12 July 1782, Elizabeth, da of George ANDERSON, in Carlungie, Angus   He was living 1823

XIII 1830?   SIR ALEXANDER WARDLAW, Baronet [S 1631], 3d but 1st surv s. and h, *b* about 1790, *suc to the Baronetcy* on the death of his father   He *d* unm 1833

XIV. 1833.   SIR WILLIAM WARDLAW, Baronet [S 1631], of Chessels Court, Canongate, Edinburgh, br and h, *b* about 1791, at Alloa, co Clackmannan, *suc to the Baronetcy* in 1833   He *d* unm 23 Dec 1863

XV 1863   SIR ARCHIBALD WARDLAW, Baronet [S 1631], br. and h, *b*. 23 Jan 1793, at Alloa aforesaid, *suc to the Baronetcy* 23 Dec 1863   He *d* s p 29 Jan 1874

XVI 1874.   SIR HENRY WARDLAW, Baronet [S 1631], of Balmule, near Tillicoultry, cousin and h male, being s and h of James WARDLAW, of the same, by his 1st wife, Margaret, da of John MONRO, of Dollar, which James (who *d* 5 March 1867, aged 80) was s of Henry WARDLAW an officer of Excise (*d*. 21 July 1820, aged 74), who was yr br of William, the 12th Baronet He was *b* 22 March 1822, *suc to the Baronetcy*, 29 Jan 1874   He *m* 24 July 1845, Christina, 3d da. of James PATON   He *d* in 1897

XVII 1897   SIR HENRY WARDLAW, Baronet [S 1631], of Balmule aforesaid, 2d but only surv. s and h, *b* 8 Feb 1867, *suc to the Baronetcy* in 1897   He *m* in 1892, Janet Montgomerie, da of James WYLIE

Residence.—Glendevon, Honor Oak Park, Forest Hill, co Kent.

---

[a] Of his four elder brothers (1) Henry, was an officer in the army, (2) Andrew, a midshipman R N, (3) David, an officer in the Dragoons.

[b] The descent of the 12th and the succeeding Baronets from this William as here given, agrees with that in Foster's *Baronetage* for 1883, wherein it is stated to have been "very courteously supplied by Messrs Duncan and Archibald, of Edinburgh, solicitors to Sir Henry Wardlaw," it being, however, added that "the information is unfortunately most meagre, and this is clearly a case for investigation prior to the title being officially acknowledged"

SINCLAIR

cr 2 June 1631, and sealed 18 June 1631(a),

afterwards, since 1789, EARLS OF CAITHNESS [S.]

I 1631   JAMES SINCLAIR, of Canisbay, co Caithness, s and h ap. of Sir William SINCLAIR,(b) of Canisbay aforesaid, of Mey in the said county, and of Cadboll, co. Ross, by Catherine, da of Sir David Ross, of Balnagowan, co Ross, was *cr a Baronet* [S] 2, the patent being sealed 18 June 1631, but not recorded in the Great Seal register [S] with rem to heirs male whatsoever, and with a grant of, presumably, 16,000 acres in Nova Scotia, called the Barony of Canisby Sinclair, of which he had seizin with "baill gold mines within the said Barony,' in July 1631 (c) He suc his father in 1643 and had, 18 July 1643, special service to his grandfather, the Hon George SINCLAIR, of Mey aforesaid (yr s of George, EARL OF CAITHNESS [S]), in the lands afterwards erected into the Barony of Cadboll He *m* Elizabeth, 3d da of Sir Patrick LESLIE, of Lindores, by Jean, da of Robert (STEWART), EARL OF ORKNEY [S.] He *d* 1662

II. 1662   SIR WILLIAM SINCLAIR, Baronet [S 1631], of Mey and Canisbay aforesaid, s and h , *suc to the Baronetcy* in 1662 He had special service, 15 April 1657 to his great uncle, Sir John(d) SINCLAIR, of Dunbeath, co Caithness, who *d* Sep 1651 He *m* (contract 4 Oct 1648) Margaret, 2d da of George (Mackenzie), 2d EARL OF SEAFORTH [S], by Barbara, da of Arthur (FORBES), 9th LORD FORBES [S] He was living 1670, but dead in 1685

III 1677?   SIR JAMES SINCLAIR, Baronet [S 1631], of Mey and Canisbay aforesaid, s and h , *suc to the Baronetcy* on the death of his father He *m* Jane,(e) sister and (in 1698) heir of George, EARL OF CAITHNESS [S], da of the Hon Francis SINCLAIR, of Keiss, Tister, and Northfield He was unjustly ejected from the Keiss and other of his wife's estates, by the Earl of Breadalbane [S], who claimed them under a disposition made in 1672, by George, the then Earl of Caithness [S] He was living 1704

IV 1710?   SIR JAMES SINCLAIR, Baronet [S 1631], of Mey and Canisbay aforesaid, s and h , *suc to the Baronetcy* on the death of his father. He *m* Mary, da of James (SUTHERLAND), 2d LORD DUFFUS [S],(f) by Margaret, da of Kenneth (MACKENZIE), 3d EARL OF SEAFORTH [S]

V 1730?   SIR JAMES SINCLAIR, Baronet [S 1631], of Mey and Canisbay aforesaid, s and h., *suc to the Baronetcy* in or before 1736 and was, on 11 Aug 1736, served heir male of entail and of provision general to his father He *m* Margaret, da of John SINCLAIR, of Barrack, by his 1st wife, Anne, d of Robert SINCLAIR, of Durran He *d* 4 Oct. 1760

(a) Milne's List , Laing's List

(b) Erroneously called a Baronet by Sir Robert Gordon in his history of the Sutherland family [*Ex inform* R R Stodart, Lyon Clerk Depute, 1863-86, by whom much else in this article was supplied]

(c) Banks's Lists

(d) This John is often, erroneously, supposed to have been *cr a Baronet* See note to Sir James Sinclair, 1st Baronet [S 1704], of Dunbeath, nephew and h male of the said John

(e) In Douglas's *Baronage* [S], his wife is given as "Frances, da of Sir John Towers, of that ilk" There never was such a family Probably it is a confusion with Jean, da and h of Sir John Towers, of Innerleith, who, about 1680, *m* Sir John Sinclair, 2d Baronet [S 1664], of Longformacus

(f) See Fraser's *Sutherland*, contradicting the account in Wood's *Douglas' Peerage* [S], which makes her da of Alexander, the 1st Lord

VI. 1760. SIR JOHN SINCLAIR, Baronet [S. 1631], of Mey and Canisbay aforesaid, s. and h., *suc. to the Baronetcy*, 4 Oct. 1760, and was, on 1 May 1765, served heir male of entail and provision special of his father in Mey, Canisbay, etc. He *m.* Charlotte, 2d da. of the Hon. Eric SUTHERLAND (who, but for his father's attainder, would have been 4th LORD DUFFUS [S.]), by Elizabeth, 3d da. of Sir James Dunbar, 1st Baronet [S. 1706], of Hempriggs. He *d.* April 1774, at Barrogill Castle, co. Caithness.

VII. 1774. SIR JAMES SINCLAIR, Baronet [S. 1631], of Mey aforesaid, s. and h., *b.* 31 Oct. 1766, at Barrogill Castle; *suc. to the Baronetcy* in April 1774, and had, on 5 Dec. 1785, special service to his father. He *m.* 2 Jan. 1784, at Thurso Castle, Jean, 2d da. of General Alexander CAMPBELL, of Barcaldine, by Helen, da. of George SINCLAIR, of Ulbster, co. Caithness. She was living, when by the death, 8 April 1789, of his distant cousin John, the 11th Earl, he became EARL OF CAITHNESS [S.]; his right, as such, being allowed 4 May 1793. In that peerage this *Baronetcy* then *merged* and still so continues.

SINCLAIR:

cr. (as alleged) 3 Jan. 1631(ª);

ex. soon after 1650.

I. 1631 SIR JOHN SINCLAIR, of Dunbeath, co. Caithness,
to 2d s. of the Hon. George SINCLAIR, of Mey, by Margaret,
1652? da. of William (FORBES) LORD FORBES [S.], which George was younger s. of George, EARL OF CAITHNESS [S.], is said to have been *cr. a Baronet* [S.] 3 Jan. 1631, with rem. to the heirs male of his body.(ª) He was M.P. [S.] for Caithness-shire 1649-50. He *m.* firstly, before 31 July 1634 (when she was living as his wife) Christian, da. of Magnus MOWAT, of Buchollie. He *m.* secondly, Catherine (*b.* 1619), da. of Hugh (FRASER) LORD LOVAT [S.], by Isabel, da. of Sir John WEMYSS. He was living May 1650 (Act Parl.) but *d.* s.p.m.(ᵇ) probably shortly afterwards, when the *Baronetcy became extinct.*(ᶜ) His widow *m.*, as his second wife, Robert (ARBUTHNOTT) 1st VISCOUNT ARBUTHNOTT [S.], who *d.* 10 Oct. 1655. She *m.* thirdly, in 1663, Andrew (FRASER) 3d LORD FRASER [S.], who *d.* 22 May 1674.

(ª) There is, however, no mention of any such creation in Milne's, Laing's, Banks's or any other List. Neither, apparently, is the supposed grantee called a Baronet in any Act of Parl. or other record. The limited remainder is an unusual one, at that date, for Nova Scotia Baronetcies, though so stated in Douglas's *Baronage* [S.], p. 252, and Playfair's *Baronetage* [S.], p. cclxviii, in which last the date of " 2 Jan." is supplied.

(ᵇ) Margaret, his da. (by his 1st wife), *m.* Hugh Rose, of Kilravock, and her eldest son, Hugh Rose, inherited £10,000 from his grandfather, Sir John Sinclair; her second son, John Rose, 5,000 merks and lands of the value of 50,000 merks; and her daughter Margaret 5,000 merks.

(ᶜ) The estate of Dunbeath was inherited by his nephew and h. male, William Sinclair, s. of his brother, Alexander Sinclair, of Latheron, co. Caithness, who *d.* before 1638. This William was a Royalist, and is incorrectly spoken of as the *second* Baronet (Burke's *Baronetage*, 1841-71, and Foster's, 1883, in the " Chaos"), but never assumed that title. He was suc. in the estate of Latheron by John Sinclair, his 2d but 1st surv. s. and h., who was suc. therein by James Sinclair, his s. and h. (*d.* 1775), who was suc. therein by another James Sinclair, who *d.* umm. 1788. The estate of Dunbeath, however, was inherited by James Sinclair, *fourth* s. of William Sinclair abovenamed, which James was *cr. a Baronet* [S.] 12 Oct. 1704. This creation, of 1704, is unnoticed in Playfair's *Baronetage* [S.], in which it is, misleadingly, said that he " appears to have claimed and used the title of Baronet under his grand-uncle's patent " of 2 Jan. 1631.

MACLELLAN :

cr (a) about 1631 ,

afterwards, 1633-1832, LORDS KIRKCUDBRIGHT [S] ,

dormant 19 April 1832

I   1631 ?   SIR ROBERT MACLELLAN, of Bombie in Galloway, s and h. of Sir Thomas MACLELLAN of the same, by Grizell, da of John (Maxwell), LORD HERRIES [S], suc. his father July 1597, was Gentleman of the Bedchamber to James VI [S], before and after his accession to the English throne, as also to Charles I , was M P   S] for Wigtonshire, 1621, and was cr a *Baronet* [S](a) about 1631, being subsequently cr , 25 June 1633, LORD KIRKCUDBRIGHT [S], in which Peerage this *Baronetcy* then *merged*, and so continued till on the death of the 10th holder, 19 April 1832, it became *dormant* He *m* three wives, as to whom, and as to other particulars about him and his successors, see *Peerage*

GORDON

cr 18 and sealed 29 June 1631(b)

I. 1631.   JOHN GORDON, of Embo, co. Sutherland, s and h of John GORDON, of the same, who, though of illegitimate descent, had acquired a great estate in that county, suc his father 23 Nov 1628, and was *cr* a *Baronet* [S] 18, the patent being sealed 29 June 1631,(b) but not recorded in the Great Seal Register [S], with rem to heirs male whatsoever, and with a grant of, presumably, 16,000 acres in Nova Scotia, entitled the Barony of New Embo, of which he had seizin in the said month of June 1631(c)   In 1634 he bought the estate of Achinnes   On 25 May 1648 he was served heir general of his father   He *m* Margaret, da of Hon Robert LESLIE, of Findrassie, co Moray, by Margaret, da of Alexander DUNBAR, of Grange, Dean of Moray, and one of the Lords of Session, which Robert was son of George, EARL OF ROTHES [S]   He *d* 1649, his estate being "much decayed."

II   1649   SIR ROBERT GORDON, Baronet [S 1631], of Embo aforesaid, s and h , *suc* to the *Baronetcy* in 1649, and was, on 5 June 1649, served heir general   His liabilities amounted to £10,862 2s 4d , and he was adjudged in 1649 to be imprisoned till that sum was paid   He was M P [S] for Sutherlandshire, 1649-50 and 1661, being in 1663 excused from attendance, as in the King's service   He *m* Jean,(d) da of Robert LESLIE, of Findrassie, co Moray, by Isabel, da of Abraham FORBES of Blackford   He *d* 16 Oct 1697

III.   1697   SIR JOHN GORDON, Baronet [S 1631], of Embo aforesaid, s and h , was (*v p*) M P [S] for Sutherlandshire, 1681-82, 1689 and 1689-1700, being in 1689 excused, as absent on the King's service, and being in 1693 ordered to sign the Assurance, on pain of forfeiting his seat   He *suc* to the *Baronetcy*, 16 Oct. 1697   He *d*. shortly before 10 May 1701

IV.   1701.   SIR WILLIAM GORDON, Baronet [S 1631], of Embo aforesaid, s. and h ; *suc.* to the *Baronetcy*, 10 May 1701, and on 10 Jan 1721, had special service to his grandfather in Embo, etc (e)   He *d* 14 April 1760

(a) The creation, without any date, is in Milne's List, being therein stated to be " in ane old list," and that " his armes as Baronet is in the Lyon's book "

(b) The date of creation in Laing's List, and that of the sealing in Milne's List.

(c) Banks's Lists

(d) She is often, though erroneously, called a sister of Lord Duffus

(e) He is often (erroneously) called M.P [S] for Cromarty and Nairn, 1741-42, but this relates to his namesake the 1st Baronet [S 1704] of Dalpholly and Invergordon

V. 1760   SIR JOHN GORDON, Baronet [S 1631], of Embo aforesaid, s and h , *suc to the Baronetcy*, 14 April 1760, and had, 19 Feb 1761, special service to his father in Embo aforesaid, etc He is said([a]) to have *m* firstly Charlotte, da of Kenneth (SUTHERLAND) 3d LORD DUFFUS [S], and secondly, in 1727, Margaret, widow of James SUTHERLAND, of Pronsy, da of William SUTHERLAND He *d* 24 Jan 1779 at Embo

VI 1779   SIR JAMES GORDON, Baronet [S 1631], of Embo aforesaid, 1st s and h , *suc to the Baronetcy*, 24 Jan 1779 He was a Colonel in the service of the States of Holland He *d* unm at Zutphen, in Guelderland, 1786

VII 1786   SIR WILLIAM GORDON, Baronet [S 1631], of Embo aforesaid, br and h , *b* 1736, entered the army 1755, becoming Captain in the 19th Foot, and subsequently in the Norfolk Militia, *suc to the Baronetcy* in 1786 He *m* 15 June 1760, Sarah, only da of Crosby WESTFIELD, an officer R N , by whom he had 14 children He *d* at Colchester, 7 Jan 1804 Will proved 1804 Will of "Dame Sarah Gordon" proved 1819

VIII 1804,   SIR JOHN GORDON, Baronet [S 1631], of Embo aforesaid, Jan 6th, but 1st surv s and h ([b]) Lieut of Engineers in the East India service, *suc to the Baronetcy*, 7 Jan 1804, and *d* unm a few months later, 12 Nov 1804, in Prince of Wales' Island

IX 1804   SIR ORFORD GORDON, Baronet [S 1631], of Embo Nov. aforesaid, only surv br and h , being 8th and yst s of the 7th Baronet, *b* at Norwich, Capt 78th Reg of Foot , *suc to the Baronetcy*, 12 Nov 1804 He *m* 20 Dec 1813, Frances, da of General Gore BROWNE, Col 44th Reg He *d* 19 June 1857, at Brighton Will proved July 1857 His widow *d* there (24 Brunswick Square), 11 Aug 1866, aged 72

X 1857   SIR WILLIAM HOME GORDON, Baronet [S 1631], of Embo aforesaid, only s and h , *b* at Devonport in 1818, educated at Trinity College, Cambridge , B A , 1839, D L for Sutherlandshire, *suc to the Baronetcy*, 19 June 1857 He *m* 26 March 1844 at Speldurst, co Kent, Ellen Harriet, yst da of Bartholomew BARNEWALL, of Weymouth Street, Marylebone, by Mary, da of John Charles LUCENA, Consul General for Portugal in London He *d* 18 Sep 1876, at (the residence of his sister) 64 Upper Brunswick Place, Brighton His widow living 1901

XI 1876   SIR HOME SETON GORDON, Baronet [S 1631], of Embo aforesaid, only s and h , *b* 21 March 1845, educated at Eton and at the Royal Military College of Sandhurst, Ensign 76th Foot, 1864, and subsequently in the 44th Foot, with which he served in India, retired 1869, Captain in the Glamorgan Light Infantry Militia till 1875 , *suc to the Baronetcy*, 18 Sep 1876 He *m* 25 Nov 1870, at Crawley, co Sussex, Mabel Montagu, only child of Montagu David SCOTT, of Hove in that county, by Margaret, da of James BRIGGS, of Oaklands, Herts

---

([a]) Burke's *Baronetage* for 1901
([b]) Of his five elder brothers, two died in infancy, but (1) William Gordon, Major 41st Foot, *d* 30 June 1794 in his 30th year, at St Domingo, (2) Paulus Æmilius Gordon, Lieut 47th Foot, *d* in the Bahama Islands, and (3) Robert Crosby Gordon, Major 85th Foot, *d* at Derby in 1797 A younger brother (the 7th son), Walter Gordon, Midshipman R N , *d* in the West Indies, all six being unm

MACLEAN

cr 3 Sep 1631, or 13 Feb 1632 , sealed 12 Jan 1632 (ᵃ)

I. 1632   SIR LAUCHLAN MACLEAN, of Morvaren, or Morven, s and h of Hector Og MACLEAN, of Duart, by his 1st wife, Jeannette, da of Colin MACKENZIE, of Kintail, suc his father in 1618, was M P [S] for Tarbert Sheriffdom, 1628-33, and was cr a Baronet [S] 3 Sep 1631, or 13 Feb 1632, the patent being sealed 12 Jan 1632,(ᴬ) but not recorded in the Great Seal Register [S], with rem to heirs male whatsoever, and with a grant of, presumably, 16,000 acres in Nova Scotia, entitled the Barony of New Morvaren, of which he had seizin in Feb 1632 (ᵇ) He was a Royalist, and, as such, was at the battles of Inverlochy and (Aug 1645) of Kilsyth He m Mary, 2d da of Roderick MACLEOD, of Macleod, by Isabel, da of Donald MACDONALD, of Glengarry He d 18 April 1649

II 1649.   SIR HECTOR MACLEAN, Baronet [S 1632], of Morven aforesaid, 1st s and h, b about 1625, suc to the Baronetcy, 18 April 1649, raised 700 men of his clan for the Royal cause, with whom he was defeated and slain at the battle of Innerkeithing in 1651 He d unm

III   SIR ALLAN MACLEAN, Baronet [S 1632], of Morven aforesaid, br and h, b about 1637, suc to the Baronetcy in 1651 He m Giles, 3d da of John MACLEOD, of Macleod, by Sybilla, da of Kenneth (MACKENZIE), 1st LORD MACKENZIE OF KINTAIL [S] He d 1674 in his 38th year His widow m (—) CAMPBELL, of Glendaroul

IV 1674   SIR JOHN MACLEAN, Baronet [S 1632], of Morven aforesaid, only surv s and h, suc to the Baronetcy in 1674, fought (with his clan) on behalf of the House of Stuart, at the battle of Killecrankie (1689), and at that of Sheriffmuir in the rising of 1715 He m in or before 1704, Mary, da of Sir Æneas MACPHERSON, of Invereshie She d before him He d in or before 1719 Admon 7 Oct 1719, as "of Gordon Castle, Scotland," granted to a creditor

V 1719?   SIR HECTOR MACLEAN, Baronet [S 1632], of Morven aforesaid, only s and h, b about 1704, suc to the Baronetcy in or before 1719 He was arrested in Edinburgh in 1745 on suspicion of treason and imprisoned two years in London He d unm at Paris, Jan or Feb 1751, aged 47,(ᶜ) when the issue male of the grantee became extinct

VI 1751.   SIR ALLAN MACLEAN, Baronet [S 1632], of Brolas in Mull, 3d cousin and h male, being only surv s and h of Donald MACLEAN, of Brolas aforesaid, by Isabella, da of Allan MACLEAN, of Ardgour, which Donald (who d 1750) was s and h of Lauchlan MACLEAN, of Brolas, by Isabella, da of Hector MACLEAN, of Torloish, which Laughlan (b 1650, M P [S] for Argyleshire, 1685-86, who d 1687), was s and h of Donald MACLEAN, also of Brolas, who was yr br (of the half blood) to the 1st Baronet, being s of Hector Og MACLEAN abovenamed, by his 2d wife, Isabella, da of Sir Archibald ACHESON He suc to the Baronetcy in 1781, was sometime Captain in the Dutch service, but afterwards served in the American war, and was finally Major in the 119th regiment He m Una, da of Hector MACLEAN, of Coll He d s p m 10 Dec 1783 Admon March and Aug 1798

(ᴬ) Milne's List for the date of sealing The date of creation is given in Laing's List as 3 Sep 1631, but in Douglas's *Baronage* [S] as 13 Feb 1632, it being there added that the charter, one to heirs male whatsoever, was in the public archives

(ᵇ) Banks's Lists

(ᶜ) Macfarlane's *Genealogical Collections* In Douglas's *Baronage* [S] he is said to have died at Rome, in Oct 1750

VII. 1783   SIR HECTOR MACLEAN, Baronet [S 1632], 2d cousin and
            h male, being s and h of Donald MACLEAN Collector of Customs
at Montego Bay, Jamaica, by his 1st wife, Mary, da of John Dickson, of Glasgow,
which Donald, was s of John MACLEAN,(a) by Florence, da of (—) MACLEAN,
the said John being s of Hector Og MACLEAN, yr br of Lauchlan MACLEAN, of
Brolas, abovementioned, the grandfather of the 6th Baronet. He was an officer
in the army, *suc to the Baronetcy* 10 Dec 1783   He *d s p*, probably unm , 2 Nov
1818, at Hatfield, co York

VIII   1818   SIR FITZROY JEFFREYS GRAFTON MACLEAN, Baronet
            [S 1632], br of the half blood and h, being s of Donald
MACLEAN abovenamed by his 2d wife, Margaret, da of James WALL, of Clonea
Castle, co Waterford, entered the army 1787, served in the West Indies at the
capture of Tobago, the attack on Martinique, Guadaloupe, etc, as also at the
capture (1808) of the islands of St Thomas and St John, of which he was made
Governor in 1808, became a full General in 1837 and Col of the 54th Foot in
1841   He *suc to the Baronetcy* 2 Nov 1818   He *m* firstly, Elizabeth, widow of
John BISHOP, of Barbadoes, only child of Charles KIDD   She *d* 1832   He *m*
secondly, 17 Sept 1838, Frances, widow of Henry CAMPION, of Malling Deanery,
co Sussex, 3d da of the Rev Henry WATKINS, of Conisbrough   She *d* 12 June
1843   Admon June 1843   He *d* 5 July 1847, at 53 Cadogan Place, Pimlico
Will pr. Aug 1847

IX   1847   SIR CHARLES FITZROY MACLEAN, Baronet [S 1632], 1st
            s and h, by 1st wife, *b* 14 Oct 1798; ed at Eton and at
Woolwich, entered the Scots Fusileer Guards, 1816, sometime, 1832-39,
Lieut -Col 81st Foot, and, subsequently, Military Sec at Gibraltar, Col in the
army 1846, *suc to the Baronetcy,* 5 July 1847   He *m* 10 May 1831, at
Wateringbury, Kent, Emily Eleanor, 4th da of the Hon Jacob MARSHAM, D D,
Canon of Windsor (yr s of Robert, 2d Baron ROMNEY), by Amelia Frances,
da and h of Joseph BULLOCK, of Caversfield, Oxon   She, who was *b* 10 Feb
1803 *d* 12 April 1838   He *d* 27 Jan 1883, at West Cliff House, Folkestone,
Kent, in his 85th year

X. 1883   SIR FITZROY DONALD MACLEAN, Baronet [S 1632], of
            Overblow, near Shorne, co Kent, only s and h, *b* 18 May 1835,
served in the Crimean war, 1854-55, being present at Alma and Sebastopol,
sometime Lieut -Col of the 13th Hussars, and Col of the West Kent Yeomanry
Cavalry, *suc to the Baronetcy* 27 Jan 1883   He *m* 17 Jan 1872, at St James',
Piccadilly, Constance Marianne, 2d and yst da and coheir of George Holland
ACKERS,(b) of Moreton Hall, Cheshire, by Harriett Susan, da of Henry William
HUTTON, of Beverley, co York

BALFOUR ·

cr 22 Dec 1633(c),

dormant since 1793

I   1633   SIR JAMES BALFOUR, of Denmiln and Kinnaird, co Fife,
            Lyon king of Arms [1630-54], 1st s and h ap of Sir Michael
BALFOUR, of Denmiln aforesaid, who was M P [S] for Fifeshire, 1643-44,

---

(a) *Account of the Clan Maclean*
(b) He died but three days afterwards, viz 20 Jan 1872, aged 59, at 15 Hyde
Park terrace
(c) Laing's List and Milne's List

and Comptroller of the Household [S] to Charles I, by Joanua, da of James DURHAM, of Pitkeiro, co Forfar,(a) was b 1603-04, probably at Denmiln, was cr 20 April 1630, LYON KING OF ARMS [S], *Knighted* 2 May, and crowned 15 June following, being subsequently *cr a Baronet* [S] 22 Dec 1633,(b) with rem to heirs male whatsoever, and with a grant of, presumably, 16,000 acres in Nova Scotia, of which, however, he appears never to have had seizin (c) He suc his father (who d aged 72) 14 Feb 1652, and was deprived of his office of "Lyon" in 1654 He *m* firstly Anne, da of Sir John AYTON, of Ayton She *d* 1644 He *m* secondly, early in 1645, Jean, widow of James SINCLAIR, of Stevenson, da of Sir James DURHAM, of Pitkerro, co Forfar She *d*, a few months later, 19 July 1645 He *m* thirdly, Margaret, da of Sir James ARNOT, of Ferney, co Fife She *d* 15 Dec 1653, aged 25 He *m* fourthly, in June 1654, Janet, da of Sir William AUCHINLECK, of Balmanno He, who was not only an author of several antiquarian works, but a most diligent collector of MSS , *d* 14 Feb 1657,(d) aged 57, and was *bur* in the church of Abdie, co Fife

II 1657   SIR ROBERT BALFOUR, Baronet [S 1633], of Denmiln aforesaid, only surv s and h by 3d wife, *b* 1652, *suc to the Baronetcy* 14 Feb 1657 He *d* s p, probably unm, being killed in a duel, 1673, by Sir James MACKGILL, of Rankeillour

III 1673.   SIR ALEXANDER BALFOUR, Baronet [S 1633], of Denmiln aforesaid, uncle and h male, being next yr br of the 1st Baronet He was a graduate of St Andrew's University 1626, and was minister of Abdie, co Fife, 1634 He *suc to the Baronetcy* in 1673 He *m* Euphemia, da of (—) CARSTAIRS She *d* Aug 1634 He is sometimes said to have subsequently *m* Janet, da of Peter HAY, of Leys

IV. 1680?   SIR MICHAEL BALFOUR, Baronet [S 1633], of Denmiln aforesaid, 1st s and h , *suc to the Baronetcy* on the death of his father He *m* (—), da of (—) AYTON, of Ayton He *d* Feb 1698

V. 1698   SIR MICHAEL BALFOUR, Baronet [S 1633], of Denmiln aforesaid, only s and h , *suc to the Baronetcy* in Feb 1698 He *m*, in 1698, Marjory, da of George MONCRIEFF, of Reidie He *d* 1709 being probably murdered, having left his house on horseback and being never again seen His widow *d* 22 or 29 Aug 1762, aged 86

VI 1709   SIR MICHAEL BALFOUR, Baronet [S 1633], of Denmiln aforesaid, only s and h , *suc to the Baronetcy* in 1709 He sold the estate of Denmiln in 1750, a few months before his death He *m* Jane, da of (—) Ross, of Invernethie He *d* 1750

VII 1750.   SIR JOHN BALFOUR, Baronet [S 1633], 1st s and h *suc to the Baronetcy* in 1750 He *d* unm 1773

(a) Several particulars in this article have been kindly supplied by Sir J Balfour Paul, Lyon King of Arms, from memoranda by R R Stodart, Lyon Clerk Depute [1863—86], and other sources
(b) See p 395, note "c"
(c) Banks's Lists
(d) So stated by R R Stodart (see note "a" above), but it is to be noted that the date of "14 Feb" is the same as that of the death of his father.

VIII 1773,   SIR PATRICK BALFOUR, Baronet [S 1633], only br and
    to   h , *suc to the Baronetcy* 1773, and was served heir to his brother
1793 20 Oct 1779   He d unm in 1793, when the *Baronetcy* became
    dormant (ª)

CUNNINGHAM, *or* CUNYNHAME,

cr 23 Dec 1633, sealed 22 April 1634 ,(ᵇ)

dormant since Feb 1658/9

I   1633,   DAVID CUNNINGHAM, of Auchinharvie, in the parish of
    to   Stewarton, co Ayr, *was cr a Baronet* [S] 23 Dec 1633, the
1659   patent being sealed 22 April 1634,(ᵇ) but not entered in the
            Great Seal Register [S], with remainder to heirs male what-
soever, and with a grant, presumably, of 16,000 acres in Nova Scotia, entitled
the Barony of Auchinharvie, in Cape Breton, of which he had seizin in June
1634 (ᶜ) He, as "*David Cunningham of the City of London, Knight and Baronet
of Scotland*," was, subsequently, *cr a Baronet* [E], 21 Jan 1641/2, which dignity
became *extinct* at his death, s p m in Feb 1658/9, when the *Baronetcy* [S 1633],
became *dormant* (ᵈ) For fuller particulars of him see page 153 above, under his
English creation

VERNATE, *or* VERNATTI

cr. 7, and sealed 30 June 1634(ᵇ),

dormant in, or shortly after, 1678

I. 1634   SIR PHILIBERT VERNATTI,(ᵉ) of Carleton [near Snaith],
            co York, br of Sir Gabriel VERNATTI, of Hatfield in that county
(d 1 Oct 1655), of Maximilian VERNATTI and Peter VERNATTI, all of them being
sons of (—) VERNATTI, of Holland, received the degree of LL D from the Univ
of Leyden, and was incorp as such at Oxford 18 March 1612/3, took, with many
others of his countrymen, an active part in the drainage of Hatfield Level in 1626
(of which, in 1635, he was one of the proprietors), and was *cr a Baronet* [S]
7, sealed 30 June 1634,(ᵇ) though not recorded in the Great Seal Register [S],
with rem to heirs male whatsoever, and with a grant of, presumably, 16,000

(ª) The heir male of the grantee must, after 1793, be sought for further back
than among the descendants of his 4 brothers, Alexander (afterwards 3d Baronet),
Michael, Andrew, and David The Rev William Balfour, 2d and yst s of
Alexander, d s p m. So also did Michael Balfour, of Randerston, the next br to
Alexander The next br , Sir David Balfour of Forret, had two sons, but the line
of each ended in daughters The yst br , Sir Andrew Balfour Physician and
Botanist (nearly 30 years younger than the grantee), m Anne Napier, but d
s p m, 10 Jan 1692, aged 62 Colonel James William Balfour, of Trenabie, co
Orkney, in a letter, dat 23 Oct 1897, to the Sec of State for Home affairs,
claimed the representation of the family, as the descendant of Michael Balfour, of
Garth, " all the senior branches " having (according to his statement) " died out "
    (ᵇ) The date of creation is given in Laing's list , that of the sealing is in
Milne's list
    (ᶜ) Banks's lists, where it is added, ' Represented, as considered, by Robert
Cunninghame, of Seabank "
    (ᵈ) Robert Conynham, of Auchinharvie aforesaid, Physician [S] to Charles II
(whose relationship to the grantee of 1633 is unknown), was *cr a Baronet* [S],
3 Aug 1673 , see under that date
    (ᵉ) See *Her & Gen*, vol v, pp 146-155, for an account of this family by
" Q F V F ," from which the above is compiled

acres in Nova Scotia, of which, however, he appears never to have had seizin ([a])
In 1637 he was employed in the King's service He m Elizabeth, da of Henry
DENTON, of Warnell Denton, co Cumberland, by Elizabeth, da of William OGLE-
THORPE He d in Scotland between 2 May and 14 June 1643 Admon 9 March
1648/9 and 11 Dec 1650 to a creditor His widow's will, as of Caversham,
Oxon (directing her burial to be at Bardsey, co York, near her mother, Elizabeth
Thorpe, widow), dat 22 Aug , pr 4 Oct 1666

II 1643,   SIR PHILIBERT VERNATTI, Baronet [S 1684], s and h,
   to   *suc to the Baronetcy* in May or June 1643, was a student at the
   1680 ?   Univ of Leyden in 1649, having been "grieved to the very heart"
              by the "murther of his Sacred Majesty", was living in Batavia
in 1658, and contributed a paper to the Royal Society, London, in Jan 1677/8
He m before July 1664, (—), da of Isaac VIGNY, a Frenchman. After Jan
1677/8 all trace of him is lost, and on his death the *Baronetcy* is presumed to
have become *dormant*

BINGHAM
cr. 7 and sealed 30 June 1634 ,([b])
afterwards, since 1776, BARONS LUCAN OF CASTLEBAR [I],
and subsequently, since 1795, EARLS OF LUCAN [I]

I 1634   HENRY BINGHAM, of Castlebar, Co Mayo, 1st s and h
             of Sir George BINGHAM,([c]) Governor of Sligo, by Cicely, da of
Robert MARTIN, of Athelhampton, Dorset was *bap* 1573 at Milton Abbas in that
county , suc his father (—), was serving in Ireland, as a Captain, in 1634, M P
[I] for Castlebar, 1634-35, and 1639-48, and was *cr a Baronet* [S], 7, sealed
30 June 1634,([b]) but not recorded in the Great Seal office [S], with rem to heirs
male whatsoever, and with a grant of, presumably, 16,000 acres in Nova Scotia, of
which, however, he never appears to have had seizin ([a]) He m before 1625
(—), da of John BYRNE of Ballinclough, co Wicklow

II 1640 ?   SIR GEORGE BINGHAM, Baronet [S 1634], of Castlebar
              aforesaid, s and h b about 1625, *suc to the Baronetcy* on the
death of his father, was M P [I] for Castlebar, 1661-66 He m firstly (—)
He m secondly 1 June 1661, at St Benet's, Paul's Wharf, London (Lic Vic Gen
31 May 1661, he about 35, widower) Anne PARGITER, of St Andrew's Holborn,
widow, about 30 She d a few months later Her admon as "of Hayes,
co Midx," 11 Sep 1661 He (very quickly) m thirdly (Lic Vic Gen 5 Dec
1661) Rebecca (aged 24, parents deceased), 2d da of Sir William MIDDLETON,
2d Baronet [1622], by Eleanor, da of Sir Thomas HARRIS, 1st Baronet [1622],
of Boreatton

([a]) Banks's Lists
([b]) The date of creation is given in Laing's List, that of the sealing is in
Milne's List The reason for conferring a Scotch, instead of an Irish, Baronetcy
on him is (as is often the case elsewhere) not obvious
([c]) This Sir George and his br , Sir Richard Bingham, the well known Marshal
of Ireland (d 19 Jan 1598, aged 70), were younger sons of Robert Bingham, of
Melcombe Bingham, Dorset, who d 1561, being ancestor of the family still (1900)
of that place He is confounded in Lodge's *Irish Peerage* [1789] with his cousin,
Capt George Bingham, who was murdered in Sligo Castle in 1595 [*ex inform*
G D Burchaell, Office of Arms, Dublin]

III   1690?   SIR HENRY BINGHAM Baronet [S 1634], of Castlebar,
            aforesaid, 1st s and h by 1st wife admitted to Middle Temple,
London, 13 Sep 1673, *suc to the Baronetcy* on the death of his father, was
M P [I] for co Mayo (4 Parls) 1692-99 and 1703-14   He m 4 Sep 1677,
Jane, da of James CUFFE, of Pakenham Hall, co Longford   He m secondly,
Lettice, da of (—)   He d s p m, in or shortly before 1714   Will pr [I] 1714
That of his widow pr [I] 1728

IV   1714?   SIR GEORGE BINGHAM Baronet [S 1634], of Castlebar
            aforesaid, br of the half blood and h male, being son of the 2d
Baronet by his 3d wife   He was an officer in the army of James II, whom,
however, he deserted at the battle of Aughrim, in 1691   He *suc to the Baronetcy*
about 1714   He m firstly, about 1688, Mary, da of (—) SCOTT   He m secondly
Phœbe, da of (—) HAWKINS   He was living in 1727 (ᵃ)

V.   1730?   SIR JOHN BINGHAM, Baronet [S 1634], of Castlebar
            aforesaid, s and h by first wife, b about 1690, admitted to the
Middle Temple, London, 27 July 1717, *suc to the Baronetcy* on the death of his
father(ᵃ), was M P [I] for co Mayo, 1727 till his death, and Governor of that
Shire   He m in or before 1730, Anne, 1st da and coheir of Agmondesham VESEY,
of Lucan, co Dublin, by Charlotte, only da of William SARSFIELD, of Lucan
aforesaid, br to the well known General, Patrick SARSFIELD, who was cr EARL
OF LUCAN [I] in 1691, by James II after his deposition   He d 21 Sep 1749,
aged 60, and was bur at Castlebar   His widow d 1762

VI   1749   SIR JOHN BINGHAM, Baronet [S 1634], of Castlebar
            aforesaid, 1st s and h, b 1730, *suc to the Baronetcy* 21 Sep 1749
He d unm 10 Oct, 1752, aged 22, and was bur at Castlebar

VII   1752   SIR CHARLES BINGHAM, Baronet [S 1634], of Castlebar
            aforesaid, br and h, b 22 Sep 1735, *suc to the Baronetcy* 10
Oct 1752, was M P [I] for co Mayo, 1761-76   He m 25 Aug 1760, at Bath,
Margaret, da and coheir of James SMITH, of St Audries, co Somerset,
and Canons Leigh, co Devon, by Grace, his wife   She was living when he was
cr, 24 July 1776, BARON LUCAN OF CASTLEBAR, co Mayo [I], being
subsequently cr, 1 Oct 1795, EARL OF LUCAN [I]   In that Barony this
Baronetcy then *merged*, and still so continues   See *Peerage*

MONRO, or MUNRO

cr. 7 June(ᵇ) and sealed 3 July 1634 (ᶜ)

I.   1634   "Colonel HECTOR MONRO, of Foulis,"(ᵇ) co Ross, br
            and h male of Colonel Robert MONRO, or MUNRO, of the same
(who served in the Swedish service in the German wars, and d s p m, at Ulm in
Germany, 1633), both being sons of Hector MUNRO, of Foulis (d 14 Nov 1603),
by his 1st wife, Anne, da of Hugh (FRASER), LORD LOVAT [S], served, like his
brother, in the Swedish service in the German wars, and attained the rank of
Colonel, and, having suc in 1634 to the family estates, was cr a Baronet [S]
7 June,(ᵇ) sealed 3 July 1634,(ᶜ) with rem to heirs male whatsoever, and with a
grant of, presumably, 16,000 acres in Nova Scotia, entitled the Barony of New
Foulis, of which he had seizin in Aug 1634 (ᵈ)   He m in 1619, Mary, sister of
Donald, 1st LORD REAY [S], da of Hugh MACKAY, of Strathnaver, by his 2d wife,
Jean, da of Alexander (GORDON), EARL OF SUTHERLAND [S]   He d April 1635,
at Hamburgh, and was bur at Buckstehood, on the Elbe

(ᵃ) John Bingham, afterwards 5th Baronet, is called "Esq" when, in 1727,
elected M P [I] for the Parl which lasted the whole reign of George II
    (ᵇ) Laing's List
    (ᶜ) Milne's List
    (ᵈ) Banks's Lists

II 1635   SIR HECTOR MUNRO, Baronet [S 1634], of Foulis aforesaid, only s and h , b about 1635, and suc to the Baronetcy
in April of that year He married,(a) but d s p Dec 1651, at the house of his
cousin, John MACKAY, afterwards 2d Lord REAY [S], at Durness in Strath-
naver,(a) in his seventeenth year

III 1651   SIR ROBERT MUNRO, Baronet [S 1634], of Foulis aforesaid, and formerly of Obsdaill, 2d consin and h male, being 2d but
1st surv s and h of Col John MUNRO, of Obsdaill (who served in the German wars
and d in Germany, March 1633), s and h of George MUNRO, of Obsdaill afsd (d
1589), who was br of the half-blood, to Hector MUNRO, of Foulis abovenamed
(d 14 Nov 1603), the father of the 1st Baronet, both being sons of Robert-More
MUNRO, of Foulis, who d 4 Nov 1588 He was M P [S] for Inverness-shire,
1649, and for Ross-shire, 1649-50 He suc to the Baronetcy, and to the family
estates in 1651 He m Jean, sister and coheir of his predecessor, 1st da of Sir
Hector MUNRO, 1st Baronet [S 1634], by Mary, da of Hugh MACKAY, abovementioned He d 14 Jan 1668 (b)

IV 1668 (b) SIR JOHN MUNRO, Baronet [S 1634], of Foulis aforesaid,
s and h , suc to the Baronetcy, 14 Jan 1668(b), was M P [S], for
Ross-shire, 1689-97, and a zealous supporter of the Revolution He m Agnes,
2d da of Sir Kenneth MACKENZIE, 1st Baronet [S 1673], of Coull, by his first
wife, Jean, da of Alexander CHISHOLM, of Comar He d shortly before 29 Sep
1697

V 1697   SIR ROBERT MUNRO, Baronet [S 1634], of Foulis aforesaid, s and h , suc to the Baronetcy in 1697, was M P [S] for Ross-
shire, 1697 1701, and a firm Presbyterian and supporter of the Protestant Succession Sheriff of the counties of Ross and Cromarty, 1725 He m in or before
1684, Jean, da of John FORBES, of Culloden, by Anne, da of Alexander DUNBAR,
of Grange He d 11 Sep 1729 Admon as " of Foulis," 16 Oct 1729

VI 1729   SIR ROBERT MUNRO, Baronet [S 1634], of Foulis aforesaid, s and h , b about 1684, served with the army in Flanders,
1705 12, as Cornet of Dragoons, and Capt of the Royal Scots, and greatly distinguished himself as Lieut Col of a Highland regiment at the battle of Fontenoy
in April 1745, was M P for the Wick Burghs (six Parls), 1710-41, Gov of
Inverness Castle, 1715, a Commissioner for forfeited estates, 1716, suc to the
Baronetcy in 1729 He m Mary, da of Henry SEYMOUR, of Woodlands, Dorset
She d 24 May or 11 June 1732 Admon as " of Kilterne, co Ross," 19 Jan
1732/3 He d 17 Jan 1745/6, being slain at the battle of Falkirk, at the head of
his regiment, by the insurgents M I at Falkirk Admon as " of Foulis,"
26 March 1747

VII 1746   SIR HARRY MUNRO, Baronet [S 1634], of Foulis afore-
said, s and h , ed at Westm School and at the Univ of Leyden ,
suc to the Baronetcy 17 Jan 1745/6, was M P for Ross-shire, 1746-47 and for the
Wick Burghs (two Parls), 1747-61 He m , in or before 1762, Anne, da of Hugh
ROSE, of Kilravock, co Nairn, by his 2d wife Jean, da of Hugh ROSE, of Broadley
He d 12 June 1781, at Edinburgh

VIII 1781   SIR HUGH MUNRO, Baronet [S 1634], of Foulis aforesaid, s and h , b 1763, suc to the Baronetcy, 12 June 1781 He
m (c) Jane, da of Alexander LAW, of London She was drowned 1 Aug 1803,
while bathing in Cromarty Firth, near Foulis He d s p m, 2 May 1848, at 22
Manchester square, Marylebone, aged 85 Will pr May 1848

(a) Macfarlane's Geneological Collections
(b) This is the date given by Macfarlane (see note " a " above), but in Mackenzie's account of the Munro family it is said to be 1666
(c) The legality of this marriage was questioned , but the da and only child
thereof was found by the House of Lords to be legitimate

X. 1848   SIR CHARLES MUNRO, Baronet [S 1634], of Foulis aforesaid, and formerly of Culrain, co Ross, 5th cousin and h male, being s and h of George MUNRO, of Culrain aforesaid, by Margaret, da of ohn MONTGOMERY of Milmount house, co Ross, which George (who d 19 Dec 845, at Edinburgh) was s and h of James MUNRO, br and h of Gustavus [UNRO, both being sons of George MUNRO (d 1724), s and h of Sir George IUNRO, Commander in Chief of the Royalist army in Ireland, all of Culrain foresaid, which Sir George (who d 1690), was yr br of Robert, the 3d Baronet, oth being sons of Col John MUNRO, of Obsdaill abovementioned, who d in termany March 1633   He was b 20 May 1795, at Culrain aforesaid, ed at the ligh School and at the Univ of Edinburgh, entered the army, 1810, Lieut .5th Foot, 1812, receiving a medal and six clasps for his conduct (1812-14) at lodrigo, Badajoz (where he was wounded), Salamanca, the Nive, Orthes, and 'oulouse, fought in the war of Independence in South America, and was in .ommand of a division of the Columbian army (under Bolivar) at the victory of Ignotmar   He *suc to the Baronetcy*, 2 May 1848   He *m* firstly, 20 June 1817, Amelia, da of Frederick BROWNE, of Dublin, sometime an officer in the 14th)ragoons   She d 14 Sep 1849   He *m* secondly, 14 Jan 1853, Harriette, da of Robert MIDGLEY, of Essington, co York   She d 17 July 1886, aged 78   He d five days afterwards), 22 July 1886, aged 91

X 1886   SIR CHARLES MUNRO, Baronet [S 1634] of Foulis aforesaid, s and h by 1st wife, b 20 Oct 1824, sometime Capt in the Ross-shire Militia, *suc to the Baronetcy*, 22 July 1886   He *m* 19 March 1847, Mary Anne, da of John NICHOLSON, of Camberwell, co Surrey   He d 29 Feb 1888, at Edinburgh, aged 63   His widow living there 1901

XI 1888   SIR HECTOR MUNRO, Baronet [S 1634], of Foulis aforesaid, s and h, b 13 Sep 1849, Lieut Col Com 3rd Seaforth Highlanders Militia, *suc to the Baronetcy*, 29 Feb 1888   Lord Lieut of the counties of Ross and Cromarty   He *m* 7 April 1880, Margaret Violet, 1st da of John STIRLING, of Fairburn, co Ross

Family Estates—These, in 1883, consisted of 4,458 acres in Ross-shire, worth £3,780 a year   *Principal Seats*—Foulis Castle, near Evanton, and Ardullie Lodge, both in co Ross

---

FOULIS.

cr. 7 June, and sealed 22 July 1634 ;[a]

afterwards, since 1843, LISTON-FOULIS

I 1634   ALEXANDER FOULIS, *"fear of Colinton,"* co Edinburgh, only s and h ap of Sir James FOULIS, of Colinton, Advocate [S] 1576, and sometime [1612] M P [S] for Edinburgh, by Mary, da of Sir John LAUDER, of Hatton, was *cr a Baronet* [S] 7 June, sealed 22 July 1634,[a] but not recorded in the Great Seal Register [S], with rem to heirs male whatsoever [b] and with a grant of, presumably, 16,000 acres in Nova Scotia, of which he had seizin in Aug 1634 [c]   He *m* v p (settlement 30 March 1619) Elizabeth, widow of Sir John STEWART, of Bute, 1st da and coheir of Robert HEPBURN, of Foord, co Edinburgh   He was living 7 Aug 1643, and probably in 1663, but was dead in 1672 [d]

(a) The date of the creation is given in Laing's List, but that of the sealing in Milne's List, in which, however, the Baronetcy is assigned [not to Alexander, but] to "Sir *James*, of Collingtoun"

(b) Douglas's *Baronage* [S]

(c) Banks's Lists

(d) The 2d Baronet is styled "knight" in the Parl of 1661-63, being first called "Baronet" in the Convention of 1672.

3 D

II   1670?   SIR JAMES FOULIS, Baronet [S 1634], of Colinton aforesaid, s and h , was *Knighted* v p 14 Nov 1641, took part in
the Civil Wars on the side of the King, was a member of the Committee of
Estates 1646, was M P [S] for co Edinburgh (in ten Parls or conventions) 1645 to
1684, was taken prisoner by Monk's forces at Alyth, 28 Sep 1651, and carried to
London, was made a Senator of the College of Justice [S] 14 Feb 1661, being
then entitled LORD COLINTON, *suc to the Baronetcy* on his father's death, probably
about 1670(·), was a Lord of the Articles and a Lord of Justiciary [S] 1671,
P C [S] 1674, Lord Justice Clerk [S] 22 Feb 1684   He *m* firstly, Barbara,
da of Andrew AYNSLEY, a magistrate of Edinburgh   He *m* secondly (contract
1 June 1661) Margaret, widow of Sir John MACKENZIE, 1st Baronet [S 1628],
of Tarbat (who *d* 10 Sep 1654), da and coheir of Sir George ERSKINE, of Innerteil,
a Lord of Session [S]   He *d* in Edinburgh, 19 Jan 1688   His widow living 1693

III   1688   SIR JAMES FOULIS, Baronet [S 1634], of Colinton aforesaid s and h by 1st wife, was Advocate [S], 8 June 1669, and
was (*v p*) a Senator of the College of Justice [S], 10 Nov 1674, being then
entitled LORD REIDFORD, M P [S] for co Edinburgh, 1685-86, 1689 and 1689-93,
when his seat was declared vacant as he had not taken the allegiance oath
He *suc* to the Baronetcy, 19 Jan 1688   P C [S], 1702   He *m* 4 Sep 1670,
Margaret da of John BOYD, Dean of Guild, of Edinburgh   He *d* 1711

IV   1711   SIR JAMES FOULIS, Baronet [S 1634], of Colinton aforesaid s and h , was *Knighted* v p before 1704 , M P [S] for co
Edinburgh, 1704-07 , *suc to the Baronetcy* in 1711   He *d* unm , July 1742

V   1742   SIR JAMES FOULIS, Baronet [S 1634], of Colinton aforesaid nephew and h , being 1st s and h of Henry FOULIS, by Jean,
da of Adam FOULIS of Edinburgh, Merchant, which Henry was 2d and yst s of the
3d Baronet   He was an Antiquary of some note and as early as 1701, wrote a
treatise on the Celtic origin of the Scots   He *suc to the Baronetcy* in July 1742
He *m* Mary, da of Archibald WIGHTMAN of Edinburgh, Writer to the Signet
[S]   He *d* 3 Jan 1791

VI   1791   SIR JAMES FOULIS aforesaid Baronet [S 1634], of Colinton 1st and only surv s and h , *suc to the Baronetcy,* 3 Jan 1791,
and, shortly afterwards, *m* , 17 June 1791, Margaret, da of William DALLAS   He
sold the estate of Colinton   He *d* s p 1825, when the issue male of the grantee
and of the grantee's father became extinct

VII 1825   SIR JAMES FOULIS, Baronet [S 1634], of Woodhall, co
Edinburgh, 6th cousin and h male being yst s of William
FOULIS, of Woodhall aforesaid by (—), da of (—) CAMPBELL, of Carsebank, co
Forfar, which William (*b* 6 Nov 1732, *d* June 1796), was only s of John FOULIS
of Woodhall (*b* 25 Feb 1709, *d* Dec 1732), s of William FOULIS, also of Woodhall,
Advocate [S], 1700 (*b* 20 May 1674, *d* June 1737), who was yst s ([b]) of Sir
John FOULIS, 1st Baronet [S 1661], of Ravelstoun (the purchaser, in 1701, of
the estate of Woodhall where he *d* 5 Aug 1707, in his 70th year), who was s
and h of George FOULIS of Ravelstoun (*b* 6 April 1606), s and h of George
FOULIS, Master of the Mint [S], the purchaser of the estate of Ravelstoun (*d*
28 May 1633, aged 64), who was yr br of Sir James FOULIS of Colinton abovenamed, the father of the 1st Baronet [S 1634], both being sons of James FOULIS
of Colinton, by Agnes, da and h of Robert HERIOT, of Lumphoy   He was *b*
9 Sep 1770, and, having first suc to his paternal estate of Woodhall, subsequently
suc to the Baronetcy in 1825   He *m* 29 Aug 1810, Agnes, 1st da of John
GRIEVE, of Edinburgh   He *d* 2 May 1842, aged 71, at Woodhall house   His
widow is said to have *d* in 1870 ([c])

([a]) See p 401, note " d "
([b]) The male issue of the eldest son became extinct, 28 Jan 1747, on the death
of the only son of the 2d Baronet (grandson of the 1st Baronet), who had been
executed, 15 Nov 1746, for high treason whereby the Baronetcy became attainted,
which otherwise would have passed to the family of Foulis of Woodhall
([c]) Foster's *Baronetage* for 1883   If 1870 was the date of her death she must
have survived her marriage some sixty years

VIII   1842   SIR WILLIAM FOULIS, *afterwards* LISTON-FOULIS, Baronet
              [S 1634], of Woodhall aforesaid s and h, b 27 July 1812, at Shen-
stone co Stafford, *suc to the Baronetcy* 22 May 1842   He m firstly, 20 June 1843,
Henrietta Ramage LISTON, of Millburn Tower, co Edinburgh, spinster, 1st da of
Ramage LISTON, Capt R N, great niece and testamentary heir of the Right Hon
Sir Robert LISTON, G C B   He thereupon assumed the name of *Liston* before that
of *Foulis*   She d 1850   He m secondly, 7 April 1852, Mary Anne, 1st da of
Robert CADELL, of Ratho   He d 22 Feb 1858   His widow living 1901, at
Edinburgh

IX   1858.   SIR   JAMES   LISTON-FOULIS, Baronet [S 1634], of
             Woodhall and Millburn Tower aforesaid, s and h by 1st
wife, b 3 July 1847, at Millburn Tower, *suc to the Baronetcy* in 1858,
ed at the Royal Mil Coll at Woolwich, Ensign 16th Foot, 1865-66   Capt
Edinburgh Militia, 1870-76   He m 8 Dec 1868, Sarah Helen, 1st da of
Sir Charles Metcalfe OCHTERLONY, 2d Baronet [1823], by Sarah, da of
William P TRIBE of Liverpool   He d at Millburn Tower, 29 Dec 1895,
aged 48   His widow, who was b 29 Sept 1846, living 1901

X   1895   SIR WILLIAM LISTON-FOULIS Baronet [S 1634], of Wood-
           hall and Millburn Tower aforesaid, s and h, b 27 Oct 1869,
suc to the Baronetcy, 29 Dec 1895

Family Estates —These, in 1883, consisted of 2,804 acres in Midlothian, valued
at £2,163 a year   *Principal Residences* —Woodhall, and Millburn Tower, near
Corstorphine, both in co Edinburgh

GIBB

cr 4 July 1634,([a])

dormant, probably, 8 April 1650;

but possibly assumed, 1650-1734,

and certainly assumed 1867-76.

I   1634,   HENRY GIBB, of Falkland, but formerly of Caribber,
    to   co Linlithgow, Groom of the Bedchamber, 2d s of Sir John
    1650   GIBB,([b]) of Knock, near Dunfermline, and of Caribber aforesaid,
            Groom of the Bedchamber to James VI [S], by Isabel LINDSAY,
his wife, accompanied that King to England in 1603, was naturalised 1610,
obtained the estate of Caribber, 22 June 1615, from his father, but disponed it,

---

([a]) Milne's List   There is no mention whatever of this creation in Laing's
List, neither is it in Ulster's List   It is, however, in Walkley's List and in
Beatson's List, being placed in each case between the creations of Munro (sealed
3 July) and Fonlis (sealed 22 July), which, as it was sealed between these dates,
seems to be the proper place

([b]) The whole of the information, as to the collateral relatives of the grantee,
is taken from a work entitled *The Life and Times of Robert Gib, Lord of Caribber,*
by "Sir George Duncan Gibb, Baronet, of Falkland and Caribber," pub 1874, in
2 vols, 8vo, by Longman & Co, London   Its author claimed to be heir male of
the grantee, but the absence of dates and of the marriages of many of the
parties concerned, constitute a great defect in the pedigree, which appears mainly
to rest on the following statement, said to be a copy of an entry (now lost), which,
it is stated, was written (in a volume of sermons) by Thomas Gibb (who, in the
text, is set forth as 4th in succession to the Baronetcy), the great grandfather
of the said George Duncan Gibb   It is dated "July 24, 1744," and is as
under —"Robert Gib, of Carieber, had two sons, John and Patrick   Patrick was
a Burgess of Linlithgow, and left a son, Robert, named after his grandfather
Robert had a twin son and daughter, the son was named after his grand-uncle,
John Gib.   John was a zealous supporter of the blessed Covenant, he was at

24 Oct. 1629, to his elder br., James GIBB,(ª) of Knock; was sometime Clerk of
the Signet; was Groom of the Bedchamber to Henry, Prince of Wales, and
subsequently to James I and Charles I, and was *cr. a Baronet* [S.], the patent
being sealed 4 July 1634(ᵇ), though not recorded in the Great Seal Register [S.],
with rem. to heirs male whatsoever, but apparently without any grant of territory
in Nova Scotia.(ᶜ)   He acquired property at Jarrow, co. Durham.   In 1645 he was
on the Committee for Estates [S.], but, nevertheless, his own were sequestrated
by Parl. 28 Aug. 1648.   He *m.* firstly, 15 Feb. 1598, Katharine GRAY, said(ᵈ) to be
a da. of the Hon. James GRAY, 2d s. of Patrick, LORD GRAY [S.]   He *m.* secondly,
in or before 1622 (a post nuptial settlement dat. 3 Aug. 1631), Anne, 3d da. of
Sir Ralph GIBBS, of Honiton, co. Warwick, by Gertrude, da. of Sir Thomas
WROUGHTON, of Broad Hinton, Wilts.   He *d.* s.p.m.(ᵉ) 8 April 1650 at Falkland,
and was buried at Kilgour.   Admon. as "of St. Martin's in the Fields, Midx.,"
18 Nov. 1650, and again 24 Nov. 1676.   His widow *d.* 30 May and was *bur.* 1 June
1658, at St. Botolph's, Bishopsgate, London, in her 54th year.   Will dat. 25 Feb.
1655, pr. 21 June 1658.

The assumption of the title and the right thereto, after 1650,
is said(ᶠ) to be as below.

II.   1660?   SIR JOHN GIBB, Baronet(ᶠ) [S. 1634], of Linlith-
              gow, cousin and h. male, being s. and h. of Robert GIBB, of
Kersiebank in Linlithgow, Burgess of that town, by (—), his wife, which
Robert was s. and h. of Patrick GIBB, of Bearcrofts, co. Stirling, also a
Burgess of Linlithgow, next br. to Sir John GIBB, of Knock, the father of
the 1st Baronet.   He was *bap.* 13 Aug. 1618, at Linlithgow, and *assumed
the Baronetcy*,(ᶠ) after the Restoration, but is said to have "abandoned it
when he got into trouble."(ʳ)   He fought on the side of the Covenant at
Bothwell Muir, 22 June 1679.   He *m.*, late in life, (—).   He *d.* 1703, aged
84, at Dairsie or Cupar Fife, and was *bur.* there.

Bothwell Muir in 1679; settled at Cupar Fife; married late, and had children
named John and Christian.   His grandson, Thomas, married Euphem Brydie, of
Leven."   It is to be observed that the writer of the memorandum makes no
mention of any Baronetcy, though, according to Sir G. D. Gibb's abovementioned
work, he himself was entitled to it, and his father, possibly, and grandfather,
certainly, assumed it.

(ª) This James is called the last Gibb of Caribber, which estate he disponed
7 March 1640, to James Menteith.   He died s.p.m. at Dunfermline, presumably
before his brother, Henry, whom else he would have succeeded in the Baronetcy.
Janet, his da. and h., *m.* in 1633, Adam French, of Thorndikes.

(ᵇ) See page 403, note "a."

(ᶜ) No such grant appears in Banks's Lists.

(ᵈ) *Query* if legitimate.   Her father's marriage is ignored in Wood's *Douglas
Peerage* [S.].

(ᵉ) Of his two surviving daughters and coheirs by his second wife, (1) Elizabeth,
b. 1622, *m.* before 1653, as his 1st wife, Sir Richard Everard, 2d Baronet [1629],
and *d.* before 1676; (2) Frances, *b.* 1626, *m.* firstly, about 1654, William Glanville,
of Broad Hinton, Wilts (who *d.* 11 Oct. 1680, aged 78), and secondly, John
Stone, of Baldwin Brightwell, Oxon, who *d.* 30 Oct. 1704, aged 78.   She *d.*
6 March 1714/5, aged 89, and was *bur.* at Broad Hinton.   There was a son,
Charles, *bap.* 19 Dec. 1624, and *bur.* 19 Feb. 1630.

(ᶠ) The assumption or non-assumption of this Baronetcy, after the death of the
grantee, is, in all cases, given on the sole authority of Sir G. D. Gibb's work [see
note "b" above].   It is to be observed, however, that the proceedings taken
to establish the right to the dignity at the court of Lyon King of Arms in 1868
were unsuccessful.   In a letter dated 27 May 1867, signed "George Duncan
Gibb, Bart.," that gentleman writes to R. R. Stodart, the then Lyon Clerk
Depute, "I have established my claim to the Baronetcy as the nearest lawful
heir male whatsoever and on 30 April by the advice of my Council, including the

III. 1703.   JOHN GIBB, of Dairsie aforesaid, s. and h. ;
            possibly, for some short period, *assumed the Baronetcy*([ˢ]).
He *m*. (—). He *d*. near Dairsie 1734.

IV. 1734.   THOMAS GIBB, s. and h., suc. his father in 1734,
            but *did not assume the Baronetcy*.([ˢ]) He, being then of
Wickham, in England, *m*. 4 Oct. 1740, at Leven, Euphemia, da. of James
BRYDIE, of Scoome, co. Fife. He *d*. in London, 1777 or 1778. His widow
d. there 1782.

V. 1777?   BENAIAH GIBB, of Montreal, in Canada, 1st surv.
            s. and h., *b*. 1756; emigrated to Montreal, 27 May 1774;
suc. his father in 1777 or 1778, but *did not assume the Baronetcy*.([ˢ])
He was a "Knight of Portugal." He *m*. firstly, in or before 1793,
Catharine, 4th da. of Moses CAMPBELL, 42d Highlanders, by Elizabeth
COOMBS, of Albany, in North America. She *d*. Jan. 1804. He *m*.
secondly, Eleanor Leech, da. of Abraham Leech PASTORIUS. She *d*.
Dec. 1821. He *d*. at Montreal 18 March 1826, aged 70.

VI. 1826.   THOMAS GIBB, s. and h. by 1st wife, *b*. Aug. 1793 ;
            a Captain in the Army; suc. his father 18 March 1826,
but *did not assume the Baronetcy*.([ˢ]) He *m*. (his 2d cousin) Magdalen, da.
of James Ellice CAMPBELL, of Hochelaga, in Canada, by Elizabeth, da. of
Capt. Joseph THURBER. He *d*. of cholera, 7 Aug. 1832, aged 39. His
widow, who was *b*. July 1799, *d*. March 1845.

VII. 1832,   SIR GEORGE DUNCAN GIBB, Baronet([ˢ]) [S. 1634],
      or   s. and h., *b*. 25 Dec. 1821, at Montreal; suc. his father
      1867,   7 Aug. 1832, but *did not assume the Baronetcy*([ˢ]) till thirty-
      to   five years later; was ed. at MacGill College; M.D. there
      1876.   1846; L.R.C.S., Dublin, 1848; practised as a Physician at
                Montreal, 1849-53; and was President of the Pathological
Society there, 1853; settled in London, 1853; M.R.C.P., London,
1859, and Assistant Physician to Westminster Hospital. On 30 April
1867 he *assumed* the *Baronetcy*([ˢ]), and in June 1874 (in a roll pedigree of
the Gibb family, compiled by himself) he styles himself "7th Baronet, of

Solicitor Gen., Sir J. B. Karslake, I assumed the title, a record of which with my
genealogy is recorded in the Court of Chancery, London. I shall be obliged if
you will kindly inform me what steps must be taken to record my succession as
the 3d Baronet in the Lyon office. The last Baronet died 1703." It must be
observed, however, that the writer does not say where this claim was "established." The Sheriff of the county where the grantee was domiciled, or the
Sheriff Court of Chancery at Edinburgh, were the two processes substituted
by the Act 10 and 11 Vict. (1847-48) for the old "brieve," with its attendant
"retour" by a jury. See *N. & Q.*, 3d S., vol. xii (*passim*), and 4th S., vol. i, p. 37,
where Sir Duncan's "agent" mentions the *quantity* of "the evidence on which
Sir Duncan relies" as "filling several volumes," but says nothing as to the *quality*
thereof. In a subsequent letter, dat. 5 Dec. 1867, Sir Duncan writes "My
petition for service in the Sheriff's Court is in abeyance" owing to "the
destruction of a large part of the ancient borough records of Linlithgow." He
adds also "with regard to the 2d Baronet, Sir John Gibb, my direct ancestor, no
proof from the public records has been found that the title was recognised by
the Crown. It was therefore left out in my petition for service. He assumed
the title and abandoned it when he got into trouble."

([ˢ]) See page 404, note "f."

Falkland, 12th Lord of Caribber,([a]) M.A., M.D., and LL.D." He *m.* Mary
Elizabeth, da. of William RUMLEY, of Ayrfield house, co. Kildare. She *d.*
Dec. 1861. He *d.* 16 Feb. 1876, at 1 Bryanston street, Portman square,
Marylebone, aged 54, when it is believed the *assumption* of this *Baronetcy*
ceased.([b])

HAMILTON :

cr. 6 Jan. 1635 ;([c])

afterwards, 1647-79, LORD BELHAVEN AND STENTON, [S.].

dormant, or *extinct*, 17 June 1679.

I. 1635.   JAMES HAMILTON, of Broomhill, s. and h. of Claud
HAMILTON([d]), of the same, by Margaret, da. of James
HAMILTON, of Kilbrackmont; suc. his father in 1605; was Sheriff of co. Perth;
and was *cr.* a Baronet [S.], 5 Jan. 1635([c]), the patent however, not being
entered in the Great Seal Register [S.], with probably (at that date) rem. to
heirs male whatsoever, and with a grant of, presumably, 16,000 acres in
Nova Scotia, of which he never had seizin([e]). He *m.* Margaret, 1st da. of
William HAMILTON, of Udston, by Margaret, da. of (—) HAMILTON, of
Longhermiston. He *m.* secondly Jean HAMILTON, spinster, heiress of Park-
head. He *d.* apparently before 1647.

II. 1645?   SIR JOHN HAMILTON, Baronet [S. 1635], of Broomhill
    to   aforesaid and afterwards, of Biel, s. and h. by 1st wife; *suc.*
1679.   to the Baronetcy, on the death of his father, in or before 1647,
and was in that year *cr.* 15 Dec. 1647, LORD BELHAVEN
AND STENTON, receiving subsequently, 10 Feb. 1675 (having no male
issue) a *novodamus* of that Peerage, with a spec. rem. in favour of the husband of
one of his grand-daughters. He *m.* Margaret HAMILTON, spinster, illegit. da.
of James (HAMILTON), 2d MARQUESS OF HAMILTON [S.], by Anne, widow
(for such she remained) of John (ABERNETHY), LORD SALTOUN [S.], da.
of Walter (STEWART), 1st LORD BLANTYRE [S.]. She was living 24 Oct.
1666. He *d.* s.p.m. 17 and was *bur.* 20 June 1679, in Holyrood Abbey Church,
when his peerage devolved according to the spec. rem. in the *novodamus*
thereof but the *Baronetcy* became *dormant* or *extinct*. For fuller particulars
of him see " Peerage."

([a]) The "last Gibb of Caribber" had, however, apparently died before 1650.
See p. 404, note "a."

([b]) In Foster's *Baronetage* for 1883, this Baronetcy is (in the " *Chaos* " of that
work) assigned to the eldest s. and h. of Sir G. D. Gibb, the late holder, *viz:* " SIR
JAMES CAMPBELL GIBB, formerly in the Crown lands department, Canada, and late
Capt. Federal army, U.S.," of whom however no further particulars are known.

([c]) Laing's List. In Milne's List, where, however, no date is given, it is said
that " Sir John Hamilton, of Beill, is designed Barronet in his title of honor who
was made Lord 15 Dec. 1647."

([d]) This Claud was grandson of John Hamilton, of Broomhill, legitimated
under the Great Seal [S.], 20 Jan. 1512/3, being one of the many illegit.
brothers of James, 1st Earl of Arran [S.].

([e]) Banks's Lists.

GASCOIGNE·

cr. 8 June 1635, (ᵃ)

dormant, or *extinct,* 11 Feb 1810

I 1635   JOHN GASCOIGNE, of Barnbow, Lasingcroft and Parlington, co York(ᵇ), s and h of John GASCOIGNE, of Parlington, (living 1584,) by Maud, da of William ARTHINGTON, of Ardwick-in-the-street, co York, suc his father (or possibly in 1592 his uncle Richard GASCOIGNE) in the family estates and was *cr* a *Buronet* [S], 8 June 1635(ᵇ), the patent not being entered in the Great Seal Register [S], with probably (at that date) rem to heirs male whatsoever and with a grant of, presumably, 16,000 acres in Nova Scotia, of which he had seizin in Aug 1685 (ᶜ) He *m* in or before 1596, Anne, da of John INGLEBY, of Lawkland, by his 2d wife Anne, da of William CLAPHAM, of Beamsey, both in co York He *d* 3 May 1637, and his widow *d* a few weeks later, 2 or 20 June 1637

II 1637   SIR THOMAS GASCOIGNE, Baronet [S 1635,] of Barnbow, etc aforesaid 1st s and h, *b* about 1596, *suc to the Baronetcy,* 3 May 1637 He entered his pedigree in the Heralds' Visitation of Yorkshire, 1666, being then aged 70 He was tried for high treason, but acquitted 24 Jan 1679/80, (being then in his 85th year) by the court of King's Bench He *m* in or before 1620, Ann, da of George SYMONDS, of Brightwell park, Oxon She *d* before him He *d* at "Lambspring" beyond the seas in or before 1686, admon 4 Jan 1686/7 and again 15 Jan 1699/1700

III 1686?   SIR THOMAS GASCOIGNE, Baronet [S 1635], of Barnbow, etc, aforesaid, 3d but 1st surv s and h, *b* about 1623, being aged 43 in 1666, *suc to the Baronetcy* about 1686 He *m*, before that date Elizabeth, da and coheir of William SHELDON, of Beoley, co Worcester He *d* s p 1698 Will dat 26 Feb 1697, pr 4 Feb 1699

IV 1698,   SIR THOMAS GASCOIGNE, Baronet [S 1635], of Barnbow, etc, aforesaid, nephew and h, being 1st s and h of George GASCOIGNE, of Parlington, by Anne, da and coheir of Ellis WOODROWE, of Helperley, which George was 2d surv s of the 2d Baronet, but *d* v p before Dec 1682 He was *b* about 1659, being aged 7 in 1666 He *suc to the Baronetcy* in

---

(ᵃ) Laing's List only, where the date "8 June" is put within brackets

(ᵇ) This appears to be the first of a series of *English* gentry, not connected with Scotland, on whom a Baronetcy of that kingdom was conferred In Wotton's *Baronetage,* 1741, is "an account of such Nova Scotia Baronets as are of English families and resident in England numbered according, to their order as Nova Scotia Baronets" These are as follow —"71, ✓Gascoigne of Barnbow, Yorkshire, [1635], 73, ✓Pilkington, of Stainley, Yorkshire, 1635, 87, Slingsby, of Scriven, Yorkshire, [1638], 91, Pickering, of Titchmarsh, Northamptonshire, [1638], 92, Longueville, of Wolverton, Buckinghamshire, 1638, 95, Musgrave, of Hayton Castle, Cumberland, 1638, 96, Meredith, of Ashley Castle, Cheshire, 1639" To these may be added (1) Norton, of Cheston, co Suffolk, 1635, (2) Widdrington, of Cartington, co Northumberland, 1635, (3) Bolles, of Osberton, Notts, 1635, (4) Rayney, of Wrotham, co Kent, 1635, (5) Fortescue, of Salden, Bucks, 1635, (6) Moir, or More, of Longford, Notts, 1636, (7) Curzon, of Kedleston, co Derby, 1636, and (8) Piers, of Stonepit, in Sele, co Kent, 1638 The grantee of the Baronetcy [S], of Thomson, *cr* 20 Feb 1635/6, is erroneously said, in Walkley's List, to have been "English" Certain *Irish* Gentry, not apparently in any way connected with Scotland, were likewise so honoured, as, for instance, the two Baronetcies granted in 1630 to the name of Crosby, in 1634, the Baronetcy of Bingham, in 1636, that of Browne of the Neale, also the three granted to the name of Bourke, the one to Macarthy, etc

(ᶜ) Banks's Lists

1698   He *m* Magdalen, da of Patricius CURWEN, of Workington, co Cumberland
He, who was living 1712, *d* s p s in or before 1718   Admon 3 Nov 1718, at York
Admon of his widow, then or St Anne's, Westminster, 22 Feb 1721/2, to Henry
Curwen, of Workington, br and next of kin

V   1718 ?   SIR JOHN GASCOIGNE, Baronet [S 1635], of Parlington,
aforesaid, br and h, *b* about 1662, being aged 4 and more in 1666,
admitted to Gray's Inn, 4 Dec 1682, *suc to the Baronetcy* about 1718   He *m*
Mary, da and coheir of Roger WIDDINGTON, of Harbottle   He *d* at Bath, 11 June,
1723   Will dat 30 March 1720/1, pr 15 Aug 1723 at York

VI   1723   SIR EDWARD GASCOIGNE, Baronet [S 1635], of Parlington
aforesaid, s and h, *suc to the Baronetcy*, 11 June 1723   He *m*
Mary (then a minor, whose wardship was granted to him as her husband, 23 Aug
1728), da and h of Sir Francis HUNGATE, 4th Baronet [1642], of Hudleston, co
York, by Elizabeth, da of William WELD, of Lulworth, Dorset   He *d* at Cambray
in Flanders, 31 May 1750   Will dat 16 Sep 1742, pr 24 March 1750/1, at York
His widow *m* 15 Nov 1753, Gerard STRICKLAND, of Sizergh, co Westmorland, who
d 1 Sep 1791, aged 87   She *d* 14 Jan 1764

VII   1750   SIR EDWARD GASCOIGNE, Baronet [S 1635], of Parlington and Hudleston aforesaid, 1st s and h, *suc to the Baronetcy*
31 May 1750   He gave, from his quarry at Hudleston, the stone for repaving
York Minster   He *d* unm at Paris, 16 Jan 1762   Will dat 31 March 1758 to
11 May 1760, pr 12 Aug 1762

VIII   1762,   SIR THOMAS GASCOIGNE, Baronet [S 1635], of Parling-
to   ton aforesaid, br and h, *b* Feb 1743, *suc to the Baronetcy*,
1810   10 Jan 1762   He renounced the Roman Catholic faith, and read
a recantation of its tenets before the Archbishop of Canterbury,
was M P for Thirsk, 1780-84, for Malton, April to Aug 1784, and for Arundel,
Feb 1795 to 1796   He *m* firstly, in 1772 (—), da of (—) Montgomery   He *m*
secondly, 4 Nov 1784, at Aston upon Trent, Mary, widow of Sir Charles TURNER,
1st Baronet [1782], of Kirkleatham, co York, da of James SHUTTLEWORTH, of
Gawthorp, co Lancaster, by Mary, da of Robert HOLDEN, of Aston Hall, co Derby.
She *d* in childbirth at Parlington, 1 Feb 1786   Admon 4 April 1786, at York
He *d* s p s,(a) 11 Feb 1810, when the *Baronetcy* became *dormant* or *extinct*
Will pr 1810 (b)

NORTON

cr 18 June 1635 ,(c)

dormant or *extinct* in or before 1673

1   1635   WALTER NORTON, of Cheston, co Suffolk,(d) and afterwards of Sibsey, co Lincoln, Sheriff of that county, 1635-36 (being
then styled, possibly erroneously, "knight"), was *cr* a *Baronet* [S], 18 June 1635,(e)
the patent not being entered in the Great Seal Register [S], with probably (at
that date), rem to heirs male whatsoever, and with a grant of, presumably, 16,000

(a) His only child, Thomas Gascoigne, *b* 7 Jan 1786, *d* unm and v p 20 Oct
1809 from a fall out hunting, aged 24
(b) Under his will the Parlington and other Gascoigne estates, went to
Richard Oliver, of Castle Oliver, Ireland, the husband of Mary, eldest da of his
late wife, by her 1st husband, Sir Charles Turner abovenamed   He took the
name of Gascoigne, was Sheriff for co York 1816, and *d* 14 April 1843, s p m s
leaving two daughters and coheirs
(c) Laing's List, but not in Milne's List
(d) One of the Nova Scotia Baronetcies conferred on Englishmen not connected
with Scotland, as to which see p 407, note "b," under 'Gascoigne'

aces in Nova Scotia, of which he had seizin in Sep 1635 (ª) He *m* Mary, da of Edward (STOURTON), BARON STOURTON, by Frances, da of Sir Thomas TRESHAM, of Rushton, co Northampton She *d* at Drury lane, in childbirth 23, and was *bur* 24 May 1633, at St Giles' in the Fields He *d* in or before 1656 Admon 22 Feb. 1655/6, as of Brackenboro', co Lincoln

II 1656 ?
to
1673 ?
SIR EDWARD NORTON, Baronet [S 1635], s and h *suc to the Baronetcy* on the death of his father He *d s p*, probably unm, in or before 1673, when the *Baronetcy* became *dormant* Will, as of St Dunstan s in the West, London, dat 29 Nov 1669, in which he devises all to his good friend, Daniel Norton, of London, merchant, pr 4 June 1673

PILKINGTON

cr. 29 June 1635 ,(ᵇ)

sometime, 1854 and 1856, MILBORNE-SWINNERTON,

subsequently MILBORNE-SWINNERTON-PILKINGTON.

I 1635. ARTHUR PILKINGTON, of Stanley (near Wakefield), and of Nether Bradley, co York(ᶜ), s and h of Frederick PILKINGTON, by Frances, da of Sir Francis RODES, of Barlborough, co Derby, Justice of the Common Pleas, (which Frederick was 2d s, but the only one whose male issue continued more than one generation, of Thomas PILKINGTON, of Bradley, Bow Bearer to Queen Elizabeth), having suc to the family estates, was *cr* a Baronet [S], 29 June 1635(ᵇ), the patent not being entered in the Great Seal Register [S], with, probably (at that date) rem to heirs male whatsoever, and with a grant of, presumably, 16,000 acres in Nova Scotia, of which he had seizin in Sep 1635(ᵈ) He *m* in or before 1613 Ellen, da of Henry LYON, of Roxby, co Lincoln, and Twyford in Willesden, co Midx, merchant She was *bur* at Wakefield, 5 Feb 1646/7 He was *bur* 5 Sep 1650, at St Mary's, Castlegate, York

II 1650 SIR LYON PILKINGTON, Baronet [S 1635], of Stanley and Bradley aforesaid, s and h, *bap* 14 Nov 1613, at Wakefield admitted to Gray's Inn, 2 March 1631/2 *suc to the Baronetcy* in Sep 1650 He *m* firstly(ᵉ), (—) da of Sir Thomas NEWTON She *d s p* He, being then of St Andrew, Holborn, "Esq, aged 26, widower,' had lic (London,) June 1639, to marry Jane ONSLOW, aged 21, spinster He *m* subsequently (Lic Fac, 15 Aug 1650, Phœbe, (then aged 30), 2d da of Capt Robert MOYLE, of Buckwell, in Boughton Aluph, co Kent, by Priscilla, da of Charles FOTHERBY, Dean of Canterbury He was *bur* 5 Nov 1684, at St John's, Hackney, co Midx His widow *d* 20 and was *bur* 25 June 1686, in York Minster Will pr 7 Jan 1686/7

(ª) Banks's Lists, the entry therein being, ' Sir Walter Norton, of one Barony of land in New Scotland, represented by the Editor of this work [who styles himself on the title page thereof "Sir T C Banks, Bart, N S "], confirmed into another charter of lands erected into the Barony of St Maur in New Scotland "
(ᵇ) Laing's List, this also being the date given in the pedigree recorded in the College of Arms In Foster's copy of Milne's List the date is given as 29 *Jan* 1635, but it is partially enclosed by *one* bracket and so may not be in Milne's original List, as those that are "within brackets" are not in that list
(ᶜ) See p 408, note " d " under " Norton "
(ᵈ) Banks's Lists
(ᵉ) This marriage is said in Foster s YORKSHIRE PEDIGREES to have taken place 31 Dec 1639, at St Benets' Pauls wharf, London, but *query*

3 E

III   1684.   SIR LYON PILKINGTON, Baronet [S 1635], of Stanley
and Bradley aforesaid, 1st s and h by last wife, b about
1660, suc to the Baronetcy in Nov 1684 He m firstly in or before 1683,
Amy, only da of Thomas EGGLETON, of Grove in Ellesborough, Bucks, by Amy,
da of Nicholas DENTON, of Barton, Beds She, who was bap 8 March 1660/1,
at Elleslow, d 4 and was bur 6 April 1695, at Wakefield, aged 36 He m
secondly (settlement 18 March 1698), Lennox, (aged 6 in 1665), widow of
George SMITH, of Osgodby, co York, da and h of Cuthbert HARRISON,
of Acaster Selby, co York, by Lennox, da of Marmaduke (Langdale), 1st
BARON LANGDALE OF HOLME He was bur 7 Aug 1714, at Wakefield,
aged 54 M I Will pr at York, 15 Jan 1714/5

IV   1714   SIR LYON PILKINGTON, Baronet [S 1635], of Stanley
and Bradley aforesaid, sometime of Hickleton, co York, 1st
s and h by 1st wife, bap 5 June 1683, at Ellesborough, suc to the
Baronetcy in Aug 1714 He m 3 Feb 1705, at Hickleton, co York, Anne,
4th da of Sir Michael WENTWORTH of Wolley, co York, by Dorothy, da of
Sir Godfrey COPLEY 1st Baronet [1611], of Sprotborough He was bur (less
than two years after his father), 26 June 1716, at Wakefield, in his 34th year
M I Will pr at York 8 Aug 1716 His widow, who was b 16 and bap
20 March 1683, at Woolley, m secondly (as his 2d wife), Sir Charles DALSTON,
3d Baronet [1641], who d 8 March 1723, aged 83 M I She m (for
her 3d husband) 1 Dec 1730, at Horbury, John MAUDE, of Alverthorpe Hall and
of Wakefield She d at Chevet, in Royston, co York, 5 and was bur 9 Aug
1764, at Wakefield

V   1716   SIR LIONEL PILKINGTON, Baronet [S 1635], of Stanley
aforesaid, afterwards of Chevet in Royston, co York, bap at
Hickleton, 20 Jan 1706/7, suc to the Baronetcy in June 1716, matric at Oxford
(Ch Ch) 14 May 1725, aged 18, was Sheriff of Yorkshire, 1740-41, M P for
Horsham (three Parls), 1748-68 He purchased the estate of Chevet, co York
(formerly belonging to the family of Neville) 4 July 1765 He d unm. at Chevet
11, and was bur 17 Aug 1778, at Wakefield Will pr 5 Oct 1778

VI   1778   SIR MICHAEL PILKINGTON, Baronet [S 1635], of Lupset
in Wakefield, co York, br and h, bap at All Saints', Wakefield,
25 May 1715, suc to the Baronetcy, 11 Aug 1778 He m firstly, 7 Dec 1738, at
West Ardsley, Judith, da and coheir of the Rev Charles NETTLETON, of Earls
Heaton, co York, Rector of Bulwick, co Northampton She d s p at Wakefield,
and was bur there 29 Jan 1772 He m secondly, 11 Nov 1772, at Badsworth
Isabella, da of the Rev William RAWSTORNE, Vicar of Badsworth, by Elizabeth,
only child of Samuel WALKER, of Stapleton park, co York He d at Lupset, 6
and was bur 18 Feb 1788, at Wakefield Will pr 20 March 1788 His widow
m, April 1791, at St James', Westm, Thomas HEWETSON, Major in the army
She d at Doncaster, 25 Feb 1823, and was bur at Wakefield, aged 75

VII   1788   SIR THOMAS PILKINGTON, Baronet [S 1635], of Chevet
aforesaid, 1st s and h, by 2d wife, b 7 Dec 1773 and bap at
Badsworth 10 Jan 1774, suc to the Baronetcy, 6 Feb 1788, matric at Oxford
(Merton Coll) 1 Aug 1791, aged 17, cr M.A 5 July 1793, Sheriff of Yorkshire,
1798-99 He m, 1 Aug 1797, at Great Waltham, Essex, Elizabeth Anne, 1st da
of William TUFNELL, of Langley, co Essex, by Anne, da of John CLOSE, of Eashy
House, co York He d s p m 9 and was bur 15 July 1811, at Wakefield, aged
37 Will, in which he devised all his estates to his daughters, pr Feb 1839 His
widow m William MULES, and d Nov 1842, being bur at Dedham, Essex

VIII   1811   SIR WILLIAM PILKINGTON, Baronet [S 1635], of Chevet
aforesaid, br and h male, bap 14 Nov 1775, at Wakefield, suc to
the Baronetcy, 9 July 1811, and purchased the estate of Chevet from his nieces soon

afterwards He m , 25 June 1825, at St Marylebone, Mary, 2d da and coheir of Thomas SWINNERTON, of Butterton Hall, in Tientham, co Stafford, by Mary, da and h of Charles MILBORNE, of Wonastow, co Monmouth, and of the Priory, Abergavenny He d at Chevet Hall, 30 Sep 1850, and was bur at Sandal Magna, in his 75th year Will pr Jan 1851 His widow, who by Act of Parl , 1836-37, took the name of Milborne-Swinnerton before that of Pilkington, d 11 and was bur 20 Dec 1854, at Butterton, aged 61 Will pr Feb 1855

IX 1850 SIR THOMAS EDWARD PILKINGTON, Baronet [S 1635], of Chevet aforesaid, 1st s and h , b 19 March and bap 9 April 1829, at Chevet Hall and was reg at Sandal Magna , matric at Oxford (Univ Coll) 16 Oct 1847, aged 18 , suc to the Baronetcy 30 Sep 1850, Capt in the West Riding Yeomanry Militia, 1852-53 He d unm at Funchal, in Madeira, 7 Jan 1854, aged 24, and was bur in the English cemetery there

X 1854 SIR WILLIAM MILBORNE-SWINNERTON, afterwards MIL-BORNE-SWINNERTON-PILKINGTON, Baronet [S 1635], of Chevet aforesaid, br and h , b 8 and bap 28 June 1831 at Chevet Hall, reg at Sandal Magna He, in infancy, took the name of Milborne-Swinnerton in lieu of that of Pilkington, by Act of Parl , 1836-37, but by another Act of Parl , 1854, resumed the final name of Pilkington, having suc to the Baronetcy 7 Feb 1854, Lieut Staffordshire Yeomanry, 1854 He d unm , 12 Nov 1855, aged 24, at Hillingdon, and was bur at Butterton Admon Jan 1856

XI. 1855 SIR LIONEL PILKINGTON, afterwards MILBORNE-SWINNER-TON and MILBORNE-SWINNERTON-PILKINGTON, Baronet [S 1635], of Chevet aforesaid, br and h , b 7 July 1835, at Chevet Hall, and bap at Sandal Magna, 4 Aug following , ed at Charterhouse school , Cornet 1st West York Yeomanry Cavalry, 1854 , suc to the Baronetcy, 12 Nov 1855, and took by royal lic , 15 Feb 1856, the name of Milborne-Swinnerton only, but subsequently resumed the final name of Pilkington , Sheriff of Yorkshire, 1859 He m 3 Feb 1857, at St Geo , Hanover sq , Isabella Elizabeth, da and h of the Rev Charles KINLESIDE, Rector of Poling, co Sussex He d at Chevet Park, 25 June 1901 Will pr at £73,017 His widow living 1902

XII. 1901 SIR THOMAS EDWARD MILBORNE-SWINNERTON-PILKINGTON, Baronet [S 1635], of Chevet aforesaid, 1st s and h , b 9 Dec 1857, at Chevet, matric at Oxford (Ch Ch) 13 Oct 1876, aged 18 , B A , 1879 , M A , 1883 , sometime Major King's Royal Rifle Corps , suc to the Baronetcy 25 June 1901 He m 23 July 1895, at St Mark's, North Audley street, Kathleen Mary Alexina, da and h of William Ulick O'Connor (CUFFE), 4th EARL OF DESART [1] by his 1st wife, Maria Emma Georgiana, da of Thomas Henry PRESTON, of Morehy, co York She was b 17 May 1872

Family Estates —These, in 1883, consisted of 4,808 acres in the West Riding of Yorkshire , 2,195 in Staffordshire , 1,457 in Monmouthshire , 149 in Hereford-shire, and 135 in Kent Total —8,744 acres, worth £13,597 a year Principal Seats —Chevet Park, near Wakefield, co York , Butterton Hall, near Newcastle-under-Lyme, co Stafford, and Wonastow Court, co Monmouth.

HAY

cr. 20 July 1635 ,(ᵃ)

dormant 1683 ? to 1805,

but assumed since 1805.

I 1635 JAMES HAY, of Smithfield, co Peebles, only surv. s
and h of John HAY, of the same (called "Dumb John"), was
made "Esquire of the Body," 1624, suc his father in 1628, was M P [S] for
Peebles-shire, 1628-33, and again 1643, and was cr a Baronet [S], 20 July 1635, by
patent dat at Oatlands,(ᵃ) but not recorded in the *Registrum Preceptorum Cartarum pro Baronettis Novæ Scotiæ,* with probably (at that date) rem to heirs male
whatsoever, and with a grant of, presumably, 16,000 acres in Nova Scotia,
"extending 3 miles along the river Grand Solbison in Capricorne and Stretchbury
and from thence northwards for 6 miles to be thenceforth called the Barony and
Regality of Smithfield,"(ᵃ) of which he had seizin in [Dec ?] 1635 (ᵇ) He m (ᶜ)
Sidney MASSEY, an English or Irish lady, who survived him (ᵈ) He d 1654
Admon (in C P C, London) 21 June 1655, to a creditor Will dat 19 Feb
1654, pr 6 April 1659, in Prerog Court [1]

II 1654 SIR JOHN HAY, Baronet [S 1635], who *suc to the
Baronetcy* in 1654, but to none of his father s estate save £1,000,
all else being left to his yr br , William He m before 1652 He d about 1659,
in Scotland Admon as "of Peebles," 24 Aug 1668, to "Sir James Douglas,
Knight," principal creditor

III 1659 ? SIR JAMES HAY, Baronet [S 1635], only s and h, b at
to Peebles, 1652, *suc to the Baronetcy* about 1659, and subsequently
1683 ? became h to his uncle, William HAY, of Smithfield, but the estates
had been wasted He m 23 July 1678, Grace, yst da of the Rev
Thomas CLAVERING, Rector of Piddlehinton, Dorset He d s p m in or soon after
1683 His widow d 1753, aged 96 After his death the *Baronetcy* became
dormant, and so remained for above 120 years

*   *   *   *   *   *

IV.(ᵉ) 1805. SIR JAMES HAY, Baronet(ᵉ) [S 1635], of Haystoun, co
Peebles, cousin and h male,(ᶠ) being 2d but 1st surv s and h of
John HAY, of the same, by Grizel THOMPSON (m 7 March 1712), which John (who

---

(ᵃ) Playfair's *Baronetage* [S], 1811 The date of creation as in Laing's List
(said therein to be given "on the authority of former lists") is *10 Dec 1635* It
is omitted in Milne's List

(ᵇ) Banks's Lists

(ᶜ) According to a note of R R Stodart (Lyon Clerk Depute, 1863-86) the
mother of his only da Anne (who m 10 Feb 1649 Sir James Douglas, afterwards
Earl of Morton [S]), was "a da of Lord Beaumont, by (—) Wilford, of
Worcestershire," as stated in the "birthbrief" (date or history not mentioned) of
the said Anne [*Ex inform* Sir J Balfour Paul, Lyon King of Arms]

(ᵈ) The funeral entry in Ulster's Office of "Lady Hay," who d 30 March and
was bur 2 April 1677 in St Bride's Church, London, may refer to her, but as it
is added that "she was married to Sir James Hay, Baronet of Scotland," it looks
as if her husband was then living, in which case she might be a *1st* wife of Sir
James, the 3d Baronet, who a year after this date m Grace Clavering The
arms entered for her are those of LAXTON, impaled with HAY [*Ex inform*
G D Burtchaell, Office of Arms, Ireland]

(ᵉ) According to the service at Peebles, 9 Nov 1805 The numbering, however,
(as given after the 3d holder) does not include those persons who, according to
such service, would have been entitled to the Baronetcy

(ᶠ) The want of any reliable proof of heirship in this somewhat dateless descent
is discussed, and the existence of other sons of this family is shown, in the *Her and
Gen*, vol iv, p. 372

d 1762) was s of John HAY, of Haystoun (living 1689), s of [another] John HAY, of Haystoun, one of the Principal Clerks of Session [S] (*d* 27 Oct 1679), 1st s and h of Andrew HAY, of Haystoun (which estate he purchased in 1635), Writer to the Signet [S], who *d* 1655, being 1st s of John HAY, of Kingsmeadows (an estate he purchased in 1570), yr br of Thomas HAY, of Smithfield aforesaid (who *d* 1570, being father of "Dumb John Hay," the father of the 1st Baronet), the said John HAY, of Kingsmeadows, and Thomas, his elder brother, both above-named, who were sons of John HAY, of Smithfield, living 1525 He suc his father in 1762 in the estate of Haystoun He was a Physician at Edinburgh On 9 Nov 1805, he was "served heir at Peebles to John HAY, of Kingsmeadows, his great-great [apparently great-great-great] grandfather and *assumed the title [of Baronet]* as heir male of the 3d Baronet "(*a*) He *m* 13 Dec 1751, Dorriel, yst da and coheir of Daniel CAMPBELL, of Greenyards, Sec to the Bank of Scotland, by Elizabeth, da of Thomas TULLOCH, Writer She *d* 28 March 1770 He *d* 21 Oct 1810

V (*b*) 1810   SIR JOHN HAY, Baronet(*b*) [S 1635], of Haystoun aforesaid, 1st s and h, *b* 15 Jan 1755, was a Banker in Edinburgh, *suc to the Baronetcy* (*b*) 21 Oct 1810 He *m*, 9 July 1785, Mary Elizabeth, yst da of James (FORBES), 16th LORD FORBES [S], by Catherine, only child of Sir Robert INNES, 6th Baronet [S 1628], of Balvenie She, by whom he had eight sons and seven daughters, *d* 2 Nov 1803 He *d* 23 May 1830 Will pr Oct 1830

VI (*b*) 1830   SIR JOHN HAY, Baronet(*b*) [S 1635], of Haystoun aforesaid, 3d but 1st surv s and h, *b* 3 Aug 1788, Advocate [S], 28 June 1811, M P for Peebles (three Parls), 1831-37, *suc to the Baronetcy,*(*b*) 23 May 1830 He *m* 6 Oct 1821, Anne, da and h of George PRESTON, Capt in the Royal Marines (*d* 1798, aged 60), 4th s of Sir George PRESTON, 4th Baronet [S 1637], of Valleyfield, co Perth He *d* s p 1 Nov 1838, at Rome, aged 50 His widow, who in April 1855, inherited the estate of Valleyfield aforesaid *d* 2 Sep 1862, in Devonshire place house, New road, Marylebone

VII (*b*) 1838   SIR ADAM HAY, Baronet(*b*) [S 1635], of Haystoun aforesaid, br and h, being the 7th s of the 5th Baronet(*b*), *b* 14 Dec 1795, in St Andrew's parish, Edinburgh, was a banker at Edinburgh, M P for Linlithgowshire, 1826 30, *suc to the Baronetcy,*(*b*) 1 Nov 1838, Vice Lieut of co Peebles, 1839 67 He *m*, 23 March 1823, Henrietta Callender, 1st da of William GRANT, of Congalton, co Haddington She *d* at Edinburgh, 6 June 1849 He *d* 18 Jan 1867, at Cannes, in France, aged 71

VIII. (*b*) 1867   SIR ROBERT HAY, Baronet (*b*) [S 1635], of Haystoun aforesaid, 2d but 1st surv s and h, *b* 8 May 1825, *suc to the Baronetcy,*(*b*) 18 Jan 1867 He *m*, 3 Aug 1853, at Castle Menzies, co Perth, Sally, da of Alexander DUNCAN, of Providence, Rhode Island, U S A and of Knossington Grange, co Leicester He *d* suddenly, 29 May 1885, at Lyons, in France, aged 60 Will pr 19 Aug 1885, over £90,000 His widow living 1902

IX   1885 (*b*)   SIR JOHN ADAM HAY, Baronet(*b*) [S 1635], of Haystoun aforesaid, 1st s and h, *b* 5 May 1854, ed at Eton, sometime Lieut in the Scots Guards, Major 3d Vol Batt Lothian Regt, *suc to the Baronetcy,*(*b*) 29 May 1885 He *m* 10 March 1885, at All Saints, Ennismore Gardens, Anne Salisbury Mary Mehora, 1st da of Sir Robert John MILLIKEN-NAPIER, 9th Baronet [S 1627], by Anne Salisbury Mehora, da of John Ladoveze ADLERCRON He *d* 4 May 1895, at his mother's residence, North House, Putney hill, co Surrey, in his 41st year His widow living 1902

(*a*) Burke's *Baronetage* for 1901
(*b*) See page 412, note "e"

X.(ᵃ) 1895.   SɪR DᴜɴᴄᴀN EᴅᴡᴀRᴅ Hᴀʏ, Baronet(ᵃ) [S. 1633], of
Haystoun aforesaid, only s. and h., b. 25 Sep. 1882; *suc. to the
Baronetcy*,(ᵃ) 4 May 1895.

Family Estates.—These, in 1883, consisted of 9,155 acres in co. Peebles, and 600
in co. Selkirk. *Total,* 9,755 acres, worth £4,514 a year. *Principal Seats.*—King's
meadows and Haystoun, co. Peebles.

WIDDRINGTON :

cr. 26 Sep. 1635 ;(ᵇ)

dormant, or *extinct,* 13 July 1671.

I. 1635,   EᴅᴡᴀRᴅ WɪᴅᴅRɪɴɢᴛᴏɴ, of Cartington, co. Northum-
    to   berland,(ᶜ) was *cr. a Baronet* [S.], 26 Sep. 1635,(ᵇ) the patent not
    1671.   being entered in the Great Seal Register [S.], with probably (at
that date) rem. to heirs male whatsoever, and with a grant
of, presumably, 16,000 acres in Nova Scotia, of which he had seizin in Dec. 1635.(ᵈ)
He was subsequently *cr. a Baronet of England,* 8 Aug. 1642, but *d.* s.p.m.s., 13 July
1671, when that Baronetcy became extinct and the *Baronetcy* [S. 1635], became
dormant or extinct. See fuller account of him on page 188.

BOLLES :

cr. 19 Dec. 1635 ;(ᵉ)

subsequently, after 1662, Jᴏᴘsᴏɴ.

dormant, or *extinct,* about 1670.

I. 1635.   MᴀRʏ Bᴏʟʟᴇs,(ᶠ) of Osberton,(ᵍ) in Worksop, co. Nottingham,(ᶜ) widow, was *cr. a Baronetess* [S.],(ᵇ) 19 Dec. 1635,(ᵉ) the
patent however not being entered in the Great Seal Register [S.], with rem. of
the dignity of a Baronet [S.], "to her heirs male and assignees,"(ⁱ) with a grant
of, presumably, 16,000 acres in Nova Scotia, of which she never had seizin.(ʲ)
She, who was *bap.* 30 June 1579, at Ledsham, co. York, was da. of William
Wʏᴛʜᴀᴍ, of Ledsham aforesaid, by Eleanor, da. of John Nᴇᴀʟᴇ, of co.

(ᵃ) See page 412, note " e."
(ᵇ) Laing's List, but not in Milne's List. In Walkley's List the 95th and last
creation therein given is "Sir William [*sic*] Witherington, English," but as there
is no Sir *Edward* Widdrington in that List, the christian name of *William* is
probably a mistake.
(ᶜ) See p. 408, note "d" under "Norton."
(ᵈ) Banks's Lists, in which however " Sir Edward " is [incorrectly] said to have
been " afterwards Lord Widdrington."
(ᵉ) Laing's List, but not in that of Milne.
(ᶠ) This is the only case of a Baronetcy having been conferred on a female, or
even enjoyed *suo jure,* by one. The rank of the *widow of a Baronet* has
occasionally been conferred, as was the case in the Baronetcy of Speelman,
9 Sep. 1686, where the mother of the grantee was so honoured.
(ᵍ) In Walkley's List the grantee is described as " Dame Mary Bolles, of
Ardworth, English." She is sometimes called " of Cudworth, co. York," the
residence of her 1st husband.
(ʰ) J. C. Brooke (Somerset Herald, 1778-94), states in his Yorkshire collections
(" I.C.B. vol. 1, p. 408, Coll. of Arms) that she purchased her title. He adds that
there is a tradition, that, after her death " she haunted her house at Heath and
parts adjacent till such time as she was conjured into a certain deep place in the
river Calder, near that town [*i.e.* Wakefield], called from thence *Lady Bolles's Pit.*"
(ⁱ) Foster's List of Nova Scotia Baronets, in his *Baronetage* for 1883.
(ʲ) Banks's Lists.

Northampton She *m* firstly Thomas JOPSON, of Cudworth, in Royston, co York
She *m* secondly (Lic at York, 1611), as his 2d wife, Thomas BOLLES, of Osberton
aforesaid, and by him had two daughters but no son He, who entered his
pedigree in the Visit of Notts, 1614, *d* 19 March 1634/5, and was *bur* at Worksop
Funeral certificate "testified by the *Lady Mary Bolles, Baronettes,* late wife and
executrix" Will dat 15 March 1634/5 Within nine months of his death she was
cr a Baronetess [S], as above mentioned She resided at Heath Hall, near
Wakefield, co York, and *d* 5 May, being *bur* 16 June 1662, at Ledsham aforesaid,
aged about 81

II 1662,   SIR WILLIAM JOPSON, Baronet [S 1635], of Cudworth and
to   of Heath Hall aforesaid, grandson and h, being 4th but only
1670 ?   surv s and h of Thomas JOPSON, of Cudworth, by his 1st wife,
Anne (*m* 31 July 1626, at Worksop), da of Nicholas STRINGER, of
Sutton-upon-Lound, co Notts, which Thomas (who *d* before his mother, 26 Aug
1653, was only s and h ap of DAME MARY BOLLES, *suo jure* Baronetess [S], by
her 1st husband, Thomas JOPSON, both abovenamed He was *b* probably about
1635 and *suc to the Baronetcy* on the death of his said grandmother, 5 May
1662 He *m* Lucy, da of Henry TINDALL, of Brotherton, co York He
d s p m (a) in or before 1673 (leaving a will, when the *Baronetcy* became *dormant*
His widow *m* between 1667 and 1673, as his 2d wife, Sir John JACKSON, 1st
Baronet [1660], of Hickleton, co York, who *d* in or before 1678

RAYNEY

cr 19 Dec, 1635 and (again) 13 Sep 1636 ,(b)

cr a Baronet [E.] 22 Jan 1641/2,

dormant, 1721

I 1635,   JOHN RAYNEY, of Wrotham, co Kent,(c) was *cr a*
and   *Baronet* [S] 19 Dec 1635, as also again (possibly owing to some
1636   defect in the former creation) on 13 Sep 1636,(b) with rem to
heirs male whatsoever, and with a grant of, presumably, 16,000
acres in Nova Scotia, of which he never had seizin (d) He was, a few years later,
cr a Baronet of England, 22 Jan 1641/2, see that creation which became *extinct*
on the death of the 5th Baronet in 1721, when the *Baronetcy* [S] became *dormant*

FORTESCUE ·

cr 17 Feb 1635/6 ;(e)

dormant, 9 Nov. 1729

I 1636   JOHN FORTESCUE, of Salden, in Mursley, Bucks,(c) s and
h of Sir Francis FORTESCUE, K.B, of the same, by Grace (*m* before
1590), da of the Hon Sir John MANNERS, of Haddon, co Derby (which Francis was
son of Sir John FORTESCUE, Chancellor of the Exchequer, who purchased the estate of
Salden in 1590 and *d* 23 Dec 1607, aged 76), was *bap* at Mursley, 1592, matric at
Oxford (Merton Coll) 11 July 1606, aged 12, admitted to Inner Temple, 1612,
suc his father in Jan 1623/4 and was *cr a Baronet* [S] 17 Feb 1635/6,(e) the

---

(a) Lucy, his da and eventually sole heir, who inherited the estate of
Cudworth, *m* in 1686, Robert (Ridgeway), 4th Earl of Londonderry [I], who
d, s p m s, 7 March 1713/4 She *d* 4 Sep 1724, leaving a da Frances (only child
who left issue) wife of Thomas (Pitt), 1st Baron and Earl of Londonderry [I],
being so created respectively in 1719 and 1726, who in her right inherited the
estate of Cudworth

(b) Laing's List for both dates and Milne s List for the latter

(c) See p 408, note "d," under "Norton"

(d) Banks's Lists

(e) Laing's List

patent not being entered in the Great Seal Register [S], with rem to heirs male whatsoever, and with a grant of, presumably, 16,000 acres in Nova Scotia, of which he never had seizin (ᵃ) In the Civil War, he was in arms on the King's side and was taken prisoner, May 1644, near Islip, Oxon He m Frances, da of Sir Edward STANLEY, K B, of Ensham, Oxon He d Sep 1656, and was bur at Mursley Admon 6 Nov 1656

II 1656   SIR JOHN FORTESCUE, Baronet [S 1636], of Salden aforesaid, 1st s and h, bap 13 July 1614, at Mursley, reverted to the ancient religion of his family, suc to the Baronetcy in Sep 1656 He m firstly, Margaret, da of Thomas (ARUNDELL), 1st BARON ARUNDELL OF WARDOUR, by his 2d wife, Ann, da of Miles PHILIPSON She d s p m 1638 He m secondly, in or before 1644, Mary, da of Sir William STONOR, of Stonor, Oxon, by Elizabeth da of Sir Thomas LAKE, Secretary of State to James I She was bap 11 Nov 1622 He m thirdly, Elizabeth, 2d da of Sir John WINTOUR, of Lydney, co Gloncester, by Mary, da of Lord William HOWARD She d s p s 1674 He was bur 14 June 1683 at Mursley

III 1683   SIR JOHN FORTESCUE, Baronet [S 1636], of Salden aforesaid, 1st and only surv s, by 2d wife, b 1644, suc to the Baronetcy in June 1683, d s p 1717, aged 73

IV 1717,   SIR FRANCIS FORTESCUE, Baronet [S 1636], of Salden
to   aforesaid, cousin and h male, being s of Francis FORTESCUE, the
1729   only surv s of Sir Edward FORTESCUE,(ᵇ) (bur at Mursley, 14 Feb 1662, yr s of the 1st Baronet He was b about 1662, suc to the Baronetcy in 1717 He m before 7 May 1713, Mary, da of Henry HUDDLESTON of Sawston, co Cambridge (who d 1714/5), by Mary, da of Richard BASTOCK, of Wixhall, Salop He d s p at Bath, 9 and was bur 11 Nov 1729, at Salden, aged 67, when the Baronetcy became dormant, he being "the last male descendant of Queen Elizabeth's minister and so far as we know of Sir Adrian Fortescue also "(ᶜ) M I Will dat 18 Sep 1724, pr 8 Jan 1729/30 The will of his widow, dat 26 Jan 1743, pr 8 Feb 1744/5

THOMSON.
cr 20 Feb 1635/6 ,(ᵈ)
dormant since Jan 1691

I 1636   SIR THOMAS THOMSON, of Duddingston, co Edinburgh,(ᵉ) br and h of John THOMSON, of the same, both being sons of Alexander THOMSON, of Easter and Wester Duddingston, Advocate (who d in or

(ᵃ) Banks's Lists
(ᵇ) There is an admon, 18 June 1651, of Dame Frances Fortescue, wife of Sir Edward Fortescue, of Salden, Bucks (who renounces), da of "Robert Brooke, Esq," and Joan his wife, both deceased, granted to "Robert Slingsby, Esq," uncle of Catherine Fortescue, minor, da of deceased A subsequent admon was granted, 11 May 1680, to Wm Waller, the said minor having died This Frances was Sir Edward's 1st wife, the 2d wife was Mary, da of Gilbert Reresby, by whom he had two sons and four daughters [Napier's Swyncombe, Oxon]
(ᶜ) Lord Clermont's Fortescue Family
(ᵈ) Laing's List and Milne's List "The Baronetcy is recorded in the Reg Mag Scot, 20 Feb 1636 grant of lands to Thomas Thomson, of Duddingston, Miles, and his heirs male and assigns whomsoever (next the lands and Barony of Salden, Nova Scotia, belonging to Sir John Fortescue, of Salden, Baronet), and creating him a Baronet [S], with rem to heirs male " [Sir J Balfour Paul, Lyon King of Arms]
(ᵉ) In Walkley's Catalogue this creation stands as being that of "Sir Thomas Tompsone of Duddingstone, English," but the word English has doubtless been inserted in error See p 407, note "b," under "Gascoigne"

shortly before May 1603), by Margaret, sister of Sir John PRESTON, L President of the Court of Session, da of Alexander PRESTON, of Edinburgh, Baker,[a] was *Knighted* before 23 Feb 1633, and was cr a *Baronet* [S], 20 Feb 1635/6,[b] with rem to heirs male whatsoever and with a grant of, presumably, 16,000 acres in Nova Scotia, of which he never had seizin[c] He m, in or before 1627,[d] Margaret, da of John SCRIMGEOUR, Constable of Dundee She was living 1654, on which date she and the heirs of her body had an annuity of £120 settled on them, her husband having been exempted from the Act of Pardon in that year He d between 1654 and March 1666

II   1666 ?   SIR PATRICK THOMSON, Baronet [S 1636], of Dudding-ston aforesaid, 1st surv s and h, b 24 Dec 1637, *suc to the Baronetcy* on the death of his father, to whom he was served heir, 13 March 1666, shortly after which date he alienated the family estates He apparently d s p His will confirmed 15 April 1674, in the Commissariat of Edinburgh

III.   1674 ?   SIR JAMES THOMSON, Baronet [S 1636], heir male,
to   presumably brother,[e] but possibly son, of the above, *suc to the*
1691   *Baronetcy*, in or before April 1674 He d, apparently s p m, in or before Jan 1691, when the *Baronetcy* became *dormant* Will confirmed, as above, 28 Jan 1691

ABERCROMBY
cr. 20 Feb 1635/6 ([f])

I   1636   ALEXANDER ABERCROMBY, of Birkenbog, co Banff, s and h ap of Alexander ABERCROMBY, of the same, Grand Falconer in Scotland to Charles I, by Elizabeth, da of (—) BETHUNE, or BEATON, of Balfour, was b about 1603, obtained, 21 April 1636 (with others) a monopoly of trading from Scotland to Africa for 15 years, and was cr a *Baronet* [S] 20 Feb 1635/6,[f] with remainder to heirs male and with a grant of, presumably, 16,000 acres in Nova Scotia, of which, however, he never had seizin[c] He suc his father between 1641 and 1648, was M P [S] for Banffshire, 1640-41, 1643 1646-47, 1648, and 1661-63 He took an active part against the King, being considered "A Main Covenanter," and in May 1645, joined the forces of Major Urry, and was present at the battle of Auldearn He m firstly, Jane, 2d da of Sir Thomas URQUHART, senior, of Cromarty, by Christian, 4th da of Alexander (ELPHINSTONE), 4th LORD ELPHINSTONE [S] She d s p He m secondly, Jane, da of (—) SUTHERLAND, of the family of Kilminty She also d s p He m thirdly,[g] Elizabeth, da of Sir James BAIRD, of Auchmedden His widow m Col Patrick OGILVIE, of Inchmartin.

---

[a] For the whole of the information as to this family the Editor is indebted to Sir J Balfour Paul, Lyon King of Arms The grandfather of the grantee was Alexander Thomson, of Duddingston, who m Catharine, da of Sir William Lawson, of Boghall, and who was s of Thomas Thomson, also of Duddingston, by Catharine, da of John Towers, of Innerleith, co Edinburgh

[b] See p 416, notes "d " and "e "

[c] Banks's Lists

[d] A son, Thomas, was *bap* 9 Dec 1627

[e] The 2d Baronet had a younger br James, born 15 July 1641

[f] The Abercromby Charter is on the same terms and of the same date as that of Thomson [*Ex inform* Sir J Balfour Paul, Lyon King of Arms] No date is given in Milne's List, but in Laing's List it is stated to be 18 June 1636, and to be "given on the authority of former lists"

[g] The date of this marriage is given as "22 Aug 1668 " in Burke's *Baronetage* (1901).

3 F

II   1670 ?   SIR JAMES ABERCROMBY, Baronet [S 1636], of Birkenbog
                 aforesaid, s. and h.,(a) by 3d wife, *suc to the Baronetcy* on the
death of his father, was M P [S] for co Banff, 1693—1702   He m 1645, Mary,
da of Arthur GORDON, of Straloch   He d 20 Sep 1734 (b)

III   1734   SIR ROBERT ABERCROMBY, Baronet [S 1636], of Birken-
                bog aforesaid, 3d but 1st surv s and h , *suc to the Baronetcy*,
20 Sep 1734   He m 1739, Helen, da of his paternal uncle, Alexander ABER-
CROMBY, of Tullibody, co Clackmannan   He d 11 March 1787.

IV.   1787   SIR GEORGE ABERCROMBY, Baronet [S 1636], of Birken-
                bog aforesaid, and subsequently [after 1803] of Forglen House, co
Banff, s and h , b 1750, Advocate [S] 4 Dec 1773, Sheriff for co Elgin and co
Nairn, 1783 , *suc to the Baronetcy*, 11 March 1787 , Clerk for the admission of
Notars, 1807   He m 1778, Jane, da of Alexander (OGILVIE), 7th LORD BANFF [S],
by Jean, da of William NISBET, of Dirleton, co Haddington   She was eldest
sister and coheir of William, the 8th Lord, on whose death, unm , 4 June 1803,
his estate of Forglen passed to this family.   Sir George d 18 July 1831

V   1831   SIR ROBERT ABERCROMBY, Baronet [S 1636], of Birkenbog
                and Forglen House aforesaid, s and h , b 4 Feb 1784, M P
for Banffshire, 1812-18 , *suc to the Baronetcy*, 18 July 1831   He m 22 Oct 1816,
Elizabeth-Stephenson, da and sole h of Samuel DOUGLAS, of Netherlaw   He d
6 July 1855   His widow d 28 Dec 1863

VI.   1855   SIR GEORGE-SAMUEL ABERCROMBY, Baronet [S 1636], of
                Birkenbog and Forglen House aforesaid, s and h , b 22 May
1824 , *suc to the Baronetcy*, 8 July 1855   He m 12 June 1849, Agnes Georgiana,
2d da of John Cavendish (BROWNE), 3d BARON KILMAINE [I], by his 1st wife,
Eliza, da of David LYON   He d 14 Nov 1872

VII   1872   SIR ROBERT JOHN ABERCROMBY, Baronet [S 1636], of
                Birkenbog and Forglen House aforesaid, s and h , b 14 June 1850
in Chester Square, Middlesex, ed at Eton, *suc to the Baronetcy* 14 Nov 1872 ,
Vice-Lieut of co Banff   He m 26 June 1883, at Apsley Guise, Beds , Florence
Anita Eyre, only da of Eyre COOTE, of West Park, Rockburne, Hants, by Jessie
Mary, da of Major-Gen Henry Lechmere WORRALL   He d at Forglen House
24 July 1895, aged 45   Will pr at £127,653   His widow, who was b 23 Dec
1860, at Florence, and bap in the English Church there, m 10 June 1899, at
St Saviour's, Walton Place, as his 2d wife, Francis George BARING, *styled*
VISCOUNT BARING, s and h ap of Thomas George, 2d EARL OF NORTHBROOK ·

VIII 1895   SIR GEORGE WILLIAM ABERCROMBY, Baronet [S 1636], of
                Birkenbog and Forglen House aforesaid, 1st s and h , b 18 March
1886 , *suc to the Baronetcy* 24 July 1895

Family Estates—These, in 1883, consisted of 8,053 acres in Banffshire, 1,942 in
Aberdeenshire , 1,339 in Kirkcudbrightshire , and 434 (worth £2,679 a year) in co
Cork   Total —11,768 acres, worth £12,395 a year   *Principal Seats*—Forglen
House (near Turriff), and Birkenbog, both in Banffshire, Castle Douglas, in
Scotland, and Fermoy, co Cork, in Ireland

(a) His next br , Alexander Abercromby, who in 1699 became of Tullibody, co
Clackmannan, was grandfather of the celebrated General SIR RALPH ABERCROMBY,
whose widow, for her late husband's services, was cr BARONESS ABERCROMBY
in 1801   Her 3d s , JAMES ABERCROMBY, was Speaker of the House of Commons
1835 to 1839, and was cr BARON DUNFERMLINE in 1839, which last peerage
became *extinct* 12 July 1868
        (b) *Query* as to his identy with "The Lord James Abercrombie," who d. at a
chateau in Westphalia, 1726, aged 98, and was *bur* there

BROWNE.

cr 21 June 1636 ,(ª)

afterwards, since 1789, BARONS KILMAINE [I.]

I 1636   JOHN BROWNE, of the Neale, near Ballinrobe, co
Mayo,(ᵇ) s and h ap of JOSIAS BROWNE, of the same, by Joan,
la of Edward BIRMINGHAM, of Carrick, co Kildare, was *cr a Baronet* [S], 21
June 1636,(¹) the patent not being recorded in the *Registrum Preceptorum
Cartarum pro Baronettis Nova Scotia* and the limitation being unknown, but,
probably (at that date), being to heirs male whatsoever, and with a grant of, presumably, 16,000 acres in Nova Scotia,(c) but no record of such grant, nor any seizin
of such lands is known (d) Possibly owing to this cause it may have been considered that the grant of the Baronetcy was not valid,(e) as he did not assume the
title, neither did any of his descendants, till about the year 1762 He suc his
father, in Dec 1634 (who was *bur* at Kilmaine, aged 55), was excepted from
pardon for life and estate by Ordinance, 1652, but restored to his estate at
the Restoration He *m* in 1626, Mary, da of Sir Dominick BROWNE, of Carra
Browne, co Galway and Castle Margarett, co Mayo, by Anastacia, da of James
DARCY He d Whitsunday 1670, and was *bur* in Ross Abbey, co Galway
Funeral certif

II 1670.   GEORGE BROWNE, of the Neale aforesaid, 1st s and h ,(f)
suc his father in 1670, but *never assumed the Baronetcy* He, in
Nov 1684, had a regrant of the Neale , was Sheriff of co Mayo, 1690 , had pardon
for himself and son in June 1693, reciting that he himself had served as Sheriff, and
that neither had ever been indicted or outlawed He *m* Alicia, only da of Sir Henry
BINGHAM, 1st Baronet [S 1634] of Castlebar, co Mayo, by Catherine, da of John
BYRNE, of Ballinclough He d May 1698 His wife survived him

III 1698   JOHN BROWNE, of the Neale aforesaid, s and h He
was sometime Captain in the Irish Army of James II, and was taken
prisoner, 6 May 1689, at the siege of Derry He suc his father in May 1698, but
never assumed the Baronetcy He *m* firstly (settl 27 and 28 May 1680), Anne, 1st da
of George (HAMILTON), 3d BARON STRABANE [I], by Elizabeth, da of Christopher
FAGAN She d s p 14 and was *bur* 17 Aug 1680, "in the country" Funeral
certif He *m* secondly, Juliana, 3d da of Sir Patrick BELLEW, 1st Baronet
[I 1688] of Barmeath by Elizabeth, 4th da of Sir Richard BARNEWALL, 2d
Baronet [I. 1622] His will dat 11 Sep 1700, pr 21 Nov 1712 in the Prerog
Court [I]. The will of his widow dat 15 Nov 1728, pr there 10 May 1729

(ª) This creation is not in Milne's Walkley's or Ulster's Lists, but it is in that
of Laing, under the date of 17 [*sic*] June 1636, and is there stated to be given
"on the authority of former Lists" There is a letter, dated 19 Dec 1776, from
the then Baronet, Sir John Browne, to Lord Charlemont, in which he writes " The
date of my patent is June 21 1632 [*sic*], so I shall be pretty forward on the
bench of Baronets, if any there be " See, however, the correct date, 21 June
1636, in the copy of the patent in Lodge's Irish Peerage, [1789], vol III, p 271

(ᵇ) See p 407, note " b," *circa finem*, *sub* Gascoigne

(c) About this date " the French, by the construction of the treaty of St
Germain [made 29 March 1632] between them and King Charles, entered upon
Nova Scotia as included therein " [Banks's *Baronia Anglica Concentrata*, vol II,
p 218, and app 45] After the year 1637 no seizin took place of lands granted in
Nova Scotia, save one in Nov 1640, *viz* , that of " Sir Robert Campbell "

(¹) No mention of such occurs in Banks's Lists

(ᵉ) Such, however, was not the case with the kindred family of Bingham, who
were similarly situated, and who certainly assumed the Baronetcy [S] granted to
them

(f) His next br , John Browne, Col. in the Irish Army of James II, and one of
the capitulators of Limerick, was grandfather of John Browne, *cr* Baron Monteagle [I], 1760 , Viscount Westport [I] 1768 , and Earl of Altamont [I], 1771,
whose grandson, the 3d Earl, was *cr* Marquess of Sligo [I] in 1800

IV. 1712?   GEORGE BROWNE, of the Neale aforesaid, s and h, suc
his father about 1712, but *never assumed the Baronetcy*, was M P
[I] for Castlebar, 1713-14   He m, in 1709, his consin Bridget, da of Edward
(BERMINGHAM), LORD ATHENRY [I], by his 2d wife, Bridget, da of Col John
BROWNE, of Westport, co Sligo, 2d s of the 1st Baronet   He d s p 8 May 1737,
at the Neale   Will dat 6 April 1737, pr 4 March 1737/8 at the Prerog Court
[I]   His widow d 25 Sep 1747

V. 1737.   JOHN BROWNE, of the Neale aforesaid, and formerly of
Rahins, co Mayo, br and h   Sheriff of co Mayo, 1731, suc his
brother 8 May 1737, but *never assumed the Baronetcy*, was M P [1] for Castlebar
(*vice* Henry Bingham) from, probably, about 1740 to 1760   He m firstly, 30 June
1722 Margaret, 1st da and coheir of Henry DODWELL, of Athlone, by his 2d
wife Cathaiine, da of Arthur ORMSBY, of Ballyvenose, co Limerick   She d 23
April 1739, and was bur in Kildare cathedral   Admon 11 June 1741, in Prerog
Court [I]   He m secondly, Catherine, widow of Denis DALY, of Carrownakelly,
da of Sir Walter BLAKE, 6th Baronet [I 1622], of Menlo, by his 2d wife, Agnes,
da of John BLAKE   He d 2 Oct 1762   His 2d wife, by whom he had no issue,
survived him

VI 1762   SIR GEORGE BROWNE, Baronet [S 1636], of the Neale
aforesaid, 1st s and h by 1st wife, b in or before 1725, Sheriff of
co Mayo, 1747, suc his father 2 Oct 1762, and *assumed the Baronetcy*
at that date, being the *first* of his family who did so   He m Oct 1761, Anastacia,
1st da of Denis DALY, of Raford, co Galway, by Anne, da of Michael (DE
BURGH), EARL OF CLANRICARDE [I]   He d s p 9 Sep 1765

VII. 1765   SIR JOHN BROWNE, Baronet [S 1636], of the Neale
aforesaid, br of the whole blood and h, b 20 May 1726, *suc to
the Baronetcy*, 9 Sep 1765, and registered his pedigree in Ulster's office, Ireland, as
such 28 Feb 1777, and in the Lyon office, Scotland, 7 April 1777, was M P [I],
for Newtown, 1777-83, and for Carlow, 1783-89, Sheriff of co Mayo, 1778 and
1788, purchased the estate of Gaulston, co Westmeath   He m 30 March 1764,
(Lords' entries, in Ulster's office), Alice, only da of James (CAULFEILD), 3d
VISCOUNT CHARLEMONT [I], by Elizabeth, da of Francis BERNARD, 3d Justice of
the Common Pleas [I]   She was living when he was cr 21 Sep 1789, BARON
KILMAINE(a) [I], in which dignity this *Baronetage then merged* and so continuos
See "*Peerage*"

MOIR, *or* MOORE·

cr 18 June 1636 ;(b)

dormant, or extinct, Aug 1644.

I   1636,   EDWARD MOIR, *or* MOORE, of Langford, Notts,(c) s. and
   to   h of William MOORE, of Thelwell, Cheshire, by Elizabeth, da of
   1644.   Alexander VAUDREY, of the Bank, co Chester, was b about
1610, suc his father about 1632, and was cr a Baronet [S] 18
June 1636(b), the patent not being in the Great Seal Register [S], with, it is
supposed, rem to heirs male whatsoever, and with a grant of, presumably, 16,000

(a) "The peerages of Kilmaine, Cloncurry and Glentworth were sold for hard
cash and the proceeds laid out in the purchase of members" [Fitzpatrick's *Secret
Service under Pitt*, p 254]

(b) Laing's List   In the copy of Milne's List in Foster's *Baronetage* for 1883,
the date is given as 18 *Feb* 1636, but it is there marked as being in Laing's List
only, where the date is 18 *June* 1636

(c) See p 408, note "d," under "Norton."

acres in Nova Scotia, of which, however, he never had seizin (ª) He who fought on the Royal side in the Civil Wars, *d* at Newark-upon-Trent of wounds received at the battle (2 July 1644) of Marston Moor, and was *bur* 1 Aug 1644 at Newark He *d* s p m ,(ᵇ) when the *Baronetcy* became *dormant* or *extinct* Admon as " of Kirtlington, Notts," 26 Feb 1657/8, to the guardian of Elizabeth Moore, da of deceased, then a minor

---

SINCLAIR

afterwards, since 1899, SINCLAIR-LOCKHART ,

cr 18 June 1636 (ᶜ)

I 1636   JOHN SINCLAIR, of Stevenston, co Haddington, s and h of George SINCLAIR(ᵈ) (who *d* about 1670), having acquired a considerable fortune as a merchant at Edinburgh, purchased in 1624 the Barony of Stevenston and lands at Wester Pencaithland, Easter Winsheills, etc , in the counties of Edinburgh, Haddington, and Berwick, and was cr a Baronet [S] 18 June 1636, the patent, not, however, being recorded in the Great Seal Register [S] with rem to heirs male whatsoever, and with a grant of, presumably, 16,000 acres in Nova Scotia, called the Barony of Stevenston and Murkle, of which he had seizin in July 1636 (ª) He *m* Margaret, da of (—) MACMATH, probably of Newbyres, but sometimes called a da of Sir John MACMATH, " of that ilk " He *d* 1648/9

II 1649   SIR JOHN SINCLAIR, Baronet [S 1636], of Stevenston aforesaid, grandson and h , being 1st s and h of John SINCLAIR, by Isabel, da of Robert (BOYD), 6th LORD BOYD [S], which John was only s and h ap of the 1st Baronet, but *d* v p in 1643 He was *b* 26 July 1642, and *suc* to *the Baronetcy* on the death of his grandfather, to whom he was served heir 24 May 1650 He *d* unm before July 1652

III. 1652   SIR ROBERT SINCLAIR, Baronet [S 1636], of Stevenston, or Stevenson aforesaid, br and h , *b* 15 Oct 1643 (posthumous), *suc* to *the Baronetcy* on the death of his brother, to whom he was served heir, 5 July 1652, was Sheriff of co Haddington, 1689, M P [S] for Haddington Constabulary, 1689-1702, P C and a Lord of the Exchequer [S] 1690, nominated a Lord of Session [S], but declined to act , P C [S] again, 1703 He *m* firstly, 10 Sep 1663, at the Chapel of Holyrood Helen, da of John (LINDSAY), EARL OF CRAWFORD [S], by Margaret, da of James (HAMILTON), 2d MARQUESS OF HAMILTON [S] He *m* secondly, Anne, widow of Sir Daniel CARMICHAEL, of Hyndford, da of Sir William SCOTT, of Ardross He *d* July 1713

(ª) Banks's Lists

(ᵇ) John Moore of Kirtlington, Notts, aged 47 in the Visit of 1662, was his next br and h male, but appears never to have assumed the Baronetcy

(ᶜ) Laing's List, as also, but with the Christian name given (erroneously) as " James," in Milne's List

(ᵈ) It seems hardly likely that the family are descended, as is often alleged, in the male line from the old race of Sinclair of Longformacus, and the arms (a saltire charged with bezants) assigned to them in 1672, were thought by R R Stodart (Lyon Clerk Depute, 1863-86), to indicate an unknown origin In the funeral escutcheon in 1713 of the 3d Baronet, his grandfather the 1st Baronet, is, however, called a son of Sir Matthew Sinclair, of Longformacus, but on the other hand, in that of the 4th Baronet in 1726, it is the *mother* (not father) of the 1st Baronet who is said to be of the family of Longformacus Father Hay, a well-known genealogist (*b* about 1650) says that the grandfather of the 1st Baronet was " a famous brewer of Leith," where " Sinclair's Society is yet extant," and that upon him the song of the " Clouting of the Caldron " was written [*Ex inform* Sir J Balfour Paul, Lyon King of Arms]

IV. 1713.   SIR JOHN SINCLAIR, Baronet [S 1636], of Stevenson
aforesaid, s and h, by 1st wife, M P [S] for Lanarkshire,
1702-07, and an opposer of the Scotch Union, *suc to the Baronetcy*, July 1713,
was a staunch supporter of the Hanoverian Succession   He *m* in 1698,
Martha, widow of Cromwell LOCKHART, of Lee, co Lanark, da and eventually
sole heir (on the death of her brother) of Sir John LOCKHART, of Castlehill, in
that county, a Lord of Session [S], under the title of LORD CASTLEHILL
He *d* 1726   His widow *d* at Stevenson, 15 May 1752

V   1726   SIR ROBERT SINCLAIR, Baronet [S 1636], of Stevenson
aforesaid, 1st s and h, *suc to the Baronetcy* in 1726   He *m*
Sep 1733, Isabella, only da of da of James KERR, Col 3rd Foot Guards   He
d 25 Oct 1754

VI 1754.   SIR JOHN SINCLAIR, Baronet [S 1636], of Stevenson,
aforesaid, 1st s and h, *suc to the Baronetcy*, 25 Oct 1754 He, on the
death, 9 Dec 1765, of Alexander (SINCLAIR), EARL OF CAITHNESS [S], suc to the
estate of Murchill or Murkley, co Caithness, and other lands, under a deed
executed in 1761 by that Earl   He *m* 12 Feb 1760, at Edinburgh, Mary, yst
da of William BLAIR, formerly SCOT, of Blair, Advocate [S], by his 2d wife,
Catharine, da of Alexander TAIT, of Edinburgh, Merchant   He *d* 13 Feb 1789

VII 1789   SIR ROBERT SINCLAIR, Baronet [S 1636], of Stevenson
and Murkley aforesaid, 1st s and h, *suc to the Baronetcy*, 13 Feb
1789, was Gov of Fort St George in Scotland   He *m*, 2 April 1789, in the house
of the Earl of Bristol, St James' square, Madelina (then a minor), 2d da of
Alexander (GORDON), 4th DUKE OF GORDON [S], by Jane, da of Sir William
MAXWELL, 3d Baronet [S 1681], of Monreith   He *d* 4 Aug 1795 at Fort St
George   His widow *m*, 25 Nov 1805, at Kimbolton Castle, Charles Fysche
PALMER, of Luckley Park, Berks, who *d* Jan 1843   She, who, on 28 May 1836,
became coheir to her brother George, 5th DUKE OF GORDON [S], *d* 1 June
1847, in Chapel street, Grosvenor place, aged 75

VIII 1795. SIR JOHN GORDON SINCLAIR, Baronet [S 1636], of
Stevenson and Murkley aforesaid, only s and h, *b* 31 July 1790
in Edinburgh, *suc to the Baronetcy*, 4 Aug 1795, when aged 5, entered the Royal
Navy, 1800, and served in "The Victory" under Nelson, was in command of
"The Redwing" at Morjean and Cassis (1813) in the Mediterranean, Capt
1814, Rear Admiral, 1849, Vice Admiral of the blue, 1856, Admiral, 1861,
was sometime Capt of the port at Gibraltar   He *m* 15 June 1812, at Stonehouse, Devon, Anne, da of Admiral the Hon Michael DE COURCY (yr s of John,
LORD KINGSALE [I]), by Anne, da of Conway BLENNERHASSETT   She *d* 23 Sep
1857, at Stevenson   He *d* there 12 Nov 1863, aged 73

IX 1863   SIR ROBERT CHARLES SINCLAIR, Baronet [S 1636], of
Stevenson and Murkley aforesaid, 1st s and h, *b* 25 Aug 1820,
in Paris, Capt 38th Foot, 1849, *suc to the Baronetcy*, 12 Nov 1863, Lieut Col
Caithness and Sutherland Vols, 1864-80   Colonel, 1880   He *m* firstly, in 1851,
Charlotte Anne, da of Lieut John COOTE, 71st Foot   She *d* 7 July 1874   He
m secondly, 5 Dec 1876, at St Andrew's Cathedral, Inverness, Louisa, 1st da
of Roderick HUGONIN, of Kinmyhes House, co Inverness   He *d* s p, 5 May
1899, at Stevenson aforesaid, in his 79th year   His widow living 1902

X. 1899.   SIR GRÆME ALEXANDER SINCLAIR-LOCKHART, Baronet
[S 1636], of Castlehill and Cambusnethan, co Lanark, cousin and
h male, being 5th but 1st surv s of Robert LOCKHART, of Castlehill and Cambusnethan aforesaid, *i e.*, his 2d s by his 2d wife Charlotte Simpson, da of Capt
William MERCER, of Potterhill, which Robert (who *d* 2 Nov 1850), was s and h
of James LOCKHART, formerly SINCLAIR, of Castlehill aforesaid (an estate he
inherited on the death, 5 May 1764, of his paternal uncle, George LOCKHART,

formerly SINCLAIR), which James was next br. to the 6th, being the 2d s. of the 5th Baronet. Major-Gen. LOCKHART (to call him by the name under which in 1899 he was known), was *b.* 23 Jan. 1820; entered the army, 1837; Capt., 1850; Major, 1858; Lieut.-Col., 1859; Col., 1866; retiring as Major-General, 1867. He served with 78th Highlanders in the Persian war, 1857, and in Indian Mutiny Campaign, 1857-58 (medal with clasp in both cases), **C.B.**. 1861; suc. to the Lanarkshire estates on the death of his brother in 1873; *suc. to the Baronetcy,* 5 May 1899 and thereupon assumed the name SINCLAIR before that of LOCKHART. He *m.* in 1861, Emily Udny, da. of James BREMBER of Aberdeen, Advocate [S.]

Family Estates.—Those in 1883 attributed to the then Baronet, were 18,874 acres in Caithness and 473 in Haddingtonshire. *Total,* 19,374 acres, worth £6,326 a year. These, however, appear to be now (1901) enjoyed by his widow or descendants. The estates in 1883 attributed to Gen. Lockhart (who, in 1899, suc. to the Baronetcy), were 4,422 acres in Lanarkshire, worth £5,250 a year. *Principal Residence,* Cambusnethan House, near Wishaw co. Lanark.

CURZON :

cr. 18 June 1636 ;[a]

cr. a Baronet [E.] 11 Aug. 1641 ;

subsequently, since 1761, BARONS SCARSDALE.

I. 1636. JOHN CURZON, of Kedleston, co. Derby,[b] was *cr. a Baronet* [S.] 18 June 1636,[a] the patent not being recorded in the Great Seal Register [S.], with, it is supposed, rem. to heirs male whatsoever and with a grant of, presumably, 16,000 acres in Nova Scotia, of which, however, he never had seizin.[c] He was subsequently, 11 Aug. 1641, *cr. a Baronet of England ;* see that dignity, pp. 132-133, the 5th Baronet being *cr.* 9 April 1761, BARON SCARSDALE, co. Derby, in which peerage these Baronetcies then *merged* and still so continue, see *Peerage.*

RAYNEY :

cr. 13 Sep. 1636 ;

and previously 19 Dec. 1635.

See that creation, p. 415.

BAILLIE :

cr. 21 Nov. 1636 ;[d]

dormant in or shortly before 1648.

I. 1636. GIDEON BAILLIE, of Lochend co. Haddington, s. and h. of Sir James BAILLIE,[e] of the same, one of the Receivers of the Crown [S.] (who in 1614 had for 1,700 marks purchased that estate), by

[a] Laing's List.
[b] See p. 408, note "d," under "NORTON."
[c] Banks's List.
[d] Laing's List and Milne's List.
[e] It is said by Lord Napier that this James was basely borne, and was educated by a butcher. [*Ex inform,* R. R. Stodart, Lyon Clerk Depute, 1863-86]. There appears, however, to be no foundation for this statement.

Jean NISBET, his wife, was b 29 Feb 1616, and was cr a Baronet [S], 21 Nov. 1636(a), with rem to heirs male whatsoever, and with a grant of, presumably, 16,000 acres, called the Barony of Lochend, in Nova Scotia, of which, however, he never had seizin (b) He m (contract 17 Feb 1636) Margaret, da and coheir of David CARNEGIE, styled LORD CARNEGIE (s and h. ap of David, 1st EARL OF SOUTHESK [S]), by Margaret, da of Thomas (HAMILTON), 1st EARL OF HADDINGTON [S] He d 30 Aug 1640 being killed at the blowing up of Douglas Castle His widow m Sir John CRAWFORD, of Kilbirnie

II.   1640,   SIR JAMES BAILLIE, Baronet [S 1636], of Lochend
        to   aforesaid, only s and h , suc to the Baronetcy, 30 Aug 1640, and
      1648 ?   was, by Act of Parl 11 Aug 1641, allowed to enter without
                    composition on the lands of his father, who had fallen in his
country's service He d s p in or shortly before 1648(c), when the Baronetcy became dormant (d)

NICOLSON
cr 16 Jan 1636/7.(e)

I   1637   " Master THOMAS NICOLSON, of Carnock " co Stirling,
                2d s of John NICOLSON, of Lasswade,(f) by Elizabeth, da of Dr
Edward HENDERSON, Advocate [S], was an Advocate [S] 1612, and was cr a Baronet [S] 16 Jan 1636/7,(e) with rem to heirs male whatsoever and with a grant of, presumably, 16,000 acres in Nova Scotia, of which he had seizin in Feb 1637 (g) He was M P [S] for Stirlingshire, 1644 He m Isabel, da of Walter HENDERSON, of Granton He d 8 Jan 1646

II   1646   SIR THOMAS NICOLSON, Baronet [S 1637], of Carnock
                aforesaid, s and h , b 10 June 1628, suc to the Baronetcy,
8 Jan 1646 (h) He m Margaret, da of Alexander (LIVINGSTONE), 2d EARL OF LINLITHGOW [S], by his 2d wife, Mary, da of William (DOUGLAS), EARL OF ANGUS [S] He d 24 July 1664 His widow m in 1666, as his 4th wife, Sir George STIRLING, of Keir, who d s p, 1667 She m thirdly, in 1668, as his 1st wife, Sir John STIRLING, of Keir and Cawder, who d 1684 She d 1674

III   1664   SIR THOMAS NICOLSON, Baronet [S 1637], of Carnock
                aforesaid, s and h , b 15 Sep 1649, suc to the Baronetcy,
24 July 1664 He m , in or before 1668, Jean, 1st da of Archibald (NAPIER), 3d LORD NAPIER OF MERCHISTOUN [S], by Elizabeth, da of John (ERSKINE), EARL OF MAR [S] He d 20 Jan 1670 His wife, who probably survived him, d before Aug 1683

(a) See p 423, note " d "
(b) Banks's Lists
(c) Margaret, his only surv sister and heir, m (contract 17 Feb 1636), as her 1st husband, Sir John Colquhoun, 2d Baronet [S 1625], of Luss, who, in 1678, sold the estate of Lochend
(d) A certain " William Baillie, of Letham," acts in some deeds with the family
(e) Laing's List and Milne's List, in which last mention is made, without, however, any date, that " Sir John [sic] Nicolson of that ilk has taken out his armes as Baronet "
(f) See p 304, note " b " and the corrigenda thereto
(g) Banks's Lists, where the Baronetcy is stated to be " represented by Sir Michael Shaw-Stewart, of Blackhall," a descendant of Eleanor, sister of the 3d and 1st da of the 2d Baronet, by her husband, Sir John Shaw, 2d Baronet [S 1687] of Greenock
(h) He is not to be confused with another Sir Thomas Nicolson, who was Lord Advocate [S] 1649

IV 1670.   Sir Thomas Nicolson, Baronet [S. 1637], of Carnock
aforesaid, only s and h, b 14 Jan 1669, suc to the Baronetcy,
20 Jan 1670, and was served heir of his father in Carnock 3 Oct 1671 He
became, in Aug 1683, LORD NAPIER OF MERCHISTOUN [S] by the
death, in Aug 1683, of his maternal uncle, the 3d Lord He d unm, 9 June
1686, in France, in his 18th year, when the peerage devolved on his maternal
aunt, and the estate of Carnock, etc, on his three paternal aunts and coheirs

V 1686   Sir Thomas Nicolson, Baronet [S 1637] of Tillicoultrie, cousin and h male, being 1st s and h of Sir John Nicolson,
also of Tillicoultrie, by Sabina (sometimes called Martha), da of Col Walter
Robertson, otherwise Colyear, which John, who d 1683, was 2d s of the 1st
Baronet He suc to the Baronetcy, 9 June 1686, and, his affairs having become
embarrassed, sold the estate of Tillicoultrie in 1697 He d 2 Jan 1699

VI 1699   Sir George Nicolson, Baronet [S 1637] only s and h,
suc to the Baronetcy, 2 Jan 1699, served in a Scotch Regiment in
the service of the States of Holland, retiring in 1746 as a Major, and residing at
the Hague He m Charlotte, 2d daughter of Edward Halket He d, at the
Hague, Oct 1771

VII 1771   Sir Walter Philip Nicolson Baronet [S 1637], 1st
s and h, suc to the Baronetcy in Oct 1771, was an officer in a
Scotch Regiment in the Dutch service He m Helen Frances Carpenter He d
s p legit, 1786 Will pr in 1786

VIII 1786   Sir David Nicolson, Baronet [S 1637], br and h,
suc to the Baronetcy in 1786, was an officer in a Scotch Regiment
in the Dutch service He d unm at Breda, 19 Oct 1808 Will pr 1809

IX 1808   Sir William Nicolson, Baronet [S 1637], cousin and h.
male, being only s and h of George Nicolson, of Tarviston co.
Lanark, by Catharine Edmondstone, which George (who d 1769), was 1st s of
William Nicolson, Lieut -Col in the service of the states of Holland (d at Ypres,
1720), yr br of the 5th Baronet, both being sons of Sir John Nicolson, of
Tillicoultrie abovenamed He was b 1758, entered the army, 1778, served in
America, India, Ireland, and the Mauritius becoming, finally, 1804, Major-Gen,
suc to the Baronetcy, 19 Oct 1808 He m, 5 July 1804, Mary, da of John
Russell, Writer to the Signet [S], by Eleanor, da of William Robertson,
D D, of Edinburgh, the well known historian He d 5 Aug 1820 Will pr
1821 His widow d 20 Feb 1853, aged 73, in Eaton terrace Admon March
1853

X 1820.   Sir Frederick William Erskine Nicolson, Baronet
[S 1637], only s and h, b 22 April 1815, at Ham Common, suc
to the Baronetcy, 5 Aug 1820, entered the navy, 1827, Capt, 1846, C B, 1859,
Commodore Superintendent of Woolwich Dockyard, 1861-64, Rear Admiral of
the Blue, 1863, Vice-Admiral, 1870-73, Admiral (retired), 1877, sometime
Chairman of the Thames Conservatory Board He m firstly, 26 May 1847 at St
Geo, Han sq, Clementina Maria Marion, 2d da of James Loch, of Drylaw, co
Edinburgh, by Ann da of Patrick Orr of Bridgeton She d 17 July 1851, at
15 William street, Knightsbridge, aged 27 He m secondly, in 1855, Augusta
Sarah, widow of Capt Hay, only da of Robert Cullington, of Old Lakenham
She d 19 April 1861, at 15 William street, aforesaid He m thirdly, 16 Aug
1867, at Lydeard Saint Lawrence, Somerset, Anne, only child of R Crosse, niece
of Rev James Crosse, M A, Rector of that parish She d 8 Jan 1896 at 26,
Ladbrooke square, Notting Hill He d 29 Dec 1899, aged 84, at 39, Egerton
gardens Will pr at £22,058

XI 1899   Sir Arthur Nicolson, Baronet [S 1637], only s and
h by 1st wife, b 19 Sep 1849, entered Foreign Office, 1870,
acting Chargé d'Affaires at Athens, 1882-85, Sec of Legation, 1885, C M G,

3 G

1886, Sec of Legation at Teheran and acting Chargé d'Affaires in Persia, 1885-88, Consul Gen for Hungary, at Buda-Pest, 1888-93, K C I E, 1888, Sec of Embassy at Constantinople, 1893-94, Consul Gen at Sofia, in Bulgaria, 1894-95, Minister at Tangier since 1895 He *m*, 20 April 1881, Mary Katharine, 3d and yst da. of Archibald Rowan HAMILTON, of Killyleagh Castle, co Down, sometime Capt 5th Dragoon Guards, by Anne, da of the Rev George CALDWELL

PRESTON.

cr. 13 March 1636/7 ,(ᵃ)

dormant since 25 Nov. 1873

I. 1637.   " Master GEORGE PRESTON, fear of Valafield " [*i e*, Valleyfield], co Perth, *i e*, s and h, ap of Sir John PRESTON, of Valleyfield aforesaid, by Grizel, da of Alexander COLVILLE, Commendator of Culross, was *cr a Baronet* [S], 13 March 1636/7,(ᵃ) the patent, however, not being entered in the Great Seal Register [S] with rem to heirs male, whatsoever, and with a grant of, presumably, 16,000 acres in Nova Scotia "with the haill gold mines therein, and power to transport thereto all gold affecting mines," of which Barony he had seizin in the same month (ᵇ) He obtained £1,000 from Parl, 6 May 1646, for payment of four Perthshire troops and was in 1649 made Colonel of them He *m*, in 1634, Marian, 1st da of Hugh (SEMPILL), 5th LORD SEMPILL [S], being the only child of his 1st wife, Anne, da of James (HAMILTON), 1st EARL OF ABERCORN [S] He *d* 26 Nov 1679

II 1679   SIR WILLIAM PRESTON, Baronet [S 1637], of Valleyfield aforesaid, 1st s and h (ᶜ), to whom his father made over certain lands there, 10 May 1663 He *suc to the Baronetcy*, 26 Nov 1679 He *m* Anne, da of Sir James LUMSDEN, of Innergelly He *d* between 1702 and 1705

III 1703 ?   SIR GEORGE PRESTON, Baronet [S 1637], of Valleyfield aforesaid, 1st s and h, *b* about 1670, *suc to the Baronetcy* about 1703 He *m* Agnes (well known for her beauty), da of Patrick MUIRHEAD, of Rashyhill He *d* Sep 1741, aged 70

IV 1741.   SIR GEORGE PRESTON, Baronet [S 1637], of Valleyfield aforesaid, 1st s and h, *suc to the Baronetcy* in 1741 He *m*, about 1730, Anne, sister of Thomas, 8th EARL OF DUNDONALD [S], 4th and yst da of William COCHRANE, of Ochiltree (grandson of the 1st Earl), by Mary, da of Alexander (BRUCE), EARL OF KINCARDINE [S] He *d* 2 March 1779, at Valleyfield His widow *d* a few months later, 7 Nov 1779

V 1779.   SIR CHARLES PRESTON, Baronet [S 1637], of Valleyfield aforesaid, 3d(ᵈ) but 1st surv s and h male, *b* probably about 1735, was Capt in the 26th Foot and distinguished himself early in 1775,

---

(ᵃ) Laing's List, but not in Milne's List

(ᵇ) Banks's Lists

(ᶜ) George Preston the 2d son (*b* 1660) was Capt in the service of the States General in 1688 ; served in the wars under Marlborough, was Gov of Edinburgh Castle in 1715 and Commander-in-Chief [S] soon afterwards He *d* at Valleyfield, 7 July 1748, in his 89th year

(ᵈ) His eldest br, Patrick Preston, Major in the British service, and Brig - General in that of Portugal, *d* v p, 25 April 1776, leaving two daughters, who successively inherited the family estate of Valleyfield On the death of the survivor, 6 April 1855, it was inherited by her cousin, Ann, da and h. of George Preston, widow of Sir John Hay, 6th Baronet [S 1635], on whose death, s p, 2 Sep 1862, it passed to the descendants of Mary, wife of Robert Wellwood, sister of the 5th and 6th, da of the 4th Baronet

being then a Major, in his defence of Fort St John against the Americans He *suc to the Baronetcy,* 2 March 1779 He was M P for Kirkcaldy Burghs, 1784-90, and was a Commissioner of Customs [S], 1798-1800. He *d* unm 23 March 1800

VI 1800   SIR ROBERT PRESTON, Baronet [S 1637], of Valleyfield aforesaid, yst br and h male, being 5th s of the 4th Baronet, was b 21 April 1740, was some time in the sea service of the East India Company and was in command of the " Asia " frigate, becoming eventually an elder brother of the Trinity House. He *suc to the Baronetcy,* 23 March 1800 He *m* Elizabeth, da of George BROWN, of Stockton He *d* s p, 7 May 1834, at Valleyfield aforesaid, aged 94 His will, as also that of his wife or widow, pr July 1834 On his death the issue male of the 1st Baronet became *extinct*

VII 1834   SIR ROBERT PRESTON, Baronet([a]) [S 1637], of Lutton, co Lincoln, and of Sydney Place, Bath, cousin and h male, being only s and h of George PRESTON, Gen in the Army, and Col of the Scots Greys, by Lucy, da of James JOHNSTONE, which George (who *d* 7 Feb 1785) was 2d and yst s of William PRESTON, of Gorton, a Major in the Army (*d* 1733), who was 5th of the six sons of Robert PRESTON, a Lord of Session [S] (*d* 1674), yr br of the 1st Baronet He was b 3 Jan 1757, *assumed the Baronetcy,* 7 May 1834, and was, in 1835, served heir male general of the 6th Baronet at the Sheriff's Court at Edinburgh He *m* about 1780 his cousin, Euphemia, da of John PRESTON, of Gorton aforesaid He *d* 30 Aug 1846, at Blackadder, aged 90 Will pr Nov 1846

VIII 1846.   SIR ROBERT PRESTON, Baronet([a]) [S 1637], of Lutton and of Sydney Place, both aforesaid, 1st s and h, b about 1780, sometime a Col in the Army, *suc to the Baronetcy,*([a]) 30 Aug 1846 He *m* in 1826 (—), widow of (—) WILLIAMS, Major E I C S, da of Charles DEANE, of Hendon, co Midx He *d* s p 23 Oct 1858, at Sydney Place aforesaid His widow *d* at Bath 15 Dec 1867, in her 89th year.

IX. 1858,   SIR HENRY LINDSAY PRESTON, Baronet([a]) [S 1637], of
to   Lutton and of Sydney Place aforesaid, only br and h, b 18 Feb
1873   1789, entered the Navy, 1801, Commander, 1830, Capt on the retired list, 1856, *suc to the Baronetcy,*([a]) 23 Oct 1858 He *d* unm at Bath, 25 Nov 1873, aged 84, when the *Baronetcy* became *dormant*

KERR, *afterwards* [1776-91] CARR ·

cr. 31 July 1637([b]),

dormant (rightfully) *since* 16 Aug 1776 ,

but assumed, in 1776, as CARR ;

till 6 March 1791.

I. 1637.   ANDREW KERR, of Greenhead, co Roxburgh, 1st of the seven sons of Sir Andrew KERR, of Greenhead, Hietoun and Prymsideloch in that county (*d* between Nov 1612 and March 1617), by Alison, da of Gilbert WAUCHOPE, of Niddrie Marischal, co Edinburgh,([c]) was served heir special to his father, 18 March 1617, and was *cr* a Baronet [S] 31 July 1637,([b]) with rem to heirs male whatsoever, and with a grant of, presumably,

([a]) According to the service in 1835
([b]) Laing's List and Milne's List.
([c]) See an article by " S " [R R Stodart] in the *Her and Gen*, vol vi, pp 231-240, as to this family See, also, *Genealogist,* orig series, vol iii, p 66.

16,000 acres, entitled the Barony of Greenhead, in Nova Scotia, of which he had seizin in Dec following (a) He was on the Committee of War, co Roxburgh, 1643-49, was M P [S] for that county 1645 and 1648-49, and [E] for the Sheriffdom of Roxburgh 1659, was on the Committee of Estates, 1649, was styled "Colonel" in 1650, and was an active supporter of the Covenant, being consequently imprisoned at Edinburgh in 1660, and fined £6000 in 1662 He *m* firstly, in 1634, Elizabeth, 1st da of Sir William SCOTT, of Harden, co Roxburgh, by his 1st wife, Agnes, da of Sir Gideon MURRAY, of Elibank He *m* secondly,(b) 16 Aug 1664, at Edinburgh, Katherine, widow of David CARNEGIE, of Craig, 5th and yst da of John (WEMYSS), 1st EARL OF WEMYSS [S], by Jean, da of Patrick (GRAY), LORD GRAY [S] He *d* May 1665 His widow *d* 24 Feb 1668 at Dysart

II 1665   SIR ANDREW KERR, Baronet [S 1637] of Greenhead
                aforesaid, 1st s and h, was M P for Roxburghshire [S], 1669-71, *suc to the Baronetcy* in May 1665 He *m*, 4 Dec 1664, Jean, da of Sir Alexander DON, 1st Baronet [S 1667], of Newton, by Isabel SMITH his wife He *d* s p m, in or before June 1676 His widow(c) *m* in 1685, Sir Roger HAY, of Harcarse, Senator of the College of Justice [S].

III 1676?   SIR WILLIAM KERR, Baronet [S 1637], of Greenhead
                aforesaid, br and h male, *suc to the Baronetcy* on the death of his brother, to whom he was served heir special 15 June 1676, was a Commissr of Supply, 1685-1704, Col of Militia, 1689, and was M P. [S] for Roxburghshire, 1685-86 and 1702-07, and [G B] 1707-08 He *m* Jean COCKBURN (c) He *d* in or before March 1718

IV 1718?   SIR WILLIAM KERR, Baronet [S 1637], of Greenhead
                aforesaid, grandson and h, being only s and h of Andrew KERR, a Commis of Supply, 1698-1704, by Helen HAY, his wife, which Andrew was 1st s and h ap of the late Baronet, but *d* v p before March 1718 His house at Bridgend, Kelso, with all its contents, was destroyed by fire in Aug 1741 He *suc to the Baronetcy* on the death of his grandfather, being served heir to his father, his grandfather, and great uncle 30 March 1721 He *d* s p,(d) Aug 1741

V 1741.   SIR ROBERT KERR, Baronet [S 1637], of Greenhead
                aforesaid, uncle and h male, *suc to the Baronetcy* in Aug 1741 and was served heir of provision to his nephew, 27 Aug 1745 He sold the estate of Greenhead and most of the other estates He *m* (—), da of Gilbert KERR, of Bamfmiln in Sprouston He *d* April 1746

VI 1746   SIR WILLIAM KERR, Baronet [S 1637], of Softlaw and
                of Bridgend aforesaid, 1st s and h, *suc to the Baronetcy* in April 1746, and was served heir special to his father, 9 Oct 1750 He sold the last of the family estates, and *d* s p at Boulogne, 8 Dec 1755

(a) Banks's Lists, it being the last entry therein of the seizins, save the somewhat unintelligible one, in Nov 1640, of "Sir Robert Campbell, of one part of Nova Scotia" who, possibly, may have been the *successor* of a grantee, and not a grantee himself

(b) See Lamont's *Diary* as to this match

(c) The widow of the 2d Baronet is, probably, the "Lady Greenhead" who was fined 16,000 Scots, 4 Sep 1684, for her adherence to the Covenant, but possibly the reference is to Jean, wife of the 3d Baronet This "Jean Cockburn" was not improbably a daughter of Sir James Cockburn, of Ryslaw, by his 2d wife, Jean, daughter of Andrew Kerr, of Lintoun

(d) His two sisters, both of whom *d* unm, were served heirs portioners general to their cousin, the 7th Baronet, 26 Jan 1779, but seem to have inherited no landed property Agnes the survivor, *d* 1 March 1785, at a great age

VII. 1755,   Sir Robert Kerr, Baronet [S. 1637], only br. and h.,
to   *suc. to the Baronetcy,* but to none of the estates, 8 Dec. 1755. He
1776.   was served heir general to Gilbert Kerr, his maternal grandfather,
27 Sep. 1768. He resided in the town of Kelso. He *d.* s.p. 16 Aug.
1776, when the male issue of the grantee became *extinct,* and when the *Baronetcy*
(no one having proved any descent in the male line from a common ancestor
of the grantee) became (rightfully) *dormant.*

VIII. 1776.   Sir William Carr, Baronet([a]) [S. 1637], of Etall,
co. Northumberland, calling himself cousin and h. male, but
whose pedigree as such is unknown.([b])   He was *s.* of (—) by (—). He,
who was *b.* about 1705,([c]) *assumed the Baronetcy* 16 April 1776. He *m.* in
or before 1742 (—). He *d.* s.p.m.([d]) 11 April 1777. Will dat. 19 Oct. 1776
to 20 Jan. 1777.

IX. 1777,   Sir Robert Carr, Baronet([a]) [S. 1637], br. and h.
to   male, *b.* about 1707 ; was sometime a Mercer on Ludgate
1791.   Hill, London, and was subsequently of Hampton, co. Midx.;
suc. to the Baronetcy([a]) but not to the family estates,
11 April 1777. He *m.* firstly, Grace, da. of Thomas Bigge, of Newcastle-
on-Tyne, by Elizabeth, da. of Edward Hindmarsh. He *m.* secondly, Mary,
da. of (—) Little. He *d.* s.p.m.([e]) 6 March 1791, in his 85th year, and was
bur. at Hampton aforesaid. M.I. Will pr. March 1790. After his death
the assumption of this Baronetcy ceased.

([a]) According to the assumption of the Baronetcy in 1776.
([b]) He was descended from Col. Sir Robert Carr, of Etal aforesaid (presumably
of Scottish descent), who obtained in 1647 two warrants of Baronetcies, of
which, owing to the Civil War, he was unable to make any use. On 8 Aug.
1661, however, Charles II, on his petition, allowed their renewal, provided " he
nominate two meete persons to His Majestie capable for their extraction and
estates of the dignity and honour of a Knight Baronett." Whether he ever did
nominate anyone is unknown, but he " certainly seems not to have thought of
appropriating one of the titles at his disposal to himself as he always styles himself, and was styled by others, *Knight.*" [See R. R. Stodart's " Notes on the
traffic in Baronetcies," in *The Genealogist,* O.S., vol. iii, pp. 65-68.] One of the six
yr. brothers of the 1st Baronet is there " *said* " to have been " ancestor of the
Carrs of Etall " in Stodart's article on the family, as on p. 427, note " c."
([c]) As to this assumption he shewed " a scrupleousness worthy of all praise,"
inasmuch as though in his will, dat. 19 Oct. 1776, he designs himself " Sir William
Carr, of Etal, Baronet," he explains in a codicil of 20 Jan. following, as under :—
" I did apprehend I was warranted in taking the title of Baronet, but as I do not
find that I can, by indisputable evidence, satisfie myself that I have undoubted
right to, and [*sic*] therefore I have declined that title." [See p. 427, note " c."]
([d]) Of his two daughters and coheirs, Isabel, the eldest (*b.* 31 March 1742), and
the only one that left issue (inheritors of the estate of Etall), *m.* 3 Aug. 1762,
at Ford, co. Northumberland, James (Hay, *formerly* Boyd), Earl of Erroll [S.],
and *d.* 3 Nov. 1808.
([e]) Of his two daughters and coheirs, Elizabeth, only child of the 1st wife, *m.*
in March 1754, Sir Richard Glyn, 1st Baronet [1759], of Ewell.

Memorandum—In and after 1638 no seizin of any land in Nova Scotia is recorded, though, apparently, five Baronets (Slingsby, Piers, Musgrave, Longueville, and Meredith, who were created from March 1637/8 to Jan 1638/9) had *grants* of land there ([a]) After Jan 1638/9, however, no such grants seem to have been made

---

SLINGSBY

cr 2 March 1637/8 ,([b])

dormant since 4 Feb 1869

I. 1638   HENRY SLINGSBY, of Scriven, near Knaresborough, co York, 2d but 1st surv s and h of Sir Henry SLINGSBY, of Scriven aforesaid, and of the Red House, near Marston Moor in that county (*d* 17 Dec 1634, aged 74), by Frances, da of William VAVASOUR, of Weston, co York, was *b* 14 Jan 1601/2, sometime (1619-21) of Queen's Coll, Cambridge, and was *cr a Baronet* [S] by patent dat at Stirling, 2 March 1637/8,([b]) not, however, recorded in the Great Seal Register [S] with rem to "heirs male," and with presumably a grant of land in Nova Scotia, of which, however, he appears to have never had seizin ([a]) He had shortly before entertained the King at Red House, in whose service he was a Colonel, and to whose cause he stedfastly adhered He was M P for Knaresborough, 1625, April to May 1640, and again 1640 (Long Parliament), till disabled in Dec 1642, and was one of the fifty-nine members who opposed the attainder of the Earl of Strafford He refused to compound, and in 1651 his estate was ordered to be sold In 1655, being implicated in a Royalist rising, he was imprisoned at Hull He *m* 7 July 1631, at Kensington, Barbara, 1st ds of Thomas (BELASYSE), 1st VISCOUNT FANCONBERG, by Barbara, da of Sir Henry CHOLMLEY, of Roxby, co York She, who was *bap* 11 Oct 1609, at Coxwold, in that county, *d* in London, 31 Dec 1641, and was *bur* at St Martin's in the Fields He, having entered into a scheme for the landing of Charles II at Hull, was executed by the then Government, 8 June 1658, on Tower Hill, being, however, *bur* with his ancestors, at Knaresborough ([c])

II. 1658.   SIR THOMAS SLINGSBY, Baronet [S 1638], of Scriven and Red House aforesaid, 1st s and h, *b* 15 June 1636, *suc* to *the Baronetcy*, 8 June 1658 Sheriff of Yorkshire, 1660-61, Governor of Scarborough Castle, 1670, M P for co York, Nov 1670 to 1678, for Knaresborough (three Parls), 1679-81, for Scarborough, 1685-87 He *m* 29 July 1658, at St Gregory's, London, Dorothy, da and coheir of George CRADOCK, of Caverswall Castle, co Stafford She *d* 24 Jan and was *bur* 2 Feb 1673, at Knaresborough M I He *d* at St Martin's in the Fields, and was *bur* 1 March 1687/8, at Knaresborough Admon 10 April 1688 and 26 March 1692 Admon at York 15 June 1692

III 1688.   SIR HENRY SLINGSBY, Baronet [S 1638], of Scriven and Red House aforesaid, 1st s and h, *b* about 1660, being aged 4 years and 6 months at the Visit of Yorkshire, 23 March 1665, was M P for Knaresborough 1685-87, and 1690 till void same year, *suc* to *the Baronetcy* in Feb 1687/8 He *d* unm and was *bur* 15 Sep 1691, at Knaresborough Admon. 19 March 1691/2

([a]) Banks's Lists   The creations of Slingsby, Piers, Musgrave, Longueville, and Meredith are the last in the list of those Baronets [S], who are said to have "obtained charters of land in Nova Scotia, which do not appear to have been followed by seisins"

([b]) Laing's List, but not in that of Milne

([c]) His *diary* is a most valuable account of the Civil War, 1638-1648, as far as it concerned Yorkshire.

IV. 1691.   SIR THOMAS SLINGSBY, Baronet [S 1638], of Scriven and Red House aforesaid, br and h, b probably about 1668, suc to the Baronetcy in Sep 1691 He m 12 April 1692, at Methley, co York, Sarah (bap there 22 June 1669), da of John SAVILE, of Methley, by Sarah, da of Peter TRYON He was bur 15 Nov 1726, at Knaresborough

V 1726   SIR HENRY SLINGSBY, Baronet [S 1638], of Scriven and Red House aforesaid, 1st s and h, b about 1693, matric at Oxford (Univ Coll), 13 Oct 1710, aged 17, M P for Knaresborough, 1714 to Jan 1715, and (seven Parls) 1722-63 He m in or before 1729, Mary, da of John AISLABIE, of Studley, Chancellor of the Exchequer She d at Beaconsfield, 31 May and was bur 7 June 1736, at Knaresborough He d, s p s legit, 18 Jan 1763 Will pr 1769

VI. 1763   SIR THOMAS SLINGSBY, Baronet [S 1638], of Scriven and Red House aforesaid, br and h, b about 1695, was, for many years, blind, suc to the Baronetcy, 18 Jan 1763 He d unm 18 Jan 1765

VII 1765   SIR SAVILE SLINGSBY, Baronet [S 1638], of Scriven and Red House aforesaid, br and h, b about 1698, suc to the Baronetcy, 18 Jan 1765 He d unm Nov 1780, aged 82 Will pr Dec 1780

VIII 1780   SIR THOMAS TURNER SLINGSBY, Baronet [S 1638], of Scriven and Red House aforesaid, nephew and h, being only s and h of Charles SLINGSBY, of Lofthouse hill, co York, Barrister, by Catherine, 1st da of John TURNER, of Stainsby, in that county, which Charles (who d Aug 1772), was yst s of the 4th Baronet He was b about 1741, matric at Oxford (Queen's Coll), 26 April 1759, aged 18, suc to the Baronetcy, Nov 1780, was Sheriff of Yorkshire, 1785 He m firstly, 28 Oct 1773, at Kippax, his maternal cousin, Catherine, yst da of George BUCKLEY, of Thurnscoe, co York, by Anne, yst da of John TURNER abovenamed She d 16 Jan 1778 He m secondly, 25 Oct 1781, at Moor Monckton, Mary Fletcher SLINGSBY, spinster, illegit da of his paternal uncle, Sir Henry SLINGSBY, the 5th Baronet He d 14 April 1806 Will pr 1806 His widow d s p 18 Feb 1815 Will pr 1816

IX. 1806   SIR THOMAS SLINGSBY, Baronet [S 1638], of Scriven and Red House aforesaid, 1st s and h, by 1st wife, b 10 Jan and bap 10 June 1775, at Knaresborough, matric at Oxford (Queen's Coll) 11 April 1793, aged 18, suc to the Baronetcy, 14 April 1806 Sheriff of Yorkshire, 1812 He d unm at Brighton, 26 Feb 1835, and was bur at Knaresborough, aged 60 Will pr July 1835

X 1835, to 1869   SIR CHARLES SLINGSBY, Baronet [S 1638], of Scriven and Red House aforesaid, nephew and h, being only s and h of Charles SLINGSBY, of Lofthouse hill aforesaid, by Emma Margaret, da of Thomas ATKINSON, of Ripley, co York, which Charles (who was b 17 March 1777 and d 20 May 1832), was 2d and yst s of the 8th Baronet, by his 1st wife He was b at Lofthouse hill, 22 and bap 23 Aug 1824 at Staveley, suc to the Baronetcy, 26 Feb 1835, entered the Royal Horse Guards 1843, retiring as a Lieut 1847 He d unm, being drowned (with four other members of the York and Ainsty hunt) while crossing the river Ure, near Ripon, 4 and was bur 11 Feb 1869, at Knaresborough, aged 44 (²) At his death, the issue male of the grantee being apparently extinct, the Baronetcy became dormant

---

(²) His only sister and sole heir, Emma Louisa Catherine, m 19 July 1860, Capt Thomas Leslie, who by Royal license, in 1869, took the name of Slingsby, and was Sheriff of Yorkshire in 1886 She d s p, at Scriven park, 29 June 1899, aged 70, when the estates descended to her maternal cousin Charles Atkinson, who accordingly took the name of Slingsby

PIERS, or PEIRS

cr. 24 March 1637/8 ,(ᵃ)

dormant since 7 May 1720

I   1638   THOMAS PIERS, or PEIRS,(ᵇ) of Stonepit, in the parish
of Seale, co Kent, s and h of Laurence PIERS, of Westheld, co
Sussex, by Catherine, da of John THEOBALD, of Stonepit aforesaid, was b about
1616 and was cr a Baronet [S], 24 March 1637/8,(ᵃ) with rem to heirs male
whatsoever,(ᵇ) and with, presumably, a grant of land in Nova Scotia, of which
he apparently never had seizin (c)   He m firstly, in or before 1643, Jane, sister
of Sir Henry OXENDEN, 1st Baronet [1678], da of Sir James OXENDEN, of Dene,
co Kent, by Mary, da of Thomas NEVINSON   He m secondly, 21 May 1649 at
St Bartholomew the Less, London (Lic Fac 19 May, he 33, widower, and she 23
spinster), Audrey, da of Sir Edward MASTER, of Ospringe, co Kent by Audrey,
da and coheir of Robert STREYNSHAM   She d 6 and was bur 9 Jan 1656/7, at
Seal   M I   He d at Stonepit 7 and was bur 10 April 1680, at Seale, aged 64
Will dat 16 to 17 April 1679, pr 24 May 1680

II   1680   SIR THOMAS PIERS, Baronet [S 1638], of Stonepit aforesaid, 1st s and h, being only s and h by 1st wife, b about 1643,
admitted to Gray's Inn, 6 April 1657, suc to the Baronetcy, 7 April 1680   He m,
9 Sep 1669, at St Bartholomew the Great, London (Lic Fac 5 July, he 26,
bachelor, and she 23, spinster), Elizabeth, da of Sir George COURTHOPE, of
Whiligh, co Sussex, by Elizabeth, da and h of Edward HAWES, of London   He
was bur 26 Aug 1693, at Seal aforesaid   Admon 3 Feb 1693/4, his widow
being then living

III   1693,   SIR GEORGE PIERS, Baronet [S 1638], of Stonepit aforeto   said, 1st s and h, bap 25 Oct 1670, at Seal, matric at Oxford
1720   (Mag Hall) 4 July 1689, and then said to be aged 16, suc to the
Baronetcy in Aug 1693   He d s p, probably unm 7 and was bur
20 May 1720, at Seal aged 50, when the issue male of the grantee was apparently
extinct,(ᵈ) and the Baronetcy became dormant   Will pr 1720

PICKERING

cr. 5 June 1638 , (ᵉ)

descent uncertain after July 1749 ,

assumed till April 1803

I   1638   " GILBERT PICKERING, of Titchmersh, co Northampton,
Esq ," s and h of Sir John PICKERING, of the same (d 29 Jan
1627/8, aged 43) by Susan, da of Sir Erasmus DRYDEN, of Canons Ashby in that

---

(ᵃ) Laing's List, but not in that of Milne.

(ᵇ) In the Privy Seal Register [S] he is styled "Thomas Peiris, of Stenypites,
Kent," and the rem is to "heirs male whatsoever"

(c) See p 430, note "a," under " Slingsby '

(ᵈ) The only br of the last Baronet, John Piers, was bap at Seal 12 Oct
1673, and bur there 9 April 1692   Of their three uncles of the half blood, sons of
the 1st Baronet by the 2d wife (1), Edward, b about 1652, was living 5 May
1681, (2), Richard, bap 1 Jan 1655/6, was a Factor at Aleppo, and d unm
between Sep 1678 and May 1680, (3), Streynsham, bap 22 Dec 1656 d unm
and was bur at Seal, 5 April 1681   Will pr 5 May 1681

(ᵉ) This is the date of the Royal warrant, given at Dalkeith, for affixing the
Great Seal   The diploma of this Baronetcy is among the MS collection entitled
the " H MSS " [vol xxi, 84], in the College of Arms, London   The creation is
not in Laing's or in Milne's List, but is in that of Walkley (1641), and the
Baronetcy is recognised in the Visitation of Northamptonshire made in 1681

county, was *b.* about March 1610/1 (being 16 years, 10 months and 18 days old at his father's death), and was *cr.* a *Baronet* [S.], 5 June 1638,(ᵃ) with possibly(ᵇ) (like other creations in that year) a grant of lands in Nova Scotia, of which, however, no record is known; admitted to Gray's Inn 16 Nov. 1629; was a Col. in the Army; M.P. for Northamptonshire (five parls.) 1640-58; a zealous Parliamentarian, serving on numerous committees, 1640-51, and on each of the five Councils of State of the Commonwealth; was one of Cromwell's *House of Lords*, Dec. 1657, and was Chamberlain to him and to his son Richard. He, though one of the Regicide Judges (not, however, one who signed the death warrant) obtained pardon at the Restoration. He *m.* in or before 1640, Sidney, sister of Edward, 1st EARL OF SANDWICH, only da. of Sir Sidney MONTAGU, of Hinchinbroke, co. Huntingdon, by his 1st wife Paulina, da. of John PEPYS, of Cottenham. By her he had twelve children. He *m.* secondly, Elizabeth, da. of John PEPYS, of Cottenham, by Edith, da. and h. of Sir Edmund TALBOT. He *d.* about Michaelmas 1668, aged 57. Admon. 5 May 1669 to Elizabeth his relict, who subsequently proved his will 4 Dec. 1672. She *d.* about 1679.

II. 1668.   SIR JOHN PICKERING, Baronet [S. 1638], of Tichmersh aforesaid, 1st s. and h. of eight sons by 1st wife; *b.* about 1640; matric. at Oxford (Ch. Ch.) 18 March 1656/7; *suc.* to the *Baronetcy* in 1668; entered his pedigree in the Visit. of Northamptonshire 1681, being then aged 41. He *m.* in or before 1670, Frances, 1st da. of Sir Thomas ALSTON, 1st Baronet [1642], of Odell, Beds, by Elizabeth, da. of Sir Rowland ST. JOHN. She was living 1681, and was *bur.* at Tichmersh. He was *bur.* there 3 April 1703. Will pr. April 1704.

III. 1703.   SIR GILBERT PICKERING, Baronet [S. 1638], of Tichmersh aforesaid, and of West Langton, co. Leicester, 1st and only surv. s. and h.; aged 11 years in 1681; *suc.* to the *Baronetcy* in April, 1703. Sheriff of Leicestershire, 1704-05; M.P., 1708-10. He *m.* in or before April 1691, Elizabeth (then aged about 14), da. and h. of Stavely STAUNTON, of Birchmore, in Woburn, Beds, by Elizabeth, da. of Sir Thomas ALSTON, 1st Baronet abovenamed. He *d.* March 1735/6, in Cavendish square, Midx. Will pr. 1736. His widow, who was *b.* 24 and *bap.* 26 Aug. 1677, at Woburn aforesaid, and who brought him a large fortune, *d.* July 1741.

IV. 1736,   SIR EDWARD PICKERING, Baronet [S. 1638], of Tichto   mersh aforesaid, only s. and h.; *b.* about 1716; matric. at Oxford
1749.   (Ch. Ch.), 25 May 1732, aged 16; *cr.* M.A. 9 June 1736, having *suc.* to the *Baronetcy* in March 1735/6; M.P., for St. Michael, Nov. 1745 to 1747. He *d. unm.* July 1749 when the issue male of the 2d Baronet became *extinct.* Admon. 17 Aug. 1749, and again 13 March 1773.

V. 1749?   SIR GILBERT PICKERING, Baronet(ᶜ) [S. 1638], *assumed the Baronetcy*, presumably in 1749 but certainly before Oct. 1762, as heir male of the grantee. He is said(ᵈ) to have been s. of John PICKERING, which John is said(ᵈ) to have been s. of Gilbert PICKERING (by Elizabeth PINCHON, his wife), the 2d s. of the 1st Baronet.(ᵉ) It is, however, much more likely that the 5th Baronet(ᶜ) was identical with the Gilbert PICKERING, *b.* after 1681 and before 1697, when he was

---

(ᵃ) See p. 432, note "e."
(ᵇ) See *Memorandum* on p. 430.
(ᶜ) According to the assumption of the Baronetcy, 1749-62.
(ᵈ) Atkins Davis' MSS. in Ulster's office, kindly inspected by G. D. Burtchaell.
(ᵉ) The Visitation of Northamptonshire in 1681 sets out the male issue of the 1st Baronet, moreover a very full account of such of his descendants as were living 30 March 1697, is given in the will of that date (proved 21 Oct. 1699) of his brother, Edward Pickering. From these and other sources it can be gathered that of the six younger sons of the 1st Baronet who survived infancy (1), Gilbert, *m.* 30 Sep. 1666, at St. Leonard's, Shoreditch (he 21 and she 26, Lic. Vic. Gen.),

3 H

living as son of the abovenamed Gilbert, the 2d s. of the 1st Baronet. He *m.* Anne, da. of Franks BERNARD, of Castlebar, King's County,(ᵃ) and of Clonmush, co. Carlow. She *d.* in New Ross, co. Wexford, 16 Oct. 1762, when, apparently, he was alive.(ᵇ)

VI. 1765?   SIR EDWARD PICKERING, Baronet(ᶜ) [S. 1638},
  to   1st s. and h.(ᵃ) ; *suc. to the Baronetcy*(ᶜ) on the death of his
  1803.   father. He was sometime Cornet in a Cavalry Regiment,
              but afterwards held a staff appointment at Duncannon
Fort, co. Wexford.(ᵇ) He *m.* 6 July 1770, at St. Mary's, New Ross aforesaid, Elizabeth, 3d da. of George GLASCOTT, of Aldertonn, by Anne, da. of William GIFFORD, of Polemalse, co. Wexford. She, who was *b.* 1745, *d.* 5 and *bur.* 20 Sep. 1791, at Whitechurch, co. Wexford. He *d. s.p.* and was *bur.* there 29 April 1803, when *the Baronetcy* became *dormant.*(ᵈ)

MUSGRAVE:

cr. 20 Oct. 1638 ;(ᵉ)

sometime, 1746-55, HYLTON ;

dormant or *extinct* since 30 Sep. 1875.

I. 1638.   EDWARD MUSGRAVE, of Scaleby and of Hayton Castle
            in Aspatria, co. Cumberland, s. and h. of William MUSGRAVE, (which William was s. and h. ap. of Sir Edward MUSGRAVE, of the same), by

---

Elizabeth Pinchon, widow, both of whom were living in 1681, with a da., Elizabeth, aged 12. Gilbert, however, had subsequently a son, Gilbert, living 1697, who presumably is the Gilbert who, 1749-62, assumed the Baronetcy. (2), Sydney, *b.* about 1647, *m.* (Lic. Vic. Gen., 19 Nov. 1673) his cousin, Honor Pickering, of Whaddon. He had a son, Sydney, living 1697. (3), Oliver, *d.* unm. before 1681. (4), Montagu, of Birchmore, Beds. *m.* 18 May 1679, at Campton, Beds, the "widow Stanton," and had a son Edward, *bap.* 31 March 1681, at Woburn in that county, who was living 1697. He himself was *bur.* at Woburn, 1 April 1694. (5), Francis, a merchant of Oporto, unm. 1681, but living 1697 with two sons, Francis and Edward. (6), Theophilus Pickering, D.D., *b.* at Tichmarsh, who *d.* unm. 20 March 1710, aged 48. M.I. there. It will thus be seen that there is no lack of persons who themselves or whose issue were in remainder to this Baronetcy. In Burke's *Commoners* (edit. 1837, vol. ii, p. 194) is a pedigree of Pickering, of Clapham, Surrey, deducing that family in the male line from Edward Pickering, said to be a son of Gilbert, the 2d s. of the 1st Baronet, and to have had for a mother Mary, da. of John Creed, of Tichmarsh. The existence of such Mary, however, is doubtful (see M.I. to John Creed in Bridges's *Northamptonshire*, vol. ii, p. 386), and that of such Edward as son of the said Gilbert, is still more so. If the pedigree there given could be established the Baronetcy of Pickering would presumably be in that family.

(ᵃ) See p. 433, note "d."
(ᵇ) An article by "Y. S. M." in *Notes and Queries* [4th S., vi, p. 47] gives many particulars as to the Baronets of this race in Ireland, among others that of the death of "the Lady of Sir Gilbert Pickering," 16 Oct. 1762, a description which implies that her husband was then living.
(ᶜ) See p. 433, note "c."
(ᵈ) His only br., Townsend Edward Pickering, *m.* Martha, 2d da. and coheir of Kennedy Cavanagh, of New Ross, and, it is presumed, *d. s.p.m.* before him. He had five sisters, of whom Frances, or Elizabeth, *m.* John Bernard, Capt. R.N.; Anne *m.* (—) Maddocks; Mary *m.*, in 1773, Henry Rudkin; and Dorothy *m.*, in 1779, Richard Baldwin Thomas.
(ᵉ) The creation is not in Laing's List, nor in that of Milne, but it is the pen-

Catharine, da and coheir of (—) SHERBURNE, of Lancashire, was b about 1621, suc his father (who d v p), 27 Jan 1633/4, matric at Oxford (Queen's Coll), 27 May 1636, aged 15, entered Gray's Inn, 19 June 1638, and was cr a Baronet [S], 20 Oct 1638,(ᶜ) with, presumably, a grant of lands in Nova Scotia, of which, apparently, he never had seizin (ᵇ) was a zealous Royalist, raising a regiment for Charles 1, for whose cause he was 18 April 1646, fined £960, and had to sell his estate of Scaleby and other lands said to be worth, in all, £2,000 a year At the battle of Worcester, 3 Sep 1651, he surrendered his horse to the young King, and escaped into Scotland and thence to the Isle of Man   He m Mary, 2d da of Sir Richard GRAHAM, 1st Baronet [1629], of Esk, by Catharine, da and coheir of Thomas MUSGRAVE, of Cumcatch   He was bur 22 Nov 1673 at Aspatria

II 1673   SIR RICHARD MUSGRAVE, Baronet [S 1638], of Hayton
            Castle aforesaid, s and h, b probably about 1650, matric at
Oxford (Queen's Coll) 25 May 1666, suc to the Baronetcy in Nov 1673 Sheriff of Cumberland, 1684-85, rebuilt Hayton Castle and Chapel about 1691, was Vice-Admiral of Cumberland and Westmorland in the reign of Queen Anne   He m, 18 Jan 1670, at Washington, co Durham, Dorothy, da and coheir of William JAMES,(ᶜ) of Washington, by Dorothy da of Leonard WASTELL, of Scorton, co York   He d 8 and was bur 11 May 1710, at Aspatria   Will dat 23 March 1709, pr at York, 25 July 1710   His widow, who was bap 30 Dec 1649 at Washington, and whose "great fortune and prudence" are said to have "redeemed the family estate," d 12 and was bur 15 Dec 1718, at Aspatria, aged 69   M I   Will dat 11 Oct 1717, pr at York

III 1710   SIR RICHARD MUSGRAVE, Baronet [S 1638], of Hayton
             Castle aforesaid, s and h, b about 1675, matric at Oxford
(Queen's Coll), 8 Dec 1697, aged 17, entered Gray's Inn, 17 July 1693, was M A of Edinburgh Univ, 9 March 1697/8, being, apparently, incorp at Oxford (St Edmund Hall) as B A, 18 July 1698   He was in attendance at the treaty of Ryswick, 1697, was M P for Cumberland 1700-02 and 1705-08, and suc to the Baronetcy 8 May 1710   He m, in or before 1701, Elizabeth, widow of Thomas RAMSDEN, of Croston in Halifax, co York, da and coheir of Joseph FINCH, of Leeds, by Judith, da of William HORTON, of Barkisland, co York   He was bur 11 Oct 1711, at Aspatria   Will dat 17 Sep 1711, pr March 1712   His widow d 1713   Her will dat 17 Feb 1713

IV 1711   SIR RICHARD MUSGRAVE, Baronet [S 1638], of Hayton
            Castle aforesaid, s and h, b about 1701 suc to the Baronetcy in
Oct 1711, matric at Oxford (Queen's Coll) 31 May 1721, aged 18, and was cr M A, 18 June 1723 Sheriff of Cumberland, 1730-31   He m 13 Jan 1723/4, at Monkwearmouth, Anne, sister and coheir [1746] of John HILTON, of Hylton Castle, co Durham, 2d da of John HILTON, of the same, by Dorothy, da of Sir Richard MUSGRAVE, 2d Baronet [S] abovementioned   He d intestate 5 and was bur 8 Oct 1739, at Aspatria, aged 38   M I   His widow, who was b 26 Jan 1697, and bap at Washington aforesaid, d in London 1 and was bur 16 Feb 1766 at Aspatria   Will pr 1766

V 1739   SIR RICHARD MUSGRAVE, afterwards, 1746-55, HYLTON,
           of Hayton Castle aforesaid, 1st s and h, bap, at Aspatria, 13 Oct
1724, suc to the Baronetcy, 5 Oct 1739, matric at Oxford (Oriel Coll) 16 Feb 1742/3, aged 18   In compliance with the will of his maternal uncle, John HYLTON abovenamed (who d unm 25 Sep 1746, aged 47), he, in 1746, took the name of Hylton in lieu of that of Musgrave, on inheriting Hylton Castle and the other

---

ultimate entry in the (dateless) List of Walkley, pub in 1641, being placed there next to that of Piers   The date, 20 Oct 1638, is assigned to it in Wotton's Baronetage [1741], vol iv, p 354
    (ᵃ) See p 434, note "e"
    (ᵇ) See p 430, note "a," under "Slingsby"
    (ᶜ) This William was s of Francis James, the yst s of William James, Bishop of Durham, 1606-17   See Surtees' Durham, vol 1, p 216

estates of that family   He *m* 17 Nov 1746, at Chester le-Street, Eleanor, da and coheir of John HEDWORTH, of that place, being only child of his 1st wife, Susanna Sophia, da of William PELSANT, of London   He *d* intestate and s p m s([a]) 16 and was *bur* 24 June 1755, at St Martin's in the Fields   His widow *d* 1 and was *bur* there 5 June 1764   Her will dat 11 Nov 1760

VI 1755   SIR WILLIAM MUSGRAVE, Baronet [S 1638], br and h
male, *b* at Hayton Castle aforesaid 8 Oct 1735, ed at Houghton-le-Spring school, entered Middle Temple, 7 April 1753, Barrister, 5 May 1758, being Bencher, 2 May 1789, Reader, and subsequently (1795) Treasurer, *suc to the Baronetcy*, but not, apparently, to the family estates, 16 June 1765, was a Commissioner of Customs, 15 March 1763, F R S, 14 March 1774, becoming V P thereof in 1780, F S A, 12 Nov 1778, becoming V P thereof 1786, a trustee of the British Museum, 1783, a Commissioner of Accounts, July 1785   He *m* 10 Dec 1759, by spec lic at Whitehall, St Margaret's, Westm, Isabella Dow COUNTESS OF CARLISLE, da of William (BYRON), 4th BARON BYRON OF ROCHDALE, by his 3d wife Frances, da of William (BERKELEY), 4th BARON BERKELEY OF STRATTON   She, who was *b* 10 Nov 1721, *d* 22 Jan 1795   He *d* s p 3 and was *bur* 16 Jan 1800, at St James', Westm, aged 65 ([b])   M I ([c])

VII 1800.   SIR THOMAS MUSGRAVE, Baronet [S 1638] only surv
br and h male, *b* 1737, was an officer in the army, becoming eventually (1802) full General, and being at his death, Colonel of the 76th foot and Governor of Gravesend and Tilbury forts   He *suc to the Baronetcy*, 3 Jan 1800   He *d* unm 31 Dec 1812

VIII 1812.   SIR JAMES MUSGRAVE, Baronet [S 1638], of Barnsley
park, near Cirencester, co Gloucester, cousin and h male, being s and h of the Rev James MUSGRAVE, D C L, Rector of Chinnor Oxon (1750-80), by (—), da of (—) HUGGINS which James last named (who *d* 7 Nov 1780, aged 70) was s of the Rev James MUSGRAVE, M A, Vicar of Kirkby Moorside, co York (1707), and Rector of Little Gransden, co Huntingdon (1714), who was *b* about 1681, and was yr s of the 2d Baronet   He was *b* about 1752, matric at Oxford (St John's Coll), 30 June 1769, aged 17, B A 1773, M A 1777, Sheriff of Gloucestershire, 1802-03, *suc to the Baronetcy*, 31 Dec 1812   He *m* in 1781, Clarissa, da of Thomas BLACKHALL, of Great Haseley, Oxon   He *d* 27 April 1814   Will pr 1814   The will of his widow was pr 1823

IX. 1814   SIR JAMES MUSGRAVE, Baronet [S 1638], of Barnsley
park aforesaid, 1st s and h, *b* 24 May 1785 in London, ed at Eton, matric at Oxford (Ch Ch), 21 Oct 1803, aged 18, B A, 1807, *suc to the Baronetcy*, 27 April 1814, Sheriff of Gloucestershire, 1825-26   He *d* unm 6 Dec 1858

X. 1858,   SIR WILLIAM AUGUSTUS MUSGRAVE, Baronet [S 1638],
to   br and h, *b* 1792, at St Marylebone, ed at Westm School,
1875.   matric at Oxford (Ch Ch), 17 May 1809, aged 17, B A, 1813, M A, 1815, in Holy Orders, Rector of Chinnor aforesaid, 1816-75, Rector of Emmington, Oxon, 1827-72   He *d* unm at Chinnor Rectory, 30 Sep 1875, when *the Baronetcy* became *dormant* or *extinct*

([a]) Eleanor, his only surv da and h, *bap* 27 June 1752, *m* 28 Aug 1769, at St Margaret's, Westm, William Jolliffe, whose grandson, the Right Hon Sir William George Hylton-Jolliffe, Baronet (so *cr* 20 Aug 1821), was raised to the peerage, 19 July 1866, as Baron Hylton

([b]) His laborious compilation, generally known as *Musgrave's Obituary*, is comprised in twenty-three vols in the British Museum (Addit MSS 5727-5749), and gives (as its compiler states) "reference to the books where the persons are mentioned," as also date and place of death   This most useful *Obituary* (which, however, of course ends *prior* to 1800) has, *as far as relates to England, Scotland, and Ireland*, been pub (1899-1901) by the Harleian Society in six vols

([c]) Printed in full in Malcolm's *Londinium Redivivum*, vol iv, p 227

LONGUEVILLE

cr 17 Dec 1638 ;(a)

extinct, or *dormant*, 1759

I 1638   EDWARD LONGUEVILLE, Esq, of Wolverton, Bucks, and of Little Billing, co Northampton, 1st s and h of Sir Henry LONGUEVILLE,(b) of the same, by Katharine, sister of Henry, 1st VISCOUNT FALKLAND [S], da of Sir Edward CARY, of Aldenham, Herts, was *bap* there 23 April 1604, suc his father (who was *bur* at Wolverton) 17 May 1621, and, having carried great sums to the King when at Edinburgh, was cr a *Boronet* [S] 17 Dec 1638,(a) with rem to heirs male and with presumably a grant of lands in Nova Scotia, of which he, apparently, never had seizin (c) The patent, however, is not recorded in the Great Seal Register [S] He *m*, in or before 1631, Hester, 8th da of Sir Thomas TEMPLE, 1st Baronet [1611], of Stowe, by (the prolific) Hester, da of Miles SANDYS, of Latimers, in that county He was *bur* 6 Aug 1661, at Wolverton (d) Admon 15 Feb 1664/5 His widow *d* at Buckingham, and was *bur* at Wolverton, 18 Aug 1665 Admon 5 Oct 1669

II 1661   SIR THOMAS LONGUEVILLE, Baronet [S 1638], of Wolverton and Little Billing aforesaid, s and h, aged 3 years in 1634 (Visit of Bucks), suc *to the Baronetcy*, in Aug 1661 He *m* firstly, in or before 1662, Mary, da and coheir of Sir William FENWICK, of co Northumberland, by Elizabeth, sister of Francis, 1st EARL OF DERWENTWATER, da of Sir Edward RADCLYFFE, 2d Baronet [1620] She was *bur* 17 Nov 1683 at Wolverton He *m* secondly, 7 May 1685 at Monken Hadley, co Middx, Katharine, 2d da and coheir of Sir Thomas PEYTON, 2d Baronet [1611], of Knowlton, co Kent by his 1st wife, Elizabeth, da of Sir Peter OSBORNE He *d*, breaking his neck, near Wolverton, by a fall from his horse, 25 and was *bur* there 29 June 1685 (only a week after his second marriage, aged 54 M I Will dat 25 June, and pr 4 Aug 1685 His widow, who probably was *bap* 10 July 1641, at St Margaret's, Westm, *d* s p 30 Dec 1715 and was *bur* 7 Jan following in Westm Abbey, aged, it is said, 70 M I

III 1685   SIR EDWARD LONGUEVILLE, Baronet [S 1638], of Wolverton and Little Billing aforesaid, only s and h by 1st wife, *bap* 27 July 1662, at Wolverton,(d) suc *to the Baronetcy*, 25 June 1685, was Sheriff of Bucks, 1687-88, in which year he sold the estate of Little Billing, selling subsequently, about 1712, that of Wolverton, with lands at Stony Stratford, for about £50,000 and lands at North Seaton, co Northumberland and elsewhere He was a zealous Roman Catholic,(e) and a firm supporter of the cause of James II He *m* Mary, 1st da of his paternal uncle, Edward LONGUEVILLE, by Mary, da of (—), SYLVESTER, of Iver, Bucks He *d* s p 19 or 28 Aug 1718, having, like his father, broken his neck by a fall from his horse, at Bicester races, and was *bur* at Fretwell, Oxon, aged 46 Will dat 7 Jan 1717/8, pr 11 Dec 1719 and 13 Oct 1727 His widow *m*, as his 2d wife, John LAWTON, of Lawton, Cheshire, who *d* 10 June 1736, aged 80 She apparently *d* about 1766

(a) Laing's List, this being the last creation recorded in that most valuable catalogue, in which, after this entry, is added, "Two blank precepts, names and dates not supplied"

(b) The printed pedigrees and references to this family are very numerous (see *N & Q*, 8th S, iv, 215), the fullest are those in Baker's *Northamptonshire*, vol i, p 27, vol ii, p 131, and in the *Her & Gen*, vol vi, pp 49-53

(c) See p 430, note 'a," under "Slingsby"

(d) No such entry, however, is among the extracts from those registers in *Mis Gen et Her*, O S, vol i, pp 64-65, which, presumably, contain all therein of the name of Longueville

(e) Although the religion of the 1st Baronet is doubtful, many of the family were of the old faith See an interesting account of some of these in Gillow's *Bibl Dict of the English Catholics*

IV 1718,   SIR THOMAS LONGUEVILLE, Baronet [S 1638], of
    to   Prestatin, co Flint, and Esclusham, co Denbigh, cousin and h
   1759   male, as also br in law to the late Baronet, being only s and h of
              Edward LONGUEVILLE and Mary, da of (—) SYLVESTER, all
three abovenamed, which Edward was 2d and yst s of the 1st Baronet He
entered the naval service, becoming Lieut in 1709 He *suc to the Baronetcy* in Aug
1718, was Sheriff of Flintshire, 1746-47 He *m* firstly, in or before 1722, his cousin,
Mary Margaretta, 1st da and coheir of Sir John CONWAY, 2d Baronet [1660] of
Bodrythan, by his 1st wife Margaretta Maria, 1st da and coheir of John DIGBY,
of Gayhurst, Bucks and Margaret, his wife, da of Sir Edward LONGUEVILLE,
1st Baronet [S 1638] abovenamed She, by whom he acquired the North
Wales estates, *d* s p m Aug 1731, and was *bur* at Rhyddlan He *m* secondly,
Elizabeth, da of Sir Robert OWEN, of Porkington, Salop, by whom he had no
issue He *d* s p m (a) at Wrexham, co Denbigh, 1759, and was *bur* there, when
the Baronetcy became *extinct* or *dormant*

MEREDITH, *or* AMEREDETH

cr 2 Jan 1638/9, *or* 2 June 1639(b),

dormant 2 Jan. 1790

I 1639   AMOS AMEREDETH, *otherwise* MEREDITH, of Marston in
              Tamerton Folliott, co Devon, and subsequently (in right of his 2d
marriage) of Ashley, co Chester s and h of Edward AMEREDETH,(c) of Marston
aforesaid, by Margaret, relict of Gamaliel SLANNING da of Edward MARIEN, of
London, was *cr a Baronet* [S] 2 Jan 1638/9, or 2 June 1639 (b) with rem to
heirs male whatsoever and with, presumably, a grant of land in Nova Scotia, of
which, however he apparently never had seizin (d) During the Civil War he was
Col of a troop of Horse and Gov of Exmouth for the King, in whose cause he is
said to have expended £20,000 At the Restoration he was made a Gent of the
Privy Chamber He was M P [I] for Ballynakill, 1661-66, and was a Commissioner of Excise and Custom [I] He *m* firstly, Elizabeth, widow of
Francis COURTENAY, of Powderham (*d* 5 June 1638), da of Sir Edward
SEYMOUR, 2d Baronet [1611], by Dorothy, da of Sir Henry KILLIGREW By her
he had no male issue He *m* secondly, 6 Feb 1664, at Bowdon, co Chester,
Anne, 2d da of Robert TATTON, of Whithenshaw, by Jane, da of William, and
sister and coheir of Thomas BRERETON, of Ashley aforesaid He *d* 5 and was
bur 8 Dec 1669 in the burial place of Sir Charles MEREDITH(e) at St Patrick's,

---

(a) Of his three daughters and coheirs, Maria Margaretta, *b* 1722, *m* 1739 for
her 1st husband John Jones, who *d* 29 Sep 1747, from whom descends the family
of Longueville-Jones, of Prestatin

(b) The date, 2 Jan 1639 [*ie*, 1638/9], is given in Wotton's *Baronetage*
(1741, vol iv, 358), but that of *2 June* 1639, as also the limitation is in the
pedigree (2 D xiv, 127) recorded in the College of Arms The creation is not in
Laing's, Milne's, or Banks's Lists, nor is it in that of Walkley published in 1641,
or of Ulster, compiled 1633-43

(c) In Ormerod's *Cheshire*, under "Henbury," is a well worked up pedigree of
this family, which is the last of the "Nova Scotia Baronets of English families
and resident in England" (*viz* Gascoigne, Pilkington, Slingsby, Pickering,
Longueville, Musgrave and Meredith) of which an account is given in Wotton's
Baronetage (1741) and in that of Kimber (1771)

(d) See p 430, note "a," under "Slingsby"

(e) This Charles, who had recently, 14 Sep 1664, been *knighted*, was a yr br
of Sir William Meredith, *cr a Baronet* [I] 20 Nov 1660 His will was pr in
England 1700 In Playfair's *Irish Baronetage* (p 100) a common, though *very*
distant, male descent of the two families is set forth

Dublin Funeral entry in Ulster's Office Will as "of Ballynekil, in Queen's County," dat 5 Dec 1669, pi in Prerog Court [I] 1669 His widow, living 2 June 1685, *m*, as his 1st wife, Sir Samuel DANIELL, of Over Tabley, co Chester, who *d s p s* 24 Dec 1726

II 1669   SIR WILLIAM MEREDITH, Baronet [S 1639], of Ashley aforesaid, and afterwards of Henbury, co Chester, 1st s and h (a) by 2d wife, *b* 6 Dec 1665, *suc to the Baronetcy*, 5 Dec 1669, sold the estate of Ashley and, in 1693, purchased that of Henbury He *m*, 2 June 1685, at St Bride's, London (Lic Vic Gen 31 May, both stated to be about 19),(b) Mary, da and h of Henry ROBINSON, of Whaplode, co Lincoln, by Elizabeth, da of Christ THURSBY, of Dorwood's hall, Essex He was *bur* 19 Jan 1752, at Prestbury Will pi 1753

III. 1752,   SIR WILLIAM MEREDITH, Baronet [S 1639], of Henbury
       to   aforesaid, grandson and h, being 1st s and h (c) of Amos MERE-
     1790   DITH, by Joanna (*m* 27 May 1718), da of Thomas CHOLMONDELEY, of Vale Royal, co Chester, which Amos was only s and h ap of the late Baronet, but *d v p* at Bath, 6 May 1744, aged 57 He was *b* about 1725, matric at Oxford (Christ Church), 24 March 1742/3, aged 18, and was *cr* D C L, 14 April 1749, *suc to the Baronetcy*, 19 Jan 1752, was M P for Wigan, 1754-61, and for Liverpool, 1761-80, a Lord of the Admiralty, 1765-66, Comptroller of the Household, 1774-77, P C 9 March 1774 He sold the estate of Henbury in 1779, and *d unm* at Lyons, in France, 2 Jan 1790, when the *Baronetcy* became *dormant*

———

COWPER, or COOPER.

cr 24 March 1638 ,(a)

afterwards, from 1642 Baronets [E]

from 1706, BARONS COWPER OF WINGHAM,

and from 1718, EARLS COWPER

I 1638.   WILLIAM COWPER, of Ratling Court, in Nonington, ✓
       co Kent, was *cr a Baronet* [S] shortly before 1641,(d) and was subsequently *cr*, 4 March 1641/2, *a Baronet* [E] See p 160 for fuller particulars of him and for the devolution of the title

———

(a) George Meredith, of Oldfield Hall, Altrincham, *b* 7 June 1667, who was his only brother, apparently *d s p m*
(b) In his case this statement is probably an error for 29
(c) The 2d and only other brother, the Rev Theophilus Meredith, matric at Oxford (Christ Church), 2 June 1707, aged 16, B A (St Edmund Hall), 1761, M A 1762, Vicar of Linton, co Hereford, 1769, Rector of Ross, 1771-75, *d s p m*, at Bristol, 26 Sep 1776, aged 43
(d) See an article by "W S Cooper, Advocate," on "Cooper of Gogar," in *The Genealogist* [O S, vol. 1, p 334]

LOWTHER

cr about 1638 , (ᵃ)

sometime 1696-1751, VISCOUNTS LONSDALE ,

afterwards, 1784-1802, EARL OF LONSDALE ,

extinct or *dormant*, 24 May 1802

I   1638 ?   JOHN LOWTHER, of Lowther, co Westmorland, 1st s
and h (ᵇ) of Sir John LOWTHER, of the same, by Eleanor, da of
William FLEMING, of Rydal in that county, was b 20 Feb 1605 was M P for Westmorland, 1628-29 (together with his father), and subsequently (as a Baronet),
1660 He suc his father 15 Sep 1637, was a great sufferer in the Royal cause,
was, 18 Aug 1646, a Compounder for £1,500, with £50 a year settled, being,
in the documents relating to such composition, styled a Baronet, having been
cr a Baronet [S] about 1638 (ᵃ) He was Sheriff of Cumberland, 1661-62 He m
firstly, in or before 1655, Mary, 3d da of Sir Richard FLETCHER, of Hutton, co
Cumberland, by his 2d wife, Barbara, da of (—) CRAKENTHORP, of Newbiggin,
in that county He m secondly, Elizabeth, widow of Woolley LEIGH, of
Addington and Thorpe, co Surrey (d 23 Dec 1644), sister of Sir Ralph HARE,
1st Baronet [1641], da of Sir John HARE, of Stow Bardolph, co Norfolk He
d 30 Nov, and was bur 4 Dec 1675, at St Michael's, Lowther M I Will pr
1676 That of his widow dat 14 July 1692, pr 21 Oct 1699

II   1675   SIR JOHN LOWTHER, Baronet [S 1638?], of Lowther
aforesaid, grandson and h, being s and h of Col John LOWTHER,
of Hackthorpe and Mauds Meaburn, by his 1st wife, Elizabeth (m in or before
1655), da and [1650] coheir of Sir Henry BELLINGHAM, 1st Baronet [1620] of
Hilsington, co Westmorland, which John (who was M P for Appleby, 1661, till his
death in or shortly before March 1867/8), d v p He was b 25 April 1655, at
Hackthorpe Hall, in Lowther, was ed at Kendal and Jedburgh, matric at Oxford
(Queen's Coll), 12 Nov 1670, suc to the Baronetcy, on the death of his grandfather, 30 Nov 1675, Barrister (Inner Temple), 1677, M P for Westmorland
(seven Parls), 1677-96, and was a zealous promoter of the Revolution, P C,
19 Feb 1688/9, Vice Chamberlain of the Household, 1689-90, L Lieut of
Cumberland and Westmorland, 1689-94, First Lord of the Treasury, March to
Nov 1690, Second Lord, Nov 1690 to Nov 1691 He m 3 Dec 1674 at Westm
Abbey, Katherine, 2d and yst da of Sir Henry Frederick THYNNE, 1st Baronet
[1641], by Mary, da of Thomas (COVENTRY), 1st BARON COVENTRY OF AYLES-
BOROUGH She was living when he was cr, 28 May 1676, BARON LOWTHER
of Lowther, co Westmorland, and VISCOUNT LONSDALE, co Westmorland
See fuller particulars in *Peerage* He d 10 July 1700

III   1700   RICHARD (LOWTHER), VISCOUNT LONSDALE AND }
BARON LOWTHER, also a Baronet [S 1638?], s. and h, b
1692, suc to the titles 10 July 1700, d unm 1 Dec 1713

IV   1713   HENRY (LOWTHER), VISCOUNT LONSDALE AND
BARON LOWTHER, also a Baronet [S 1638?], br and h, b
1694, suc to the titles 1 Dec 1713, L Privy Seal, 1732-35, d unm
12 March 1750/1, when the *peerage dignities* became *extinct*

See fuller particulars in Peerage

(ᵃ) The limitation is not known The creation is not in Milne's or Laing's List,
but is in that of Walkley, being among the last entries therein That most
useful list, published in 1642, and containing, in all, ninety-five Baronetcies [S],
has (with this article) been now exhausted, though (no dates being therein given)
the order of it has not in this work been strictly followed, the last ten entries
therein being Slingsby, Cowper, Sinclair, Lowther, Pickering, Longueville,
Piers, Musgrave, and Witherington

(ᵇ) The second son, Christopher Lowther, of Whitehaven, was cr a Baronet [E]
11 June 1642, a dignity which became *extinct* 2 Jan 1755

V. 1751   SIR JAMES LOWTHER, Baronet [S 1638 ?], of Lowther
aforesaid, cousin and h male, being 2d but 1st surv s and h of
Robert LOWTHER of Mauds Meaburn, co Westmorland, Gov of Barbadoes, by
Catharine, da of Sir Joseph PENNINGTON, 2d Baronet [1676], of Muncaster, and
Margaret his wife, sister to Henry (LOWTHER), 3d Viscount LONSDALE abovenamed,
which Robert (who d Sep 1745, aged 63) was s and h of Richard LOWTHER, of
Mauds Meaburn aforesaid (b 1638), who was 2d surv s of the 1st Baronet   He was
b 5 Aug and bap 6 Sep 1736, at St George's Bloomsbury, suc to the Baronetcy,
12 March 1750/1, on the death of his 2d cousin and great uncle, Henry,
Viscount LONSDALE, abovenamed, whose vast estates he also inherited, as subsequently, 2 Jan 1755, he did the valuable estate of Whitehaven and about £2,000,000
on the death of his cousin, Sir James LOWTHER, 4th and last Baronet [1642],
of Whitehaven   He was ed at Cambridge, was M P for Cumberland, 1757-61,
for Westmorland, 1761-63; for Cumberland (again), 1763-68, for Cockermouth,
1769-74, and for Cumberland (the 3d term), 1774-84   He m 7 Sep 1761, at
St Geo Han sq; Mary, 1st da of John (STUART), 3d EARL OF BUTE [S], by
Mary, da of Edward WORTLEY-MONTAGU   She, who was b 20 Jan 1738, was living
when he was cr, 24 May 1784, EARL OF LONSDALE, etc   He was subsequently cr, 26 Oct 1797, VISCOUNT LOWTHER OF WHITEHAVEN, with
a spec rem in favour of his distant kinsman, Sir William LOWTHER, of Swil-
lington   In these peerages this Baronetcy then merged till on his death s p,
24 May 1806, aged 65, the peerage of 1797 devolved according to the spec
remainder, but that of 1784 became extinct, and the issue male of the grantee of
this Baronetcy having failed, the Baronetcy became either extinct or dormant

MACCARTY

cr. about 1638 ; (ª)

afterwards, 1640-91, VISCOUNTS MUSKERRY [I],

and subsequently, 1658-91, EARLS of CLANCARTY [I],

forfeited 11 May 1691

I   1638?   DONOGH MACCARTY, 2d but 1st surv s and h ap of
Cormac Oge (MACCARTY), 1st VISCOUNT MUSKERRY [I], by his 1st
wife, Margaret, da of Donogh (O'BRIEN), was b 1594, was Knighted before 1634,
being (as a Knight) M P [I] for co Cork 1634-35 and 1639-40, and was cr a Baronet
[S] probably about 1638,(ª) but there is no record thereof in the Great Seal Register
[S], and the limitation is unknown, suc his father, 20 Feb 1640, as VISCOUNT
MUSKERRY [I], and was cr 27 Nov 1658, EARL OF CLANCARTY [I], in
which peerages this Baronetcy consequently merged, till it and the peerage
honours became forfeited, 11 May 1691, on the attainder of the 4th Earl   See
Peerage

WALLACE ·

cr about 1638(ᵇ),

resigned 1659

I   1638?   SIR HUGH WALLACE, of Craigie Wallace and Newton,
to   both in co Ayr, s and h of John WALLACE, of the same, by
1659.   Margaret, da of John (MAXWELL), LORD MAXWELL [S], and at one
time EARL OF MORTON [S], was b about 1600, suc his father
before July 1614, sold the office of Heritable Baillie of Kyle in 1626, for

(ª) Milne's List, but without the date of creation ; not, however, in the lists
of Laing or Walkley, but in that of Ulster, shewing thereby the date of creation to
be previous to 1643, the date of the death of its compiler, Thomas Preston, Ulster
King of Arms, 1633-43.

(ᵇ) This creation is not in the List of Laing or Walkley, nor in that of Milne,

£10,000, is styled "Sir Hugh" in 1631, having possibly been, at or before that date, cr a *Baronet* [S], as certainly he was before 1642, and as he is styled in 1649 in certain pleadings before Parliament He was taken prisoner, fighting in the Royal cause, 1645 He m Hester, da of John KER, of Littledean, co Roxburgh She was an Anabaptist, and was, in 1653, "dipped" by the English in the Leith In 1649 he accused his two sons, Hugh(ᵃ) and William, of robbing and endeavouring to murder him He accordingly disinherited his children in favour of his cousin, Thomas Wallace, and executed a *resignation of the Baronetcy* in his favour (ᵇ) He was alive 1659, but d before 8 March 1660 (ᶜ)

HOME, *or* HUME :
cr. about 1638 ,(ᵈ)
forfeited about 1716

I 1638 ? SIR DAVID(ᵉ) HOME, *or* HUME, of Wedderburn, only s and h of SIR George HOME, of the same, by Jean, da of John HALDANE of Gleneagles, suc his father in Nov 1616, being retoured heir special 10 April 1617, and was, presumably, cr a *Baronet* [S] apparently about 1638,(ᵈ) but there is no entry in the Great Seal Register [S], and no particulars of the creation are known He was M P [S] for Berwickshire, 1639, 1640-41, 1645-46 and 1649-50, being, however, always styled "Knight" He m Margaret, widow of Sir Mark KER, of Dolphinston, da of Sir John HOME, of Coldingknows He, with his eldest son, George, was slain fighting for the Royal cause, 3 Sep 1650, at the battle of Dunbar

II 1650, GEORGE HOME, *or* HUME, of Wedderburn aforesaid,
  to   grandson and h, being s and h of George HOME, *or* HUME, by
1716 ? Katharine (mar lic 16 Aug 1635), da of Alexander MORISON, of Preston Grange, a Lord of Session [S] 1626-32, which George (who was M P [S] for North Berwick, three Parls, 1639-45) was s and h of Sir David HOME abovenamed, and was slain with him 3 Sep 1650, as above stated He was b 1641, and suc, presumably, *to the Baronetcy*, 3 Sep 1650, but does not appear to have ever assumed the same He m Isobel, da of Sir Francis LIDDELL, of Ravensworth He d about 1716, when *the Baronetcy* or the right thereto, devolved on George HOME,(ᶠ) his 1st s and h, who had been convicted of high treason for taking part in the rising of 1715, and became consequently *forfeited*

---

save that, under the patent, 8 March 1670, to Sir Thomas Wallace, it is there incidentally mentioned that "He seems to have a former patent disponed to him by the last Sir Hugh Wallace, which is ratifyed, 8 March 1670, but maketh him not to take place conforme to date of the said patent" The name, of "Sir Hugh Wallace of Cragie Wallace" appears 7th in Ulster's List of Scotch Baronets, made before 1643

(ᵃ) This Hugh mentions that, owing to his father's treatment, he had for a time become deranged and had fled with his wife to Ireland, where he was in such a state of poverty as to be unable to maintain his children It is not known what became of him or of his brothers William and John

(ᵇ) The creation of 1670, as it did not convey the precedence of this one (see p 441, note "b") must be considered as a new one, and is accordingly dealt with under the date of 1670, being that of its grant

(ᶜ) Much of the information in this article was supplied by R. R Stodart, Lyon Clerk Depute (1863-86)

(ᵈ) See p 441, note "a"

(ᵉ) He is however, called "Sir *James* Home, of Wedderburn," in Ulster's List, apparently by mistake

(ᶠ) This George d at Wedderburn 1720, leaving issue Some account of this family is in Wood's *Douglas' Peerage* [S], vol ii, pp 175-176, under "Marchmont," but there is no mention therein of the grant or assumption of any Baronetcy

HOME, or HUME:

cr about 1638 ,(ᵃ)

extinct or dormant April 1747

I 1638? GEORGE HOME, or HUME, of North Berwick, in
Scotland, s and h ap of Sir John HOME, of North Berwick
aforesaid (which estate he sold in 1633), and of Ardgorte, co Fermanagh
M P [I] for that county,(ᵇ) was cr a Baronet [S], apparently about 1638
(possibly, however, before 1633, the date of the sale of the North Berwick
estate), but there is no entry of such creation in the Great Seal Register [S],
and no particulars of it are known   He suc his father (who was bur at
St Michan's, Dublin) 26 Sep 1639, in whose inq p mortem, 23 March 1639/40
he is styled "Baronet" and to whom he was served heir, 10 Feb 1642   He
obtained in 1641 a grant of the manor of Tully, co Fermanagh, and is consequently spoken of as being of Castle Tully   He m Mary, 1st da of Sir William
MAYNARD, of Curriglasse, co Cork, by Mary, da of Samuel NEWCE, of Brickend-
bury, Serj -at-arms of the province of Munster   He d in Edinburgh intestate
in or about 1657, before 15 June 1657   The will of his widow, dat 30 Aug 1699,
pr 12 July 1705 [I]

II 1657? SIR JOHN HUME, Baronet [S 1638?], of Castle Hume,
presumably the same as Castle Tully aforesaid, s and h , suc to
the Baronetcy on the death of his father, was Sheriff of co Fermanagh 1662, and
Governor thereof during the wars of 1689, and, being a zealous partizan of King
William, was attainted in the Irish parl of James II   He m Sidney, yr da and
coheir of James HAMILTON, of Manor Hamilton, co Leitrim, by Catharine, da of
Claud (HAMILTON), 1st BARON STRABANE [I]   She, by whom he had ten children,
d 10 and was bur 23 Jan 1685 in St Michael's [sic, but probably St Michan's],
Dublin   Funeral certificate [I.]   He d Midsummer eve 1695   Will dat 12
June 1690, pr 1695 [I]

III 1695 SIR GUSTAVUS HUME, Baronet [S 1638?], of Castle
Hume aforesaid, 3d but only surv s and h ,(ᶜ) b about 1670, suc
to the Baronetcy, 23 June 1695, was Sheriff for co Fermanagh, 1701, M P [I]
thereof 1713-14, 1715-27 and 1727 till his death, P C [I] to George I, 1714   He
m 11 Sep 1697, at St Michan's, Dublin (Lic dat 10 Sep 1697), Alice, 1st da of
Henry (MOORE) 3d EARL OF DROGHEDA [I], by Mary, da of Sir John COLE, 1st
Baronet [I 1660], of Newland, co Dublin   He d s p m s (ᵈ) 25 Oct 1731   Will
dat 18 Aug 1729, pr 21 Feb 1731/2 [I], and 1732 [E.]   His widow, who was bap
29 Dec 1679, d at Dublin 13 April 1750   Will dat 18 April 1740, pr 20 April
1750 [I]

IV. 1731, SIR CHARLES HUME, Baronet [S 1638?], cousin and
  to   h male, being only surv s of the Rev George HUME, of Tully, co
1747   Fermanagh, by Dorothy, his wife, which George (whose admon
       [I] was dated 6 May 1699) was 2d son of the 1st Baronet   He
suc to the Baronetcy, 25 Oct 1731   He d s p April 1747 (Pue's Occurrences),
when the Baronetcy became extinct or dormant

(ᵃ) See p 441, note "a"
(ᵇ) G W Burtchaell, of the Office of Arms, Dublin, has kindly supplied most
of the information in this article   The estate of North Berwick devolved on
the Baronet's father, Sir John Home, on the death of Alexander Home uncle of
the said John, in or before Sep 1608   See Wood's Douglas Peerage [S] vol ii,
p 178
(ᶜ) Of his two brothers, James d 1689, and John, who ent Trin Coll , Dublin,
30 May 1685, aged 18, d 1690
(ᵈ) An account of his six children, his three brothers (who all d unm), and six
sisters is given in Archall's Lodge's Peerage [I], vol ii, p 112, under "Drogheda"
To this it may be added that Moore, the 1st son, ent Trin Coll , Dublin, 28 Oct
1721, aged 17
(ᵉ) Of his two brothers, John, ent Trin Coll , Dublin, 27 Oct. 1708, aged 18,
and James, 14 Dec 1711, aged 15.

BOURKE, Viscount Mayo [I.] :

cr. about 1638 ; (ᵃ)

extinct or *dormant* 12 Jan. 1767.

I. 1638 ?   MILES (BOURKE), VISCOUNT MAYO [I.], who succeeded
to that title (*cr.* 21 June 1627) as 2d Viscount 13 June 1629, was
(*apparently* on the same date as was his s. and h. ap.) *cr. a* Baronet [S.], probably
about 1630,(ᵃ) but there is no record of such creation in the Great Seal Register
[S.], and the limitation is unknown. In the abovenamed peerage this *Baronetcy*
continued *merged*, till on the death of the 8th Viscount and 7th Baronet, 12 Jan.
1767, both became *extinct* or *dormant*. See *Peerage.*

BOURKE :

cr. about 1638 ; (ᵃ)

afterwards, 1649-1767, VISCOUNTS MAYO [I.] ;

extinct or *dormant* 12 Jan. 1767.

I. 1638 ?   THE HON. THEOBALD BOURKE, s. and h. ap. of Miles
(BOURKE) 2d VISCOUNT MAYO [I.] next abovenamed, by his 2d wife
Elizabeth, da. of (—) FREKE, was v.p. (apparently on the same date as was his said
father), *cr. a* Baronet [S], probably about 1638,(ᵃ) but there is no record of such
creation in the Great Seal Register [S.], and the limitation is unknown. The
date was certainly before 1639 when, as "Knt. and Baronet," he was M.P. [I.]
for co. Mayo. He *m.* firstly, Elizabeth (*b.* 1613), widow of Thomas LEWIS, of
Marr, co. York, da. and coheir of Thomas TALBOT, of Bashall, in that county, by
Anne, sister of John Rushworth. She *d.* s.p. He *m.* secondly, Eleanor, da. of Sir
Luke FITZ-GERALD, of Tecroghan, co. Meath. This marriage was presumably before
1649, when he suc. to his father's honours becoming thus the 3d VISCOUNT
MAYO [I.]. In that peerage this *Baronetcy* then *merged*, and so continued till
on the death of the 8th Viscount, 12 Jan. 1767, both became *extinct* or *dormant.*
See *Peerage.*

> *Memorandum.*—Each successive eldest son and heir ap. of these Viscounts
> appears to have been, anomalously, considered as entitled to the style of
> a Baronet in his father's lifetime ; on the ground, apparently, of such son
> of the 2d Viscount having been created a Baronet in the lifetime of *his*
> father.(ᵇ) In some instances it probably was, for various reasons, not
> assumed, but it is as well to set out each of the five cases in which it was
> or might have been so assumed.
>   (1) Theobald Bourke, a minor when he suc. his father, 12 Jan. 1652/3,
> as 4th Viscount Mayo [I.].

(ᵃ) See p. 441, note "a."

(ᵇ) The fact that the father having (though a Viscount) been *cr. a* Baronet (as
well as, and probably at the same time as the son) may possibly have somewhat
contributed to this extraordinary opinion. In Archdall's *Lodge's Peerage* [I.], vol.
iv, 236, note, it is stated that "Mr. Lodge" (after stating that the creation by
Charles I. of this Baronetcy must have been after that of the Viscountcy) says
"certain it is that the eldest son of the Viscount Mayo enjoys the title of
Baronet, and is stiled *Sir*, during his father's lifetime." The notion that the son
and heir ap. of a Peer, who was also a Baronet, was entitled v.p. to his father's
Baronetcy, was apparently held by Francis Holles, who was *cr. a* Baronet, 27 June
1660, and who subsequently, 17 Feb. 1679/80, suc. his father as the 2d Baron
Holles of Ifield. He, in his will, dat. 3 Sep. 1680, speaks of his only surv. son
(who, subsequently, 1 March 1689/90, succeeded to his titles) as being "called Sir
Denzell Holles, *Baronet.*" See *Complete Peerage*, by G. E. C., vol. iv, p. 245,
note "c."

(2) Miles Bourke, br. and h. to the above, who, having been in his brother's lifetime heir *presumptive* (not *apparent*), is not likely to have assumed the Baronetcy before he suc. to the peerage, as 5th Viscount, 5 June 1676.

(3) Theobald Bourke, only s. and h. of the above; *b.* 6 Jan. 1681, who but three months later, in March 1681, suc. to his father's dignities as 6th Viscount.

(4) Theobald Bourke, 1st s. of the above; *b.* probably in or shortly after 1703. He was unquestionably *styled Baronet*(a) in his father's lifetime, to which title as also to the peerage he suc. 25 June 1741, as 7th Viscount.

(5) John Bourke, br. and h. to the above, to whom the same remark applies as to Miles, the 5th Viscount. He suc. to his brother's titles 7 Jan. 1741/2, but *d. s.p.m.s.*, 12 Jan. 1767, when they became *extinct* or *dormant*.

BOURKE:

cr. about 1638 : (b)

subsequently BARONS BOURKE OF BRITTAS [I] :

forfeited 1691.

I. 1638? THE HON. JOHN BOURKE, s. and h. ap. of Theobald (BOURKE), 1st BARON BOURKE OF BRITTAS [I.], by Margaret, da. of Richard (BOURKE) 2d EARL OF CLANRICARDE [I.]; was v.p. *cr. a Baronet* [S.], probably about 1638,(b) but there is no record of such creation in the Great Seal Register [S.], and the limitation is unknown. He *m.* in or after 1638, Margaret, widow of Walter BERMINGHAM (who *d.* 13 June 1638), da. of Thomas (FITZ-MAURICE), LORD KERRY [I.], by his 2d wife, Gillies, da. of Richard (POWER) BARON POWER OF CURRAGHMORE. He suc. his father in 1654 as the 2d BARON BOURKE OF BRITTAS [I.], in which peerage this *Baronetcy* then *merged*, and became forfeited therewith in 1691, on the attainder of his successor, the 3d Baron. See *Peerage*.

COOPER, *or* COUPER:

stated to be a Baronetcy [S.] ; (c)

created about 1638, or 1646.(d)

I. 1638? JOHN COOPER, *or* COUPER, of Gogar, co. Midlothian, only s. and h. of Adam COOPER, Clerk of Session [S.], by Katharine DENNISTOUN, his wife, suc. his father (who had purchased the estate of Gogar in or shortly before 1601) in 1608, and is said to have been *cr. a Baronet* [S.],(c) probably about 1638,(d) but "no patent is entered in the Great Seal Register, and it does not seem anywhere to be asserted that the original exists."(c) He *m.* in or before 1620, Helen SKENE, said to have been da. of Robert SKENE, of Halyards. He *d.* 30 Aug. 1640, at the blowing up of Dunglas Castle. His testament (Comm. Reg. Edinburgh) describes him as "John Coupar, of Gogar," the cautioner for the widow being "David Gray, Tailor, Burgess of Edinburgh." His widow, "Helen Skene, widow of John Coupar, of Gogar," was *bur.* 21 July 1667, at the Greyfriars, Edinburgh.

(a) "There is among the Prerog. [Marriage] Licences [I.] one, 29 Nov. 1723, for Theobald Bourke, of the parish of St. Andrew, Dublin, *Baronet*, and Sibilla Blake of same parish, spinster. But on examining the grant book, I find he is there designated *Honblem* as well as *Baronettum*, so I conclude that this refers to

(b) (c) (d) See these notes on p. 446.

II 1640,   JOHN, *afterwards* (1643) SIR JOHN COOPER, *or*
   to   COUPER, of Gogar aforesaid, s and h , *bap* 18 March 1621;
1686 ?   served heir to his father 27 Oct 1640, and then styled
           "John Couper, of Nether Gogar," was *Knighted* before
26 Aug 1643, and appears as *Knight*, but never as *Baronet*, in various
commissions; was M P [S] for co Edinburgh, 1681-82 , He *m* 15 March
1661, Margaret INGLIS, of the family of Inglis of Otterston   He *d*
s p m ,([e]) in or shortly after 1686, when the estate of Gogar was sold to
pay his debts

     *   *   *   *   *   *   *

[Nothing was heard of this (supposed) Baronetcy for upwards of one
hundred and thirty years, when it was assumed as under]

III ([f]) 1775.   SIR GREY COOPER, Baronet [S 1638 ?],([g]) claim-
           ing to be cousin and h male   He was s and h of William
GREY, M D , who practised as a physician at Newcastle-upon-Tyne, by
Mary (*m* in or before 1726), da of Edward GREY, of Alnwick, which
William([h]) (who *d* 5 May 1758), was only s of another William COOPER,([h])
M D , who practised as a Physician at Berwick-upon-Tweed, who was s of
the Rev James COOPER,([h]) Minister of Wigton, 1664 , of Mochrum, 1666,
and of Humbie 1681 till deprived as a non juror in 1695 when he became
Curate of Holyisland, near Berwick (where he died early in 1701), which
James (though not licensed as a minister([i]) till 16 Feb 1663) is stated([g])
to be identical with James (seemingly([i]) born 1622), 2d s of the 1st
Baronet ([k]) He was *b* about 1726 at Newcastle-upon-Tyne , was admitted

---

Theobald [afterwards 7th Viscount], 1st s and h of Theobald, 6th Viscount Mayo
This marriage licence, however has never been noticed in any peerage   Certain
it is that [the future 7th Viscount] Theobald Bourke of Ballintubber, co Mayo,
Baronet, is so described in his mar lic with Ellis Agar, of Gowran, co Kilkenny,
spinster, 18 March 1726 " [G D Burtchaell, Ulster's office]

([b]) See p 441, note " a."

([c]) An article on "Cooper of Gogar," by "S***," in *The Genealogist* [O S ,
vol i, pp 257-266 and 334], supplementing one in the *Her and Gen* [vol viii,
p 193], deals fully with this family, and "furnishes a negative reply" to the two
questions—(1), "Was a Baronetcy ever conferred on a Cooper, of Gogar ? " and
(2), "Is Mr [William] Cooper, of Failford [in 1876], the heir male of the Gogar
family ? "

([d]) The date of 1638 and the remainder to heirs male, are given in Playfair's
Baronetage [S]   In Paterson's *Ayrshire*, it is stated that the first Baronet "does
not appear to have assumed the title   It is, however, sometimes alleged that
the Baronetcy was not created till 1646 in the person of the son "   This date,
"1646," is the one given in Edmondson's List of Scotch Baronetcies.

([e]) He left two daughters and coheirs, viz , (1), Mary, who *m* Thomas Chalmers,
and had issue , and (2), Margaret, *m* 28 Oct 1680, Archibald Graham, Bishop
of the Isles, by whom she had two daughters and coheirs

([f]) This numbering is exclusive of any who might have had a right to the
(supposed) Baronetcy, after the death, about 1686, of Sir John Cooper, the s. and
h of John, the presumed grantee

([g]) According to the service of 1 Aug 1775

([h]) None of these three persons assumed the Baronetcy, which, in the case of
James, who for many years survived the 2d Baronet (said to be his brother), is
(to say the least of it) very remarkable

([i]) See note " c " above

([k]) "One would expect to find the son of a gentleman, who had a residence in
the town of Edinburgh, and whose estate was only at a distance of five miles, a
graduate of the University there, but the name of this James is not on the list
Then he was not licensed till 16 Feb 1663, when James, the son of Gogar would
have been over 40 years   It is not impossible that [James] the clergyman was
the James yr br of Sir John, but it seems unlikely, and one would like to see
the proofs that satisfied the jury "   [See note " c' above].

to the Temple, and became a Barrister ; was M.P. for Rochester, 1765-68 ;
for Grampound, 1768-74 ; for Saltash, 1774-84 ; and for Richmond, 1786-90 ;
was a zealous supporter of the Rockingham Ministry [1765-66], and was
Joint Sec. of the Treasury (under three Ministries), 1765-82 ; was a Lord
of the Treasury, April to Dec. 1783 ; P.C., 29 April 1796. Having suc. his
father 5 May 1758, he was, 1 Aug. 1775, served heir male to Sir John
COOPER, of Gogar, called the 2d Baronet and stated to have been brother of
his great grandfather, James COOPER, by a service before the Sheriff of
Edinburgh, which was, however, "never retoured to Chancery, and [even] if it
had been, could have conveyed no right to a title which had no existence."(ª)
He accordingly after that date *assumed the Baronetcy*, that was ascribed
in that service to the family of COOPER, of Gogar. He *m.* firstly, 5 Oct. 1753,
Margaret, sister of Charles, 1ST EARL GREY, da. of Sir Henry GREY, 1st
Baronet [1746] of Howick, by Hannah, da. of Thomas WOOD, of Falloden,
co. Northumberland. She, who was *bap.* 8 Dec. 1726, *d.* s.p. in 1755.
He *m.* secondly, 19 July 1762, Elizabeth, da. of (—) KENNEDY, of Newcastle-
upon-Tyne. He *d.*, suddenly, 30 July 1801 at his seat at Worlington, co.
Suffolk, aged 75, and was *bur.* in the church there. M.I. Will pr. 1801.
His widow *d.* there, 3 Nov. 1809, aged (also) 75.

IV.(ᵇ) *1801.* SIR WILLIAM HENRY COOPER, Baronet [S. 1638 ?],(ᶜ)
1st s. and h. by 2d wife ; *b.* 29 May 1766 ; took Holy
Orders ; was a Prebend of Rochester Cathedral, 1793-97 ; *suc. to the
Baronetcy*,(c) 30 July 1801, was sometime detained prisoner in France by
Napoleon. He *m.*, 21 May 1787, Isabella Ball, only da. of Moses FRANKS,
of Teddington, co. Midx. He *d.* about 1834. Will pr. Jan. 1835. His
widow *d.* 27 Jan. 1855, at Isleworth House, co. Midx., aged 85. Will pr.
Feb. 1855.

V.(ᵇ) *1834?* SIR WILLIAM HENRY COOPER, Baronet [S. 1638 ?],(ᶜ)
only s. and h., *b.* 28 March 1788 ; *suc. to the Baronetcy*,(ᵛ)
about 1834. He *m.* 10 April 1827, at St. Geo., Han. sq., Anne, 1st da. of
Charles KEMEYS-TYNTE, of Kevenmably, co. Glamorgan, by Anne, da. of
the Rev. Thomas LEYSON, Vicar of Bossaleg, co. Monmouth. He *d.*, s.p.s.,
14 Jan. 1836, at Chilton Lodge (near Andover), Berks, aged 47. Will pr.
Feb. 1836. His widow *d.* 17 Sep. 1880, at Leversdown, Bridgwater.

VI.(ᵇ) *1836.* SIR FREDERICK GREY COOPER, Baronet [S. 1638 ?],(ᶜ)
uncle and h. ; *b.* 19 March 1769 ; was a "Colonel" before
1805 ; *suc. to the Baronetcy*,(c) 14 Jan. 1836. He *m.* 7 Jan. 1805, at St. Geo.,
Han. sq., Charlotte Dorothea (then a minor), 2d da. of Sir John HONYWOOD,
4th Baronet [1660], by Frances, da. of William (COURTENAY), 2d VISCOUNT
COURTENAY OF POWDERHAM. She *d.* July 1811. He *d.* 23 Feb. 1840, at
Barton Grange, Somerset, aged 71. Will pr. April 1840.

VII.(ᵇ) *1840,* SIR FREDERICK COOPER, Baronet [S. 1638 ?],(ᶜ)
to only s. and h., *b.* probably about 1808 ; *suc. to the
1850.* Baronetcy,(ᵉ) 23 Feb. 1840. He *d.* unm. 1850, when the
issue male of his grandfather, Grey COOPER, became
extinct, and the *assumption of the Baronetcy*(c) (commenced by his said
grandfather in 1775) *ceased.*(ᵈ)

(ª) See p. 446, note "c."
(ᵇ) See p. 446, note "f."
(ᶜ) See p. 446, note "g."
(ᵈ) The notice in Debrett's *Baronetage* for 1870, that William Cooper, of
Failford, co. Ayr, claims this Baronetcy "as representative of the 3d son of the
1st Baronet," is not correct as far as such claim goes, though apparently the
pedigree is correct. The matter is very fully discussed in *The Genealogist* [O.S.,
vol. i, pp. 257-266, corrected by p. 334], and in the *Her. and Gen.* [vol. viii,
pp. 193-196], where is a quotation that the Rev. John Cooper, formerly Couper (who

DICK :

stated to be a Baronetcy [S.] ; (ᵃ)

created about 1638, 1642, or 1646.

I. 1638 ?   SIR WILLIAM DICK, of Braid, co. Edinburgh,(ᵇ) s. of John DICK, Merchant Burgess of Edinburgh, by Margaret, da. of William STEWART, of Edinburgh, Writer, was b. 1580, and acquired a considerable fortune (estimated in 1642, at £222,166) as a merchant and Banker in that city; was Provost thereof, 1638-39; was a zealous Covenanter, advancing enormous sums for that cause, as, on the other hand, did he, in 1641, for Charles 1, and subsequently, in 1650 (to the extent of £20,000), for Charles II. He was *Knighted* between 10 Aug. and 17 Nov. 1641, and is (apparently in error) *supposed* to have been *cr.* a *Baronet* [S.] about 1638, 1642 or 1646.(ᵃ) He was a member of the Committee of Estates, 1644-51, but, having incurred the displeasure of the then Government, was fined £64,934, and reduced to poverty. He m. Elizabeth, da. of John MORISON, of Preston Grange. He d. at his lodgings (according to some, in the debtor's prison) in Westminster, 19 Dec. 1655, aged 75.

II. 1655.   WILLIAM DICK, of Braid aforesaid, grandson and h., being s. and h. of John DICK, "fiar of Braid" and (1628), Sheriff-Depute of Orkney, by Nicholas, da. of Sir George BRUCE, of Carnock, which John was s. and h., ap. of Sir William abovenamed, but d., v.p., 1642. He suc. his grandfather, 19 Dec. 1655, but *never styled himself a Baronet*, which he undoubtedly would have done, after the Restoration, had such title ever been conferred. He, who was *bap.* 10 Aug. 1631, sold the estate of Braid in 1676, and, in a petition, dated 1681, states he had sacrificed £8,000, for payment of his grandfather's creditors. He m., in 1678, Elizabeth DUNCAN. He d. in or before 1695, when his widow was living. Her will (as Elizabeth Duncan, widow of Mr. William Dick, of Braid) pr. 24 April 1697, in the Edinburgh Commissariat Court.

III. 1695 ?   WILLIAM DICK, s. and h., aged 16 in 1695, being the son of "a poor widow"; was in 1707 an Ensign in the Foot Guards; was at the battle of Almanza; but afterwards settled in America, and was styled "Captain in the independant army of the State of New York." He is stated, as heir male of his great grandfather, to have *assumed the title of Baronet*, but such "is *not the case*."(ᵇ) He m. (—), widow of Capt. FOULIS, but d. s.p.m., in 1733, his only child, Agnes, being served his heir general.

died s.p. 1789, aged 80), "considered himself entitled to the Baronetcy of Gogar, and was proceeding to claim it, but desisted therefrom on the appearance of Sir Grey Cooper, claiming descent from an elder branch." This John was elder brother to William Cooper, formerly Couper, of Curries' Close, High Street, Glasgow, merchant, who, in 1786, purchased the estate of Failford, which his descendants still hold.

(ᵃ) In Milne's List it is given without any date, and as "only in ano old list." In Beatson's List the date is 1638; in Debrett's *Baronetage* (1873) it is 1642; and in Dod's (1876) it is 1646.

(ᵇ) An accurate and very full account of this family and of "the pretensions to a Baronetcy" by the descendants of Sir William Dick, of Braid, is given by "S***," [i.e., R. R. Stodart, Lyon Clerk Depute, 1863-86], in the *Her. and Gen.*, vol. viii, pp. 257-269. The singular career of this Sir William is mentioned in Scott's *Heart of Mid-Lothian.* See also *The Grange of St. Giles*, by Mrs. J. Stewart Smith [Edinburgh, 1898].

IV.   *1733.*   ROBERT DICK, of Frackafield, near Lerwick in
Shetland, cousin and h. male. He was s. and h. of William
DICK, of Frackafield aforesaid (*bap.* 5 Nov. 1679, at Kirkwall) who was s.
of Capt. Andrew DICK, M.P. [S.], for the Orkney and Zetland Stewartry,
1678 (*bap.* 12 Dec. 1637, and living 1700), who was yr. br. to William DICK,
of Braid. He became the "head of the family"(ᵃ) in 1733, but *never
assumed the title of Baronet.* He *m.*, in or before 1738, Jane DICKSON. He
d. a bankrupt in 1743.

V.   1743.   CHARLES DICK, of Frackafield aforesaid, s. and h.,
bap. 13 Oct. 1736. He never made up any title to the
estate (which was sold by the creditors in 1770), and *never assumed the title
of Baronet,* though in consequence of the assumption thereof in 1768 by
his cousin (as below mentioned), he took steps to prove his position as
heir male to Sir William DICK, of Braid, his grandfather's grandfather's
father. He *m.* 11 Oct. 1760, Martha MONTGOMERIE. He was living in
London 1805.

*   *   *   *   *   *   *

V *bis.* 1768,   SIR JOHN DICK, Baronet [S. 1638?],(ᵇ) after having
to   been served, 14 or 21 March 1768, by a Jury in Edinburgh,
1804.   heir male to Sir William DICK, of Braid, abovenamed,
assumed the style of a Baronet,(ᶜ) on the supposition that
such dignity had been granted to the abovenamed William, and that
he himself was the heir male of the said grantee's body. He was 2d but
1st surv. s. and h. of Andrew DICK, of West Newton, co. Northumberland,
by Janet, da. of Roger DURHAM, of Newcastle-upon-Tyne, which Andrew
(who *d.* 1744, in his 68th year) was s. of Andrew DICK, of Newton aforesaid, s. of Louis DICK, 5th and yst. s. of Sir William DICK abovenamed. He
was *b.* 1720; was a merchant residing in Holland in or soon after 1739;
was British Consul at Leghorn, 1754 to 1771 and probably later, when for
his services there to the Russian fleet, the Empress Catherine made him a
Knight of the Russian Order of St. Alexander Newski.(ᵈ) He finally
obtained the lucrative post of Head Auditor and Comptroller of the Army
Accounts in London. He *m.* Anne, sister of General BRAGG, and da. of
Joseph BRAGG, of Somerset. She, who was *b.* 13 Oct. 1720, *d.* 31 Jan. 1781.
He *d. s.p.* 3 Dec. 1804, at Mount Clare, Roehampton, co. Surrey, in his 85th
year. M.I. at Eastham, Essex. He left no portion of his fortune (above
£70,000) to any of his relatives.(ᵉ) Will pr. Dec. 1804.

*   *   *   *   *   *   *

(ᵃ) See p. 448, note "b."

(ᵇ) According to the service of 14 March 1768.

(ᶜ) He was a descendant, but certainly not the heir male of Sir William Dick,
of Braid. See p. 448, note "b."

(ᵈ) This, presumably, is the reason why he is stated in Playfair's *Baronetage* [S].
(appendix ccxviii) to have obtained from George III "the distinguished honour
of Knight of the Bath," an honour which he certainly did *not* obtain.

(ᵉ) *Annual Register,* 1804, where the residuary legatees, in four equal divisions,
are stated to be (1), Mr. Carr; (2), Mr. Simons, of Carlisle street, Soho, testator's
apothecary; (3), the Rev. Mr. Cleaver; and (4), Dr. Vaughan, testator's physician.
Playfair (as in note "d" above) writes that " Sir John's nearest relations and
heirs were the Prestonfield family [*i.e.,* the descendants of Sir James Dick, 1st
Baronet (S. 1677) of Prestonfield, son of Alexander, 4th s. of Sir William Dick, of
Braid], who would have succeeded to a large fortune, but Sir John was induced in
his old age to leave almost the whole to a stranger and three of that stranger's
friends."

3 K

VI. *1810?*   Sir William Dick Baronet [S 1638 ?],(ᵃ) 1st s. and h of Charles Dick, of Frackafield and Martha his wife,

1821   both abovenamed, *b* 8 Dec 1765, was sometime a Major in the East India Company's Service, suc his father between 1805 and 1820, and was 15 Jan 1821, served heir male of his lineal ancestor, Sir William Dick, of Braid, abovenamed, when he *assumed the Baronetcy*,(ᵃ) supposed to have been conferred on the said Sir William He *m*, 27 April 1821, Caroline, widow of Lieut.-Col Alexander Fraser (76th Regiment), da of John Kingston, of Rickmansworth, Herts He *d*, s p m, 17 Dec 1840 The will of his widow (who *d* at Bath), pr Jan 1843.

VII 1840   Sir Page Keble Dick, Baronet [S 1638],(ᵃ) br and h male, *b* 29 Sep 1769, suc his brother, 17 Dec 1840, and *assumed the presumed Baronetcy* (ᵃ) He was of Port Hall, near Brighton He *m*, 1795, Nancy, da of Richard Partridge, of Birmingham She *d* 1850 He *d* in London, 27 July 1851, aged 81 Admon, Jan 1852

VIII. 1851   Sir Charles William Hockaday Dick, Baronet [S 1638?],(ᵃ) only s and h, *b*, 1802, suc his father, 27 July 1851, and *assumed the presumed Baronetcy* (ᵃ) He *m*, in 1835, Elizabeth, da of George Chasserau, of Brighton He *d*, in straightened circumstances,(ᵇ) 3 Dec 1876, at his residence, 42 Elm Grove, Brighton, aged 74 His widow *d*, apparently, in 1880

IX 1876   Sir Henry Page Dick, Baronet [S 1638?],(ᶜ) only s and h, *b* 1853, suc his father 3 Dec 1876, and *assumed the presumed Baronetcy*(ᵃ), was sometime in the London and County Bank He *m* in 1880, Eliza, da of J Hylden, of Brighton (-)

SETON

cr 1638?

"Seton of Tough [*i e*, Touch], now of Culbeg," is said in Beatson's List of Scotch Baronets to have been *cr* a Baronet [S] in 1638 No such creation, however, is known (ᵈ)

(ᵃ) According to the service of 15 Jan 1821, "The evidence in support of *descent* is satisfactory" [see p 448, note "b"], but, of course, it could not convey the right to a title that had no existence

(ᵇ) It is stated that "in extreme old age" he was "so entirely destitute" as to be "unable to do more than keep the sticks and umbrellas of visitors" at the Brighton Museum Two pamphlets were published at Brighton in 1864, on "the claims of Sir Charles W H Dick, Baronet" (as to £52,418, £83,988, etc), on Government, and it is remarked thereon (see p 448, note "b"), that "surely Government could not be blamed if some provision were made, even at this date, for the descendant of one [Sir William Dick, of Braid], who was ruined by his trust in the good faith of the authorities of his time "

(c) On 30 March 1881 was born "a son and heir" of "Sir Henry Dick, Baronet," at Islip street, Kentish Town He received the name of Charles Henry Chasserau

(ᵈ) Walter Seton, of Abercorn, was *cr* a Baronet [S], 3 June 1663 His grandson, the 3d Baronet, on the death of James Seton, of *Touch*, became the representative of that family, whose son, the 4th Baronet, was of *Culbeg*

PRETYMAN

often (erroneously) considered as *cr* about 1638,
see under 1660

GUTHRIE

date unknown   *Qy* about 1638

"SIR HARIE GUTHRIE, of Kingsward" [*Qy* King Edward, co
Banff], appears without date, in Milne's List of Scotch Baronets, but
nothing is known of this creation

GORDON

cr. 13 Aug 1642, (ᵃ)

afterwards, since 1682, EARLS OF ABERDEEN [S]

I   1642   SIR JOHN GORDON, of Haddo, only s. and h of George
GORDON, by Margaret, da of Sir Alexander BANNERMAN, of Elsick,
which George (who *d* v p Oct 1610) was 1st s and h ap of James GORDON, of
Methlic and Haddo, was *b* early in 1610, suc his grandfather in Nov 1624, was
next in command of the Royal forces to oppose the Covenanters, and was in the
action at Turreff in 1639 He joined the King at Newark, and was by him *cr a
Baronet* [S], 13 Aug 1642,(ᵃ) with remainder to the heirs male of his body In
Oct 1643 he protested against the Covenant, was besieged in his house at Kelly,
and taken prisoner at its surrender, 8 May 1644, was found guilty of treason and
accordingly beheaded at Edinburgh, 19 July following, aged 34 He *m*, in 1630,
Mary, da of William FORBES, of Tolquhoun She survived him

II   1644   SIR JOHN GORDON, Baronet, [S 1642], of Haddo aforesaid, 1st s and h, *b* about 1632, *suc to the Baronetcy*, 19 July 1644,
which was, however, owing to his father's attainder, under forfeiture till the Restora
tion in 1660 He *m* Mary, only da of Alexander (FORBES), 1st LORD FORBES OF
PITSLIGO [S], by Jean, da of William (KEITH), 5th EARL MARISCHAL [S] He
d s p m 1665

III   1665   SIR GEORGE GORDON, Baronet [S 1642], of Haddo
aforesaid br and h male, *b* 3 Oct 1637, *suc to the Baronetcy*
in 1665 Advocate, 7 Feb 1668, M P [S] for co Aberdeen, 1669-74, 1678 and
1681-82 P C, 1678, one of the Lords of Session, 1 June 1680, President,
1 Nov 1681 High Chancellor [S], 1 May 1682 He *m*, Anne, 1st da of George
LOCKHART, of Torbrecks, by Anne, da of Sir James LOCKHART, of Lee She, who
became, in 1672, heir to her br, William LOCKHART, was living when her
husband, six months after having been made High Chancellor [S], was *cr*,
30 Nov 1682, EARL OF ABERDEEN, etc [S] In that peerage *this Baronetcy*
then *merged*, and still so continues See *Peerage*

TURING.

cr about 1642

I   1642 ?   SIR JOHN TURING, of Foveran, co Aberdeen, s of James
TURING,(ᵇ) of the same, was *b* about 1595, espoused the royal
cause, and, having previously been *Knighted*, obtained in, or shortly before, 1641

(ᵃ) Milne's List
(ᵇ) "The Lay of the Turings," by H McK [i e, Mackenzie], pub in 1849
which besides a tabular pedigree, contains notes illustrative thereof

a warrant for the creation of a Baronet [S], which warrant he on 7 Aug 1641 held, "to bestow to the best advantage,"(ᵃ) though it is *presumed* that he not long afterwards *nominated himself as such Baronet* [S] (ᵇ) He was taken prisoner by the Covenanters, 27 May 1639, by whom his house of Foveran was subsequently sacked He fought on behalf of the young King at the battle of Worcester, 3 Sep 1651 He *m* about 1620, Barbara, da of George GORDON, of Gight She *d* Feb 1639 He *d* 1662

II 1662   JOHN TURING, of Foveran aforesaid, grandson and h, being s and h of George TURING, by Margaret (marr contract, 18 June 1652), da of John FORBES, of Leslie, which George was only s and h ap, of Sir John Turing abovenamed, but *d*, *v p*, between 1652 and 14 Feb 1657. He suc his grandfather in 1662, but *never assumed the Baronetcy*, to which he was heir, presuming the said Sir John Turing to have nominated himself as a Baronet He sold the estate of Foveran, and *d* unm in the Canongate of Edinburgh, Feb 1682, when *the Baronetcy* remained dormant for about 100 years

*   *   *   *   *   *   *

III *1682*   JOHN TURING, 2d cousin and h male, being s of John TURING, by JANET SEATON, his wife, which John (b 1650) was s of Henry TURING, next br to Sir John TURING (who *d* 1662) first abovenamed, to whose male representation he succeeded in 1682, when possibly, though not probably, he *assumed the Baronetcy* (ᶜ) He was *b* 1680 was in Holy Orders, and was sometime, 1703-33, Minister of Drumblade He *m*, Dec 1700, Jean, da of Rev John DUNBAR, of Forglen He *d* 1733

IV 1733   ALEXANDER TURING, 1st s. and h, *bap* 9 Aug 1702, was in Holy Orders, and was sometime, 1729-82, Minister of Oyne, suc his father in 1733, when possibly, but not probably, he *assumed the Baronetcy* (ᶜ) He *m*, in 1740, Anna BROWN He *d* 1782, aged 80

V 1782   SIR INGLIS TURING, Baronet(ᶜ) [S 1642?] 1st surv. s. and h, *bap* 4 Dec 1743, suc his father in 1782, when probably (as certainly he did subsequently) he *assumed the Baronetcy* (ᶜ) He, also, was in Holy Orders, and was Rector of St Thomas in-the-Vale, Jamaica, where he *d* unm in 1791

(ᵃ) See *Genealogist* (O S, vol III, pp 65-68), in an article by "S * * *" (i e, R R Stodart, Lyon Clerk Depute, 1863-86), on the "Traffic in Baronetcies in the seventeenth century," where it is stated that Sir John Turing, of Foverne, for £180 paid him by John Turing, of Covent Garden, Midx, agrees on 7 Aug 1641, to give half of any money that should be paid for the Baronetcy by his nominee, to the said John, with whom for security he "leaveth the patent for yᵉ said Knight Barronett until we both jointly can find a seasonable opportunity to bestow it to the best advantage" This is conclusive evidence that, as late as Aug 1641, he had not nominated *himself* as a Baronet, though the date of 1638 is positively assigned to the creation in Mackenzie's "Lay of the Turings"

(ᵇ) In like manner Sir Robert Carr, of Etal, co Northumb, had, in 1647, two warrants of Baronetcy [S], which he still held in 1661, when he asks for and obtains their renewal What however, was their ultimate fate is unknown A like warrant was obtained for John Bannatine, Minister of Lanark, who sold it (1676?) to his parishioner, Carmichael of Bonnington, who and whose issue male, held the title without dispute, till their extinction in July 1738, see *Genealogist*, as in note "a" above

(ᶜ) This is on the supposition that the grant of the Baronetcy was to heirs male whatsoever

VI 1791.   SIR ROBERT TURING, Baronet(ᵃ) [S 1642 ?], of Banff
            Castle, co Banff, hr and h , bap 25 Dec 1745, suc to the
Baronetcy(ᵃ) in 1791, as to which " a service was expede at Banff " 9 July 1792 (ᵇ)
He, who had acquired a fortune in India, returned thence in 1792 and settled at
Banff Castle   He m 12 Oct 1797, at Edinburgh, Anne, da of Col Donald
CAMPBELL, of Glensaddel   She d 7 Dec 1809   He d s p m 21 Oct 1831 (ᶜ)
Will pr June 1832 and Nov 1851

VII 1831   SIR JAMES HENRY TURING, Baronet(ᵃ) [S 1642 ?], cousin
            and h male, being s and h of John TURING, of Campvere in
Zealand, Factor, by Margaret, da of Smart TENNENT, of Musselburgh, Scotland,
which John (who d , 1798, aged 48), was s of James TURING, also of Campvere,
Factor, which James (who d , 1788, aged 74), was s of the Rev Walter TURING,
Minister of Rayne, co Aberdeen, yr br of John TURING (d , 1738, aged 58),
numbered (above) as the 3d Baronet   He was b 10 Dec 1791 , suc to the Baronetcy,(ᵃ)
21 Oct 1831 , was British Consul at Rotterdam, 1845-60, having previously been
Vice-Consul there   He m in 1821, Antoinette, 3d da of Sir Alexander FERRIER, K H
British Consul for the Hague,(ᵈ) by Antoinette JONES his wife   He d at Rotterdam,
13 Feb 1860, aged 68   His widow d , 9 April 1884, at Rotterdam, aged 80

VIII. 1860   SIR ROBERT FRASER TURING, Baronet,(ᵃ) [S 1642 ?], 3d
              but 1st surv s and h , b 29 Aug 1827, British Vice-Consul at
Rotterdam, 1852-60, Consul, 1860-74, having suc to the Baronetcy,(ᵃ) 13 Feb
1860, his claim thereto being admitted by the Lyon office in 1882   He m , 29 June
1853, at the British Legation, at the Hague, Catherine Georgiana, da of Walter
S DAVIDSON, of Saxonbury, Kent and of Lowndes square

HAMILTON
cr about 1646 (ᵉ)

I 1646 ?   ROBERT HAMILTON, of Silvertonhill, co Lanark, s. and
            h ap of Edward HAMILTON, formerly of Balgiay, but subsequently
of Silvertonhill aforesaid, by Marion, da of James MURE, of Caldwell, was a
steady Loyalist, and is said to have been cr a Baronet [S], by Charles I about

---

(ᵃ) See p 452, note " c "
(ᵇ) See Genealogist as on p 452, note " a ", it being there added as to the statement that this Robert had been " served heir in 1792," that " no such service was
retoured to Chancery, and no record of it exists in the Sheriff Court books of
Banffshire where Sir Robert resided '   This Robert appears as the " present [1811]
Baronet " in Playfair's Baronetage [S], where, however, its Editor adds that we
are totally unable to trace any of the intermediate generations ' from the 1st
Baronet to him
(ᶜ) The title was claimed in 1831 by John Turing, who, however, gave up his
claim to James Henry Turing   [Pall Mall Budget, 13 July 1878]
(ᵈ) He died at Rotterdam in 1845, aged 72
(ᵉ) The date of 1646 is usually assigned for this creation, though 1642 is a more
probable one   There is no entry thereof in the Great Seal Register, or, apparently,
elsewhere , neither is it in Milne's List, or even in that of Beatson   The grantee,
Robert Hamilton, in his service to his uncle, William, in 1655, is not given any
title at all, and in his service to his father, Edward, in 1666, is simply called
Dominus, with no addition of Miles or Miles Baronettus, which last is usual in the
case of a Baronet   On the other hand, Sir Frederic Hamilton recorded arms in
the Lyon office in 1790, being styled in the entry in the Register, grandson and
heir of Sir Robert Hamilton, 4th Baronet, who was great grandson and
representative of Sir Robert Hamilton, cr a Baronet of Nova Scotia, by patent,
anno 1646, under the great seal of Charles I [ex inform , Sir J Balfour Paul, Lyon
King of arms]   The Baronetcy is omitted by Playfair in his existing Baronetage
[S] of 1811

1646 (ᵃ) He suc his father in 1649, sold the estate of Provan,(ᵇ) and burdened his other estates   He was M P [S] for Lanarkshire, 1661-63, as (possibly) also 1678   He *m* Anne, 2d da of John (HAMILTON), 1st LORD BELHAVEN [S] (who *d* s p m, 17 June 1679) by Margaret, illegit da of James (HAMILTON), 2d MARQUESS OF HAMILTON [S]

II   1670?   SIR ROBERT HAMILTON, Baronet(ᶜ) [S 1646?], of Silverstonhill aforesaid, s and h , *suc to the Baronetcy*(ᶜ) on the death of his father   He (or, possibly his father) was M P [S] for Lanarkshire, 1678,(ᵈ) served in the army of Holland, under the Prince of Orange, was subsequently Capt (1688) and Major (1700), in the Earl of Leven's Foot   He *m* firstly in Holland, Aurelia Katharine VAN HEFTINGEN, of Friesland   He *m* secondly, Isabel, da of John HAMILTON, of Boggs, in Scotland   He *d* at Fort William, 1708

III   1708   SIR JOHN HAMILTON, Baronet(ᶜ) [S 1646?], s and h by 1st wife , *suc to the Baronetcy* in 1708 (ᶜ)   He *m* firstly, Mary, da of (—) LEWERS   He *m* secondly, Rachael, da of (—) LEMPRIERE   He *d* in Jersey in 1748   Admon, 21 Jan , 1748/9, to a creditor   His 2d wife survived him   Her will pr 1751

IV   1748.   SIR ROBERT HAMILTON, Baronet(ᶜ) [S 1646?], s and h by 1st wife , *suc to the Baronetcy*(ᶜ) in 1748 , was an officer in the army, becoming eventually, 1777, Lieut -Gen , was sometime Col of the 108th and subsequently, 1770, of the 40th Foot   He *m* firstly, Louisa,(ᵉ) sister of Sir Hutchins WILLIAMS, 1st Baronet [1747], da of William Peere WILLIAMS, Barrister, by Anne, da of Sir George HUTCHINS   She *d* 15 Jan 1777   He *m* secondly, 6 Feb 1778, Anne, da of Sir John HEATHCOTE, 2d Baronet [1733], of Normanton, by Bridget, da of Thomas WHITE   He *d* in Grosvenor street, 10 Aug 1786   Will pr Aug 1786   The will of Dame Anne HAMILTON was pr 1816

V   1786   SIR FREDERIC HAMILTON, Baronet(ᶜ) [S 1646], grandson and h, being only s and h of John William HAMILTON, Capt 54th Regiment, by Mary Anne, da of Richard ST GEORGE, of Kilrush, co Kilkenny, which John William was 1st s and h ap , by his 1st wife, of the late Baronet, but *d* v p   He was *b* 14 Dec 1777, in Dublin, *suc to the Baronetcy*,(ᶜ) 10 Aug , 1786, and was in the East India Company service, 1792-1833, being sometime Collector of Revenues for the district of Benares   He *m* , 20 Aug 1800, Eliza Ducarel, yst da of John COLLIE, M D , of Calcutta   She *d* 11 Feb 1841   He *d* 14 Aug 1853, aged 76   Will pr Nov 1853

VI   1853   SIR ROBERT NORTH COLLIE HAMILTON, Baronet [S 1646?], 1st s and h, *b* at Benares aforesaid, 7 April 1802 , was in the Bengal Civil Service, 1819-1860, Magistrate and Collector of Meerut, 1834 , Civil and Session Judge of Delhi, 1837 , Sec to the Lieut Gov of the N W Provinces, 1841 , *suc to the Baronetcy*, 14 Aug 1853, Agent to the Gov Gen in Central India, 1854 , was thanked by Parl for his services during the Indian mutiny, and made provisional member of the Council of the Gov Gen in 1859, K C B , 1860, Sheriff of Warwickshire, 1866   He *m* 9 Oct 1831, at St Marylebone, his cousin, Constantia, 3d da of Gen Sir George ANSON, G C B , by Frances, sister of Sir Frederic HAMILTON, 5th Baronet [S] abovenamed   She *d* 28 Nov 1842   He *d* at Avoncliffe, near Stratford-on-Avon, co Warwick, 30 May 1887, in his 86th year   Will pr 26 Sep 1887, above £18,000

VII.   1887   SIR FREDERIC HARDING ANSON HAMILTON, Baronet [S 1646?], 2d but 1st surv s and h , *b* 24 Sep 1836 , ed at Eton , sometime Major 60th Rifles , *suc to the Baronetcy*, 30 May 1887   He *m* 18 Sep 1865, Mary Jane, da of H WILLAN

(ᵃ) See p 453, note " e "

(ᵇ) His grandmother, Elizabeth, wife of Sir Robert Hamilton, was da and heir of Sir William Baillie, of Provan, President of the Court of Session

(ᶜ) According to the entry in the Lyon office   See p 453, note " e "

(ᵈ) Both in 1661 and 1678 the M P is styled " Knight " only

(ᵉ) In Anderson's *House of Hamilton* she is called " Mary "

Supplemental Creations by Charles I.

A search, kindly made by J Horace Round through the Signet office Docquet Books (vols 12 and 13) from the beginning of the year 1642, discloses some creations of Baronetcies by Charles I, which are not in the list given in the "appendix to the 47th report of the Deputy Keeper of the Public Records" or in the extracts from *Black's Docquets*(ᵃ) printed at the end thereof (ᵇ) The date of the month is not given in these books

These creations are eight in number, *viz* ,

1643, Oct	"EDWARD BATHURST, of Lechlade, co Gloucester, Esq" [See this creation set out on page 237]
1643/4, Feb	"ROBERT DALLISON, of Greetwell, co. Lincoln, Esq" [As to this creation, which, apparently, is nowhere else noticed, see p 456 below]
1644, April	"SIR JOHN AWBREY [AUBREY], of Llantrithed, co Glamorgan, Knt" [See under 1660, in which year the grantee(ᵇ) obtained a *patent* of Baronetcy]
1644, April	"FRANCIS GAMULL, of Chester, co Cheshire, Esq" [As to this creation, which, apparently, is nowhere else noticed, see p 456 below]
1644, April	"EVAN LLOYD, of Yale, co Denbigh, Esq." [See this creation set out on page 246]
1644/5, Feb	"WILLIAM COURTNAY [COURTENAY], of Powderham, co Devon, Esq" [See this creation set out on page 241, where, however, the date is given as "Feb 1644," instead of "Feb 1644/5"]
1644/5, March	"WOLSTAN DIXIE, of Market Bosworth, co Leicester" [See under 1660, in which year the grantee(ᵇ) obtained a *patent* of Baronetcy]
1645, July	"JOHN KNIGHTLEY, of Offchurch, co Warwick, Esq" [See under 1660, in which year the grantee(ᵇ) obtained a *patent* of Baronetcy]

"These creations are described as *By warrant under His Majesties signe Manuall procured by Mr Secretary Nicholas, Lord Digby, or some other*"

It may be noted that the creation of JOHN PRESTON [of Furness co Lancaster], given as 1 April 1644 in *Black's Docquets* occurs as early as May 1643 in the Signet Office Docquet Book, this being an earlier stage in the process of creation" [J Horace Round]

(ᵃ) "The Ashmolean MS from which *Black's Docquets* are printed has now been ascertained to be only the draft The fair copy of it has been found in the *Crown Office* at the House of Lords" [J Horace Round]

(ᵇ) Three Baronetcies, of which no patents exist, were conferred, as under, viz, 24 Nov 1644, on JOHN ACLAND, of Columb John, Devon, 5 Nov 1644, on HENRY BOOTHBY, of Clattercote, Oxon and 21 March 1644/5, on THOMAS EDWARDS, of Grete, Salop, but though these grants were followed by patents from Charles II, such patent in each case was *not to the original grantee*, who had died before that event, but to his son Those persons, therefore, that held that dignity before the patentee of Charles II (in the case of Acland these were as many as four) are dealt with in this Volume, pp 236, 239, and 243

DALLISON

cr Feb. 1643/4

existing as late as April 1714

I   1644   ROBERT DALLISON, of Greetwell, co Lincoln, s and h.
of William DALLISON, of the same, by Hester, da and h of George
BLESBY, of Blesby in that county, was admitted to Gray's Inn 17 Aug 1632,
and, again, 23 June 1637, was aged 17 in 1634 (*Visit of Lincolnshire*), matric
at Oxford (Christ Church), 20 May 1636 aged 18, raised a regiment of horse[a]
at his own charge for the King, and was cr a Baronet, the docquet being dated
Feb 1643/4 (see p 455) He, with his father, was at the siege of Newark in
March 1644, and both were living 1650, when discharged of their amercement
He was living after the Restoration

II   1670 ?   SIR ROBERT DALLISON, Baronet [1644], apparently s
and h, presumed to be identical with the "Sir Robert Dallyson,
Baronet, of Greetwell,[b] co Lincoln," who had lic (Vic Gen) 17 April 1677 to
marry at Swinderly, co Lincoln, Mrs Alice ANDREWES, of Lincoln, widow

III   1680 ?   SIR THOMAS DALLISON, Baronet [1644] apparently s
and h, presumed to be identical with "Sir Thomas Dallison
Baronet of St Paul's, Covent Garden, Midx, Bachelor," administration of whose
goods was granted 25 June 1713, to a creditor, "Dame Alice Dallison," the mother
of deceased, having renounced

IV   1713,   SIR JAMES DALLISON, Baronet [1644], possibly br and h
to   male, supposed to be identical with "Sir James Dalyson, Baronet,
1720 ?   of Chelsea, Midx about 25 and a Bachelor" 13 April 1714, when
he had lic (Vic Gen) to marry Anne SYMONDS, of the same
aged 18, spinster, with consent of her mother, Anne, wife of John SYMONDS, then
at Barbadoes

GAMULL.

cr April 1644,

ex or dormant Nov 1654

I   1644,   FRANCIS GAMULL, of Chester, s and h of Thomas
to   GAMULL, Recorder of that city, by Alice, da of Richard BAVAND,
1654.   was *bap* at St Oswald's, Chester, 25 Nov 1606, suc his father
11 Aug 1613, was *Knighted* at Oxford, 25 April 1644, and was
cr a Baronet, the docquet bearing date that same month (see p 455) He was
Alderman of Chester, Mayor, 1634-35, and M P thereof 1640, till disabled
22 Jan 1643/4 He was a Royalist delinquent, and fled the kingdom, his estate
being sequestrated in July 1649 He m firstly, Oct 1624, at Eccleston, Christiana,
da of Sir Richard GROSVENOR, 1st Baronet [1622] by his 2d wife, Lettice, da of
Sir Hugh CHOLMONDELEY She was *bur* 11 June 1640, at St Mary's, Chester
He m secondly, Elizabeth, widow of Robert RAVENSCROFT, da of Sir Randle

---

(a) See *Mis Her & Gen*, 2d S, Vol II, p 289, in a petition (without date) to
the King from "Sir Robert Dalyson, Baronet" At p 259 thereof is an extract
from "*Lloyd's Memories*," stating that besides "Sir Thomas Dallison, a Lancashire
[*Qy* Lincolnshire] gentleman   whose loyalty cost him his life at Nazeby
and £12,000 in his estate   there were in the King's army three Colonels
more of that name, viz, Sir Charles, *Sir Robert*, and Sir William, who spent
£130,000 therein "

(b) The parish registers of Greetwell do not begin till 1723, after which date
there are no Dallison entries in them

MAINWARING, of Over Peover, by Jane, da of Sir Thomas SMITH, of Hough, co Chester By her he had no issue He d 27 Nov 1654, and was *bur* at St Mary's aforesaid, *when the Baronetcy* presumably became *extinct*, and certainly was never subsequently assumed (ᵃ) Admon 12 Dec 1660 to his da, Sidney BREREWOOD, *otherwise* GAMULL His widow d at Chester, 13 Aug 1661, and was *bur* at Harden with her first husband

---

(ᵃ) According to the pedigree in Ormerod's *Cheshire* (edit 1882, vol iii, p 475), he had three sons, viz (1), Thomas Gamull, slain in the Civil Wars, v p, and *bur* 12 June 1644 at St Mary's, Chester, (2), Edward Gamull, and (3), Edmund, who died s p It is there stated that Edward, the 2d son, was *bur* 16 Feb 1663/4, at St Mary's, in which case he would have been entitled to his father's Baronetcy during the ten years that he survived him It is, however, not unlikely that the Edmund who died in 1664 was only a relation not a son, of Sir Francis See particulars as to the career and estates of this Francis in the Royalist Composition papers, where it is to be noted he is occasionally styled " Baronet "

CORRIGENDA ET ADDENDA

p 8, note (ᵇ), *for* "Sir John Winter," *read* " (as his 2d wife) Sir George Wintour, Baronet [1642], and *d s p*"

p 17, line 4, *after* "Goodwyns," *add* "[in Hoo]", line 7, *for* "about 1585," *read* "6 and *bap* 27 March 1607, at Letheringham", *for* "1609," *read* '1609/10", line 10, *for* "aged 53," *read* "was *bur* 31, at Letheringham, in his 33d year M I", line 11, *after* "1642," *add* "She was *bur* 6 April 1642, at Letheringham", line 15, *after* "HALLIDAY," *add* "She was *bur* 22 June 1652, at Letheringham", line 18, *after* "1657," *add* "She was *bur* 13 Nov 1656, at St Giles' in the Fields"

p 25, 3d and 2d lines from bottom, *for* "*d s p*, being killed," *read* "who was a Jesuit Priest (though he obtained a dispensation to marry), *d s p*, being killed near Dartford"

p 26, line 23, *after* "was" *read* "*b* 10 March 1606, being"

p 31, line 26, *after* "Chichester," *add* "She was *bur* 18 June 1623, at North Mundham", line 27, *for* "before 1634," *read* '4 June 1624, at St Mary le Strand, Midx", line 30, *for* "1650," *read* "1649/50", line 37, *after* "1648," *add* "Her admon 13 March 1655", line 38, *dele* "(ᵃ)", line 39, *after* "widow," *add* "She was *bur* 31 July 1687, at North Mundham" Note (ᵃ), *for* "136," *read* "137"

p. 32, line 17, *for* "William," *read* "Robert", line 18 *for* "1655," *read* "1657"

p 36, line 31, *for* "William ATHERTON, of Skelton, co York," *read* 'John ATHERTON, by Anne, da of Sir John BYRON (Visit of Lanc 1665)", line 33, *after* "widow," *add* "who was *b* at Newstead, Notts", line 37, *for* "pr Feb 1645," *read* "dat 8 July 1644, pr 26 Feb 1644/5."

p 37, note (ᵃ), line 1, *after* "adjudged," *add* "in 1678", line 3, *before* "invalid," *insert* "apparently"

p 49, line 37, *after* "London" *add* "He *d* 1 Jan 1691/2", line 44, *after* "by," *add* "apparently"

p 56, line 43, *for* "about 1730," *read* "presumably 4 May 1761"

p 66, in margin, *for* "1669," *read* "1670", line 13, *after* "m", *add* "7 May 1668", lines 17 and 20, *for* "1669," *read* "1669/70", line 22, *after* "m" *add* "in or shortly before June 1689"

p. 67, in margin, *for* "1630," *read* "1629", *for* "1700?" *read* "1706", line 12, *for* "1629/30," *read* "1628/9", line 13, *for* "presumably about 1700," *read* "Sep 1706", line 18, *after* "1602," *add* "suc his father 18 Sep 1629", *dele* "1615-16, and", line 19, *for* "Margaret," *read* "Catharine", line 21, *after* "Hooton," *add* "She was *bur* 12 Sep 1639, at St Mary's Chester", line 23, *for* "1630," *read* "1629", line 27, *for* "father," *read* 'grandfather", line 28, *dele* "in or" *to* 'Mary," *and insert* "8 May 1649, Mary (*b* 26 June 1626)", line 29, *for* "Carnarvon," *read* 'Flint She was living 9 Jan 1652/3 ", *for* "Jane," *read* "in or before 1657, Jane, widow of Col John MARRON (*d* Aug 1644) and previously of Henry HARDWARE, of Peel, co Lanc", line 30, *after* "Flint," *add* "She was *bur* at Gresford, 17 Feb 1684/5", lines 31 and 32, *dele* "it is" *to end and insert* "and was *bur* at Gresford 28 Sep 1706, when the *Baronetcy* became *extinct* (ᵈ) Will dat 11 Feb 1705/6" Note (ᵇ), *dele* the whole of this note Note (ᶜ), lines 3 and 6, *dele* "before 1694" *to the end*, *and insert* "and was *bur* at Gresford, 16 April 1689, aged 39, leaving four surviving children, viz, two daughters by his 1st wife, and one son and one daughter by his 2d The son, Samuel, *bap* at Gresford 18 July 1682, was living 11 Feb. 1705/6, but *d s p* a few months later, as, had he survived to Sep 1706, he would have inherited the Baronetcy, whereas Winifred (the heiress of Horsley) then wife of " Edward Lloyd, Esq ," is spoken of, 19 Sep 1707, at a Court Baron of Horsley, as sister and next heir of Samuel Powell, *Esquire*, decd " [*Mem.*—These valuable corrections to the Powell family were furnished by H R Hughes, of Kinmel Park, co Denbigh]

p 69 , line 39, *dele* " of Eske, co Cumberland [E] "

p 72 , note (ᶜ), *conclude* " In Oct following, Alderman Sir Robert Ducie (who had been Sheriff, 1620-21, and Lord Mayor, 1630-31) was similarly honoured , as, in Dec 1641, was Sir Richard Gurney, the then Lord Mayor, he being the first person who received a Baronetcy during his Mayoralty [See W D Pink's *Citizen Baronets* in *N & Q*, 9th S , ix, 61]

p. 73 , line 13, *after* " firstly," *add* " 1 April 1656, at Holkham "

p 77 , lines 2 and 12, *for* " 1629," *read* " 1629(ᵛ) " Note (ᵛ), *conclude* " As to these Citizen Baronetcies, see p 72, note ' c, ' and the *addenda* thereto "

p 79 , lines 2 and 8, *for* " 9," *read* " 19 "

p 81 , line 43, *for* " 1663," *read* " 1683 "

p 89 , line 31, *for* " Besilden Lee," *read* " Besselsleigh ", line 32, *after* " there," *add* " before him, who d 9 Nov 1581 "

p 93 , note (ᵃ), *conclude* " He petitions in Dec 1696, to surrender his Baronetcy for one to be granted to himself for life, with rem to his kinsman, John Thornicroft, of Gray's Inn, stating that he is in years and unmarried, and is anxious to prevent its descent to any person not qualified to support the dignity [*Rawlinson's MSS*] A Baronetcy in 1701 was conferred on this John Thornicroft "

p 96 , line 28, *for* " Telton," *read* " Teston "

p 98 , line 29, *for* " 29 July 1811," *read* " 26 June 1811, aged 52, at Ballogie, of which he was tenant (under the designation of Mr Brown, an Irish gentleman, his real name being unknown till after his death), and was *bur* at Birse, co Aberdeen M I ", line 32, *for* " 29 July," *read* " 26 June "

p 120 , line 8, *after* " 1875-76," *add* " He m 18 March 1902, at Christ Church, Folkestone, Margaret Elizabeth widow of John Dillon BROWNE, 100th Regiment ", line 18, *after* " firstly," *add* " 28 Jan 1646/7, at Wrotham, Kent ", line 20, *after* " She," *add* " who was *bap* 27 April 1626, at St Dionis Backchurch, London ", line 26, *for* " of the," *read* " of Stidulfe's Place, i e , the "

p 126 , line 23, *for* " b about," *read* " bap at Werrington aforesaid, 24 Jan '

p 147 , line 30, *for* " Baronet," *read* " Baronet(ᵈ)," *and insert as note* (ᵈ) " He was the first Lord Mayor or a Baronet during his term of office "

p 148 , line 8, *after* " 1628," *add* " admitted to Gray's Inn (with his brother Richard) 2 Feb 1630/1, as of St John's, Herts ", line 10, *after* " 1665-66," *add* " named, in 1660 as a Knight of the intended order of the Royal Oak, his estate being then valued at £1,000 a year " Note (ᵃ), *conclude* " It is sometimes said that about 1658, he received a Baronetcy from Oliver Cromwell, but this presumably is an error It would, in any case, have been unnecessary, as his creation in 1641 was previous to the date (4 Jan 1641/2) on and after which the King's creations were disallowed, and his fidelity to the Royal cause seems evidenced by his being nominated in 1660 among the projected Knights of the Royal Oak "

p. 153 , lines 9 and 10, *for* " about 1626," *read* " 23 Dec 1633 ", *dele* " said to be "

p 154 ; line 1, *after* " [S]," *add* " 19 Dec 1635 and again ", *for* ' was," *read* " and with a grant, presumably, of 16,000 acres in Nova Scotia (of which, however, he never had seizin), being ", lines 3 and 4, *for* " in or before 1627," *read* " 21 Dec 1624, at St Dionis Backchurch, London ", *for* " Backchurch London " *read* " aforesaid ", lines 14, 15, and 16, *for* " b about," *read* " bap, at St Dionis aforesaid, 28 Aug ", *after* " firstly," *add* " in or before 1670 ", *dele* " or Mary ", *after* " London," *add* " She was *bur* 27 Aug 1663, at

Wrotham", *after* "secondly," *add* "in or before 1666", line 20, *after* "firstly," *add* "in or about 1683", line 31, *for* "s and h," *read* "2d but 1st surv s and h", *for* "b about 1688," *read* "bap 12 March 1685/6, at Wrotham", line 36, *for* "b," *read* "bap at Wrotham, 10 June"

p 156, line 13, *after* "at," *add* "Exeter House", *after* "40," *add* "and was bur 21 Jan 1656/7, at Moreton Corbet", line 24, *for* "1670," *read* "1668", line 25, *after* "d," *add* "in London", *after* "4,' *add* ' and was bur at Moreton Corbet, 24", line 26, *for* "living Sep 1688, d about," *read* "was bur at Moreton Corbet, 16 Nov", line 28, *for* "b," *read* 'bap at Moreton Corbet" Note (ᵇ), line 3, *dele* ' the", note (ᵈ), line 1, *for* "b 1669," *read* "bap 4 Dec 1668, at Moreton Corbet"

p 166, note (ᵈ), line 1, *after* "omission," *add* "(made 19 Dec 1827)"

p 168, line 26, *after* "1680," *add* "16 Dec 1689 and 31 Oct 1699" Note (ᶜ), line 4, *for* ' Bradwardine," *read* "Bredwardine"

p 186, line 8, *for* "in or before 1664," *read* "5 July 1662, at Langton", line 10, *after* "abovenamed," *add* "She was bur 18 Jan 1670/1, at Bugthorpe", line 15, *for* "2 Nov 1643," *read* "1643—1716"

p 187, in margin, *for* "1680 ?" *read* "1680", line 25, *conclude* thus "He was bur 20 Aug 1680 in the church of the Augustine Convent, Louvain", line 28, *for* "on his father's death," *read* "Aug 1680"

p 194, line 33, *for* "Katharine, da and h," *read* "1679/80, at Westow, co York, Katharine, 2d da and coheir", *for* "co York and" *read* "aforesaid, by Mary, da of Sir Thomas GOWER, of Stittenham She was aged 14, in 1666 He"

p 196, line 39, *for* "b about 1614," *read* "bap 2 Jan 1616/7, at Kippax", line 47, *for* "1617, m Walter WALSH, of Houghton and," *read* "1617(ᶜ)" *Add* as note (ᶜ) "The marriage at Kippax 25 Jan 1654/5, of 'Walter Walsh and Dame Katherine Bland,' refers presumably to the Baronet's mother, who, however, must then have been about sixty years old", line 49, *for* "b about," *read* "bap at Kippax, 6 June"

p 197, in margin, *for* "1668," *read* "1667", line 2, *for* "1662," *read* "1661 and bap at Kippax 2 Jan 1661/2", line 3, *for* "1668," *read* "1667", line 5, *after* "2," *add* "and bap at Kippax, 8", line 15, *for* "b about," *read* "bap at Kippax, 10 Sep", line 24, *for* "b about 1722," *read* "bap at Kippax, 13 Jan 1721/2", line 32, *for* "b about," *read* "bap at Kippax, 7 Sep"

p 207, line 2, *after* ' Devon," *add* "one of the Baronets created by Oliver Cromwell"

p 220, note (ᵃ), *conclude* "The docquet is dated as early as May 1643 See p 455 below"

p 227, line 6, *for* "yᵉ," *read* "the", line 20, *for* "1644( )," *read* "1644(ᵈ)" line 25, *after* "Penelope," *add* "sister of John, 1st VISCOUNT SCUDAMORE [1]", line 26, *after* "Hereford" *add* "by Ann, da of Sir Thomas THROG-MORTON", *after* "1649," *add* "at Ballingham", lines 31 and 32, *for* ' George " *read* "Thomas", *dele* "by Ahoe" *as far as* "Norfolk," *and insert* ' 2d Baronet [1652 ?], by Mary, da of Thomas BOND(ᶜ)," *and add as note* (ᶜ) "Dame Margaret Scudamore is generally said to have been Margaret, bap 1 May 1640, at Camberwell, Surrey, sister of Sir Thomas, the 2d Baronet, but the will (dat 1 Sep 1708, pr 16 Nov 1709) of her brother Edmund, shews her to be da of the 2d and sister of the 3d Baronet", last line, *for* "extinct," *read* "extinct(ᶠ)" *and add as note* (ᶠ) "Robert Scudamore, who as Baronetti filius, matric at Oxford (Trin Coll), 7 May 1695, B A 4 Feb 1698 9, M A, 23 March 1701/2, Vicar of West Malling, Kent, 1704-17, was presumably a son of this Sir Barnabas He m Martha, da of Sir Felix Wild, 2d Baronet [1660], and was living 1709, s p, but presumably must have d v p"

p 233, line 14, *for* "Owen," *read* "Onen", line 15, *after* "DOWSE," *add* "of Wallop, Hants", *after* "70," *add* "and was bur 12 Feb at Hawnes, Beds", line 18, *after* "husband" *add* "She was bur 19 March 1696, at Hawnes" p 234, line 36, *for* "Sir Richard," *read* "Sir Thomas", last line, *after* "1615," *add* "was (with his said br Thomas) admitted to Gray's Inn, 2 Feb 1630/1, being then of St John's, Herts"

p 237, note (d), line 1, *for* "notes a and b," *read* "note (b), and p 215, note (b); see also p 455 as to the date of the docquet being in Oct 1643"

p 239, line 3, *for* "Bart," *read* "Bart (d)," *and add*, as note (d) "He is said to have had a da who m (—) Woodman, and was mother of Charles Bathurst Woodman [ex inform H Gough], line 23, *for* "Clote," *read* "Cote"

p 241, in margin, *for* "1644," *read* "1645", lines 23 and 30, *for* "1644," *read* "1644/5" Note (c), *for* "236, note 'a,'" *read* "215, note 'b'", note (d), *commence* "See p 455 as to the date of the docquet being in Feb 1644/5"

p 242, lines 8, 21, 34, and 41, *for* "1644," *read* "1645"

p 245, line 11, *after* "MIDLETON," *add* "or MIDDLETON", line 12, *after* "aforesaid," *add* "by his 2d wife, Elizabeth, da, of Marmaduke (LANGDALE), 3d BARON LANGDALE", line 13, *for* "Dec 1769," *read* "1 and was bur 4 Jan 1770, at Spofforth"

p. 246, note (b), line 1, *for* "236, note (a)," *read* "215, note (b), and p 455, as to the date in the Signet office docquet book being in April 1644"

p 257, line 39, *after* "Elinor," *add* "(b about 1640)", line 42, *after* "Cork," *add* "(who d 12 April 1638)", *after* "s p," *add* "He also (or possibly a successor of the same name) m Joan, da of Theobald ROCHE (a minor in 1642), of Ballamagooly, in the Barony of Fermoy, by Ann, da of John BOYLE"

p 259, lines 4 and 5, *for* "Archdeacon of Ardfert and Dean," *read* "Dean of Ardfert and Archdeacon"

p 261; line 6, *after* "s and h," *add* "admitted to Gray's Inn 23 June 1628 as, s. and h of Richard Osborn, of Capagh, co Waterford, Esq"

p 262, note (b), *conclude* "The said Charles, moreover, is described as the *fifth son* when admitted to Lincoln's Inn, 16 Dec 1780"

p 272 line 28, *dele* "of whom", line 29, *after* "Papists," *add* "He was one of the Aldermen of Limerick, appointed 1687 by James II"

p 278, line 19, *for* "1644," *read* "1643/4", line 24, *for* "1647," *read* "1646/7"

p 280, line 2 from bottom, *for* "20," *read* "28" Note (d), lines 4 and 5, *dele* from "Douglas" to end

p 246, note (b), line 2, *for* "as to whom see," *read* "the great champion of the Kirk, who was bur 13 Nov 1652, at Leith, 'excommunicate because he came into the English' See N & Q, 9th s, vii, 446 and"

p. 294, line 16, *dele* "and h", *after* "1636]," *add* "of Lochend aforesaid", line 18, *after* "widow," *add* "(who was h to her br the 2d Baronet)"

p 304, note (b), line 3, *for* "was of," *read* "who inherited", line 4, *conclude* "and who was cr a Baronet [S] 16 Jan 1636/7, as of Carnock, co Stirling"

p 305 line 6, *after* "death," *add* "10 Jan 1794"

p 314; line 3 from bottom, *after* "Fife," *add* "and afterwards of Blebo"

p 319, line 18, *for* "living 1901," *read* "d 5 Jan 1902, at Penicuik House, Penicuik, Scotland"

p 325, line 8, *for* "1732," *read* "1722"

p 336, note ('), *for* "5th," *read* "6th"

p 341, line 27, *conclude* "He d s p m, 25 Dec 1900, at Waipukuran, Hawkes Bay, New Zealand"

p 349, in margin, *for* "1638," *read* "1628"

p 355, between lines 10 and 11, *insert* "Forfeited 14 Sep 1763"

p 374, line 32, *for* "sometimes," *read* "sometime."

INDEX

TO THE SURNAMES OF THE SEVERAL HOLDERS OF THE
BARONETCIES CREATED BY CHARLES I.

including not only those of the grantees themselves but of their successors, to which is added the local or, failing that, personal description of each grantee The name of any Peerage dignity held with such Baronetcy is not included in the alphabetical arrangement, neither is the surname of the holder of any such peerage, when different(ª) from that of any Baronet who was a Commoner

(ª) See vol 1, p 263, note " a "

3 M

3 N

PROSPECTUS

OF THE

Complete Baronetage,

EXTANT, EXTINCT, OR DORMANT

EDITED BY

G. E. C.

EDITOR OF THE

"Complete Peerage."

Vol I BARONETCIES (English and Irish) created by JAMES I, 1611 to 1625, issued at 14s to Subscribers, June 1900, price, after publication, £1 1s. net.

Vol II, BARONETCIES (English, Irish, and Scotch) created by CHARLES I, 1625 to 1649, issued at £1 1s to Subscribers, May 1902, price, after publication, £1 11s. 6d net

Vols III and IV will contain BARONETCIES (English, Irish, and Scotch), created 1649 to 1 May 1707 (the date of the Union with Scotland), each Vol to be issued on the same terms as Vol. ii.

Vols V and VI will contain the BARONETCIES of Great Britain and those of Ireland, 1707 to 1 Jan 1801 (the date of the Union with Ireland), while the remaining Vols. will deal with those of the United Kingdom, viz, from 1801 to the date of publication.

All applications to be made to

Messrs W POLLARD & CO Ltd,
Publishers,
North Street,
EXETER

[MAY 1902]

CPSIA information can be obtained at www.ICGtesting.com
228407LV00003B/155/P